ILYA is a professional comic book creator (writer and artist). Since 1987 his work has appeared internationally, published by Marvel, DC and Dark Horse in the USA, Kodansha in Japan and by numerous independent companies worldwide. In 2005 he created the *Manga Drawing Kit* for Thunder Bay Press. Other bookwork includes: *Countdown* and *Time Warp*, two collections of his award-winning graphic novel series *The End of the Century Club*; *A Bowl of Rice*, for Amnesty International; *It's Dark in London*, a noir anthology from Serpent's Tail; and *Skidmarks*, a charming kitchen-sink drama series. ILYA also designs and tutors workshops and courses on the art of comics and manga for colleges, galleries, libraries, schools and prisons, across the UK as well as abroad.

ILYA's very favourite mangas include *Akira*, Hideki Arai's *Miyamoto Kara Kimie* and Yasuhito Yamamoto's *Tetsuo the Iron Man* (a crazed family comedy strip, nothing to do with the movies). The last two have never been translated into English, so he can only look at the pictures and dream. For anime, he says, 'You can't beat Studio Ghibli'.

Also available

The Mammoth Book of 20th Century Science Fiction
The Mammoth Book of Best New Horror 16
The Mammoth Book of Best New Science Fiction 18
The Mammoth Book of Celebrity Murder
The Mammoth Book of Celtic Myths and Legends
The Mammoth Book of Chess
The Mammoth Book of Comic Fantasy
The Mammoth Book of Comic Quotes
The Mammoth Book of Egyptian Whodunnits
The Mammoth Book of Extreme Science Fiction
The Mammoth Book of Famous Trials
The Mammoth Book of Great Detective Stories
The Mammoth Book of Great Inventions
The Mammoth Book of Haunted House Stories
The Mammoth Book of Historical Whodunnits
The Mammoth Book of Illustrated True Crime
The Mammoth Book of IQ Puzzles
The Mammoth Book of How It Happened: Ancient Egypt
The Mammoth Book of How It Happened: Ancient Rome
The Mammoth Book of How It Happened: Battles
The Mammoth Book of How It Happened: Trafalgar
The Mammoth Book of How It Happened: WWI
The Mammoth Book of How It Happened: WW II
The Mammoth Book of Jacobean Whodunnits
The Mammoth Book of Jokes
The Mammoth Book of Kakuro, Worduko and Super Sudoku
The Mammoth Book of King Arthur
The Mammoth Book of Maneaters
The Mammoth Book of Mountain Disasters
The Mammoth Book of New Terror
The Mammoth Book of New Jules Verne Adventures
The Mammoth Book of On The Edge
The Mammoth Book of On the Road
The Mammoth Book of Pirates
The Mammoth Book of Private Eye Stories
The Mammoth Book of Roaring Twenties Whodunnits
The Mammoth Book of Roman Whodunnits
The Mammoth Book of Secret Codes and Cryptograms
The Mammoth Book of Seriously Comic Fantasy
The Mammoth Book of Sex, Drugs & Rock 'n' Roll
The Mammoth Book of Short Spy Novels
The Mammoth Book of Sorcerers' Tales
The Mammoth Book of Space Exploration and Disasters
The Mammoth Book of SAS & Special Forces
The Mammoth Book of Shipwrecks & Sea Disasters
The Mammoth Book of Sudoku
The Mammoth Book of Travel in Dangerous Places
The Mammoth Book of True Crime
The Mammoth Book of True War Stories
The Mammoth Book of Unsolved Crimes
The Mammoth Book of Vampires
The Mammoth Book of Vintage Whodunnits
The Mammoth Book of Wild Journeys
The Mammoth Book of Women's Fantasies
The Mammoth Book of Women Who Kill
The Mammoth Book of the World's Greatest Chess Games
The Mammoth Encyclopedia of Unsolved Mysteries

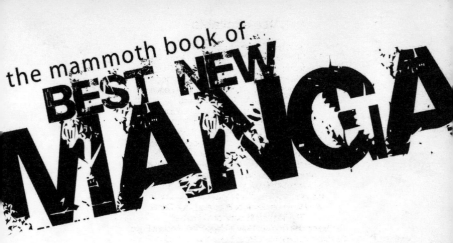

the mammoth book of
BEST NEW
MANGA

edited by ILYA

CARROLL & GRAF PUBLISHERS
New York

Carroll & Graf Publishers
An imprint of Avalon Publishing Group, Inc.
245 W. 17th Street
11th Floor
New York NY 10011-5300
www.carrollandgraf.com

AVALON
publishing group incorporated

First published in the UK by Robinson,
an imprint of Constable & Robinson Ltd 2006

First Carroll & Graf edition 2006

ISBN-13: 978-0-78671-838-2
ISBN-10: 0-7867-1838-2

Printed and bound in the EU

Contents

omake (Extras)

Introduction

Welcome to *Best New Manga*, and what is hopefully just the first of many volumes of new and original manga comic strips. You may have been attracted by the title, the cover image – or the look of what's inside (and if you haven't already done so, go on, take a good look. We've got time, and we'll be waiting right here for when you get back).

First up, a quickie definition of terms…

'MANGA = Comics from Japan: the term also refers to various styles and influences from Japanese comics.'
To that, you may as well add 'and / or animation – also known as anime', as it is in the form of these cartoon movies and TV serials, such as *Akira* and *Dragonball Z*, that many folk get their first taste of manga.

For the purposes of this book, *Best New Manga*, it's the second part of that definition we're most interested in. That is, comic strips inspired by – or showing the obvious influence of – Japanese comics (and anime), but which build from there to create and become their own animal. Neither fake manga, nor a pale imitation of existing material, but something else again, something entirely unique and original – that's what you will find within the pages of *Best New Manga!* It's manga that hasn't been imported, flipped, or translated, because it isn't necessarily Japanese (and nor is it pretending to be). The UK, the USA, Thailand, Sweden, Libya and, hey, Japan too – the creators of *Best New Manga* come from all over the world.

What Goes Around Comes Around

America was the birthplace of the comic book medium, and for decades American comic books dominated the worldwide comics market.

Manga, the Japanese art of comics, is stylistically distinct – not only from American comics, but equally as much, from indigenous European, Indian or South America comic books. Yet Japanese manga itself would not exist in the first place without the influence and inspiration of American cartoon and comic book culture.

The history of comics, and in particular manga, is one of cultural exchange. Turn back time sixty or so years, and the form of comic strip we call manga has its origins in some unexpected places. At the end of the Second World War, from 1945–51, Japan is briefly occupied by US armed forces. Imported American comic books give the GI Joes (General Infantrymen) a chuckle, and are then chucked away – inevitably falling into the hands of young Japanese. Meanwhile, the animated cartoon adventures of Disney and Fleischer Studios characters such as *Popeye* are playing on Japanese cinema screens. The Godfather of manga, Osamu Tezuka, takes these influences, and merges them with aspects of his own heritage (principally, the narrative prints of Hokusai) to create manga.

Back then, sixty years ago, before the rise of television and other visual media, almost everybody read comics (mostly in the form of newspaper strips) – and in Japan, oh boy, do they still: but they read them in the form of manga. You cannot underestimate the popularity of manga in Japan. They have manga titles that appeal to all ages and types of reader – every genre, and any subject matter you can conceive of, and in combinations you would probably never expect! If you were living in Japan, and you read and loved comics, you wouldn't be the only one: not only your kid brother or sister, but your mum and dad would collect comics, and they'd have their own favourite titles. And so would your granny!

At present, aside from a few honourable exceptions, most of the manga material that gets translated and imported into the West is restricted to one of two types – either *shojo*, for teenage girls, or *shonen*, for teenage boys. This has given rise to a limited conception of what manga actually is. There's a lot more to it than big eyes, wee noses and oops-you-can-see-my-panties. It's still early days for the cultivation of manga reading habits outside Japan, but their growth in popularity is something of a phenomenon, and one that shows signs of only continuing to snowball. As the younger readers who have latched onto manga in a big way grow up, they have begun to demand a wider range of material – and to create manga of their own!

Which is where, incidentally, *Best New Manga* comes in.

Manga Style – Influence and Inspiration

The first thing you should know about 'manga style' is that there is NO SUCH THING. Manga is just a Japanese word for comics – they can, and do, come in an infinite variety of drawing styles. There's the photo-real 'advertising art' of *Mai, the Psychic Girl* or *Crying Freeman* (both Ryoichi Ikegami); the loose brush-line evoking smoke, wind and motion in Koike and Kojima's *Lone Wolf & Cub*; the all-out pop art action of the likes of *Yaiba* or *Dragonball*; – and thousands more. Some of the strips you will see in *Best New Manga* haven't even been drawn, but were created with the aid of various computer programs!

When imagining what makes manga unique you may think of a blizzard of visual signatures – speedlines, sweatdrops, extreme foreshortening, and everyone and everything appearing to 'shout'. It's true to some extent – they spend much of their time and energy in evoking (what often seem to our eyes) extremes of emotional expression, as well as hi-speed, exquisitely choreographed action. This sort of visual shorthand was largely refined and defined by the work of one man, Osamu Tezuka (although not necessarily originating with him – being more of a distillation of pre-existing cartoon form and influence). And it has been proliferating and developing in the hands of thousands ever since.

So, there are aspects of the surface styling we can immediately identify, but not so easily what goes on between panels and behind the lines. In their art, as in their language, the Japanese like to concentrate on mood and feeling (one of the reasons why many, but by no means all, manga feature those great big eyes, since they are the windows to the soul): it's all in aid of generating empathy, an intimacy between reader and character, in order to tell a compelling story. Outside of the more manic *shojo* and *shonen*, you can find a great deal that involves equal subtlety, contemplation, and stillness.

Consider also the circumstances surrounding the birth of manga. You are in a country undergoing a super-swift industrial revolution. That means modernization, urbanization (an overnight move from the country into a big city), and the ecological and psychological stresses and strains of pollution, overcrowding, and so on, which that entails. Look again at certain scenes in the recent anime hit *Spirited Away* in such a light. Also, more importantly, you have just suffered a catastrophic defeat in a world war. Having two atomic bombs dropped on you does tend to leave a lasting imprint on the national psyche! Thus, manga is largely characterised by certain prevailing themes, both underlying and overarching – DESTRUCTION, MUTATION, MECHANIZATION (all those monsters, and robots with feelings) – all, essentially, forms of TRANSFORMATION. You can see this clearly in *Akira*, many Studio Ghibli films, or even the arc of evolution as played out through *Gon*. Japanese society is constantly changing, always testing its own cultural boundaries as to what's permissible – what may be portrayed, or openly discussed, within its media. Finally, consider what is happening in your own life and the world around you, and you will see why the themes of manga speak so directly to so many of us – both inside and outside Japan itself.

Ultimately, then, 'manga style artwork' is not limited by appearance – it can look like anything. The essence of manga, and of manga influence, is most crucially of all to be found in the pacing and the storytelling. By their nature they are long-form, stories often numbering thousands of pages before they are complete. What's the difference between a manga and a graphic novel? Not much, except manga is itself Japanese, or displays the implicit influence of Japanese comics or anime as outlined above. Manga traditionally enjoy the luxury of space afforded by their huge popularity: they can relax the action across many more pages than traditional western comics – fewer panels per page, and fewer words per panel (but again, this is a tendency, not necessarily the standard). As a result, action sequences of every sort (large and small, quiet or loud) go both faster and slower at the same time: manga storytelling deals in what could be called 'exploded moments' – but that is an editorial in itself, for another time. For now, a flick through the pages of *Best New Manga* can tell you all you need to know.

And What Genre Would You Like to Read Today?

Not only can manga be created in any style, they also cover the total spectrum when it comes to genre (or category of story). We have already mentioned many of the classics of the medium, old and new, that have so far been translated: *Akira* (seen the film? read the comic, 4,000+ pages written and drawn by the film's director, Katsuhiro Otomo), *Gon* (no words necessary!), Studio Ghibli anime (*Princess*

Mononoke, *Spirited Away*, *Howl's Moving Castle* and many more – all excellent), anything by Tezuka (try *Buddha*). Then there's *Dragonball Z*, *Barefoot Gen*, big monster fun such as *Godzilla*, hordes of giant robot mecha *Transformers*; the more girly *Sailormoon* and *Swan; Hino Horror* and *Spiral*, or *Parasyte*, for those who like to be creeped out; tournament or combat based computer game fare such as *Tekken*, cyberpunk futures, and to a lesser extent the historical chambara 'fencing' dramas – epics such as *Lone Wolf & Cub*, and *Samurai Executioner*. Many of these titles will have been prime or secondary influences on most of the creators of *Best New Manga* – all of whom will have their own particular favourites. We recommend you try them all!

There are many further classics that haven't and may never be translated – there's sixty years' worth of a mass-market phenomenon to catch up on, and much of it seems just too weird! Nothing stops you (like many fans before you) tracking down the imported Japanese title you like the look of best, and studying the images to work out the stories for yourself, even when you can't read the actual words – and then dreaming up your own.

Meanwhile, within these pages you will find...

Fantastical Drama (*Jinn Narration, Bad Luck and Princess at Midnight*), Bizarre Funny Animal and Cute Robot Comedy (*Big Bam Boo, Carlos & Sakura* and *Magic Science Robot Zappy*), Mythical Action Heroes (*Bulldog : Empire* and *Outlaw Wu*), Horror Fantasy (*The Healing*), Psycho-Cosmic Science Fiction (*Ongoing Mission*), plus more Romantic Drama than you can shake a stick at (*Station, Instant Noodles* and *New Shoes*), as well as a healthy dose of the Indescribably Odd (*The House That Wasn't Her* and *Advent*). And there are over 500 pages of it, at a very reasonable price! We're spoiling you.

The only thing we seem to be missing is Crime and Zombies... Hmm, maybe next time!

'Not Real Manga' – Dispelling the Myth

A minor controversy currently rages over the spread of manga to the west, and the legitimacy of manga that is created outside of Japan. A few editors and publishers have taken the position that the term 'manga' means 'Japanese comic' (1), and should not be applied to anything originating elsewhere. Some people are fond of insisting – 'If it's not back to front (2), and it isn't in black and white (3), then it isn't really manga.' Others see its surging popularity as a threat to the survival of our own indigenous comics (4).

WRONG! WRONG! WRONG! On Every Single Count.

(1) In actual fact the term 'manga' dates back to 1814, and Hokusai's satirical prints. Literally translated, about the closest we can get is the phrase 'Irresponsible Pictures'. In context, Hokusai was presumably cocking a snook at his critics by getting in there first. This aspect of his work featured scurrilous caricature or pornographic rudeness, and was unashamedly populist, as well as being somewhat 'underground'. Much of this fits with the general conception of comics as 'pulp', low fiction, and counter-cultural fare as much as a culture unto themselves. Most cartoonists (or 'mangaka'), the world over, are only too happy to be thought of as 'irresponsible', while many others strive for respect and acceptance – and so it goes. The term has been wholeheartedly embraced.

(2) Somewhere down the line, back in Japan, 'manga' became synonymous with comics. The material within these pages might perhaps be defined (broadly) as not just 'comics', but western manga.

Some of it started out in another language than English, but all of it has been created according to our preferred reading direction in the West, left to right. (In Japan, and some other cultures, they read in the opposite direction, from right to left. Original Japanese manga is best enjoyed read back to front, even when translated, as flipping the artwork does not always work – as an early, colourized translation of *Akira* showed.) Except... *Best New Manga* includes the work of international creators from as far afield as Libya and Thailand, so it can't even properly be called 'western manga'. Doh!

Tell you what, to make things easy – let's just call it MANGA, and leave it at that!

Best New Manga is Definitive Manga

None of the work by the new wave of young manga creators represented within the pages of *Best New Manga* would look or read how it does without the influence of Japanese manga and anime, and the love of those forms that both informs and inspires it (and them!). But beyond that – Anything Goes!

In assembling the book we have been truly spoiled for choice, there is so much activity going on in this area. With *Best New Manga* we are taking that title literally, choosing to zero in on the most original talents, those who are doing it their way (rather than imitating anyone else's idea of 'manga style'), and who have something to say that is very much personal to them.

When thinking in manga terms, even with 500+ pages to play with, the stories that appear here are equivalent to little more than shorts, brief scenes or *haiku*. Given the opportunity, every person whose work appears in *Best New Manga* is more than capable of filling a book of this same size by themselves, with much longer stories – the further adventures of their very own character creations. Everyone represented here is by rights a future star in their chosen field, which is manga. Remember their names – and watch for them!

If and when their work becomes popular, they will be able to concentrate on making their manga pages full-time – which means more fabulous manga stories for us all to read! So, go on, help to give them that chance. If you like *Best New Manga* (and how could you NOT!) help to make it the success it deserves to be by spreading the word. Buy lots of copies to give to your family and friends as presents, or cajole them into going out and buying their own – they too will love it. The more copies sold of this first volume of *Best New Manga*, the better its chances of being just the first of many – and if it sells really well, then next time, we hope to introduce colour!

(3) That's right. There is no earthly reason manga should be only black and white. It's been that way in Japan for decades due to the economics of bulk printing on cheap paper – which was necessary with a readership in the millions. That isn't the case in the West, and seems increasingly less necessary even in the home of manga: new print technology is bringing the costs of colour print down (although paper shortage is a problem!). In the future, manga will most likely turn full colour. Most of our featured artists already work in colour, as you can readily see if you check out their websites (see the individual introduction pages before each story for URL addresses). We heartily recommend that you do – there's a wealth of material available to read and enjoy online, far beyond what has so far made it into print. The nascent new manga scene is still waiting for the world to catch up! But it will…

Global Domination – Nyahh, hahh, haah!

Today, you! Tomorrow, the world! Not only in Japan, comic strips have also stayed at the top of the publishing game, widely read and produced by the million, in the Philippines, India, and some South American countries such as Brazil. In their birthplace, the USA, things have slipped a bit, although comics' cultural influence in other media (principally movies and computer games) has never been stronger. The ever-growing popularity of manga, worldwide, and the resurgence of the graphic novel may actually be unrelated phenomena, at least commercially speaking, but even that is open to debate: it is thanks to manga, at least in part, that the habit and enthusiasm for reading comics (of every sort) is returning all over. Yay!

In the brave new world ahead the future is always up for grabs, but it will almost certainly come with speech balloons attached, and have panel borders around it. Manga is a truly pan-cultural, international, pro-literacy language. In the West, the comic book medium is about to regain the mass audience potential it once had for the first time in, ooh, decades (4). And that's what's Best about *Best New Manga!*

Enjoy the book!
ILYA

Advent

by

Michiru Morikawa

Date of Birth: 31 July 1973

Michiru Morikawa

Although Japanese, Michiru currently lives in the UK. Her manga influences are, she says, too numerous to mention, but she loves to read – anything – from sci-fi to dog breed catalogues.

A wordless strip, **Advent** is the story of one man's encounter with his inner child, and won 2005's International Manga and Animation Festival competition (see details on page 538). 'This manga was clever and magical at the same time,' say the Festival organizers. 'With delightful artwork and confident storytelling it had an audacious perspective on the old idea of lost, childhood innocence and fully deserved to win the Grand Prize.' We are delighted, therefore, to present it within the pages of **Best New Manga**.

Among Michiru's many plans for the future are manga adaptations of the short stories of H.G. Wells, and also well-known fairy stories.

You can check out more of her work online at:
http://photos.yahoo.com/michirumorikawa

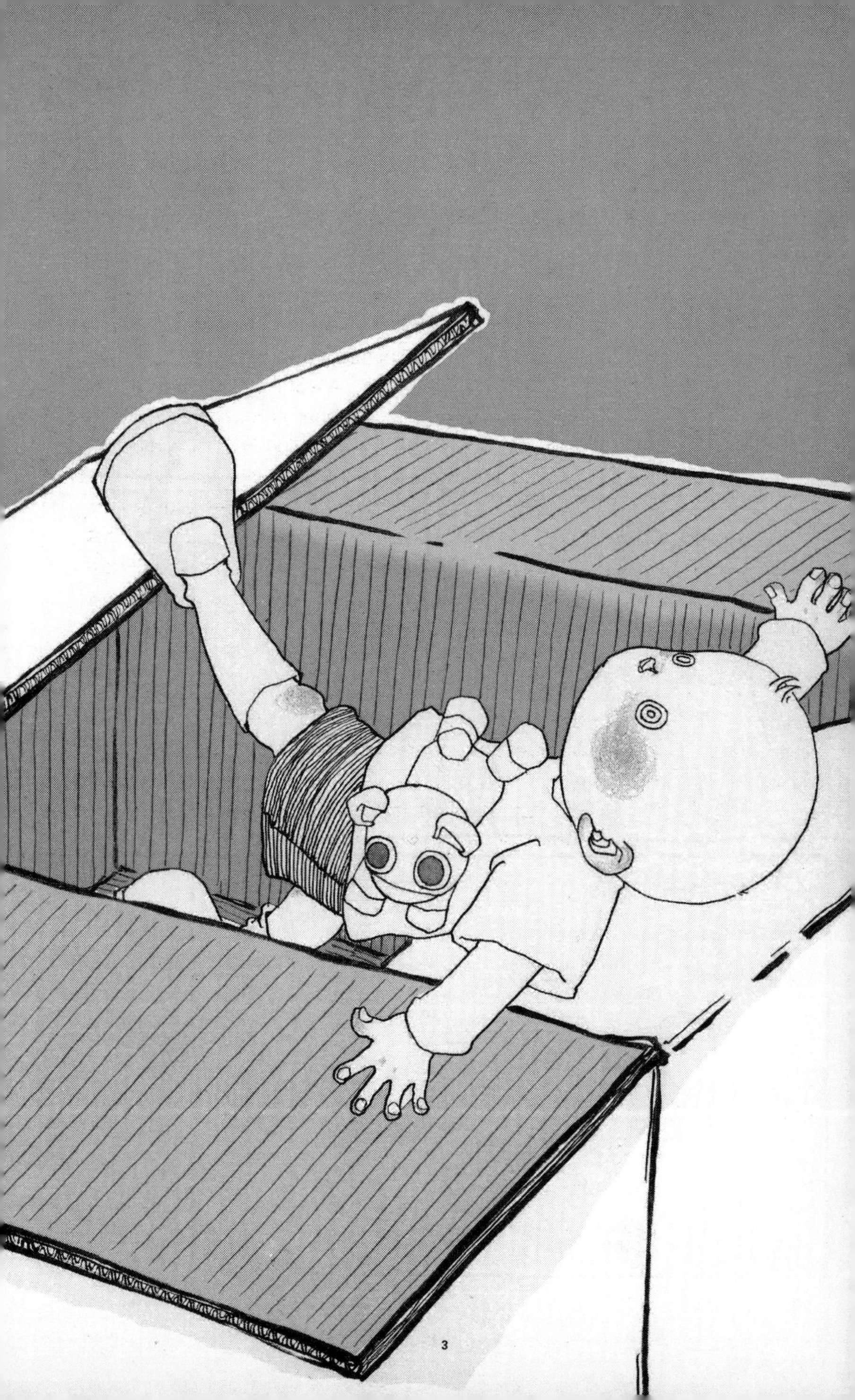

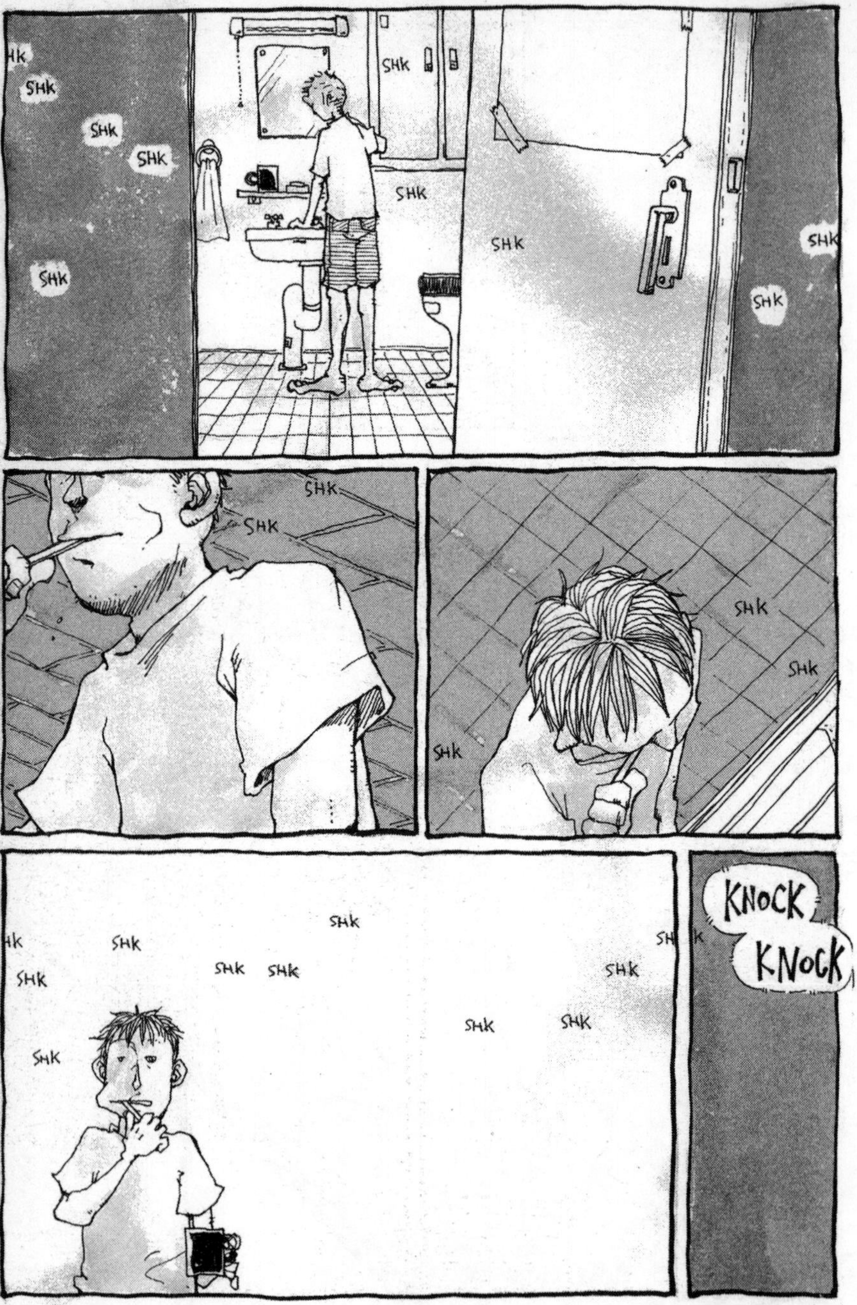
SHK
SHK
SHK
SHK
SHK
SHK
SHK
SHK
SHK
SHK
SHK
SHK
SHK
SHK
SHK
SHK
SHK
SHK
SHK
SHK
SHK
SHK
SHK
SHK
SHK
KNOCK
KNOCK

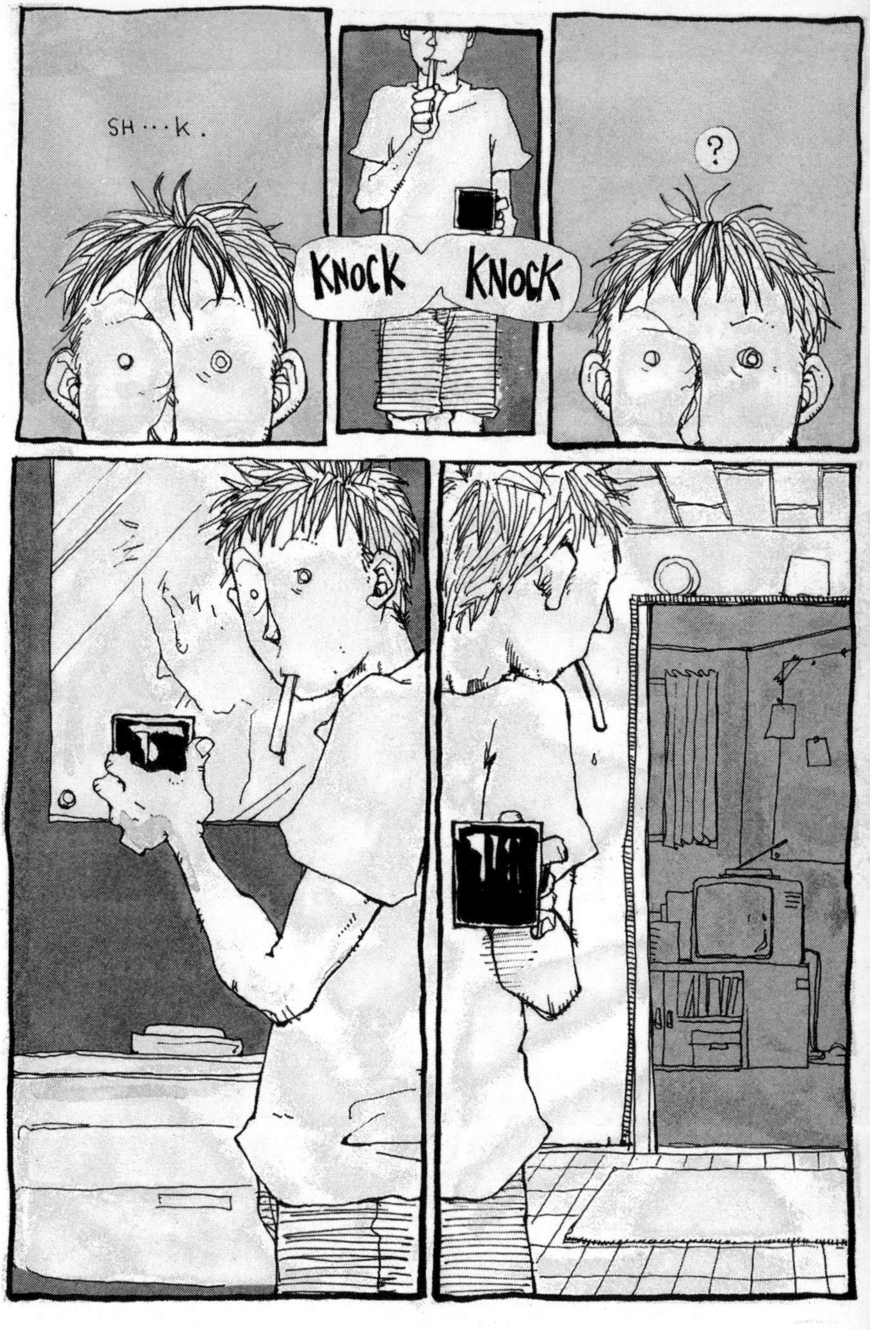
SH···K.
KNOCK KNOCK
?

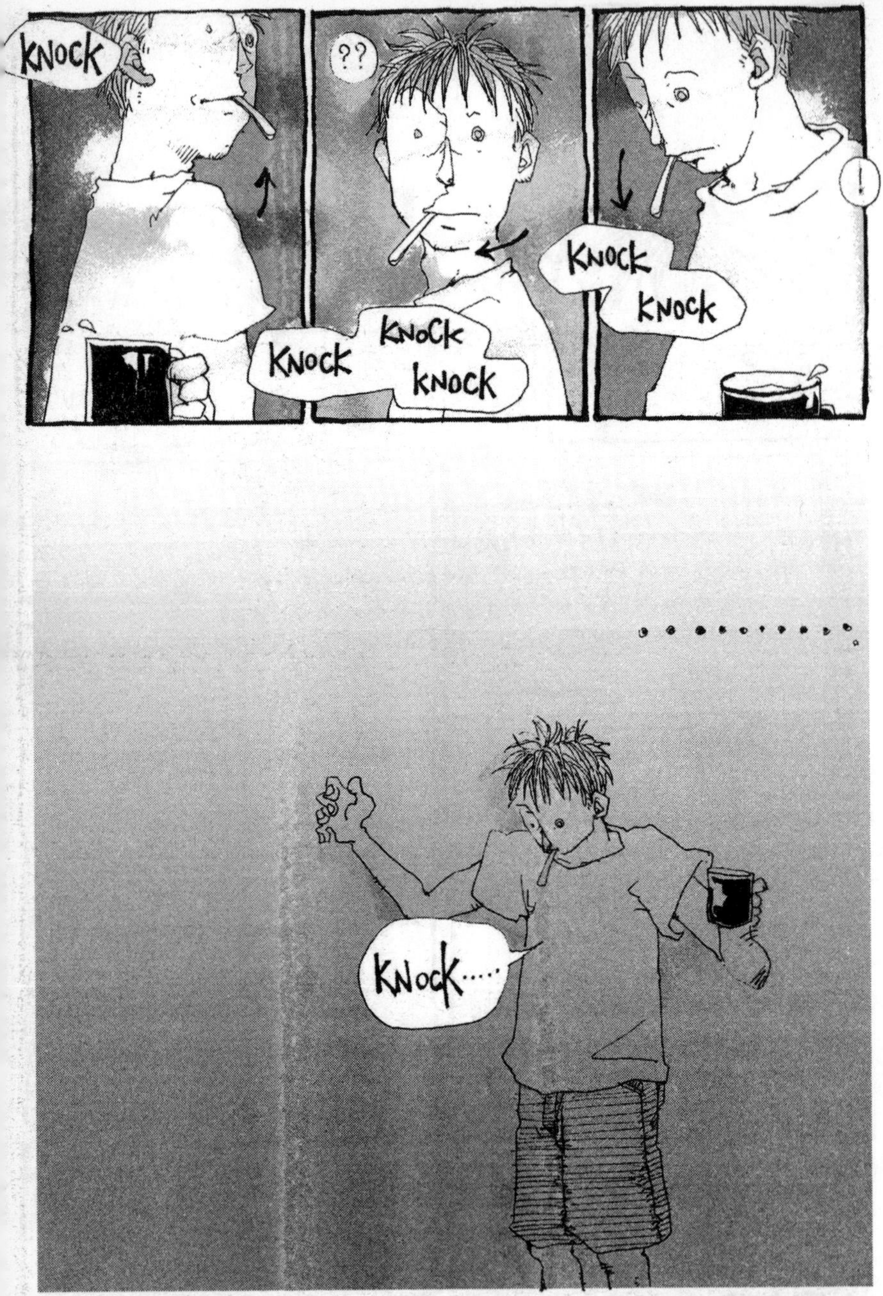
KNOCK
??
KNOCK
KNOCK
KNOCK
KNOCK
KNOCK
!
....
KNOCK.....

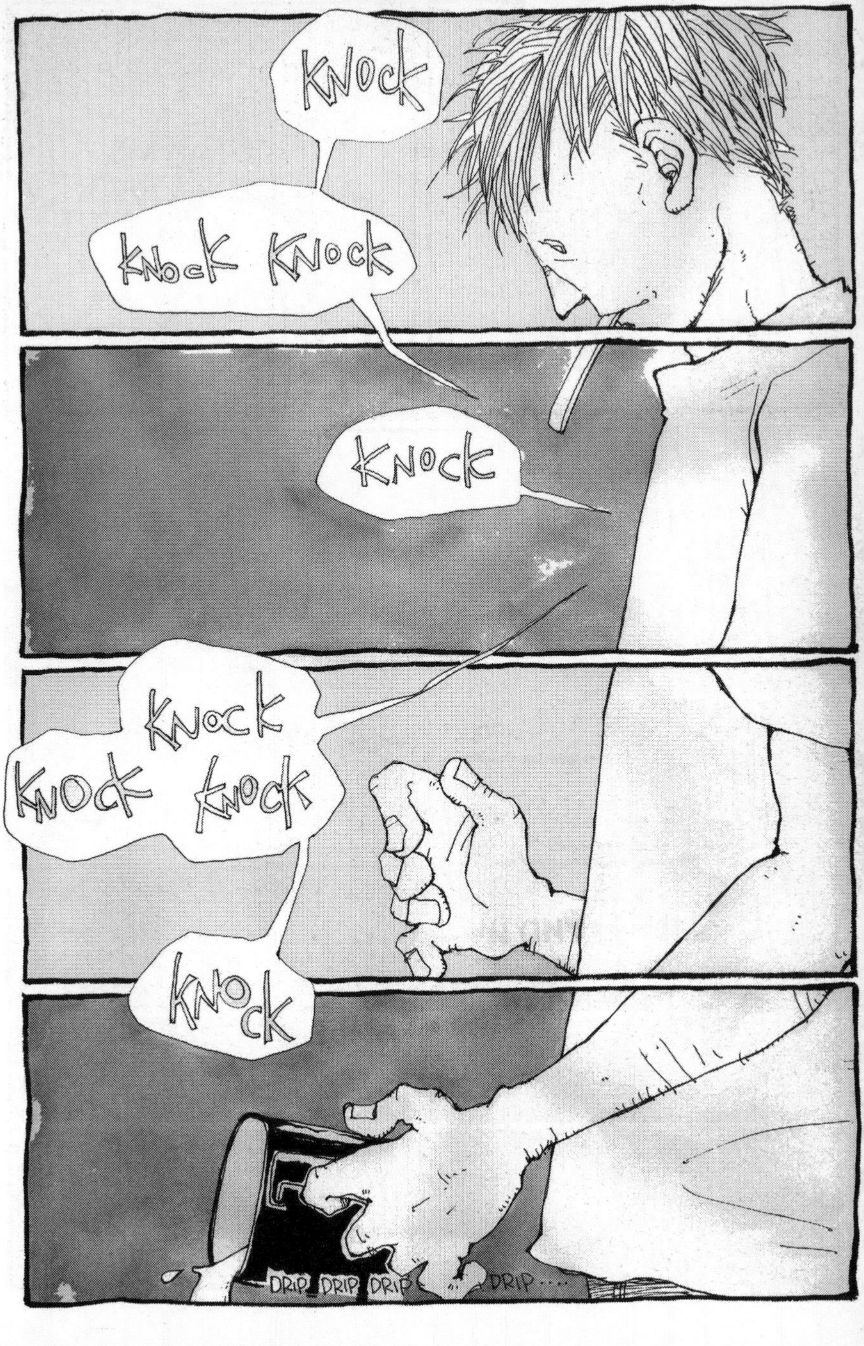
KNOCK
KNOCK KNOCK
KNOCK
KNOCK
KNOCK KNOCK
KNOCK
DRIP DRIP DRIP DRIP....

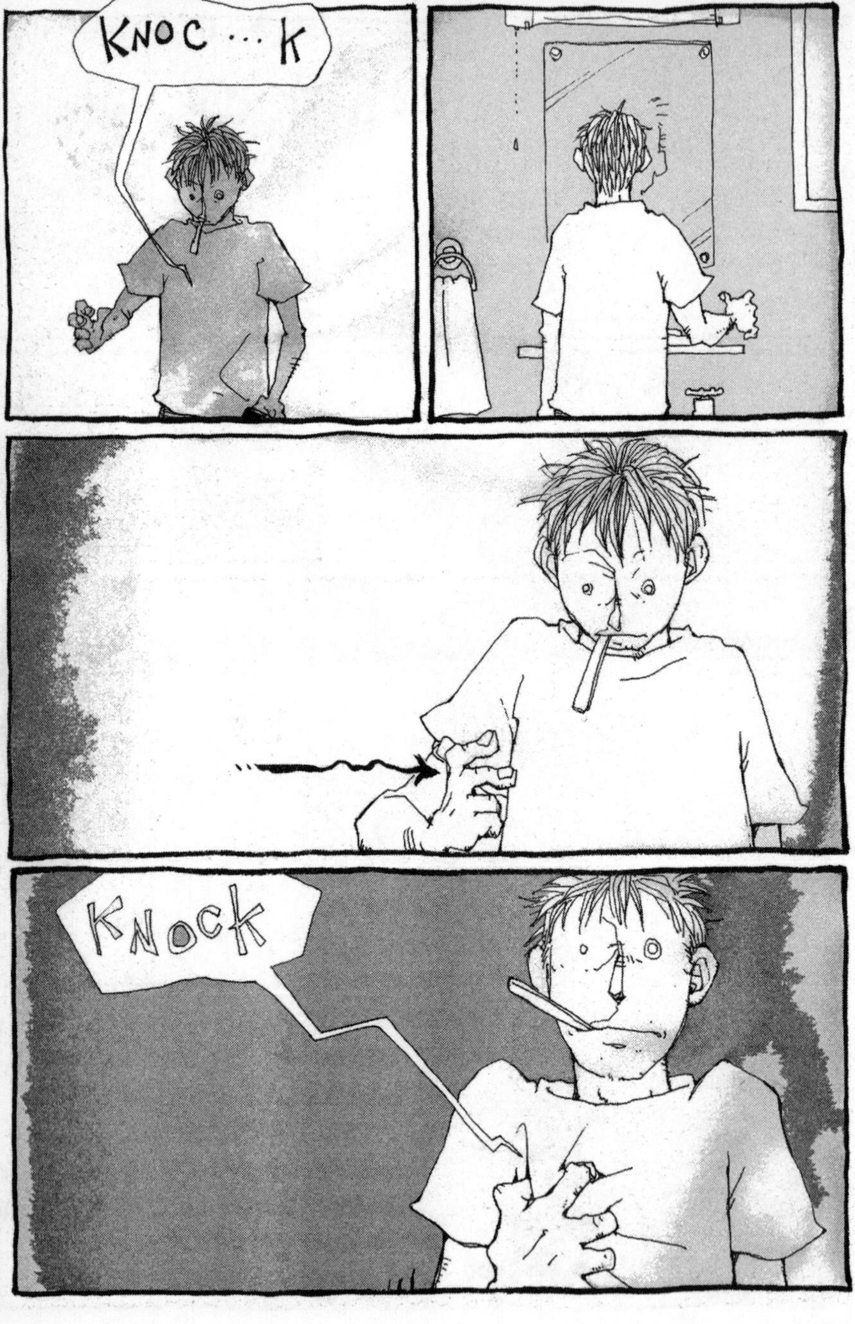
KNOC ... K
KNOCK

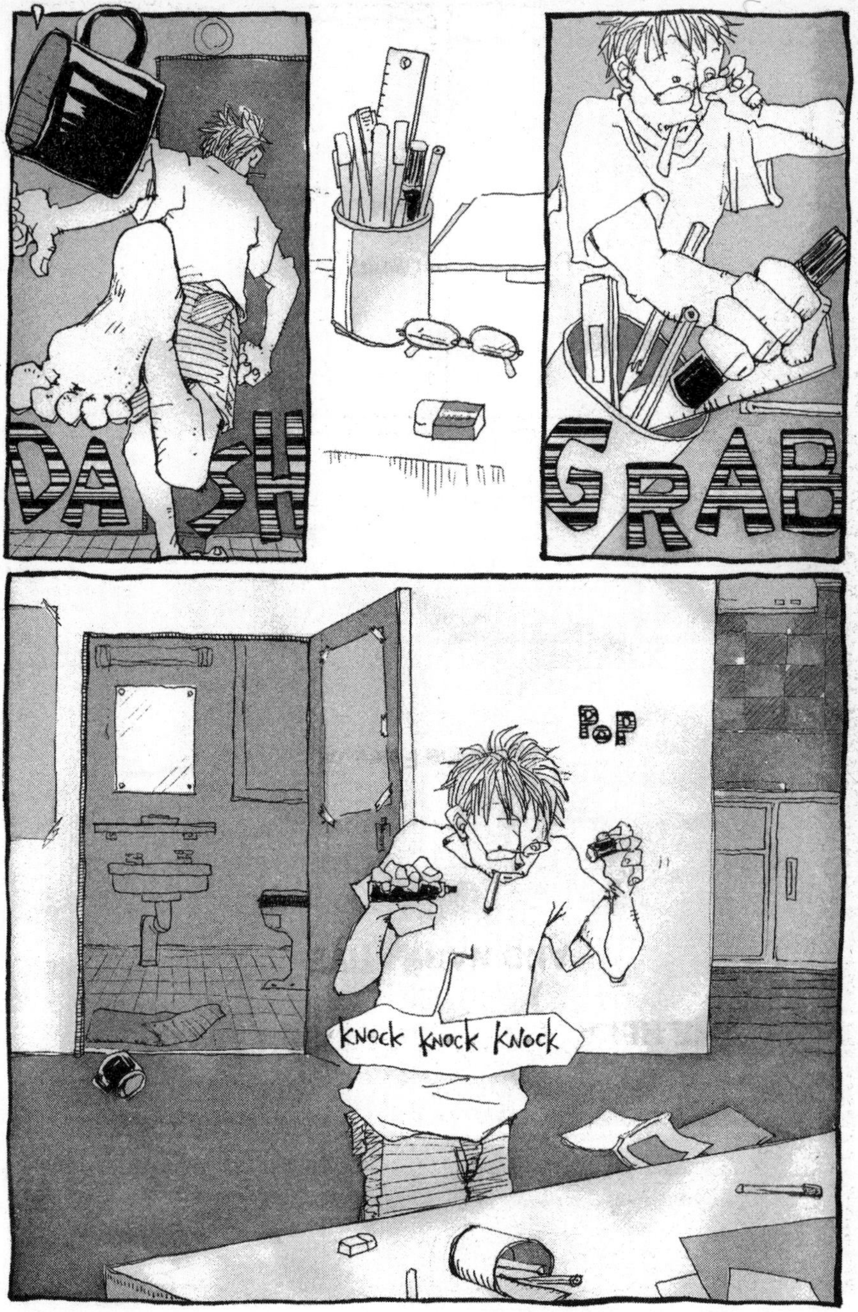
DASH
GRAB
PoP
KNOCK KNOCK KNOCK

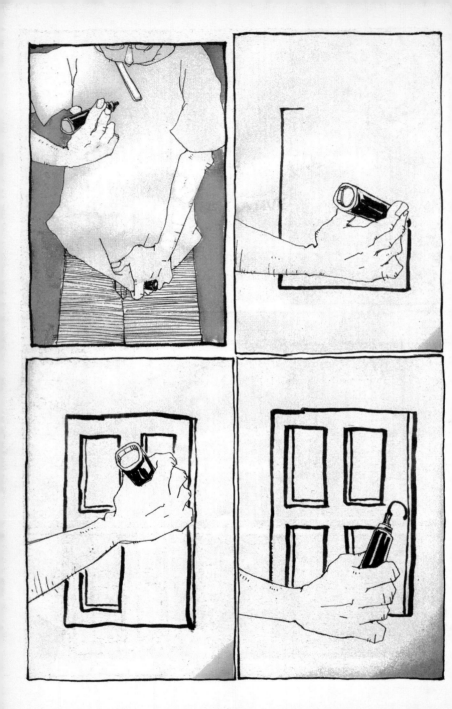

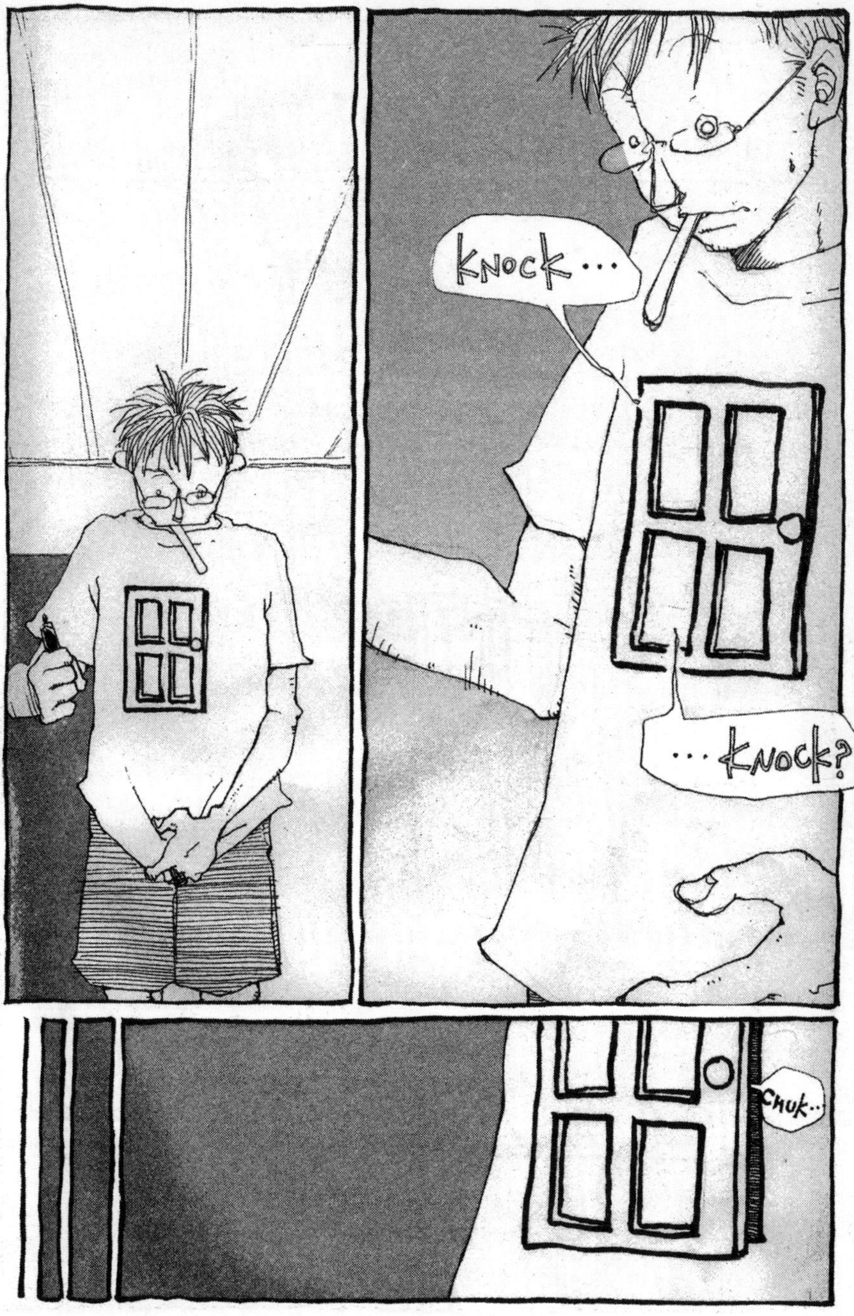
KNOCK...
...KNOCK?
CHUK..

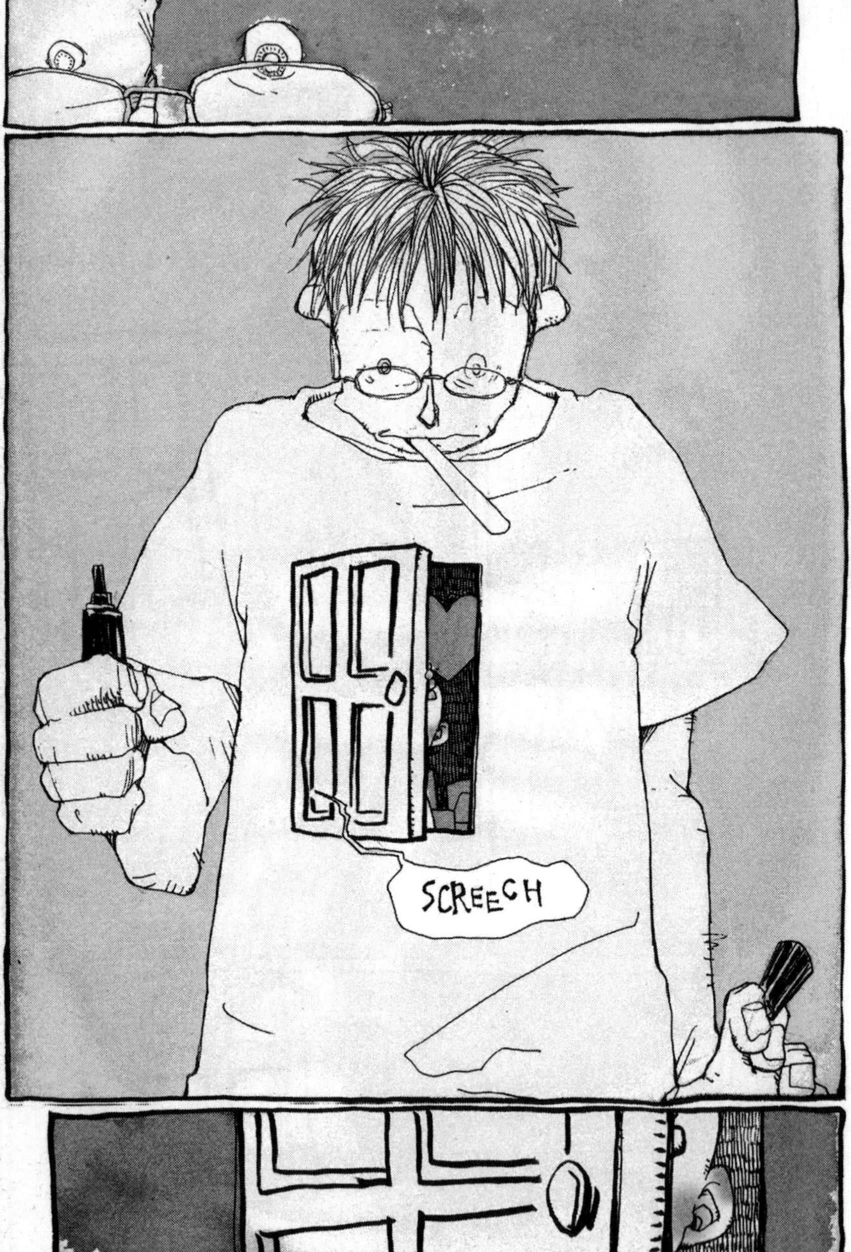
SCREECH

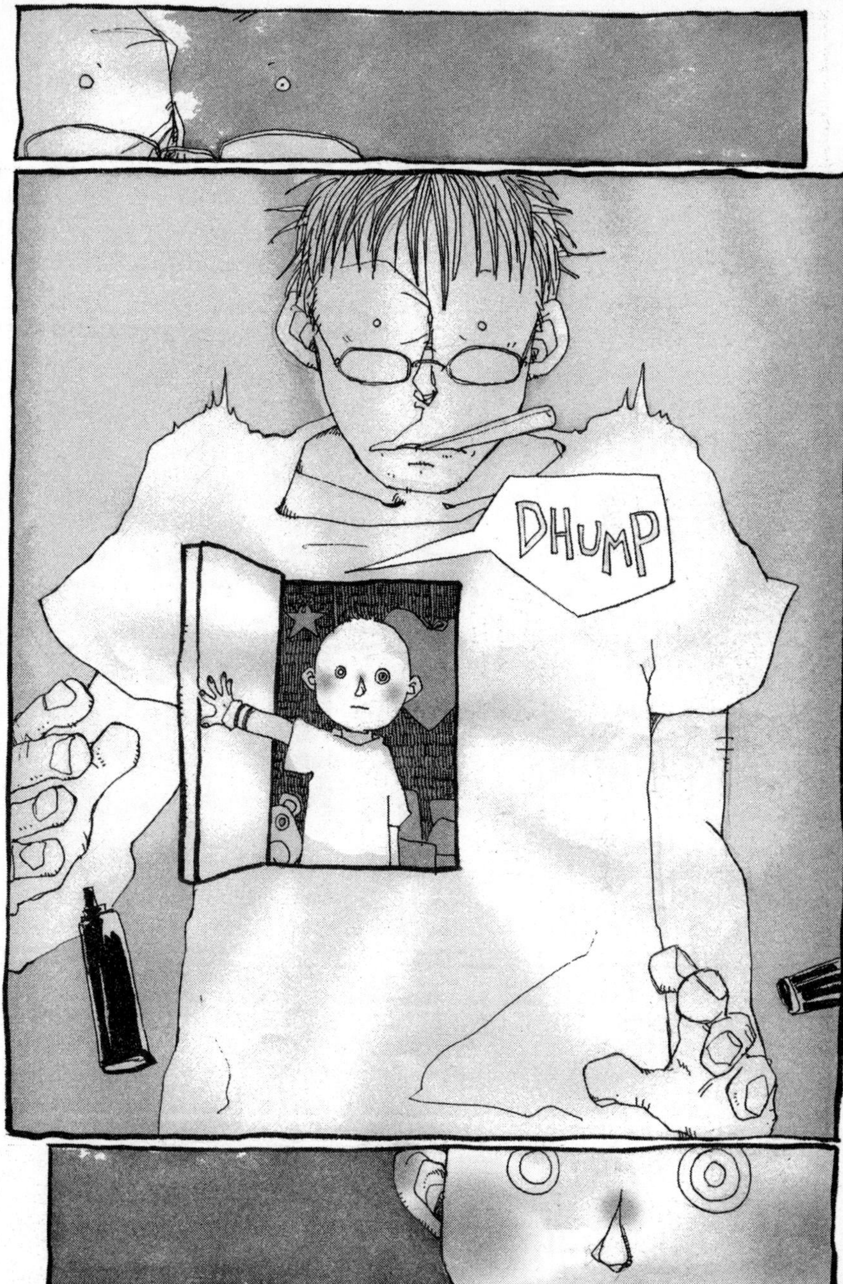
DHUMP

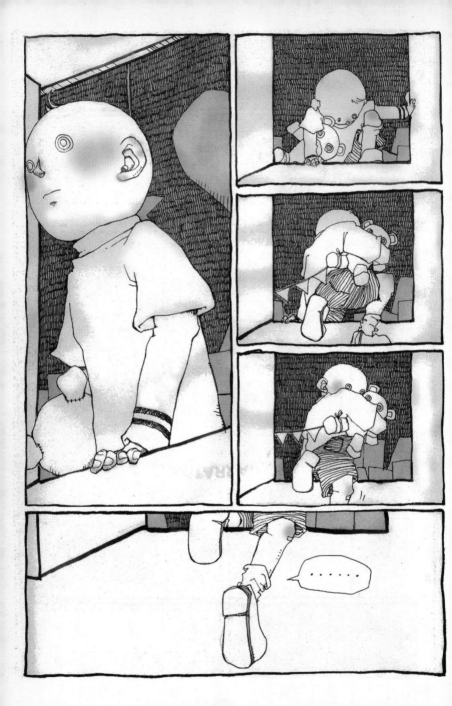

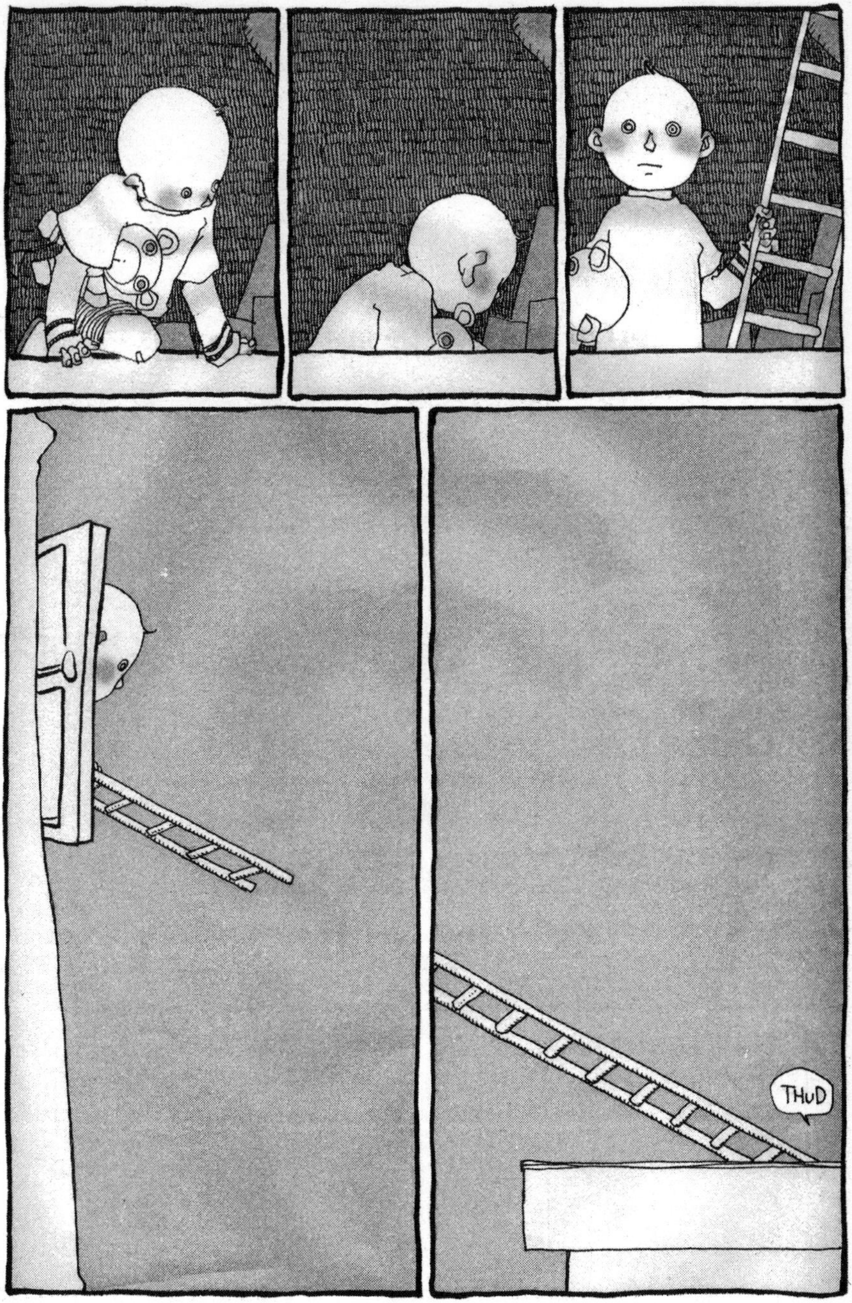
THUD

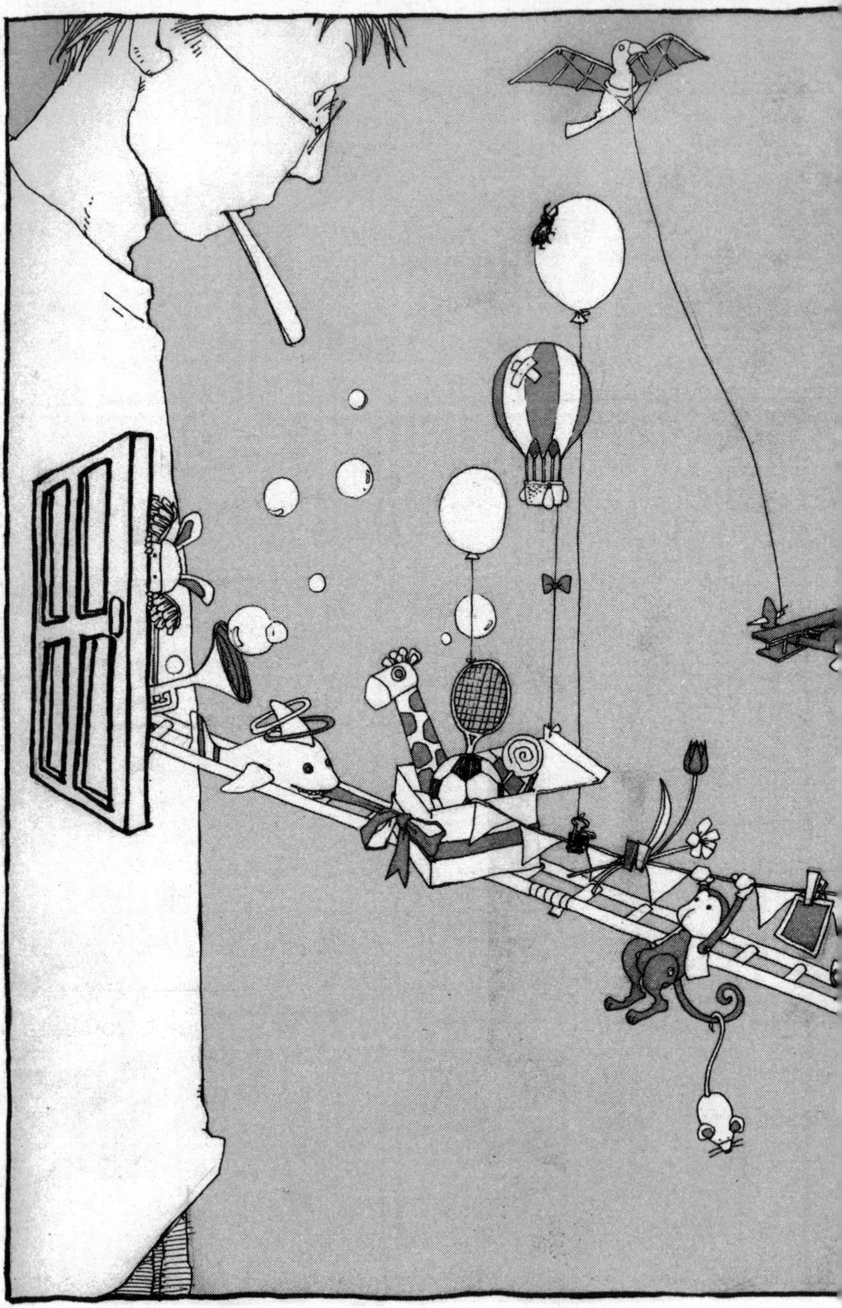

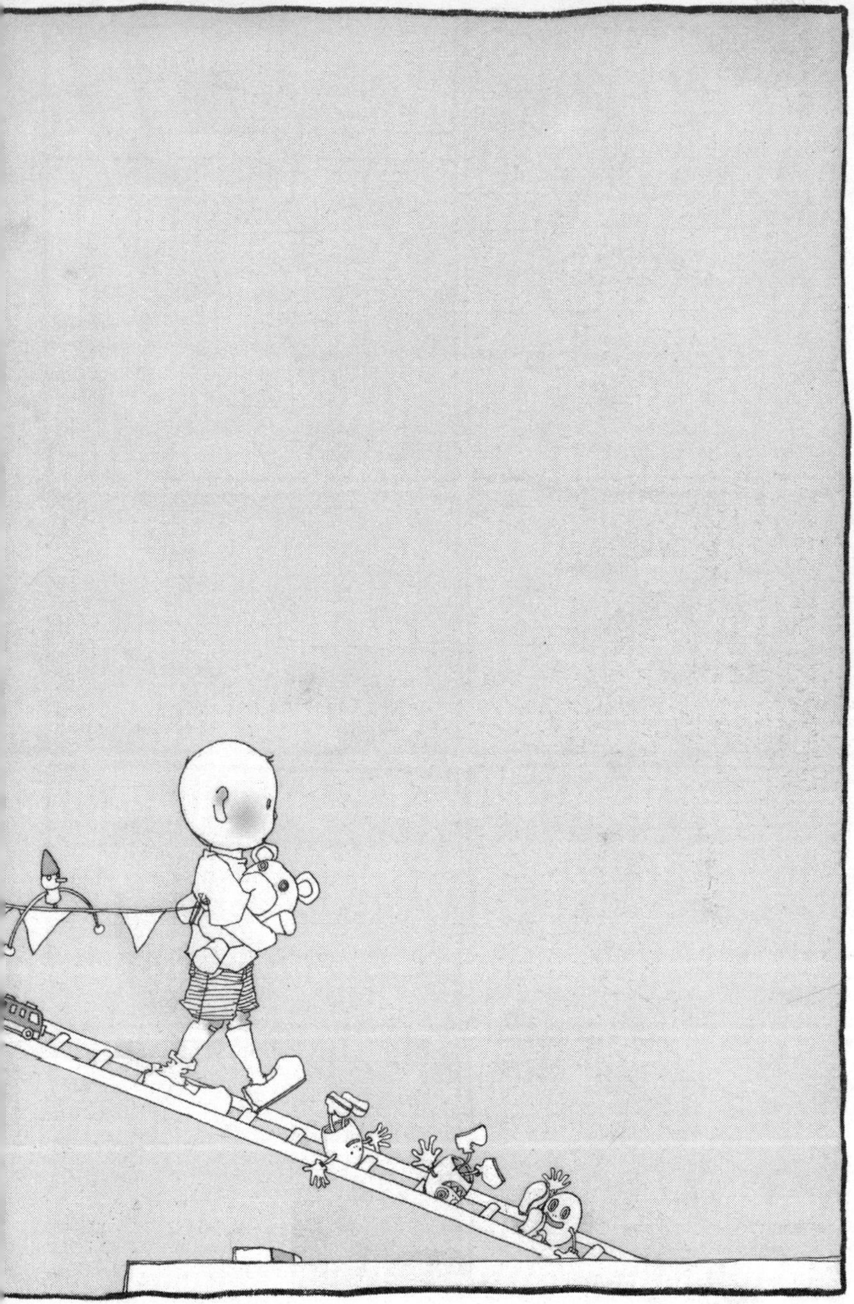

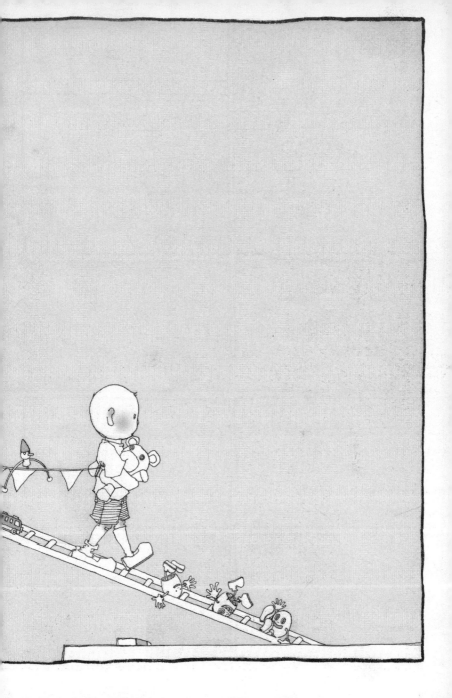

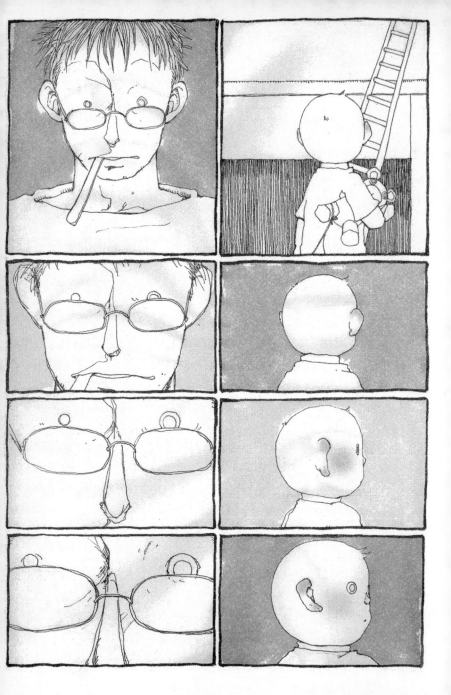

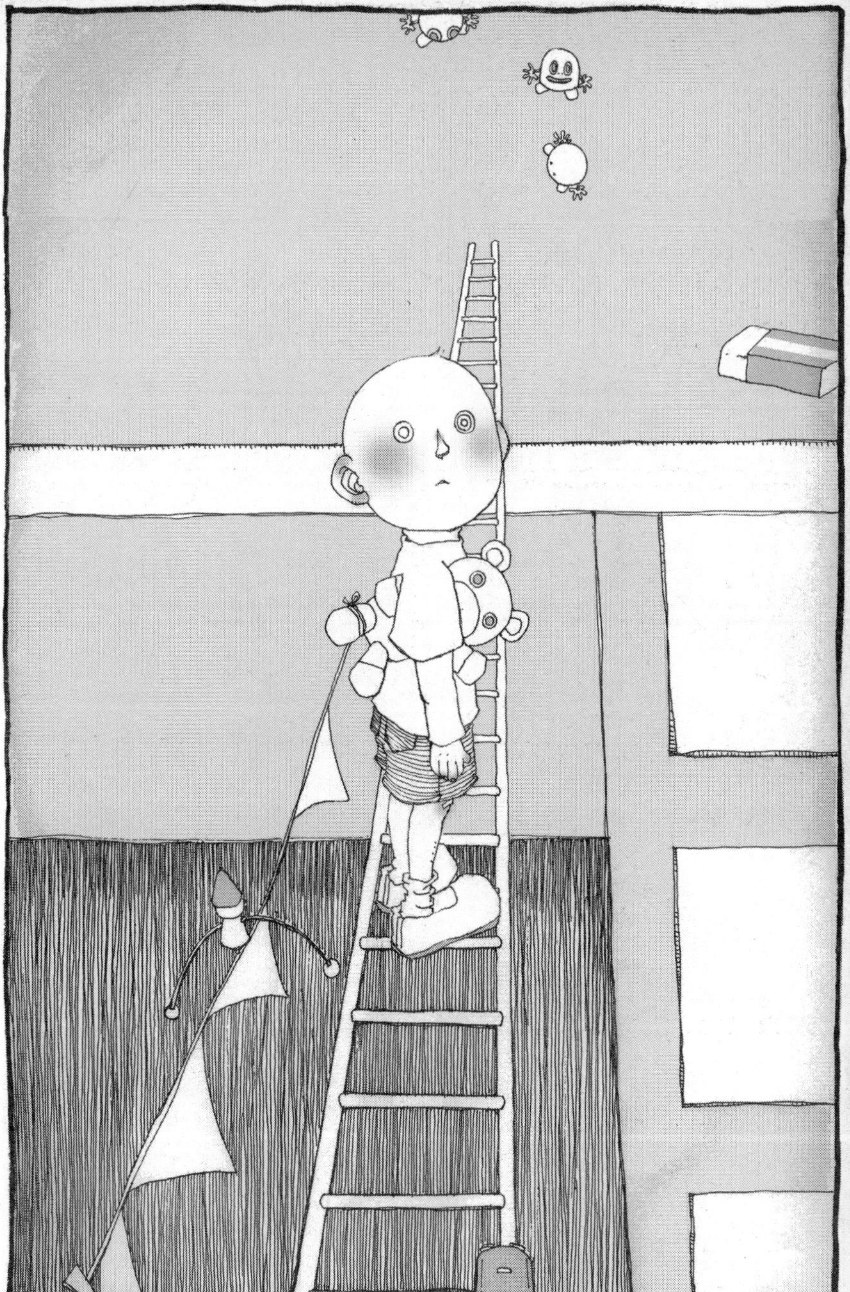

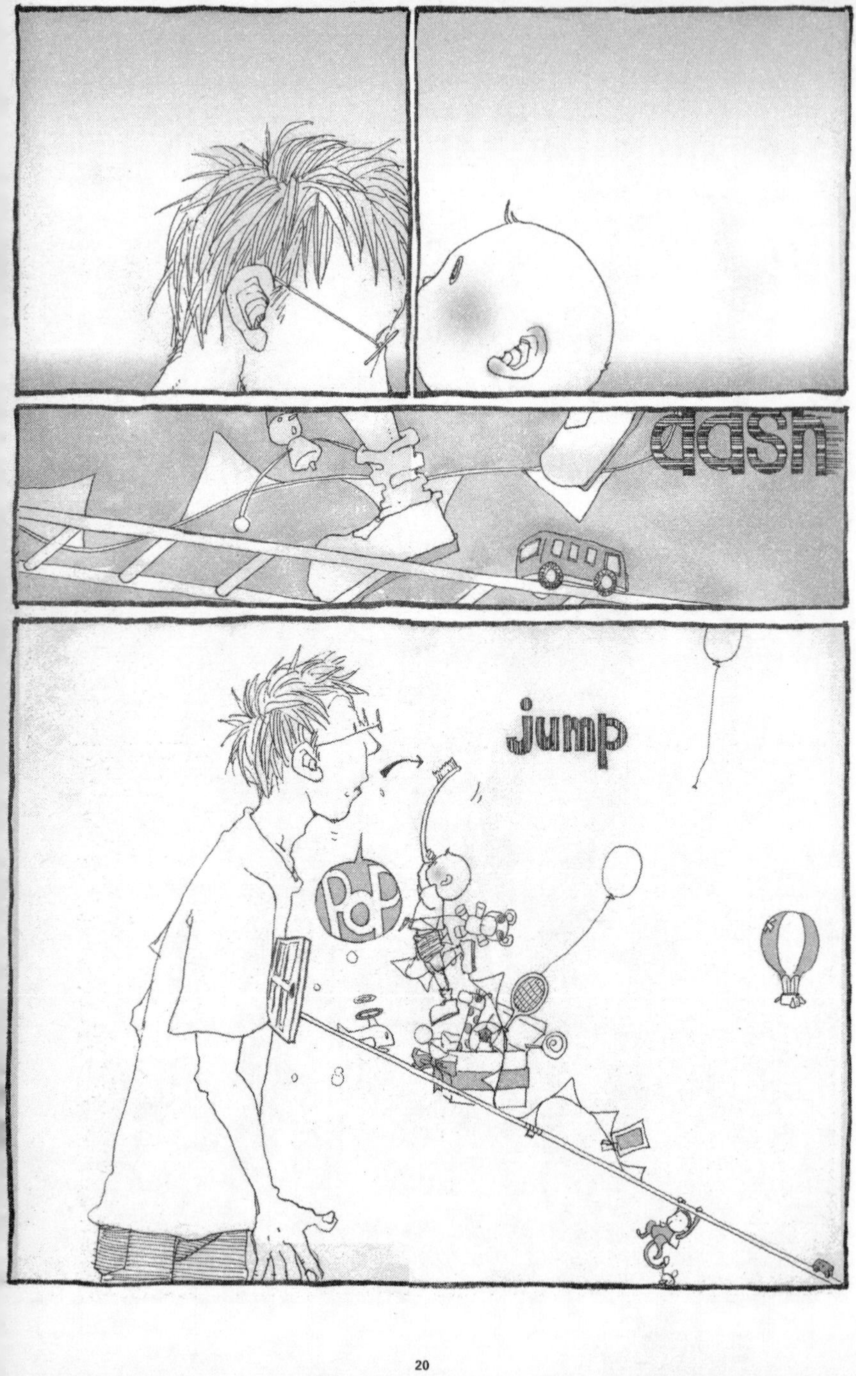
dash
jump
PoP

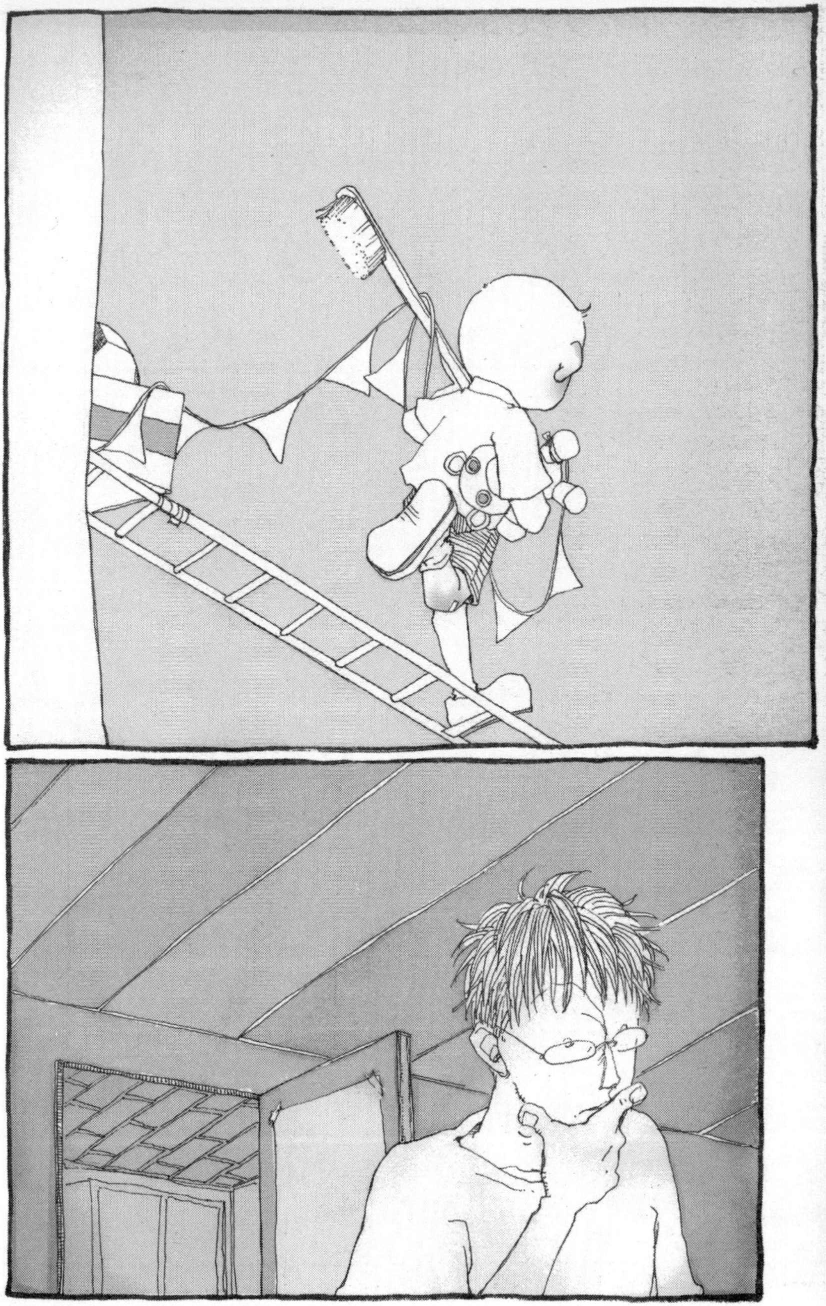

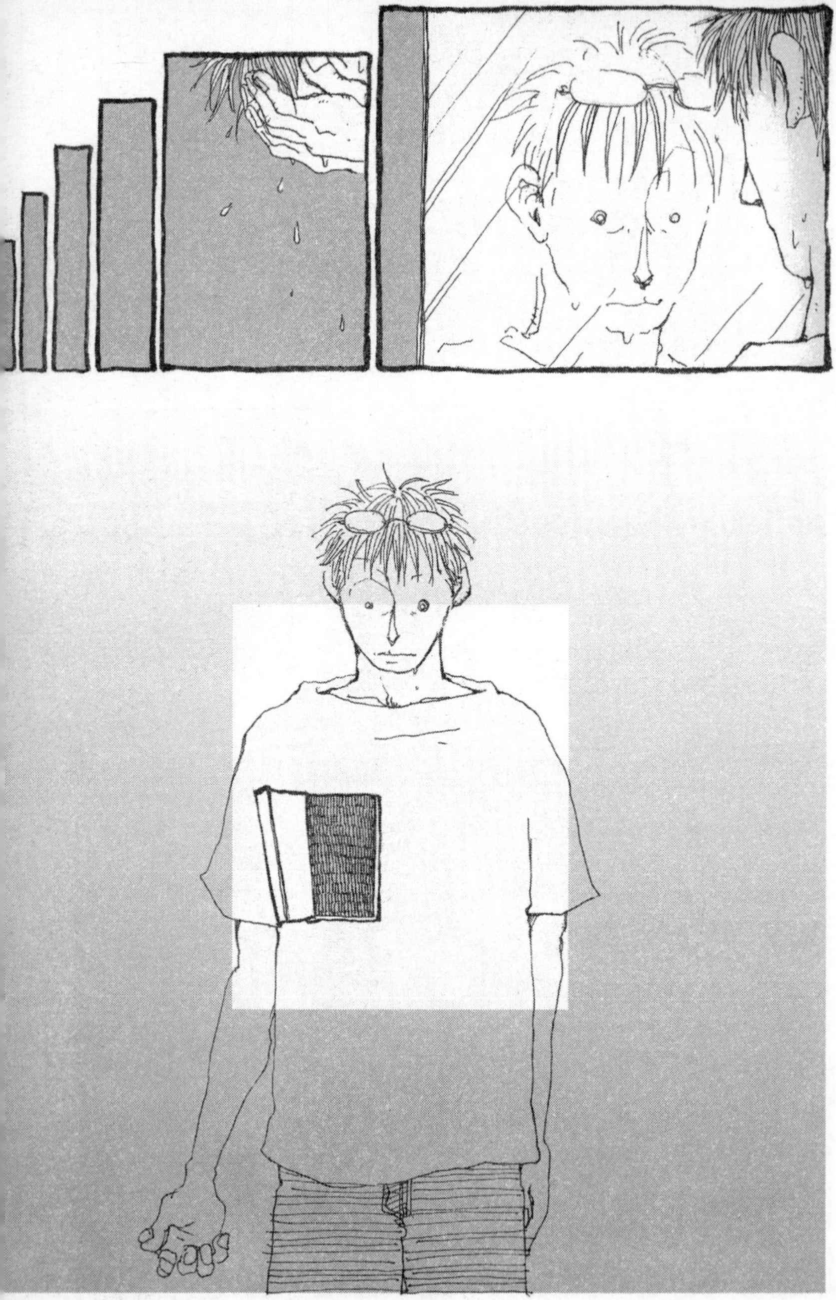

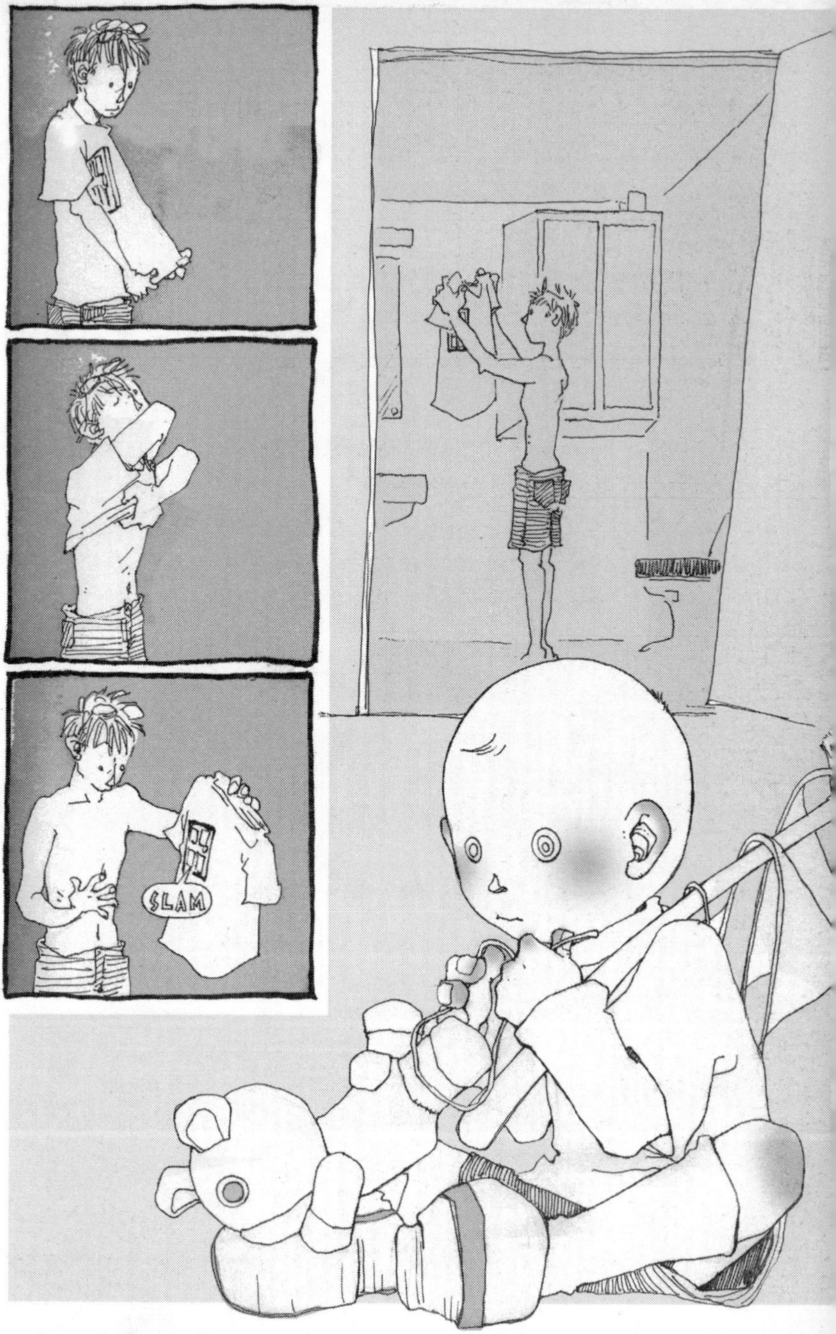
SLAM

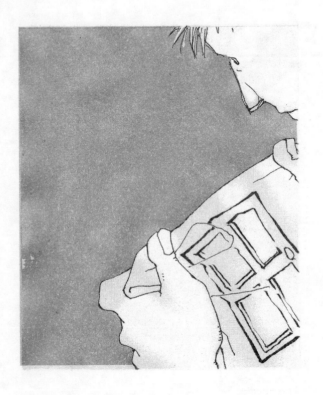

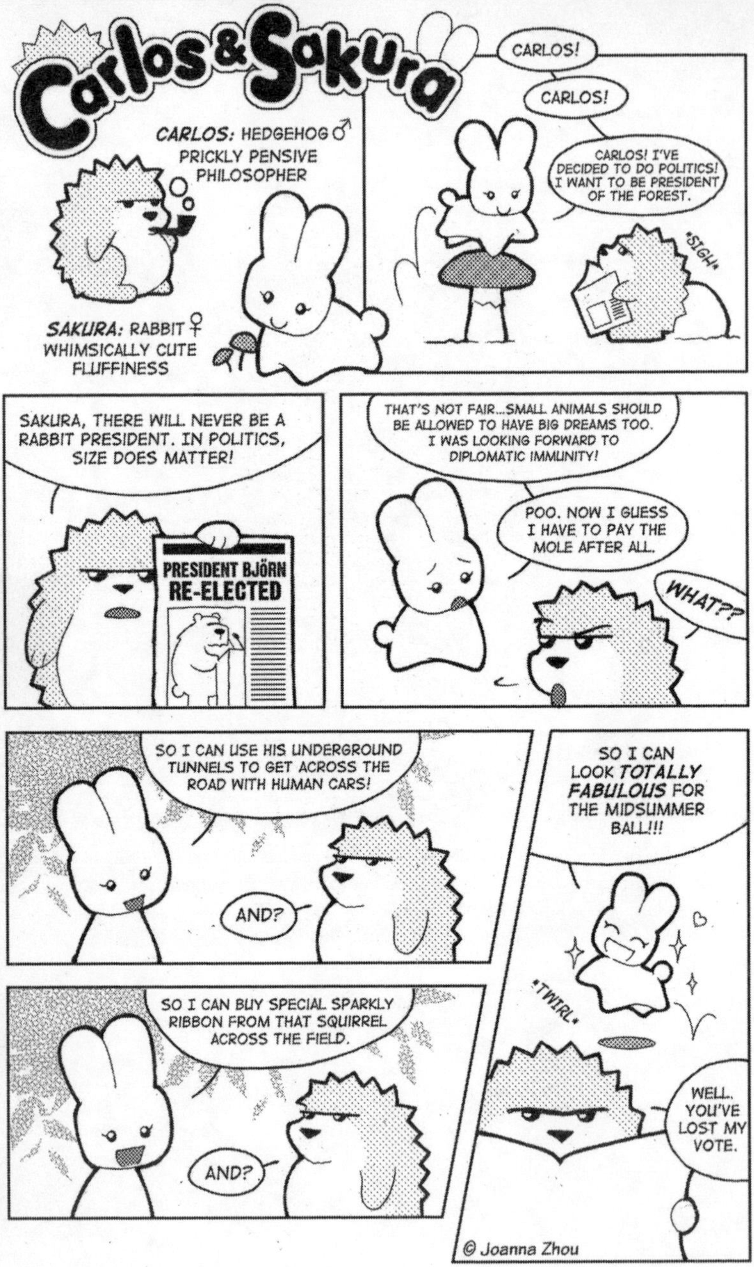
Carlos & Sakura
CARLOS: HEDGEHOG ♂
PRICKLY PENSIVE PHILOSOPHER
SAKURA: RABBIT ♀
WHIMSICALLY CUTE FLUFFINESS
CARLOS!
CARLOS!
CARLOS! I'VE DECIDED TO DO POLITICS! I WANT TO BE PRESIDENT OF THE FOREST.
SIGH
SAKURA, THERE WILL NEVER BE A RABBIT PRESIDENT. IN POLITICS, SIZE DOES MATTER!
PRESIDENT BJÖRN RE-ELECTED
THAT'S NOT FAIR...SMALL ANIMALS SHOULD BE ALLOWED TO HAVE BIG DREAMS TOO. I WAS LOOKING FORWARD TO DIPLOMATIC IMMUNITY!
POO. NOW I GUESS I HAVE TO PAY THE MOLE AFTER ALL.
WHAT??
SO I CAN USE HIS UNDERGROUND TUNNELS TO GET ACROSS THE ROAD WITH HUMAN CARS!
AND?
SO I CAN BUY SPECIAL SPARKLY RIBBON FROM THAT SQUIRREL ACROSS THE FIELD.
AND?
SO I CAN LOOK TOTALLY FABULOUS FOR THE MIDSUMMER BALL!!!
TWIRL
WELL. YOU'VE LOST MY VOTE.
© Joanna Zhou

Jinn Narration

by

Asia Alfasi

Date of birth: 20 April 1984

ASIA ALFASI

Born of Libyan parents, Asia moved to Scotland when she was eight, and currently lives in Birmingham. The first manga she ever read, which started it all for her, was *Iron Fist Chinmi*. Also, she says, 'I deeply admire Inoue Takehiko's work (*Slam Dunk, Vagabond*) for his amazing artistry – he manages both minimalist manga and intricate realism and switches between them effortlessly.'

Like Michiru (*Advent*) Morikawa, Asia was a participant in comic strip workshops run as part of the Midlands' *Hi8us Stripsearch* Scheme.

As an Arab Muslim girl living in the UK, she draws on some of her own experience in the creation of her manga series *Jinn Narration*, making its debut here. 'The recent avalanche of negativity between the Muslim world and the West has pushed me further, to try and reconcile the two. I understand both cultures and there is no need for a culture clash at all.'

'This is the first time (in my experience) that a Muslim girl wearing a *hijab* is a manga hero,' says Asia, understandably nervous. But also: 'The manga will explain better than I.'

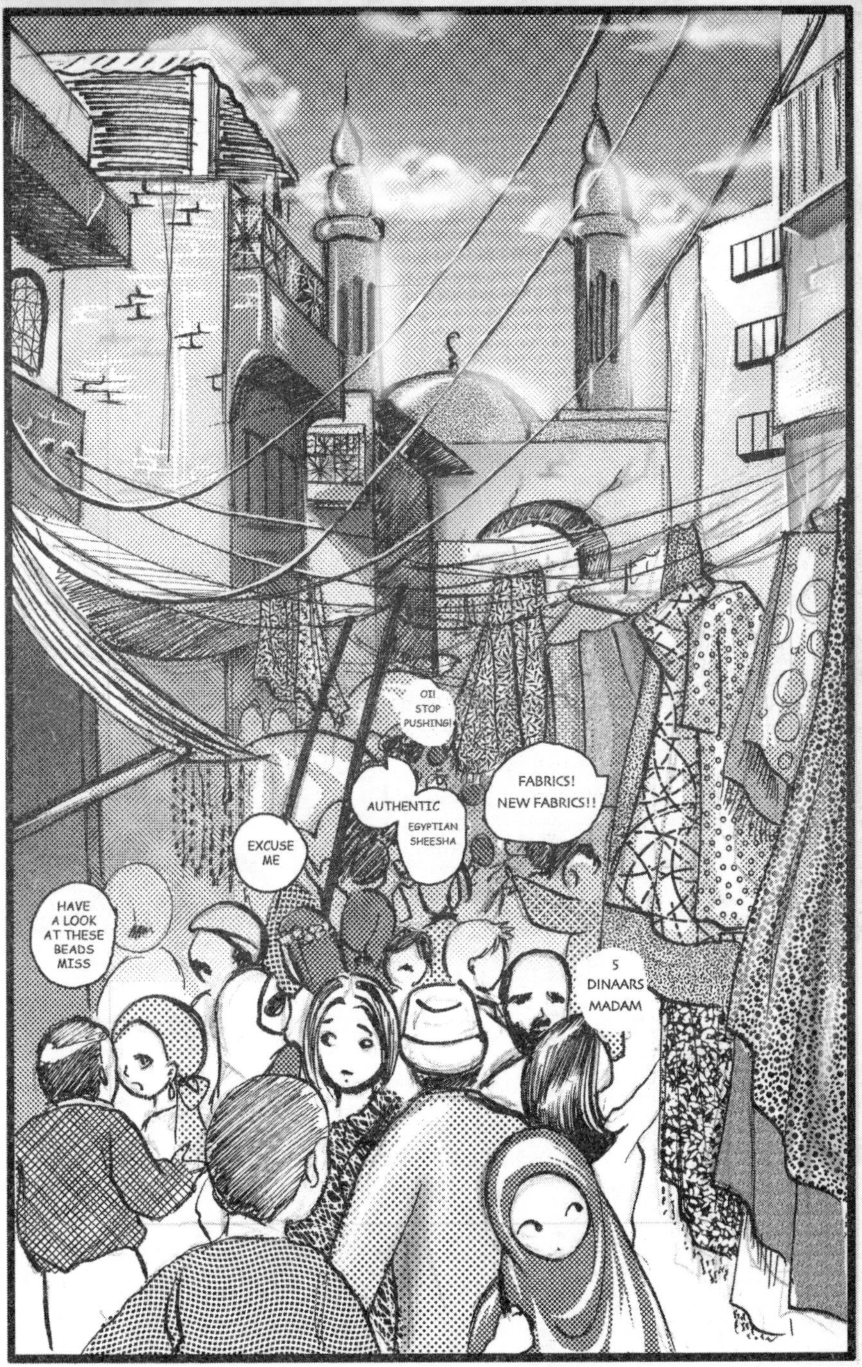
OI! STOP PUSHING!
AUTHENTIC EGYPTIAN SHEESHA
FABRICS! NEW FABRICS!!
EXCUSE ME
HAVE A LOOK AT THESE BEADS MISS
5 DINAARS MADAM

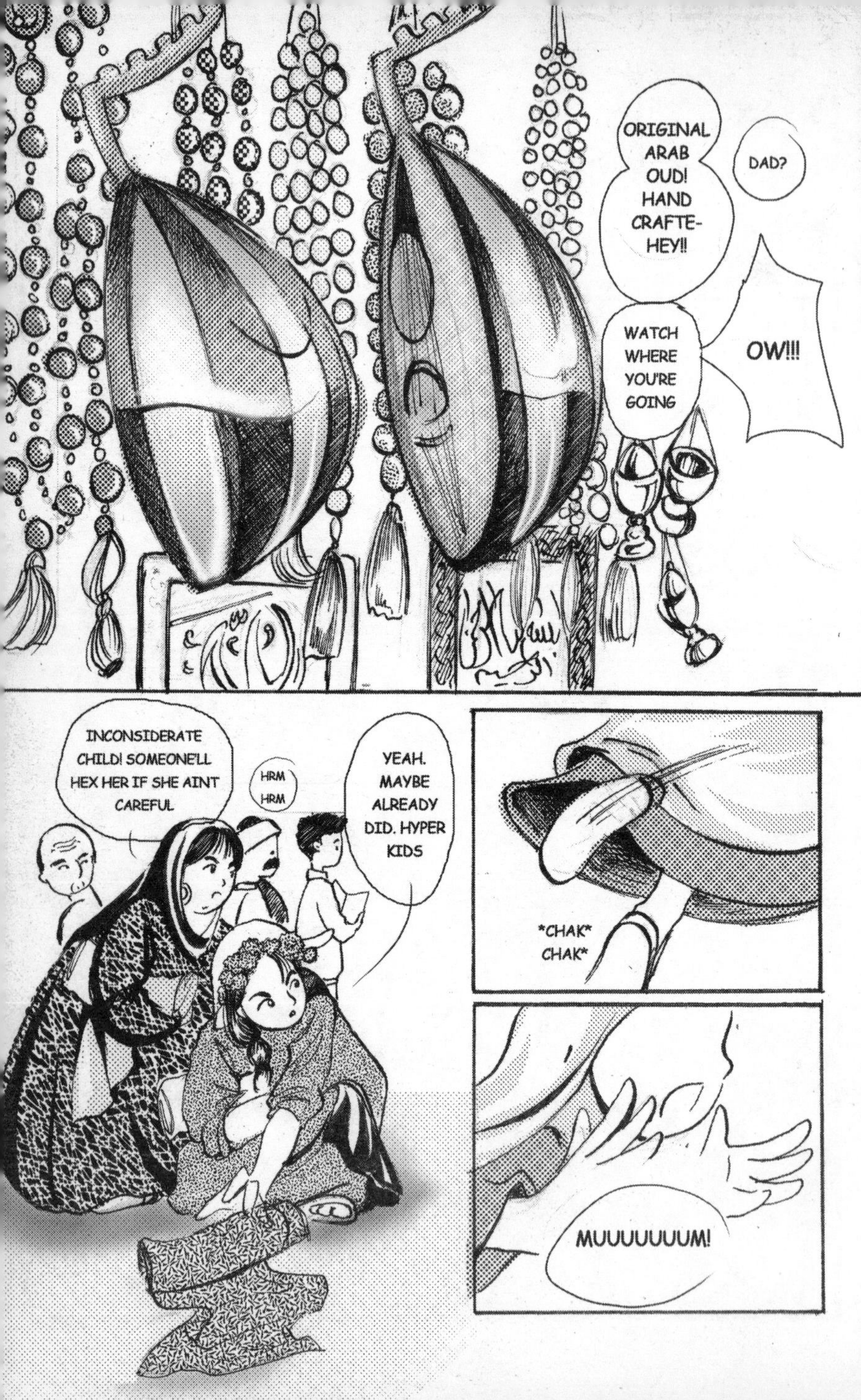
ORIGINAL ARAB OUD! HAND CRAFTE- HEY!!
DAD?
WATCH WHERE YOU'RE GOING
OW!!!
INCONSIDERATE CHILD! SOMEONE'LL HEX HER IF SHE AINT CAREFUL
HRM HRM
YEAH. MAYBE ALREADY DID. HYPER KIDS
CHAK CHAK*
MUUUUUUUM!

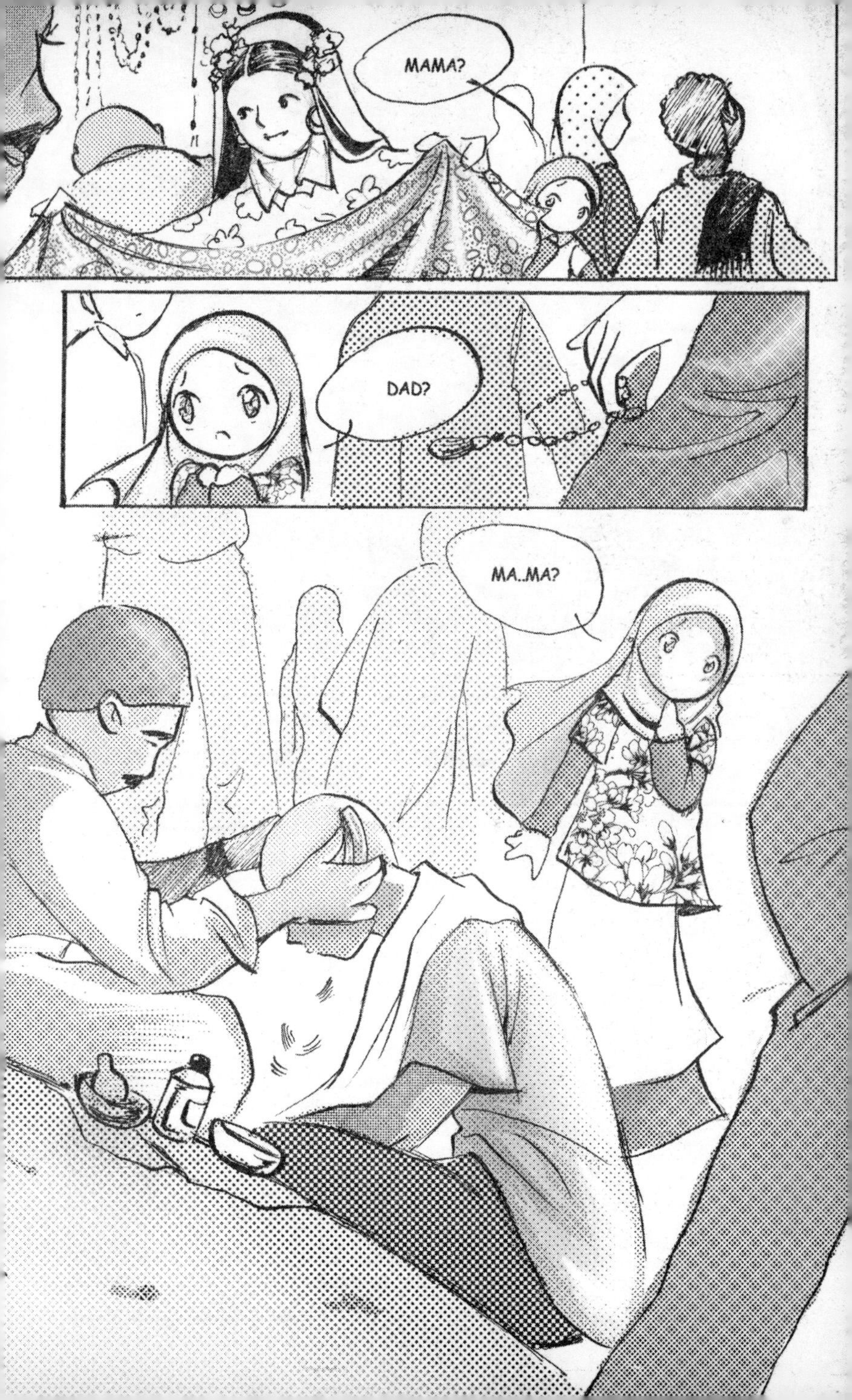
MAMA?
DAD?
MA..MA?

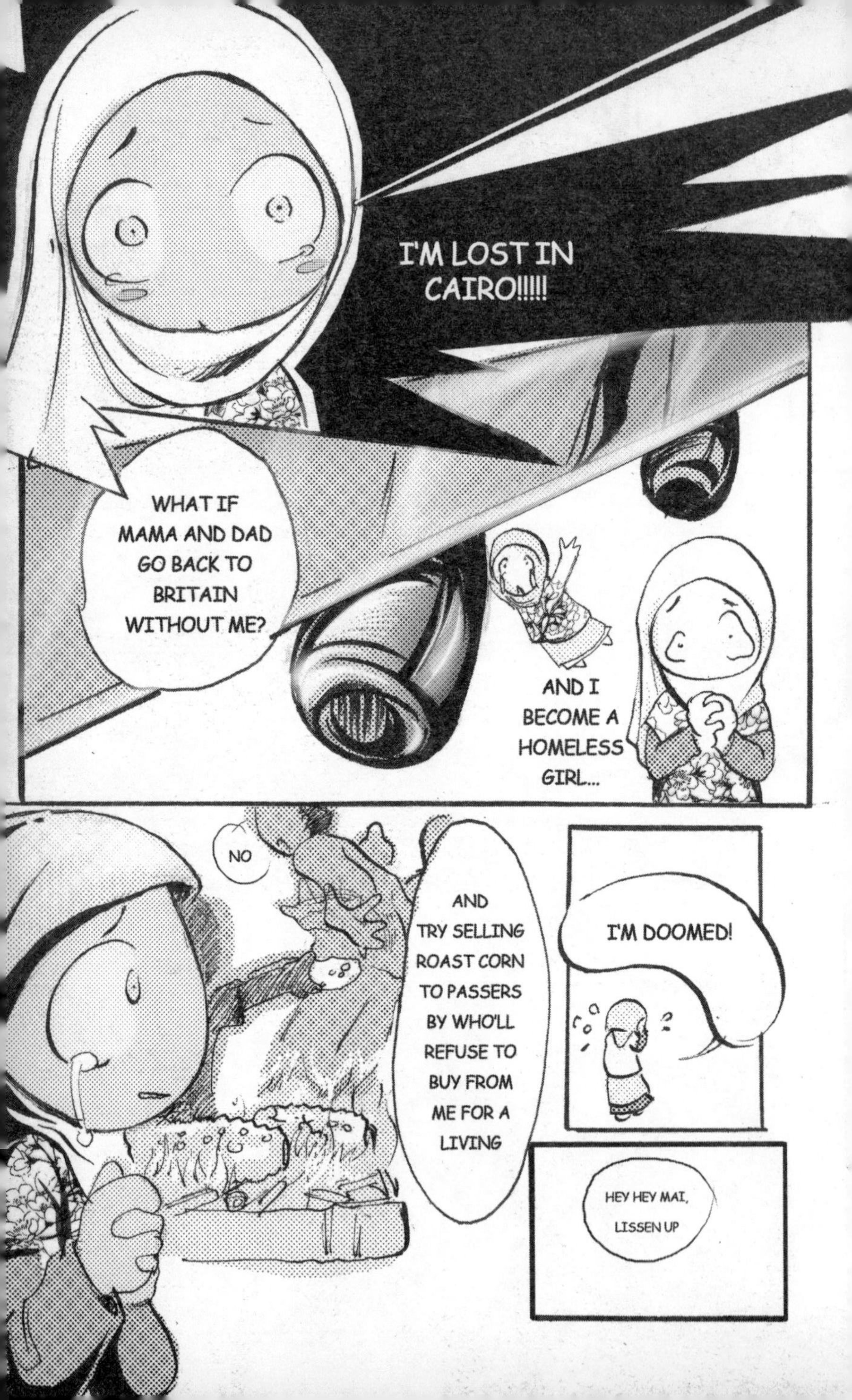
I'M LOST IN CAIRO!!!!!
WHAT IF MAMA AND DAD GO BACK TO BRITAIN WITHOUT ME?
AND I BECOME A HOMELESS GIRL...
NO
AND TRY SELLING ROAST CORN TO PASSERS BY WHO'LL REFUSE TO BUY FROM ME FOR A LIVING
I'M DOOMED!
HEY HEY MAI, LISSEN UP

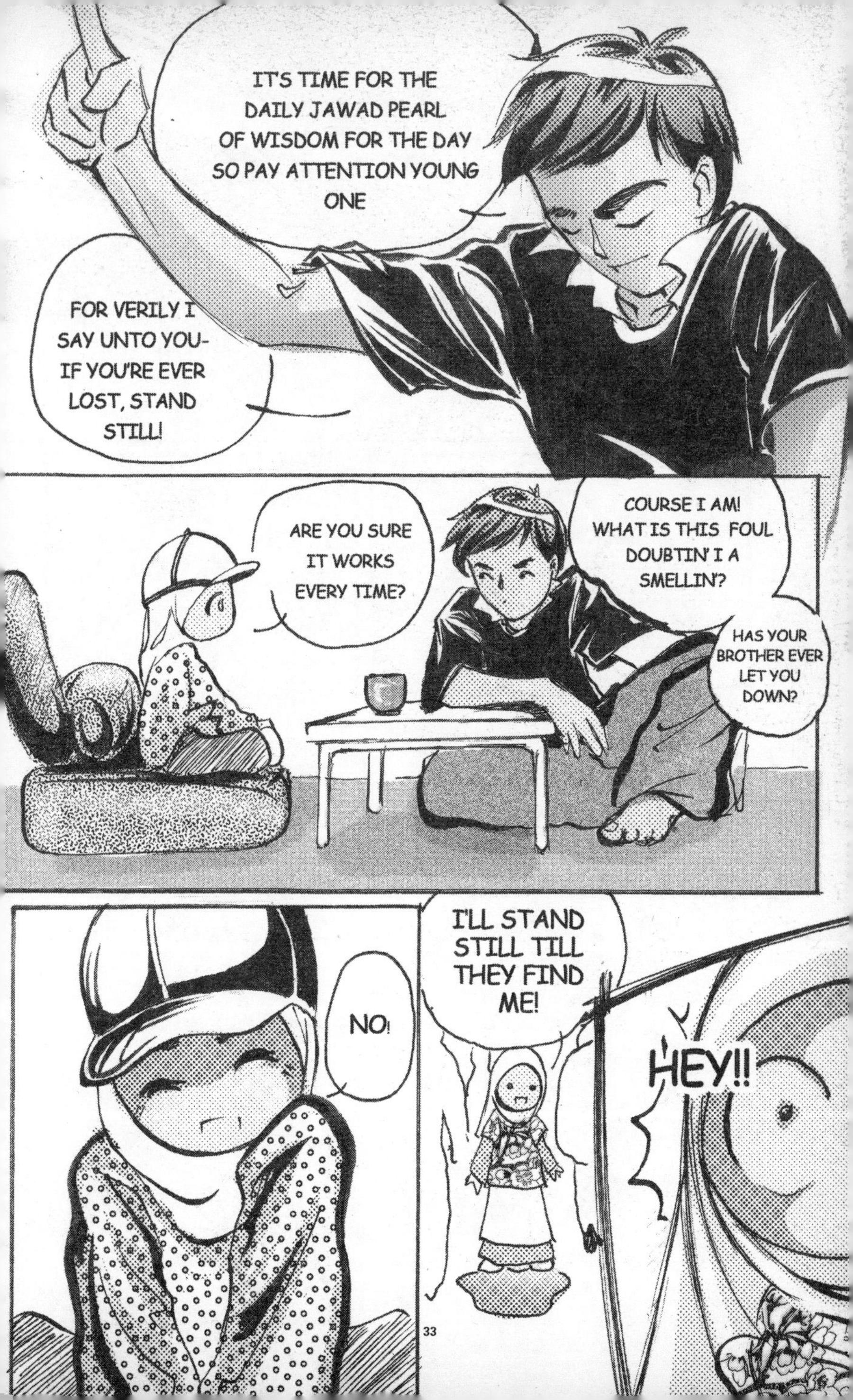
IT'S TIME FOR THE DAILY JAWAD PEARL OF WISDOM FOR THE DAY SO PAY ATTENTION YOUNG ONE
FOR VERILY I SAY UNTO YOU- IF YOU'RE EVER LOST, STAND STILL!
ARE YOU SURE IT WORKS EVERY TIME?
COURSE I AM! WHAT IS THIS FOUL DOUBTIN' I A SMELLIN'?
HAS YOUR BROTHER EVER LET YOU DOWN?
NO!
I'LL STAND STILL TILL THEY FIND ME!
HEY!!

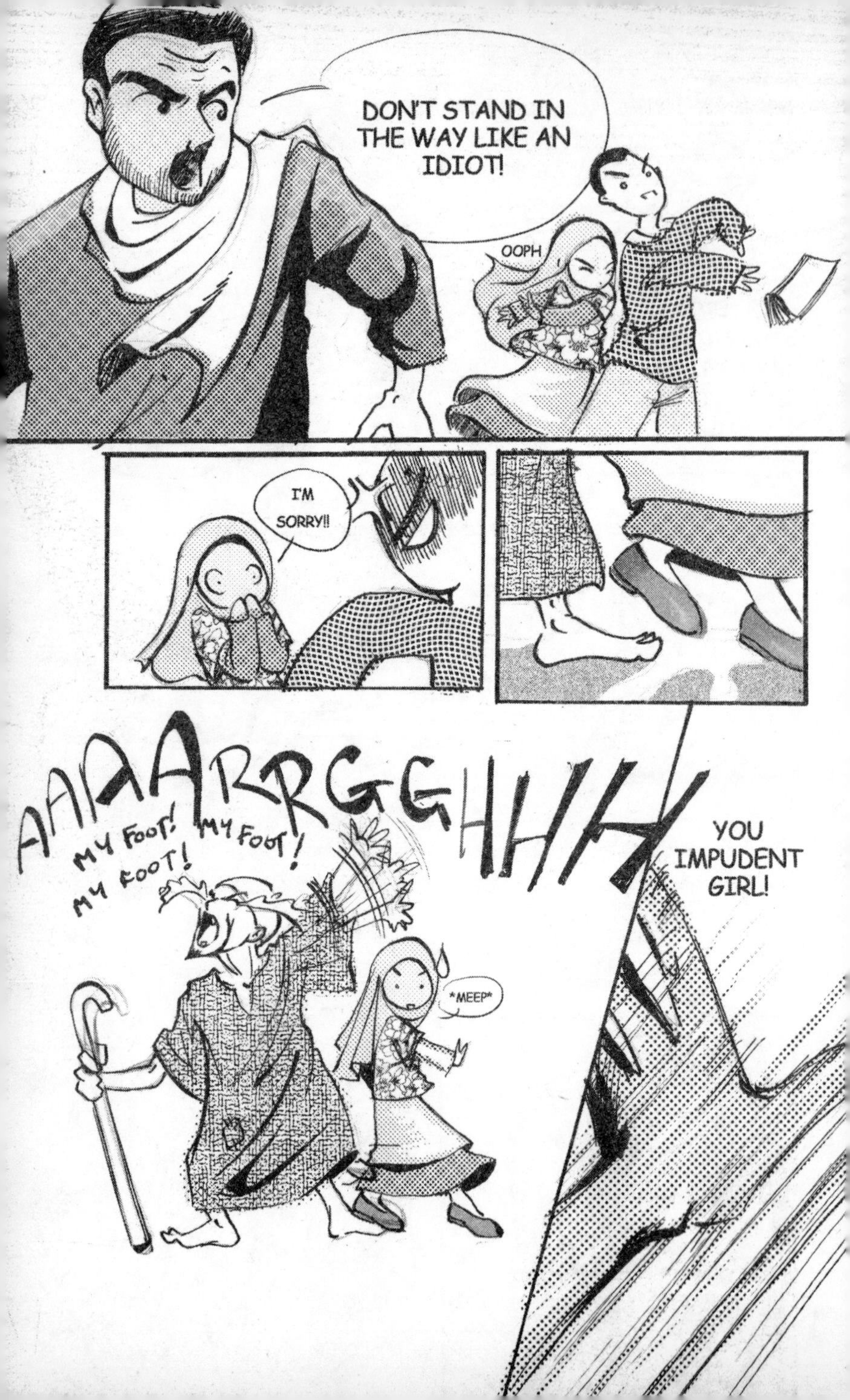
DON'T STAND IN THE WAY LIKE AN IDIOT!
OOPH
I'M SORRY!!
AAAARRGGHHHH
MY FOOT! MY FOOT! MY FOOT!
MEEP
YOU IMPUDENT GIRL!

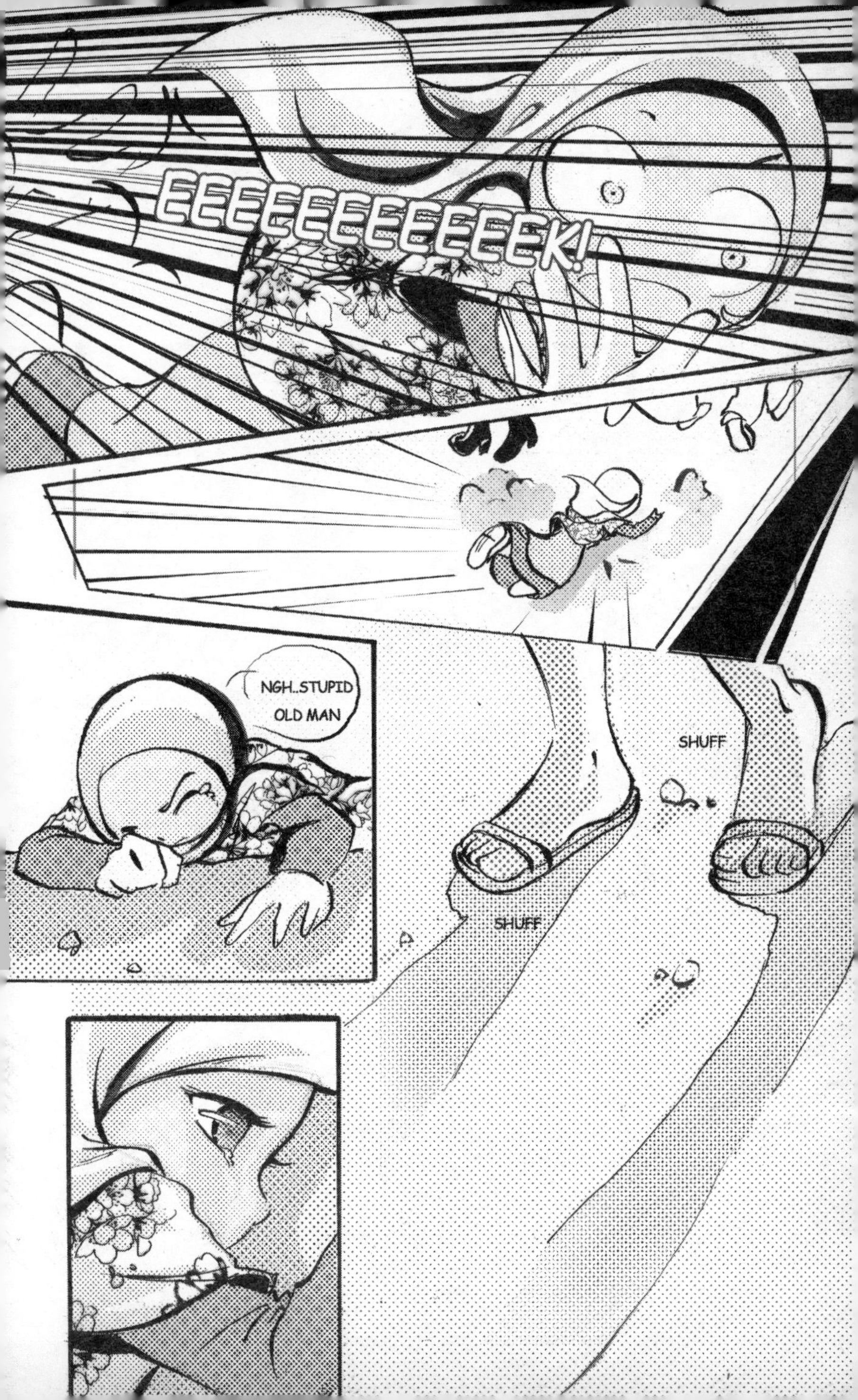
EEEEEEEEEEEEEK!
NGH..STUPID OLD MAN
SHUFF
SHUFF

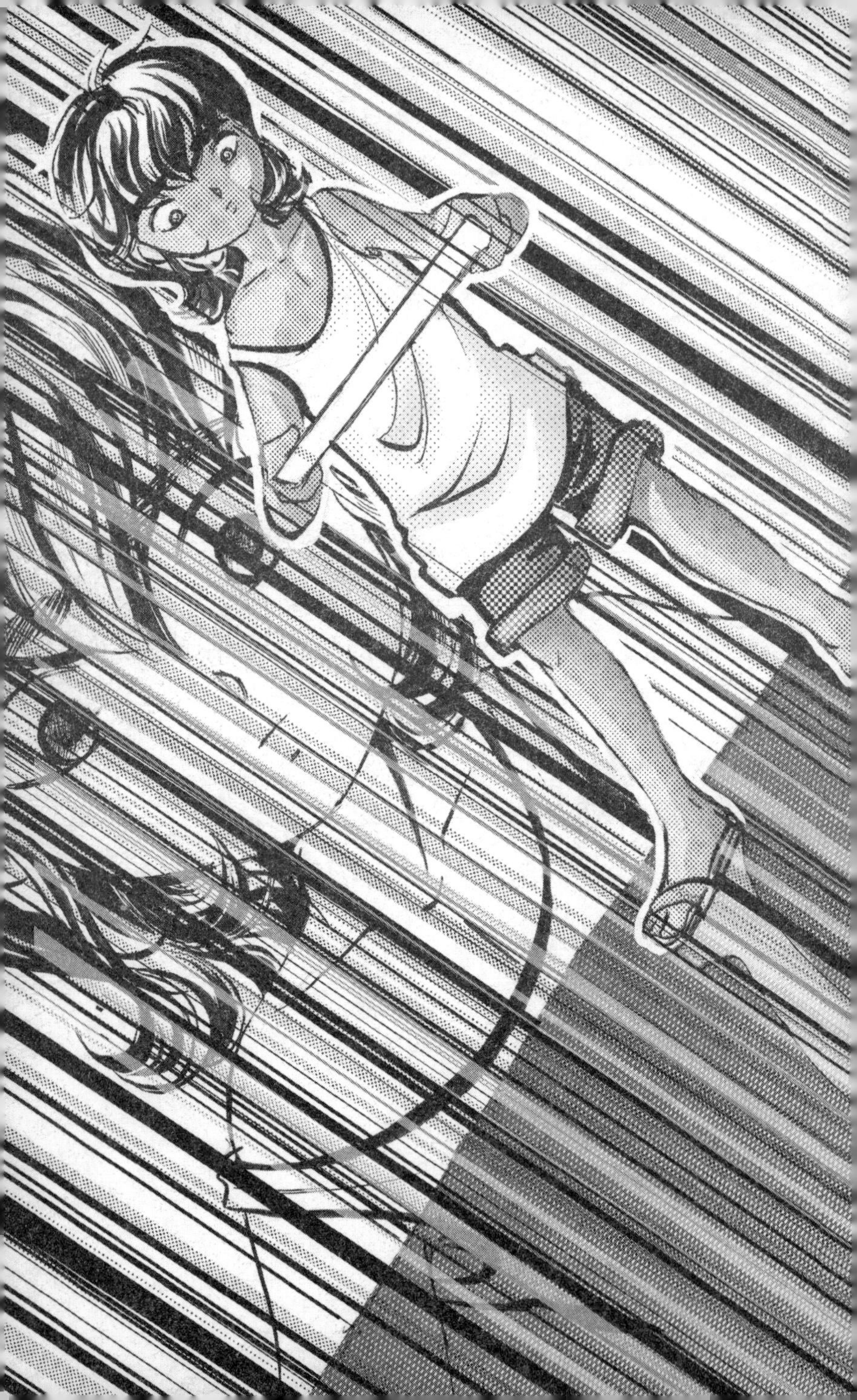

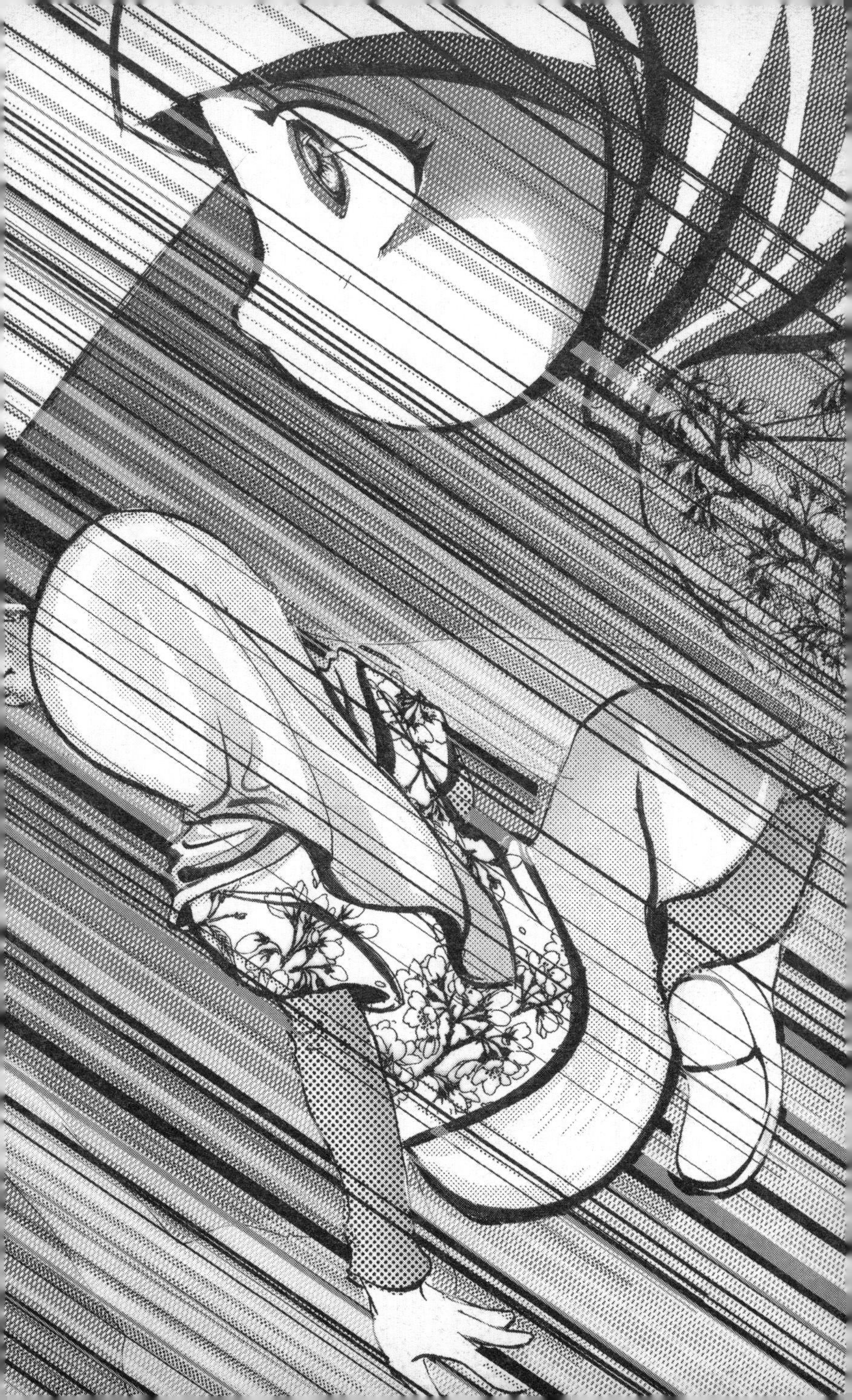

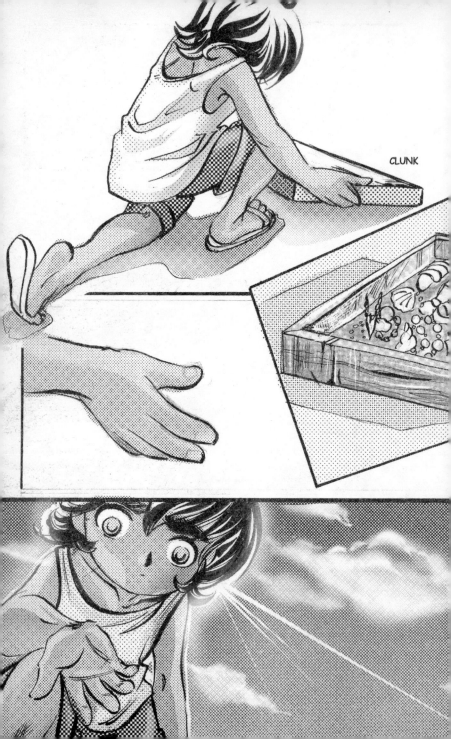

CLUNK

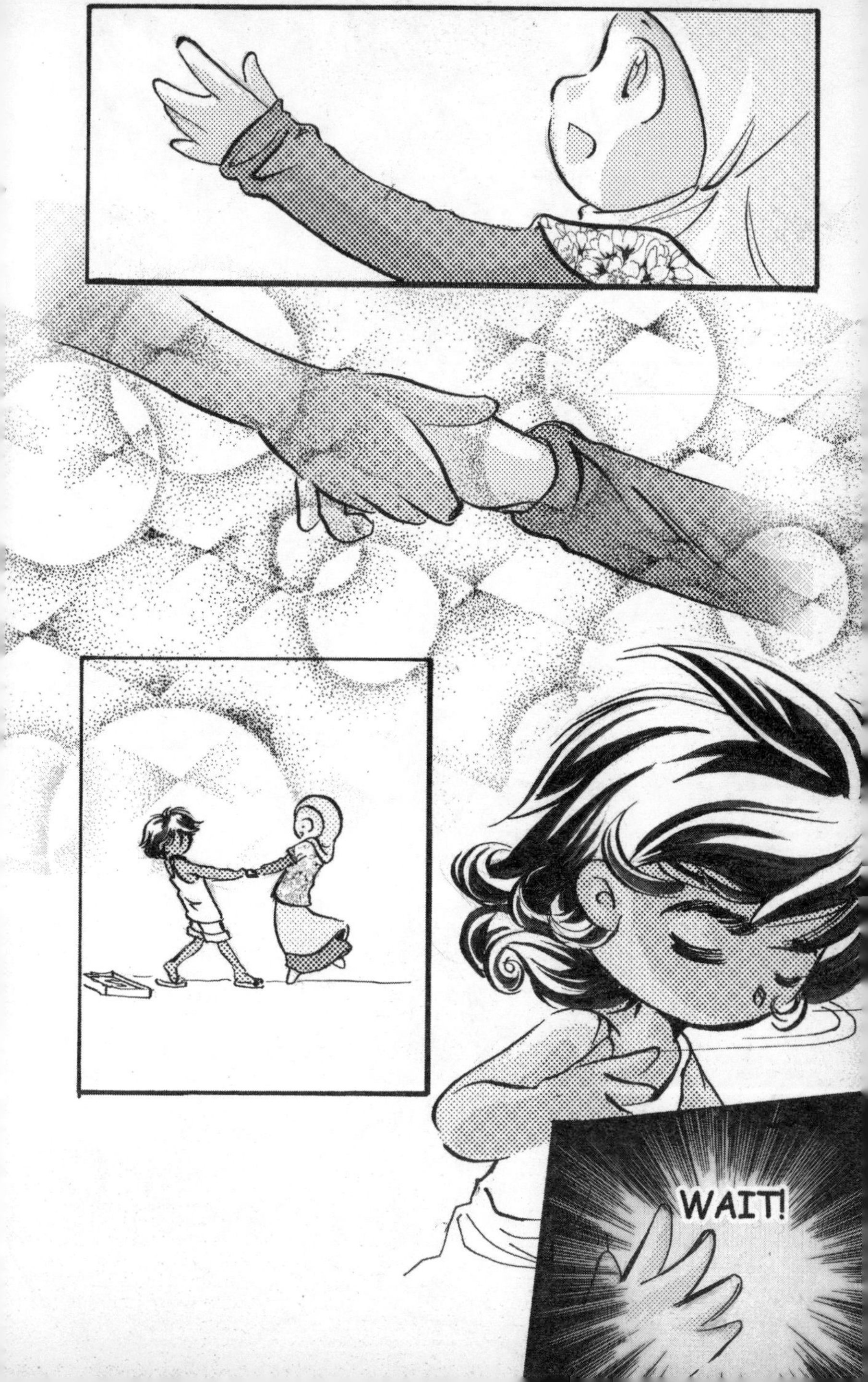
WAIT!

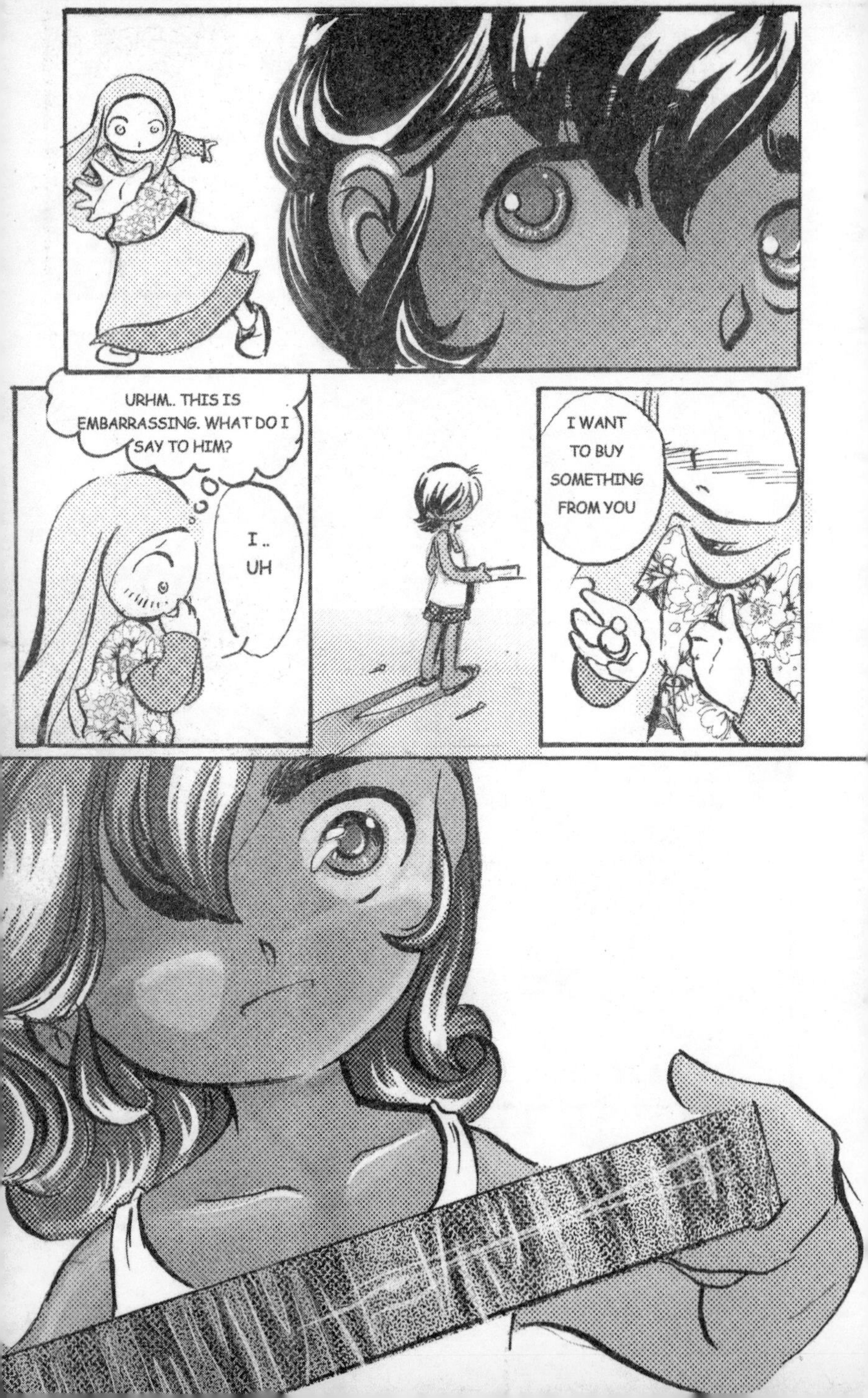
URHM.. THIS IS EMBARRASSING. WHAT DO I SAY TO HIM?
I .. UH
I WANT TO BUY SOMETHING FROM YOU

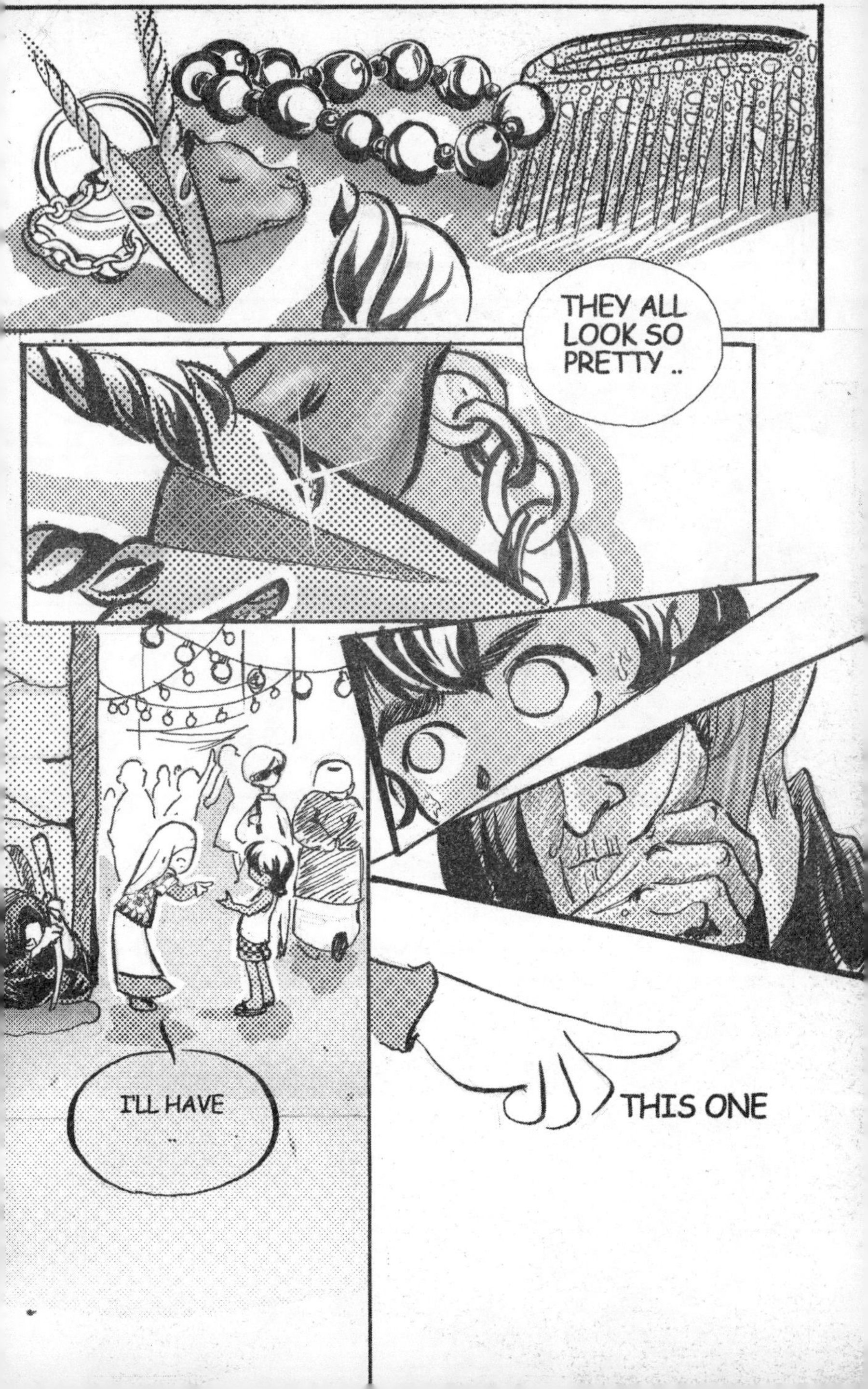
THEY ALL LOOK SO PRETTY ..
I'LL HAVE ..
THIS ONE

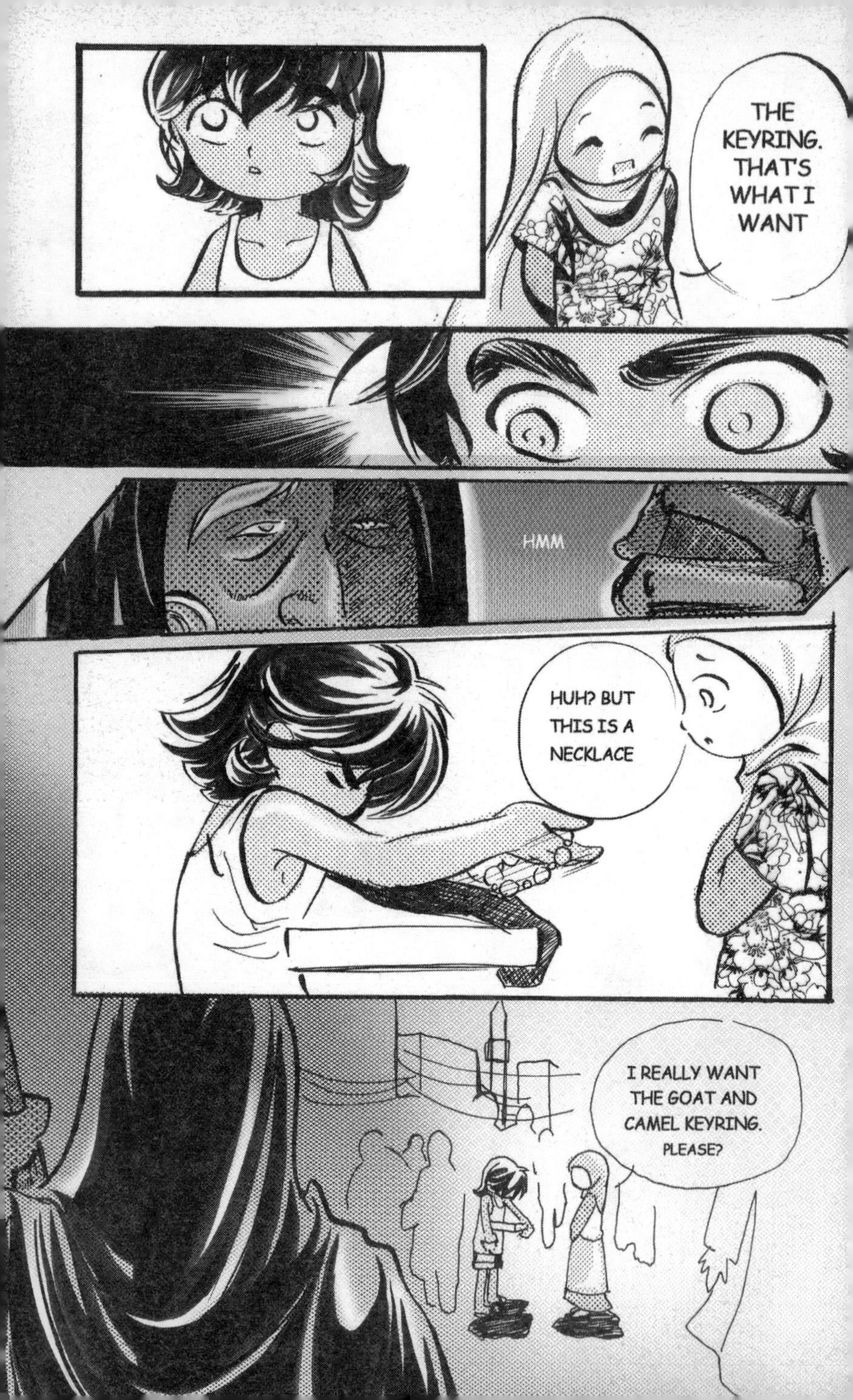
THE KEYRING. THAT'S WHAT I WANT
HMM
HUH? BUT THIS IS A NECKLACE
I REALLY WANT THE GOAT AND CAMEL KEYRING. PLEASE?

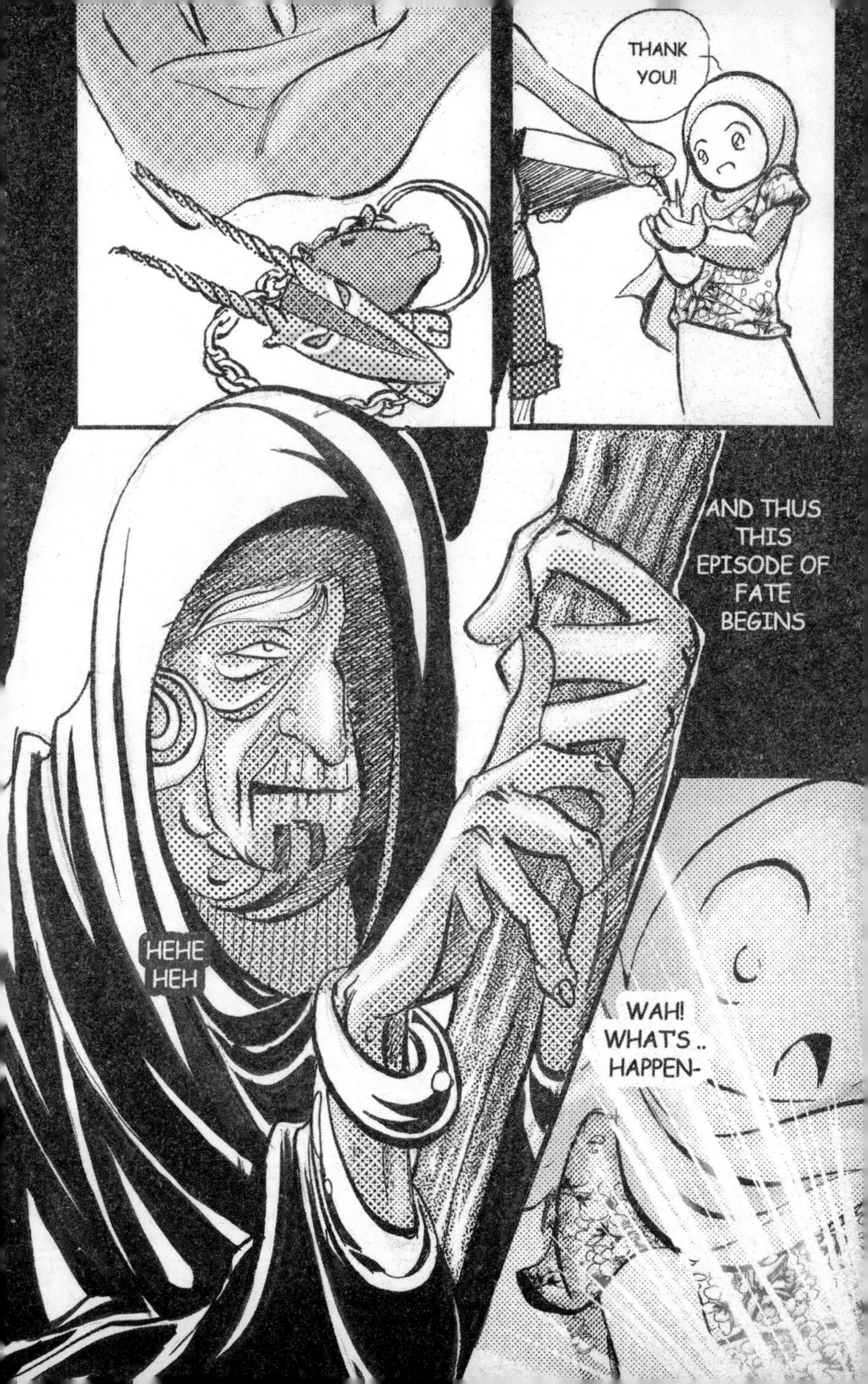
THANK YOU!
AND THUS THIS EPISODE OF FATE BEGINS
HEHE HEH
WAH! WHAT'S .. HAPPEN-

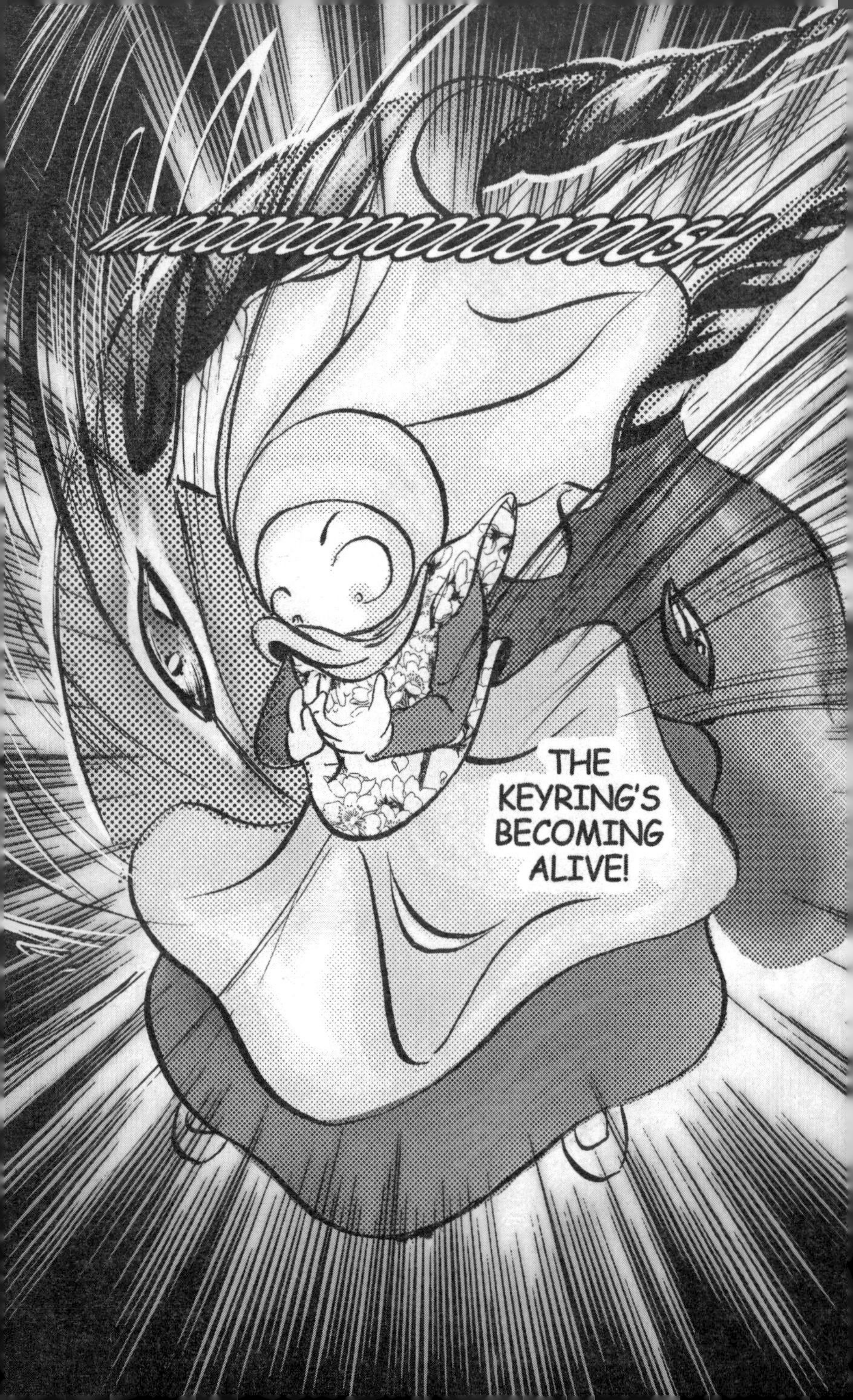
WHOOOOOOOOOOOOOOOSH
THE KEYRING'S BECOMING ALIVE!

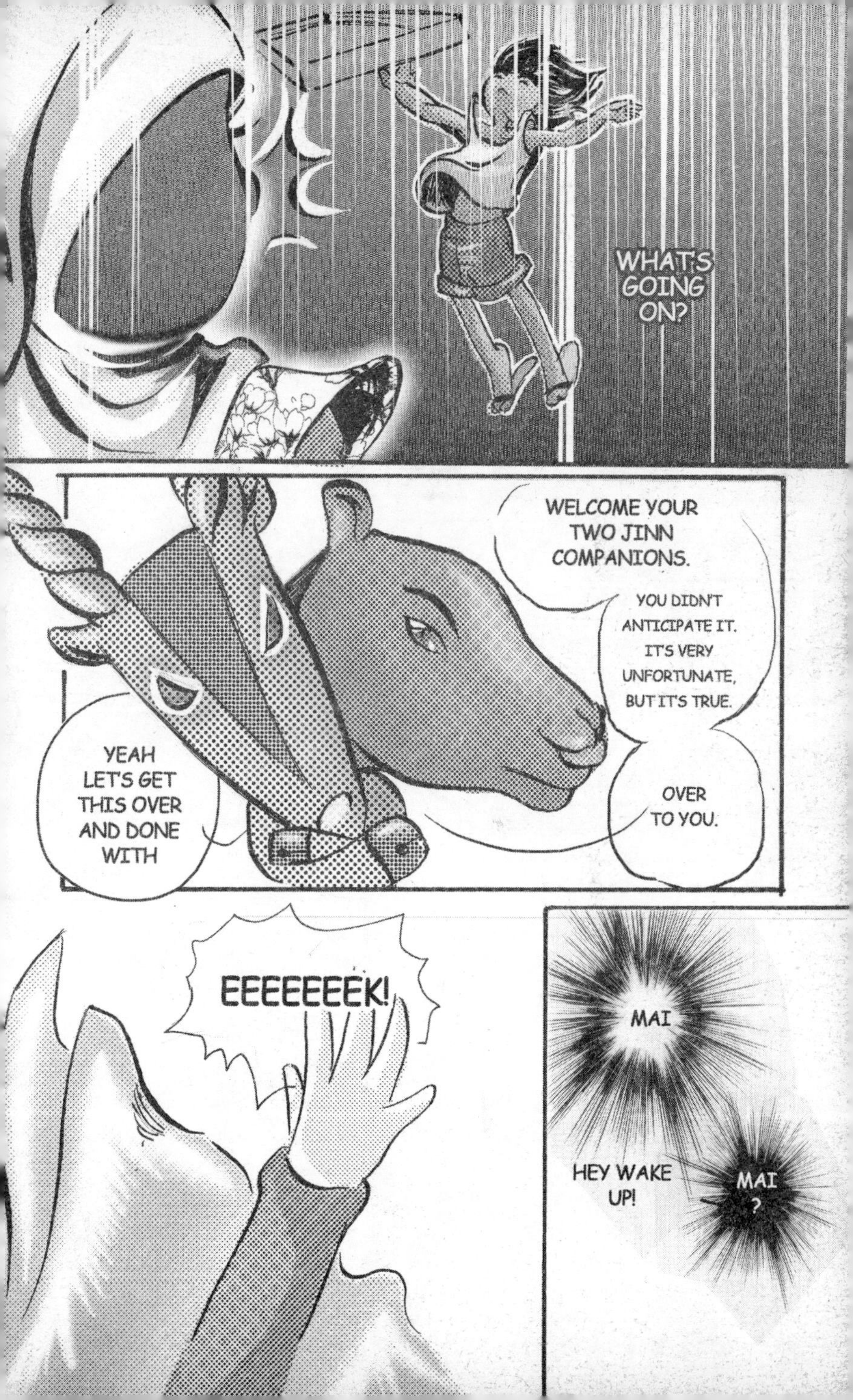
WHAT'S GOING ON?
YEAH LET'S GET THIS OVER AND DONE WITH
WELCOME YOUR TWO JINN COMPANIONS.
YOU DIDN'T ANTICIPATE IT. IT'S VERY UNFORTUNATE, BUT IT'S TRUE.
OVER TO YOU.
EEEEEEEK!
MAI
HEY WAKE UP!
MAI ?

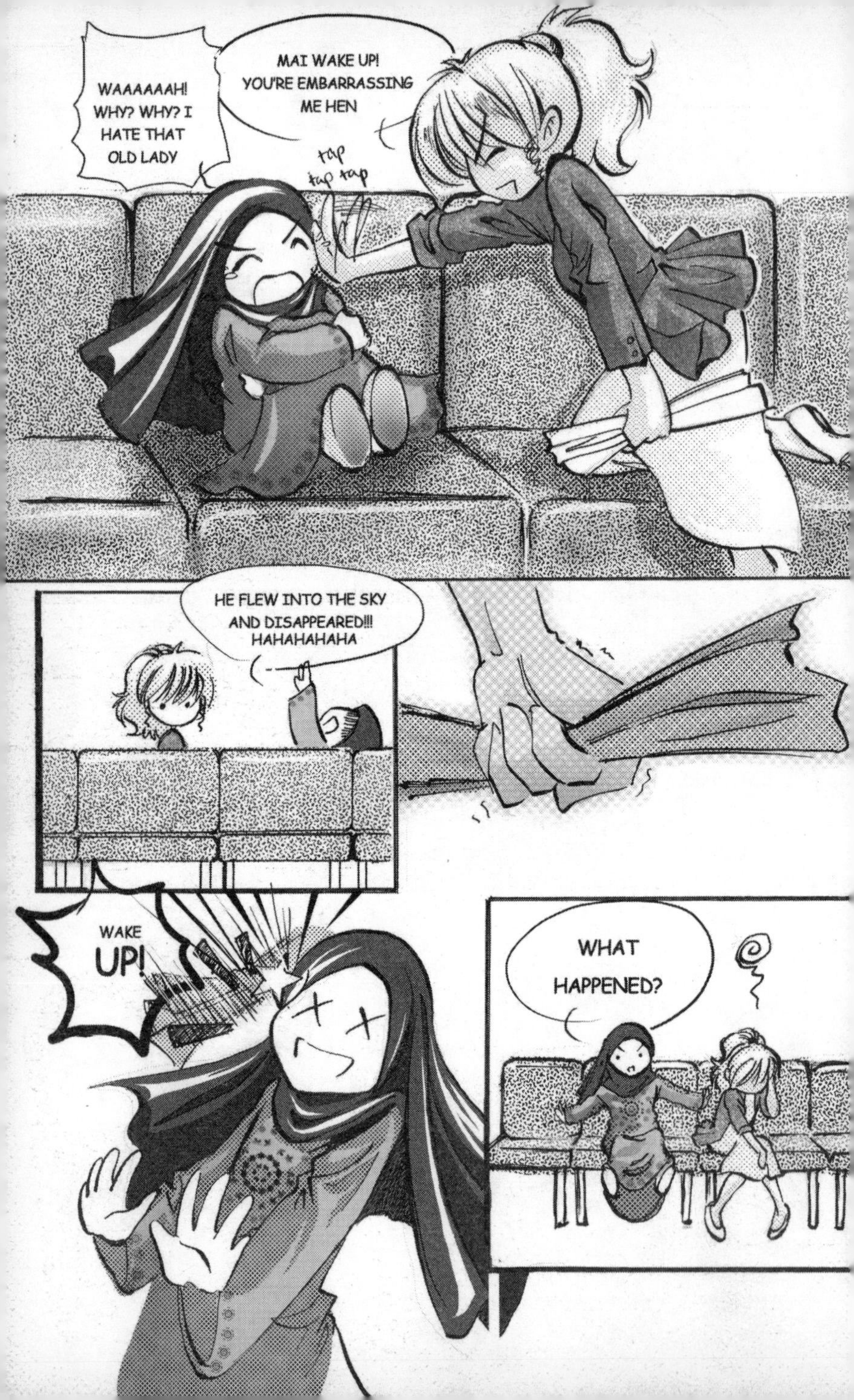
WAAAAAAH! WHY? WHY? I HATE THAT OLD LADY
MAI WAKE UP! YOU'RE EMBARRASSING ME HEN
tap tap tap
HE FLEW INTO THE SKY AND DISAPPEARED!!! HAHAHAHAHA
WAKE UP!
WHAT HAPPENED?

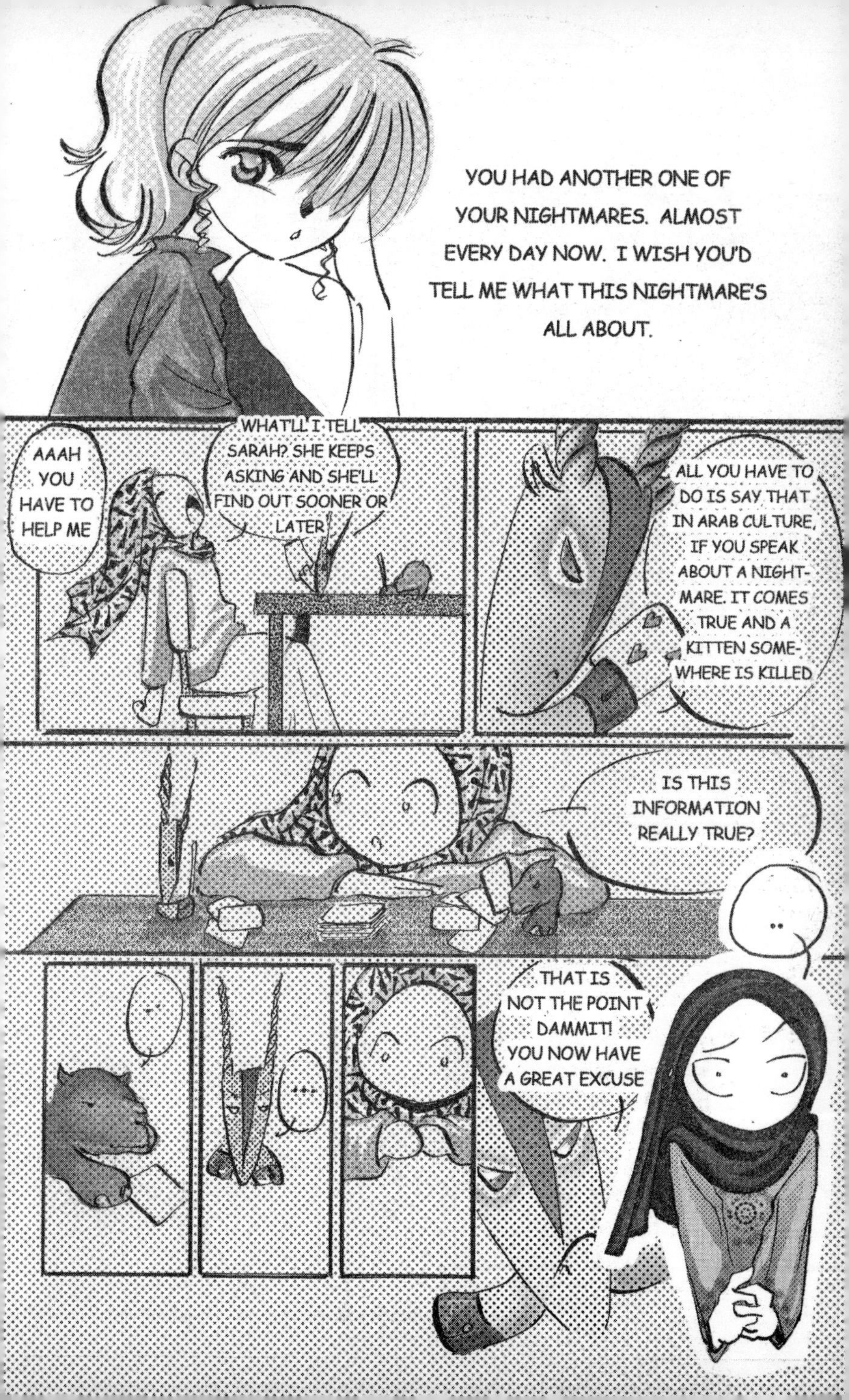
YOU HAD ANOTHER ONE OF YOUR NIGHTMARES. ALMOST EVERY DAY NOW. I WISH YOU'D TELL ME WHAT THIS NIGHTMARE'S ALL ABOUT.
AAAH YOU HAVE TO HELP ME
WHAT'LL I TELL SARAH? SHE KEEPS ASKING AND SHE'LL FIND OUT SOONER OR LATER
ALL YOU HAVE TO DO IS SAY THAT IN ARAB CULTURE, IF YOU SPEAK ABOUT A NIGHT-MARE. IT COMES TRUE AND A KITTEN SOME-WHERE IS KILLED
IS THIS INFORMATION REALLY TRUE?
THAT IS NOT THE POINT DAMMIT! YOU NOW HAVE A GREAT EXCUSE

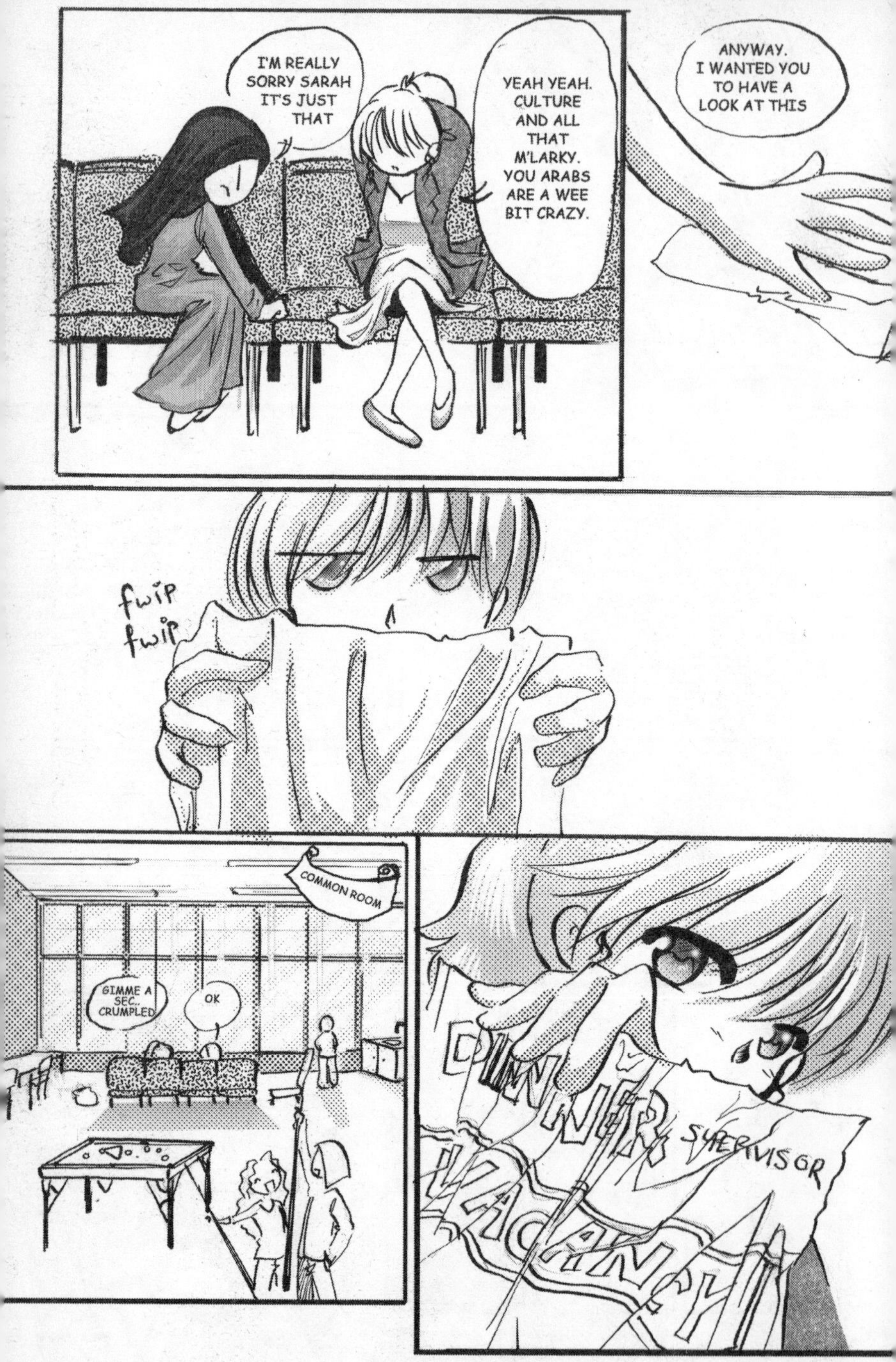
I'M REALLY SORRY SARAH IT'S JUST THAT
YEAH YEAH. CULTURE AND ALL THAT M'LARKY. YOU ARABS ARE A WEE BIT CRAZY.
ANYWAY. I WANTED YOU TO HAVE A LOOK AT THIS
fwip fwip
COMMON ROOM
GIMME A SEC. CRUMPLED
OK
DINNER SUPERVISOR VACANCY

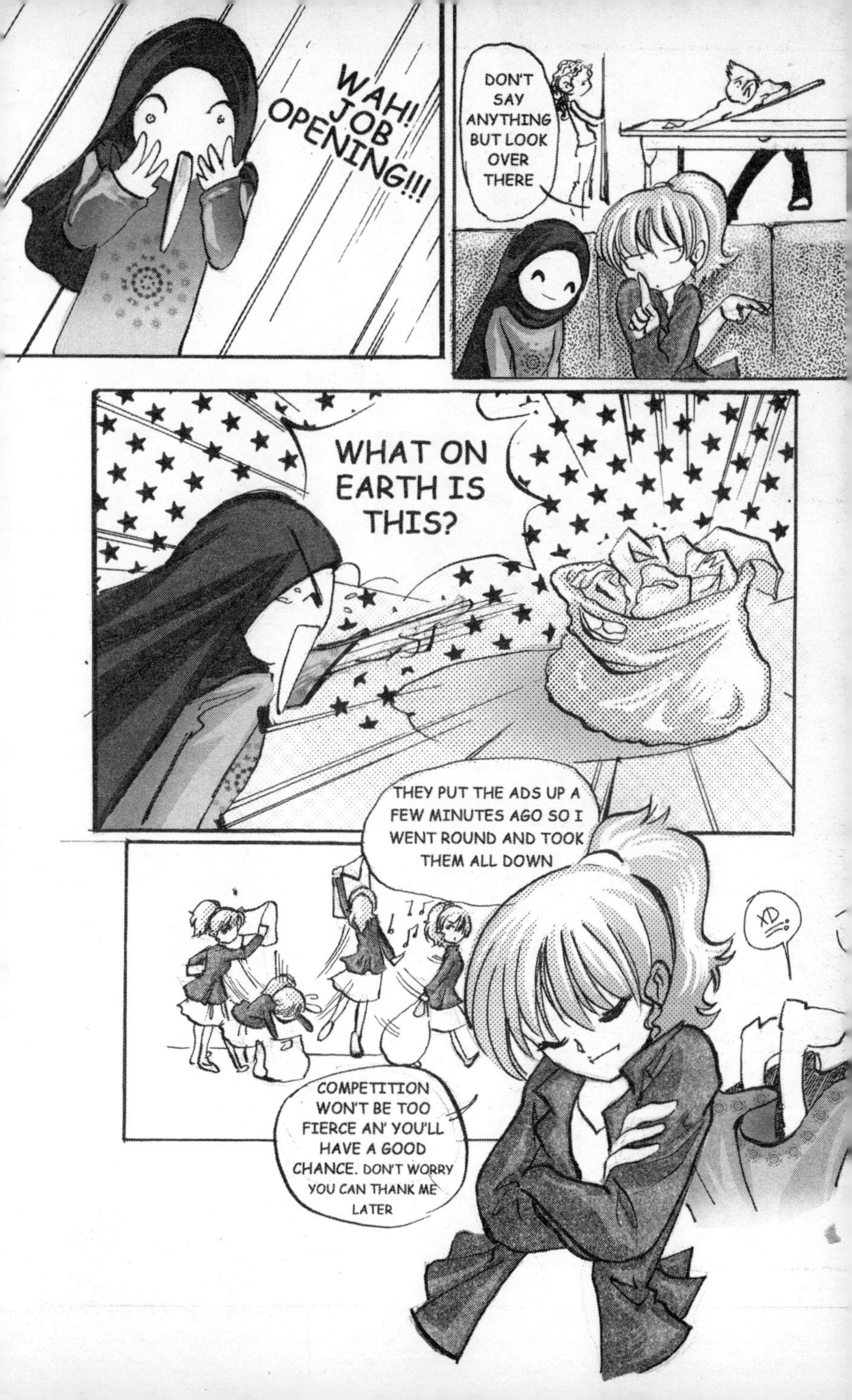
WAH! JOB OPENING!!!
DON'T SAY ANYTHING BUT LOOK OVER THERE
WHAT ON EARTH IS THIS?
THEY PUT THE ADS UP A FEW MINUTES AGO SO I WENT ROUND AND TOOK THEM ALL DOWN
XD
COMPETITION WON'T BE TOO FIERCE AN' YOU'LL HAVE A GOOD CHANCE. DON'T WORRY YOU CAN THANK ME LATER

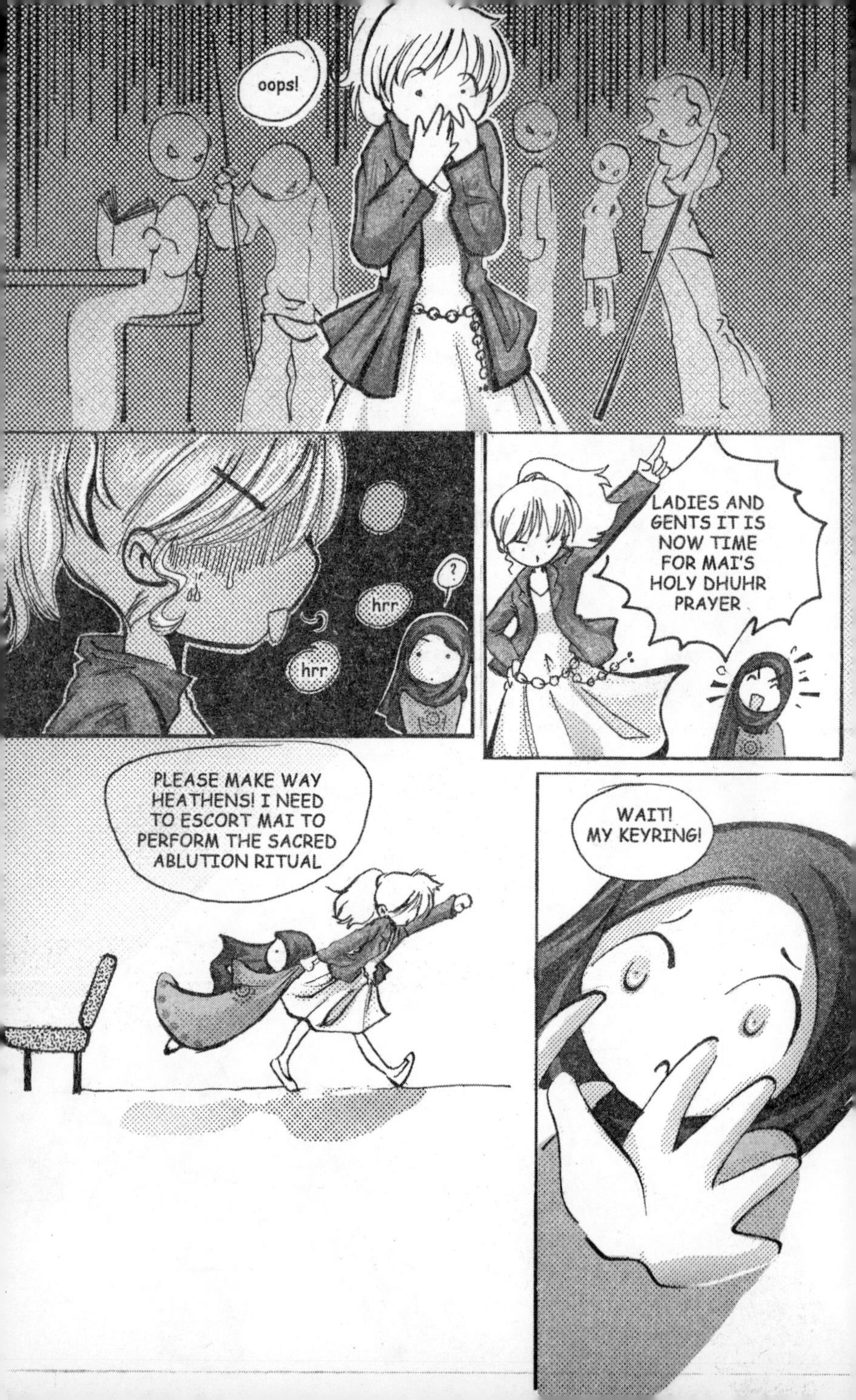
oops!
?
hrr
hrr
LADIES AND GENTS IT IS NOW TIME FOR MAI'S HOLY DHUHR PRAYER
PLEASE MAKE WAY HEATHENS! I NEED TO ESCORT MAI TO PERFORM THE SACRED ABLUTION RITUAL
WAIT! MY KEYRING!

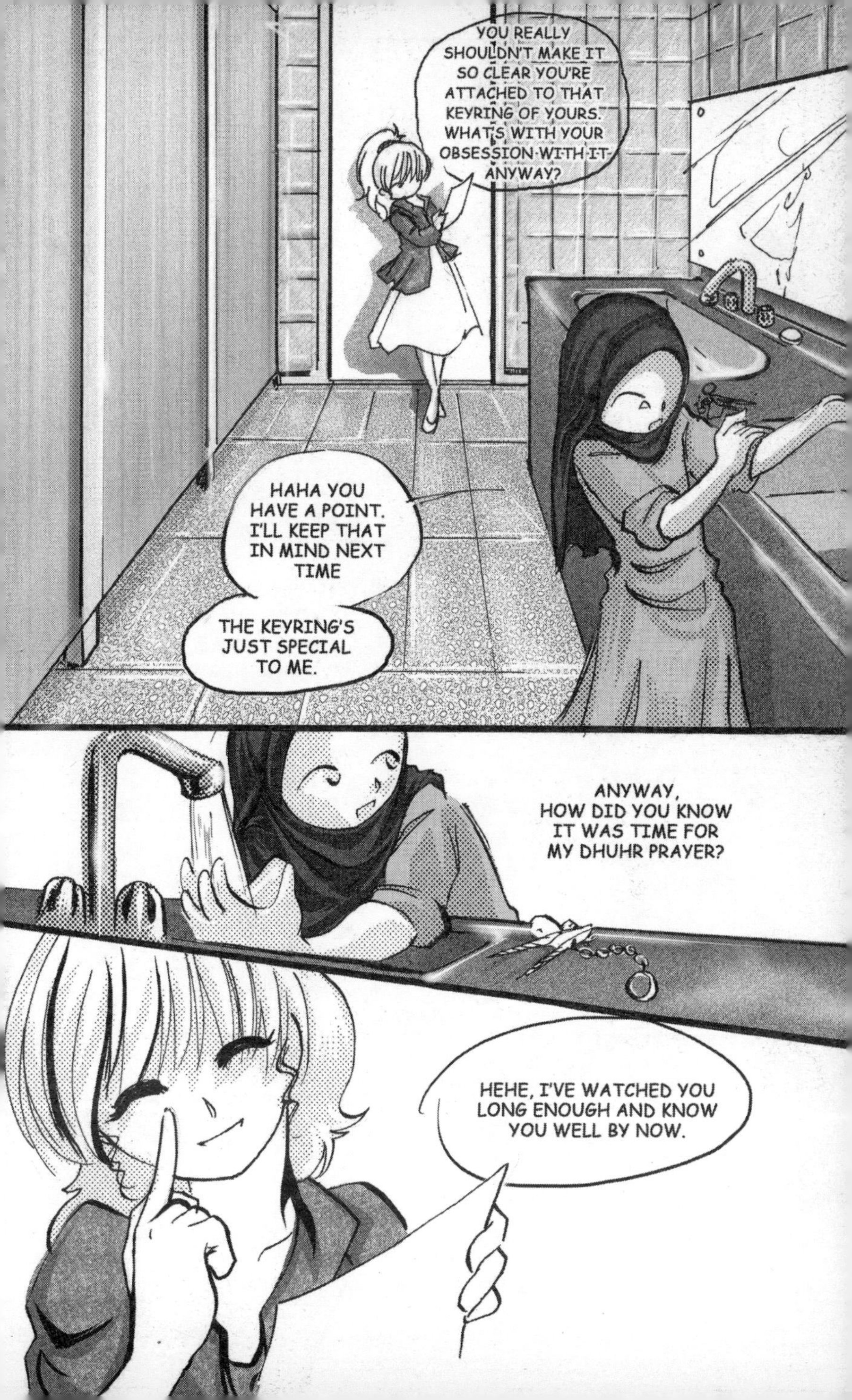
YOU REALLY SHOULDN'T MAKE IT SO CLEAR YOU'RE ATTACHED TO THAT KEYRING OF YOURS. WHAT'S WITH YOUR OBSESSION WITH IT ANYWAY?
HAHA YOU HAVE A POINT. I'LL KEEP THAT IN MIND NEXT TIME
THE KEYRING'S JUST SPECIAL TO ME.
ANYWAY, HOW DID YOU KNOW IT WAS TIME FOR MY DHUHR PRAYER?
HEHE, I'VE WATCHED YOU LONG ENOUGH AND KNOW YOU WELL BY NOW.

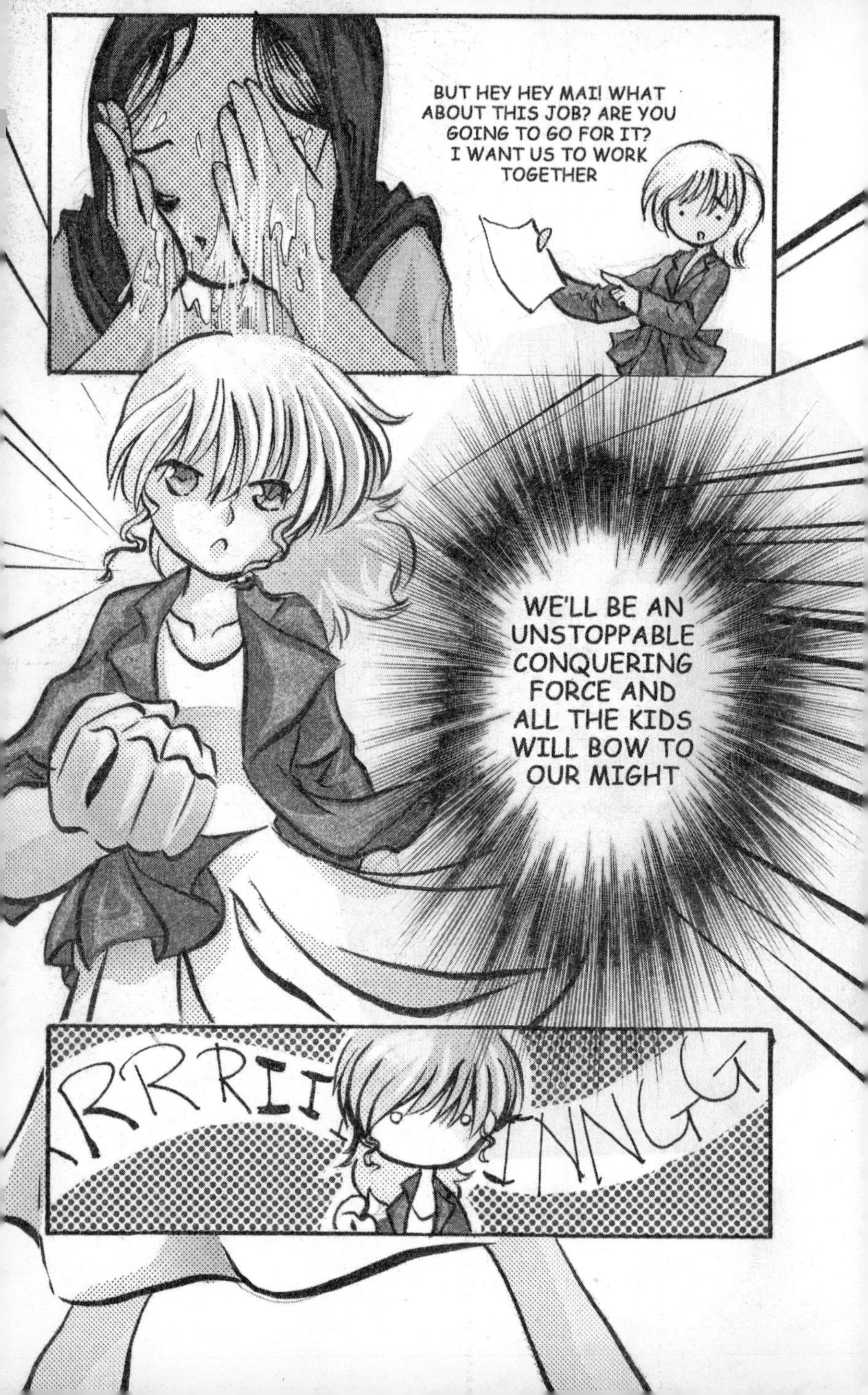
BUT HEY HEY MAI! WHAT ABOUT THIS JOB? ARE YOU GOING TO GO FOR IT? I WANT US TO WORK TOGETHER
WE'LL BE AN UNSTOPPABLE CONQUERING FORCE AND ALL THE KIDS WILL BOW TO OUR MIGHT
RRRIIIINNGG

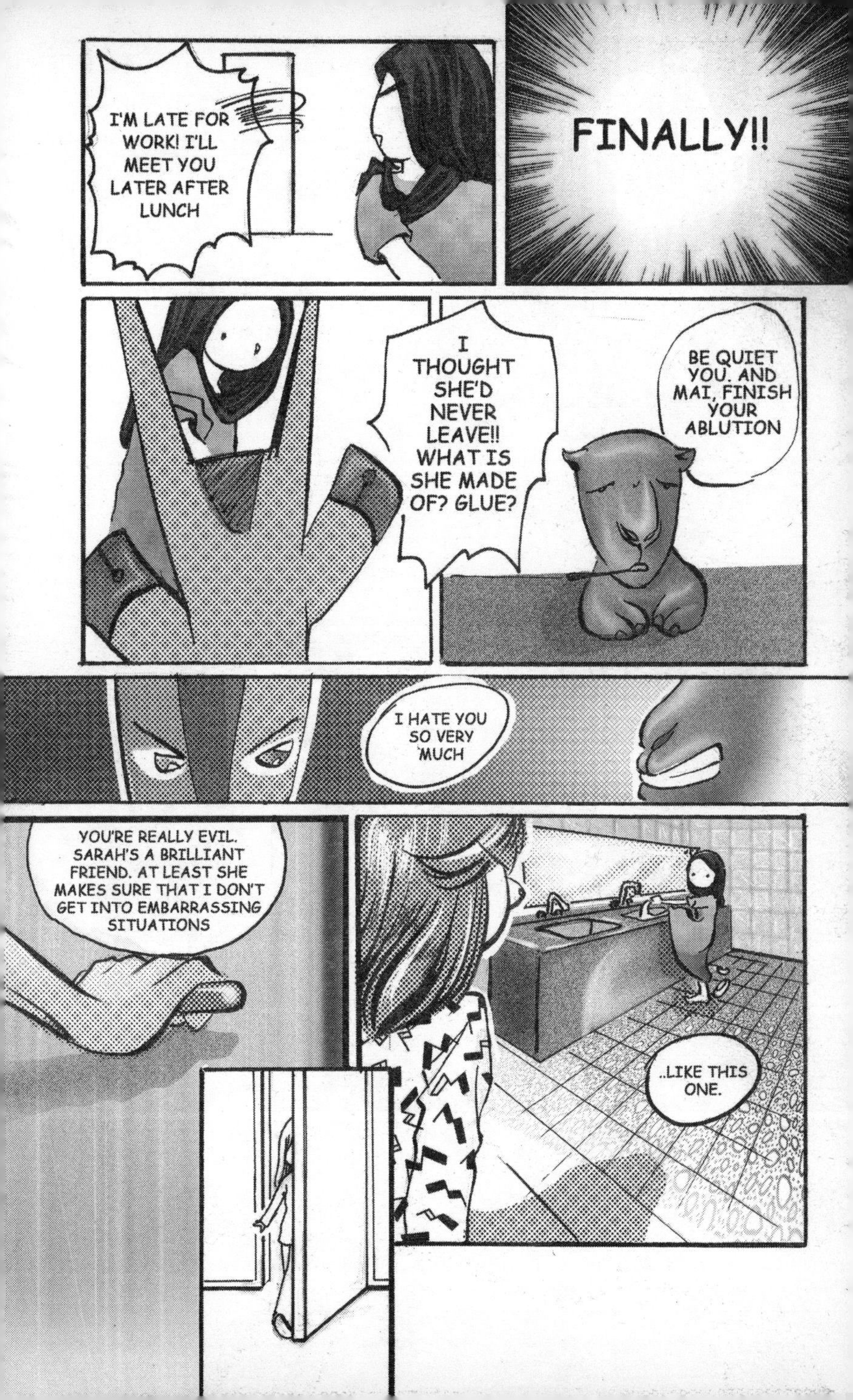
I'M LATE FOR WORK! I'LL MEET YOU LATER AFTER LUNCH
FINALLY!!
I THOUGHT SHE'D NEVER LEAVE!! WHAT IS SHE MADE OF? GLUE?
BE QUIET YOU. AND MAI, FINISH YOUR ABLUTION
I HATE YOU SO VERY MUCH
YOU'RE REALLY EVIL. SARAH'S A BRILLIANT FRIEND. AT LEAST SHE MAKES SURE THAT I DON'T GET INTO EMBARRASSING SITUATIONS
..LIKE THIS ONE.

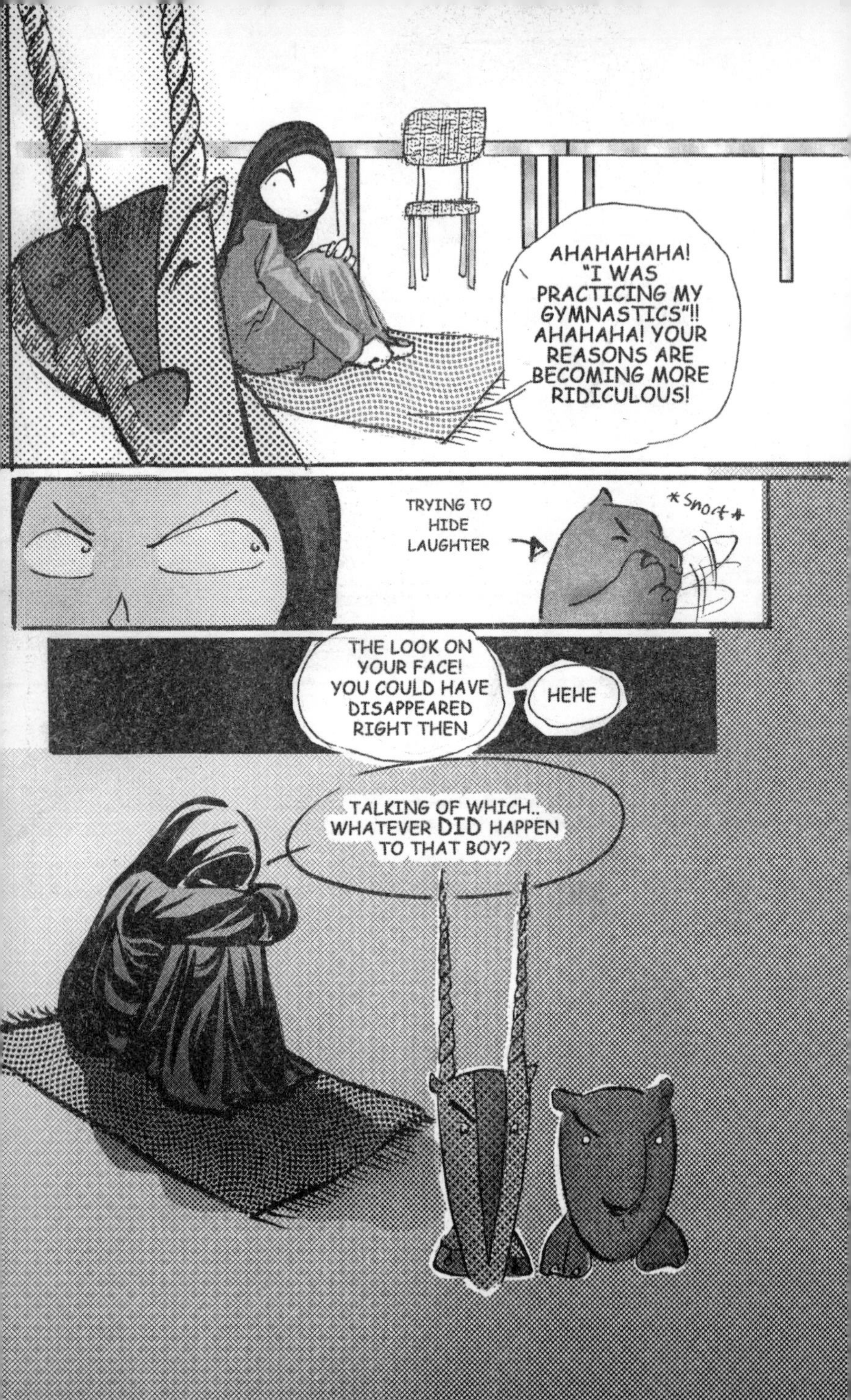
AHAHAHAHA! "I WAS PRACTICING MY GYMNASTICS"!! AHAHAHA! YOUR REASONS ARE BECOMING MORE RIDICULOUS!
TRYING TO HIDE LAUGHTER
Snort
THE LOOK ON YOUR FACE! YOU COULD HAVE DISAPPEARED RIGHT THEN
HEHE
TALKING OF WHICH.. WHATEVER DID HAPPEN TO THAT BOY?

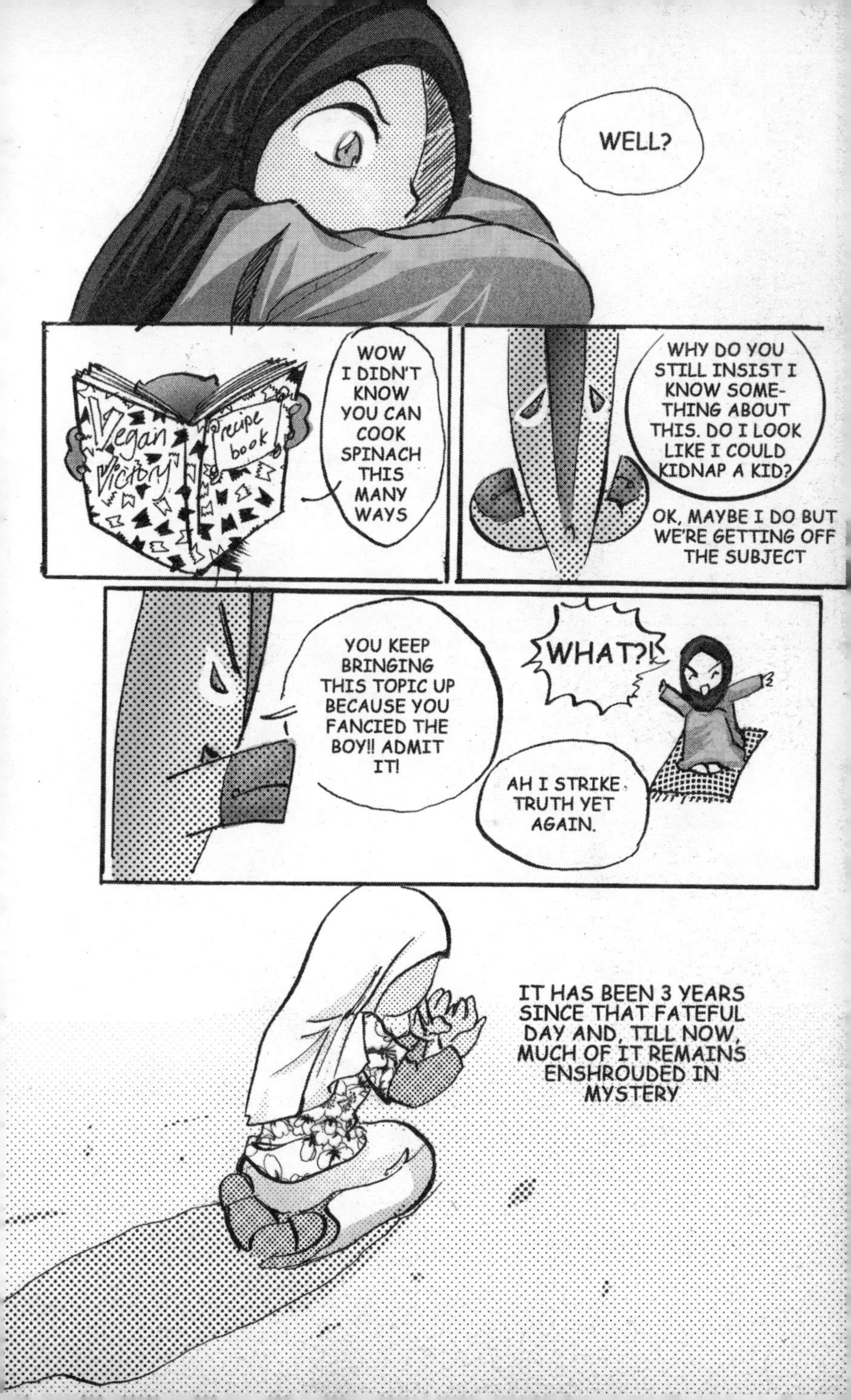
WELL?
WOW I DIDN'T KNOW YOU CAN COOK SPINACH THIS MANY WAYS
Vegan Victory
recipe book
WHY DO YOU STILL INSIST I KNOW SOME-THING ABOUT THIS. DO I LOOK LIKE I COULD KIDNAP A KID?
OK, MAYBE I DO BUT WE'RE GETTING OFF THE SUBJECT
YOU KEEP BRINGING THIS TOPIC UP BECAUSE YOU FANCIED THE BOY!! ADMIT IT!
WHAT?!
AH I STRIKE TRUTH YET AGAIN.
IT HAS BEEN 3 YEARS SINCE THAT FATEFUL DAY AND, TILL NOW, MUCH OF IT REMAINS ENSHROUDED IN MYSTERY

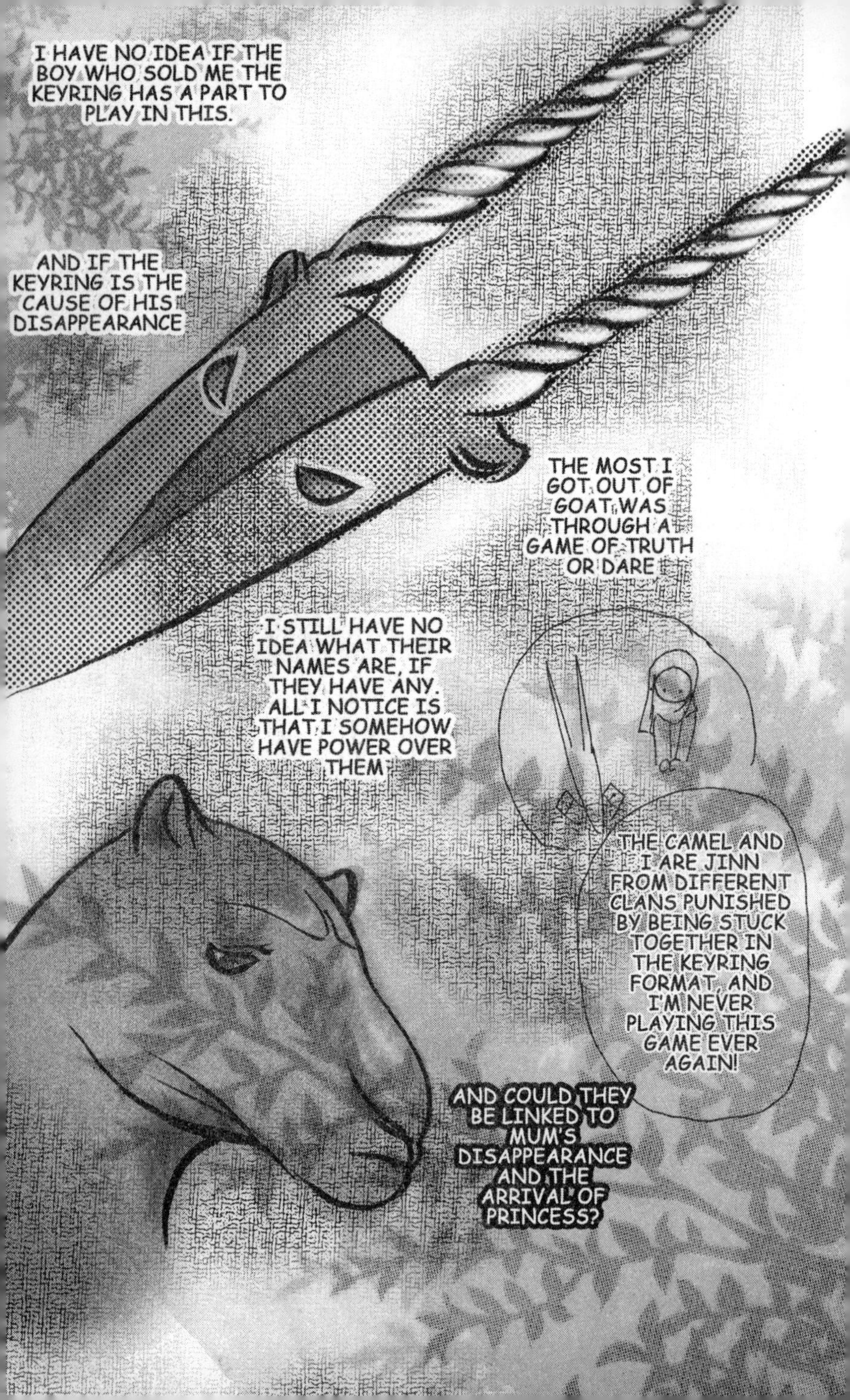
I HAVE NO IDEA IF THE BOY WHO SOLD ME THE KEYRING HAS A PART TO PLAY IN THIS.
AND IF THE KEYRING IS THE CAUSE OF HIS DISAPPEARANCE
THE MOST I GOT OUT OF GOAT WAS THROUGH A GAME OF TRUTH OR DARE
I STILL HAVE NO IDEA WHAT THEIR NAMES ARE, IF THEY HAVE ANY. ALL I NOTICE IS THAT I SOMEHOW HAVE POWER OVER THEM
THE CAMEL AND I ARE JINN FROM DIFFERENT CLANS PUNISHED BY BEING STUCK TOGETHER IN THE KEYRING FORMAT, AND I'M NEVER PLAYING THIS GAME EVER AGAIN!
AND COULD THEY BE LINKED TO MUM'S DISAPPEARANCE AND THE ARRIVAL OF PRINCESS?

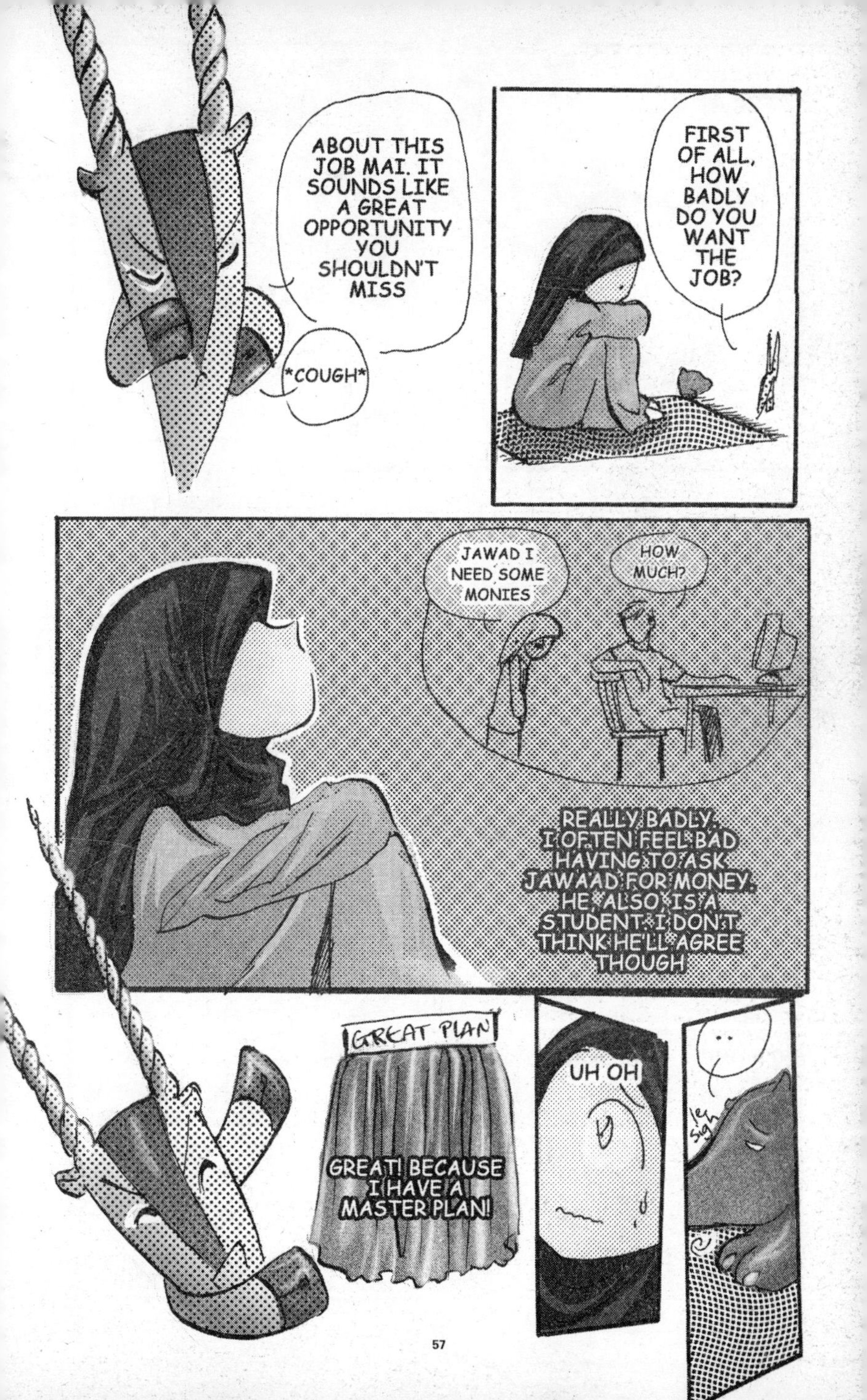
ABOUT THIS JOB MAI. IT SOUNDS LIKE A GREAT OPPORTUNITY YOU SHOULDN'T MISS
COUGH
FIRST OF ALL, HOW BADLY DO YOU WANT THE JOB?
JAWAD I NEED SOME MONIES
HOW MUCH?
REALLY BADLY. I OFTEN FEEL BAD HAVING TO ASK JAWAAD FOR MONEY. HE ALSO IS A STUDENT. I DON'T THINK HE'LL AGREE THOUGH
GREAT PLAN
GREAT! BECAUSE I HAVE A MASTER PLAN!
UH OH
..
le sigh

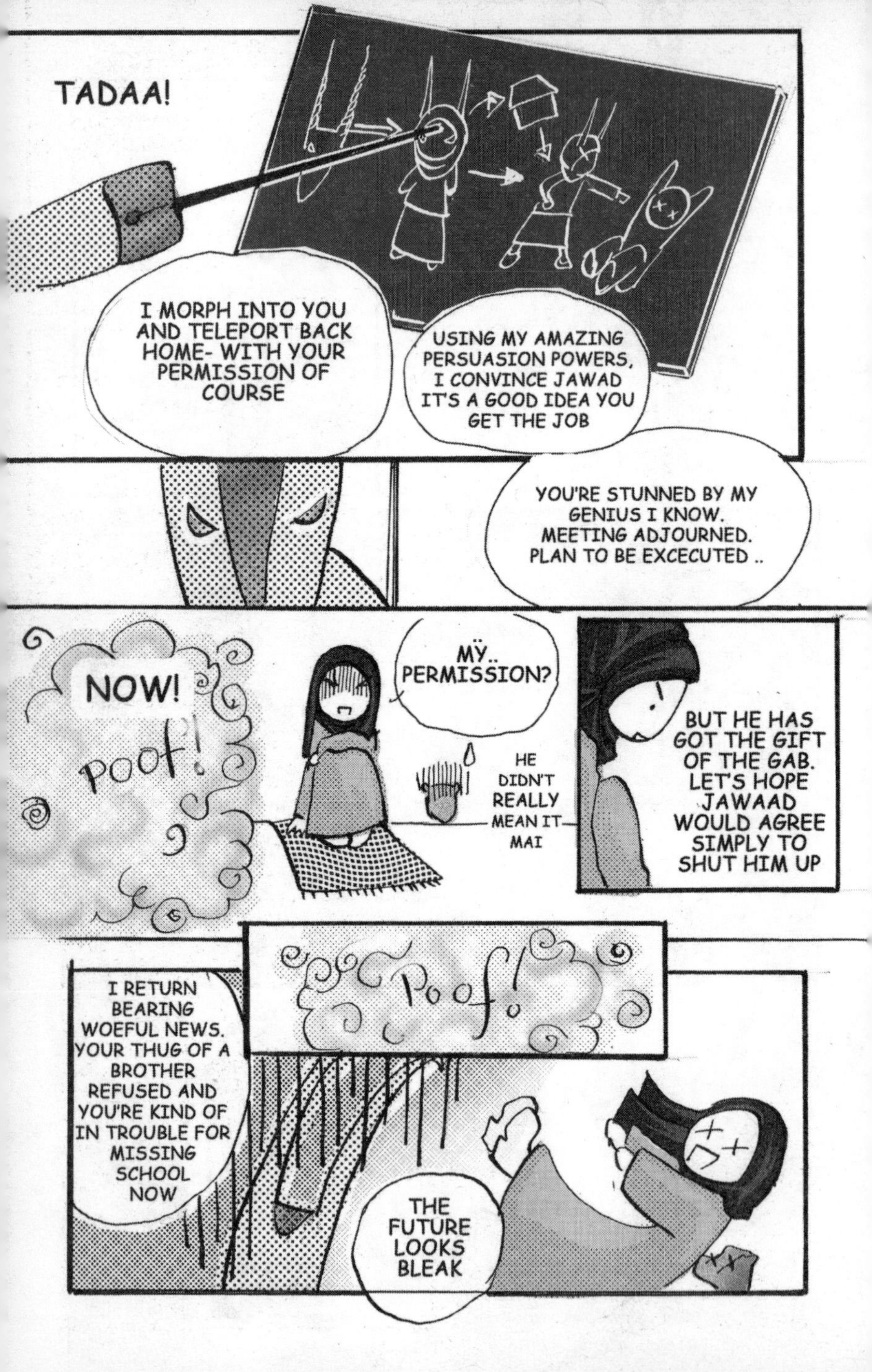
TADAA!
I MORPH INTO YOU AND TELEPORT BACK HOME- WITH YOUR PERMISSION OF COURSE
USING MY AMAZING PERSUASION POWERS, I CONVINCE JAWAD IT'S A GOOD IDEA YOU GET THE JOB
YOU'RE STUNNED BY MY GENIUS I KNOW. MEETING ADJOURNED. PLAN TO BE EXCECUTED ..
NOW!
POOF!
MY.. PERMISSION?
HE DIDN'T REALLY MEAN IT MAI
BUT HE HAS GOT THE GIFT OF THE GAB. LET'S HOPE JAWAAD WOULD AGREE SIMPLY TO SHUT HIM UP
POOF!
I RETURN BEARING WOEFUL NEWS. YOUR THUG OF A BROTHER REFUSED AND YOU'RE KIND OF IN TROUBLE FOR MISSING SCHOOL NOW
THE FUTURE LOOKS BLEAK

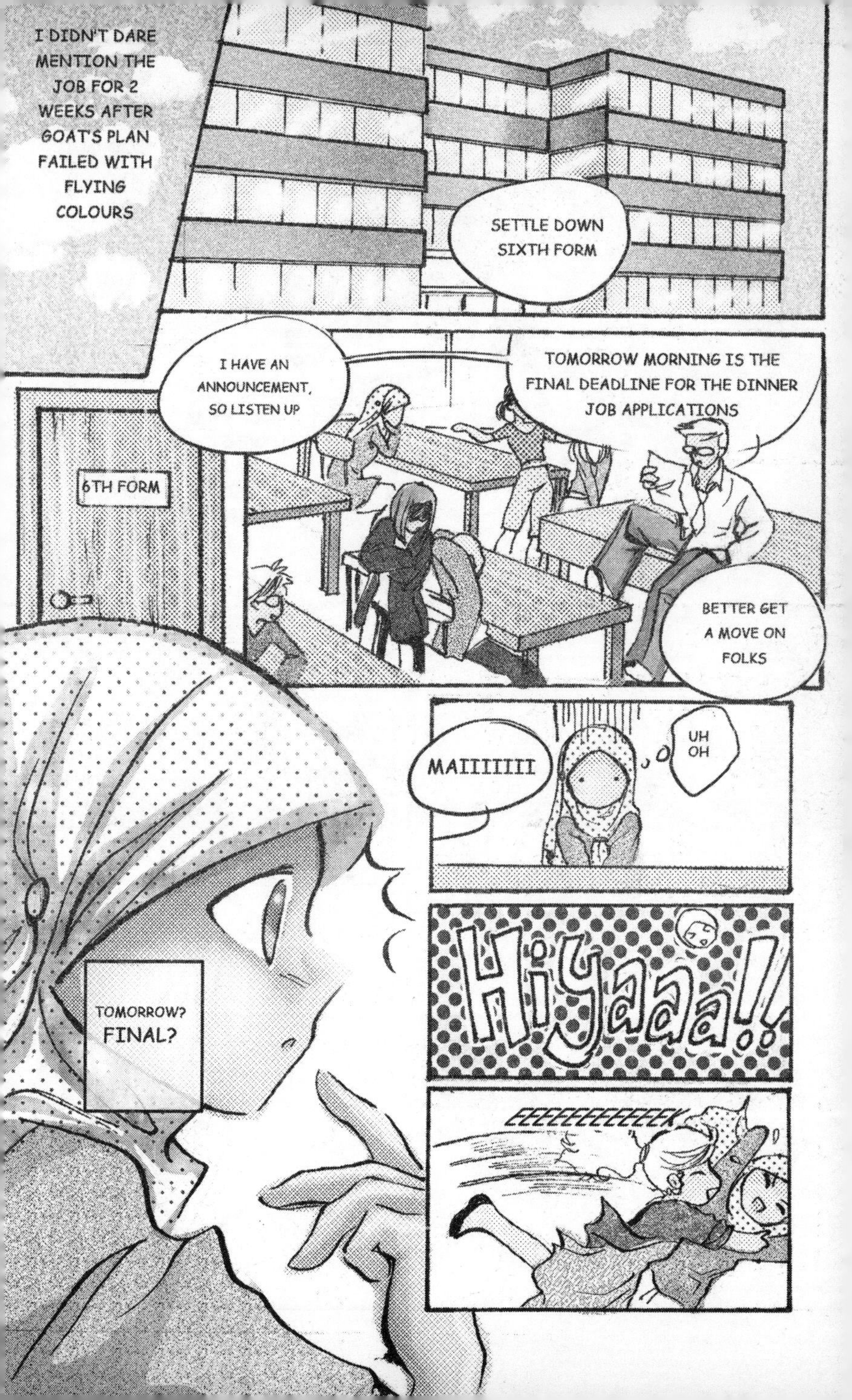
I DIDN'T DARE MENTION THE JOB FOR 2 WEEKS AFTER GOAT'S PLAN FAILED WITH FLYING COLOURS
SETTLE DOWN SIXTH FORM
I HAVE AN ANNOUNCEMENT, SO LISTEN UP
TOMORROW MORNING IS THE FINAL DEADLINE FOR THE DINNER JOB APPLICATIONS
6TH FORM
BETTER GET A MOVE ON FOLKS
TOMORROW? FINAL?
MAIIIIIII
UH OH
Hiyaaa!!
EEEEEEEEEEEEK

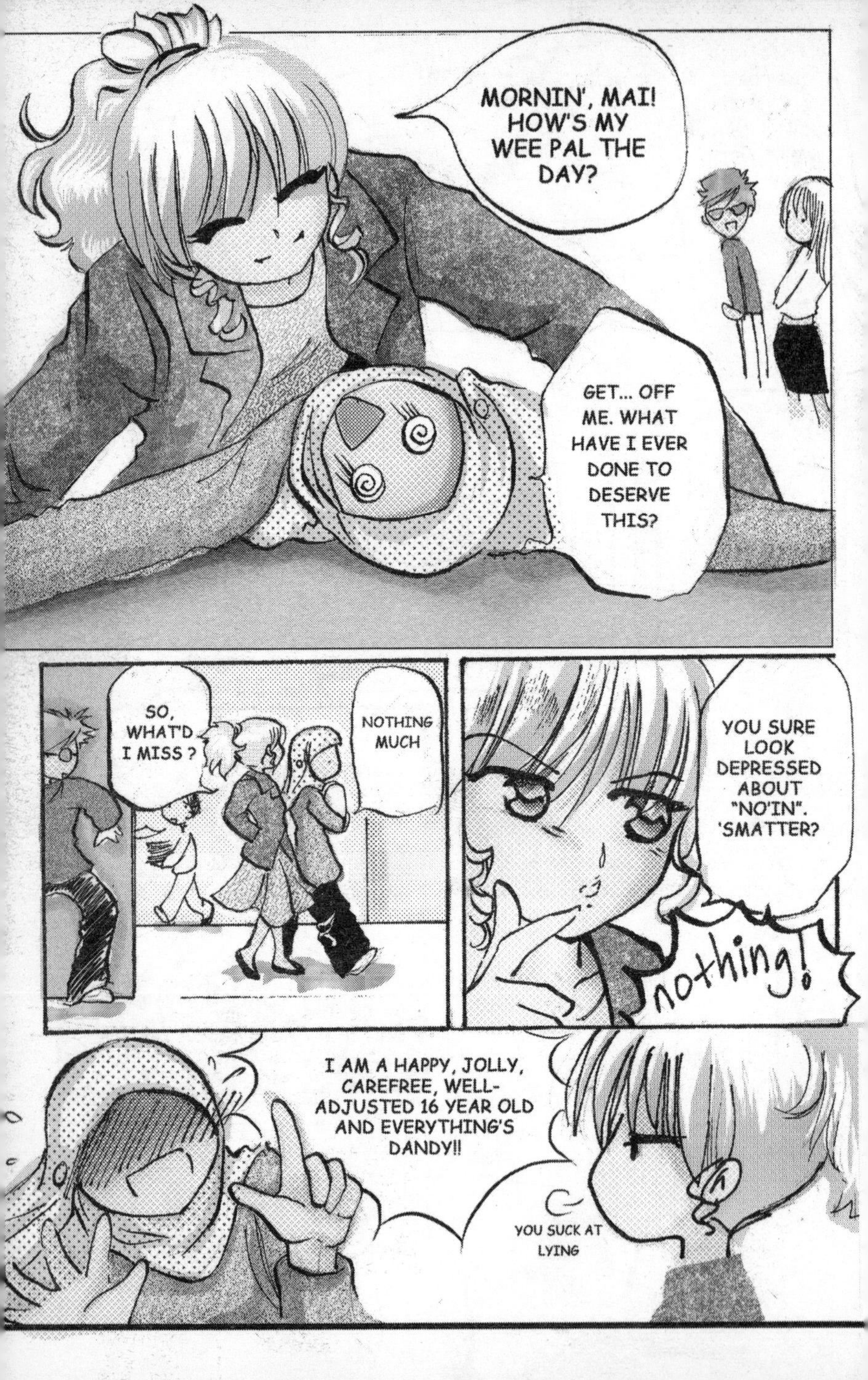
MORNIN', MAI! HOW'S MY WEE PAL THE DAY?
GET... OFF ME. WHAT HAVE I EVER DONE TO DESERVE THIS?
SO, WHAT'D I MISS ?
NOTHING MUCH
YOU SURE LOOK DEPRESSED ABOUT "NO'IN". 'SMATTER?
nothing!
I AM A HAPPY, JOLLY, CAREFREE, WELL-ADJUSTED 16 YEAR OLD AND EVERYTHING'S DANDY!!
YOU SUCK AT LYING

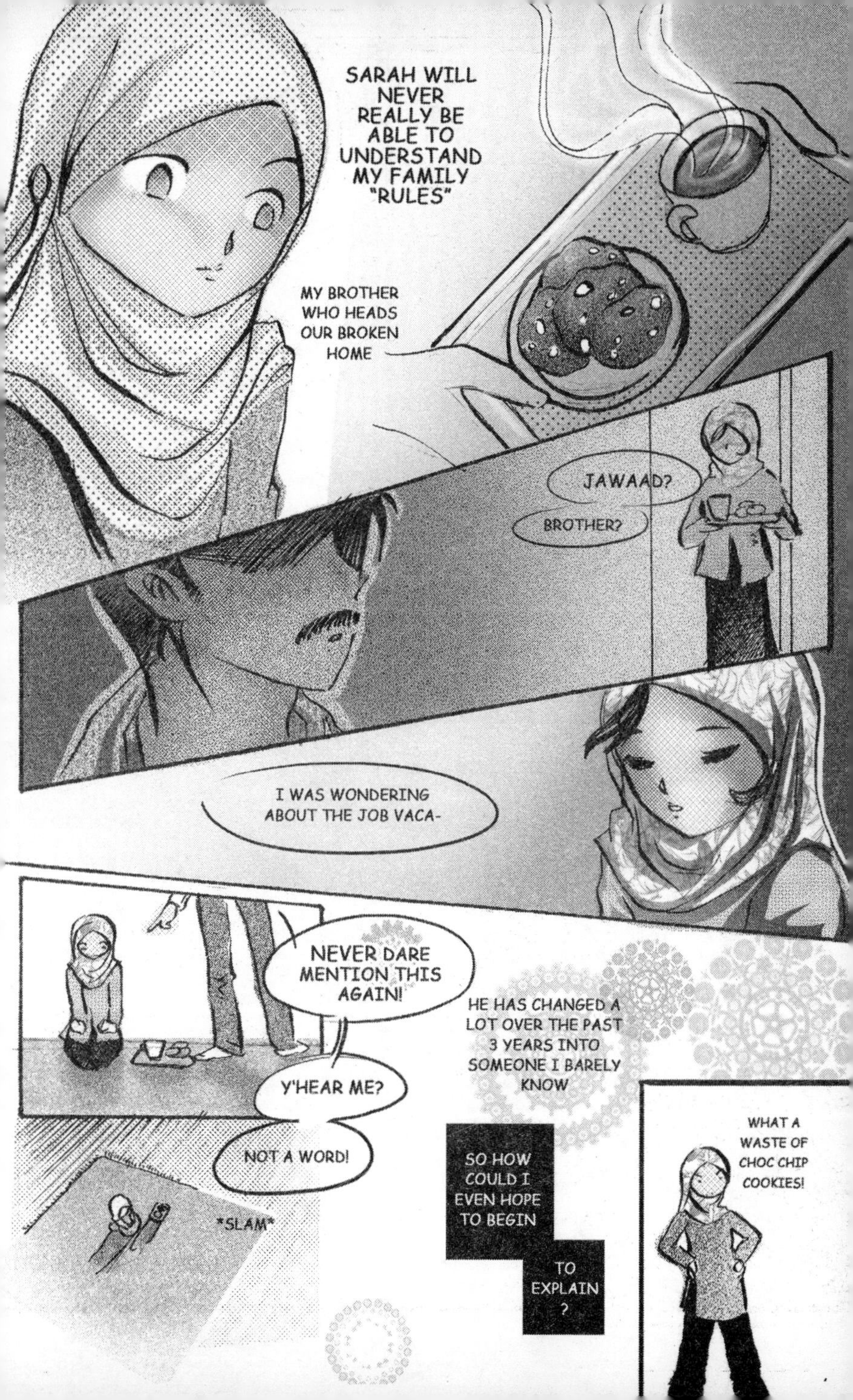
SARAH WILL NEVER REALLY BE ABLE TO UNDERSTAND MY FAMILY "RULES"
MY BROTHER WHO HEADS OUR BROKEN HOME
JAWAAD?
BROTHER?
I WAS WONDERING ABOUT THE JOB VACA-
NEVER DARE MENTION THIS AGAIN!
Y'HEAR ME?
NOT A WORD!
SLAM
HE HAS CHANGED A LOT OVER THE PAST 3 YEARS INTO SOMEONE I BARELY KNOW
SO HOW COULD I EVEN HOPE TO BEGIN
TO EXPLAIN ?
WHAT A WASTE OF CHOC CHIP COOKIES!

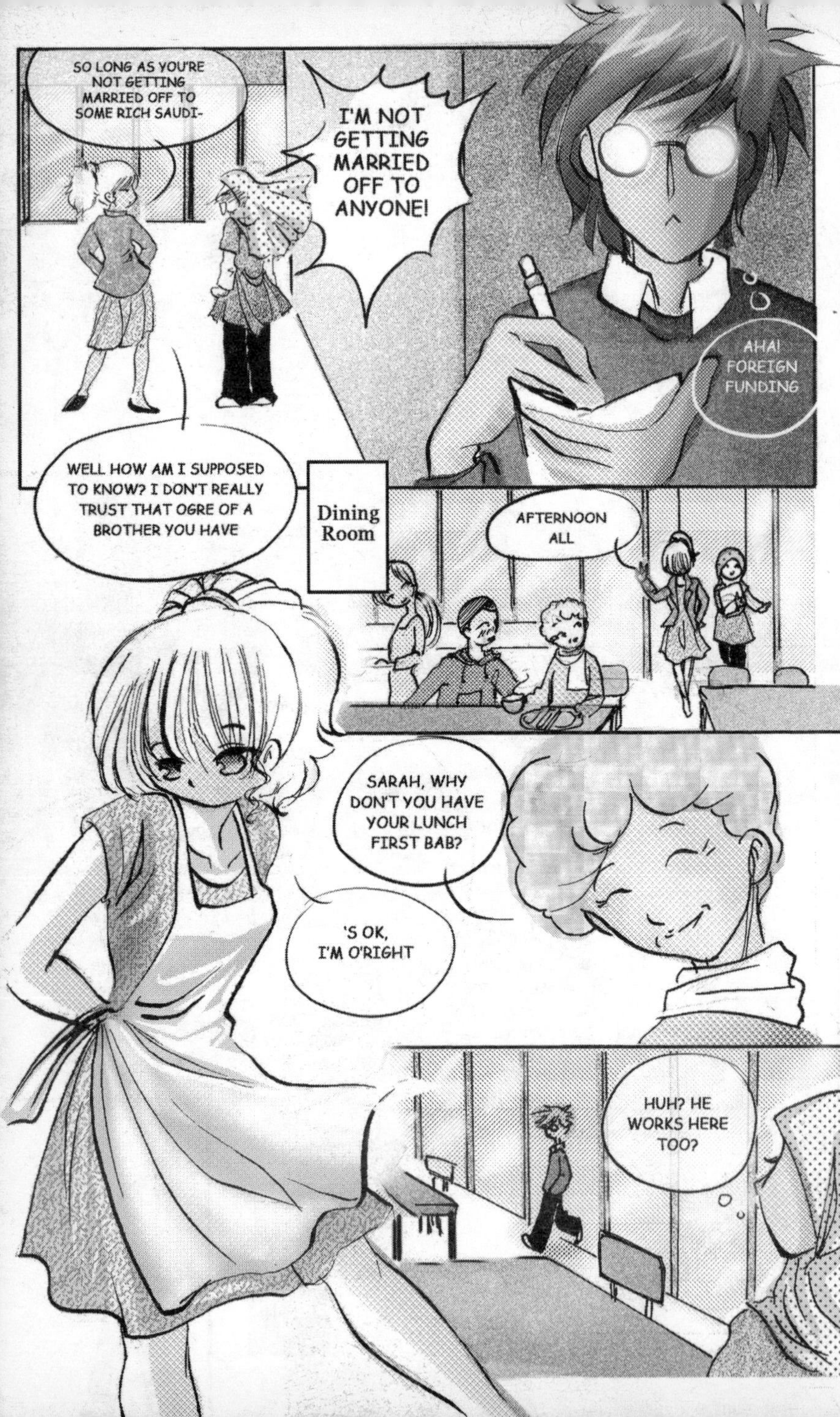
SO LONG AS YOU'RE NOT GETTING MARRIED OFF TO SOME RICH SAUDI-
I'M NOT GETTING MARRIED OFF TO ANYONE!
WELL HOW AM I SUPPOSED TO KNOW? I DON'T REALLY TRUST THAT OGRE OF A BROTHER YOU HAVE
AHA! FOREIGN FUNDING
Dining Room
AFTERNOON ALL
SARAH, WHY DON'T YOU HAVE YOUR LUNCH FIRST BAB?
'S OK, I'M O'RIGHT
HUH? HE WORKS HERE TOO?

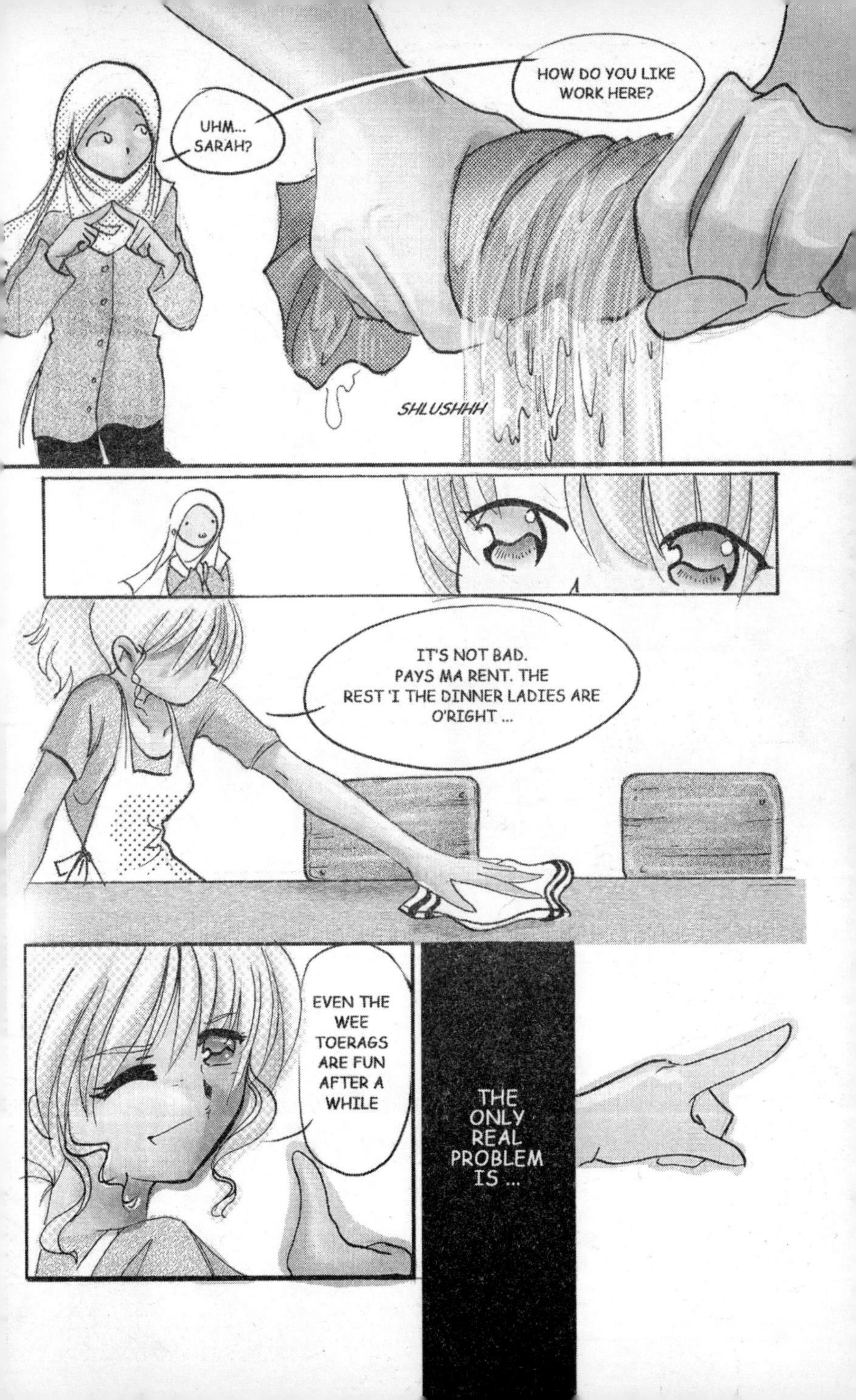
UHM... SARAH?
HOW DO YOU LIKE WORK HERE?
SHLUSHHH
IT'S NOT BAD. PAYS MA RENT. THE REST 'I THE DINNER LADIES ARE O'RIGHT ...
EVEN THE WEE TOERAGS ARE FUN AFTER A WHILE
THE ONLY REAL PROBLEM IS ...

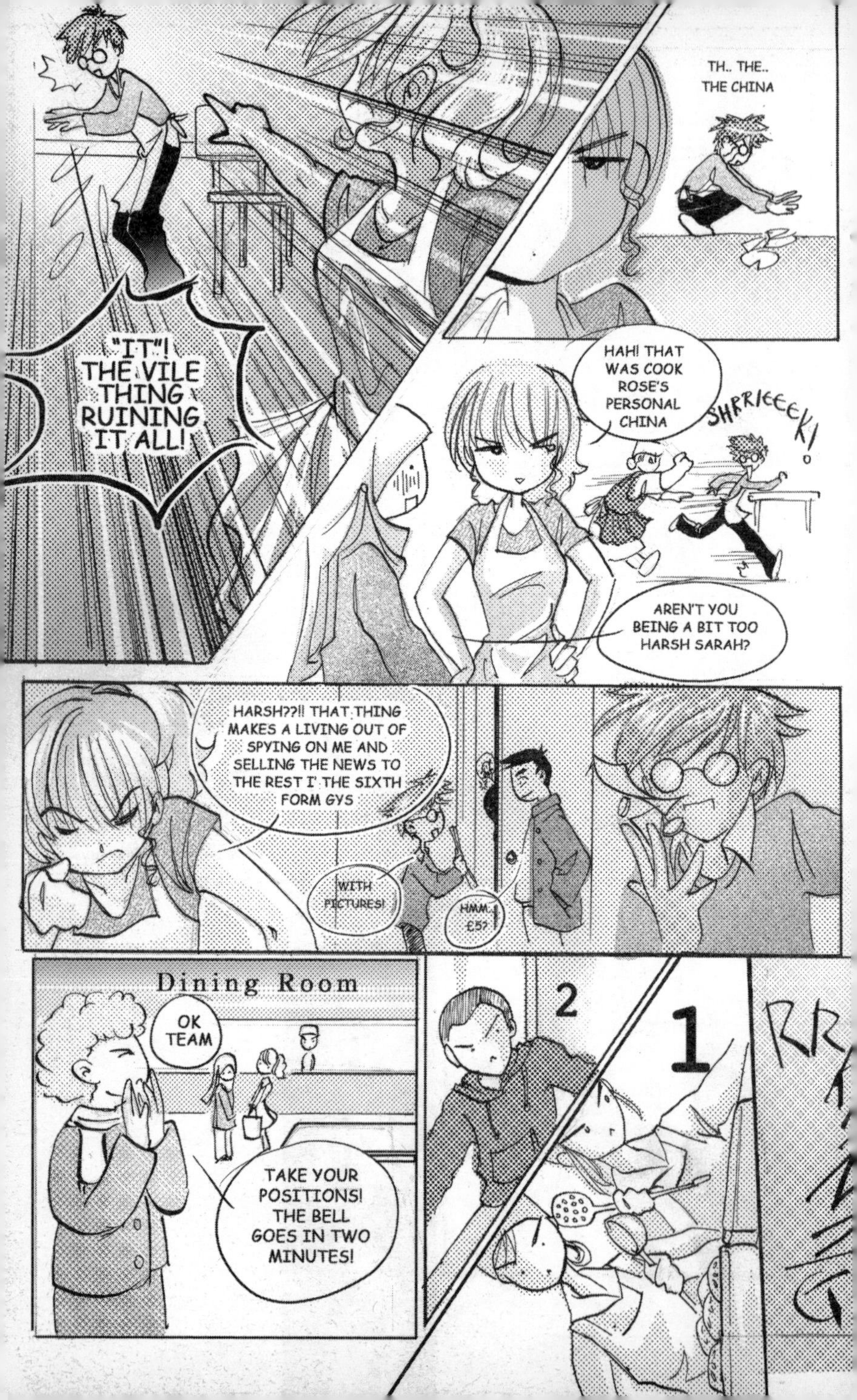
"IT"! THE VILE THING RUINING IT ALL!
TH.. THE.. THE CHINA
HAH! THAT WAS COOK ROSE'S PERSONAL CHINA
SHRRIEEEEK!
AREN'T YOU BEING A BIT TOO HARSH SARAH?
HARSH??!! THAT THING MAKES A LIVING OUT OF SPYING ON ME AND SELLING THE NEWS TO THE REST I' THE SIXTH FORM GYS
WITH PICTURES!
HMM. £5?
Dining Room
OK TEAM
TAKE YOUR POSITIONS! THE BELL GOES IN TWO MINUTES!
2
1
RRRING

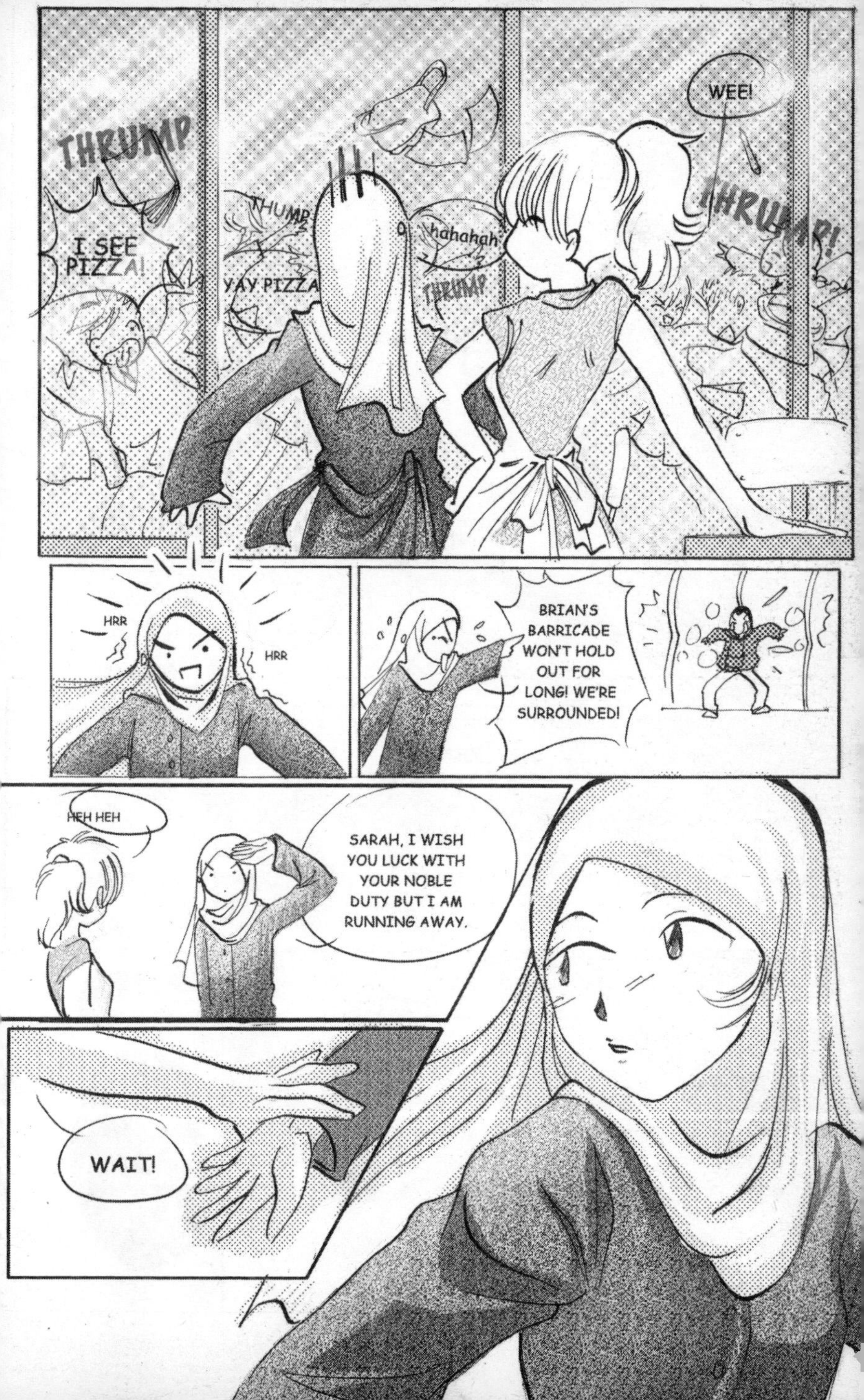
THRUMP
I SEE PIZZA!
THUMP
YAY PIZZA
hahahah
THRUMP
WEE!
THRUMP!
HRR
HRR
BRIAN'S BARRICADE WON'T HOLD OUT FOR LONG! WE'RE SURROUNDED!
HEH HEH
SARAH, I WISH YOU LUCK WITH YOUR NOBLE DUTY BUT I AM RUNNING AWAY.
WAIT!

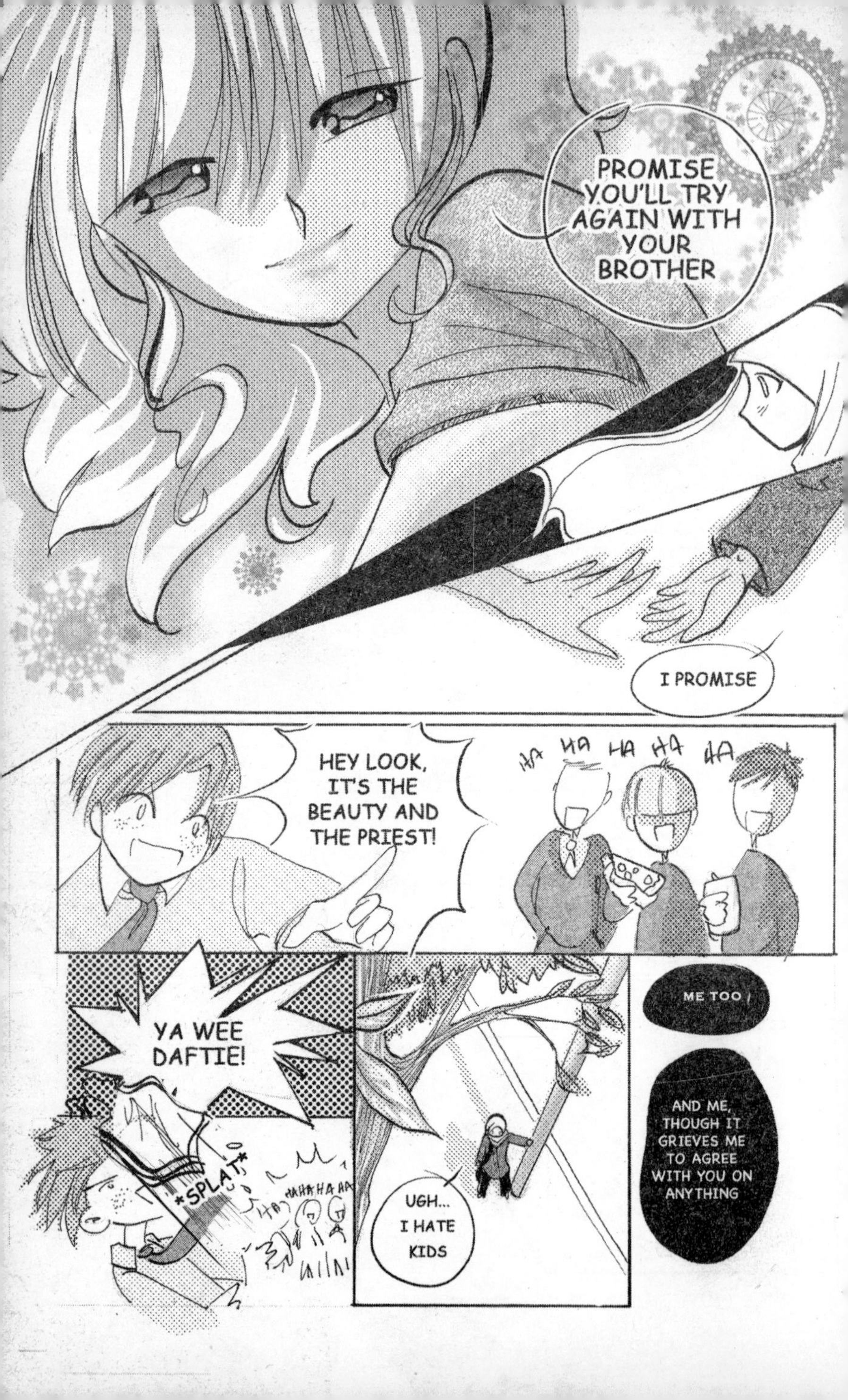
PROMISE YOU'LL TRY AGAIN WITH YOUR BROTHER
I PROMISE
HEY LOOK, IT'S THE BEAUTY AND THE PRIEST!
HA HA HA HA HA
YA WEE DAFTIE!
SPLAT
HA HA HA HA
UGH... I HATE KIDS
ME TOO!
AND ME, THOUGH IT GRIEVES ME TO AGREE WITH YOU ON ANYTHING

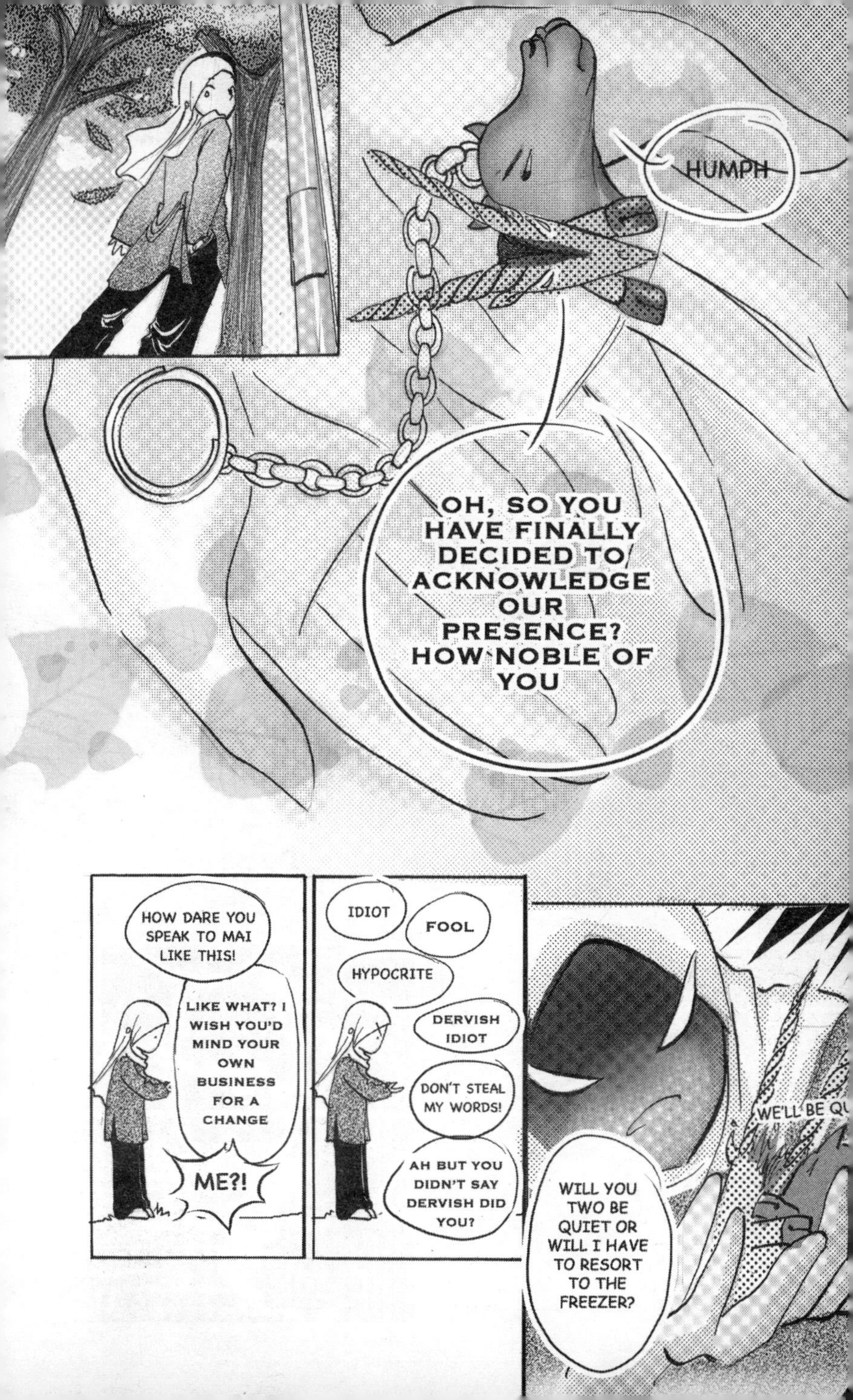
HUMPH
OH, SO YOU HAVE FINALLY DECIDED TO ACKNOWLEDGE OUR PRESENCE? HOW NOBLE OF YOU
HOW DARE YOU SPEAK TO MAI LIKE THIS!
LIKE WHAT? I WISH YOU'D MIND YOUR OWN BUSINESS FOR A CHANGE
ME?!
IDIOT
FOOL
HYPOCRITE
DERVISH IDIOT
DON'T STEAL MY WORDS!
AH BUT YOU DIDN'T SAY DERVISH DID YOU?
WE'LL BE QU
WILL YOU TWO BE QUIET OR WILL I HAVE TO RESORT TO THE FREEZER?

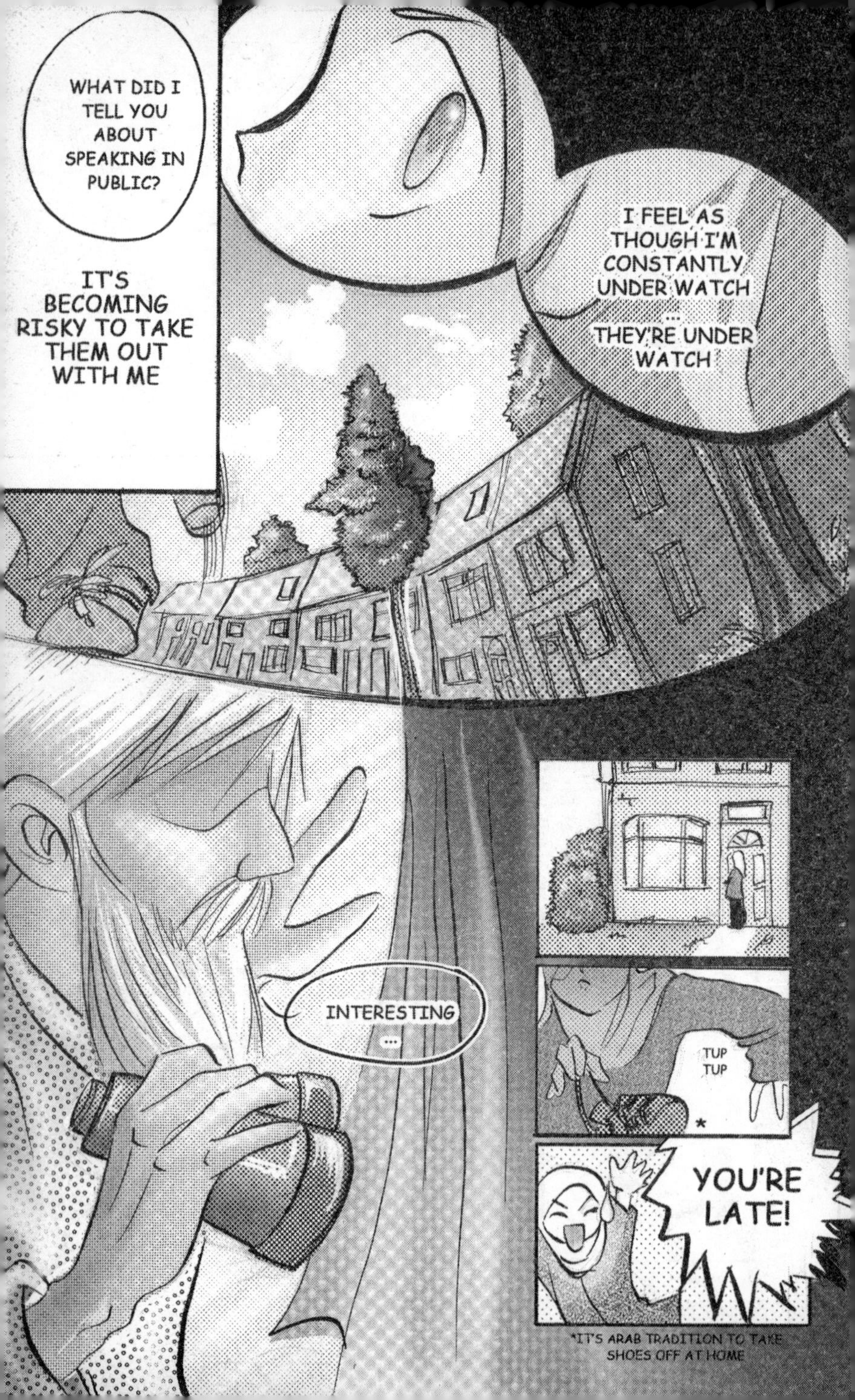
WHAT DID I TELL YOU ABOUT SPEAKING IN PUBLIC?
IT'S BECOMING RISKY TO TAKE THEM OUT WITH ME
I FEEL AS THOUGH I'M CONSTANTLY UNDER WATCH ... THEY'RE UNDER WATCH
INTERESTING ...
TUP TUP
*
YOU'RE LATE!
*IT'S ARAB TRADITION TO TAKE SHOES OFF AT HOME

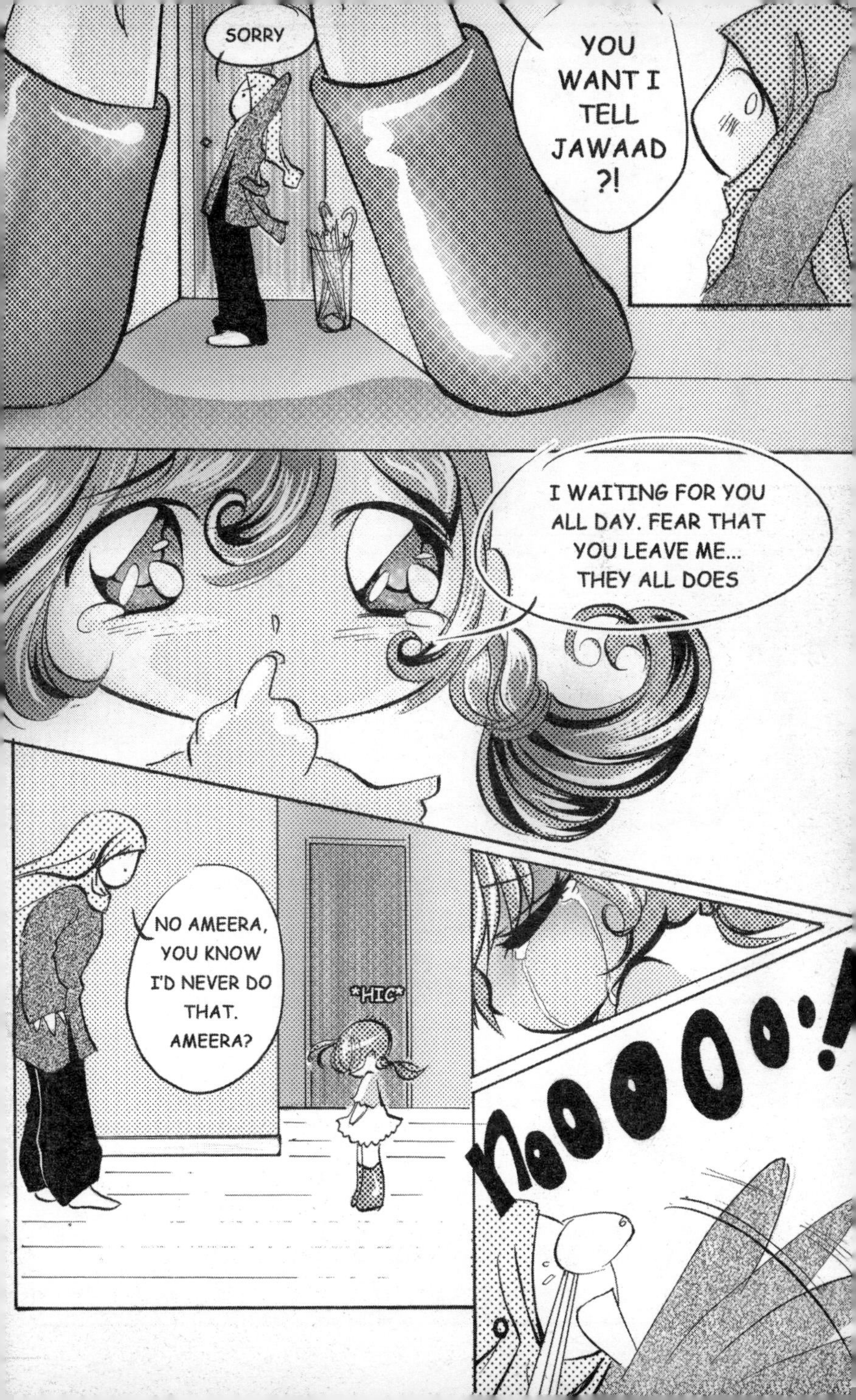
SORRY
YOU WANT I TELL JAWAAD ?!
I WAITING FOR YOU ALL DAY. FEAR THAT YOU LEAVE ME... THEY ALL DOES
NO AMEERA, YOU KNOW I'D NEVER DO THAT. AMEERA?
HIC
NoOOOO:!

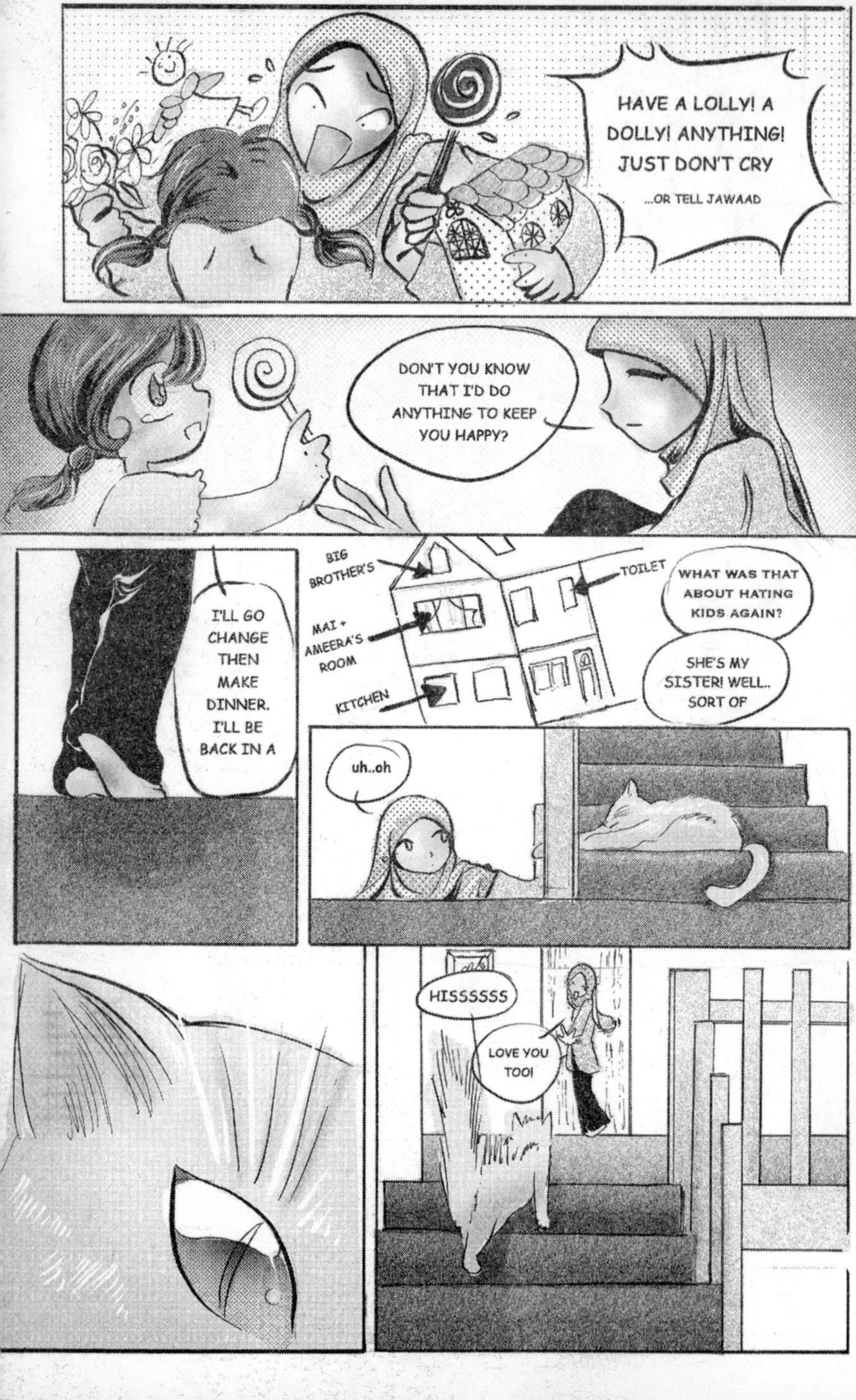
HAVE A LOLLY! A DOLLY! ANYTHING! JUST DON'T CRY
...OR TELL JAWAAD
DON'T YOU KNOW THAT I'D DO ANYTHING TO KEEP YOU HAPPY?
I'LL GO CHANGE THEN MAKE DINNER. I'LL BE BACK IN A
BIG BROTHER'S
TOILET
MAI + AMEERA'S ROOM
KITCHEN
WHAT WAS THAT ABOUT HATING KIDS AGAIN?
SHE'S MY SISTER! WELL.. SORT OF
uh..oh
HISSSSSS
LOVE YOU TOO!

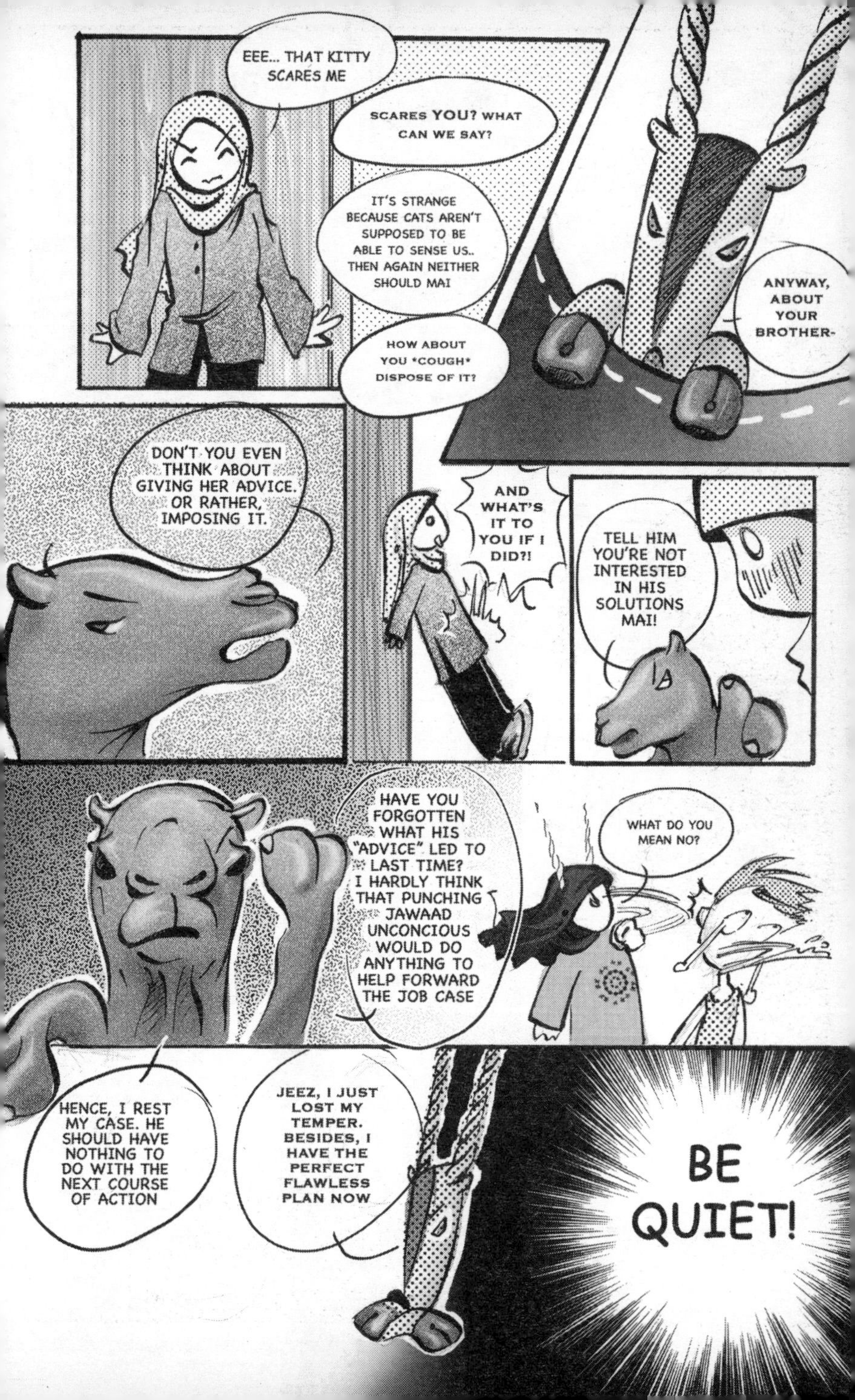
EEE... THAT KITTY SCARES ME
SCARES YOU? WHAT CAN WE SAY?
IT'S STRANGE BECAUSE CATS AREN'T SUPPOSED TO BE ABLE TO SENSE US.. THEN AGAIN NEITHER SHOULD MAI
HOW ABOUT YOU *COUGH* DISPOSE OF IT?
ANYWAY, ABOUT YOUR BROTHER-
DON'T YOU EVEN THINK ABOUT GIVING HER ADVICE. OR RATHER, IMPOSING IT.
AND WHAT'S IT TO YOU IF I DID?!
TELL HIM YOU'RE NOT INTERESTED IN HIS SOLUTIONS MAI!
HAVE YOU FORGOTTEN WHAT HIS "ADVICE" LED TO LAST TIME? I HARDLY THINK THAT PUNCHING JAWAAD UNCONCIOUS WOULD DO ANYTHING TO HELP FORWARD THE JOB CASE
WHAT DO YOU MEAN NO?
HENCE, I REST MY CASE. HE SHOULD HAVE NOTHING TO DO WITH THE NEXT COURSE OF ACTION
JEEZ, I JUST LOST MY TEMPER. BESIDES, I HAVE THE PERFECT FLAWLESS PLAN NOW
BE QUIET!

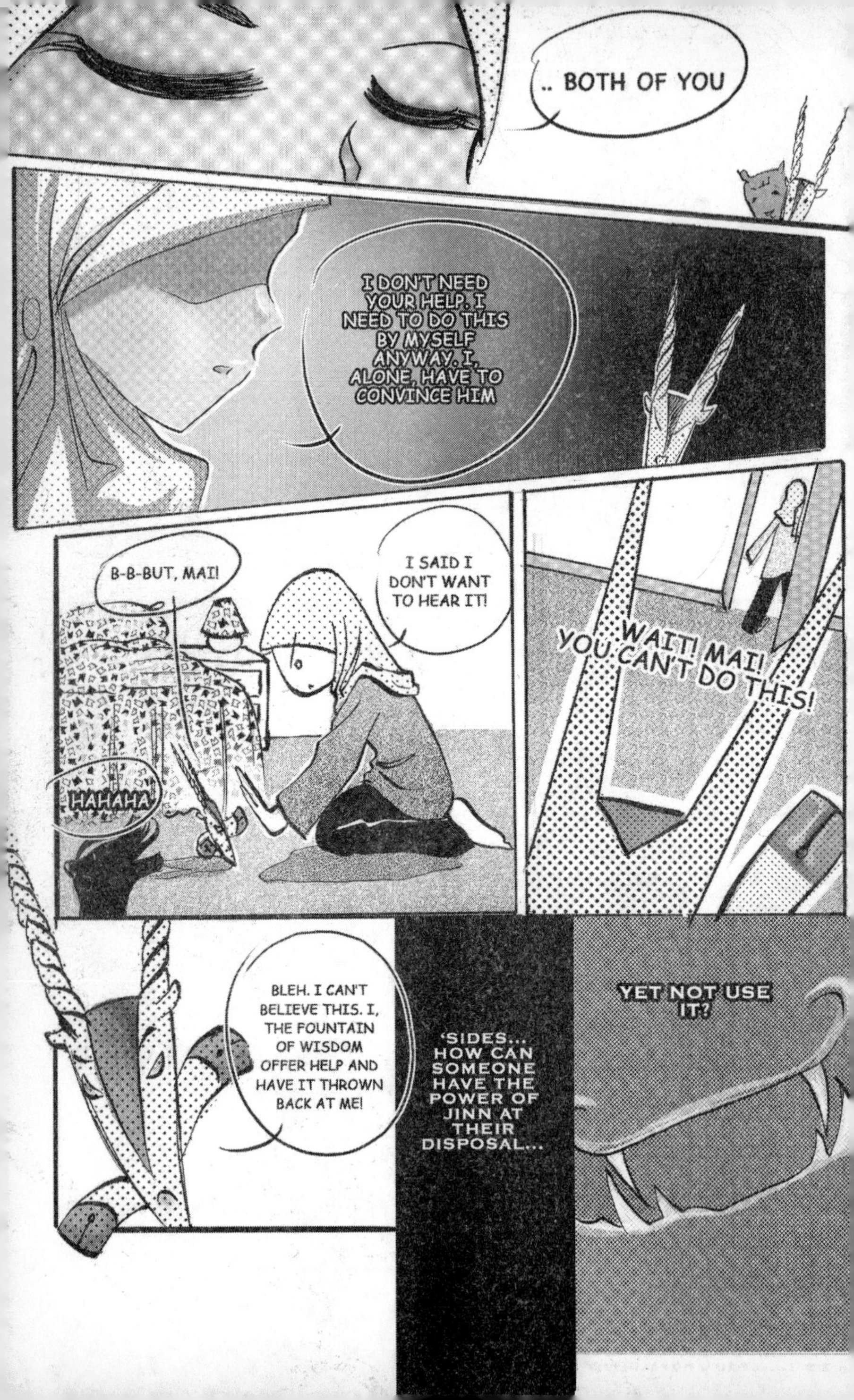
.. BOTH OF YOU
I DON'T NEED YOUR HELP. I NEED TO DO THIS BY MYSELF ANYWAY. I, ALONE, HAVE TO CONVINCE HIM
B-B-BUT, MAI!
I SAID I DON'T WANT TO HEAR IT!
HAHAHA
WAIT! MAI! YOU CAN'T DO THIS!
BLEH. I CAN'T BELIEVE THIS. I, THE FOUNTAIN OF WISDOM OFFER HELP AND HAVE IT THROWN BACK AT ME!
'SIDES... HOW CAN SOMEONE HAVE THE POWER OF JINN AT THEIR DISPOSAL...
YET NOT USE IT?

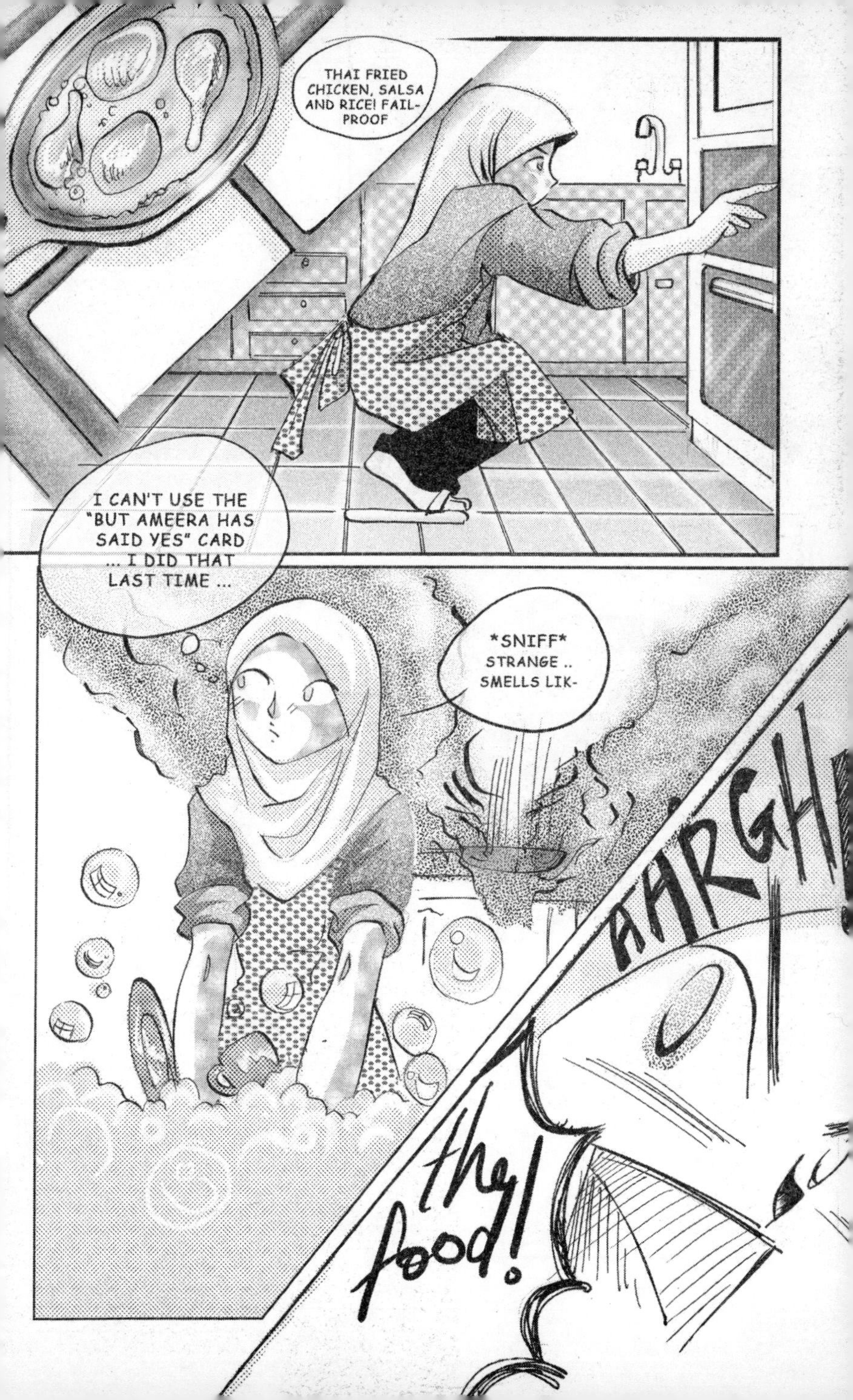
THAI FRIED CHICKEN, SALSA AND RICE! FAIL-PROOF
I CAN'T USE THE "BUT AMEERA HAS SAID YES" CARD ... I DID THAT LAST TIME ...
SNIFF STRANGE .. SMELLS LIK-
AHRGH
the food!

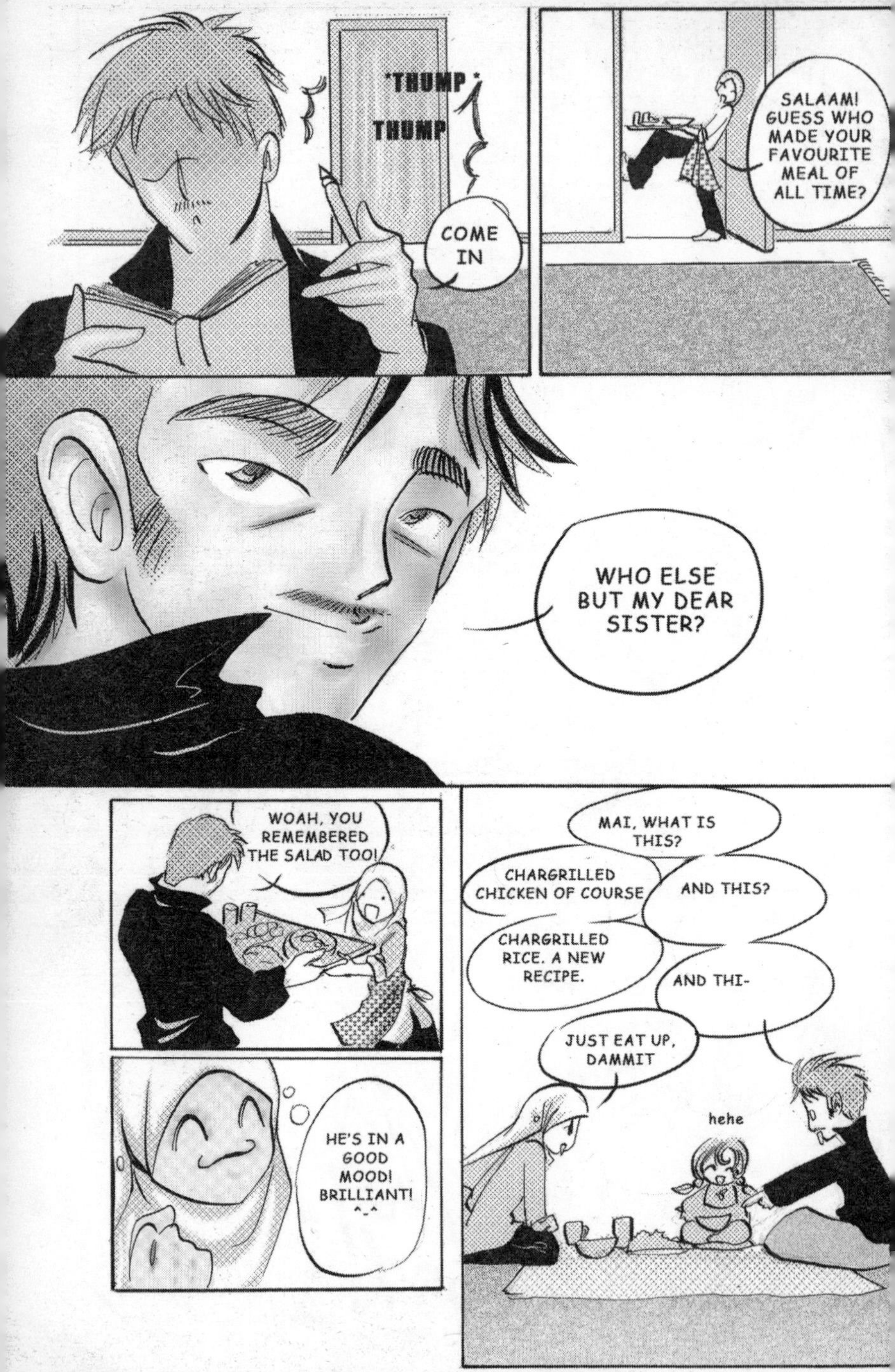
THUMP
THUMP
COME IN
SALAAM! GUESS WHO MADE YOUR FAVOURITE MEAL OF ALL TIME?
WHO ELSE BUT MY DEAR SISTER?
WOAH, YOU REMEMBERED THE SALAD TOO!
HE'S IN A GOOD MOOD! BRILLIANT! ^-^
MAI, WHAT IS THIS?
CHARGRILLED CHICKEN OF COURSE
AND THIS?
CHARGRILLED RICE. A NEW RECIPE.
AND THI-
JUST EAT UP, DAMMIT
hehe

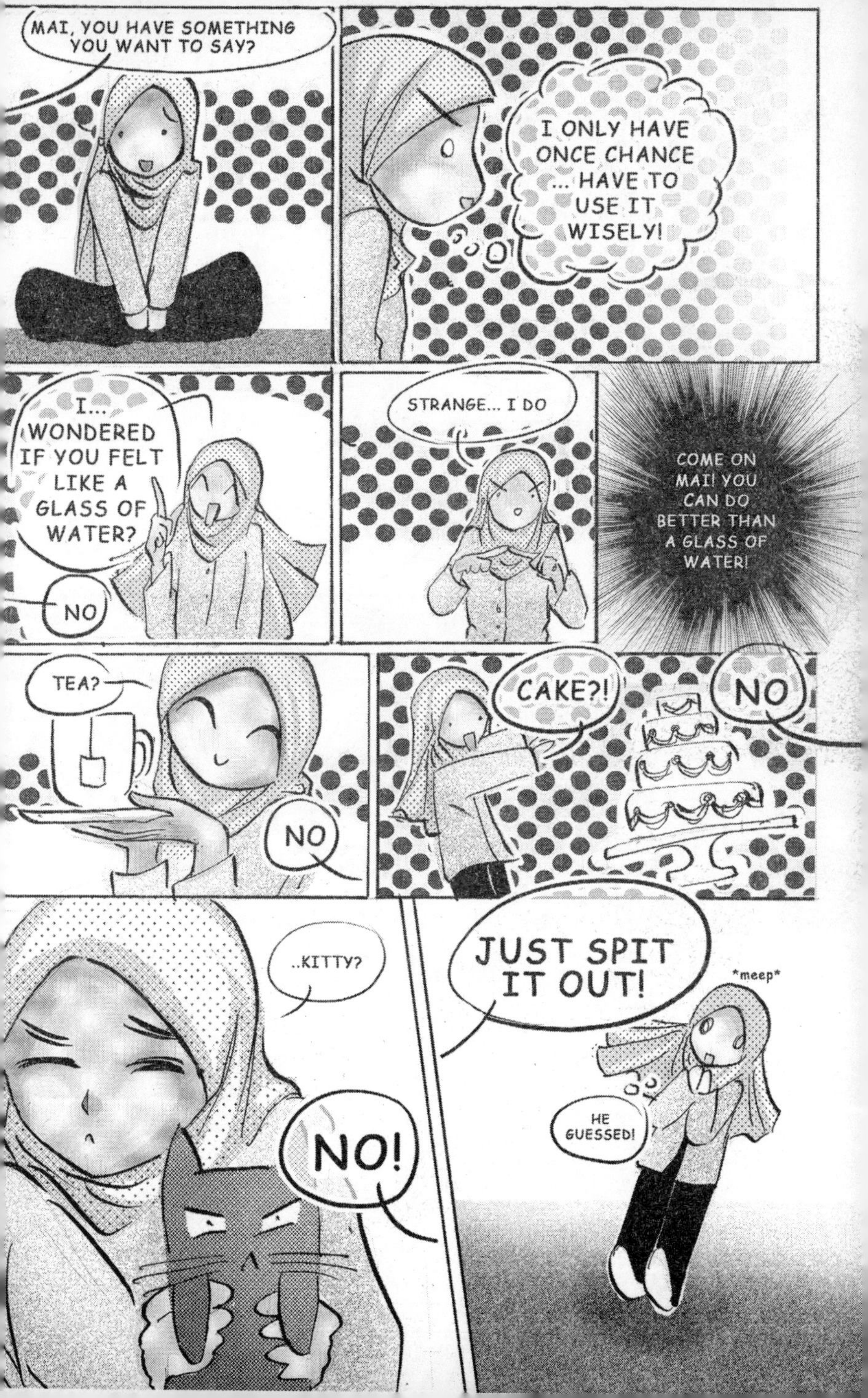
MAI, YOU HAVE SOMETHING YOU WANT TO SAY?
I ONLY HAVE ONCE CHANCE ... HAVE TO USE IT WISELY!
I... WONDERED IF YOU FELT LIKE A GLASS OF WATER?
NO
STRANGE... I DO
COME ON MAI! YOU CAN DO BETTER THAN A GLASS OF WATER!
TEA?
NO
CAKE?!
NO
..KITTY?
NO!
JUST SPIT IT OUT!
meep
HE GUESSED!

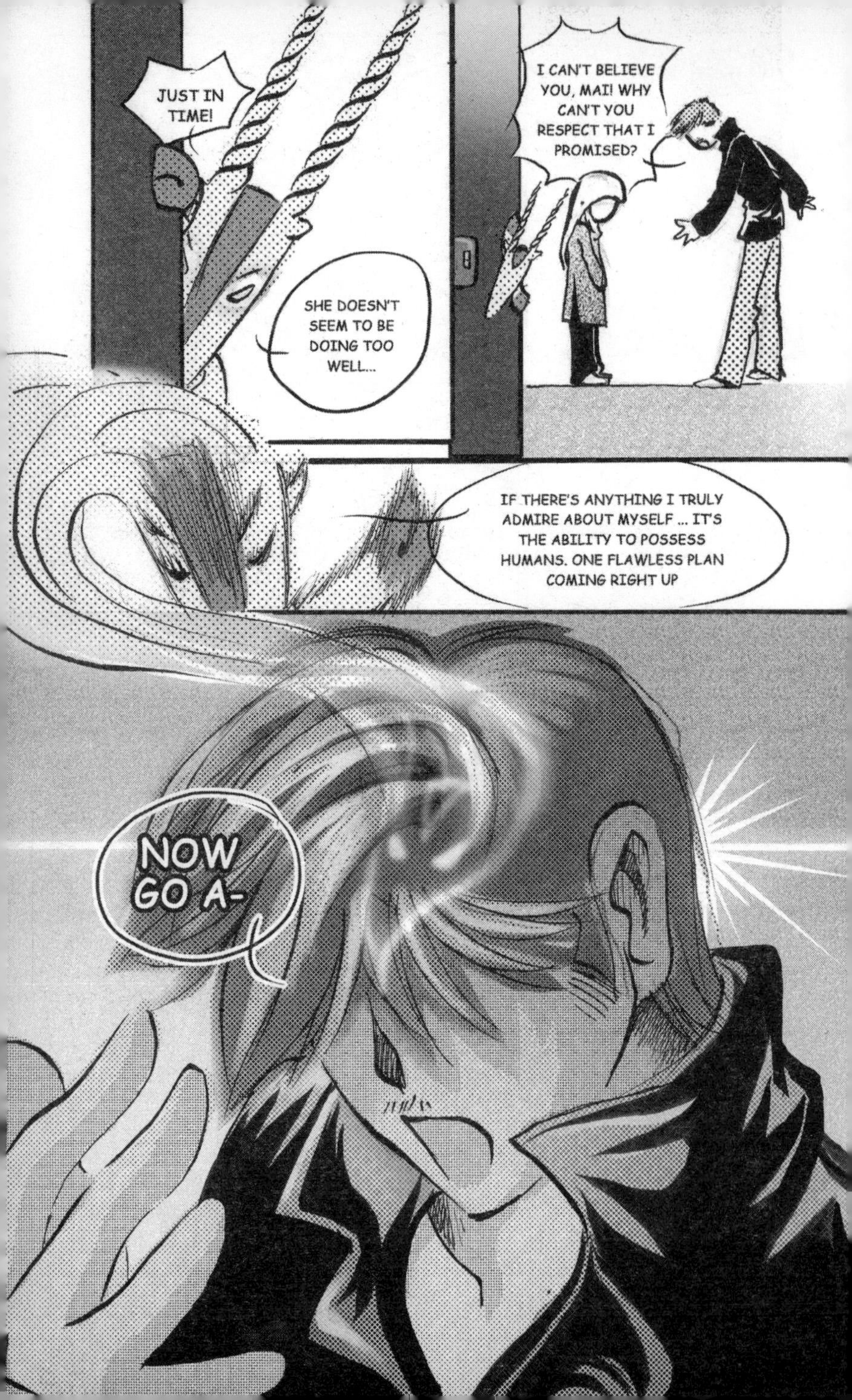
JUST IN TIME!
I CAN'T BELIEVE YOU, MAI! WHY CAN'T YOU RESPECT THAT I PROMISED?
SHE DOESN'T SEEM TO BE DOING TOO WELL...
IF THERE'S ANYTHING I TRULY ADMIRE ABOUT MYSELF ... IT'S THE ABILITY TO POSSESS HUMANS. ONE FLAWLESS PLAN COMING RIGHT UP
NOW GO A-

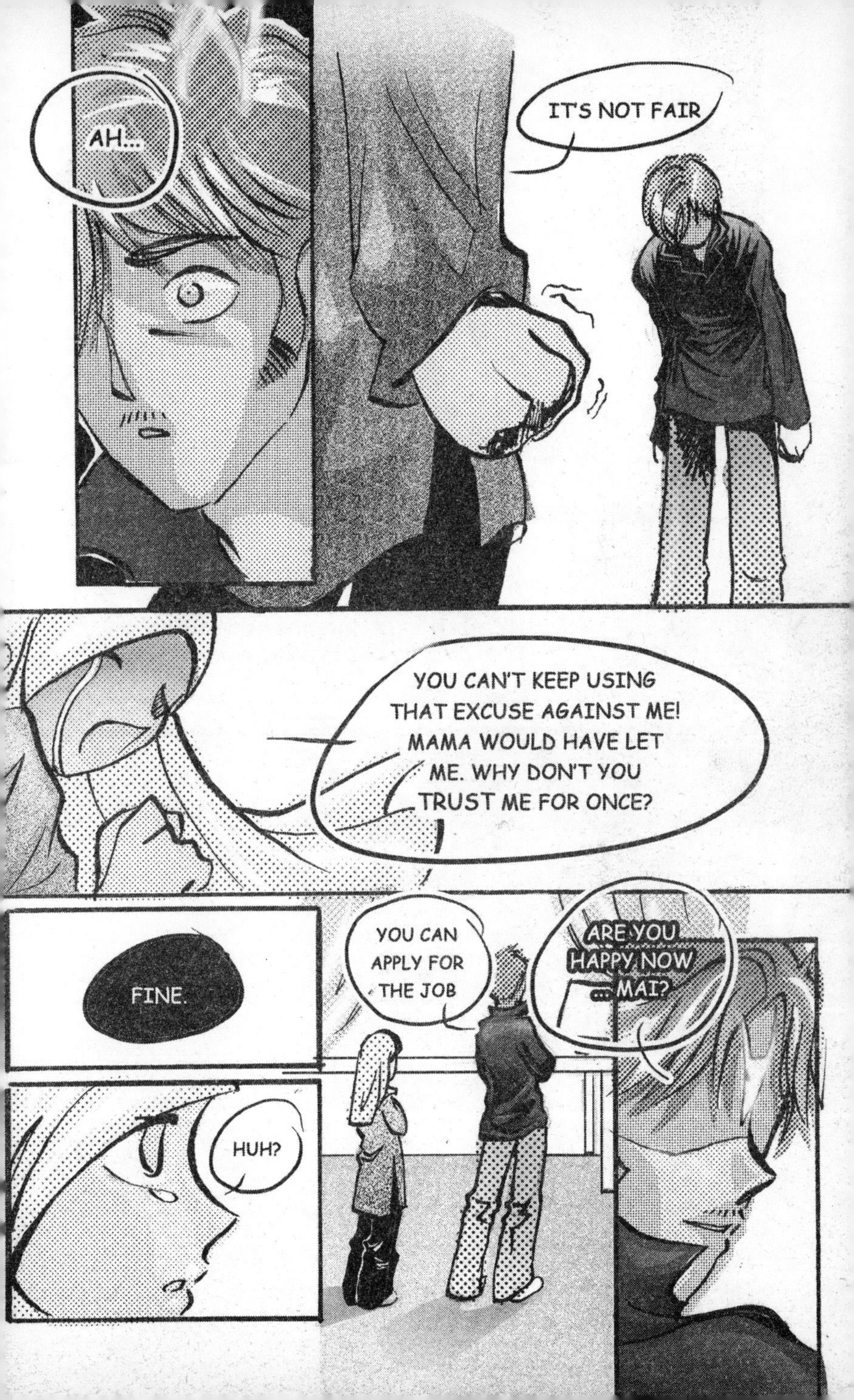
AH...
IT'S NOT FAIR
YOU CAN'T KEEP USING THAT EXCUSE AGAINST ME! MAMA WOULD HAVE LET ME. WHY DON'T YOU TRUST ME FOR ONCE?
FINE.
HUH?
YOU CAN APPLY FOR THE JOB
ARE YOU HAPPY NOW ...MAI?

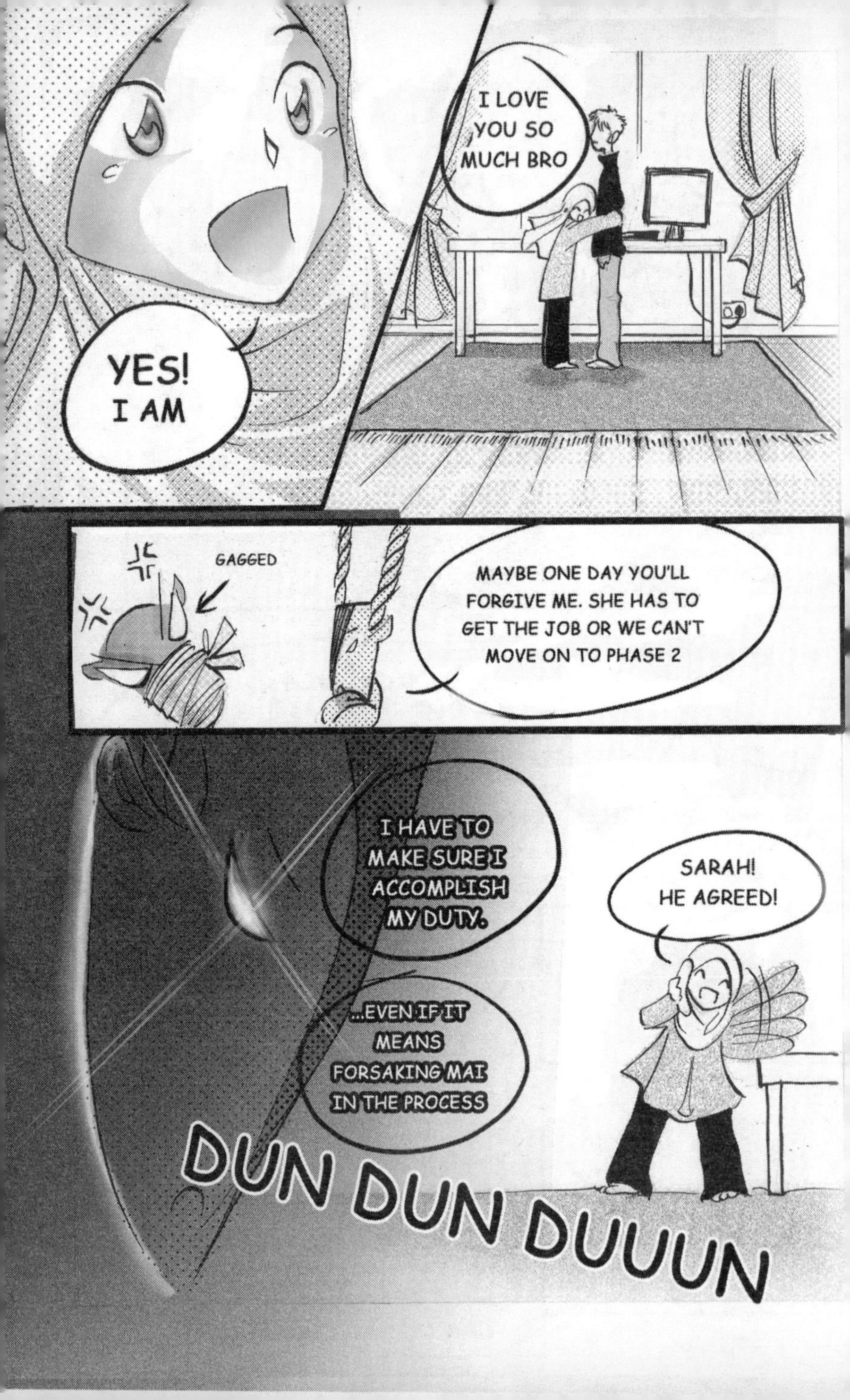
YES! I AM
I LOVE YOU SO MUCH BRO
GAGGED
MAYBE ONE DAY YOU'LL FORGIVE ME. SHE HAS TO GET THE JOB OR WE CAN'T MOVE ON TO PHASE 2
I HAVE TO MAKE SURE I ACCOMPLISH MY DUTY.
...EVEN IF IT MEANS FORSAKING MAI IN THE PROCESS
SARAH! HE AGREED!
DUN DUN DUUUN

station

by

Kate Brown

Date of birth: 16 January 1984

KATE BROWN

Half English, half Welsh, Kate lists among her influences everything from the music of Trent Reznor (Nine Inch Nails), to J.M. Barrie (creator of *Peter Pan*); from the school playground to 'beer, Boursin and baths' – hopefully, not all at the same time! She thrives on controversy, but hates hearing other people eat and drink (slurp! smack!): and anticipation ('then getting things and realising that the wait was probably better') drives her up the wall.

'*Station*', she says, 'was inspired by real events,' springing from the sighting of a carved love-heart, 'but I think that reader interpretation is (perhaps!) more valuable than author intent.'

Kate declares that she doesn't draw any more (NOOOO! Say it ain't so, Kate!), but that she is working up a few full-length stories: *Silver Sun*, about ignorance, *Rolighed*, about the inability to communicate, and *Joe*, which is about the apocalypse. What was that bit about anticipation again?

http://danse-macabre.nu
http://kandinsky-prince.deviantart.com

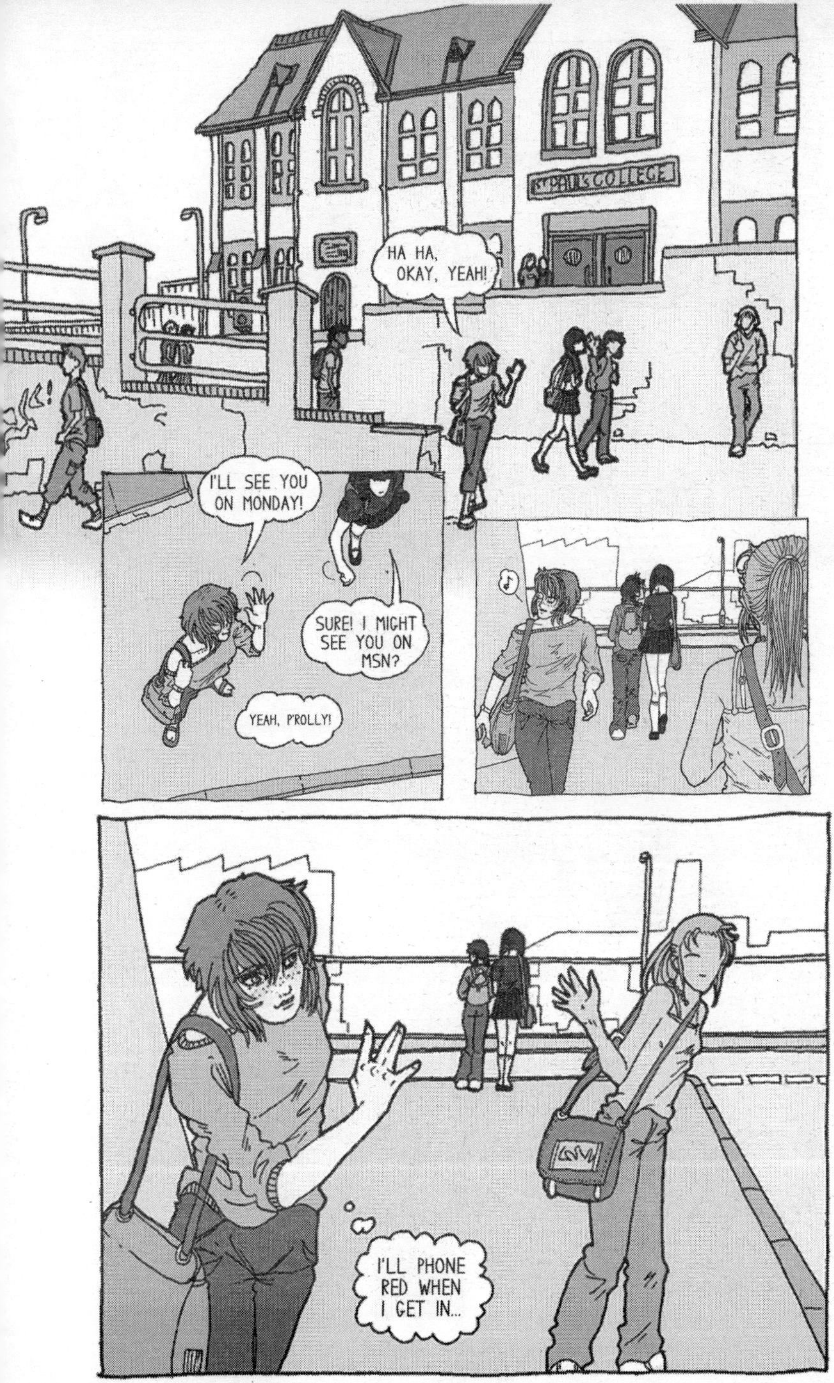
ST PAUL'S COLLEGE
HA HA, OKAY, YEAH!
I'LL SEE YOU ON MONDAY!
SURE! I MIGHT SEE YOU ON MSN?
YEAH, P'ROLLY!
I'LL PHONE RED WHEN I GET IN...

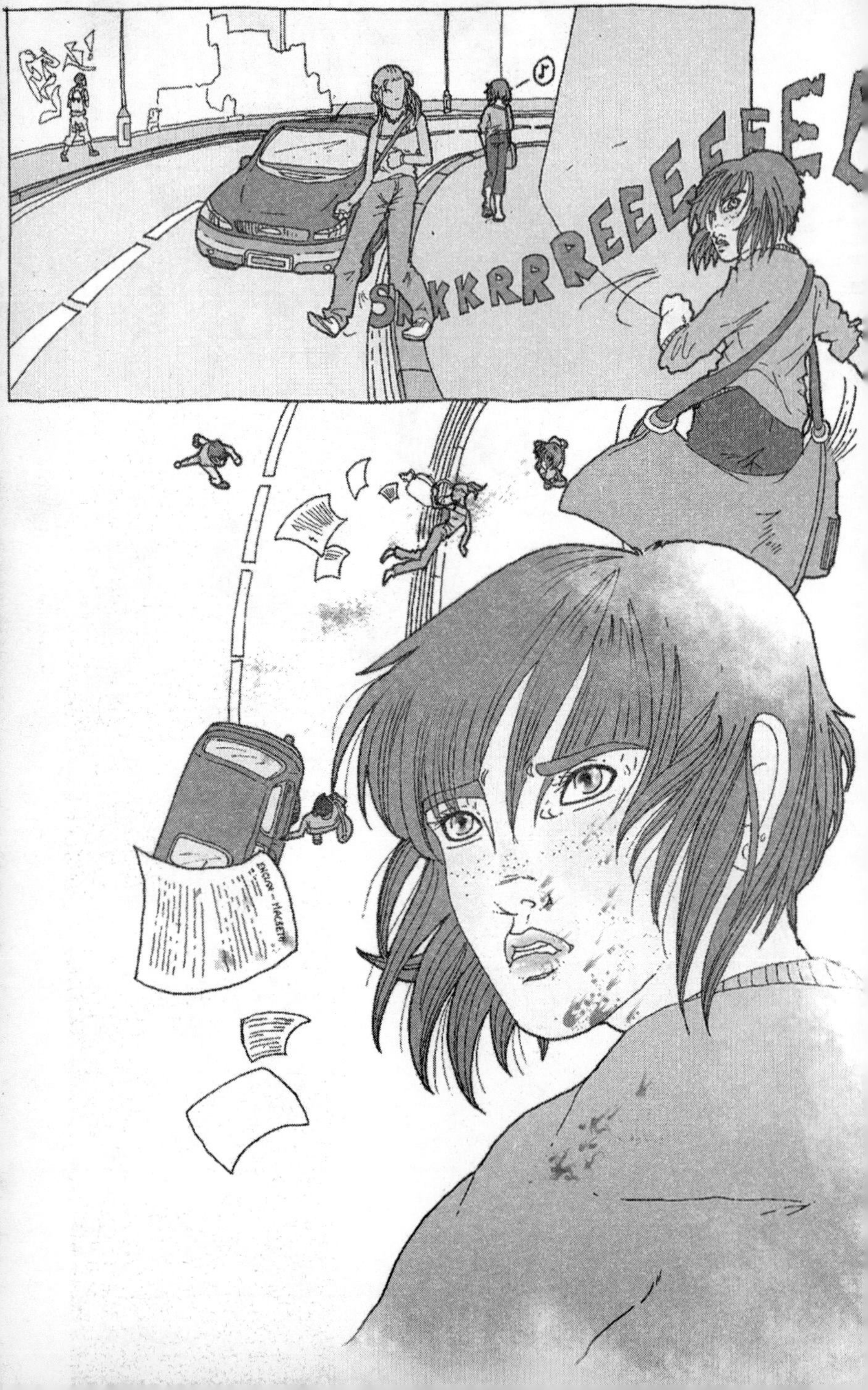
♪
SKKRRREEEEEEC
ENGLISH - MACBETH

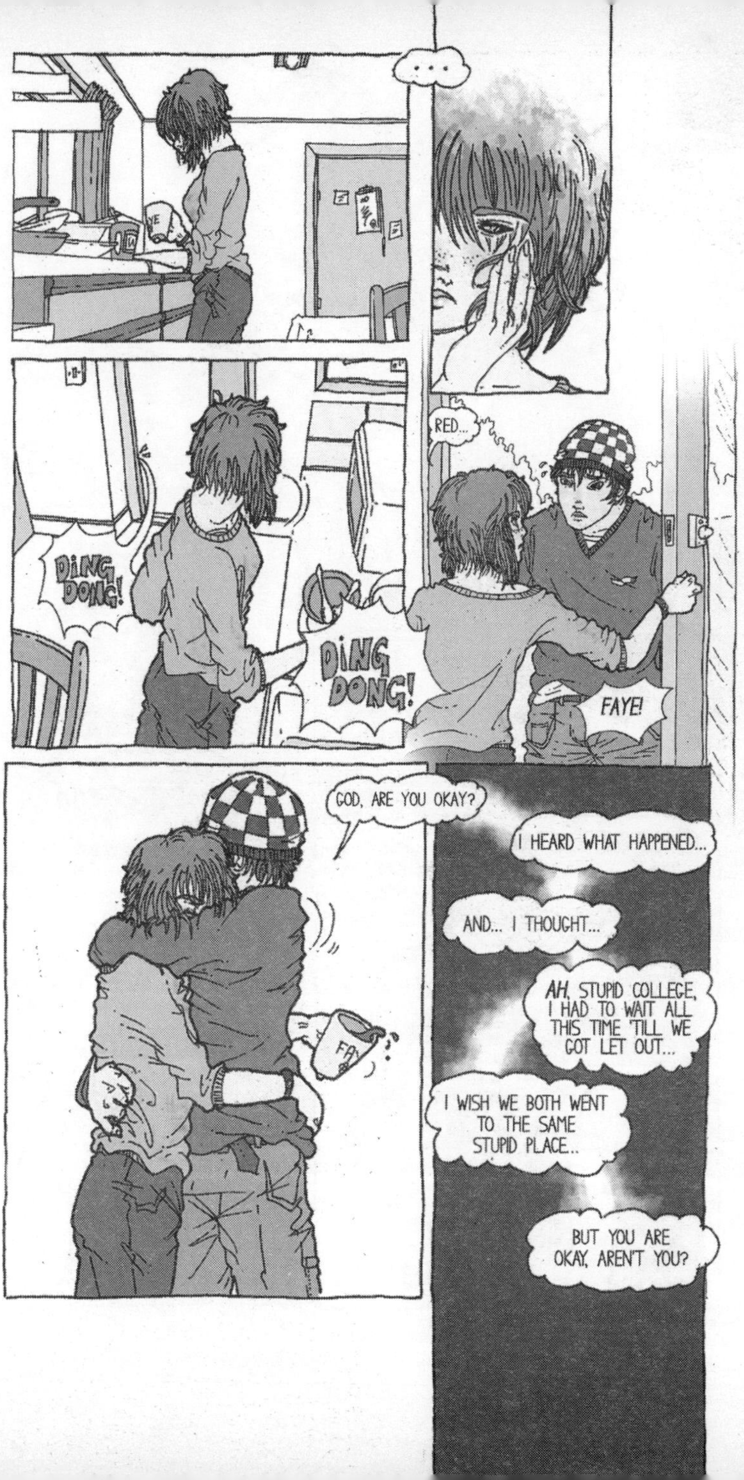

...
DING DONG!
DING DONG!
RED...
FAYE!
GOD, ARE YOU OKAY?
I HEARD WHAT HAPPENED...
AND... I THOUGHT...
AH, STUPID COLLEGE, I HAD TO WAIT ALL THIS TIME 'TILL WE GOT LET OUT...
I WISH WE BOTH WENT TO THE SAME STUPID PLACE..
BUT YOU ARE OKAY, AREN'T YOU?

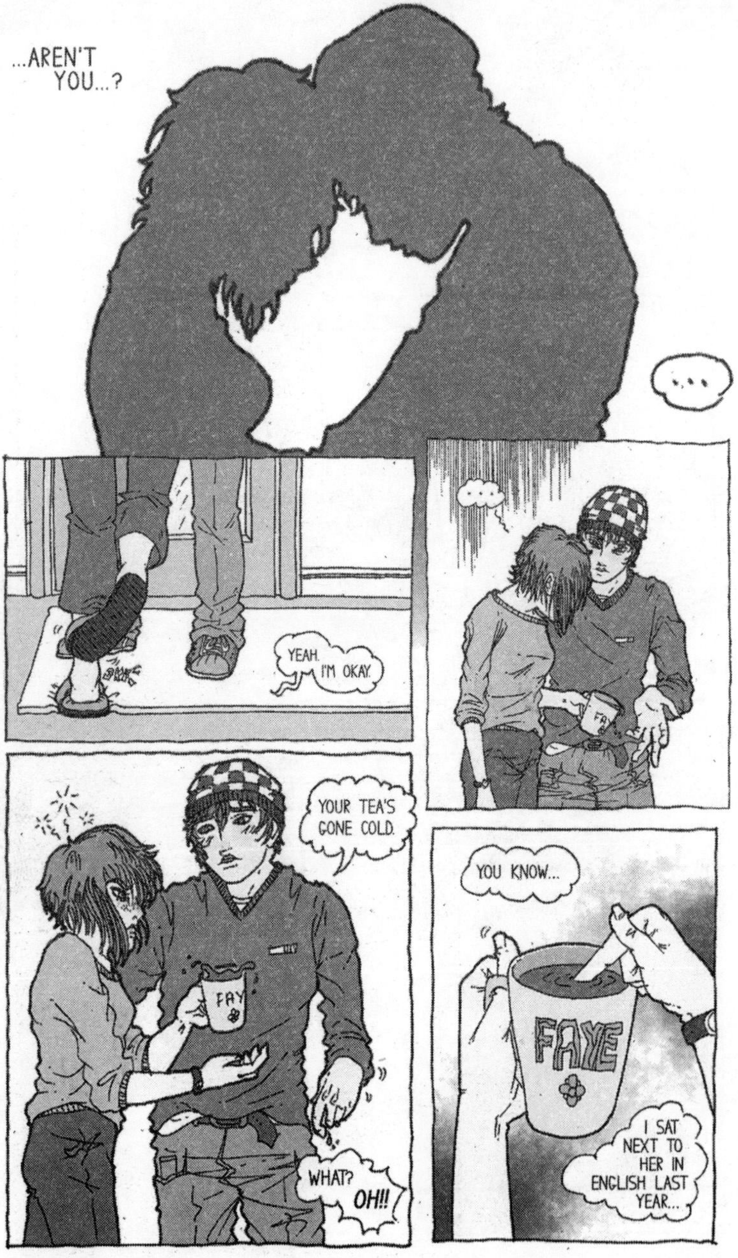
...AREN'T YOU...?
...
YEAH. I'M OKAY.
...
YOUR TEA'S GONE COLD.
WHAT? OH!!
YOU KNOW...
FAYE
I SAT NEXT TO HER IN ENGLISH LAST YEAR...

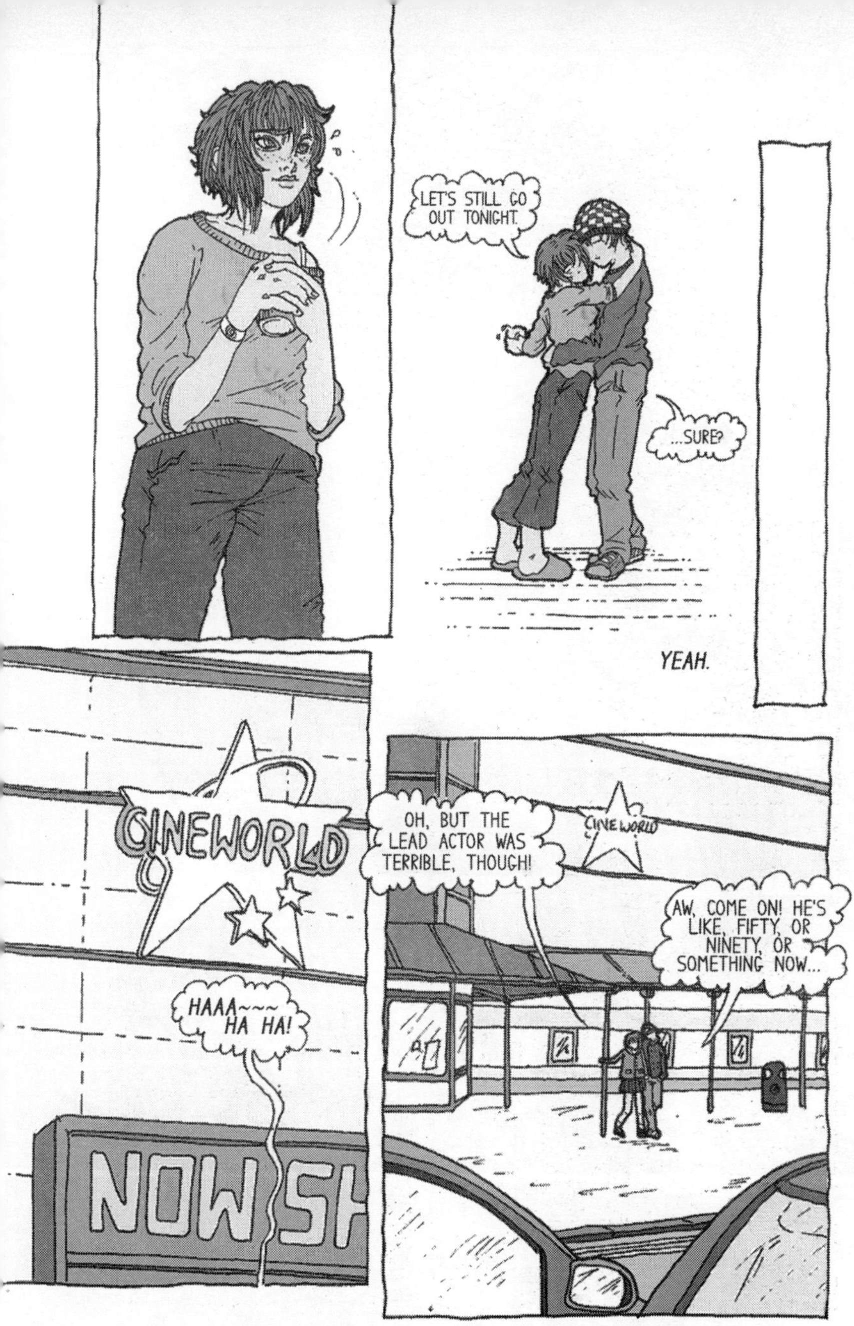
LET'S STILL GO OUT TONIGHT.
...SURE?
YEAH.
CINEWORLD
HAAA~~~ HA HA!
NOW SH
OH, BUT THE LEAD ACTOR WAS TERRIBLE, THOUGH!
CINEWORLD
AW, COME ON! HE'S LIKE, FIFTY, OR NINETY, OR SOMETHING NOW...

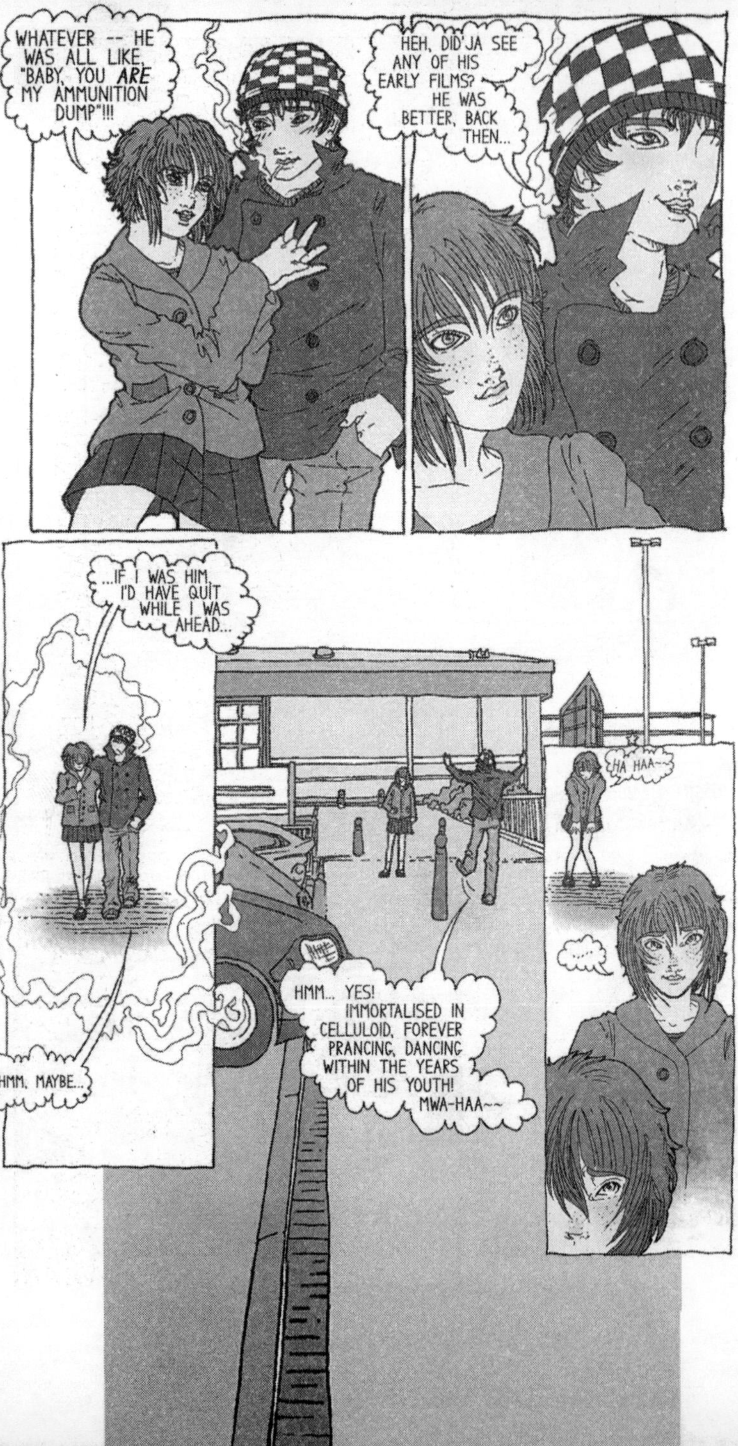
WHATEVER -- HE WAS ALL LIKE, "BABY, YOU *ARE* MY AMMUNITION DUMP"!!!
HEH, DID'JA SEE ANY OF HIS EARLY FILMS? HE WAS BETTER, BACK THEN...
...IF I WAS HIM, I'D HAVE QUIT WHILE I WAS AHEAD...
HMM, MAYBE...
HMM... YES! IMMORTALISED IN CELLULOID, FOREVER PRANCING, DANCING WITHIN THE YEARS OF HIS YOUTH! MWA-HAA~~
HA HAA~~
.....

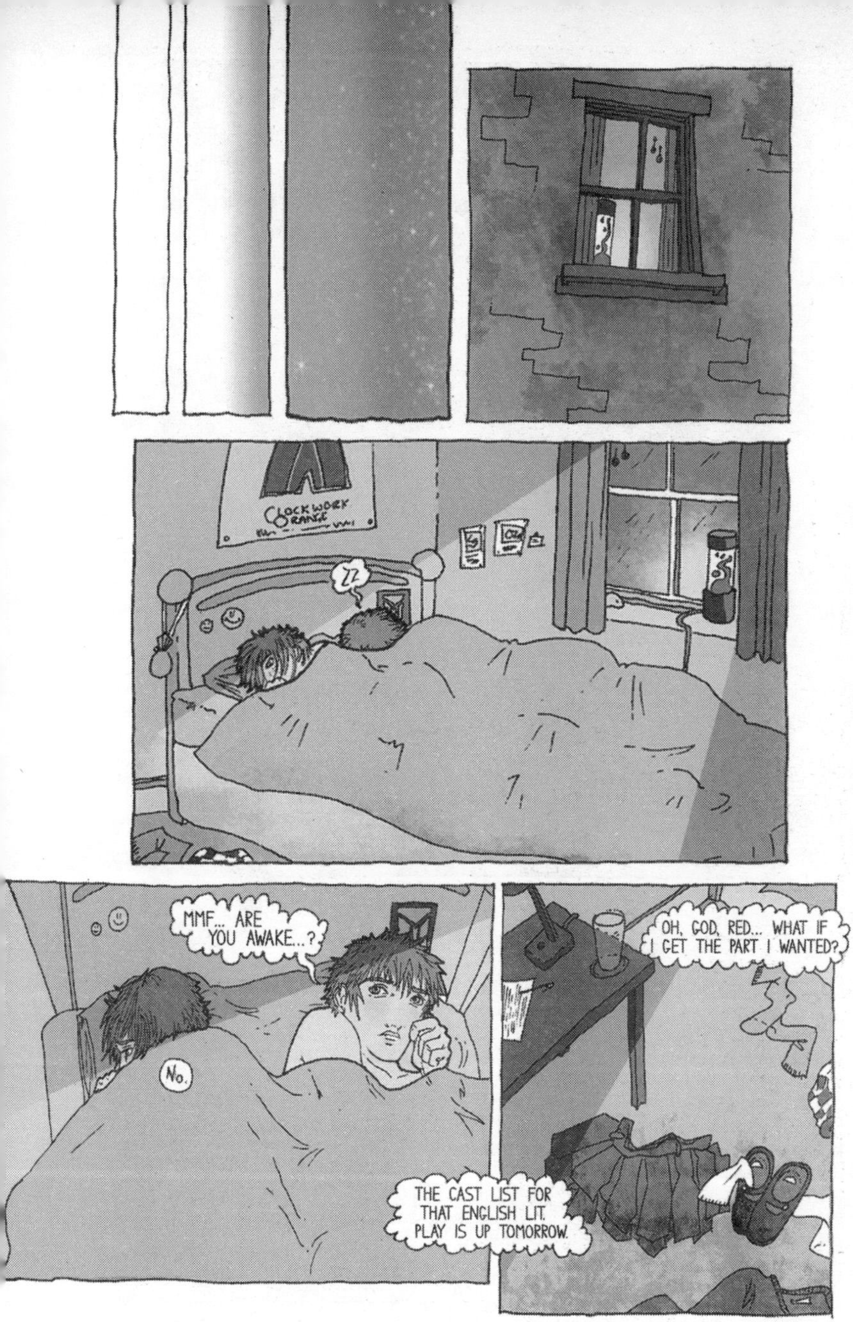
CLOCKWORK ORANGE
ZZ
MMF... ARE YOU AWAKE...?
No.
THE CAST LIST FOR THAT ENGLISH LIT. PLAY IS UP TOMORROW.
OH, GOD, RED... WHAT IF I GET THE PART I WANTED?

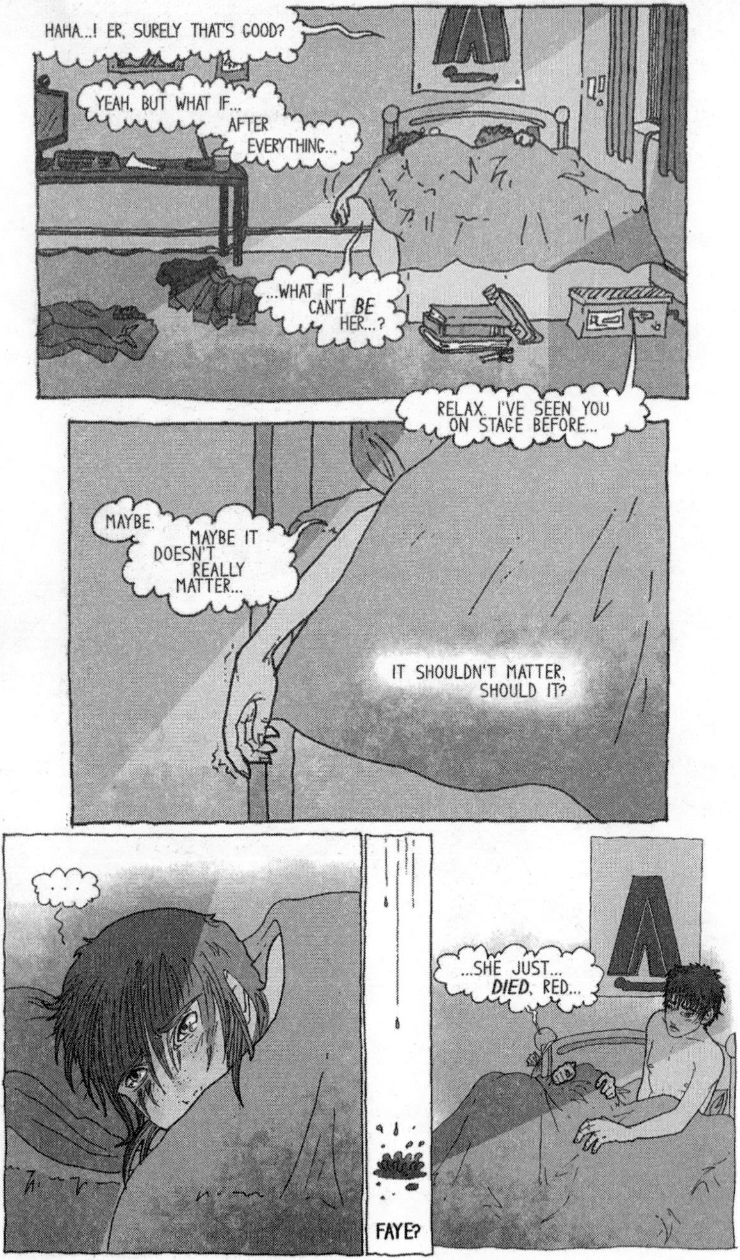
HAHA...! ER, SURELY THAT'S GOOD?
YEAH, BUT WHAT IF... AFTER EVERYTHING...
...WHAT IF I CAN'T *BE* HER...?
RELAX. I'VE SEEN YOU ON STAGE BEFORE...
MAYBE. MAYBE IT DOESN'T REALLY MATTER...
IT SHOULDN'T MATTER, SHOULD IT?
...
FAYE?
...SHE JUST... *DIED*, RED...

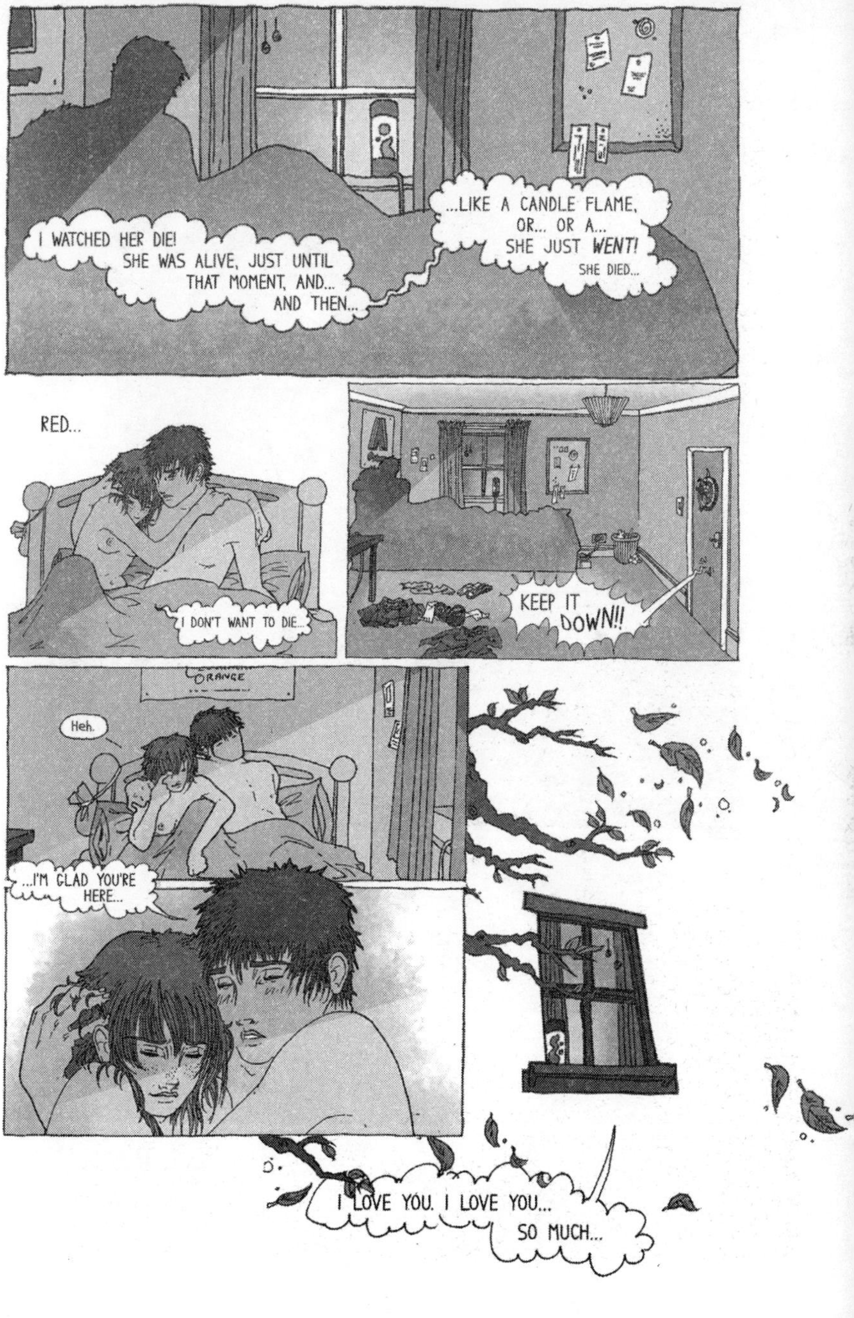
I WATCHED HER DIE! SHE WAS ALIVE, JUST UNTIL THAT MOMENT, AND... AND THEN...
...LIKE A CANDLE FLAME, OR... OR A... SHE JUST WENT! SHE DIED...
RED...
I DON'T WANT TO DIE...
KEEP IT DOWN!!
ORANGE
Heh.
...I'M GLAD YOU'RE HERE...
I LOVE YOU. I LOVE YOU... SO MUCH...

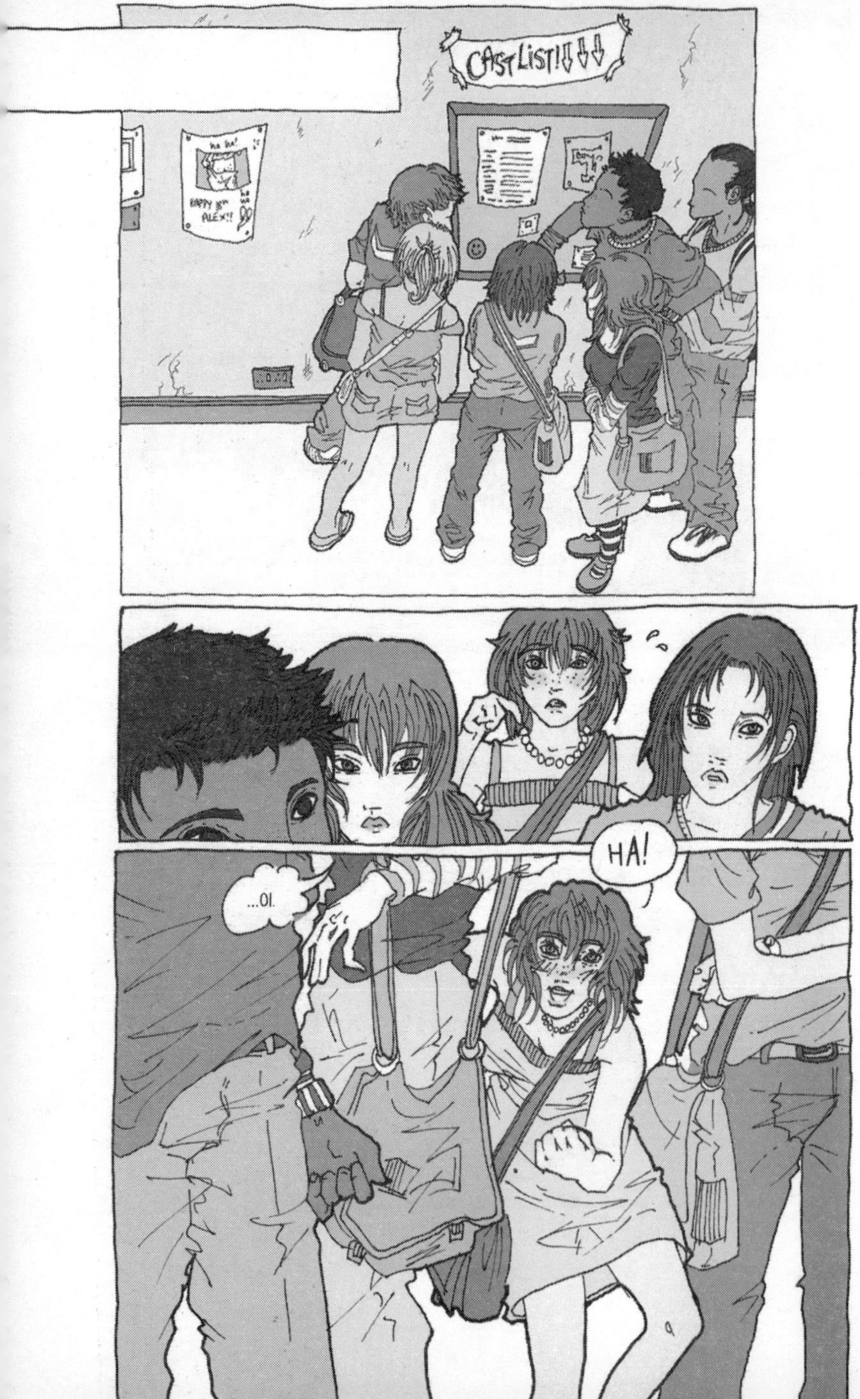
CAST LIST!
...OI.
HA!

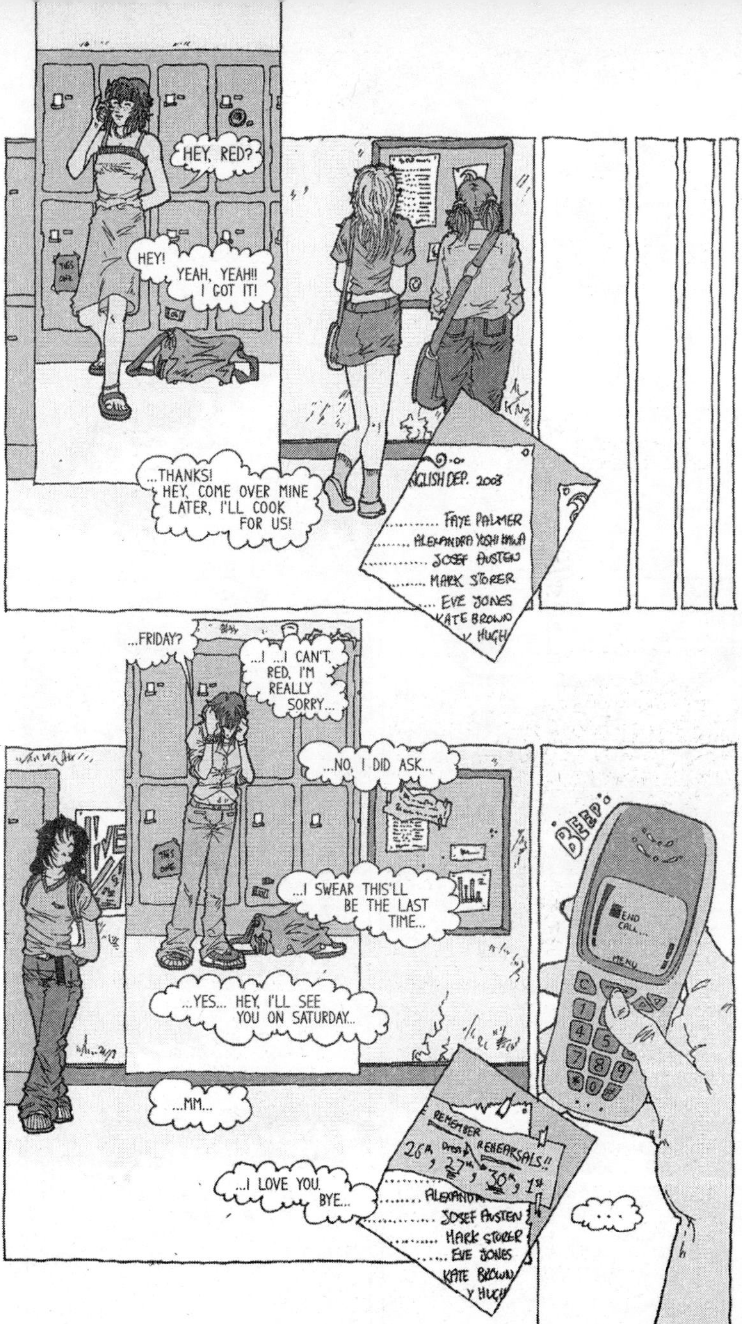
HEY, RED?
HEY!
YEAH, YEAH!! I GOT IT!
...THANKS! HEY, COME OVER MINE LATER, I'LL COOK FOR US!
NGLISH DEP. 2003
FAYE PALMER
ALEXANDRA YOSHIKAWA
JOSEF AUSTEN
MARK STORER
EVE JONES
KATE BROWN
...FRIDAY?
...I ...I CAN'T, RED, I'M REALLY SORRY...
...NO, I DID ASK...
...I SWEAR THIS'LL BE THE LAST TIME...
...YES... HEY, I'LL SEE YOU ON SATURDAY...
...MM...
...I LOVE YOU. BYE...
REMEMBER REHEARSALS!!
JOSEF AUSTEN
MARK STORER
EVE JONES
KATE BROWN
BEEP
END CALL...
MENU
...

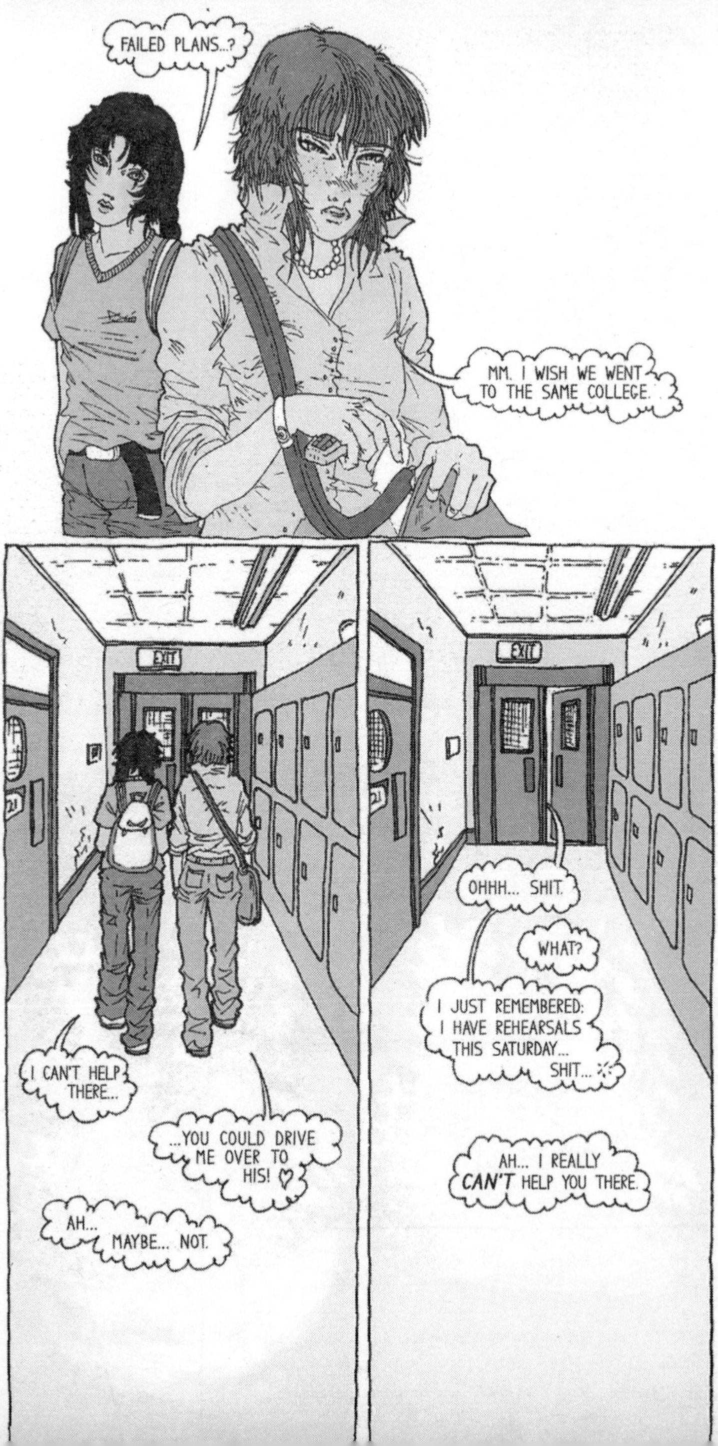
FAILED PLANS...?
MM. I WISH WE WENT TO THE SAME COLLEGE.
I CAN'T HELP THERE...
...YOU COULD DRIVE ME OVER TO HIS! ♡
AH... MAYBE... NOT.
EXIT
OHHH... SHIT.
WHAT?
I JUST REMEMBERED: I HAVE REHEARSALS THIS SATURDAY... SHIT...
AH... I REALLY ***CAN'T*** HELP YOU THERE.

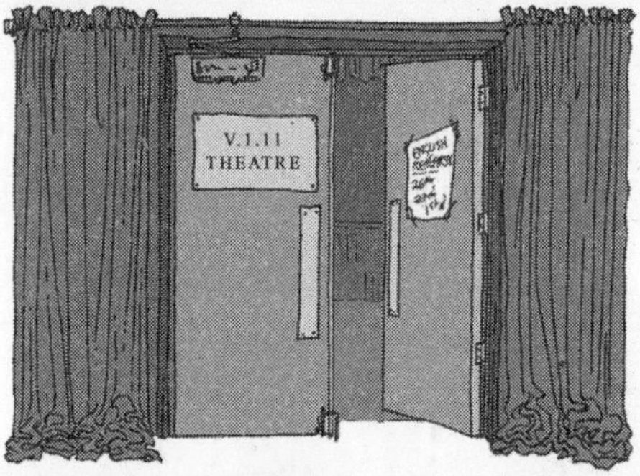
V.1.11
THEATRE

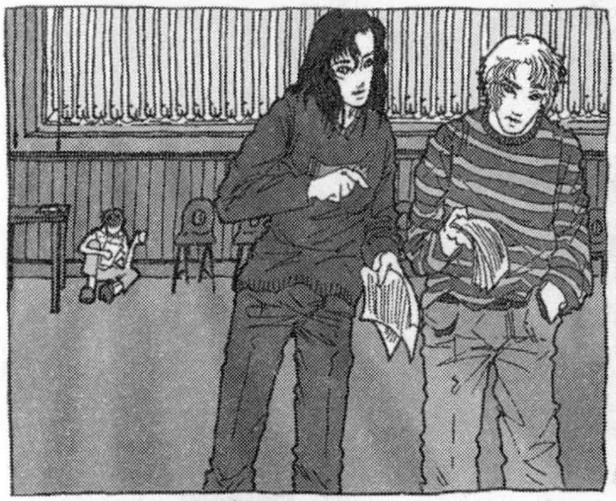

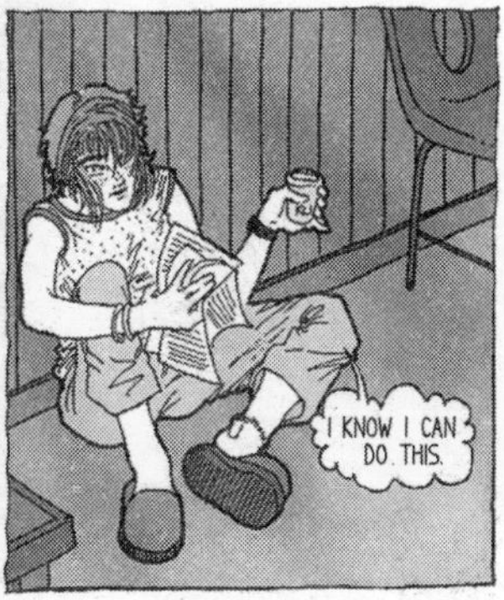
I KNOW I CAN DO THIS.

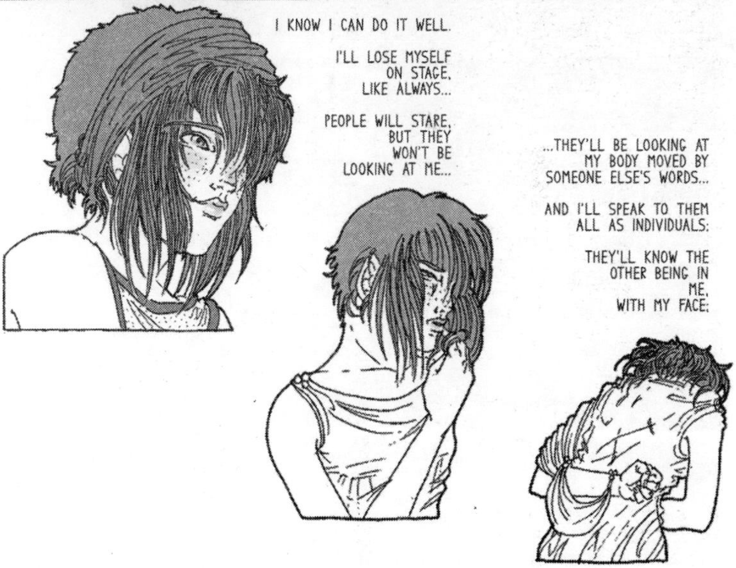
I KNOW I CAN DO IT WELL.
I'LL LOSE MYSELF ON STAGE, LIKE ALWAYS...
PEOPLE WILL STARE, BUT THEY WON'T BE LOOKING AT ME...
...THEY'LL BE LOOKING AT MY BODY MOVED BY SOMEONE ELSE'S WORDS...
AND I'LL SPEAK TO THEM ALL AS INDIVIDUALS:
THEY'LL KNOW THE OTHER BEING IN ME, WITH MY FACE;

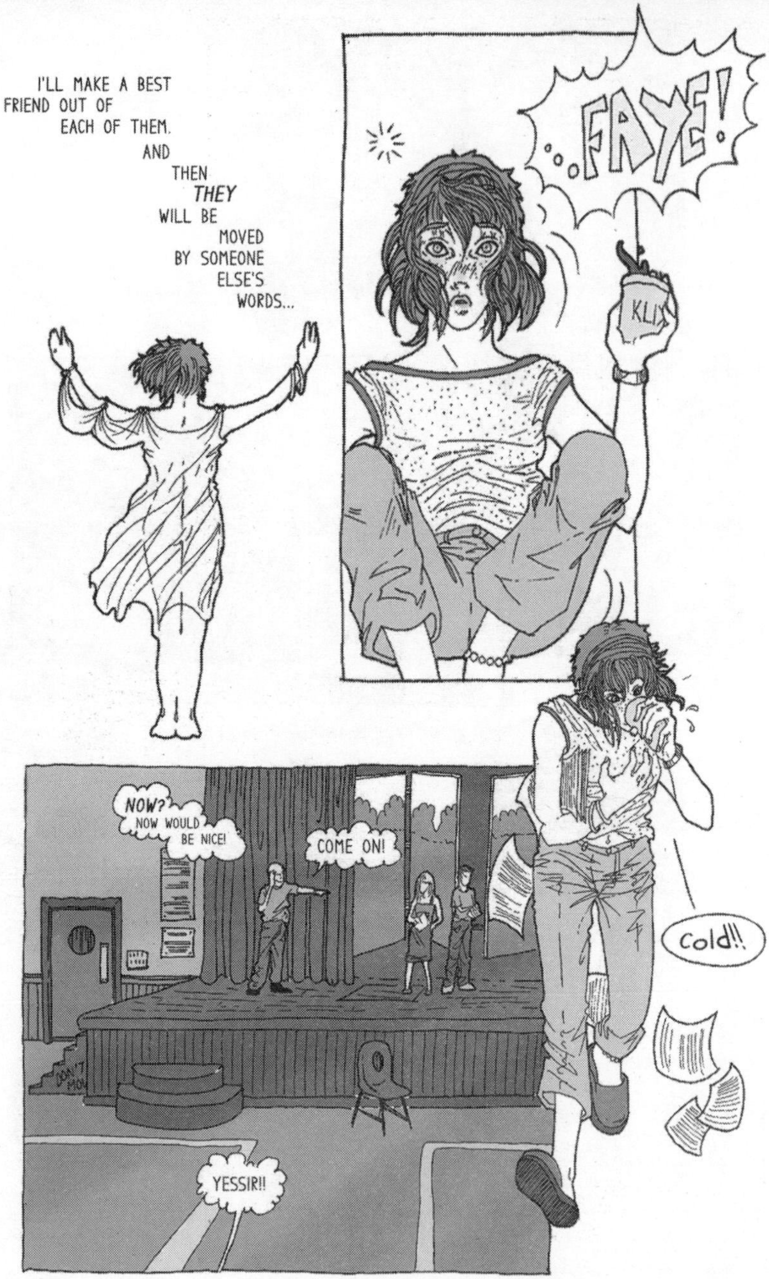
I'LL MAKE A BEST FRIEND OUT OF EACH OF THEM. AND THEN *THEY* WILL BE MOVED BY SOMEONE ELSE'S WORDS...
...FAYE!
KLI
NOW? NOW WOULD BE NICE!
COME ON!
YESSIR!!
Cold!!

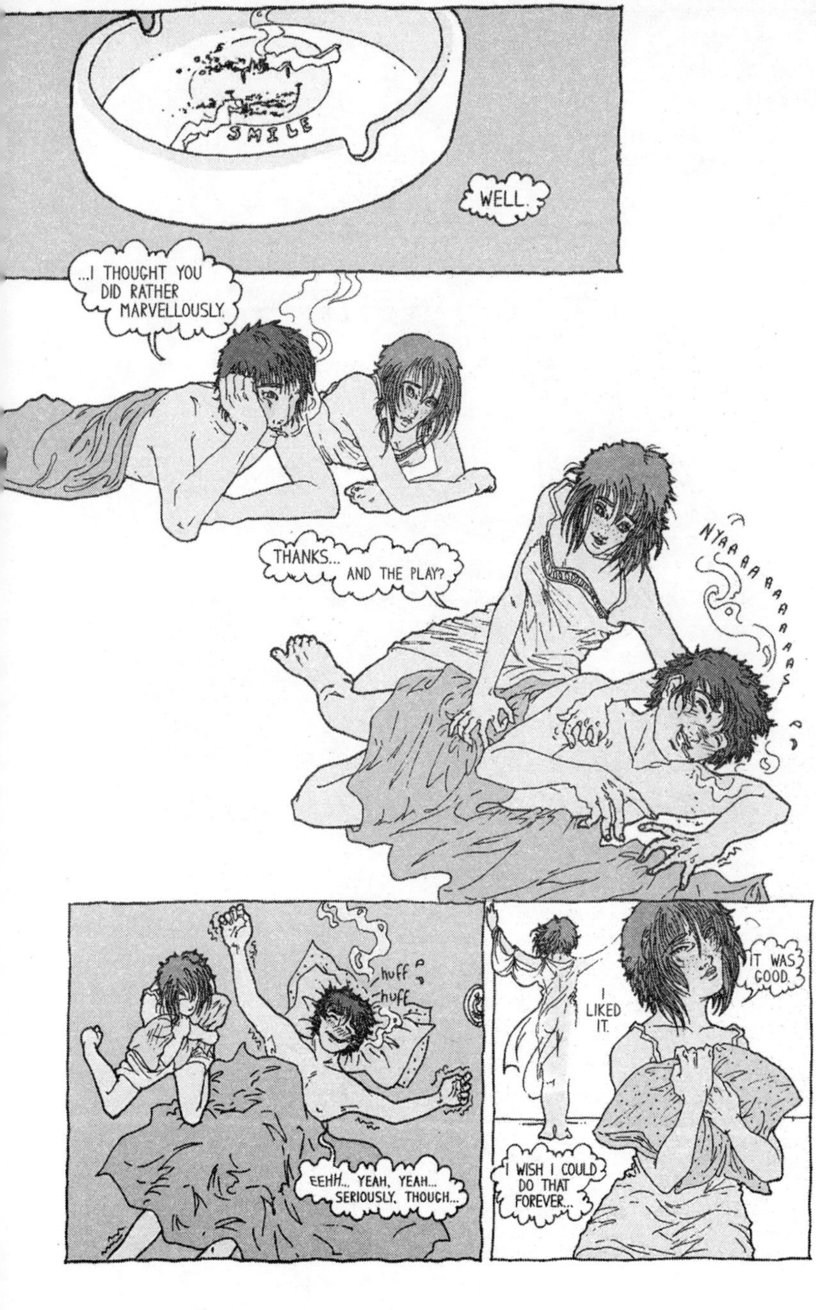
SMILE
WELL.
...I THOUGHT YOU DID RATHER MARVELLOUSLY.
THANKS... AND THE PLAY?
NYAAAAAAAAAAS!
huff huff
EEHH... YEAH, YEAH... SERIOUSLY, THOUGH...
I LIKED IT.
IT WAS GOOD.
I WISH I COULD DO THAT FOREVER...

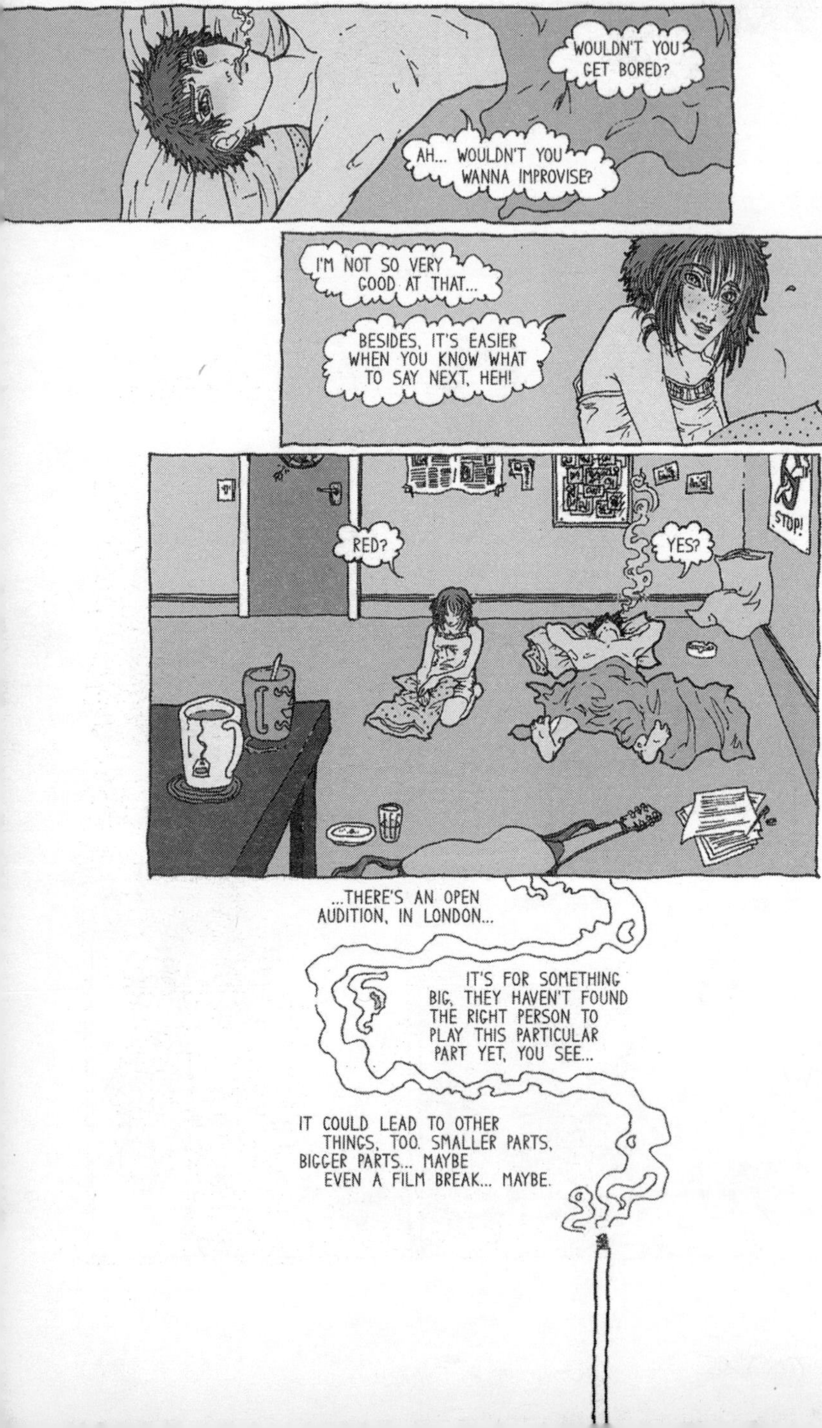
WOULDN'T YOU GET BORED?
AH... WOULDN'T YOU WANNA IMPROVISE?
I'M NOT SO VERY GOOD AT THAT...
BESIDES, IT'S EASIER WHEN YOU KNOW WHAT TO SAY NEXT, HEH!
STOP!
RED?
YES?
...THERE'S AN OPEN AUDITION, IN LONDON...
IT'S FOR SOMETHING BIG, THEY HAVEN'T FOUND THE RIGHT PERSON TO PLAY THIS PARTICULAR PART YET, YOU SEE...
IT COULD LEAD TO OTHER THINGS, TOO. SMALLER PARTS, BIGGER PARTS... MAYBE EVEN A FILM BREAK... MAYBE.

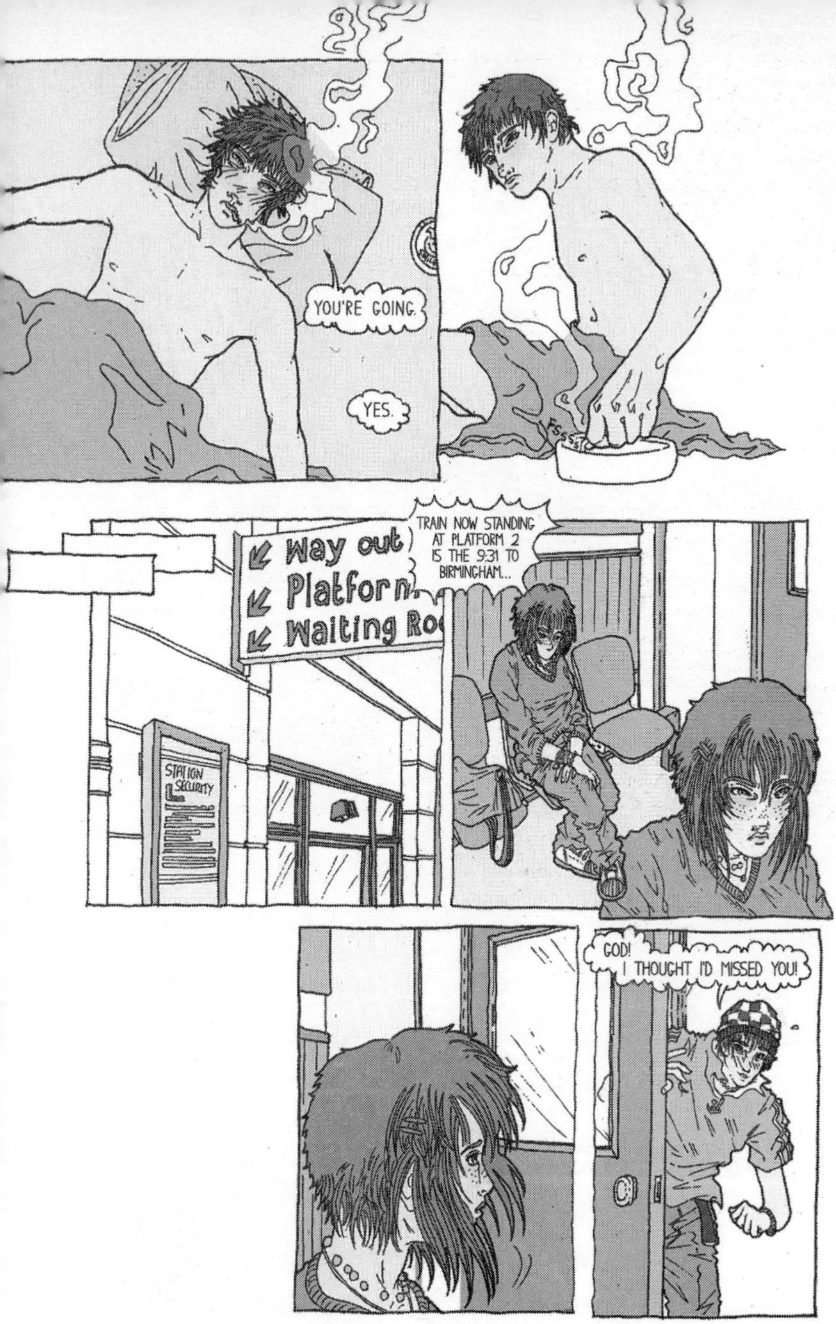
YOU'RE GOING.
YES.
FSSS
Way out
Platform
Waiting Ro
STATION SECURITY
TRAIN NOW STANDING AT PLATFORM 2 IS THE 9:31 TO BIRMINGHAM...
GOD! I THOUGHT I'D MISSED YOU!

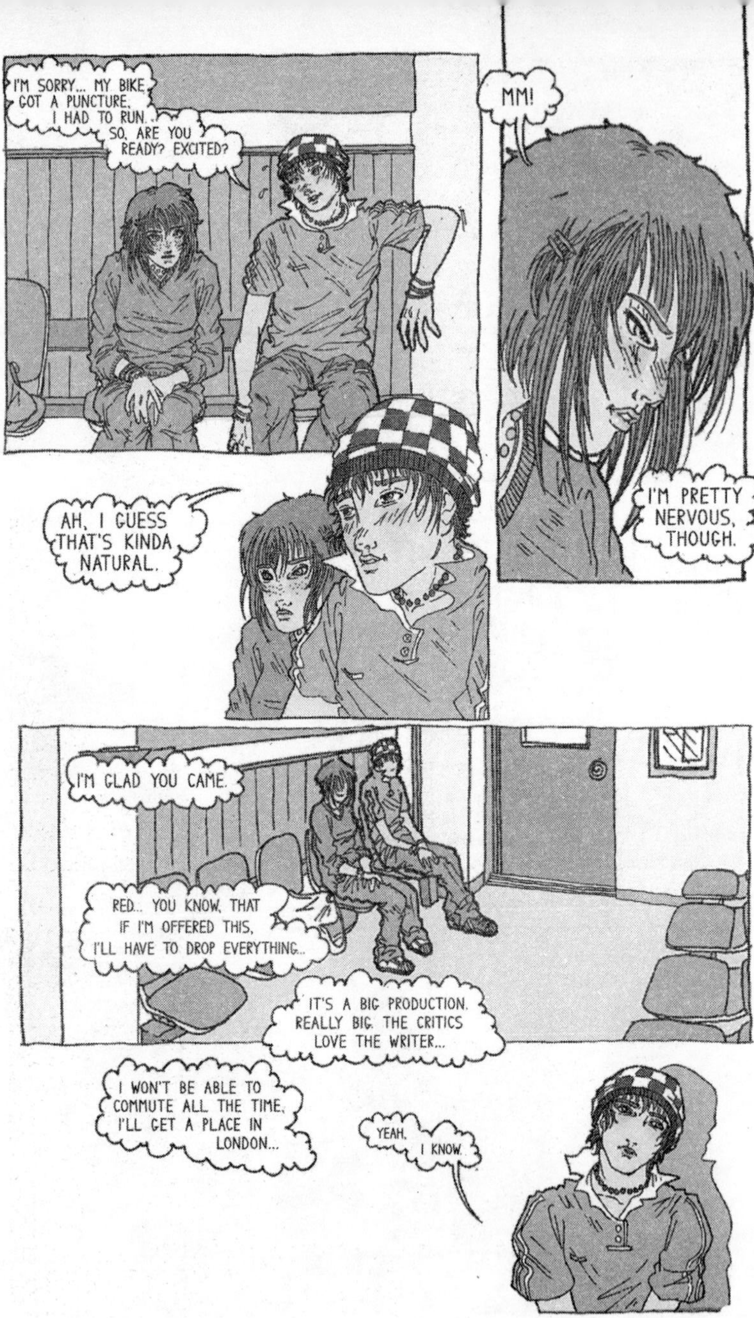
I'M SORRY... MY BIKE GOT A PUNCTURE, I HAD TO RUN...
SO, ARE YOU READY? EXCITED?
MM!
AH, I GUESS THAT'S KINDA NATURAL.
I'M PRETTY NERVOUS, THOUGH.
I'M GLAD YOU CAME.
RED... YOU KNOW, THAT IF I'M OFFERED THIS, I'LL HAVE TO DROP EVERYTHING...
IT'S A BIG PRODUCTION. REALLY BIG. THE CRITICS LOVE THE WRITER...
I WON'T BE ABLE TO COMMUTE ALL THE TIME, I'LL GET A PLACE IN LONDON...
YEAH, I KNOW.

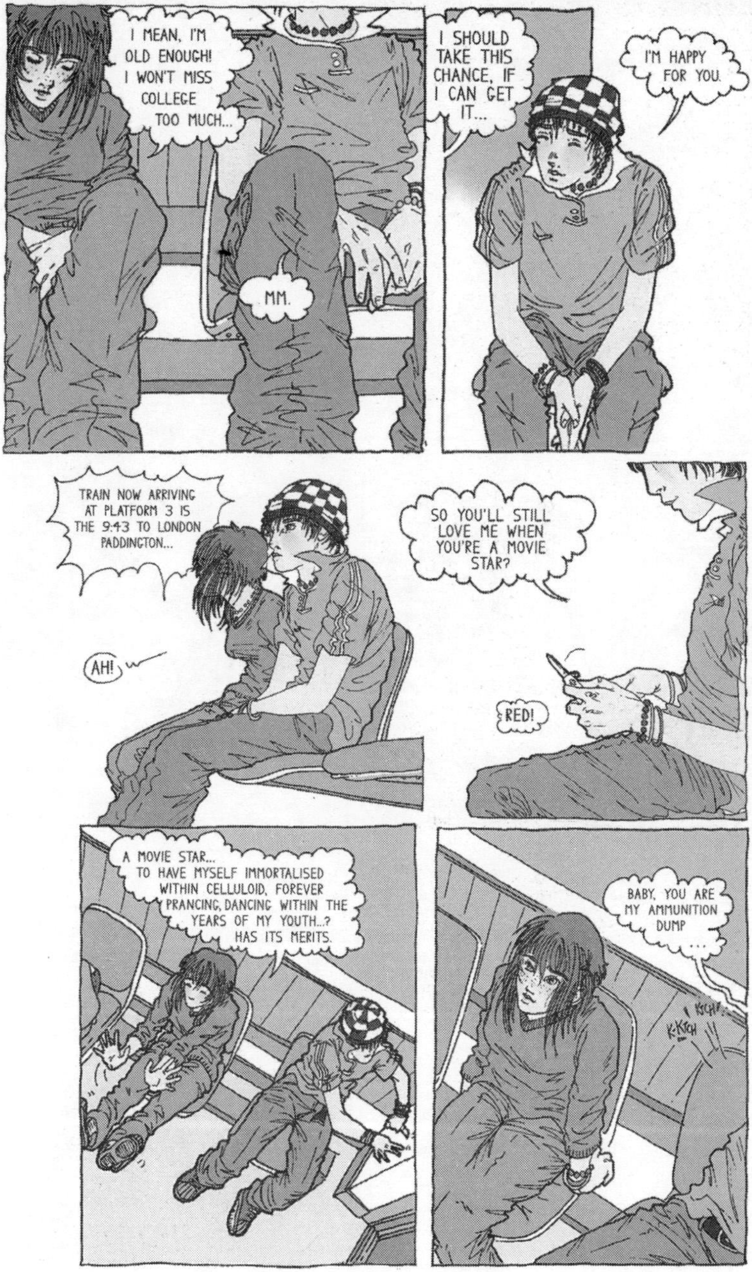
I MEAN, I'M OLD ENOUGH! I WON'T MISS COLLEGE TOO MUCH...
MM.
I SHOULD TAKE THIS CHANCE, IF I CAN GET IT...
I'M HAPPY FOR YOU.
TRAIN NOW ARRIVING AT PLATFORM 3 IS THE 9:43 TO LONDON PADDINGTON...
AH!
SO YOU'LL STILL LOVE ME WHEN YOU'RE A MOVIE STAR?
RED!
A MOVIE STAR... TO HAVE MYSELF IMMORTALISED WITHIN CELLULOID, FOREVER PRANCING, DANCING WITHIN THE YEARS OF MY YOUTH...? HAS ITS MERITS.
BABY, YOU ARE MY AMMUNITION DUMP
...
K-KTCH

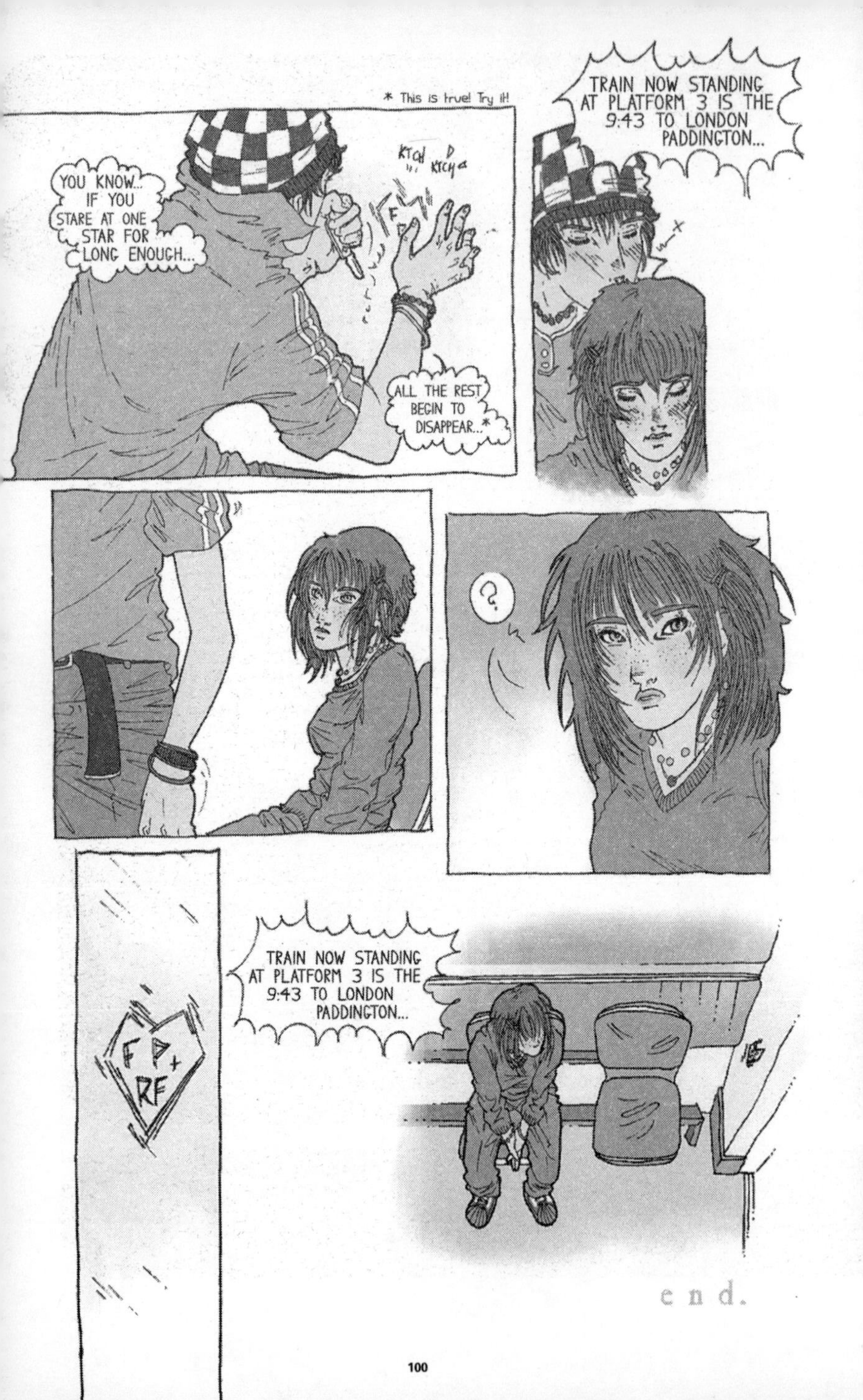
* This is true! Try it!
YOU KNOW... IF YOU STARE AT ONE STAR FOR LONG ENOUGH...
KTCH KTCH
ALL THE REST BEGIN TO DISAPPEAR...*
TRAIN NOW STANDING AT PLATFORM 3 IS THE 9:43 TO LONDON PADDINGTON...
?
FP + RF
TRAIN NOW STANDING AT PLATFORM 3 IS THE 9:43 TO LONDON PADDINGTON...
end.

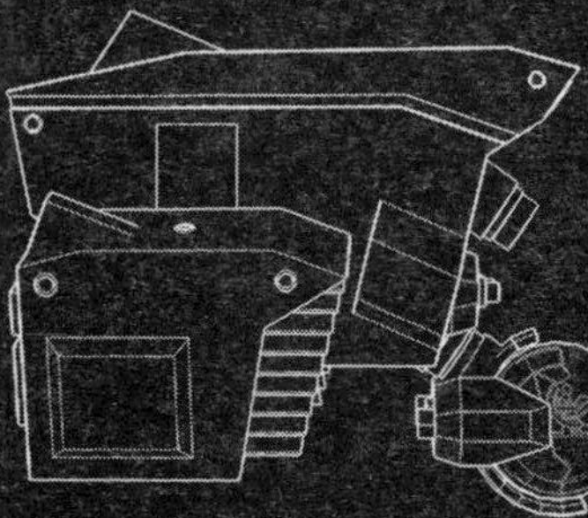

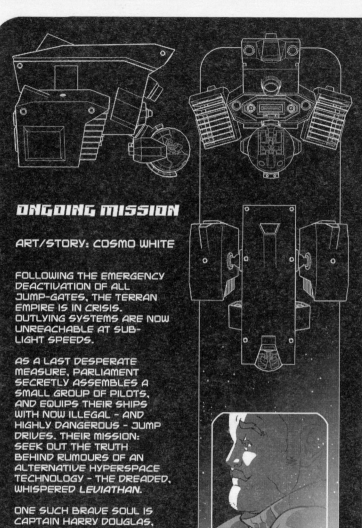

ONGOING MISSION

ART/STORY: COSMO WHITE

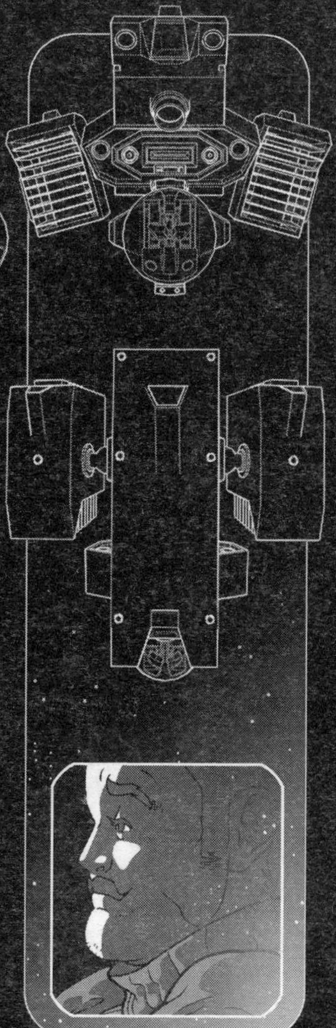

FOLLOWING THE EMERGENCY DEACTIVATION OF ALL JUMP-GATES, THE TERRAN EMPIRE IS IN CRISIS. OUTLYING SYSTEMS ARE NOW UNREACHABLE AT SUB-LIGHT SPEEDS.

AS A LAST DESPERATE MEASURE, PARLIAMENT SECRETLY ASSEMBLES A SMALL GROUP OF PILOTS, AND EQUIPS THEIR SHIPS WITH NOW ILLEGAL - AND HIGHLY DANGEROUS - JUMP DRIVES. THEIR MISSION: SEEK OUT THE TRUTH BEHIND RUMOURS OF AN ALTERNATIVE HYPERSPACE TECHNOLOGY - THE DREADED, WHISPERED *LEVIATHAN*.

ONE SUCH BRAVE SOUL IS CAPTAIN HARRY DOUGLAS, PILOT OF THE MOTOR VESSEL *ERRANT*...

Date of birth: 26 September 1972

COSMO WHITE

Born in Manchester, living in Brighton, Cosmo grooves on anime – the likes of *Ghost in the Shell* and *Battle of the Planets*. The influence of animation is clearly visible in all of his work, from its careful and clean delineation, right down to his deceptively simple use of tones of light and dark when modelling shapes. Old Filmation series figure in there (*Tarzan, He-man*), as well as the fine art of Gustav Klimt and Aubrey Beardsley, and – 'Blistering Barnacles!' – Herge's *Adventures of Tintin*. He loves Christmas, *Star Wars* and ham (naturally); but hates working, people who walk too slowly and, uh, Brighton!

Ongoing Mission is 'an attempt to build suspense primarily through sound effects and pacing; the resolution is ambiguous, but it's the journey to the resolution which is the thing.' It is also part of a proposed series of stories under the general heading, *Leviathan*.

http://www.underfire-comics.com

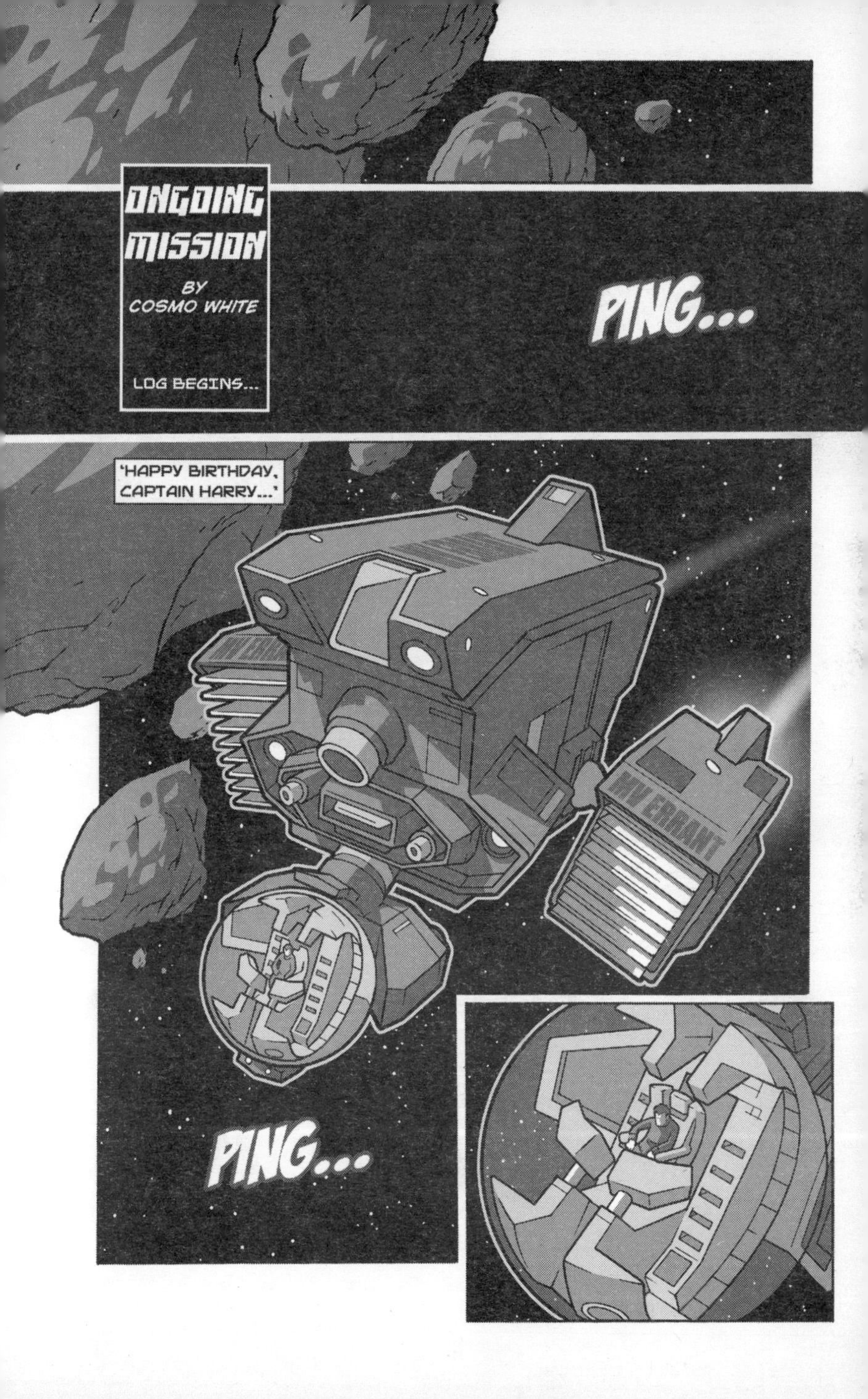
ONGOING MISSION
BY COSMO WHITE
LOG BEGINS...
PING...
'HAPPY BIRTHDAY, CAPTAIN HARRY...'
MV ERRANT
PING...

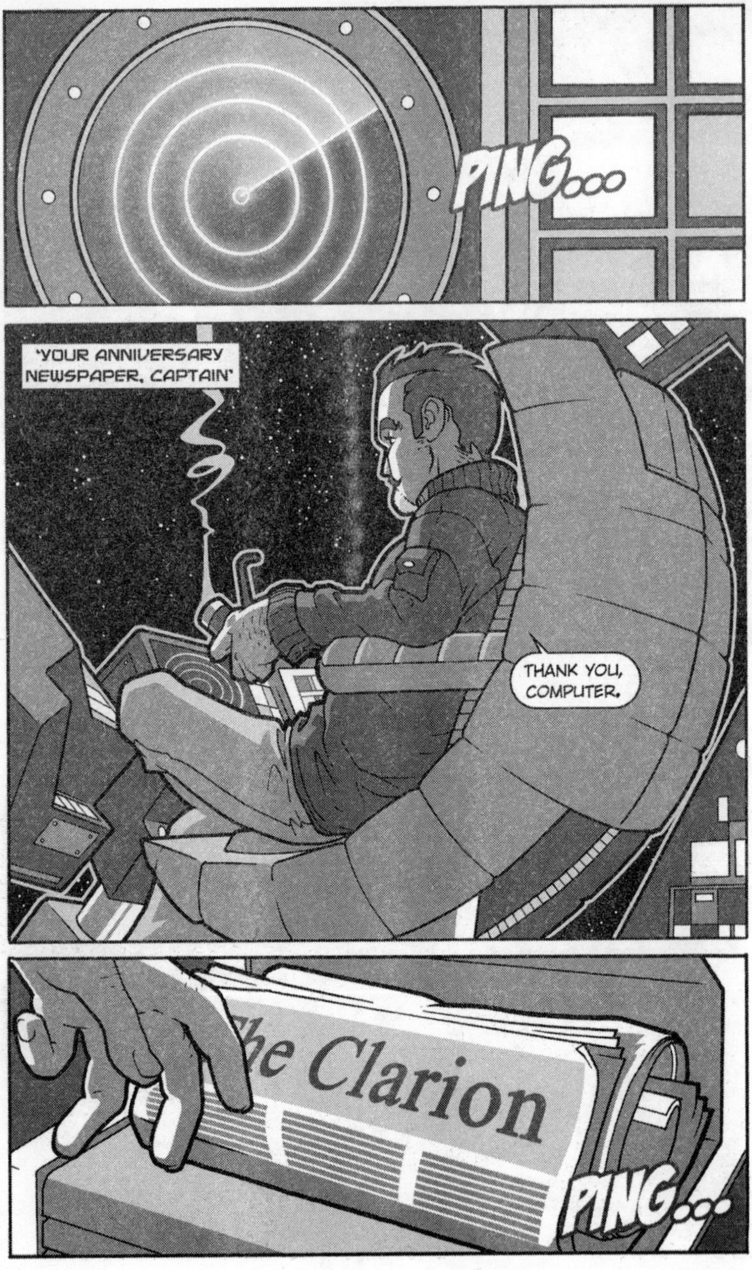
PING...
'YOUR ANNIVERSARY NEWSPAPER, CAPTAIN'
THANK YOU, COMPUTER.
The Clarion
PING...

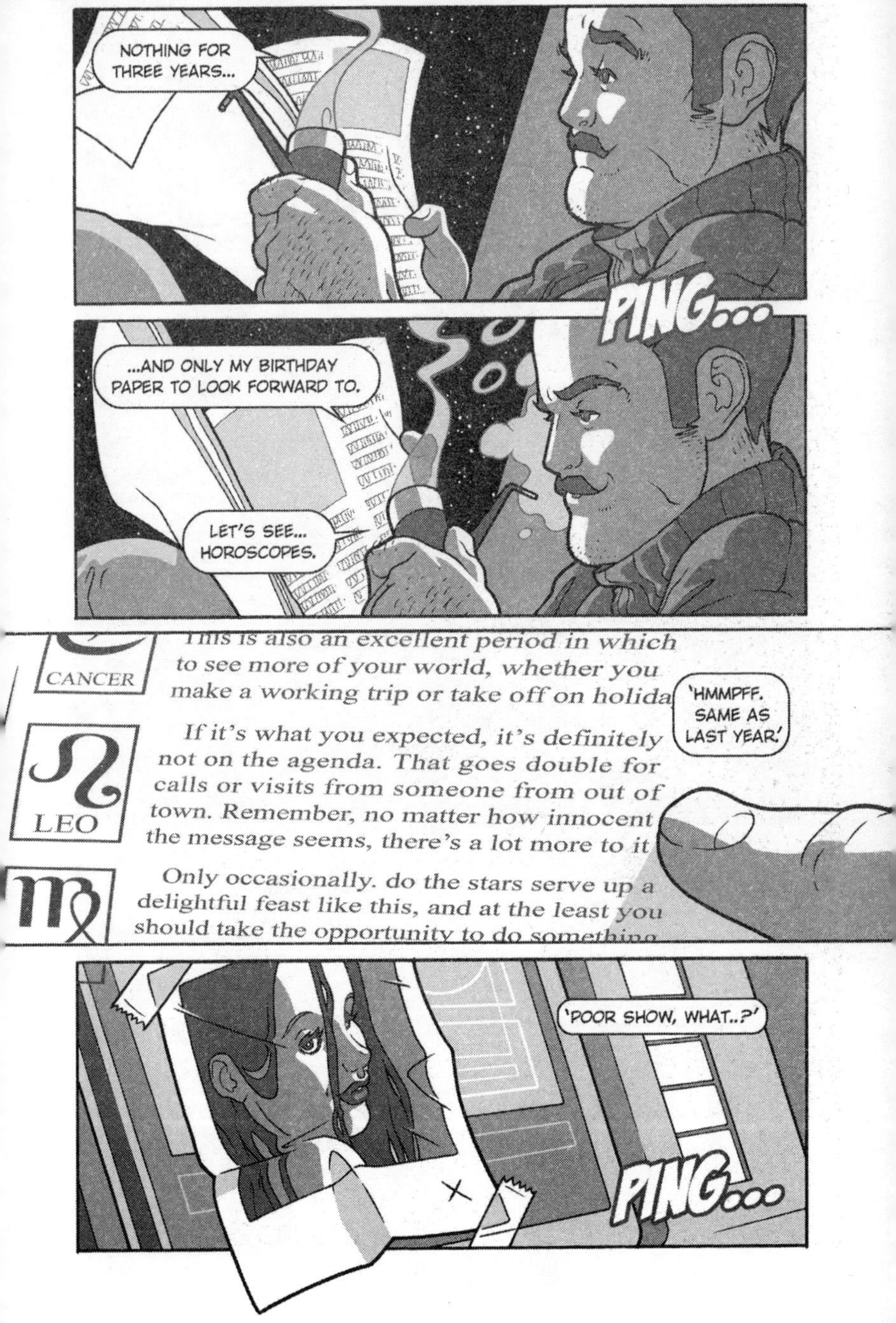
NOTHING FOR THREE YEARS...
PING...
...AND ONLY MY BIRTHDAY PAPER TO LOOK FORWARD TO.
LET'S SEE... HOROSCOPES.
CANCER
This is also an excellent period in which
to see more of your world, whether you
make a working trip or take off on holida
'HMMPFF. SAME AS LAST YEAR.'
LEO
If it's what you expected, it's definitely
not on the agenda. That goes double for
calls or visits from someone from out of
town. Remember, no matter how innocent
the message seems, there's a lot more to it
Only occasionally. do the stars serve up a
delightful feast like this, and at the least you
should take the opportunity to do somethin
'POOR SHOW, WHAT..?'
PING...

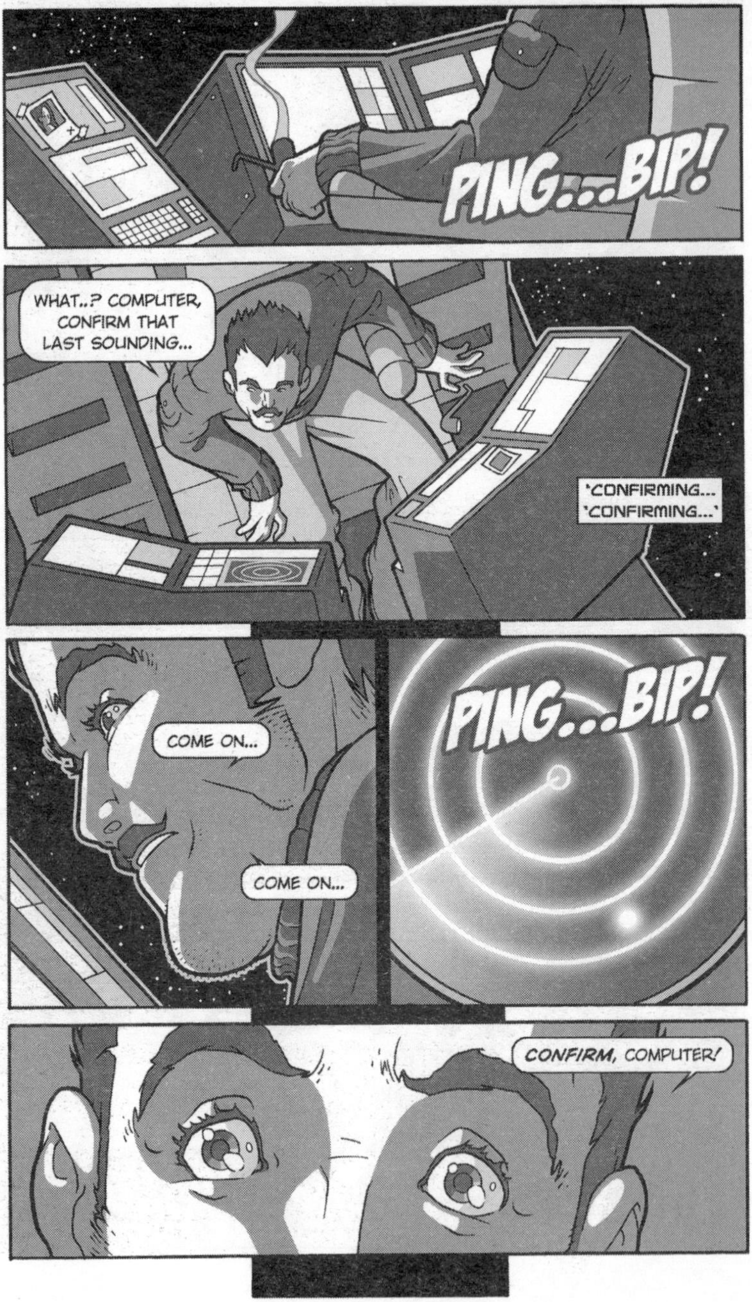

PING...BIP!
WHAT..? COMPUTER, CONFIRM THAT LAST SOUNDING...
'CONFIRMING... 'CONFIRMING...'
COME ON...
COME ON...
PING...BIP!
CONFIRM, COMPUTER!

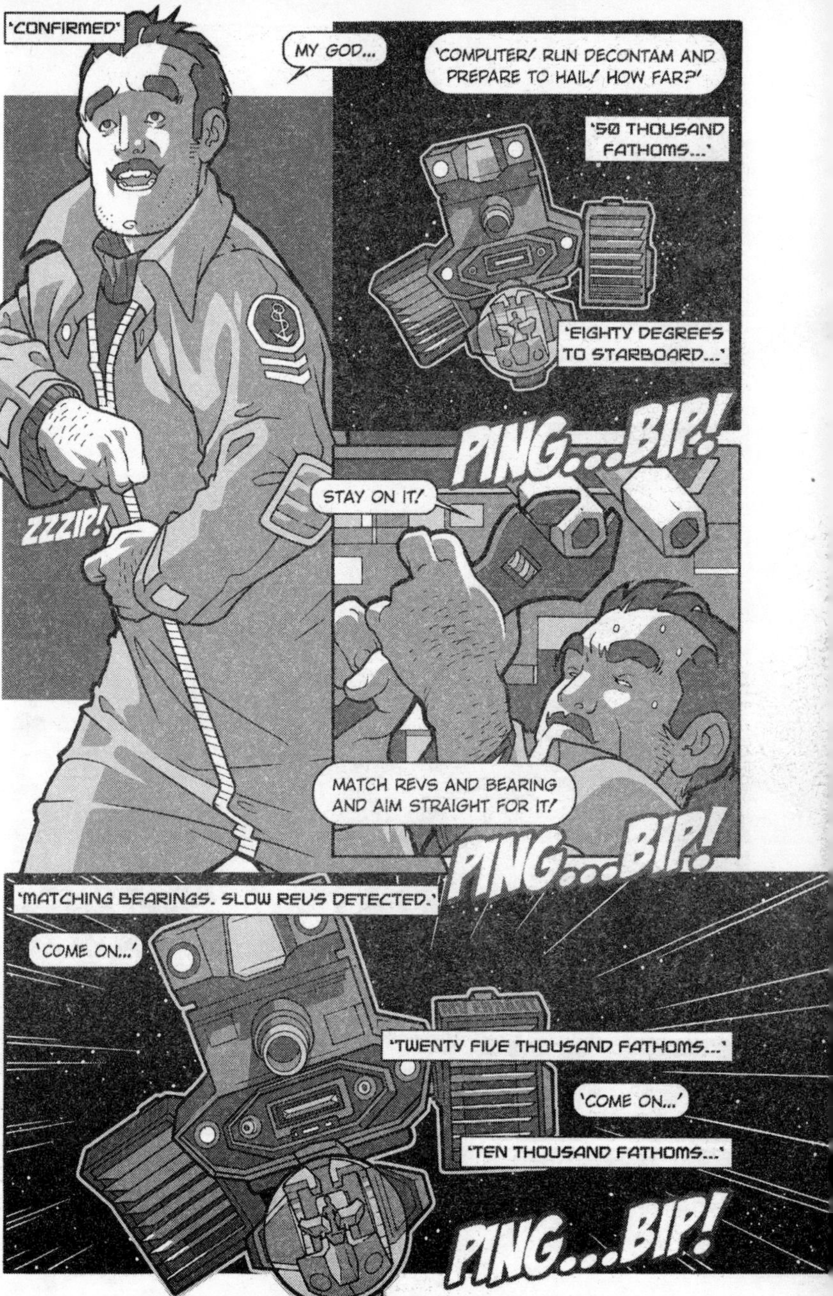
'CONFIRMED'
MY GOD...
'COMPUTER! RUN DECONTAM AND PREPARE TO HAIL! HOW FAR?'
'50 THOUSAND FATHOMS...'
'EIGHTY DEGREES TO STARBOARD...'
ZZZIP!
PING....BIP!
STAY ON IT!
MATCH REVS AND BEARING AND AIM STRAIGHT FOR IT!
PING....BIP!
'MATCHING BEARINGS. SLOW REVS DETECTED.'
'COME ON...'
'TWENTY FIVE THOUSAND FATHOMS...'
'COME ON...'
'TEN THOUSAND FATHOMS...'
PING....BIP!

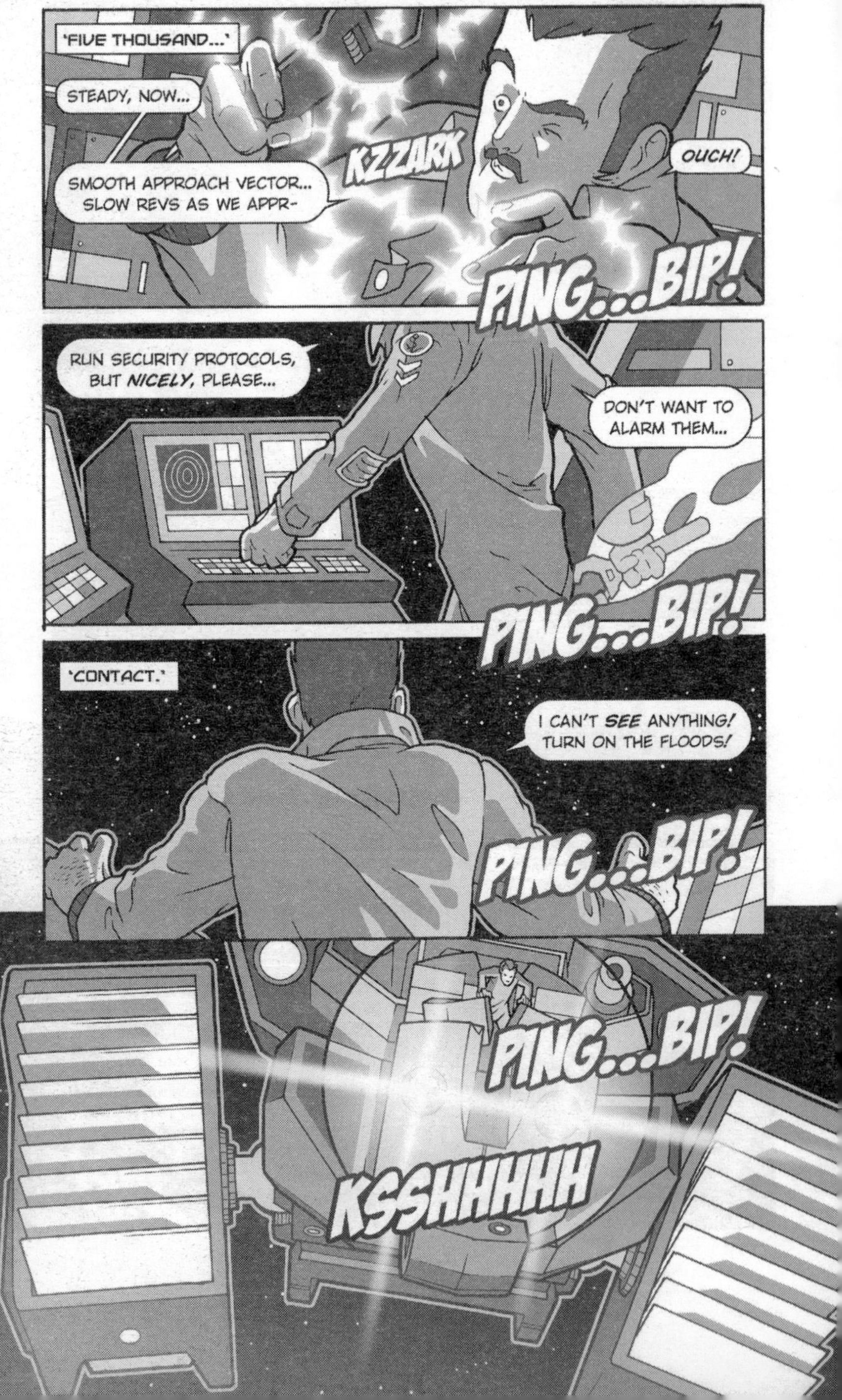
'FIVE THOUSAND...'
STEADY, NOW...
SMOOTH APPROACH VECTOR... SLOW REVS AS WE APPR-
KZZARK
OUCH!
PING...BIP!
RUN SECURITY PROTOCOLS, BUT NICELY, PLEASE...
DON'T WANT TO ALARM THEM...
PING...BIP!
'CONTACT.'
I CAN'T SEE ANYTHING! TURN ON THE FLOODS!
PING...BIP!
PING...BIP!
KSSHHHHH

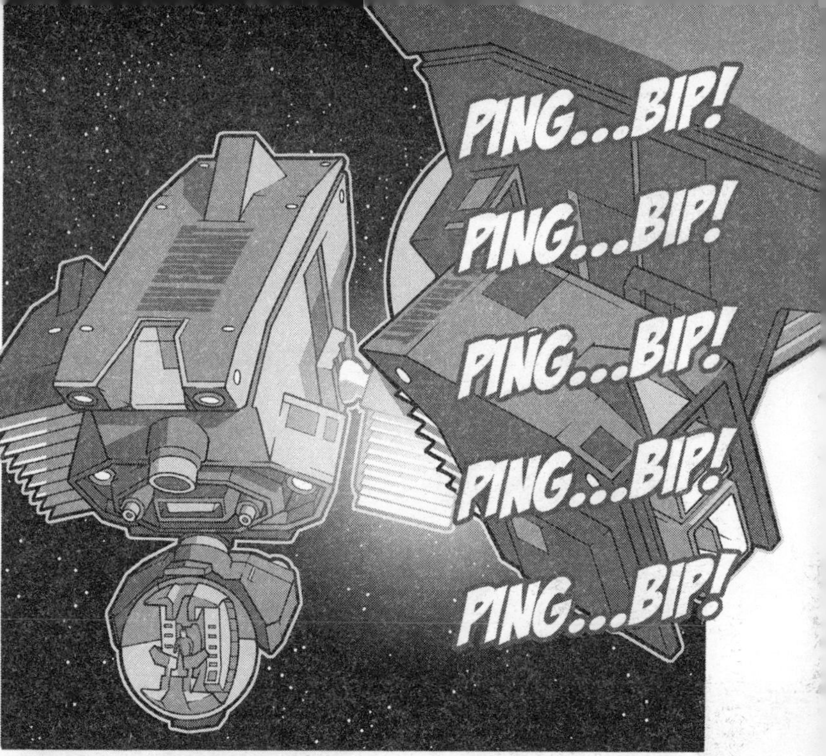
PING...BIP!
PING...BIP!
PING...BIP!
PING...BIP!
PING...BIP!

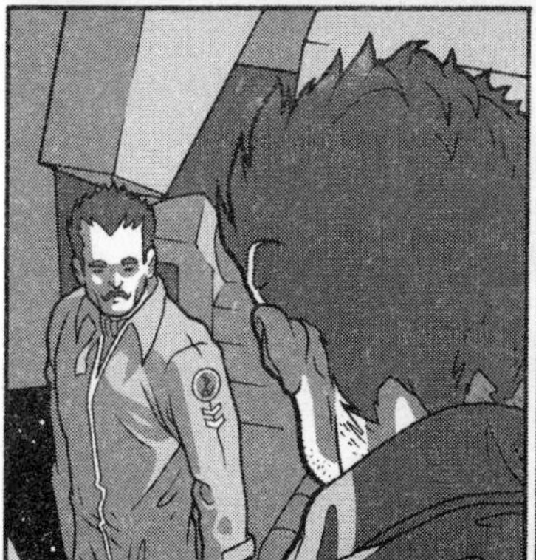

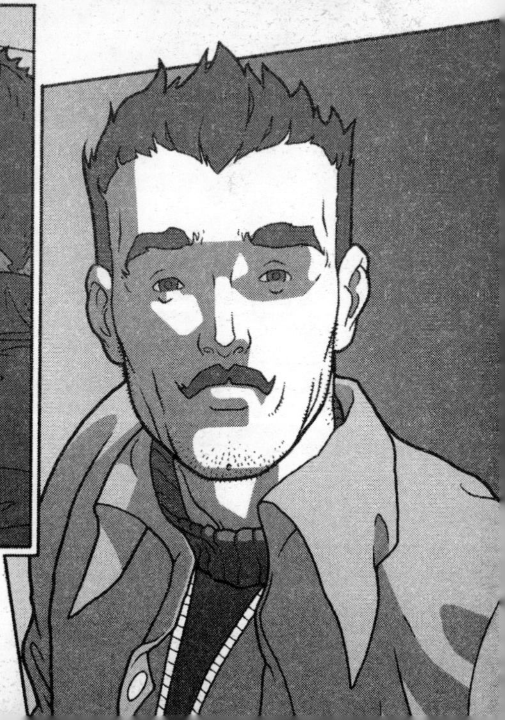

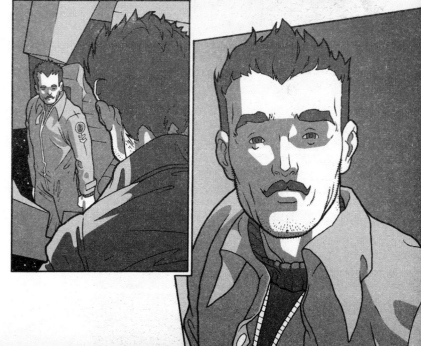

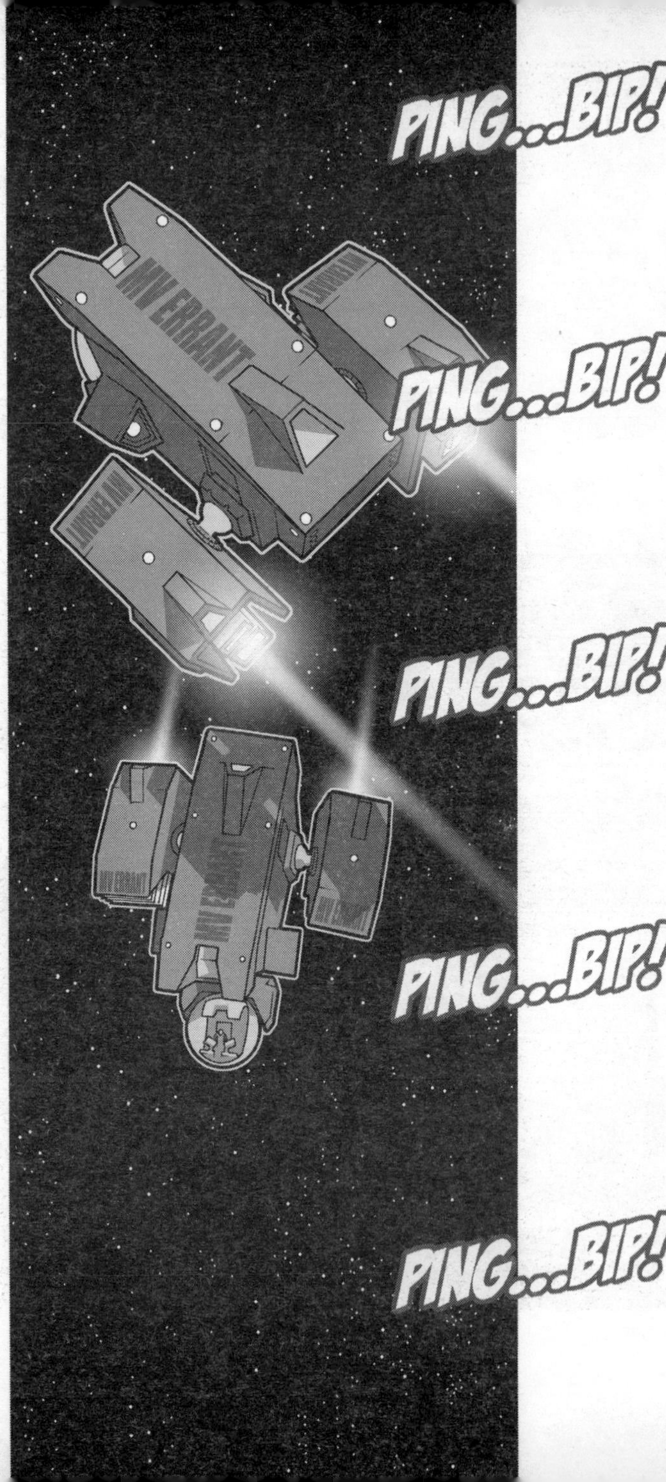
PING...BIP!
MV ERRANT
PING...BIP!
PING...BIP!
PING...BIP!
PING...BIP!

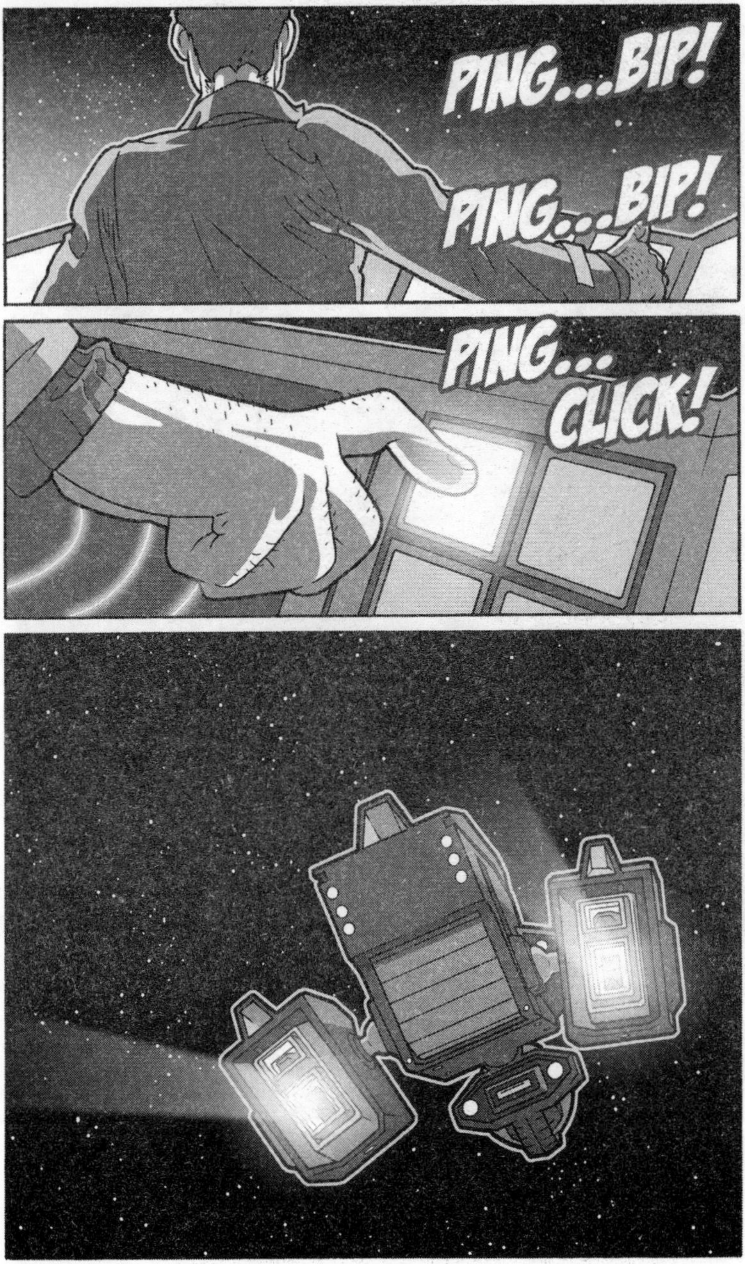
PING...BIP!
PING...BIP!
PING...
CLICK!

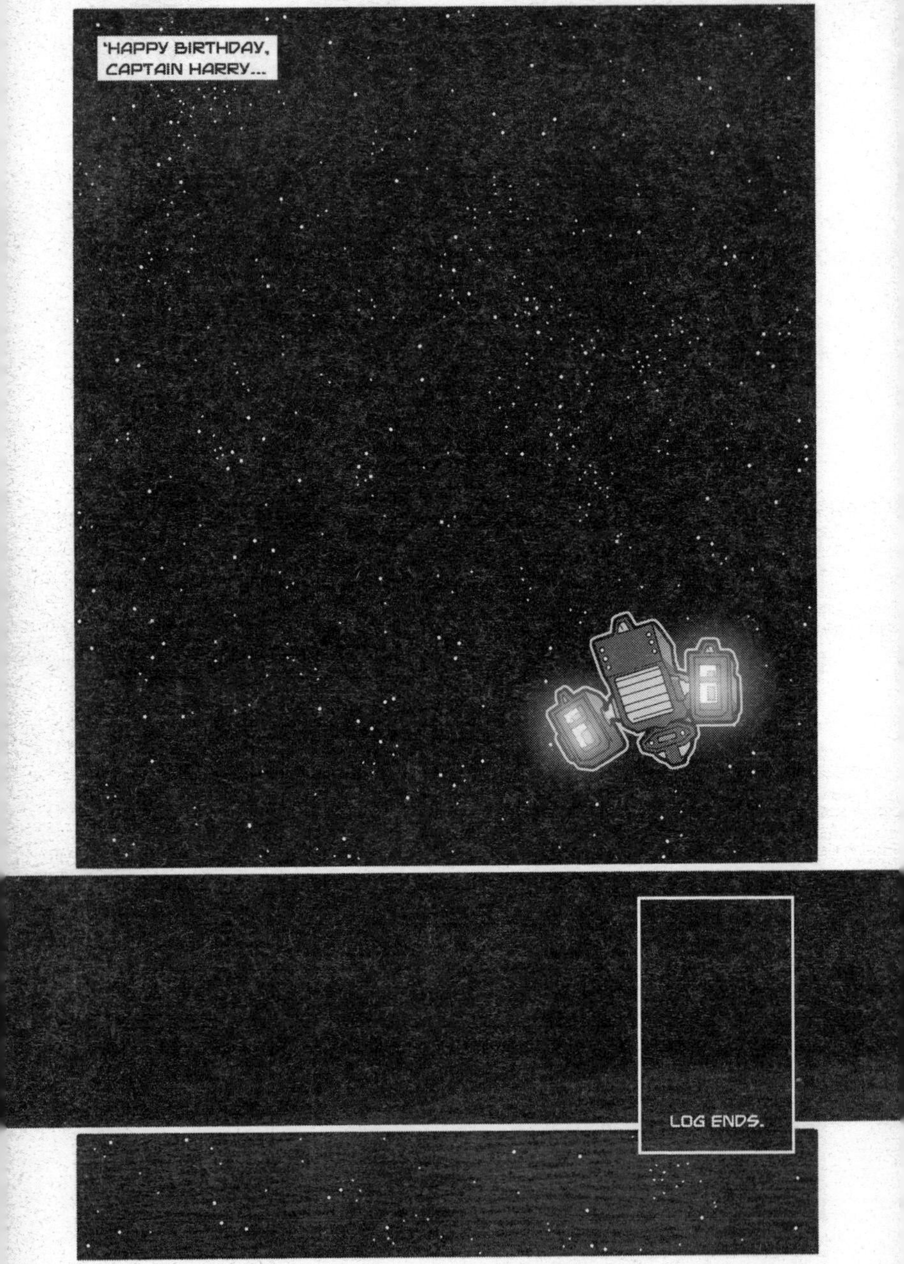
'HAPPY BIRTHDAY, CAPTAIN HARRY...
LOG ENDS.

THE HEALING

STORY
FEHED SAID

ART
SHARI CHANKHAMMA

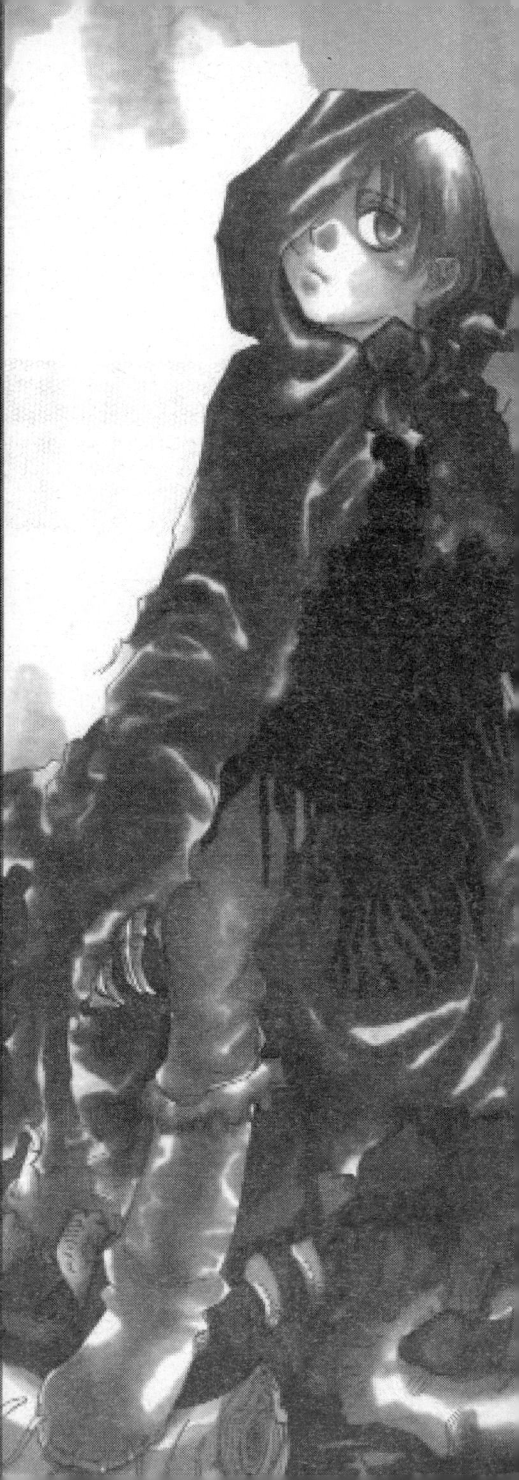

FEHED SAID

Date of birth: 12 April 1979

Fehed, originally from Palestine, is now resident in the UK, and counts movies and the manga of *Akira* and *Domu* (Katsuhiro Otomo) as major personal influences. He hates paper cuts and raisins, but ice cream and the internet make it all better.

The Healing is his first attempt at writing an action / fantasy – and, let's hope, not the last!

SHARI CHANKHAMMA

Date of birth: 6 September 1980

Shari, from Thailand, is Fehed's frequent collaborator. She likes the *Lord of the Rings* films (principally for Elijah Wood), and manga such as *Lum* and *Cobra*. Her favourite kind of character is an underdog who kills.

Together, they are working on a feature-length story entitled *The Clarence Principle*, in which the central character wakes up to the aftermath of his own suicide. Best described as 'a twisted tale that encompasses dark humour and light drama', a preview is available online.

http://sixkillerbunnies.com
http://sweatdrop.com
http://shariot.deviantart.com

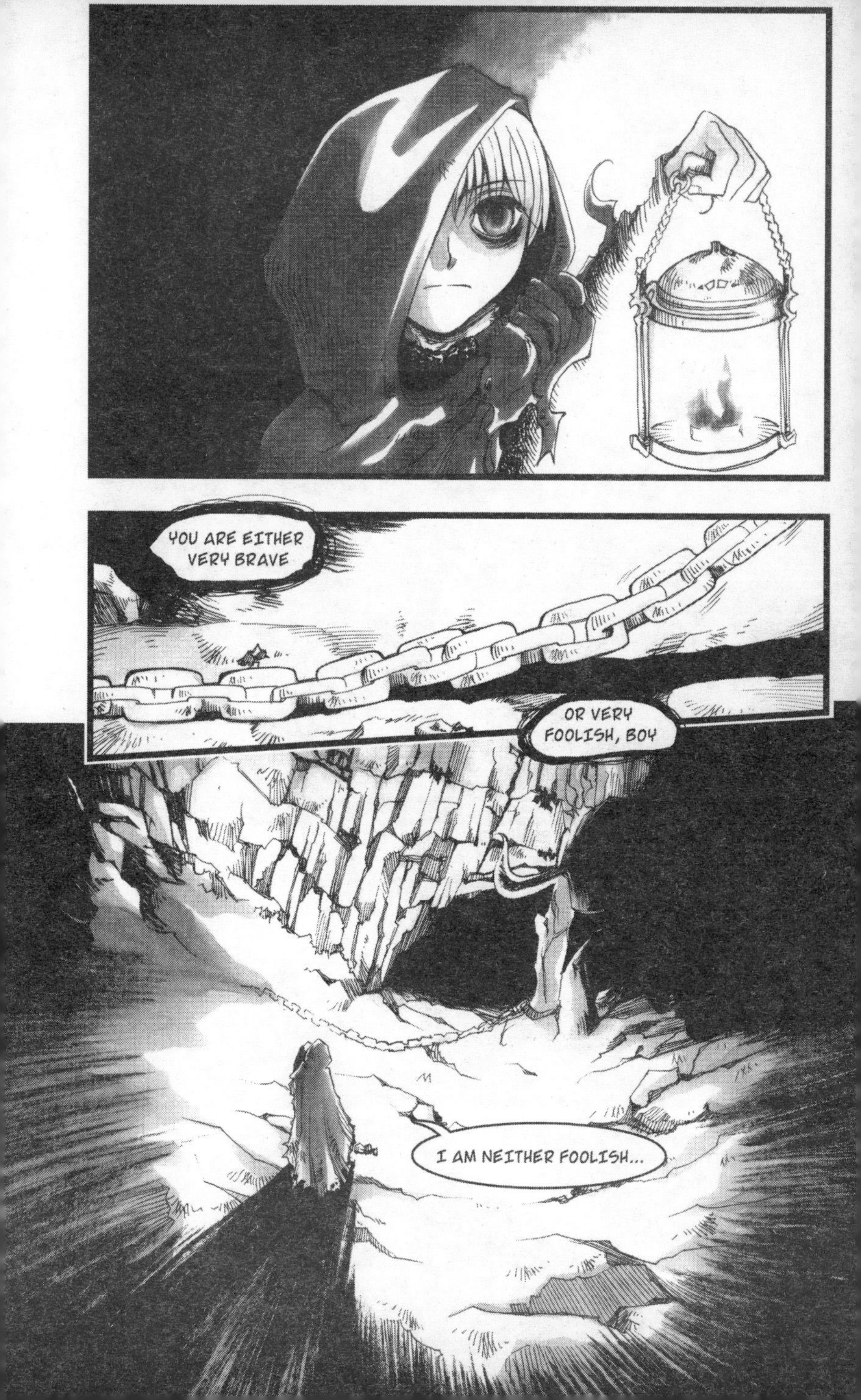
YOU ARE EITHER VERY BRAVE
OR VERY FOOLISH, BOY
I AM NEITHER FOOLISH...

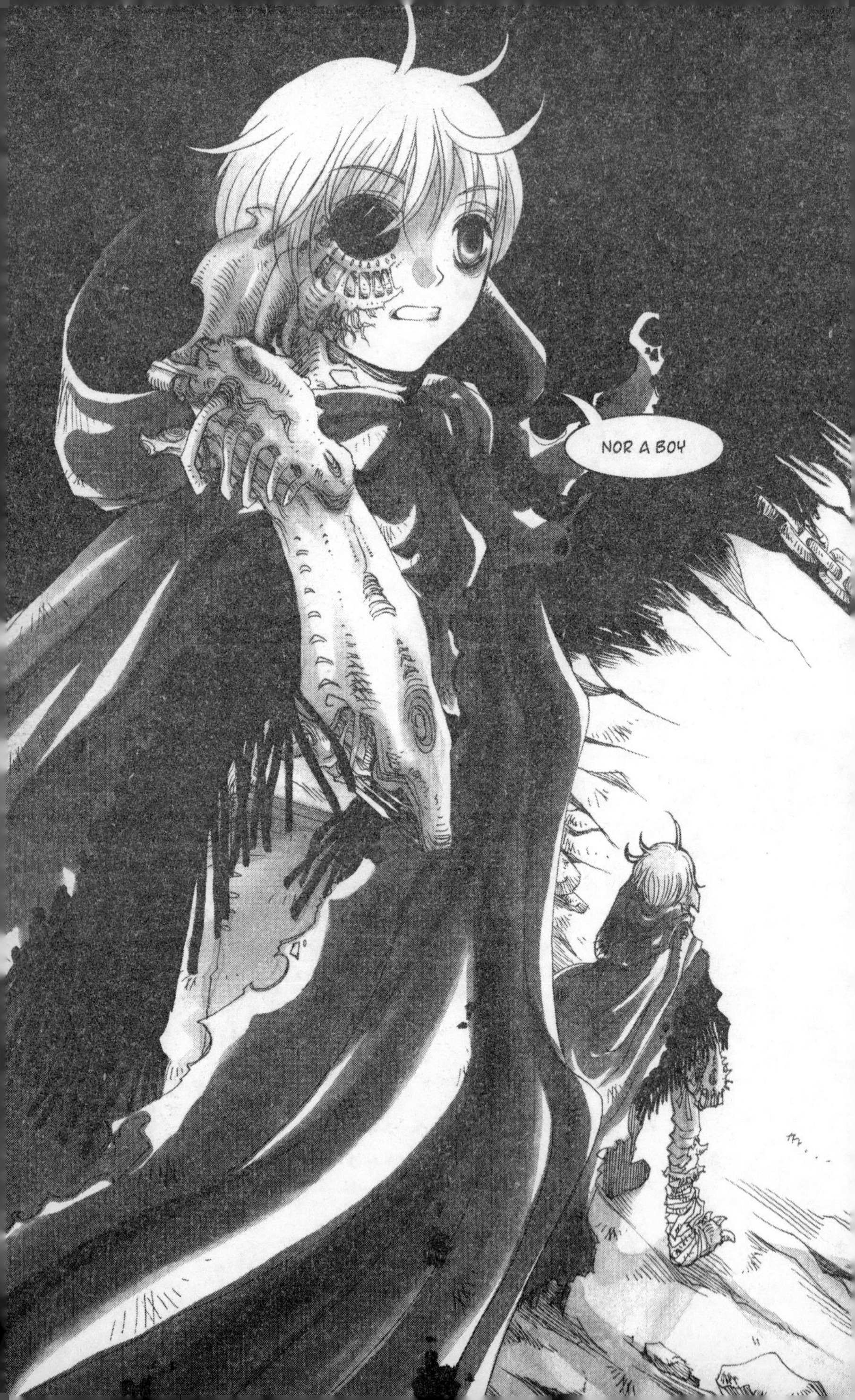
NOR A BOY

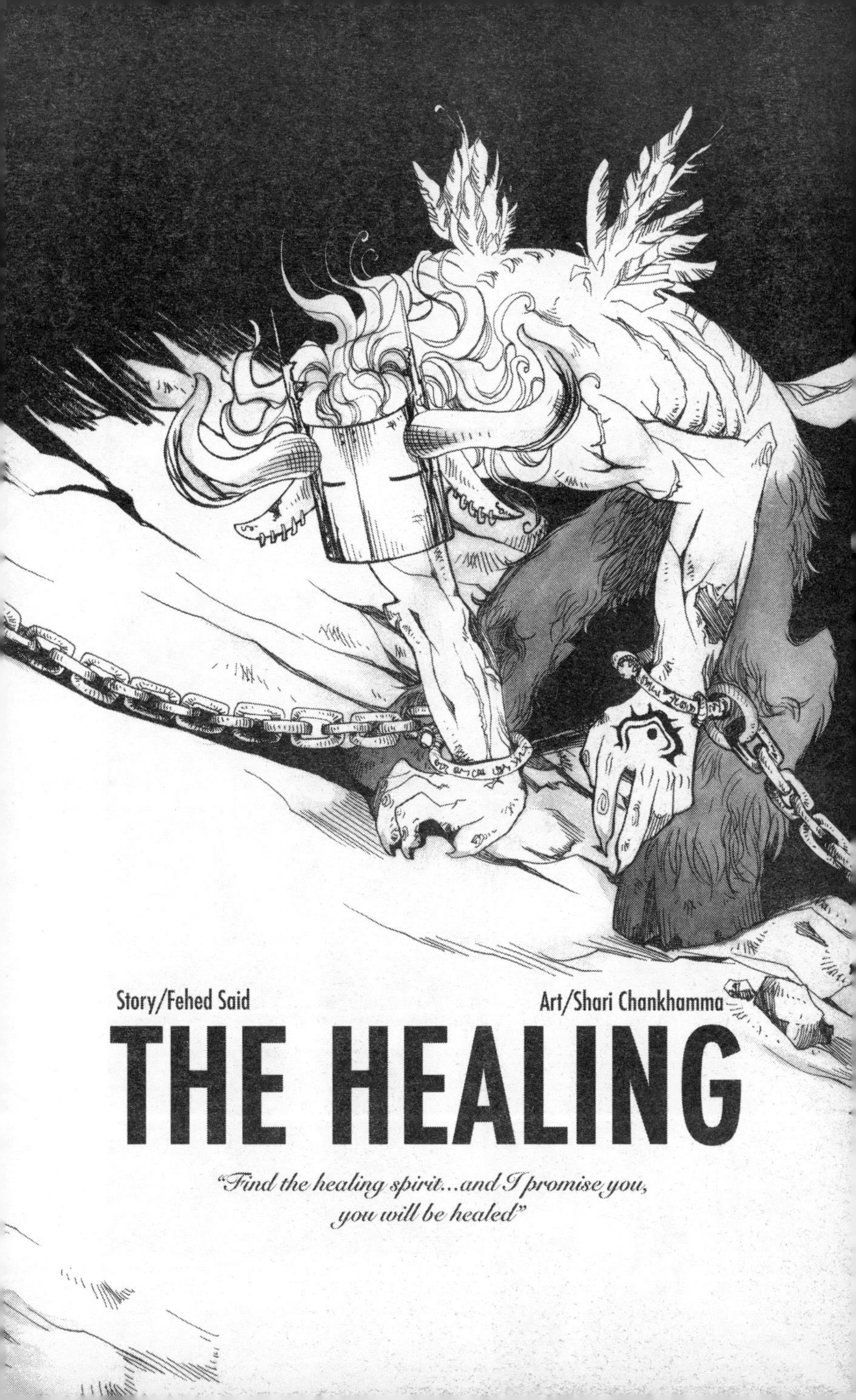
Story/Fehed Said
Art/Shari Chankhamma
THE HEALING
"Find the healing spirit...and I promise you,
you will be healed"

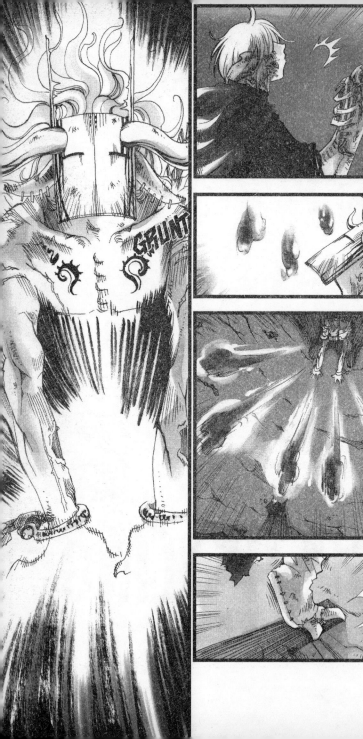

GRUNT

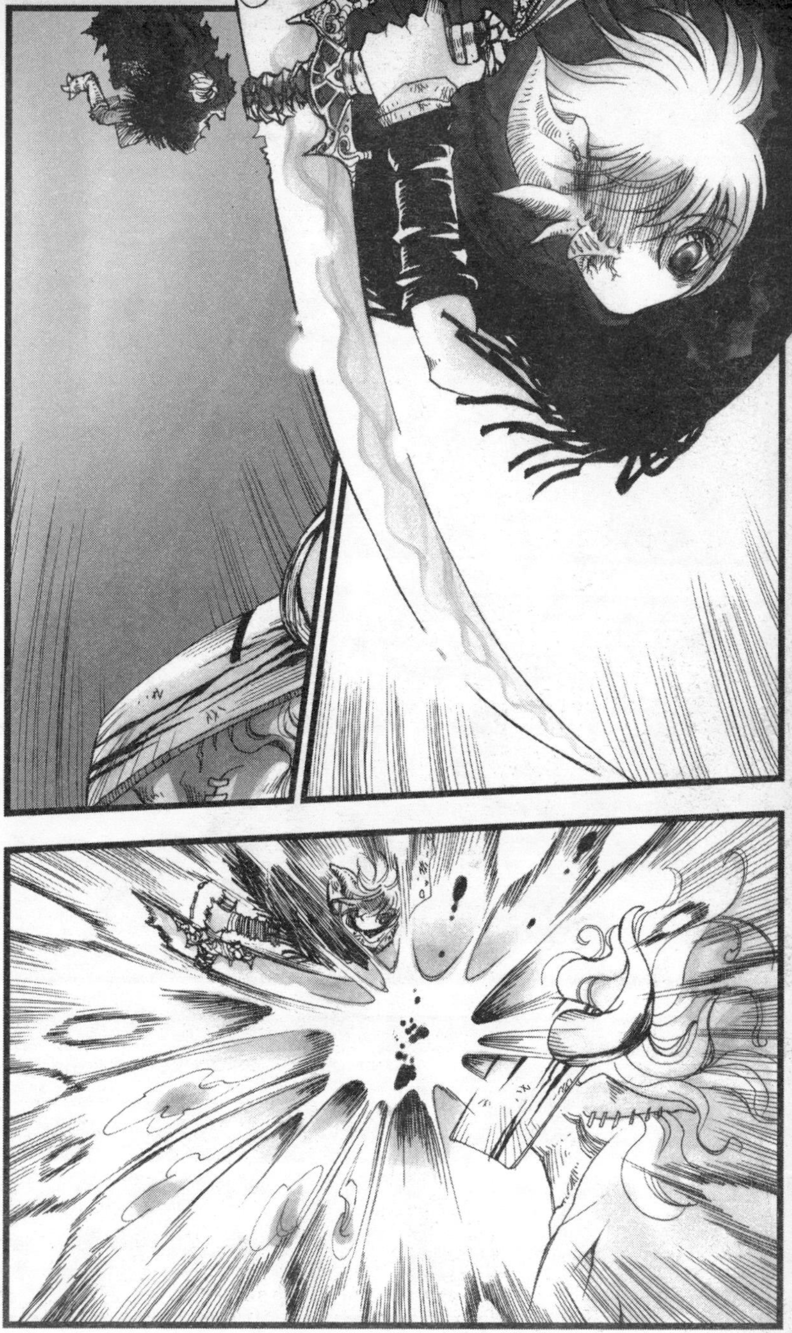

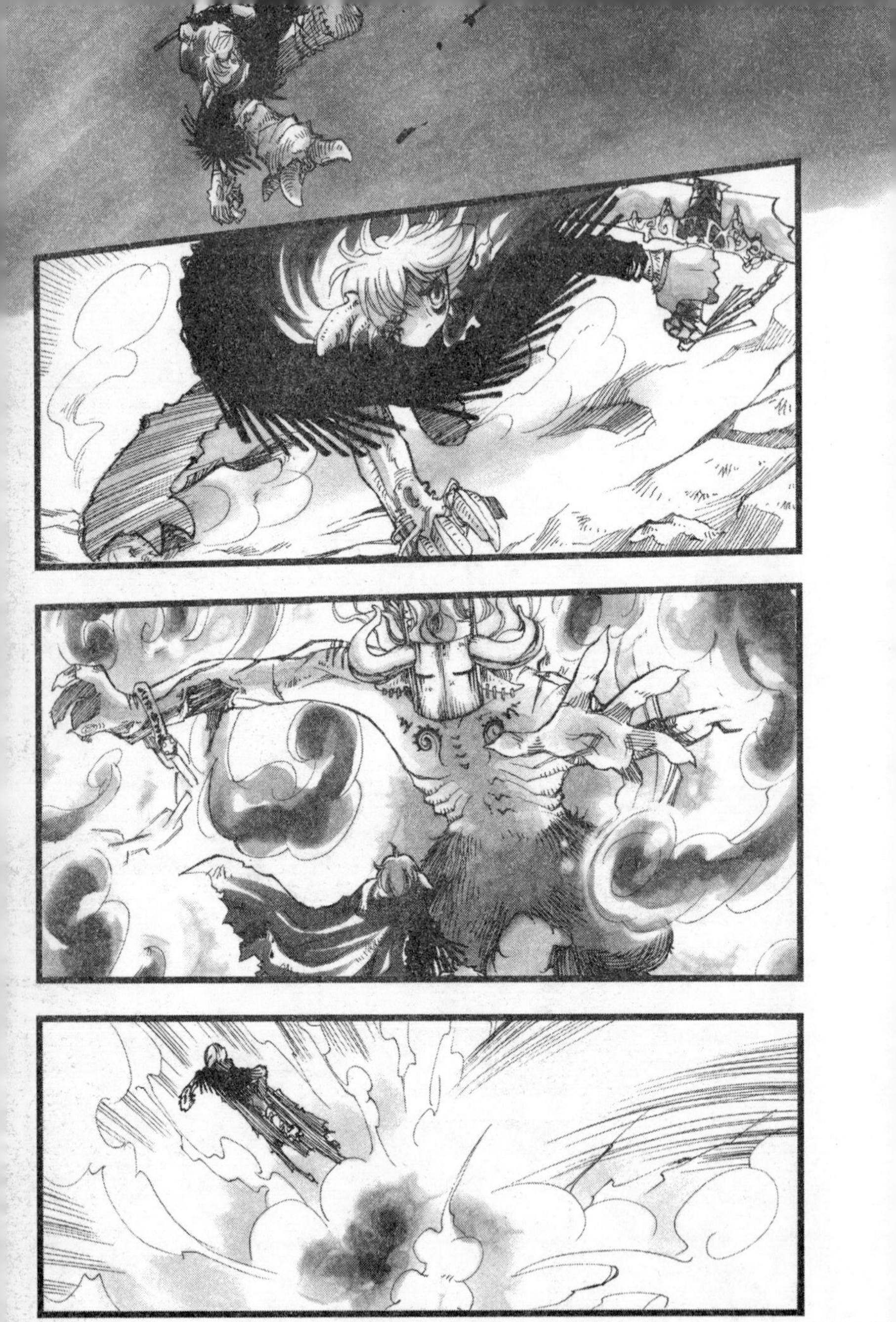

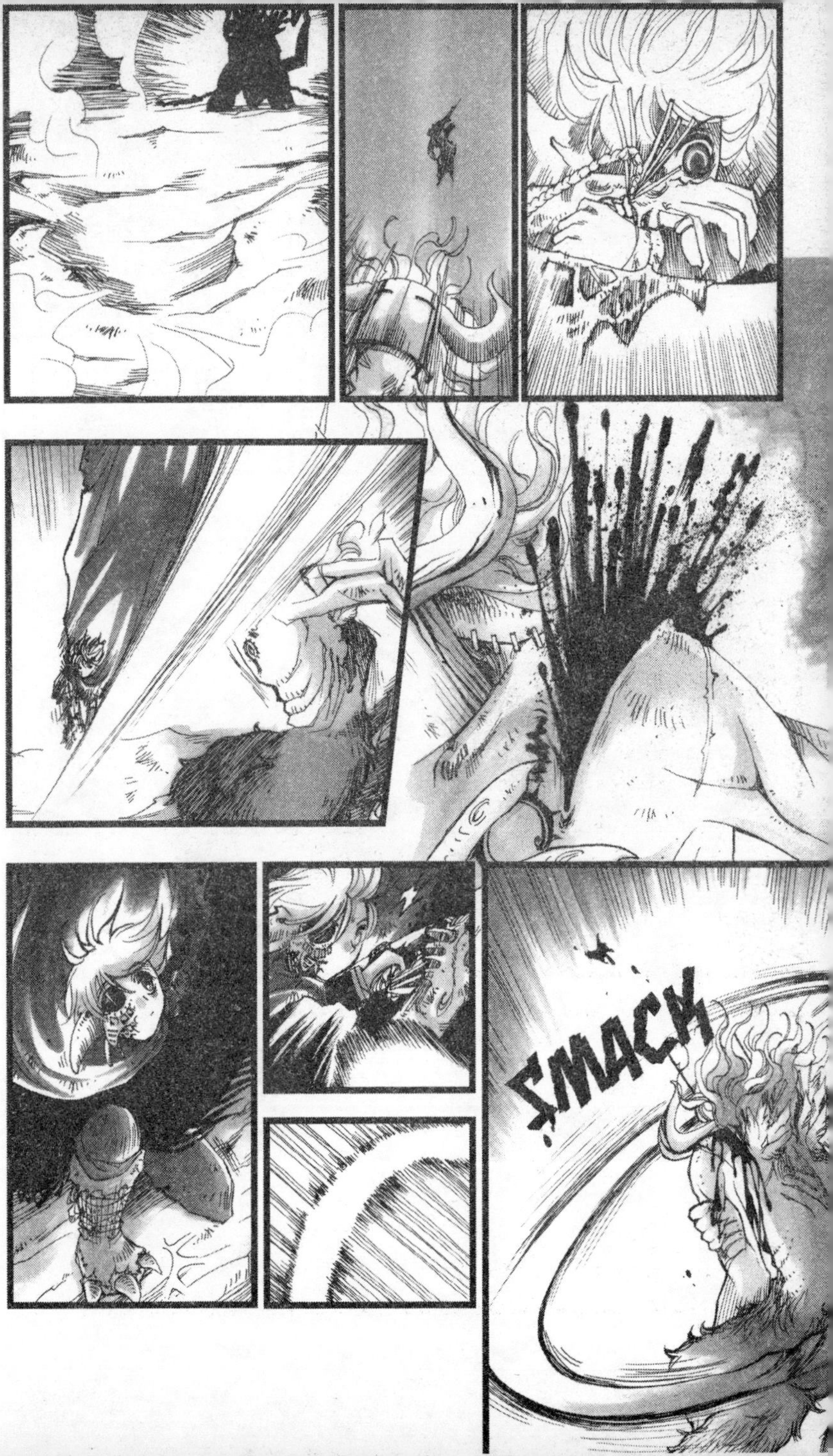
SMACK

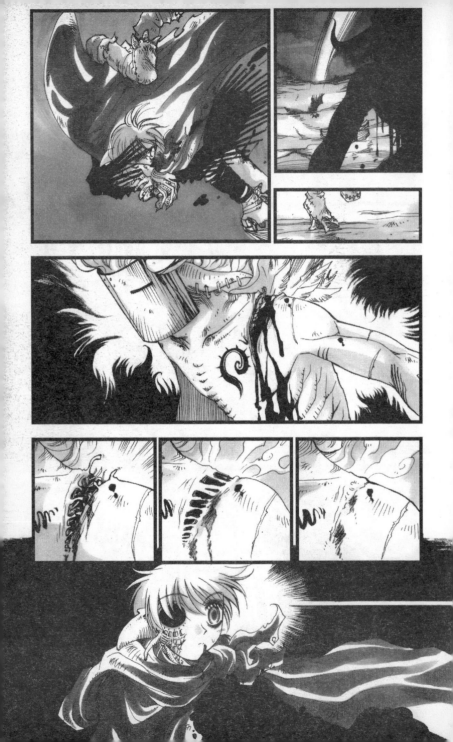

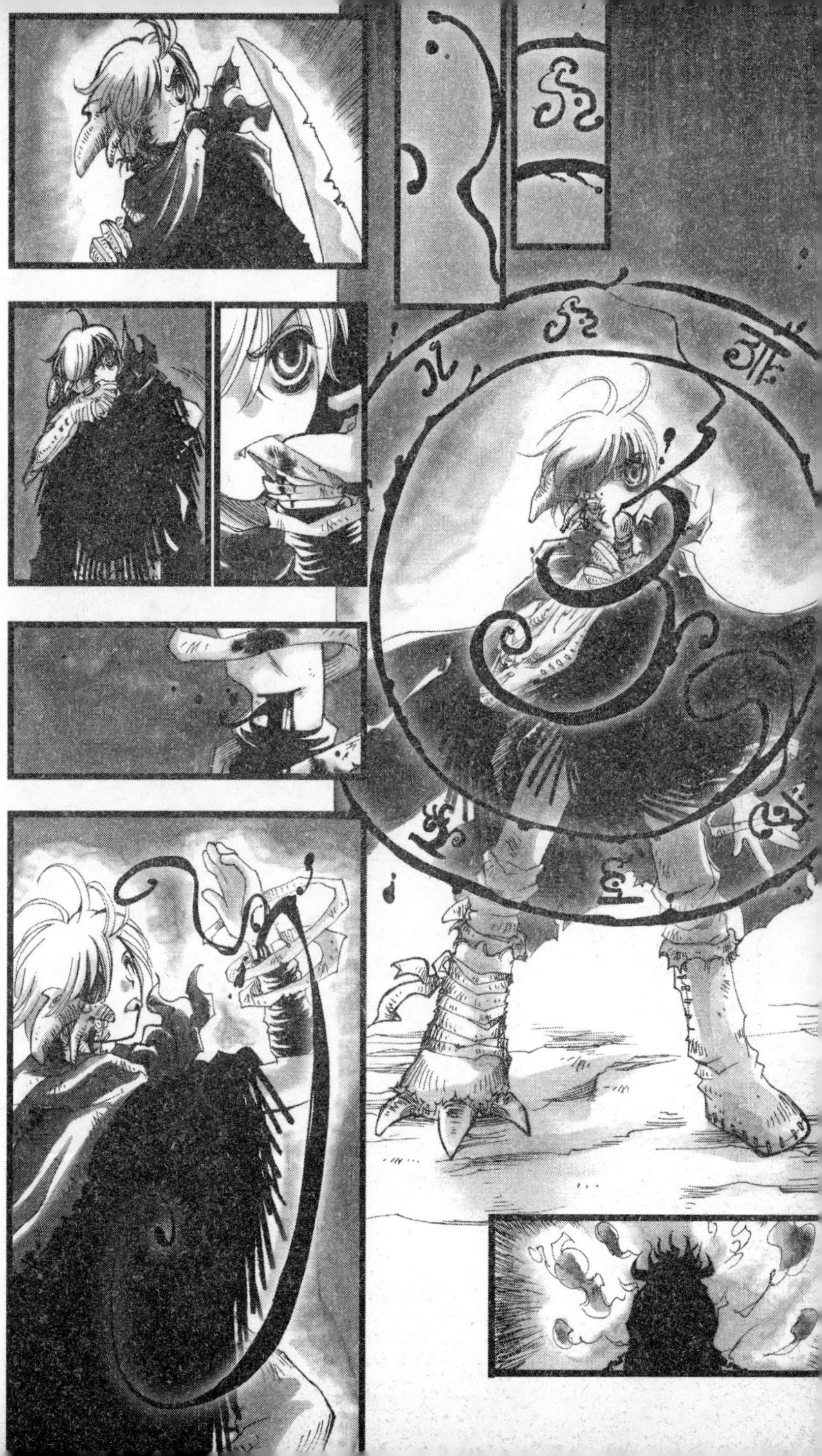

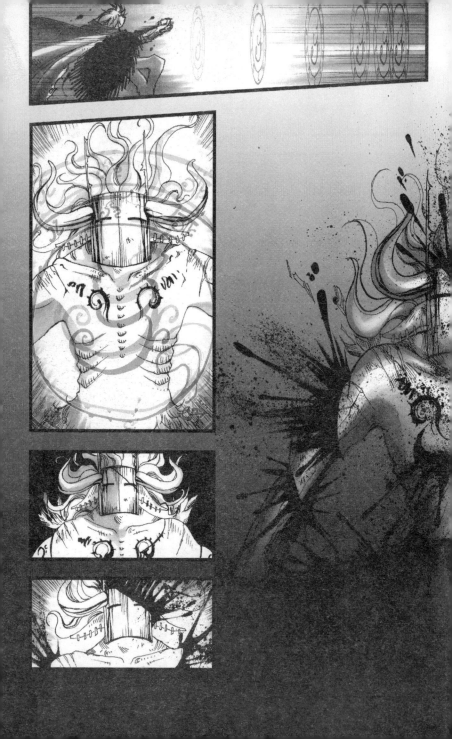

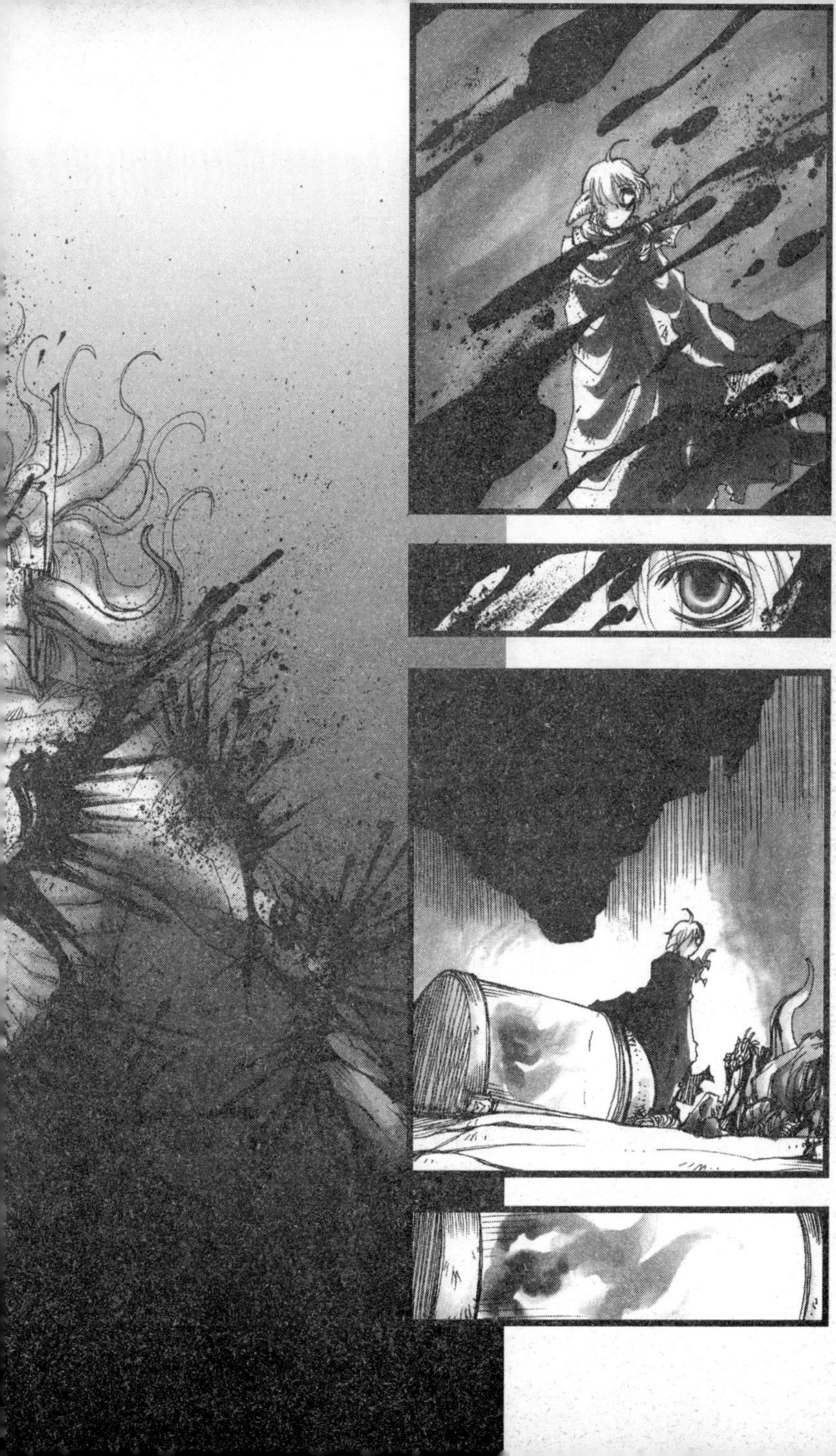

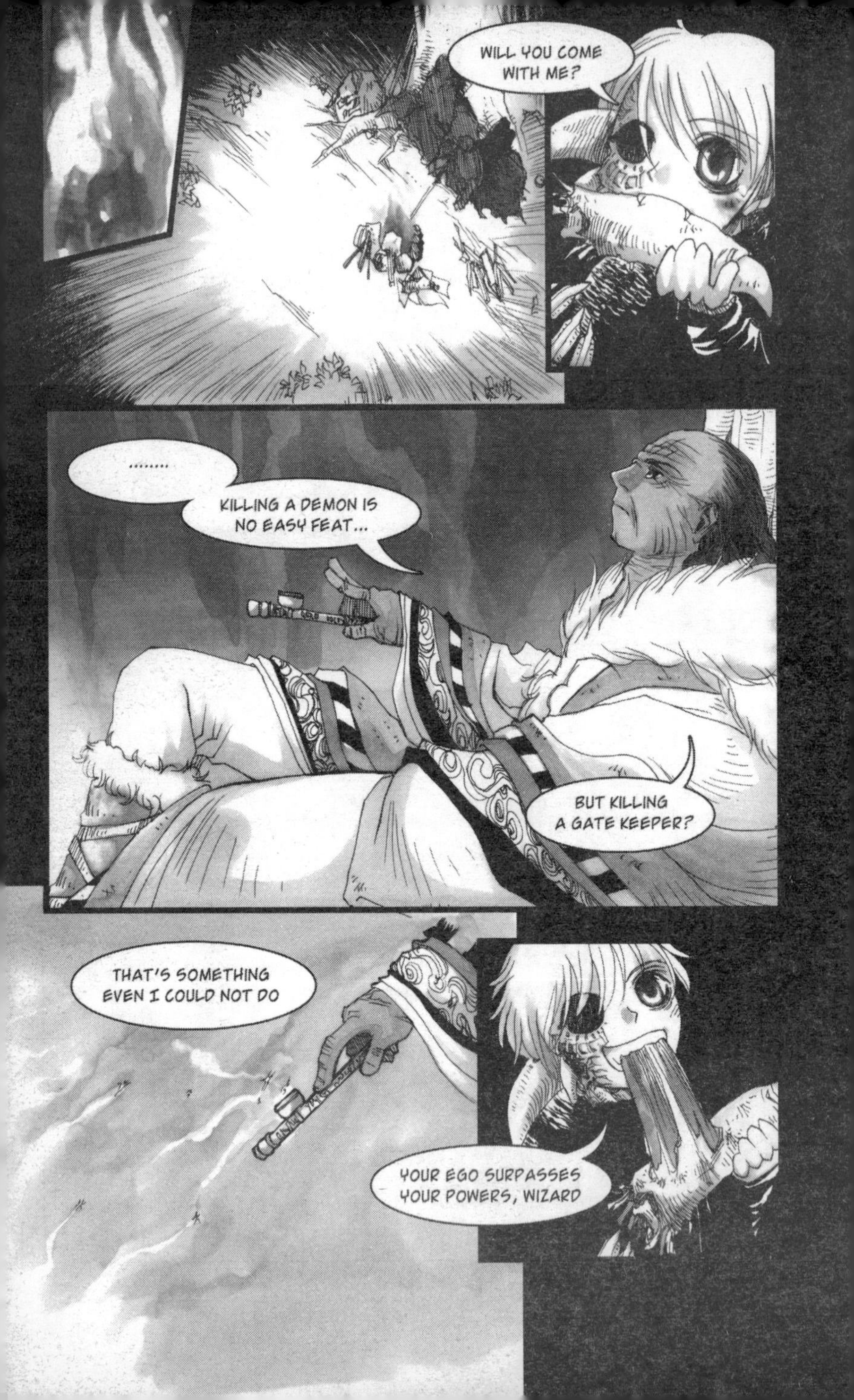
WILL YOU COME WITH ME?
....
KILLING A DEMON IS NO EASY FEAT...
BUT KILLING A GATE KEEPER?
THAT'S SOMETHING EVEN I COULD NOT DO
YOUR EGO SURPASSES YOUR POWERS, WIZARD

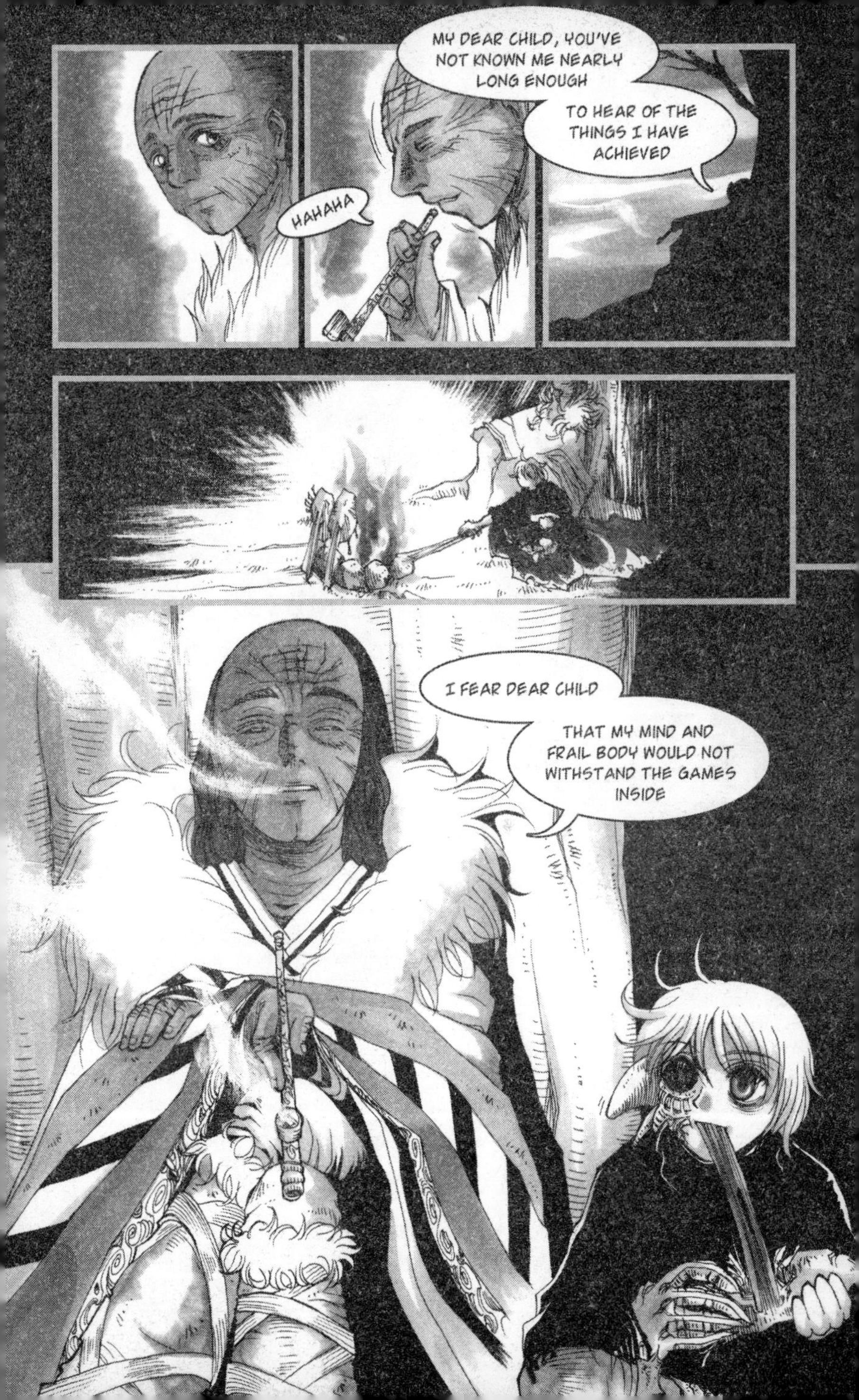
HAHAHA
MY DEAR CHILD, YOU'VE NOT KNOWN ME NEARLY LONG ENOUGH
TO HEAR OF THE THINGS I HAVE ACHIEVED
I FEAR DEAR CHILD
THAT MY MIND AND FRAIL BODY WOULD NOT WITHSTAND THE GAMES INSIDE

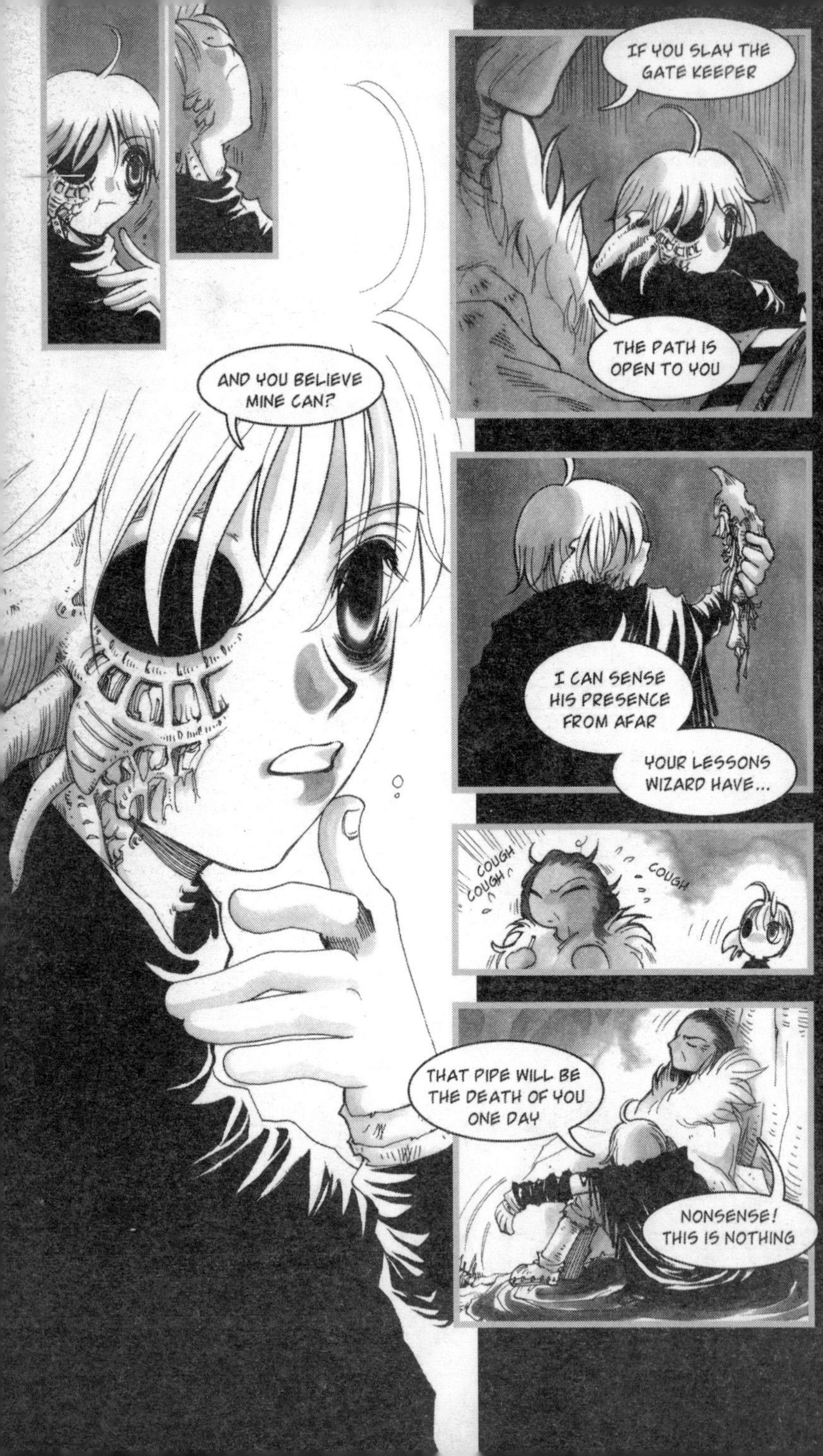
AND YOU BELIEVE MINE CAN?
IF YOU SLAY THE GATE KEEPER
THE PATH IS OPEN TO YOU
I CAN SENSE HIS PRESENCE FROM AFAR
YOUR LESSONS WIZARD HAVE...
COUGH COUGH
COUGH
THAT PIPE WILL BE THE DEATH OF YOU ONE DAY
NONSENSE! THIS IS NOTHING

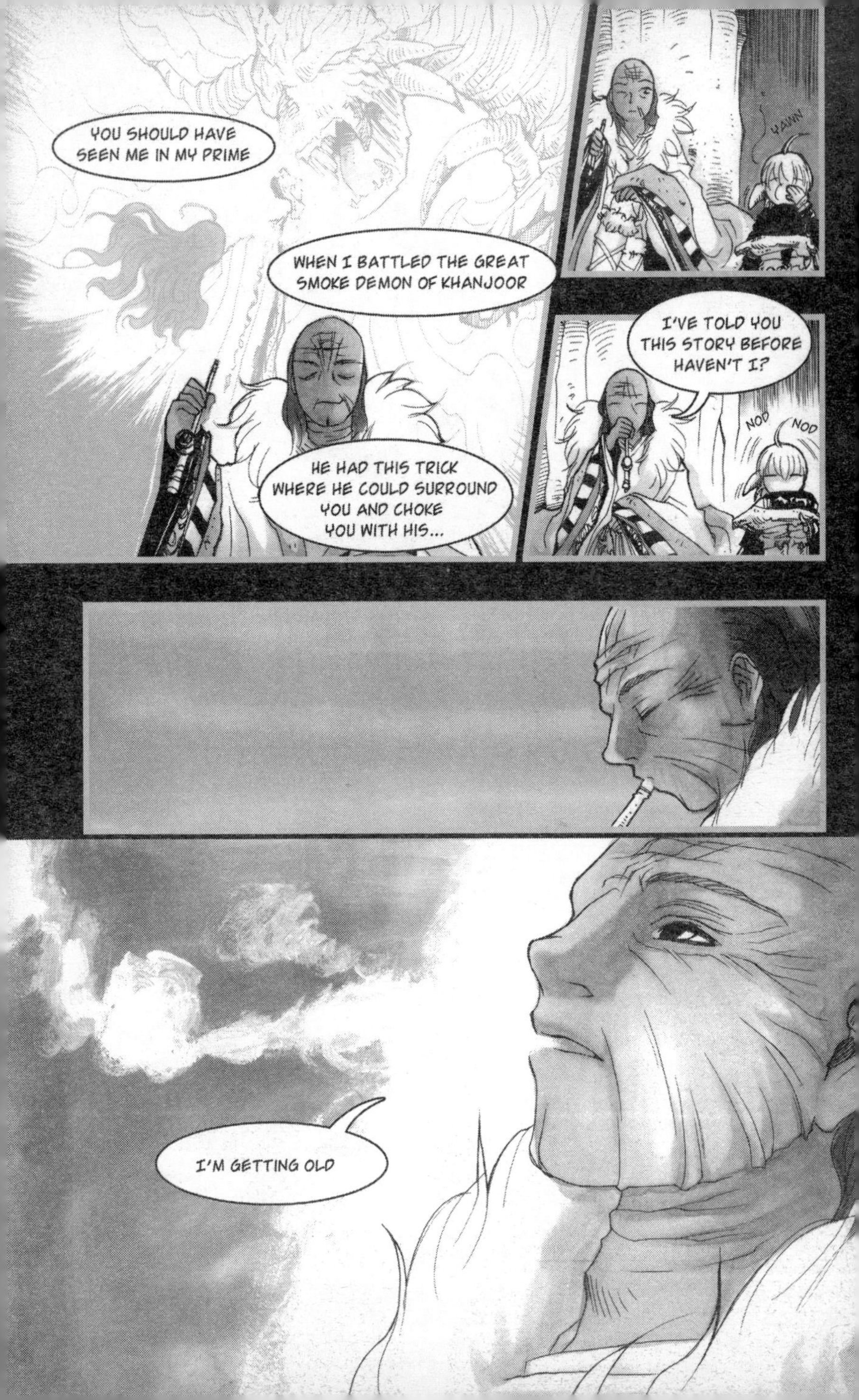
YOU SHOULD HAVE SEEN ME IN MY PRIME
WHEN I BATTLED THE GREAT SMOKE DEMON OF KHANJOOR
HE HAD THIS TRICK WHERE HE COULD SURROUND YOU AND CHOKE YOU WITH HIS...
YAWN
I'VE TOLD YOU THIS STORY BEFORE HAVEN'T I?
NOD
NOD
I'M GETTING OLD

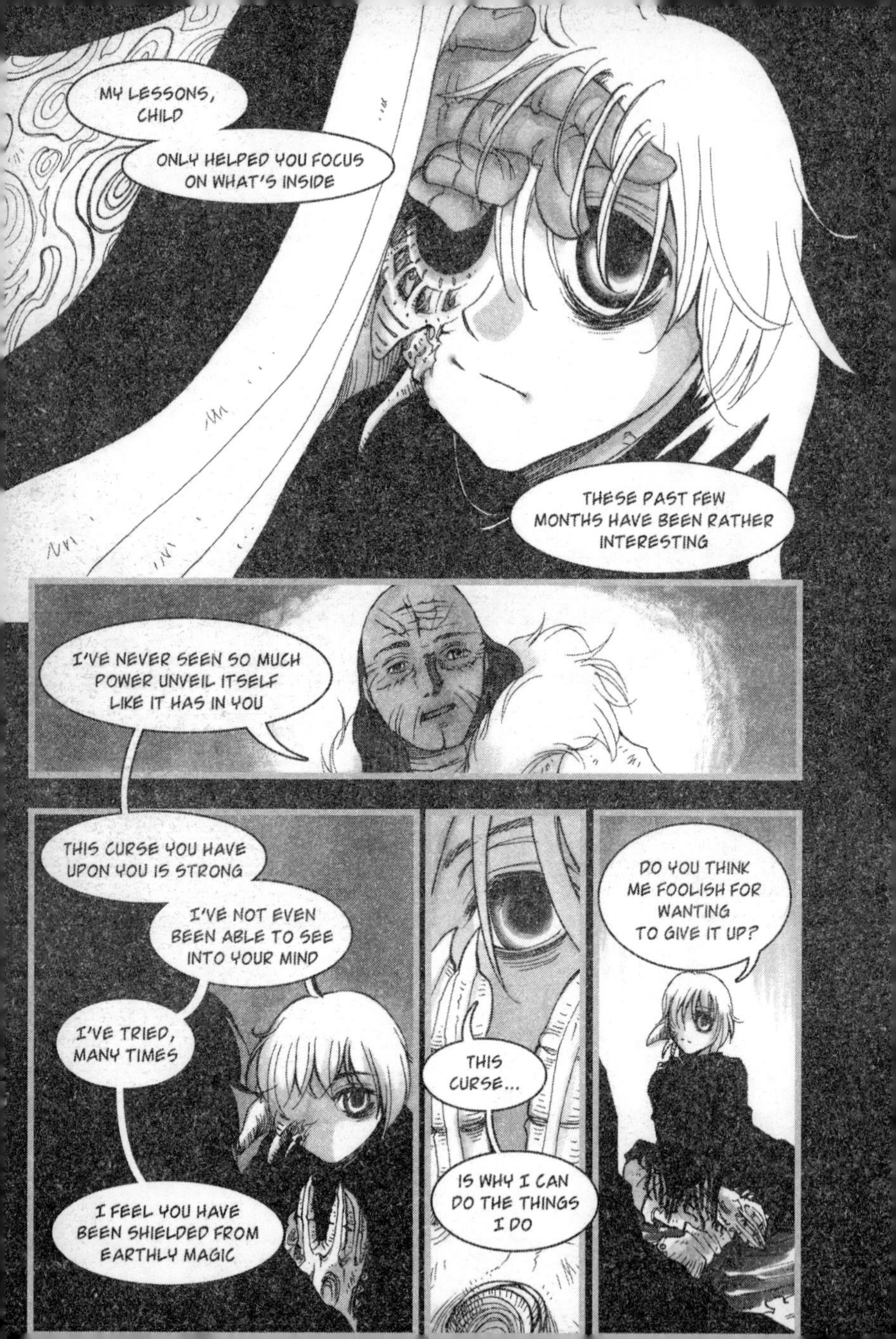
MY LESSONS, CHILD
ONLY HELPED YOU FOCUS ON WHAT'S INSIDE
THESE PAST FEW MONTHS HAVE BEEN RATHER INTERESTING
I'VE NEVER SEEN SO MUCH POWER UNVEIL ITSELF LIKE IT HAS IN YOU
THIS CURSE YOU HAVE UPON YOU IS STRONG
I'VE NOT EVEN BEEN ABLE TO SEE INTO YOUR MIND
I'VE TRIED, MANY TIMES
I FEEL YOU HAVE BEEN SHIELDED FROM EARTHLY MAGIC
THIS CURSE...
IS WHY I CAN DO THE THINGS I DO
DO YOU THINK ME FOOLISH FOR WANTING TO GIVE IT UP?

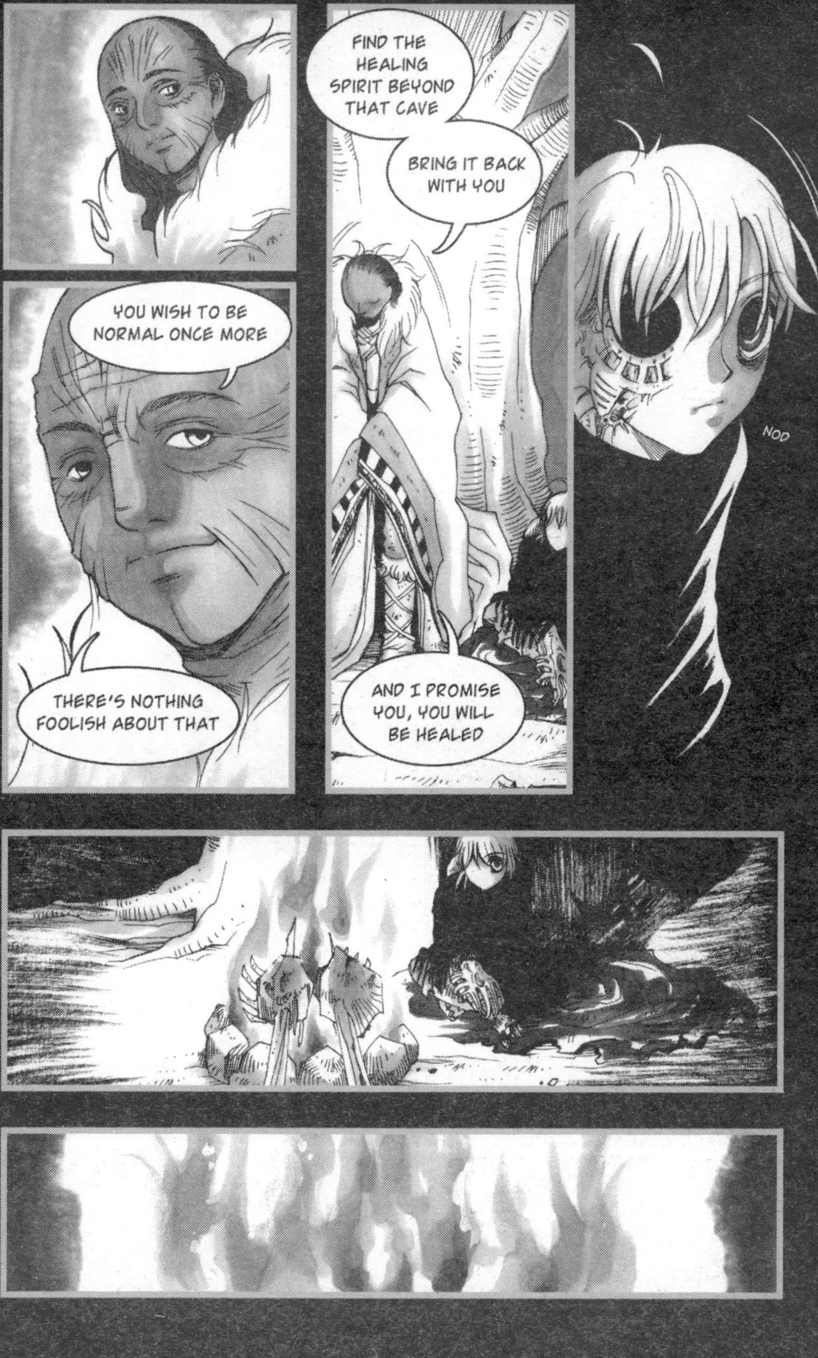
YOU WISH TO BE NORMAL ONCE MORE
THERE'S NOTHING FOOLISH ABOUT THAT
FIND THE HEALING SPIRIT BEYOND THAT CAVE
BRING IT BACK WITH YOU
AND I PROMISE YOU, YOU WILL BE HEALED
NOD

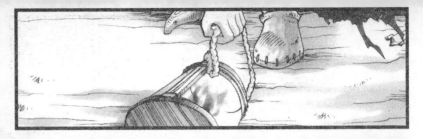

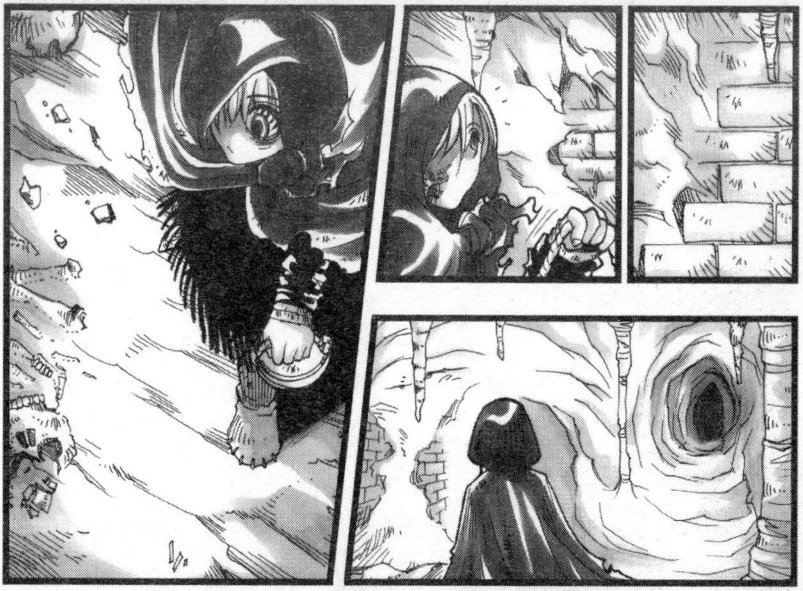
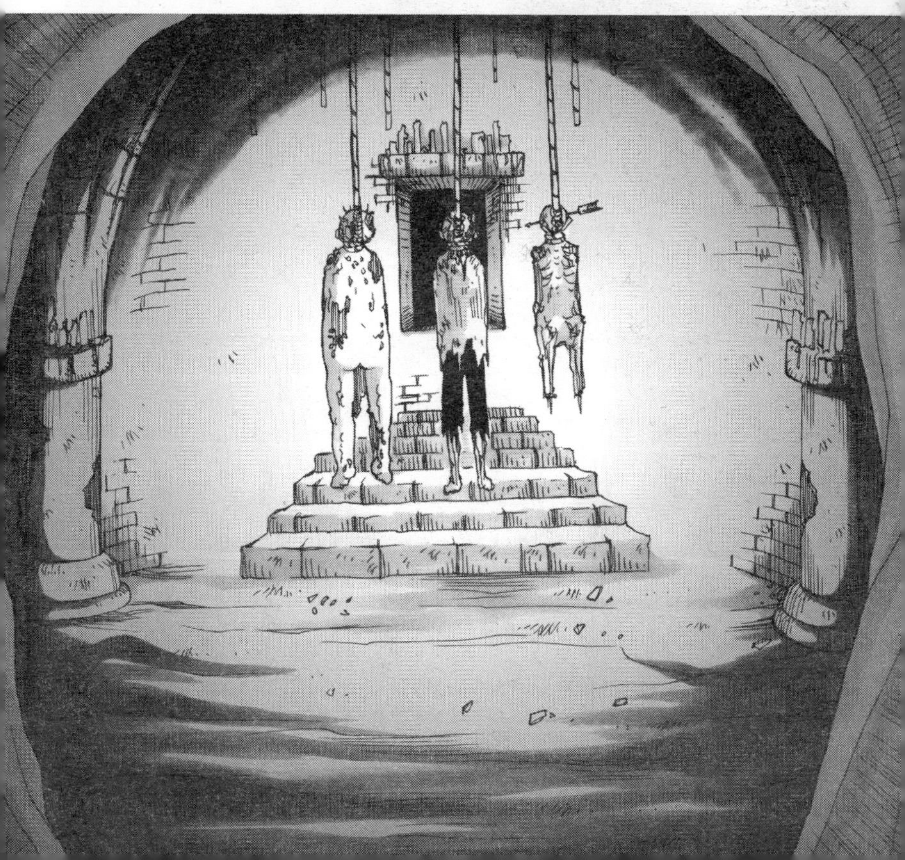

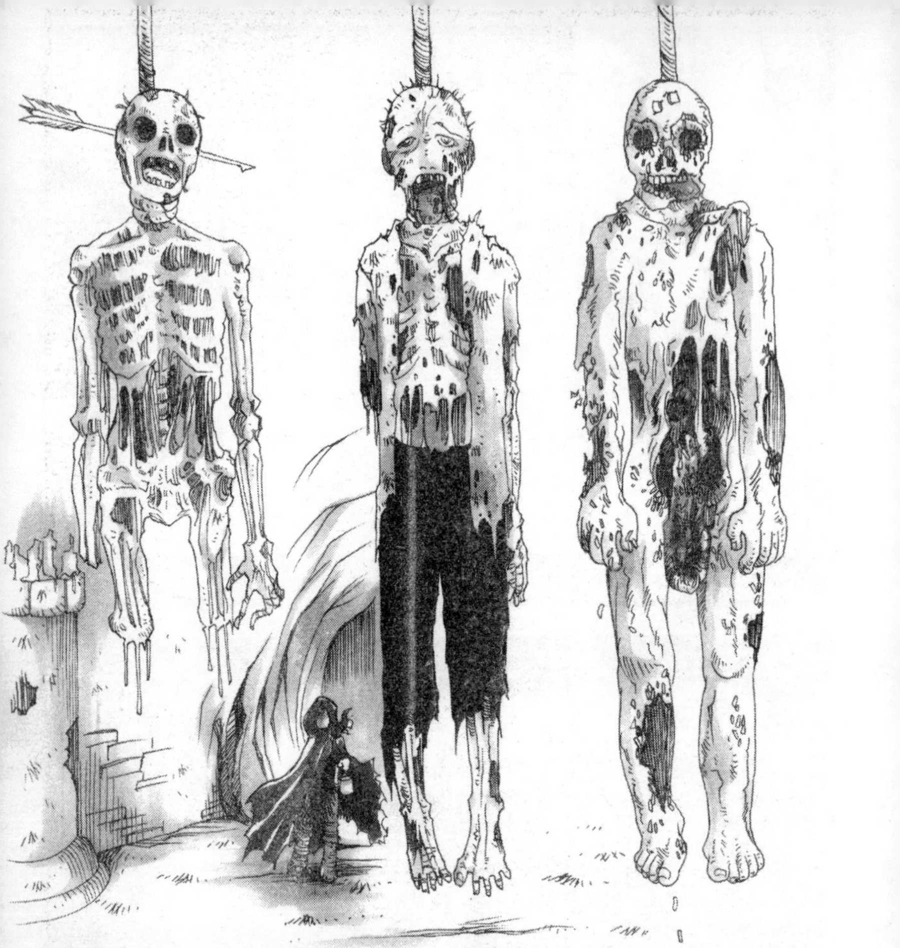

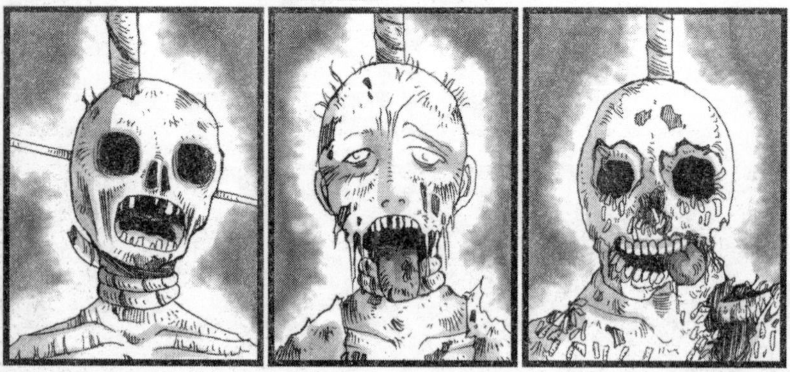

SALUTATIONS, CHILD
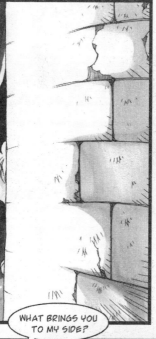

WHAT BRINGS YOU TO MY SIDE?

I SEEK GUIDANCE

IT'S SO EASY TO LOSE THE WAY VENTURING INTO THE DARKNESS

I'M LOOKING FOR A PATH TO THE HEALING SPIRIT

THOUGH I FEEL I'M AT A DEAD END

YOU'RE MERELY STANDING BEFORE A LOCKED DOOR

DO YOU WISH TO PASS?

I DO

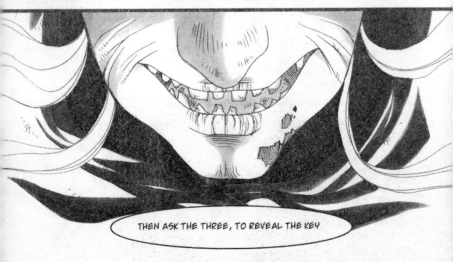

THEN ASK THE THREE, TO REVEAL THE KEY

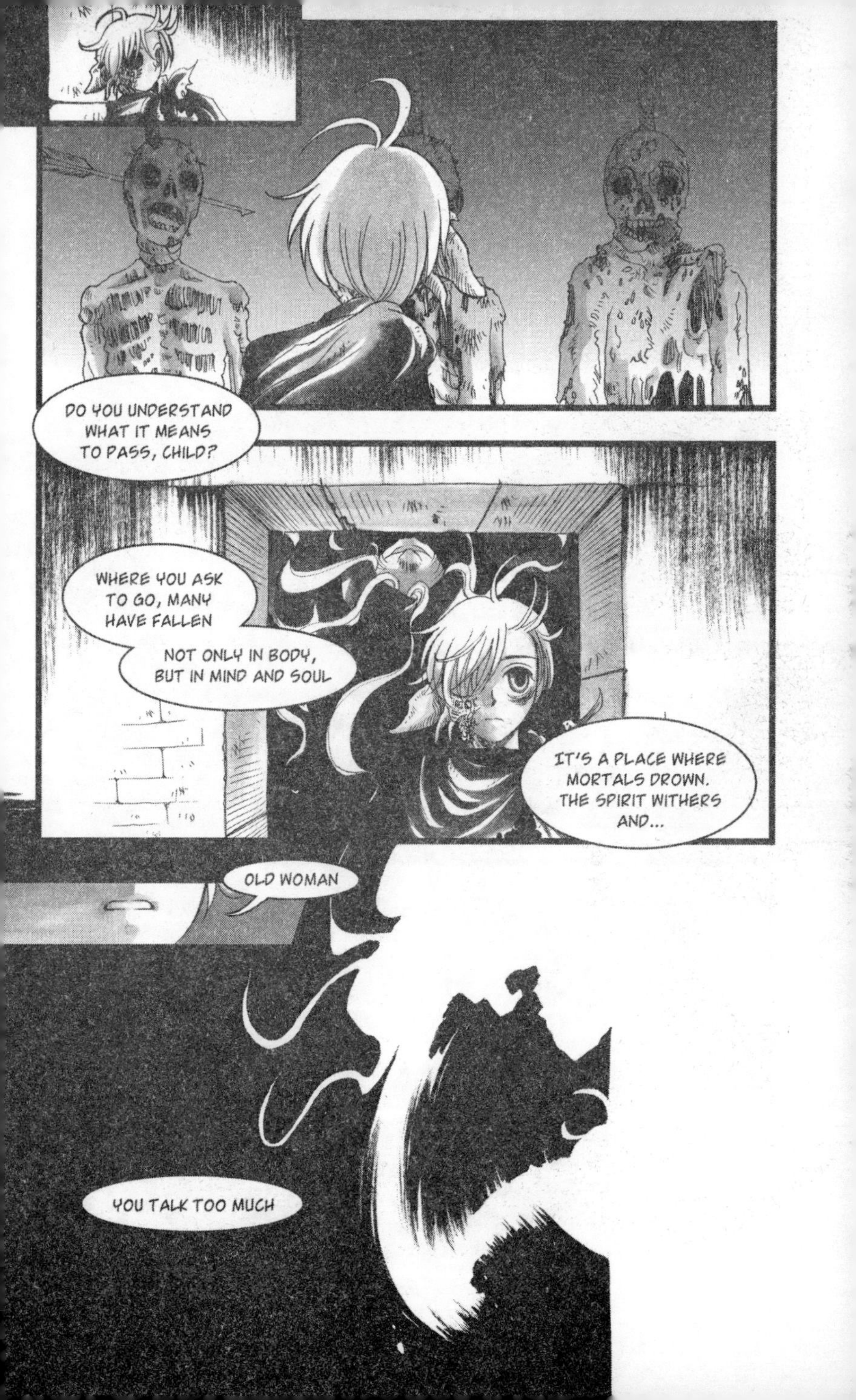
DO YOU UNDERSTAND WHAT IT MEANS TO PASS, CHILD?
WHERE YOU ASK TO GO, MANY HAVE FALLEN
NOT ONLY IN BODY, BUT IN MIND AND SOUL
IT'S A PLACE WHERE MORTALS DROWN. THE SPIRIT WITHERS AND...
OLD WOMAN
YOU TALK TOO MUCH

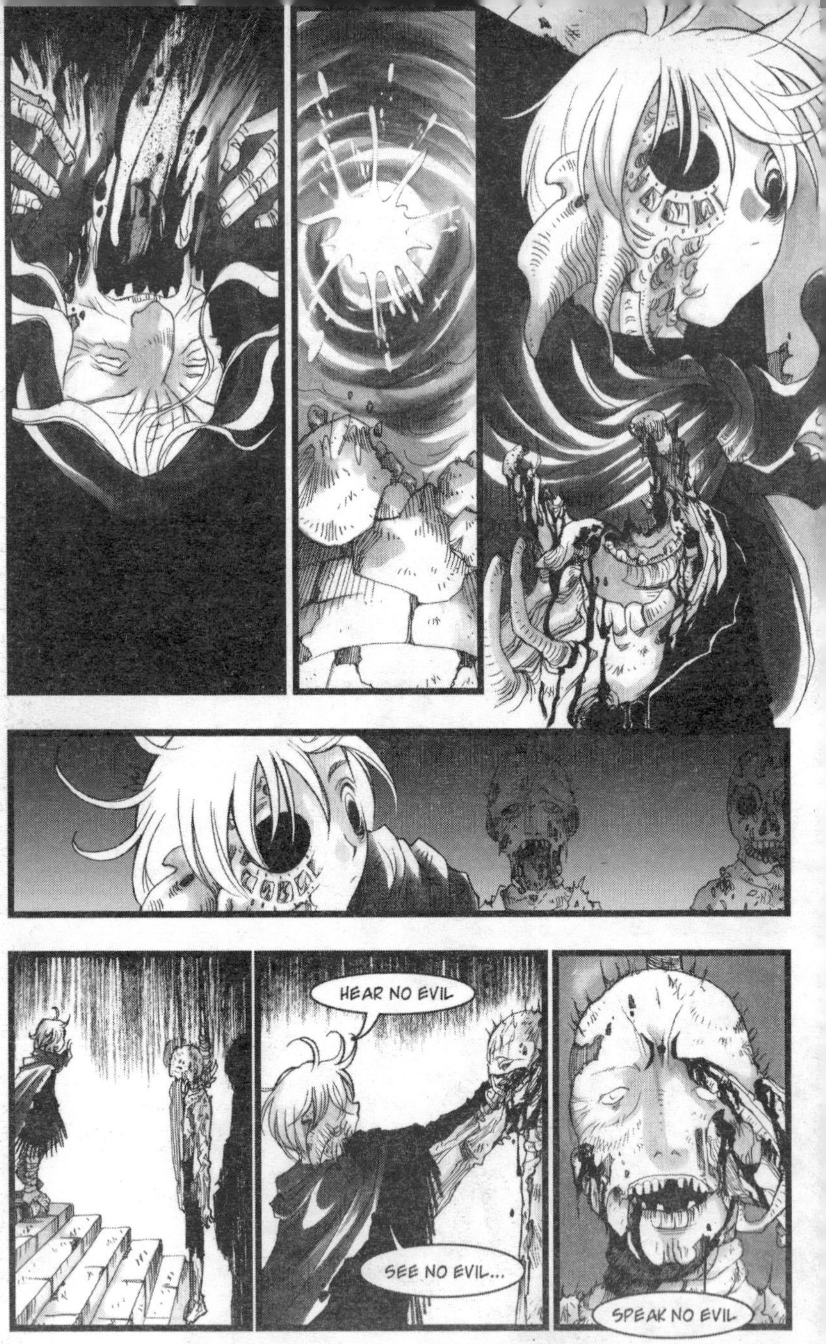
HEAR NO EVIL
SEE NO EVIL...
SPEAK NO EVIL

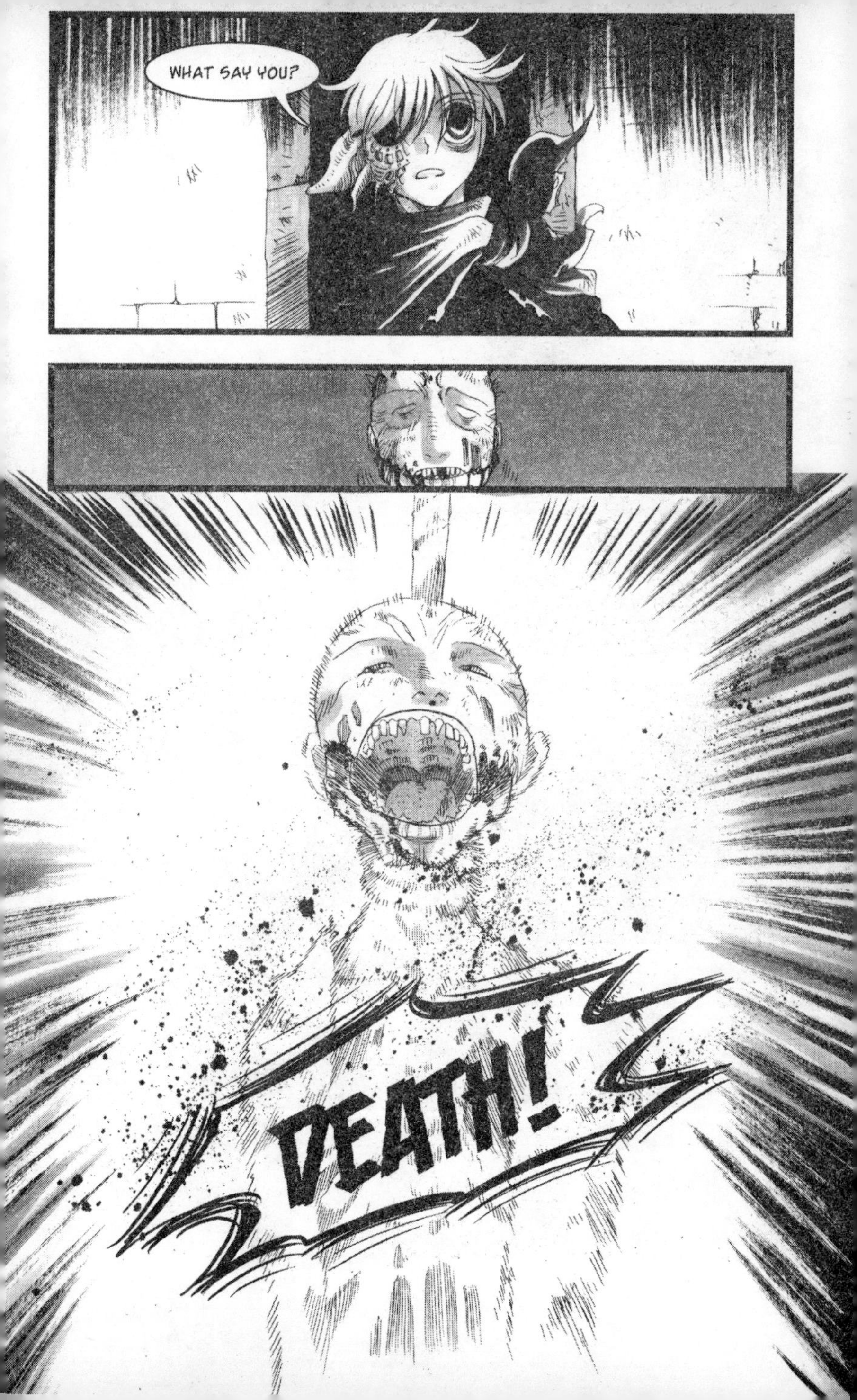
WHAT SAY YOU?
DEATH!

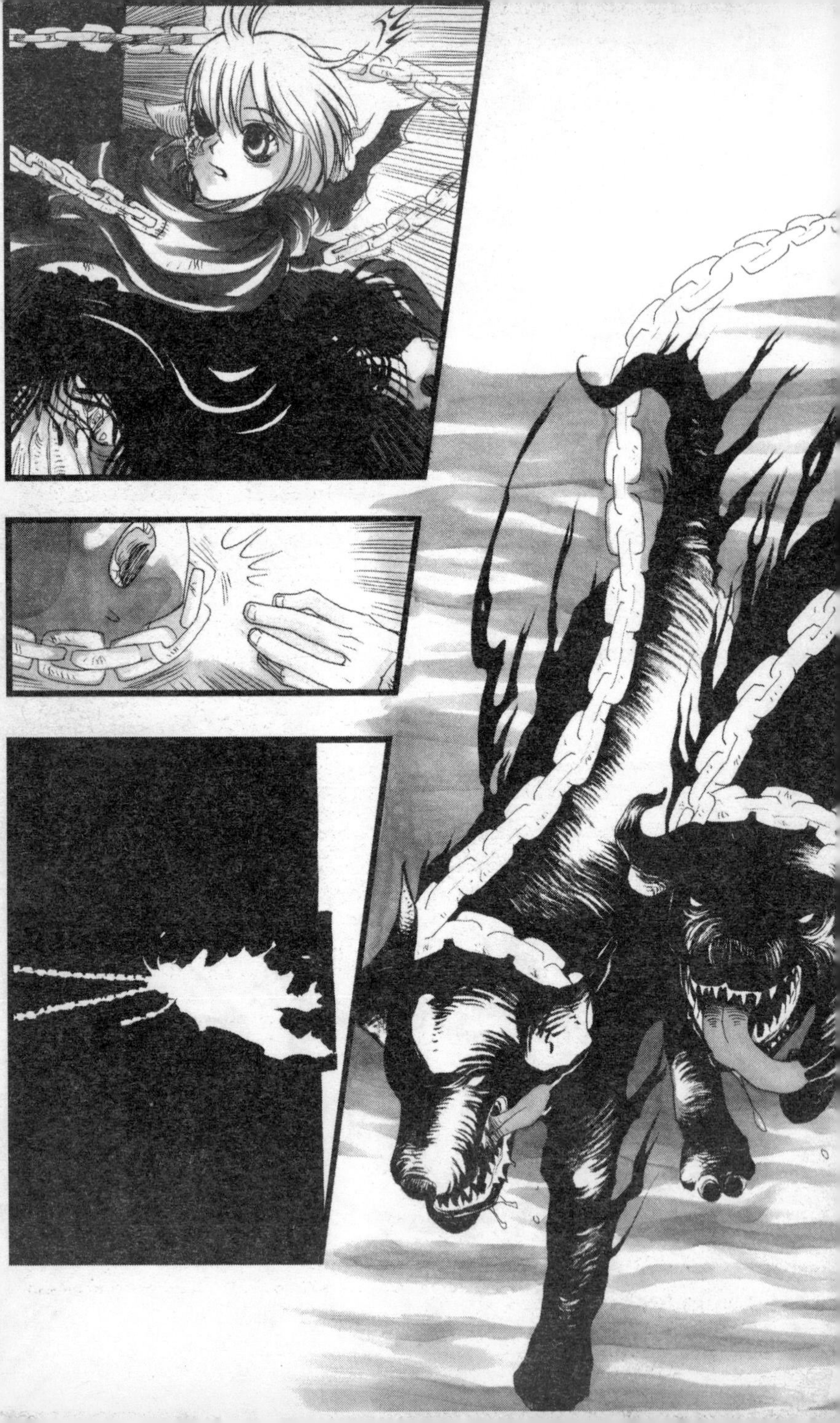

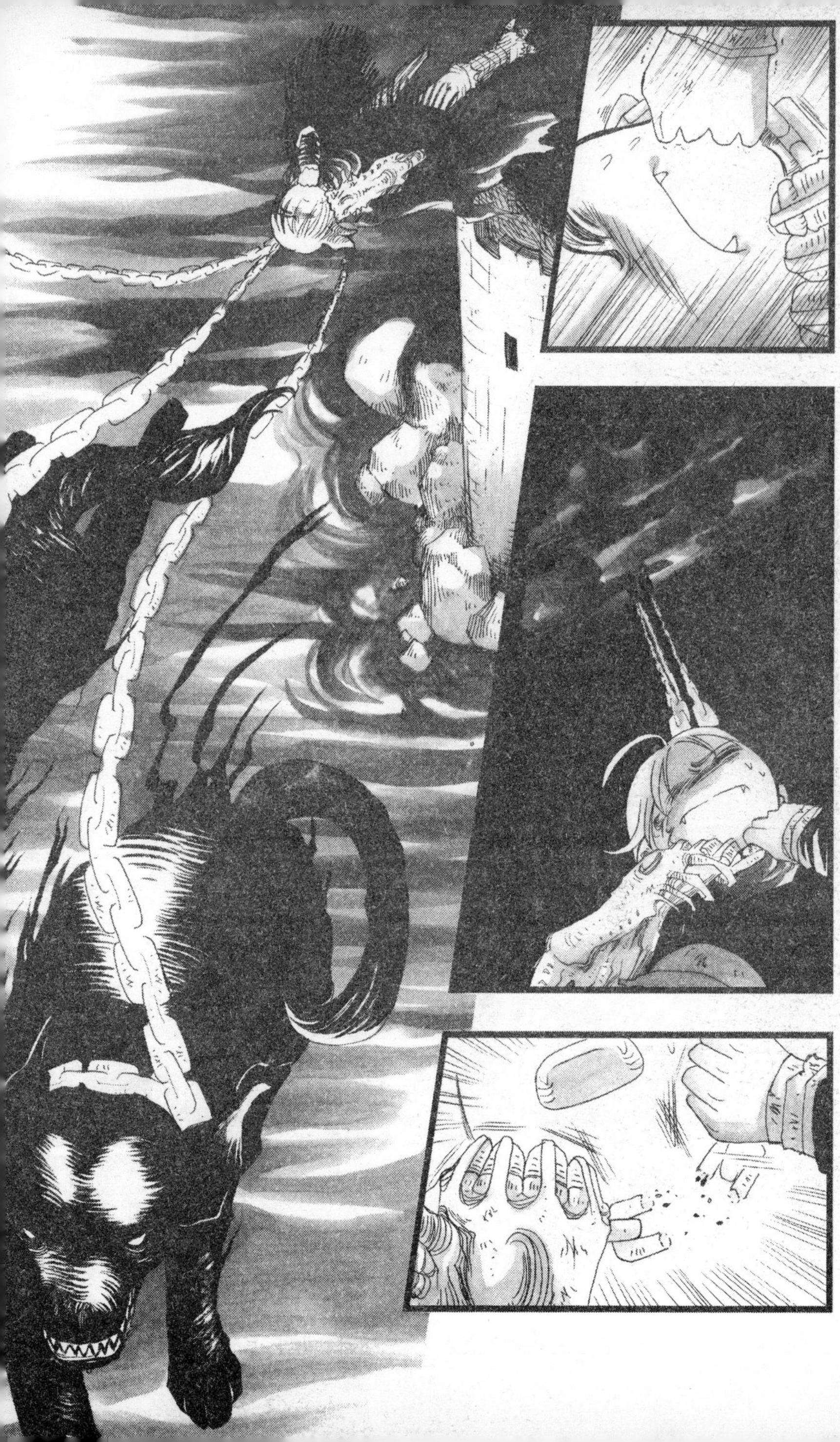

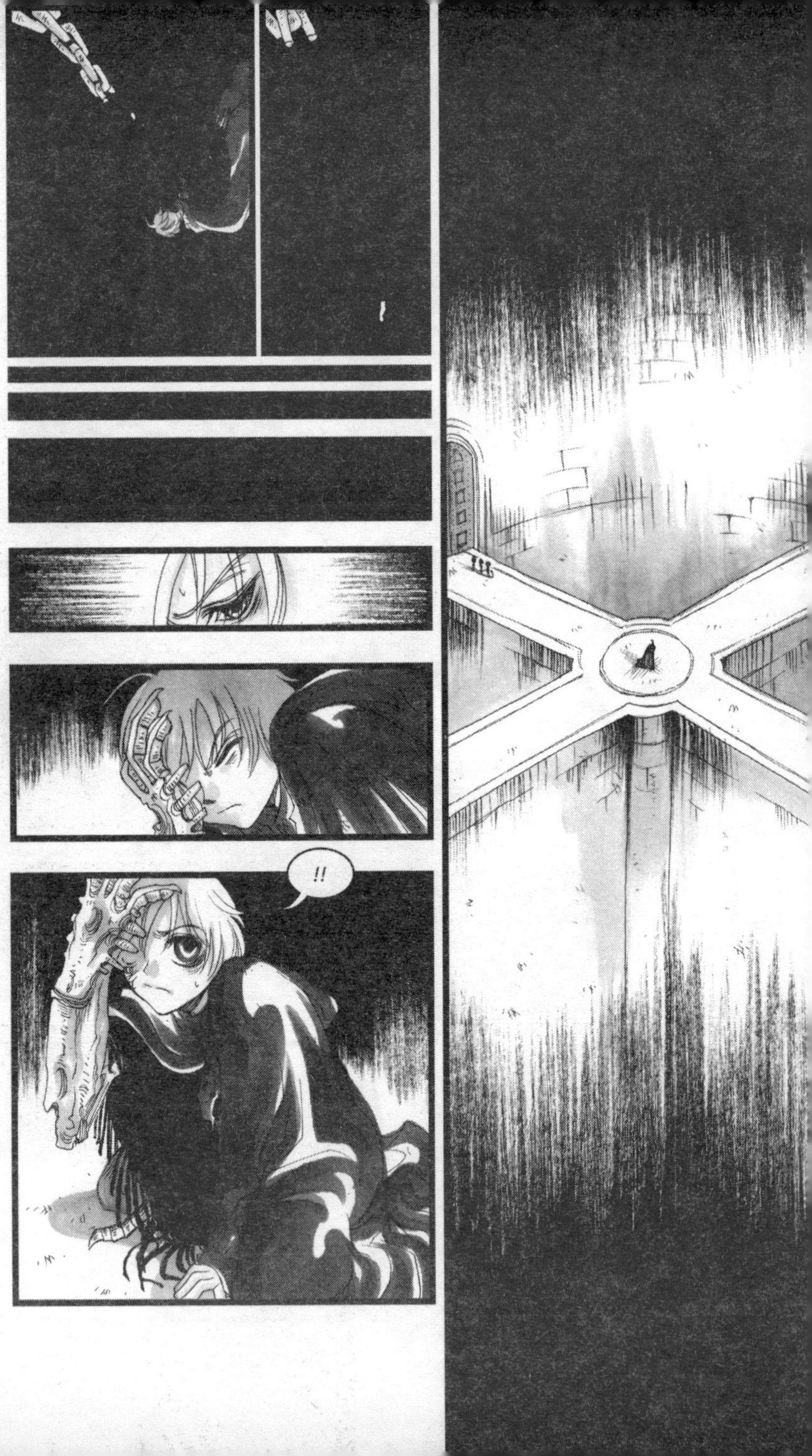
!!

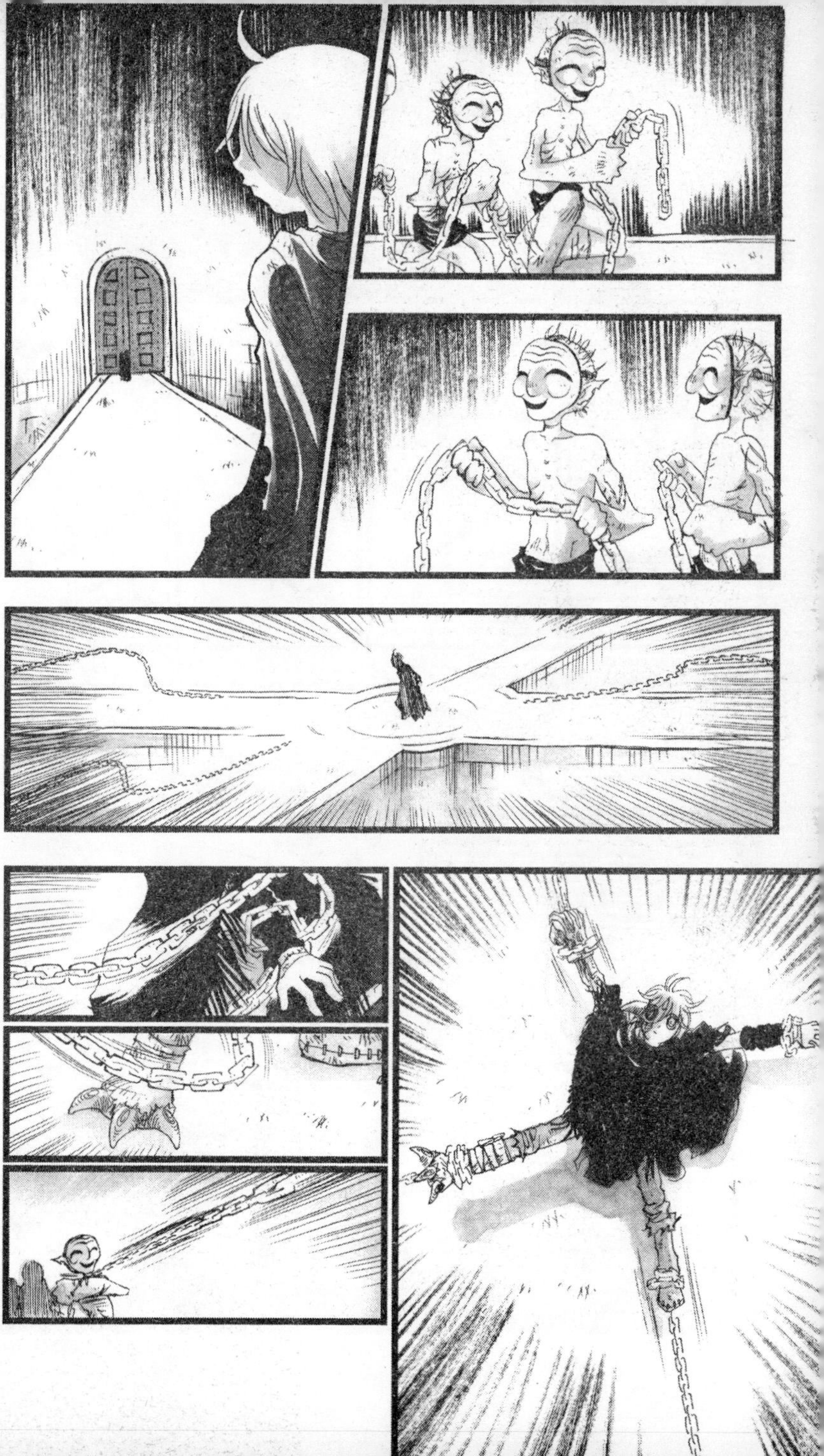

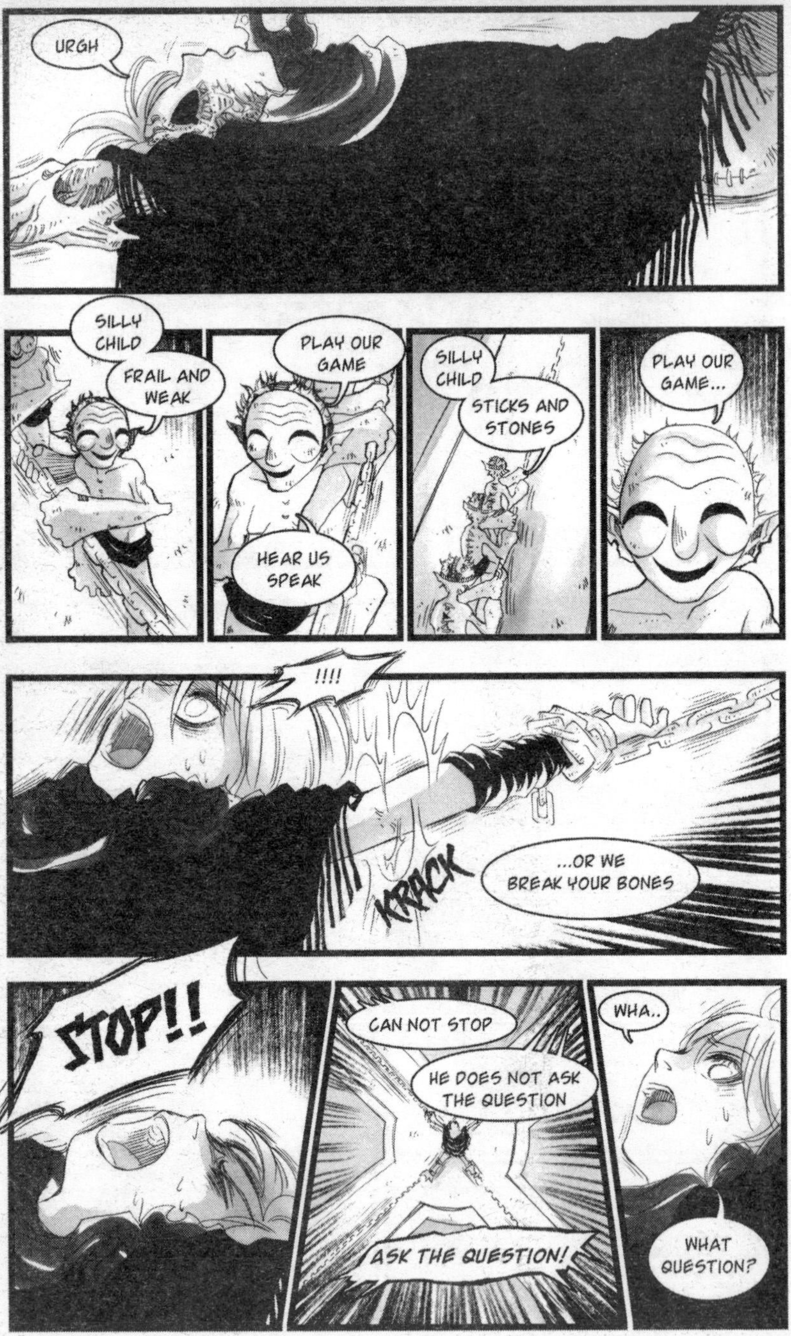
URGH
SILLY CHILD
FRAIL AND WEAK
PLAY OUR GAME
HEAR US SPEAK
SILLY CHILD
STICKS AND STONES
PLAY OUR GAME...
!!!!
KRACK
...OR WE BREAK YOUR BONES
STOP!!
CAN NOT STOP
HE DOES NOT ASK THE QUESTION
ASK THE QUESTION!
WHA..
WHAT QUESTION?

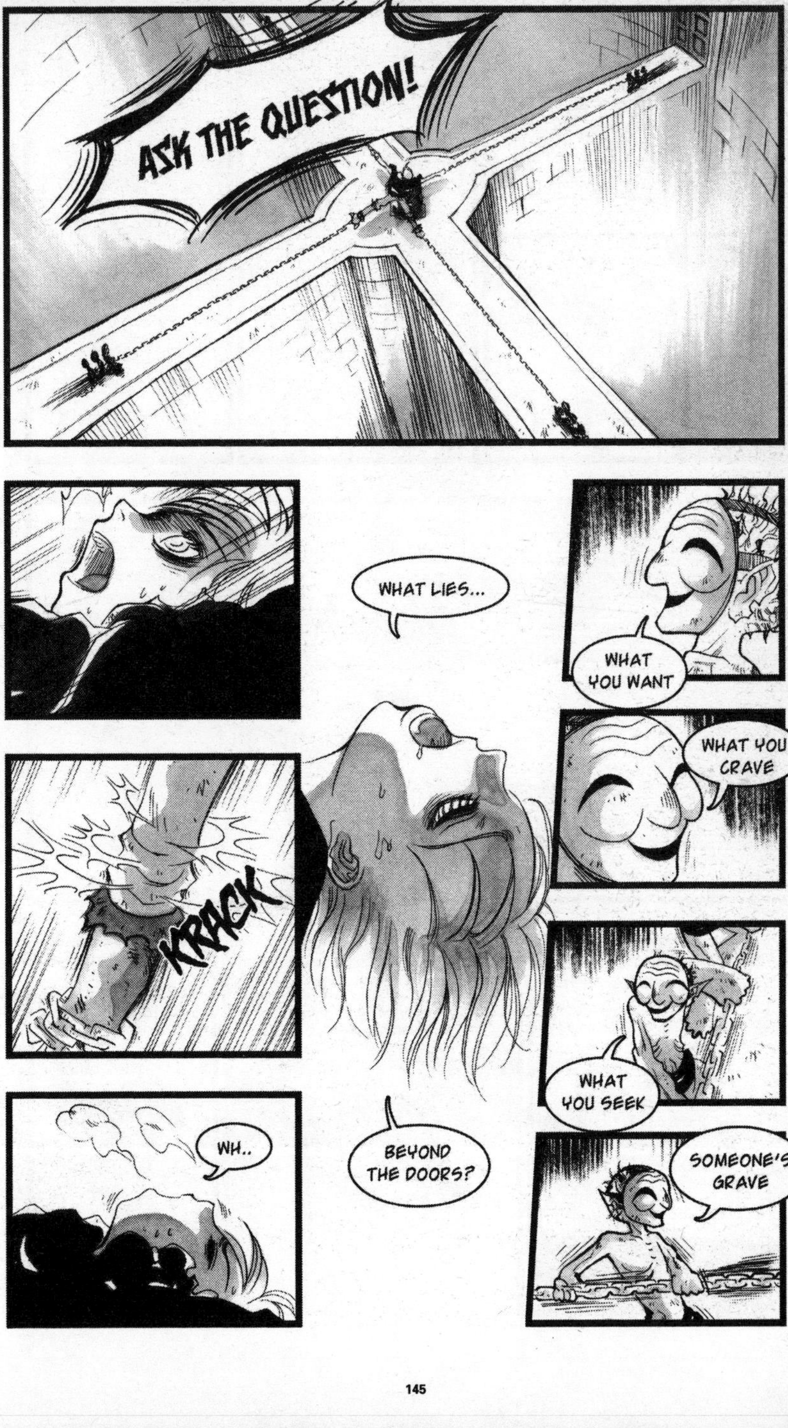
ASK THE QUESTION!
WHAT LIES...
WHAT YOU WANT
KRACK
WHAT YOU CRAVE
WHAT YOU SEEK
WH..
BEYOND THE DOORS?
SOMEONE'S GRAVE

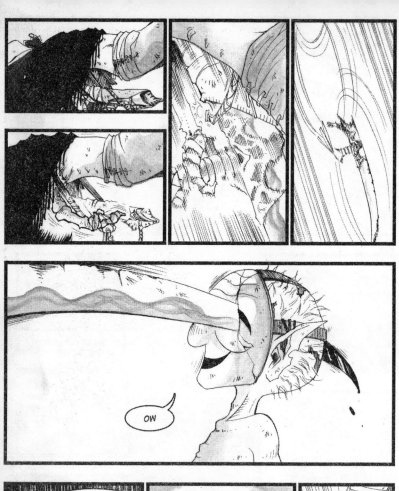

OW

EEEEEEEEEEE

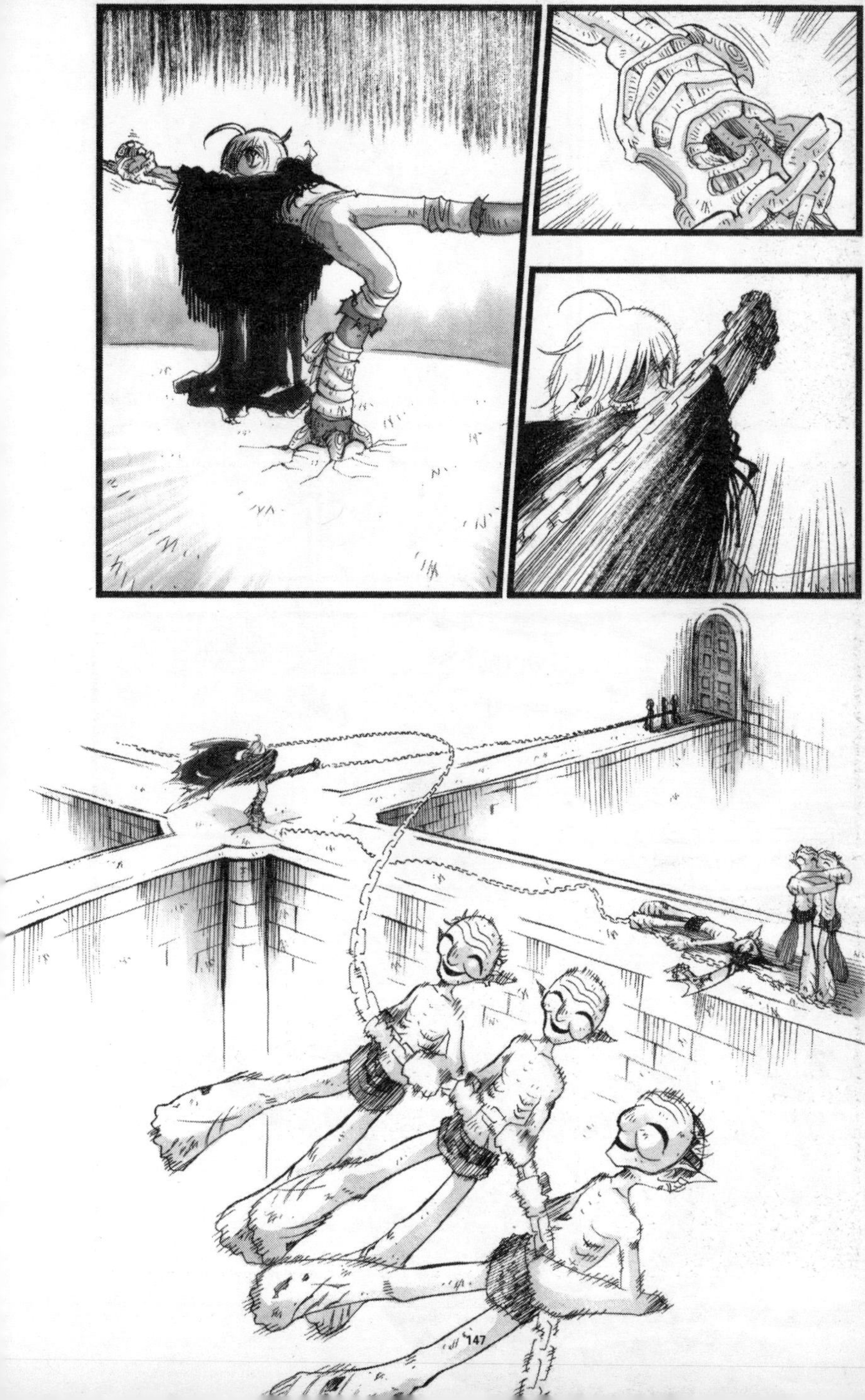

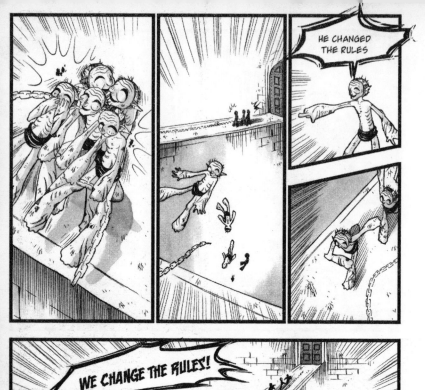

HE CHANGED
THE RULES

WE CHANGE THE RULES!

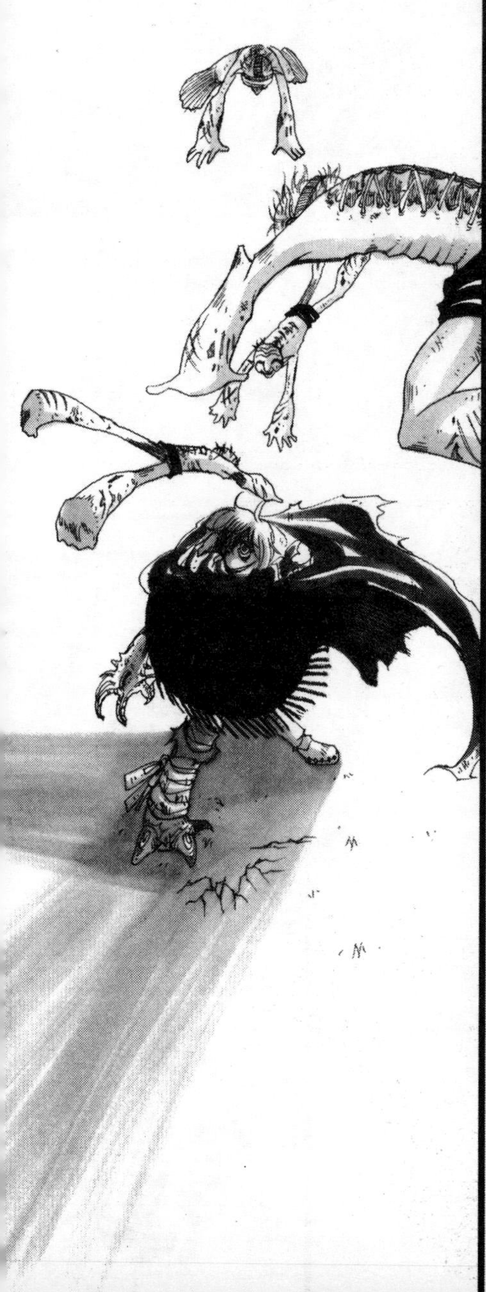
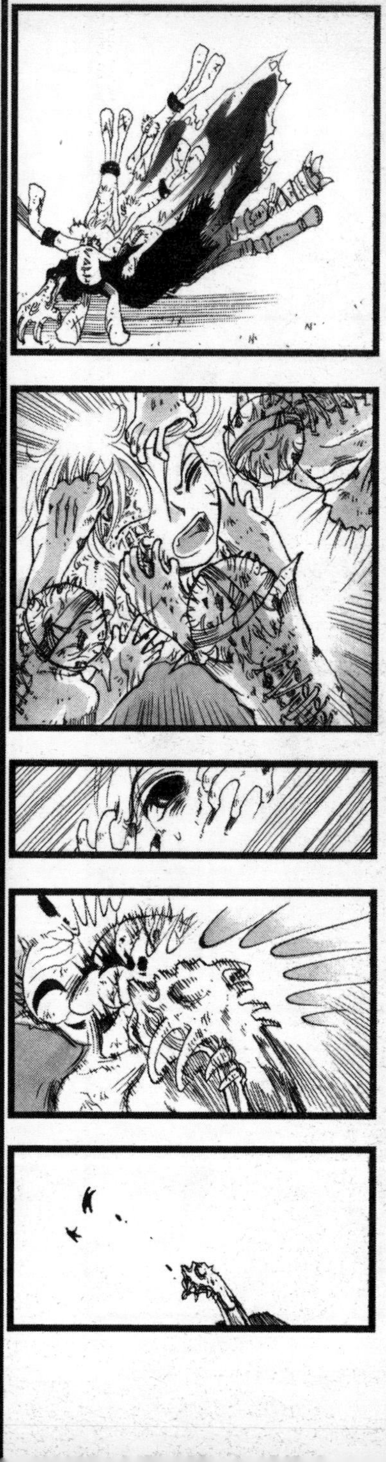

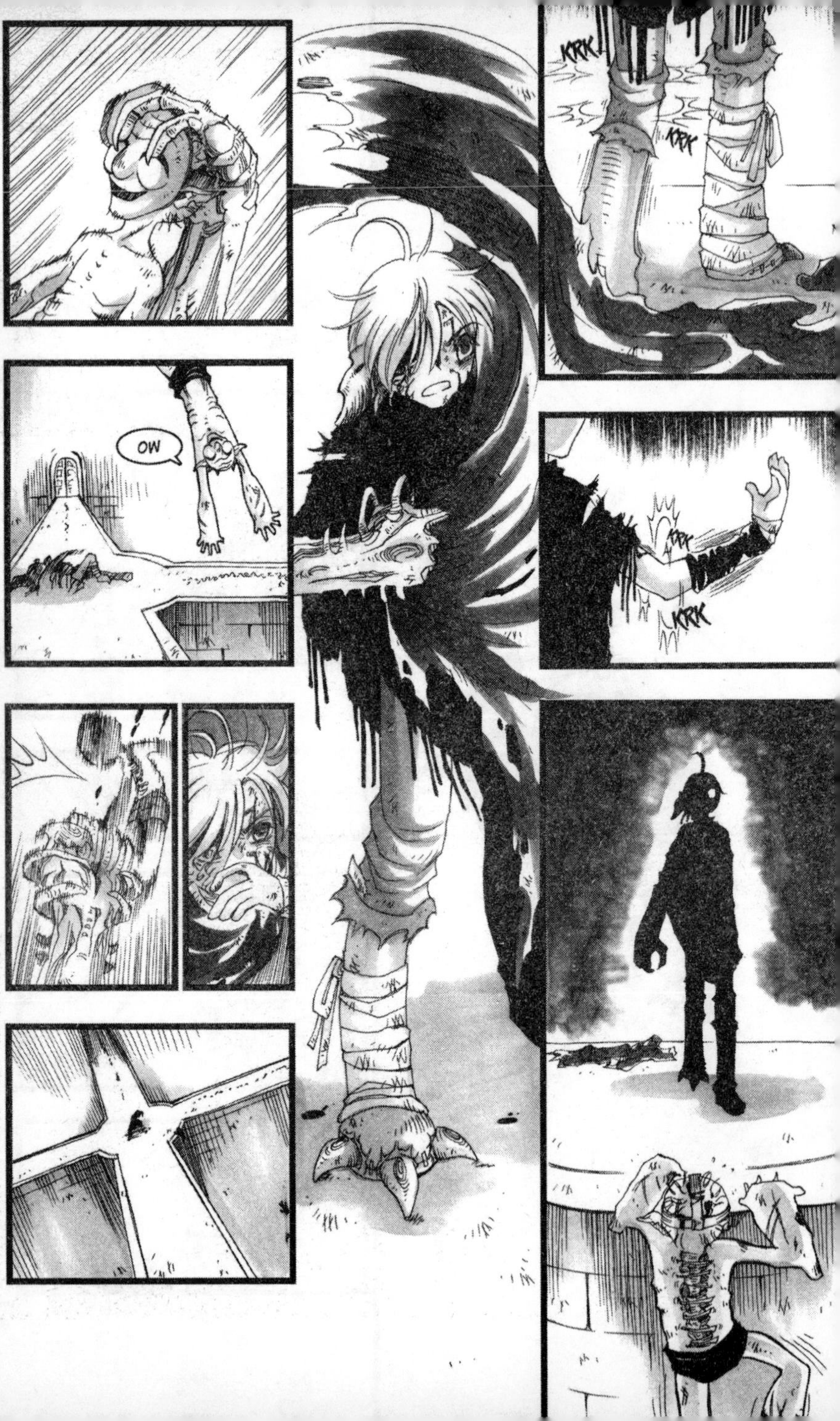
KRK
KRK
OW
KRK
KRK

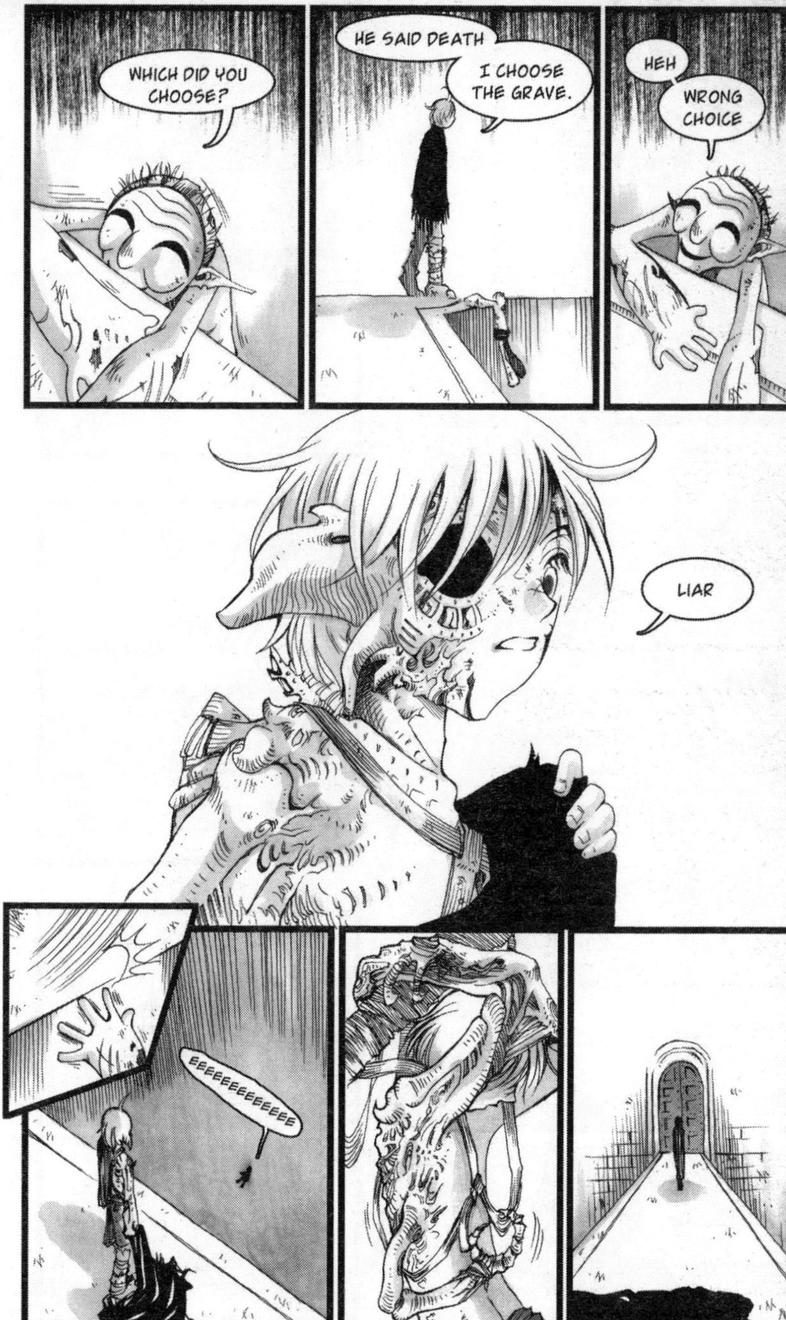
WHICH DID YOU CHOOSE?
HE SAID DEATH
I CHOOSE THE GRAVE.
HEH
WRONG CHOICE
LIAR
EEEEEEEEEEEEE

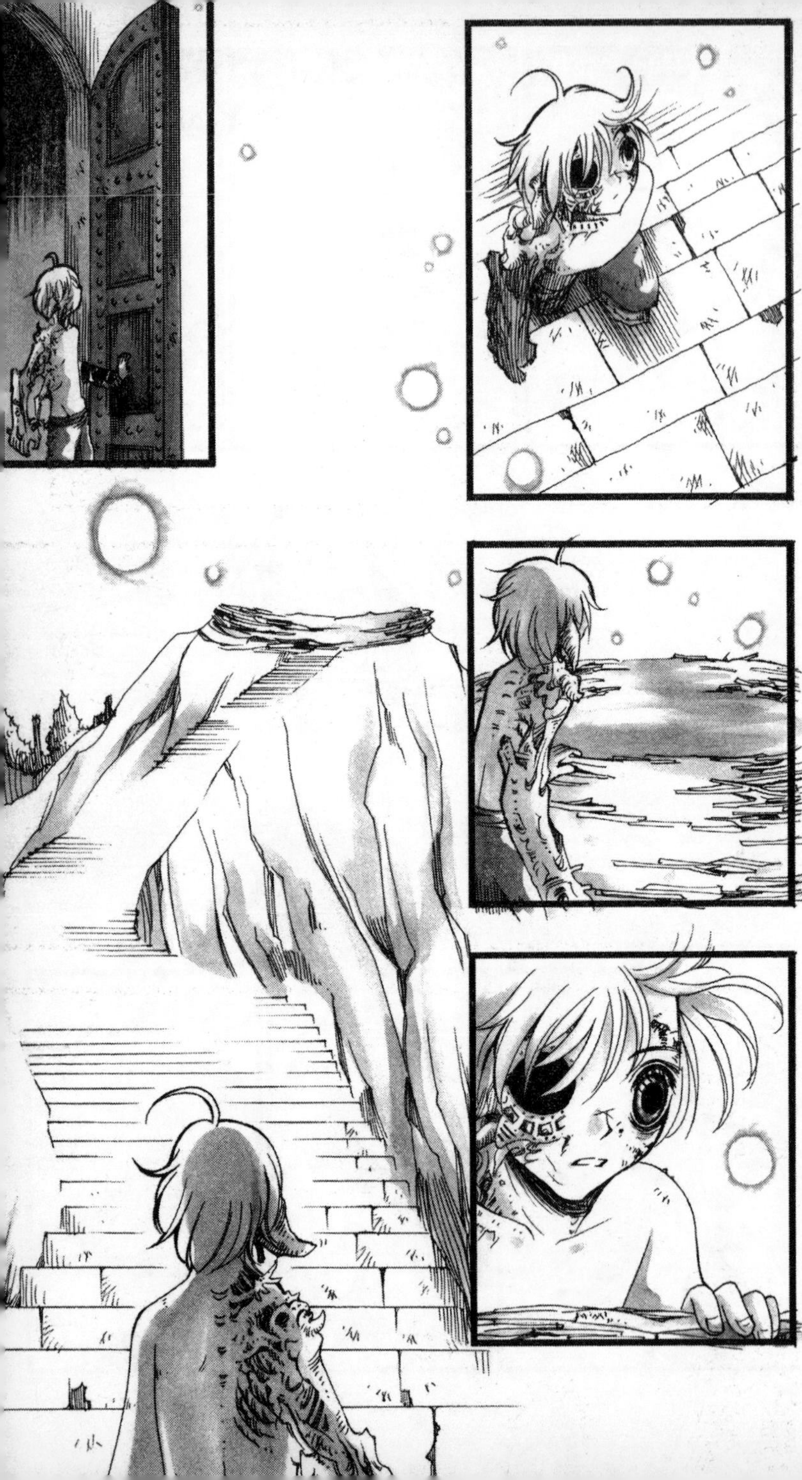

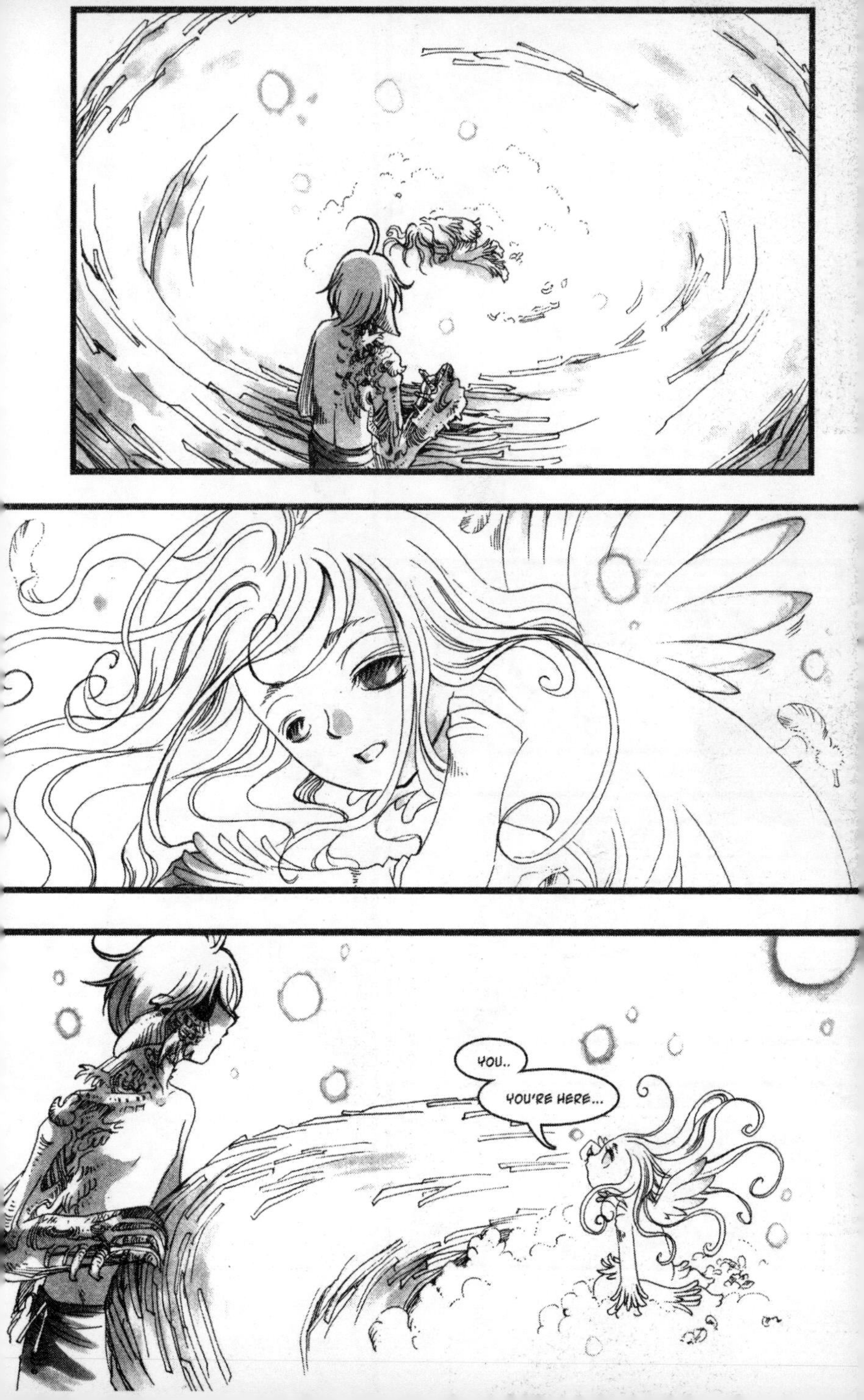
YOU..
YOU'RE HERE...

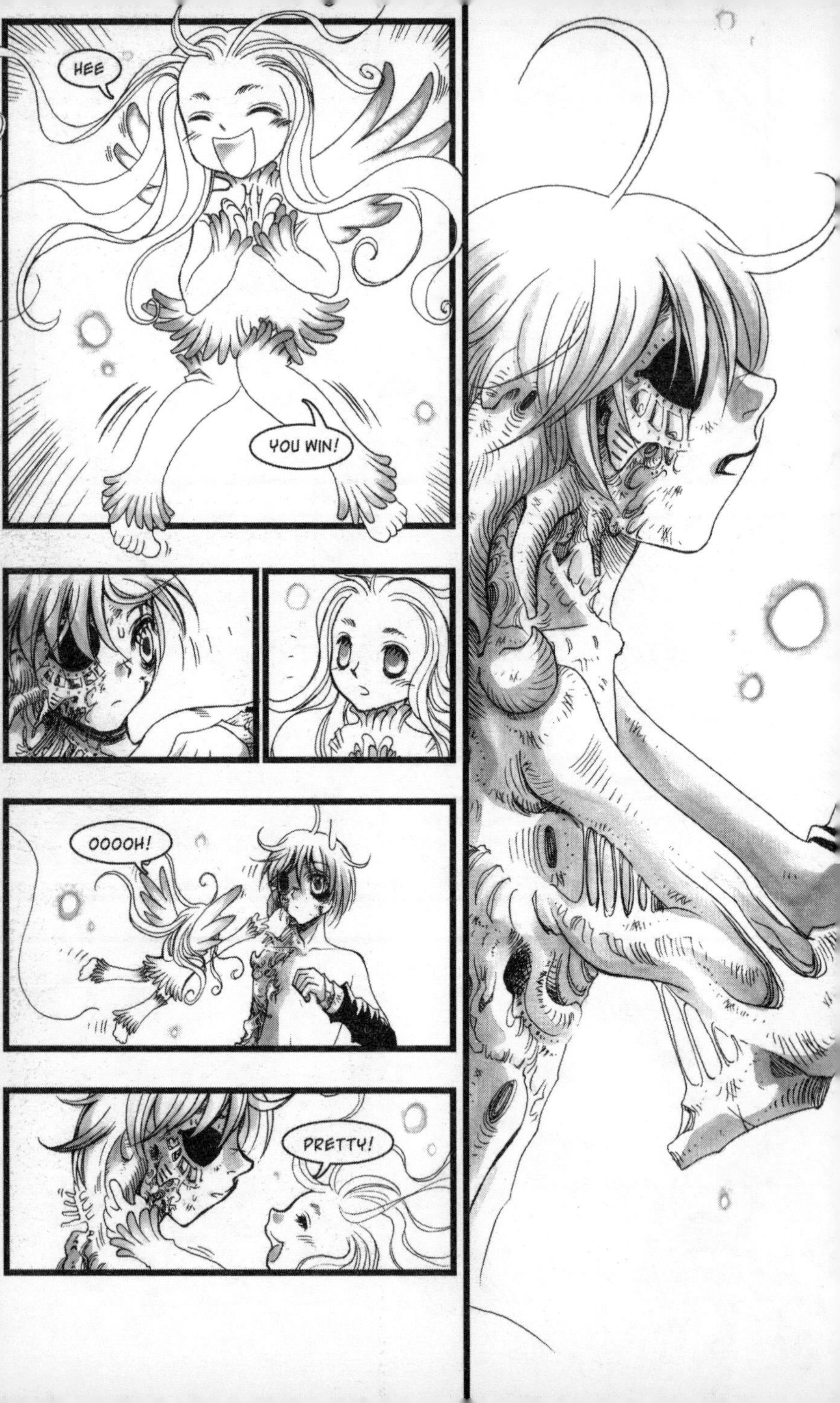
HEE
YOU WIN!
OOOOH!
PRETTY!

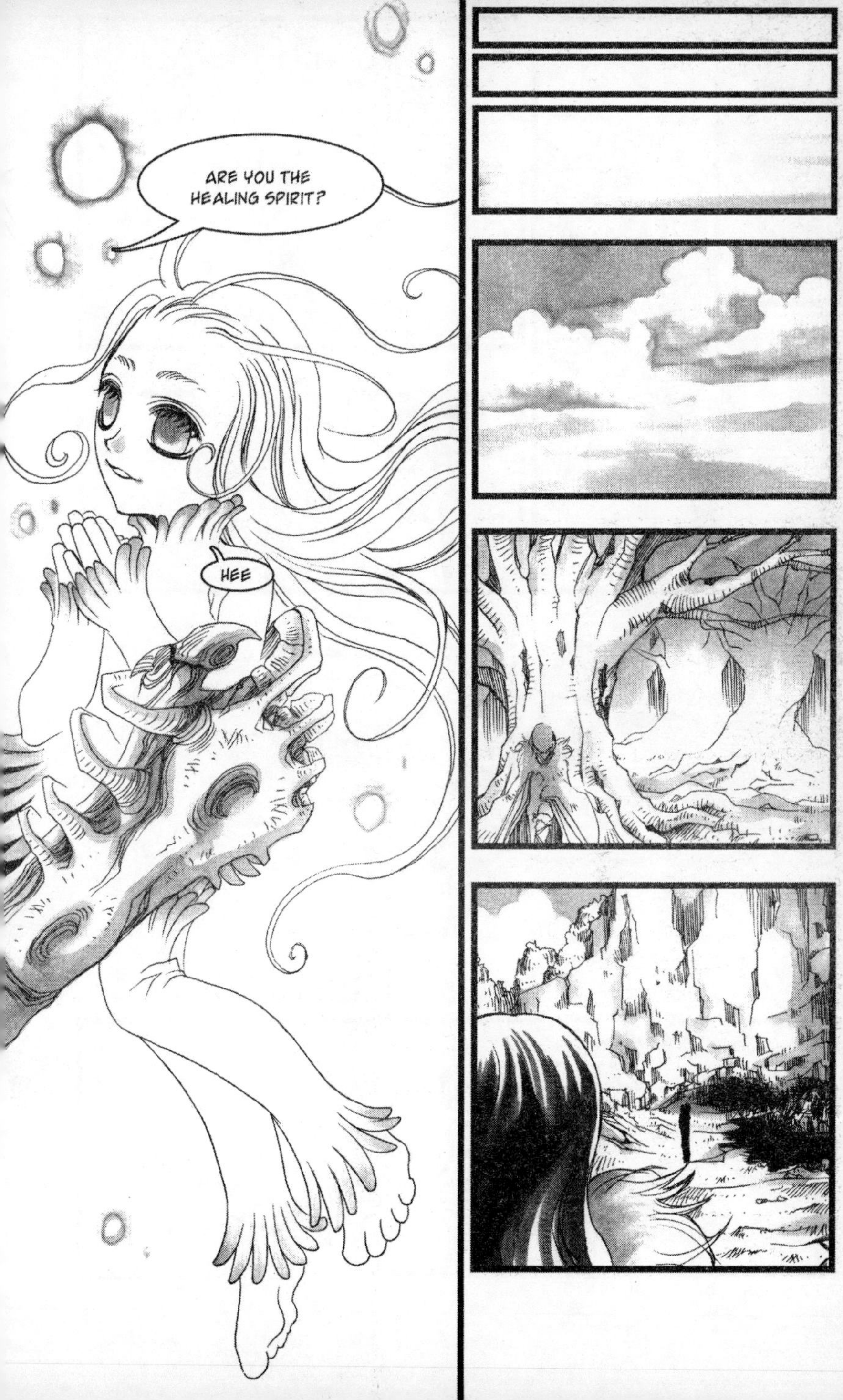
ARE YOU THE HEALING SPIRIT?
HEE

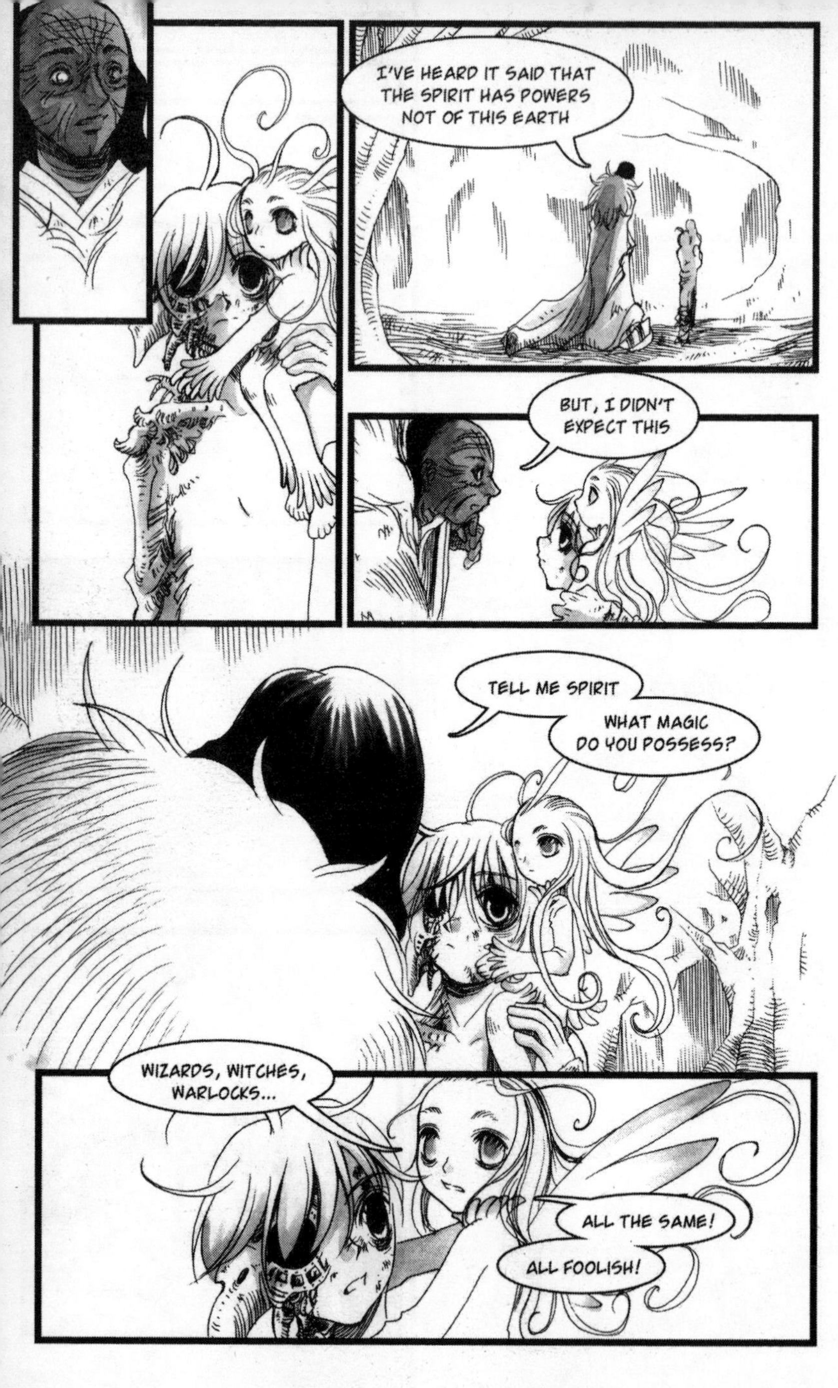
I'VE HEARD IT SAID THAT THE SPIRIT HAS POWERS NOT OF THIS EARTH
BUT, I DIDN'T EXPECT THIS
TELL ME SPIRIT
WHAT MAGIC DO YOU POSSESS?
WIZARDS, WITCHES, WARLOCKS...
ALL THE SAME!
ALL FOOLISH!

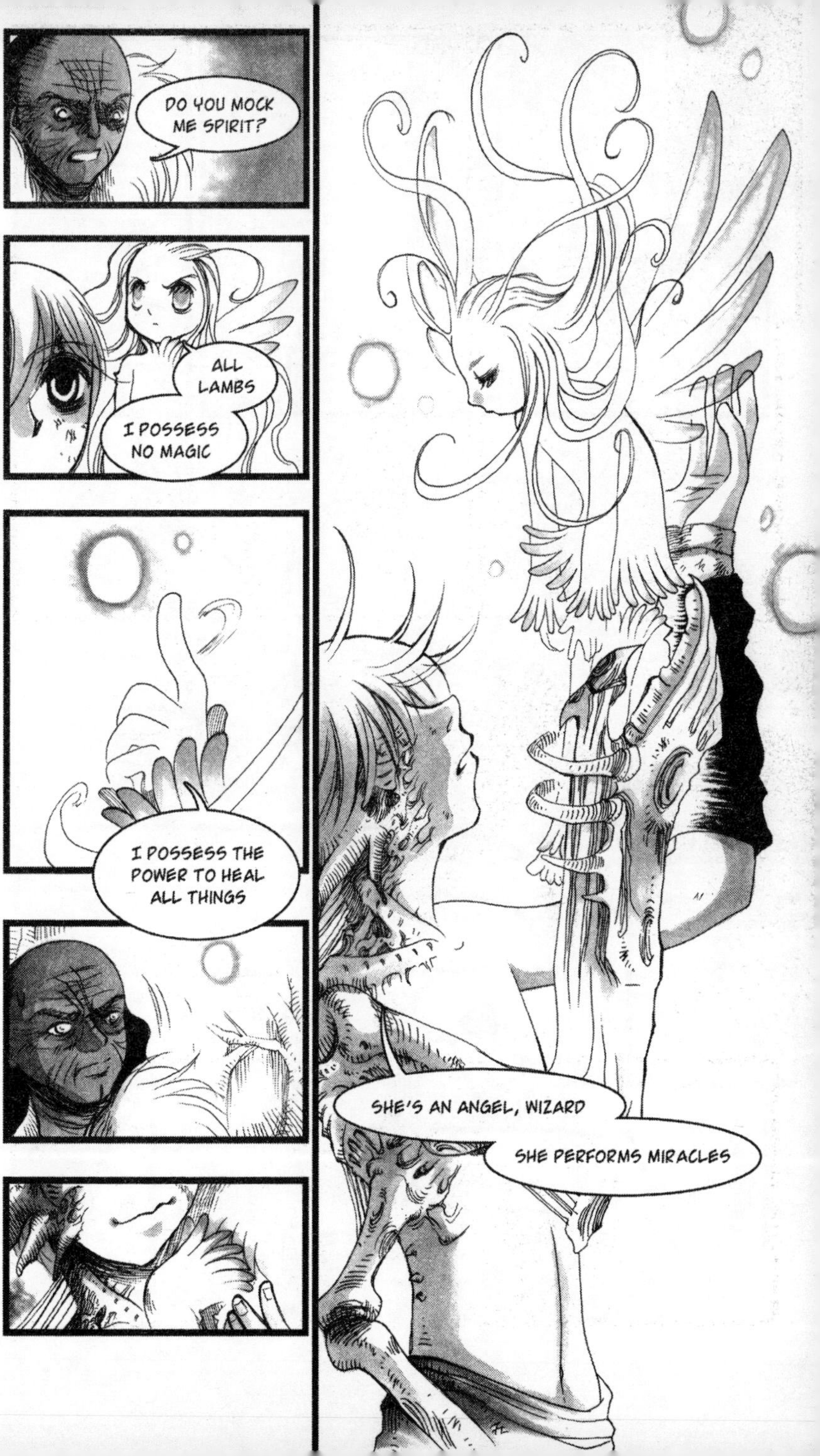
DO YOU MOCK ME SPIRIT?
ALL LAMBS
I POSSESS NO MAGIC
I POSSESS THE POWER TO HEAL ALL THINGS
SHE'S AN ANGEL, WIZARD
SHE PERFORMS MIRACLES

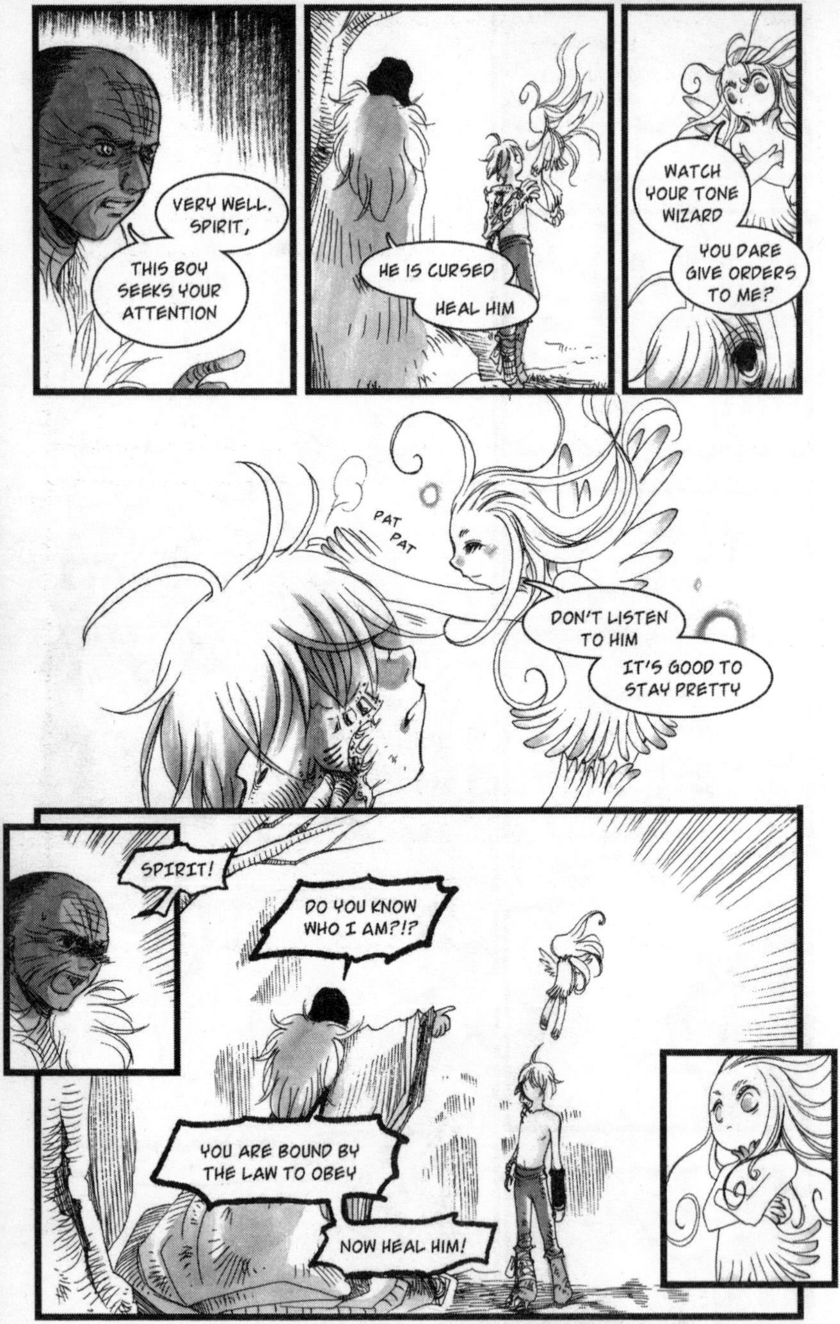
VERY WELL. SPIRIT,
THIS BOY SEEKS YOUR ATTENTION
HE IS CURSED
HEAL HIM
WATCH YOUR TONE WIZARD
YOU DARE GIVE ORDERS TO ME?
PAT PAT
DON'T LISTEN TO HIM
IT'S GOOD TO STAY PRETTY
SPIRIT!
DO YOU KNOW WHO I AM?!?
YOU ARE BOUND BY THE LAW TO OBEY
NOW HEAL HIM!

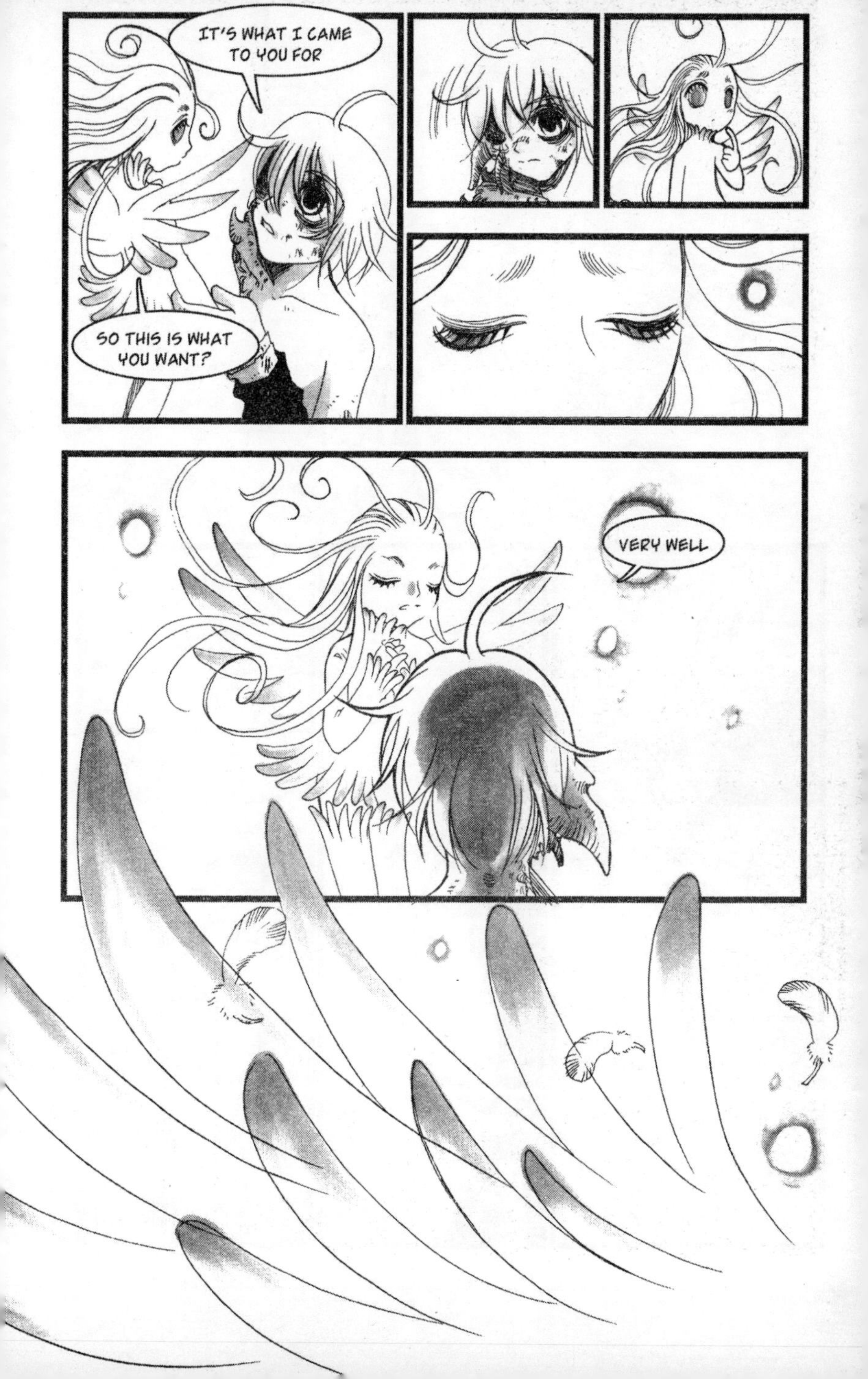
IT'S WHAT I CAME TO YOU FOR
SO THIS IS WHAT YOU WANT?
VERY WELL

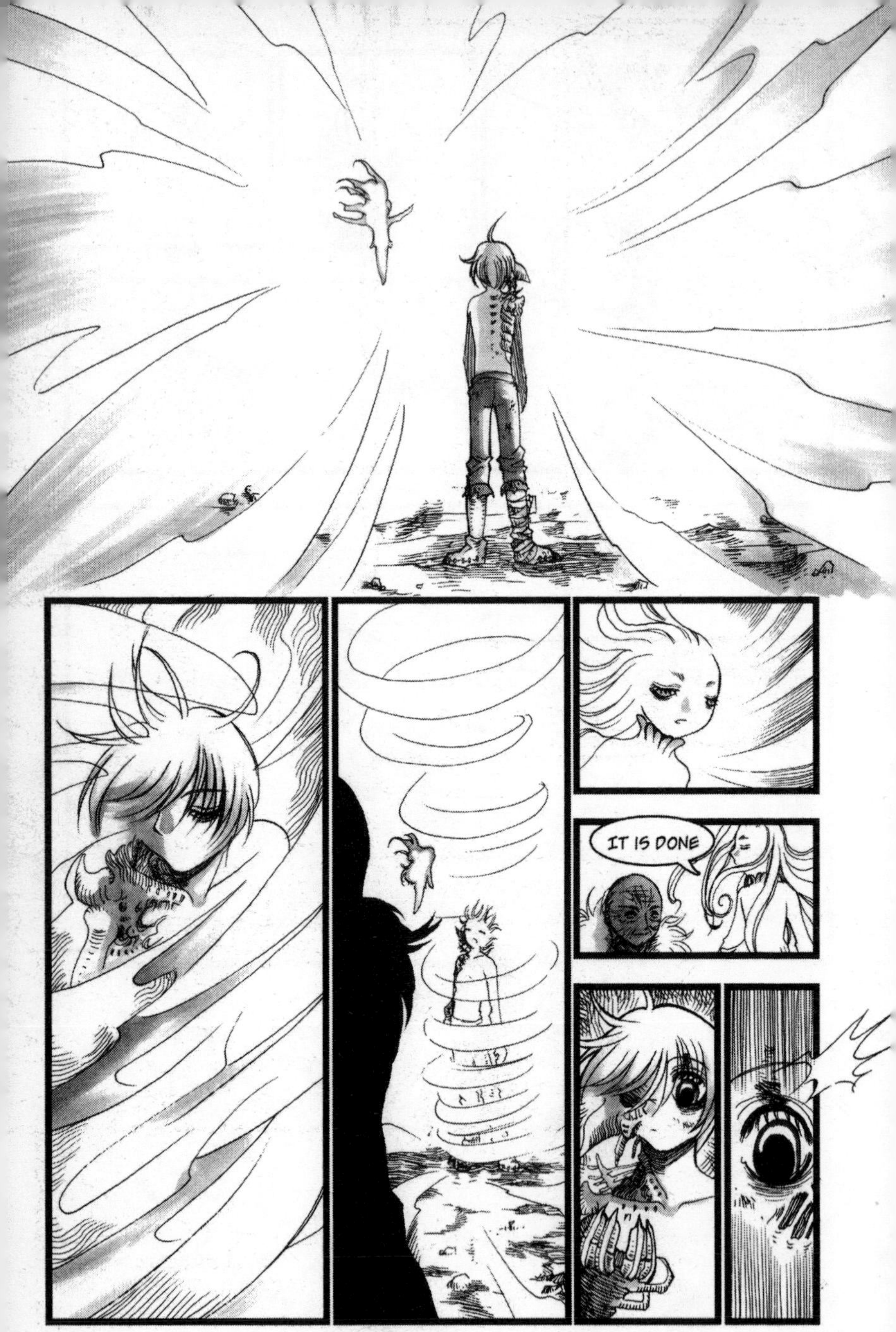
IT IS DONE

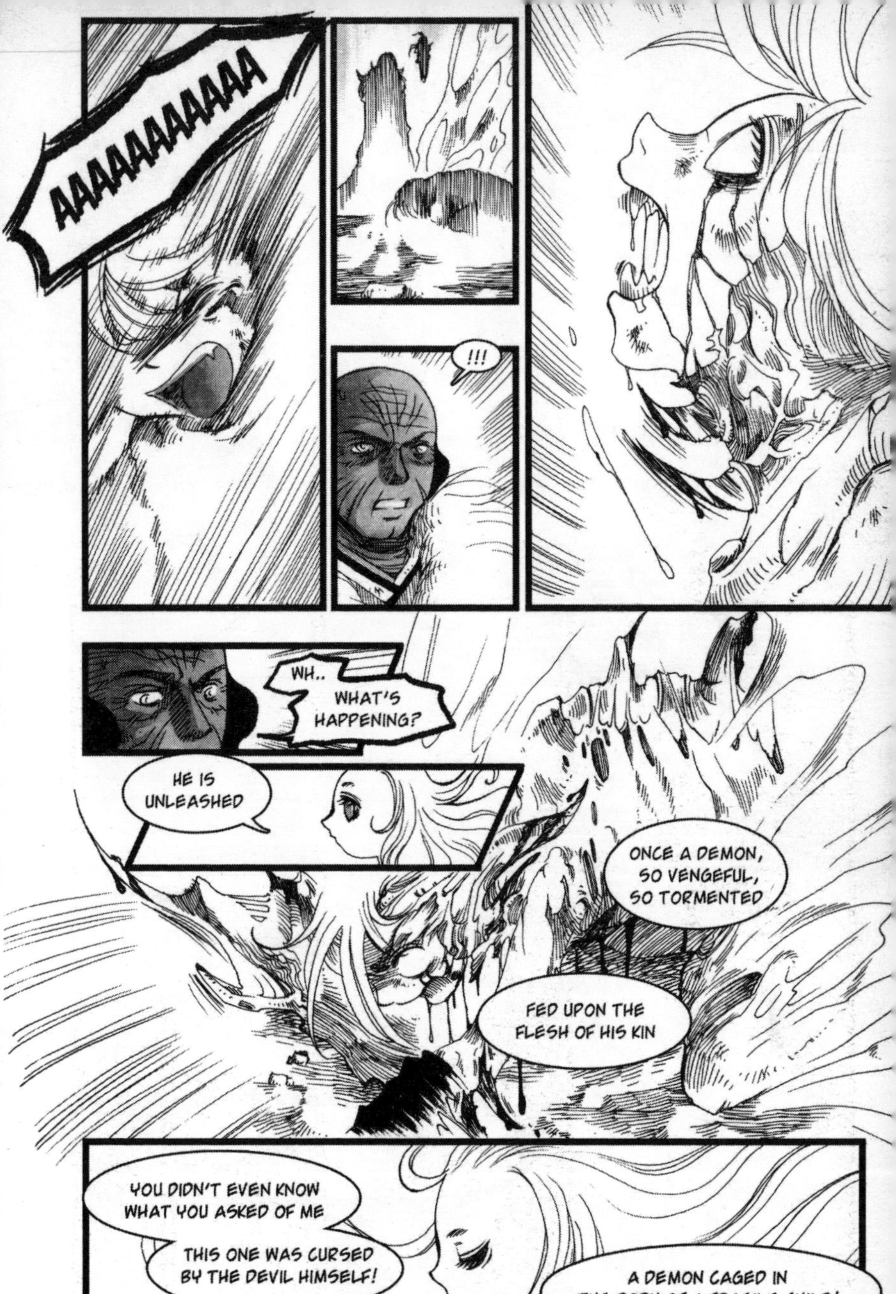

AAAAAAAAAA
!!!
WH.. WHAT'S HAPPENING?
HE IS UNLEASHED
ONCE A DEMON, SO VENGEFUL, SO TORMENTED
FED UPON THE FLESH OF HIS KIN
YOU DIDN'T EVEN KNOW WHAT YOU ASKED OF ME
THIS ONE WAS CURSED BY THE DEVIL HIMSELF!
A DEMON CAGED IN THE BODY OF A FRAGILE CHILD!

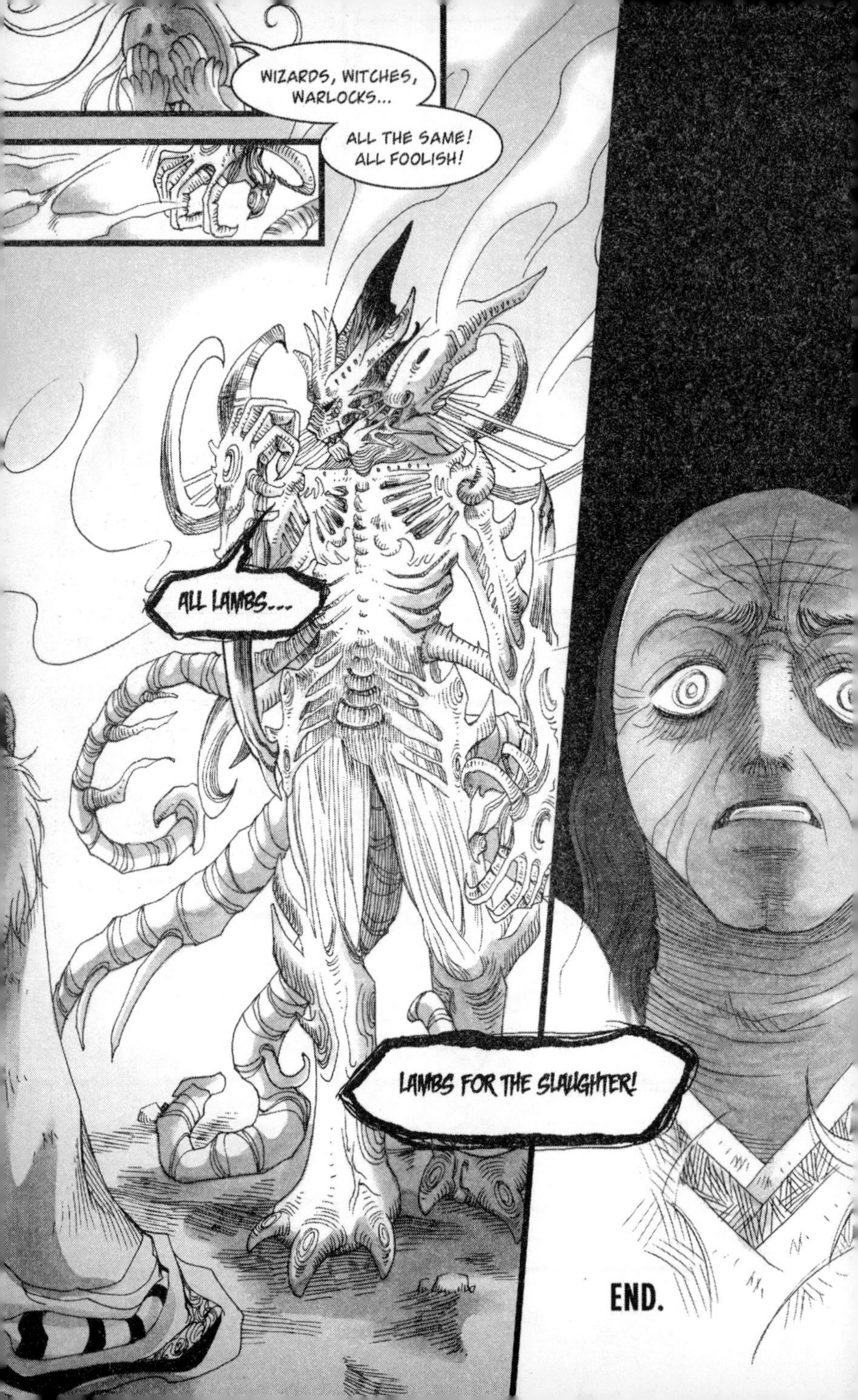
WIZARDS, WITCHES, WARLOCKS...
ALL THE SAME! ALL FOOLISH!
ALL LAMBS...
LAMBS FOR THE SLAUGHTER!
END.

Omake ('Extras')

In the West we are used to seeing manga published as paperback book collections, roughly equivalent to the original Japanese formats known as *tankobon*, and the slightly smaller *bunkobon*. In Japan, however, most longer comic strip stories make their first appearance serialized in 20–30 page chunks, within one of the hundreds of anthology titles, or *zasshi*. Containing at least 400 pages, they would look a bit like this book does – but coming out every week, not just once a year! *Zasshi* sell by the million, and are hugely popular with commuters – a deliberately disposable magazine format intended to be thrown away at the end of any journey, unlike their more collectable comic book cousins. They will usually feature a colour section (as we hope to, in future editions), and some short newspaper-style 'gag' strips, or one-page funnies, in a section termed omake, or 'extras'.

Taking an ordinary *zasshi* title such as *Comic Morning* as our inspiration for *Best New Manga*, we are happy to share with you some of these entertaining extras, which you will find scattered throughout the main body of contents.

VIVA BATATA!

DAVID GOODMAN
WWW.BAHALA-NA.CO.UK

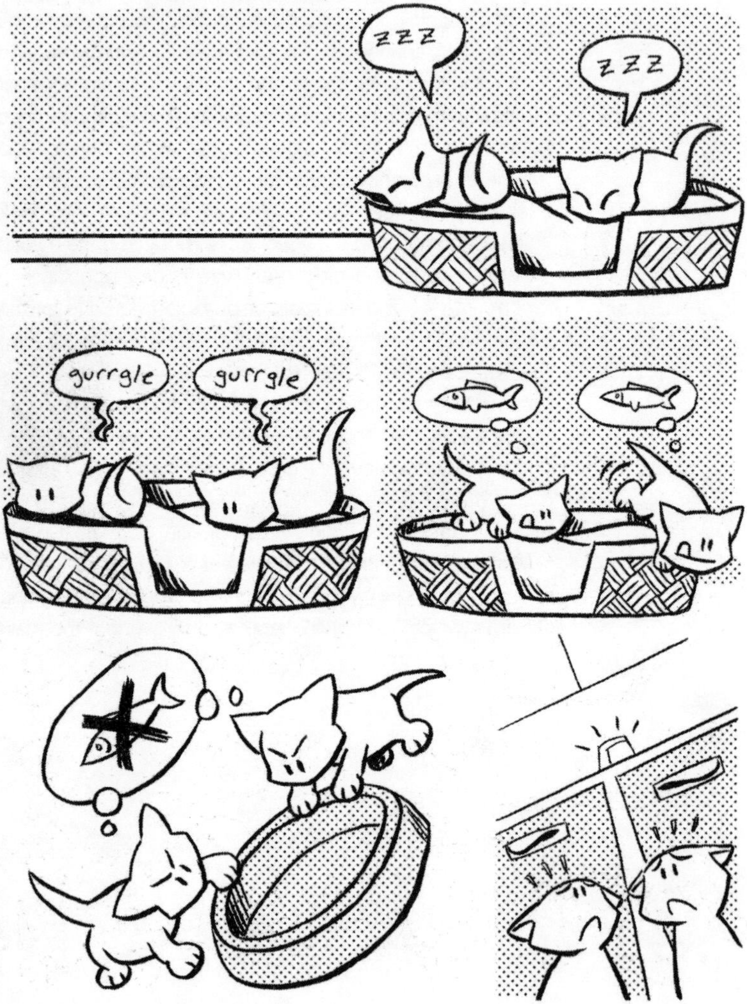
ZZZ
ZZZ
gurrgle
gurrgle

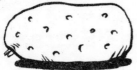

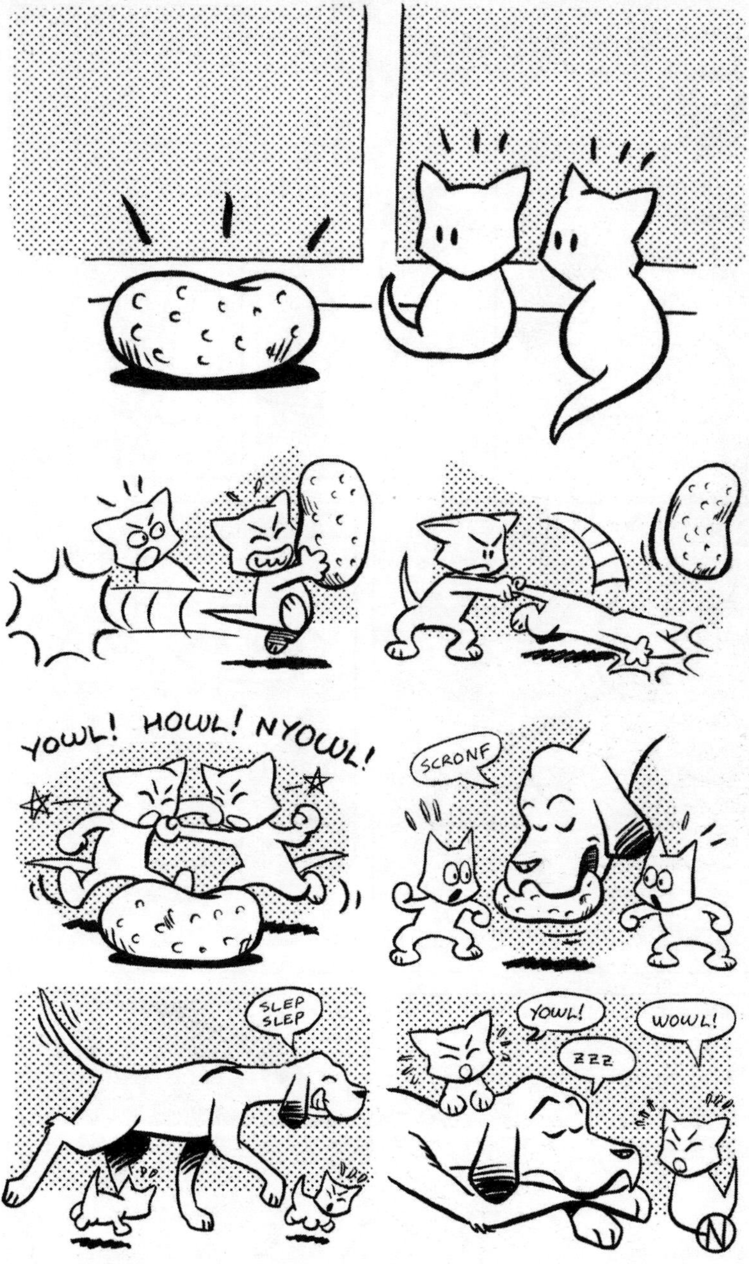
YOWL! HOWL! NYOWL!
SCRONF
SLEP SLEP
YOWL!
WOWL!
ZZZ

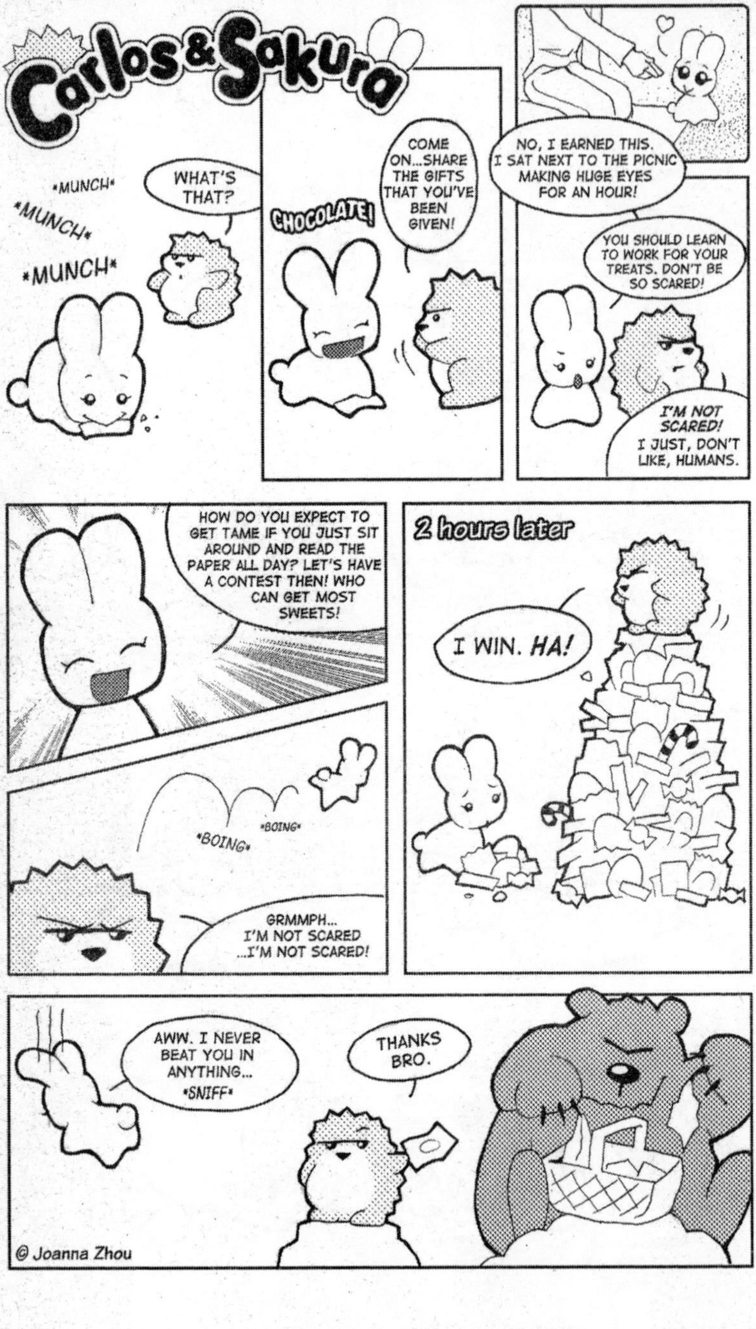
Carlos & Sakura
MUNCH
MUNCH
MUNCH
WHAT'S THAT?
CHOCOLATE!
COME ON...SHARE THE GIFTS THAT YOU'VE BEEN GIVEN!
NO, I EARNED THIS. I SAT NEXT TO THE PICNIC MAKING HUGE EYES FOR AN HOUR!
YOU SHOULD LEARN TO WORK FOR YOUR TREATS. DON'T BE SO SCARED!
I'M NOT SCARED! I JUST, DON'T LIKE, HUMANS.
HOW DO YOU EXPECT TO GET TAME IF YOU JUST SIT AROUND AND READ THE PAPER ALL DAY? LET'S HAVE A CONTEST THEN! WHO CAN GET MOST SWEETS!
BOING
BOING
GRMMPH... I'M NOT SCARED ...I'M NOT SCARED!
2 hours later
I WIN. HA!
AWW. I NEVER BEAT YOU IN ANYTHING... *SNIFF*
THANKS BRO.
© Joanna Zhou

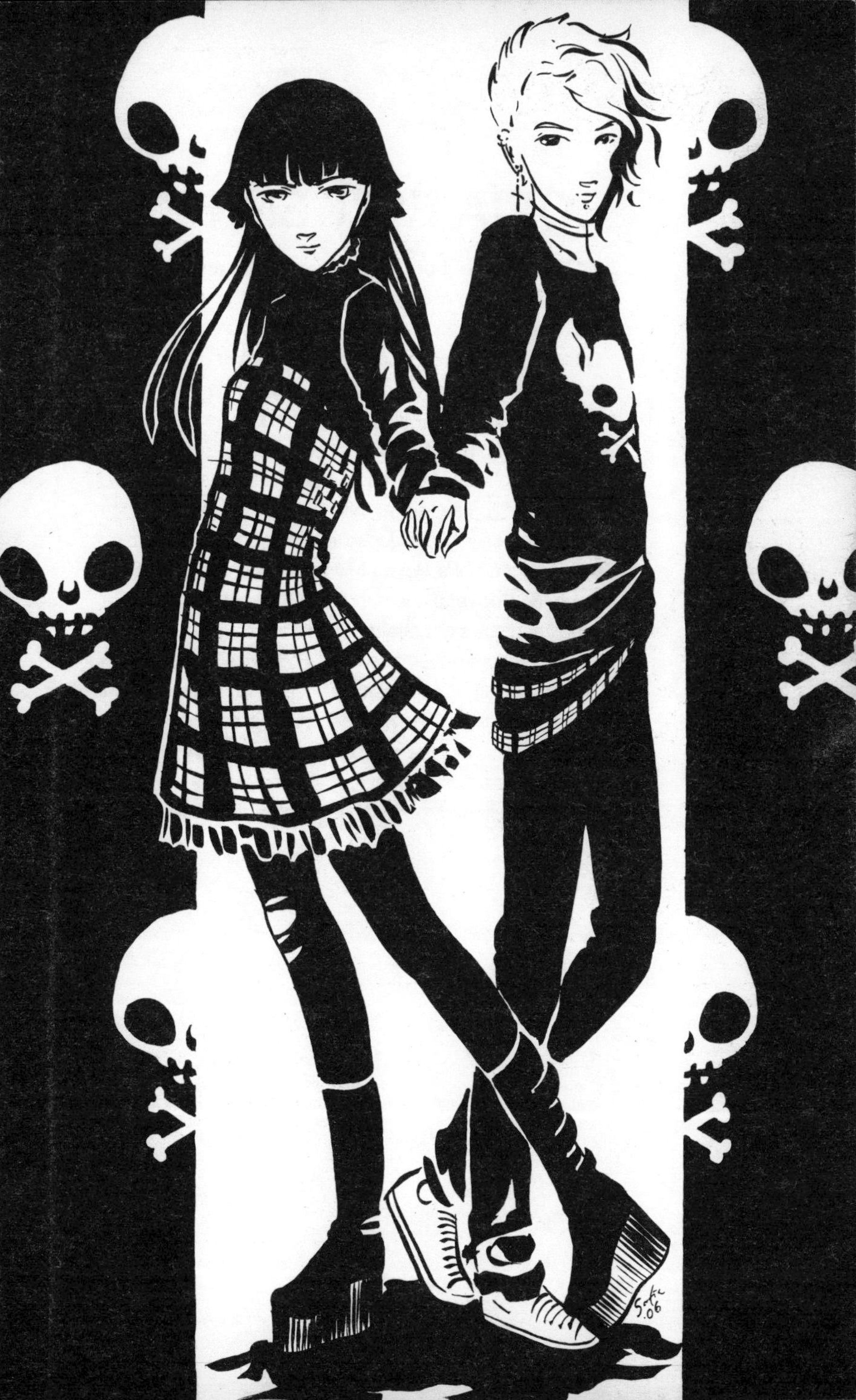

Date of birth: 6 October 1982

SOFIA FALKENHEM

Sofia was born in Kristinehamn, and currently resides in Malmö (both in Sweden). Some of her favourite things include foxes, coffee (but NOT instant, blech!), and 'little old ladies asking me if I think they would look good in my haircut'. She thinks that PCs suck (they do, Macs are way better), and so does the music from the apartment next door (why is that people who play their music the loudest also have the worst taste?). Her prime influences in terms of manga and anime styling are Junko Mizuno, Erica Sakurazawa and Studio Ghibli's Hayao Miyazaki; otherwise, Los Bros (***Love & Rockets***) Hernandez, 16 Horsepower (great band), and she's not afraid of Virginia Woolf, either.

For its appearance here, Sofia was good enough to translate the first part of her strip serial ***Instant Noodles*** into English. She describes it as 'the story of Kim, Mathias and the people around them. About their life, love and art. Mostly love...'

Check out her elegant black and white brush style. We love it!

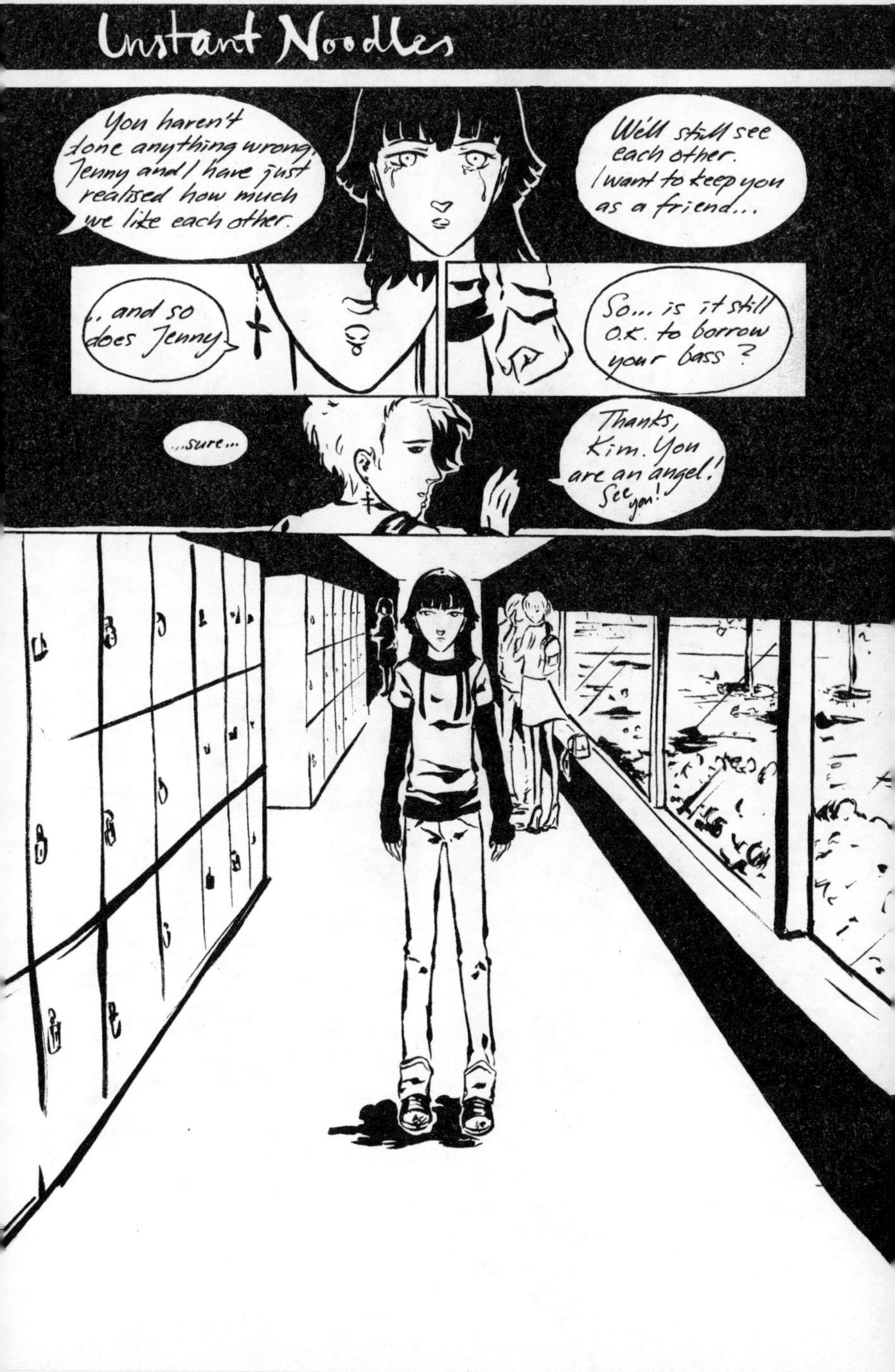
Instant Noodles
You haven't done anything wrong. Jenny and I have just realised how much we like each other.
We'll still see each other. I want to keep you as a friend...
.. and so does Jenny
So... is it still O.K. to borrow your bass?
...sure...
Thanks, Kim. You are an angel! See you!

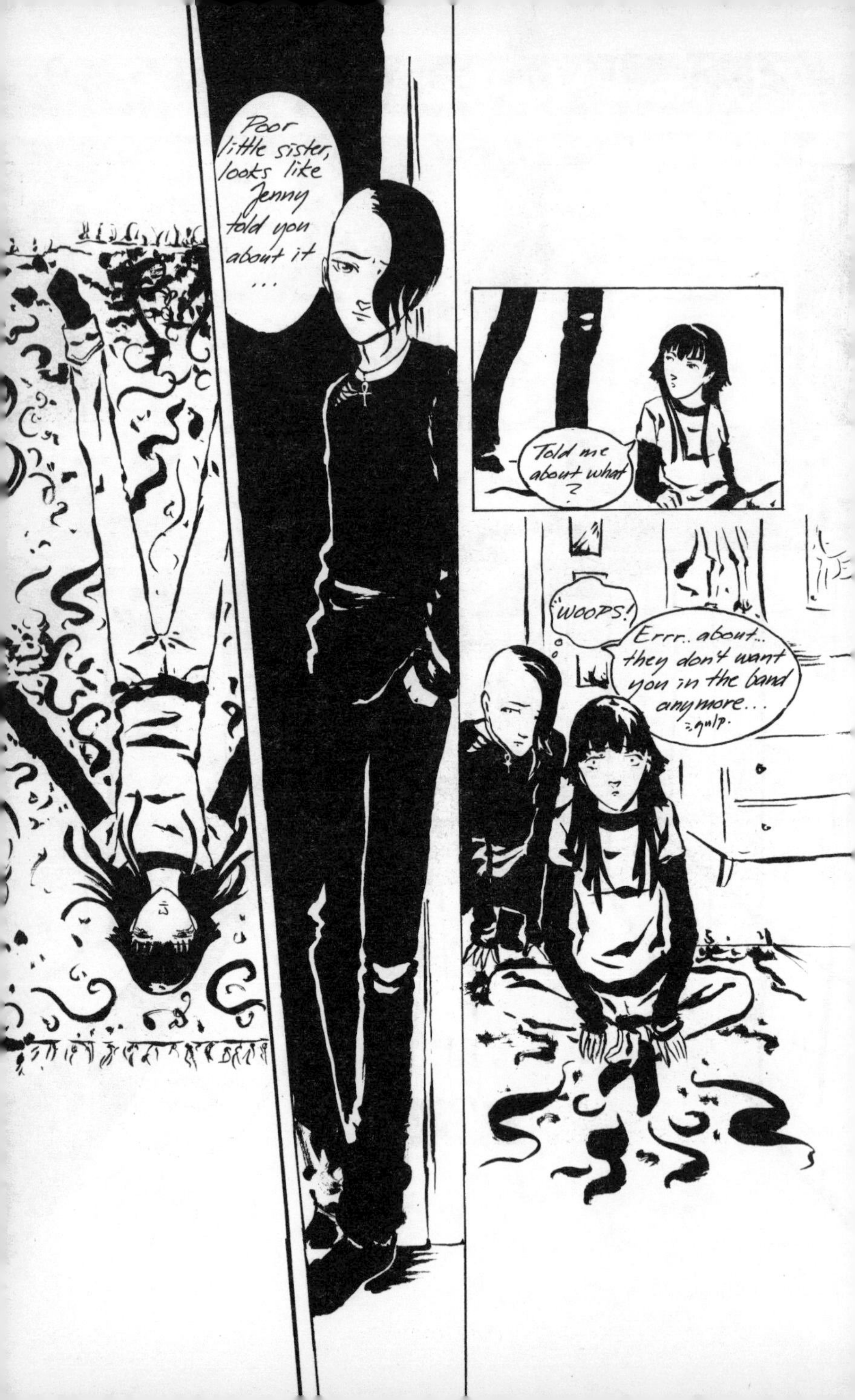
Poor little sister, looks like Jenny told you about it ...
Told me about what ?
WOOPS!
Errr.. about... they don't want you in the band anymore...
gulp.

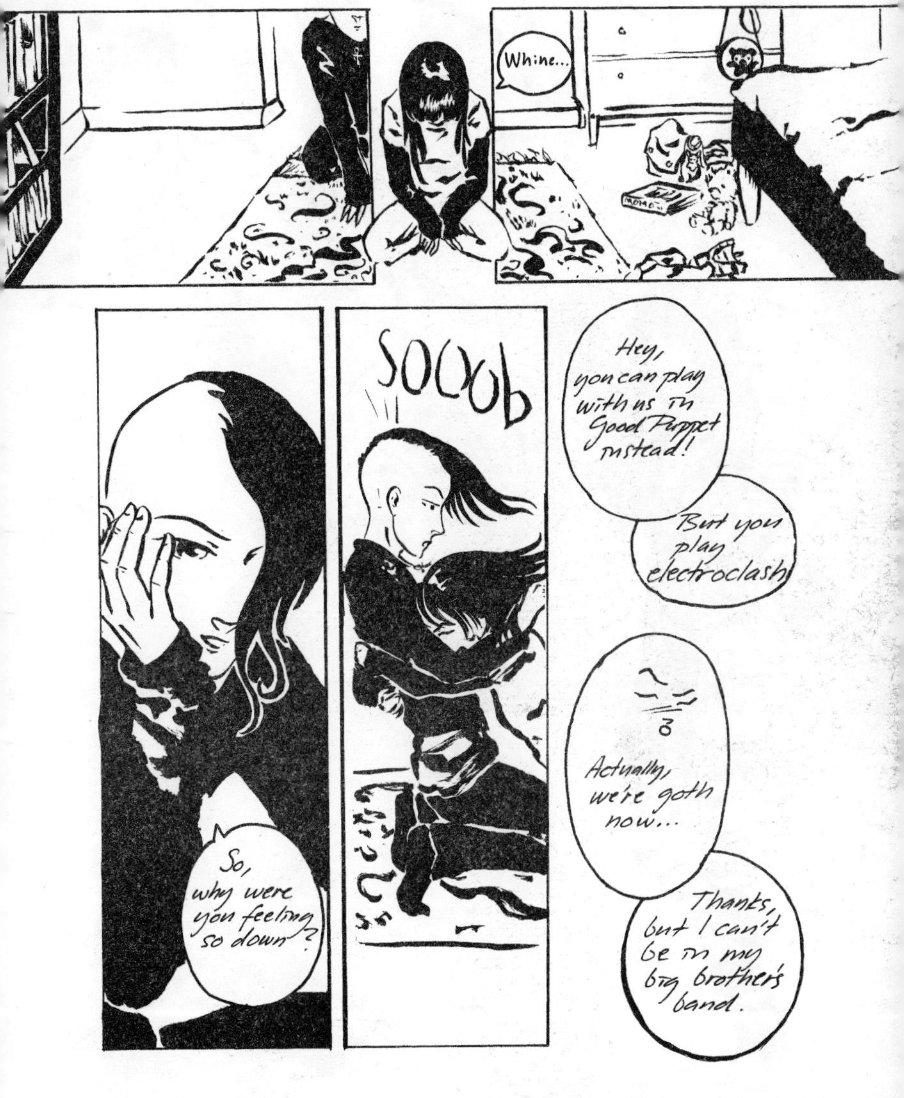
Whine...
So, why were you feeling so down?
SOOOb
Hey, you can play with us in Good Puppet instead!
But you play electroclash
Actually, we're goth now...
Thanks, but I can't be in my big brother's band.

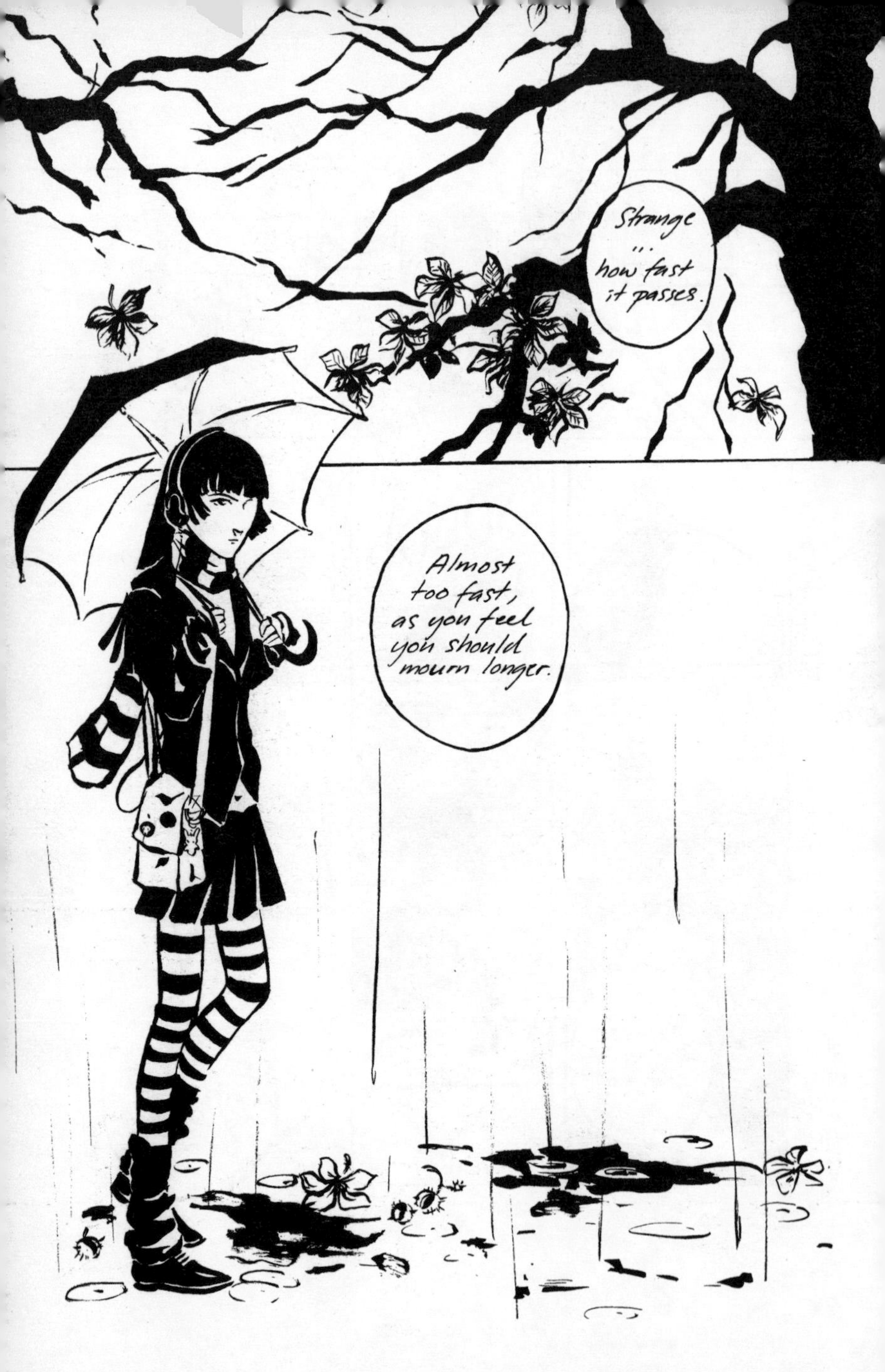
Strange ... how fast it passes.
Almost too fast, as you feel you should mourn longer.

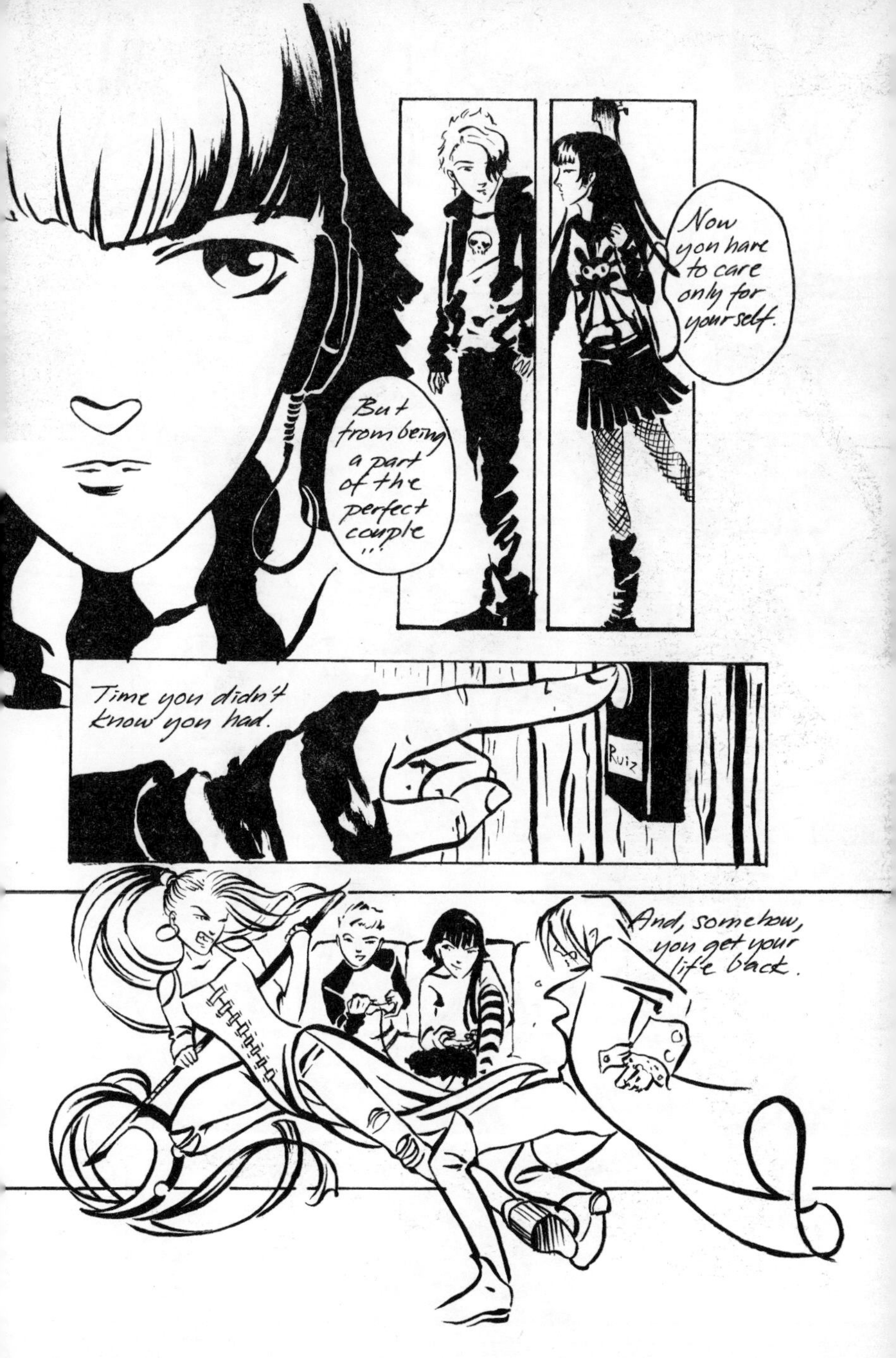
But from being a part of the perfect couple...
Now you have to care only for yourself.
Time you didn't know you had.
Ruiz
And, somehow, you get your life back.

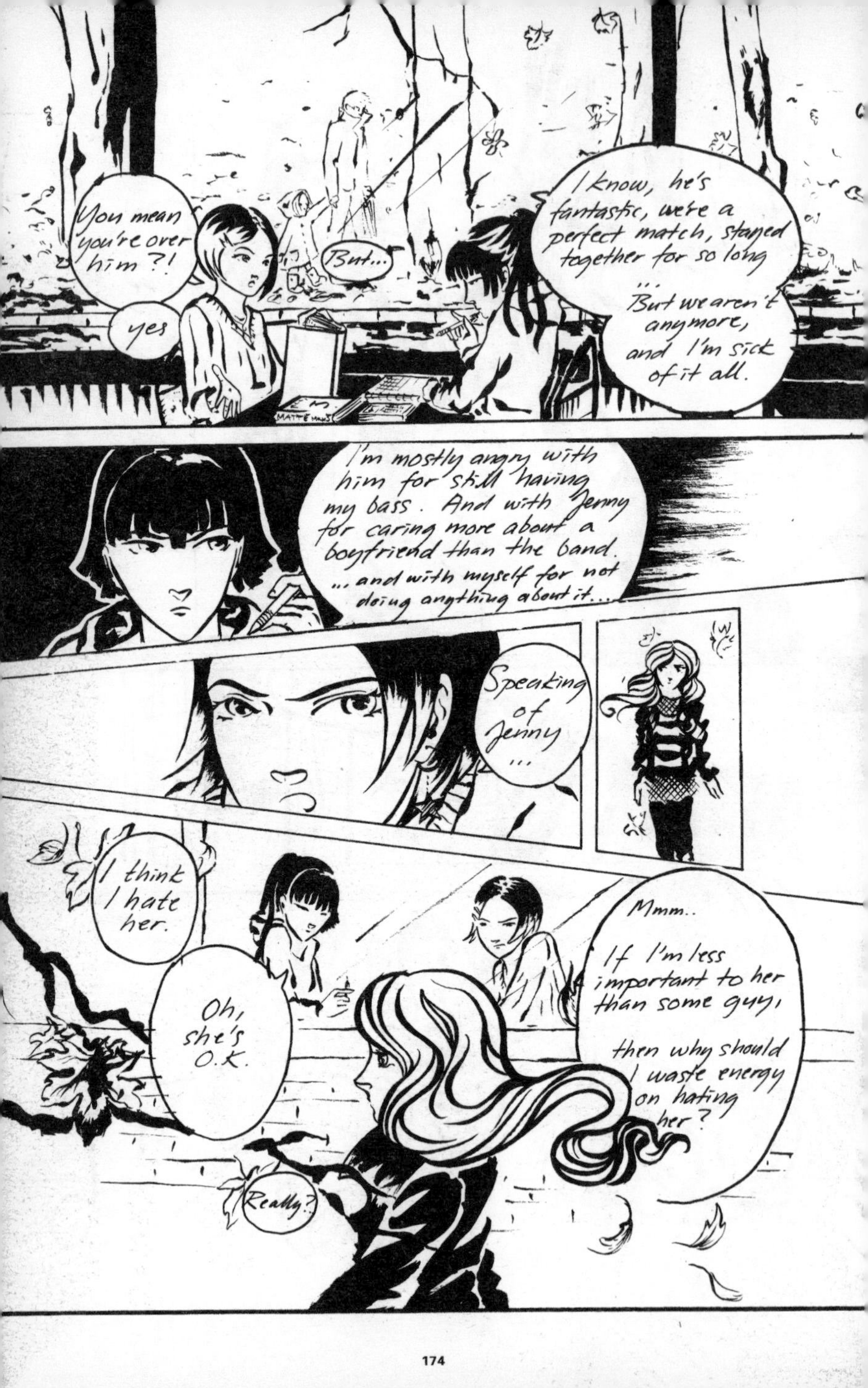
You mean you're over him?!
yes
But...
I know, he's fantastic, we're a perfect match, stayed together for so long
... But we aren't anymore, and I'm sick of it all.
I'm mostly angry with him for still having my bass. And with Jenny for caring more about a boyfriend than the band.
... and with myself for not doing anything about it...
Speaking of Jenny ...
I think I hate her.
Oh, she's O.K.
Really?
Mmm..
If I'm less important to her than some guy,
then why should I waste energy on hating her?

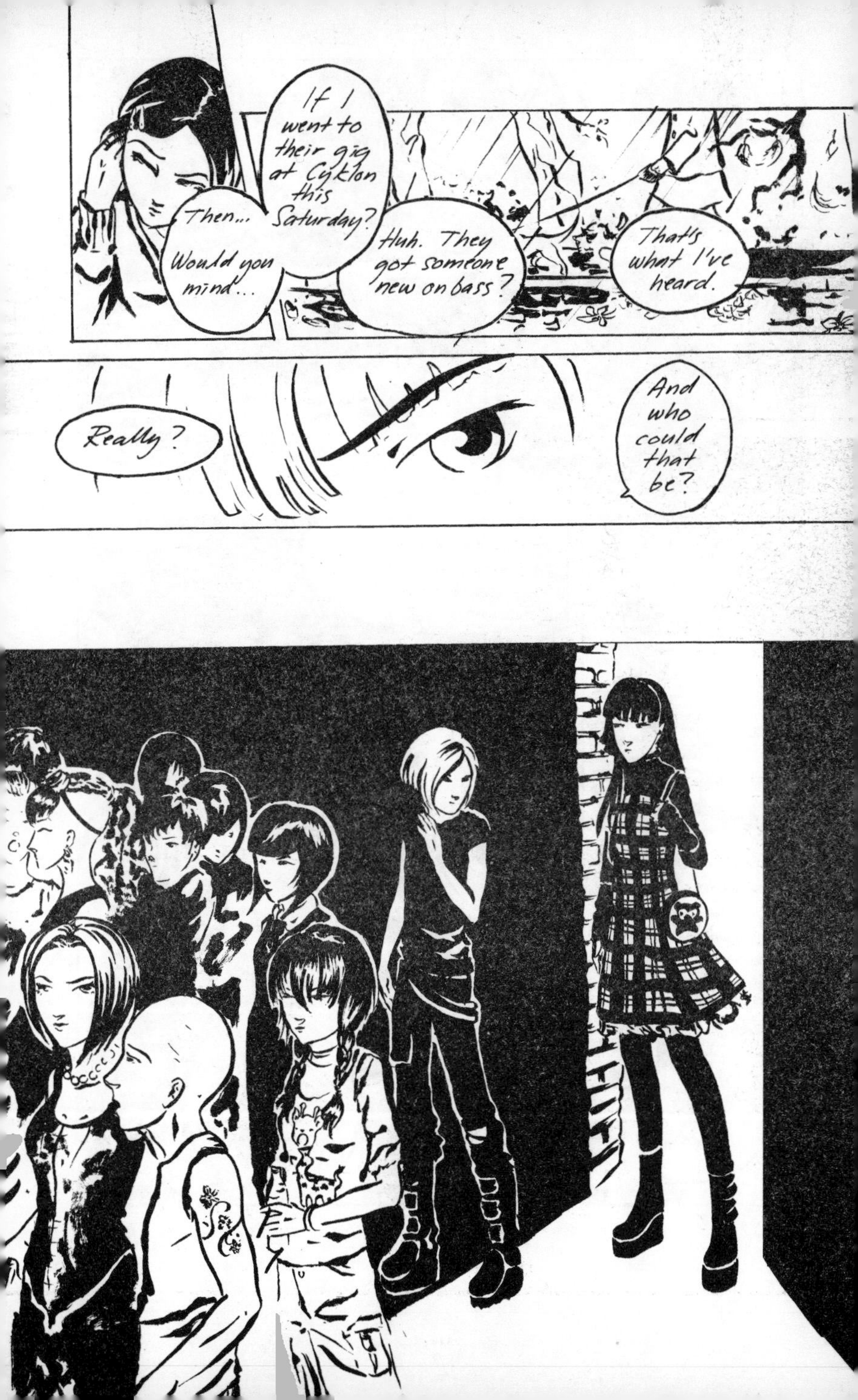
Then...
Would you mind...
If I went to their gig at Cyklon this Saturday?
Huh. They got someone new on bass?
That's what I've heard.
Really?
And who could that be?

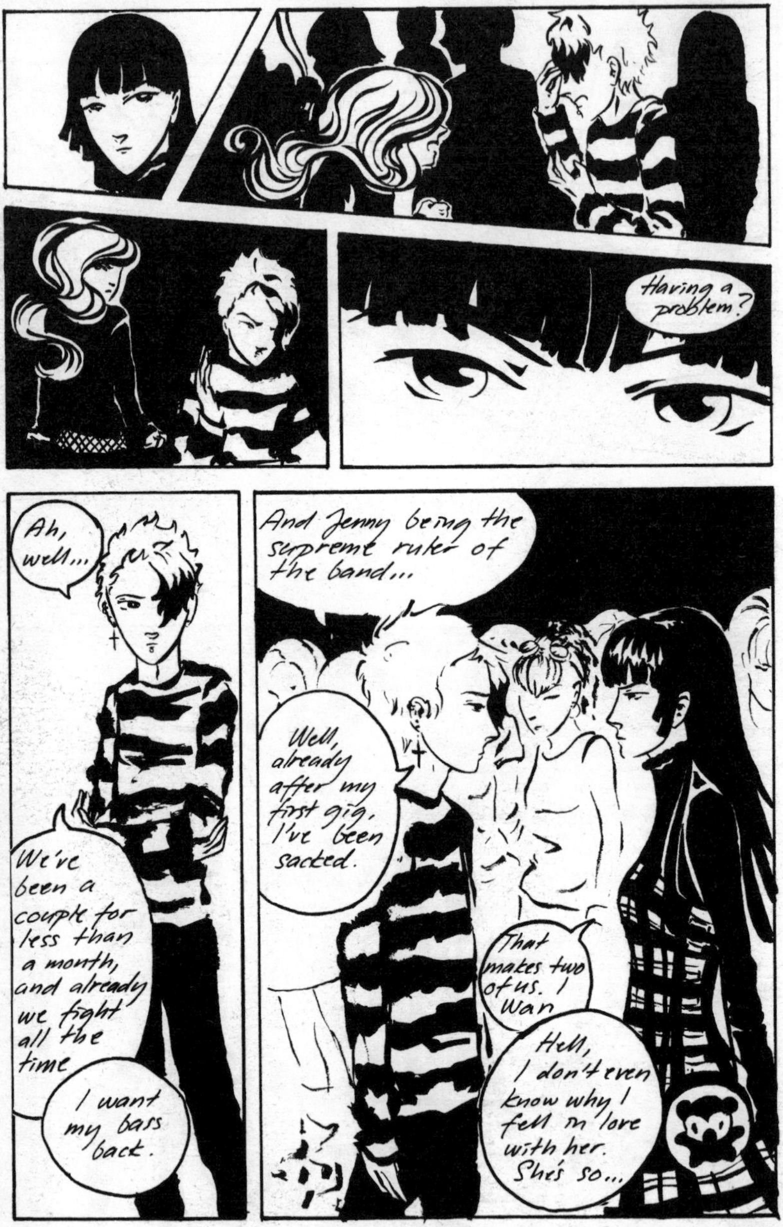
Having a problem?
Ah, well...
We've been a couple for less than a month, and already we fight all the time
I want my bass back.
And Jenny being the supreme ruler of the band...
Well, already after my first gig, I've been sacked.
That makes two of us. I wan
Hell, I don't even know why I fell in love with her. She's so...

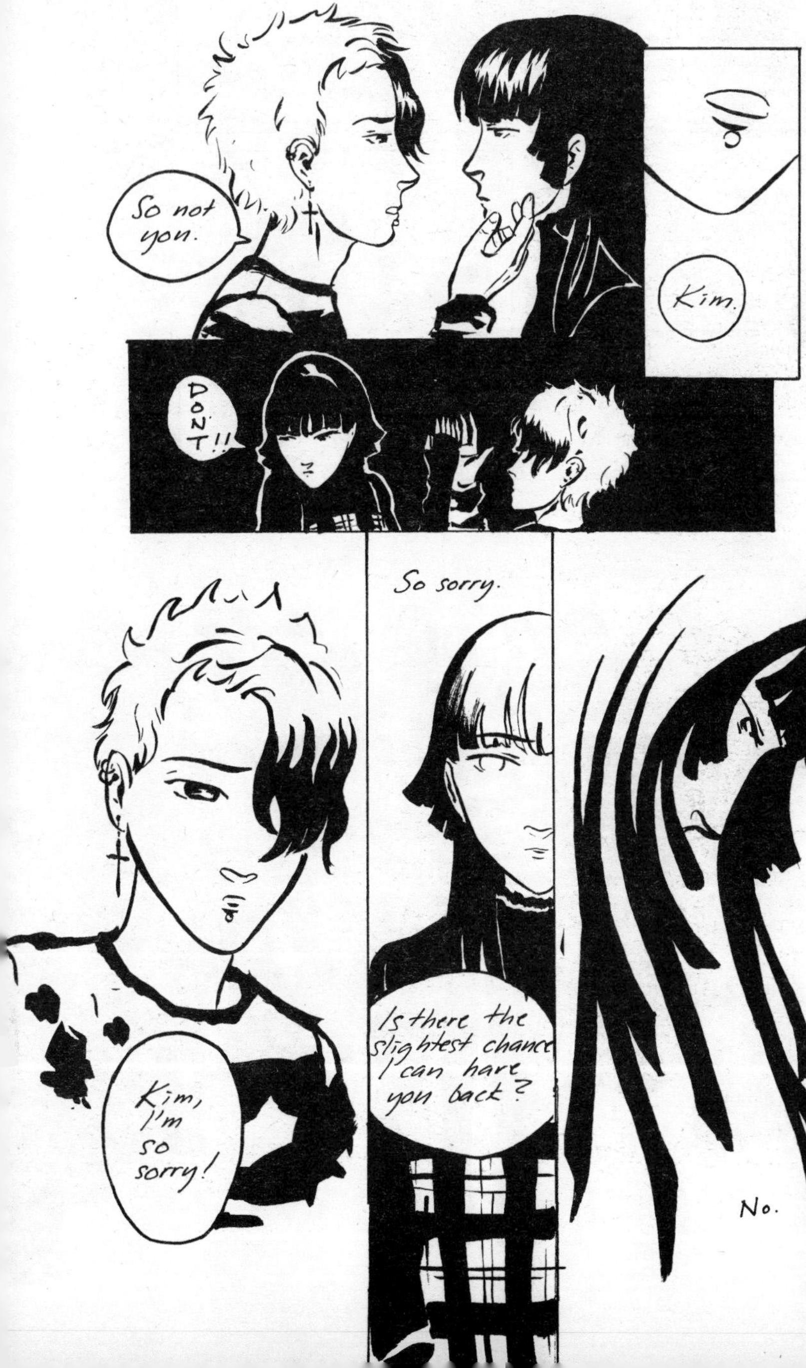

So not you.
Kim.
DON'T!!
Kim, I'm so sorry!
So sorry.
Is there the slightest chance I can have you back?
No.

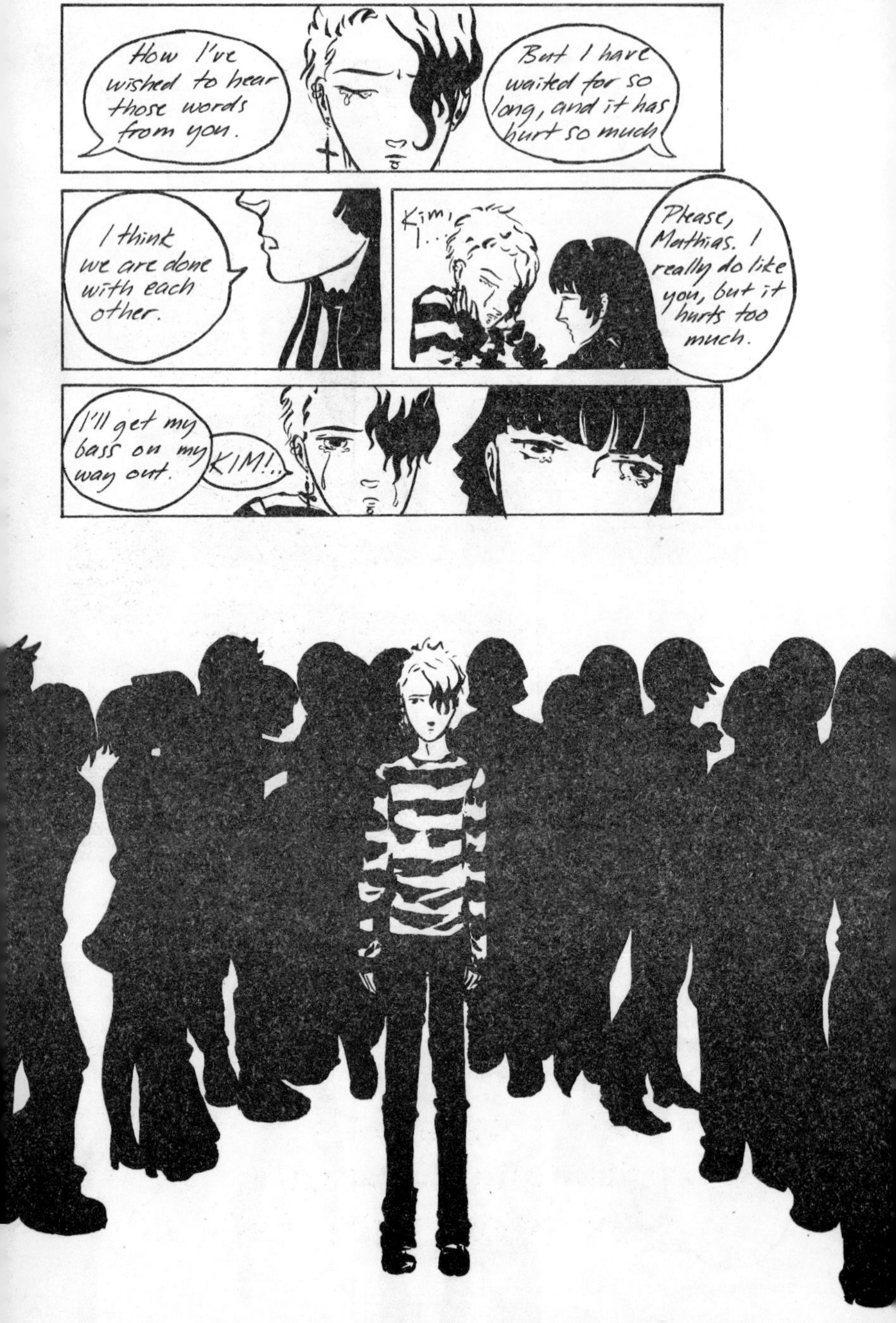
How I've wished to hear those words from you.
But I have waited for so long, and it has hurt so much
I think we are done with each other.
Kim!...
Please, Mathias. I really do like you, but it hurts too much.
I'll get my bass on my way out.
KIM!..

Storyteller   drawn by
Jay Eales Toby Ford

Date of birth: 7 January 1968

JAY EALES

Jay is from the Midlands, UK, but his dreams lie far to the East. **Outlaw Wu** is his homage to the enthusiasms of his formative years, 'steeped in slabs of eastern culture like **Battle of the Planets**, **Monkey** and, most of all, **The Water Margin**. Outlaw Wu is only one out of 108 heroes from the mystical mountain of Liangshan Po, as found in the Chinese classic **Outlaws of the Marsh**. To get his teeth into Wu's greater saga (with the titles of future instalments reflecting his current status, such as **Constable Wu, Brigand Wu**), would be Jay's 'dream come true'.

Lone Wolf & Cub is an obvious manga touchstone, and he loves the anime series **Samurai Champloo**, Simon (**Spaced**, **Shaun of the Dead**) Pegg, and (yay!) **Fight Club** (but we can't talk about that).

Check out his contribution to the Region 2 DVD of **American Splendor**.

http://www.factorfictionpress.co.uk

TOBY FORD

Date of birth: 7 August 1975

Toby Ford is from the obscure UK town of Redditch. He loves the works of Junko Mizuno, Genndy (**Samurai Jack**) Tartakovsky, and Craig (**Powderpuff Girls**) McCraken. If you ask us, **Captain Pugwash** has just got to be in there somewhere too!

He likes puppets, snowboarding, and horse-trading on eBay, and has his own band (and brand), **Hey Pablo!**. Toby confesses that this is the first strip he's done over four pages long – and we can copper-bottom guarantee, you won't have seen anything quite like it before! Here's looking at **Wu**, kid.

http://www.heypablo.com
http://www.omarthemystic.com

outlaw WU

虎

The only constant in life is
that all things change.

A boy, beaten for making mischief,
becomes a village tough,
But he is good to his mother.
Youth gives way to maturity,
and the shrimp becomes a giant.
No more beatings for Little Wu,
unless he hands them out.
Wu Sung discovers wine,
and wine is his undoing.
A simple misunderstanding.
A single blow, delivered in anger,
and a man hits the ground.

Believing himself a killer,
Wu flees the city and goes into hiding.
He hides too well,
and it is over a year before he learns
that the man recovers,
and he has run away without reason.
So Wu is coming home. But first, a little drink.
Some things never change.

STORYTELLER JAY EALES
ART BY TOBY FORD

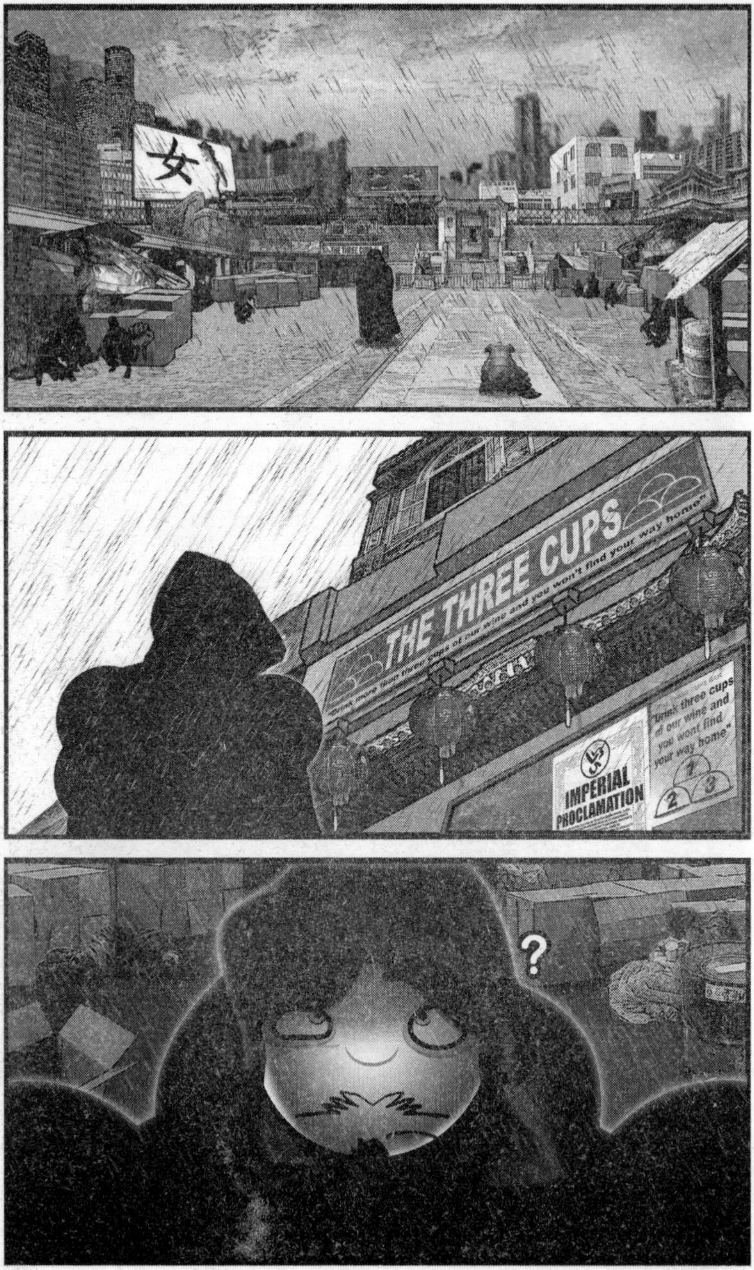
女
THE THREE CUPS
"Drink more than three cups of our wine and you won't find your way home"
IMPERIAL
PROCLAMATION
"Drink three cups of our wine and you wont find your way home"
?

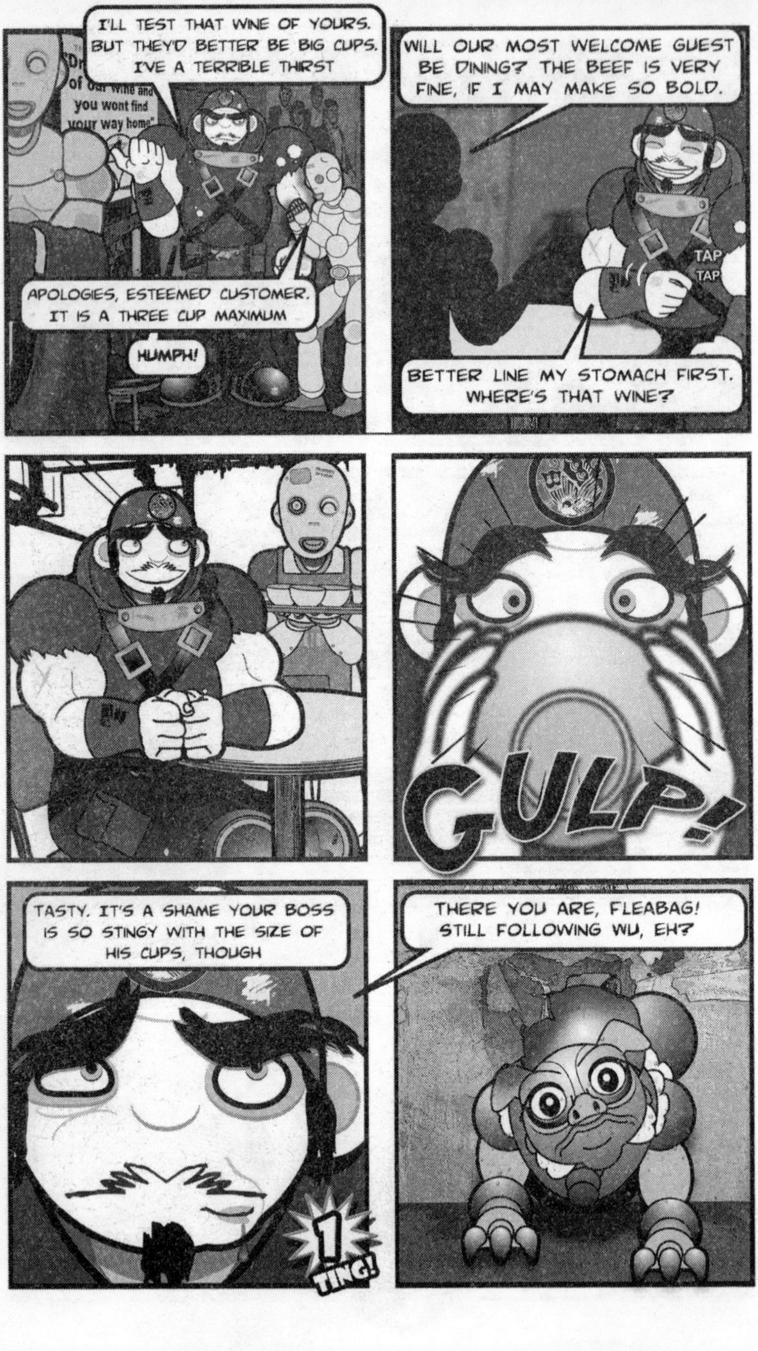
"Drink three cups of our wine and you wont find your way home"
I'LL TEST THAT WINE OF YOURS. BUT THEY'D BETTER BE BIG CUPS. I'VE A TERRIBLE THIRST
APOLOGIES, ESTEEMED CUSTOMER. IT IS A THREE CUP MAXIMUM
HUMPH!
WILL OUR MOST WELCOME GUEST BE DINING? THE BEEF IS VERY FINE, IF I MAY MAKE SO BOLD.
TAP
TAP
BETTER LINE MY STOMACH FIRST. WHERE'S THAT WINE?
GULP!
TASTY. IT'S A SHAME YOUR BOSS IS SO STINGY WITH THE SIZE OF HIS CUPS, THOUGH
1
TING!
THERE YOU ARE, FLEABAG! STILL FOLLOWING WU, EH?

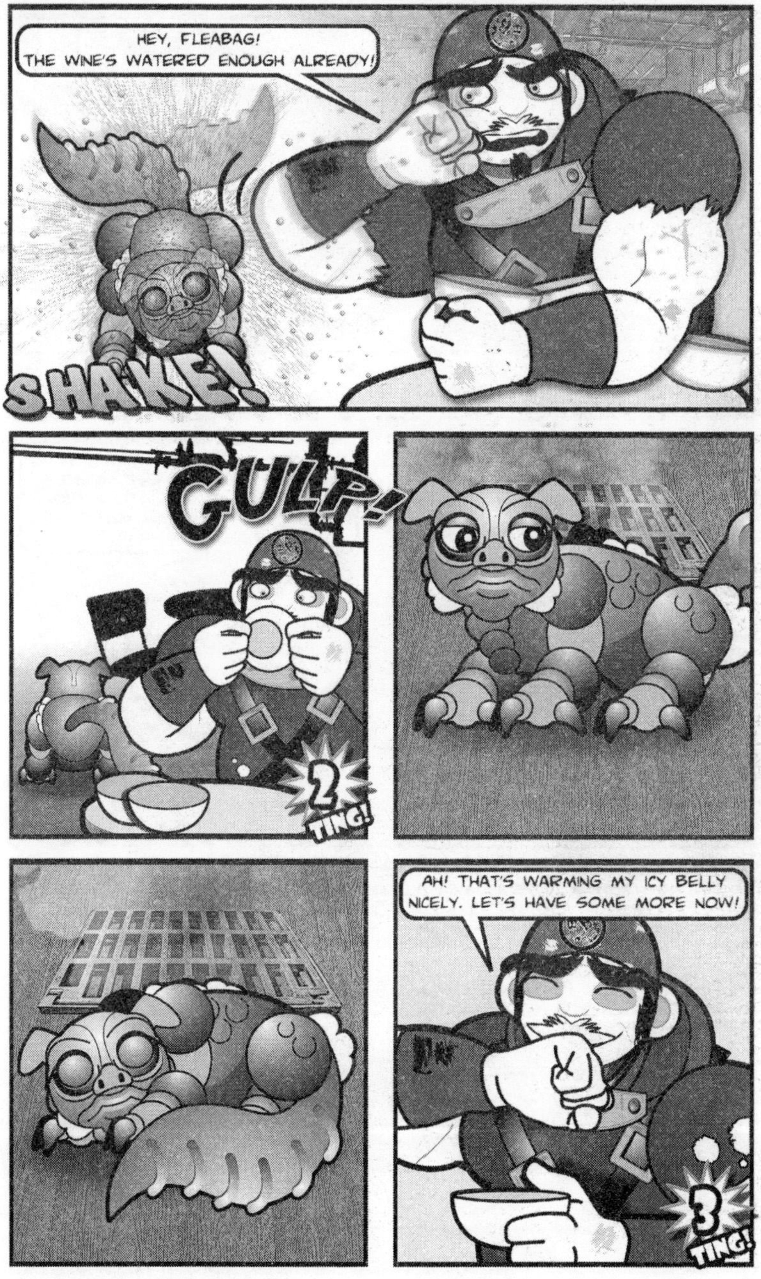
HEY, FLEABAG!
THE WINE'S WATERED ENOUGH ALREADY!
SHAKE!
GULP!
2
TING!
AH! THAT'S WARMING MY ICY BELLY NICELY. LET'S HAVE SOME MORE NOW!
3
TING!

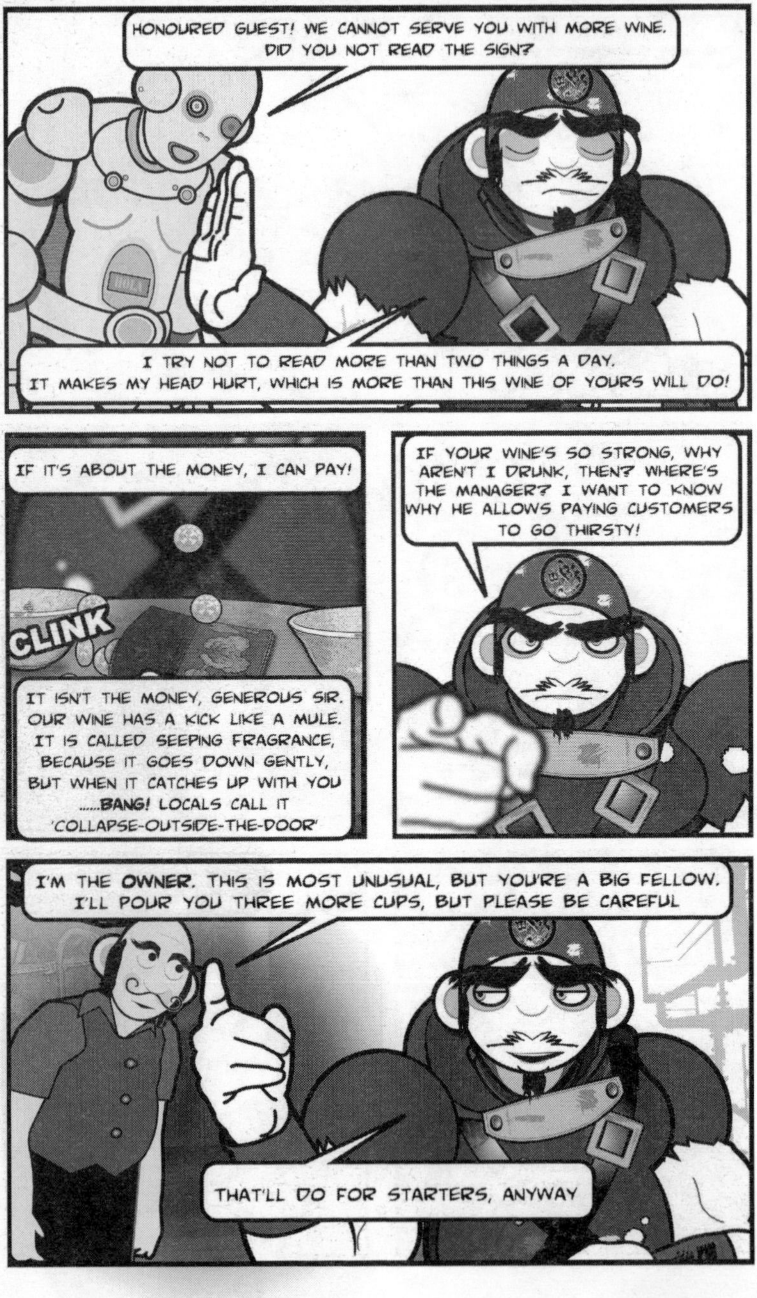
HONOURED GUEST! WE CANNOT SERVE YOU WITH MORE WINE. DID YOU NOT READ THE SIGN?
I TRY NOT TO READ MORE THAN TWO THINGS A DAY. IT MAKES MY HEAD HURT, WHICH IS MORE THAN THIS WINE OF YOURS WILL DO!
IF IT'S ABOUT THE MONEY, I CAN PAY!
CLINK
IT ISN'T THE MONEY, GENEROUS SIR. OUR WINE HAS A KICK LIKE A MULE. IT IS CALLED SEEPING FRAGRANCE, BECAUSE IT GOES DOWN GENTLY, BUT WHEN IT CATCHES UP WITH YOU ......BANG! LOCALS CALL IT 'COLLAPSE-OUTSIDE-THE-DOOR'
IF YOUR WINE'S SO STRONG, WHY AREN'T I DRUNK, THEN? WHERE'S THE MANAGER? I WANT TO KNOW WHY HE ALLOWS PAYING CUSTOMERS TO GO THIRSTY!
I'M THE OWNER. THIS IS MOST UNUSUAL, BUT YOU'RE A BIG FELLOW. I'LL POUR YOU THREE MORE CUPS, BUT PLEASE BE CAREFUL
THAT'LL DO FOR STARTERS, ANYWAY

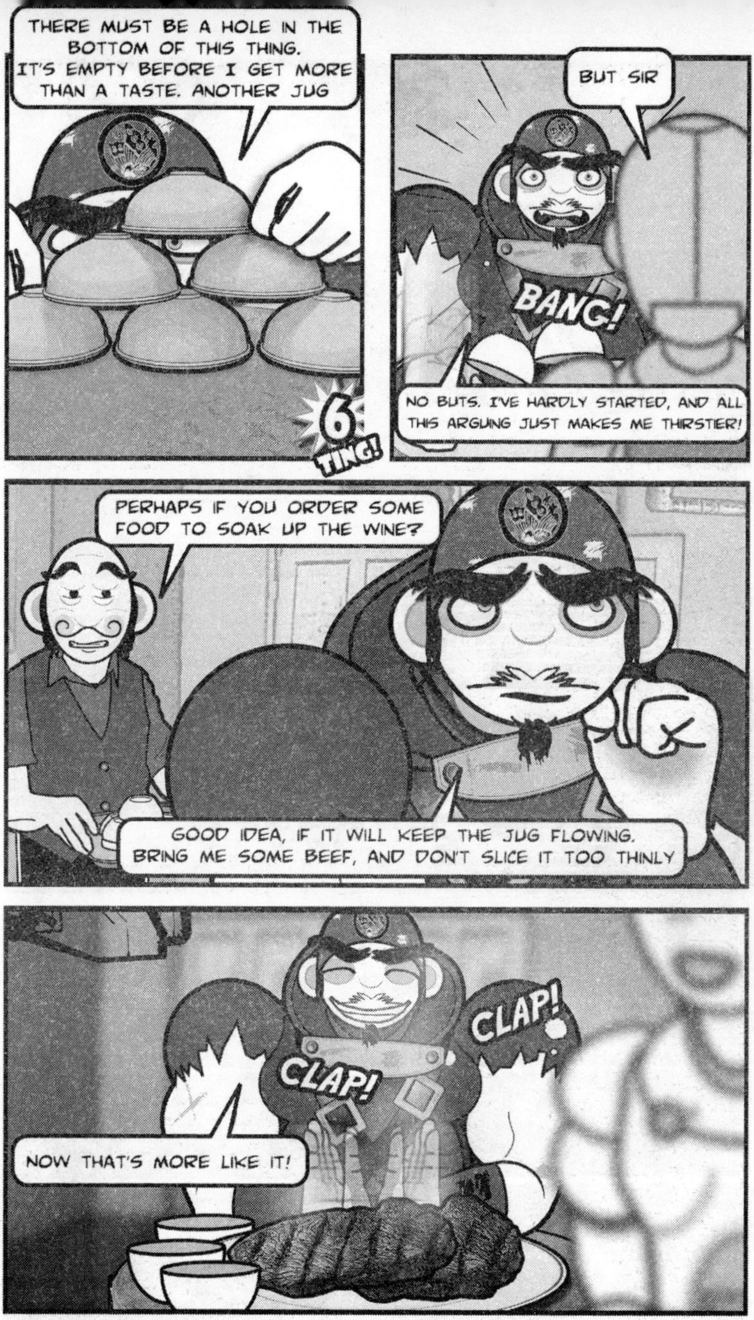
THERE MUST BE A HOLE IN THE BOTTOM OF THIS THING. IT'S EMPTY BEFORE I GET MORE THAN A TASTE. ANOTHER JUG
6
TING!
BUT SIR
BANG!
NO BUTS. I'VE HARDLY STARTED, AND ALL THIS ARGUING JUST MAKES ME THIRSTIER!
PERHAPS IF YOU ORDER SOME FOOD TO SOAK UP THE WINE?
GOOD IDEA, IF IT WILL KEEP THE JUG FLOWING. BRING ME SOME BEEF, AND DON'T SLICE IT TOO THINLY
CLAP!
CLAP!
NOW THAT'S MORE LIKE IT!

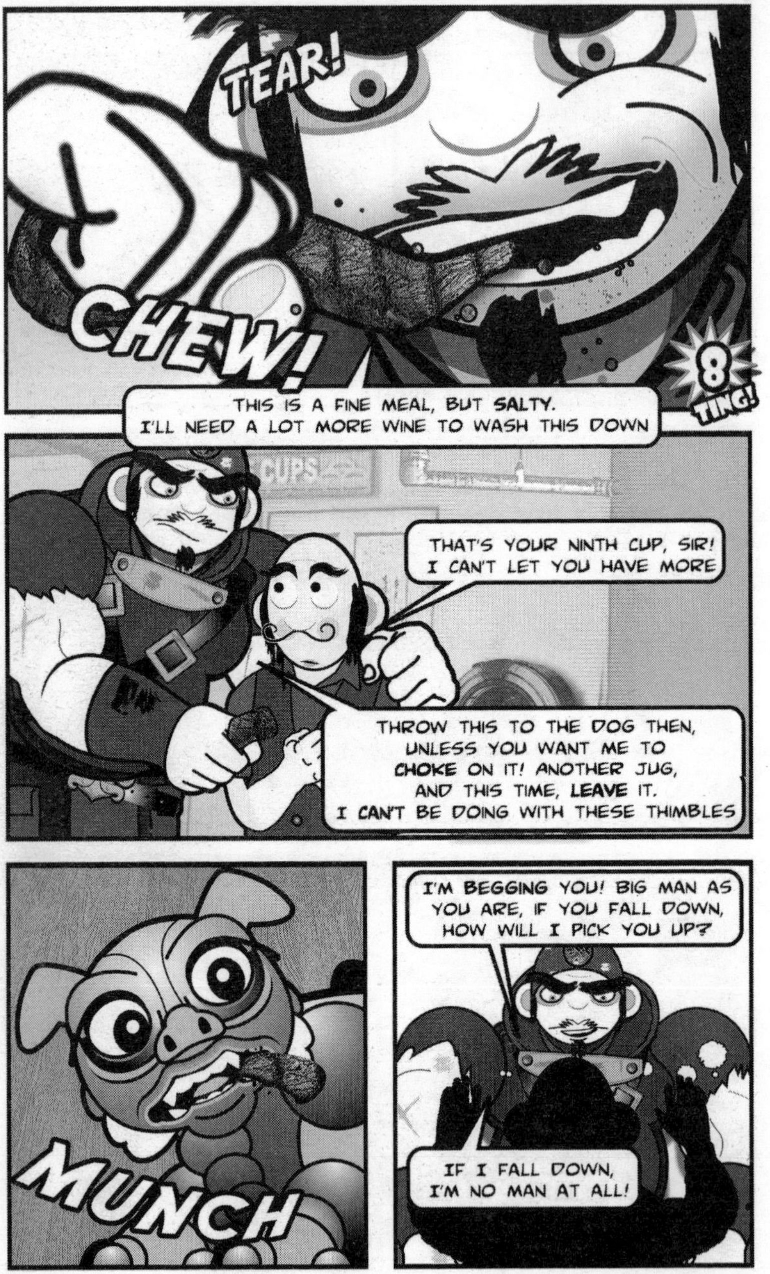
TEAR!
CHEW!
8
TING!
THIS IS A FINE MEAL, BUT SALTY. I'LL NEED A LOT MORE WINE TO WASH THIS DOWN
CUPS
THAT'S YOUR NINTH CUP, SIR! I CAN'T LET YOU HAVE MORE
THROW THIS TO THE DOG THEN, UNLESS YOU WANT ME TO CHOKE ON IT! ANOTHER JUG, AND THIS TIME, LEAVE IT. I CAN'T BE DOING WITH THESE THIMBLES
MUNCH
I'M BEGGING YOU! BIG MAN AS YOU ARE, IF YOU FALL DOWN, HOW WILL I PICK YOU UP?
IF I FALL DOWN, I'M NO MAN AT ALL!

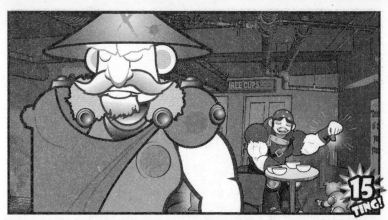

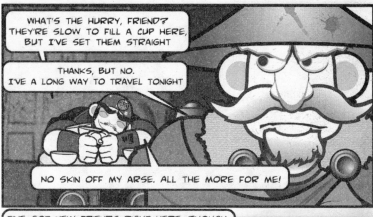

IREE CUPS
15
TING!
WHAT'S THE HURRY, FRIEND? THEY'RE SLOW TO FILL A CUP HERE, BUT I'VE SET THEM STRAIGHT
THANKS, BUT NO. I'VE A LONG WAY TO TRAVEL TONIGHT
NO SKIN OFF MY ARSE. ALL THE MORE FOR ME!
I'VE GOT NEW FRIENDS RIGHT HERE. THOUGH, WHAT KIND OF A JOB IS IT WHERE THEY MAKE YOU DRESS UP AS A SERVO? THAT.......THAT CAN'T BE HEALTHY
THE THREE CUPS
I.....I COULD NOT POSSIBLY COMMENT, SAGACIOUS SIR
17
TING!

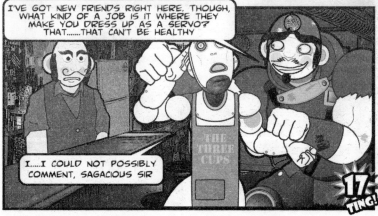

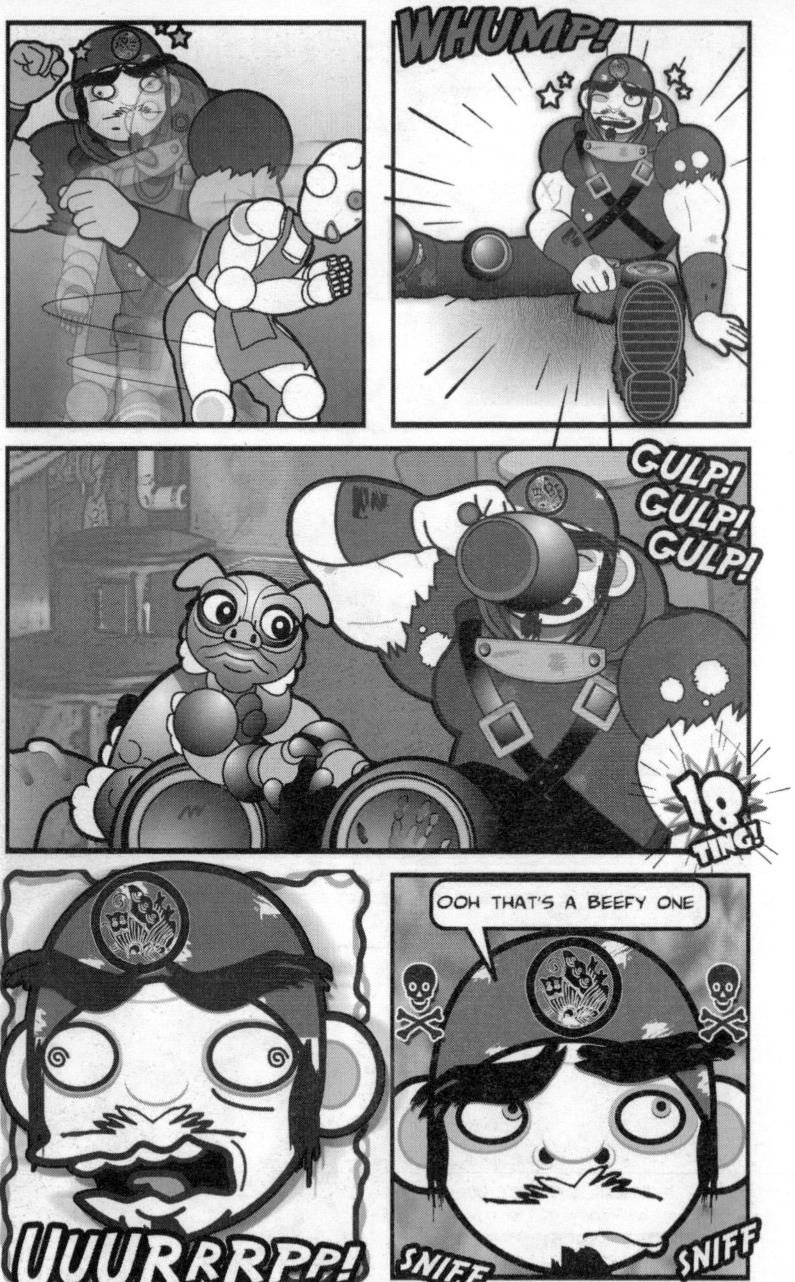
WHUMP!
GULP!
GULP!
GULP!
18
TING!
UUURRRPP!
OOH THAT'S A BEEFY ONE
SNIFF
SNIFF

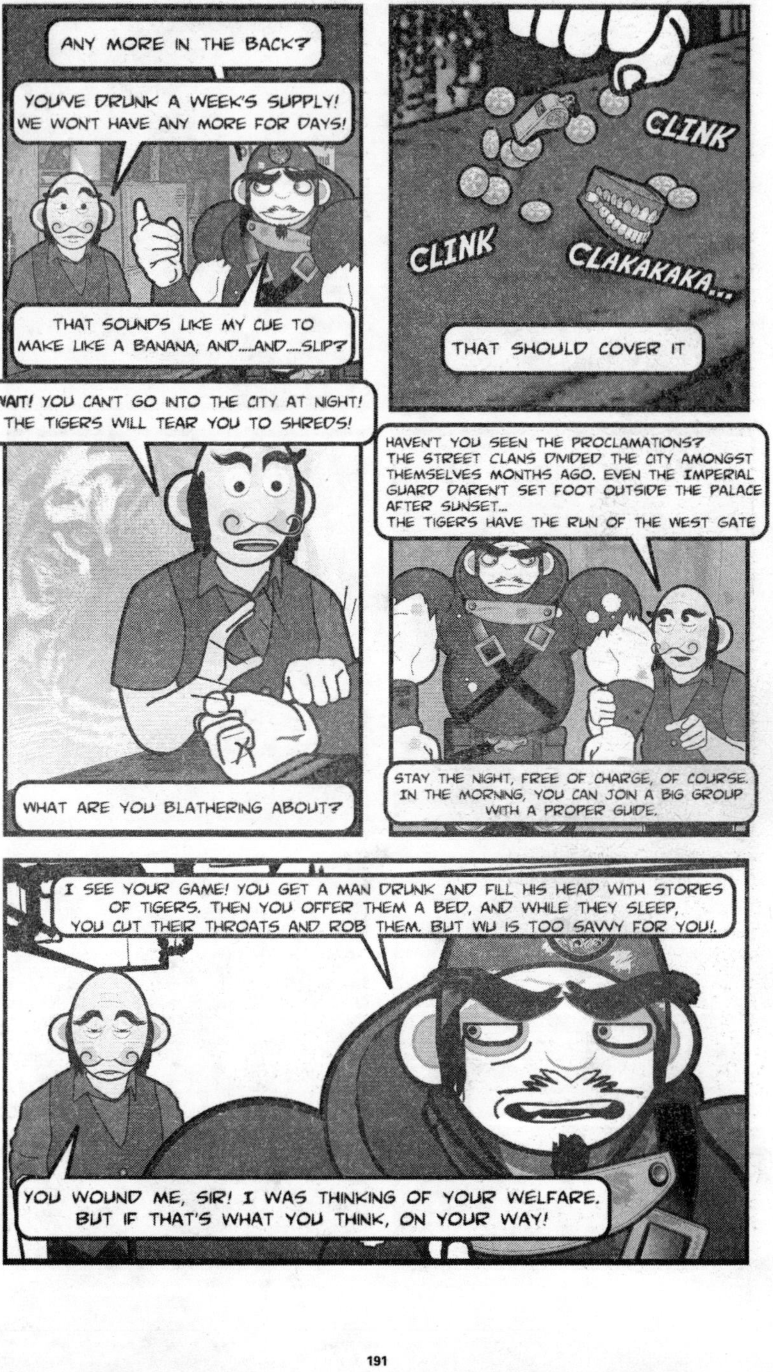
ANY MORE IN THE BACK?
YOU'VE DRUNK A WEEK'S SUPPLY! WE WON'T HAVE ANY MORE FOR DAYS!
THAT SOUNDS LIKE MY CUE TO MAKE LIKE A BANANA, AND.....AND.....SLIP?
CLINK
CLINK
CLAKAKAKA...
THAT SHOULD COVER IT
WAIT! YOU CAN'T GO INTO THE CITY AT NIGHT! THE TIGERS WILL TEAR YOU TO SHREDS!
WHAT ARE YOU BLATHERING ABOUT?
HAVEN'T YOU SEEN THE PROCLAMATIONS? THE STREET CLANS DIVIDED THE CITY AMONGST THEMSELVES MONTHS AGO. EVEN THE IMPERIAL GUARD DAREN'T SET FOOT OUTSIDE THE PALACE AFTER SUNSET... THE TIGERS HAVE THE RUN OF THE WEST GATE
STAY THE NIGHT, FREE OF CHARGE, OF COURSE. IN THE MORNING, YOU CAN JOIN A BIG GROUP WITH A PROPER GUIDE.
I SEE YOUR GAME! YOU GET A MAN DRUNK AND FILL HIS HEAD WITH STORIES OF TIGERS. THEN YOU OFFER THEM A BED, AND WHILE THEY SLEEP, YOU CUT THEIR THROATS AND ROB THEM. BUT WU IS TOO SAVVY FOR YOU!.
YOU WOUND ME, SIR! I WAS THINKING OF YOUR WELFARE. BUT IF THAT'S WHAT YOU THINK, ON YOUR WAY!

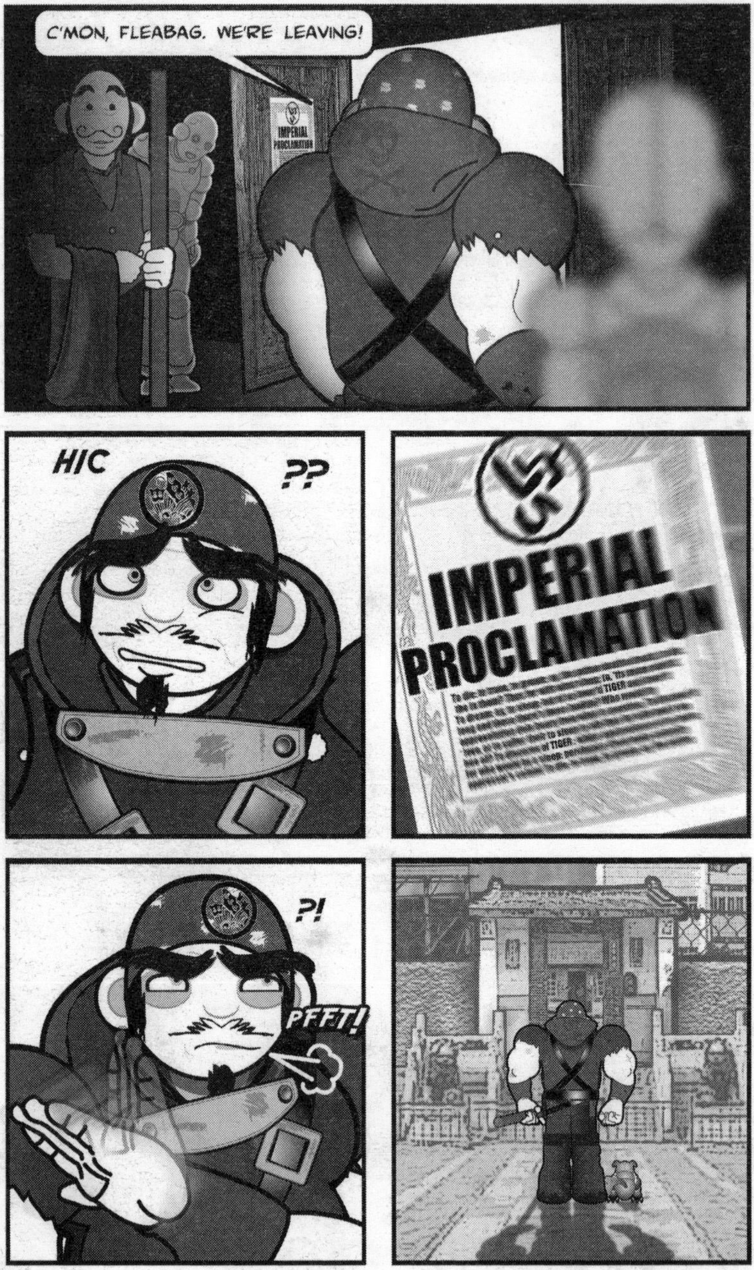
C'MON, FLEABAG. WE'RE LEAVING!
IMPERIAL PROCLAMATION
HIC
??
IMPERIAL PROCLAMATION
?!
PFFT!

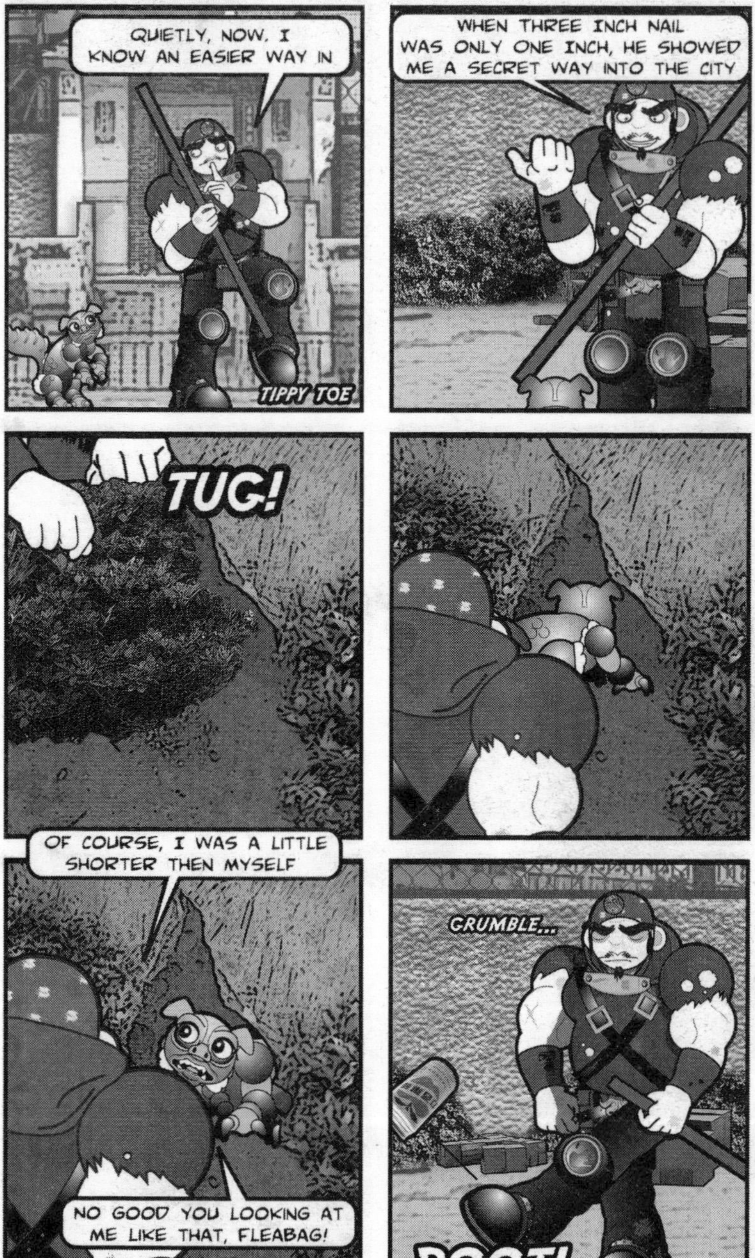
QUIETLY, NOW. I KNOW AN EASIER WAY IN
TIPPY TOE
WHEN THREE INCH NAIL WAS ONLY ONE INCH, HE SHOWED ME A SECRET WAY INTO THE CITY
TUG!
OF COURSE, I WAS A LITTLE SHORTER THEN MYSELF
NO GOOD YOU LOOKING AT ME LIKE THAT, FLEABAG!
GRUMBLE...
BOOT!

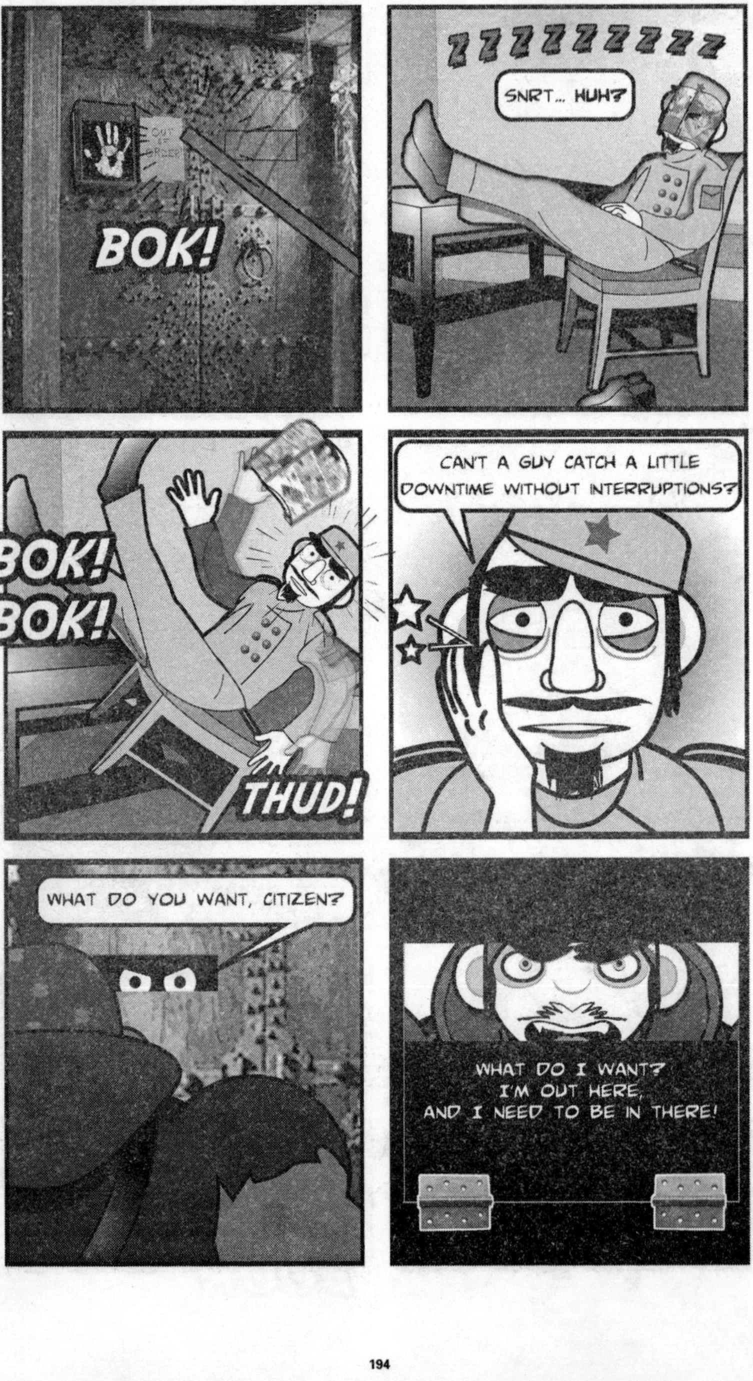

BOK!
ZZZZZZZZZZ
SNRT... HUH?
BOK!
BOK!
THUD!
CAN'T A GUY CATCH A LITTLE DOWNTIME WITHOUT INTERRUPTIONS?
WHAT DO YOU WANT, CITIZEN?
WHAT DO I WANT? I'M OUT HERE, AND I NEED TO BE IN THERE!

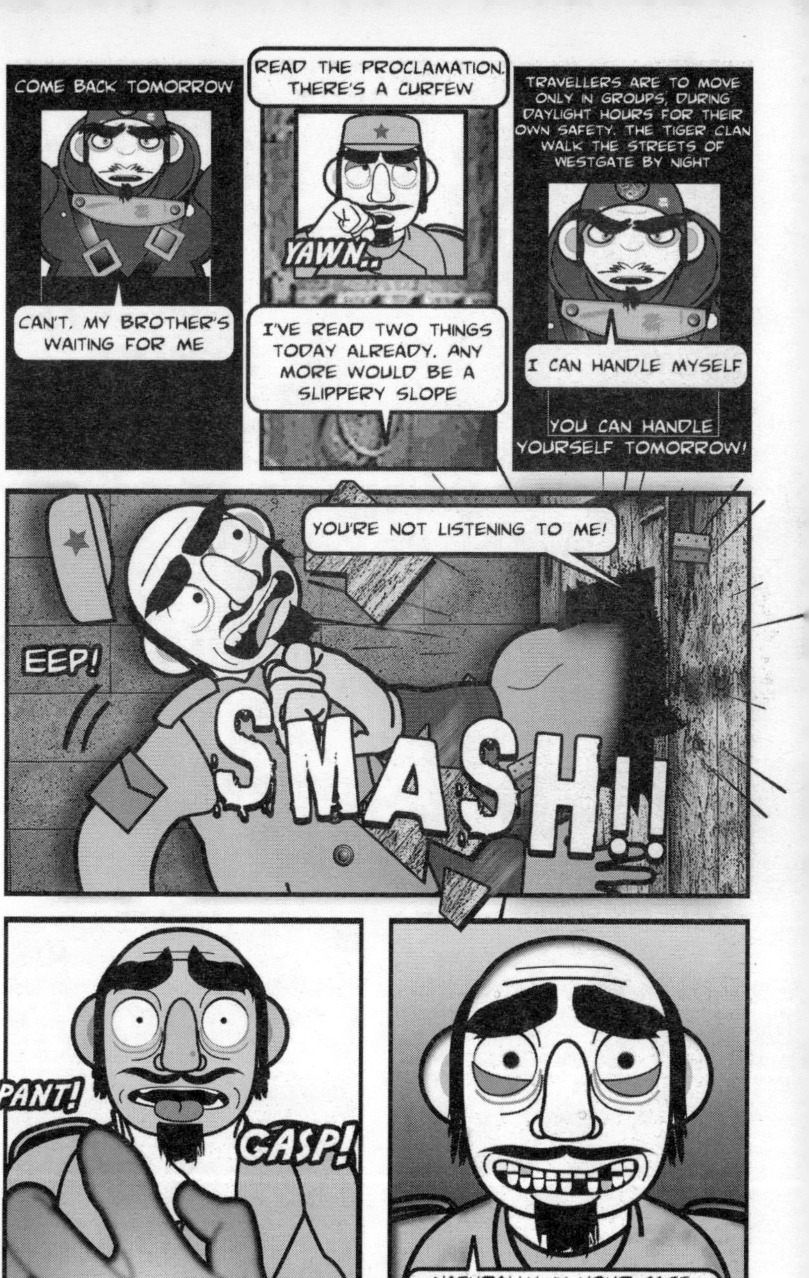
COME BACK TOMORROW
CAN'T. MY BROTHER'S WAITING FOR ME
READ THE PROCLAMATION. THERE'S A CURFEW
YAWN..
I'VE READ TWO THINGS TODAY ALREADY. ANY MORE WOULD BE A SLIPPERY SLOPE
TRAVELLERS ARE TO MOVE ONLY IN GROUPS, DURING DAYLIGHT HOURS FOR THEIR OWN SAFETY. THE TIGER CLAN WALK THE STREETS OF WESTGATE BY NIGHT
I CAN HANDLE MYSELF
YOU CAN HANDLE YOURSELF TOMORROW!
YOU'RE NOT LISTENING TO ME!
EEP!
SMASH!!!
PANT!
GASP!
NATURALLY, IN YOUR CASE WE CAN MAKE AN EXCEPTION!

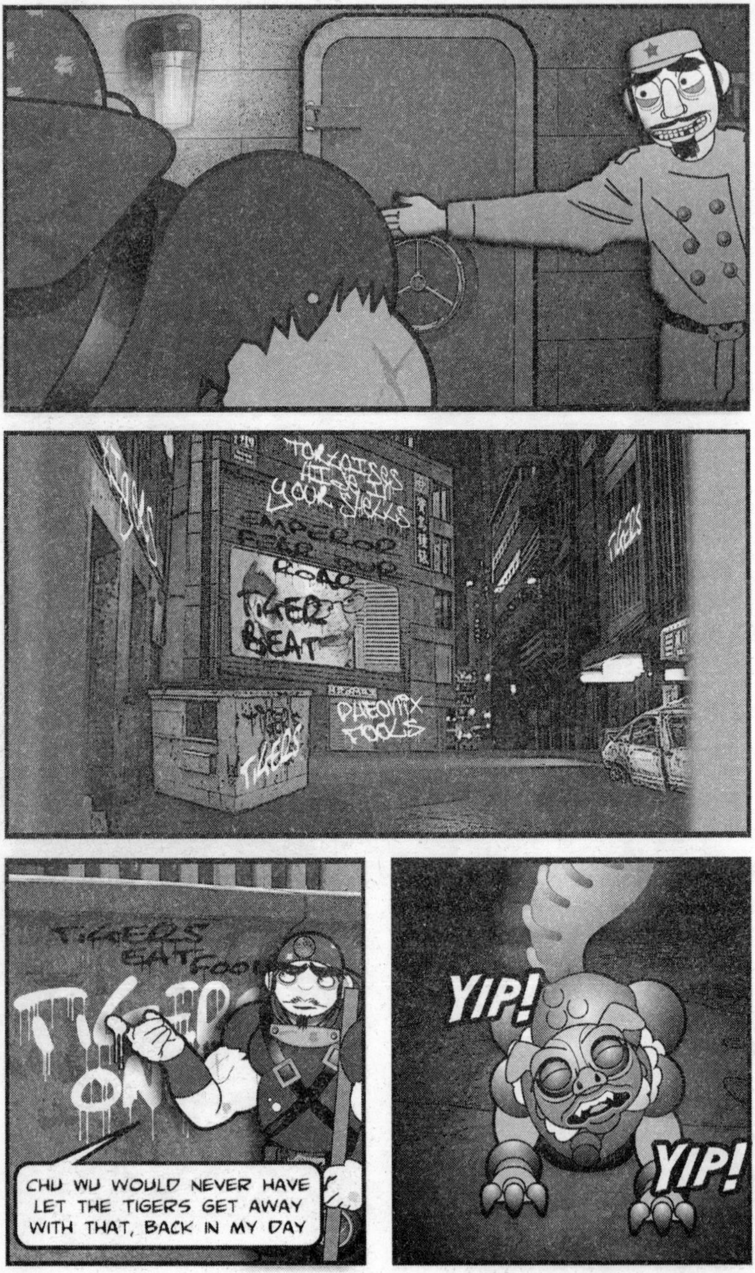
TORTOISES HIDE IN YOUR SHELLS
TIGER BEAT
TIGERS
TIGERS EAT FOOLS
CHU WU WOULD NEVER HAVE LET THE TIGERS GET AWAY WITH THAT, BACK IN MY DAY
YIP!
YIP!

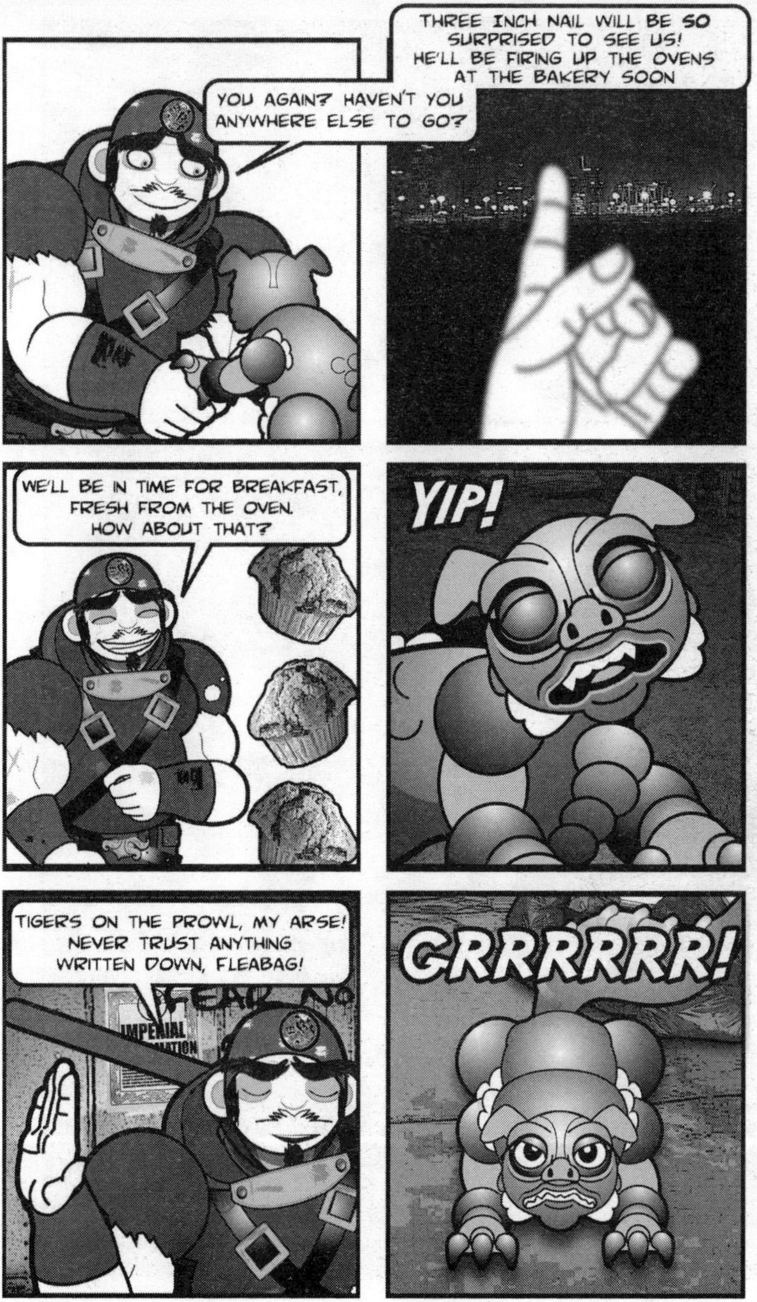
YOU AGAIN? HAVEN'T YOU ANYWHERE ELSE TO GO?
THREE INCH NAIL WILL BE SO SURPRISED TO SEE US! HE'LL BE FIRING UP THE OVENS AT THE BAKERY SOON
WE'LL BE IN TIME FOR BREAKFAST, FRESH FROM THE OVEN. HOW ABOUT THAT?
YIP!
TIGERS ON THE PROWL, MY ARSE! NEVER TRUST ANYTHING WRITTEN DOWN, FLEABAG!
IMPERIAL
GRRRRRRR!

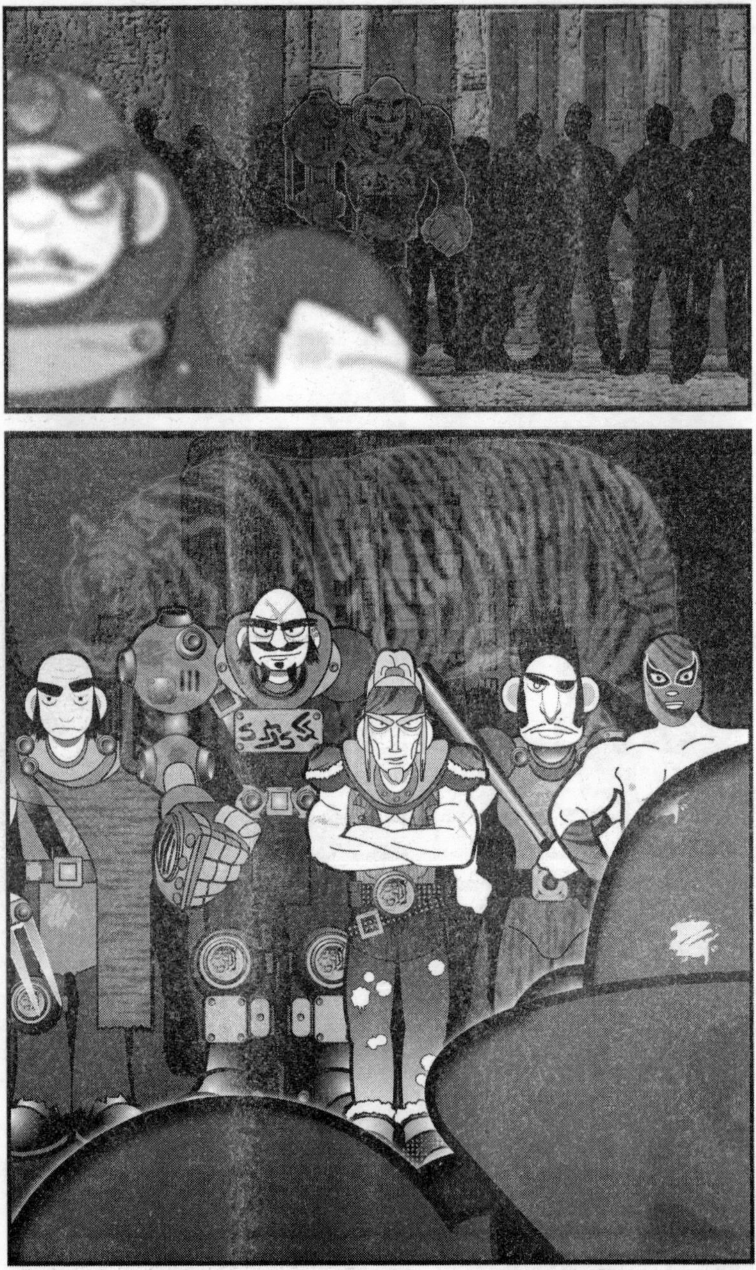

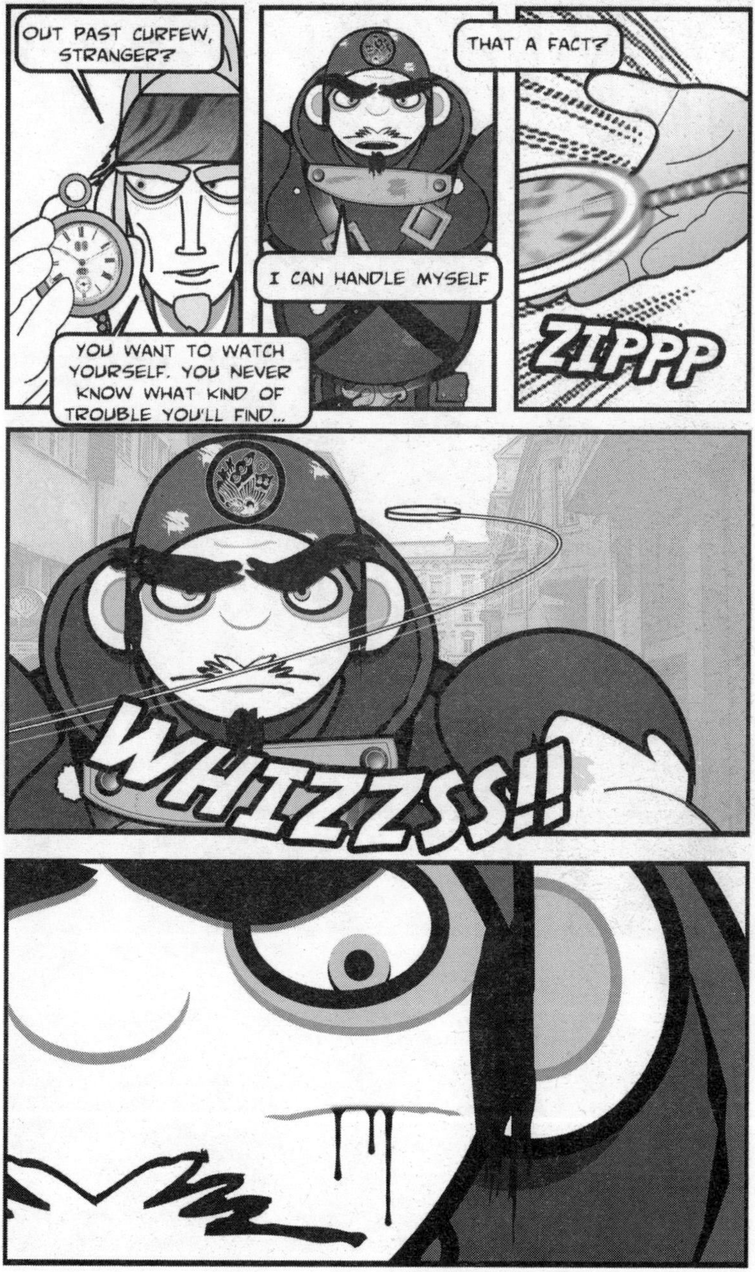
OUT PAST CURFEW, STRANGER?
YOU WANT TO WATCH YOURSELF. YOU NEVER KNOW WHAT KIND OF TROUBLE YOU'LL FIND...
I CAN HANDLE MYSELF
THAT A FACT?
ZIPPP
WHIZZSS!!

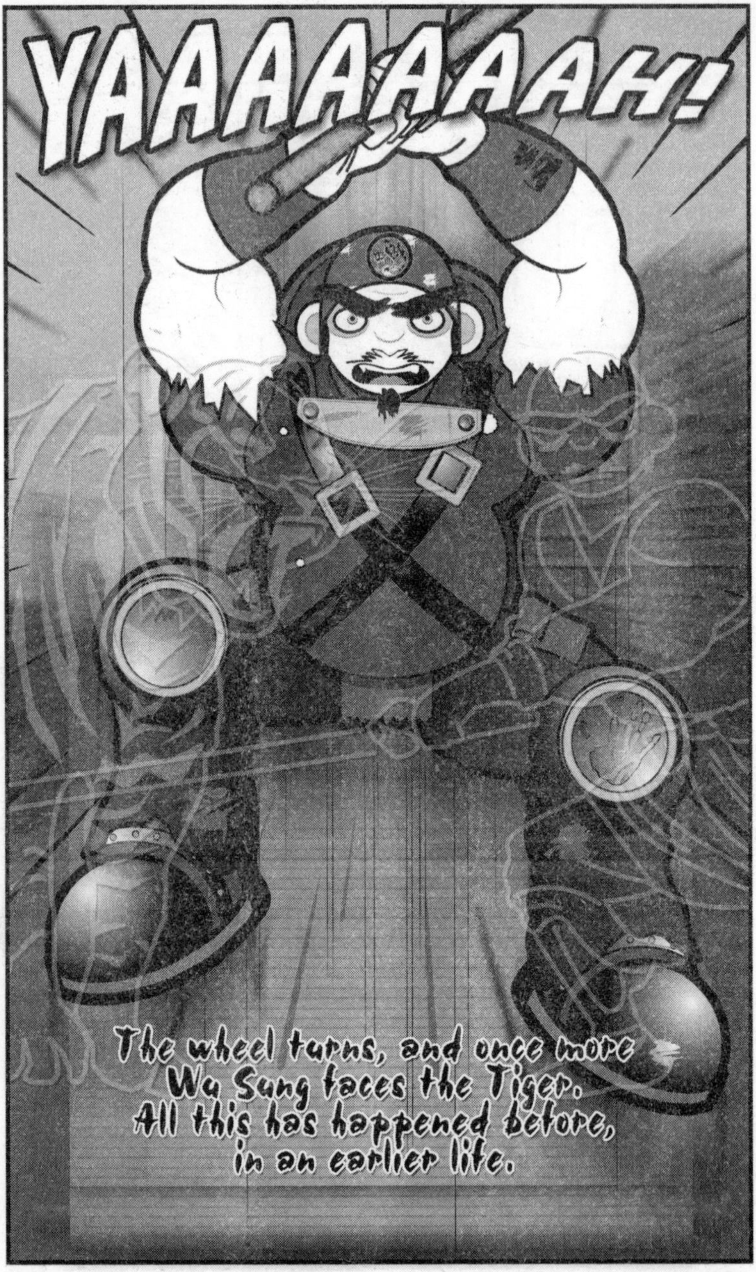
YAAAAAAAAH!
The wheel turns, and once more Wu Sung faces the Tiger. All this has happened before, in an earlier life.

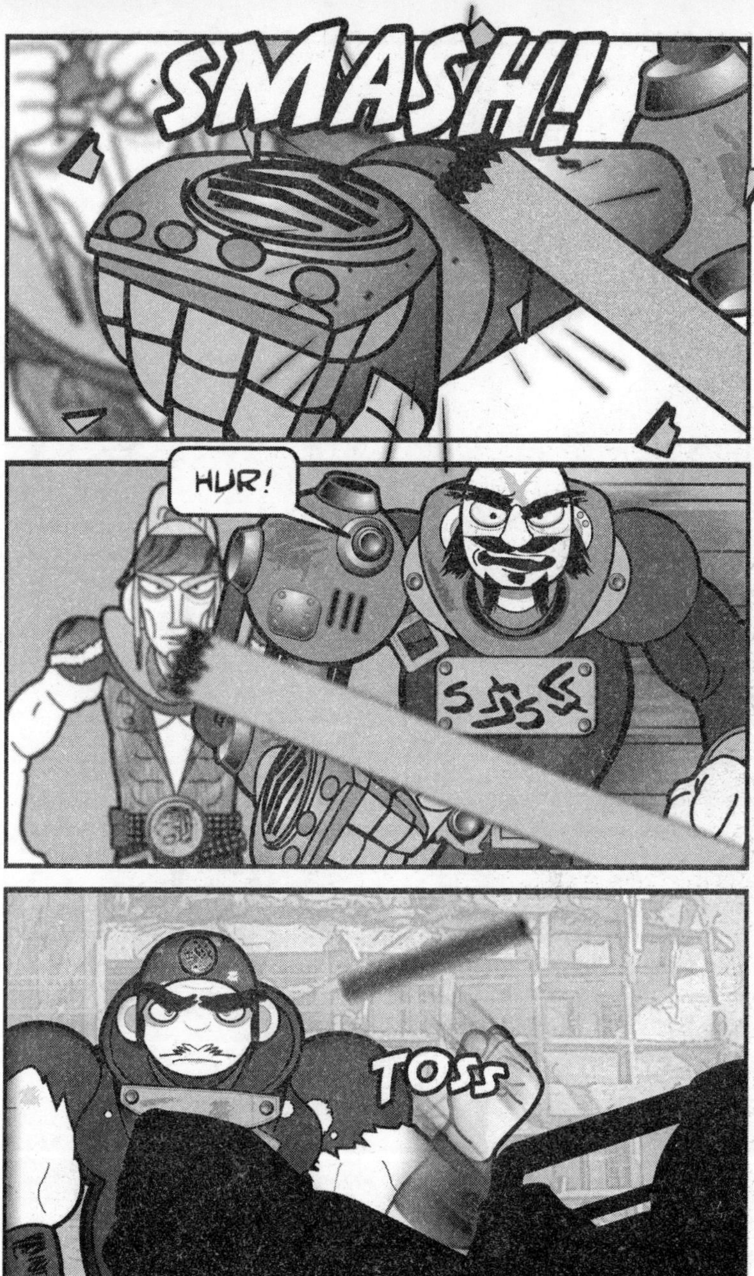
SMASH!
HUR!
TOSS

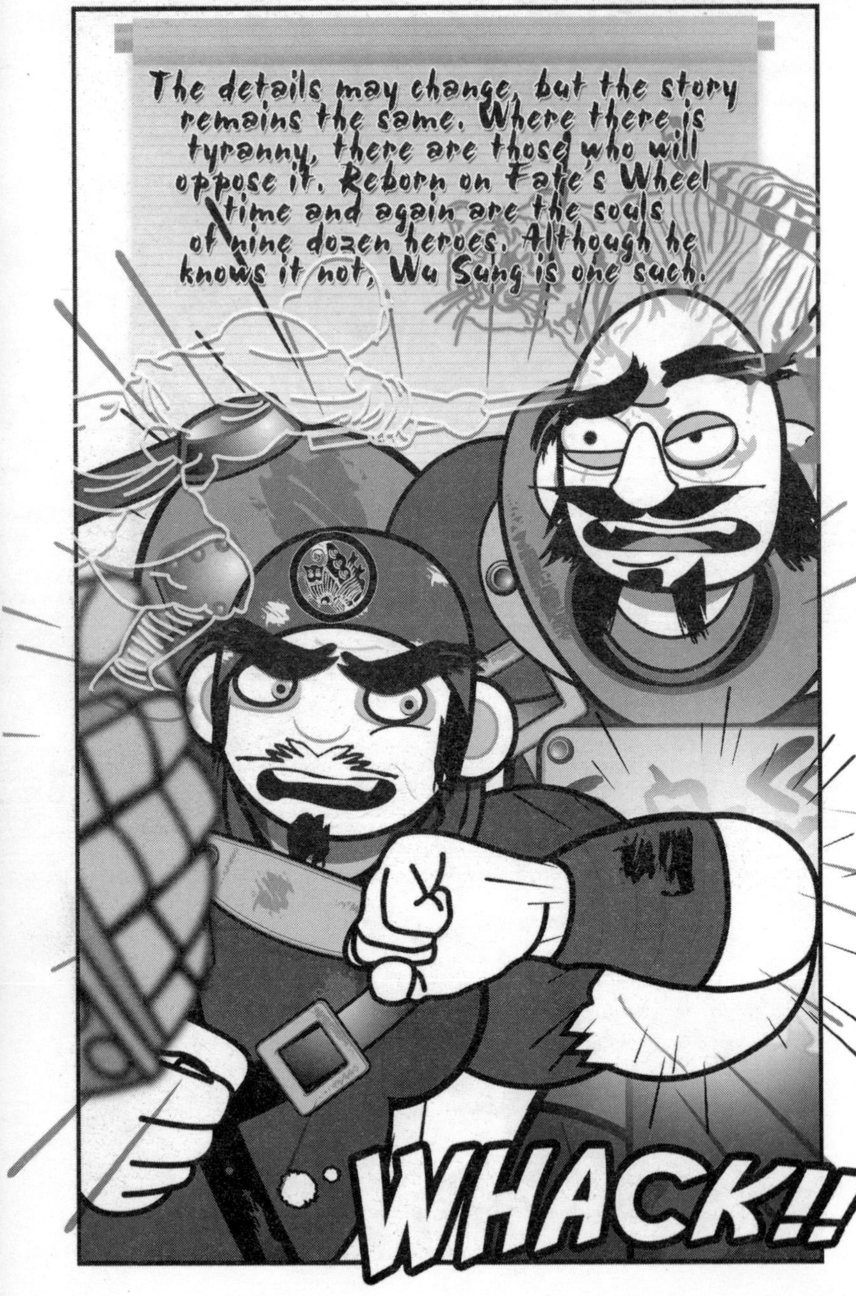
The details may change, but the story remains the same. Where there is tyranny, there are those who will oppose it. Reborn on Fate's Wheel time and again are the souls of nine dozen heroes. Although he knows it not, Wu Sung is one such.
WHACK!!

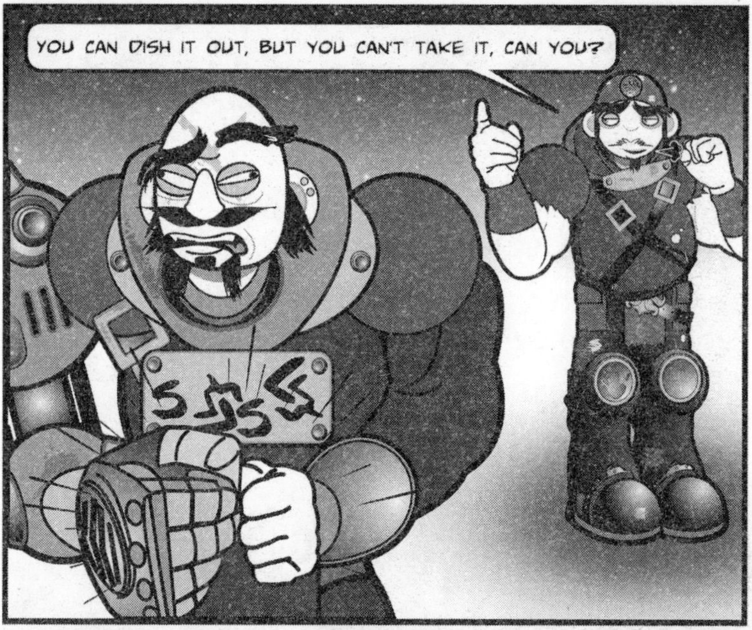
YOU CAN DISH IT OUT, BUT YOU CAN'T TAKE IT, CAN YOU?
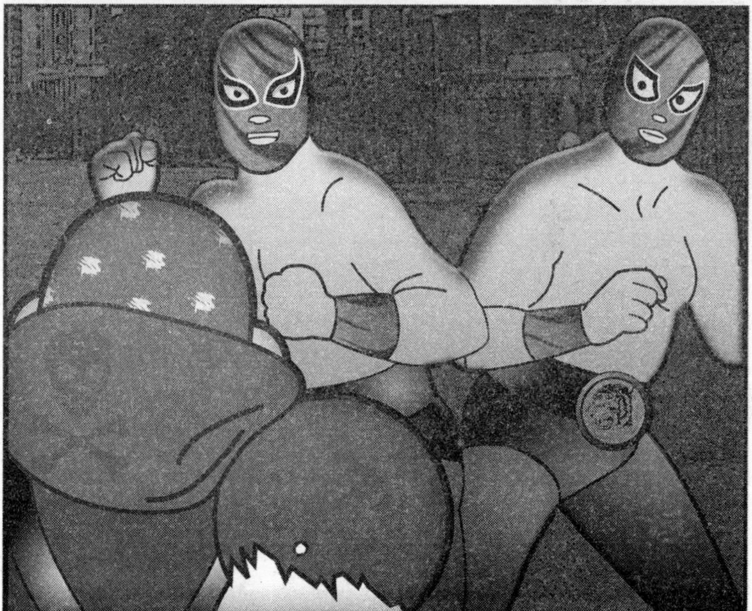

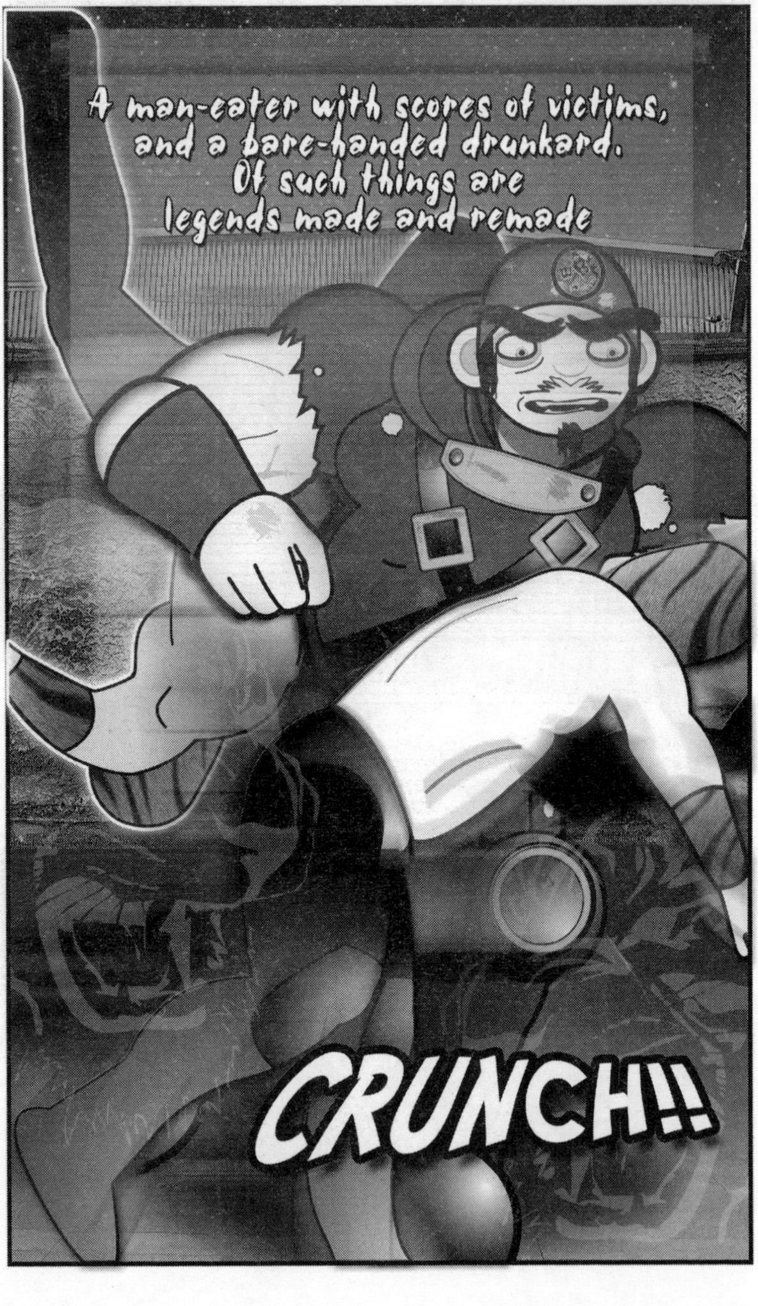
A man-eater with scores of victims,
and a bare-handed drunkard.
Of such things are
legends made and remade
CRUNCH!!

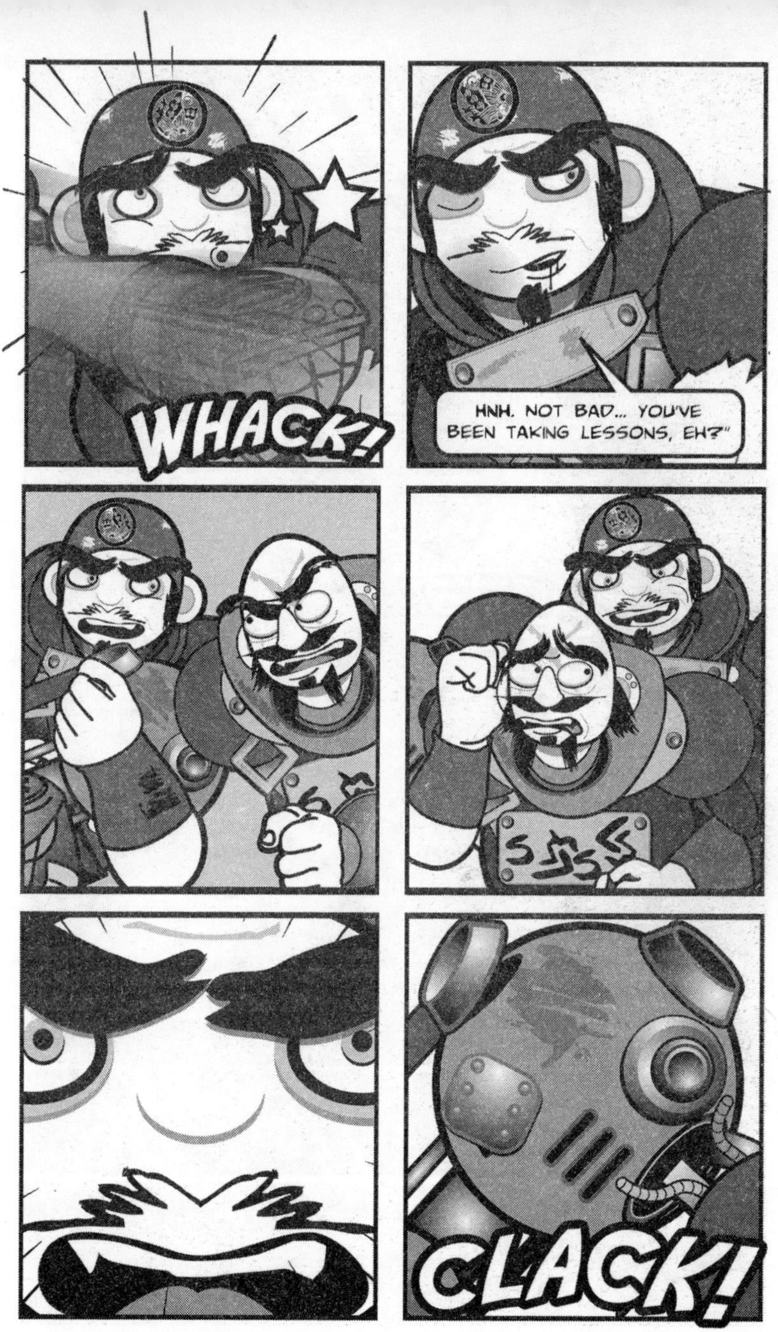
WHACK!
HNH. NOT BAD... YOU'VE BEEN TAKING LESSONS, EH?"
CLACK!

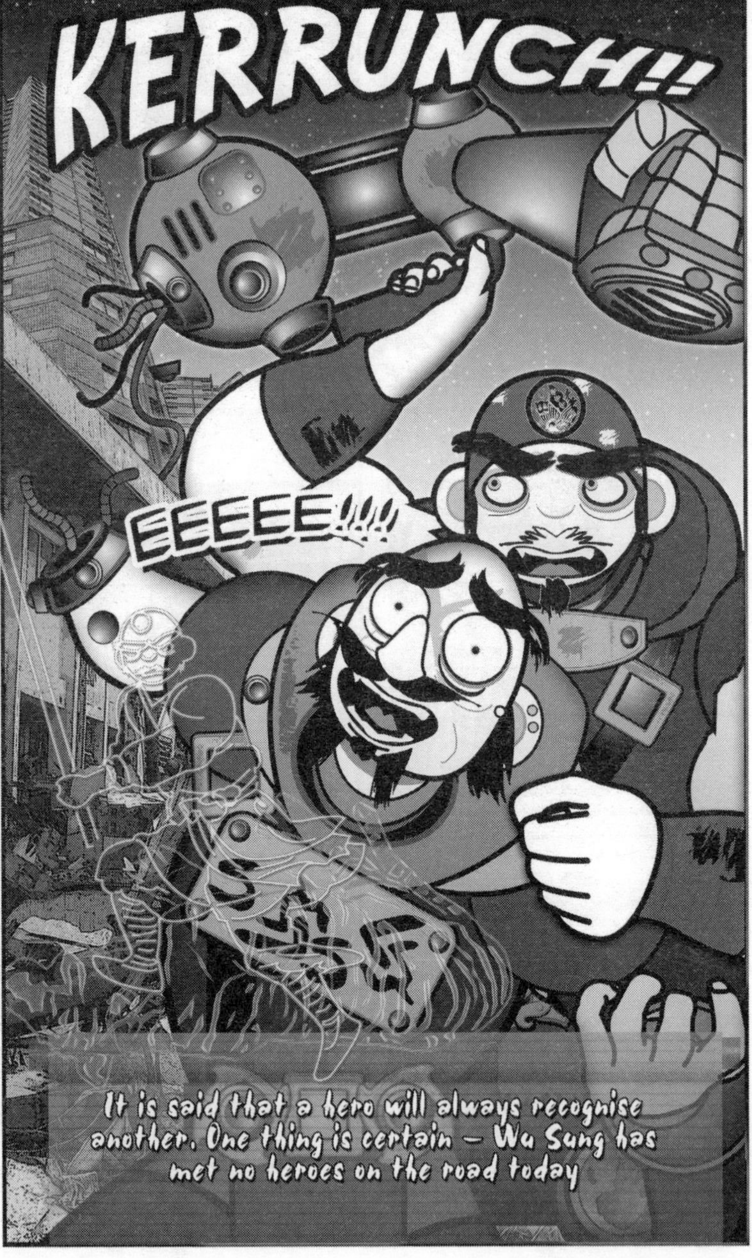
KERRUNCH!!
EEEEEE!!!!
It is said that a hero will always recognise another. One thing is certain – Wu Sung has met no heroes on the road today

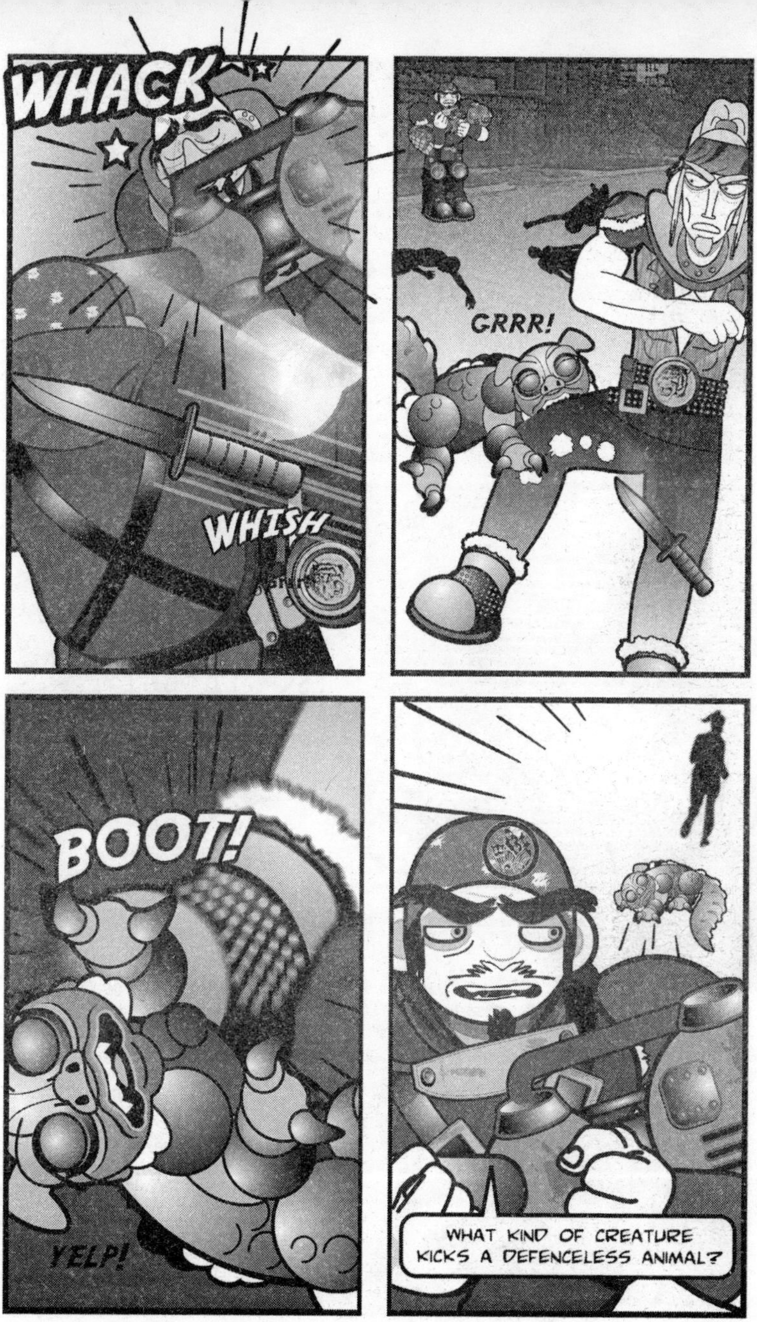
WHACK
WHISH
GRRR!
BOOT!
YELP!
WHAT KIND OF CREATURE KICKS A DEFENCELESS ANIMAL?

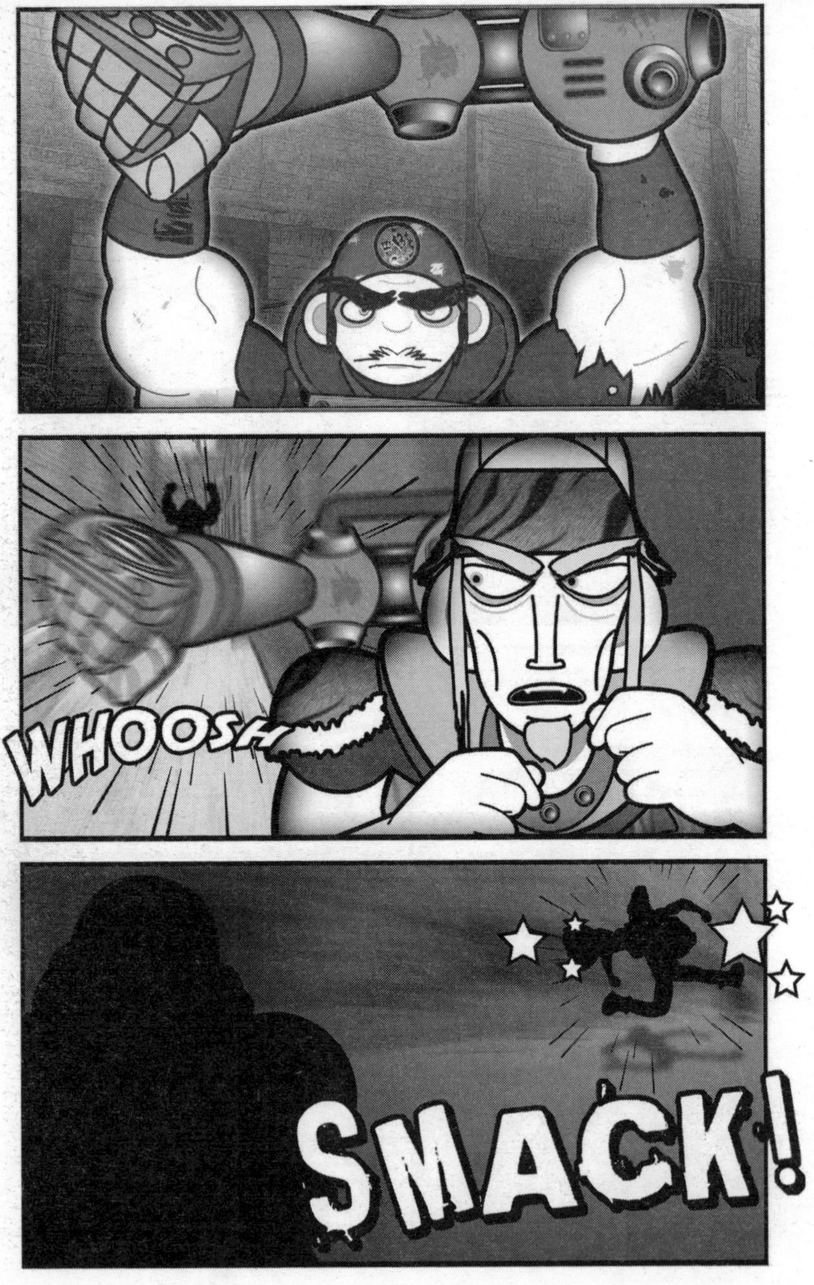
WHOOSH
SMACK!

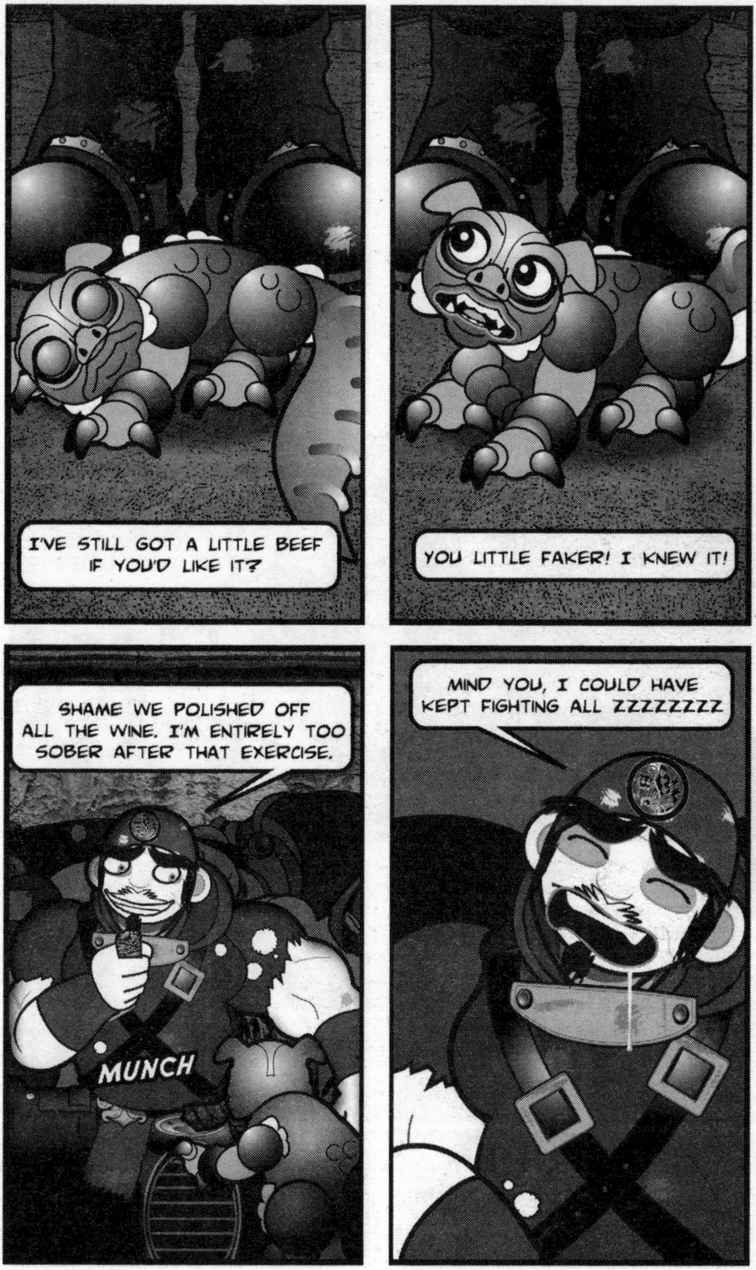

I'VE STILL GOT A LITTLE BEEF IF YOU'D LIKE IT?
YOU LITTLE FAKER! I KNEW IT!
SHAME WE POLISHED OFF ALL THE WINE. I'M ENTIRELY TOO SOBER AFTER THAT EXERCISE.
MUNCH
MIND YOU, I COULD HAVE KEPT FIGHTING ALL ZZZZZZZZ

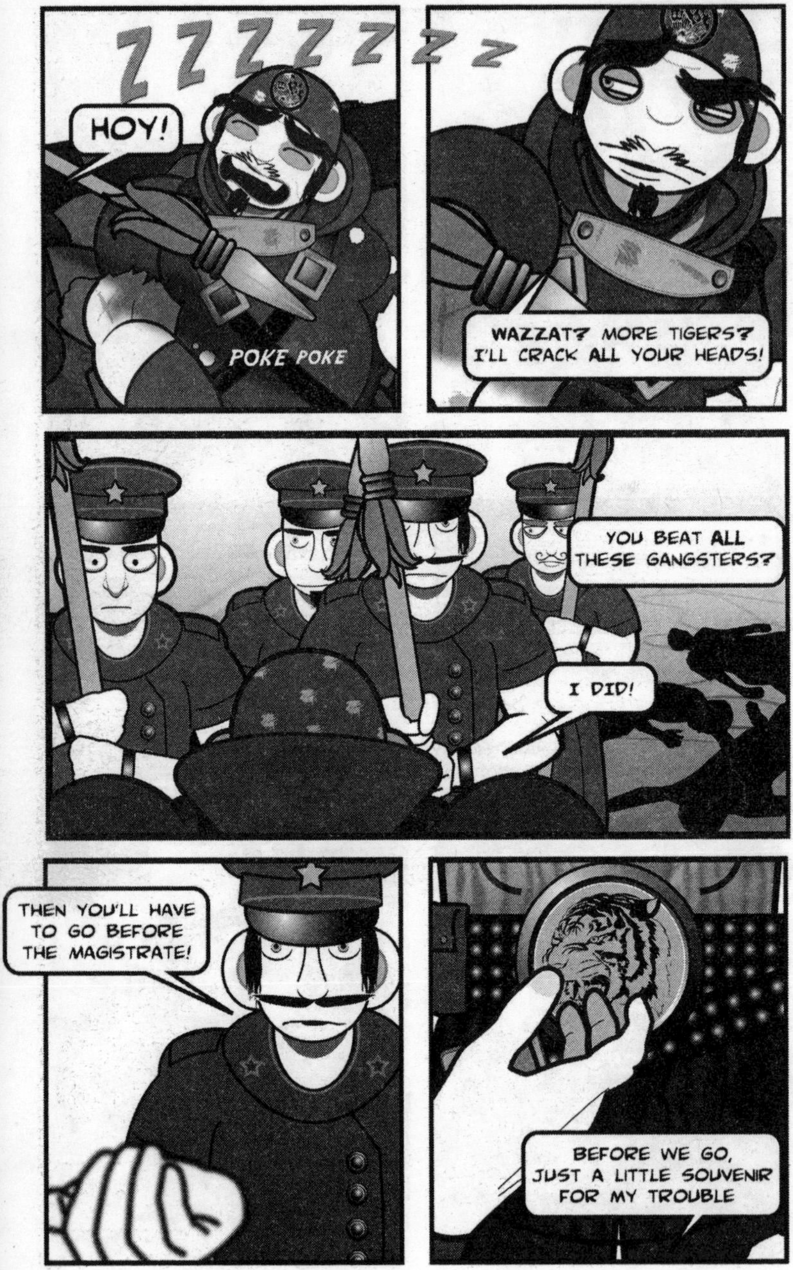
ZZZZZZZZ
HOY!
POKE POKE
WAZZAT? MORE TIGERS? I'LL CRACK ALL YOUR HEADS!
YOU BEAT ALL THESE GANGSTERS?
I DID!
THEN YOU'LL HAVE TO GO BEFORE THE MAGISTRATE!
BEFORE WE GO, JUST A LITTLE SOUVENIR FOR MY TROUBLE

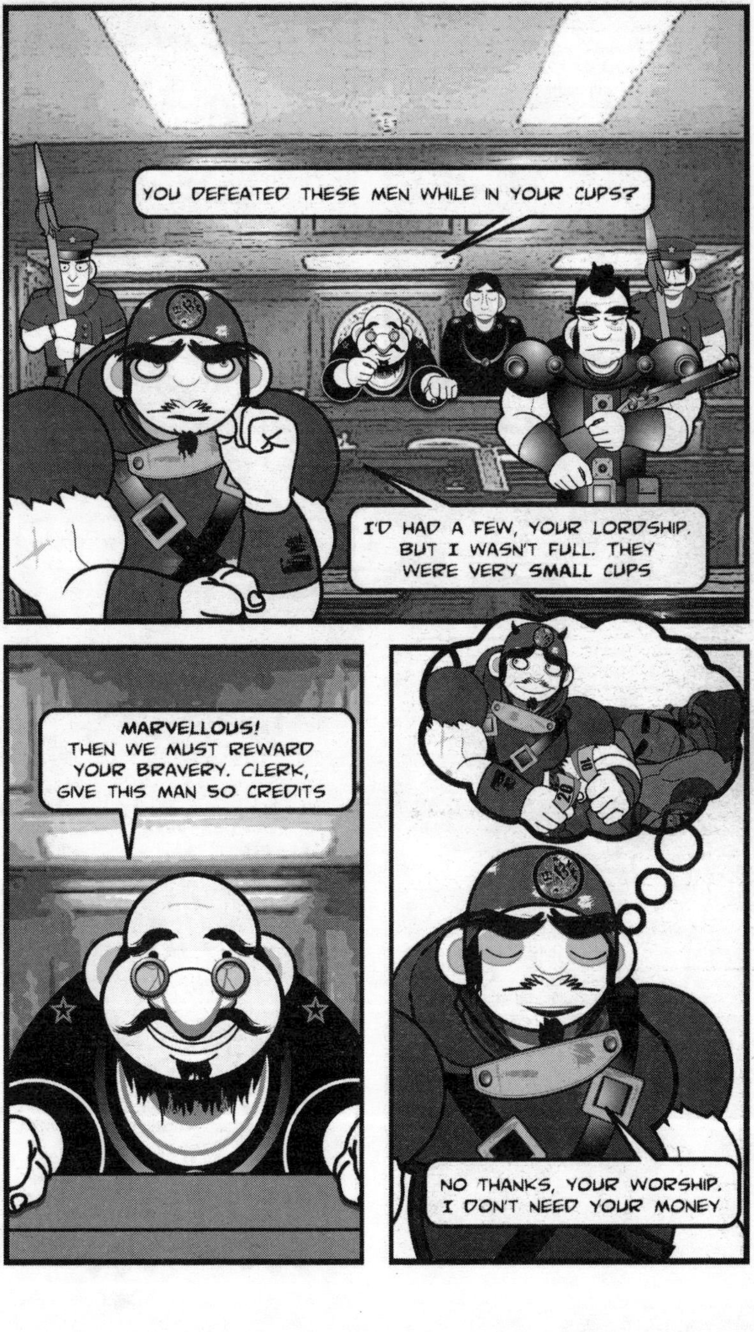
YOU DEFEATED THESE MEN WHILE IN YOUR CUPS?
I'D HAD A FEW, YOUR LORDSHIP. BUT I WASN'T FULL. THEY WERE VERY SMALL CUPS
MARVELLOUS! THEN WE MUST REWARD YOUR BRAVERY. CLERK, GIVE THIS MAN 50 CREDITS
NO THANKS, YOUR WORSHIP. I DON'T NEED YOUR MONEY

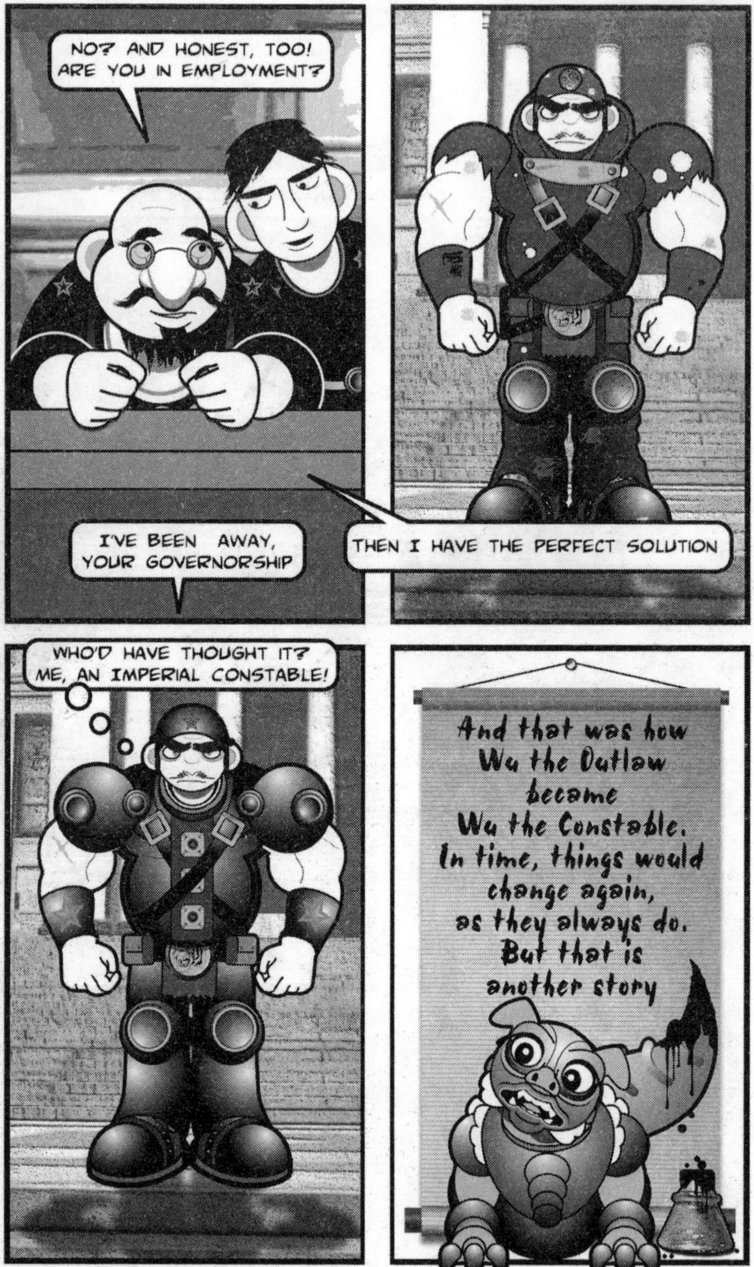
NO? AND HONEST, TOO! ARE YOU IN EMPLOYMENT?
I'VE BEEN AWAY, YOUR GOVERNORSHIP
THEN I HAVE THE PERFECT SOLUTION
WHO'D HAVE THOUGHT IT? ME, AN IMPERIAL CONSTABLE!
And that was how Wu the Outlaw became Wu the Constable. In time, things would change again, as they always do. But that is another story

Bad Luck

BY SELINA DEAN

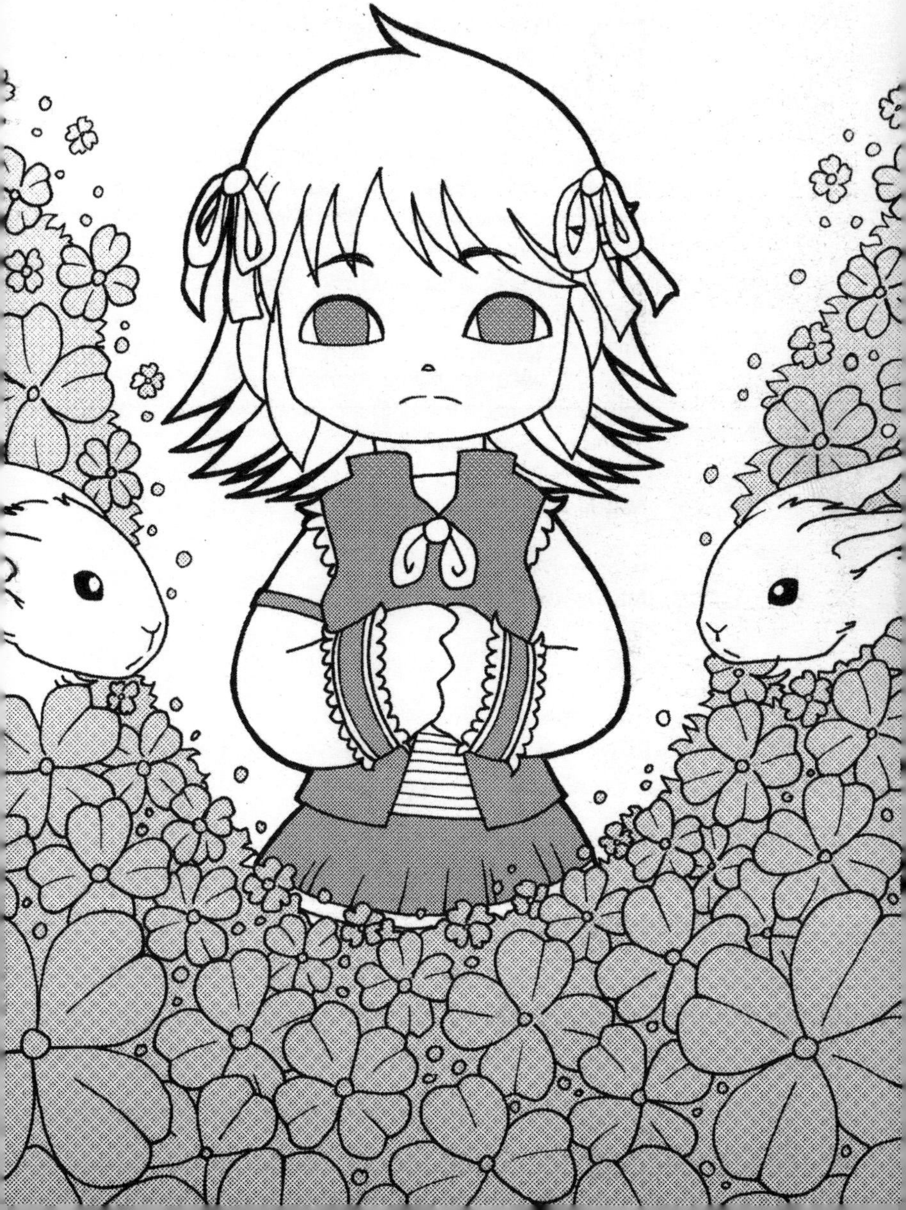

Date of birth: 4 June 1982

SELINA DEAN

Bad Luck is the first of two strips from Selina 'cute but strange' Dean, a founder member of the international manga-mad Sweatdrop collective. Hailing from the university town of Cambridge in the UK, Selina's fave raves include classic manga strips such as **Astroboy** and **Barefoot Gen**; also, the works of Taiyo Matsumoto, Junko Mizuno and Usamaru Furuya; quirky Japanese computer games, fairy tales, 'anything cute or a bit weird'. She's a cat person, not a mean dog person, hates anything with tentacles, and wishes she had more time to do the things she likes, like drinking tea.

'I want to create comics which are cool, entertaining and thought provoking,' says Selina. 'Perhaps one day I will!'

Well despite what she says, we here at **Best New Manga** think that day has come!

http://www.sweatdrop.com
http://www.noddingcat.net

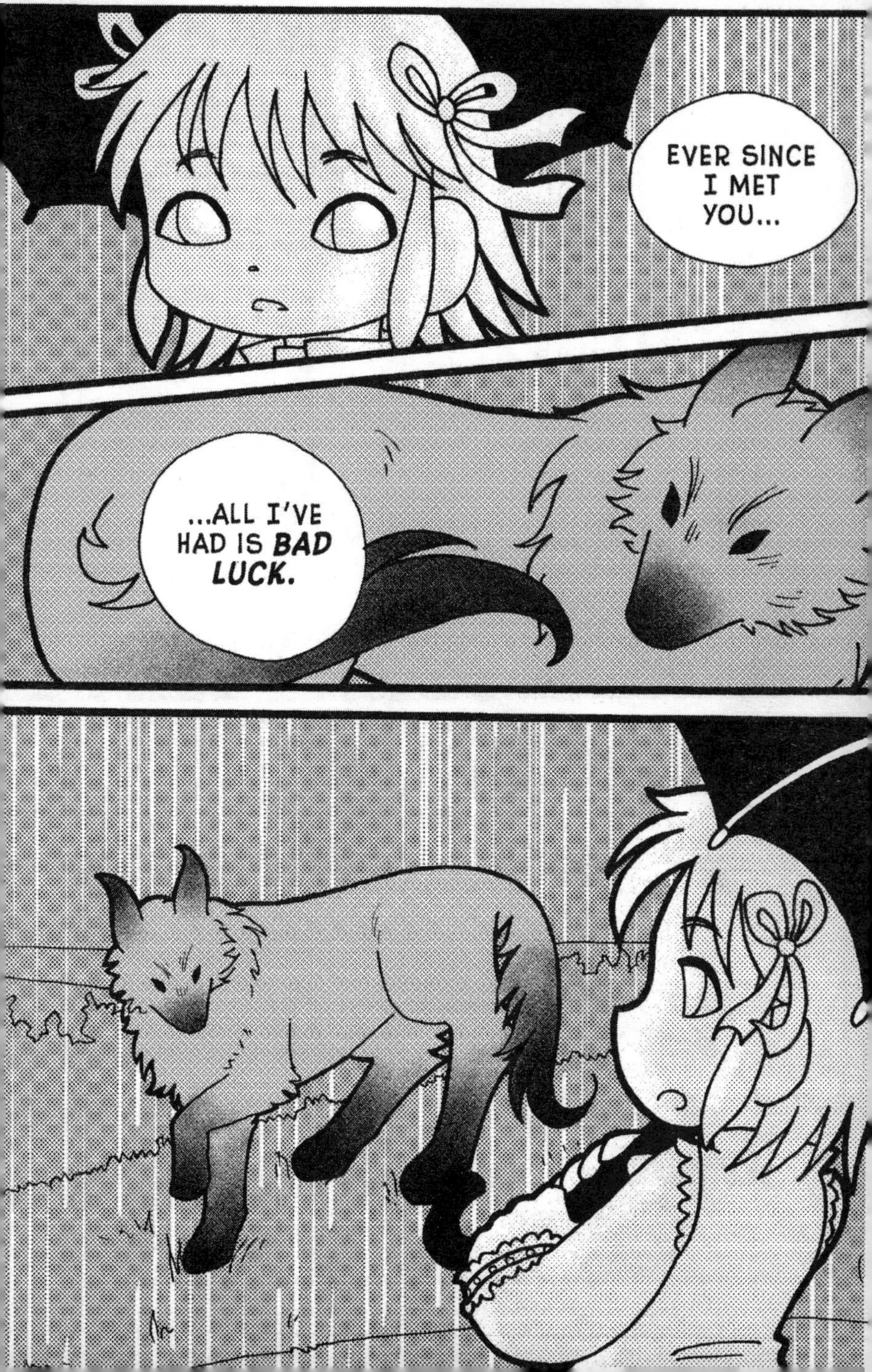
EVER SINCE I MET YOU...
...ALL I'VE HAD IS **BAD LUCK.**

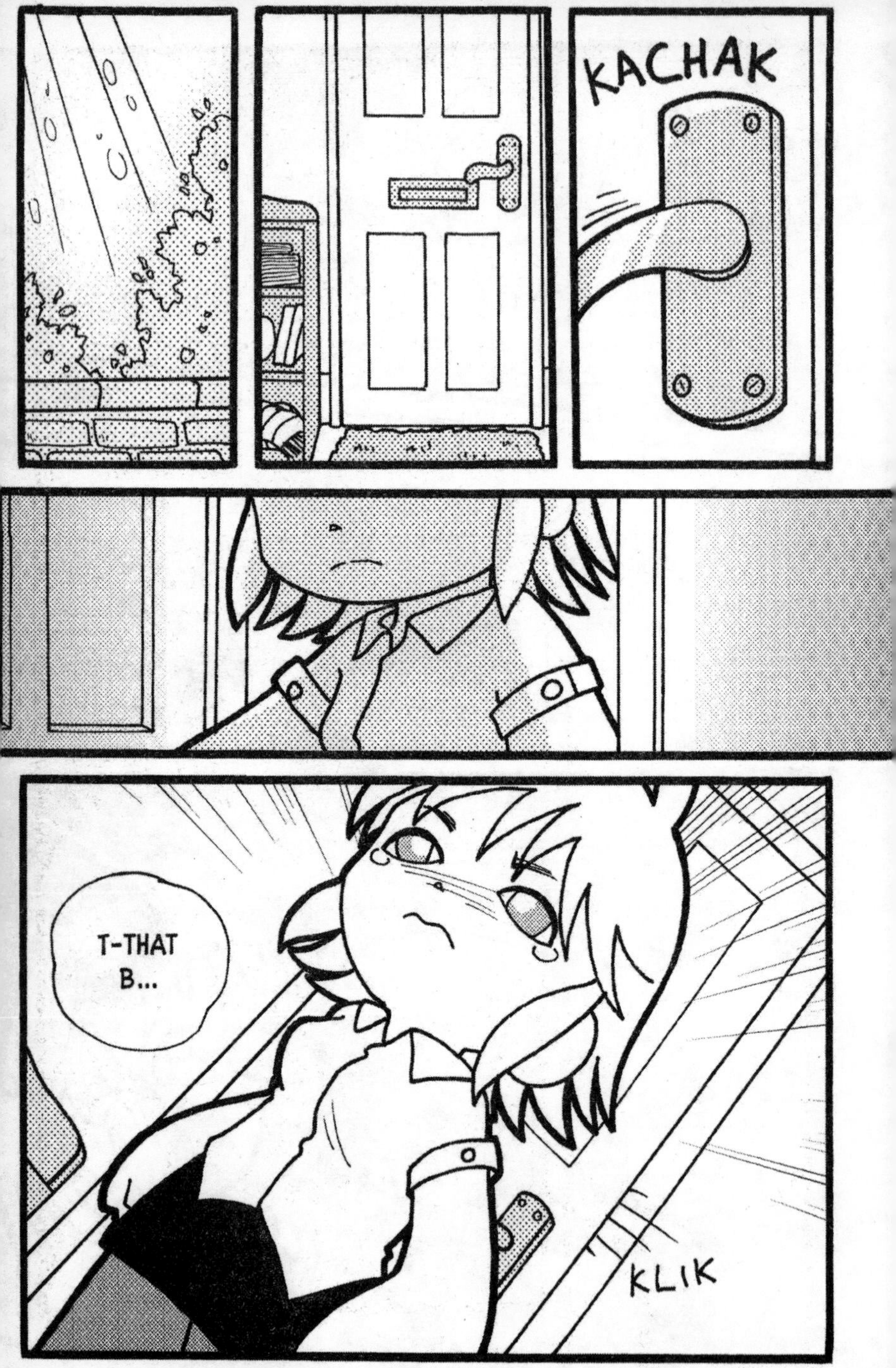
KACHAK
T-THAT B...
KLIK

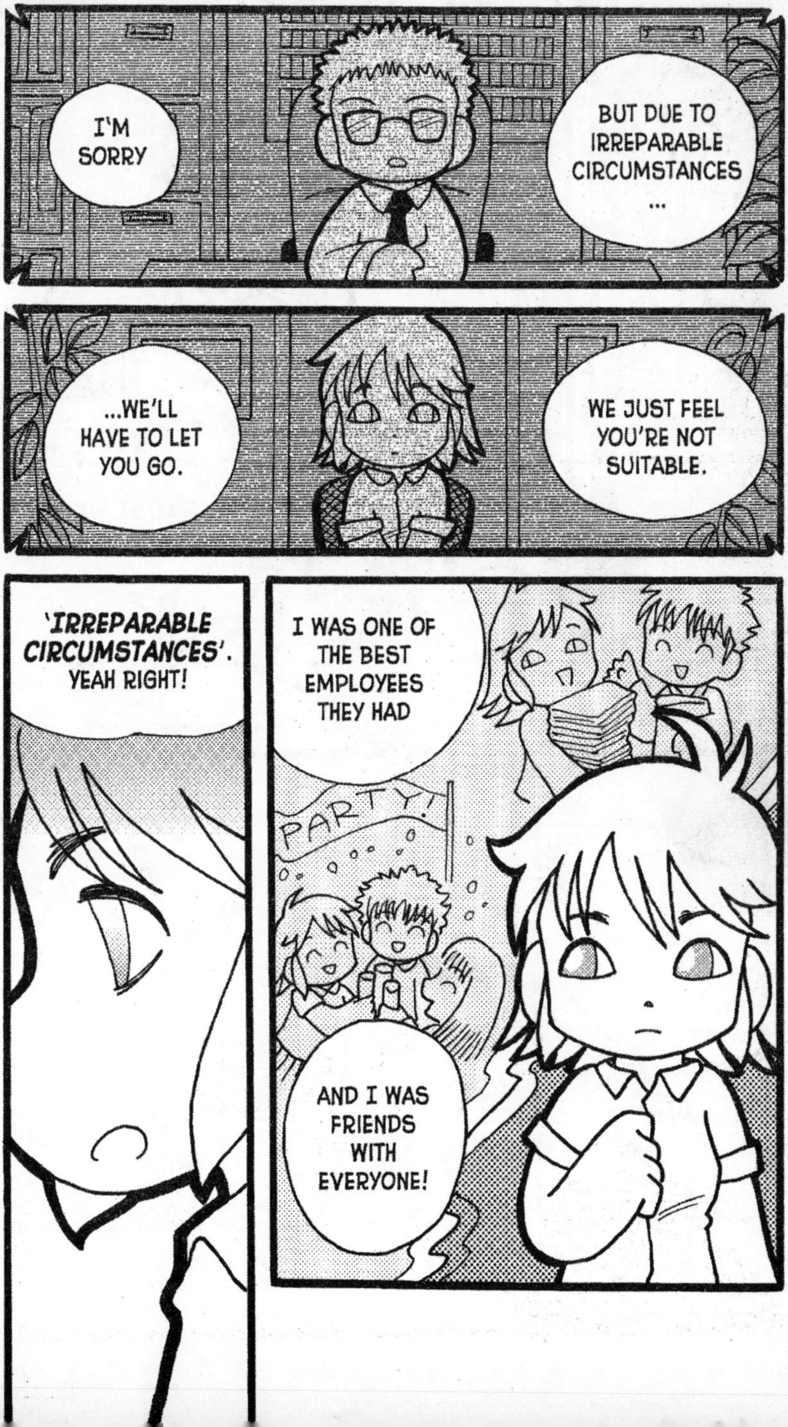
I'M SORRY
BUT DUE TO IRREPARABLE CIRCUMSTANCES ...
...WE'LL HAVE TO LET YOU GO.
WE JUST FEEL YOU'RE NOT SUITABLE.
'IRREPARABLE CIRCUMSTANCES'. YEAH RIGHT!
I WAS ONE OF THE BEST EMPLOYEES THEY HAD
PARTY!
AND I WAS FRIENDS WITH EVERYONE!

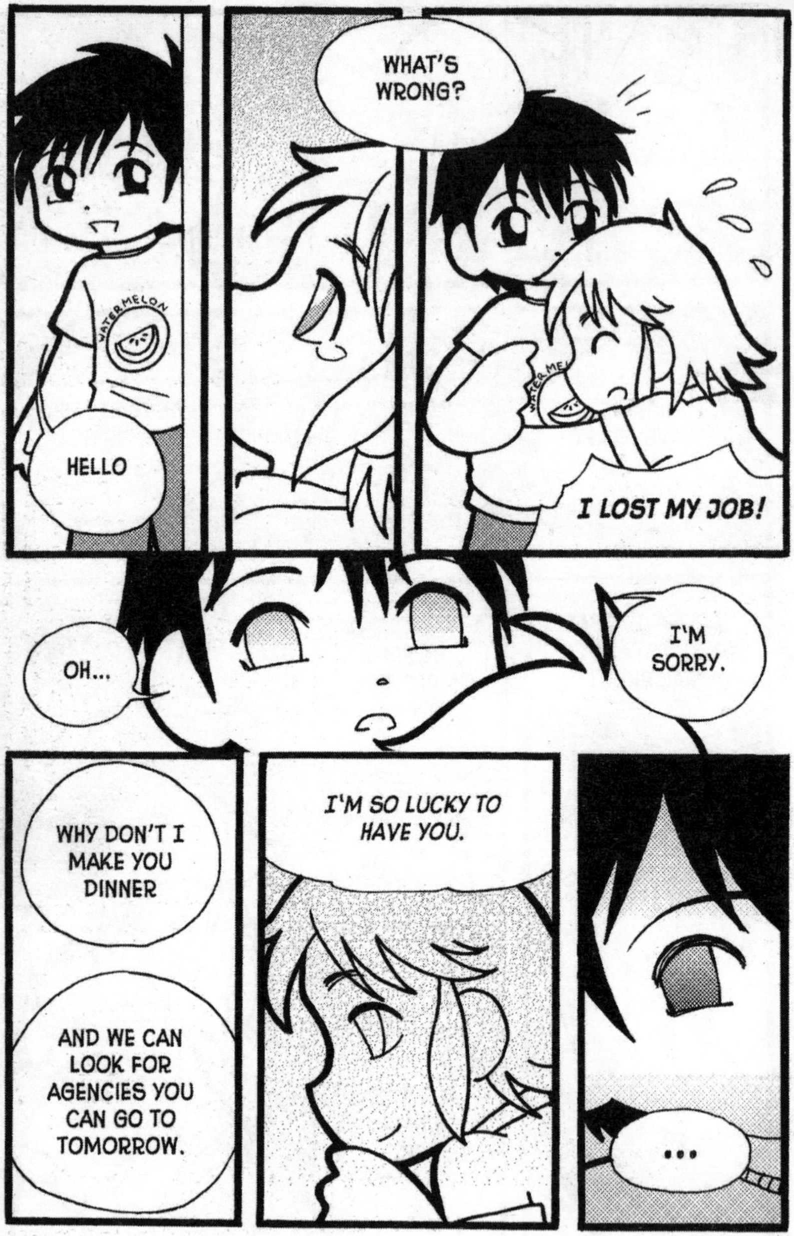
HELLO
WHAT'S WRONG?
I LOST MY JOB!
OH...
I'M SORRY.
WHY DON'T I MAKE YOU DINNER
AND WE CAN LOOK FOR AGENCIES YOU CAN GO TO TOMORROW.
I'M SO LUCKY TO HAVE YOU.
...

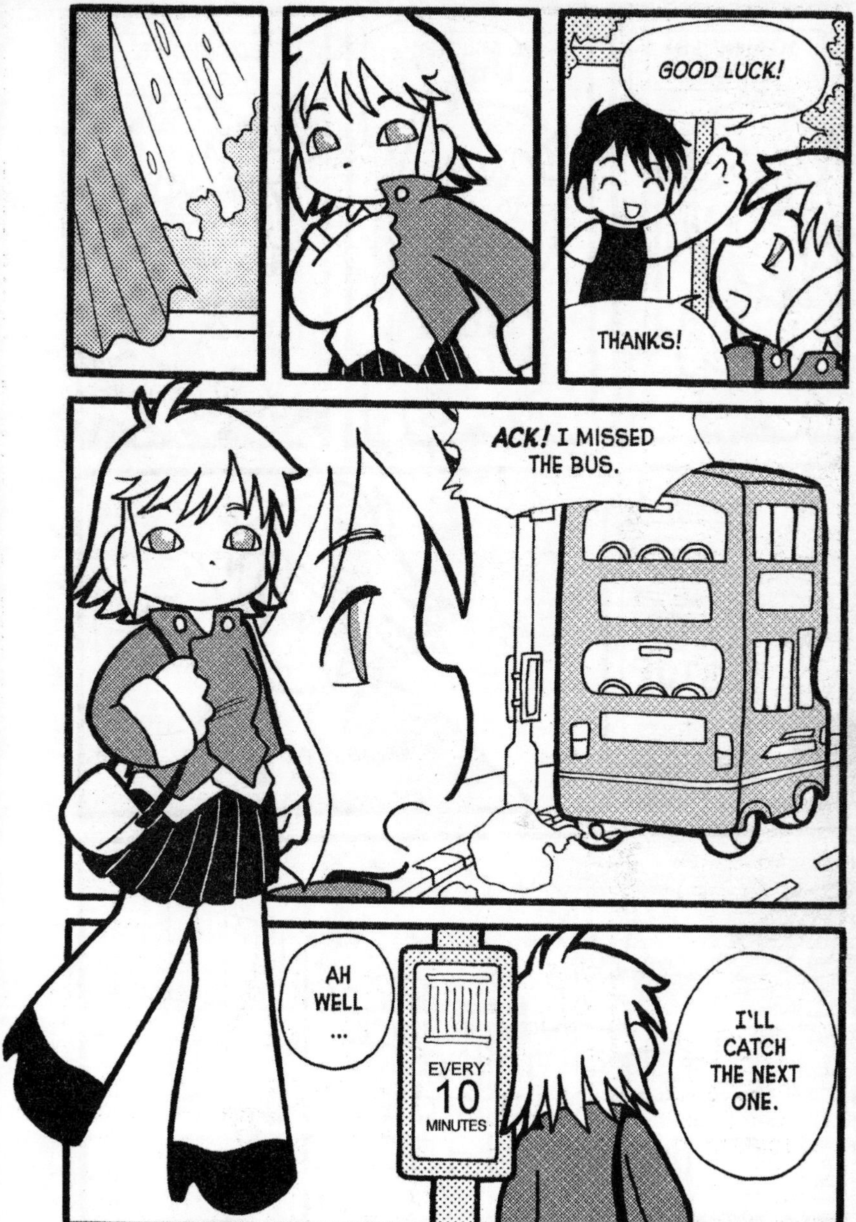
GOOD LUCK!
THANKS!
ACK! I MISSED THE BUS.
AH WELL ...
EVERY 10 MINUTES
I'LL CATCH THE NEXT ONE.

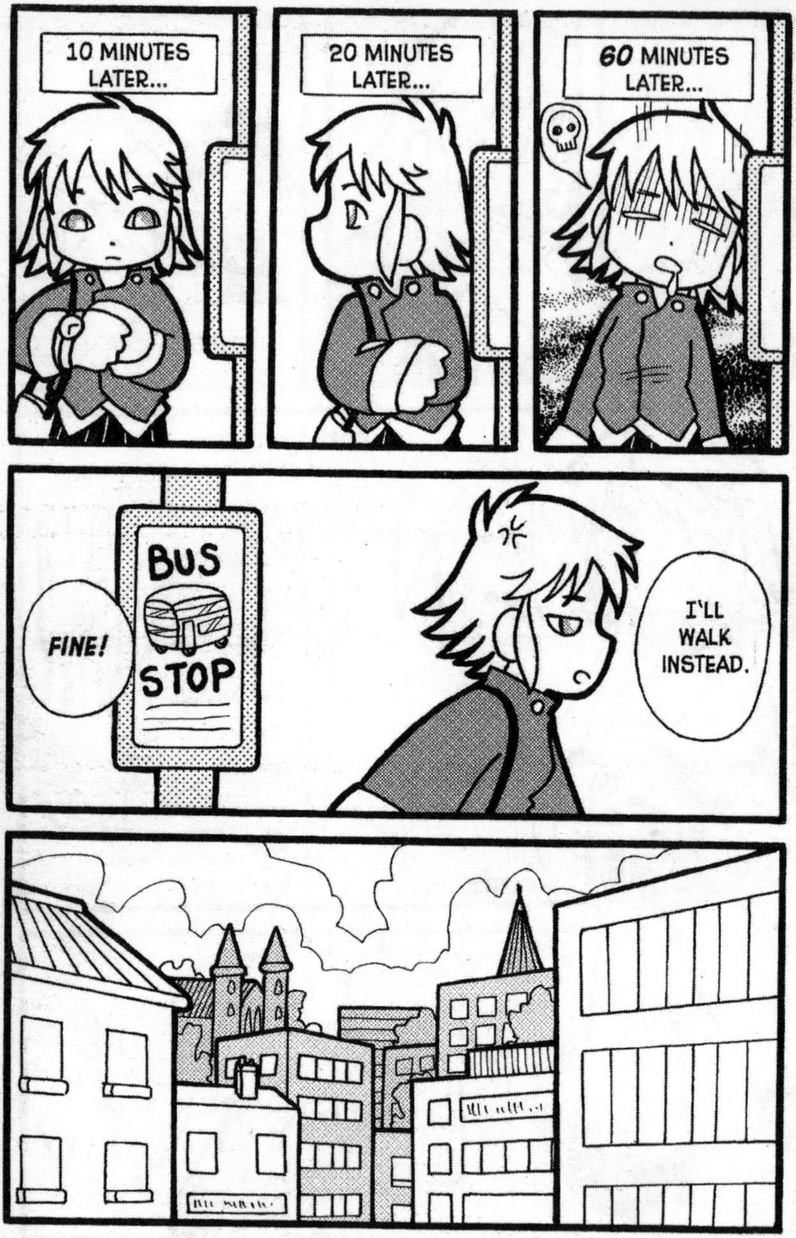
10 MINUTES LATER...
20 MINUTES LATER...
60 MINUTES LATER...
FINE!
BUS STOP
I'LL WALK INSTEAD.

SORRY, BUT...

...OUR BOOKS

ARE CURRENTLY FULL.

WE DON'T HAVE ANY WORK FOR YOU.

I DON'T UNDERSTAND. USUALLY AGENCIES HAVE LOTS OF WORK GOING.

A-Z Recruitment
Office Recruits
Z Agency
Jobs 'n' Th

ONLY ONE MORE PLACE LEFT TO TRY

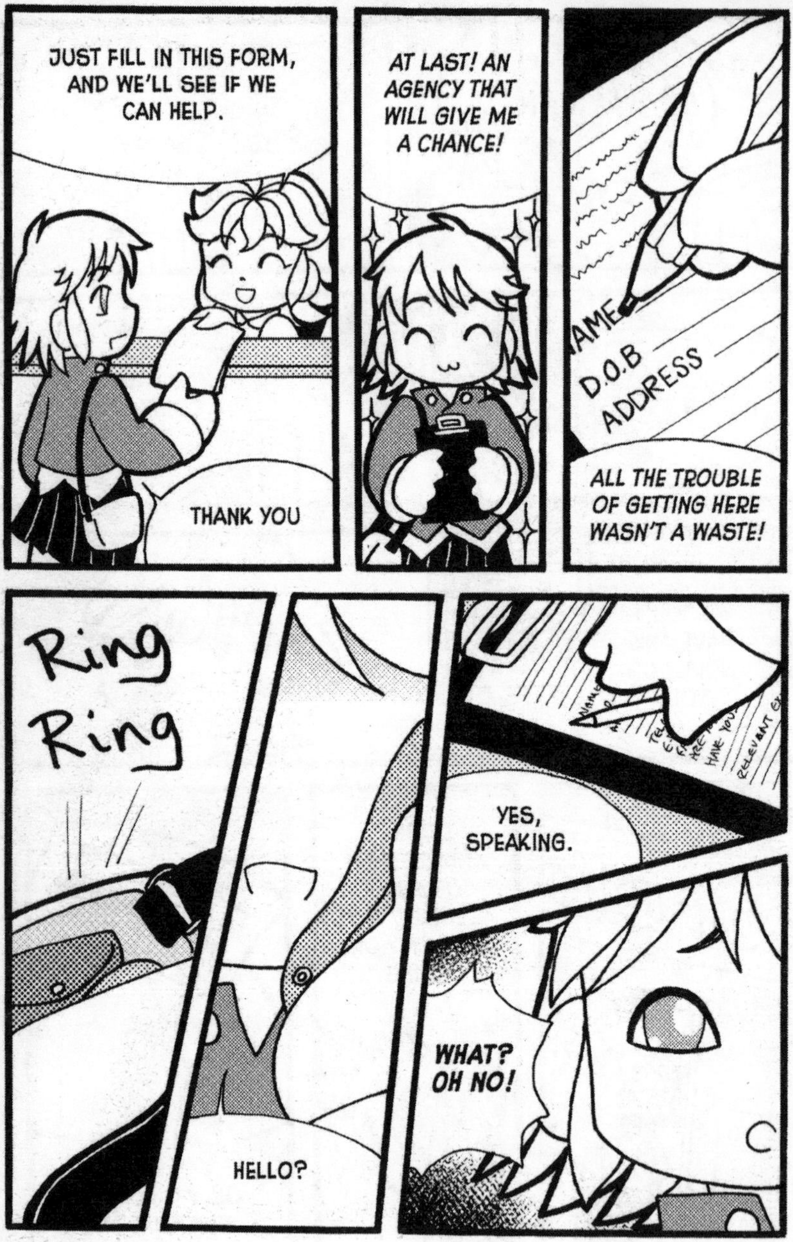
JUST FILL IN THIS FORM, AND WE'LL SEE IF WE CAN HELP.
THANK YOU
AT LAST! AN AGENCY THAT WILL GIVE ME A CHANCE!
AME
D.O.B
ADDRESS
ALL THE TROUBLE OF GETTING HERE WASN'T A WASTE!
Ring Ring
HELLO?
YES, SPEAKING.
WHAT? OH NO!

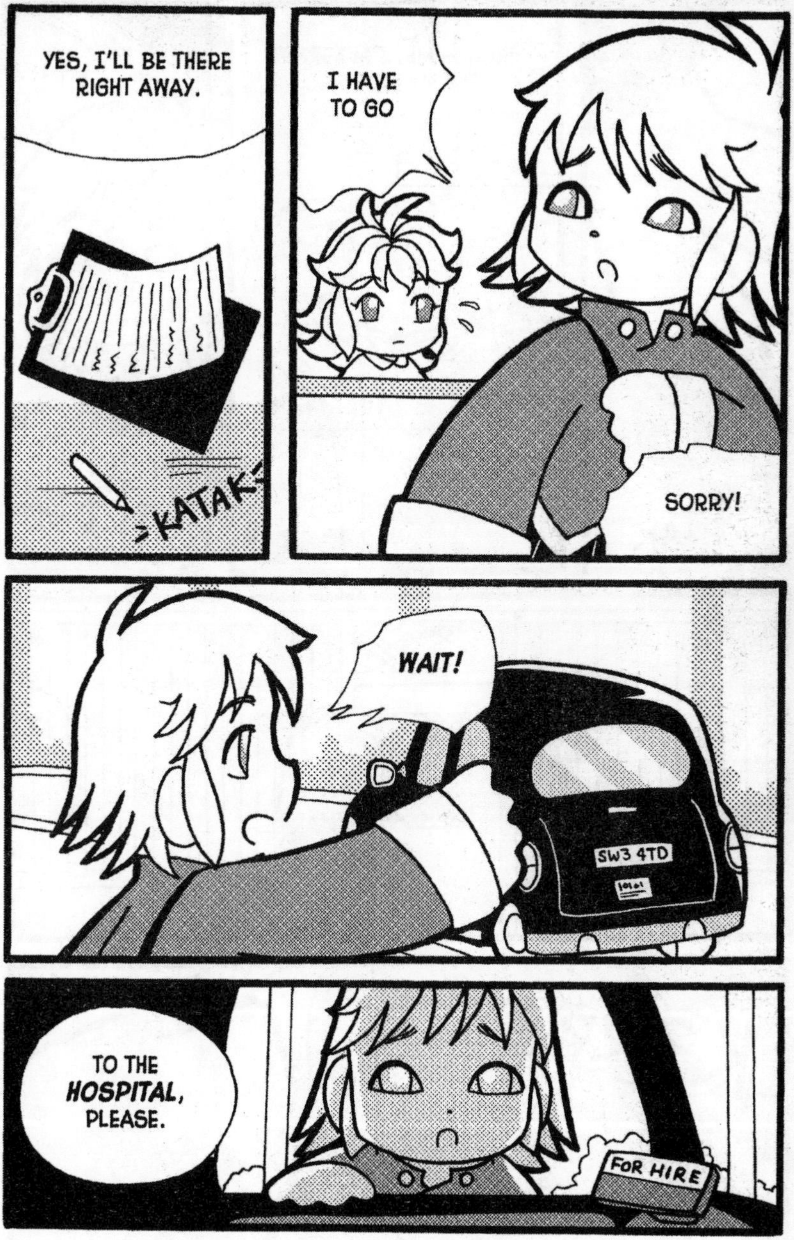
YES, I'LL BE THERE RIGHT AWAY.
KATAK
I HAVE TO GO
SORRY!
WAIT!
SW3 4TD
TO THE *HOSPITAL*, PLEASE.
FOR HIRE

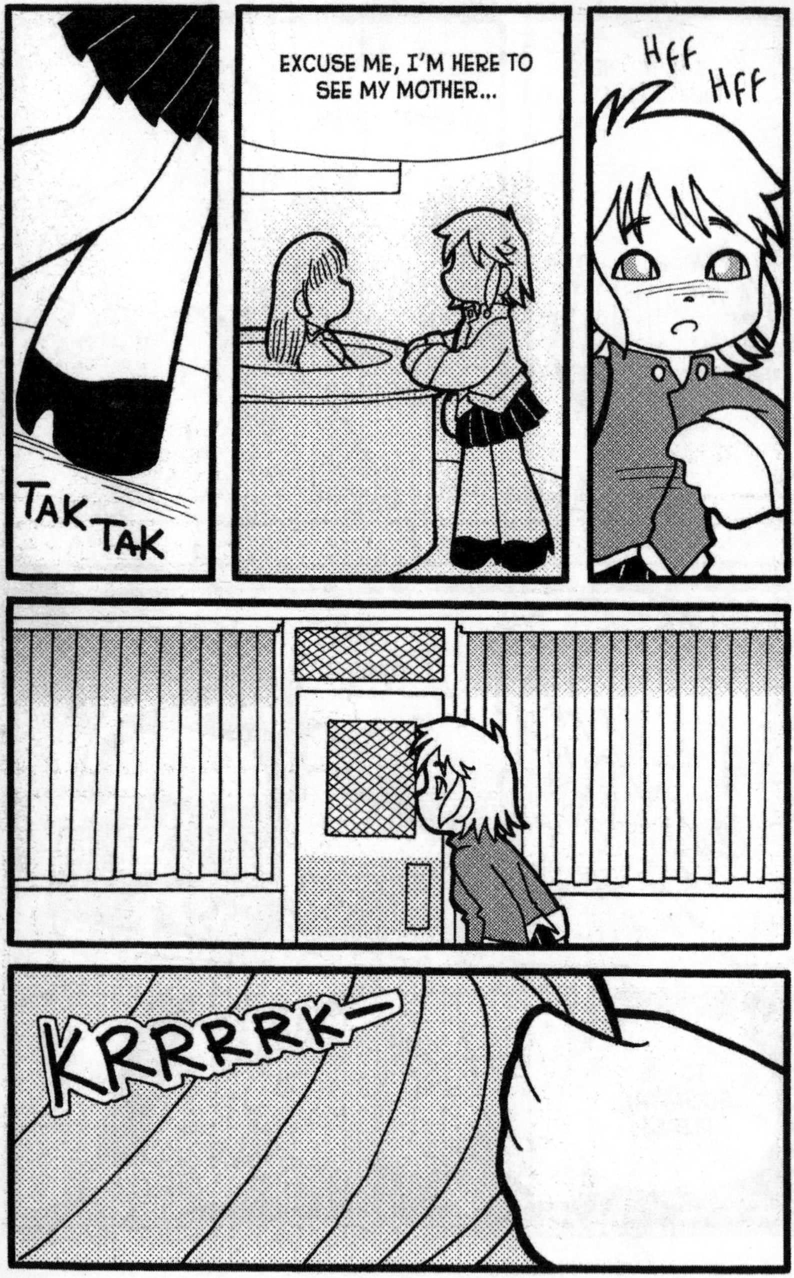
TAK TAK
EXCUSE ME, I'M HERE TO SEE MY MOTHER...
Hff Hff
KRRRRK—

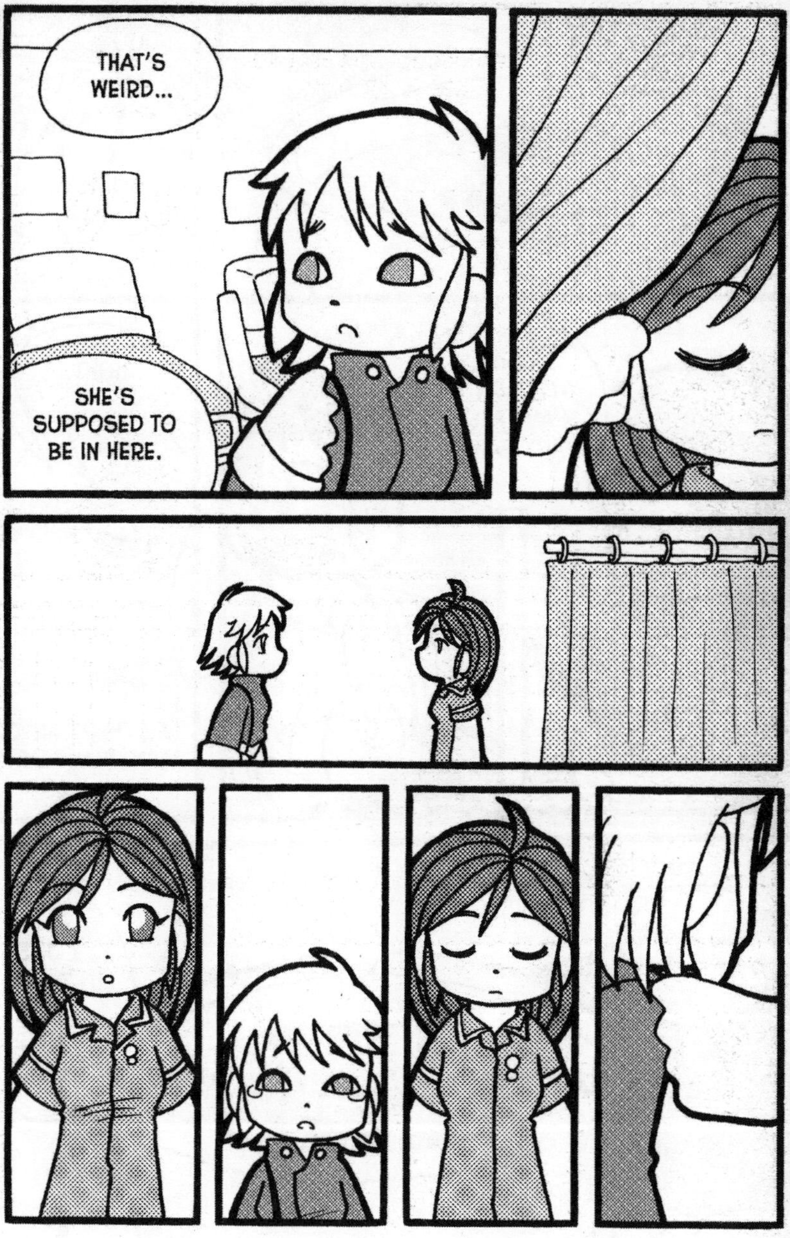
THAT'S WEIRD...
SHE'S SUPPOSED TO BE IN HERE.

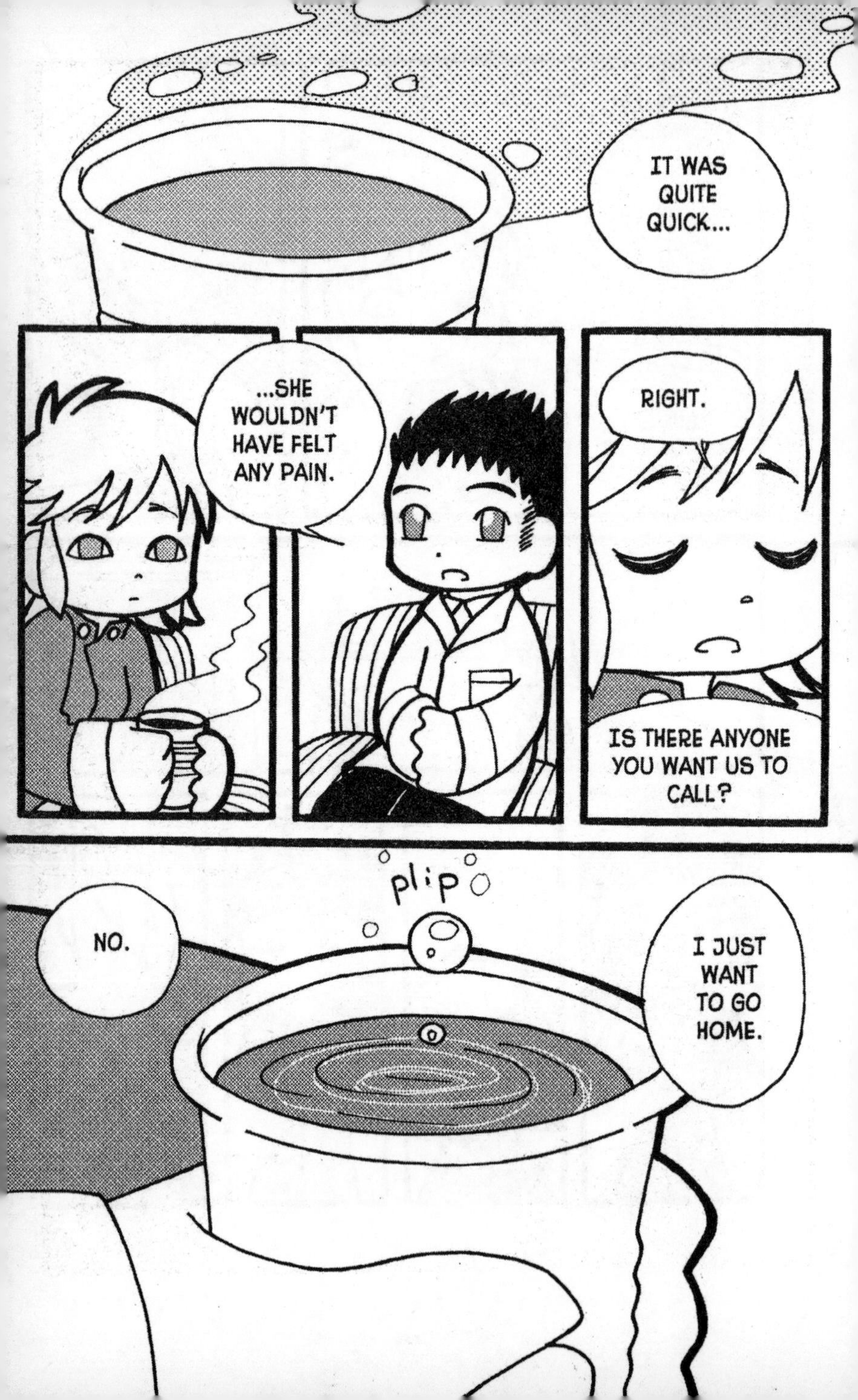
IT WAS QUITE QUICK...
...SHE WOULDN'T HAVE FELT ANY PAIN.
RIGHT.
IS THERE ANYONE YOU WANT US TO CALL?
plip
NO.
I JUST WANT TO GO HOME.

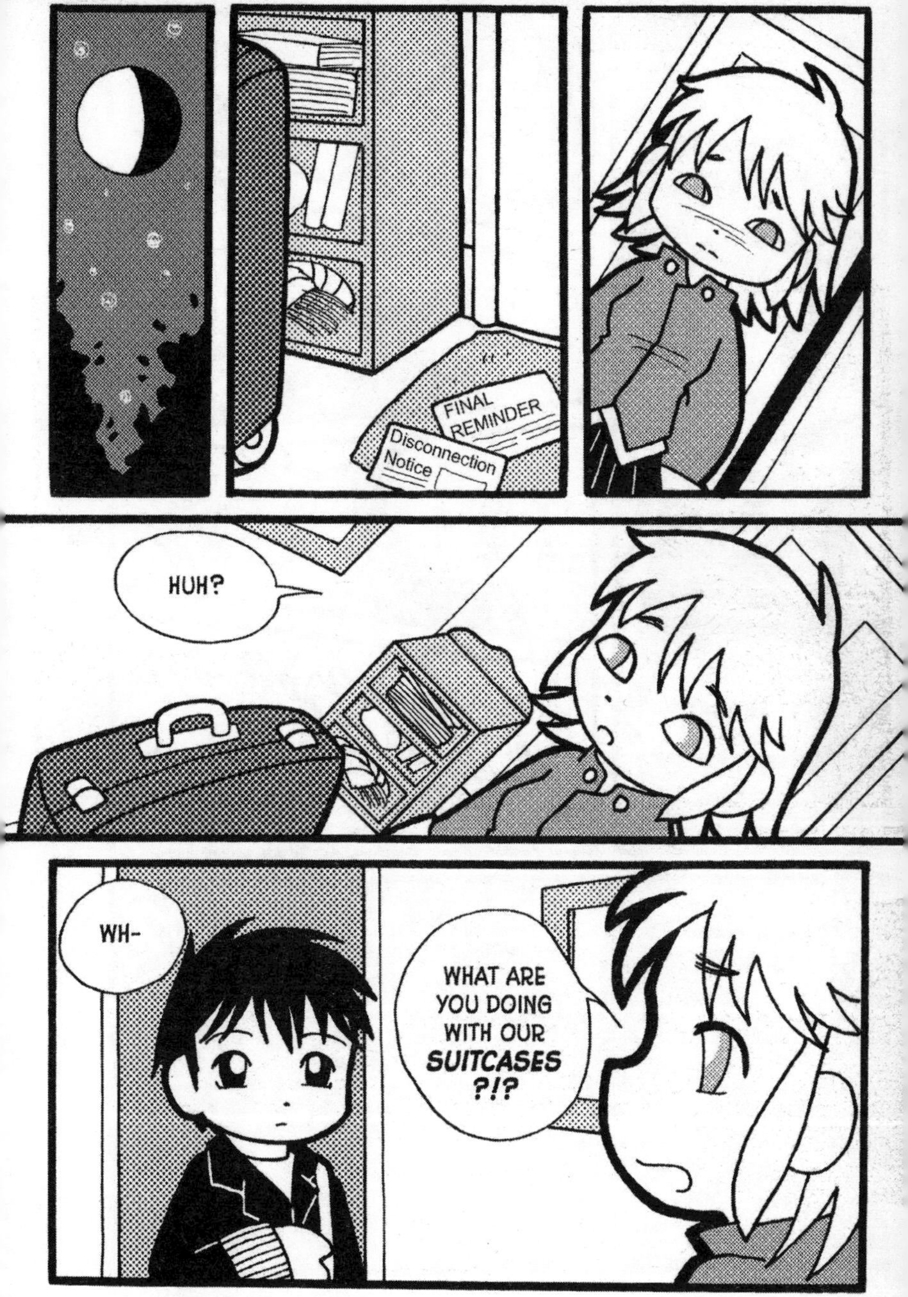
FINAL REMINDER
Disconnection Notice
HUH?
WH-
WHAT ARE YOU DOING WITH OUR **SUITCASES** ?!?

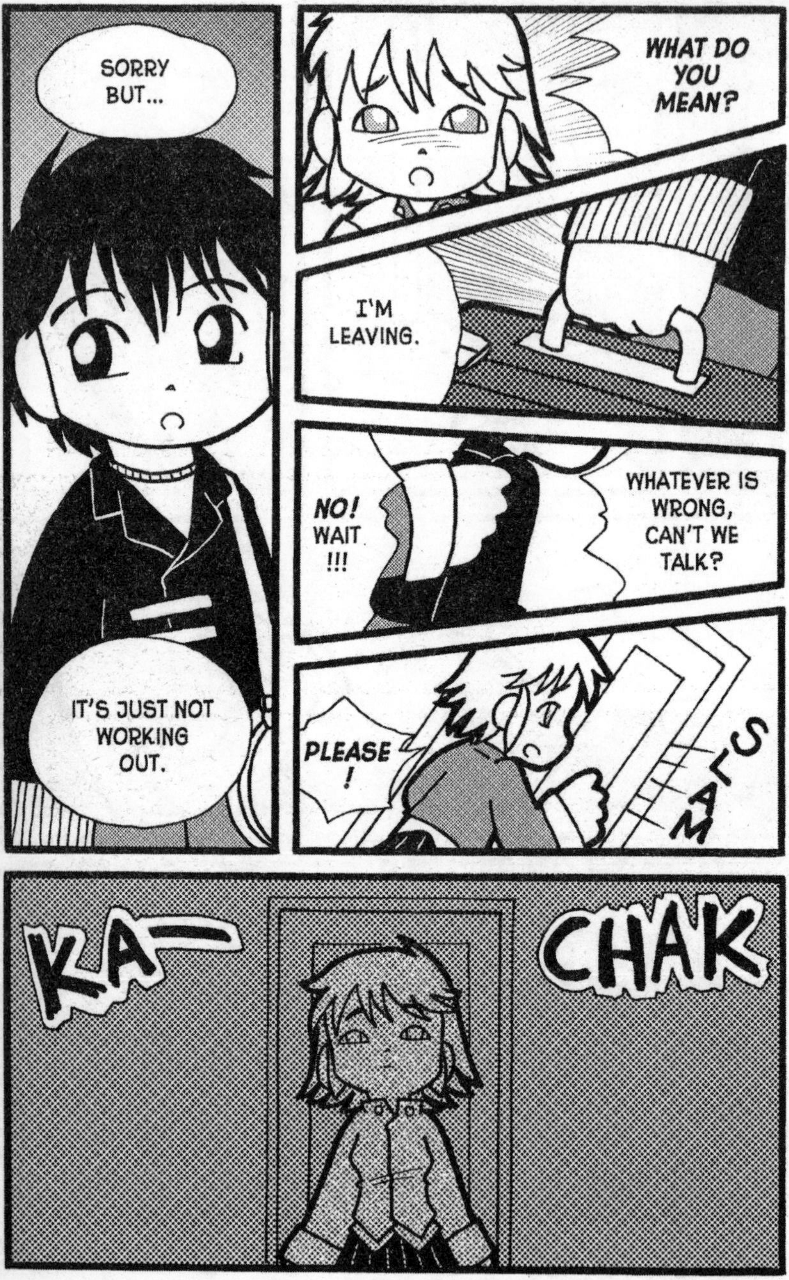
SORRY BUT...
IT'S JUST NOT WORKING OUT.
WHAT DO YOU MEAN?
I'M LEAVING.
NO! WAIT !!!
WHATEVER IS WRONG, CAN'T WE TALK?
PLEASE !
SLAM
KA— CHAK

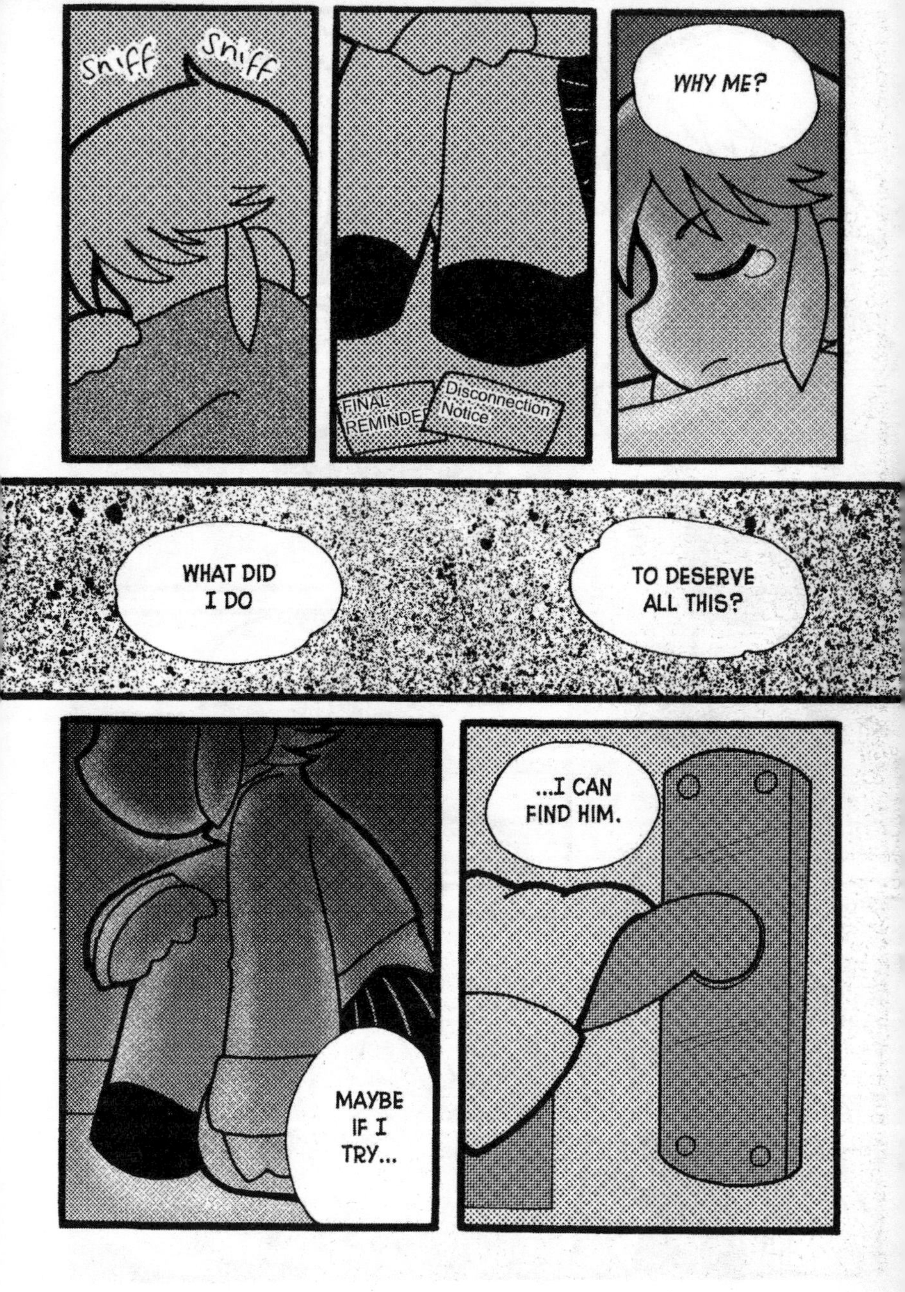
Sniff Sniff
FINAL REMINDE
Disconnection Notice
WHY ME?
WHAT DID I DO
TO DESERVE ALL THIS?
MAYBE IF I TRY...
...I CAN FIND HIM.

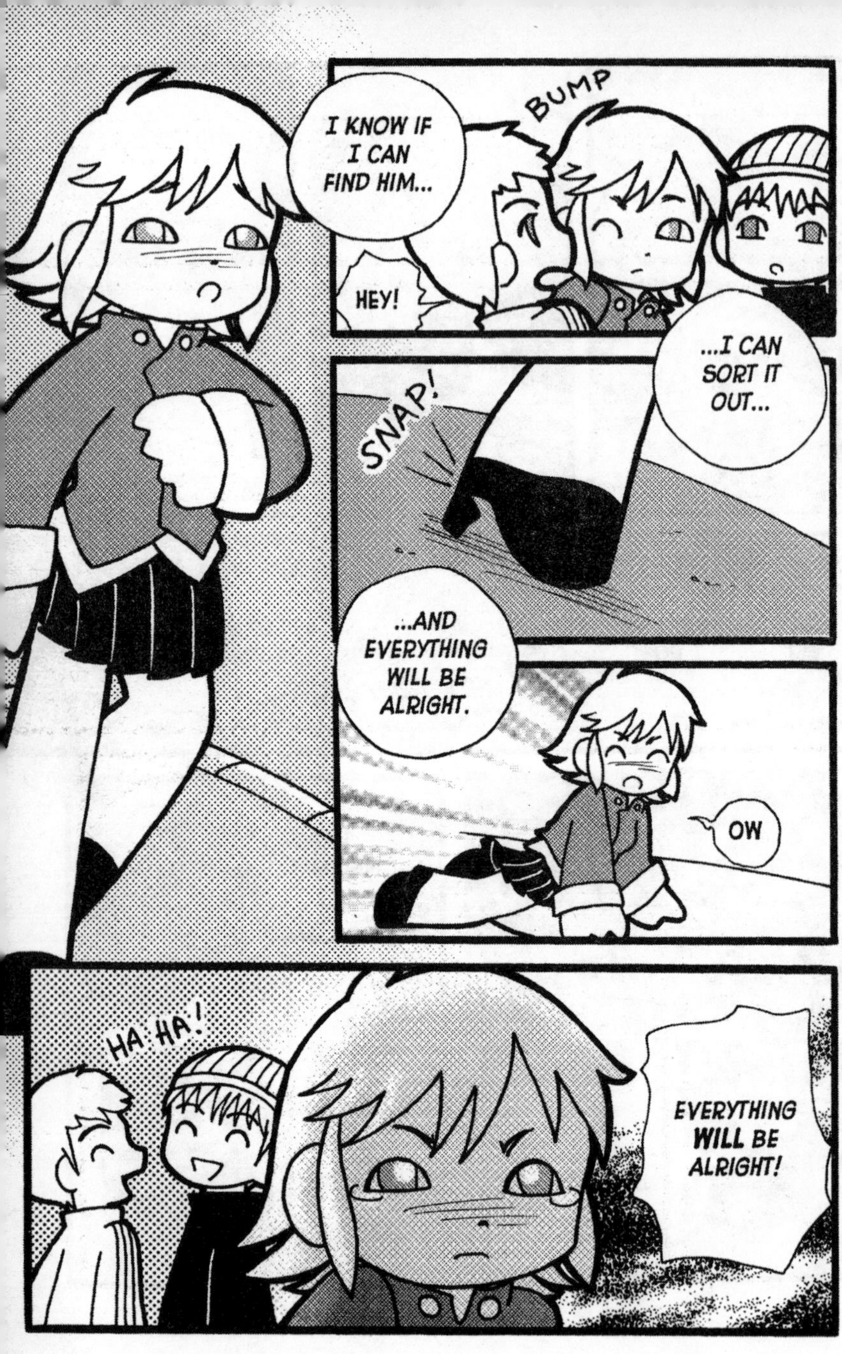
I KNOW IF I CAN FIND HIM...
BUMP
HEY!
...I CAN SORT IT OUT...
SNAP!
...AND EVERYTHING WILL BE ALRIGHT.
OW
HA HA!
EVERYTHING WILL BE ALRIGHT!

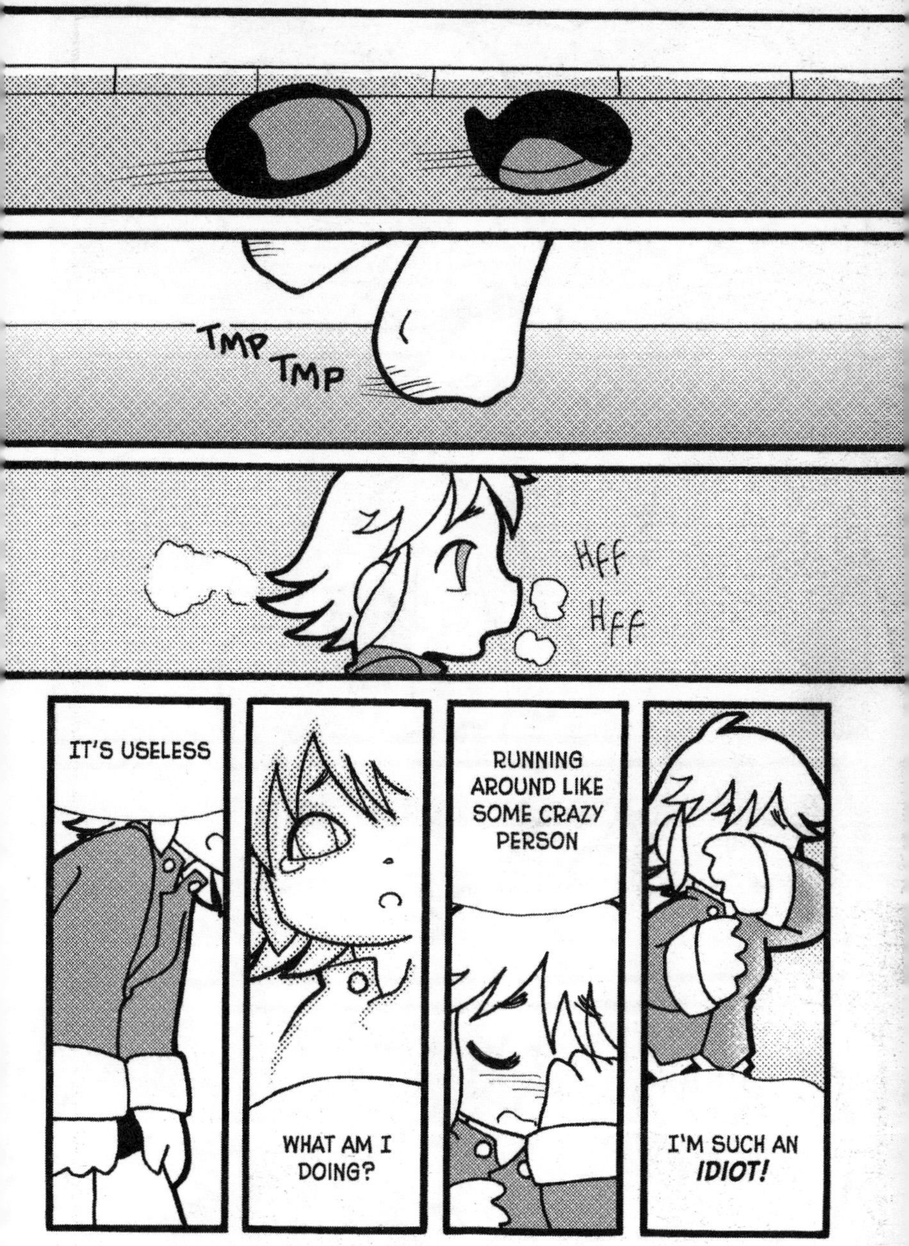
TMP TMP
Hff Hff
IT'S USELESS
WHAT AM I DOING?
RUNNING AROUND LIKE SOME CRAZY PERSON
I'M SUCH AN *IDIOT!*

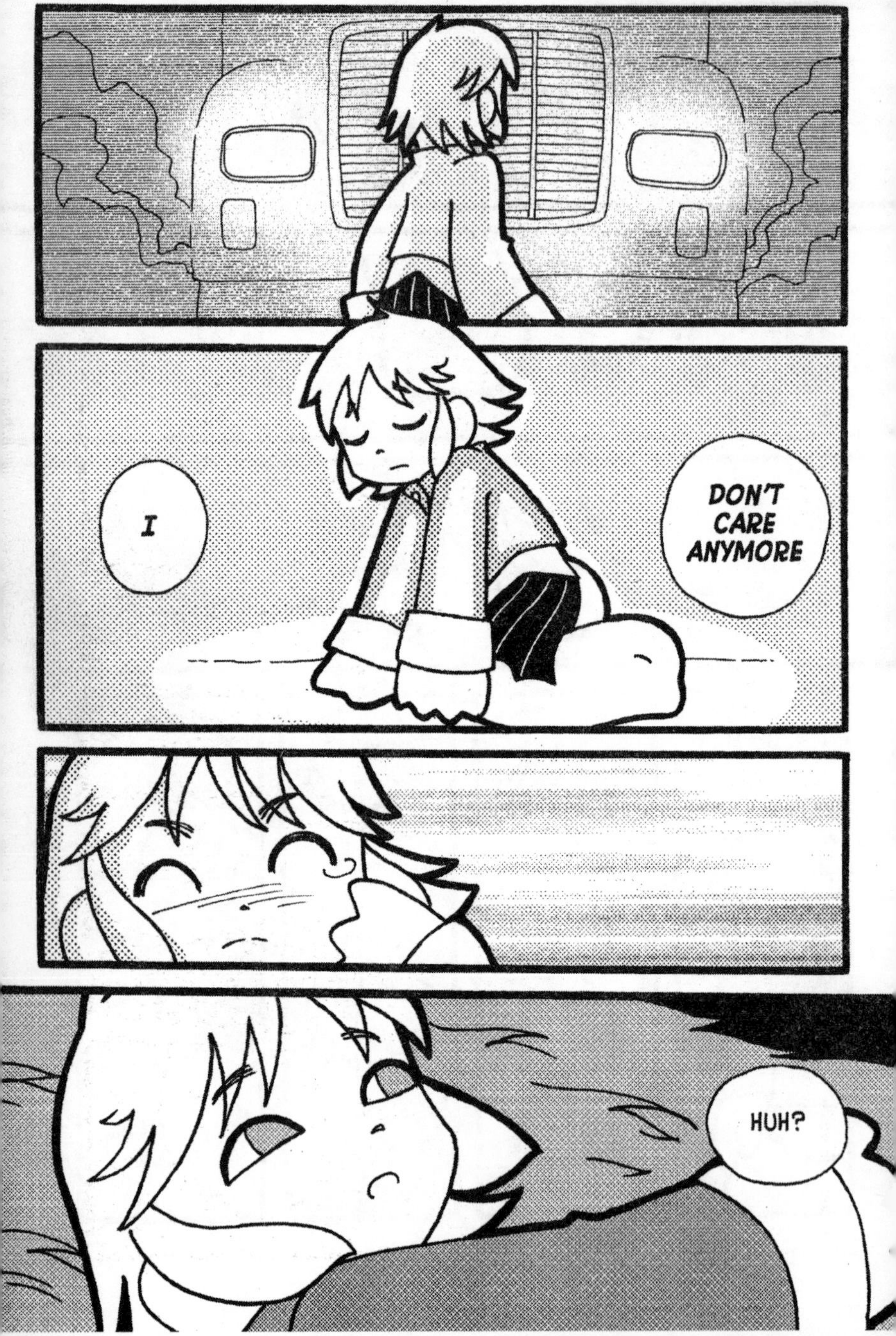
I
DON'T CARE ANYMORE
HUH?

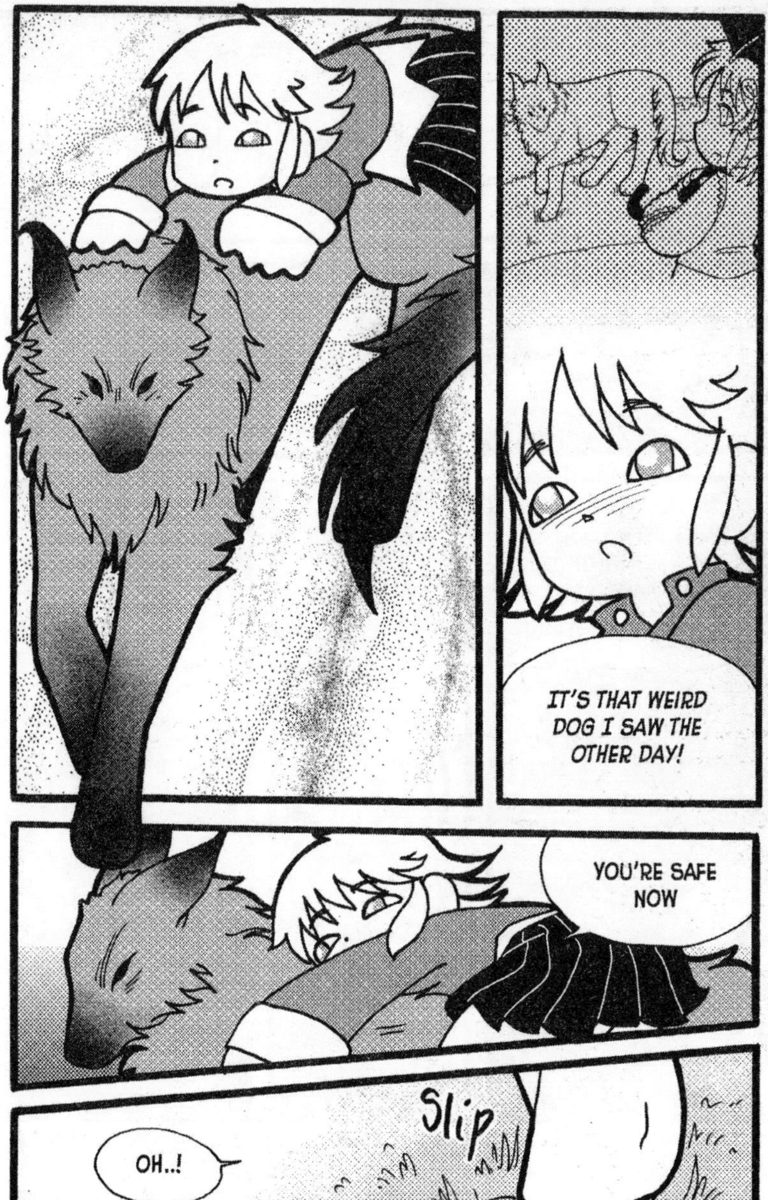
IT'S THAT WEIRD DOG I SAW THE OTHER DAY!
YOU'RE SAFE NOW
OH..!
Slip

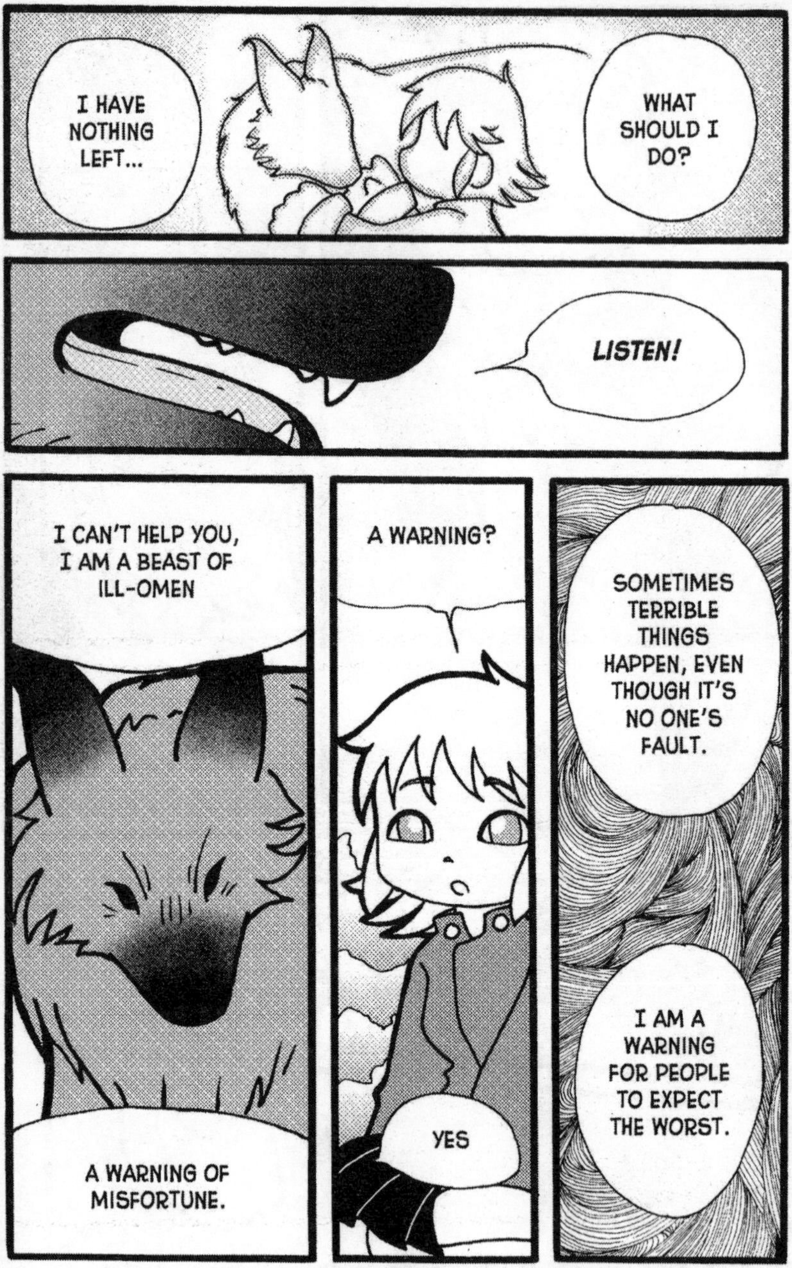
I HAVE NOTHING LEFT...
WHAT SHOULD I DO?
LISTEN!
I CAN'T HELP YOU, I AM A BEAST OF ILL-OMEN
A WARNING OF MISFORTUNE.
A WARNING?
YES
SOMETIMES TERRIBLE THINGS HAPPEN, EVEN THOUGH IT'S NO ONE'S FAULT.
I AM A WARNING FOR PEOPLE TO EXPECT THE WORST.

BUT CAN'T YOU DO *ANYTHING* ABOUT IT?

YOU HELPED ME JUST NOW, AFTER ALL!

TWITCH

TWITCH

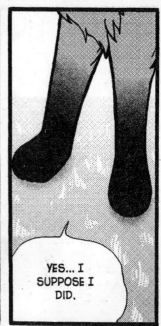

YES... I SUPPOSE I DID.

BUT ONCE ISN'T ENOUGH. IF ONLY IT WERE SO SIMPLE.

YOUR *BAD LUCK* WILL CATCH UP WITH YOU EVENTUALLY.

UNLESS...

IF YOU STAY WITH ME, I WILL PROTECT YOU.

PERHAPS YOUR LUCK WILL CHANGE.

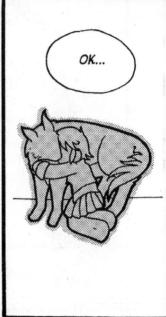

OK...

SOMETIMES, LATE AT NIGHT, YOU MIGHT SEE A STRANGE GIRL WITH A STRANGE DOG...

...BUT ONLY IF YOU'RE REALLY UNLUCKY.

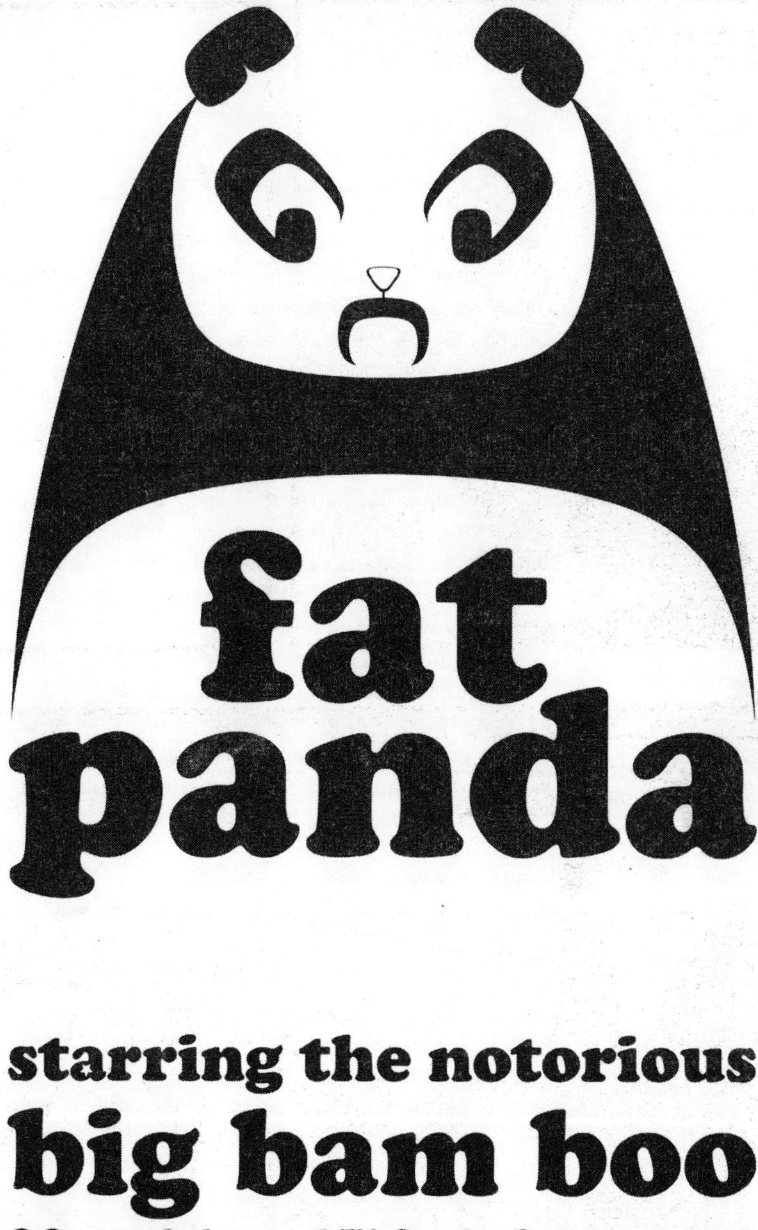

fat panda

starring the notorious big bam boo

Date of birth: 22 May 1971

CRAIG CONLAN

Craig is Scottish, but emigrated to London a long time ago. He lists an enormous number of names he considers influential on his life and work: Osama Tezuka, Hiroyuki Takei, Aya Takano, Taiyo Matsumoto, Junko Mizuno (again!), Jamie Hewlett, Jaime Hernandez, John Waters, Grant Morrison, Brendan McCarthy and, uh, Frankenstein. Kirsten Ulve is just about his favourite illustrator.

Craig is filled with great ideas for both characters and stories – just poke him and one pops out. '**Fat Panda** is about someone concerned with their size. As obesity levels balloon in the West, more people than ever will identify with Big Bam Boo's attempts to reach his "ideal weight". Join Boo on a journey full of cabbage soup lunches, overpriced carb-free chocolate and a string of lapsed gym memberships." Craig hopes what worked for diet gurus Gillian McKeith and Dr Atkins will work for him – a book on dieting may not help anyone get thinner, but he can get fat on the proceeds!

Want to see more?
http://www.craigconlan.com 'will show you the way'.
http://www.kirstenulve.com

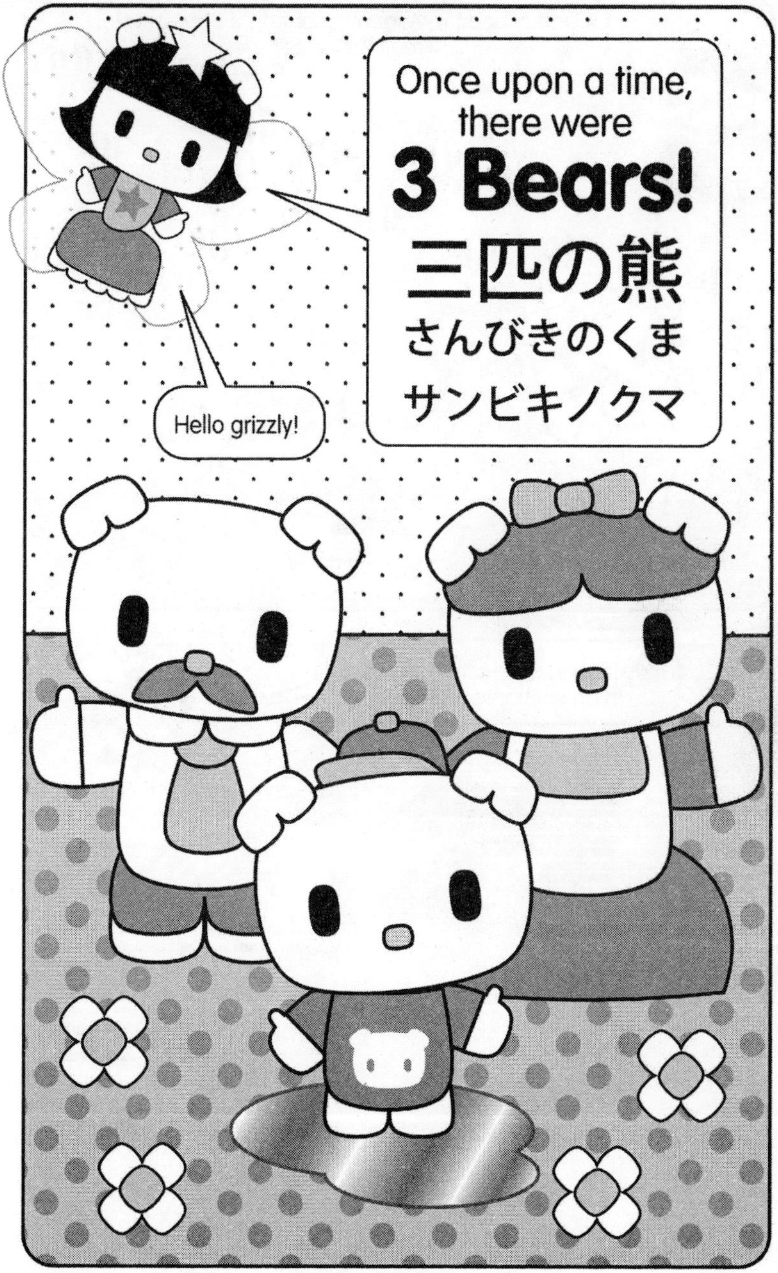
Once upon a time, there were
3 Bears!
三匹の熊
さんびきのくま
サンビキノクマ
Hello grizzly!

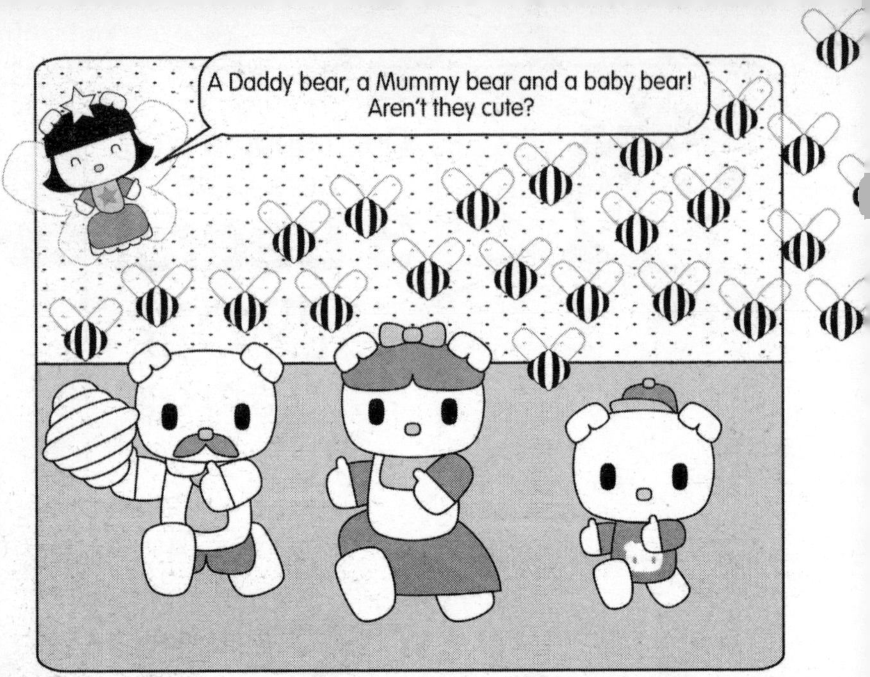
A Daddy bear, a Mummy bear and a baby bear! Aren't they cute?

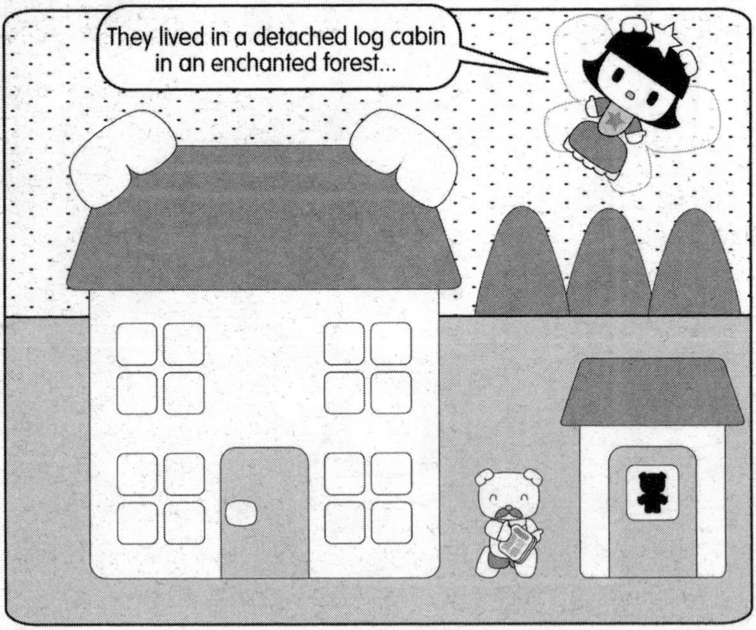
They lived in a detached log cabin in an enchanted forest...

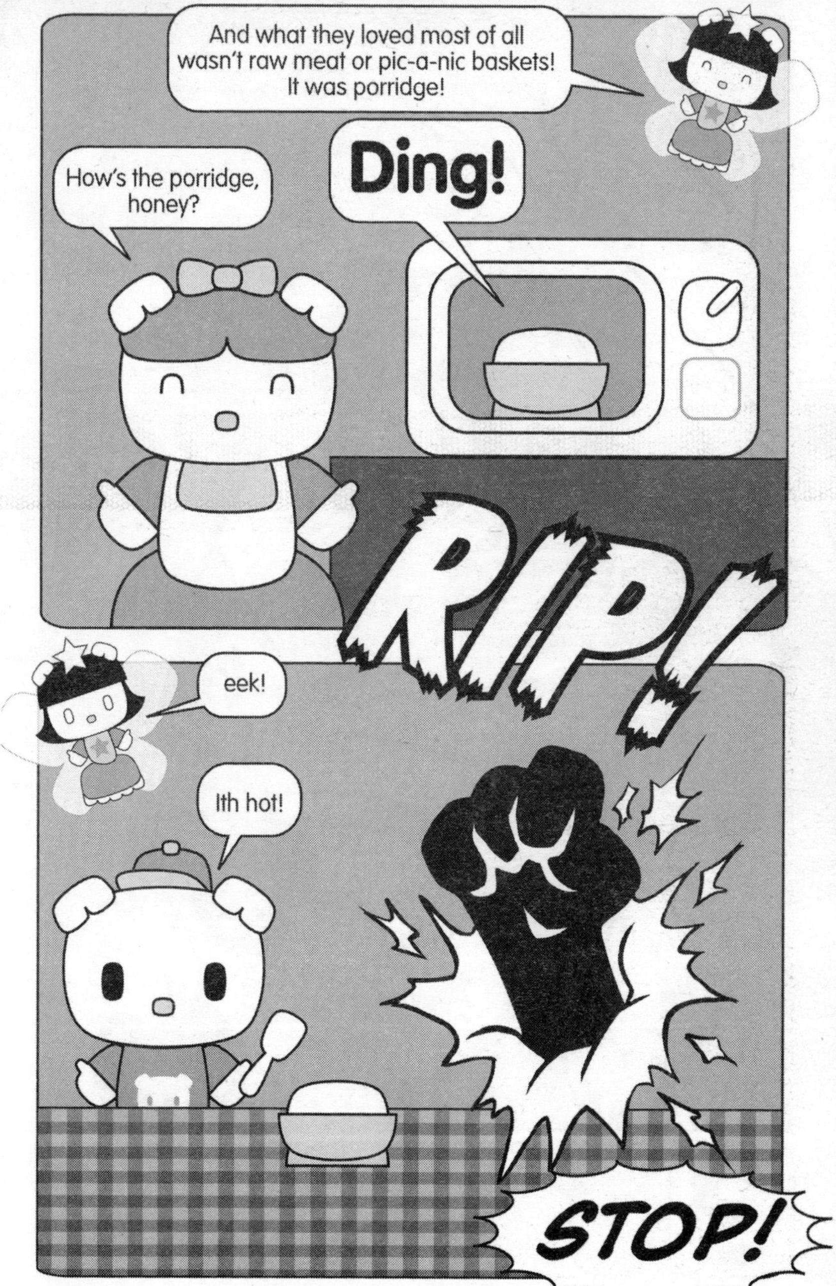
And what they loved most of all wasn't raw meat or pic-a-nic baskets! It was porridge!
How's the porridge, honey?
Ding!
RIP!
eek!
Ith hot!
STOP!

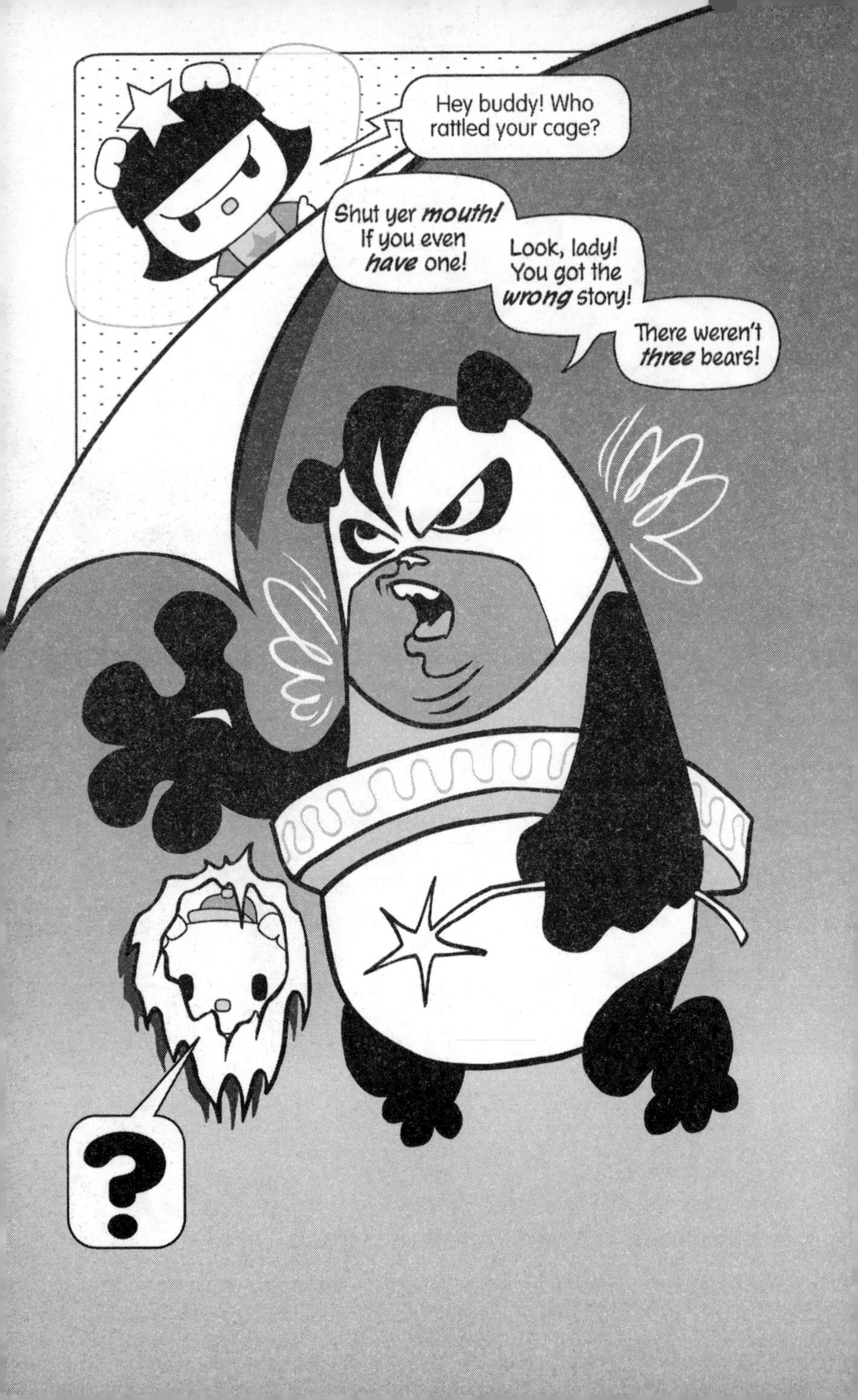
Hey buddy! Who rattled your cage?
Shut yer *mouth!* If you even *have* one!
Look, lady! You got the *wrong* story!
There weren't *three* bears!
?

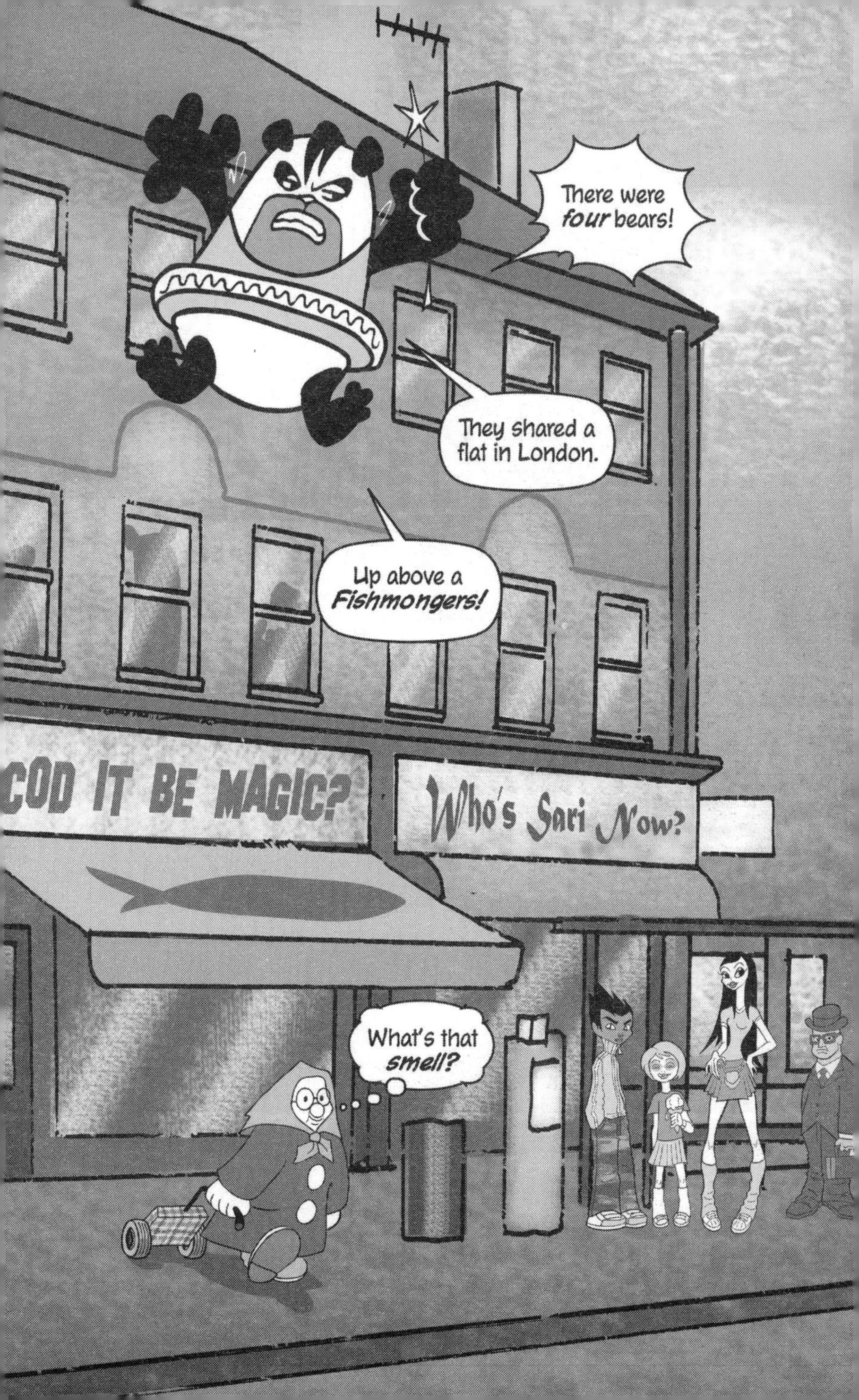
There were *four* bears!
They shared a flat in London.
Up above a *Fishmongers!*
COD IT BE MAGIC?
Who's Sari Now?
What's that *smell?*

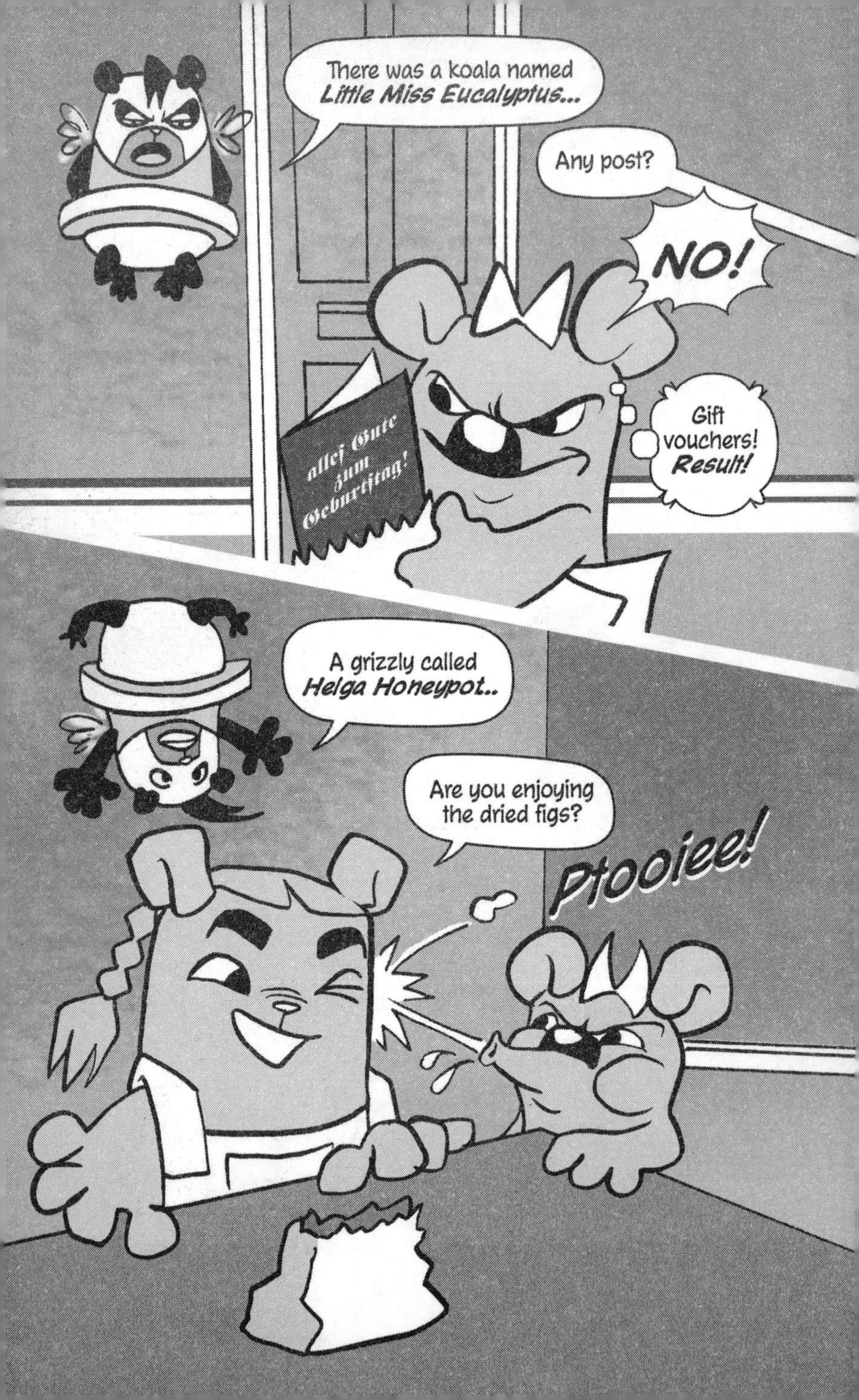
There was a koala named *Little Miss Eucalyptus...*
Any post?
NO!
alleſ Gute zum Geburtſtag!
Gift vouchers! *Result!*
A grizzly called *Helga Honeypot..*
Are you enjoying the dried figs?
Ptooiee!

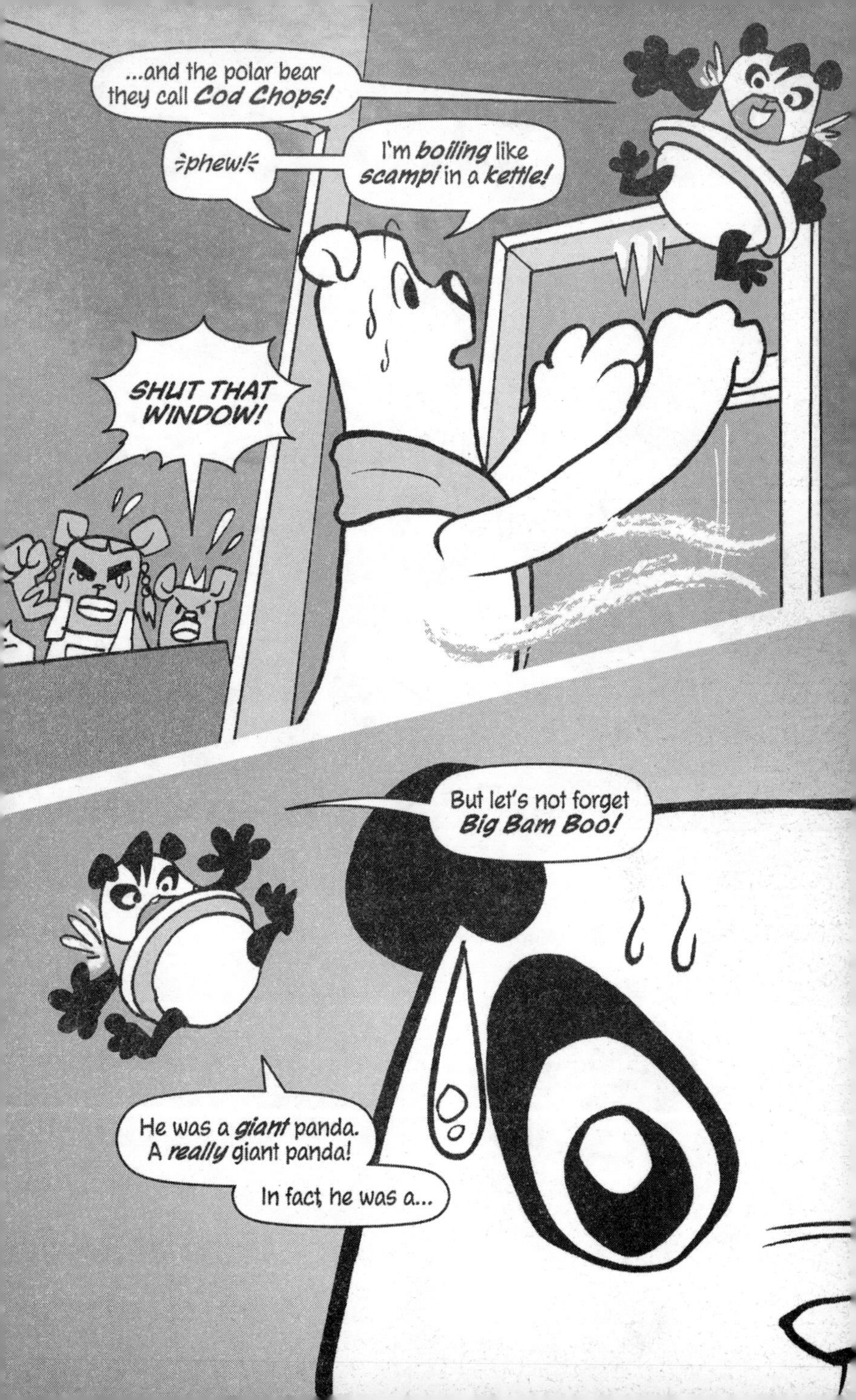
...and the polar bear they call Cod Chops!
phew!
I'm boiling like scampi in a kettle!
SHUT THAT WINDOW!
But let's not forget Big Bam Boo!
He was a giant panda. A really giant panda!
In fact, he was a...

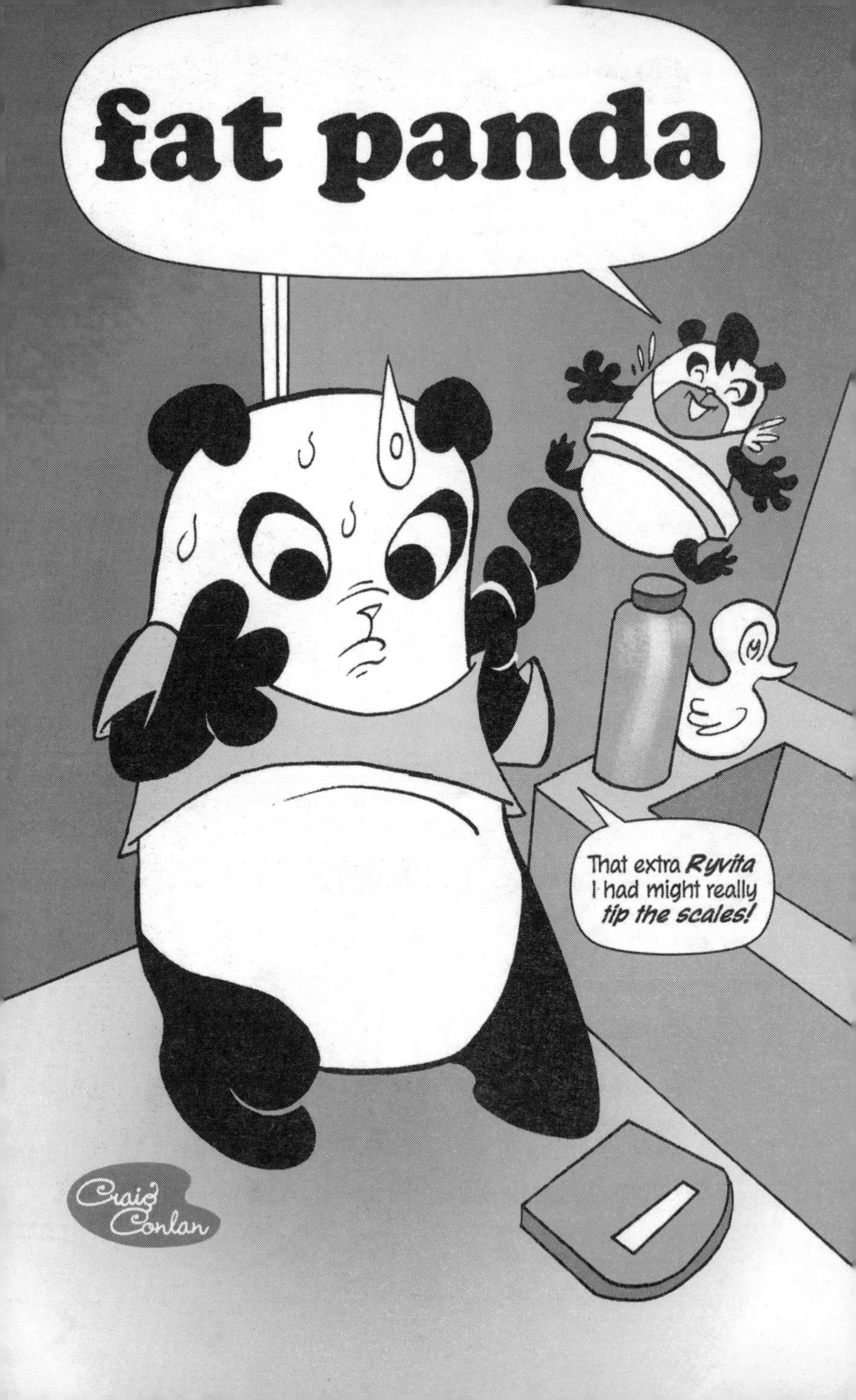
fat panda
That extra *Ryvita* I had might really *tip the scales!*
Craig Conlan

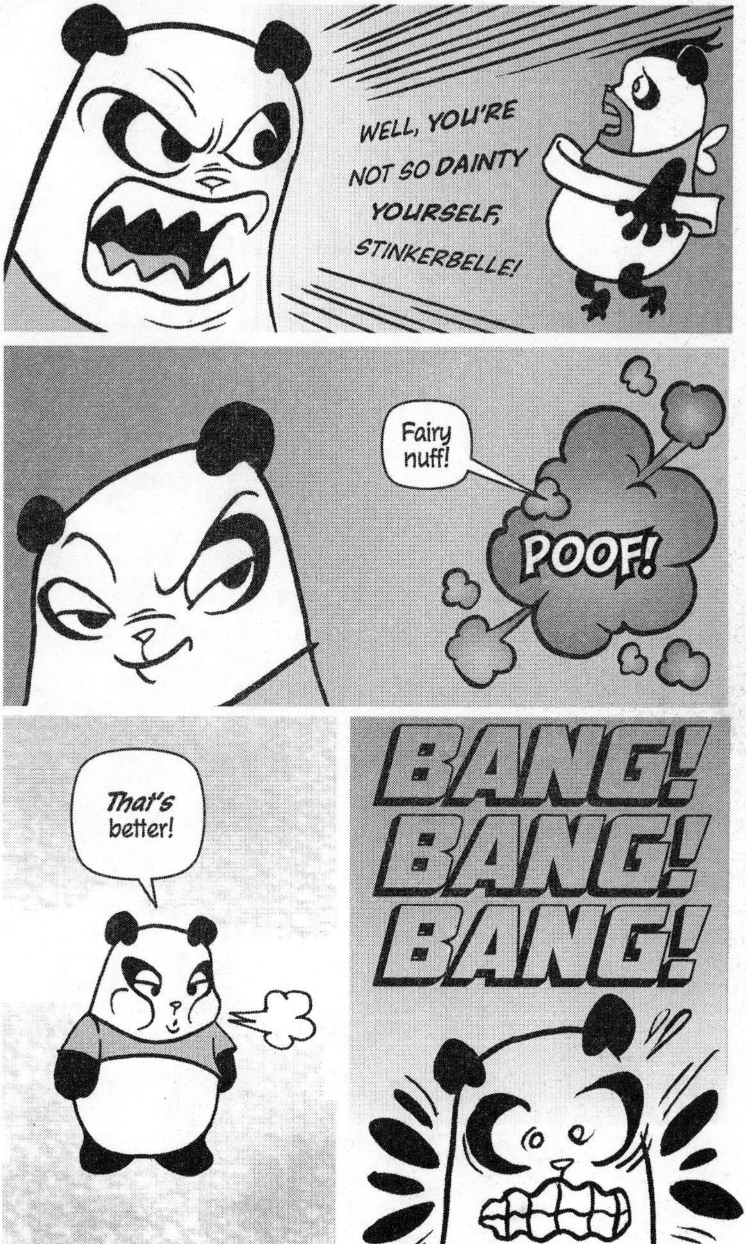
WELL, YOU'RE NOT SO DAINTY YOURSELF, STINKERBELLE!
Fairy nuff!
POOF!
That's better!
BANG! BANG! BANG!

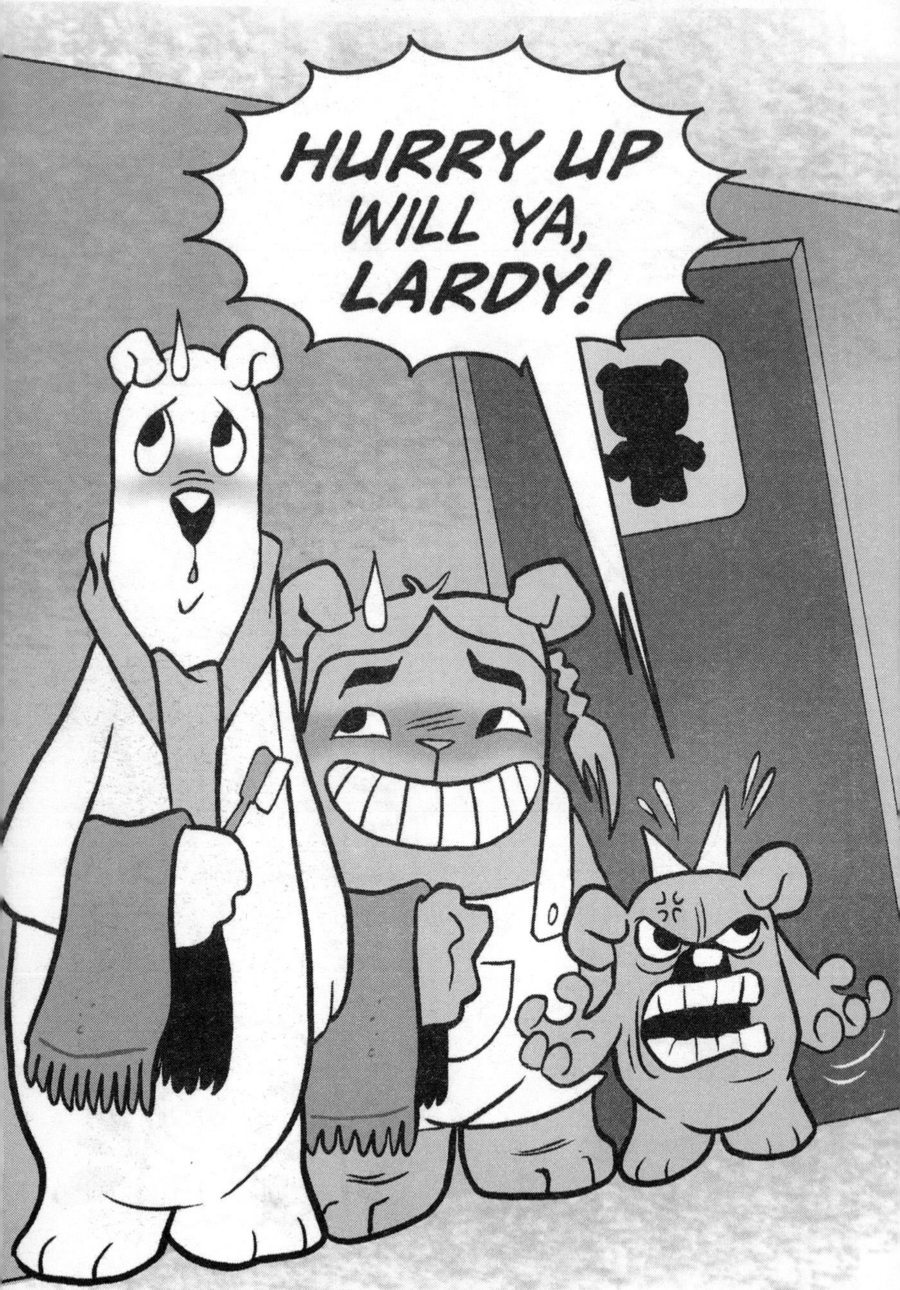
HURRY UP WILL YA, LARDY!

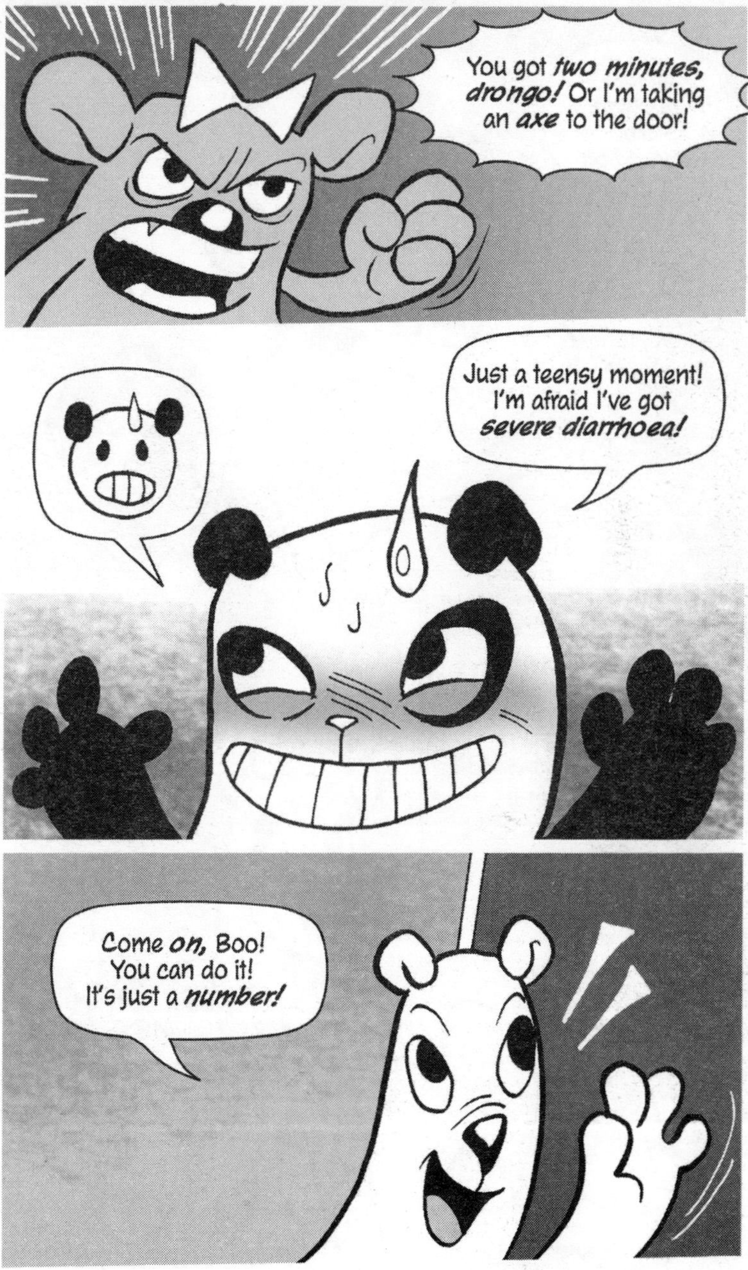
You got *two minutes, drongo!* Or I'm taking an *axe* to the door!
Just a teensy moment! I'm afraid I've got *severe diarrhoea!*
Come *on,* Boo! You can do it! It's just a *number!*

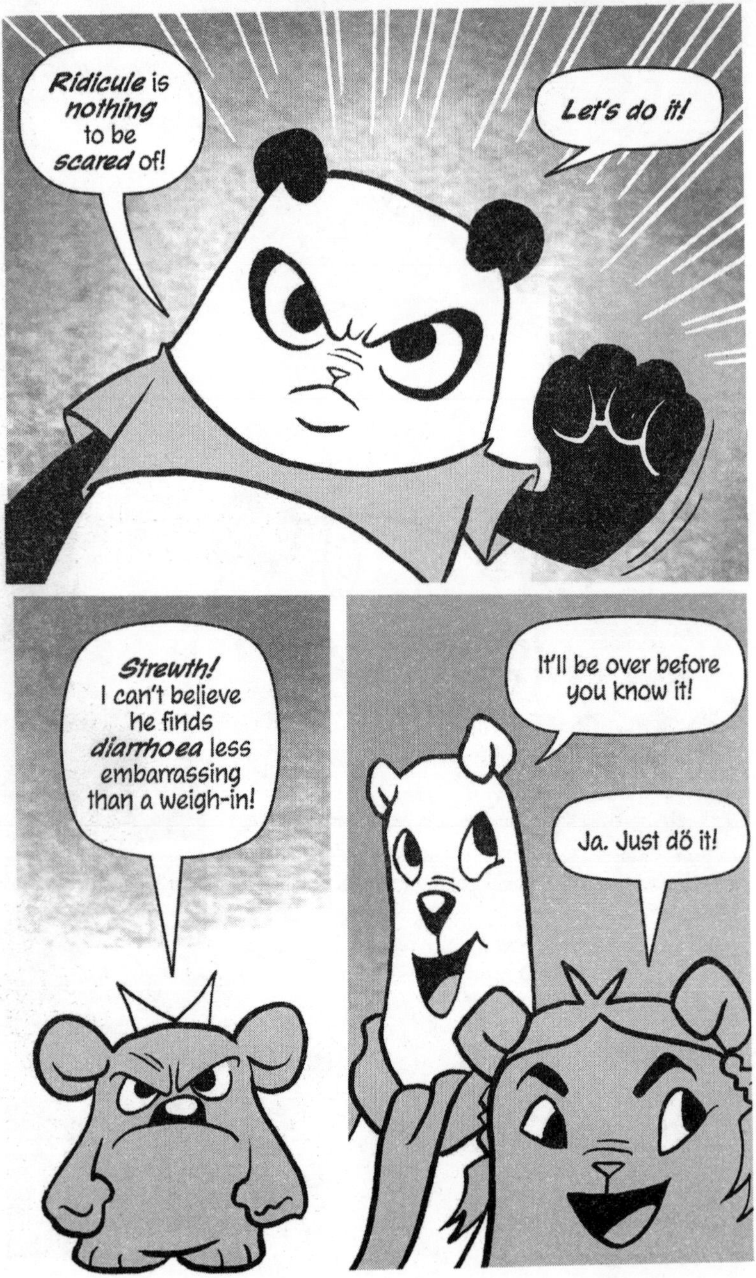
Ridicule is *nothing* to be *scared* of!
Let's do it!
Strewth! I can't believe he finds *diarrhoea* less embarrassing than a weigh-in!
It'll be over before you know it!
Ja. Just dö it!

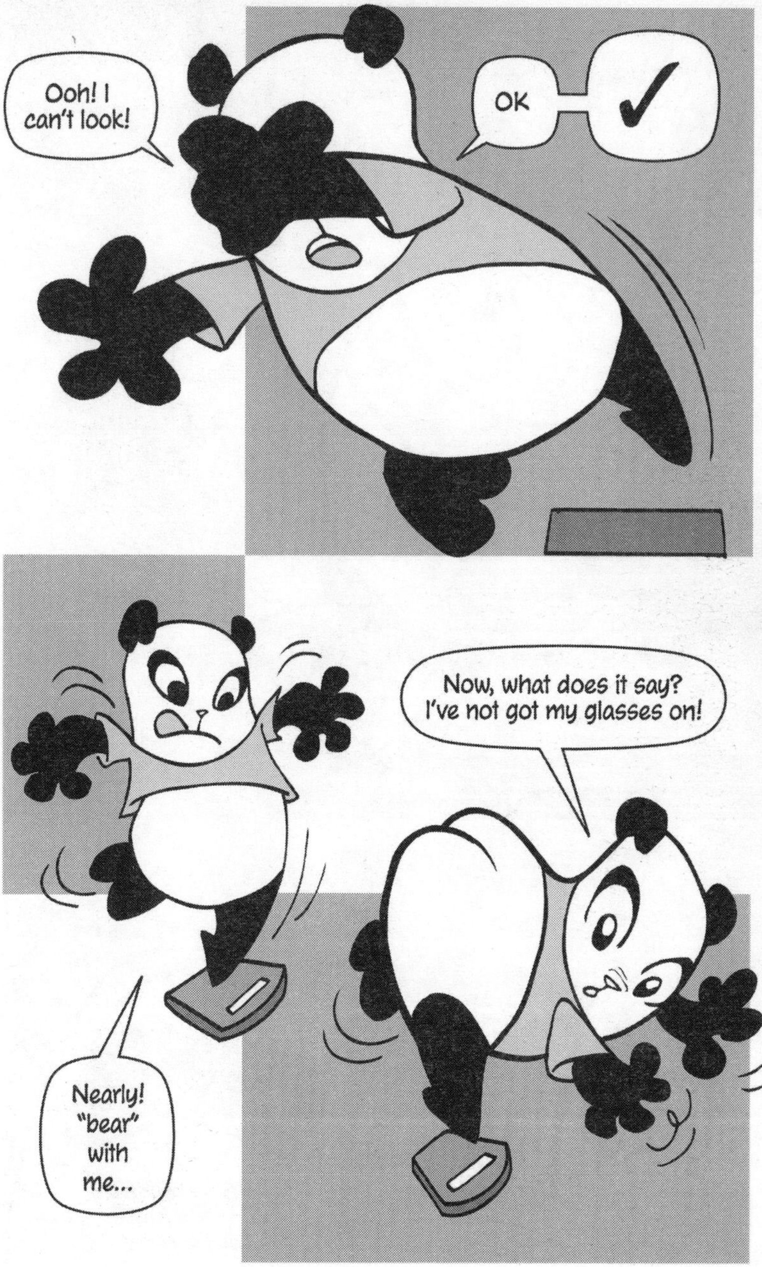
Ooh! I can't look!
OK
Nearly! "bear" with me...
Now, what does it say? I've not got my glasses on!

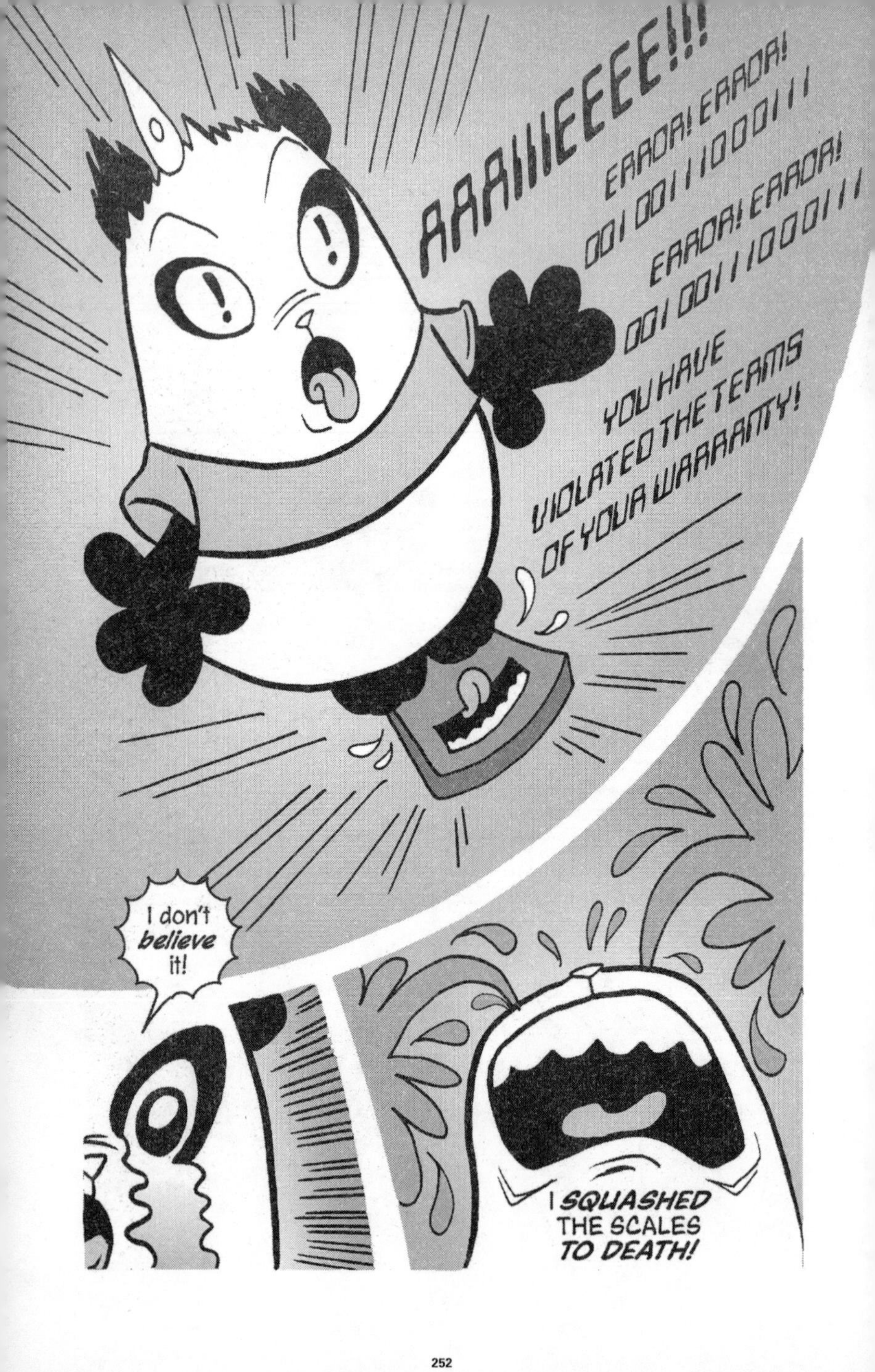
AAAIIIEEEE!!!
ERROR! ERROR! 001 001 1 1 0 0 0 1 1 1
ERROR! ERROR! 001 001 1 1 0 0 0 1 1 1
YOU HAVE VIOLATED THE TERMS OF YOUR WARRANTY!
I don't *believe* it!
I ***SQUASHED*** THE SCALES ***TO DEATH!***

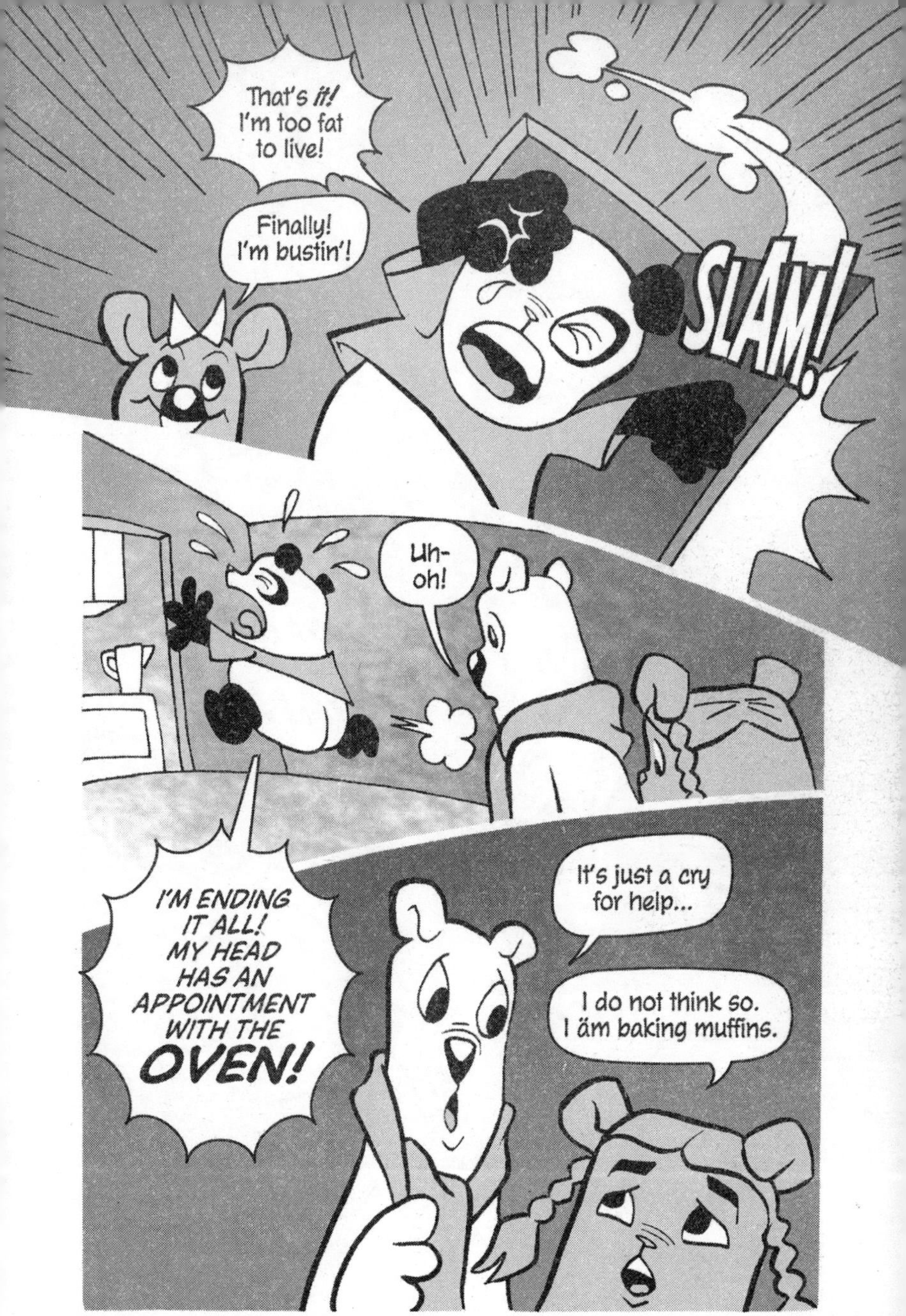
That's *it!* I'm too fat to live!
Finally! I'm bustin'!
SLAM!
Uh-oh!
I'M ENDING IT ALL! MY HEAD HAS AN APPOINTMENT WITH THE **OVEN!**
It's just a cry for help...
I do not think so. I äm baking muffins.

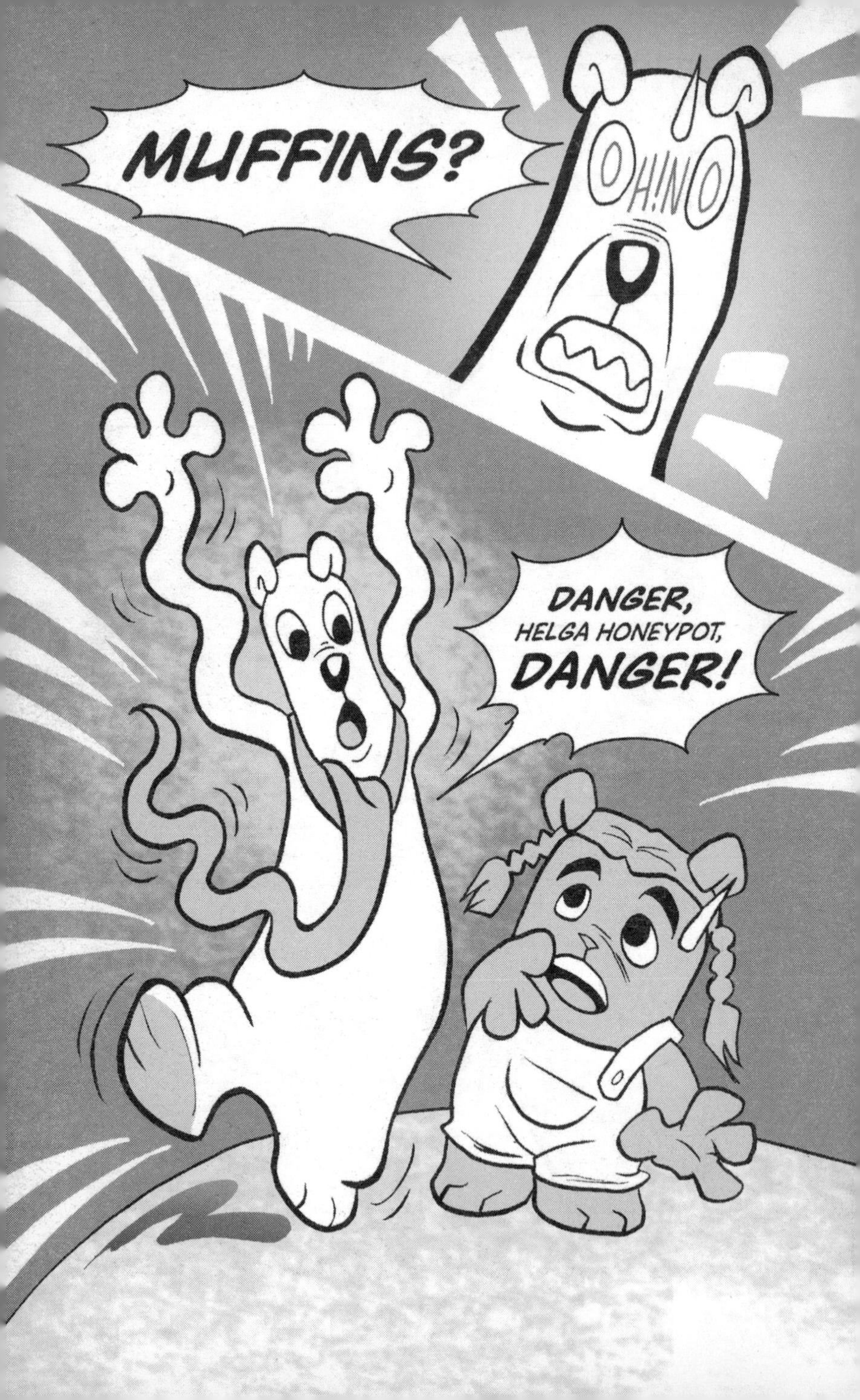
MUFFINS?
OH!NO
DANGER, HELGA HONEYPOT, DANGER!

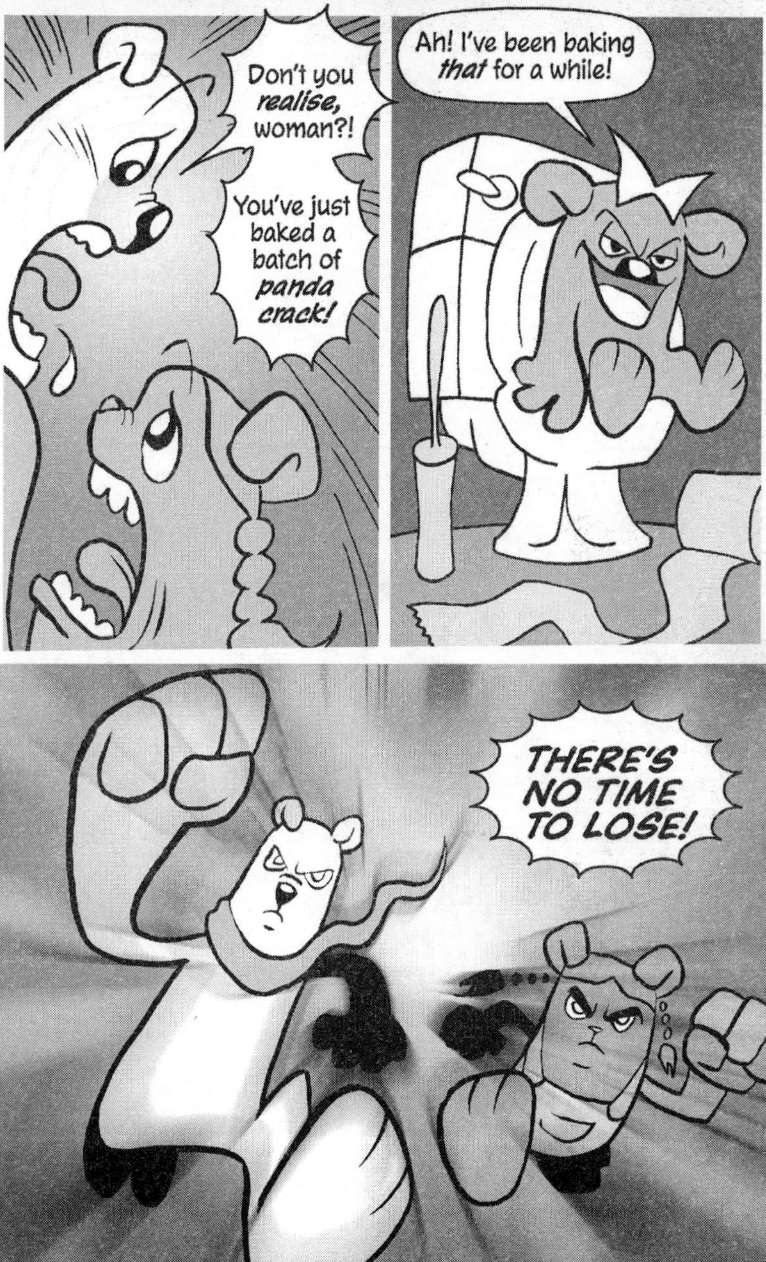
Don't you *realise,* woman?!
You've just baked a batch of *panda crack!*
Ah! I've been baking *that* for a while!
THERE'S NO TIME TO LOSE!

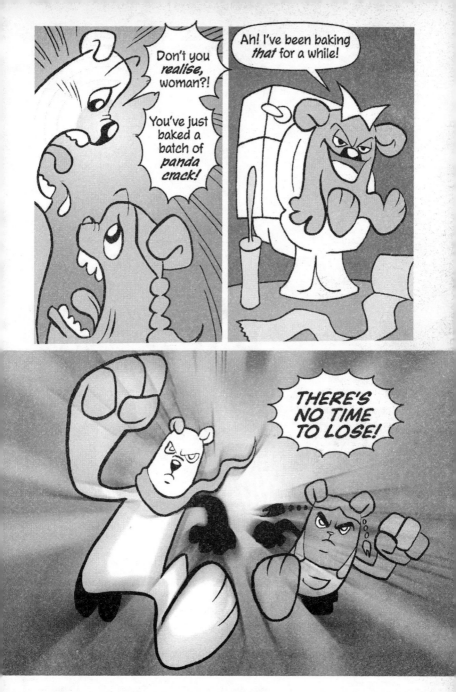

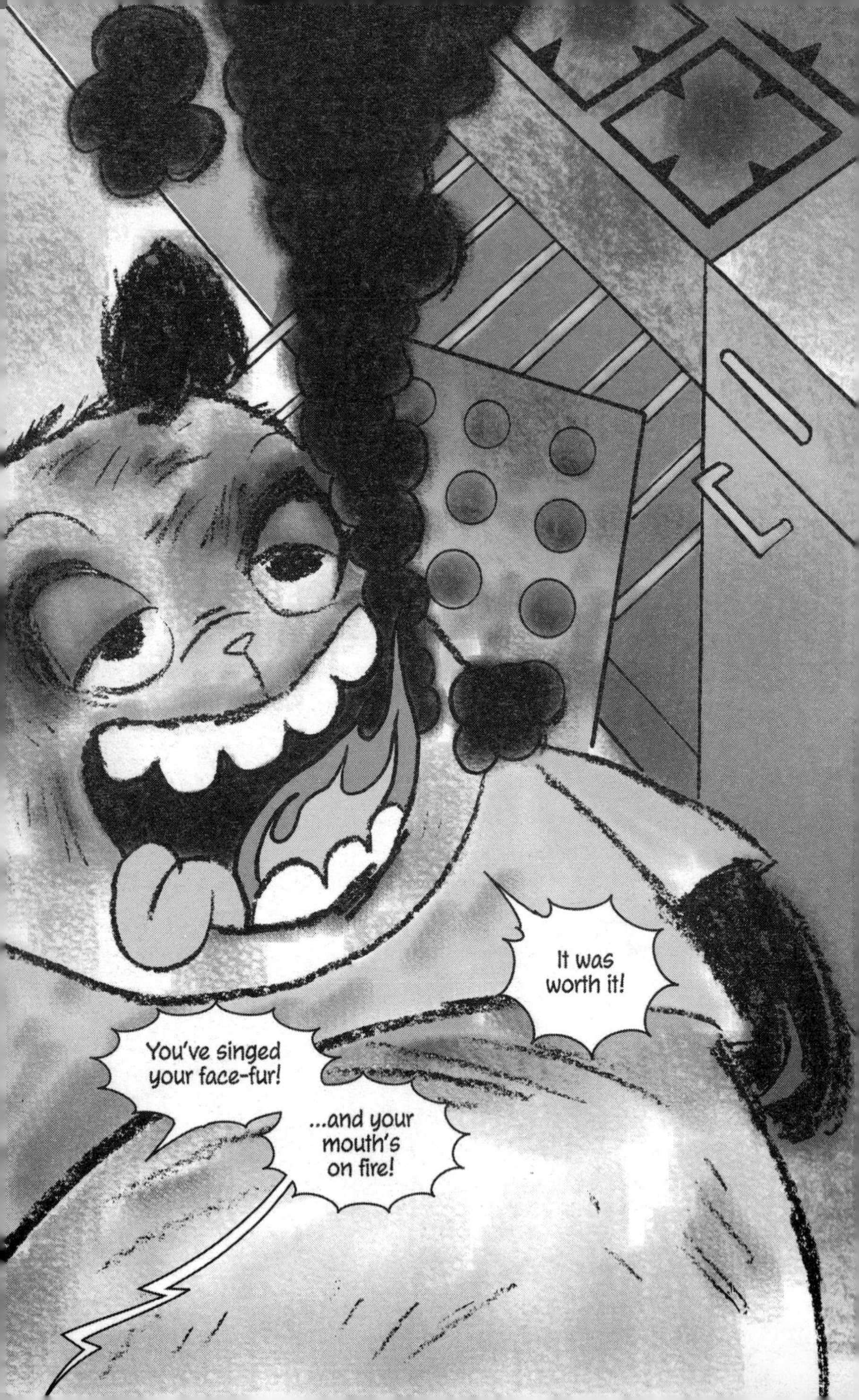

It was worth it!
You've singed your face-fur!
...and your mouth's on fire!

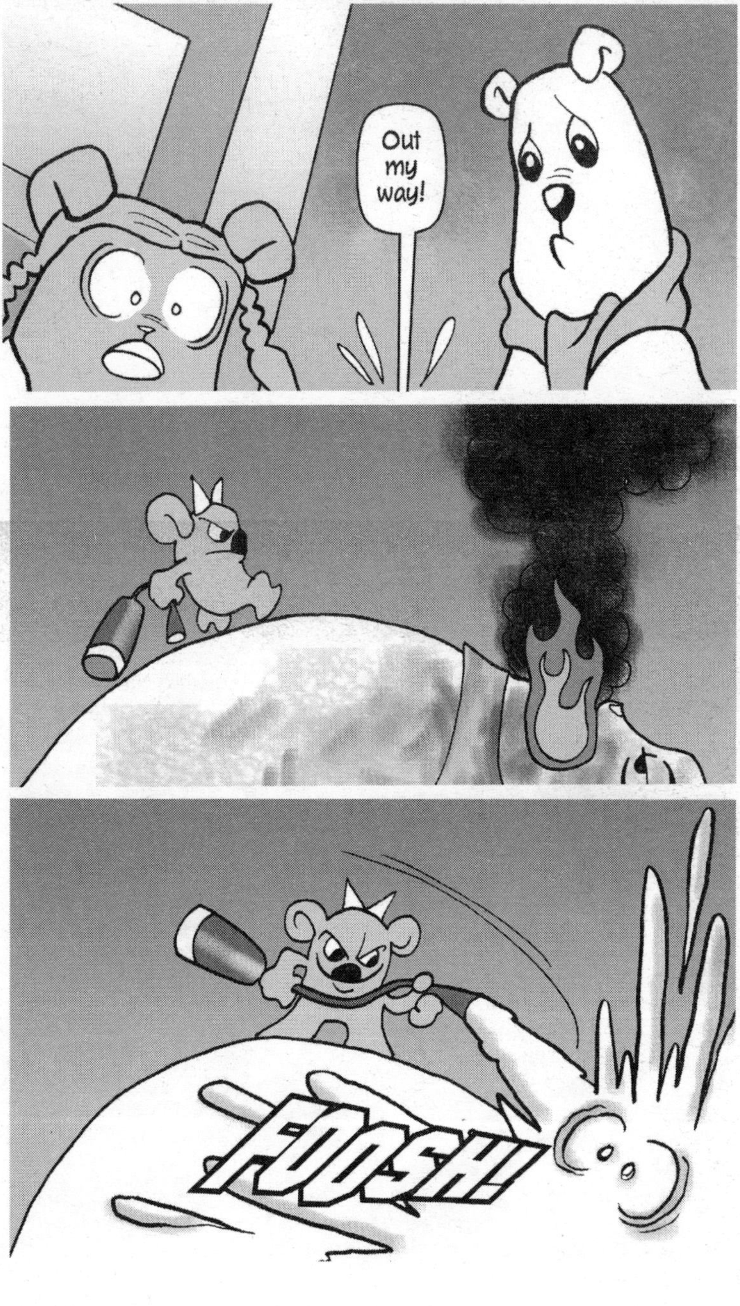
Out my way!
FOOSH!

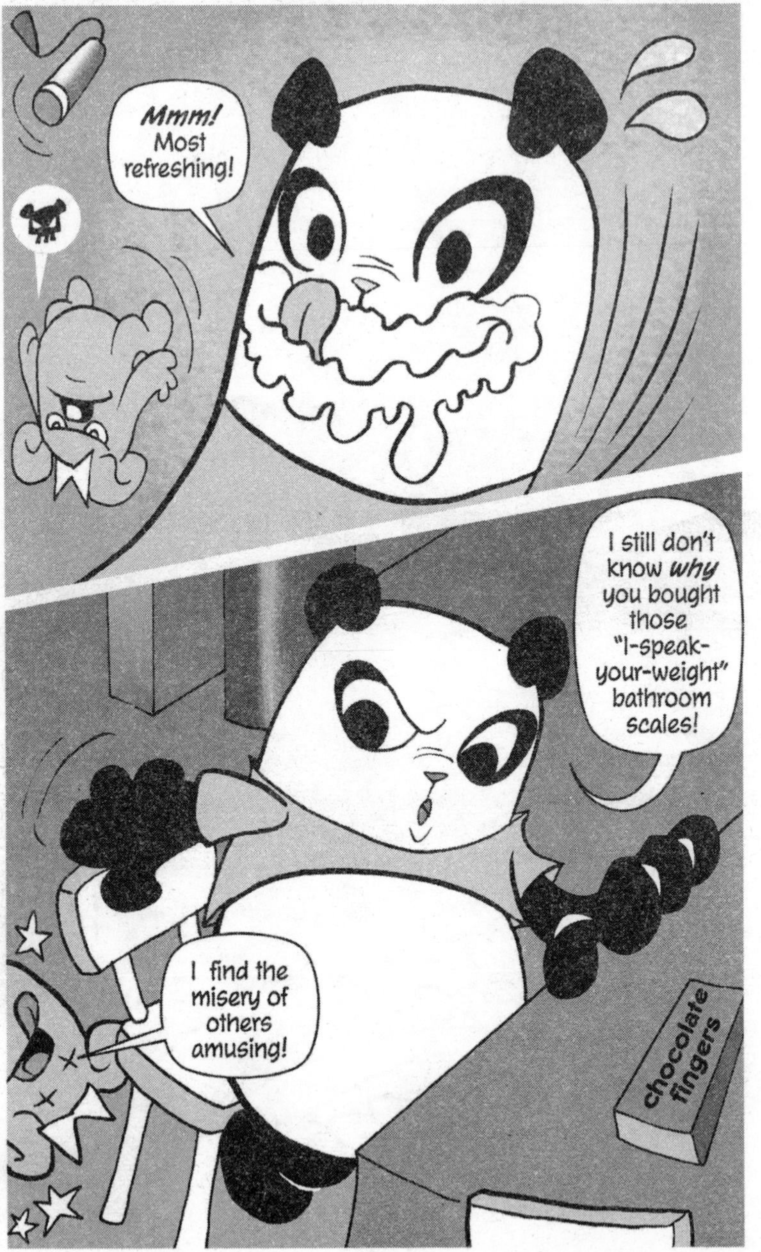

Mmm! Most refreshing!
I still don't know *why* you bought those "I-speak-your-weight" bathroom scales!
I find the misery of others amusing!
chocolate fingers

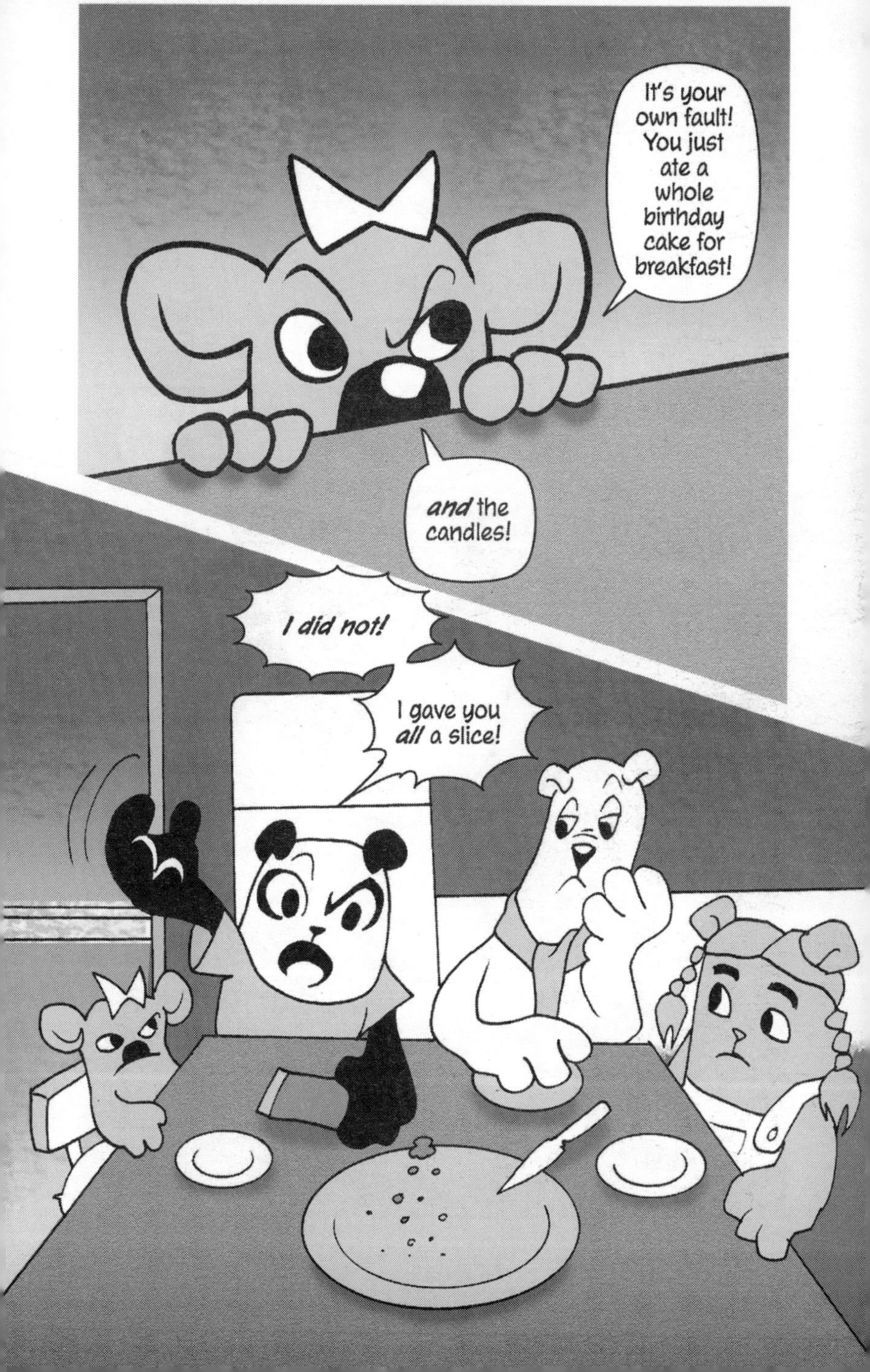
It's your own fault! You just ate a whole birthday cake for breakfast!
and the candles!
I did not!
I gave you *all* a slice!

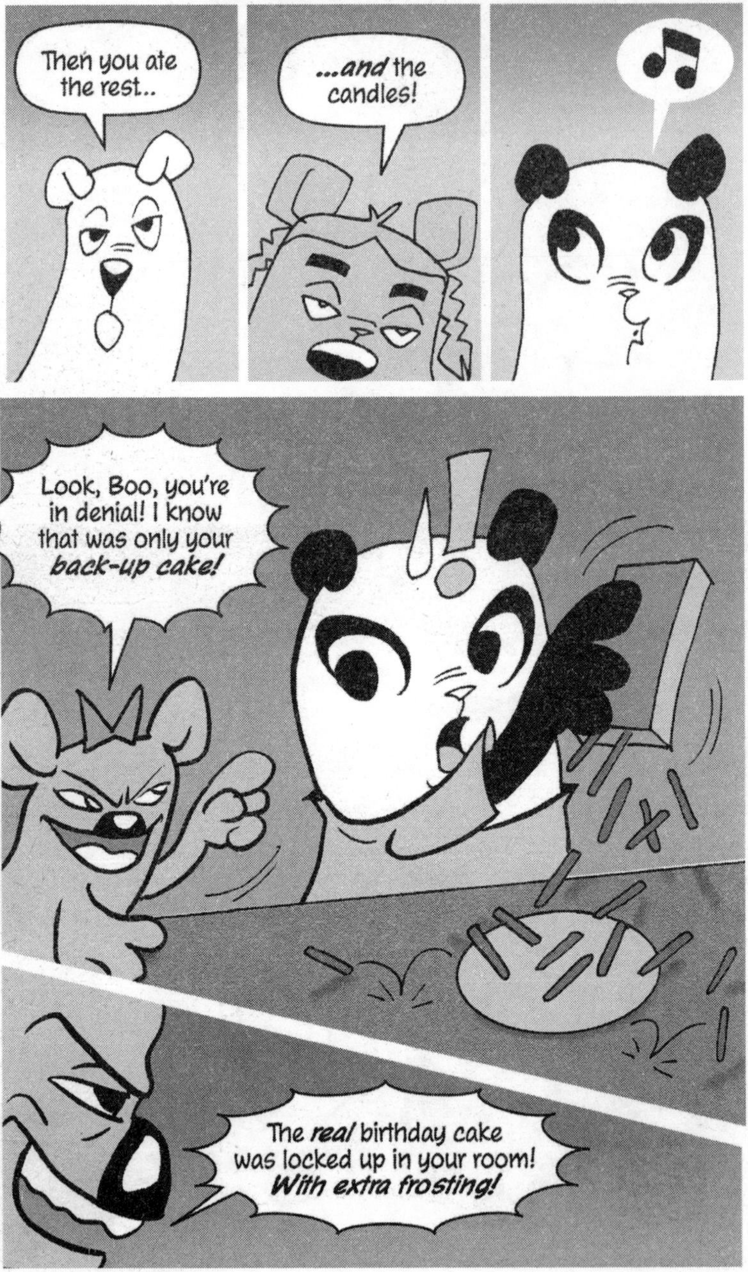
Then you ate the rest..
...*and* the candles!
♫
Look, Boo, you're in denial! I know that was only your *back-up cake!*
The *real* birthday cake was locked up in your room! *With extra frosting!*

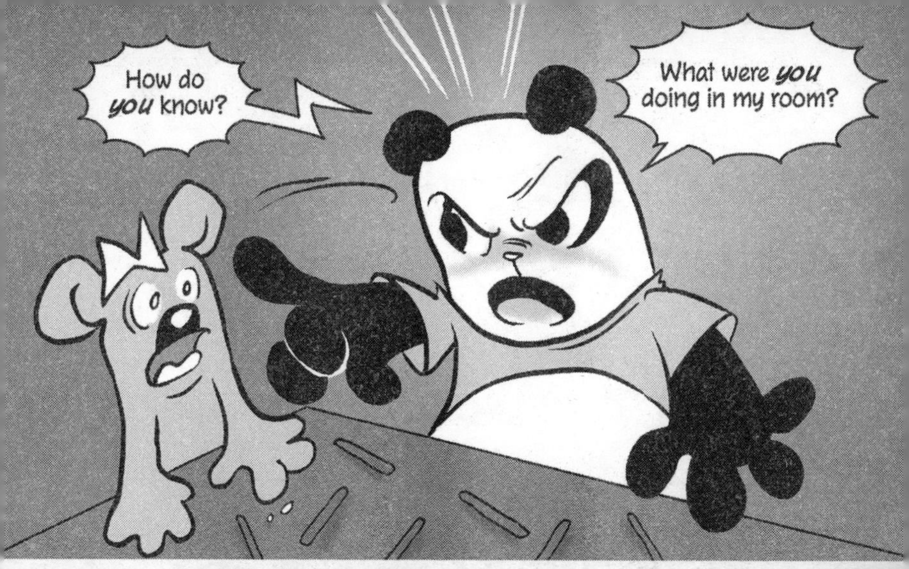
How do *you* know?
What were *you* doing in my room?
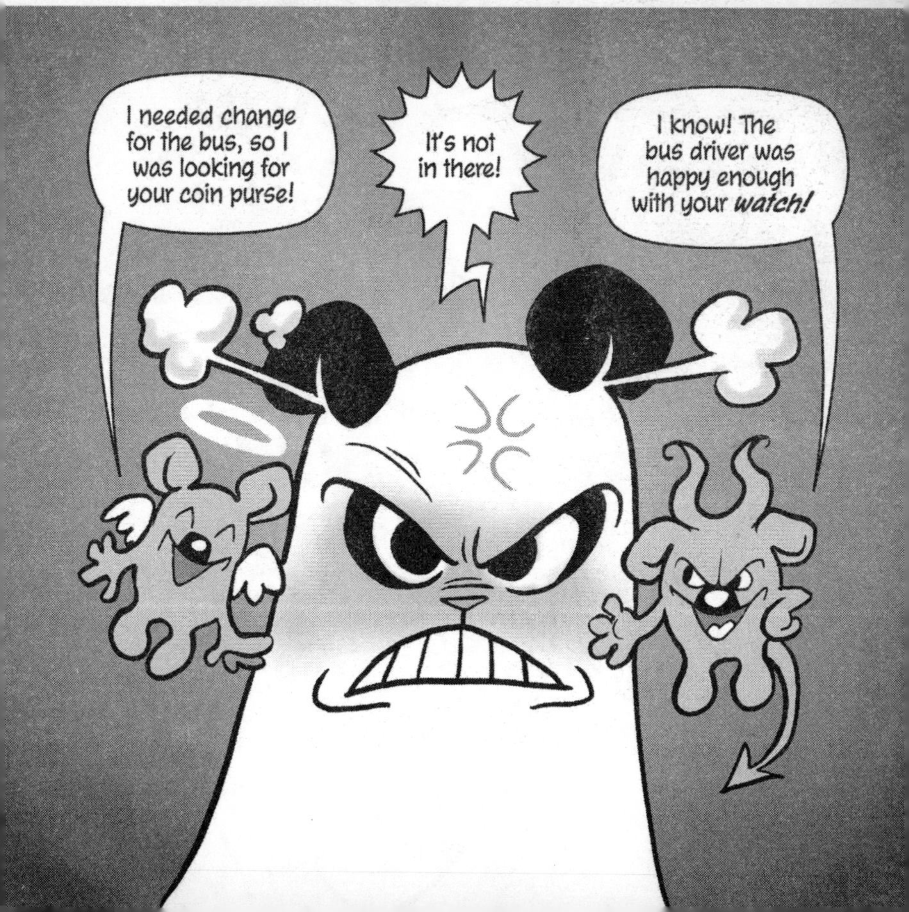
I needed change for the bus, so I was looking for your coin purse!
It's not in there!
I know! The bus driver was happy enough with your *watch!*

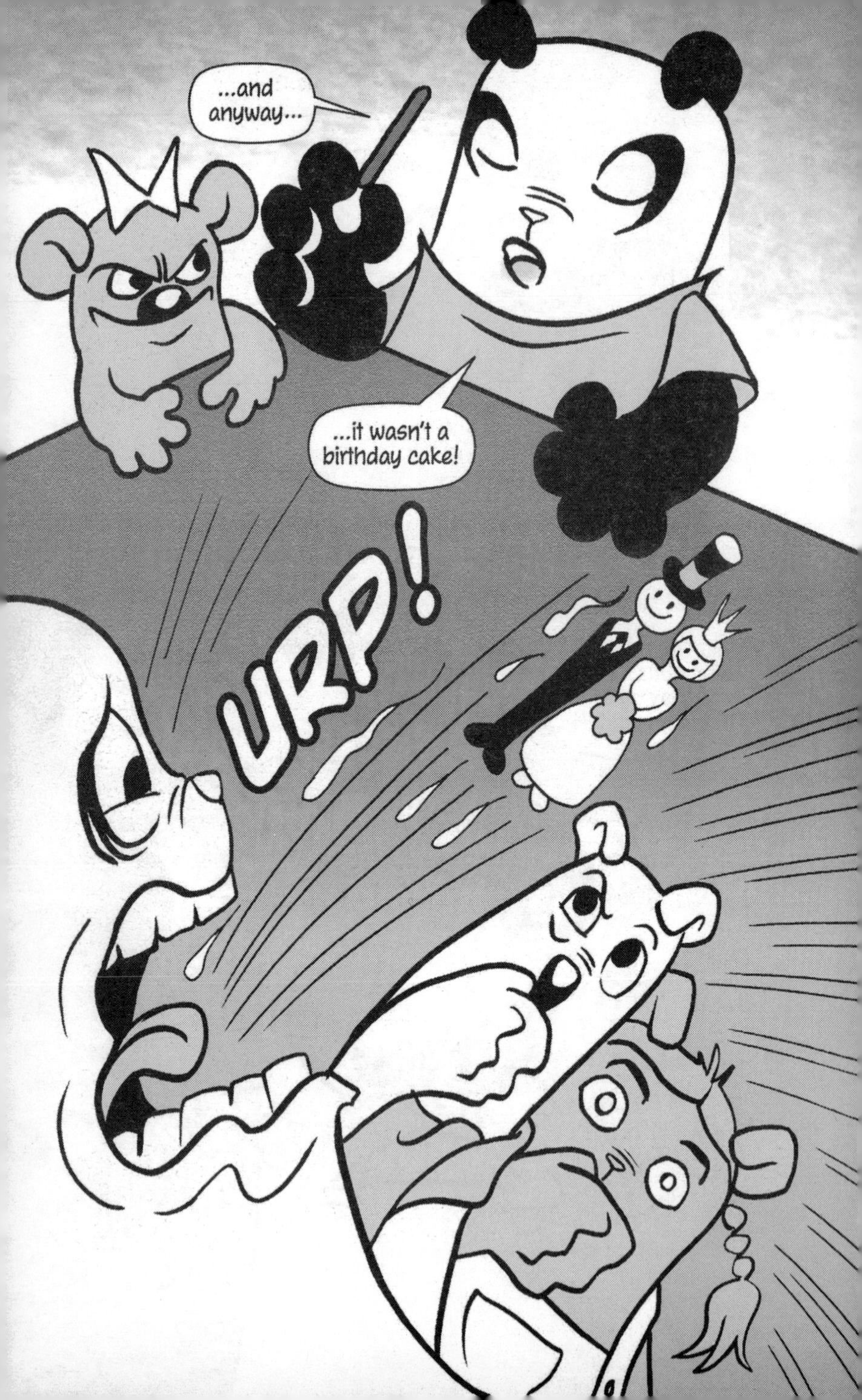
...and anyway...
...it wasn't a birthday cake!
URP!

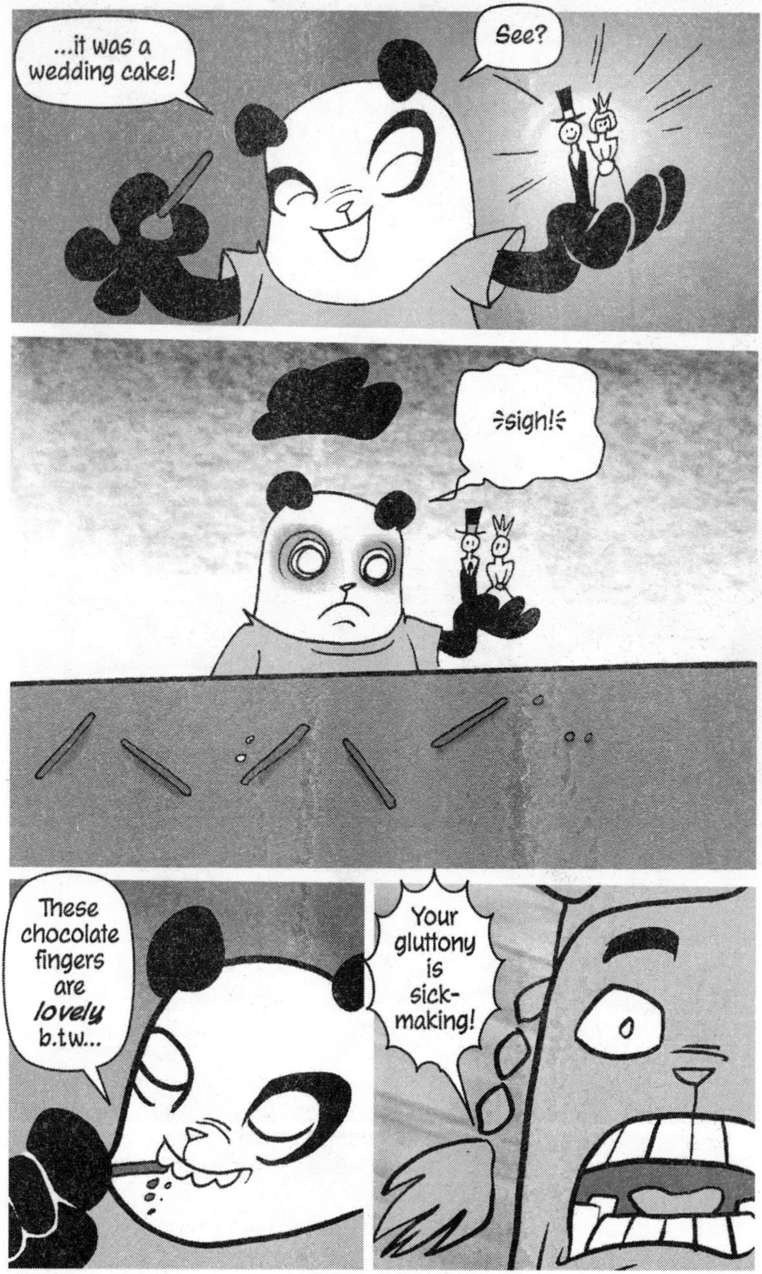
...it was a wedding cake!
See?
sigh!
These chocolate fingers are lovely b.t.w...
Your gluttony is sick-making!

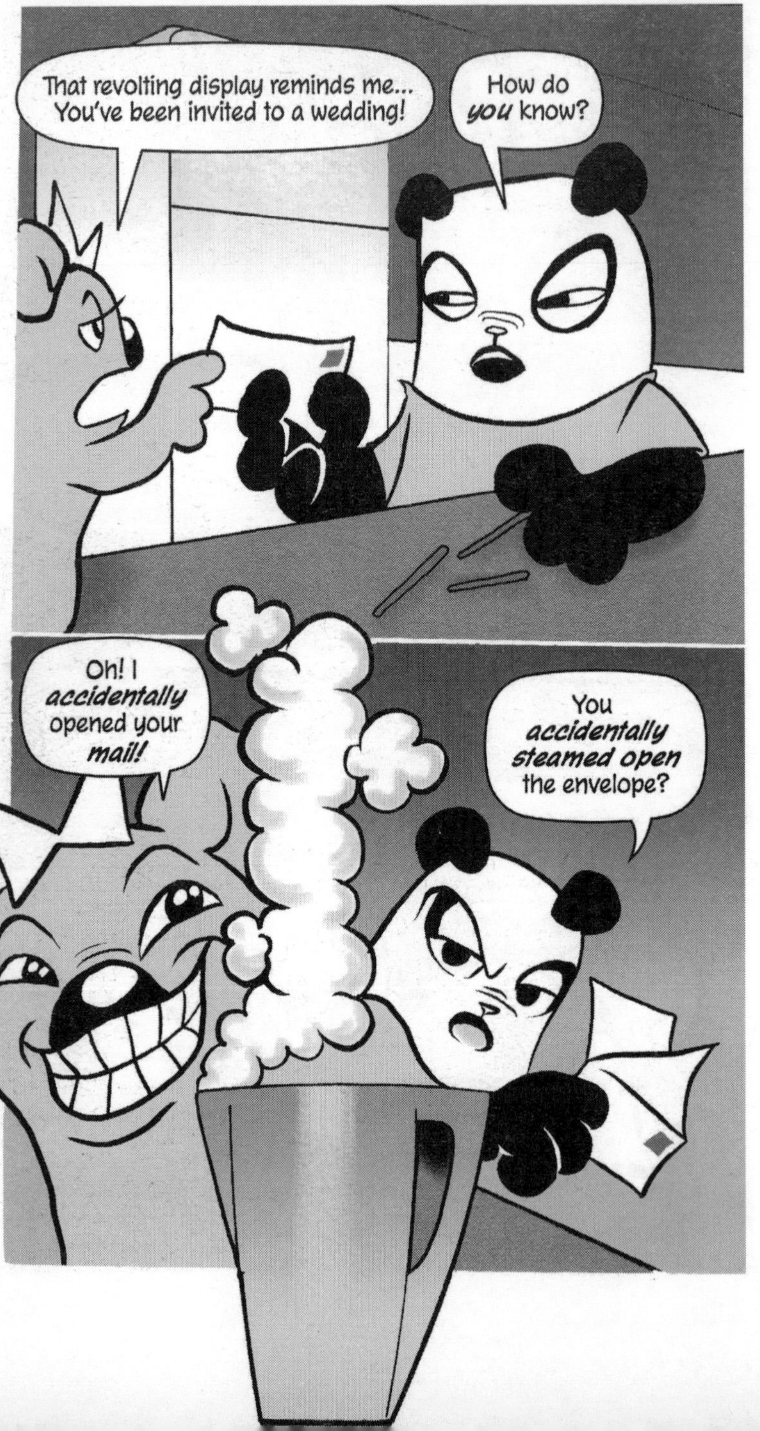
That revolting display reminds me... You've been invited to a wedding!
How do *you* know?
Oh! I *accidentally* opened your *mail!*
You *accidentally steamed open* the envelope?

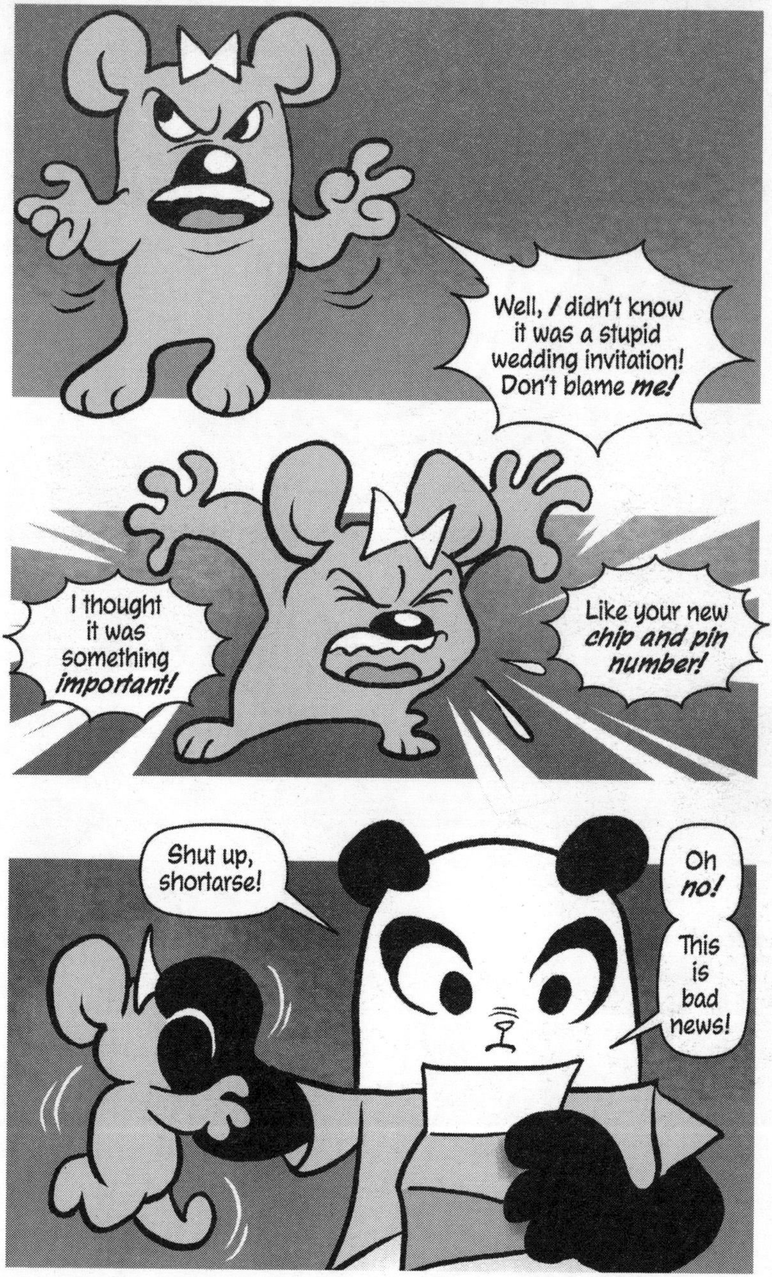
Well, I didn't know it was a stupid wedding invitation! Don't blame me!
I thought it was something important!
Like your new chip and pin number!
Shut up, shortarse!
Oh no!
This is bad news!

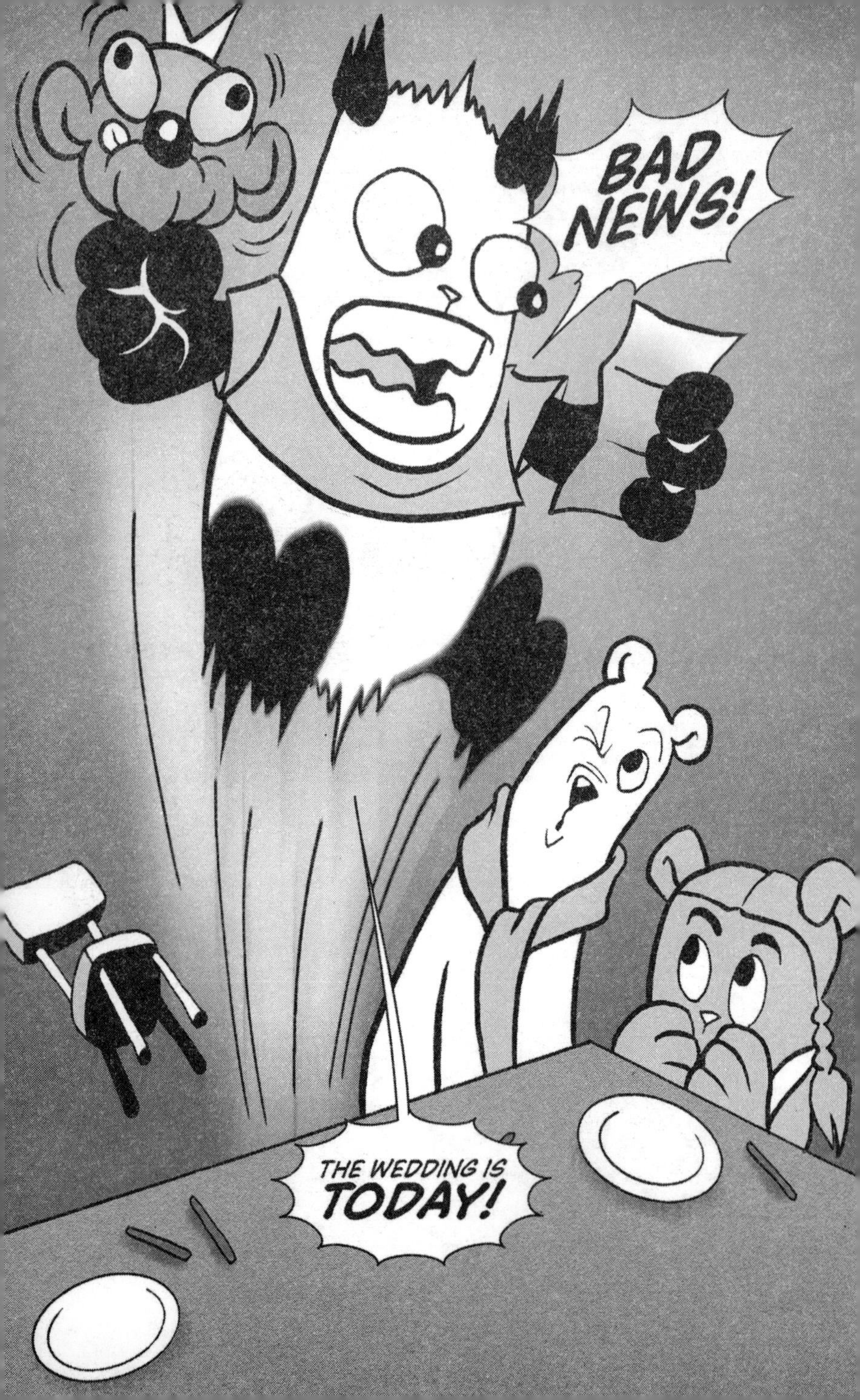
BAD NEWS!
THE WEDDING IS TODAY!

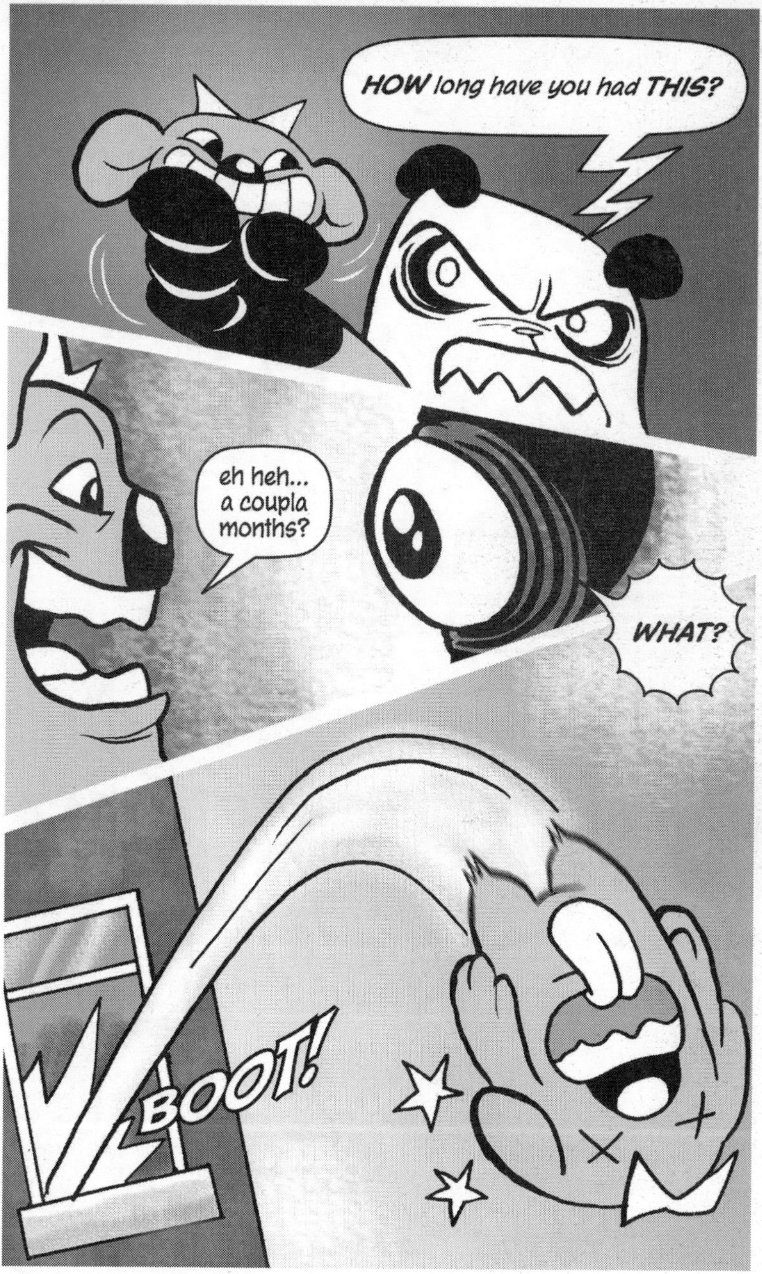
HOW long have you had THIS?
eh heh... a coupla months?
WHAT?
BOOT!

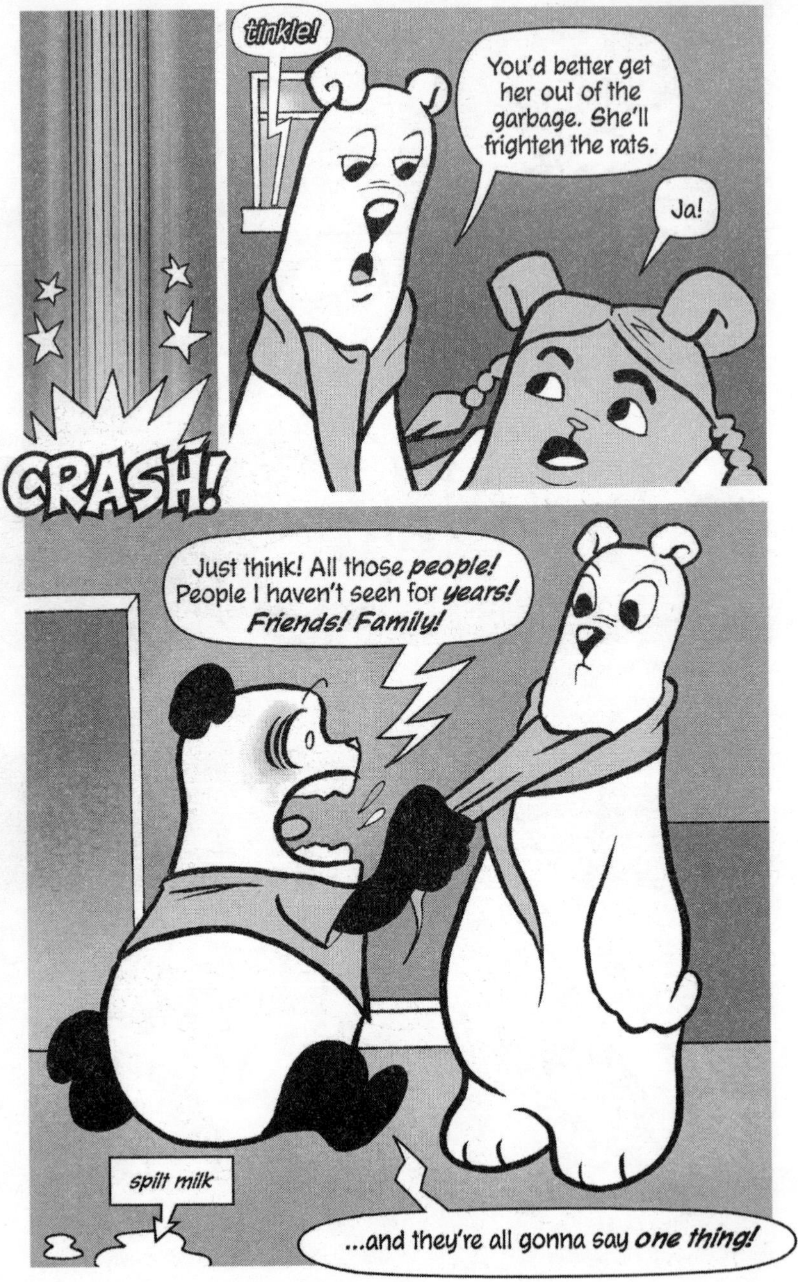
CRASH!
tinkle!
You'd better get her out of the garbage. She'll frighten the rats.
Ja!
Just think! All those *people!* People I haven't seen for *years!* ***Friends! Family!***
spilt milk
...and they're all gonna say ***one thing!***

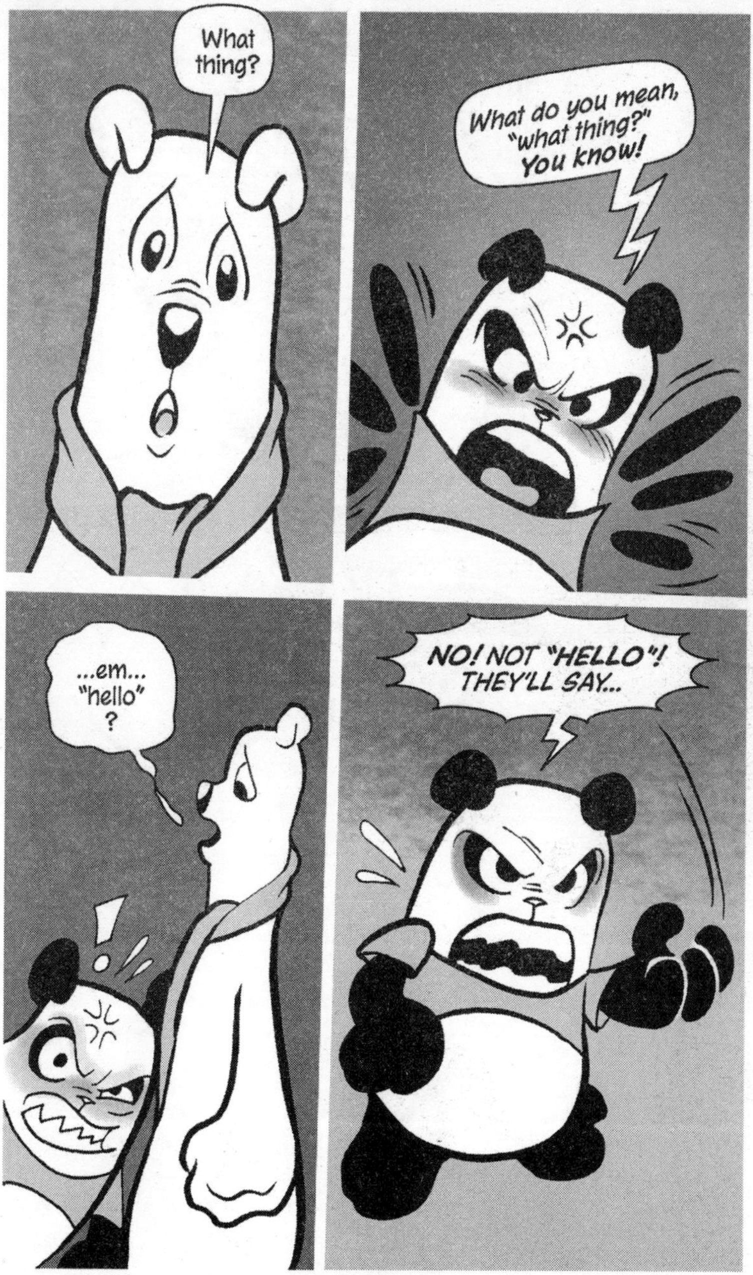
What thing?
What do you mean, "what thing?" You know!
...em... "hello" ?
NO! NOT "HELLO"! THEY'LL SAY...

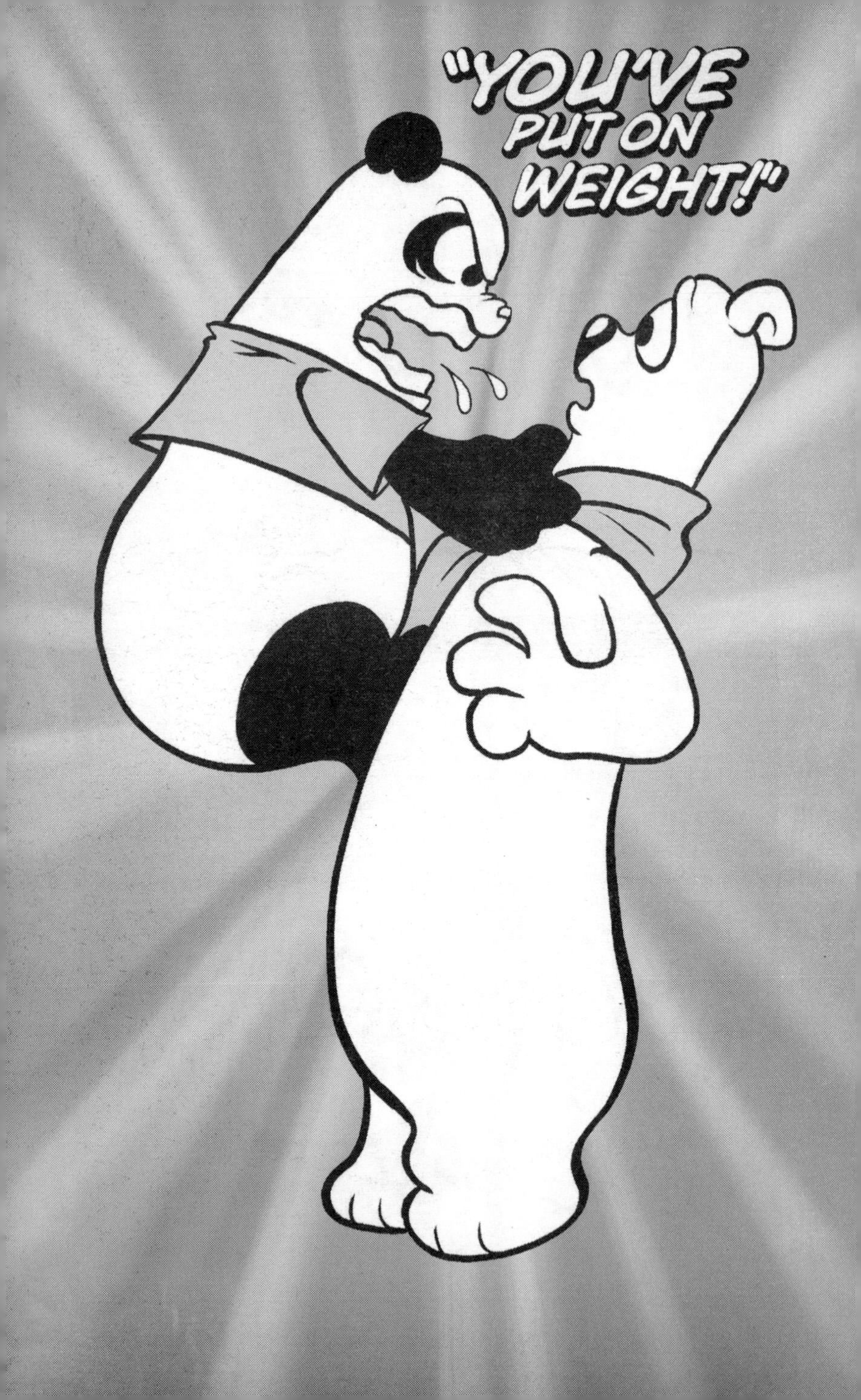
"YOU'VE PUT ON WEIGHT!"

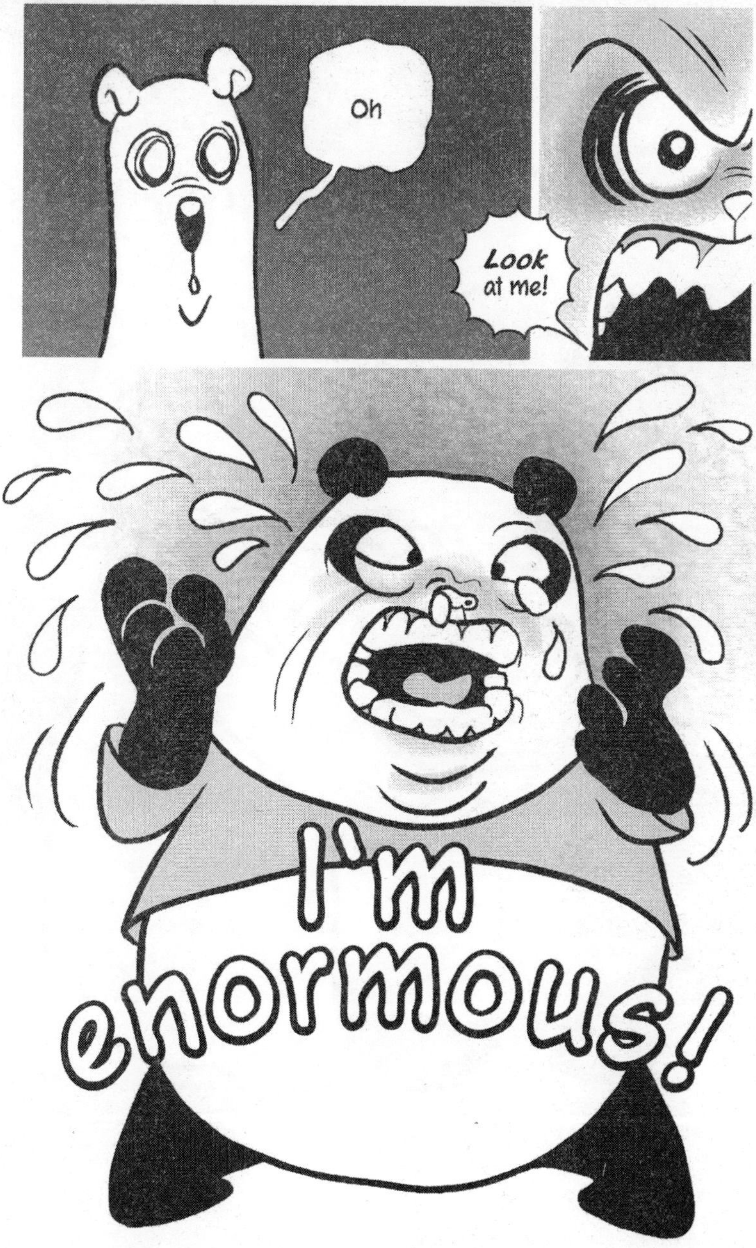
Oh
Look at me!
I'm enormous!

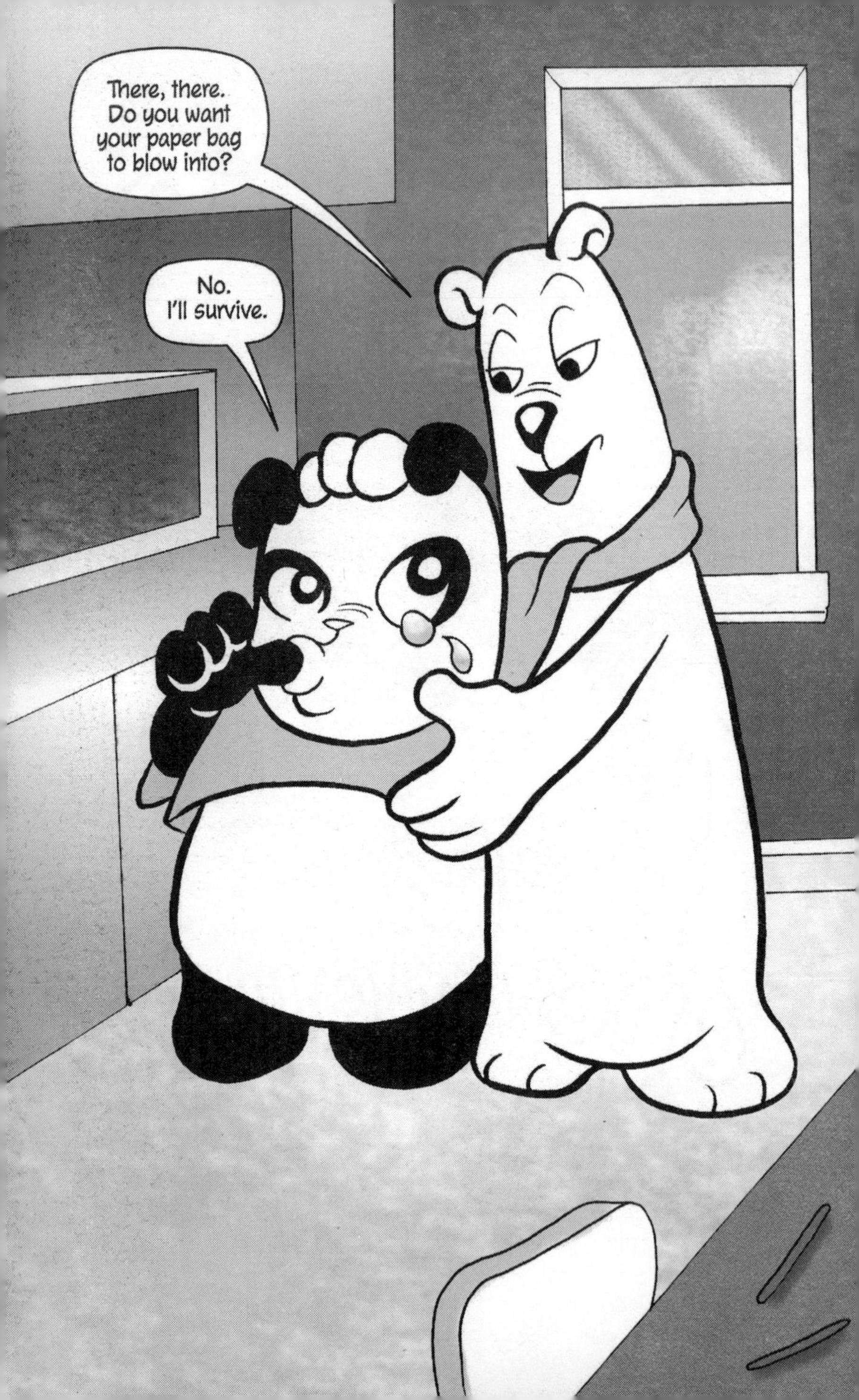
There, there. Do you want your paper bag to blow into?
No. I'll survive.

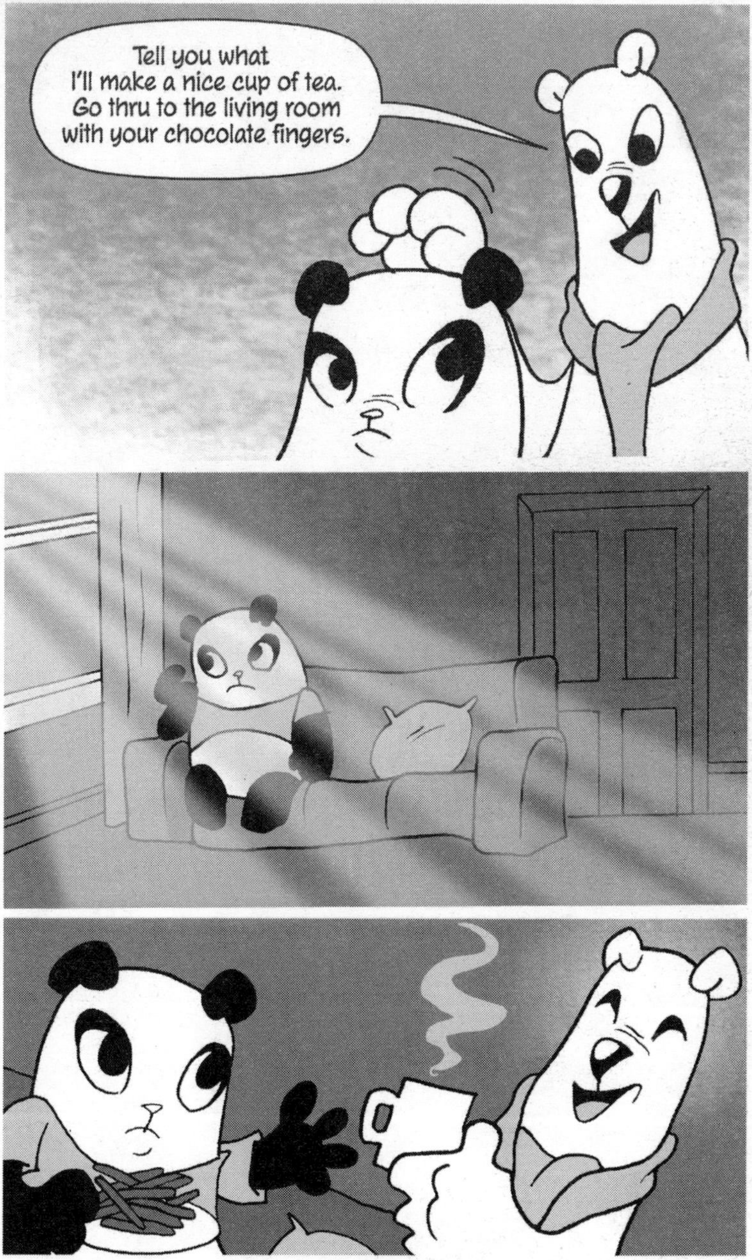
Tell you what
I'll make a nice cup of tea.
Go thru to the living room
with your chocolate fingers.

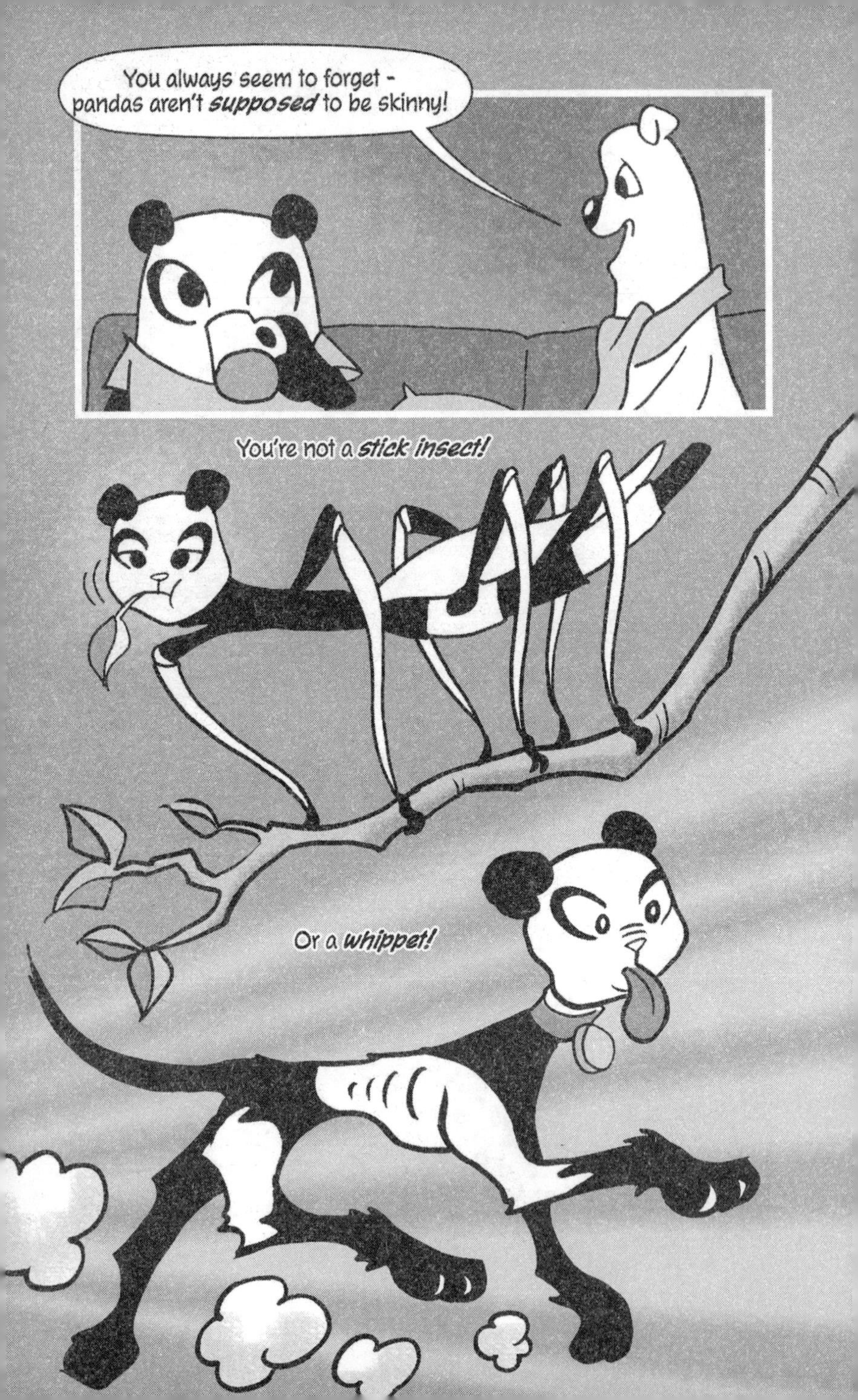
You always seem to forget - pandas aren't *supposed* to be skinny!
You're not a *stick insect!*
Or a *whippet!*

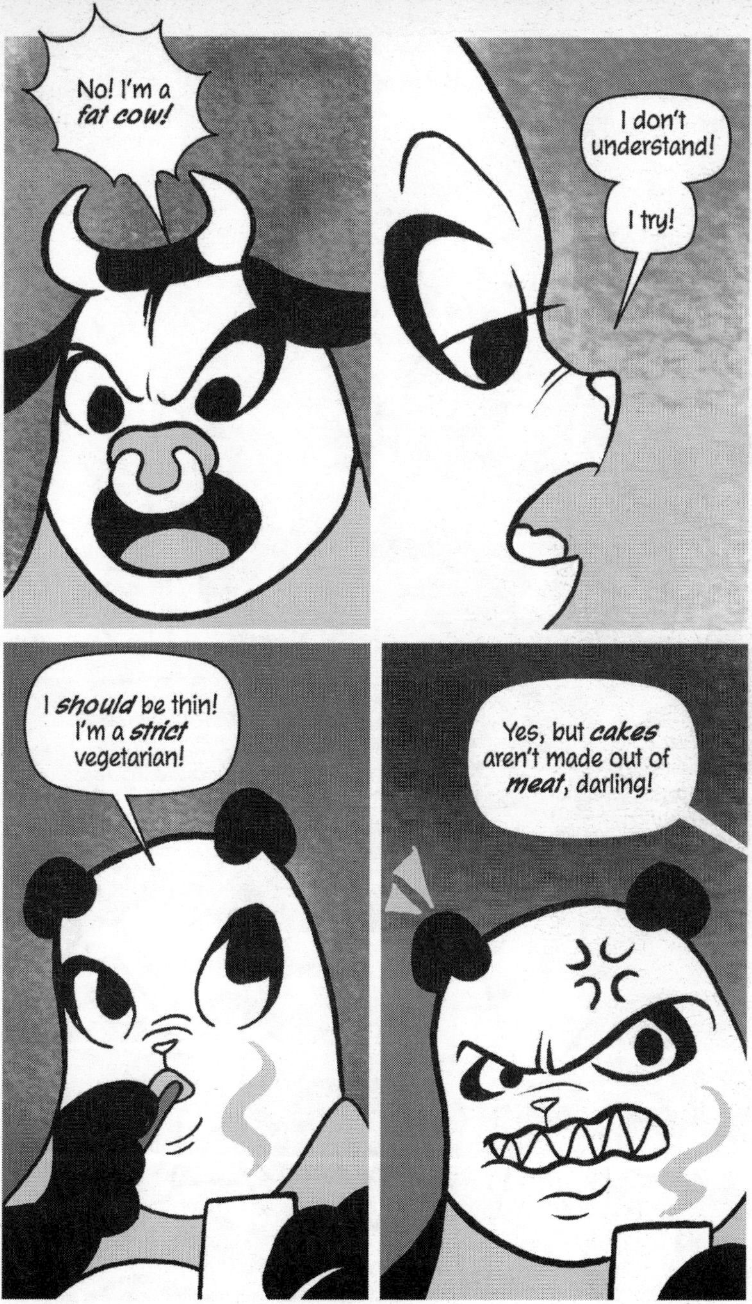
No! I'm a *fat cow!*
I don't understand!
I try!
I *should* be thin! I'm a *strict* vegetarian!
Yes, but *cakes* aren't made out of *meat*, darling!

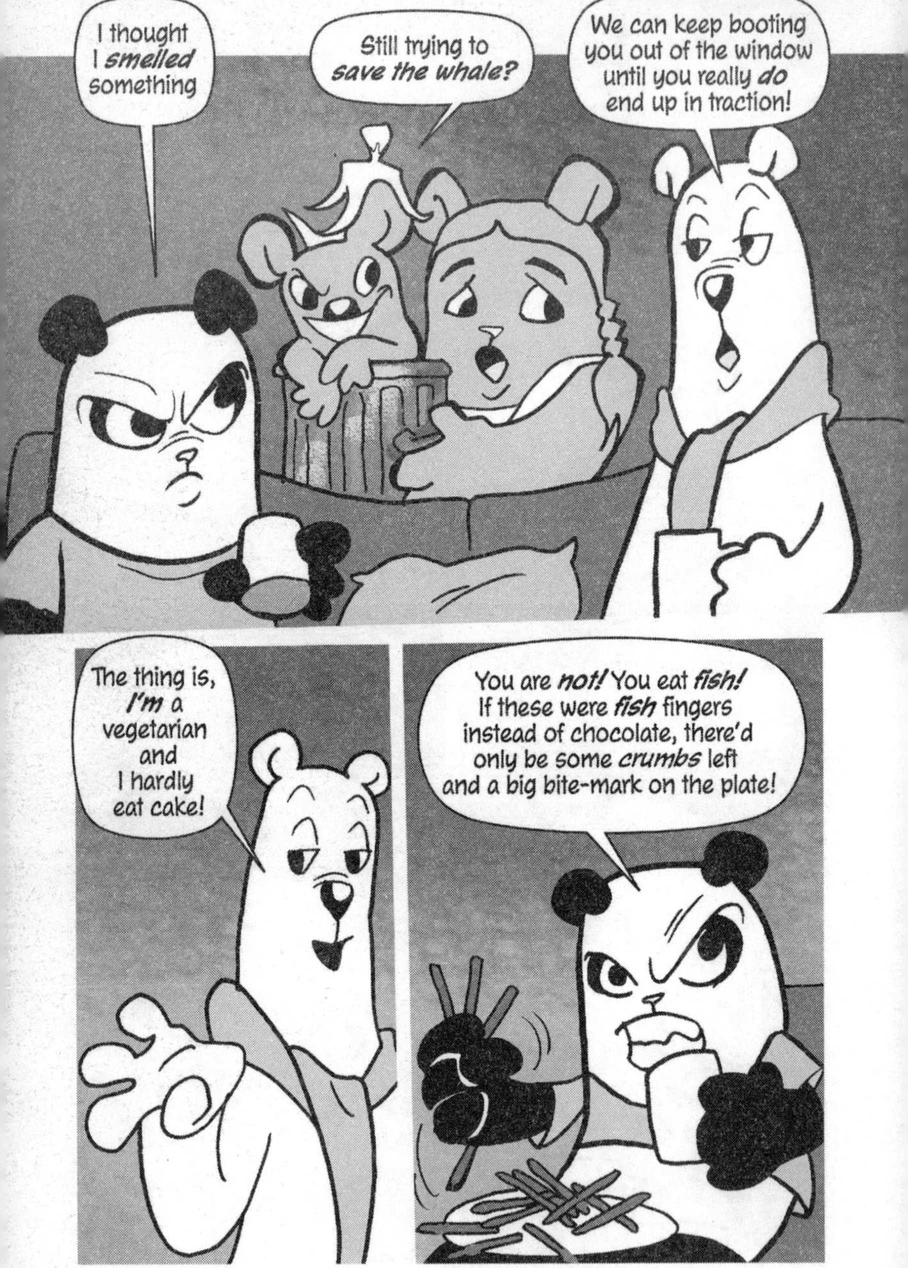
I thought I *smelled* something
Still trying to *save the whale?*
We can keep booting you out of the window until you really *do* end up in traction!
The thing is, *I'm* a vegetarian and I hardly eat cake!
You are *not!* You eat *fish!* If these were *fish* fingers instead of chocolate, there'd only be some *crumbs* left and a big bite-mark on the plate!

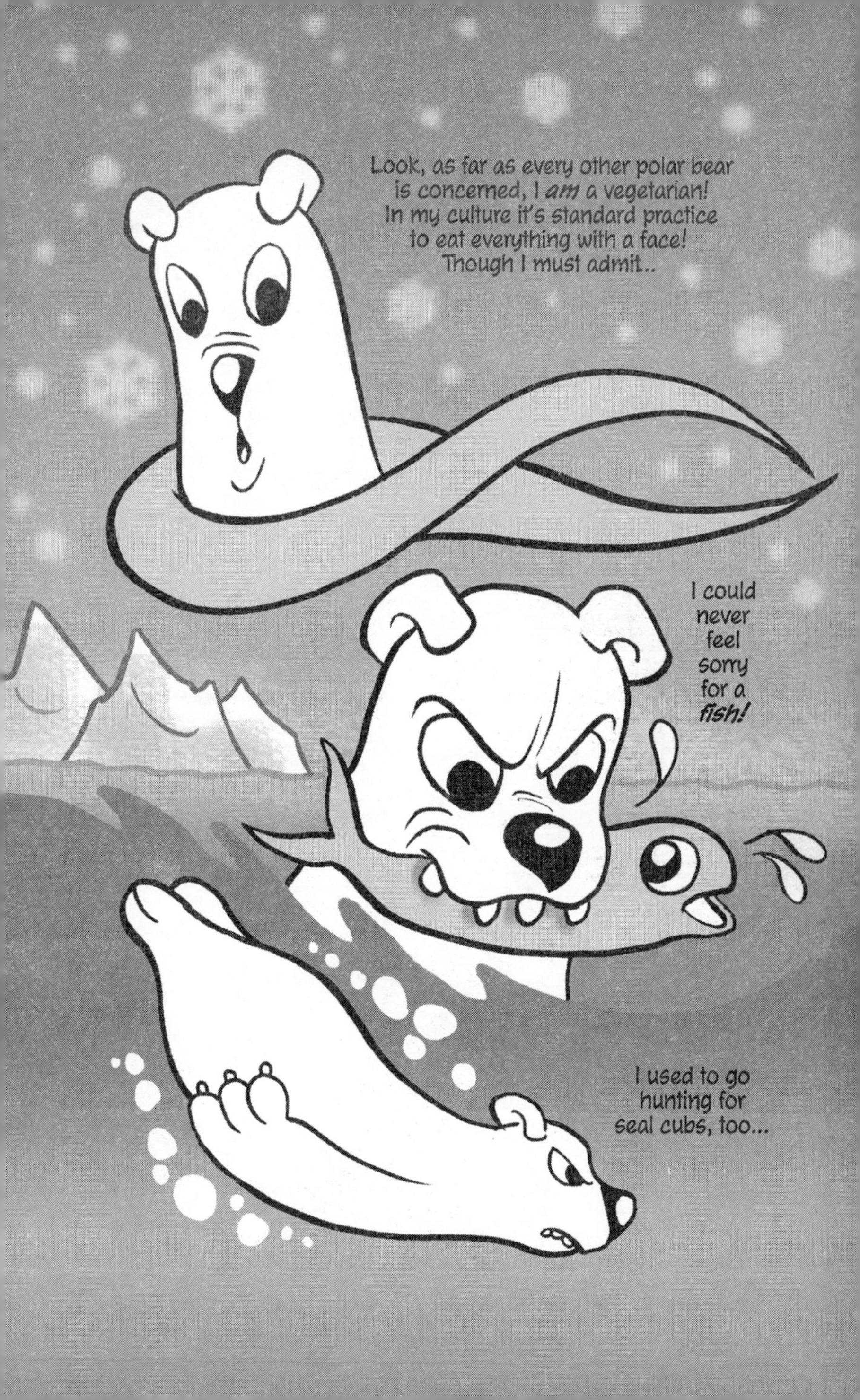
Look, as far as every other polar bear is concerned, I *am* a vegetarian! In my culture it's standard practice to eat everything with a face! Though I must admit..
I could never feel sorry for a *fish!*
I used to go hunting for seal cubs, too...

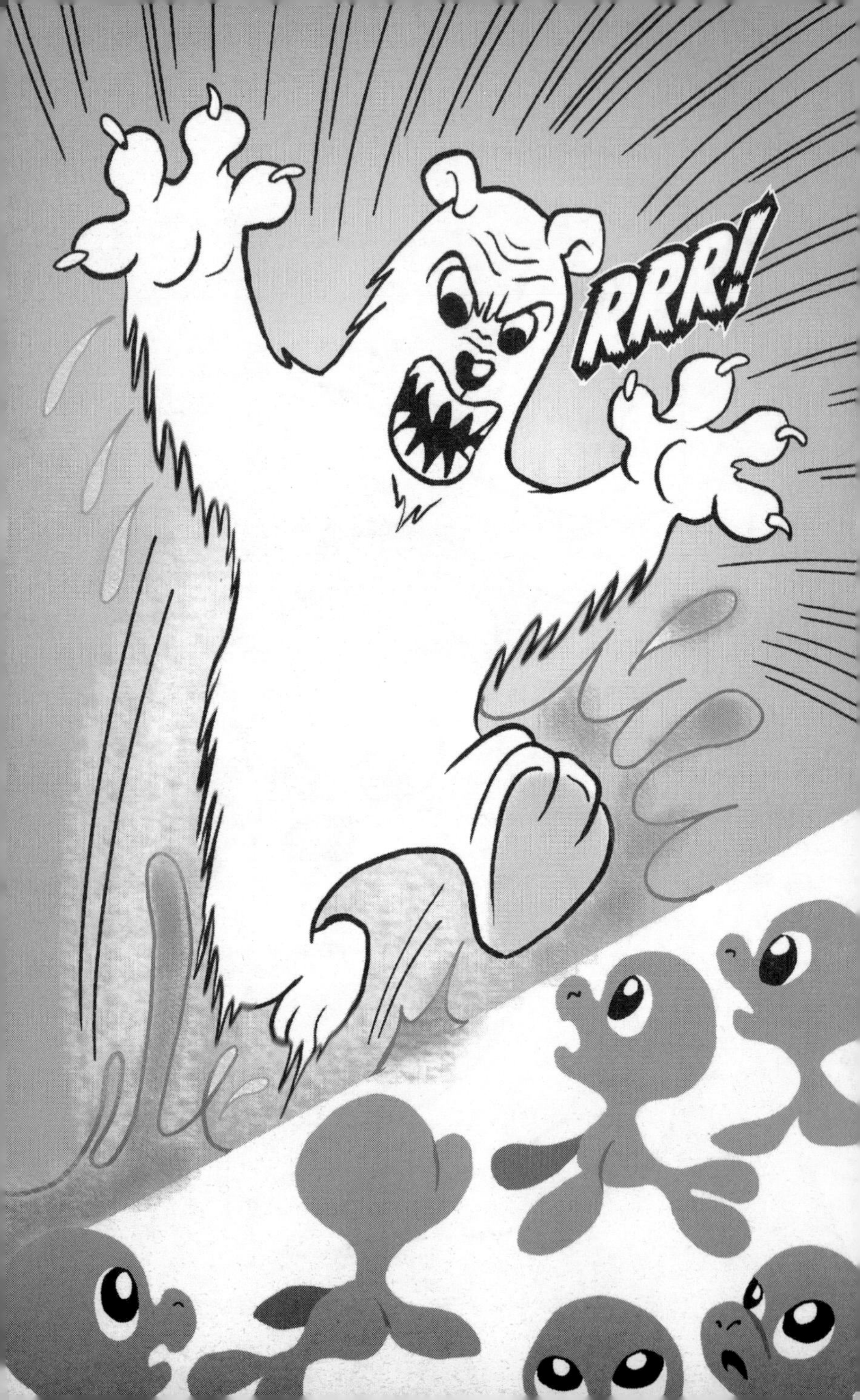
RRR!

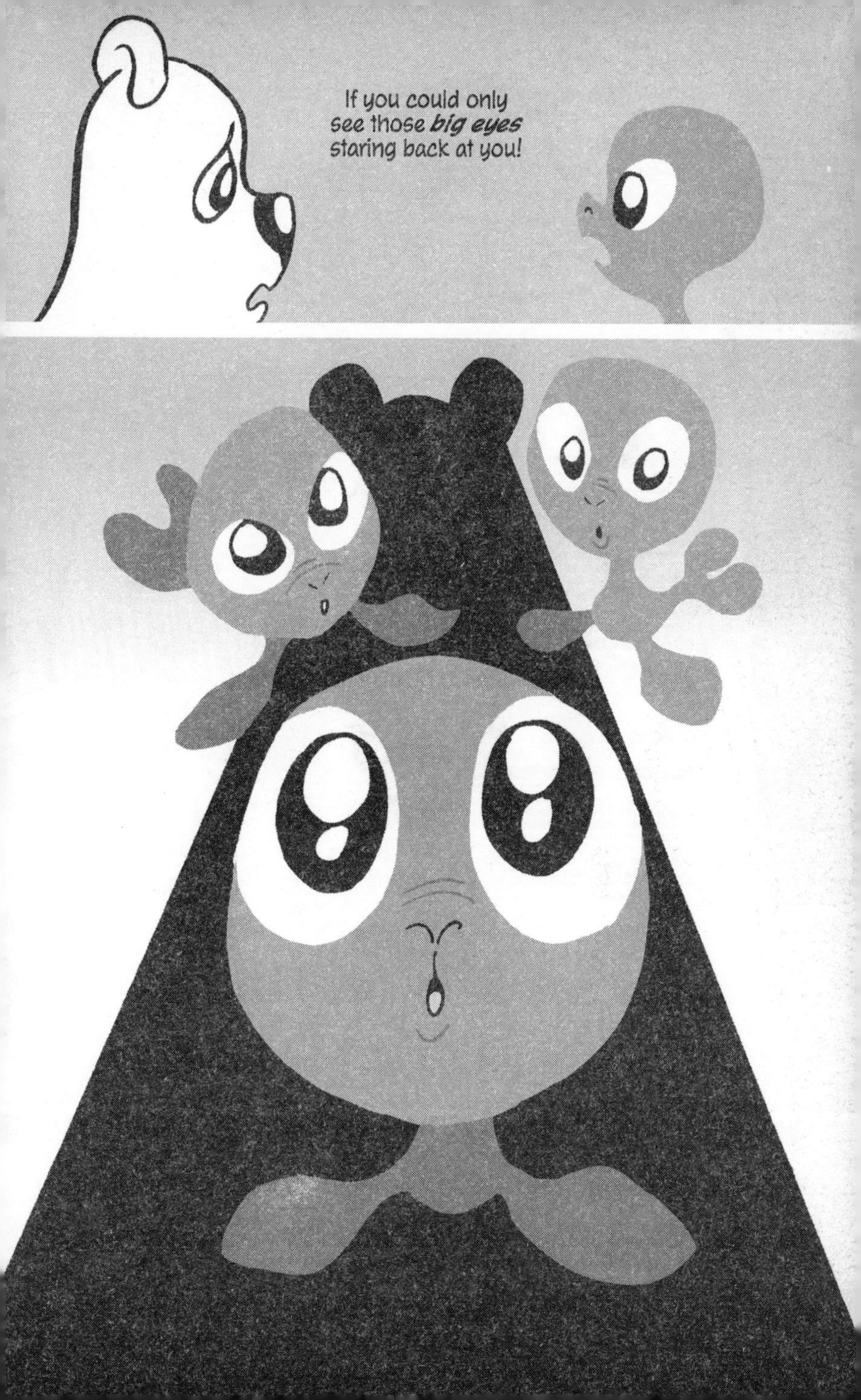
If you could only see those *big eyes* staring back at you!

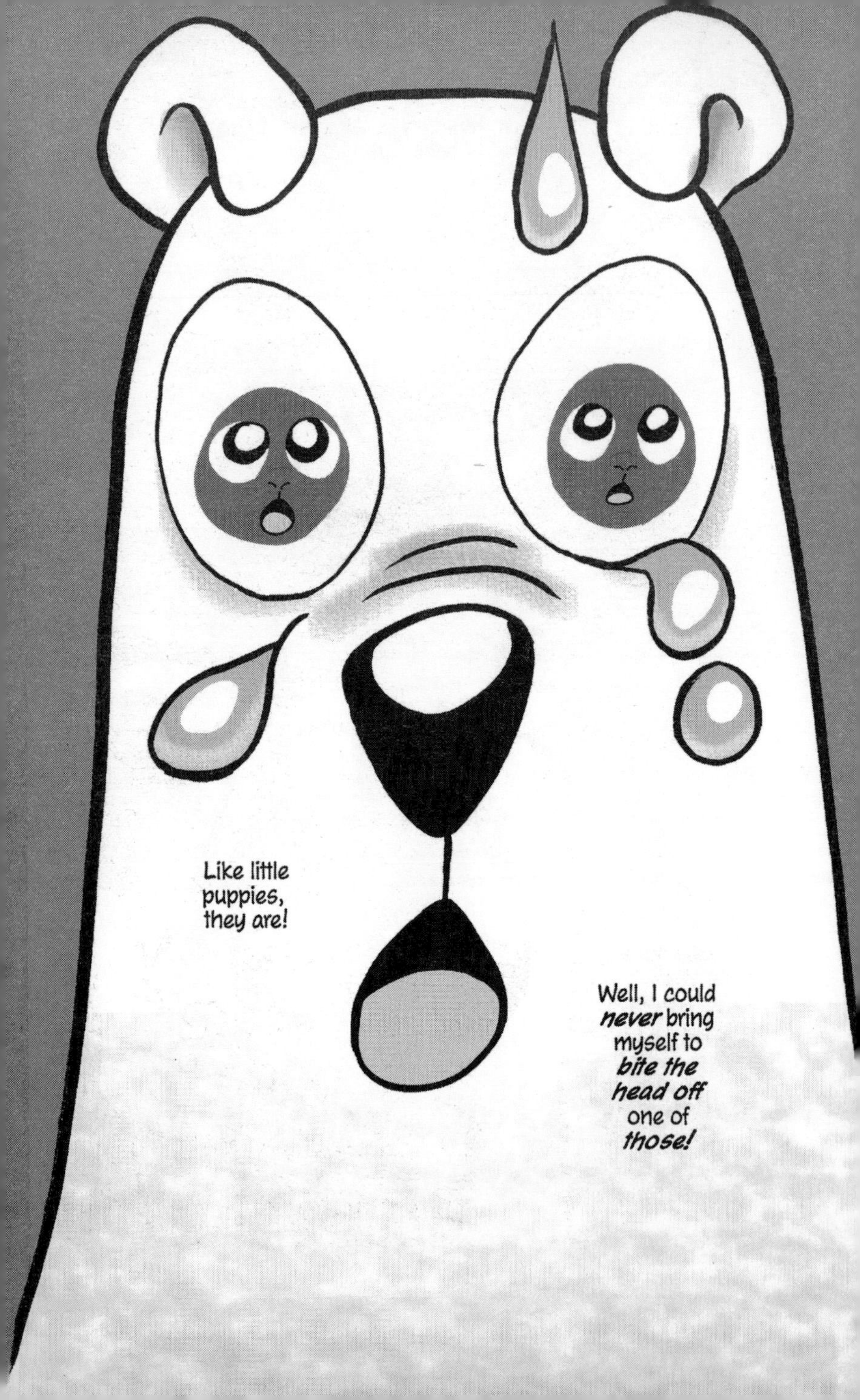
Like little puppies, they are!
Well, I could *never* bring myself to *bite the head off* one of *those!*

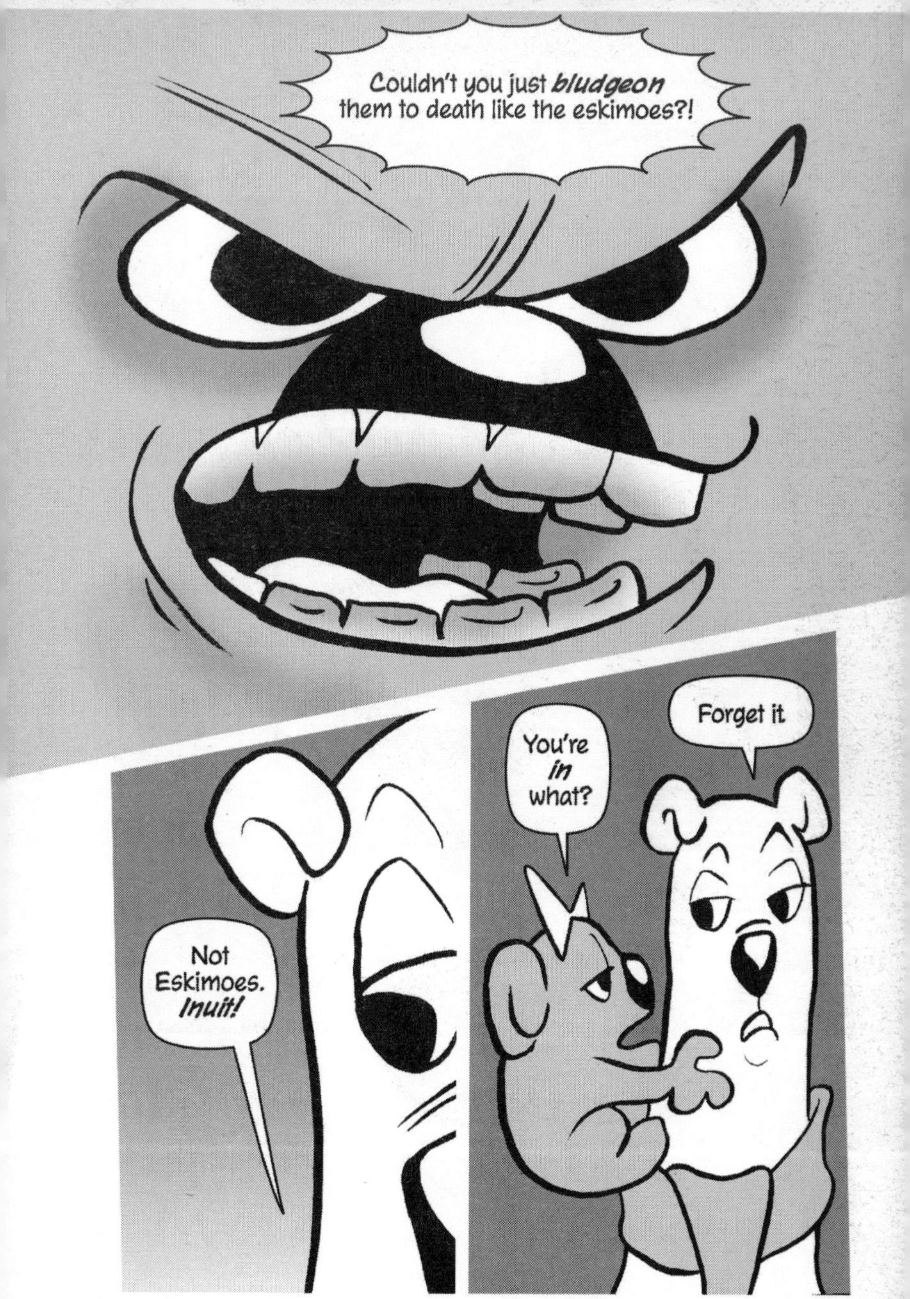
Couldn't you just *bludgeon* them to death like the eskimoes?!
Not Eskimoes. *Inuit!*
You're *in* what?
Forget it

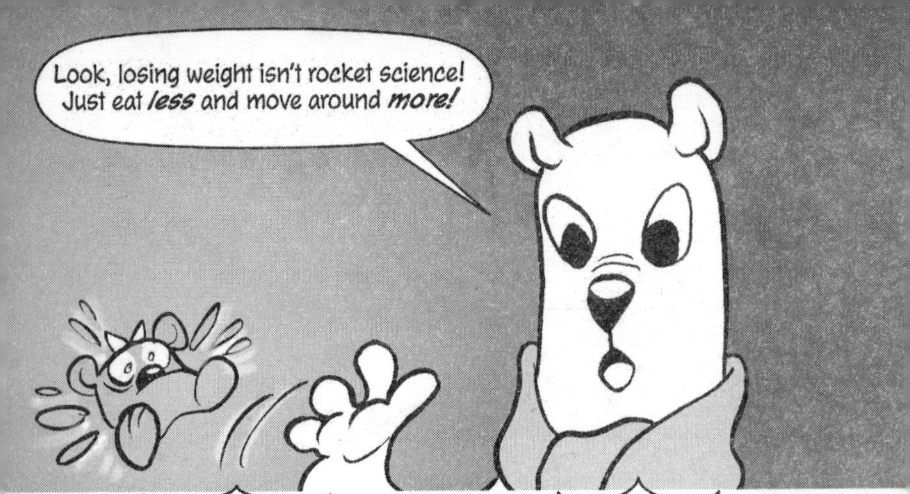
Look, losing weight isn't rocket science! Just eat *less* and move around *more!*
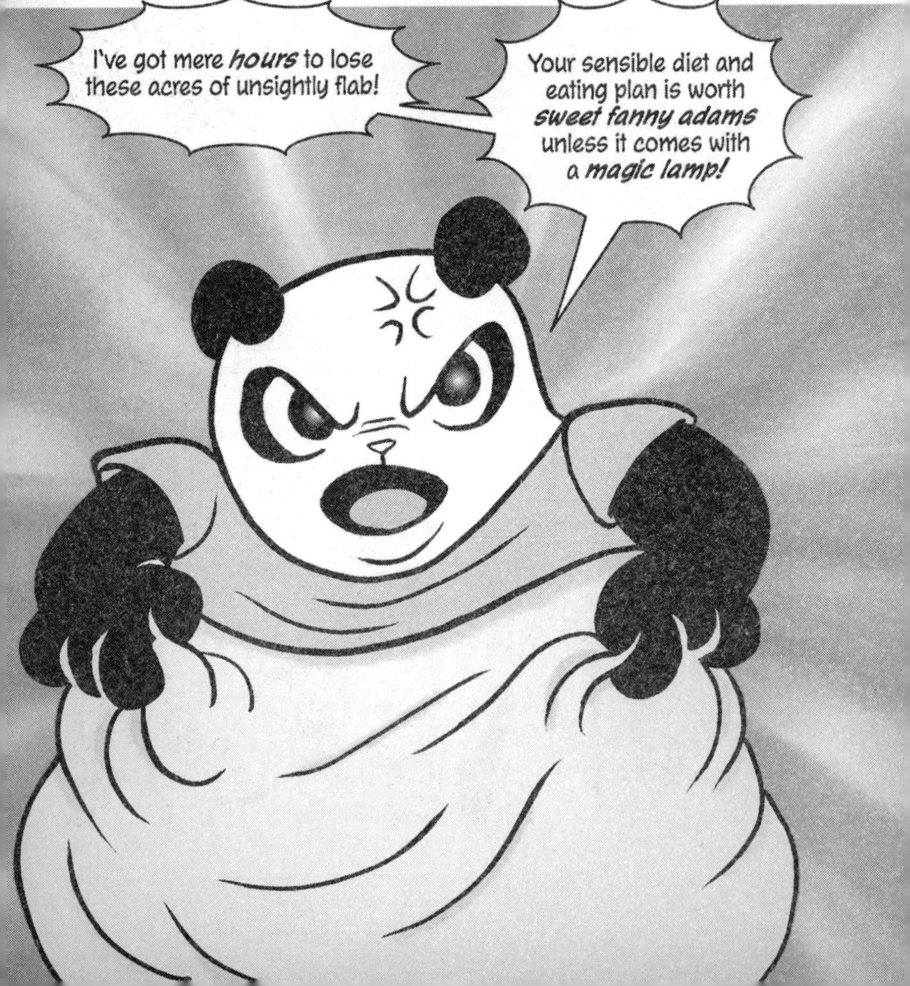
I've got mere *hours* to lose these acres of unsightly flab!
Your sensible diet and eating plan is worth *sweet fanny adams* unless it comes with a *magic lamp!*

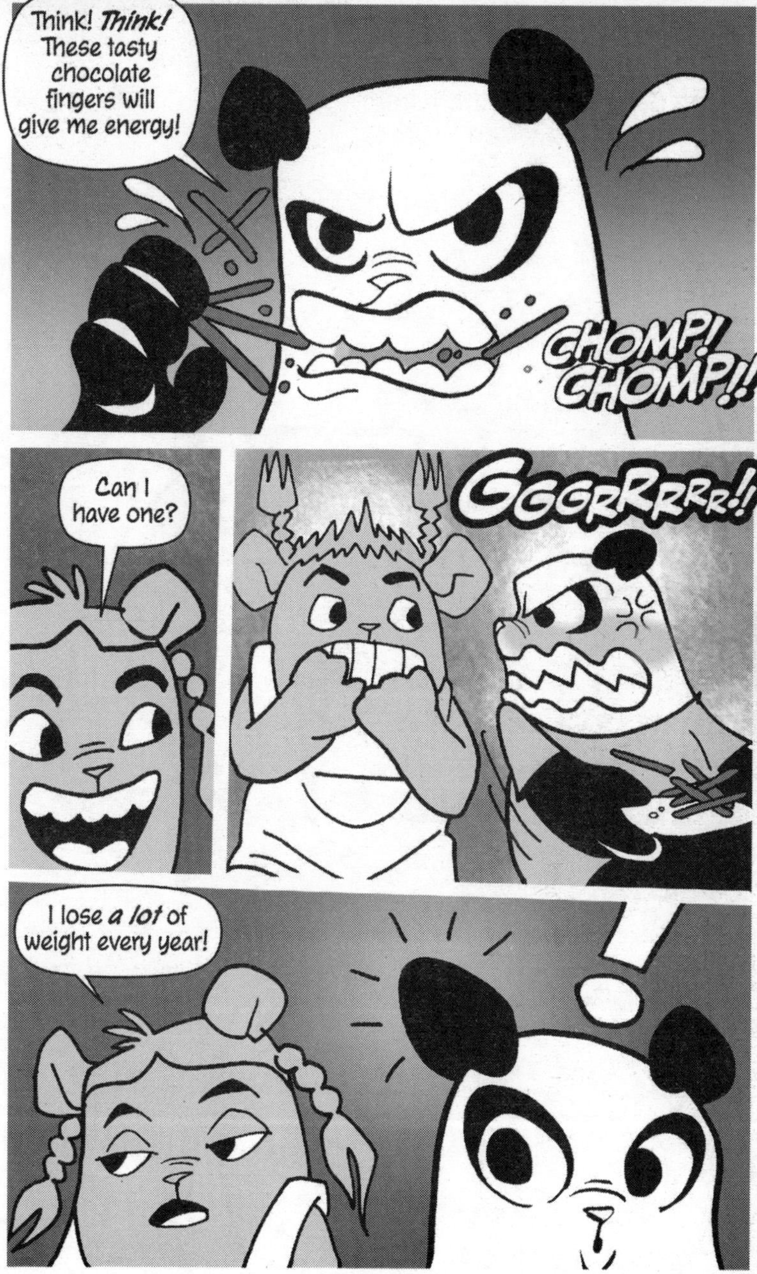
Think! *Think!* These tasty chocolate fingers will give me energy!
CHOMP! CHOMP!!
Can I have one?
GGGRRRRR!!
I lose *a lot* of weight every year!
!

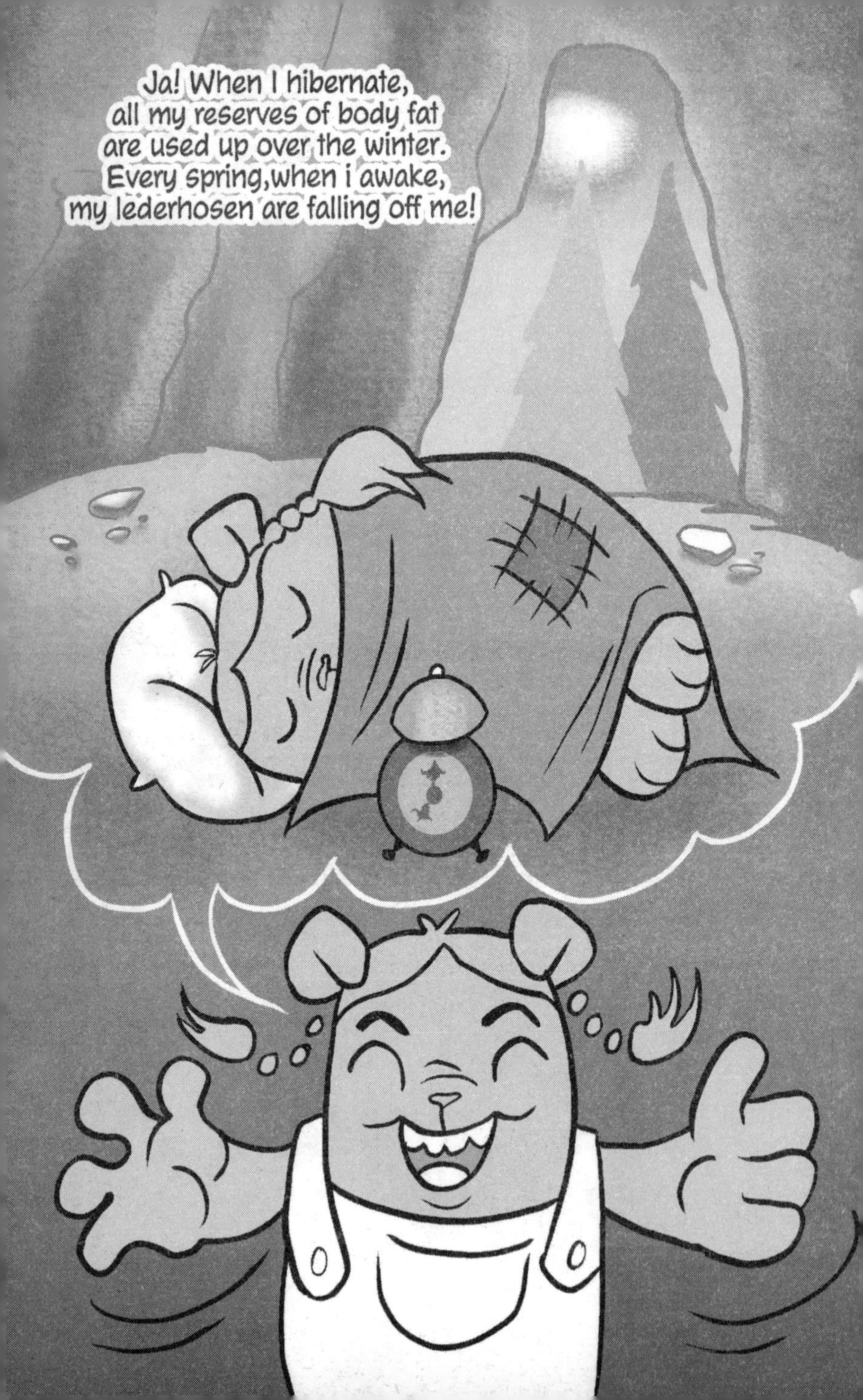
Ja! When I hibernate, all my reserves of body fat are used up over the winter. Every spring,when i awake, my lederhosen are falling off me!

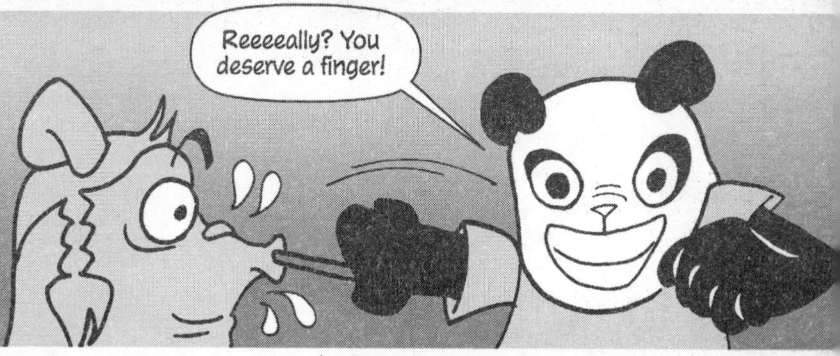
Reeeeally? You deserve a finger!

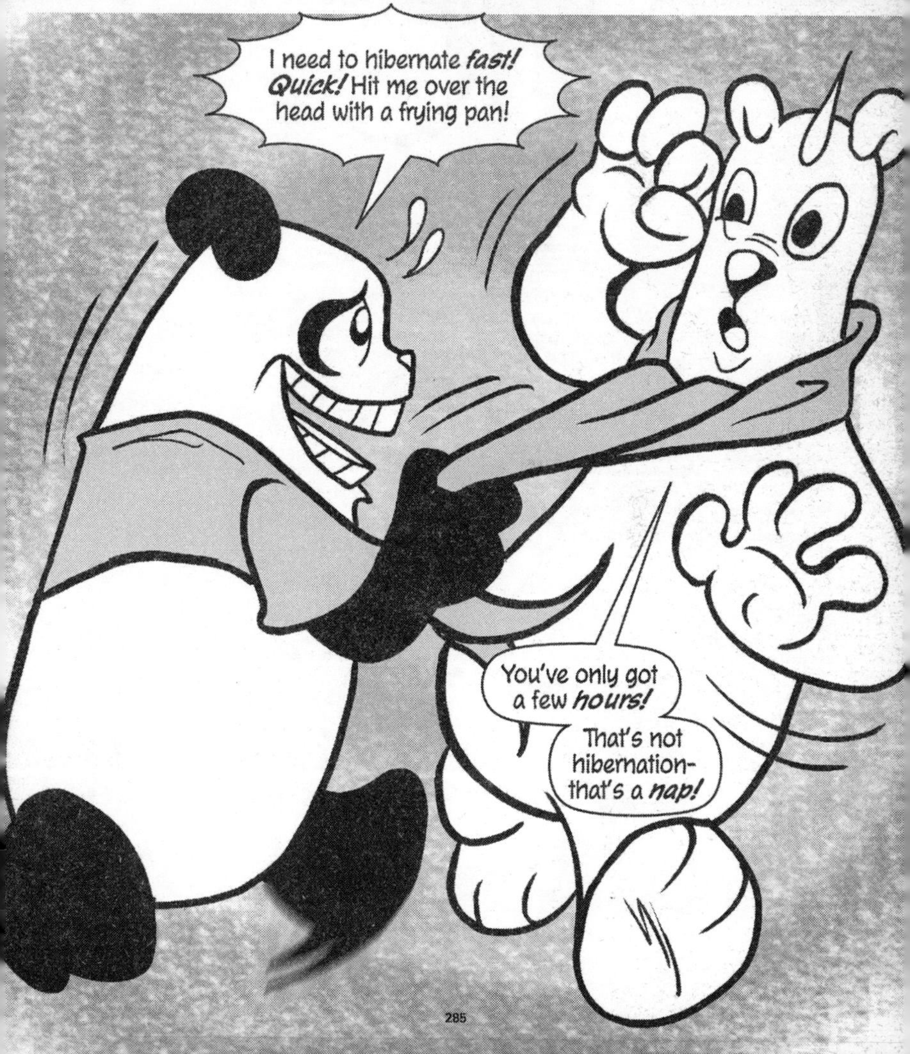
I need to hibernate *fast!* *Quick!* Hit me over the head with a frying pan!
You've only got a few *hours!*
That's not hibernation- that's a *nap!*

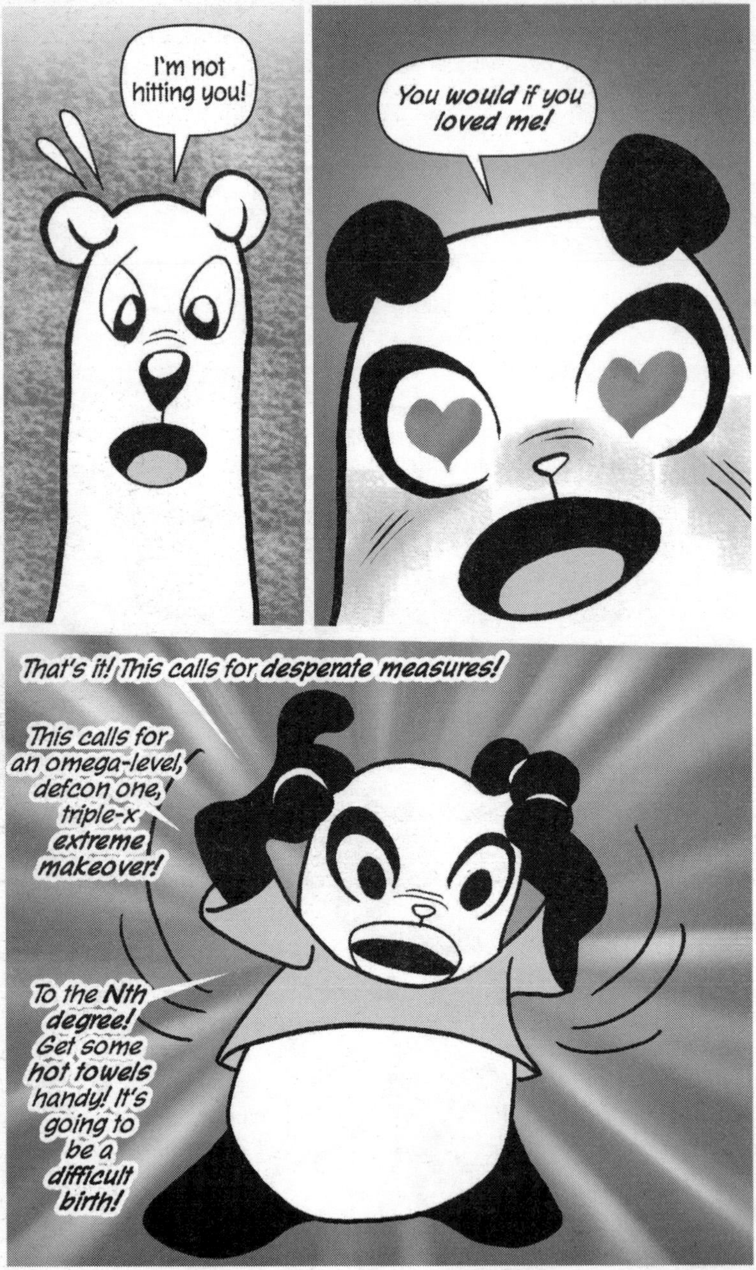
I'm not hitting you!
You would if you loved me!
That's it! This calls for desperate measures!
This calls for an omega-level, defcon one, triple-x extreme makeover!
To the Nth degree! Get some hot towels handy! It's going to be a difficult birth!

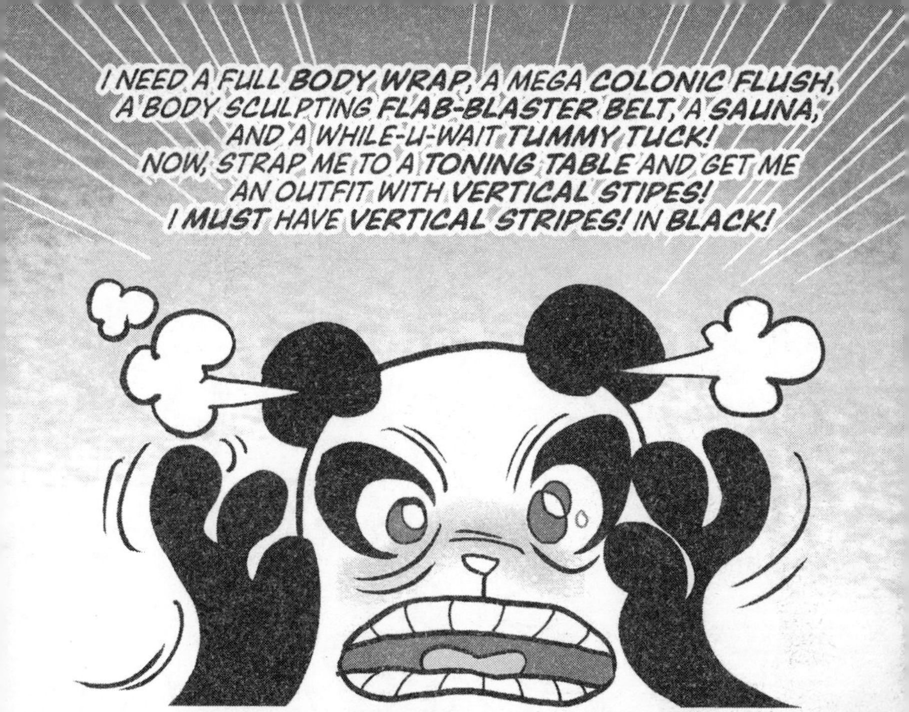
I NEED A FULL BODY WRAP, A MEGA COLONIC FLUSH, A BODY SCULPTING FLAB-BLASTER BELT, A SAUNA, AND A WHILE-U-WAIT TUMMY TUCK! NOW, STRAP ME TO A TONING TABLE AND GET ME AN OUTFIT WITH VERTICAL STIPES! I MUST HAVE VERTICAL STRIPES! IN BLACK!
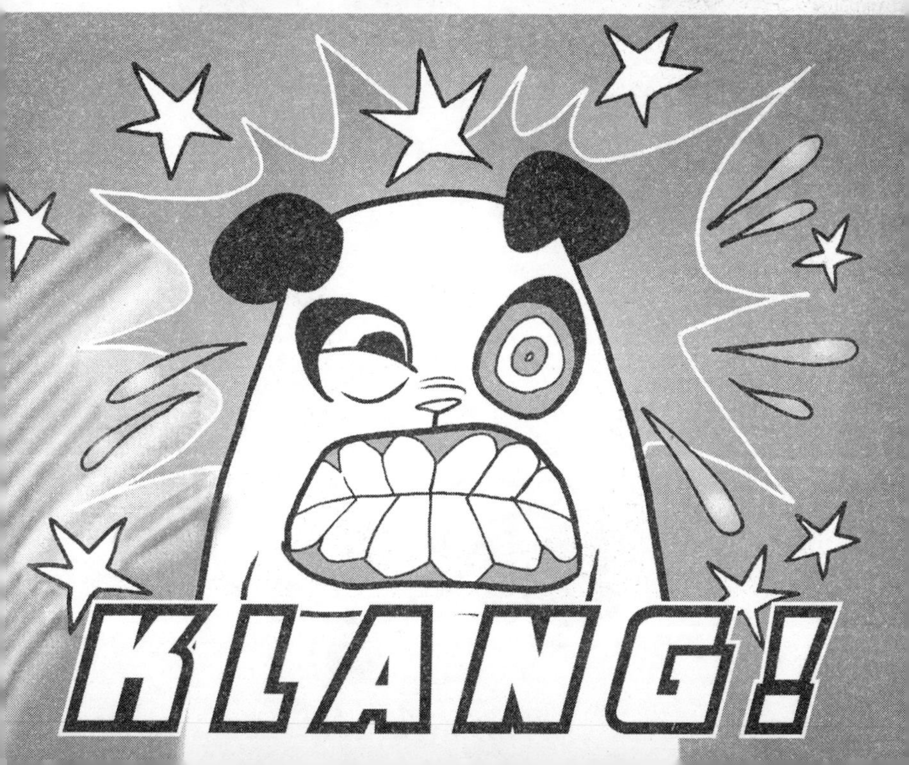
KLANG!

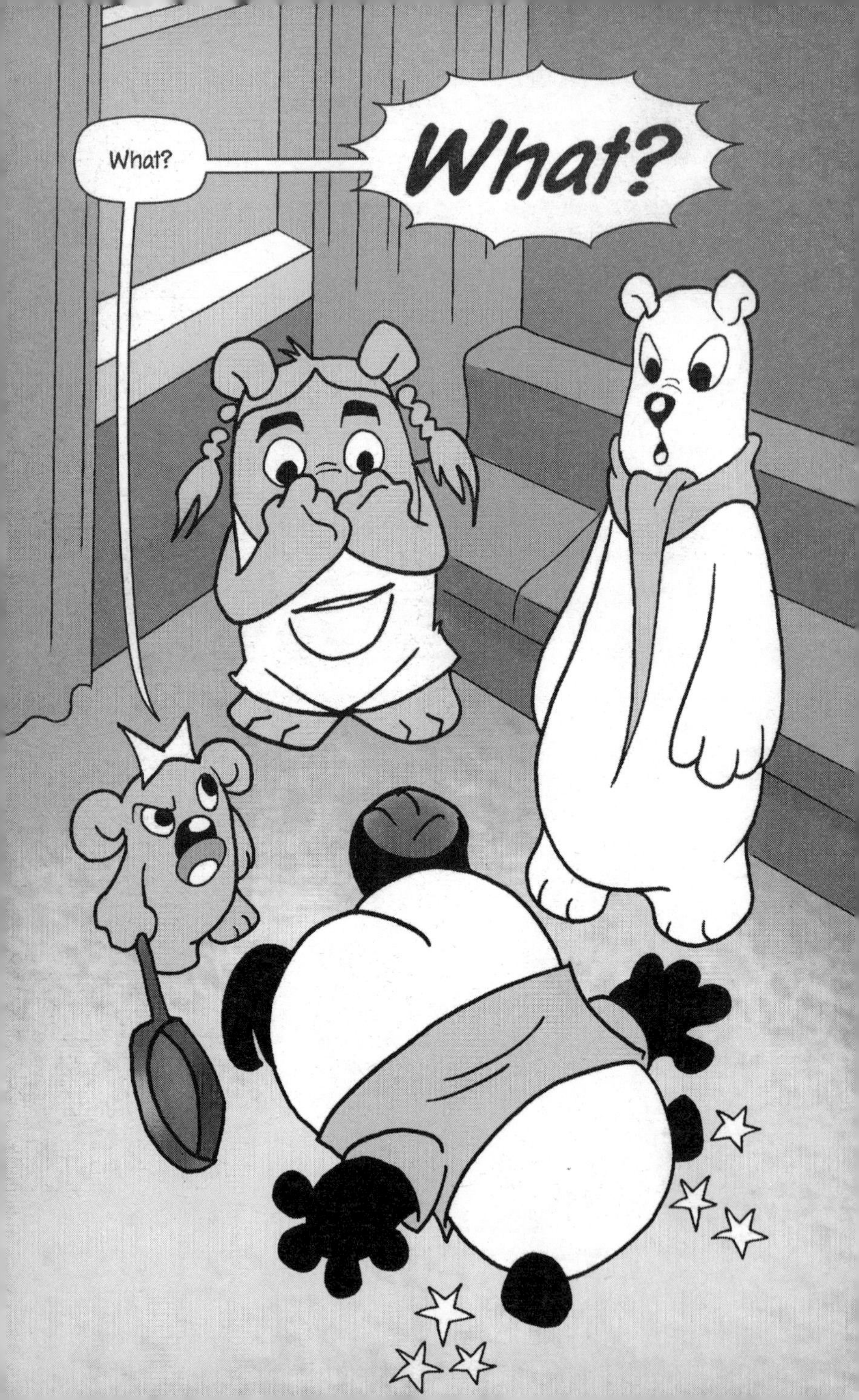
What?
What?

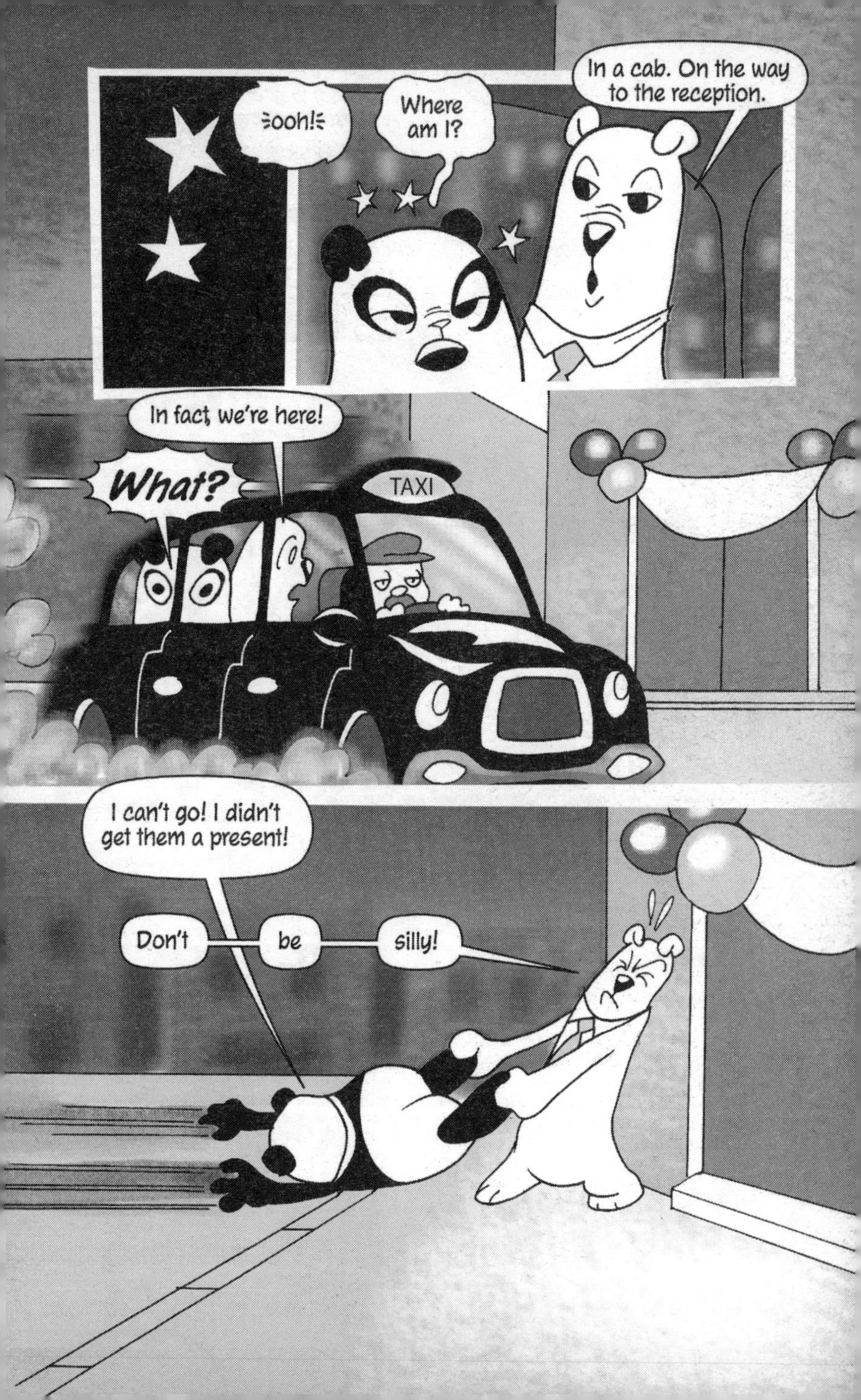
ooh!
Where am I?
In a cab. On the way to the reception.
What?
In fact, we're here!
TAXI
I can't go! I didn't get them a present!
Don't be silly!

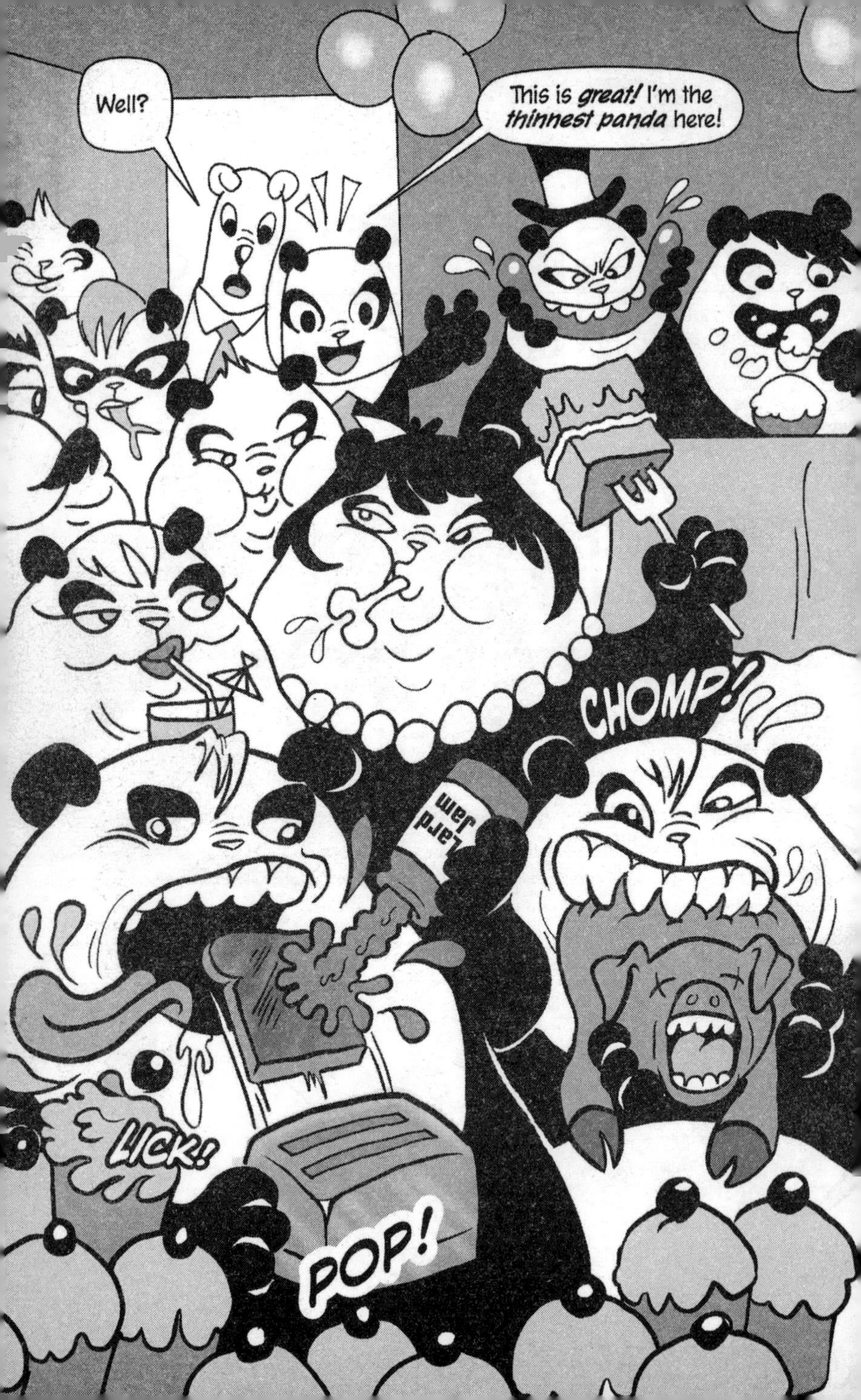

Well?
This is *great!* I'm the *thinnest panda* here!
CHOMP!
Lard Jam
LICK!
POP!

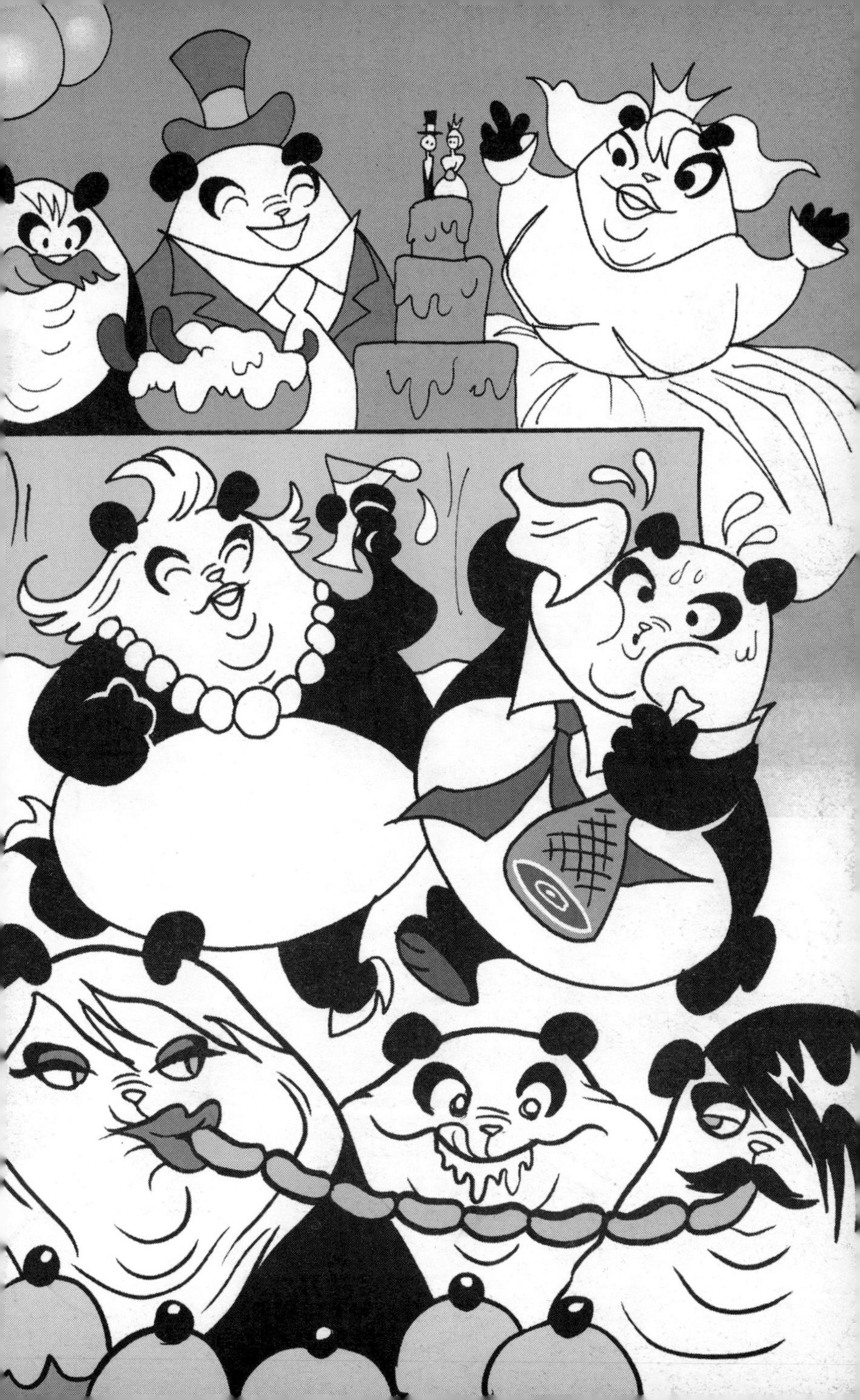

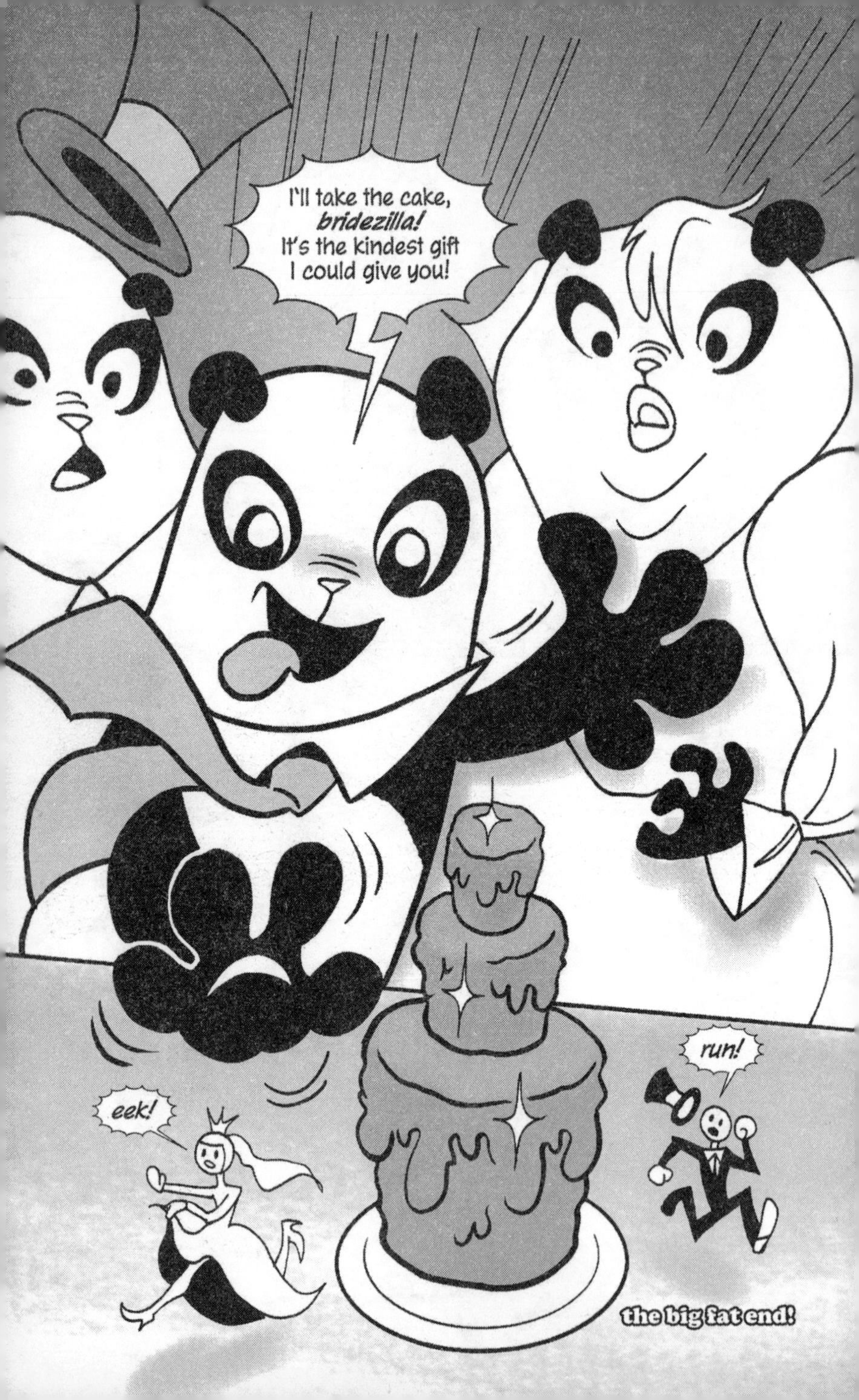

I'll take the cake, *bridezilla!* It's the kindest gift I could give you!
eek!
run!
the big fat end!

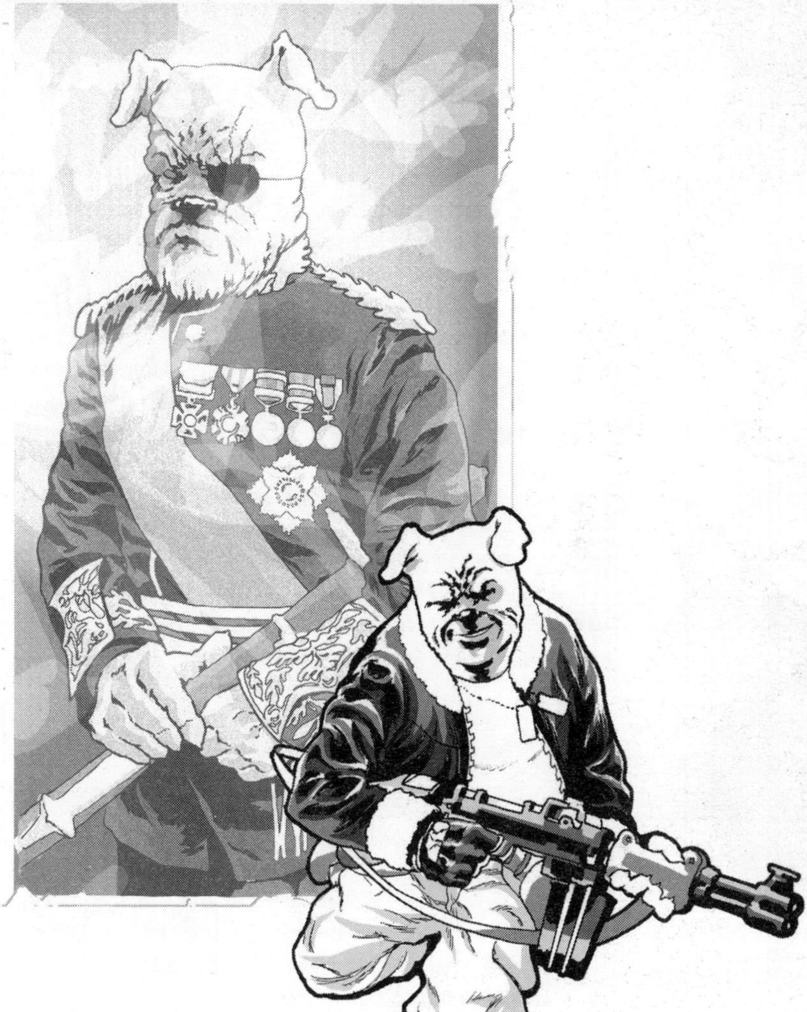

BULLDOG:

EMPIRE

by

Jason Cobley
&
Neill Cameron

JASON COBLEY

Date of birth: 7 June 1968

Jason comes from East Anglia, a UK region that is very, very flat. There, he patiently sits and waits for the seas to rise and claim him. While waiting, he watches anime – all the old favourites, plus newer ones such as *Spirited Away* and *Steamboy*. He likes his coffee strong and Italian, his ale real and despises Brussels sprouts, with their 'smell of damp washing'. 'People who make a virtue out of not reading' also earn his ire – and rightly so, the stupids. He's been crafting the chronicle of Captain Winston Bulldog for many years now, on the UK small press scene (plenty more where this came from), and hopes to one day see 'mecha transforming biplanes and Bulldog action figures in your local toyshop'. Yes, please!

http://www.jasoncobley.blogspot.com

NEILL CAMERON

Date of birth: 8 June 1977

Hip-hop, Giant Robots and his very own Lady Di do it for Neill, for whom working in an office is a major drag. He also hates 'stupid idiotic people with their hateful ignorant opinions' and, um, 'negativity'! Just take a look at his mind-boggling work, wherein early 2000AD meets Rupert Bear, Winsor (*Little Nemo in Slumberland*) McCay, the widescreen carnage of Marvel's *The Ultimates*, and the animation excellence of Studio Ghibli – *From Hell!* He badly wants to share his major manga series with you, the schoolgirl mecha *DMC:Riot* and combat tournament *ThumpCulture*.

http://www.neillcameron.com
http://www.bulldogempire.com

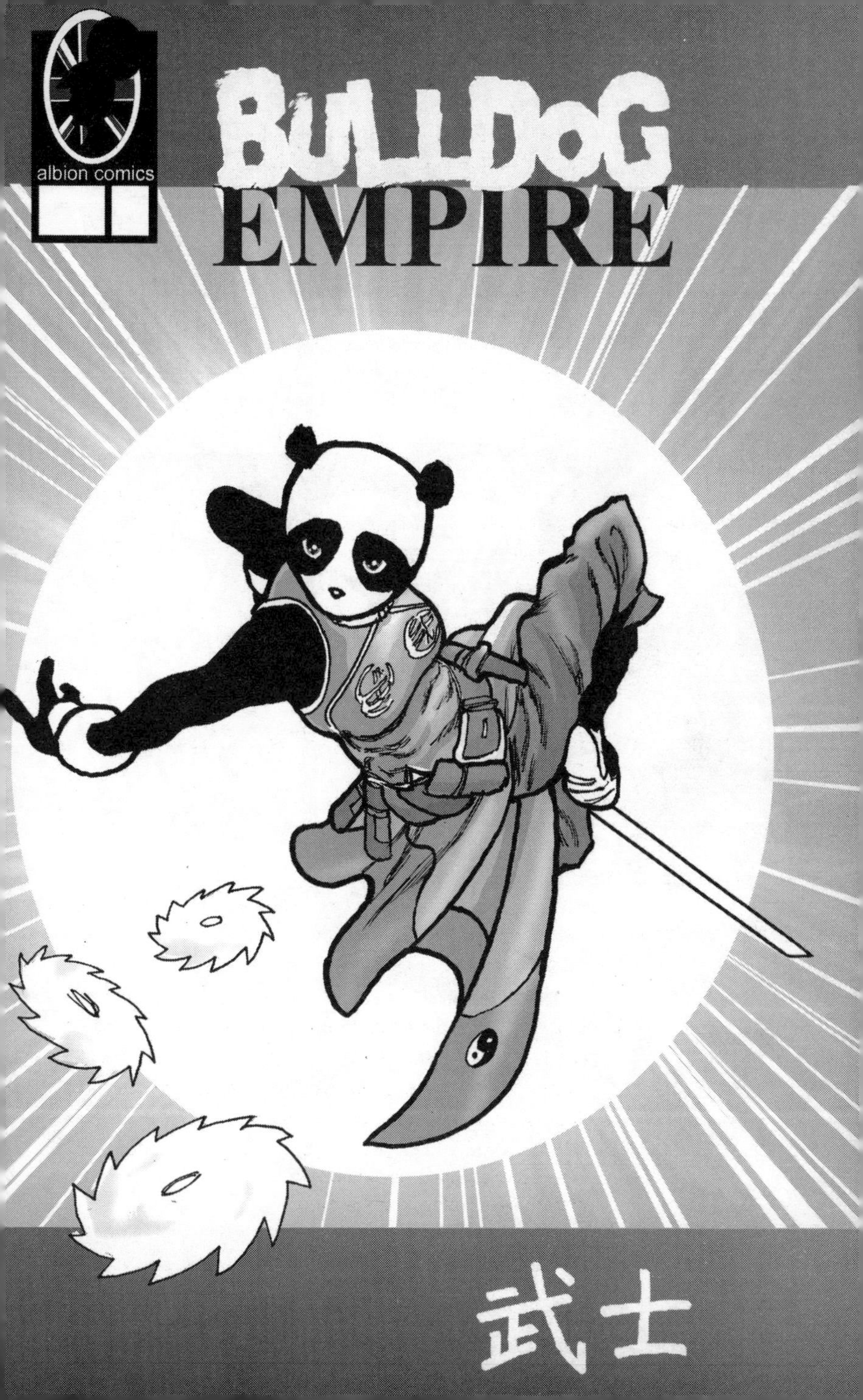
albion comics
BULLDOG
EMPIRE
武士

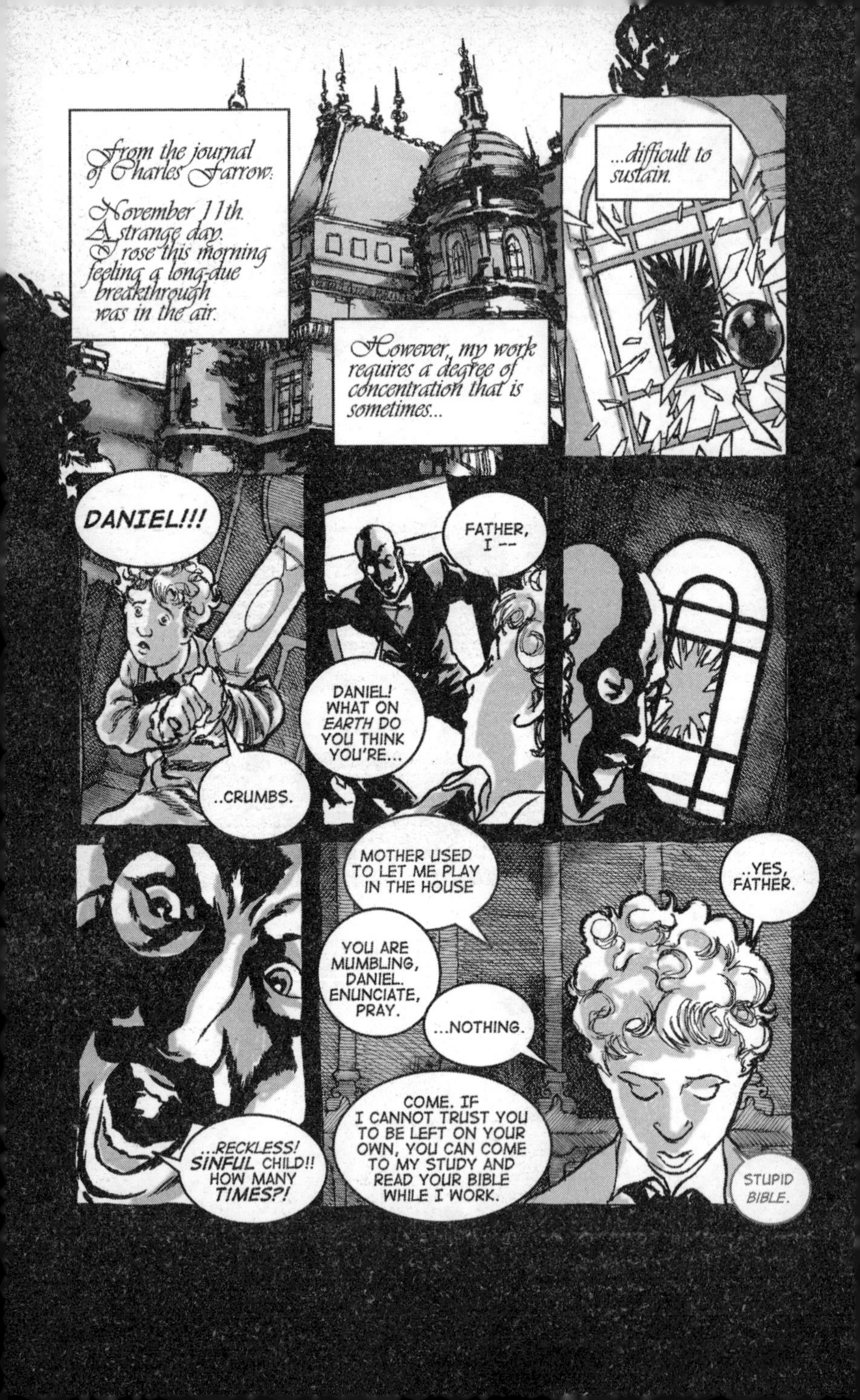
From the journal of Charles Farrow:
November 11th. A strange day. I rose this morning feeling a long-due breakthrough was in the air.
However, my work requires a degree of concentration that is sometimes...
...difficult to sustain.
DANIEL!!!
..CRUMBS.
FATHER, I --
DANIEL! WHAT ON EARTH DO YOU THINK YOU'RE...
...RECKLESS! SINFUL CHILD!! HOW MANY TIMES?!
MOTHER USED TO LET ME PLAY IN THE HOUSE
YOU ARE MUMBLING, DANIEL. ENUNCIATE, PRAY.
...NOTHING.
COME. IF I CANNOT TRUST YOU TO BE LEFT ON YOUR OWN, YOU CAN COME TO MY STUDY AND READ YOUR BIBLE WHILE I WORK.
..YES, FATHER.
STUPID BIBLE.

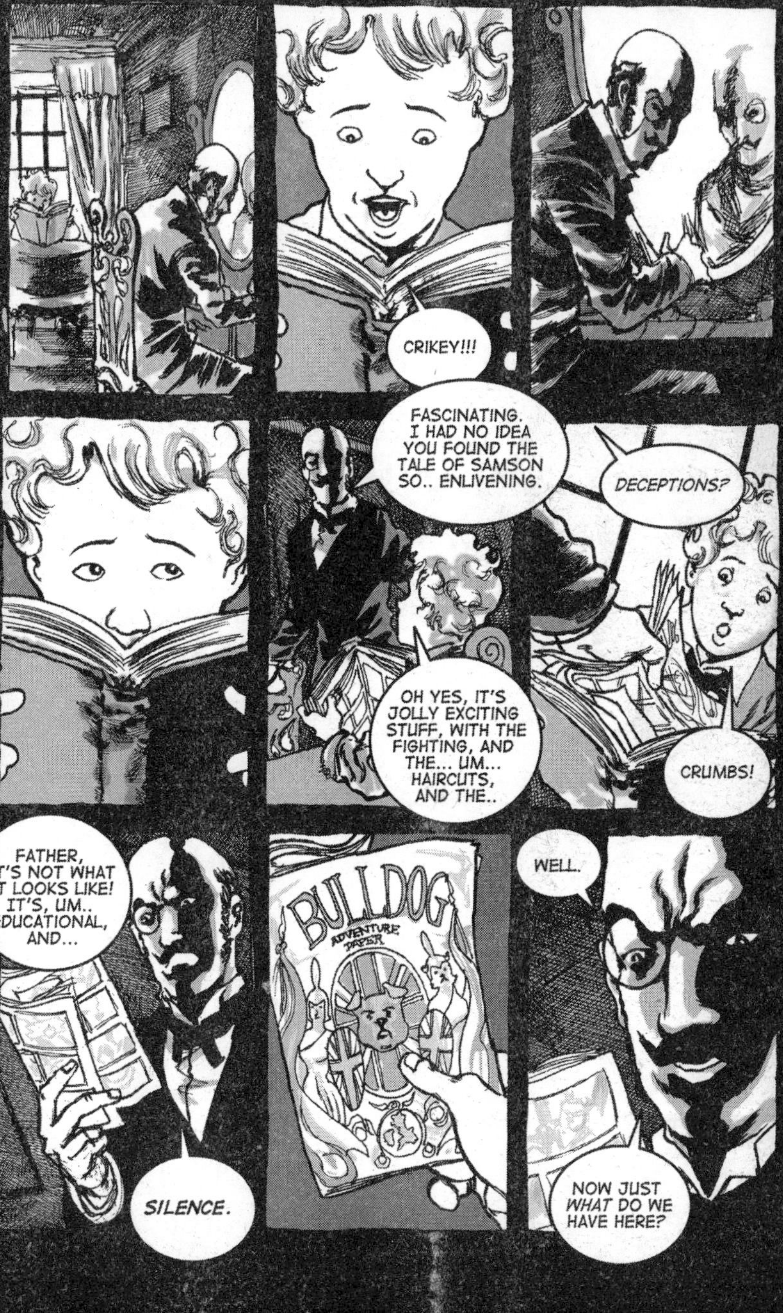
CRIKEY!!!
FASCINATING. I HAD NO IDEA YOU FOUND THE TALE OF SAMSON SO.. ENLIVENING.
OH YES, IT'S JOLLY EXCITING STUFF, WITH THE FIGHTING, AND THE... UM... HAIRCUTS, AND THE..
DECEPTIONS?
CRUMBS!
FATHER, IT'S NOT WHAT IT LOOKS LIKE! IT'S, UM.. EDUCATIONAL, AND...
SILENCE.
BULLDOG
ADVENTURE PAPER
WELL.
NOW JUST *WHAT* DO WE HAVE HERE?

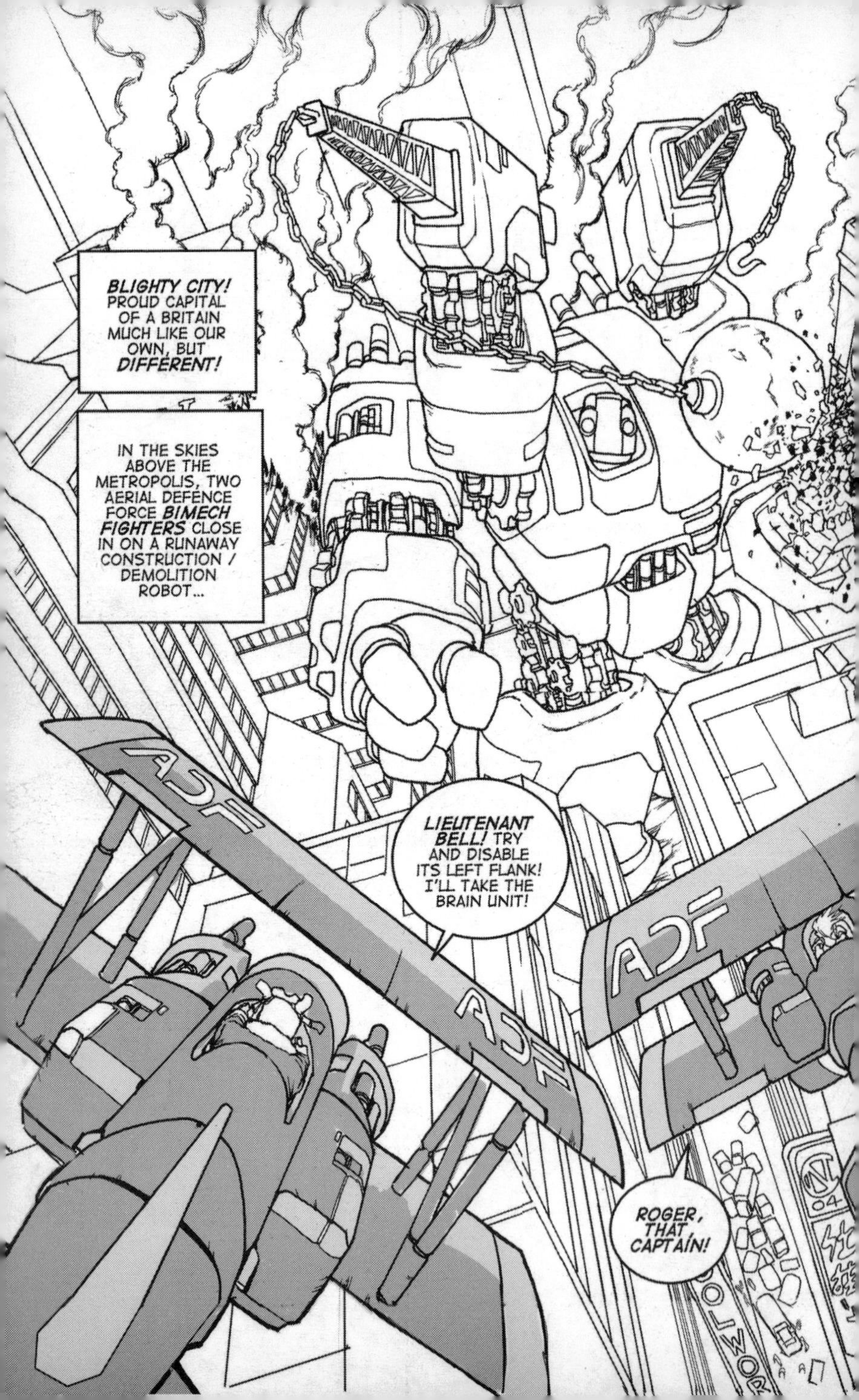
BLIGHTY CITY! PROUD CAPITAL OF A BRITAIN MUCH LIKE OUR OWN, BUT DIFFERENT!
IN THE SKIES ABOVE THE METROPOLIS, TWO AERIAL DEFENCE FORCE BIMECH FIGHTERS CLOSE IN ON A RUNAWAY CONSTRUCTION / DEMOLITION ROBOT...
LIEUTENANT BELL! TRY AND DISABLE ITS LEFT FLANK! I'LL TAKE THE BRAIN UNIT!
ADF
ADF
ADF
ROGER, THAT CAPTAIN!

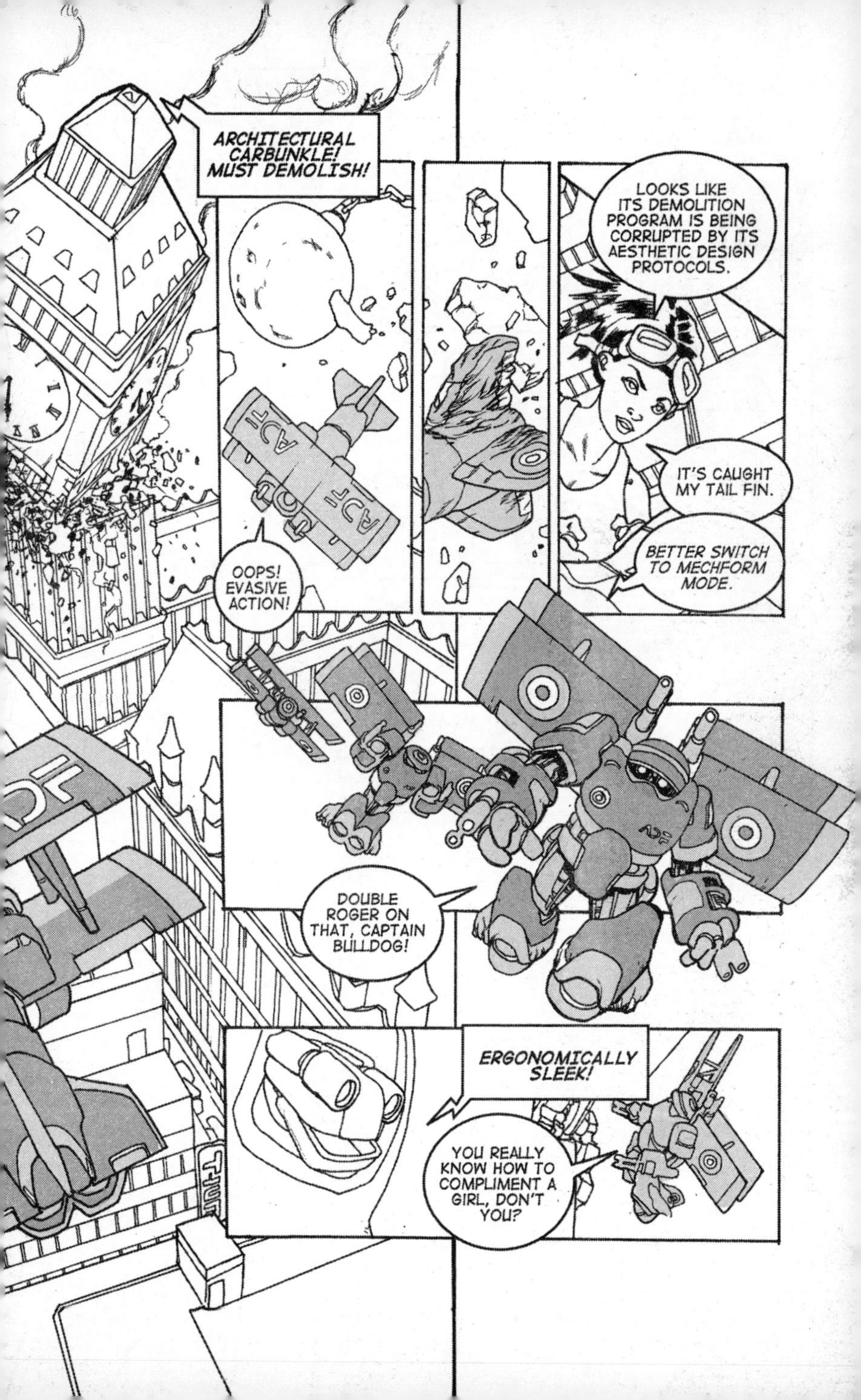
ARCHITECTURAL CARBUNKLE! MUST DEMOLISH!
OOPS! EVASIVE ACTION!
LOOKS LIKE ITS DEMOLITION PROGRAM IS BEING CORRUPTED BY ITS AESTHETIC DESIGN PROTOCOLS.
IT'S CAUGHT MY TAIL FIN.
BETTER SWITCH TO MECHFORM MODE.
DOUBLE ROGER ON THAT, CAPTAIN BULLDOG!
ERGONOMICALLY SLEEK!
YOU REALLY KNOW HOW TO COMPLIMENT A GIRL, DON'T YOU?

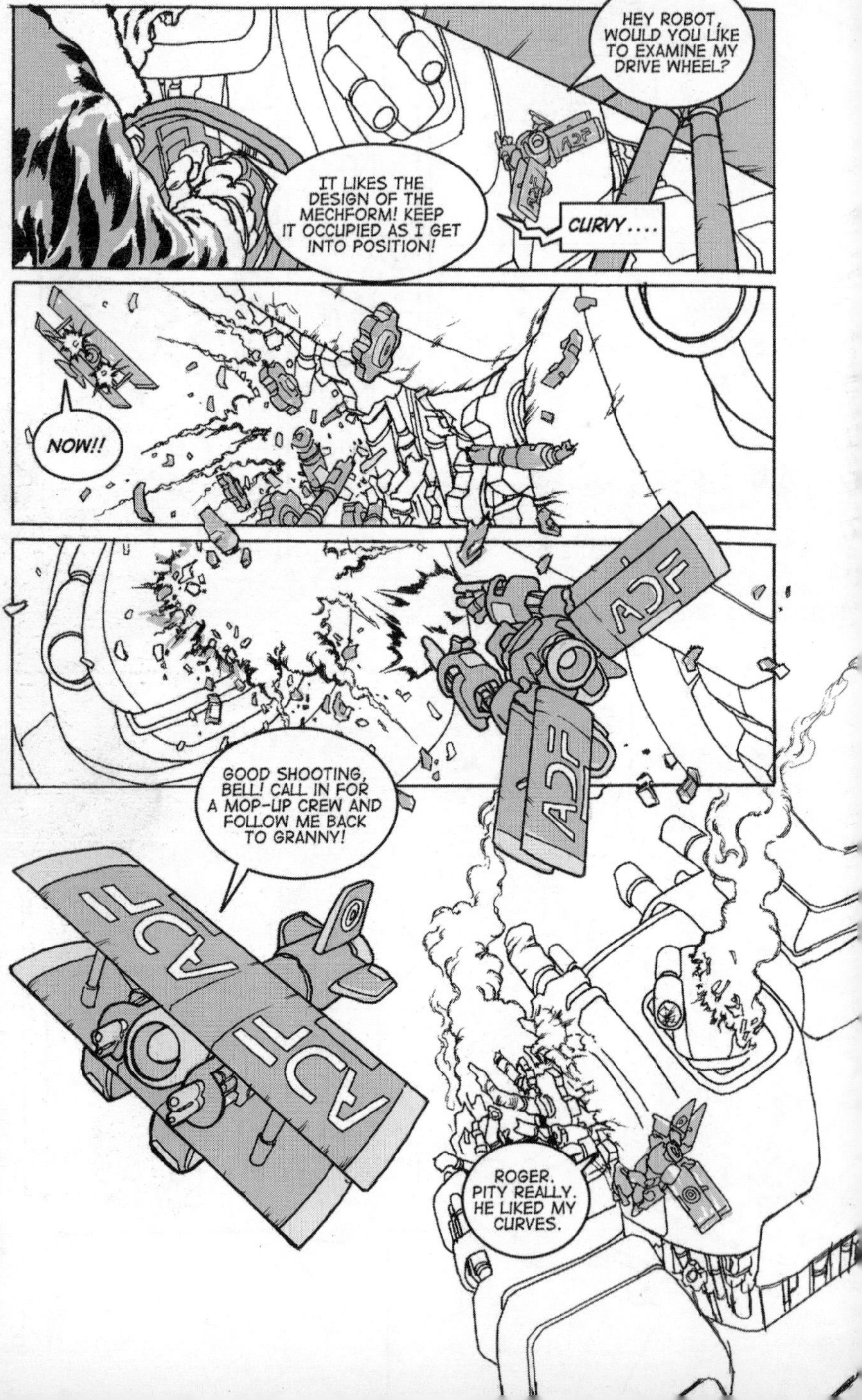
HEY ROBOT, WOULD YOU LIKE TO EXAMINE MY DRIVE WHEEL?
CURVY....
IT LIKES THE DESIGN OF THE MECHFORM! KEEP IT OCCUPIED AS I GET INTO POSITION!
NOW!!
GOOD SHOOTING, BELL! CALL IN FOR A MOP-UP CREW AND FOLLOW ME BACK TO GRANNY!
ROGER. PITY REALLY. HE LIKED MY CURVES.

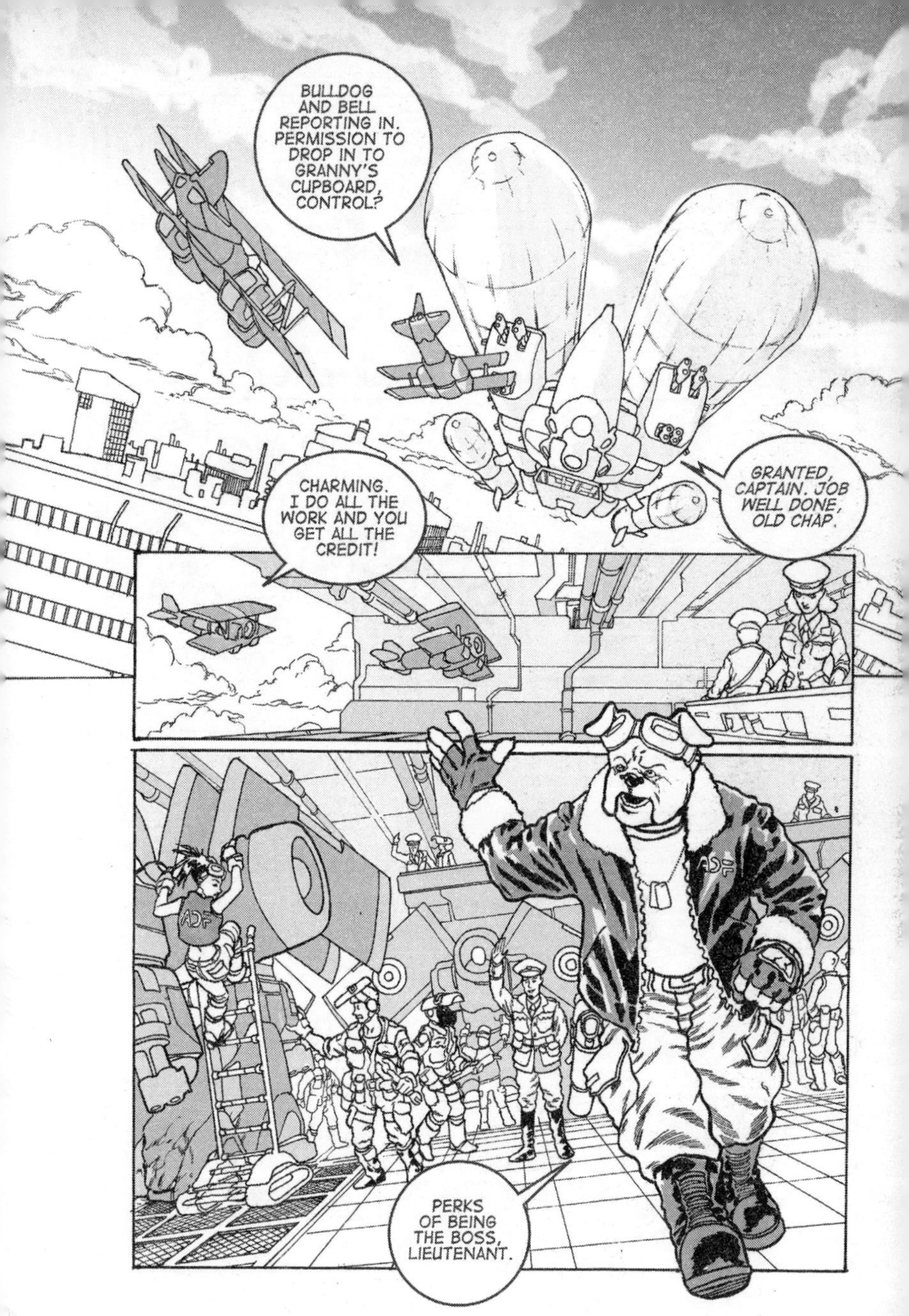
BULLDOG AND BELL REPORTING IN. PERMISSION TO DROP IN TO GRANNY'S CUPBOARD, CONTROL?
CHARMING. I DO ALL THE WORK AND YOU GET ALL THE CREDIT!
GRANTED, CAPTAIN. JOB WELL DONE, OLD CHAP.
ADF
ADF
PERKS OF BEING THE BOSS, LIEUTENANT.

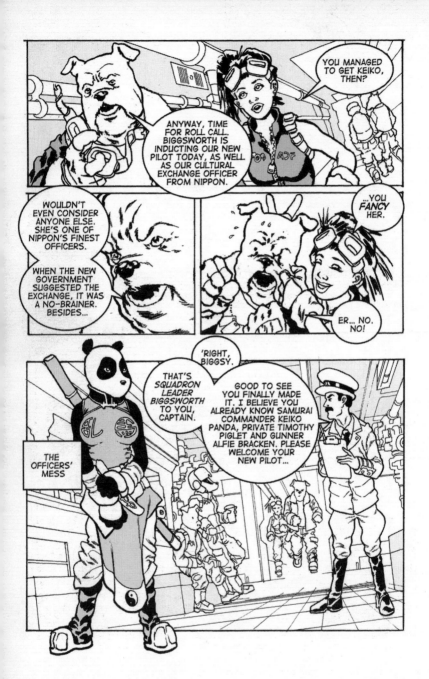

YOU MANAGED TO GET KEIKO, THEN?
ANYWAY, TIME FOR ROLL CALL. BIGGSWORTH IS INDUCTING OUR NEW PILOT TODAY, AS WELL AS OUR CULTURAL EXCHANGE OFFICER FROM NIPPON.
WOULDN'T EVEN CONSIDER ANYONE ELSE. SHE'S ONE OF NIPPON'S FINEST OFFICERS.
WHEN THE NEW GOVERNMENT SUGGESTED THE EXCHANGE, IT WAS A NO-BRAINER. BESIDES...
...YOU *FANCY* HER.
ER... NO. NO!
'RIGHT, BIGGSY.
THAT'S *SQUADRON LEADER BIGGSWORTH* TO YOU, CAPTAIN.
GOOD TO SEE YOU FINALLY MADE IT. I BELIEVE YOU ALREADY KNOW SAMURAI COMMANDER KEIKO PANDA, PRIVATE TIMOTHY PIGLET AND GUNNER ALFIE BRACKEN. PLEASE WELCOME YOUR NEW PILOT...
THE OFFICERS' MESS

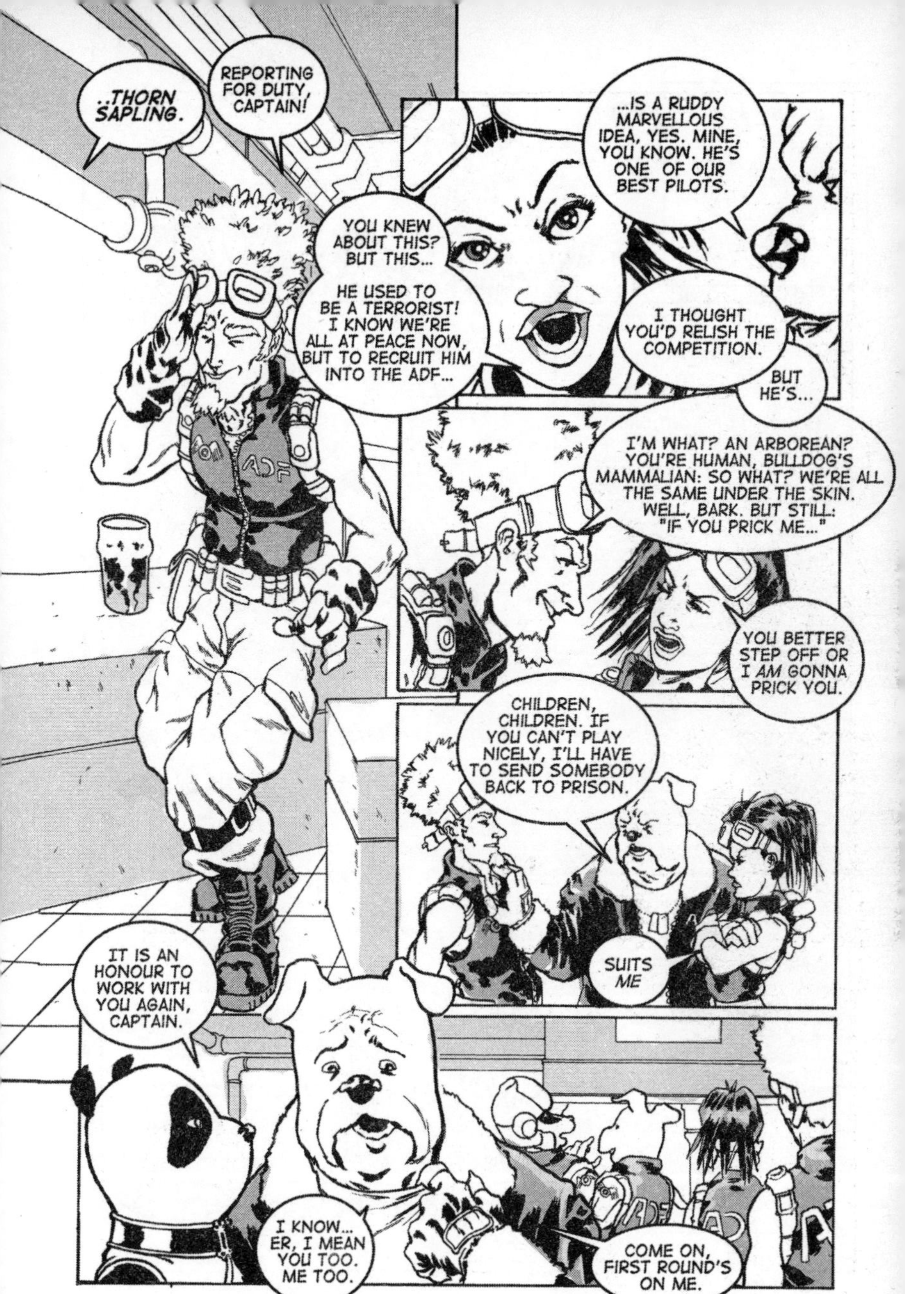
..THORN SAPLING.
REPORTING FOR DUTY, CAPTAIN!
YOU KNEW ABOUT THIS? BUT THIS...
...IS A RUDDY MARVELLOUS IDEA, YES. MINE, YOU KNOW. HE'S ONE OF OUR BEST PILOTS.
HE USED TO BE A TERRORIST! I KNOW WE'RE ALL AT PEACE NOW, BUT TO RECRUIT HIM INTO THE ADF...
I THOUGHT YOU'D RELISH THE COMPETITION.
BUT HE'S...
I'M WHAT? AN ARBOREAN? YOU'RE HUMAN, BULLDOG'S MAMMALIAN: SO WHAT? WE'RE ALL THE SAME UNDER THE SKIN. WELL, BARK. BUT STILL: "IF YOU PRICK ME..."
YOU BETTER STEP OFF OR I *AM* GONNA PRICK YOU.
CHILDREN, CHILDREN. IF YOU CAN'T PLAY NICELY, I'LL HAVE TO SEND SOMEBODY BACK TO PRISON.
SUITS *ME*
IT IS AN HONOUR TO WORK WITH YOU AGAIN, CAPTAIN.
I KNOW... ER, I MEAN YOU TOO. ME TOO.
COME ON, FIRST ROUND'S ON ME.

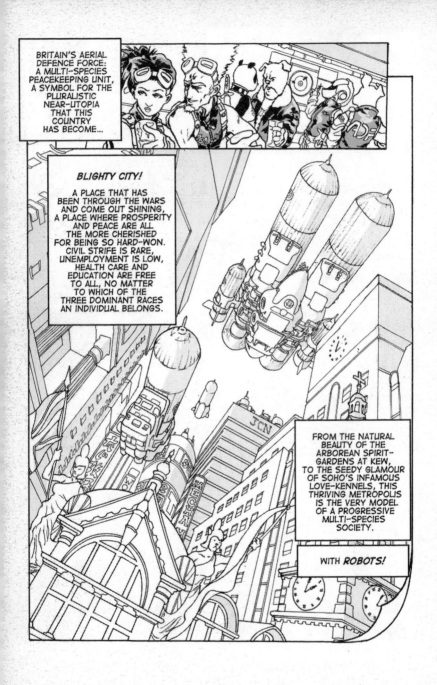

BRITAIN'S AERIAL DEFENCE FORCE: A MULTI-SPECIES PEACEKEEPING UNIT, A SYMBOL FOR THE PLURALISTIC NEAR-UTOPIA THAT THIS COUNTRY HAS BECOME...

BLIGHTY CITY!

A PLACE THAT HAS BEEN THROUGH THE WARS AND COME OUT SHINING, A PLACE WHERE PROSPERITY AND PEACE ARE ALL THE MORE CHERISHED FOR BEING SO HARD-WON. CIVIL STRIFE IS RARE, UNEMPLOYMENT IS LOW, HEALTH CARE AND EDUCATION ARE FREE TO ALL, NO MATTER TO WHICH OF THE THREE DOMINANT RACES AN INDIVIDUAL BELONGS.

FROM THE NATURAL BEAUTY OF THE ARBOREAN SPIRIT-GARDENS AT KEW, TO THE SEEDY GLAMOUR OF SOHO'S INFAMOUS LOVE-KENNELS, THIS THRIVING METROPOLIS IS THE VERY MODEL OF A PROGRESSIVE MULTI-SPECIES SOCIETY.

WITH *ROBOTS!*

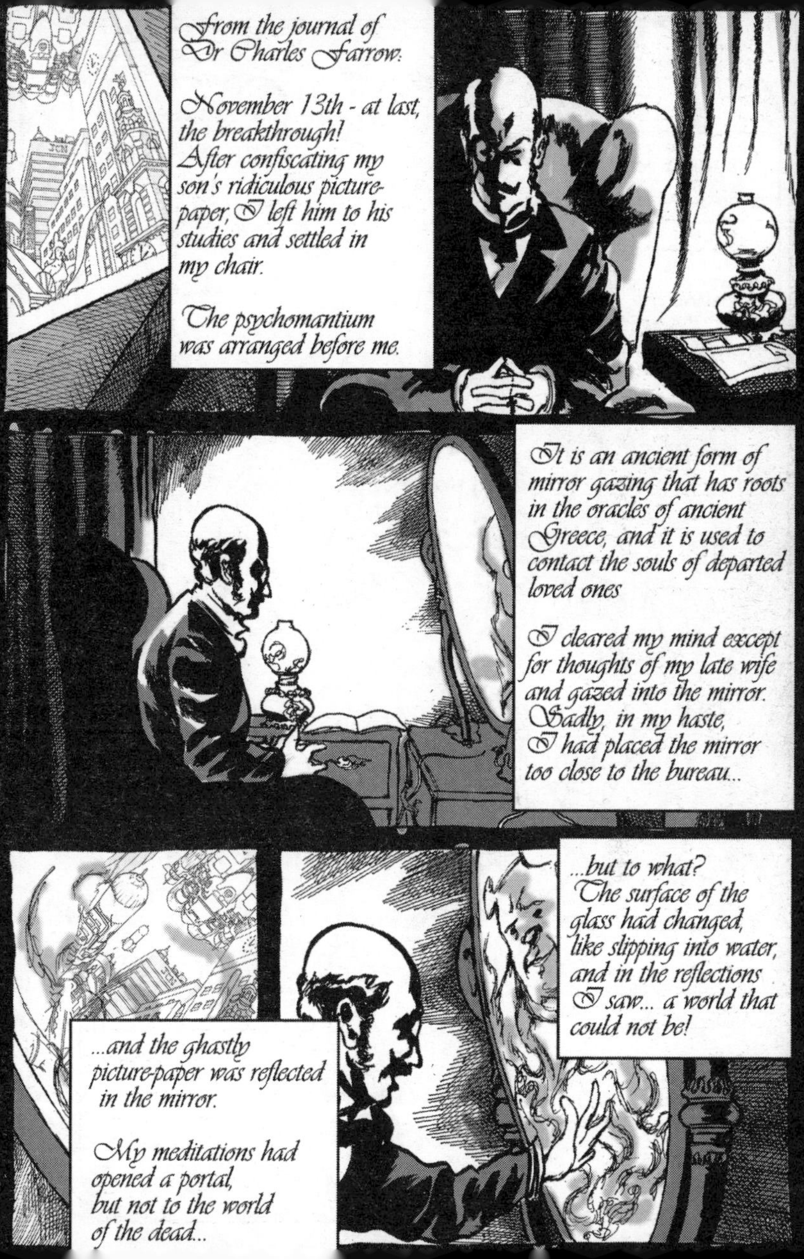
From the journal of Dr Charles Farrow:
November 13th - at last, the breakthrough! After confiscating my son's ridiculous picture-paper, I left him to his studies and settled in my chair.
The psychomantium was arranged before me.
It is an ancient form of mirror gazing that has roots in the oracles of ancient Greece, and it is used to contact the souls of departed loved ones
I cleared my mind except for thoughts of my late wife and gazed into the mirror. Sadly, in my haste, I had placed the mirror too close to the bureau...
...and the ghastly picture-paper was reflected in the mirror.
My meditations had opened a portal, but not to the world of the dead...
...but to what? The surface of the glass had changed, like slipping into water, and in the reflections I saw... a world that could not be!

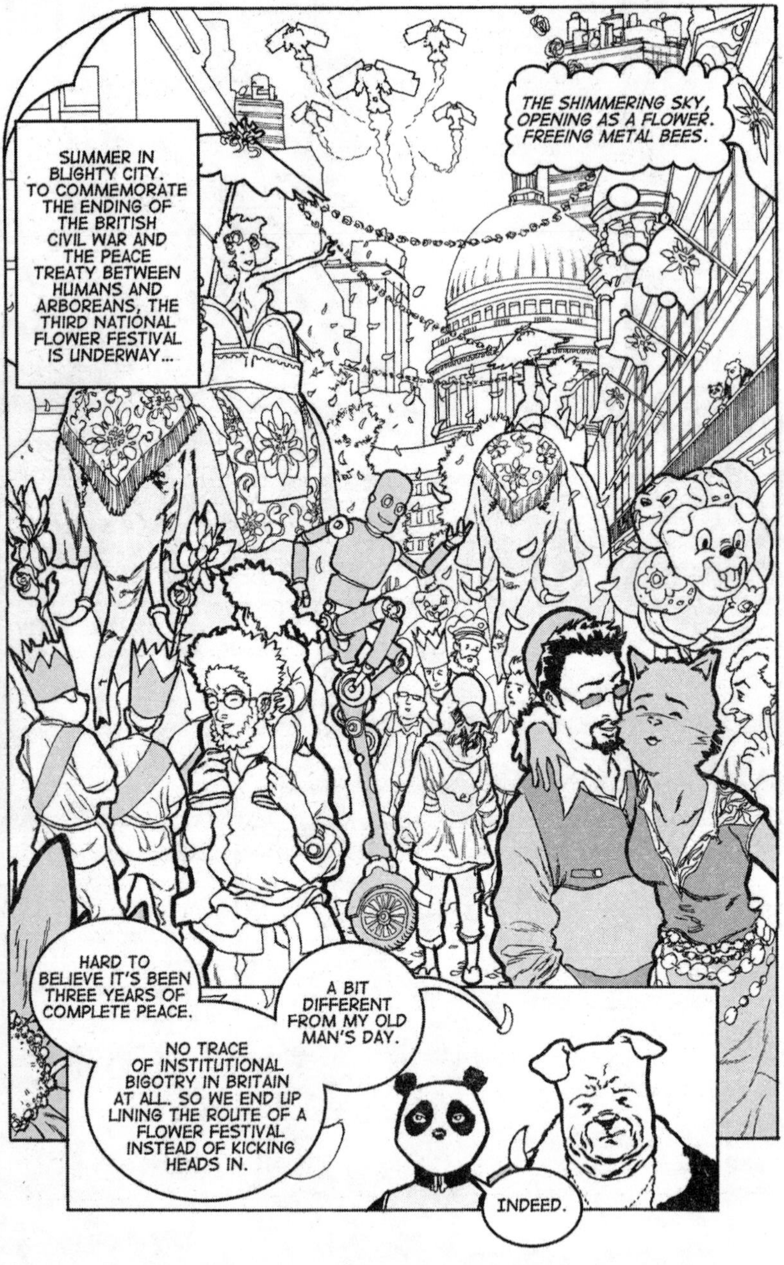
SUMMER IN BLIGHTY CITY. TO COMMEMORATE THE ENDING OF THE BRITISH CIVIL WAR AND THE PEACE TREATY BETWEEN HUMANS AND ARBOREANS, THE THIRD NATIONAL FLOWER FESTIVAL IS UNDERWAY...
THE SHIMMERING SKY, OPENING AS A FLOWER. FREEING METAL BEES.
HARD TO BELIEVE IT'S BEEN THREE YEARS OF COMPLETE PEACE.
A BIT DIFFERENT FROM MY OLD MAN'S DAY.
NO TRACE OF INSTITUTIONAL BIGOTRY IN BRITAIN AT ALL. SO WE END UP LINING THE ROUTE OF A FLOWER FESTIVAL INSTEAD OF KICKING HEADS IN.
INDEED.

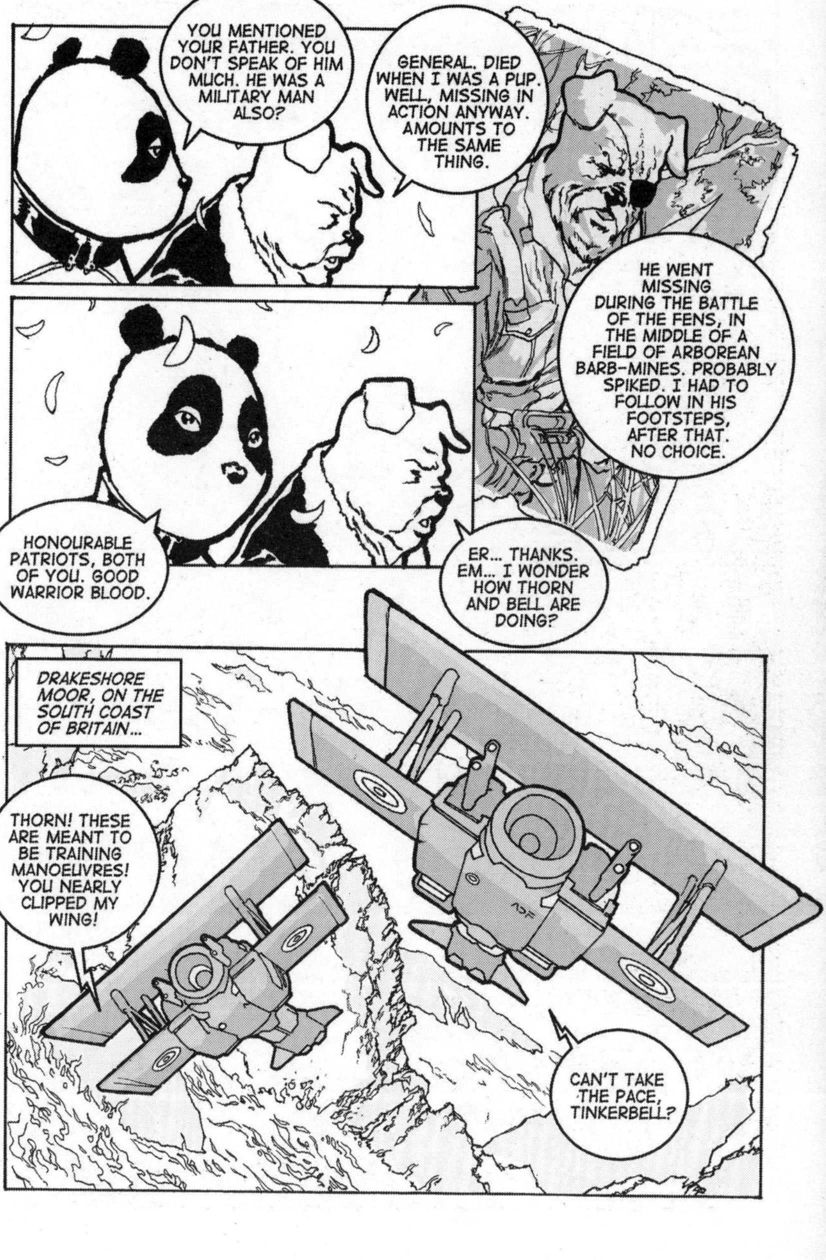
YOU MENTIONED YOUR FATHER. YOU DON'T SPEAK OF HIM MUCH. HE WAS A MILITARY MAN ALSO?
GENERAL. DIED WHEN I WAS A PUP. WELL, MISSING IN ACTION ANYWAY. AMOUNTS TO THE SAME THING.
HE WENT MISSING DURING THE BATTLE OF THE FENS, IN THE MIDDLE OF A FIELD OF ARBOREAN BARB-MINES. PROBABLY SPIKED. I HAD TO FOLLOW IN HIS FOOTSTEPS, AFTER THAT. NO CHOICE.
HONOURABLE PATRIOTS, BOTH OF YOU. GOOD WARRIOR BLOOD.
ER... THANKS. EM... I WONDER HOW THORN AND BELL ARE DOING?
DRAKESHORE MOOR, ON THE SOUTH COAST OF BRITAIN...
THORN! THESE ARE MEANT TO BE TRAINING MANOEUVRES! YOU NEARLY CLIPPED MY WING!
CAN'T TAKE THE PACE, TINKERBELL?

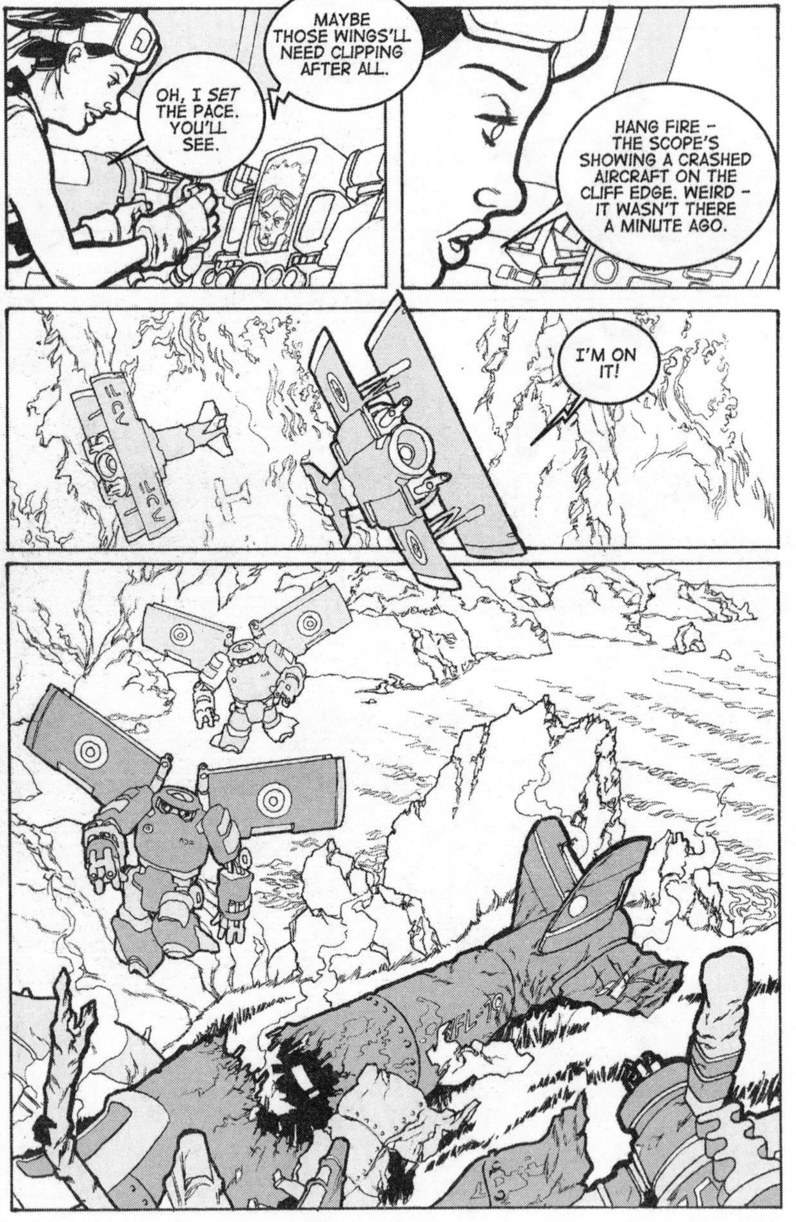
OH, I *SET* THE PACE. YOU'LL SEE.
MAYBE THOSE WINGS'LL NEED CLIPPING AFTER ALL.
HANG FIRE – THE SCOPE'S SHOWING A CRASHED AIRCRAFT ON THE CLIFF EDGE. WEIRD – IT WASN'T THERE A MINUTE AGO.
I'M ON IT!

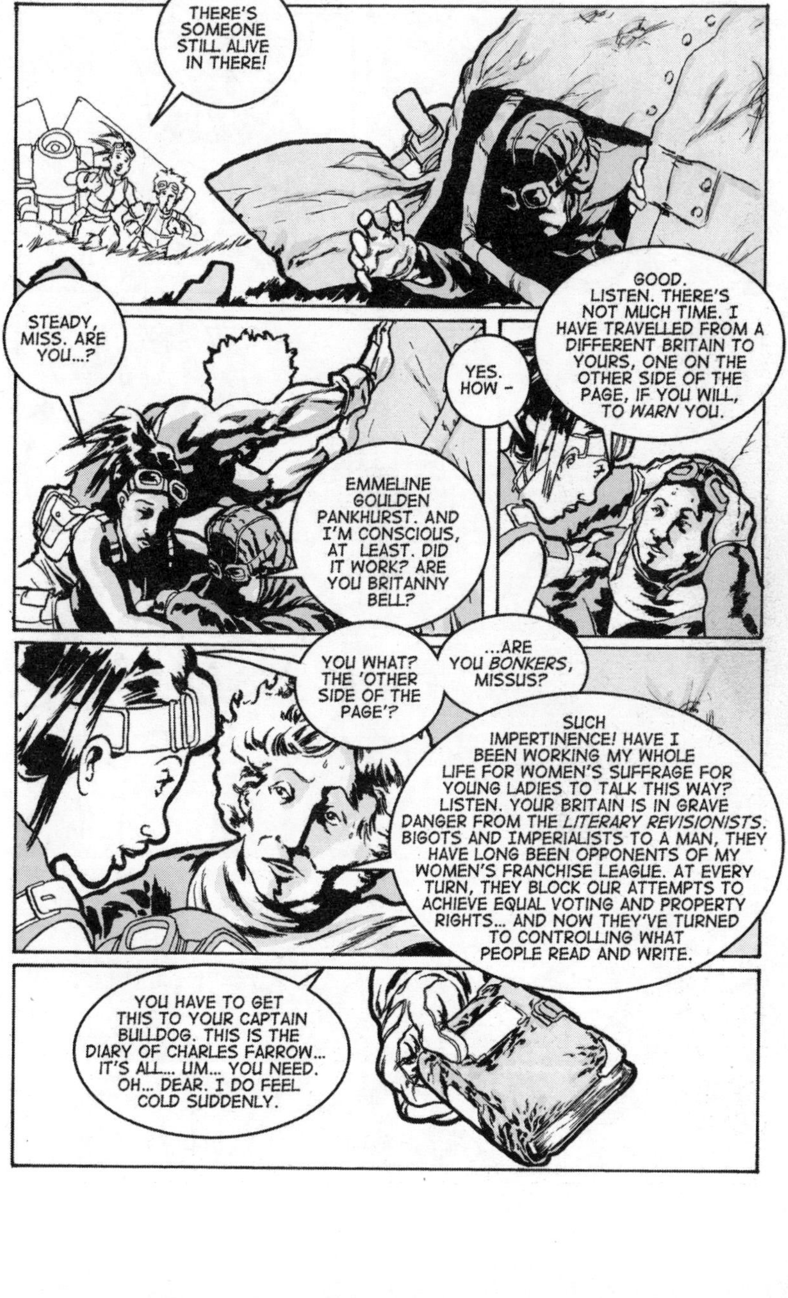
THERE'S SOMEONE STILL ALIVE IN THERE!
STEADY, MISS. ARE YOU...?
EMMELINE GOULDEN PANKHURST. AND I'M CONSCIOUS, AT LEAST. DID IT WORK? ARE YOU BRITANNY BELL?
YES. HOW -
GOOD. LISTEN. THERE'S NOT MUCH TIME. I HAVE TRAVELLED FROM A DIFFERENT BRITAIN TO YOURS, ONE ON THE OTHER SIDE OF THE PAGE, IF YOU WILL, TO *WARN* YOU.
YOU WHAT? THE 'OTHER SIDE OF THE PAGE'?
...ARE YOU *BONKERS*, MISSUS?
SUCH IMPERTINENCE! HAVE I BEEN WORKING MY WHOLE LIFE FOR WOMEN'S SUFFRAGE FOR YOUNG LADIES TO TALK THIS WAY? LISTEN. YOUR BRITAIN IS IN GRAVE DANGER FROM THE *LITERARY REVISIONISTS*. BIGOTS AND IMPERIALISTS TO A MAN, THEY HAVE LONG BEEN OPPONENTS OF MY WOMEN'S FRANCHISE LEAGUE. AT EVERY TURN, THEY BLOCK OUR ATTEMPTS TO ACHIEVE EQUAL VOTING AND PROPERTY RIGHTS... AND NOW THEY'VE TURNED TO CONTROLLING WHAT PEOPLE READ AND WRITE.
YOU HAVE TO GET THIS TO YOUR CAPTAIN BULLDOG. THIS IS THE DIARY OF CHARLES FARROW... IT'S ALL... UM... YOU NEED. OH... DEAR. I DO FEEL COLD SUDDENLY.

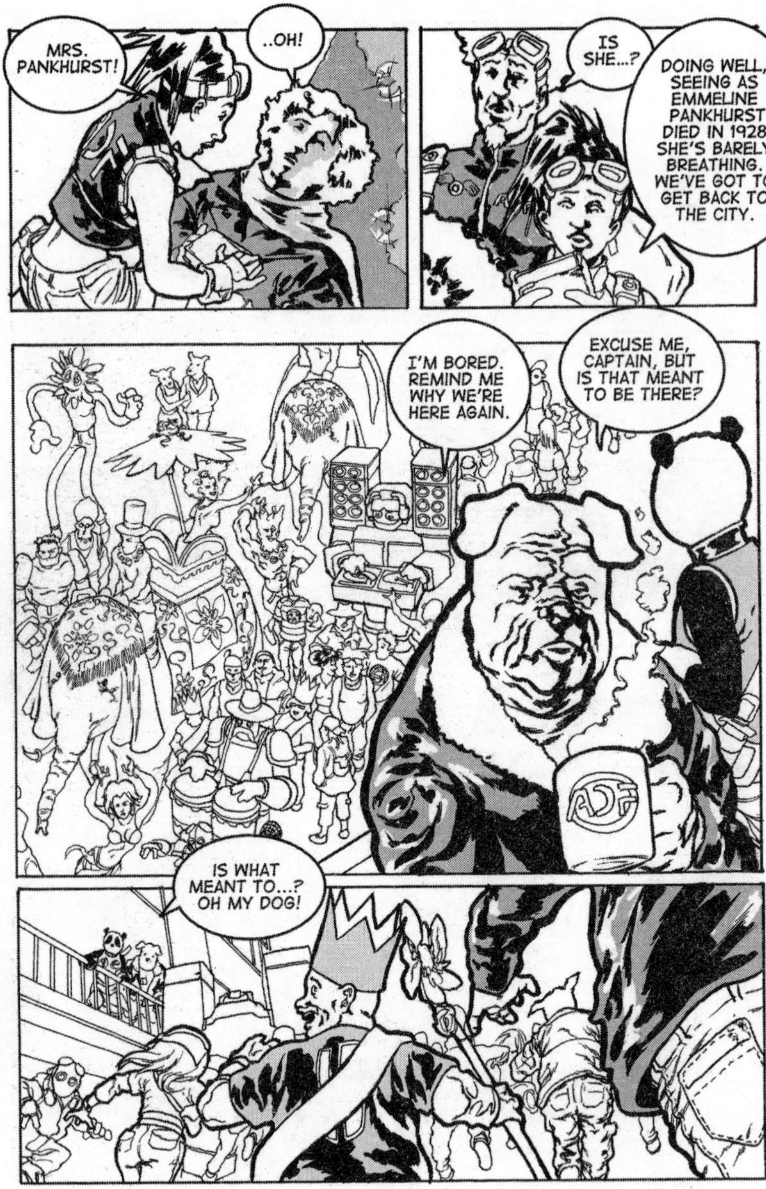
MRS. PANKHURST!
..OH!
IS SHE...?
DOING WELL, SEEING AS EMMELINE PANKHURST DIED IN 1928. SHE'S BARELY BREATHING. WE'VE GOT TO GET BACK TO THE CITY.
I'M BORED. REMIND ME WHY WE'RE HERE AGAIN.
EXCUSE ME, CAPTAIN, BUT IS THAT MEANT TO BE THERE?
ADF
IS WHAT MEANT TO...? OH MY DOG!

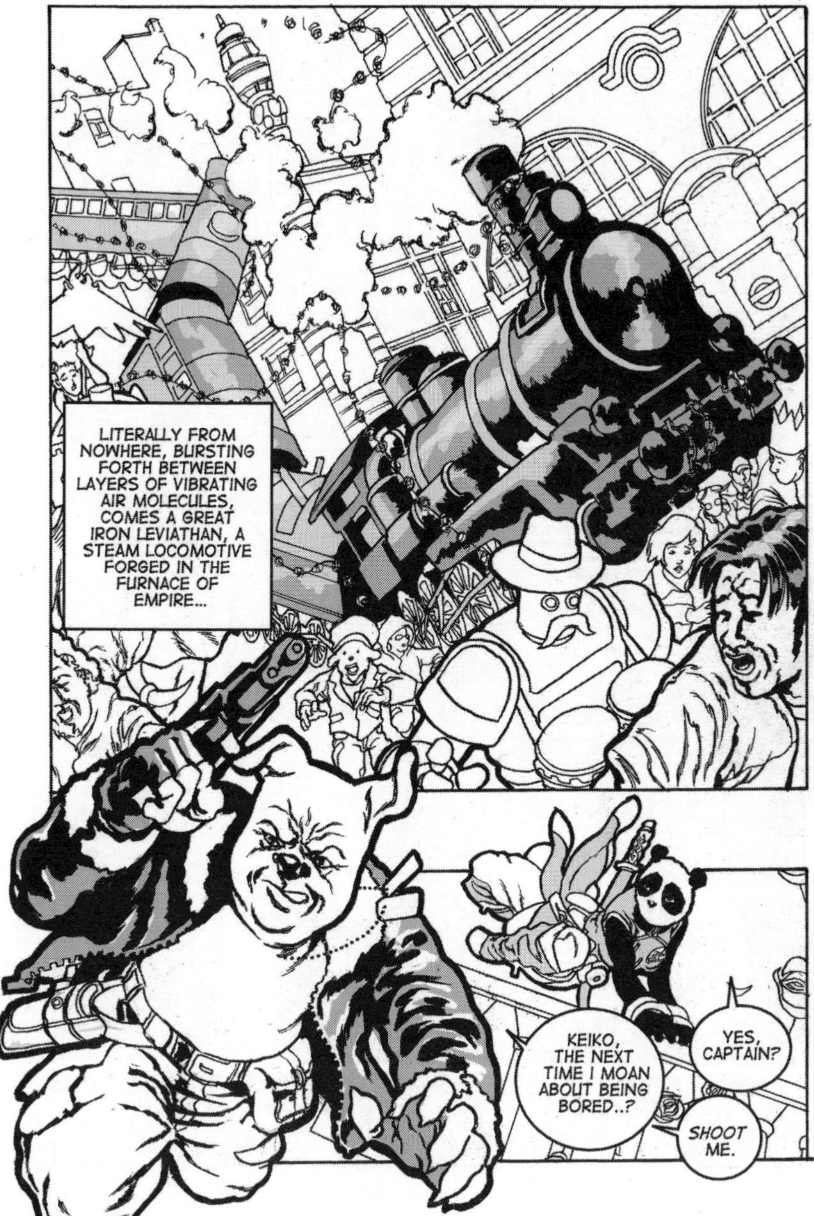
LITERALLY FROM NOWHERE, BURSTING FORTH BETWEEN LAYERS OF VIBRATING AIR MOLECULES, COMES A GREAT IRON LEVIATHAN, A STEAM LOCOMOTIVE FORGED IN THE FURNACE OF EMPIRE...
KEIKO, THE NEXT TIME I MOAN ABOUT BEING BORED..?
YES, CAPTAIN?
SHOOT ME.

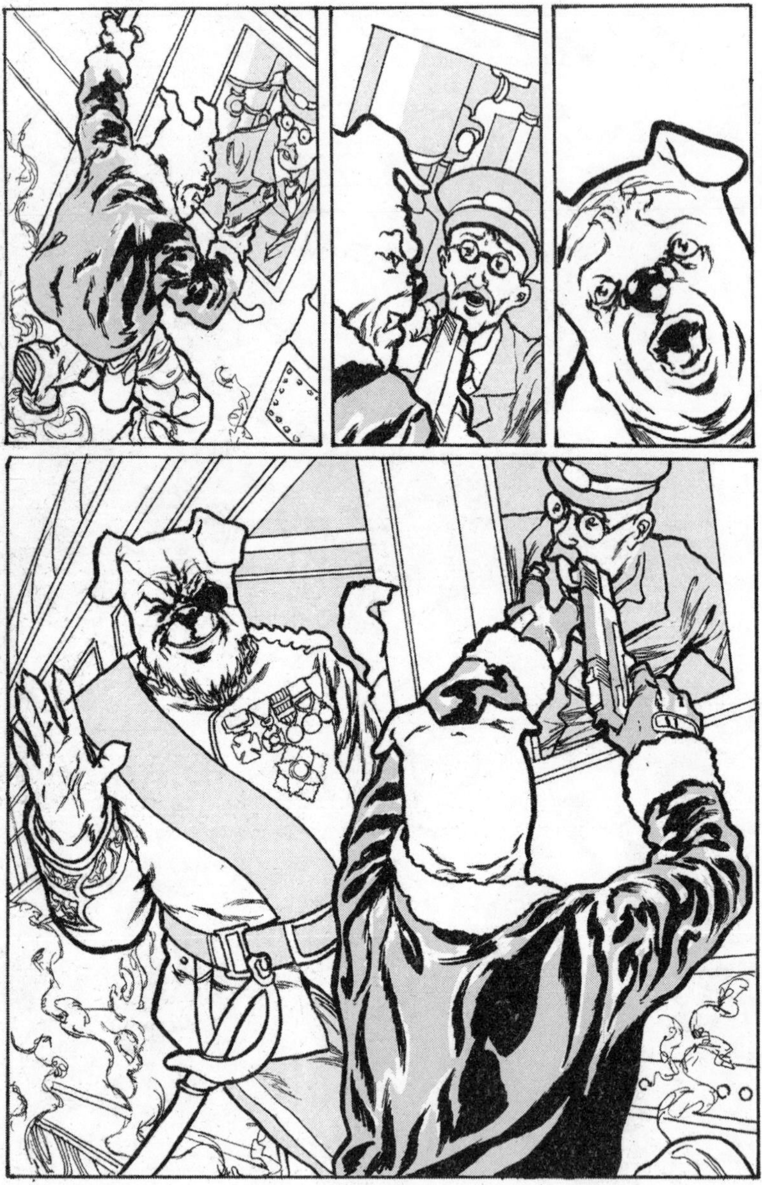

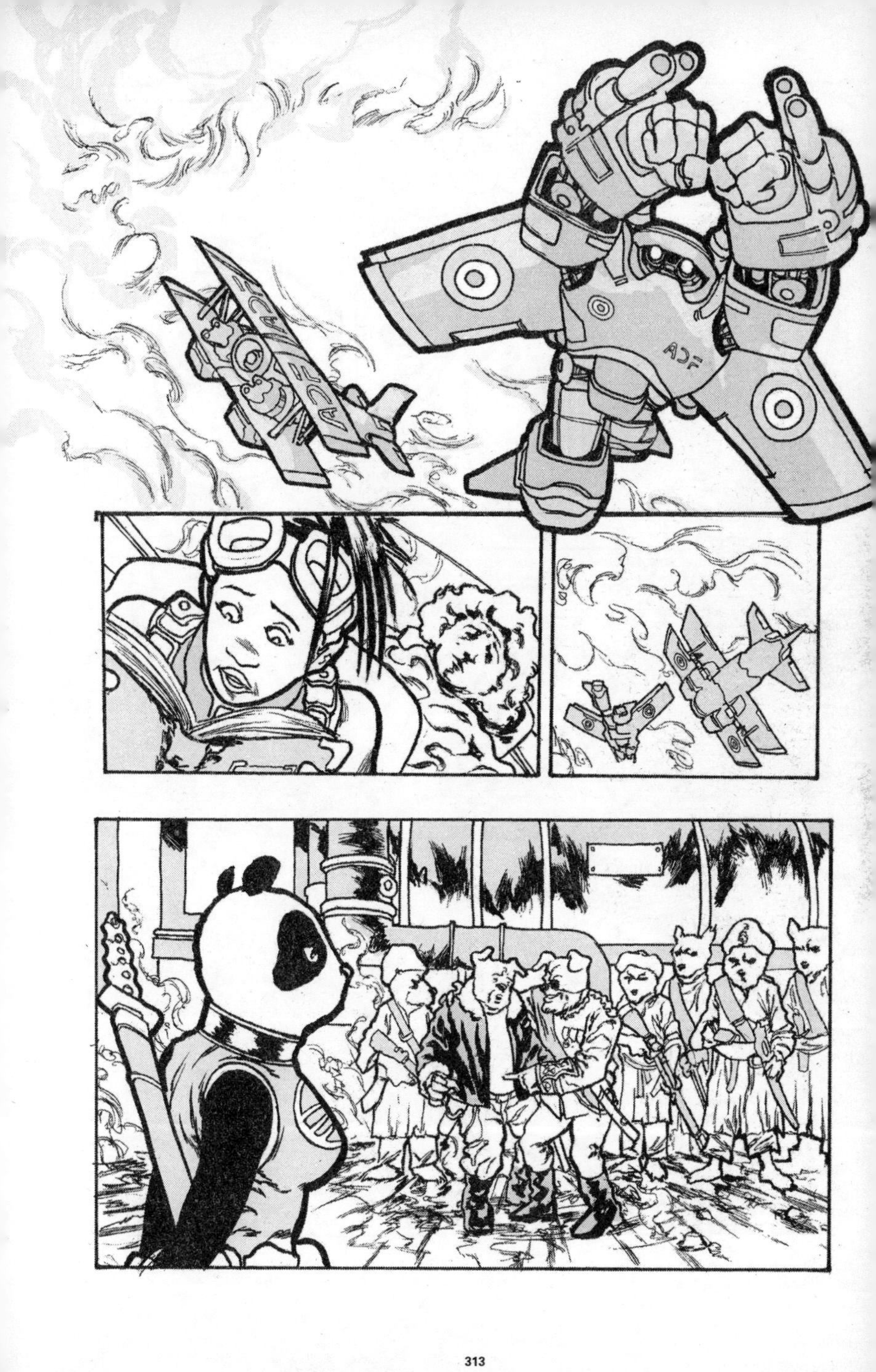

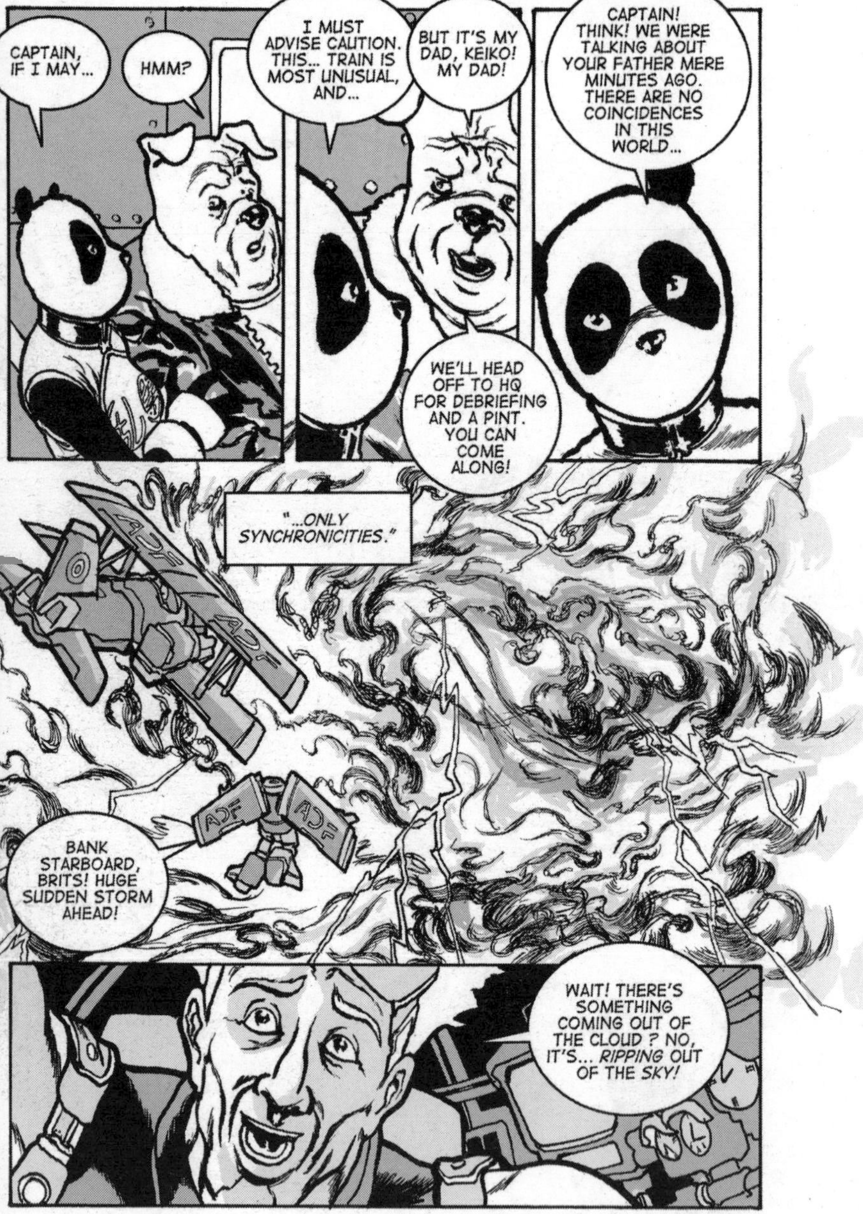
CAPTAIN, IF I MAY...
HMM?
I MUST ADVISE CAUTION. THIS... TRAIN IS MOST UNUSUAL, AND...
BUT IT'S MY DAD, KEIKO! MY DAD!
WE'LL HEAD OFF TO HQ FOR DEBRIEFING AND A PINT. YOU CAN COME ALONG!
CAPTAIN! THINK! WE WERE TALKING ABOUT YOUR FATHER MERE MINUTES AGO. THERE ARE NO COINCIDENCES IN THIS WORLD...
"...ONLY SYNCHRONICITIES."
ADF
ADF
ADF
ADF
BANK STARBOARD, BRITS! HUGE SUDDEN STORM AHEAD!
WAIT! THERE'S SOMETHING COMING OUT OF THE CLOUD ? NO, IT'S... *RIPPING* OUT OF THE *SKY!*

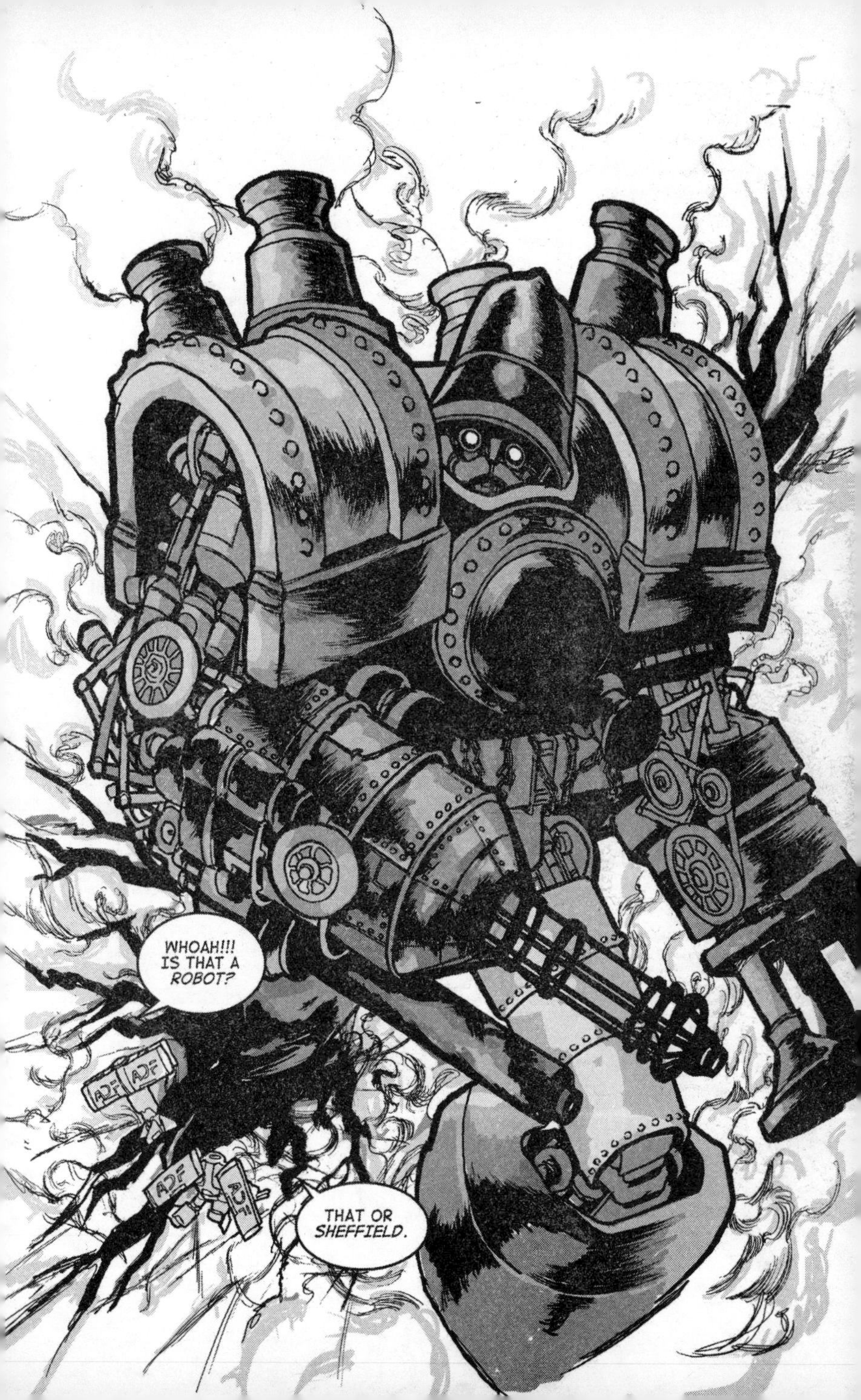
WHOAH!!! IS THAT A *ROBOT?*
THAT OR *SHEFFIELD.*
ADF
ADF
ADF
ADF

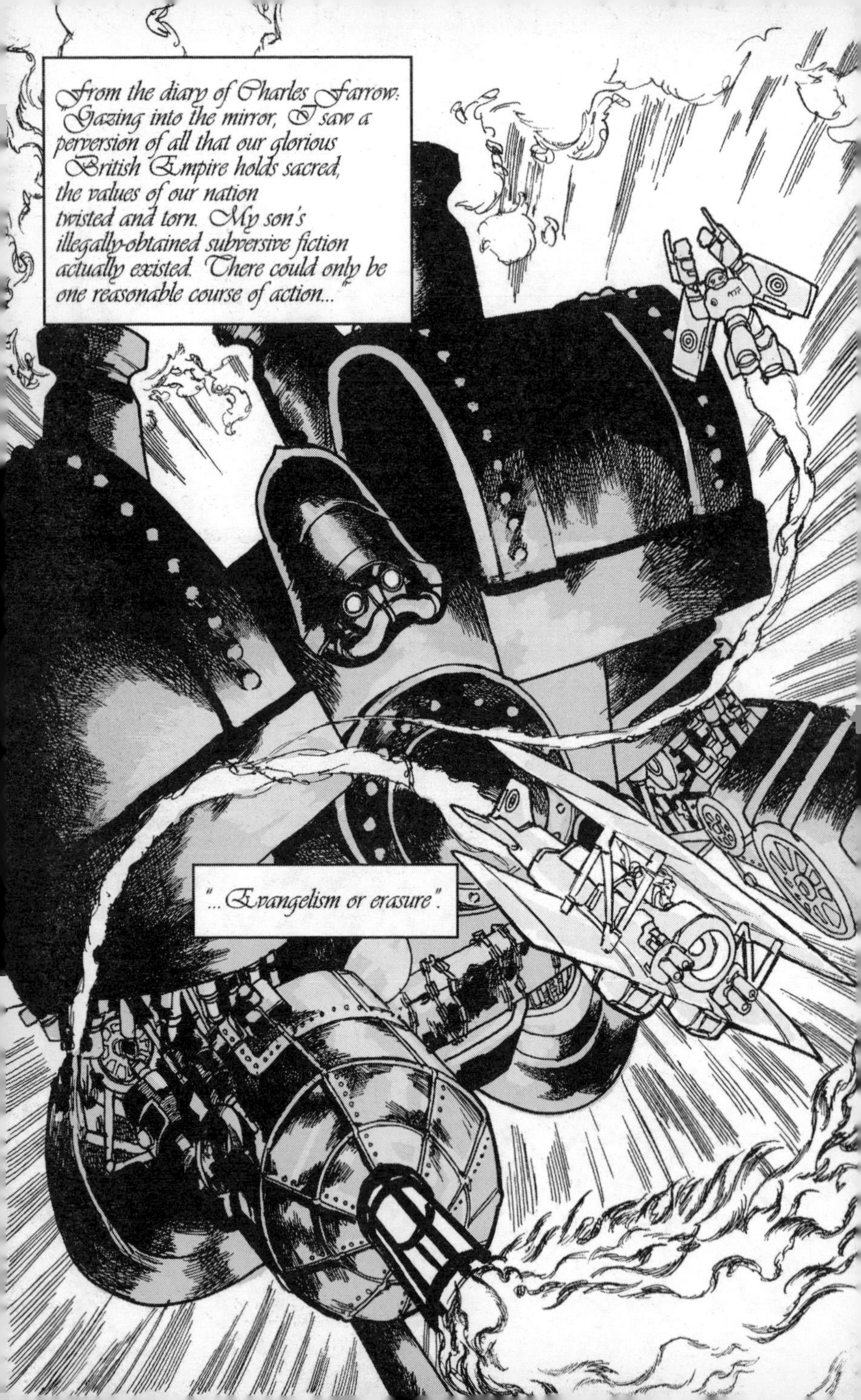
From the diary of Charles Farrow: Gazing into the mirror, I saw a perversion of all that our glorious British Empire holds sacred, the values of our nation twisted and torn. My son's illegally-obtained subversive fiction actually existed. There could only be one reasonable course of action...
"...Evangelism or erasure".

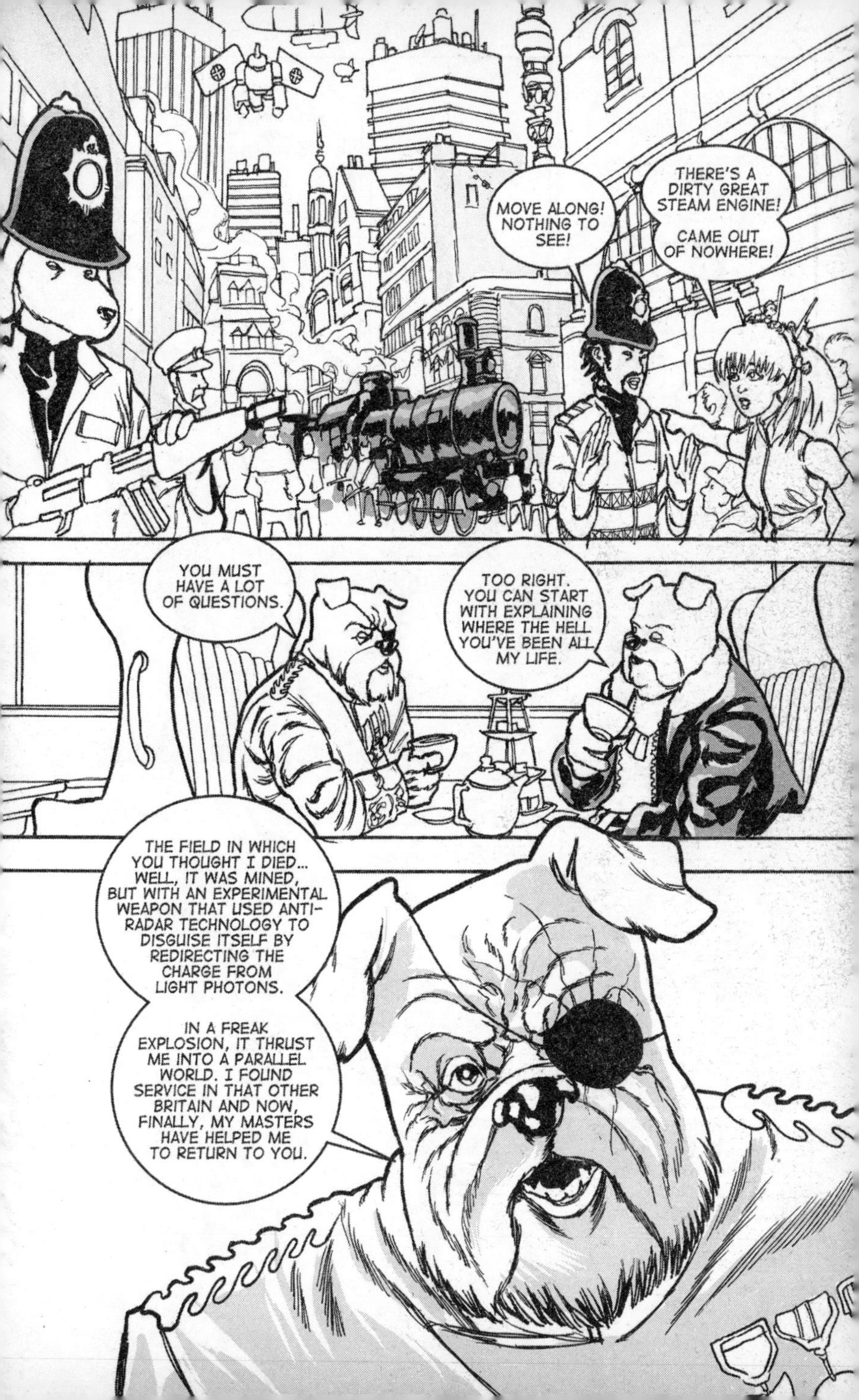
MOVE ALONG! NOTHING TO SEE!
THERE'S A DIRTY GREAT STEAM ENGINE!
CAME OUT OF NOWHERE!
YOU MUST HAVE A LOT OF QUESTIONS.
TOO RIGHT. YOU CAN START WITH EXPLAINING WHERE THE HELL YOU'VE BEEN ALL MY LIFE.
THE FIELD IN WHICH YOU THOUGHT I DIED... WELL, IT WAS MINED, BUT WITH AN EXPERIMENTAL WEAPON THAT USED ANTI-RADAR TECHNOLOGY TO DISGUISE ITSELF BY REDIRECTING THE CHARGE FROM LIGHT PHOTONS.
IN A FREAK EXPLOSION, IT THRUST ME INTO A PARALLEL WORLD. I FOUND SERVICE IN THAT OTHER BRITAIN AND NOW, FINALLY, MY MASTERS HAVE HELPED ME TO RETURN TO YOU.

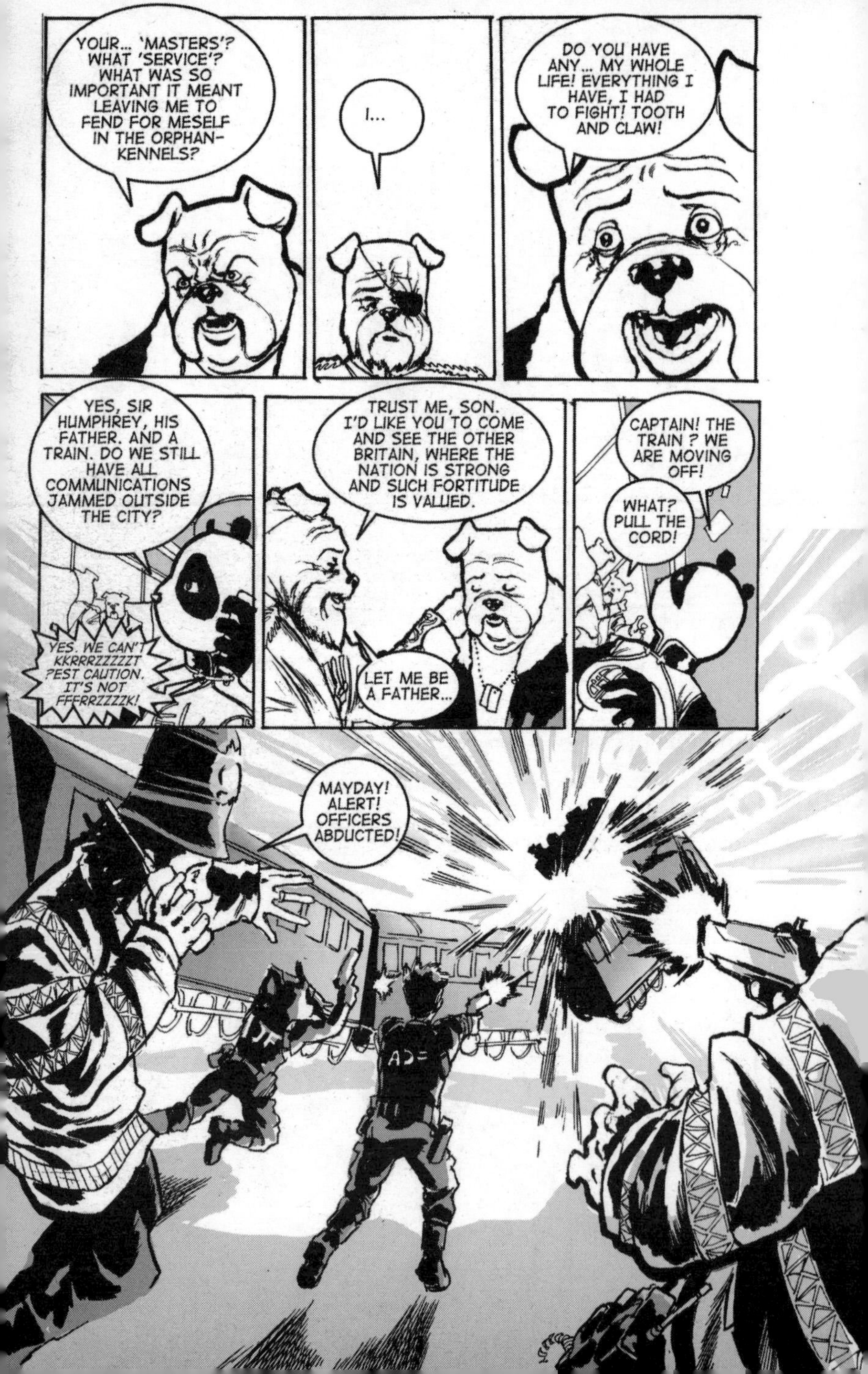
YOUR... 'MASTERS'? WHAT 'SERVICE'? WHAT WAS SO IMPORTANT IT MEANT LEAVING ME TO FEND FOR MESELF IN THE ORPHAN-KENNELS?
I...
DO YOU HAVE ANY... MY WHOLE LIFE! EVERYTHING I HAVE, I HAD TO FIGHT! TOOTH AND CLAW!
YES, SIR HUMPHREY, HIS FATHER. AND A TRAIN. DO WE STILL HAVE ALL COMMUNICATIONS JAMMED OUTSIDE THE CITY?
YES. WE CAN'T KKRRRZZZZZT ?EST CAUTION. IT'S NOT FFFRRZZZZK!
TRUST ME, SON. I'D LIKE YOU TO COME AND SEE THE OTHER BRITAIN, WHERE THE NATION IS STRONG AND SUCH FORTITUDE IS VALUED.
LET ME BE A FATHER...
CAPTAIN! THE TRAIN ? WE ARE MOVING OFF!
WHAT? PULL THE CORD!
MAYDAY! ALERT! OFFICERS ABDUCTED!

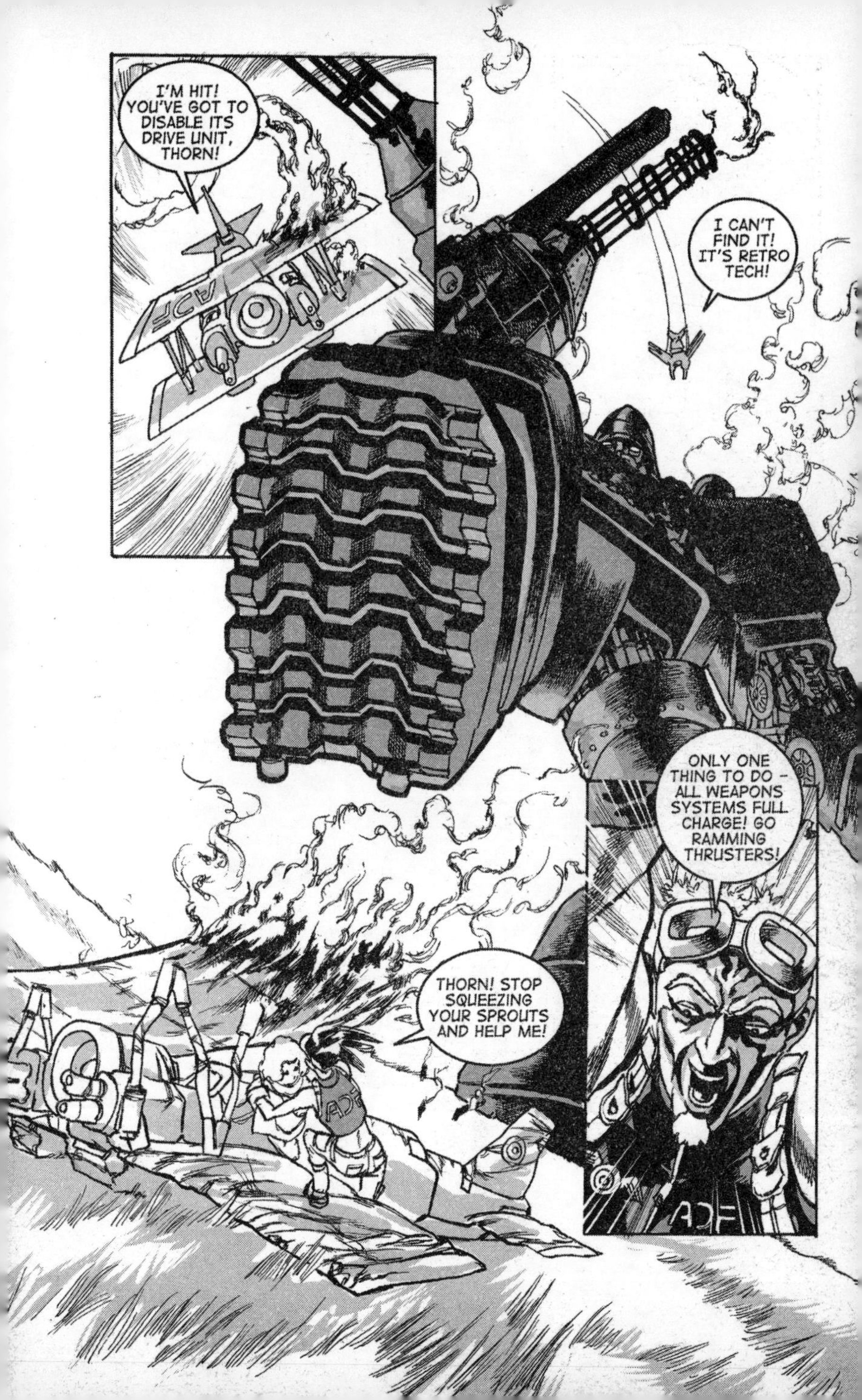
I'M HIT! YOU'VE GOT TO DISABLE ITS DRIVE UNIT, THORN!
I CAN'T FIND IT! IT'S RETRO TECH!
THORN! STOP SQUEEZING YOUR SPROUTS AND HELP ME!
ONLY ONE THING TO DO - ALL WEAPONS SYSTEMS FULL CHARGE! GO RAMMING THRUSTERS!
ADF

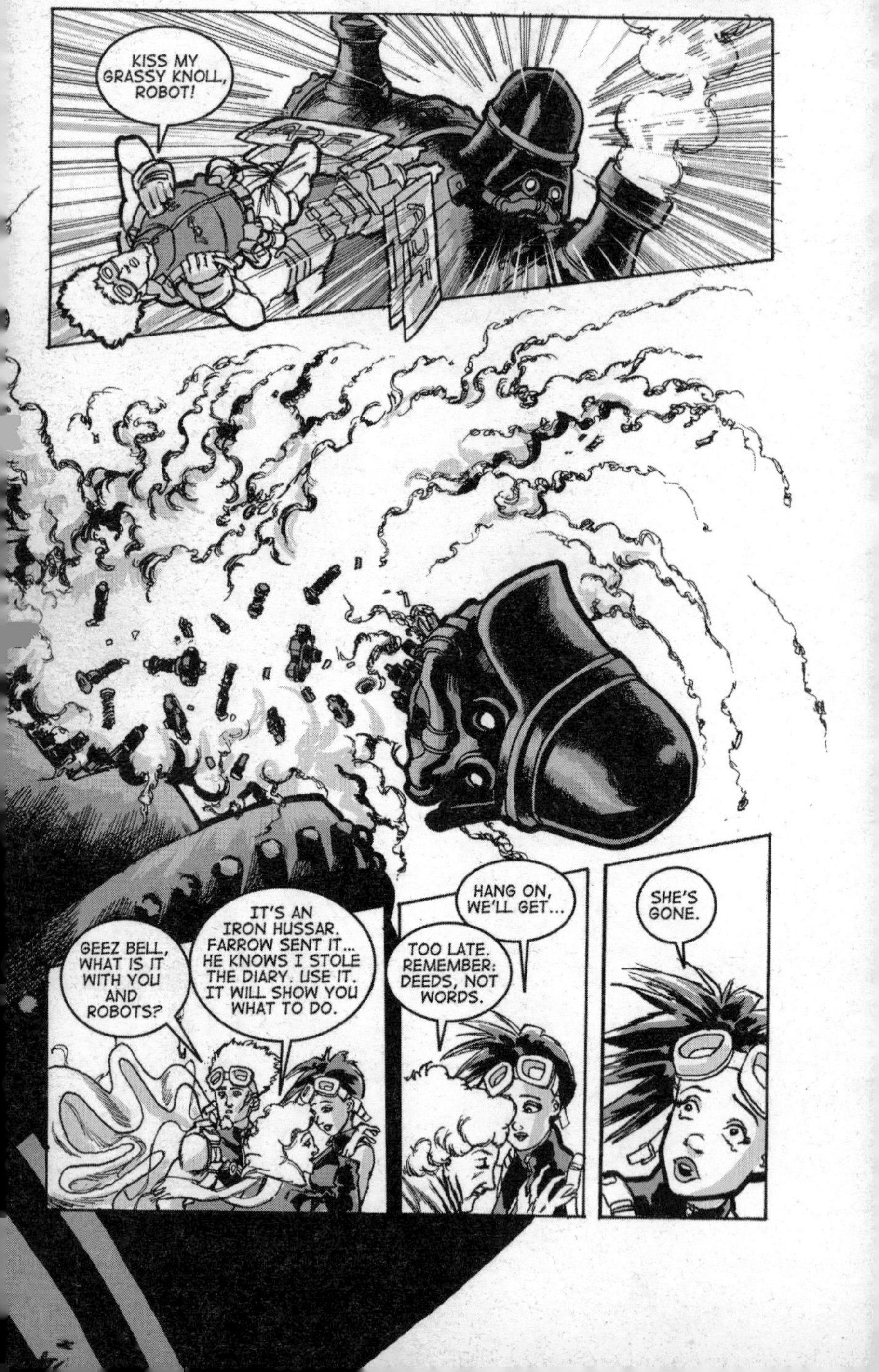
KISS MY GRASSY KNOLL, ROBOT!
GEEZ BELL, WHAT IS IT WITH YOU AND ROBOTS?
IT'S AN IRON HUSSAR. FARROW SENT IT... HE KNOWS I STOLE THE DIARY. USE IT. IT WILL SHOW YOU WHAT TO DO.
HANG ON, WE'LL GET...
TOO LATE. REMEMBER: DEEDS, NOT WORDS.
SHE'S GONE.

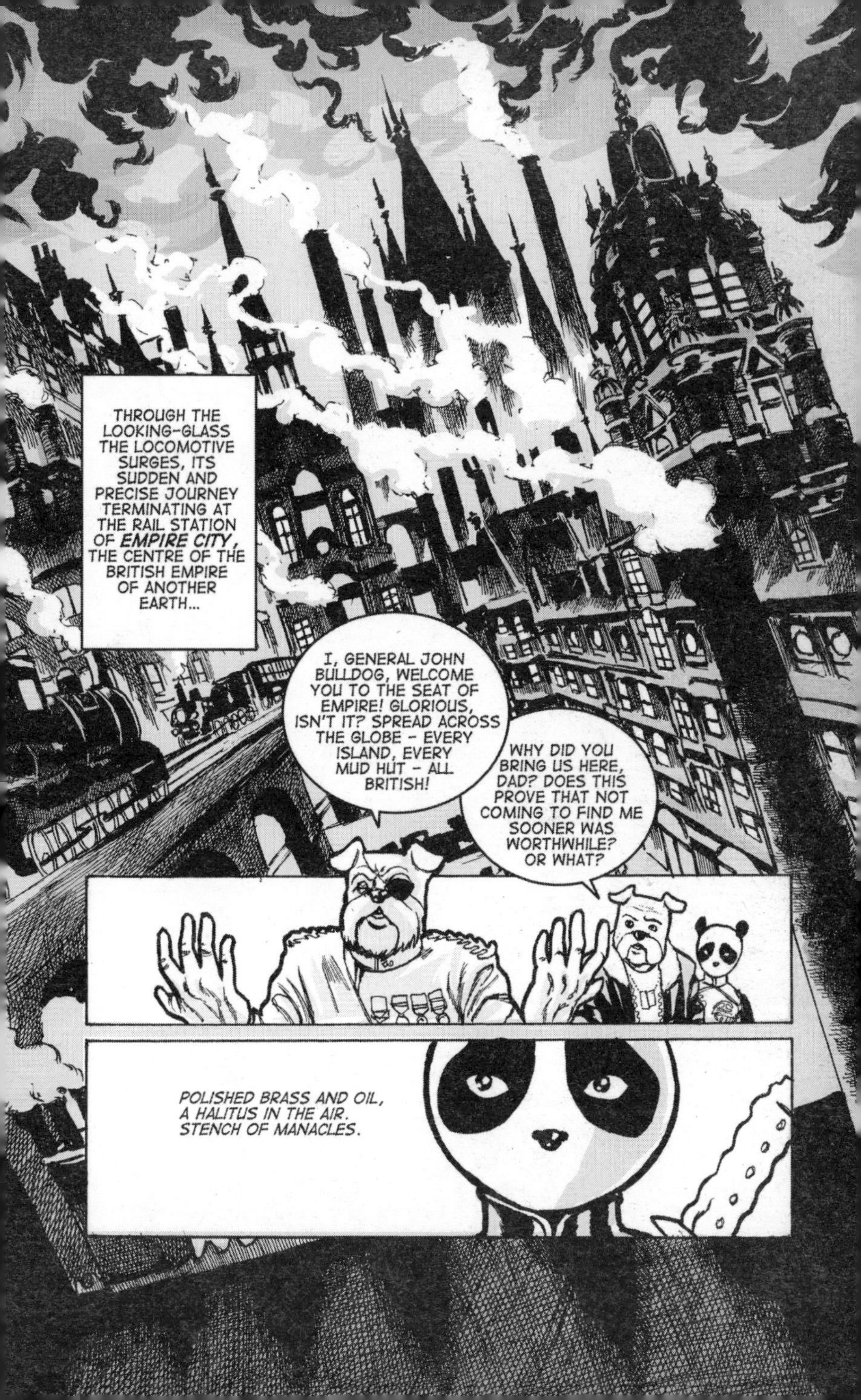
THROUGH THE LOOKING-GLASS THE LOCOMOTIVE SURGES, ITS SUDDEN AND PRECISE JOURNEY TERMINATING AT THE RAIL STATION OF EMPIRE CITY, THE CENTRE OF THE BRITISH EMPIRE OF ANOTHER EARTH...
I, GENERAL JOHN BULLDOG, WELCOME YOU TO THE SEAT OF EMPIRE! GLORIOUS, ISN'T IT? SPREAD ACROSS THE GLOBE - EVERY ISLAND, EVERY MUD HUT - ALL BRITISH!
WHY DID YOU BRING US HERE, DAD? DOES THIS PROVE THAT NOT COMING TO FIND ME SOONER WAS WORTHWHILE? OR WHAT?
POLISHED BRASS AND OIL, A HALITUS IN THE AIR. STENCH OF MANACLES.

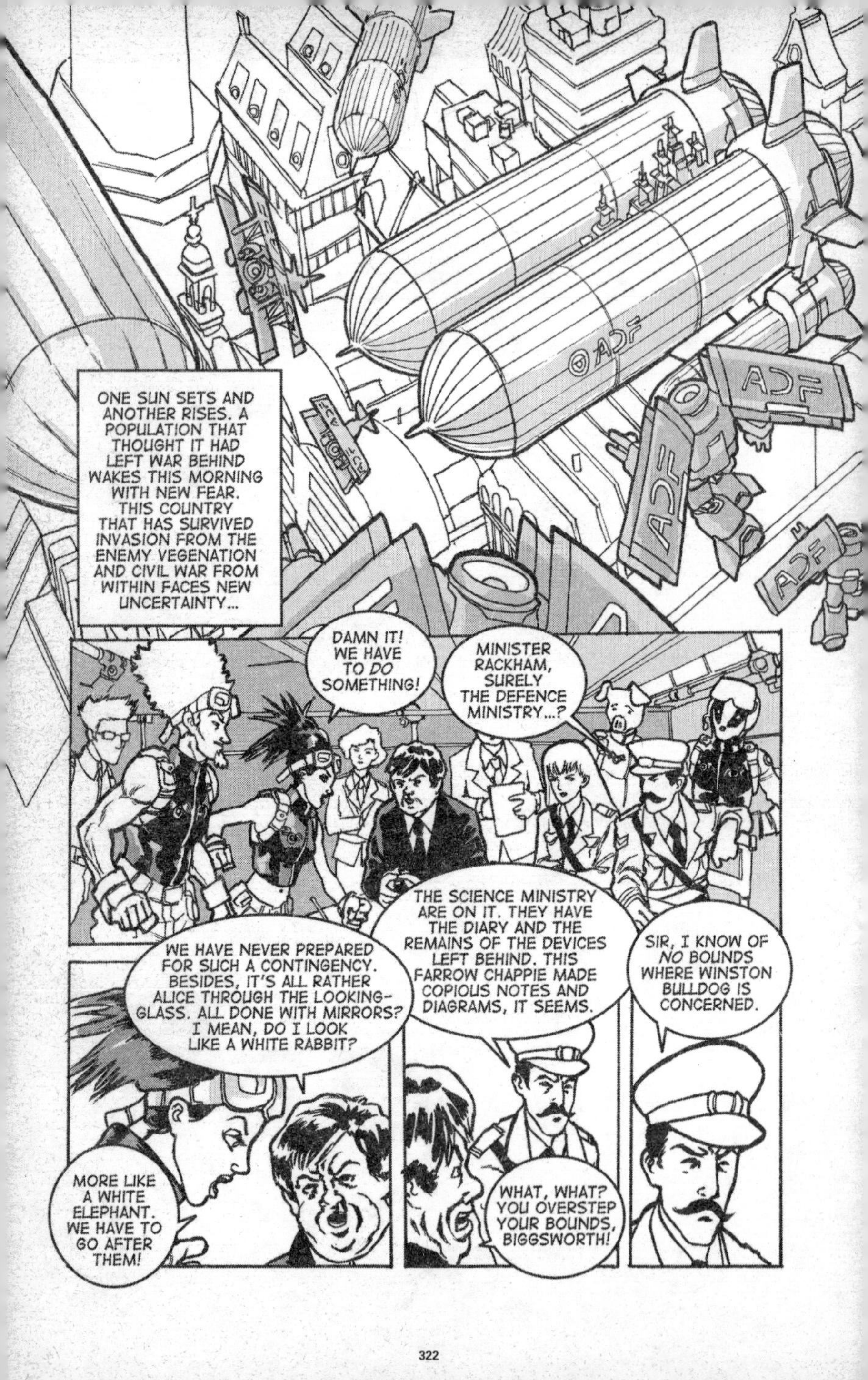
ONE SUN SETS AND ANOTHER RISES. A POPULATION THAT THOUGHT IT HAD LEFT WAR BEHIND WAKES THIS MORNING WITH NEW FEAR. THIS COUNTRY THAT HAS SURVIVED INVASION FROM THE ENEMY VEGENATION AND CIVIL WAR FROM WITHIN FACES NEW UNCERTAINTY...
DAMN IT! WE HAVE TO DO SOMETHING!
MINISTER RACKHAM, SURELY THE DEFENCE MINISTRY...?
WE HAVE NEVER PREPARED FOR SUCH A CONTINGENCY. BESIDES, IT'S ALL RATHER ALICE THROUGH THE LOOKING-GLASS. ALL DONE WITH MIRRORS? I MEAN, DO I LOOK LIKE A WHITE RABBIT?
MORE LIKE A WHITE ELEPHANT. WE HAVE TO GO AFTER THEM!
THE SCIENCE MINISTRY ARE ON IT. THEY HAVE THE DIARY AND THE REMAINS OF THE DEVICES LEFT BEHIND. THIS FARROW CHAPPIE MADE COPIOUS NOTES AND DIAGRAMS, IT SEEMS.
WHAT, WHAT? YOU OVERSTEP YOUR BOUNDS, BIGGSWORTH!
SIR, I KNOW OF NO BOUNDS WHERE WINSTON BULLDOG IS CONCERNED.

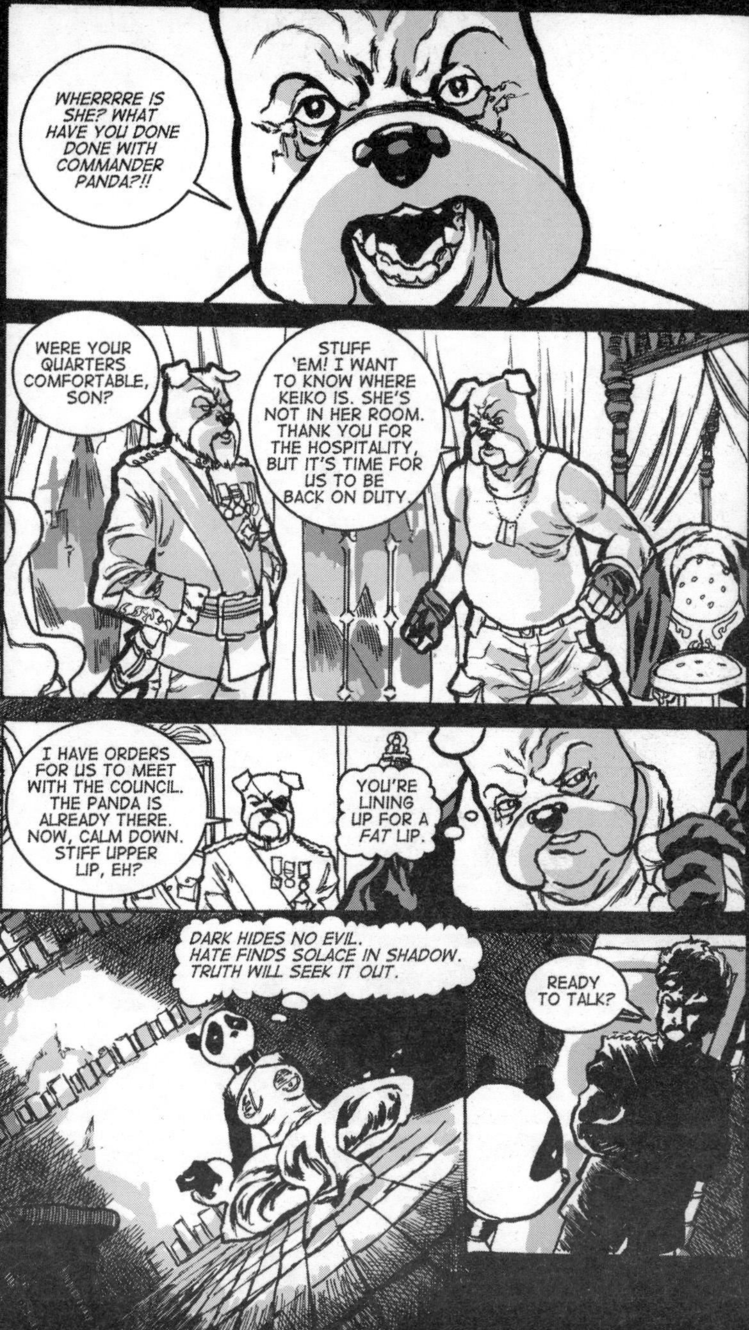
WHERRRRE IS SHE? WHAT HAVE YOU DONE DONE WITH COMMANDER PANDA?!!
WERE YOUR QUARTERS COMFORTABLE, SON?
STUFF 'EM! I WANT TO KNOW WHERE KEIKO IS. SHE'S NOT IN HER ROOM. THANK YOU FOR THE HOSPITALITY, BUT IT'S TIME FOR US TO BE BACK ON DUTY.
I HAVE ORDERS FOR US TO MEET WITH THE COUNCIL. THE PANDA IS ALREADY THERE. NOW, CALM DOWN. STIFF UPPER LIP, EH?!
YOU'RE LINING UP FOR A *FAT* LIP.
DARK HIDES NO EVIL. HATE FINDS SOLACE IN SHADOW. TRUTH WILL SEEK IT OUT.
READY TO TALK?

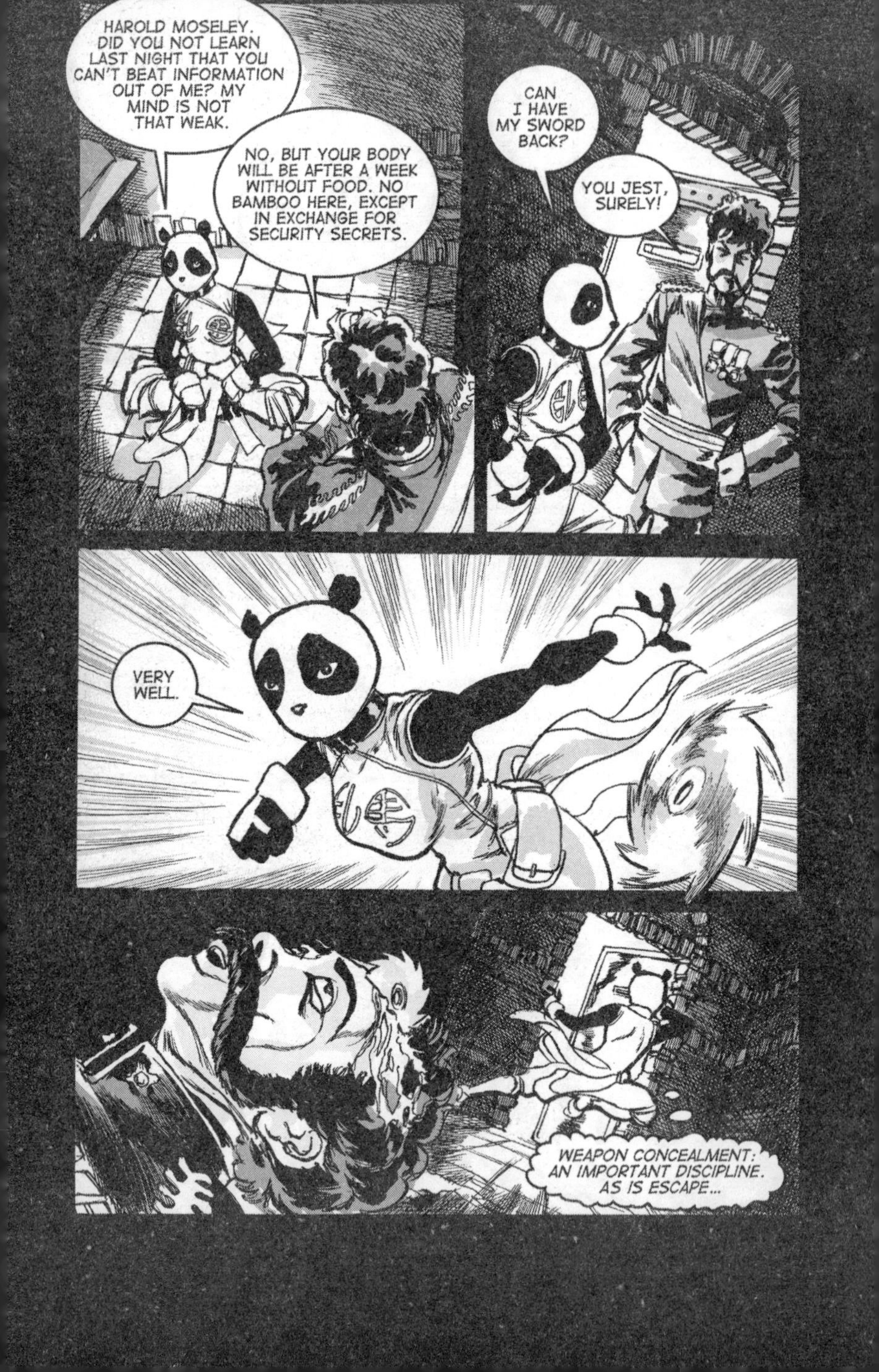
HAROLD MOSELEY. DID YOU NOT LEARN LAST NIGHT THAT YOU CAN'T BEAT INFORMATION OUT OF ME? MY MIND IS NOT THAT WEAK.
NO, BUT YOUR BODY WILL BE AFTER A WEEK WITHOUT FOOD. NO BAMBOO HERE, EXCEPT IN EXCHANGE FOR SECURITY SECRETS.
CAN I HAVE MY SWORD BACK?
YOU JEST, SURELY!
VERY WELL.
WEAPON CONCEALMENT: AN IMPORTANT DISCIPLINE. AS IS ESCAPE...

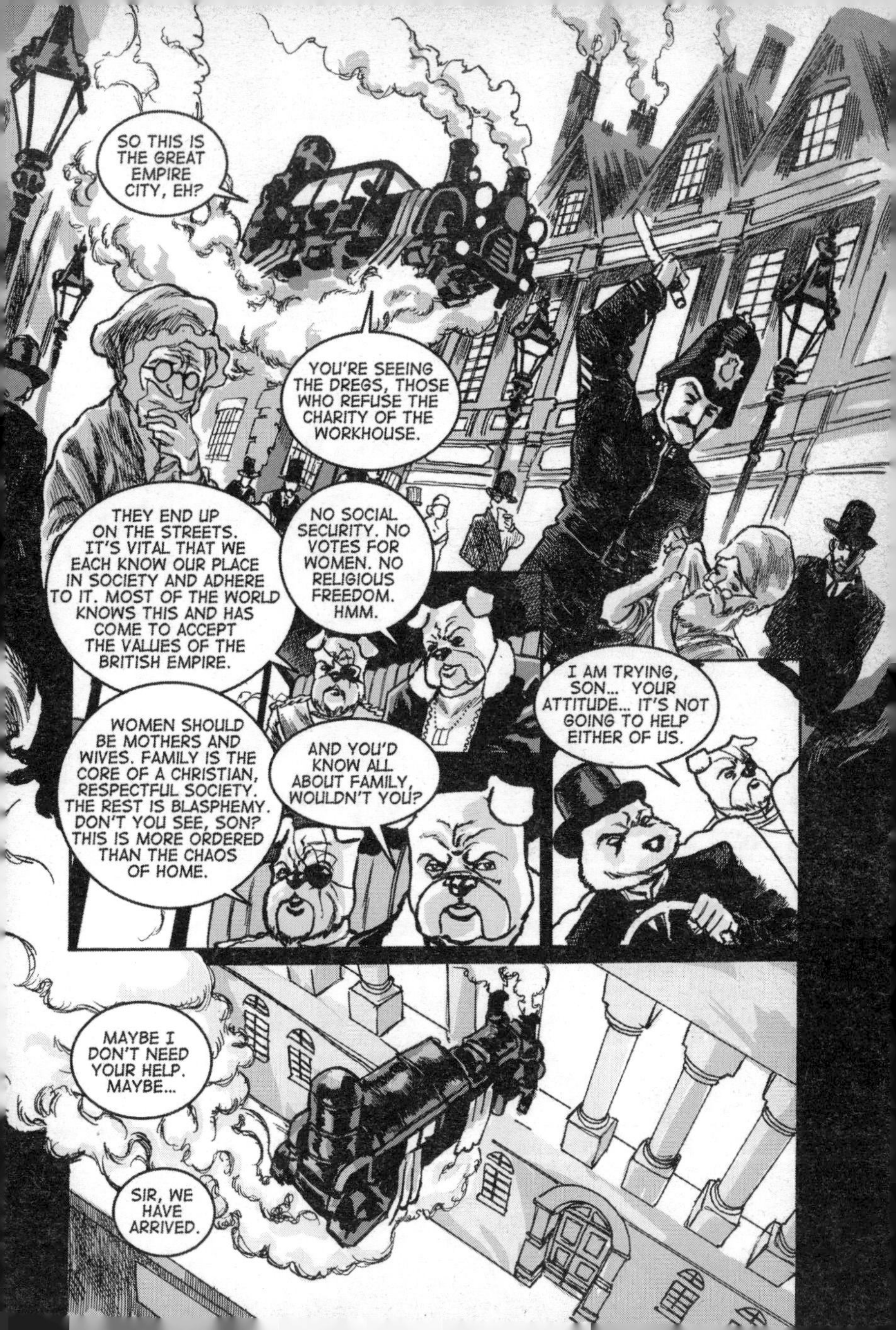
SO THIS IS THE GREAT EMPIRE CITY, EH?
YOU'RE SEEING THE DREGS, THOSE WHO REFUSE THE CHARITY OF THE WORKHOUSE.
THEY END UP ON THE STREETS. IT'S VITAL THAT WE EACH KNOW OUR PLACE IN SOCIETY AND ADHERE TO IT. MOST OF THE WORLD KNOWS THIS AND HAS COME TO ACCEPT THE VALUES OF THE BRITISH EMPIRE.
NO SOCIAL SECURITY. NO VOTES FOR WOMEN. NO RELIGIOUS FREEDOM. HMM.
WOMEN SHOULD BE MOTHERS AND WIVES. FAMILY IS THE CORE OF A CHRISTIAN, RESPECTFUL SOCIETY. THE REST IS BLASPHEMY. DON'T YOU SEE, SON? THIS IS MORE ORDERED THAN THE CHAOS OF HOME.
AND YOU'D KNOW ALL ABOUT FAMILY, WOULDN'T YOU?
I AM TRYING, SON... YOUR ATTITUDE... IT'S NOT GOING TO HELP EITHER OF US.
MAYBE I DON'T NEED YOUR HELP. MAYBE...
SIR, WE HAVE ARRIVED.

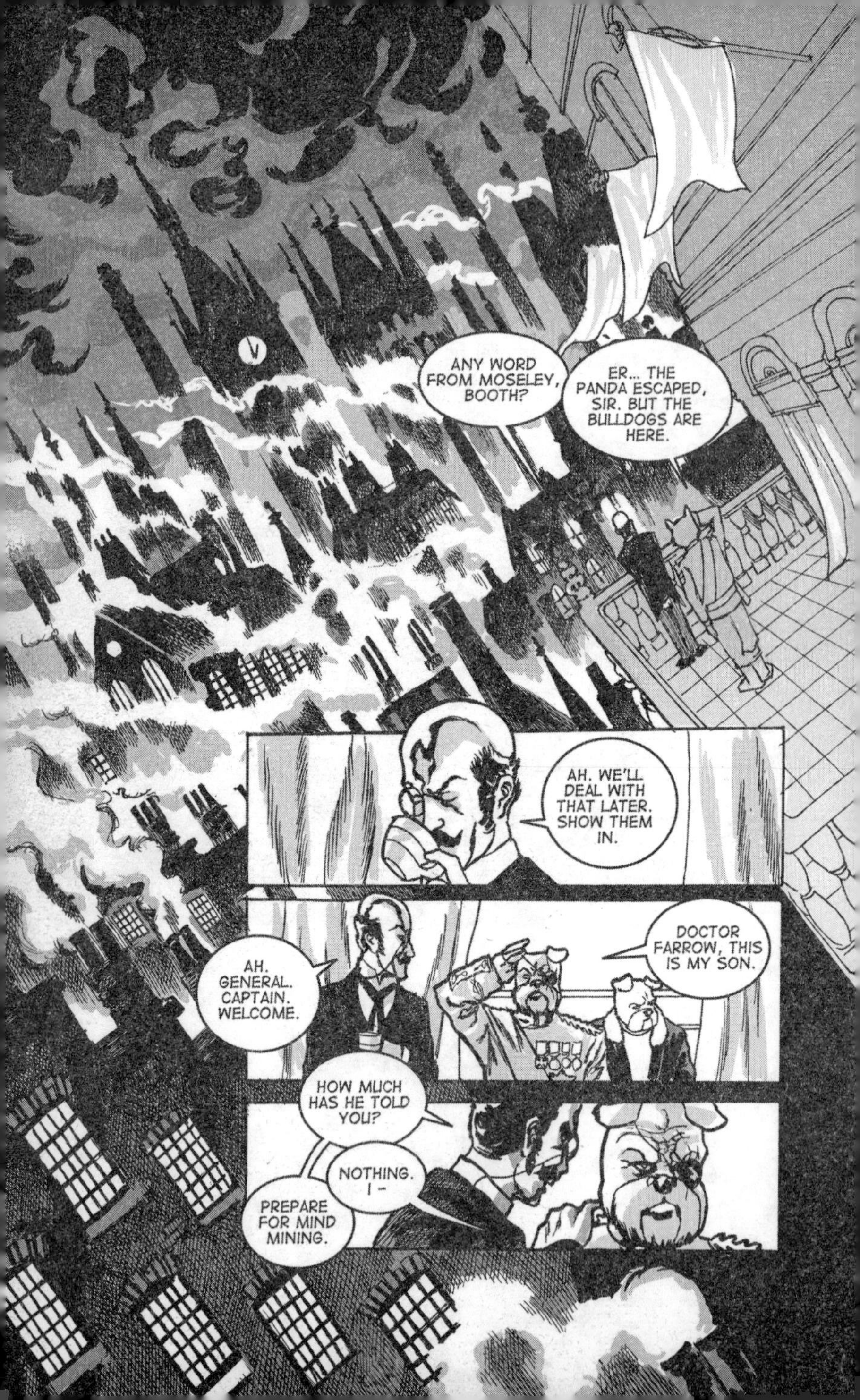
ANY WORD FROM MOSELEY, BOOTH?
ER... THE PANDA ESCAPED, SIR. BUT THE BULLDOGS ARE HERE.
AH. WE'LL DEAL WITH THAT LATER. SHOW THEM IN.
AH. GENERAL. CAPTAIN. WELCOME.
DOCTOR FARROW, THIS IS MY SON.
HOW MUCH HAS HE TOLD YOU?
NOTHING. I -
PREPARE FOR MIND MINING.

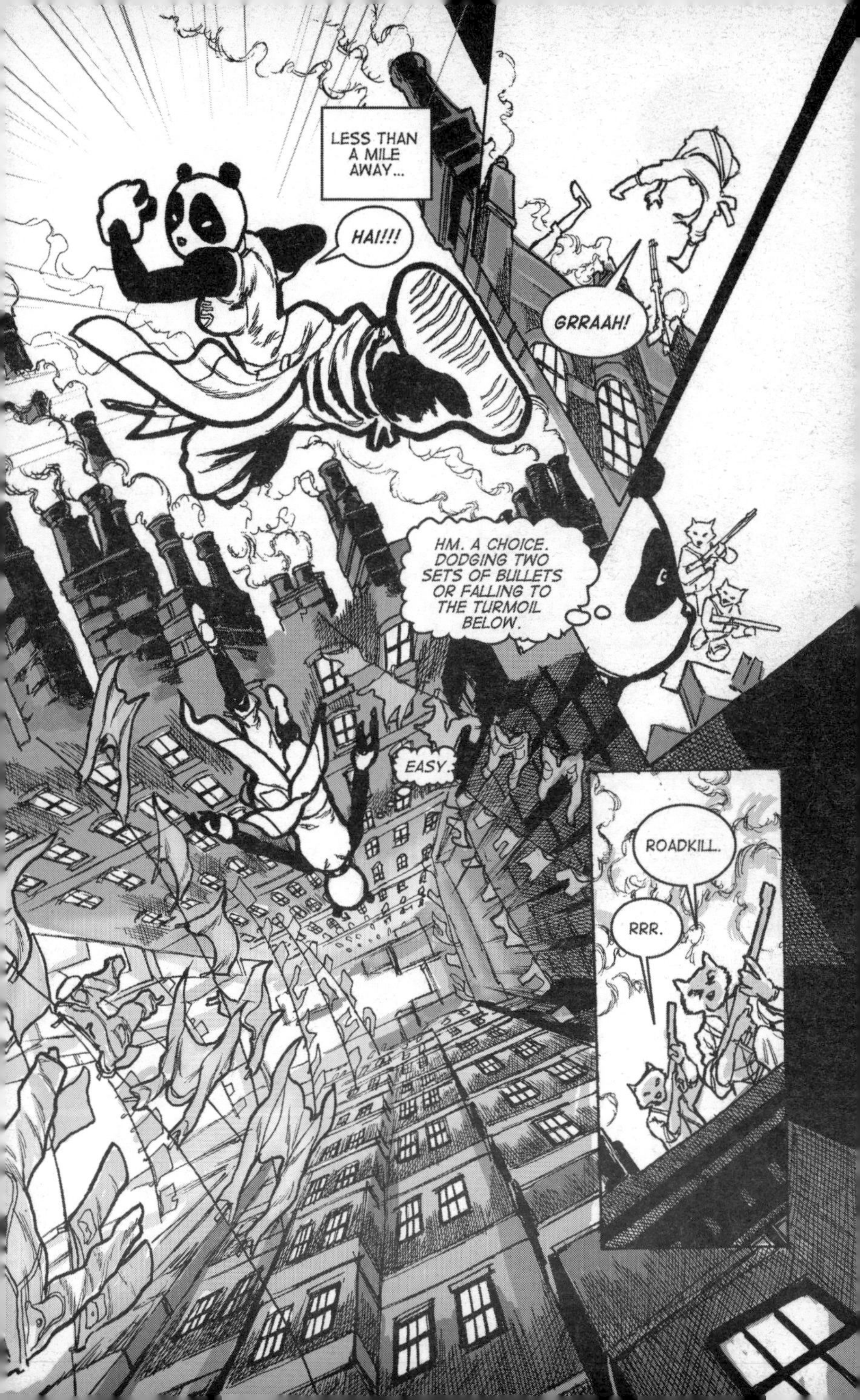
LESS THAN A MILE AWAY...
HAI!!!
GRRAAH!
HM. A CHOICE. DODGING TWO SETS OF BULLETS OR FALLING TO THE TURMOIL BELOW.
EASY.
ROADKILL.
RRR.

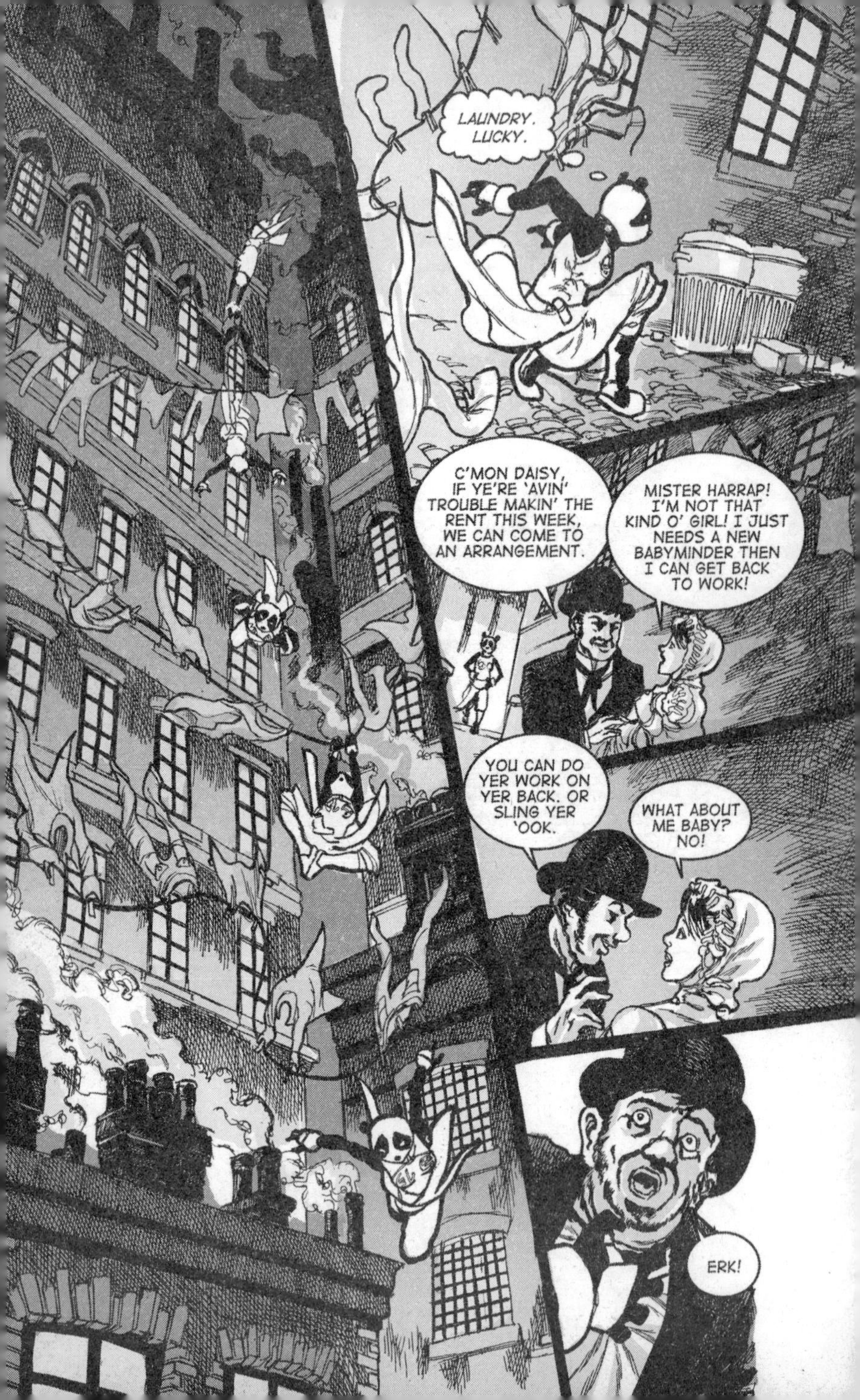
LAUNDRY. LUCKY.
C'MON DAISY, IF YE'RE 'AVIN' TROUBLE MAKIN' THE RENT THIS WEEK, WE CAN COME TO AN ARRANGEMENT.
MISTER HARRAP! I'M NOT THAT KIND O' GIRL! I JUST NEEDS A NEW BABYMINDER THEN I CAN GET BACK TO WORK!
YOU CAN DO YER WORK ON YER BACK. OR SLING YER 'OOK.
WHAT ABOUT ME BABY? NO!
ERK!

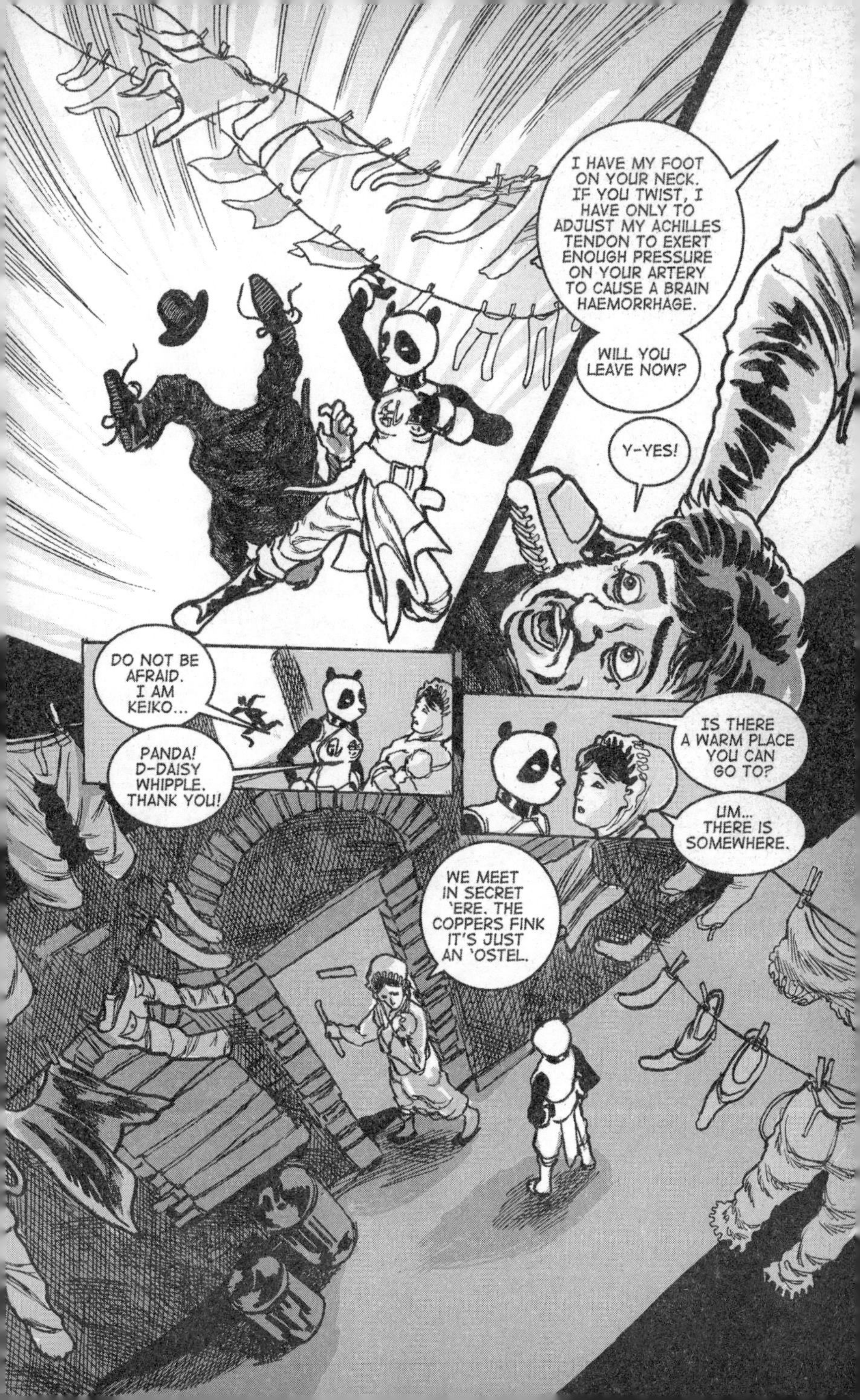
I HAVE MY FOOT ON YOUR NECK. IF YOU TWIST, I HAVE ONLY TO ADJUST MY ACHILLES TENDON TO EXERT ENOUGH PRESSURE ON YOUR ARTERY TO CAUSE A BRAIN HAEMORRHAGE.
WILL YOU LEAVE NOW?
Y-YES!
DO NOT BE AFRAID. I AM KEIKO...
PANDA! D-DAISY WHIPPLE. THANK YOU!
IS THERE A WARM PLACE YOU CAN GO TO?
UM... THERE IS SOMEWHERE.
WE MEET IN SECRET 'ERE. THE COPPERS FINK IT'S JUST AN 'OSTEL.

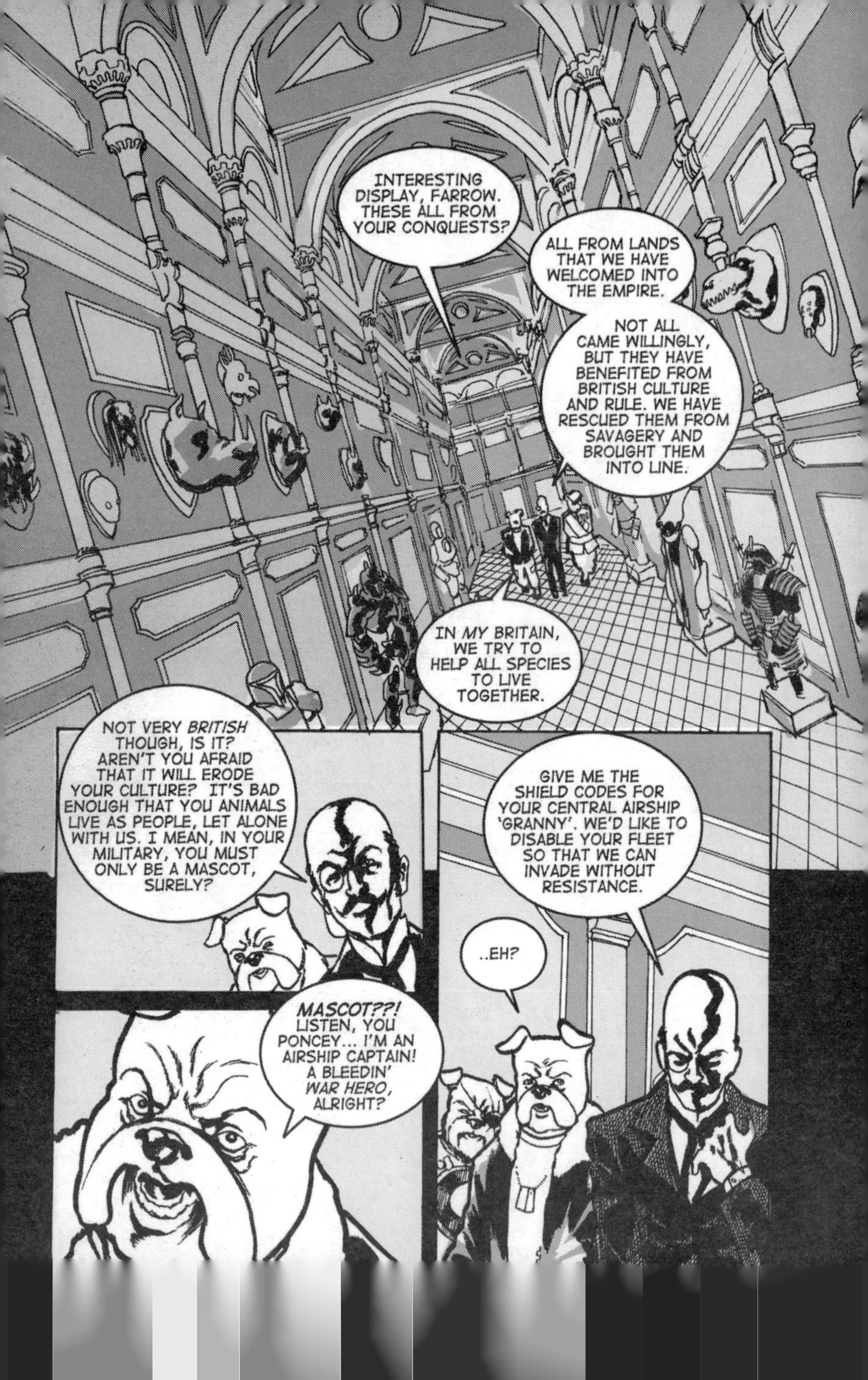
INTERESTING DISPLAY, FARROW. THESE ALL FROM YOUR CONQUESTS?
ALL FROM LANDS THAT WE HAVE WELCOMED INTO THE EMPIRE.
NOT ALL CAME WILLINGLY, BUT THEY HAVE BENEFITED FROM BRITISH CULTURE AND RULE. WE HAVE RESCUED THEM FROM SAVAGERY AND BROUGHT THEM INTO LINE.
IN *MY* BRITAIN, WE TRY TO HELP ALL SPECIES TO LIVE TOGETHER.
NOT VERY *BRITISH* THOUGH, IS IT? AREN'T YOU AFRAID THAT IT WILL ERODE YOUR CULTURE? IT'S BAD ENOUGH THAT YOU ANIMALS LIVE AS PEOPLE, LET ALONE WITH US. I MEAN, IN YOUR MILITARY, YOU MUST ONLY BE A MASCOT, SURELY?
MASCOT??! LISTEN, YOU PONCEY... I'M AN AIRSHIP CAPTAIN! A BLEEDIN' *WAR HERO*, ALRIGHT?
GIVE ME THE SHIELD CODES FOR YOUR CENTRAL AIRSHIP 'GRANNY'. WE'D LIKE TO DISABLE YOUR FLEET SO THAT WE CAN INVADE WITHOUT RESISTANCE.
..EH?

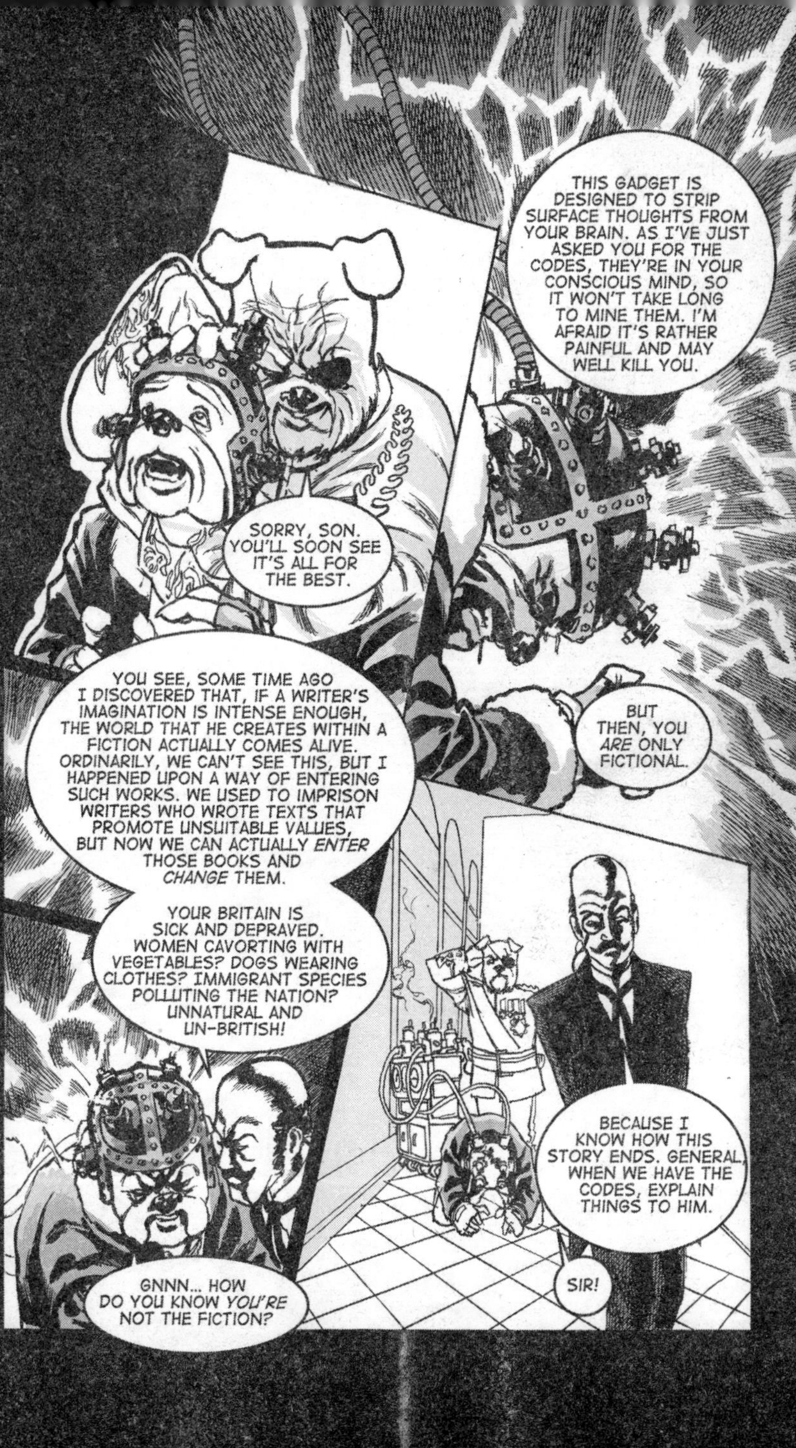
SORRY, SON. YOU'LL SOON SEE IT'S ALL FOR THE BEST.
THIS GADGET IS DESIGNED TO STRIP SURFACE THOUGHTS FROM YOUR BRAIN. AS I'VE JUST ASKED YOU FOR THE CODES, THEY'RE IN YOUR CONSCIOUS MIND, SO IT WON'T TAKE LONG TO MINE THEM. I'M AFRAID IT'S RATHER PAINFUL AND MAY WELL KILL YOU.
BUT THEN, YOU *ARE* ONLY FICTIONAL.
YOU SEE, SOME TIME AGO I DISCOVERED THAT, IF A WRITER'S IMAGINATION IS INTENSE ENOUGH, THE WORLD THAT HE CREATES WITHIN A FICTION ACTUALLY COMES ALIVE. ORDINARILY, WE CAN'T SEE THIS, BUT I HAPPENED UPON A WAY OF ENTERING SUCH WORKS. WE USED TO IMPRISON WRITERS WHO WROTE TEXTS THAT PROMOTE UNSUITABLE VALUES, BUT NOW WE CAN ACTUALLY *ENTER* THOSE BOOKS AND *CHANGE* THEM.
YOUR BRITAIN IS SICK AND DEPRAVED. WOMEN CAVORTING WITH VEGETABLES? DOGS WEARING CLOTHES? IMMIGRANT SPECIES POLLUTING THE NATION? UNNATURAL AND UN-BRITISH!
GNNN... HOW DO YOU KNOW *YOU'RE* NOT THE FICTION?
BECAUSE I KNOW HOW THIS STORY ENDS. GENERAL, WHEN WE HAVE THE CODES, EXPLAIN THINGS TO HIM.
SIR!

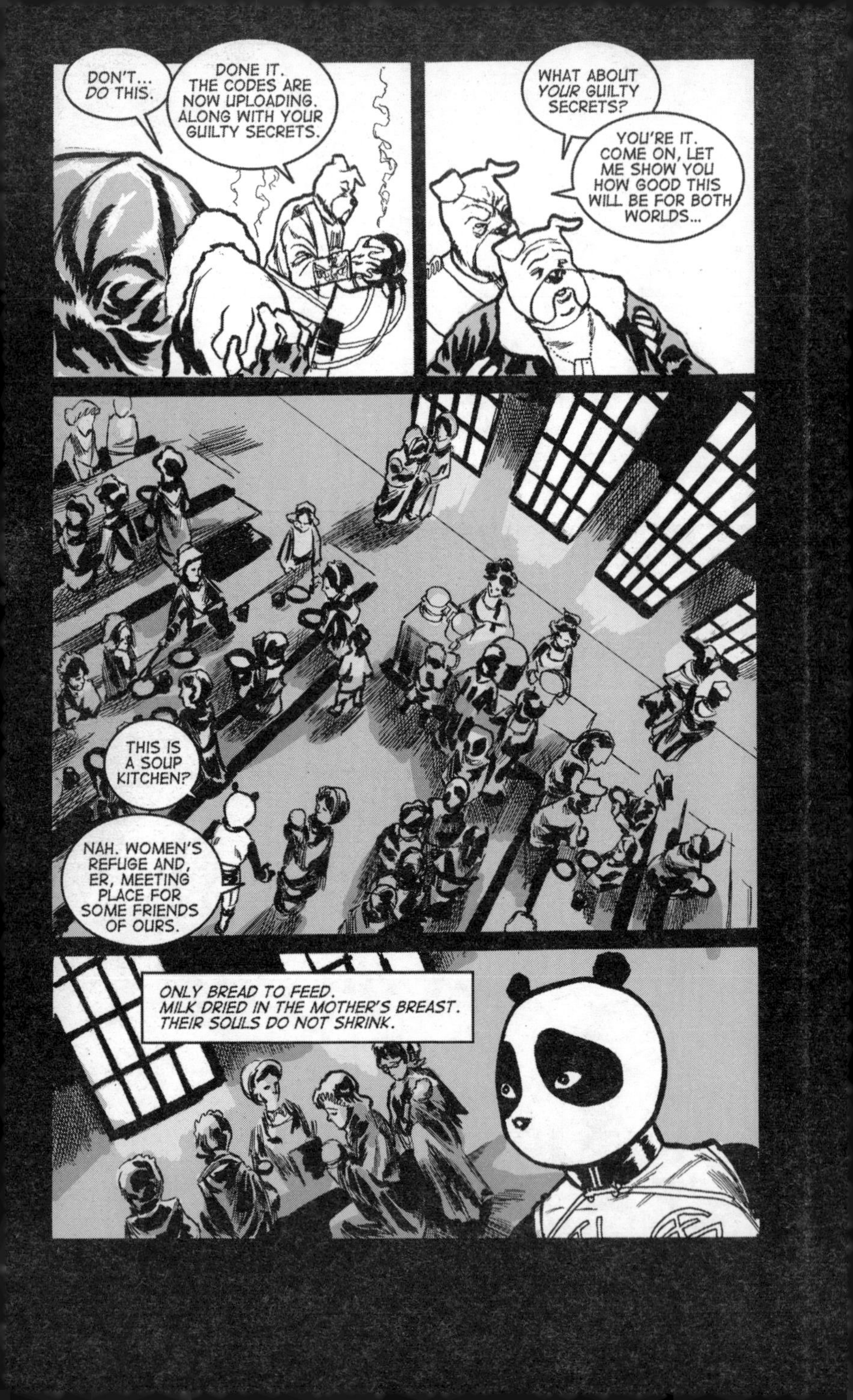
DON'T... DO THIS.
DONE IT. THE CODES ARE NOW UPLOADING. ALONG WITH YOUR GUILTY SECRETS.
WHAT ABOUT YOUR GUILTY SECRETS?
YOU'RE IT. COME ON, LET ME SHOW YOU HOW GOOD THIS WILL BE FOR BOTH WORLDS...
THIS IS A SOUP KITCHEN?
NAH. WOMEN'S REFUGE AND, ER, MEETING PLACE FOR SOME FRIENDS OF OURS.
ONLY BREAD TO FEED.
MILK DRIED IN THE MOTHER'S BREAST.
THEIR SOULS DO NOT SHRINK.

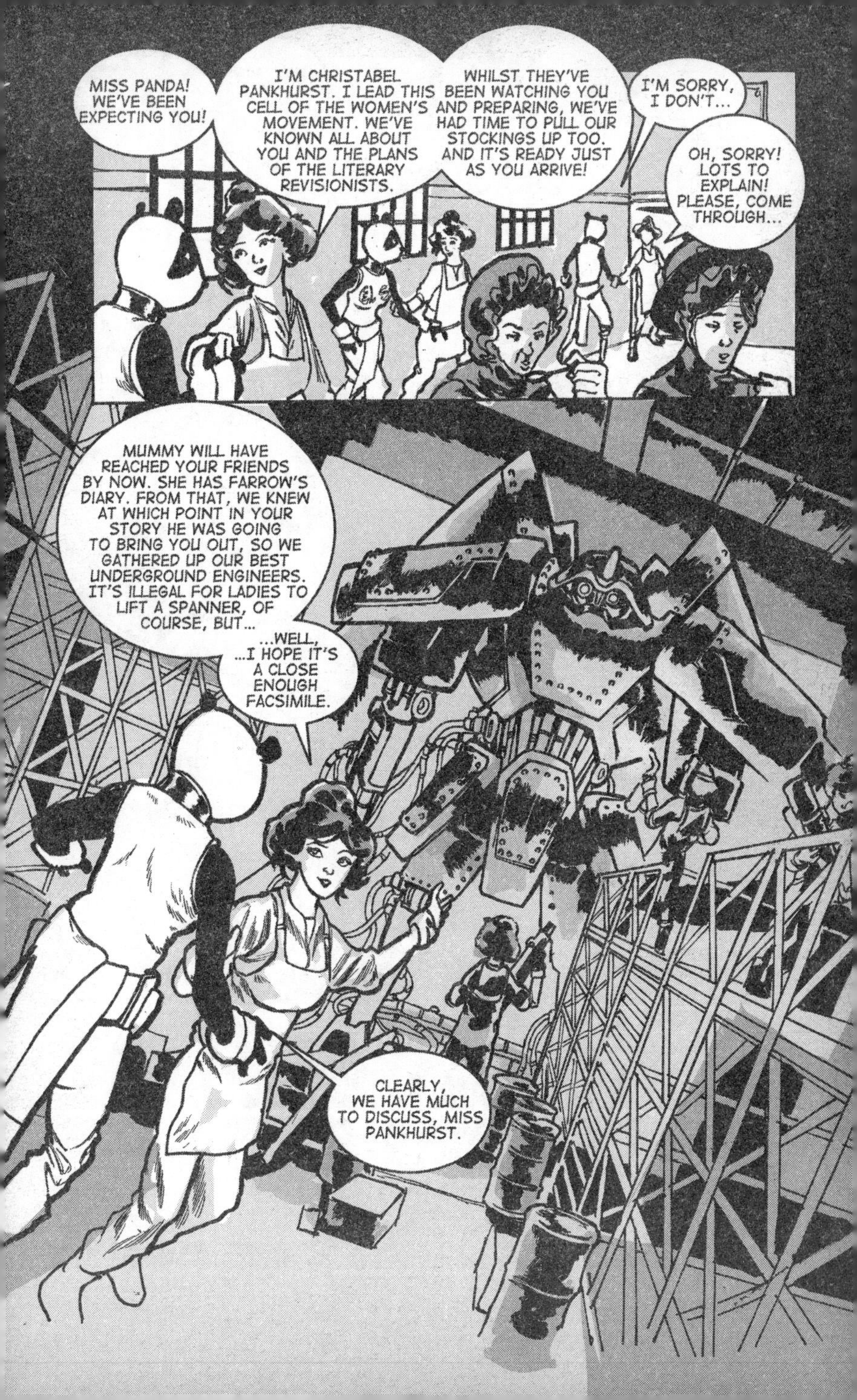
MISS PANDA! WE'VE BEEN EXPECTING YOU!
I'M CHRISTABEL PANKHURST. I LEAD THIS CELL OF THE WOMEN'S MOVEMENT. WE'VE KNOWN ALL ABOUT YOU AND THE PLANS OF THE LITERARY REVISIONISTS.
WHILST THEY'VE BEEN WATCHING YOU AND PREPARING, WE'VE HAD TIME TO PULL OUR STOCKINGS UP TOO. AND IT'S READY JUST AS YOU ARRIVE!
I'M SORRY, I DON'T...
OH, SORRY! LOTS TO EXPLAIN! PLEASE, COME THROUGH...
MUMMY WILL HAVE REACHED YOUR FRIENDS BY NOW. SHE HAS FARROW'S DIARY. FROM THAT, WE KNEW AT WHICH POINT IN YOUR STORY HE WAS GOING TO BRING YOU OUT, SO WE GATHERED UP OUR BEST UNDERGROUND ENGINEERS. IT'S ILLEGAL FOR LADIES TO LIFT A SPANNER, OF COURSE, BUT...
...WELL, ...I HOPE IT'S A CLOSE ENOUGH FACSIMILE.
CLEARLY, WE HAVE MUCH TO DISCUSS, MISS PANKHURST.

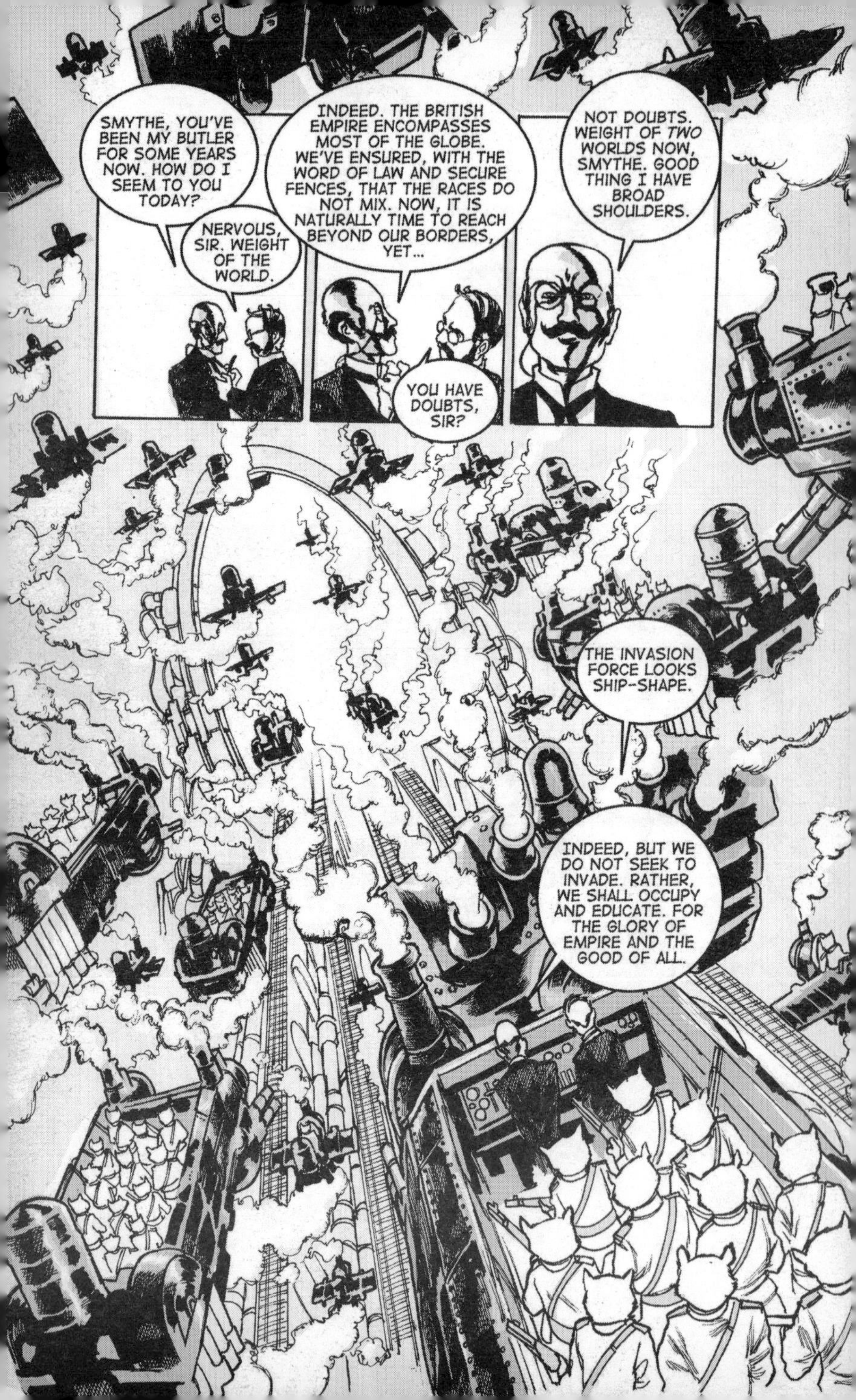
SMYTHE, YOU'VE BEEN MY BUTLER FOR SOME YEARS NOW. HOW DO I SEEM TO YOU TODAY?
NERVOUS, SIR. WEIGHT OF THE WORLD.
INDEED. THE BRITISH EMPIRE ENCOMPASSES MOST OF THE GLOBE. WE'VE ENSURED, WITH THE WORD OF LAW AND SECURE FENCES, THAT THE RACES DO NOT MIX. NOW, IT IS NATURALLY TIME TO REACH BEYOND OUR BORDERS, YET...
YOU HAVE DOUBTS, SIR?
NOT DOUBTS. WEIGHT OF *TWO* WORLDS NOW, SMYTHE. GOOD THING I HAVE BROAD SHOULDERS.
THE INVASION FORCE LOOKS SHIP-SHAPE.
INDEED, BUT WE DO NOT SEEK TO INVADE. RATHER, WE SHALL OCCUPY AND EDUCATE. FOR THE GLORY OF EMPIRE AND THE GOOD OF ALL.

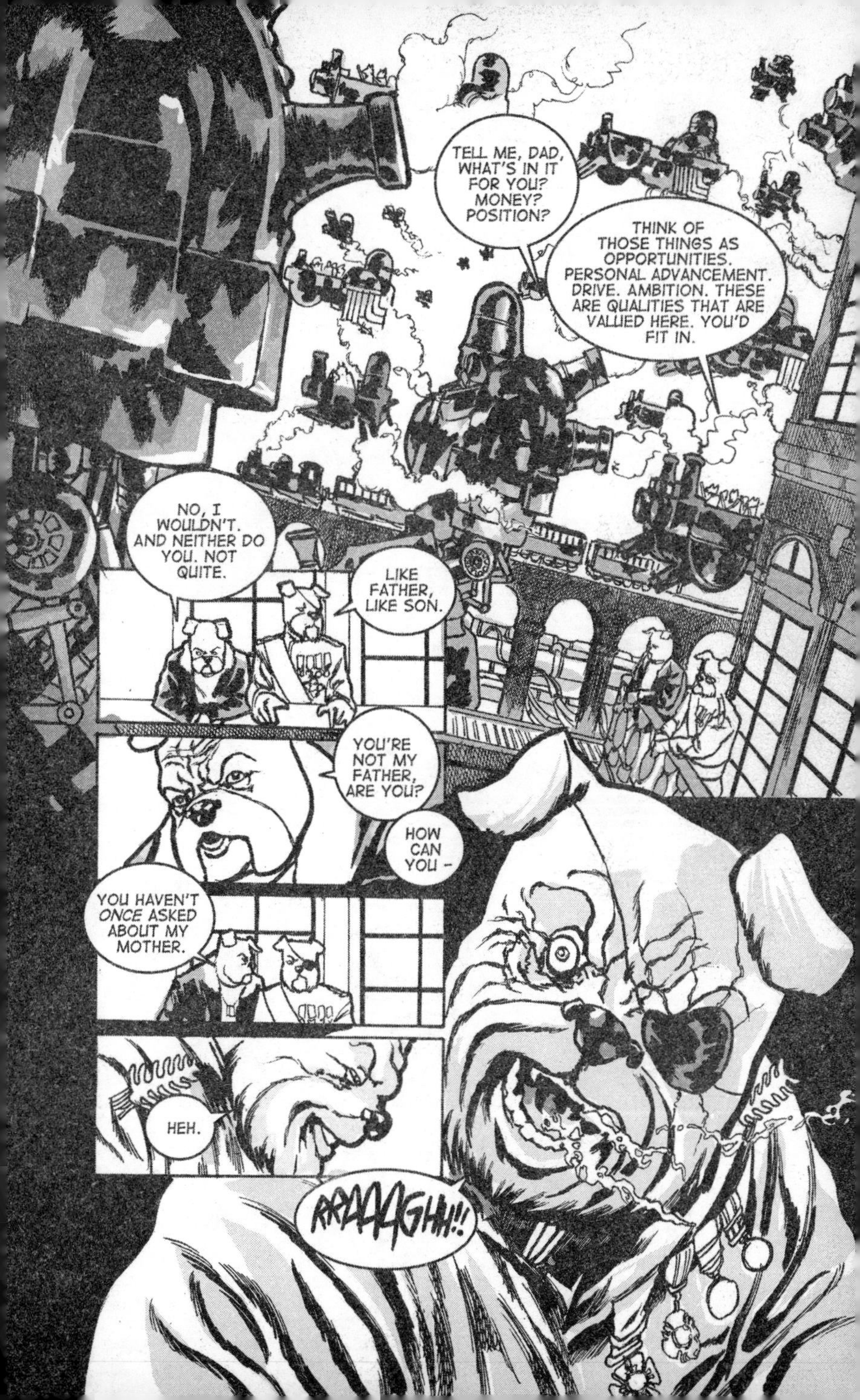
TELL ME, DAD, WHAT'S IN IT FOR YOU? MONEY? POSITION?
THINK OF THOSE THINGS AS OPPORTUNITIES. PERSONAL ADVANCEMENT. DRIVE. AMBITION. THESE ARE QUALITIES THAT ARE VALUED HERE. YOU'D FIT IN.
NO, I WOULDN'T. AND NEITHER DO YOU. NOT QUITE.
LIKE FATHER, LIKE SON.
YOU'RE NOT MY FATHER, ARE YOU?
HOW CAN YOU -
YOU HAVEN'T *ONCE* ASKED ABOUT MY MOTHER.
HEH.
RRAAAGHH!!

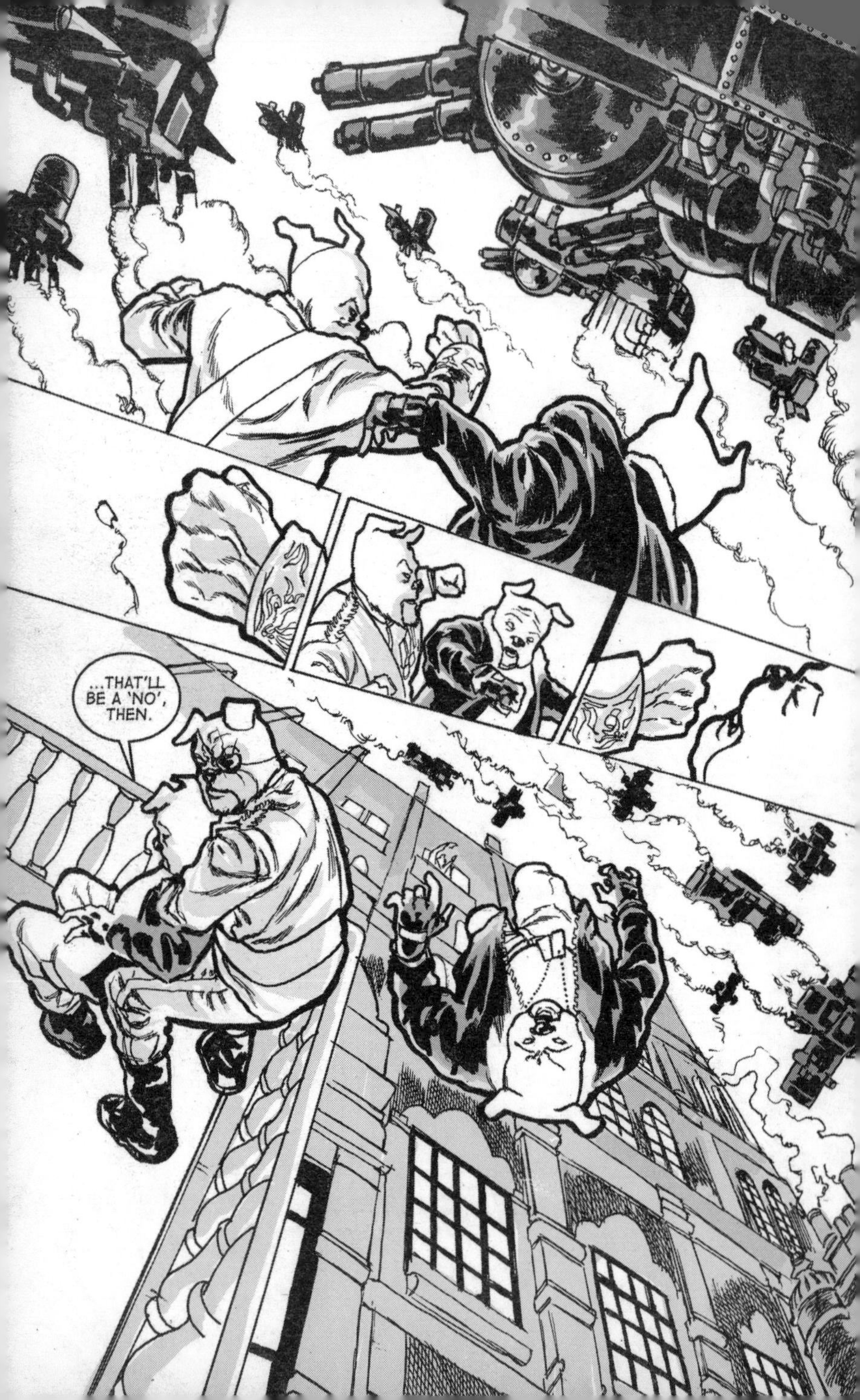
...THAT'LL BE A 'NO', THEN.

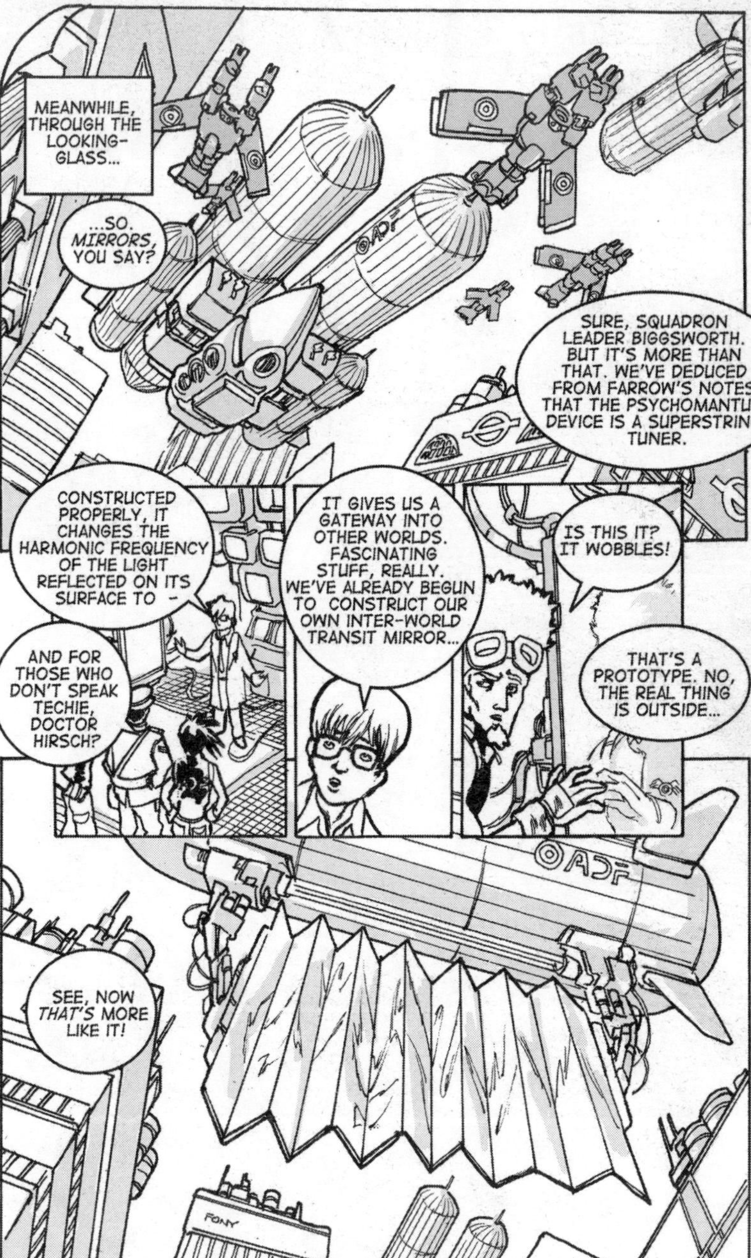
MEANWHILE, THROUGH THE LOOKING-GLASS...
...SO. *MIRRORS*, YOU SAY?
SURE, SQUADRON LEADER BIGGSWORTH. BUT IT'S MORE THAN THAT. WE'VE DEDUCED FROM FARROW'S NOTES THAT THE PSYCHOMANTUM DEVICE IS A SUPERSTRING TUNER.
CONSTRUCTED PROPERLY, IT CHANGES THE HARMONIC FREQUENCY OF THE LIGHT REFLECTED ON ITS SURFACE TO -
AND FOR THOSE WHO DON'T SPEAK TECHIE, DOCTOR HIRSCH?
IT GIVES US A GATEWAY INTO OTHER WORLDS. FASCINATING STUFF, REALLY. WE'VE ALREADY BEGUN TO CONSTRUCT OUR OWN INTER-WORLD TRANSIT MIRROR...
IS THIS IT? IT WOBBLES!
THAT'S A PROTOTYPE. NO, THE REAL THING IS OUTSIDE...
SEE, NOW *THAT'S* MORE LIKE IT!

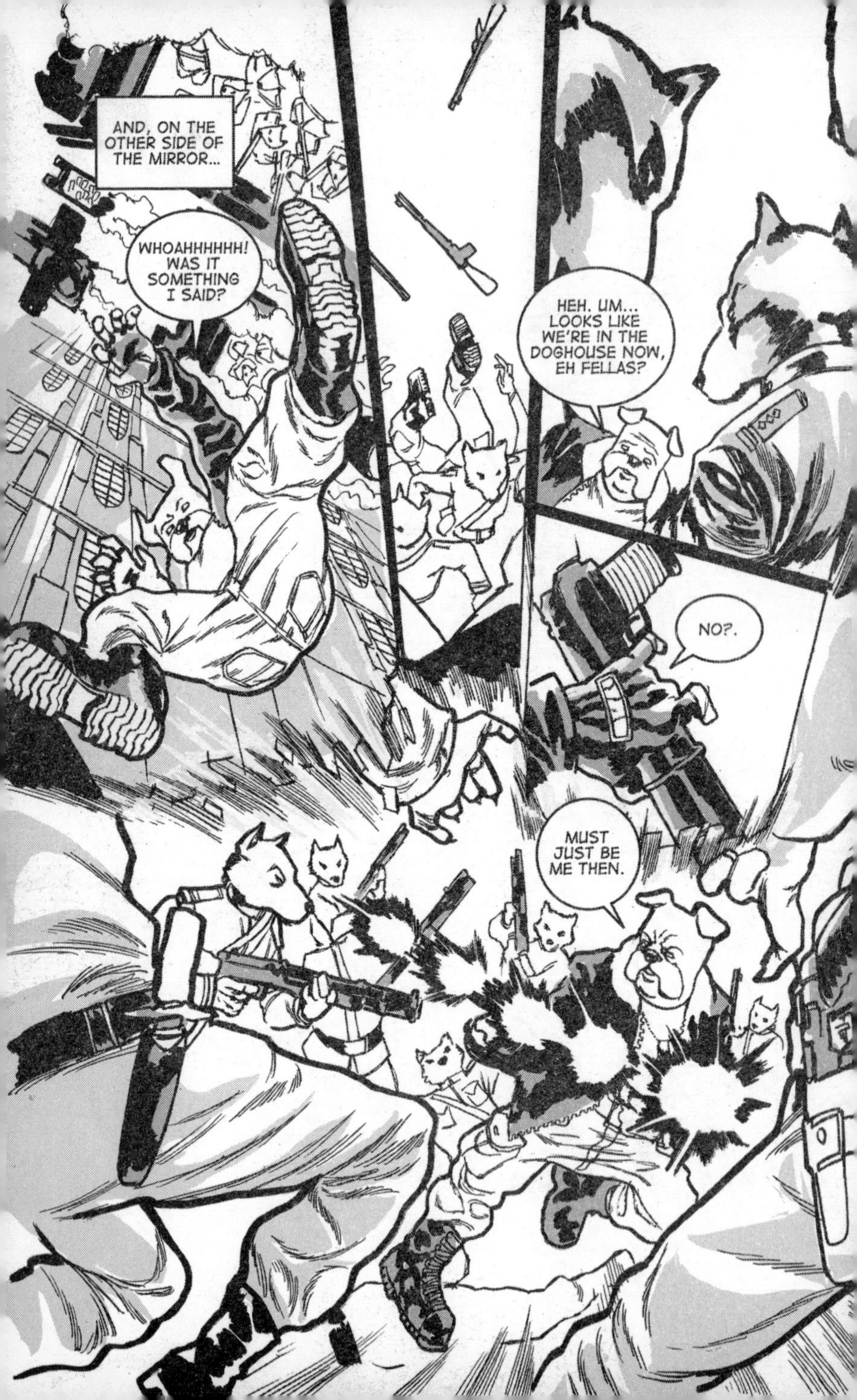
AND, ON THE OTHER SIDE OF THE MIRROR...
WHOAHHHHHH! WAS IT SOMETHING I SAID?
HEH. UM... LOOKS LIKE WE'RE IN THE DOGHOUSE NOW, EH FELLAS?
NO?.
MUST JUST BE ME THEN.

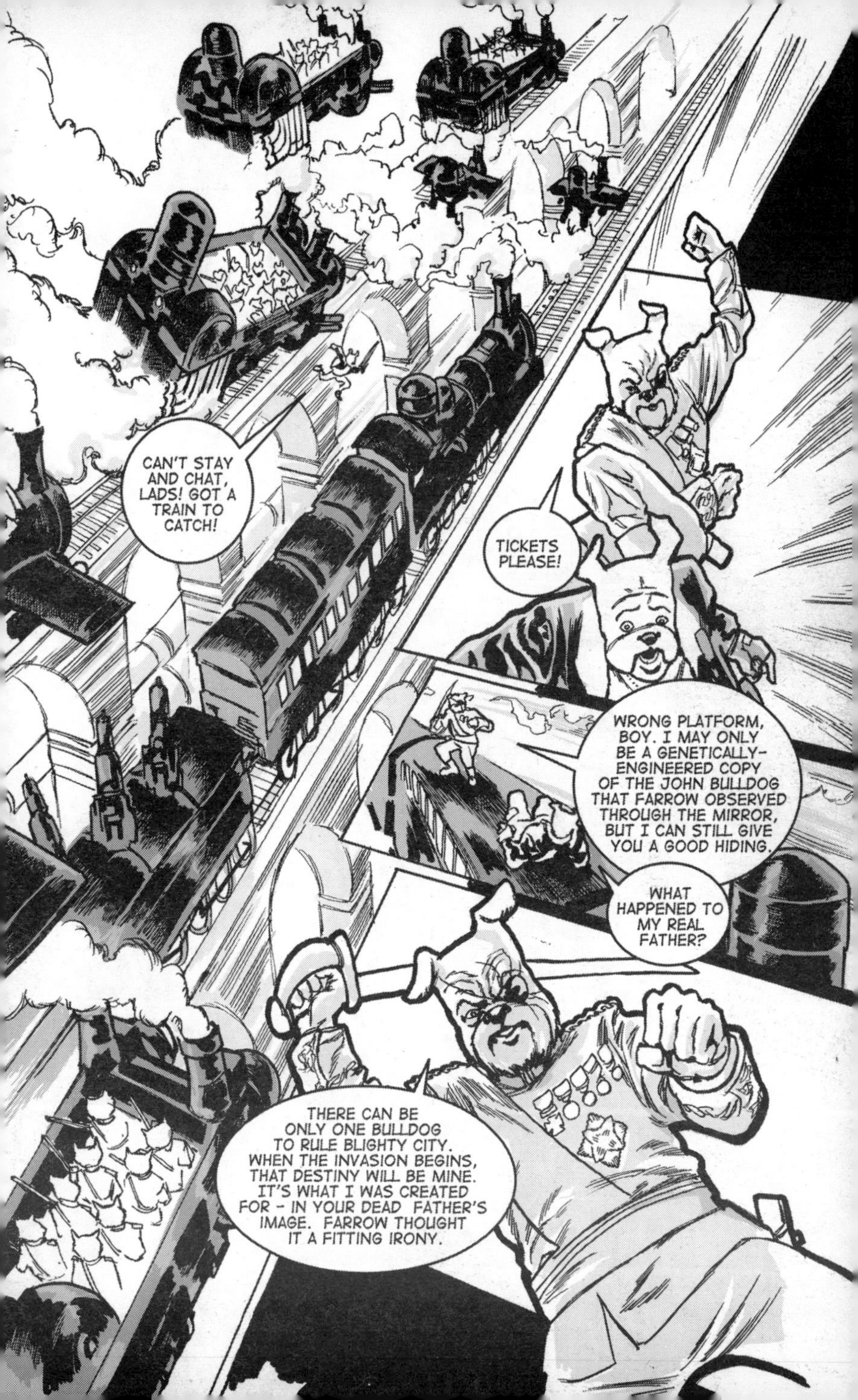
CAN'T STAY AND CHAT, LADS! GOT A TRAIN TO CATCH!
TICKETS PLEASE!
WRONG PLATFORM, BOY. I MAY ONLY BE A GENETICALLY-ENGINEERED COPY OF THE JOHN BULLDOG THAT FARROW OBSERVED THROUGH THE MIRROR, BUT I CAN STILL GIVE YOU A GOOD HIDING.
WHAT HAPPENED TO MY REAL FATHER?
THERE CAN BE ONLY ONE BULLDOG TO RULE BLIGHTY CITY. WHEN THE INVASION BEGINS, THAT DESTINY WILL BE MINE. IT'S WHAT I WAS CREATED FOR - IN YOUR DEAD FATHER'S IMAGE. FARROW THOUGHT IT A FITTING IRONY.

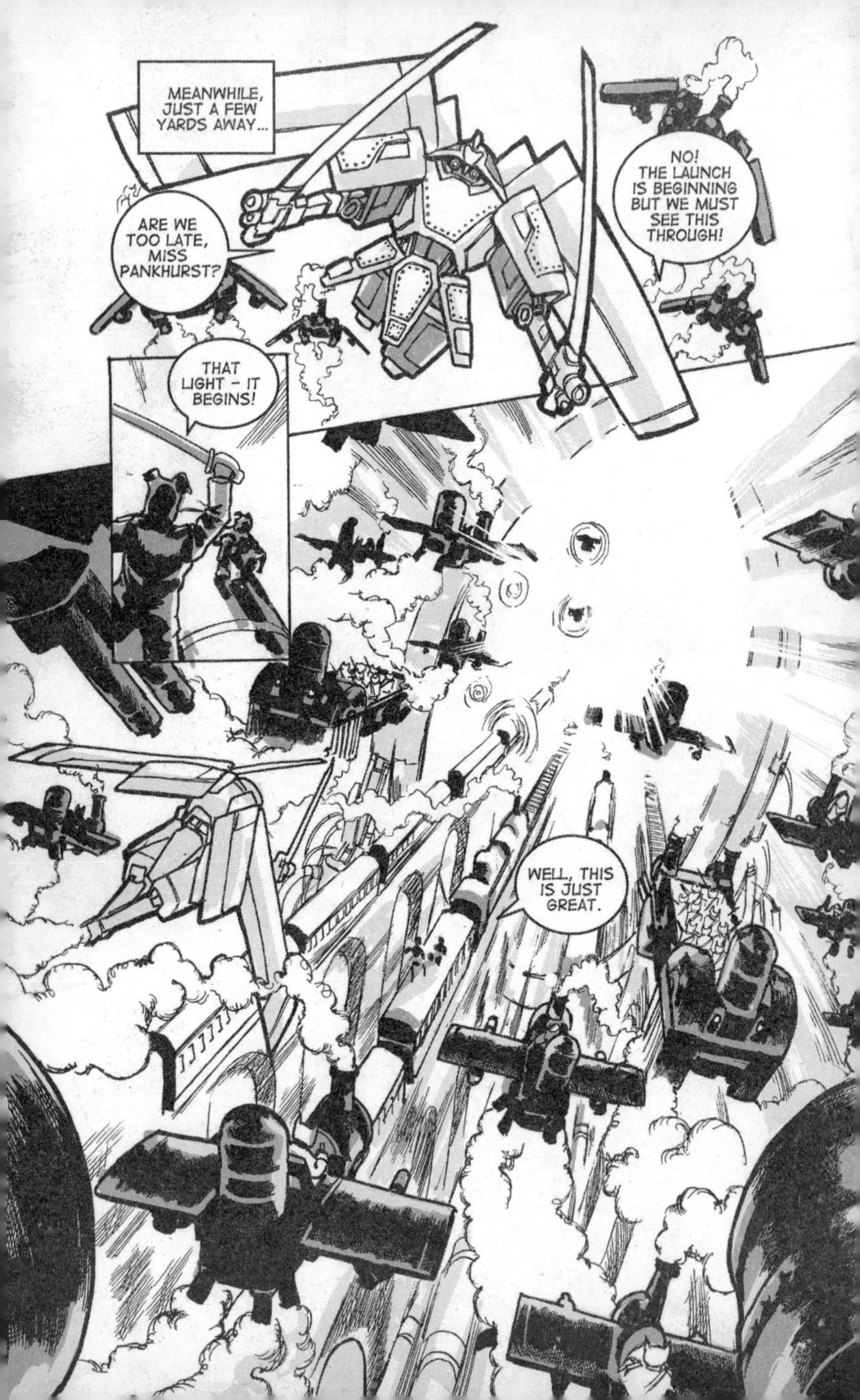
MEANWHILE, JUST A FEW YARDS AWAY...
ARE WE TOO LATE, MISS PANKHURST?
NO! THE LAUNCH IS BEGINNING BUT WE MUST SEE THIS THROUGH!
THAT LIGHT - IT BEGINS!
WELL, THIS IS JUST GREAT.

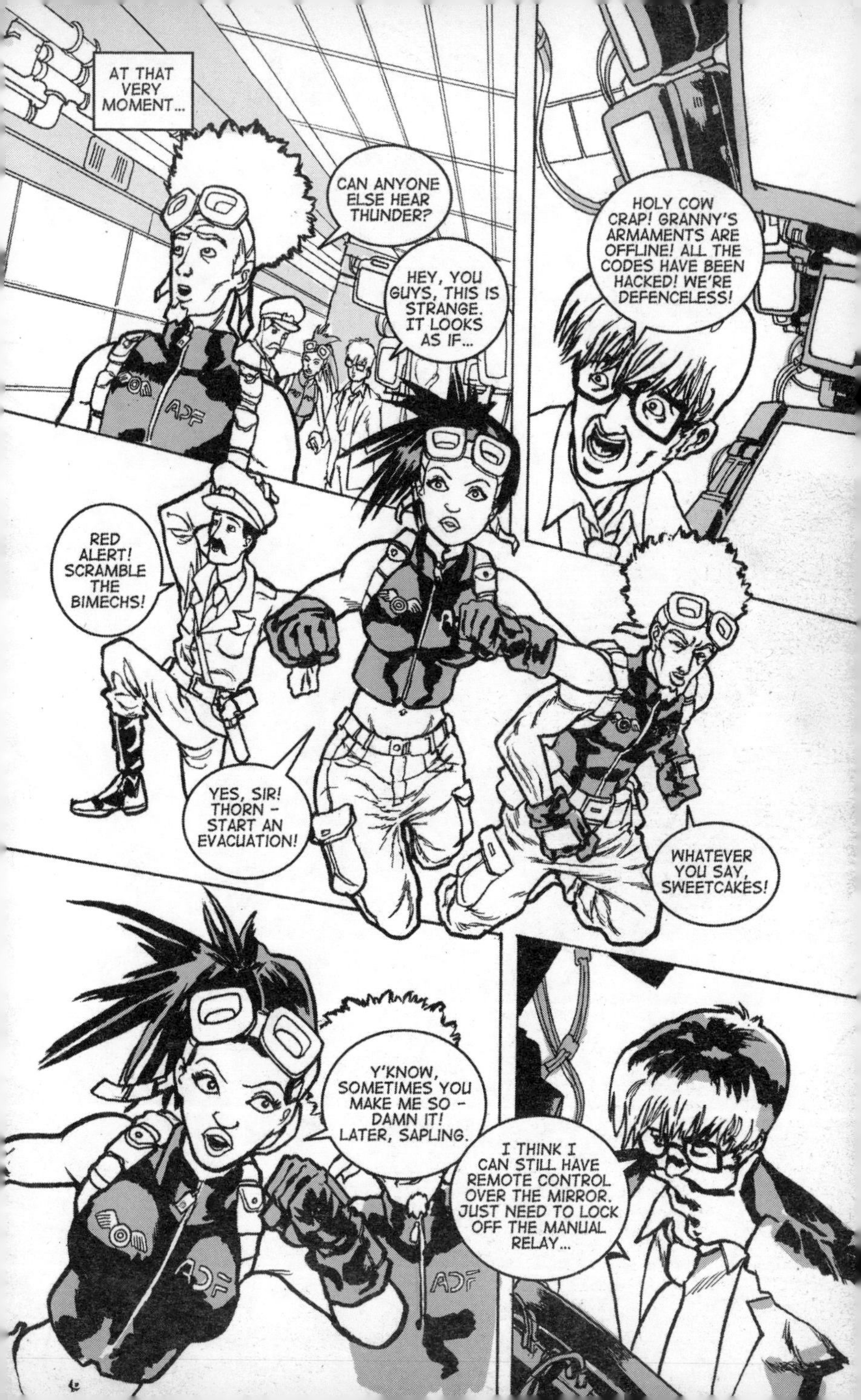
AT THAT VERY MOMENT...
CAN ANYONE ELSE HEAR THUNDER?
HEY, YOU GUYS, THIS IS STRANGE. IT LOOKS AS IF...
HOLY COW CRAP! GRANNY'S ARMAMENTS ARE OFFLINE! ALL THE CODES HAVE BEEN HACKED! WE'RE DEFENCELESS!
RED ALERT! SCRAMBLE THE BIMECHS!
YES, SIR! THORN - START AN EVACUATION!
WHATEVER YOU SAY, SWEETCAKES!
Y'KNOW, SOMETIMES YOU MAKE ME SO - DAMN IT! LATER, SAPLING.
I THINK I CAN STILL HAVE REMOTE CONTROL OVER THE MIRROR. JUST NEED TO LOCK OFF THE MANUAL RELAY...

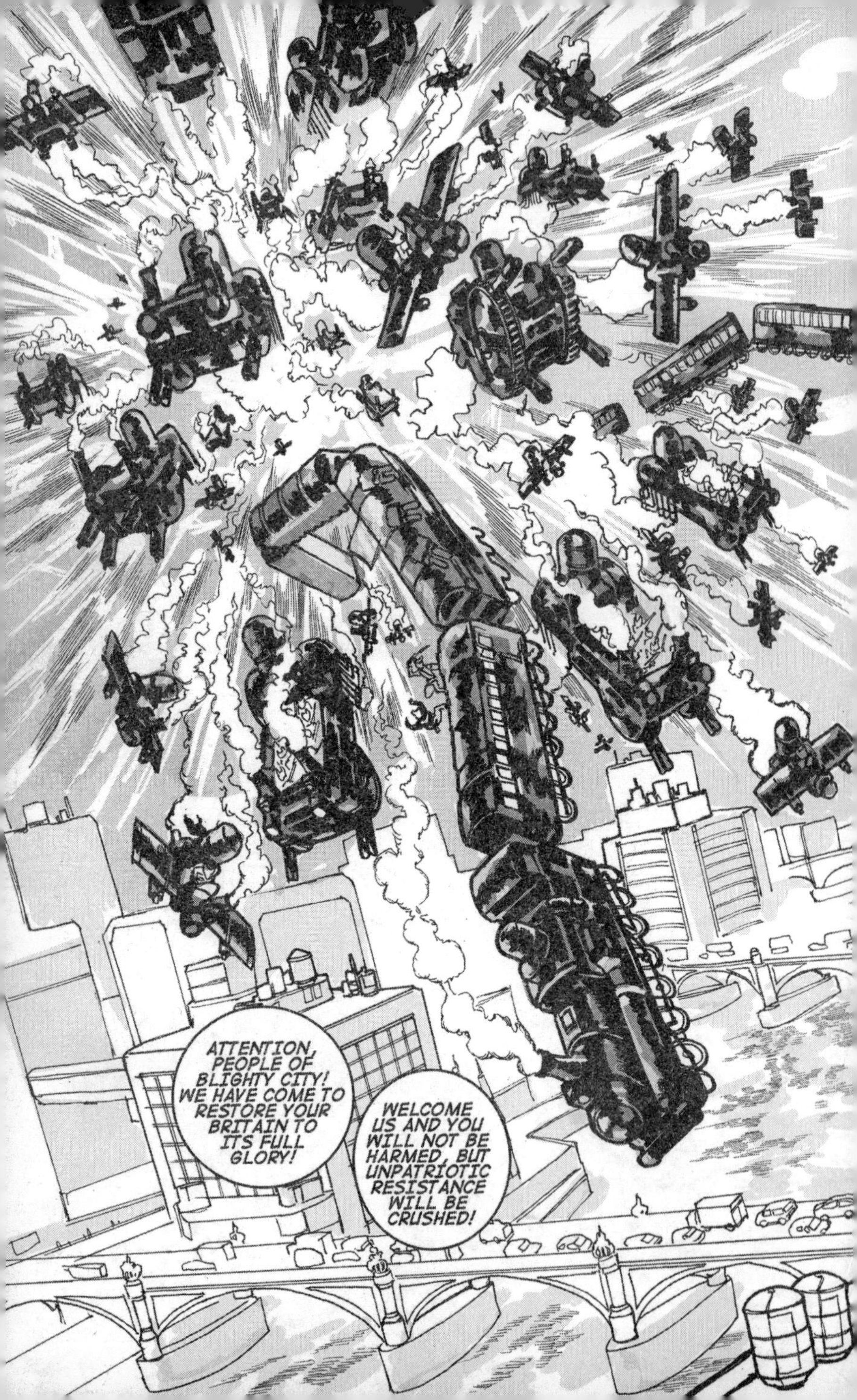
ATTENTION, PEOPLE OF BLIGHTY CITY! WE HAVE COME TO RESTORE YOUR BRITAIN TO ITS FULL GLORY!
WELCOME US AND YOU WILL NOT BE HARMED, BUT UNPATRIOTIC RESISTANCE WILL BE CRUSHED!

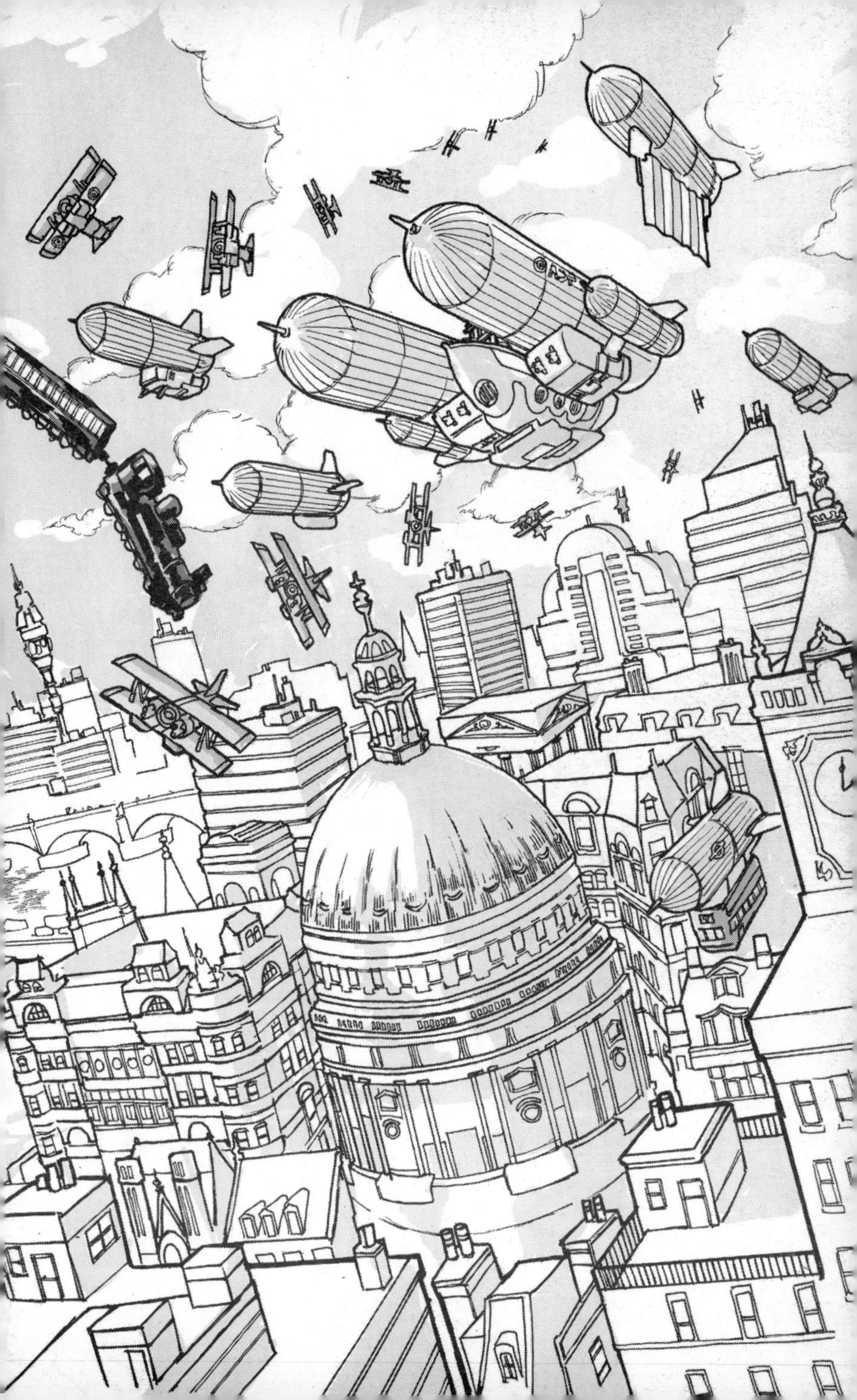

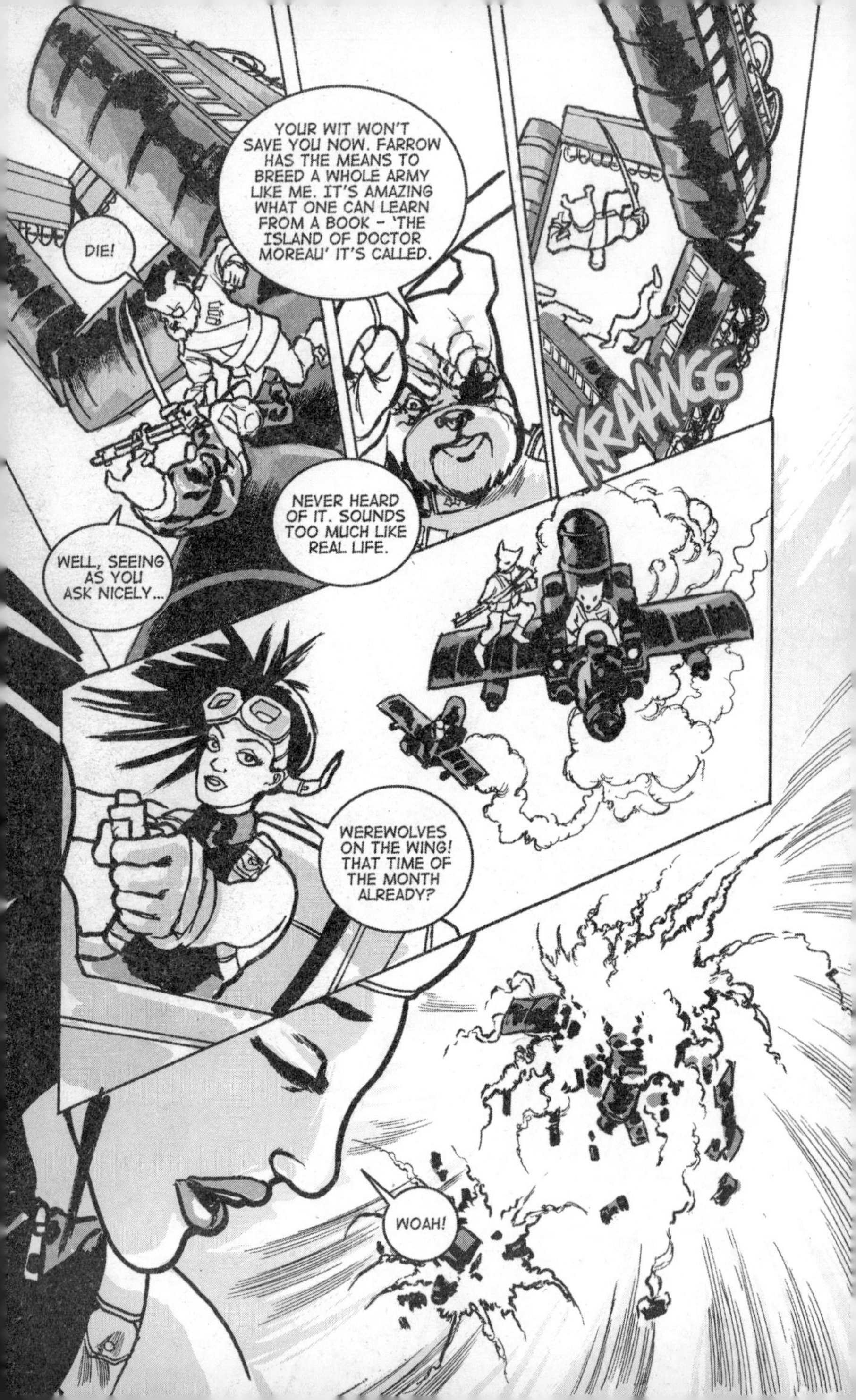
DIE!
YOUR WIT WON'T SAVE YOU NOW. FARROW HAS THE MEANS TO BREED A WHOLE ARMY LIKE ME. IT'S AMAZING WHAT ONE CAN LEARN FROM A BOOK – 'THE ISLAND OF DOCTOR MOREAU' IT'S CALLED.
KRAANGG
WELL, SEEING AS YOU ASK NICELY...
NEVER HEARD OF IT. SOUNDS TOO MUCH LIKE REAL LIFE.
WEREWOLVES ON THE WING! THAT TIME OF THE MONTH ALREADY?
WOAH!

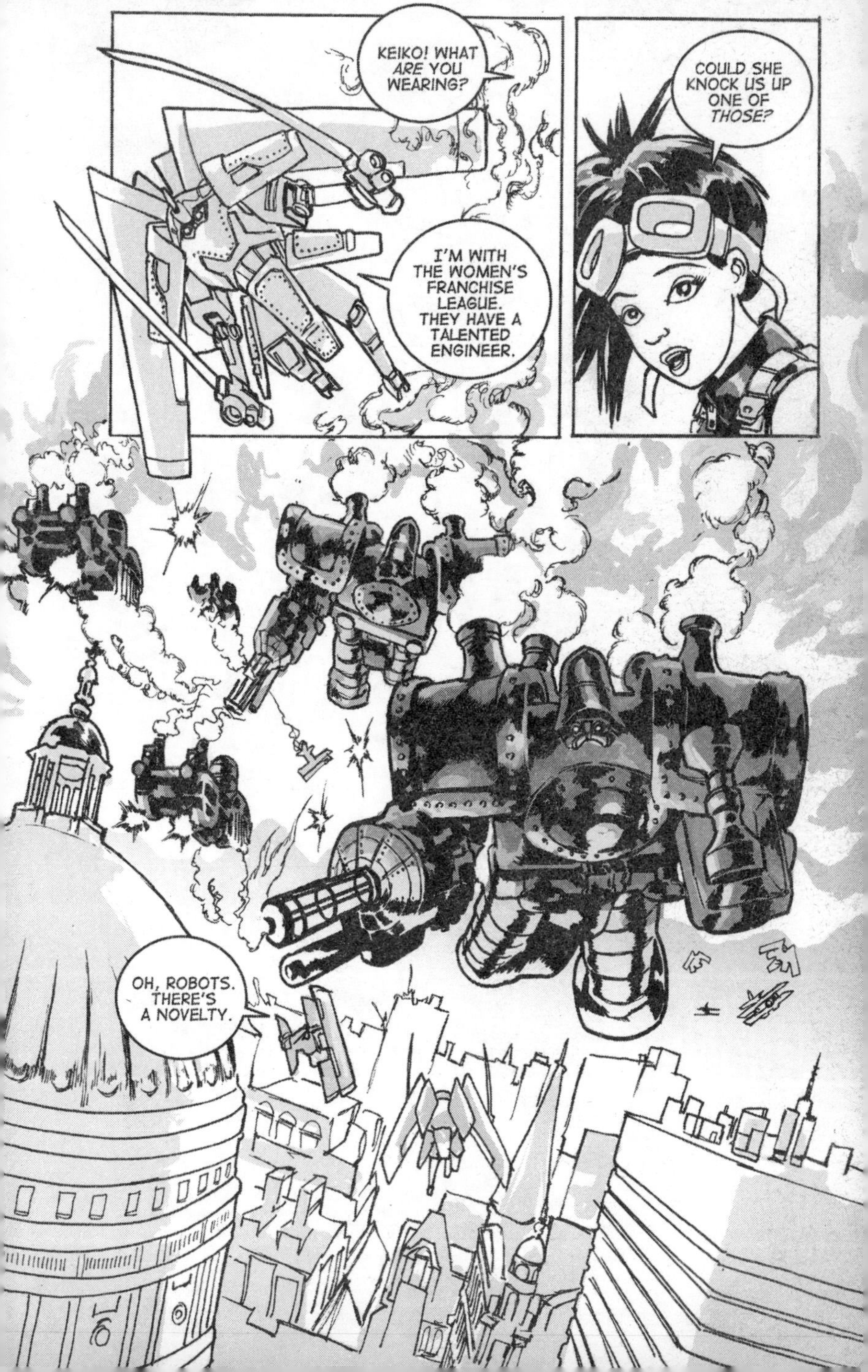
KEIKO! WHAT *ARE* YOU WEARING?
I'M WITH THE WOMEN'S FRANCHISE LEAGUE. THEY HAVE A TALENTED ENGINEER.
COULD SHE KNOCK US UP ONE OF *THOSE?*
OH, ROBOTS. THERE'S A NOVELTY.

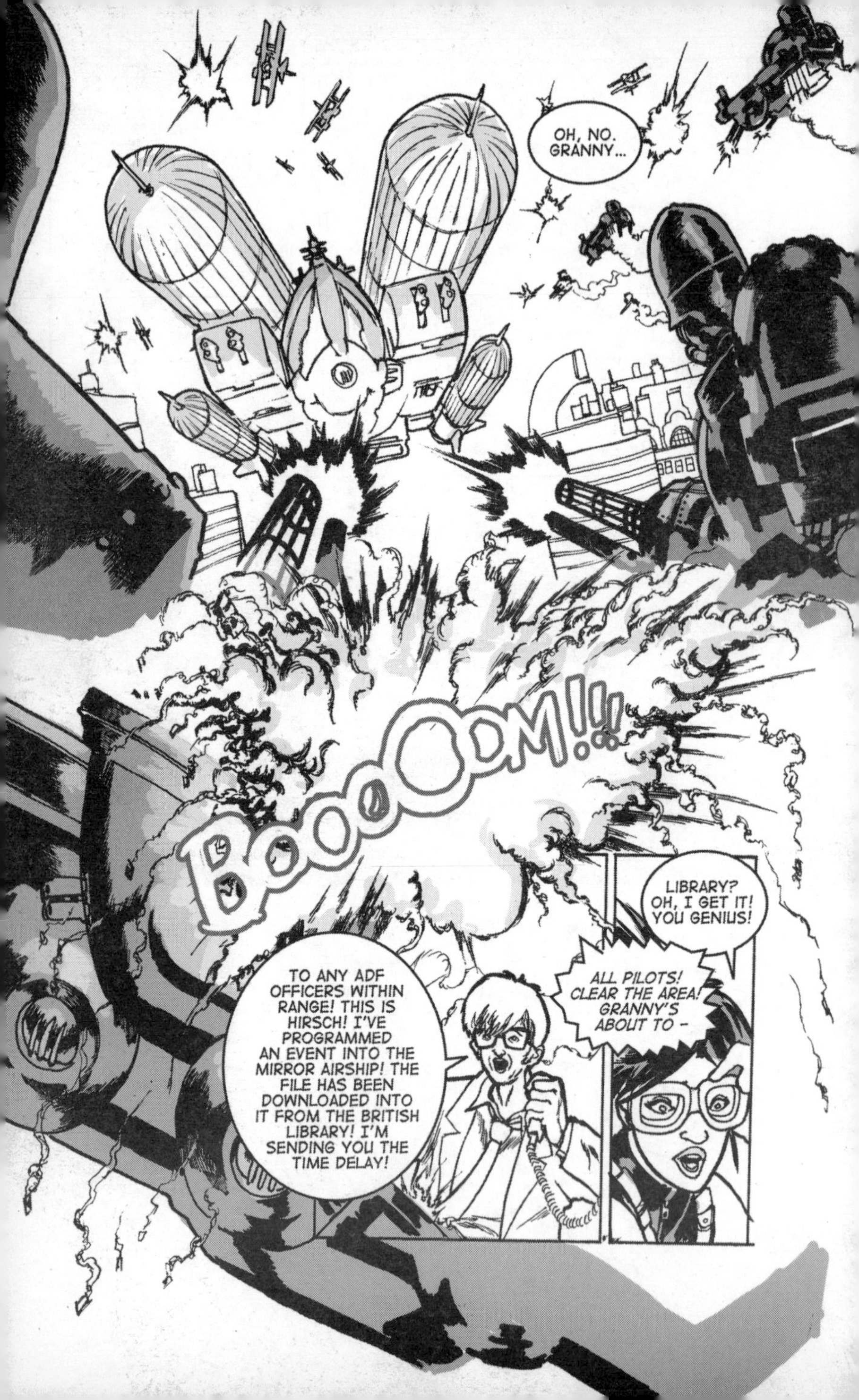
OH, NO. GRANNY...
BOOOOOOM!!!
TO ANY ADF OFFICERS WITHIN RANGE! THIS IS HIRSCH! I'VE PROGRAMMED AN EVENT INTO THE MIRROR AIRSHIP! THE FILE HAS BEEN DOWNLOADED INTO IT FROM THE BRITISH LIBRARY! I'M SENDING YOU THE TIME DELAY!
LIBRARY? OH, I GET IT! YOU GENIUS!
ALL PILOTS! CLEAR THE AREA! GRANNY'S ABOUT TO -

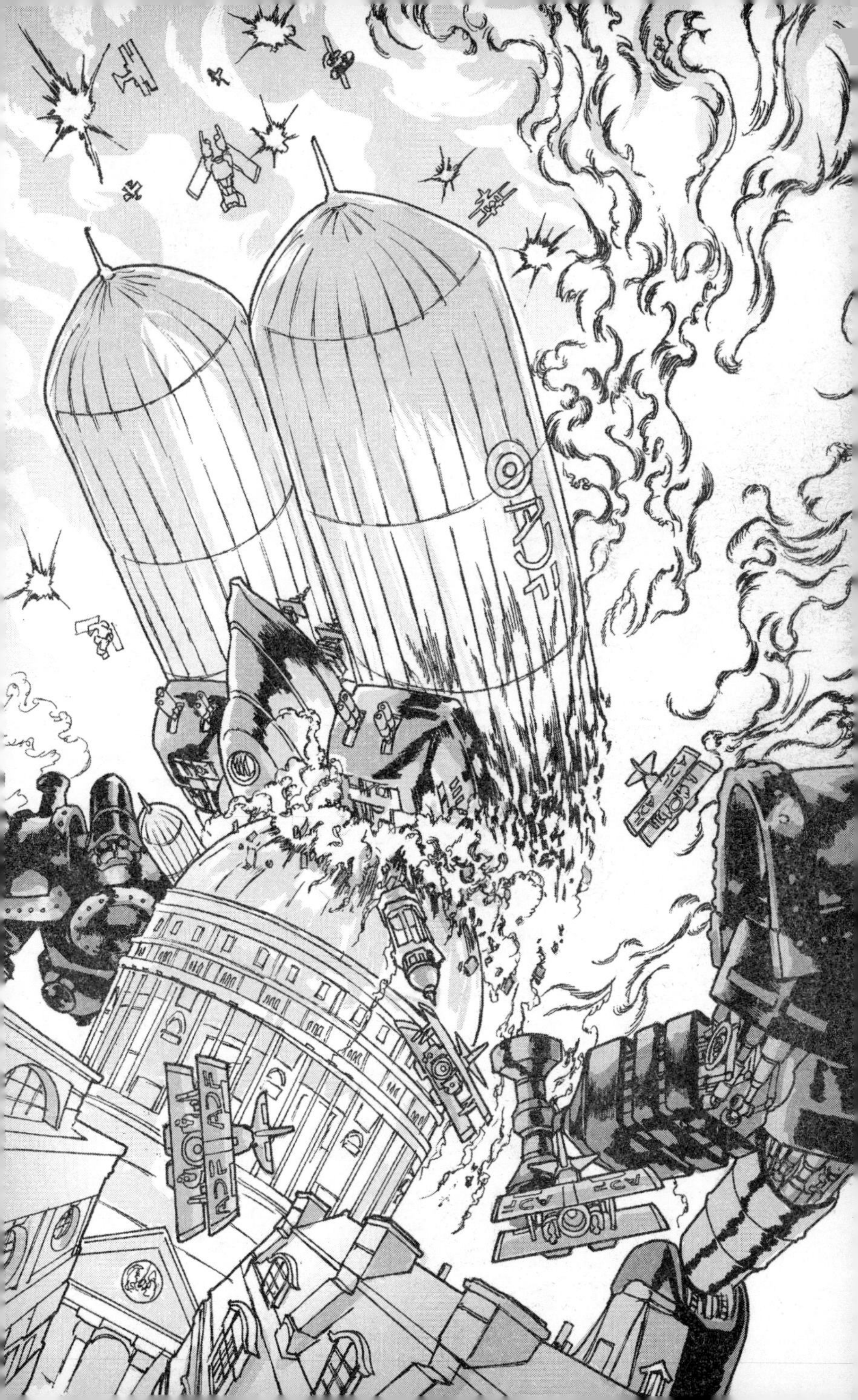

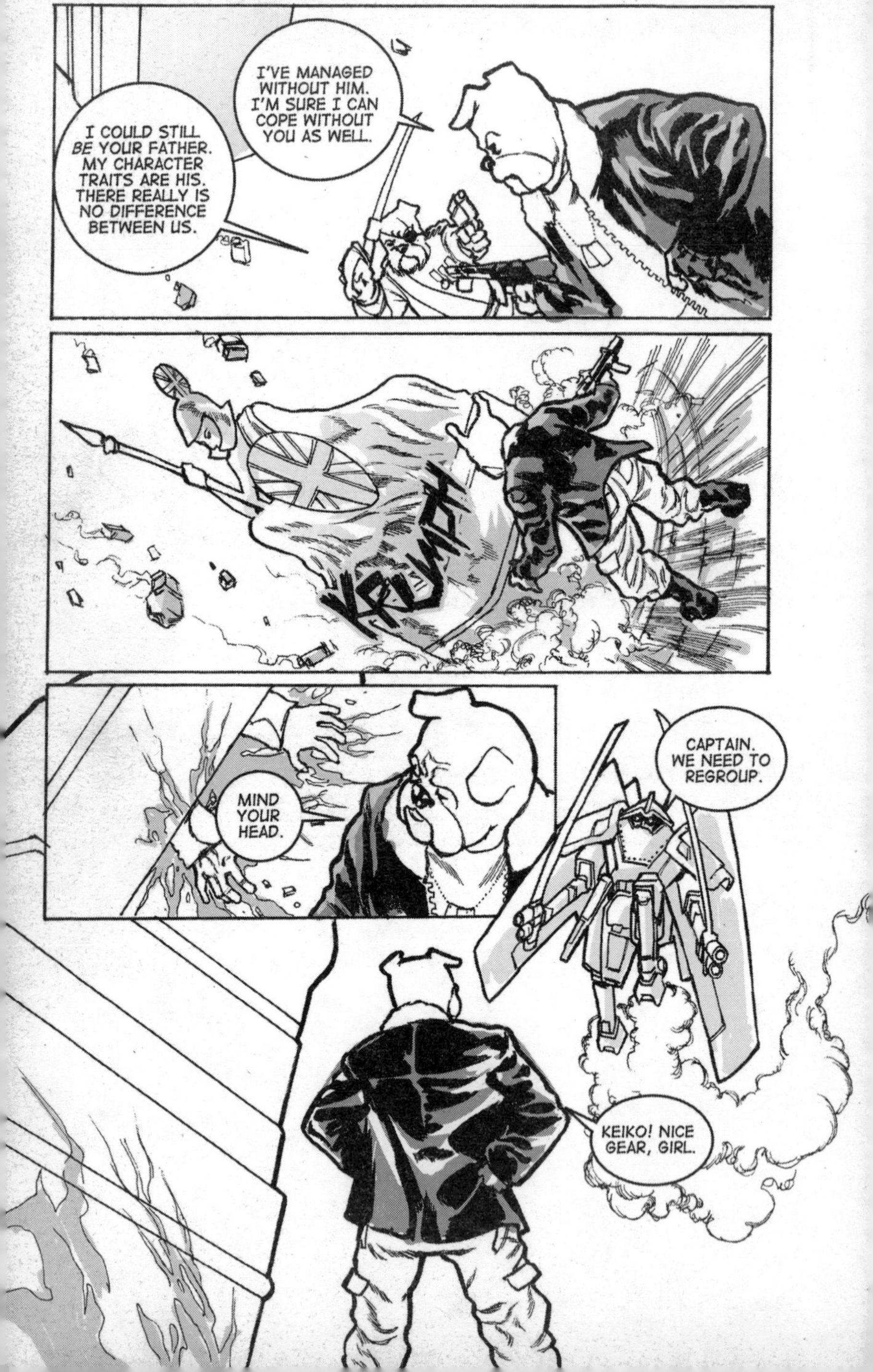
I COULD STILL *BE* YOUR FATHER. MY CHARACTER TRAITS ARE HIS. THERE REALLY IS NO DIFFERENCE BETWEEN US.
I'VE MANAGED WITHOUT HIM. I'M SURE I CAN COPE WITHOUT YOU AS WELL.
KRUNCH
MIND YOUR HEAD.
CAPTAIN. WE NEED TO REGROUP.
KEIKO! NICE GEAR, GIRL.

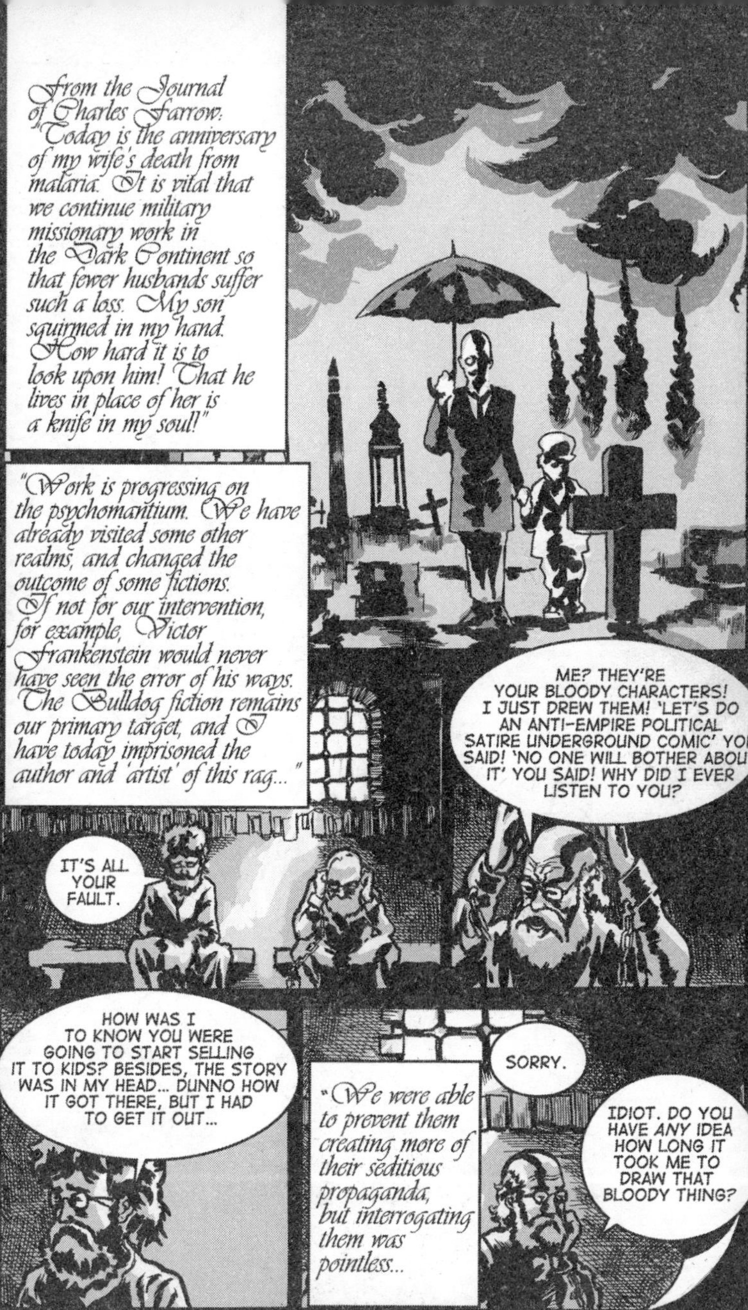

From the Journal of Charles Farrow: "Today is the anniversary of my wife's death from malaria. It is vital that we continue military missionary work in the Dark Continent so that fewer husbands suffer such a loss. My son squirmed in my hand. How hard it is to look upon him! That he lives in place of her is a knife in my soul!"
"Work is progressing on the psychomantium. We have already visited some other realms, and changed the outcome of some fictions. If not for our intervention, for example, Victor Frankenstein would never have seen the error of his ways. The Bulldog fiction remains our primary target, and I have today imprisoned the author and 'artist' of this rag..."
IT'S ALL YOUR FAULT.
ME? THEY'RE YOUR BLOODY CHARACTERS! I JUST DREW THEM! 'LET'S DO AN ANTI-EMPIRE POLITICAL SATIRE UNDERGROUND COMIC' YOU SAID! 'NO ONE WILL BOTHER ABOUT IT' YOU SAID! WHY DID I EVER LISTEN TO YOU?
HOW WAS I TO KNOW YOU WERE GOING TO START SELLING IT TO KIDS? BESIDES, THE STORY WAS IN MY HEAD... DUNNO HOW IT GOT THERE, BUT I HAD TO GET IT OUT...
"We were able to prevent them creating more of their seditious propaganda, but interrogating them was pointless...
SORRY.
IDIOT. DO YOU HAVE *ANY* IDEA HOW LONG IT TOOK ME TO DRAW THAT BLOODY THING?

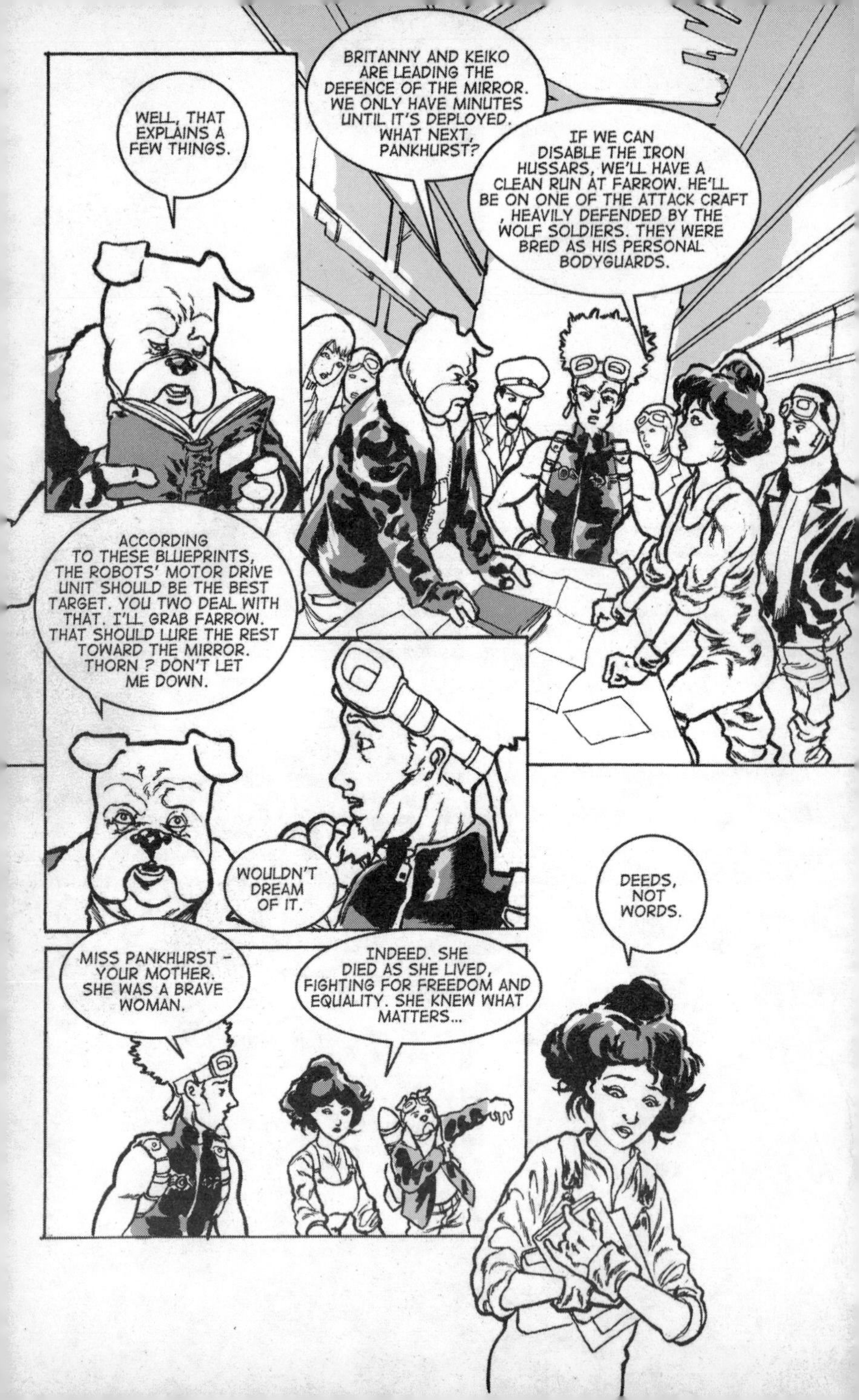
WELL, THAT EXPLAINS A FEW THINGS.
BRITANNY AND KEIKO ARE LEADING THE DEFENCE OF THE MIRROR. WE ONLY HAVE MINUTES UNTIL IT'S DEPLOYED. WHAT NEXT, PANKHURST?
IF WE CAN DISABLE THE IRON HUSSARS, WE'LL HAVE A CLEAN RUN AT FARROW. HE'LL BE ON ONE OF THE ATTACK CRAFT , HEAVILY DEFENDED BY THE WOLF SOLDIERS. THEY WERE BRED AS HIS PERSONAL BODYGUARDS.
ACCORDING TO THESE BLUEPRINTS, THE ROBOTS' MOTOR DRIVE UNIT SHOULD BE THE BEST TARGET. YOU TWO DEAL WITH THAT. I'LL GRAB FARROW. THAT SHOULD LURE THE REST TOWARD THE MIRROR. THORN ? DON'T LET ME DOWN.
WOULDN'T DREAM OF IT.
MISS PANKHURST - YOUR MOTHER. SHE WAS A BRAVE WOMAN.
INDEED. SHE DIED AS SHE LIVED, FIGHTING FOR FREEDOM AND EQUALITY. SHE KNEW WHAT MATTERS...
DEEDS, NOT WORDS.

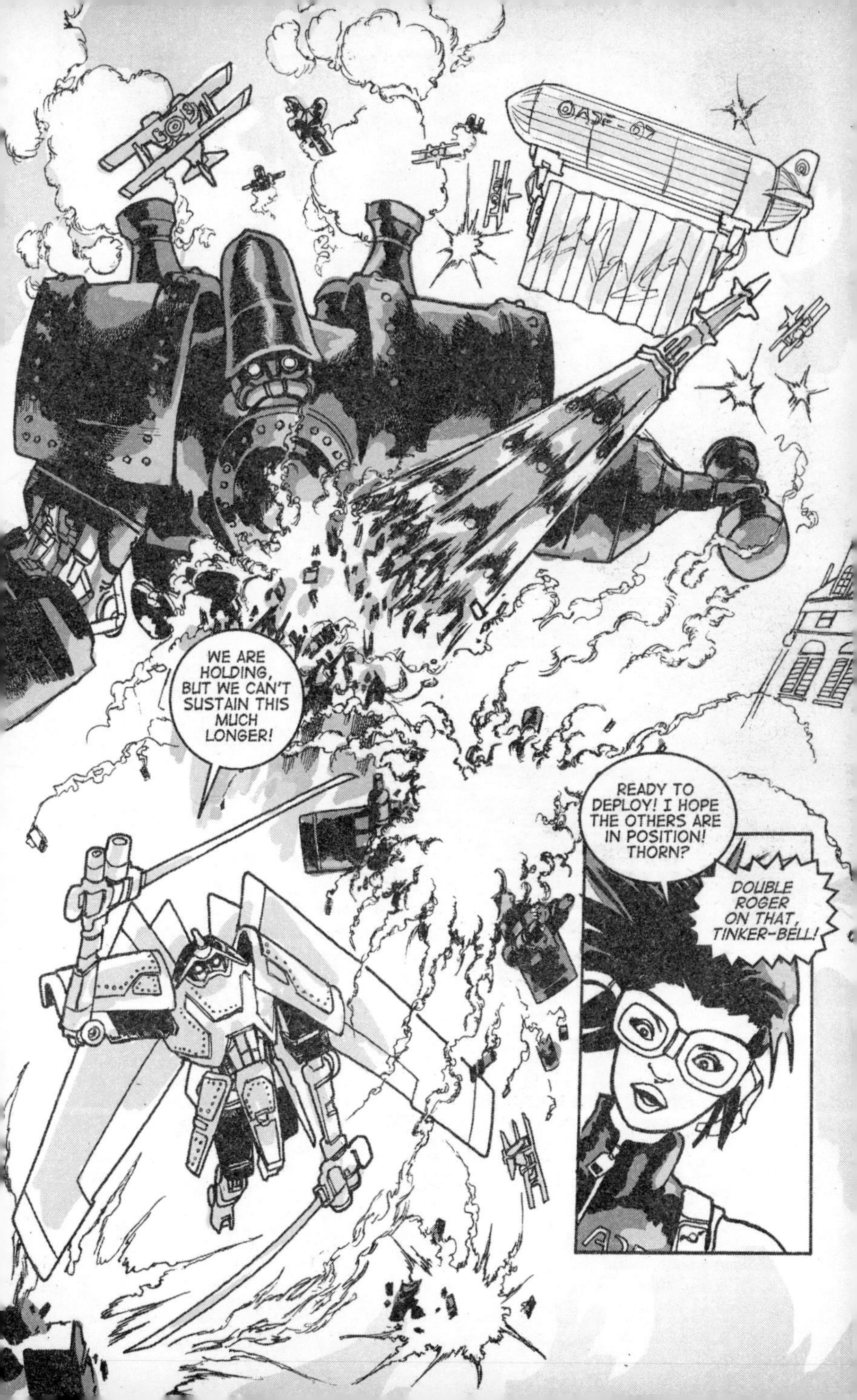
WE ARE HOLDING, BUT WE CAN'T SUSTAIN THIS MUCH LONGER!
READY TO DEPLOY! I HOPE THE OTHERS ARE IN POSITION! THORN?
DOUBLE ROGER ON THAT, TINKER-BELL!

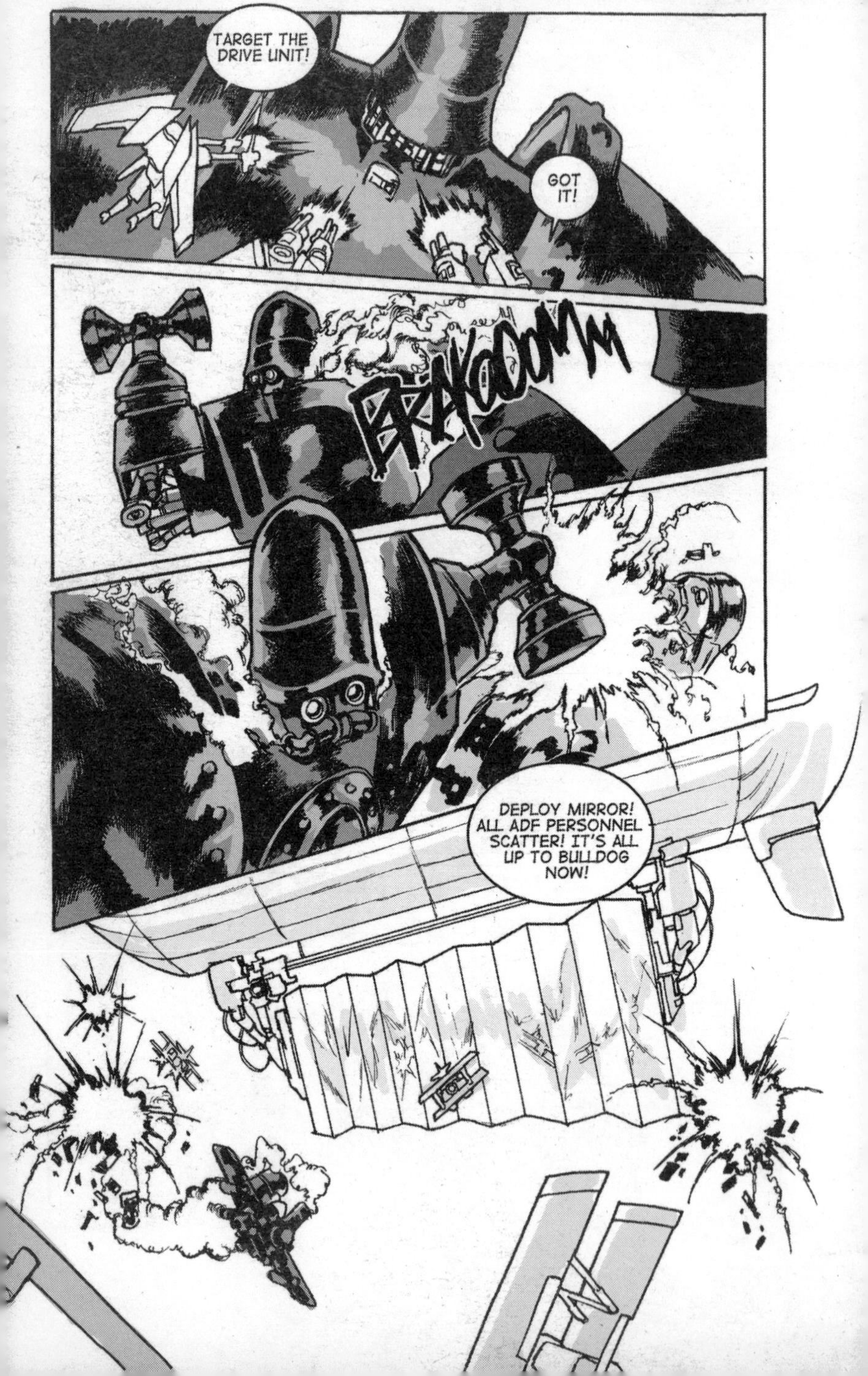
TARGET THE DRIVE UNIT!
GOT IT!
BRAKOOOM
DEPLOY MIRROR! ALL ADF PERSONNEL SCATTER! IT'S ALL UP TO BULLDOG NOW!

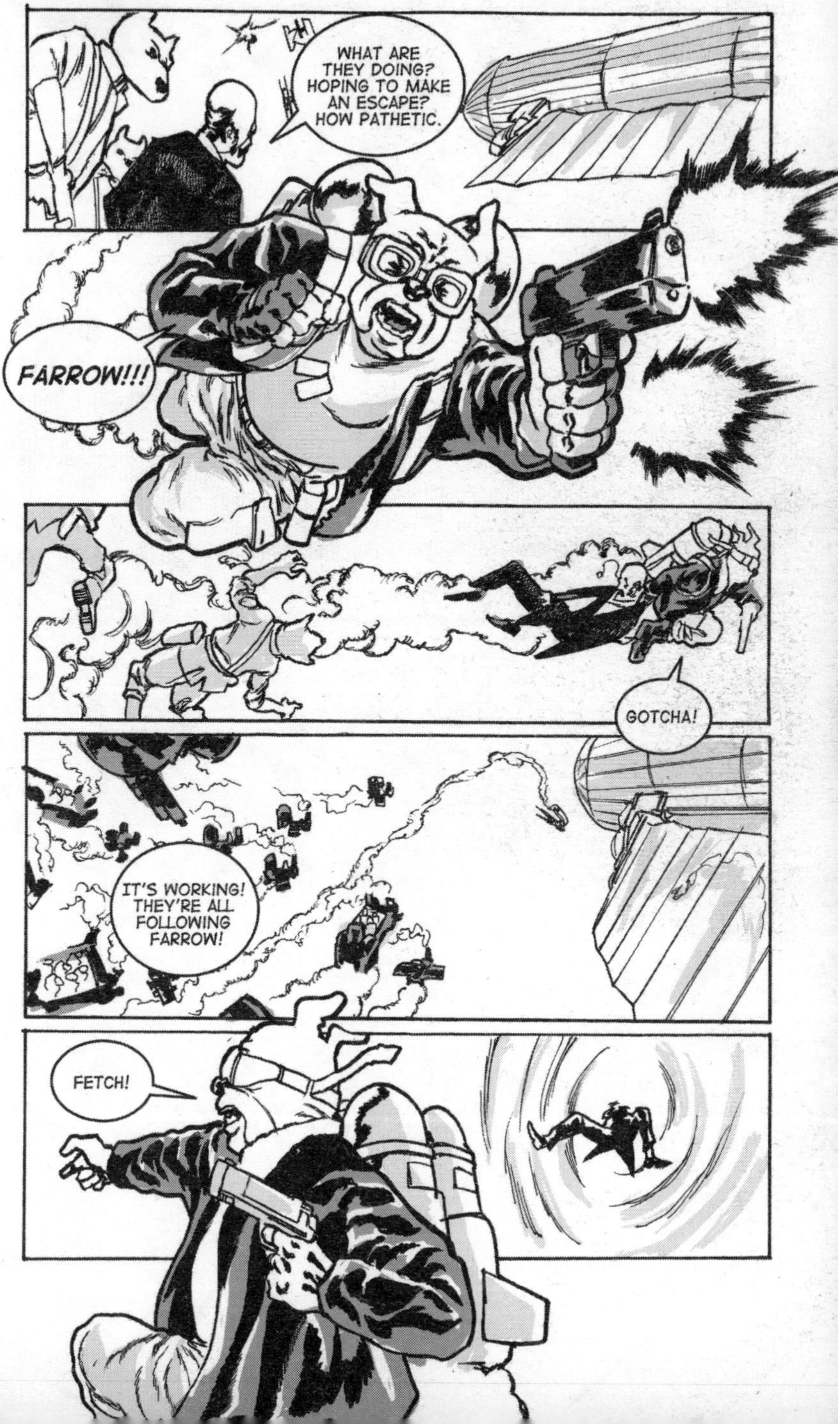
WHAT ARE THEY DOING? HOPING TO MAKE AN ESCAPE? HOW PATHETIC.
FARROW!!!!
GOTCHA!
IT'S WORKING! THEY'RE ALL FOLLOWING FARROW!
FETCH!

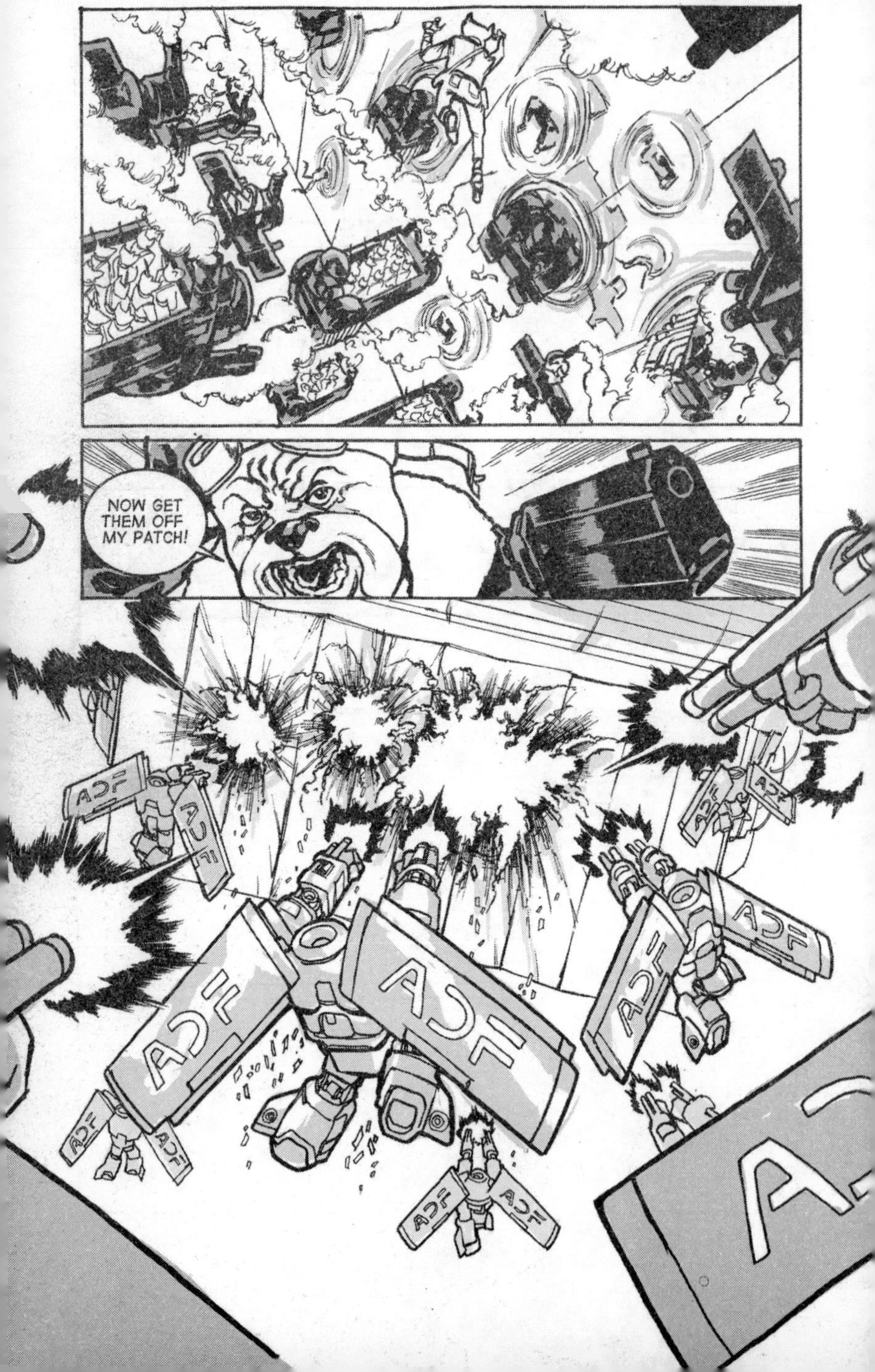
NOW GET THEM OFF MY PATCH!
ADF

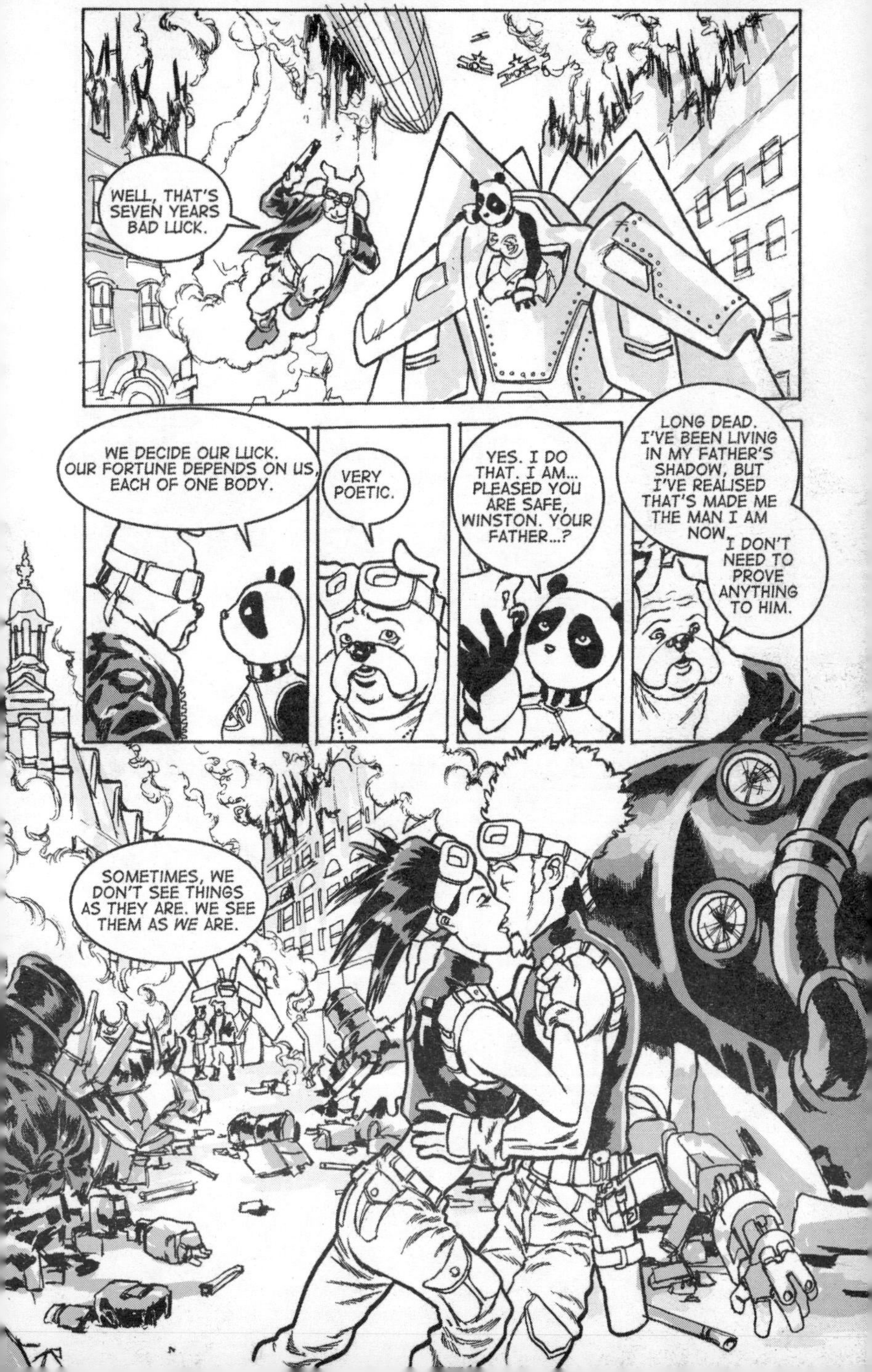

WELL, THAT'S SEVEN YEARS BAD LUCK.
WE DECIDE OUR LUCK. OUR FORTUNE DEPENDS ON US, EACH OF ONE BODY.
VERY POETIC.
YES. I DO THAT. I AM... PLEASED YOU ARE SAFE, WINSTON. YOUR FATHER...?
LONG DEAD. I'VE BEEN LIVING IN MY FATHER'S SHADOW, BUT I'VE REALISED THAT'S MADE ME THE MAN I AM NOW.
I DON'T NEED TO PROVE ANYTHING TO HIM.
SOMETIMES, WE DON'T SEE THINGS AS THEY ARE. WE SEE THEM AS *WE* ARE.

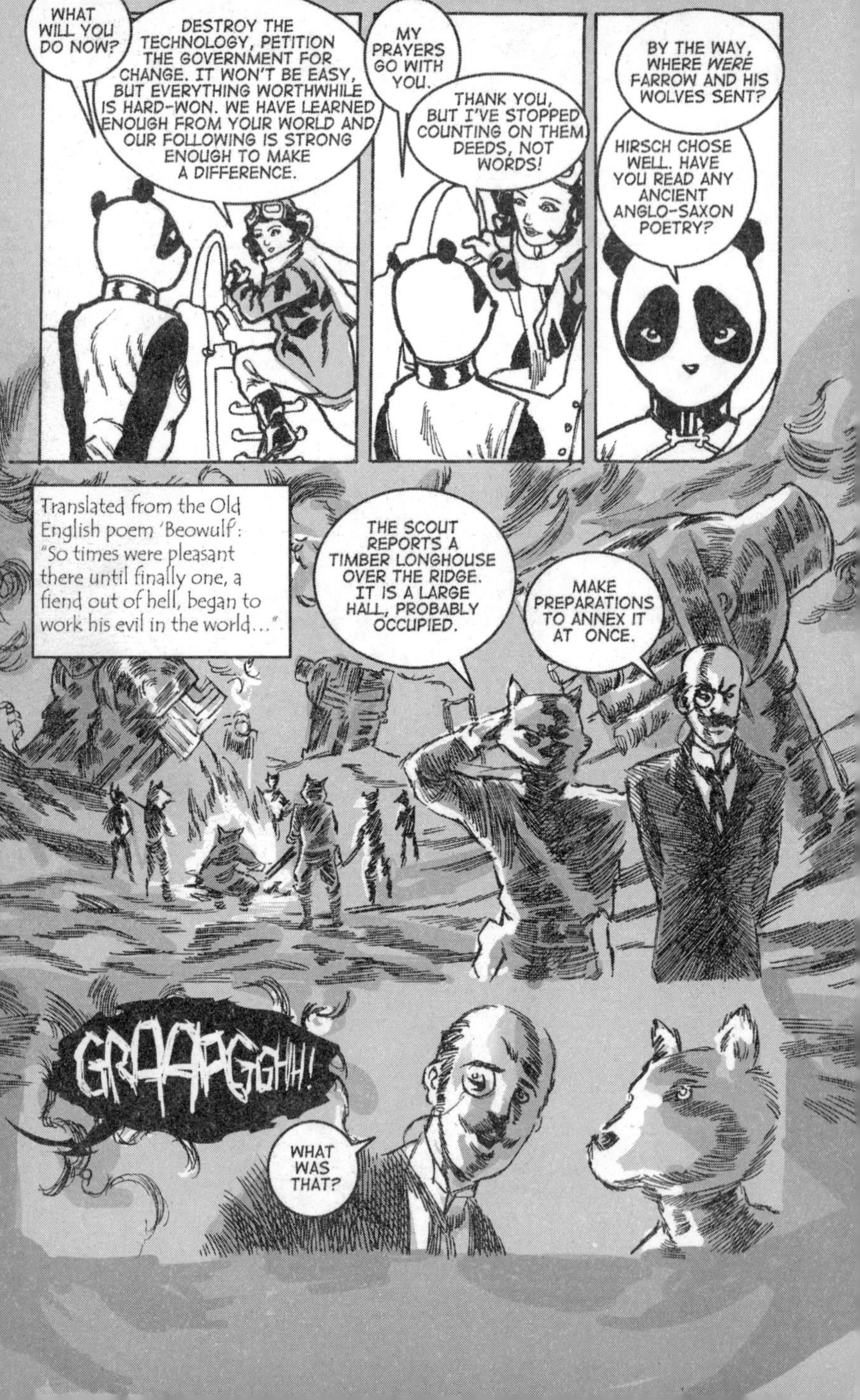
WHAT WILL YOU DO NOW?
DESTROY THE TECHNOLOGY, PETITION THE GOVERNMENT FOR CHANGE. IT WON'T BE EASY, BUT EVERYTHING WORTHWHILE IS HARD-WON. WE HAVE LEARNED ENOUGH FROM YOUR WORLD AND OUR FOLLOWING IS STRONG ENOUGH TO MAKE A DIFFERENCE.
MY PRAYERS GO WITH YOU.
THANK YOU, BUT I'VE STOPPED COUNTING ON THEM. DEEDS, NOT WORDS!
BY THE WAY, WHERE *WERE* FARROW AND HIS WOLVES SENT?
HIRSCH CHOSE WELL. HAVE YOU READ ANY ANCIENT ANGLO-SAXON POETRY?
Translated from the Old English poem 'Beowulf': "So times were pleasant there until finally one, a fiend out of hell, began to work his evil in the world..."
THE SCOUT REPORTS A TIMBER LONGHOUSE OVER THE RIDGE. IT IS A LARGE HALL, PROBABLY OCCUPIED.
MAKE PREPARATIONS TO ANNEX IT AT ONCE.
GRAAAGGHH!
WHAT WAS THAT?

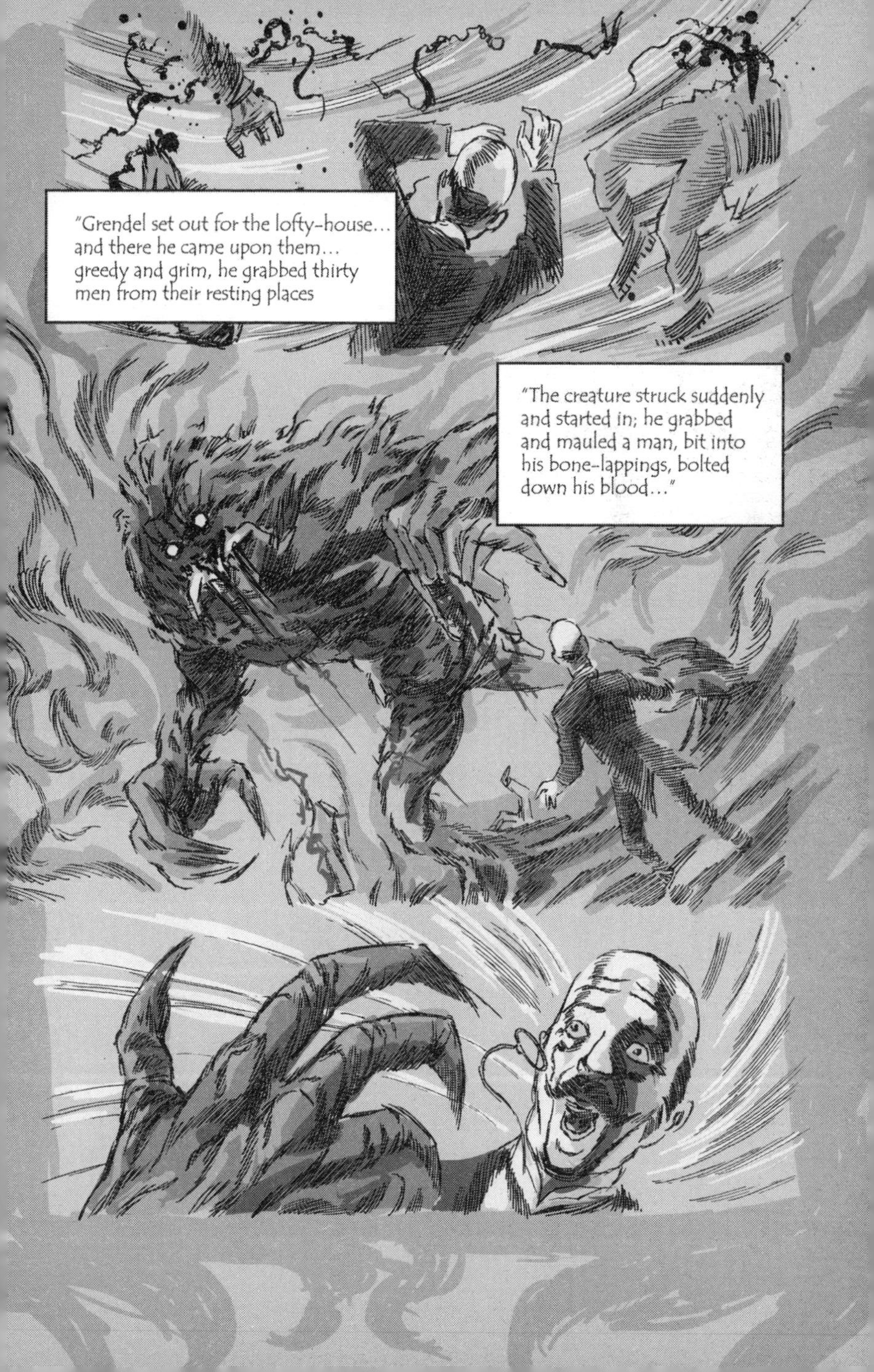
"Grendel set out for the lofty-house… and there he came upon them… greedy and grim, he grabbed thirty men from their resting places
"The creature struck suddenly and started in; he grabbed and mauled a man, bit into his bone-lappings, bolted down his blood…"

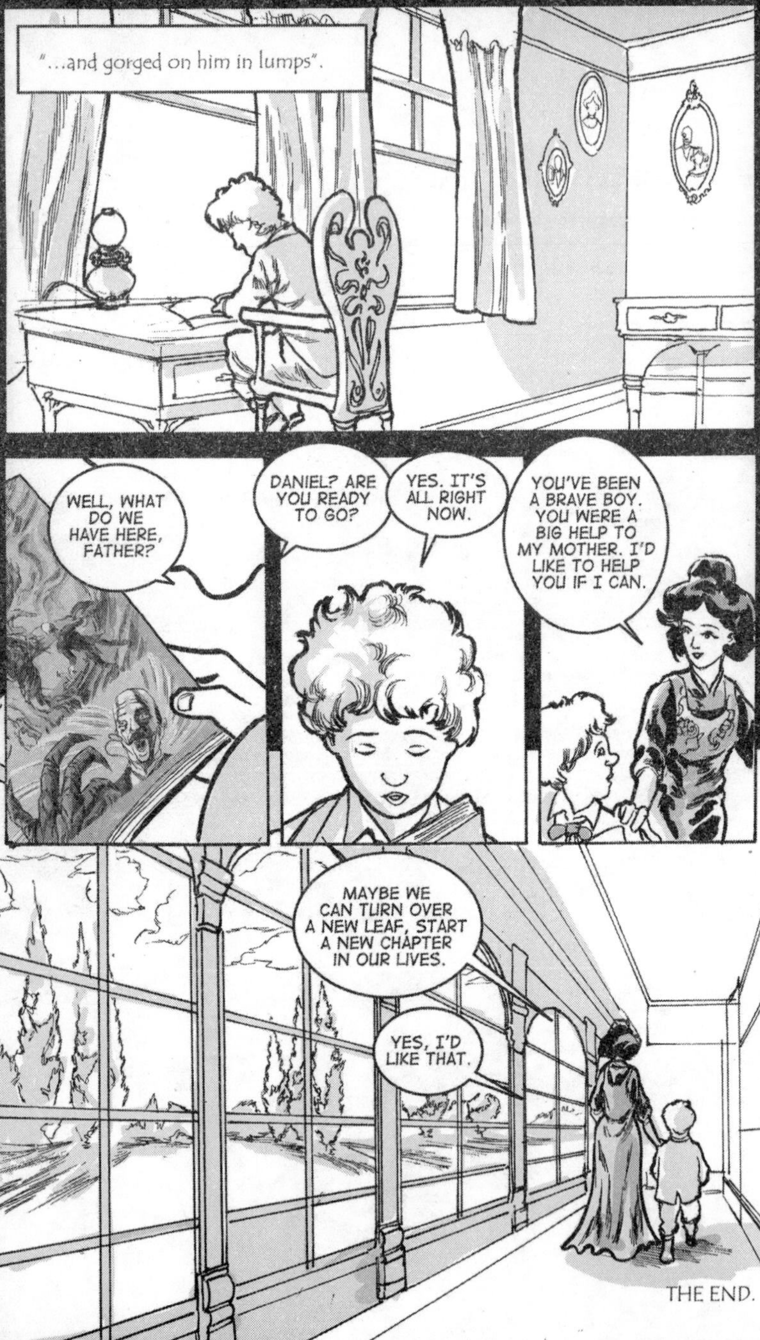
"...and gorged on him in lumps".
WELL, WHAT DO WE HAVE HERE, FATHER?
DANIEL? ARE YOU READY TO GO?
YES. IT'S ALL RIGHT NOW.
YOU'VE BEEN A BRAVE BOY. YOU WERE A BIG HELP TO MY MOTHER. I'D LIKE TO HELP YOU IF I CAN.
MAYBE WE CAN TURN OVER A NEW LEAF, START A NEW CHAPTER IN OUR LIVES.
YES, I'D LIKE THAT.
THE END.

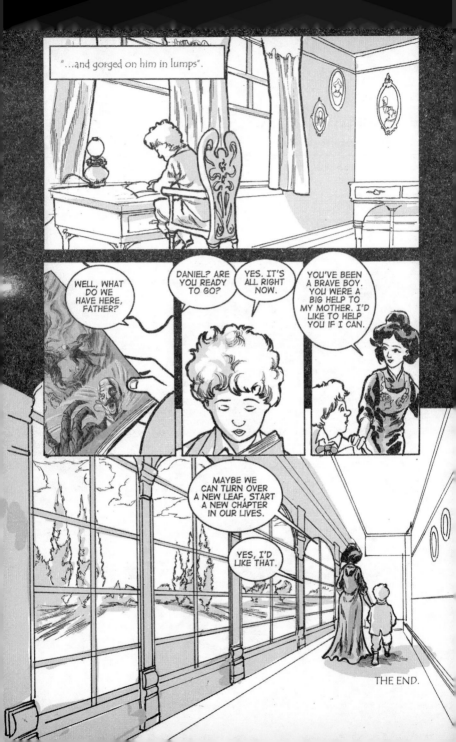

New Shoes

by

Asa Ekström

Åsa Ekström

Date of birth: 10 October 1983

Åsa is from Sweden. Her all-time favourite anime is *Shoujo Kakumei Utena*, and her all-time favourite manga are *Nana* by Ai Yazawa and *Ayashi no Ceres* by Yuu Watase. She loves the Japanese designer toy *Gloomy the bear*, and cookies (but hey, who doesn't?), but she dreads writer's block.

The original version of this story is in colour and can be seen on her website. Luckily, translating it from Swedish was very easy (: >). Asa's current major project is called *Sayonara September*; the bittersweet story of a girl who has to make peace with her sad past, and will probably end up as three volumes in total. She hopes to see it published internationally.

Åsa says she loves drinking with friends, but hates hangovers. But hey, who doesn't?

http://www.asaekstrom.com

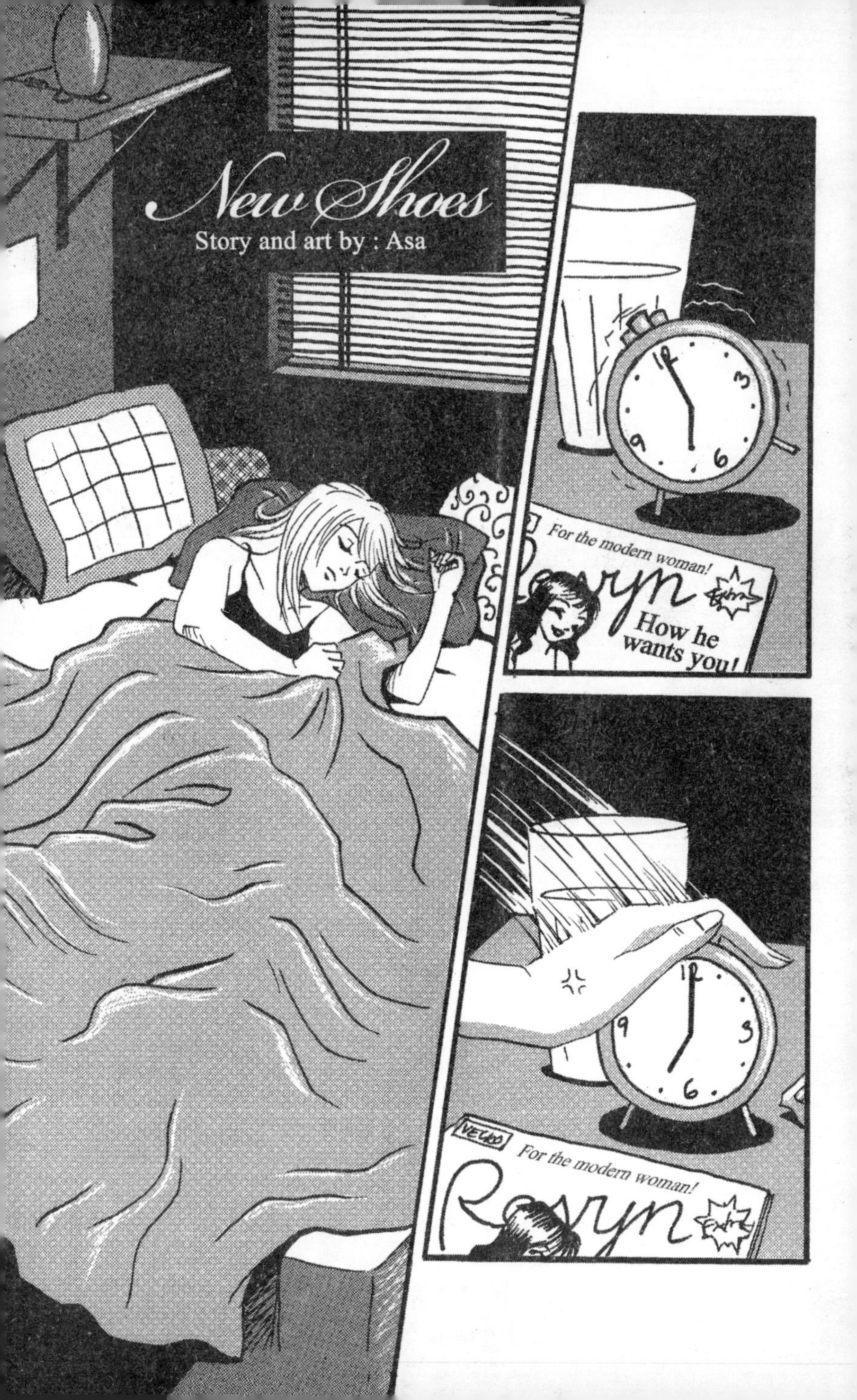
New Shoes
Story and art by : Asa
For the modern woman!
How he wants you!
For the modern woman!

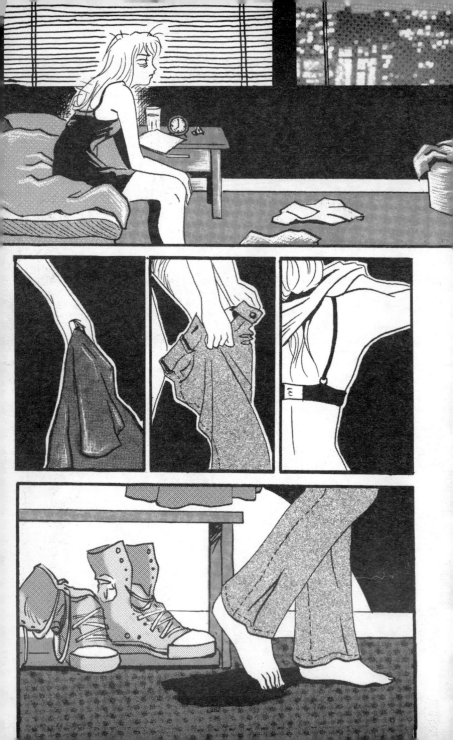

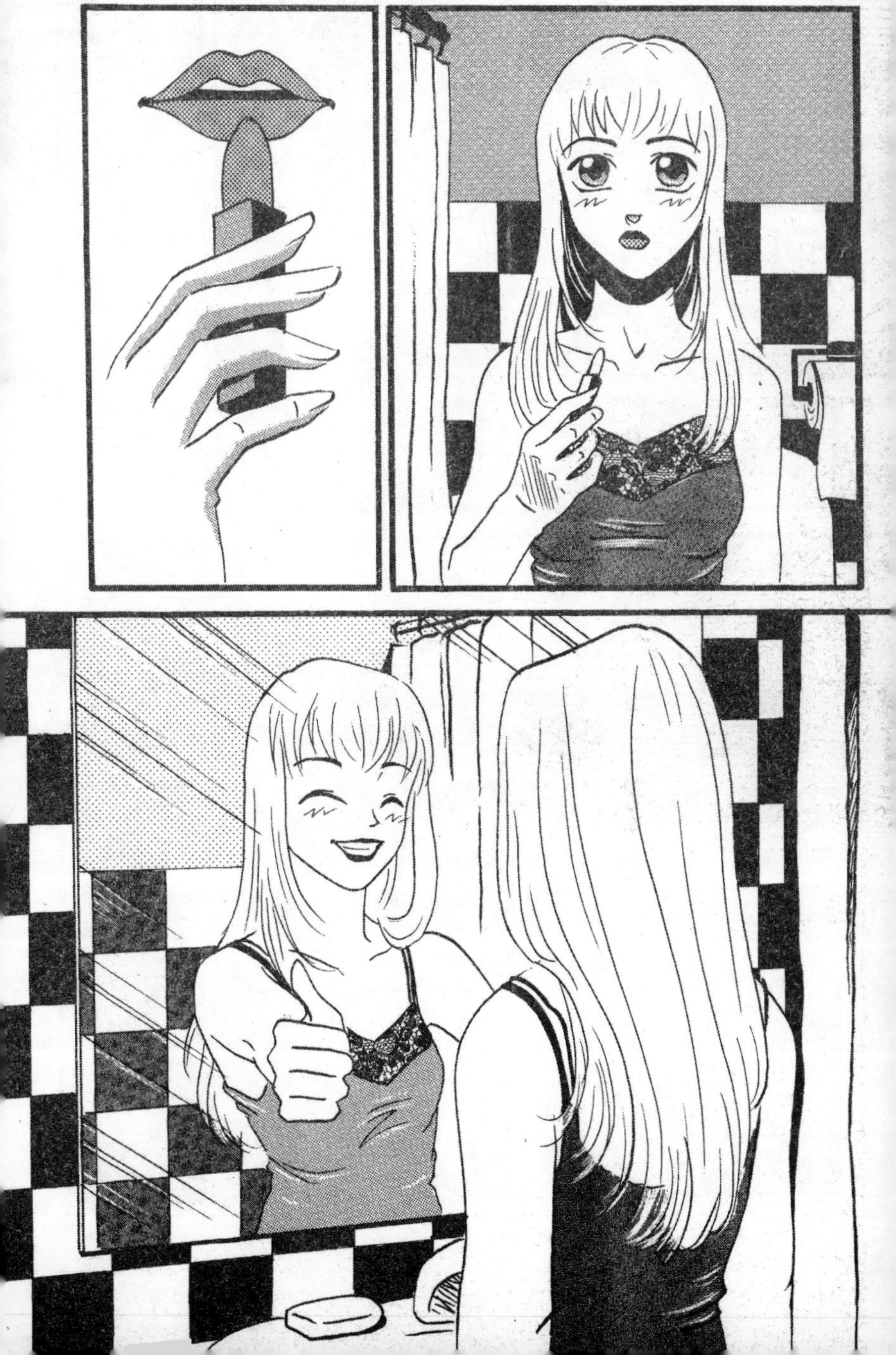

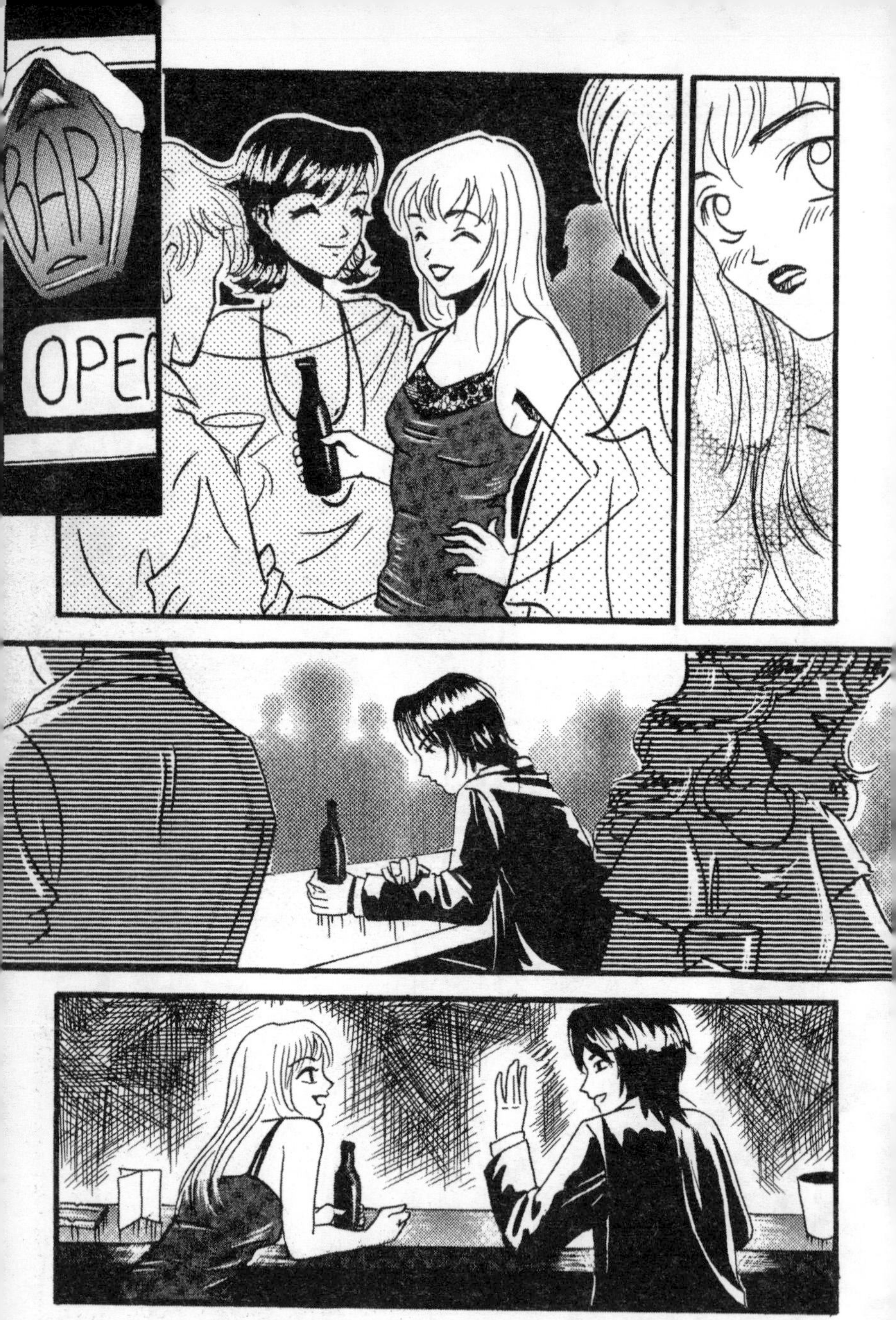
BAR
OPE

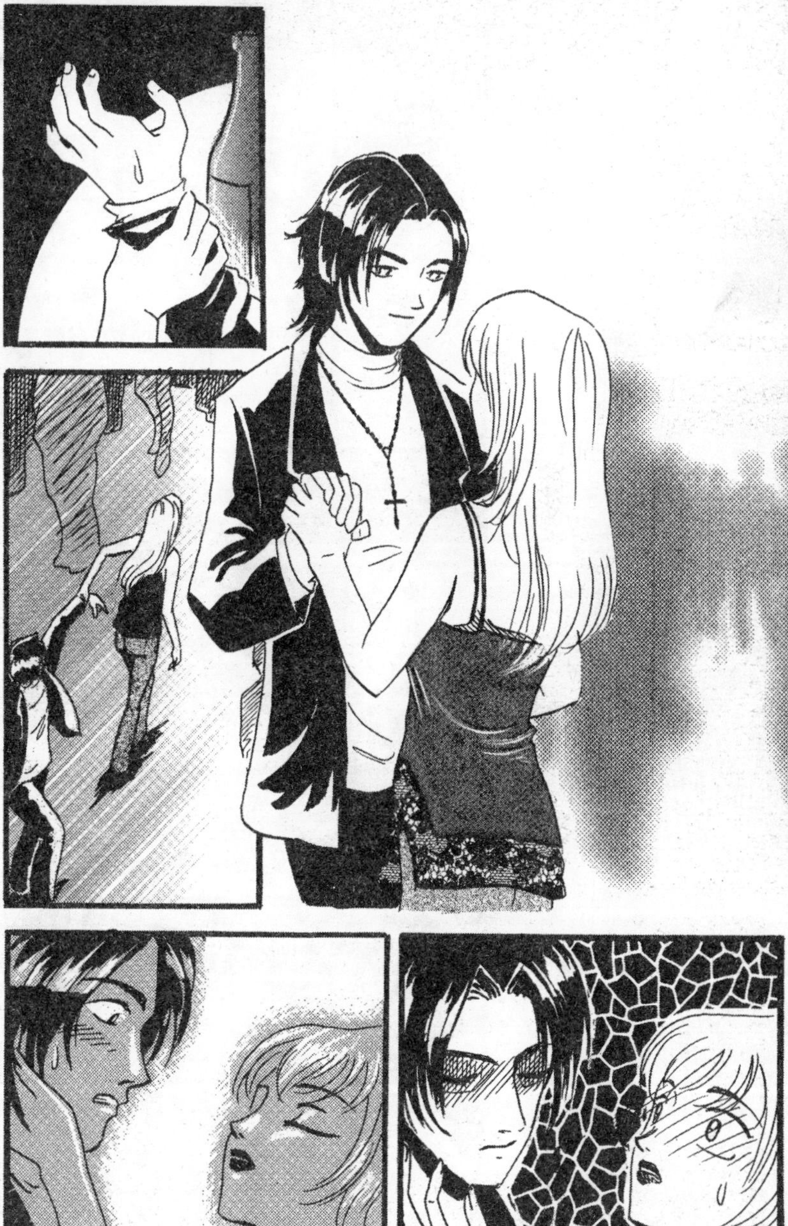

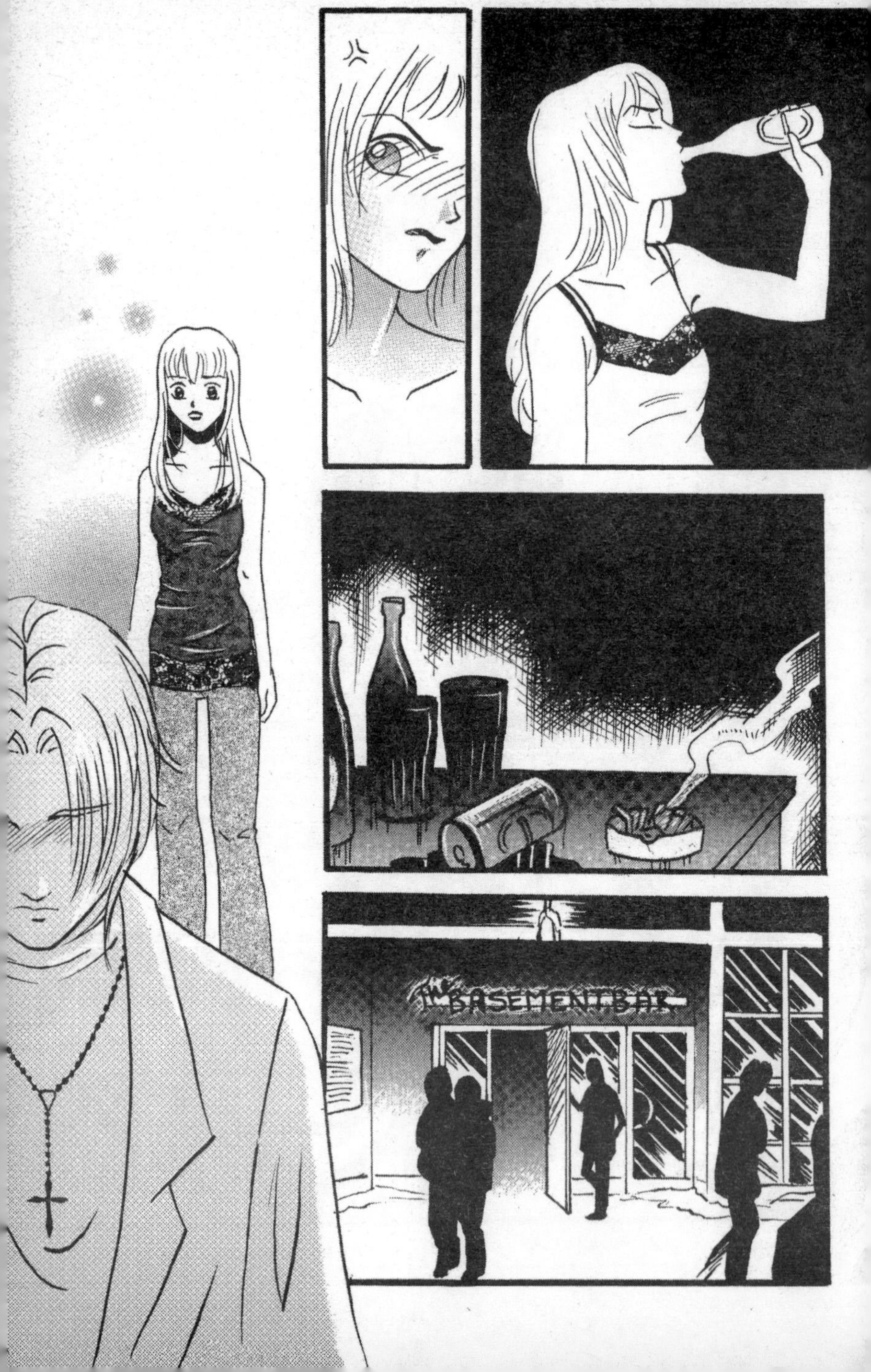
BASEMENT BAR

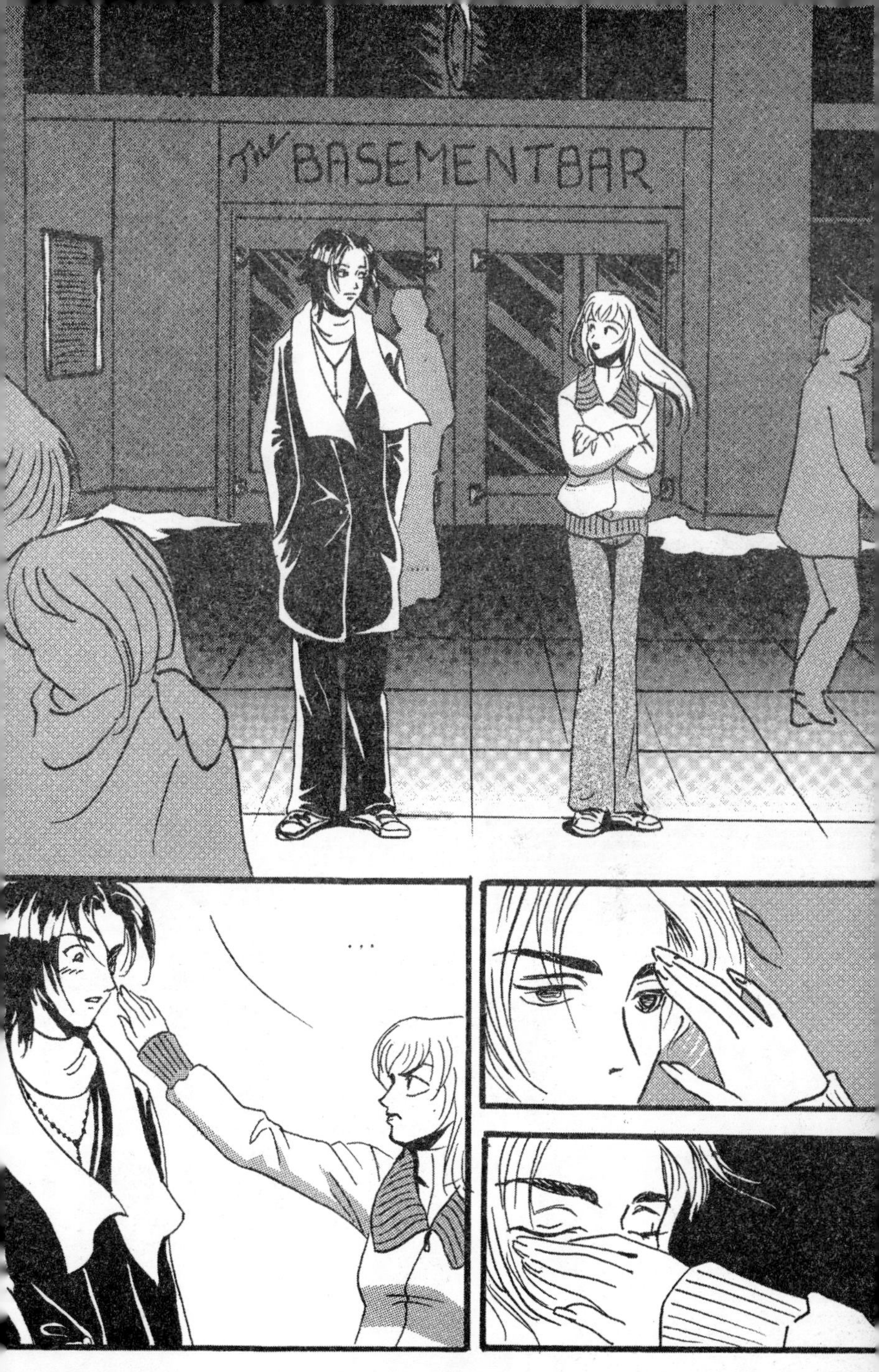
The BASEMENTBAR
...

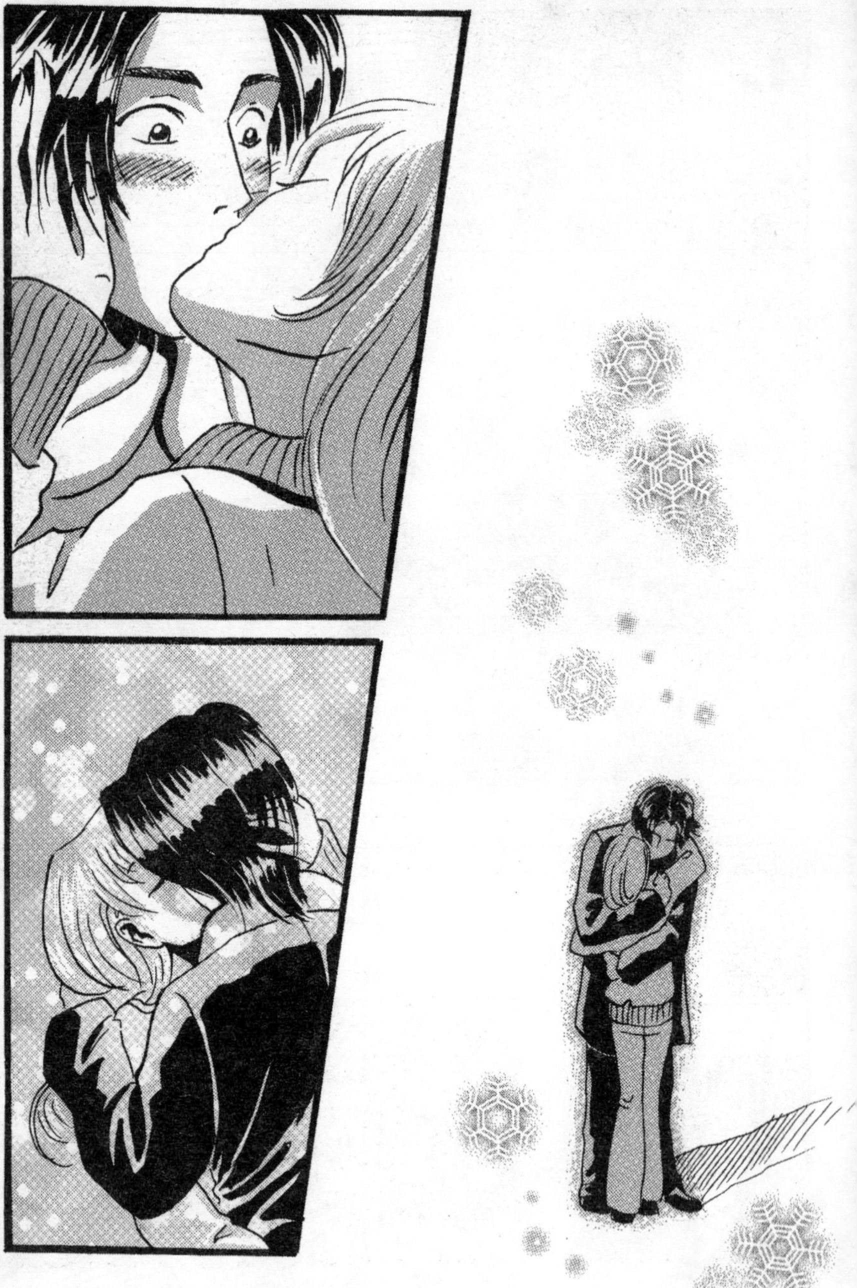

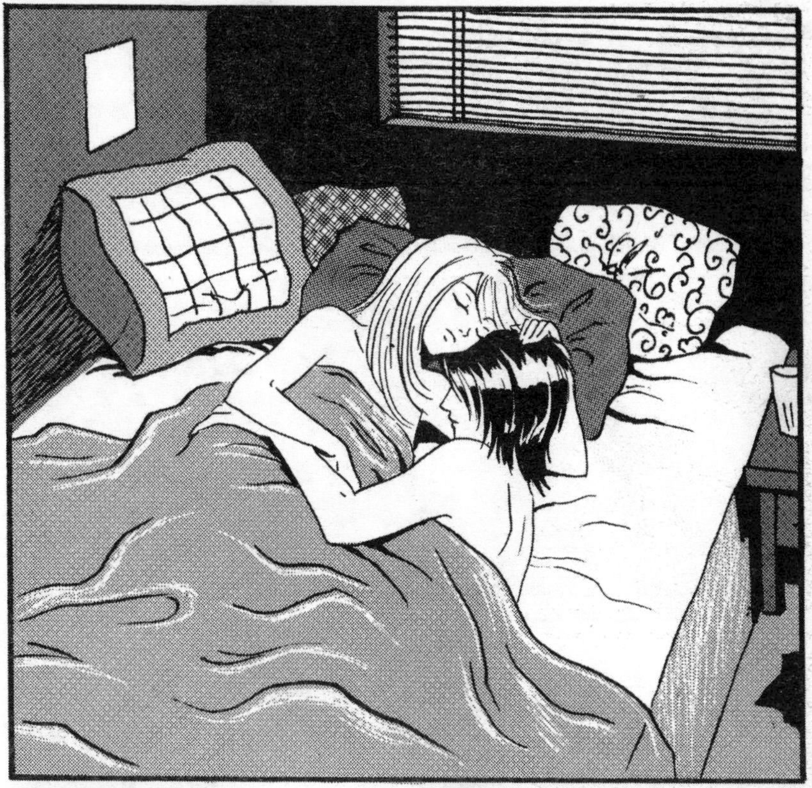

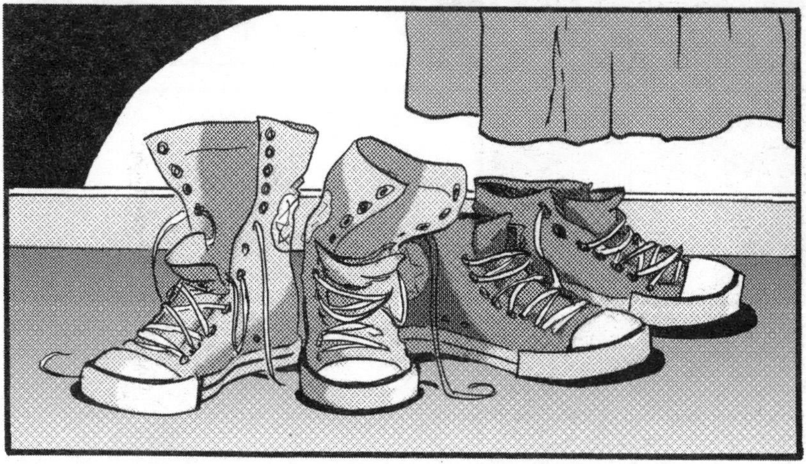

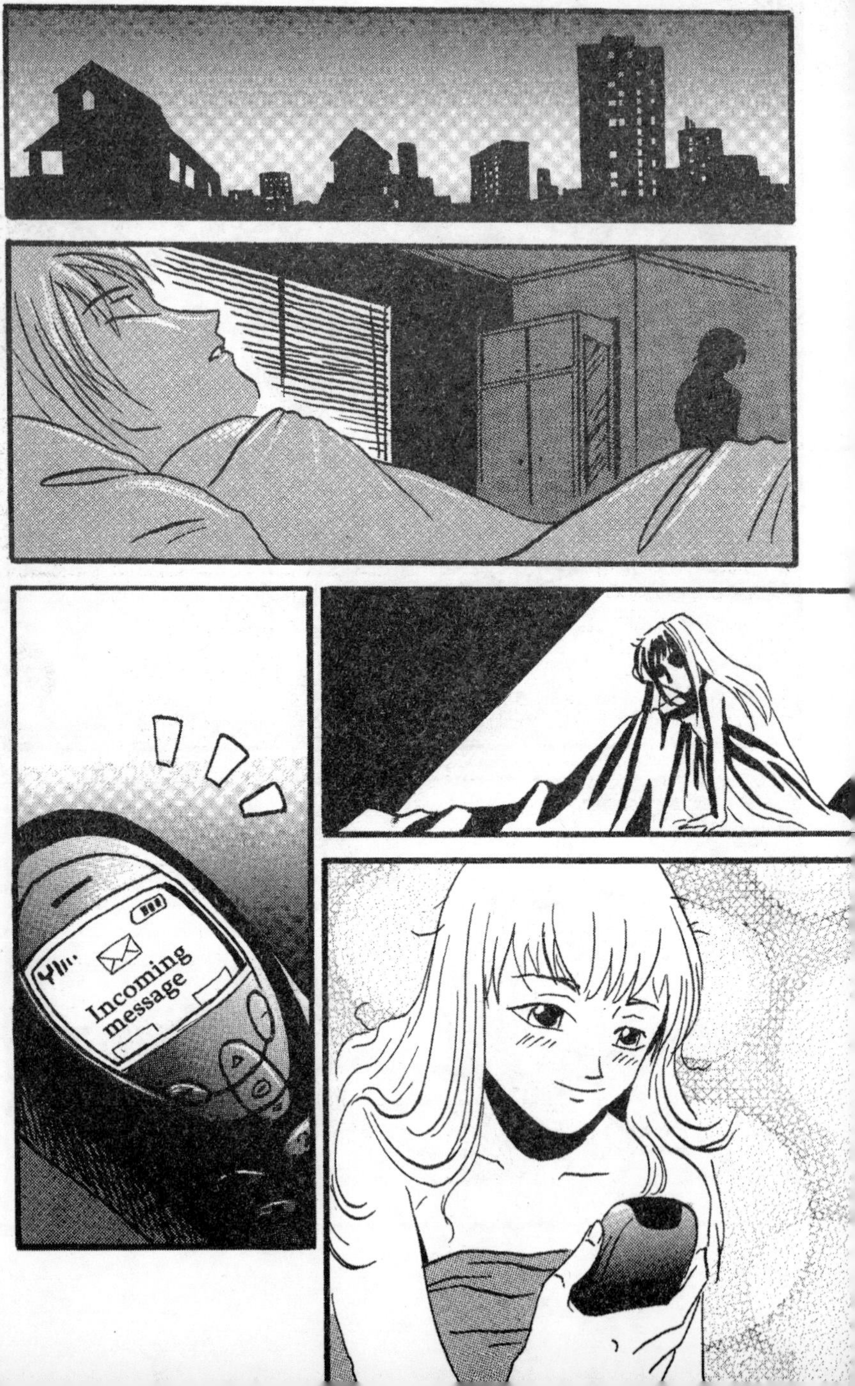
Incoming message

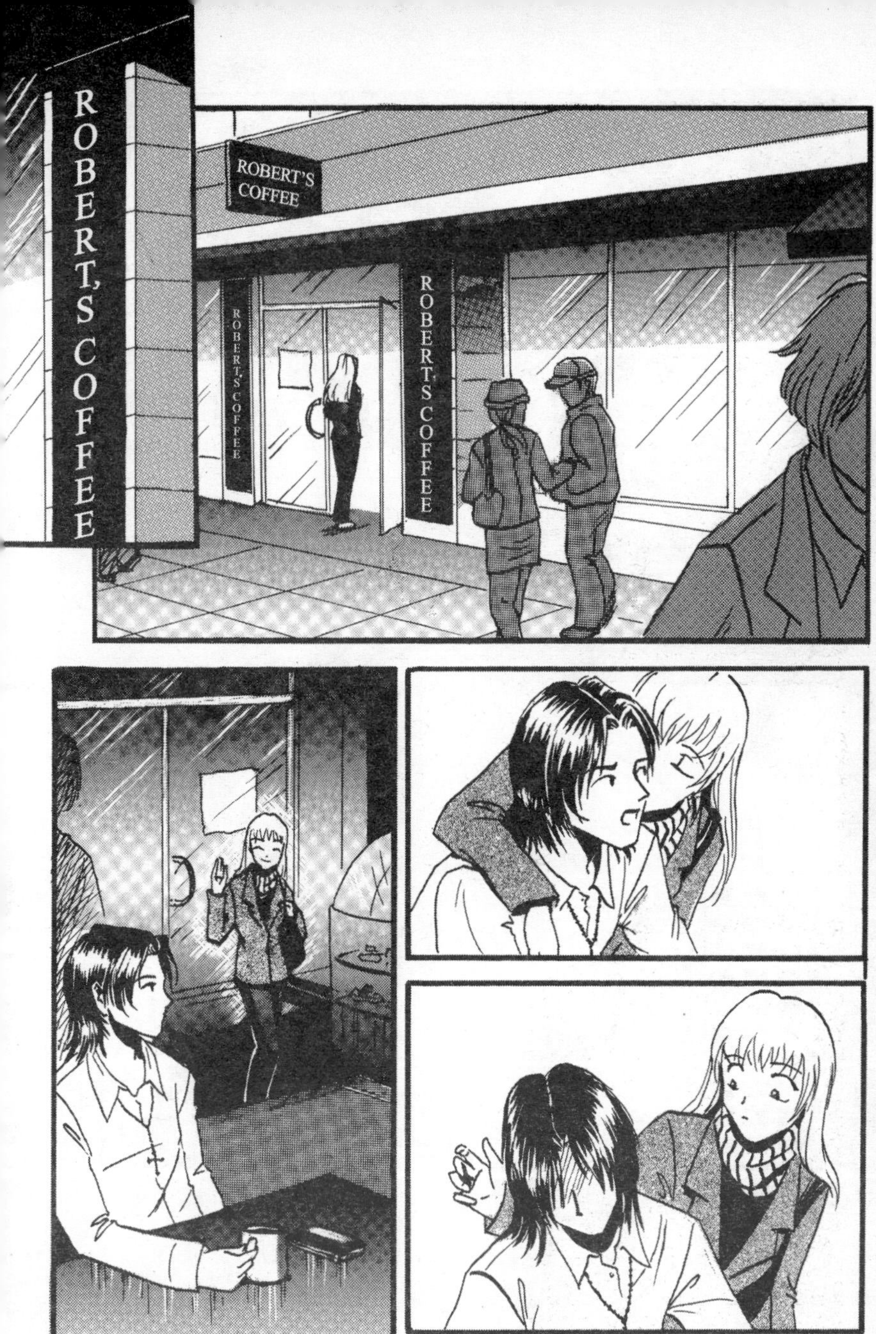
ROBERT'S COFFEE
ROBERT'S COFFEE
ROBERT'S COFFEE
ROBERT'S COFFEE

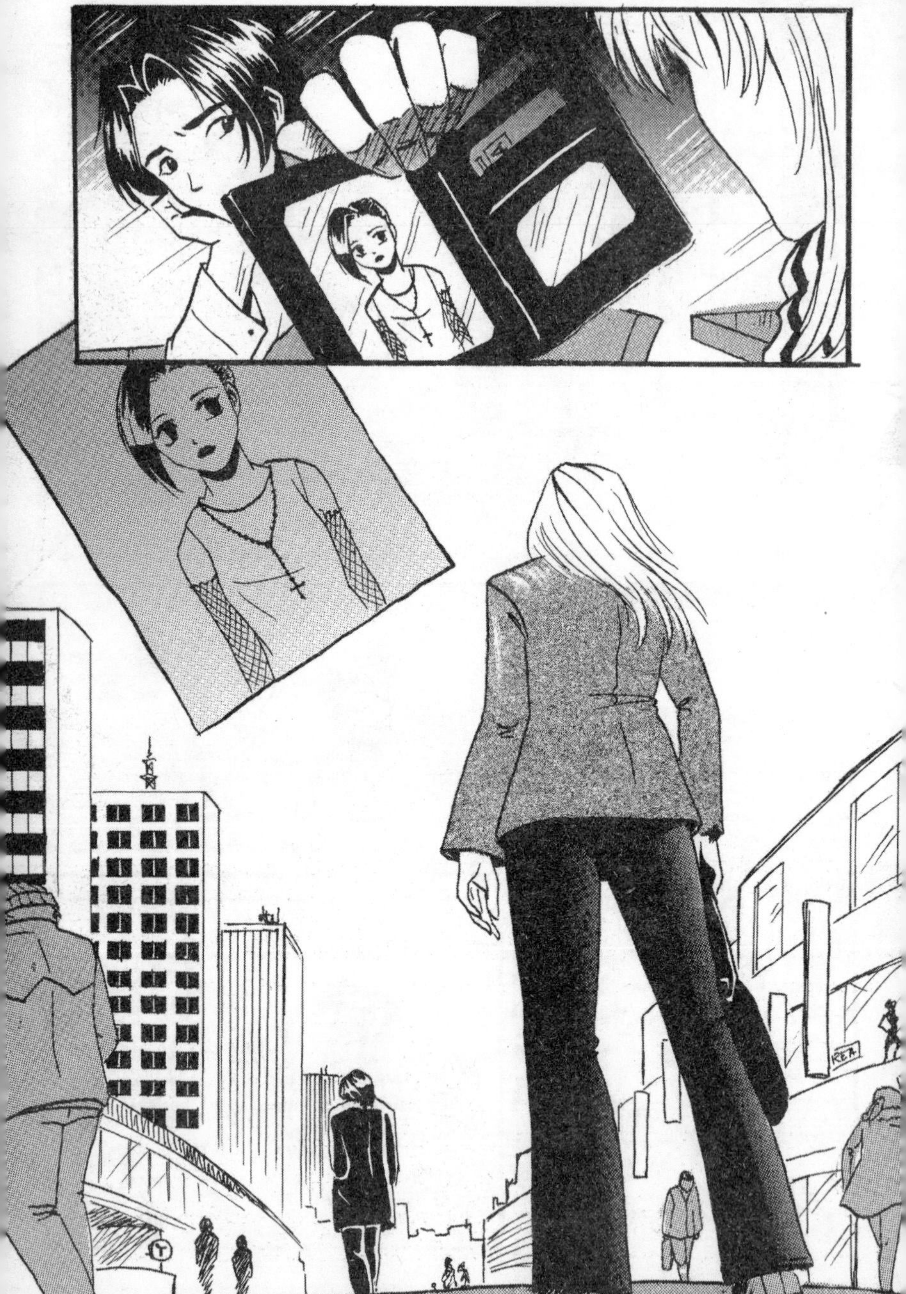

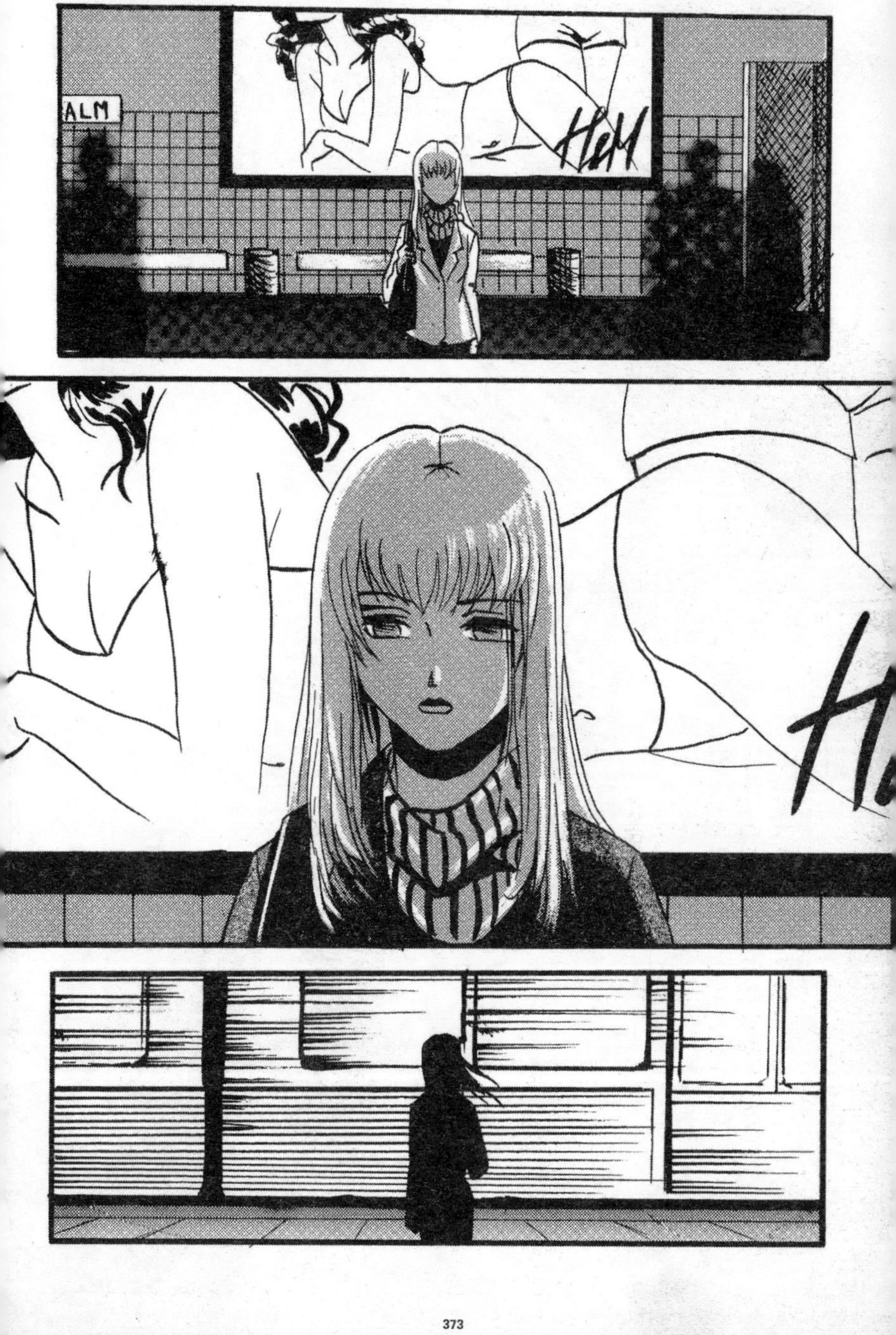
ALM

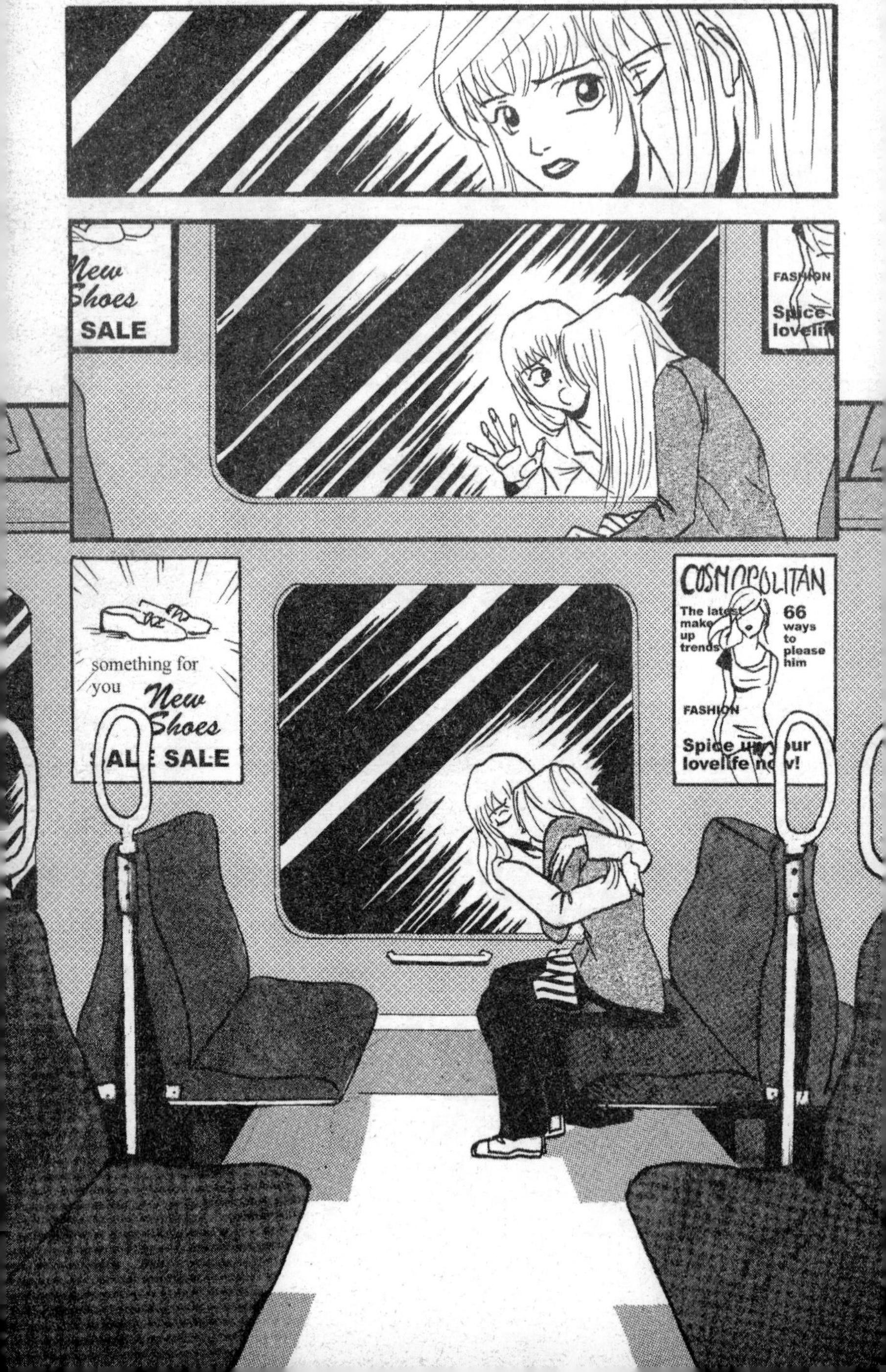
New Shoes
SALE
FASHION
something for you
New Shoes
SALE SALE
COSMOPOLITAN
The latest make up trends
66 ways to please him
FASHION

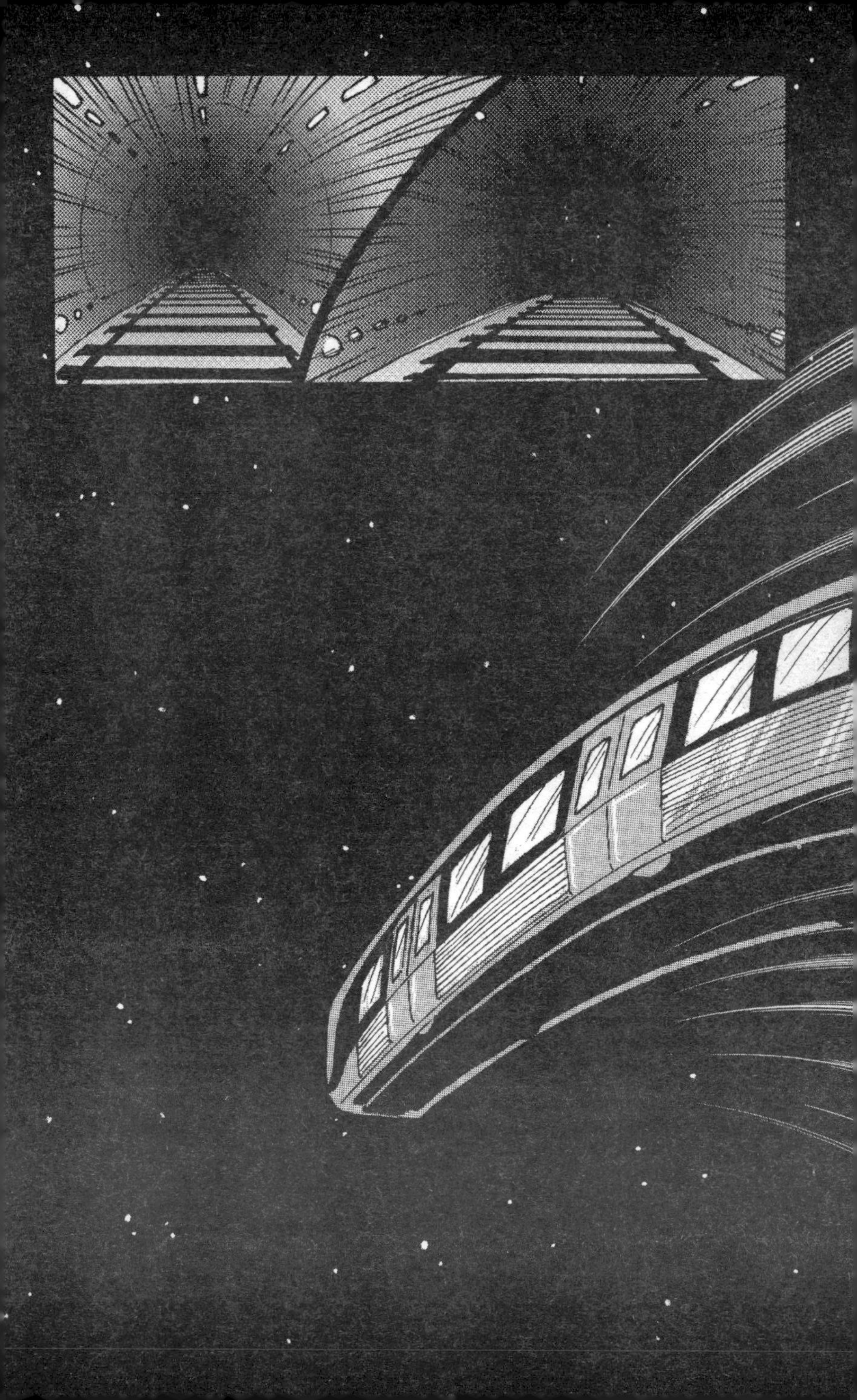

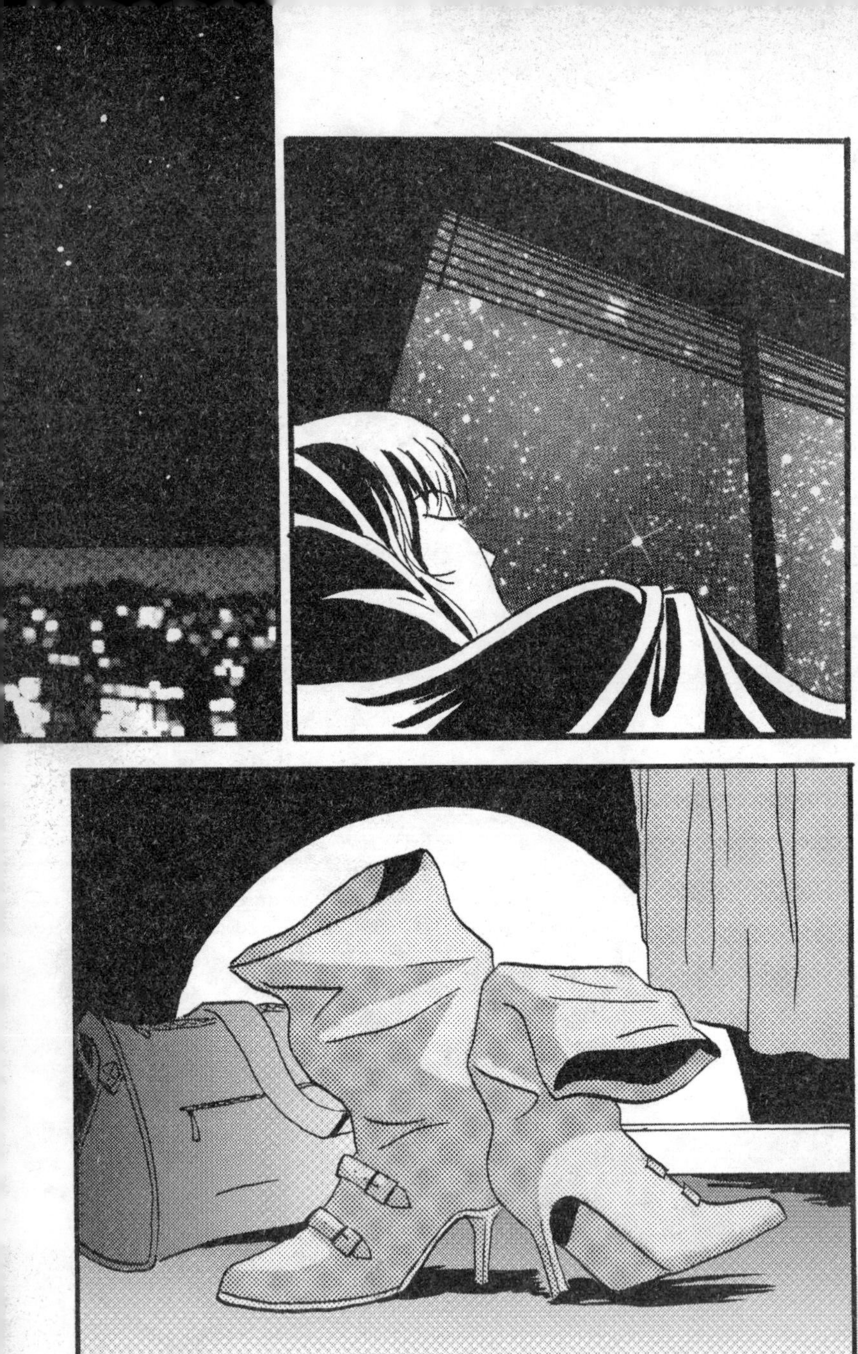

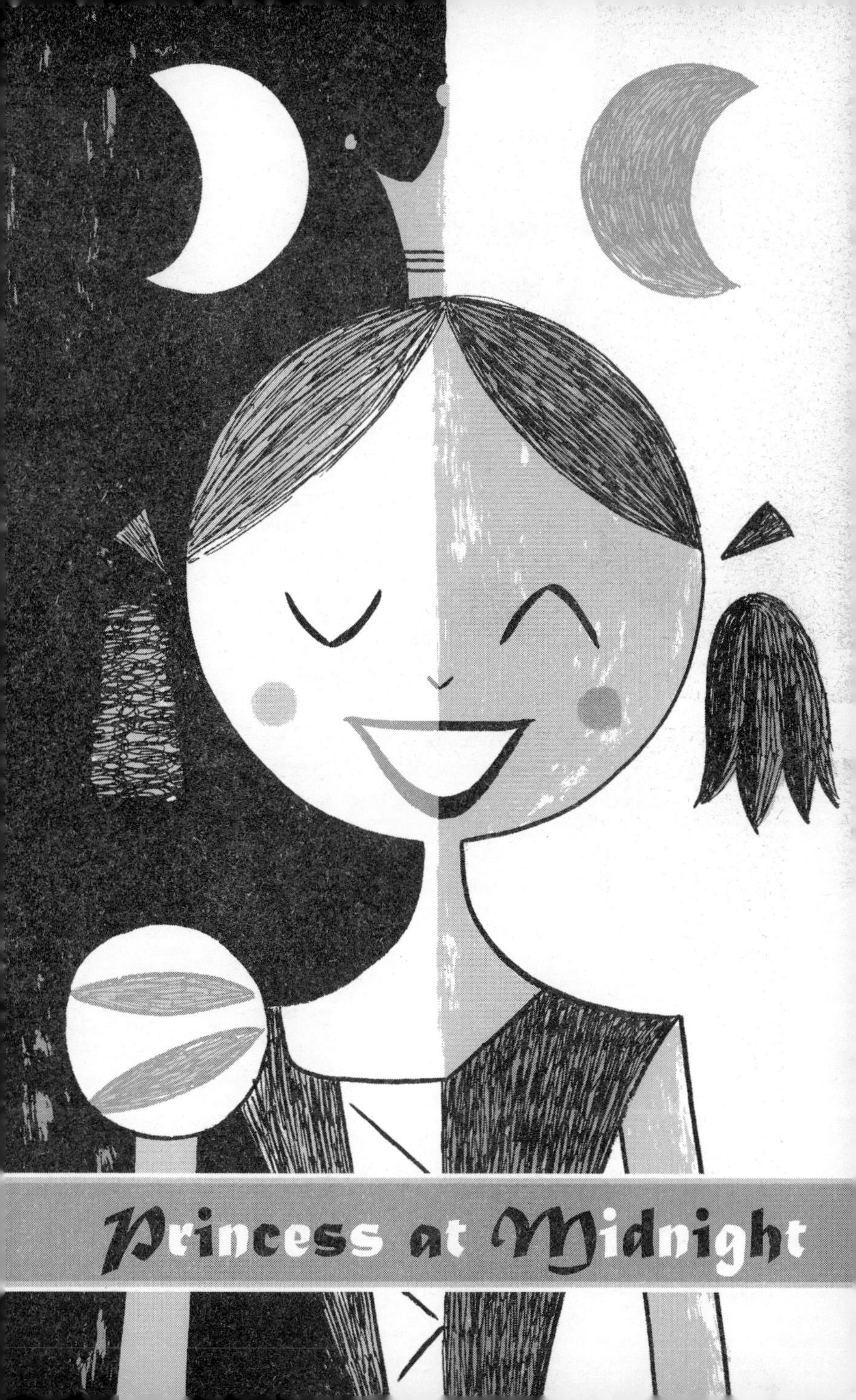
Princess at Midnight

ANDI WATSON

Date of birth: 28 October 1969

A veteran within the independent comics industry, even though still comparatively young, Andi was one of the UK's first comics creators to make a virtue out of an obvious manga influence. His earliest strips, the 'super-deformed' or *chibi*-styled **Samurai Jam**, led on to copious experimentation in style within the pages of his long-running series **Skeleton Key**. Even there, the Japanese influence shone through, not least in the person of Kitsune (a fox spirit based on traditional myth), the cuddly-toy tearaway Mr Raccoon, and a plague of Chinese hopping vampires.

These days, he draws as much inspiration from Europe as Japan in his fluid and expressive linework, to produce a truly original hybrid style.

Andi has very kindly agreed to share with us the opening chapter of his brand new magnum opus, **Princess At Midnight**, an all ages fantasy romp which makes its debut here. Expect to be seeing a lot more, soon – and quite possibly, in full colour.

http://www.andiwatson.biz

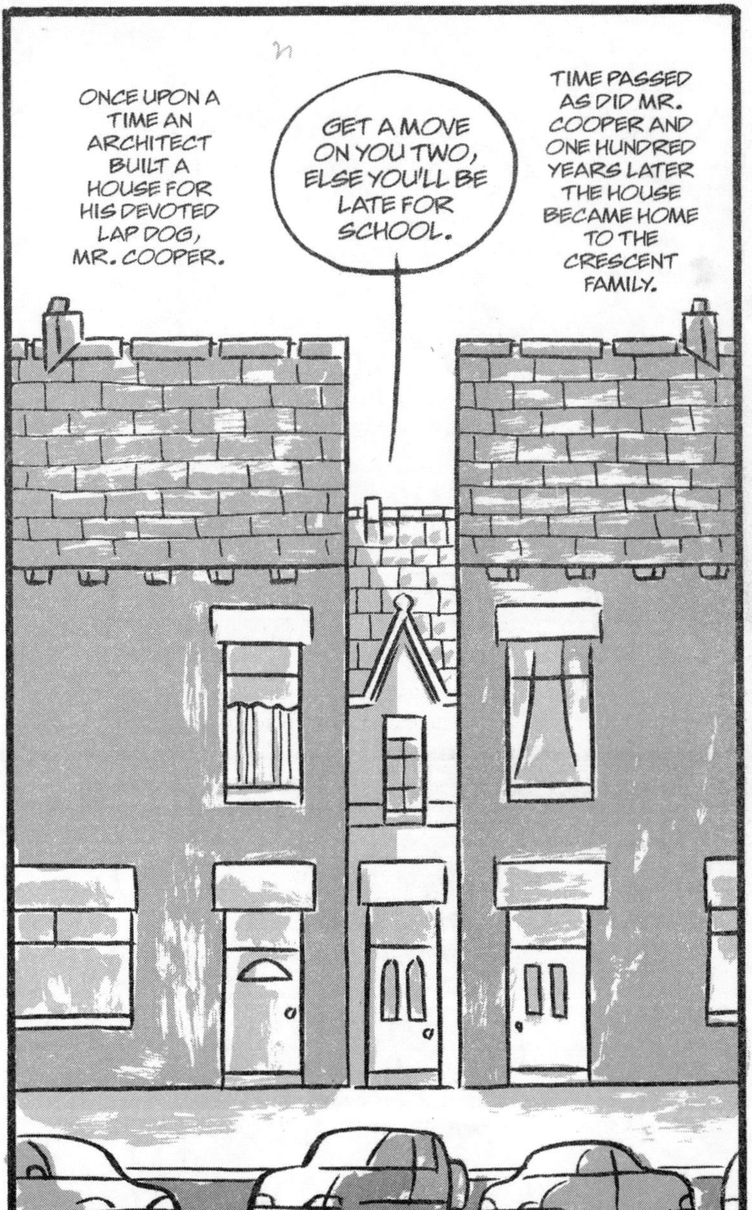
ONCE UPON A TIME AN ARCHITECT BUILT A HOUSE FOR HIS DEVOTED LAP DOG, MR. COOPER.
GET A MOVE ON YOU TWO, ELSE YOU'LL BE LATE FOR SCHOOL.
TIME PASSED AS DID MR. COOPER AND ONE HUNDRED YEARS LATER THE HOUSE BECAME HOME TO THE CRESCENT FAMILY.

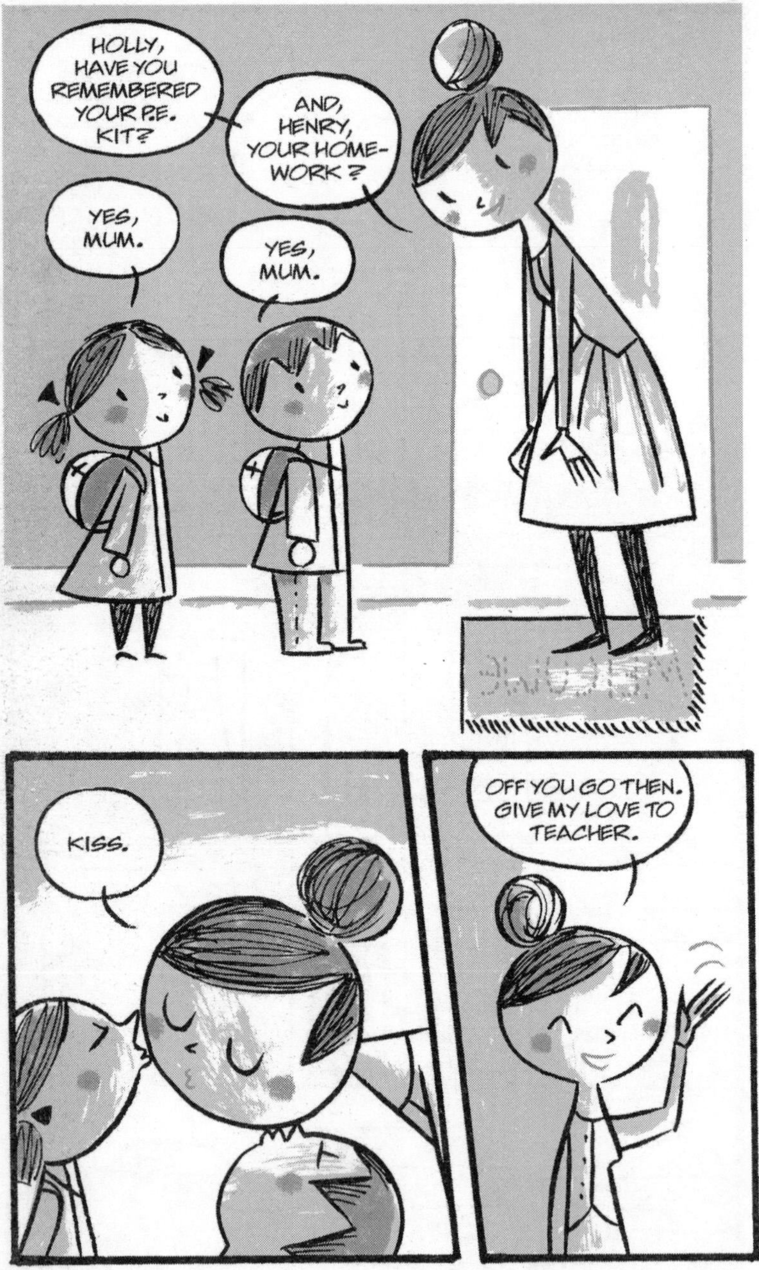
HOLLY, HAVE YOU REMEMBERED YOUR P.E. KIT?
AND, HENRY, YOUR HOME-WORK?
YES, MUM.
YES, MUM.
KISS.
OFF YOU GO THEN. GIVE MY LOVE TO TEACHER.

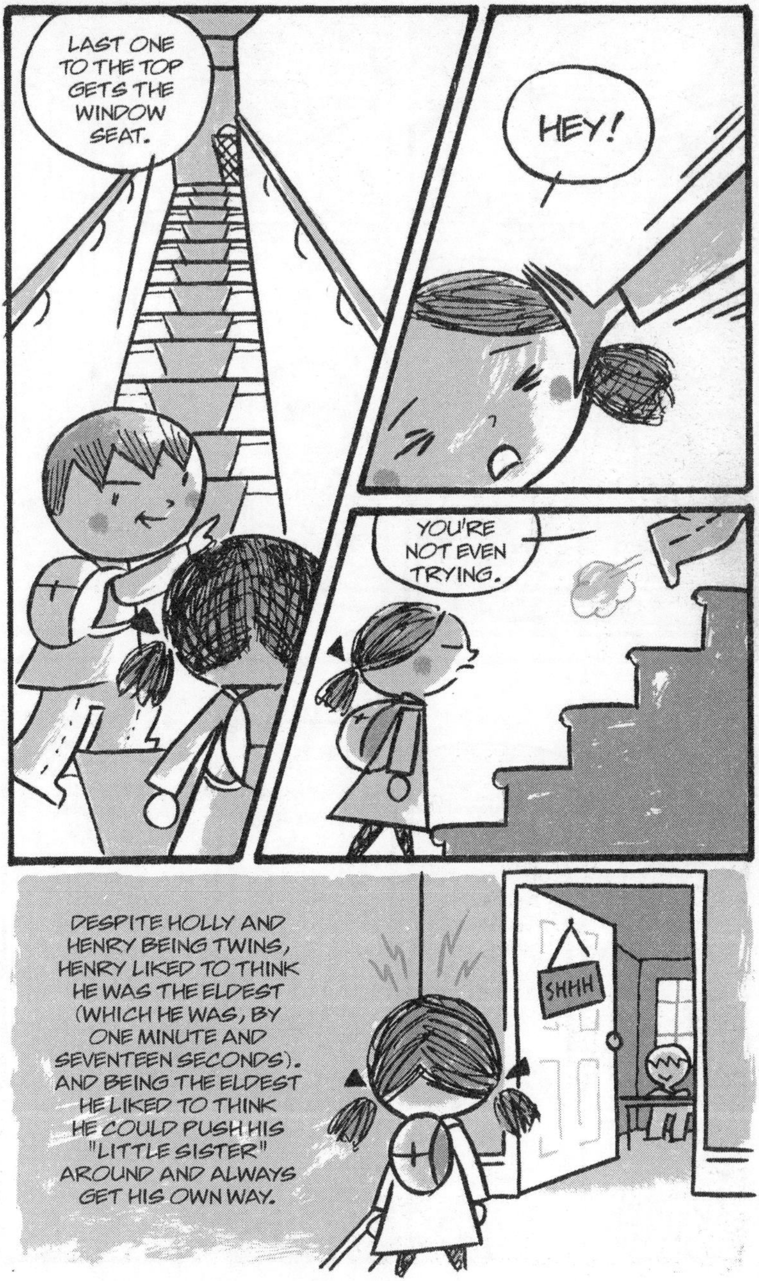
LAST ONE TO THE TOP GETS THE WINDOW SEAT.
HEY!
YOU'RE NOT EVEN TRYING.
DESPITE HOLLY AND HENRY BEING TWINS, HENRY LIKED TO THINK HE WAS THE ELDEST (WHICH HE WAS, BY ONE MINUTE AND SEVENTEEN SECONDS). AND BEING THE ELDEST HE LIKED TO THINK HE COULD PUSH HIS "LITTLE SISTER" AROUND AND ALWAYS GET HIS OWN WAY.
SHHH

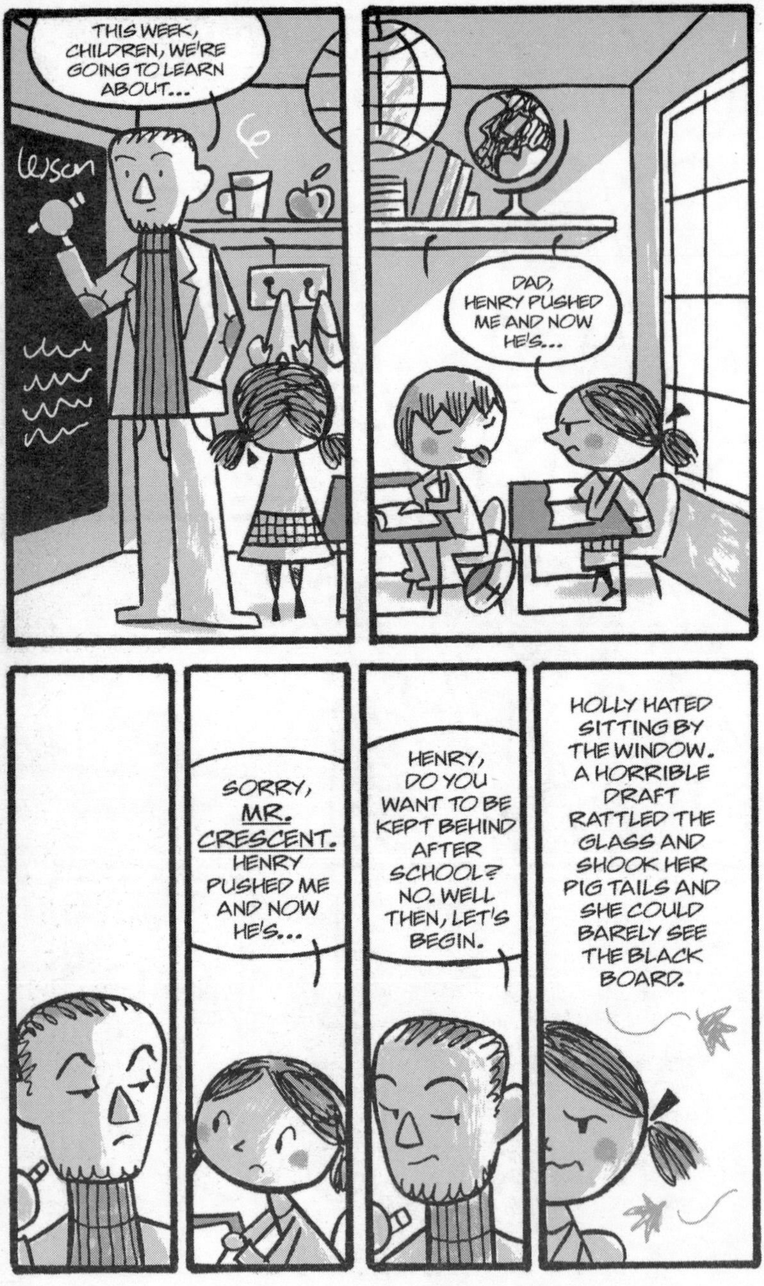
THIS WEEK, CHILDREN, WE'RE GOING TO LEARN ABOUT...
DAD, HENRY PUSHED ME AND NOW HE'S...
SORRY, MR. CRESCENT. HENRY PUSHED ME AND NOW HE'S...
HENRY, DO YOU WANT TO BE KEPT BEHIND AFTER SCHOOL? NO. WELL THEN, LET'S BEGIN.
HOLLY HATED SITTING BY THE WINDOW. A HORRIBLE DRAFT RATTLED THE GLASS AND SHOOK HER PIG TAILS AND SHE COULD BARELY SEE THE BLACK BOARD.

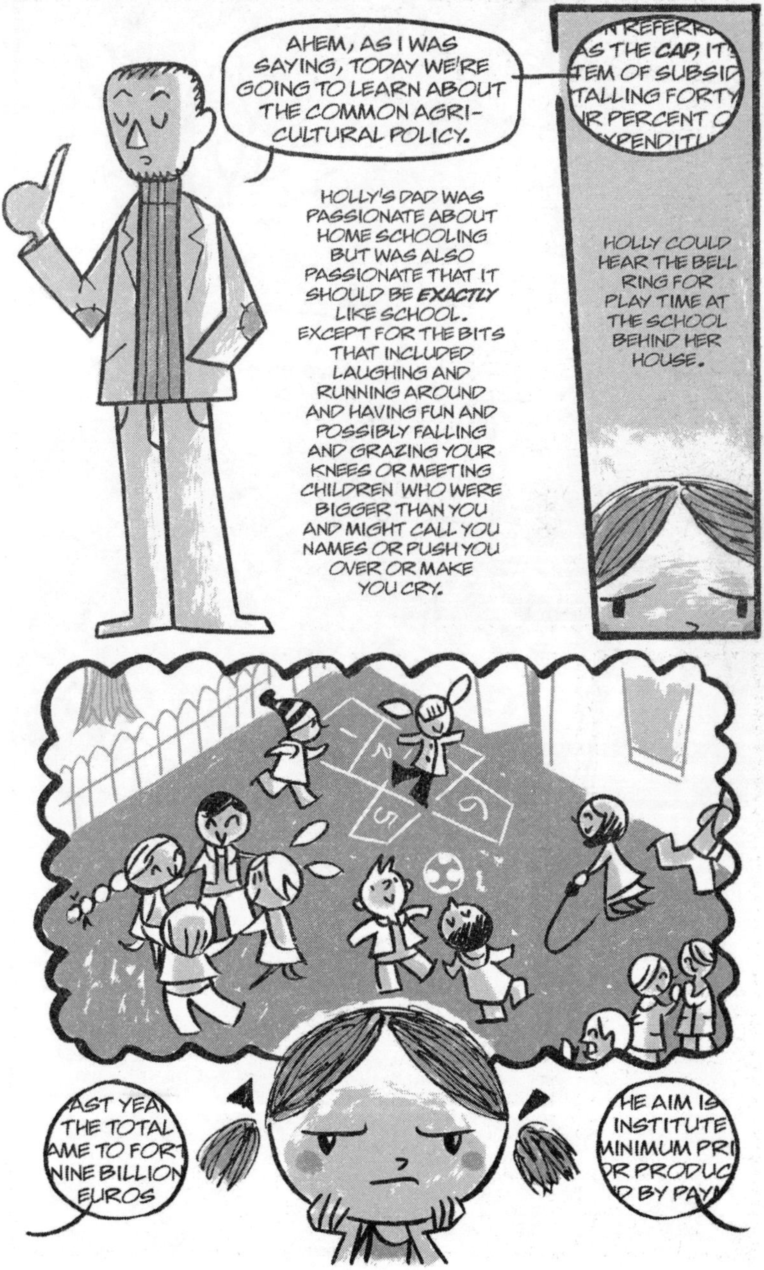
AHEM, AS I WAS SAYING, TODAY WE'RE GOING TO LEARN ABOUT THE COMMON AGRI-CULTURAL POLICY.
HOLLY'S DAD WAS PASSIONATE ABOUT HOME SCHOOLING BUT WAS ALSO PASSIONATE THAT IT SHOULD BE EXACTLY LIKE SCHOOL. EXCEPT FOR THE BITS THAT INCLUDED LAUGHING AND RUNNING AROUND AND HAVING FUN AND POSSIBLY FALLING AND GRAZING YOUR KNEES OR MEETING CHILDREN WHO WERE BIGGER THAN YOU AND MIGHT CALL YOU NAMES OR PUSH YOU OVER OR MAKE YOU CRY.
N REFERR AS THE CAP, IT'S TEM OF SUBSID TALLING FORTY R PERCENT O XPENDITU
HOLLY COULD HEAR THE BELL RING FOR PLAY TIME AT THE SCHOOL BEHIND HER HOUSE.
AST YEA THE TOTAL AME TO FORT NINE BILLION EUROS
HE AIM IS INSTITUTE MINIMUM PRI R PRODUC D BY PAY

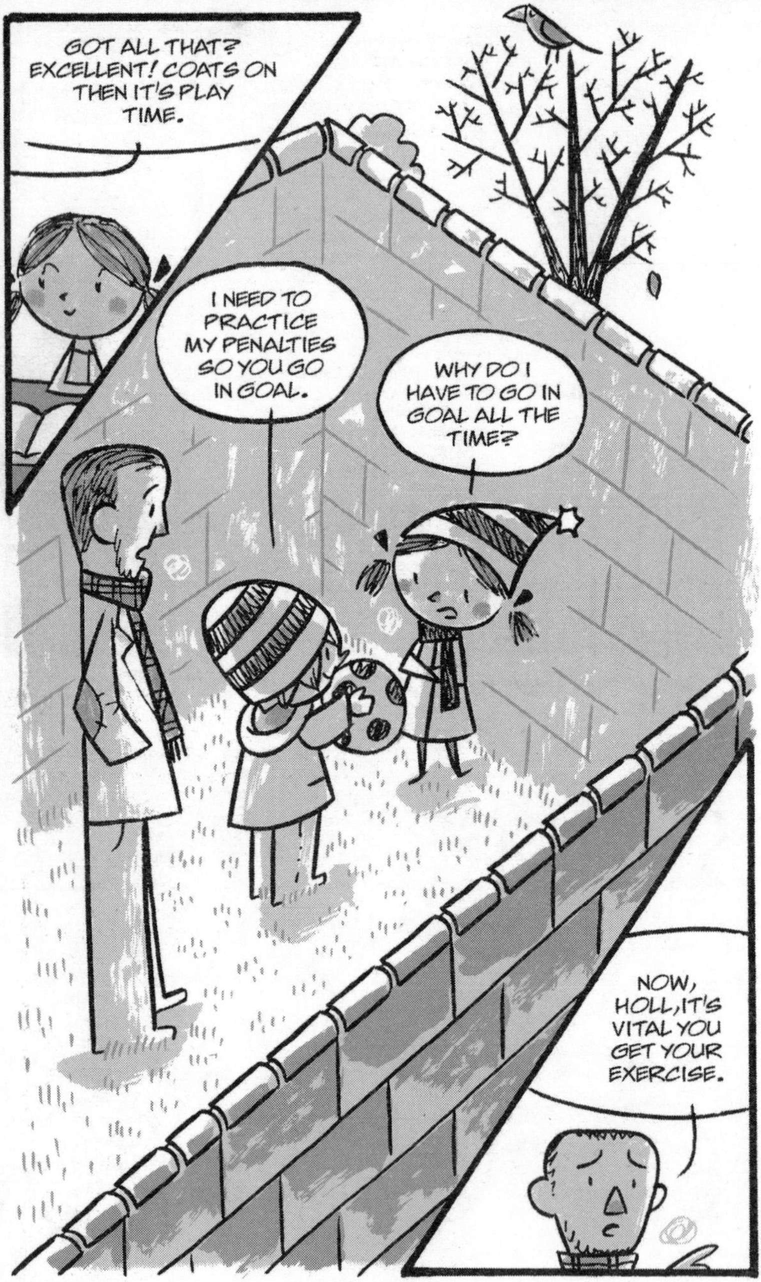
GOT ALL THAT? EXCELLENT! COATS ON THEN IT'S PLAY TIME.
I NEED TO PRACTICE MY PENALTIES SO YOU GO IN GOAL.
WHY DO I HAVE TO GO IN GOAL ALL THE TIME?
NOW, HOLL, IT'S VITAL YOU GET YOUR EXERCISE.

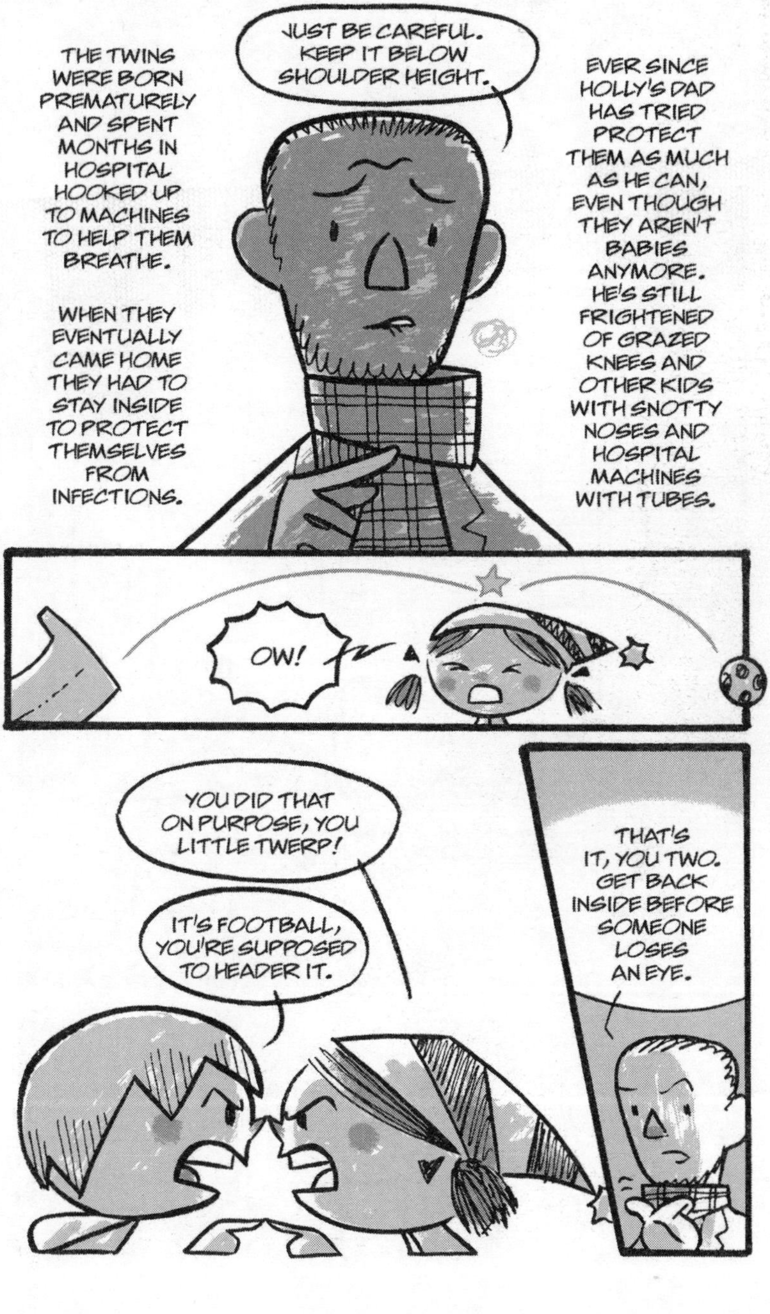
THE TWINS WERE BORN PREMATURELY AND SPENT MONTHS IN HOSPITAL HOOKED UP TO MACHINES TO HELP THEM BREATHE.
WHEN THEY EVENTUALLY CAME HOME THEY HAD TO STAY INSIDE TO PROTECT THEMSELVES FROM INFECTIONS.
JUST BE CAREFUL. KEEP IT BELOW SHOULDER HEIGHT.
EVER SINCE HOLLY'S DAD HAS TRIED PROTECT THEM AS MUCH AS HE CAN, EVEN THOUGH THEY AREN'T BABIES ANYMORE. HE'S STILL FRIGHTENED OF GRAZED KNEES AND OTHER KIDS WITH SNOTTY NOSES AND HOSPITAL MACHINES WITH TUBES.
OW!
YOU DID THAT ON PURPOSE, YOU LITTLE TWERP!
IT'S FOOTBALL, YOU'RE SUPPOSED TO HEADER IT.
THAT'S IT, YOU TWO. GET BACK INSIDE BEFORE SOMEONE LOSES AN EYE.

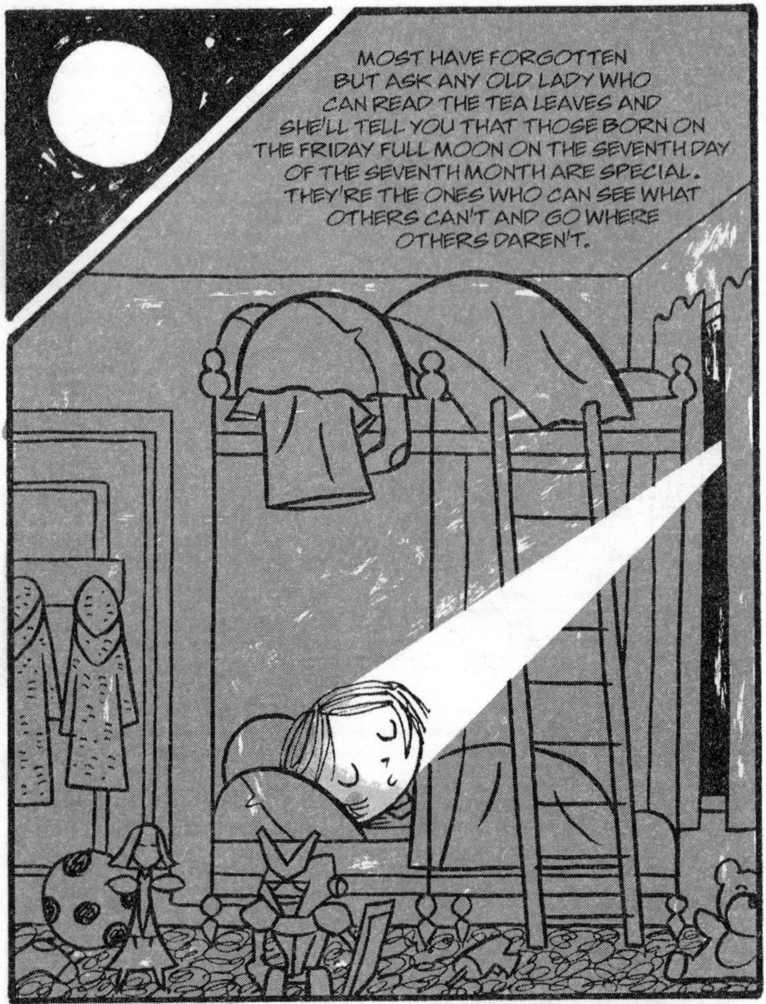
MOST HAVE FORGOTTEN BUT ASK ANY OLD LADY WHO CAN READ THE TEA LEAVES AND SHE'LL TELL YOU THAT THOSE BORN ON THE FRIDAY FULL MOON ON THE SEVENTH DAY OF THE SEVENTH MONTH ARE SPECIAL. THEY'RE THE ONES WHO CAN SEE WHAT OTHERS CAN'T AND GO WHERE OTHERS DAREN'T.

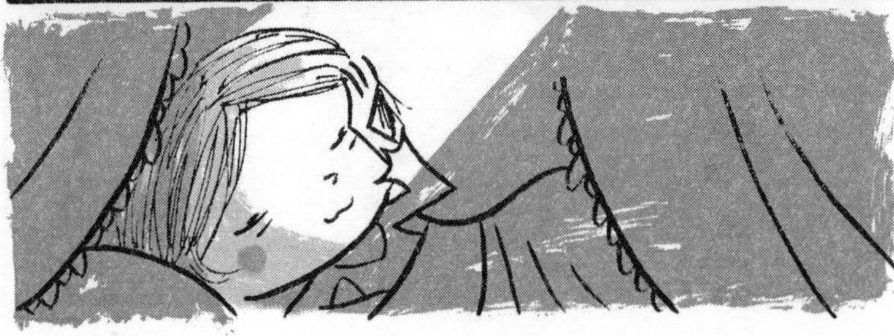

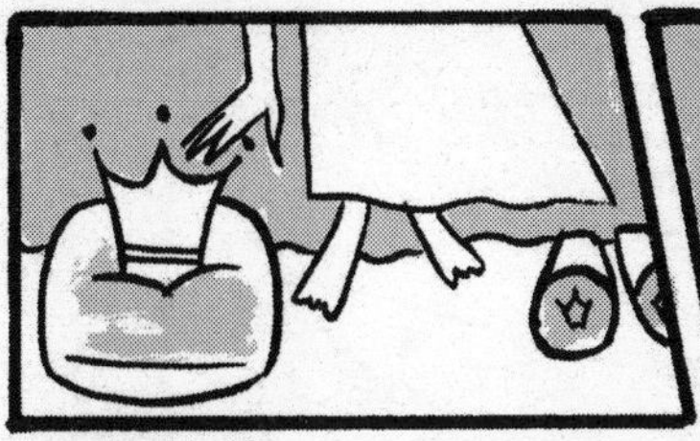

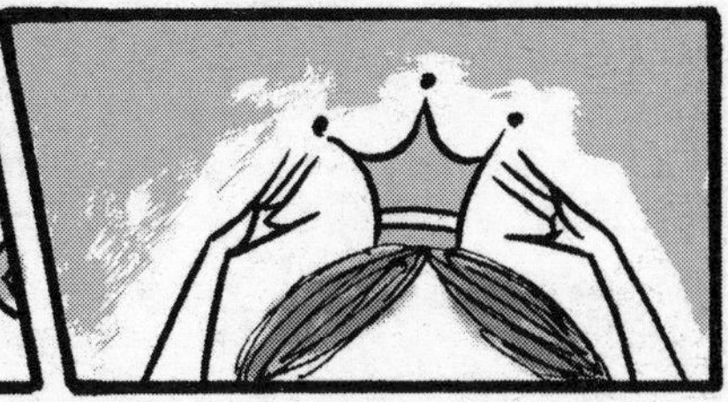

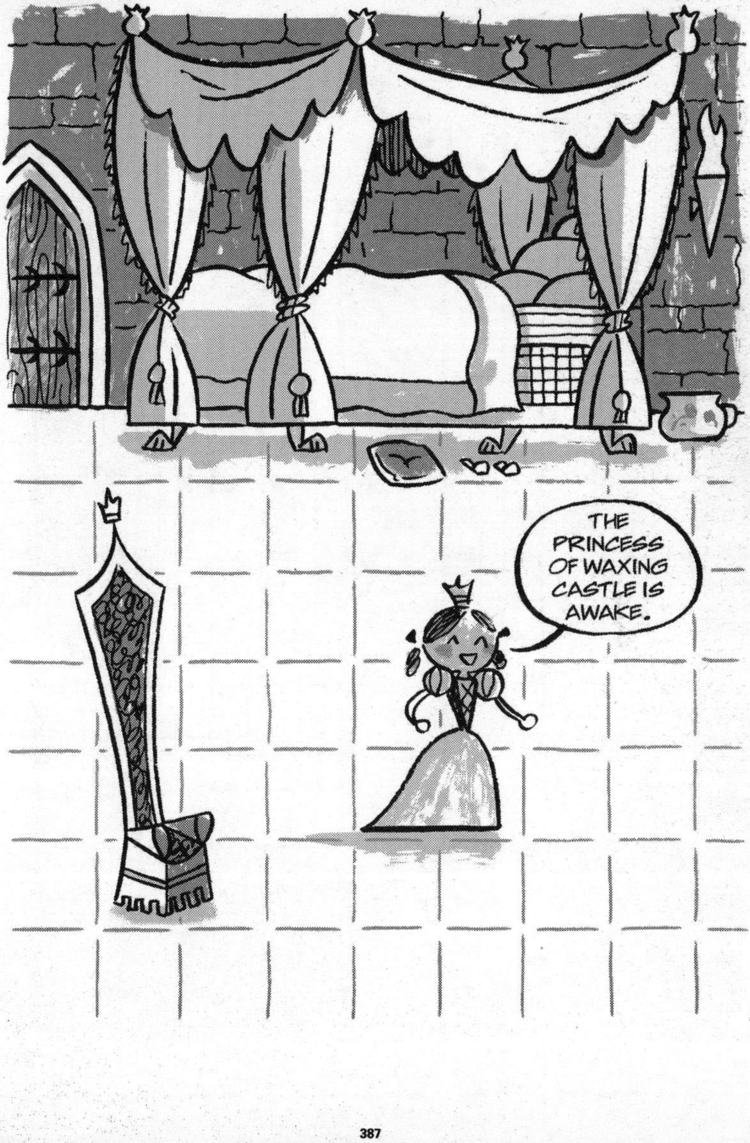
THE PRINCESS OF WAXING CASTLE IS AWAKE.

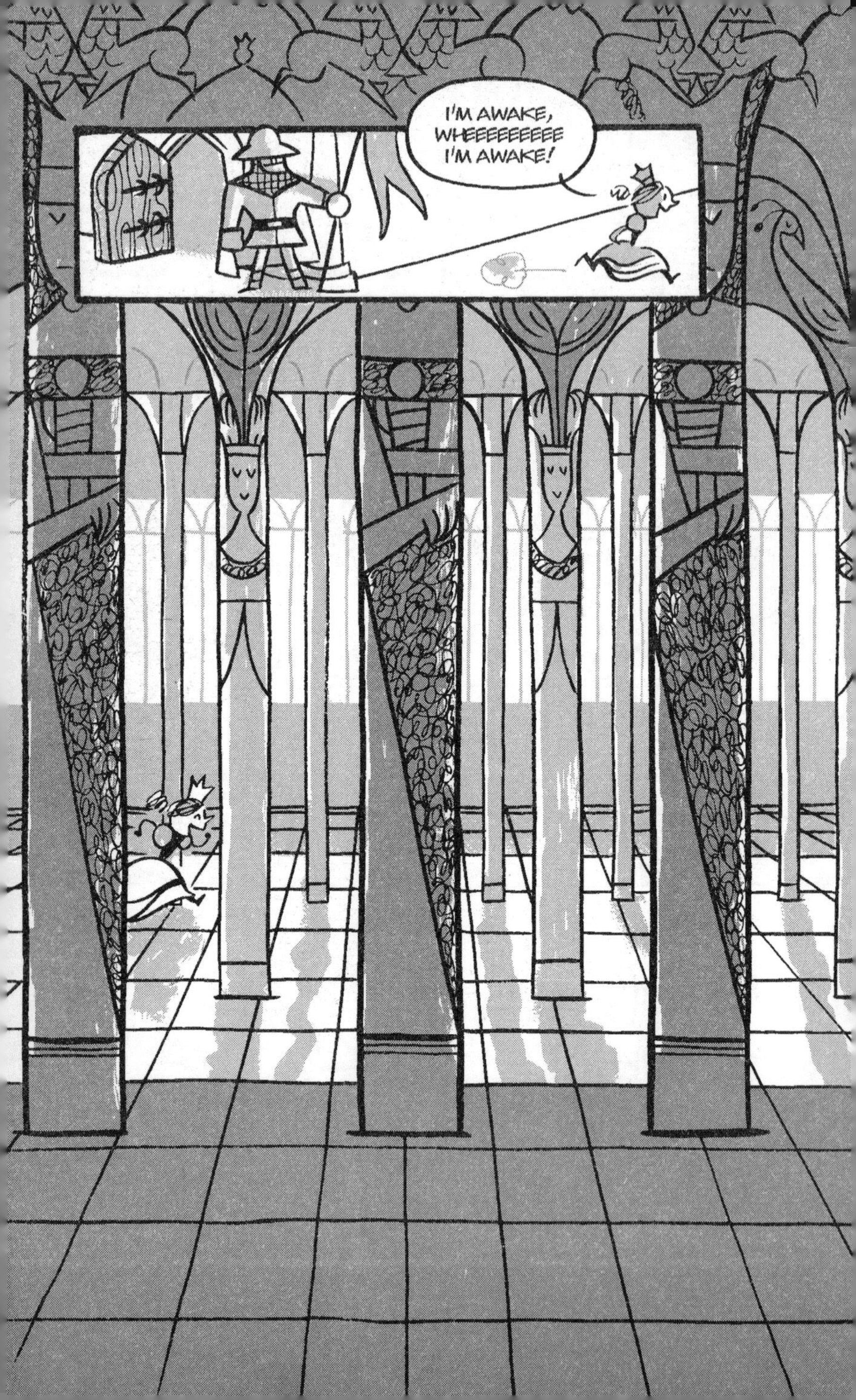
I'M AWAKE, WHEEEEEEEEE I'M AWAKE!

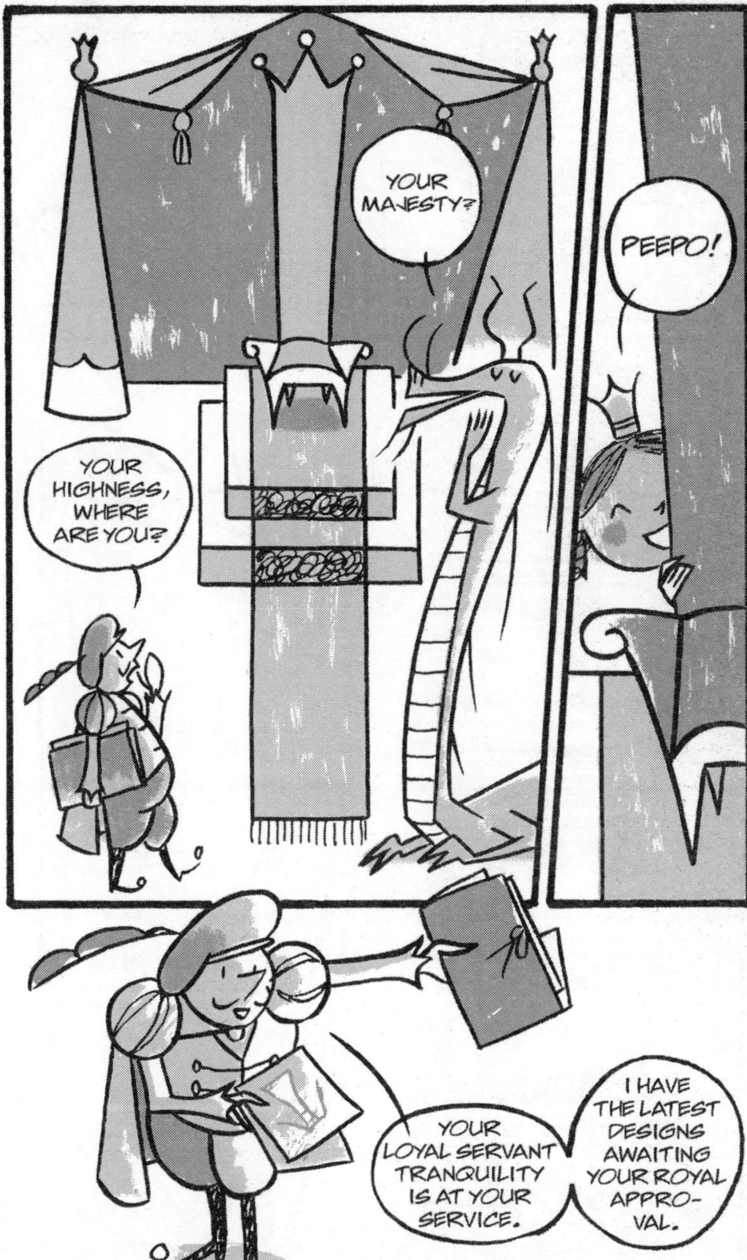
YOUR MAJESTY?
YOUR HIGHNESS, WHERE ARE YOU?
PEEPO!
YOUR LOYAL SERVANT TRANQUILITY IS AT YOUR SERVICE.
I HAVE THE LATEST DESIGNS AWAITING YOUR ROYAL APPRO- VAL.

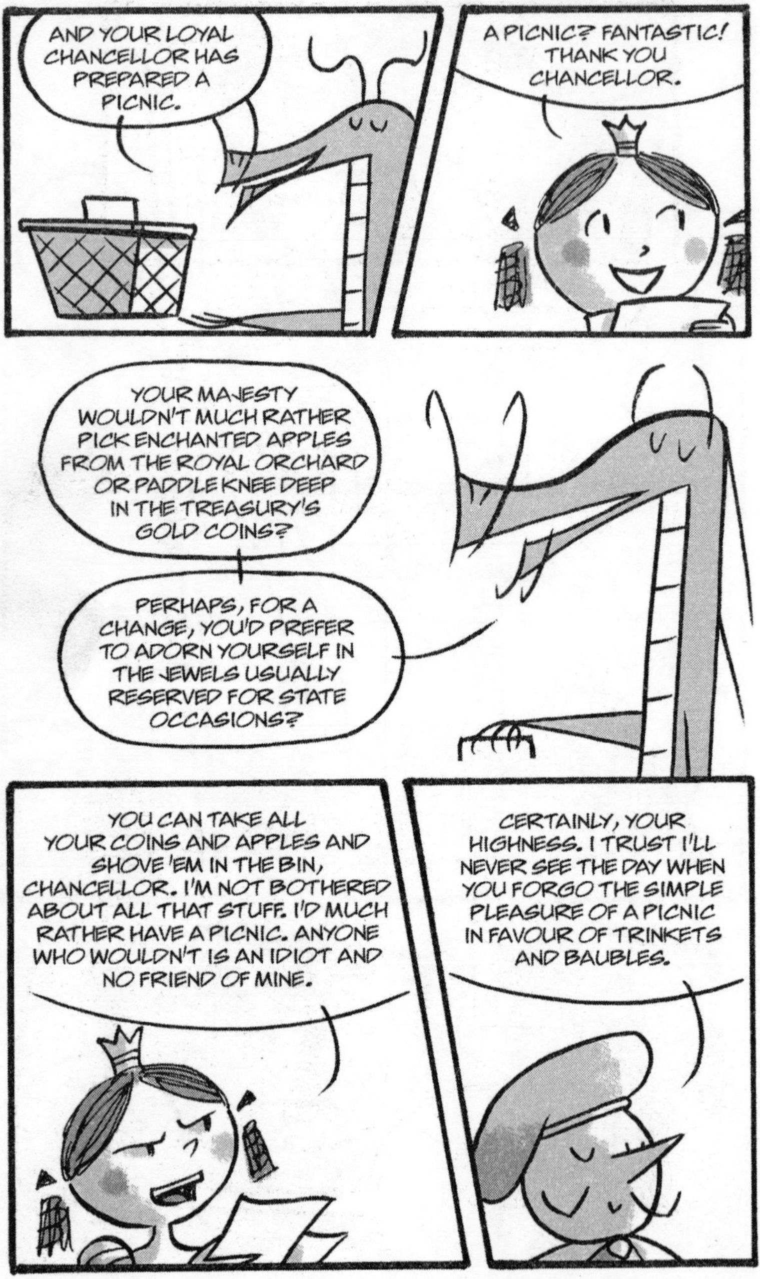
AND YOUR LOYAL CHANCELLOR HAS PREPARED A PICNIC.
A PICNIC? FANTASTIC! THANK YOU CHANCELLOR.
YOUR MAJESTY WOULDN'T MUCH RATHER PICK ENCHANTED APPLES FROM THE ROYAL ORCHARD OR PADDLE KNEE DEEP IN THE TREASURY'S GOLD COINS?
PERHAPS, FOR A CHANGE, YOU'D PREFER TO ADORN YOURSELF IN THE JEWELS USUALLY RESERVED FOR STATE OCCASIONS?
YOU CAN TAKE ALL YOUR COINS AND APPLES AND SHOVE 'EM IN THE BIN, CHANCELLOR. I'M NOT BOTHERED ABOUT ALL THAT STUFF. I'D MUCH RATHER HAVE A PICNIC. ANYONE WHO WOULDN'T IS AN IDIOT AND NO FRIEND OF MINE.
CERTAINLY, YOUR HIGHNESS. I TRUST I'LL NEVER SEE THE DAY WHEN YOU FORGO THE SIMPLE PLEASURE OF A PICNIC IN FAVOUR OF TRINKETS AND BAUBLES.

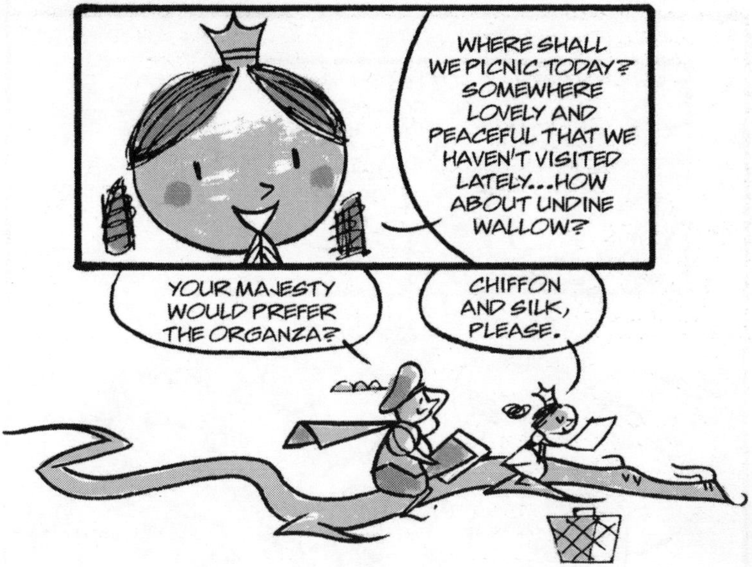
WHERE SHALL WE PICNIC TODAY? SOMEWHERE LOVELY AND PEACEFUL THAT WE HAVEN'T VISITED LATELY...HOW ABOUT UNDINE WALLOW?
YOUR MAJESTY WOULD PREFER THE ORGANZA?
CHIFFON AND SILK, PLEASE.

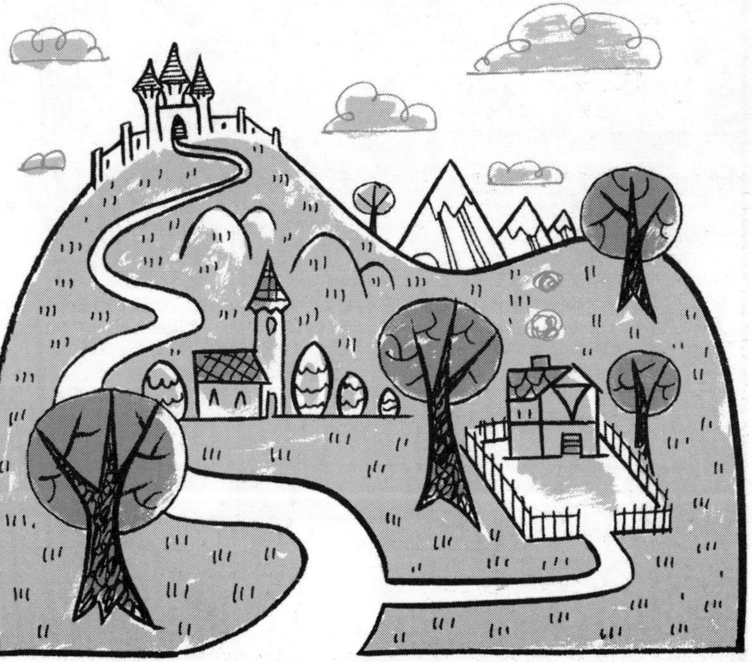

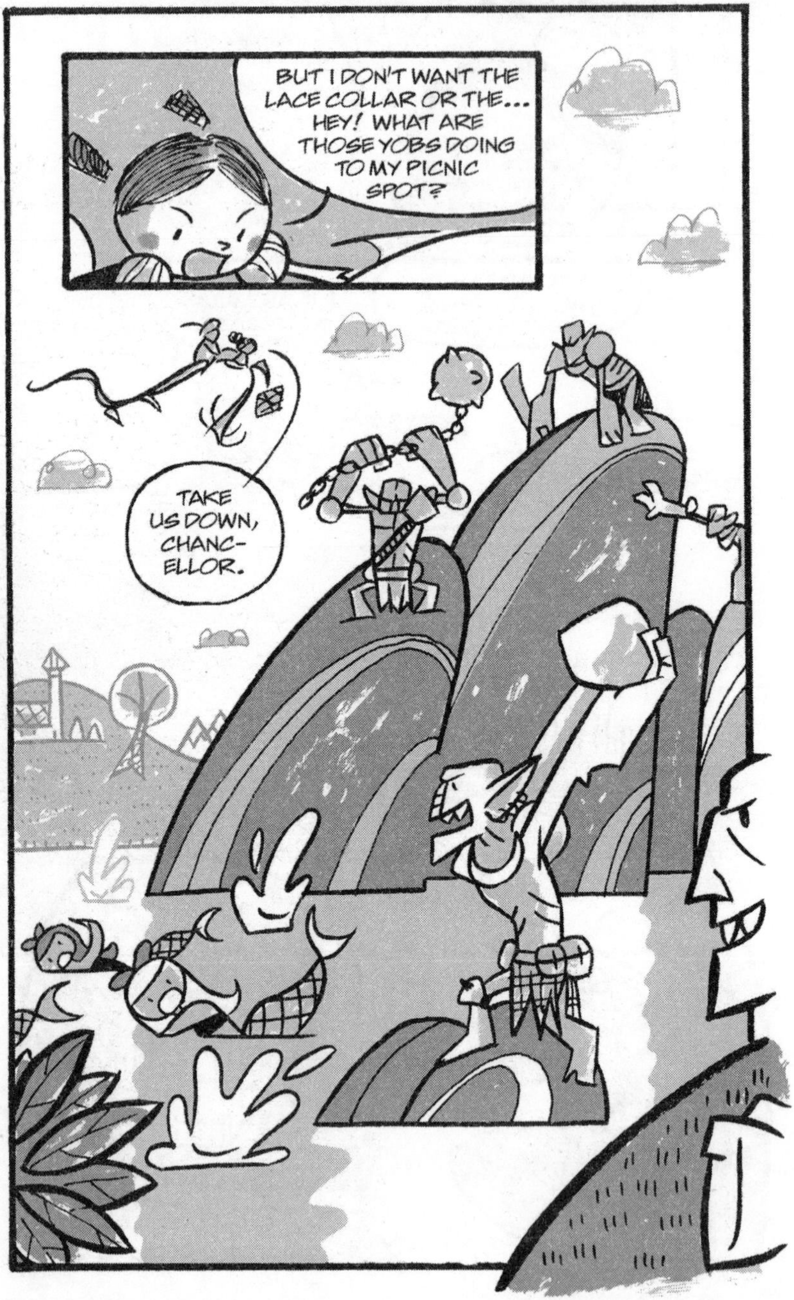
BUT I DON'T WANT THE LACE COLLAR OR THE... HEY! WHAT ARE THOSE YOBS DOING TO MY PICNIC SPOT?
TAKE US DOWN, CHANCELLOR.

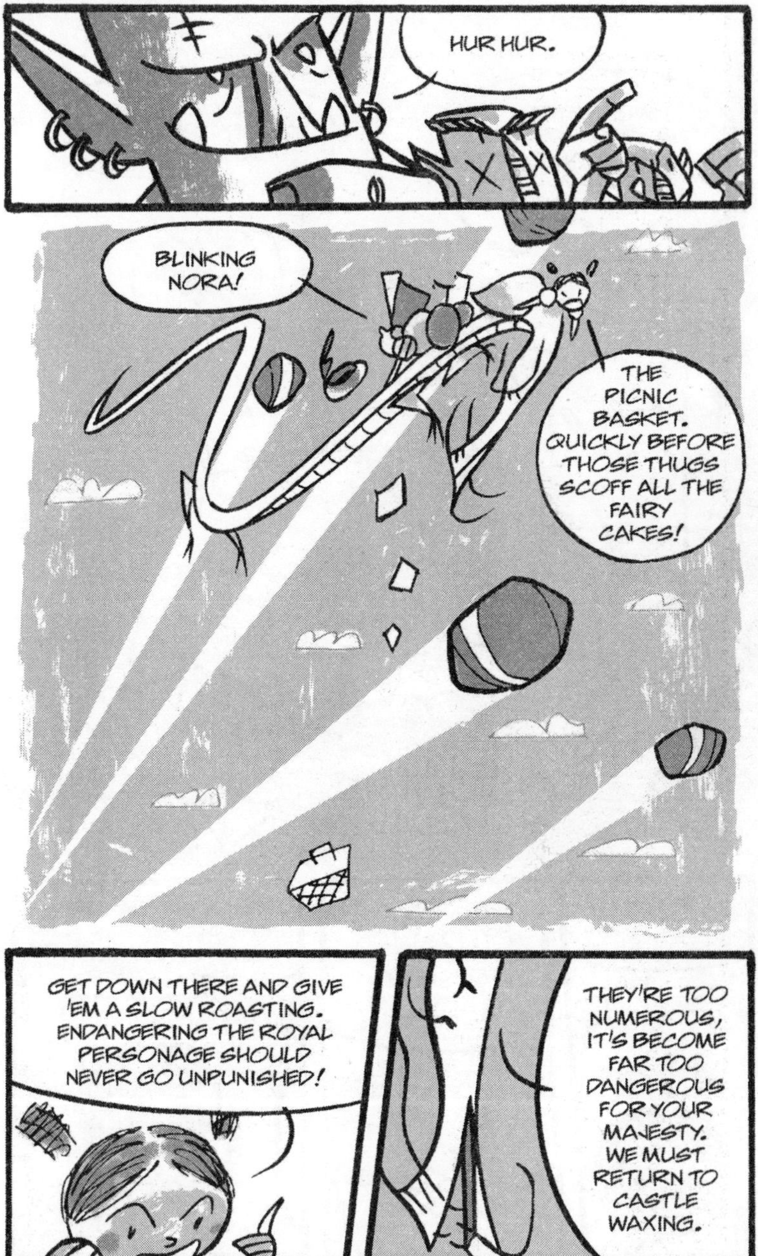
HUR HUR.
BLINKING NORA!
THE PICNIC BASKET. QUICKLY BEFORE THOSE THUGS SCOFF ALL THE FAIRY CAKES!
GET DOWN THERE AND GIVE 'EM A SLOW ROASTING. ENDANGERING THE ROYAL PERSONAGE SHOULD NEVER GO UNPUNISHED!
THEY'RE TOO NUMEROUS, IT'S BECOME FAR TOO DANGEROUS FOR YOUR MAJESTY. WE MUST RETURN TO CASTLE WAXING.

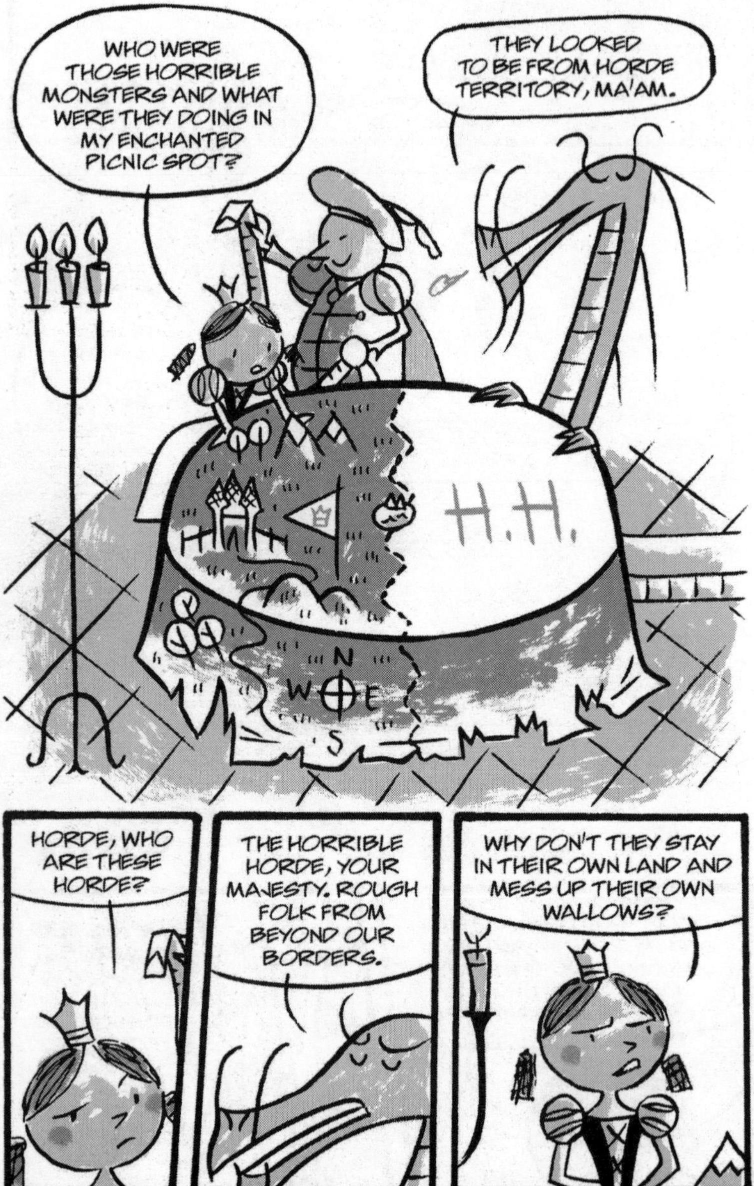
WHO WERE THOSE HORRIBLE MONSTERS AND WHAT WERE THEY DOING IN MY ENCHANTED PICNIC SPOT?
THEY LOOKED TO BE FROM HORDE TERRITORY, MA'AM.
H.H.
N
W
E
S
HORDE, WHO ARE THESE HORDE?
THE HORRIBLE HORDE, YOUR MAJESTY. ROUGH FOLK FROM BEYOND OUR BORDERS.
WHY DON'T THEY STAY IN THEIR OWN LAND AND MESS UP THEIR OWN WALLOWS?

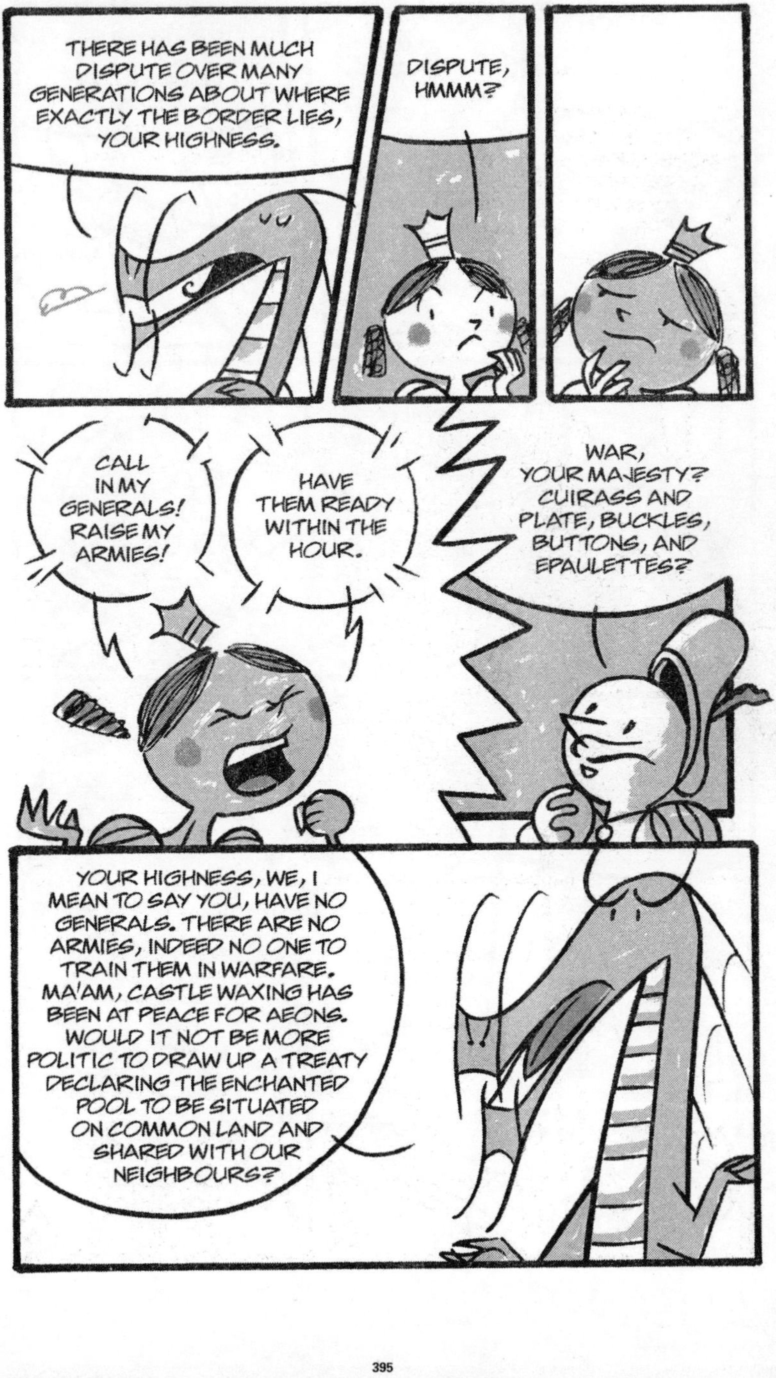
THERE HAS BEEN MUCH DISPUTE OVER MANY GENERATIONS ABOUT WHERE EXACTLY THE BORDER LIES, YOUR HIGHNESS.
DISPUTE, HMMM?
CALL IN MY GENERALS! RAISE MY ARMIES!
HAVE THEM READY WITHIN THE HOUR.
WAR, YOUR MAJESTY? CUIRASS AND PLATE, BUCKLES, BUTTONS, AND EPAULETTES?
YOUR HIGHNESS, WE, I MEAN TO SAY YOU, HAVE NO GENERALS. THERE ARE NO ARMIES, INDEED NO ONE TO TRAIN THEM IN WARFARE. MA'AM, CASTLE WAXING HAS BEEN AT PEACE FOR AEONS. WOULD IT NOT BE MORE POLITIC TO DRAW UP A TREATY DECLARING THE ENCHANTED POOL TO BE SITUATED ON COMMON LAND AND SHARED WITH OUR NEIGHBOURS?

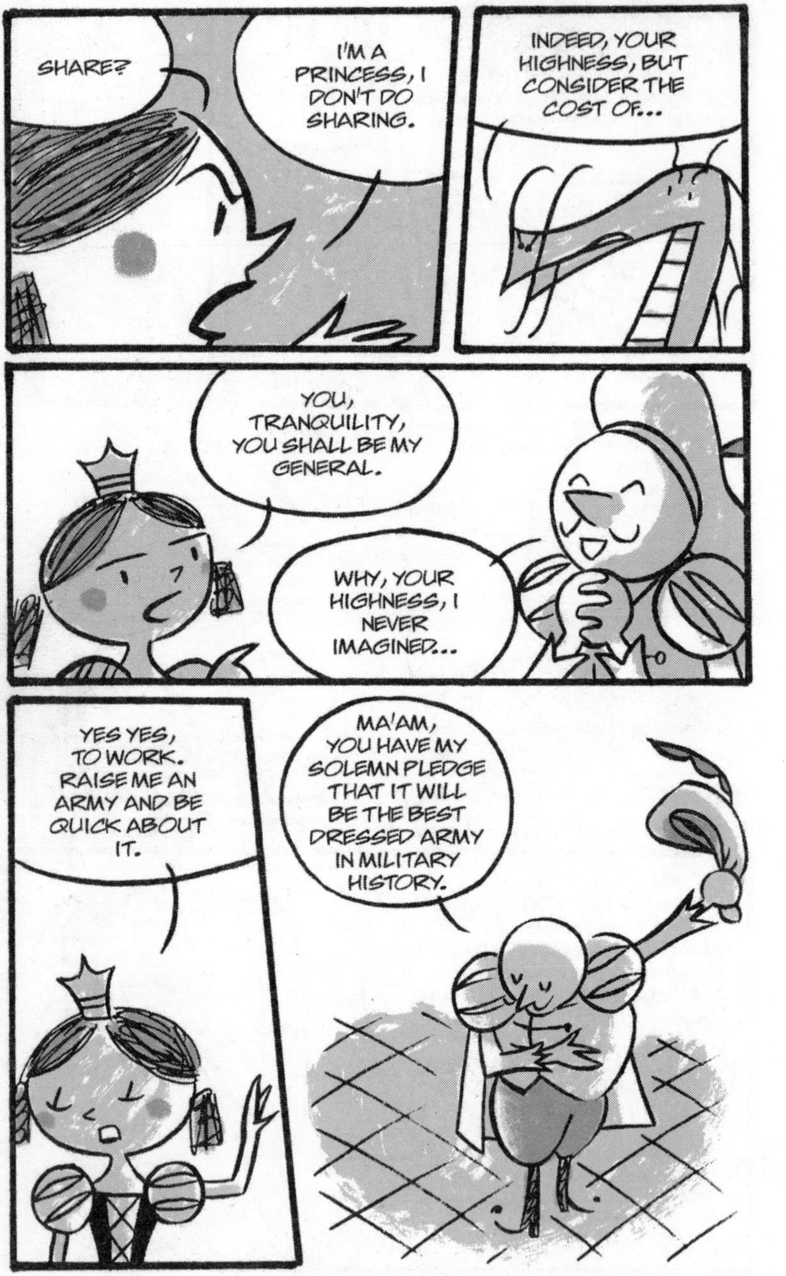
SHARE?
I'M A PRINCESS, I DON'T DO SHARING.
INDEED, YOUR HIGHNESS, BUT CONSIDER THE COST OF...
YOU, TRANQUILITY, YOU SHALL BE MY GENERAL.
WHY, YOUR HIGHNESS, I NEVER IMAGINED...
YES YES, TO WORK. RAISE ME AN ARMY AND BE QUICK ABOUT IT.
MA'AM, YOU HAVE MY SOLEMN PLEDGE THAT IT WILL BE THE BEST DRESSED ARMY IN MILITARY HISTORY.

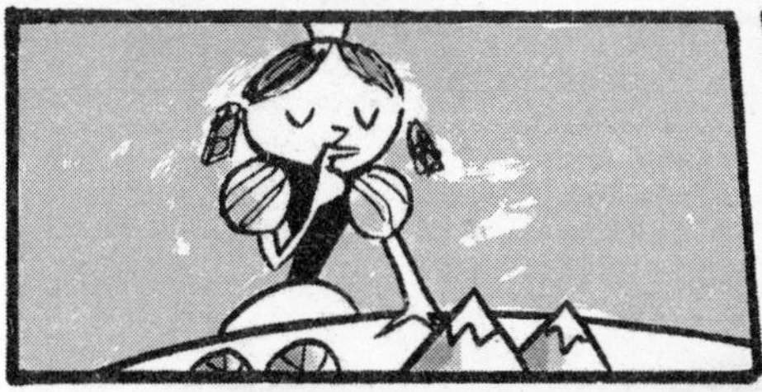

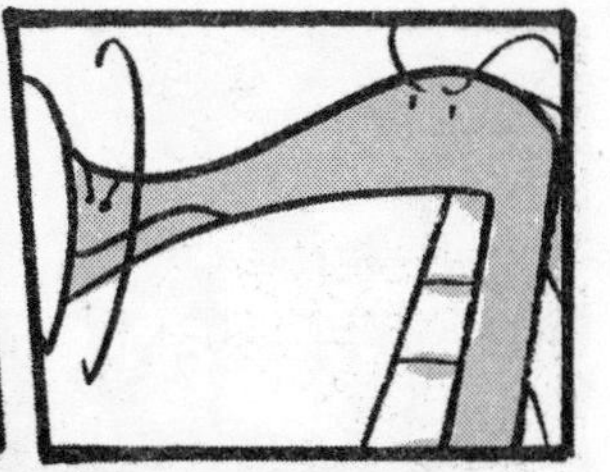

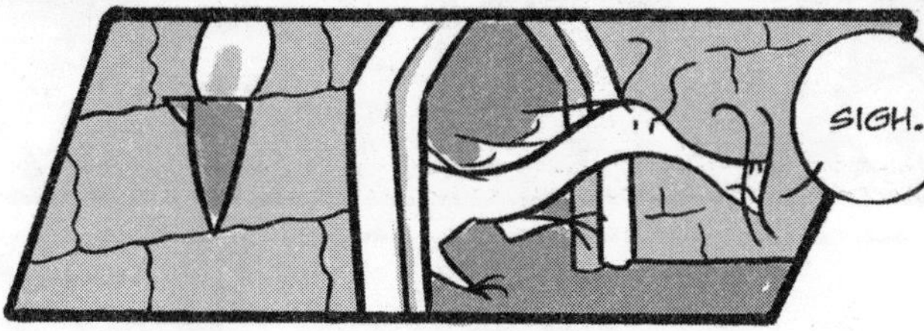
SIGH.

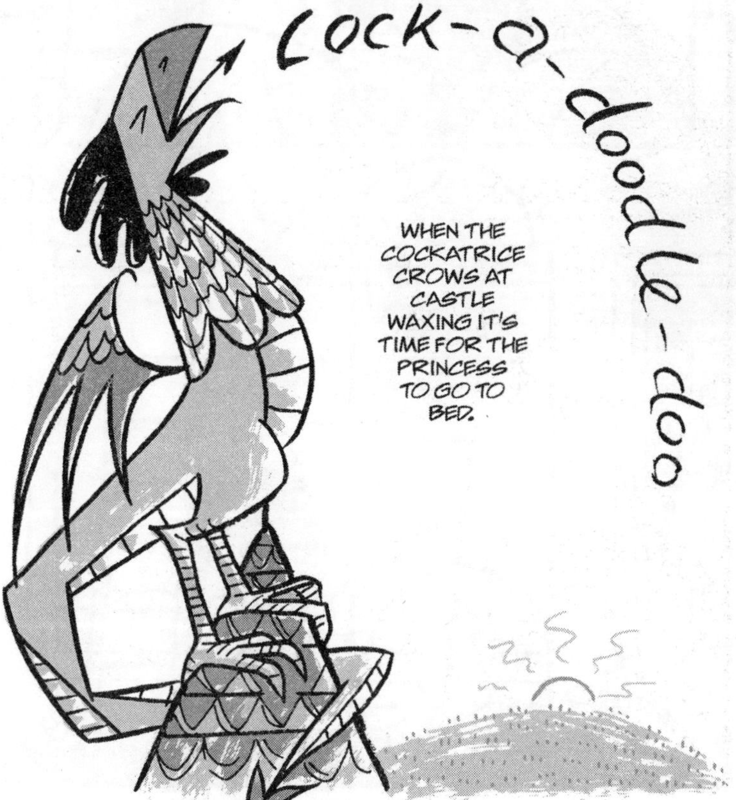
COCK-A-doodle-doo
WHEN THE COCKATRICE CROWS AT CASTLE WAXING IT'S TIME FOR THE PRINCESS TO GO TO BED.

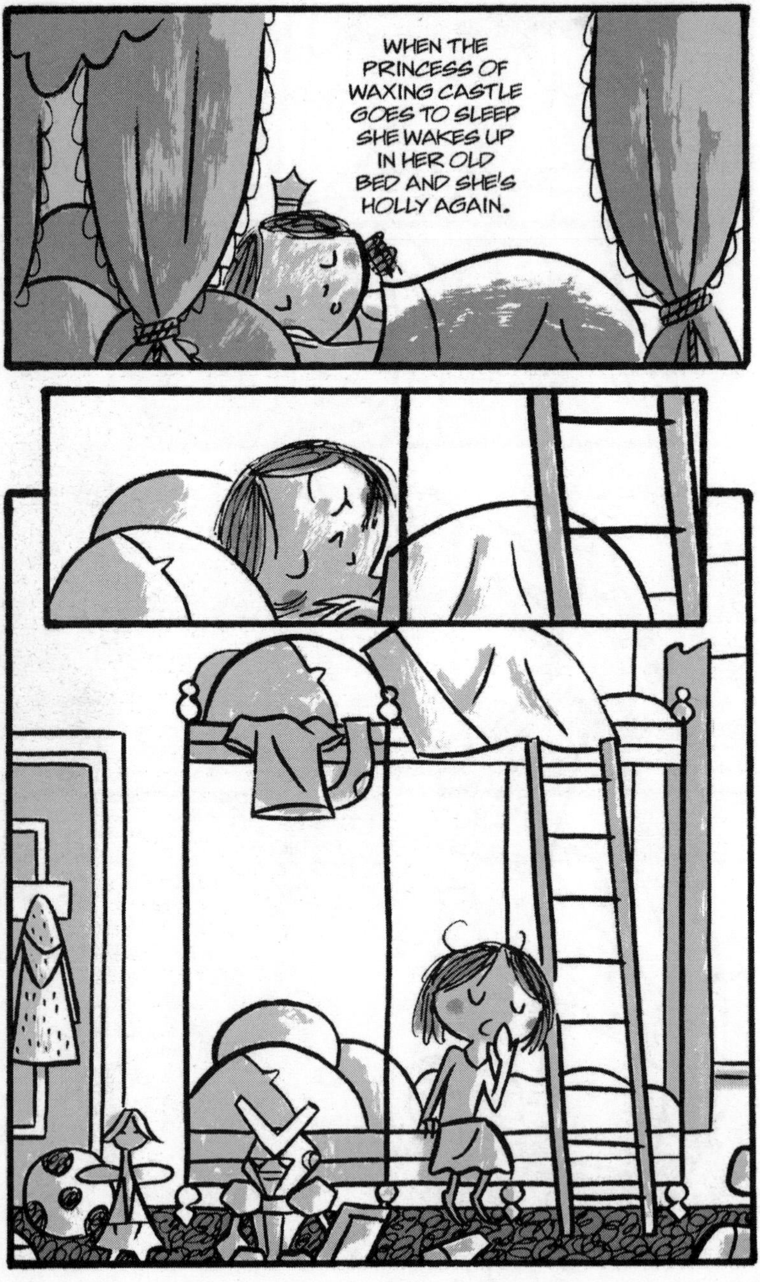
WHEN THE PRINCESS OF WAXING CASTLE GOES TO SLEEP SHE WAKES UP IN HER OLD BED AND SHE'S HOLLY AGAIN.

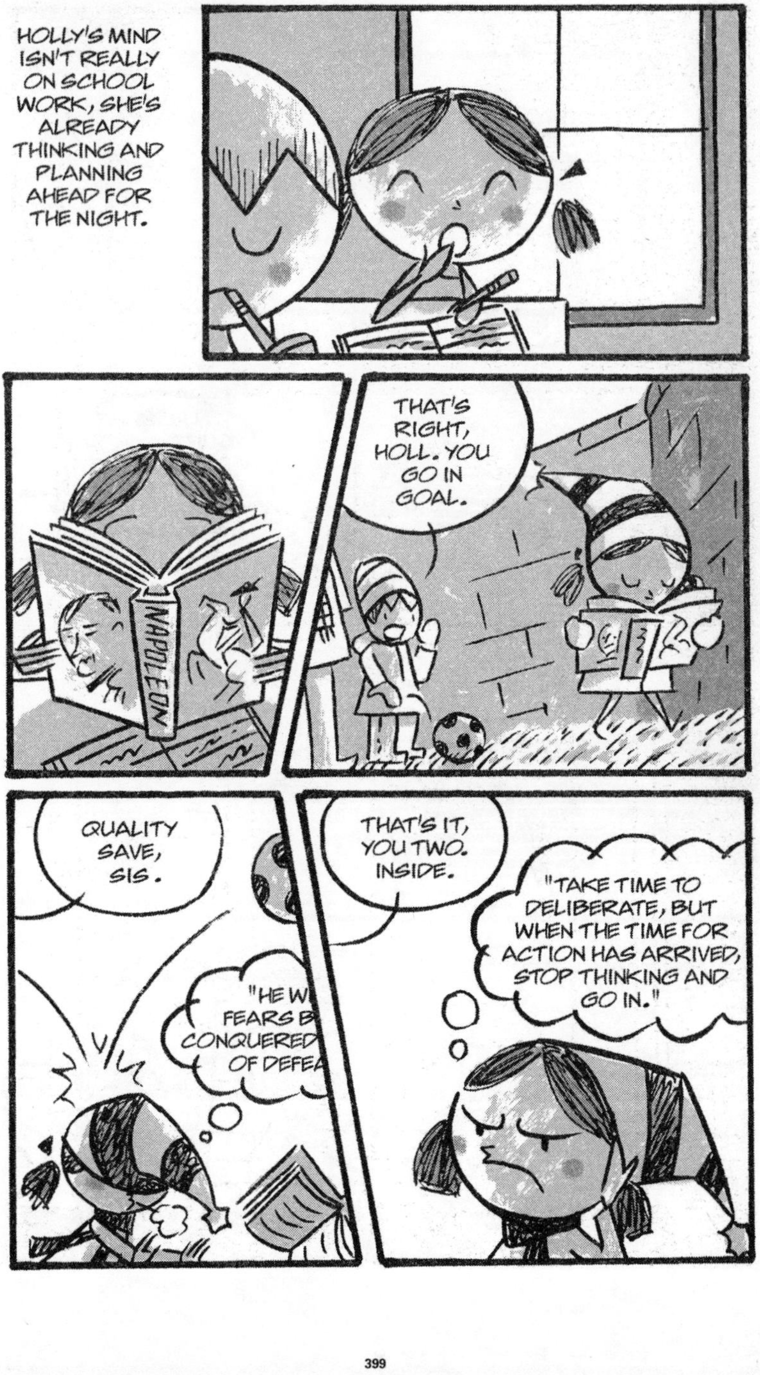
HOLLY'S MIND ISN'T REALLY ON SCHOOL WORK, SHE'S ALREADY THINKING AND PLANNING AHEAD FOR THE NIGHT.
NAPOLEON
THAT'S RIGHT, HOLL. YOU GO IN GOAL.
QUALITY SAVE, SIS.
"HE W FEARS B CONQUERED OF DEFEA
THAT'S IT, YOU TWO. INSIDE.
"TAKE TIME TO DELIBERATE, BUT WHEN THE TIME FOR ACTION HAS ARRIVED, STOP THINKING AND GO IN."

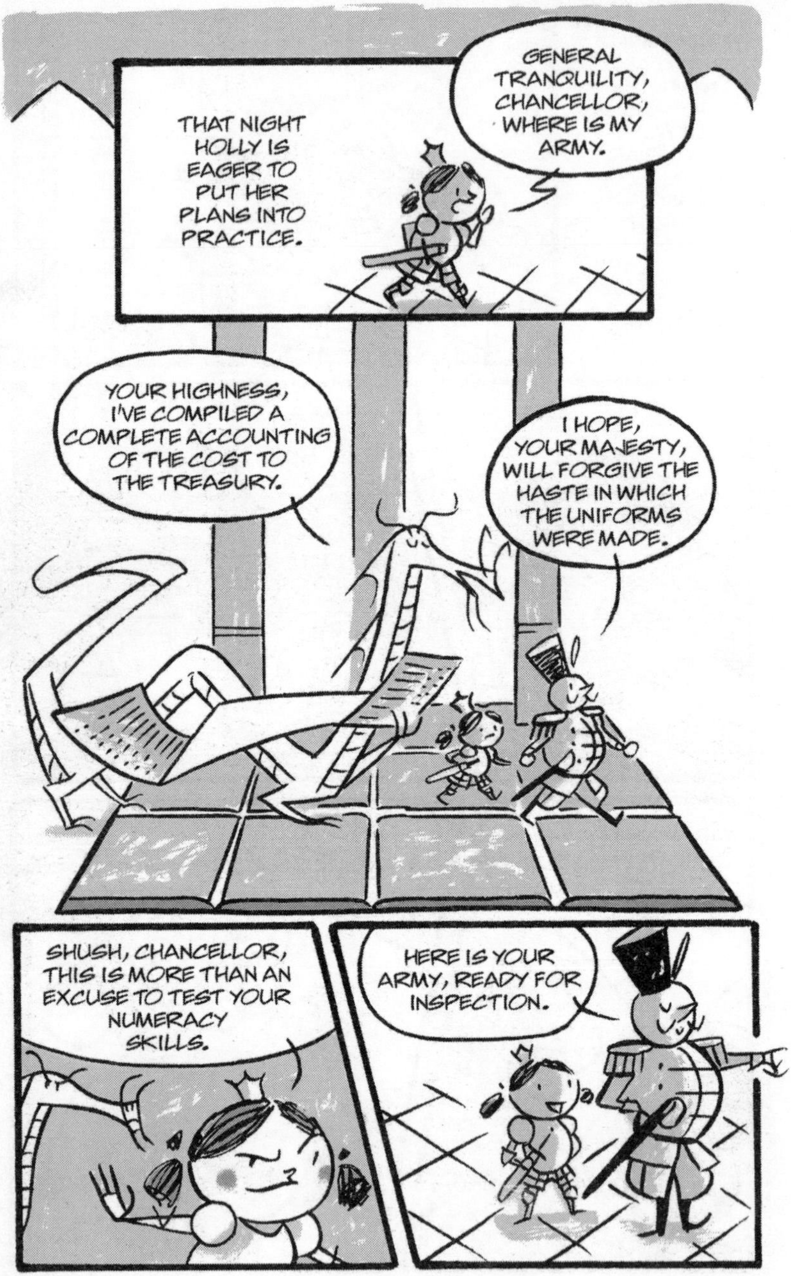

THAT NIGHT HOLLY IS EAGER TO PUT HER PLANS INTO PRACTICE.
GENERAL TRANQUILITY, CHANCELLOR, WHERE IS MY ARMY.
YOUR HIGHNESS, I'VE COMPILED A COMPLETE ACCOUNTING OF THE COST TO THE TREASURY.
I HOPE, YOUR MAJESTY, WILL FORGIVE THE HASTE IN WHICH THE UNIFORMS WERE MADE.
SHUSH, CHANCELLOR, THIS IS MORE THAN AN EXCUSE TO TEST YOUR NUMERACY SKILLS.
HERE IS YOUR ARMY, READY FOR INSPECTION.

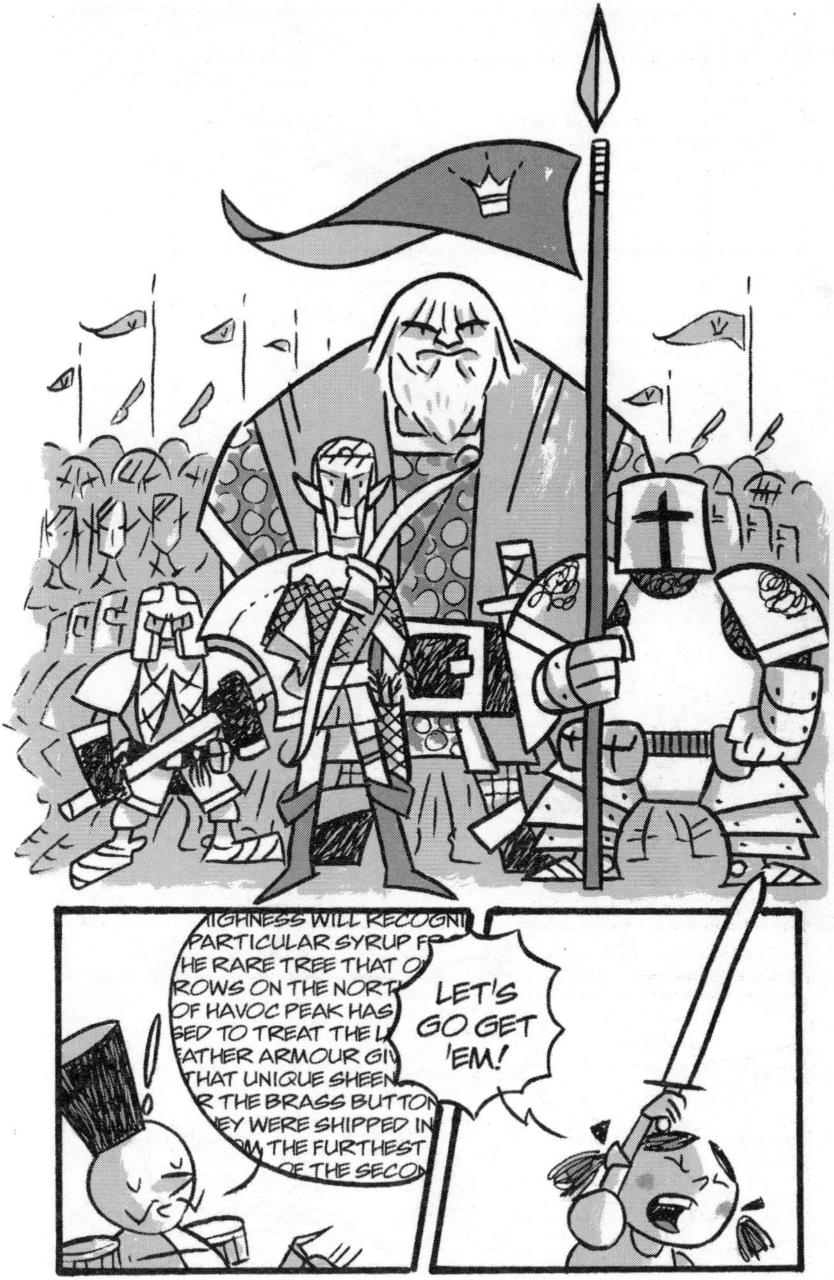
IGHNESS WILL RECOGNI
PARTICULAR SYRUP FR
HE RARE TREE THAT O
ROWS ON THE NORT
OF HAVOC PEAK HAS
SED TO TREAT THE L
EATHER ARMOUR GIV
THAT UNIQUE SHEEN
R THE BRASS BUTTON
EY WERE SHIPPED IN
OM THE FURTHEST
OF THE SECON
LET'S GO GET 'EM!

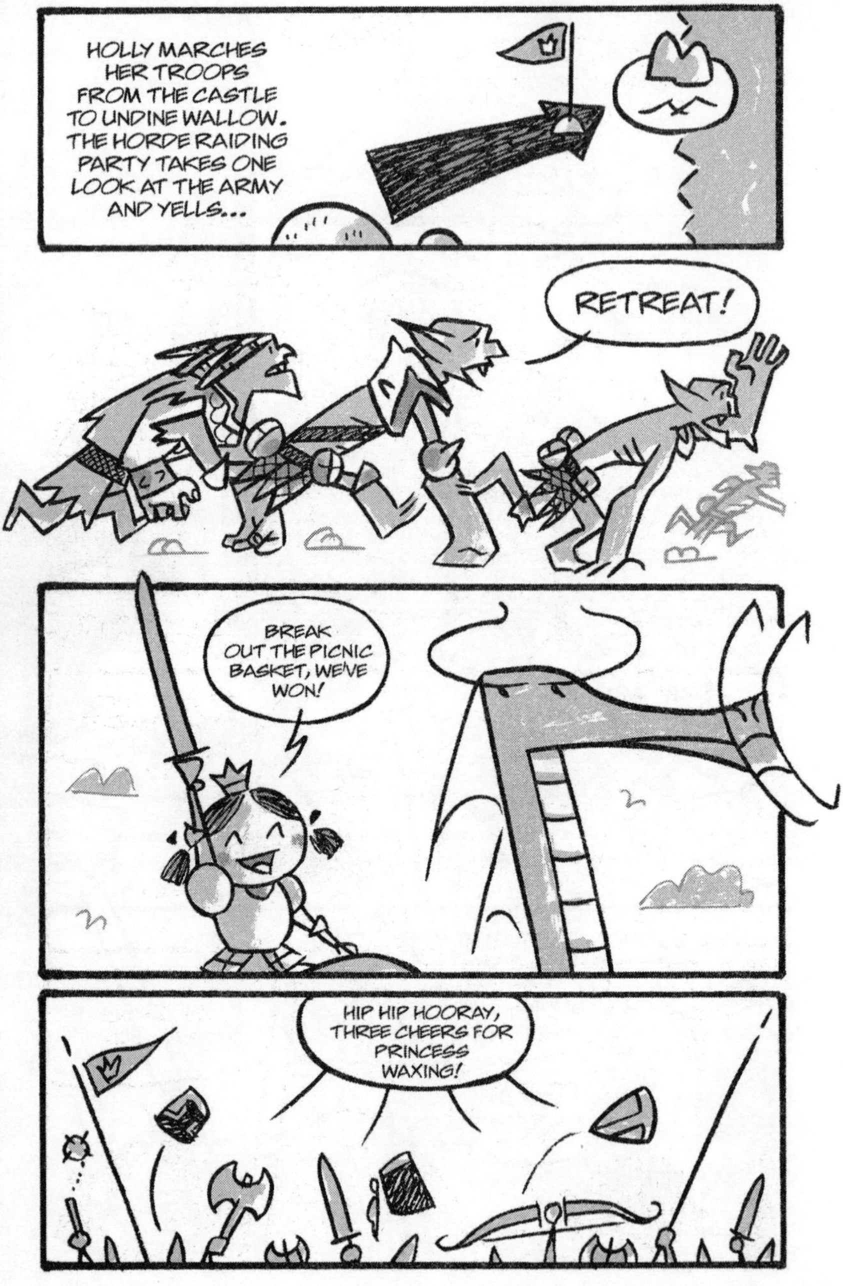
HOLLY MARCHES HER TROOPS FROM THE CASTLE TO UNDINE WALLOW. THE HORDE RAIDING PARTY TAKES ONE LOOK AT THE ARMY AND YELLS...
RETREAT!
BREAK OUT THE PICNIC BASKET, WE'VE WON!
HIP HIP HOORAY, THREE CHEERS FOR PRINCESS WAXING!

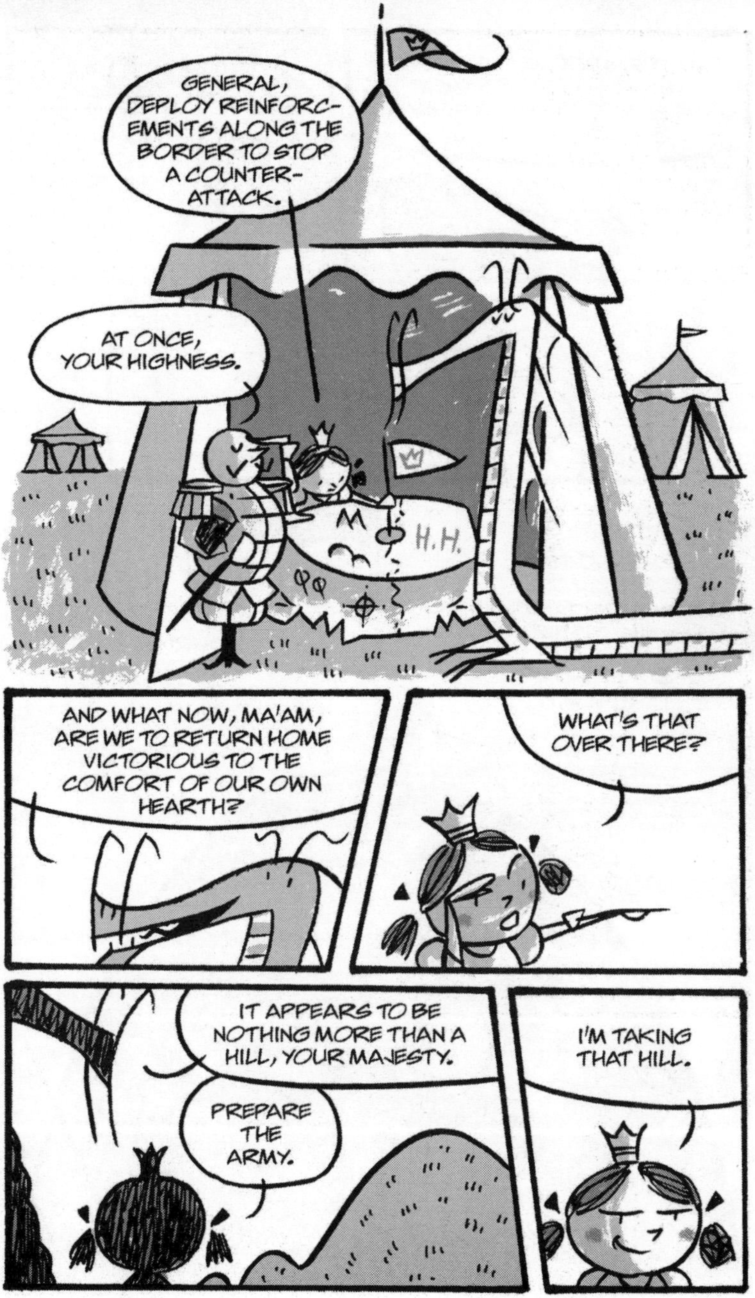
GENERAL, DEPLOY REINFORCEMENTS ALONG THE BORDER TO STOP A COUNTER-ATTACK.
AT ONCE, YOUR HIGHNESS.
H.H.
AND WHAT NOW, MA'AM, ARE WE TO RETURN HOME VICTORIOUS TO THE COMFORT OF OUR OWN HEARTH?
WHAT'S THAT OVER THERE?
IT APPEARS TO BE NOTHING MORE THAN A HILL, YOUR MAJESTY.
PREPARE THE ARMY.
I'M TAKING THAT HILL.

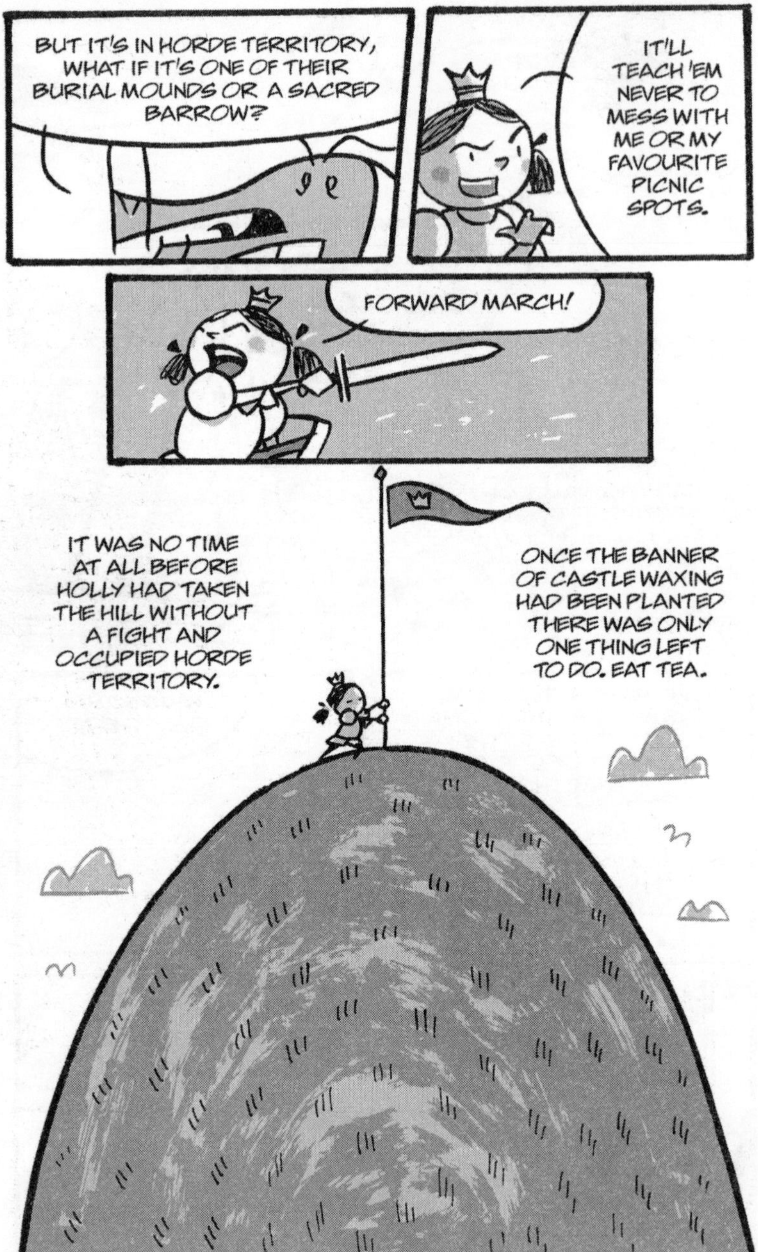
BUT IT'S IN HORDE TERRITORY, WHAT IF IT'S ONE OF THEIR BURIAL MOUNDS OR A SACRED BARROW?
IT'LL TEACH 'EM NEVER TO MESS WITH ME OR MY FAVOURITE PICNIC SPOTS.
FORWARD MARCH!
IT WAS NO TIME AT ALL BEFORE HOLLY HAD TAKEN THE HILL WITHOUT A FIGHT AND OCCUPIED HORDE TERRITORY.
ONCE THE BANNER OF CASTLE WAXING HAD BEEN PLANTED THERE WAS ONLY ONE THING LEFT TO DO. EAT TEA.

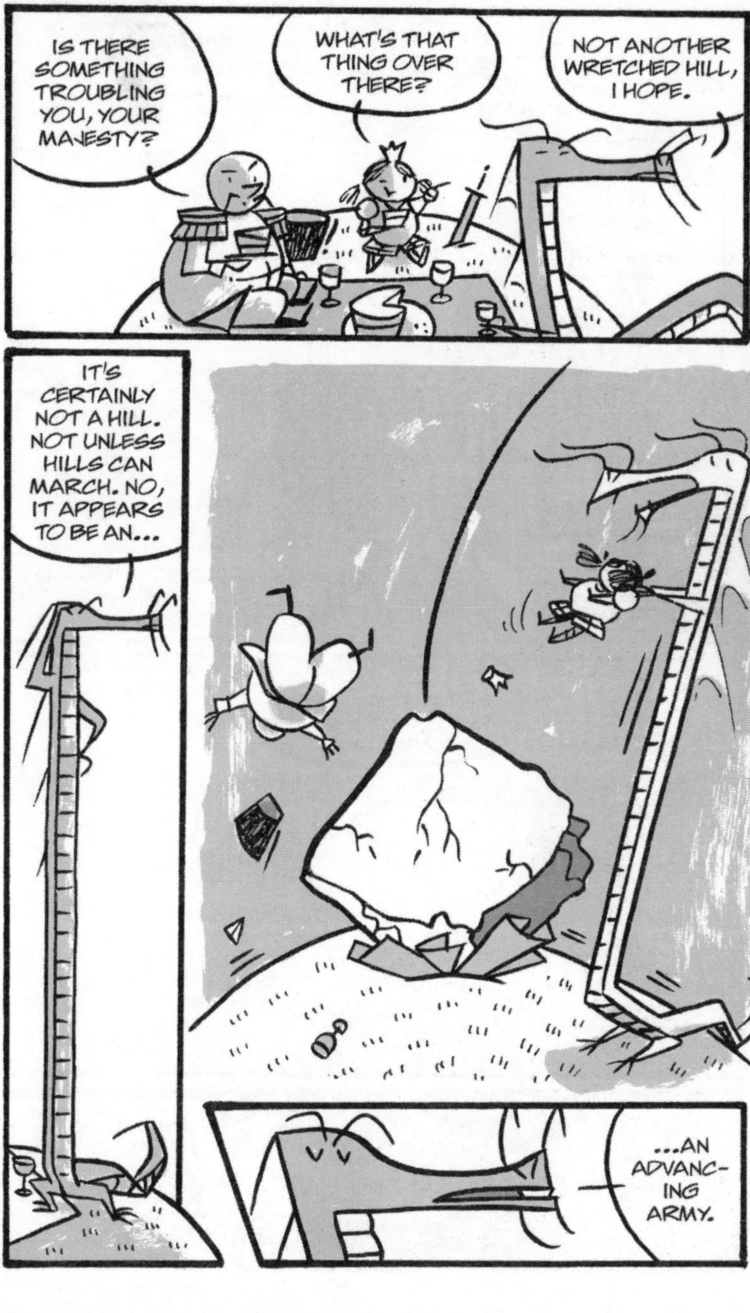
IS THERE SOMETHING TROUBLING YOU, YOUR MAJESTY?
WHAT'S THAT THING OVER THERE?
NOT ANOTHER WRETCHED HILL, I HOPE.
IT'S CERTAINLY NOT A HILL. NOT UNLESS HILLS CAN MARCH. NO, IT APPEARS TO BE AN...
...AN ADVANCING ARMY.

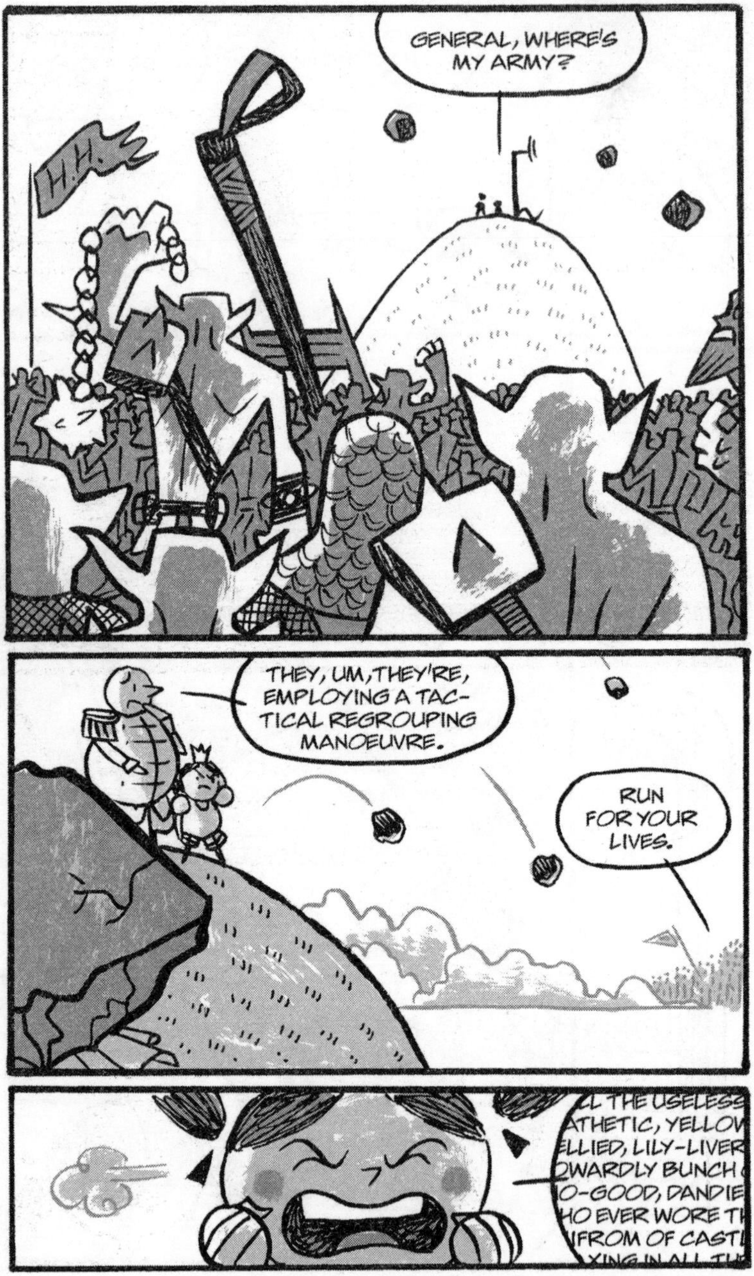
GENERAL, WHERE'S MY ARMY?
H.H.
THEY, UM, THEY'RE, EMPLOYING A TACTICAL REGROUPING MANOEUVRE.
RUN FOR YOUR LIVES.
LL THE USELESS ATHETIC, YELLOW ELLIED, LILY-LIVER OWARDLY BUNCH O-GOOD, DANDIE HO EVER WORE TH IFROM OF CASTL

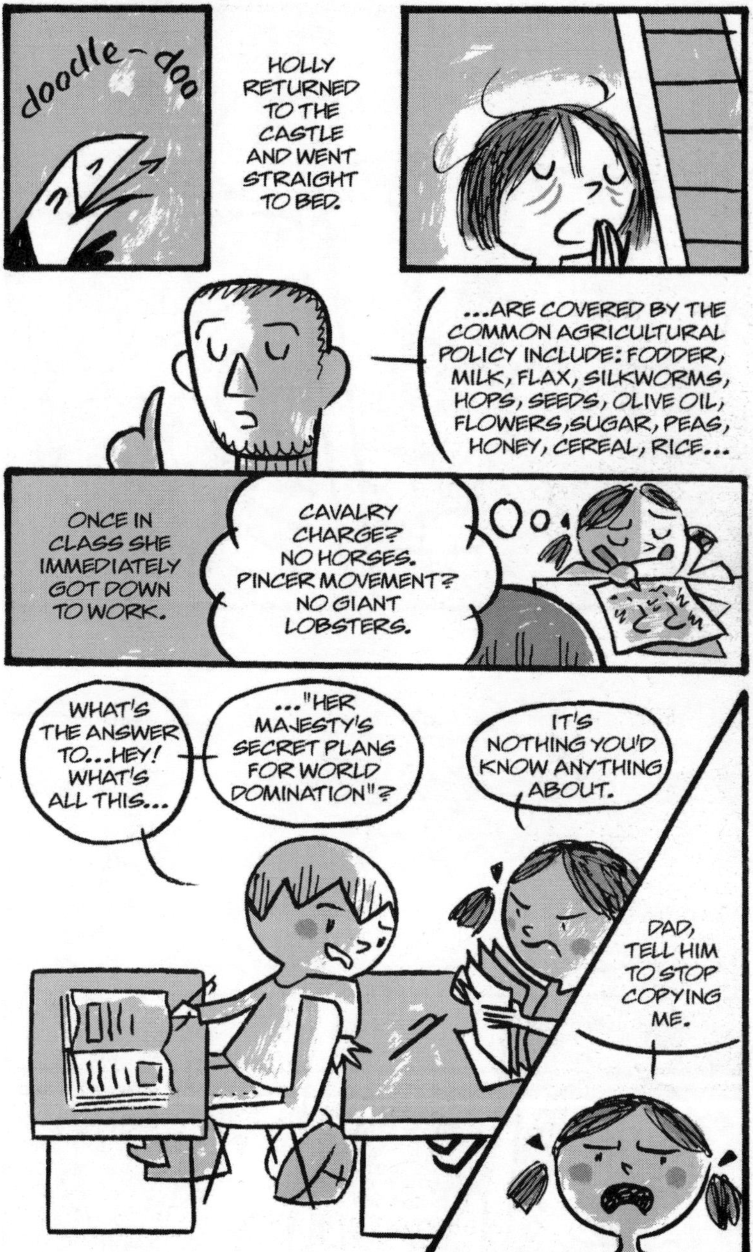
doodle-doo
HOLLY RETURNED TO THE CASTLE AND WENT STRAIGHT TO BED.
...ARE COVERED BY THE COMMON AGRICULTURAL POLICY INCLUDE: FODDER, MILK, FLAX, SILKWORMS, HOPS, SEEDS, OLIVE OIL, FLOWERS, SUGAR, PEAS, HONEY, CEREAL, RICE...
ONCE IN CLASS SHE IMMEDIATELY GOT DOWN TO WORK.
CAVALRY CHARGE? NO HORSES. PINCER MOVEMENT? NO GIANT LOBSTERS.
WHAT'S THE ANSWER TO...HEY! WHAT'S ALL THIS...
..."HER MAJESTY'S SECRET PLANS FOR WORLD DOMINATION"?
IT'S NOTHING YOU'D KNOW ANYTHING ABOUT.
DAD, TELL HIM TO STOP COPYING ME.

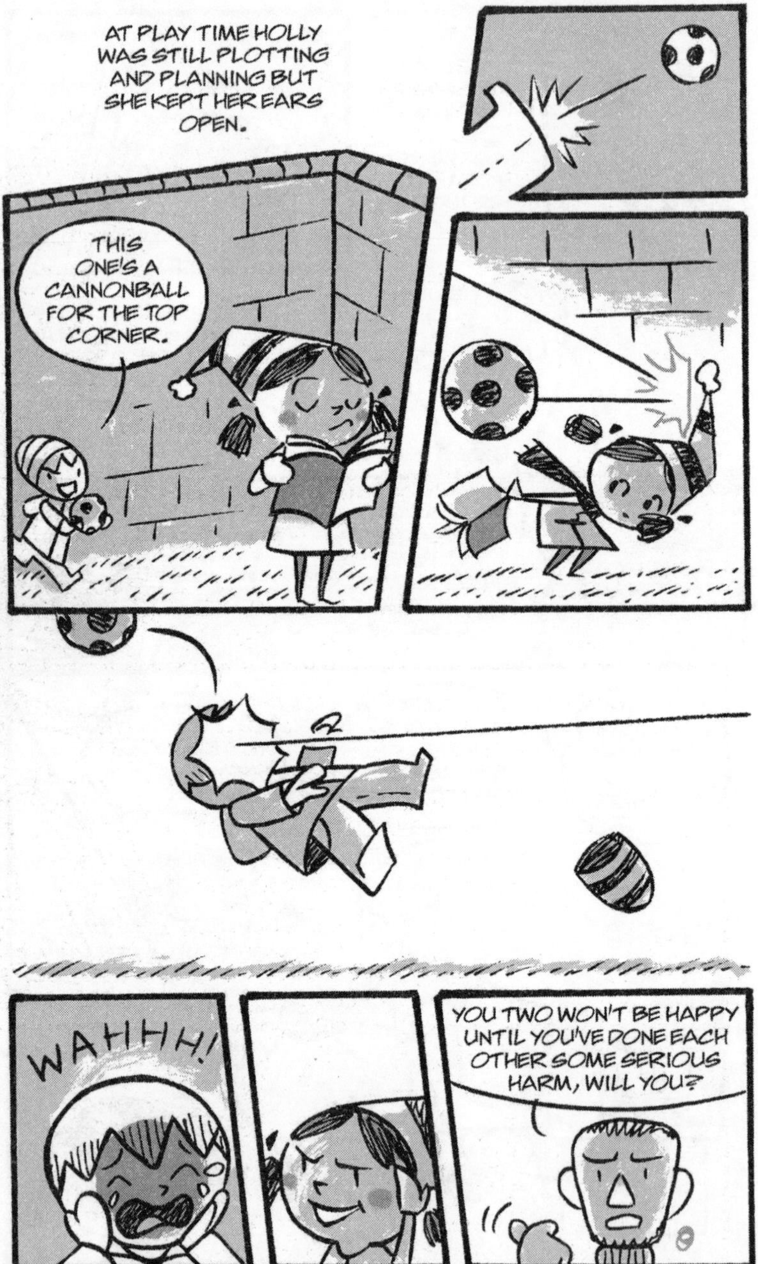
AT PLAY TIME HOLLY WAS STILL PLOTTING AND PLANNING BUT SHE KEPT HER EARS OPEN.
THIS ONE'S A CANNONBALL FOR THE TOP CORNER.
WAHHH!
YOU TWO WON'T BE HAPPY UNTIL YOU'VE DONE EACH OTHER SOME SERIOUS HARM, WILL YOU?

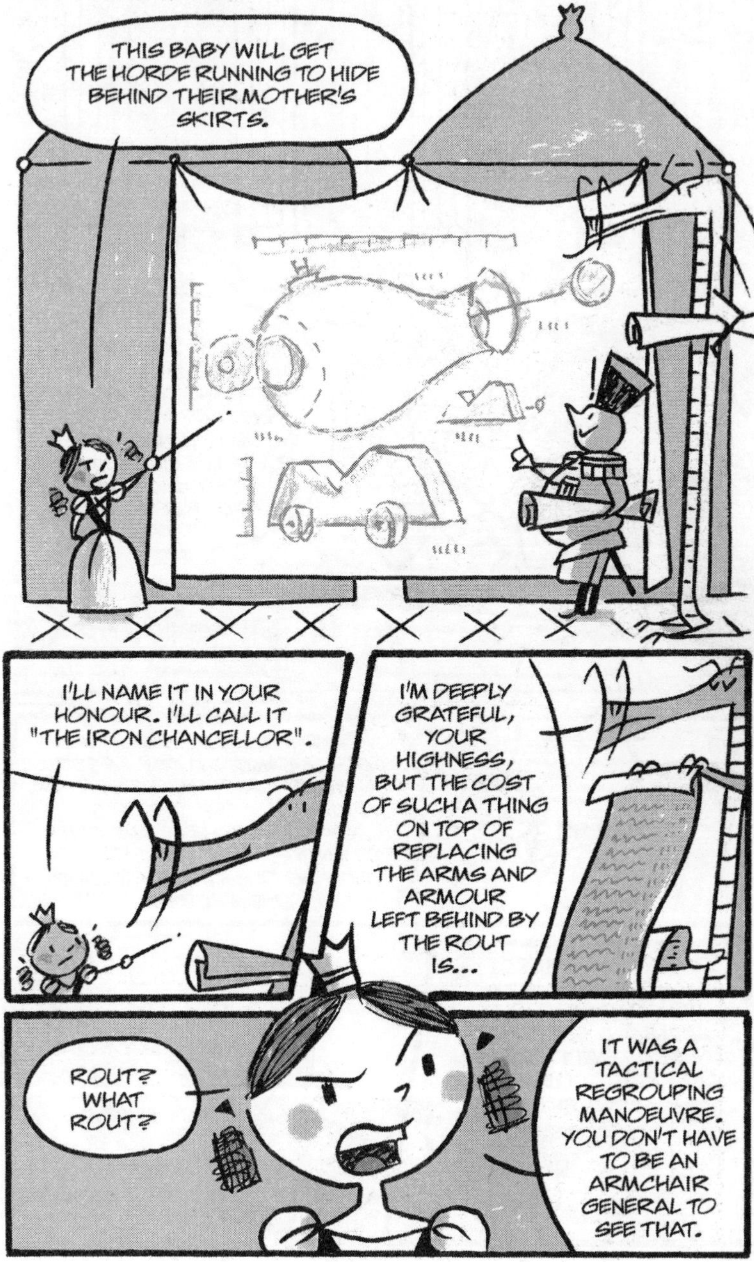
THIS BABY WILL GET THE HORDE RUNNING TO HIDE BEHIND THEIR MOTHER'S SKIRTS.
I'LL NAME IT IN YOUR HONOUR. I'LL CALL IT "THE IRON CHANCELLOR".
I'M DEEPLY GRATEFUL, YOUR HIGHNESS, BUT THE COST OF SUCH A THING ON TOP OF REPLACING THE ARMS AND ARMOUR LEFT BEHIND BY THE ROUT IS...
ROUT? WHAT ROUT?
IT WAS A TACTICAL REGROUPING MANOEUVRE. YOU DON'T HAVE TO BE AN ARMCHAIR GENERAL TO SEE THAT.

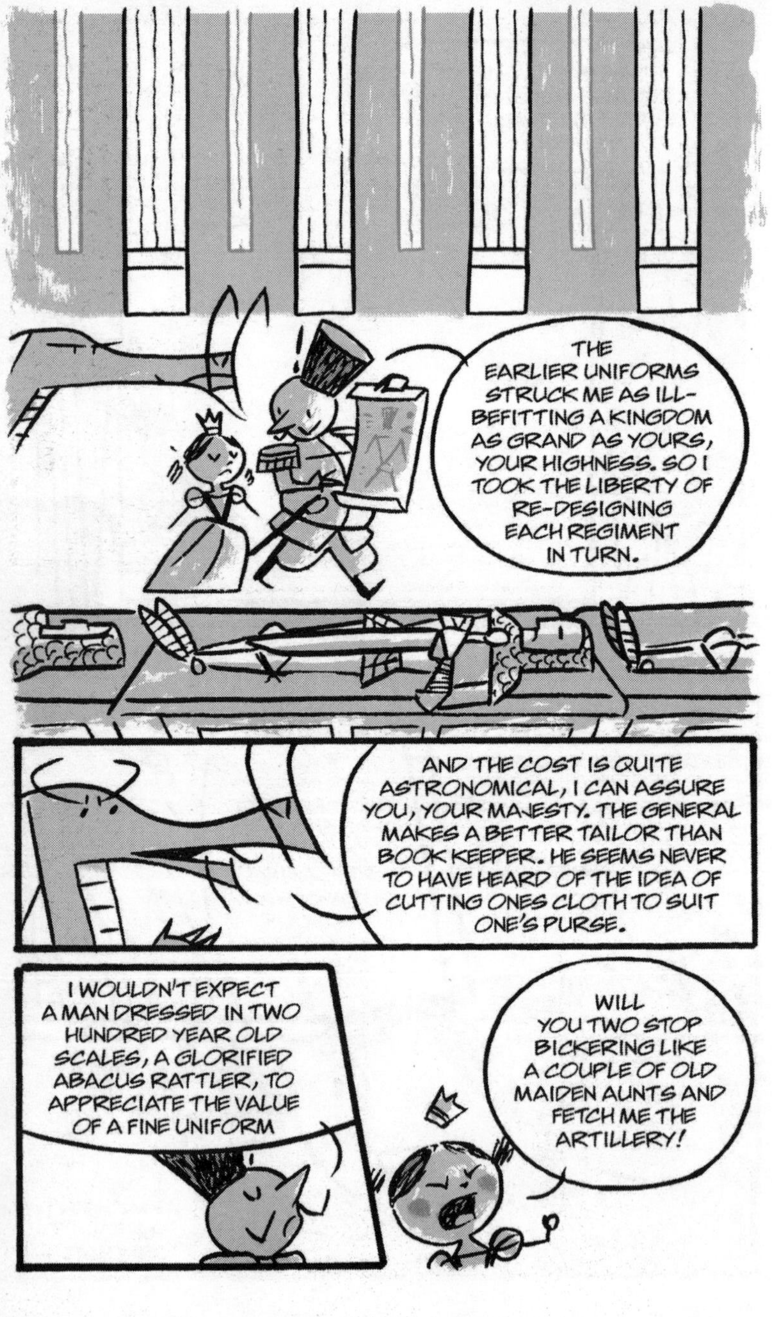
THE EARLIER UNIFORMS STRUCK ME AS ILL-BEFITTING A KINGDOM AS GRAND AS YOURS, YOUR HIGHNESS. SO I TOOK THE LIBERTY OF RE-DESIGNING EACH REGIMENT IN TURN.
AND THE COST IS QUITE ASTRONOMICAL, I CAN ASSURE YOU, YOUR MAJESTY. THE GENERAL MAKES A BETTER TAILOR THAN BOOK KEEPER. HE SEEMS NEVER TO HAVE HEARD OF THE IDEA OF CUTTING ONES CLOTH TO SUIT ONE'S PURSE.
I WOULDN'T EXPECT A MAN DRESSED IN TWO HUNDRED YEAR OLD SCALES, A GLORIFIED ABACUS RATTLER, TO APPRECIATE THE VALUE OF A FINE UNIFORM
WILL YOU TWO STOP BICKERING LIKE A COUPLE OF OLD MAIDEN AUNTS AND FETCH ME THE ARTILLERY!

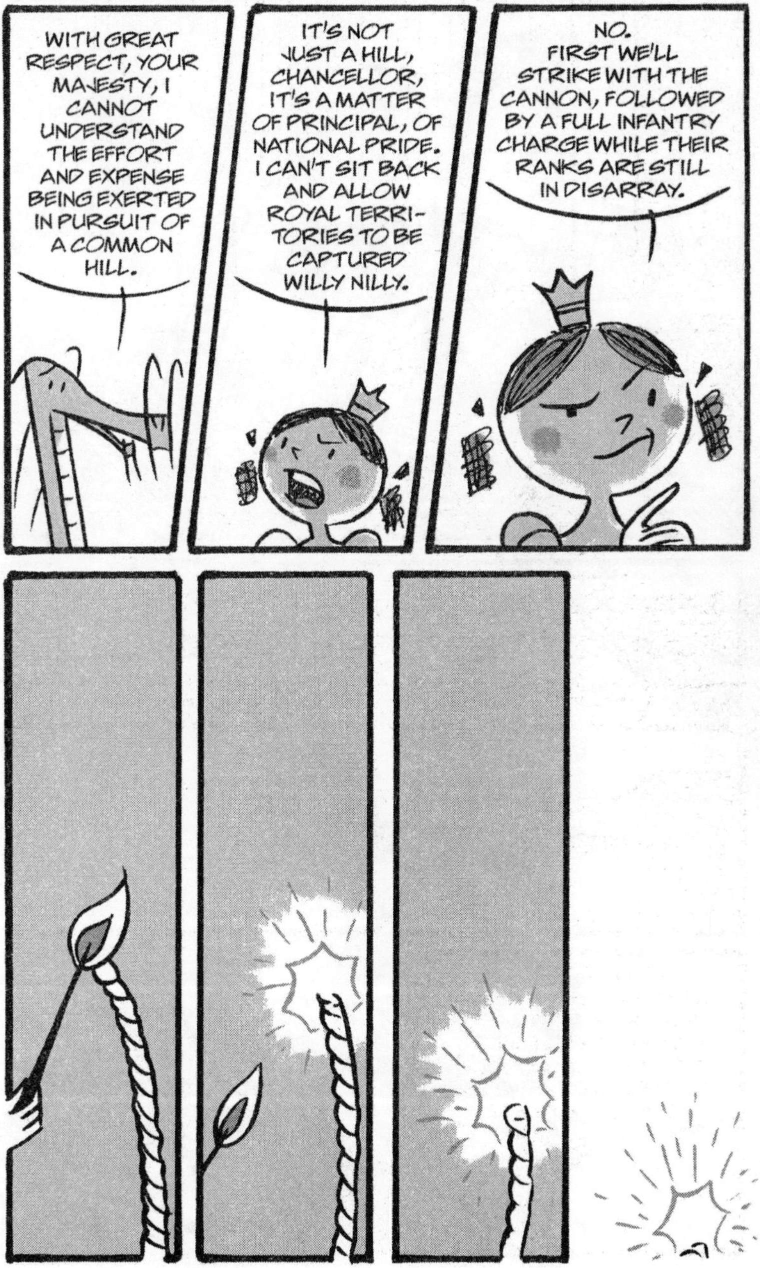
WITH GREAT RESPECT, YOUR MAJESTY, I CANNOT UNDERSTAND THE EFFORT AND EXPENSE BEING EXERTED IN PURSUIT OF A COMMON HILL.
IT'S NOT JUST A HILL, CHANCELLOR, IT'S A MATTER OF PRINCIPAL, OF NATIONAL PRIDE. I CAN'T SIT BACK AND ALLOW ROYAL TERRITORIES TO BE CAPTURED WILLY NILLY.
NO. FIRST WE'LL STRIKE WITH THE CANNON, FOLLOWED BY A FULL INFANTRY CHARGE WHILE THEIR RANKS ARE STILL IN DISARRAY.

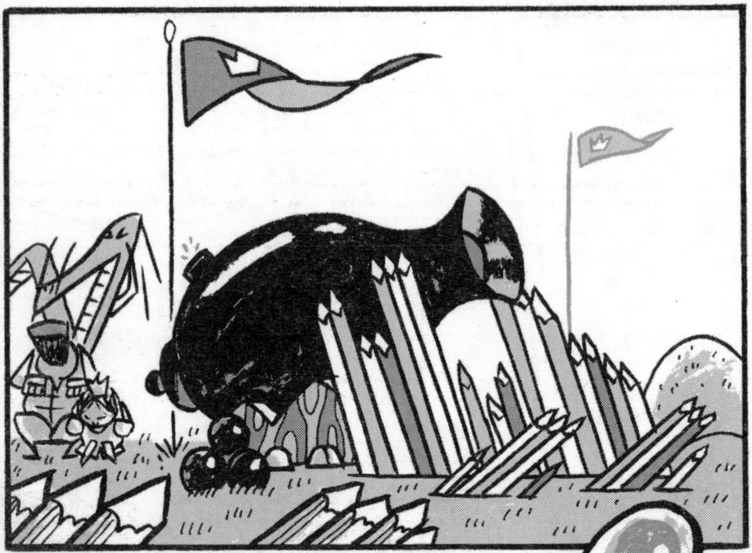
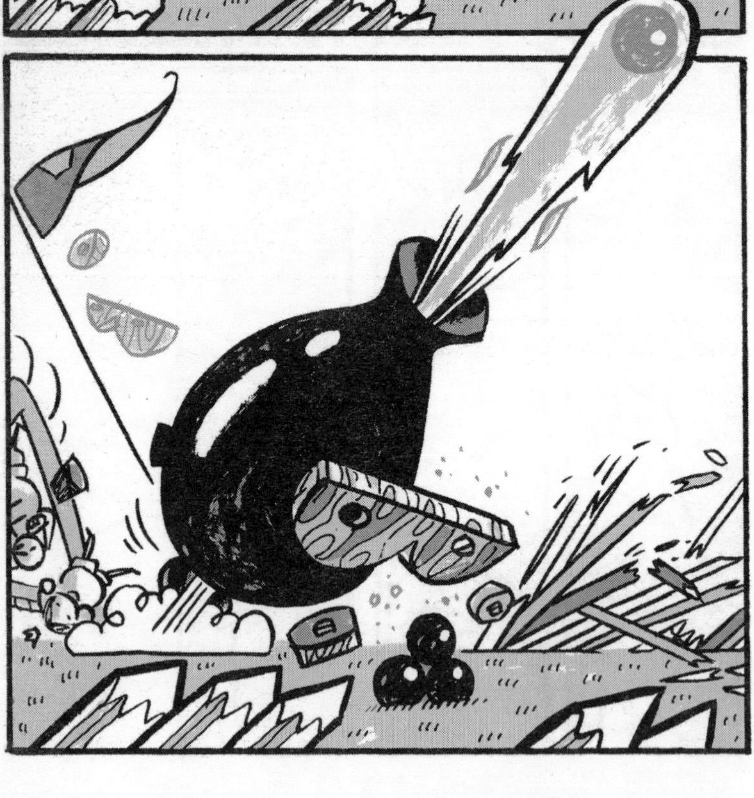

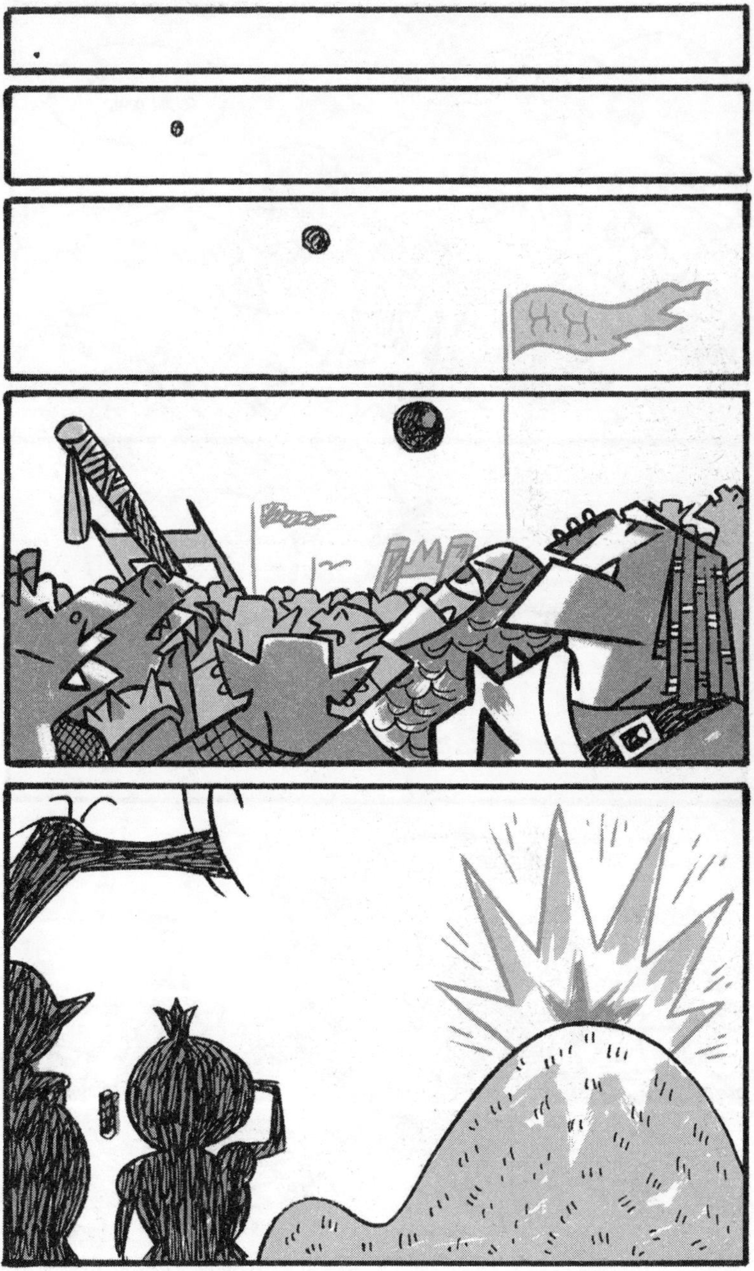
H.H.

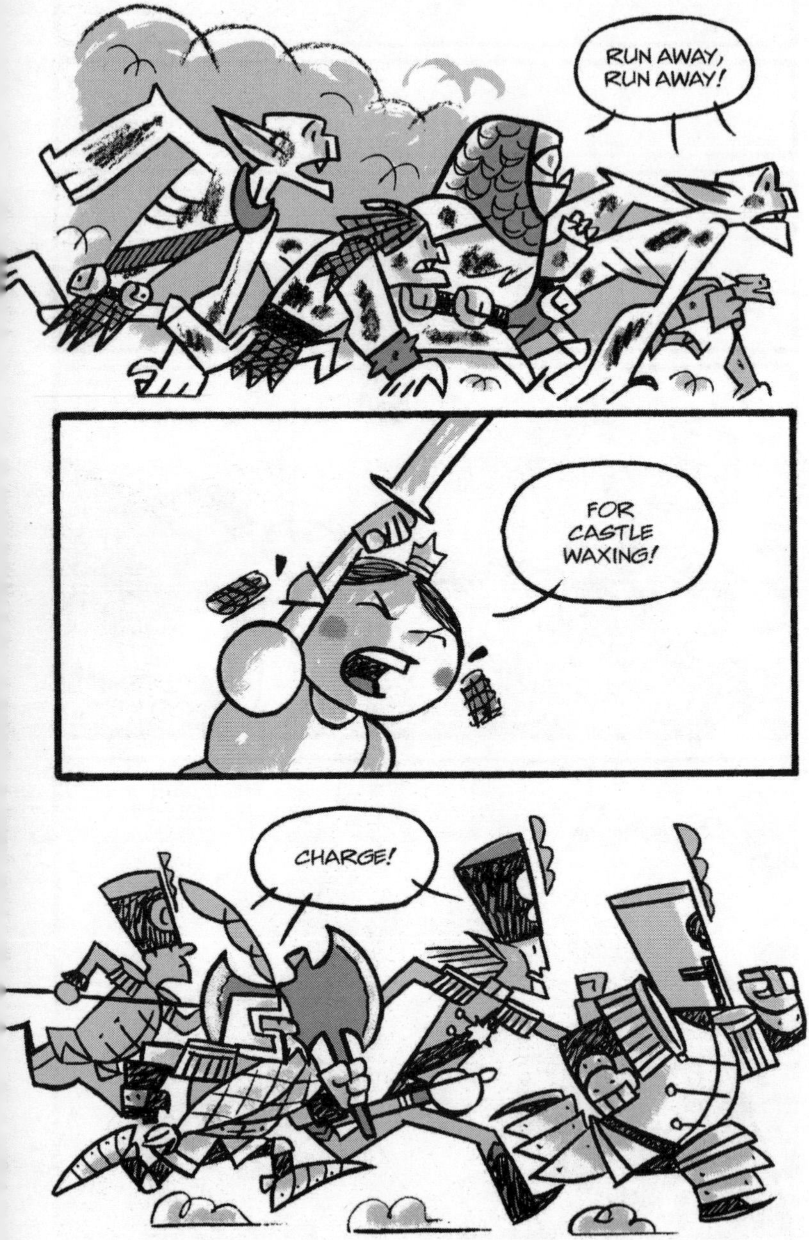
RUN AWAY, RUN AWAY!
FOR CASTLE WAXING!
CHARGE!

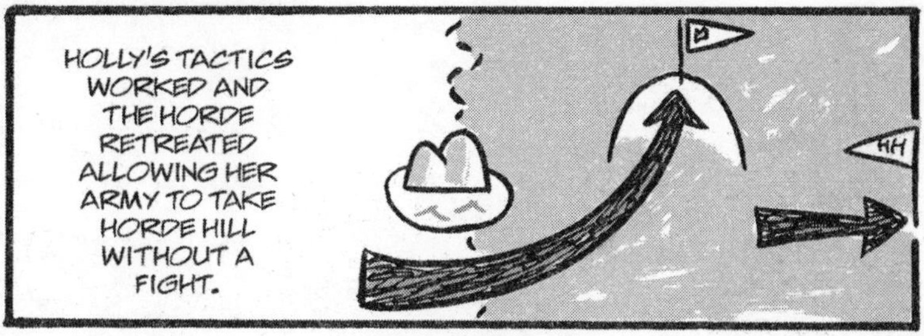
HOLLY'S TACTICS WORKED AND THE HORDE RETREATED ALLOWING HER ARMY TO TAKE HORDE HILL WITHOUT A FIGHT.
HH

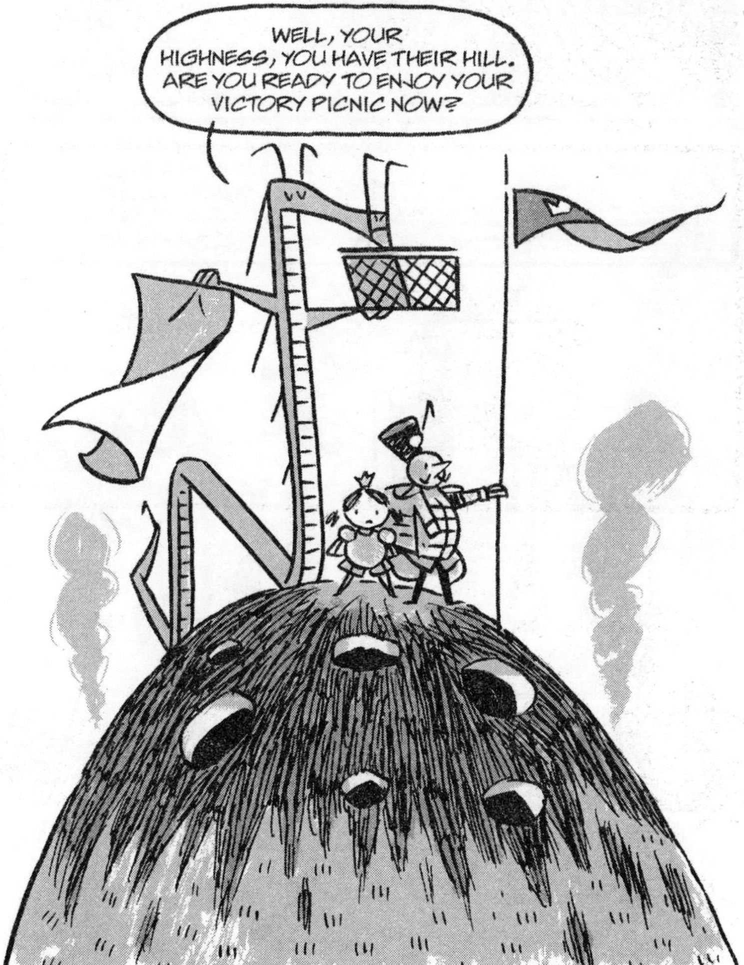
WELL, YOUR HIGHNESS, YOU HAVE THEIR HILL. ARE YOU READY TO ENJOY YOUR VICTORY PICNIC NOW?

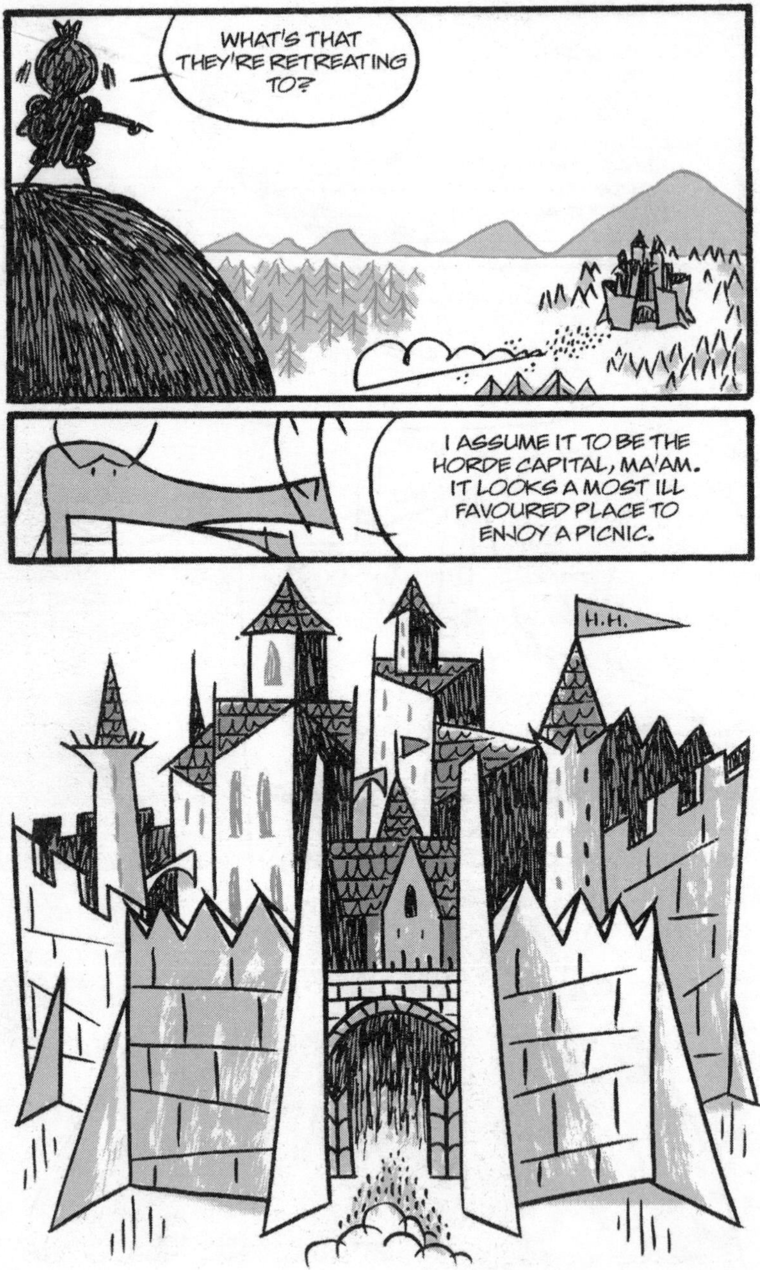
WHAT'S THAT THEY'RE RETREATING TO?
I ASSUME IT TO BE THE HORDE CAPITAL, MA'AM. IT LOOKS A MOST ILL FAVOURED PLACE TO ENJOY A PICNIC.
H.H.

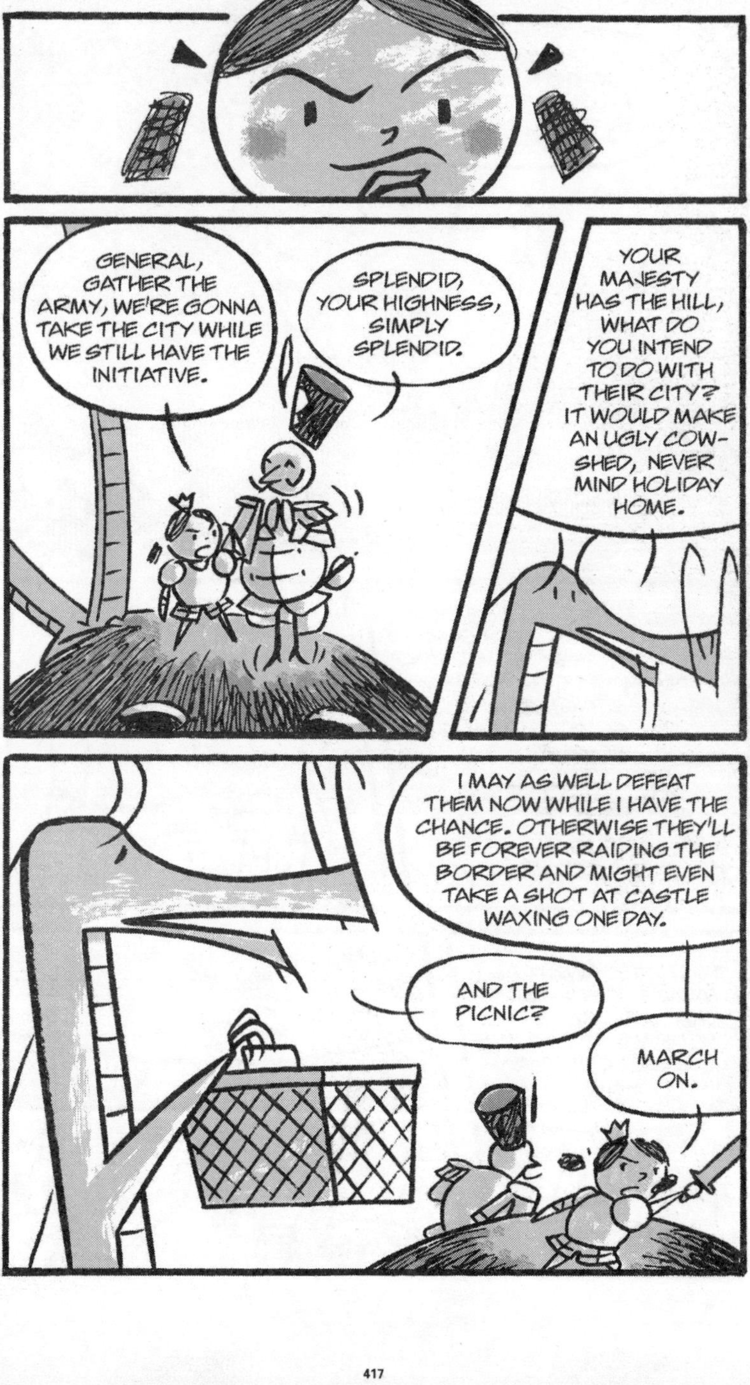
GENERAL, GATHER THE ARMY, WE'RE GONNA TAKE THE CITY WHILE WE STILL HAVE THE INITIATIVE.
SPLENDID, YOUR HIGHNESS, SIMPLY SPLENDID.
YOUR MAJESTY HAS THE HILL, WHAT DO YOU INTEND TO DO WITH THEIR CITY? IT WOULD MAKE AN UGLY COW-SHED, NEVER MIND HOLIDAY HOME.
I MAY AS WELL DEFEAT THEM NOW WHILE I HAVE THE CHANCE. OTHERWISE THEY'LL BE FOREVER RAIDING THE BORDER AND MIGHT EVEN TAKE A SHOT AT CASTLE WAXING ONE DAY.
AND THE PICNIC?
MARCH ON.

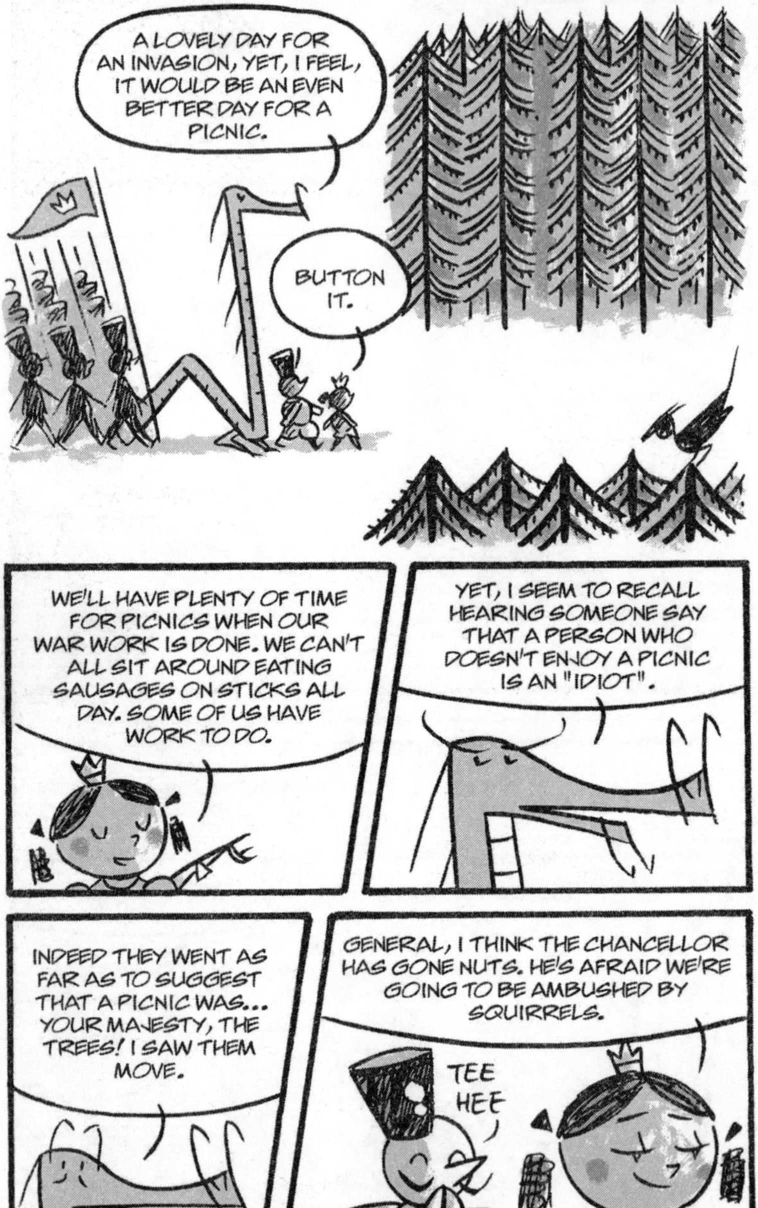
A LOVELY DAY FOR AN INVASION, YET, I FEEL, IT WOULD BE AN EVEN BETTER DAY FOR A PICNIC.
BUTTON IT.
WE'LL HAVE PLENTY OF TIME FOR PICNICS WHEN OUR WAR WORK IS DONE. WE CAN'T ALL SIT AROUND EATING SAUSAGES ON STICKS ALL DAY. SOME OF US HAVE WORK TO DO.
YET, I SEEM TO RECALL HEARING SOMEONE SAY THAT A PERSON WHO DOESN'T ENJOY A PICNIC IS AN "IDIOT".
INDEED THEY WENT AS FAR AS TO SUGGEST THAT A PICNIC WAS... YOUR MAJESTY, THE TREES! I SAW THEM MOVE.
GENERAL, I THINK THE CHANCELLOR HAS GONE NUTS. HE'S AFRAID WE'RE GOING TO BE AMBUSHED BY SQUIRRELS.
TEE HEE

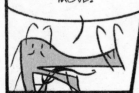

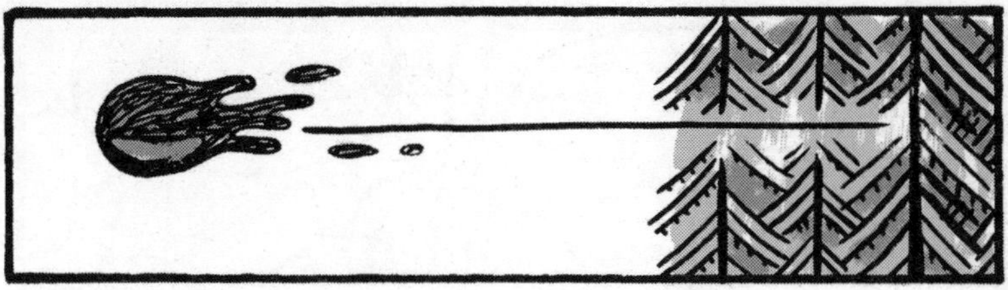

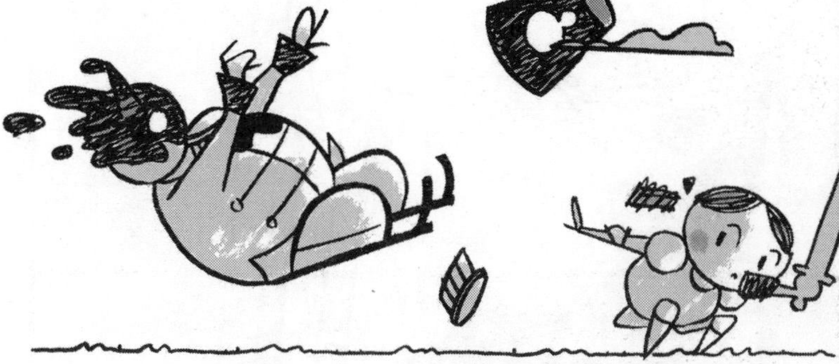

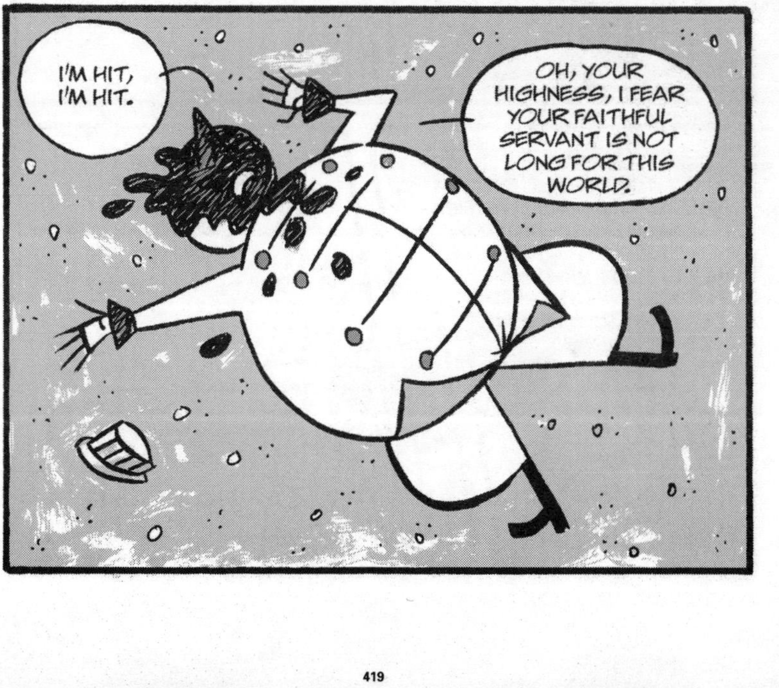
I'M HIT, I'M HIT.
OH, YOUR HIGHNESS, I FEAR YOUR FAITHFUL SERVANT IS NOT LONG FOR THIS WORLD.

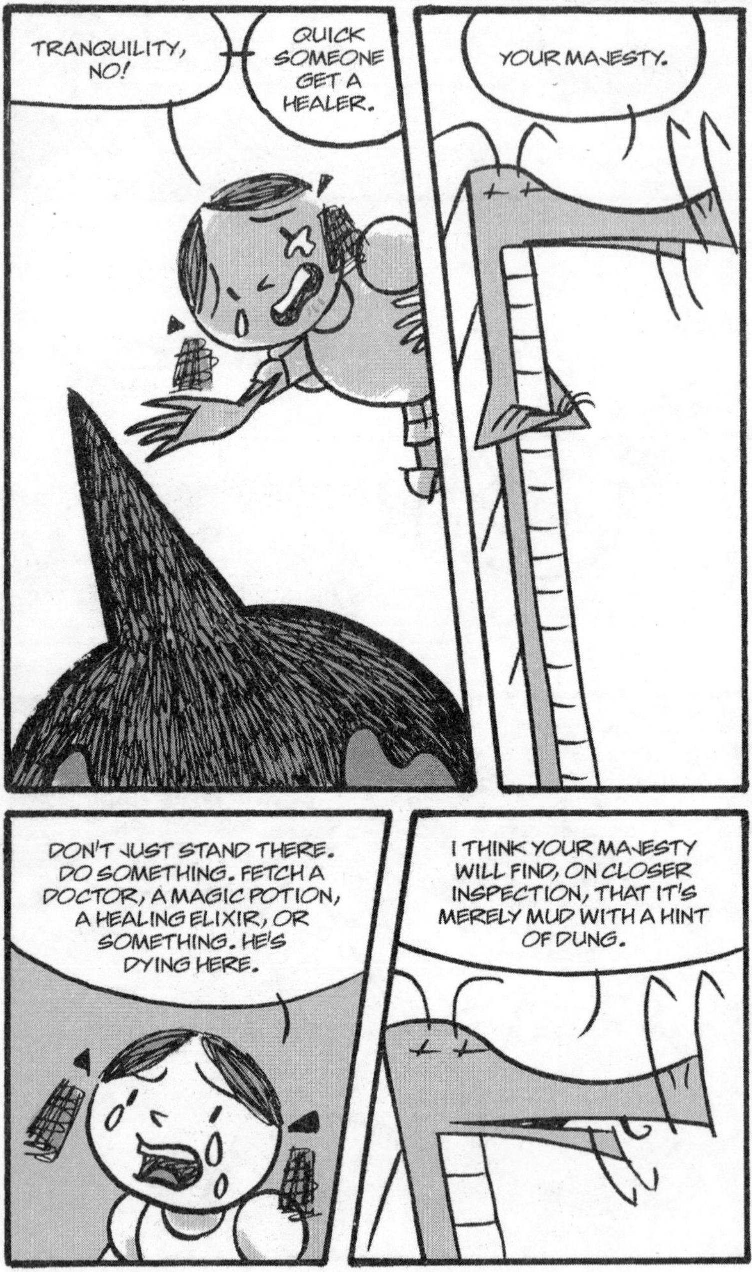
TRANQUILITY, NO!
QUICK SOMEONE GET A HEALER.
YOUR MAJESTY.
DON'T JUST STAND THERE. DO SOMETHING. FETCH A DOCTOR, A MAGIC POTION, A HEALING ELIXIR, OR SOMETHING. HE'S DYING HERE.
I THINK YOUR MAJESTY WILL FIND, ON CLOSER INSPECTION, THAT IT'S MERELY MUD WITH A HINT OF DUNG.

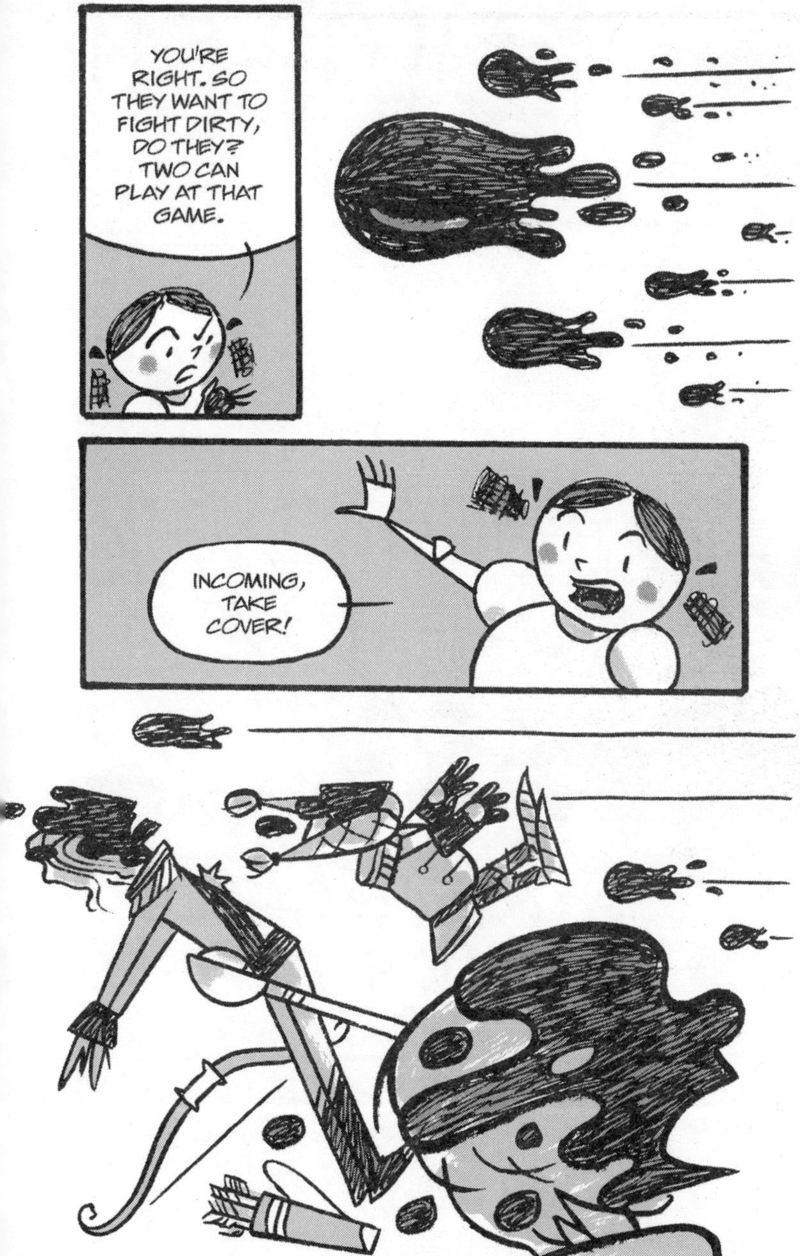
YOU'RE RIGHT. SO THEY WANT TO FIGHT DIRTY, DO THEY? TWO CAN PLAY AT THAT GAME.
INCOMING, TAKE COVER!

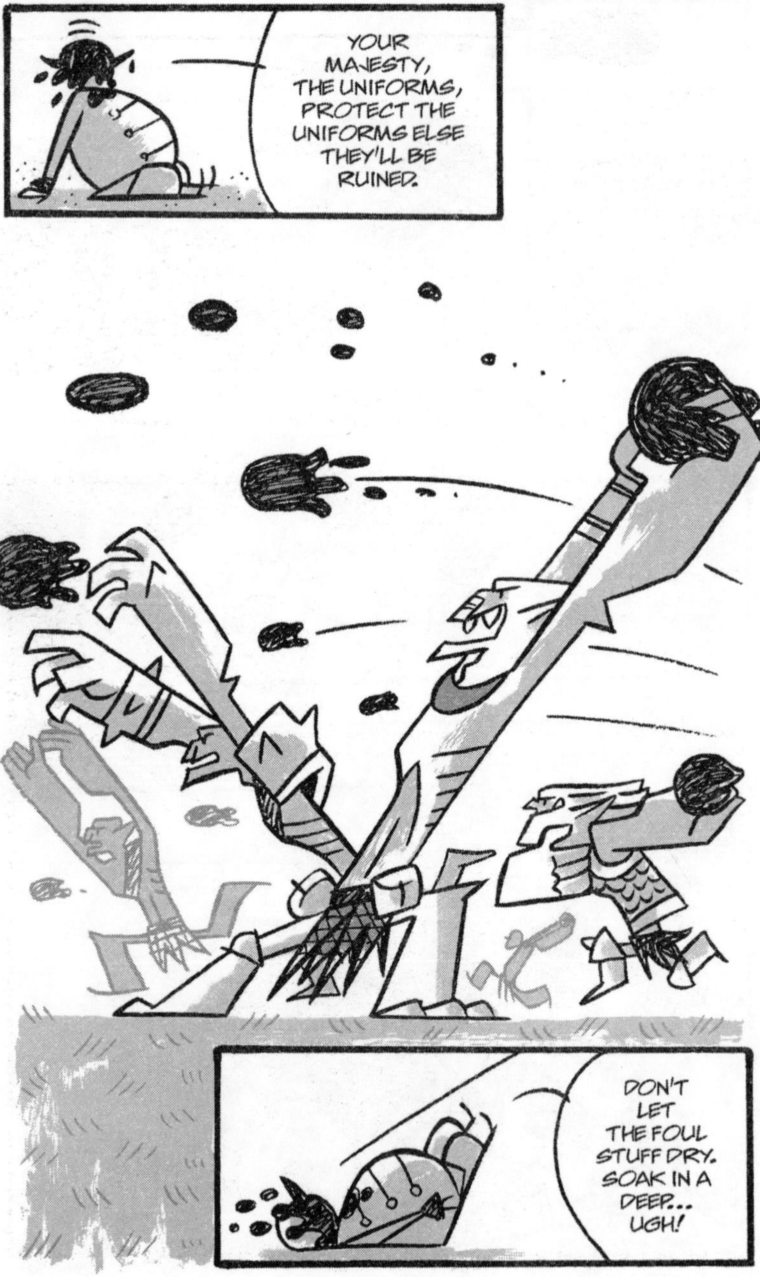
YOUR MAJESTY, THE UNIFORMS, PROTECT THE UNIFORMS ELSE THEY'LL BE RUINED.
DON'T LET THE FOUL STUFF DRY. SOAK IN A DEEP... UGH!

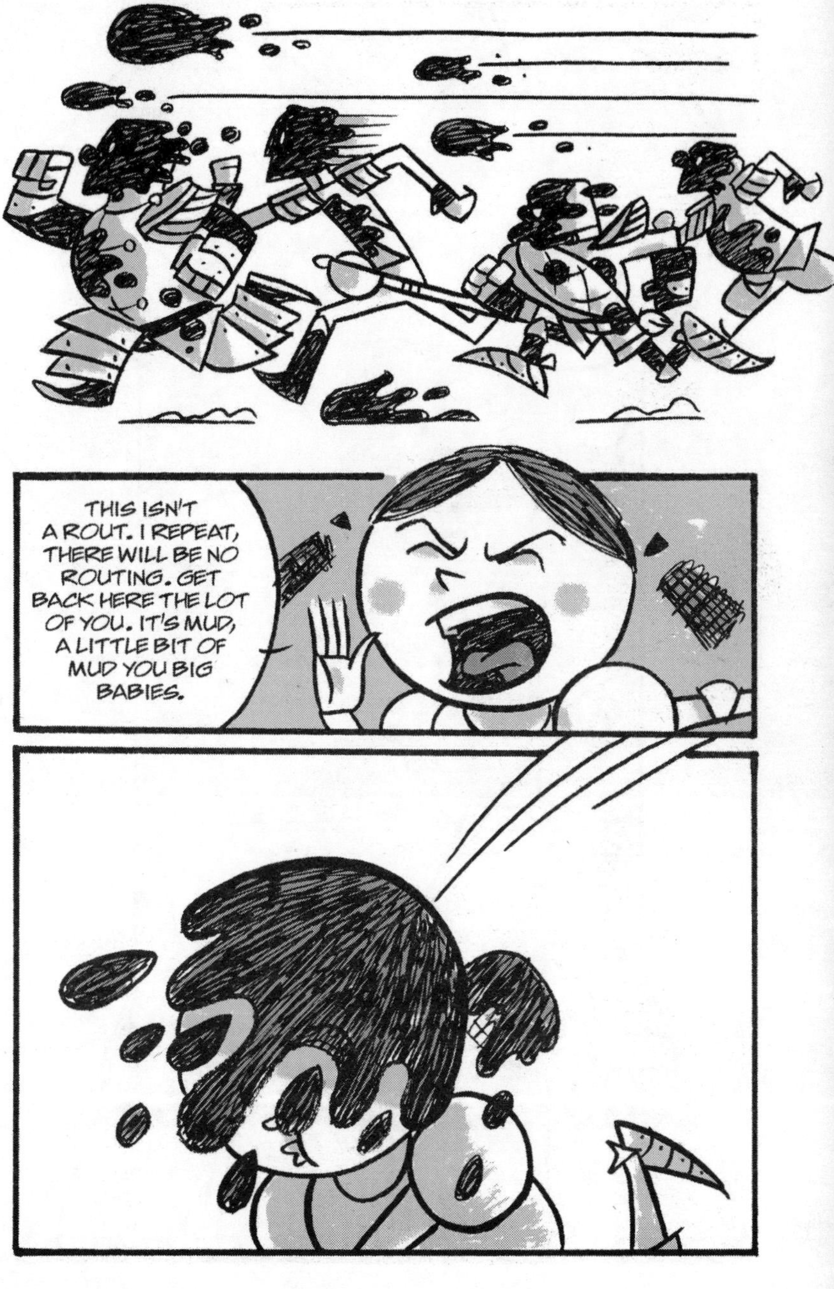
THIS ISN'T A ROUT. I REPEAT, THERE WILL BE NO ROUTING. GET BACK HERE THE LOT OF YOU. IT'S MUD, A LITTLE BIT OF MUD YOU BIG BABIES.

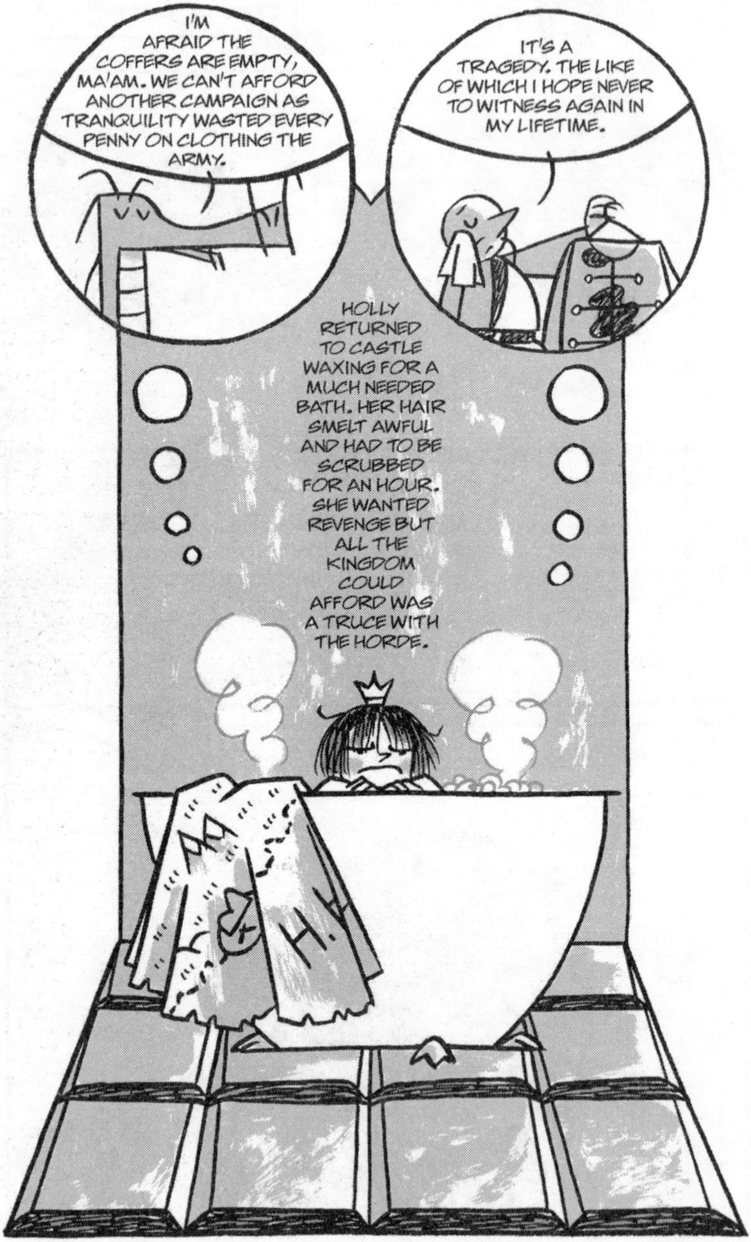
I'M AFRAID THE COFFERS ARE EMPTY, MA'AM. WE CAN'T AFFORD ANOTHER CAMPAIGN AS TRANQUILITY WASTED EVERY PENNY ON CLOTHING THE ARMY.
IT'S A TRAGEDY. THE LIKE OF WHICH I HOPE NEVER TO WITNESS AGAIN IN MY LIFETIME.
HOLLY RETURNED TO CASTLE WAXING FOR A MUCH NEEDED BATH. HER HAIR SMELT AWFUL AND HAD TO BE SCRUBBED FOR AN HOUR. SHE WANTED REVENGE BUT ALL THE KINGDOM COULD AFFORD WAS A TRUCE WITH THE HORDE.

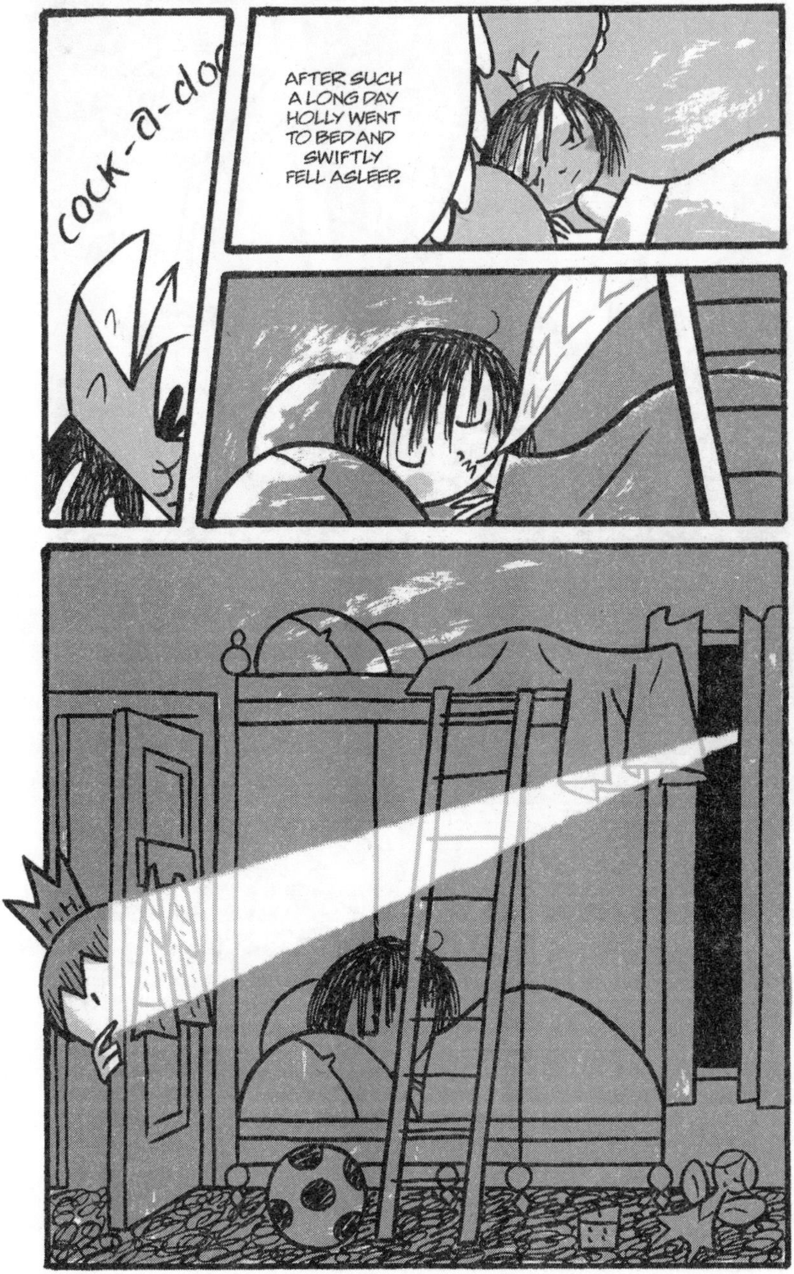
cock-a-doo
AFTER SUCH A LONG DAY HOLLY WENT TO BED AND SWIFTLY FELL ASLEEP.
H.H.

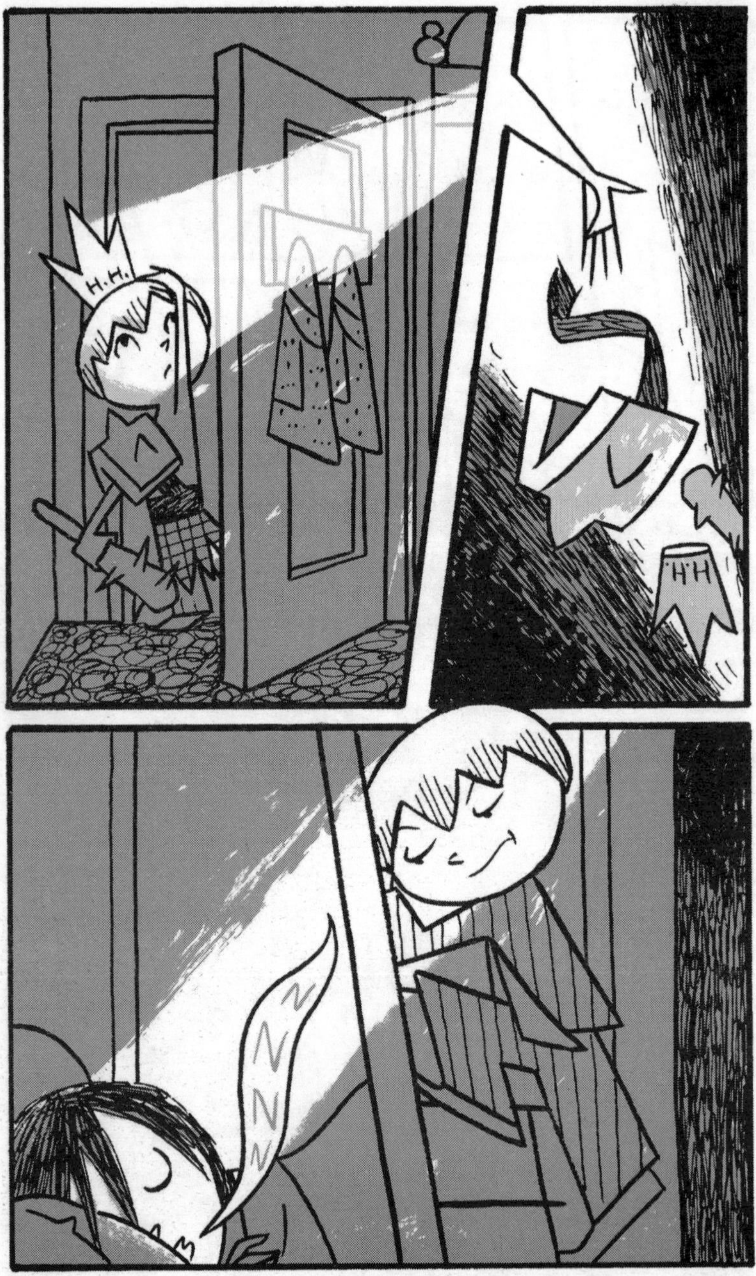
H.H.
H H

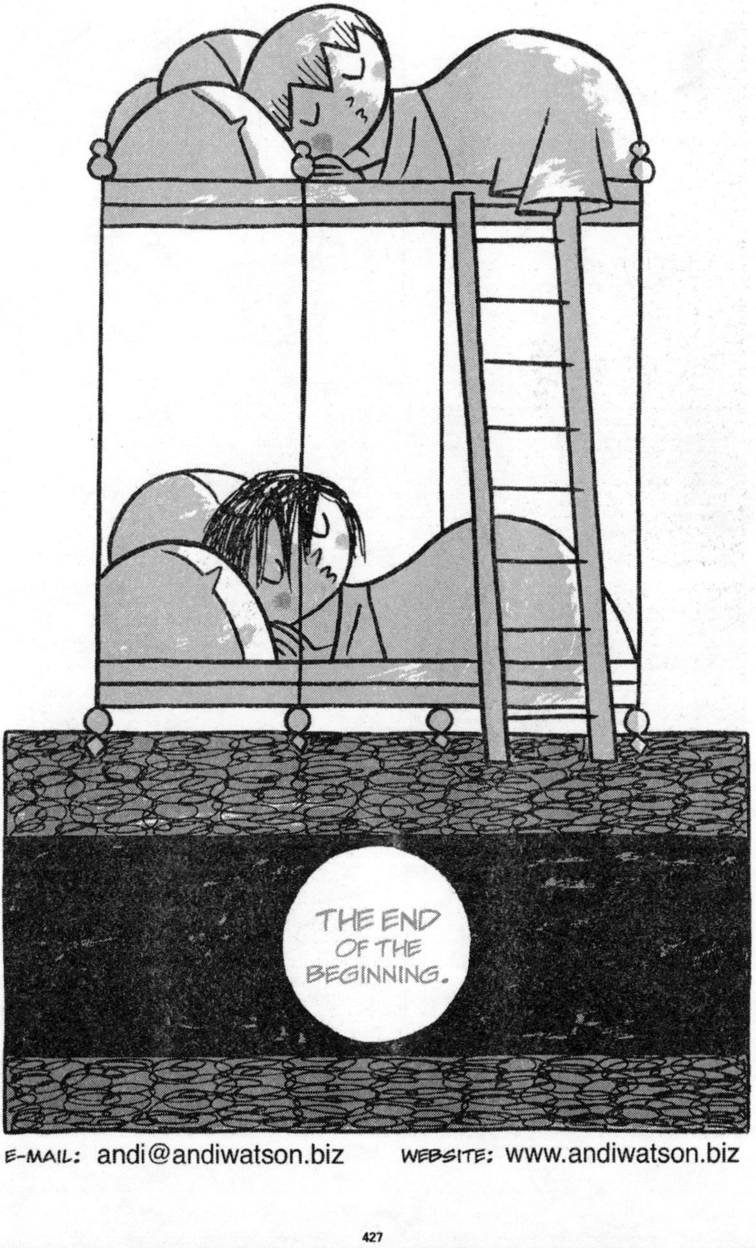
THE END
OF THE
BEGINNING.

E-MAIL: andi@andiwatson.biz WEBSITE: www.andiwatson.biz

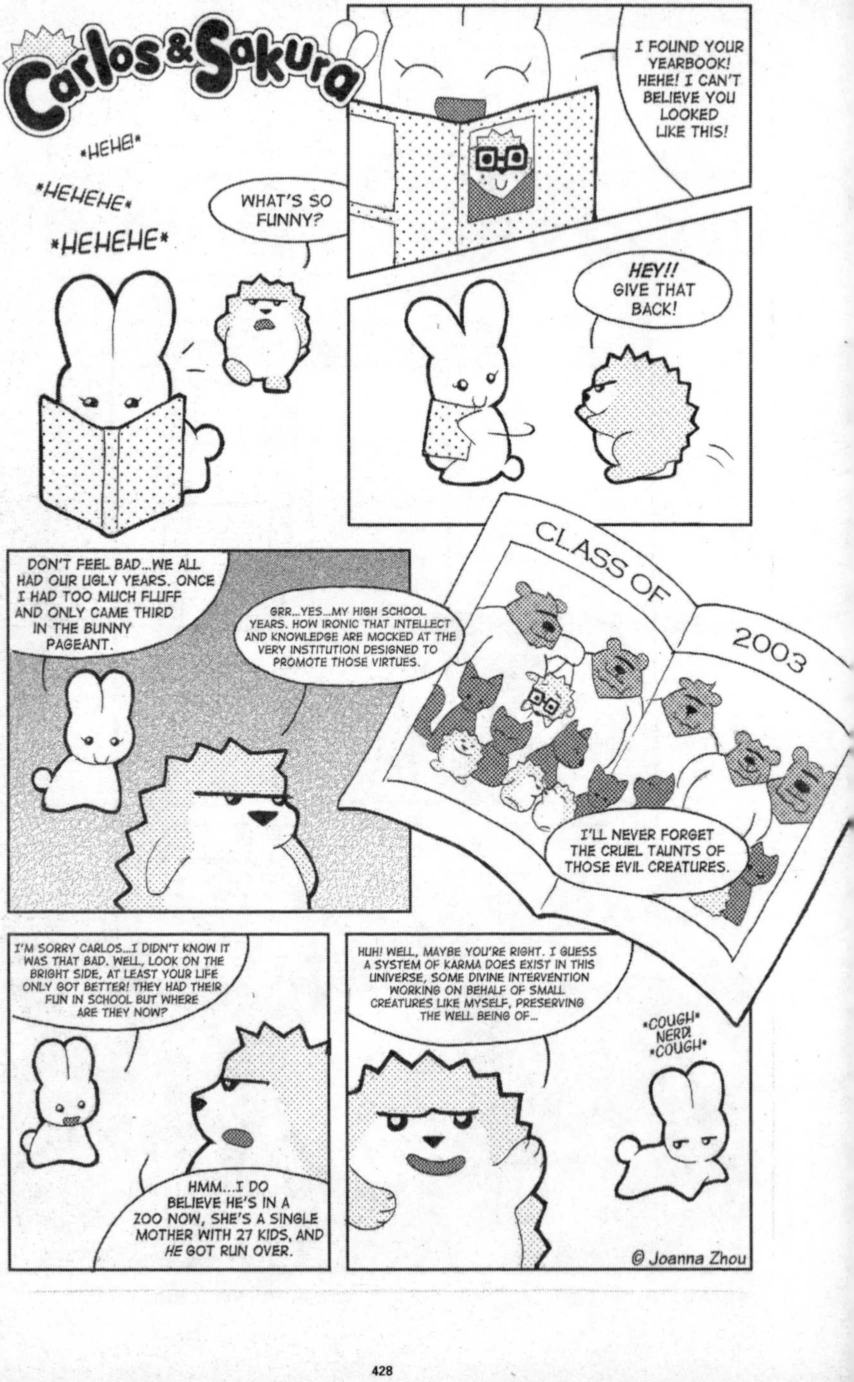
Carlos & Sakura
HEHE!
HEHEHE
HEHEHE
WHAT'S SO FUNNY?
I FOUND YOUR YEARBOOK! HEHE! I CAN'T BELIEVE YOU LOOKED LIKE THIS!
HEY!! GIVE THAT BACK!
DON'T FEEL BAD...WE ALL HAD OUR UGLY YEARS. ONCE I HAD TOO MUCH FLUFF AND ONLY CAME THIRD IN THE BUNNY PAGEANT.
GRR...YES...MY HIGH SCHOOL YEARS. HOW IRONIC THAT INTELLECT AND KNOWLEDGE ARE MOCKED AT THE VERY INSTITUTION DESIGNED TO PROMOTE THOSE VIRTUES.
CLASS OF 2003
I'LL NEVER FORGET THE CRUEL TAUNTS OF THOSE EVIL CREATURES.
I'M SORRY CARLOS...I DIDN'T KNOW IT WAS THAT BAD. WELL, LOOK ON THE BRIGHT SIDE, AT LEAST YOUR LIFE ONLY GOT BETTER! THEY HAD THEIR FUN IN SCHOOL BUT WHERE ARE THEY NOW?
HMM...I DO BELIEVE HE'S IN A ZOO NOW, SHE'S A SINGLE MOTHER WITH 27 KIDS, AND HE GOT RUN OVER.
HUH! WELL, MAYBE YOU'RE RIGHT. I GUESS A SYSTEM OF KARMA DOES EXIST IN THIS UNIVERSE, SOME DIVINE INTERVENTION WORKING ON BEHALF OF SMALL CREATURES LIKE MYSELF, PRESERVING THE WELL BEING OF...
COUGH NERD! *COUGH*
© Joanna Zhou

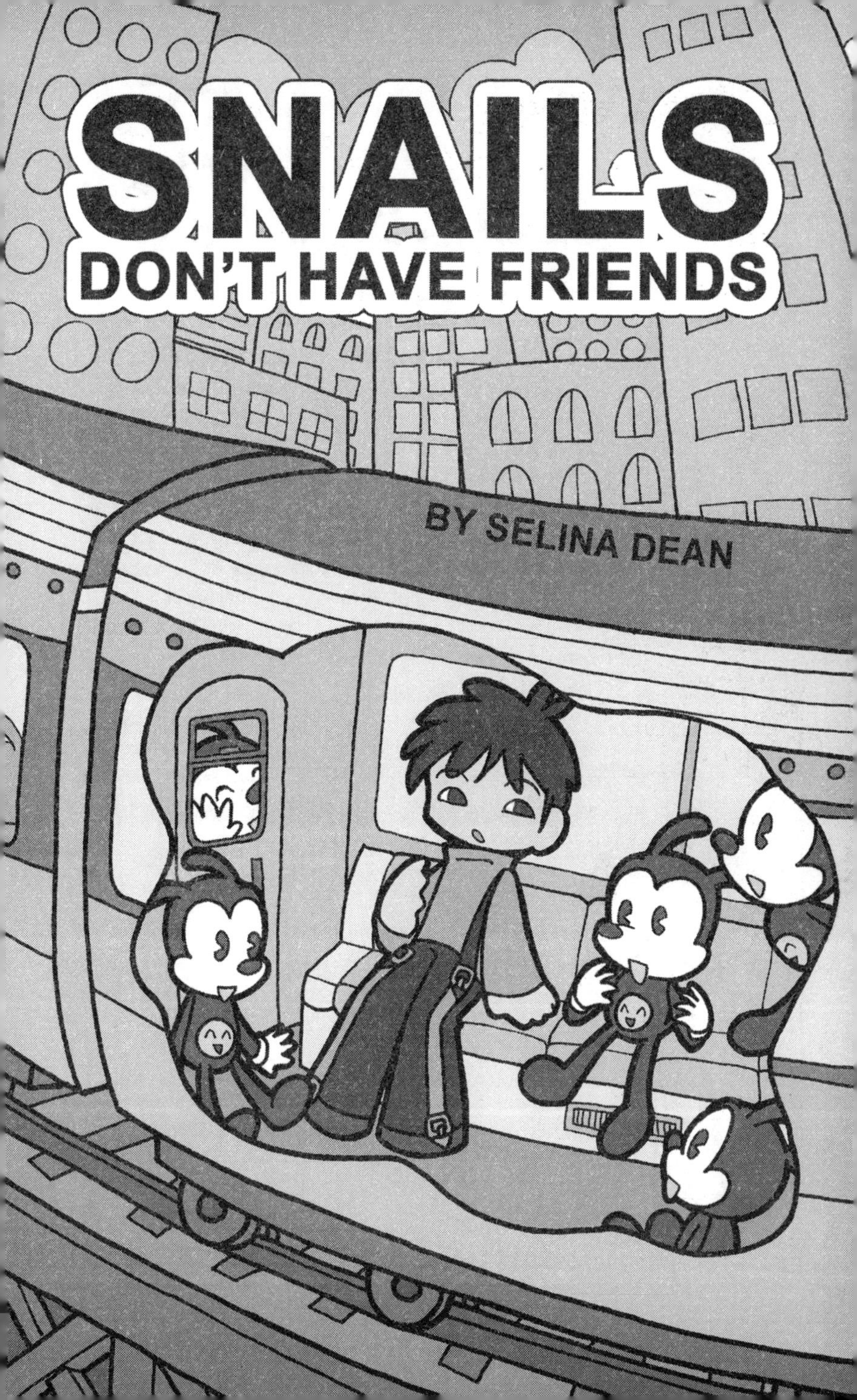

SNAILS
DON'T HAVE FRIENDS
BY SELINA DEAN

Date of birth: 4 June 1982

SELINA DEAN

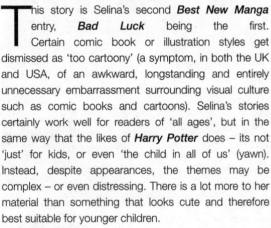

This story is Selina's second **Best New Manga** entry, **Bad Luck** being the first. Certain comic book or illustration styles get dismissed as 'too cartoony' (a symptom, in both the UK and USA, of an awkward, longstanding and entirely unnecessary embarrassment surrounding visual culture such as comic books and cartoons). Selina's stories certainly work well for readers of 'all ages', but in the same way that the likes of **Harry Potter** does – its not 'just' for kids, or even 'the child in all of us' (yawn). Instead, despite appearances, the themes may be complex – or even distressing. There is a lot more to her material than something that looks cute and therefore best suitable for younger children.

Selina has one of the most original styles around. As long as other folks can get beyond the limits of their own preconceptions, we predict a very bright comic-book future indeed for this prolific and talented young cartoonist.

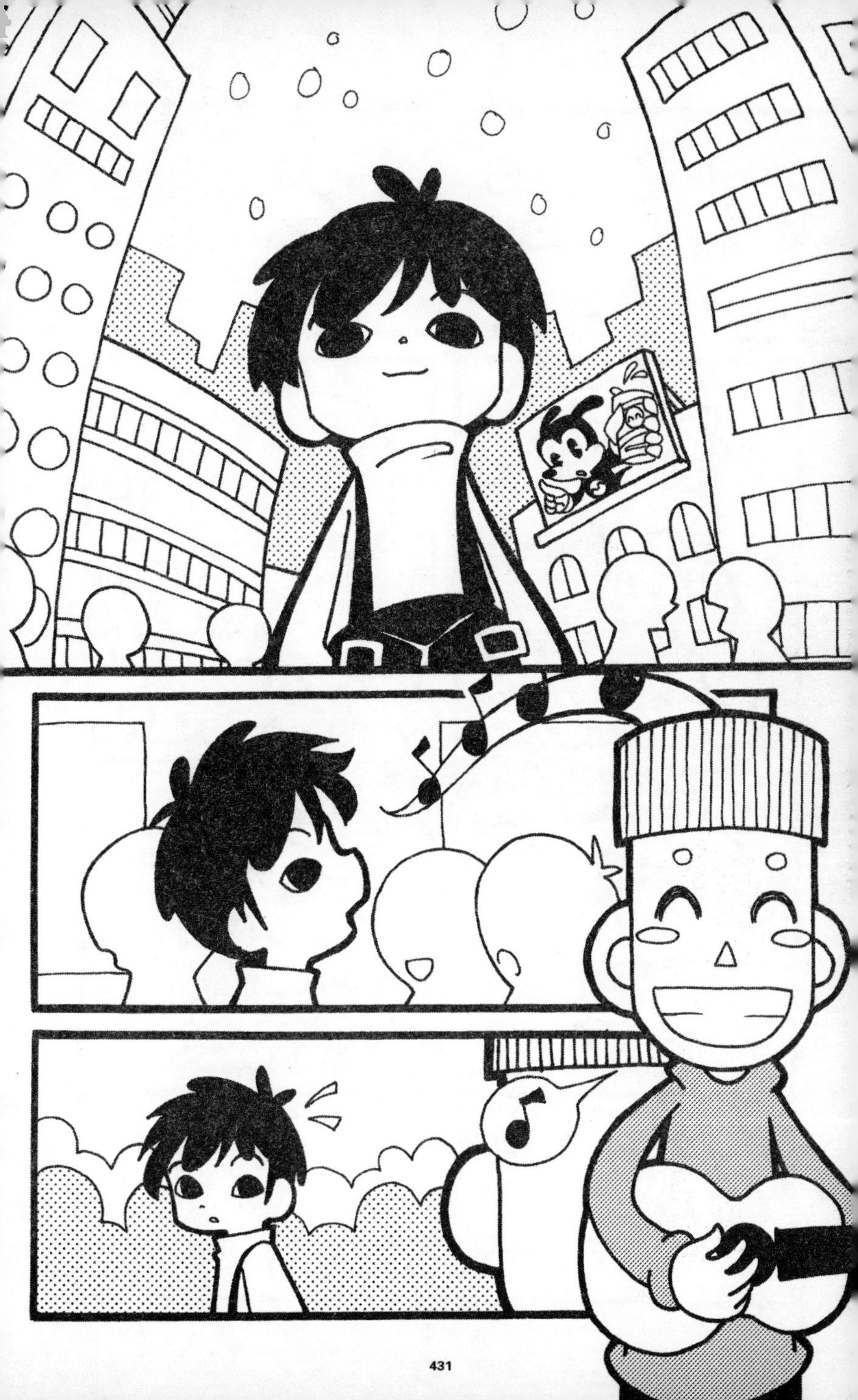

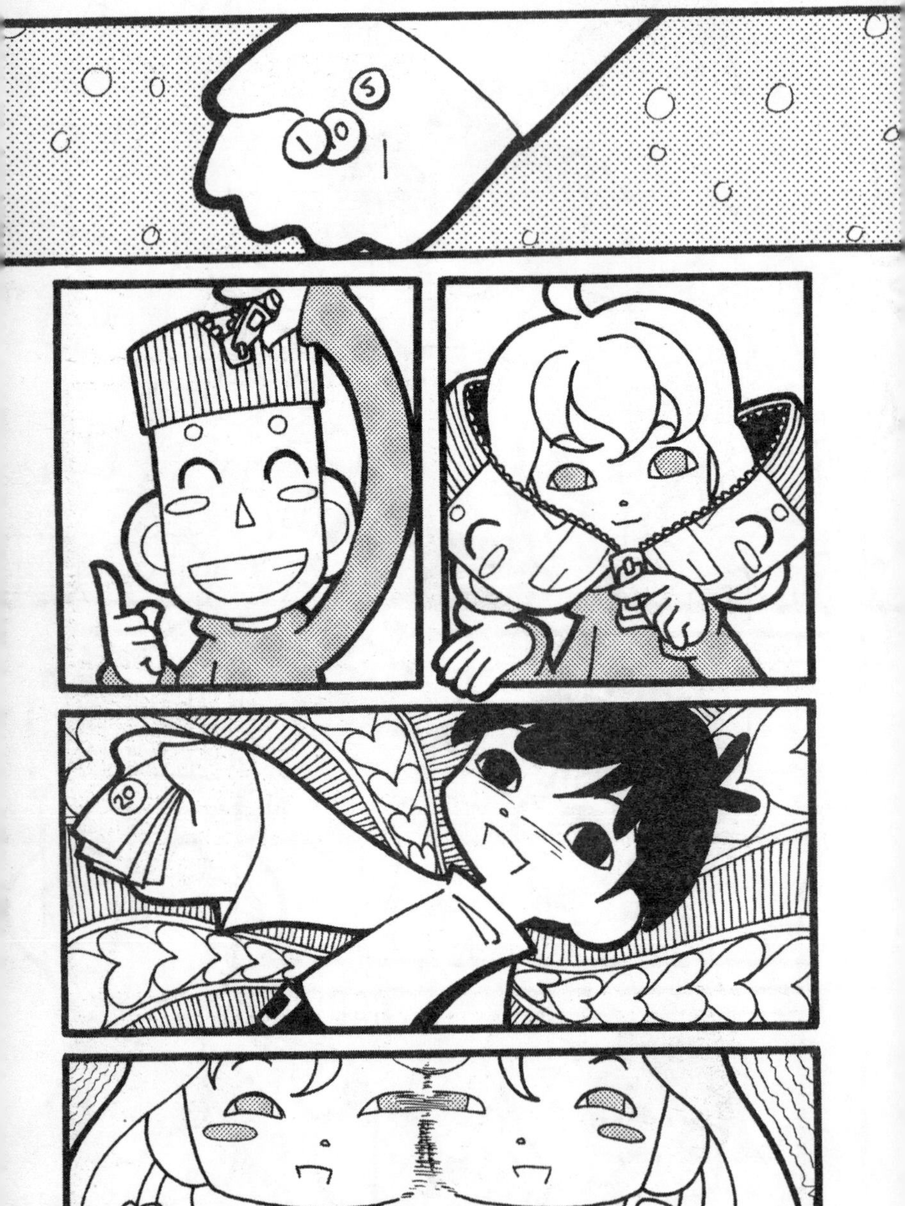

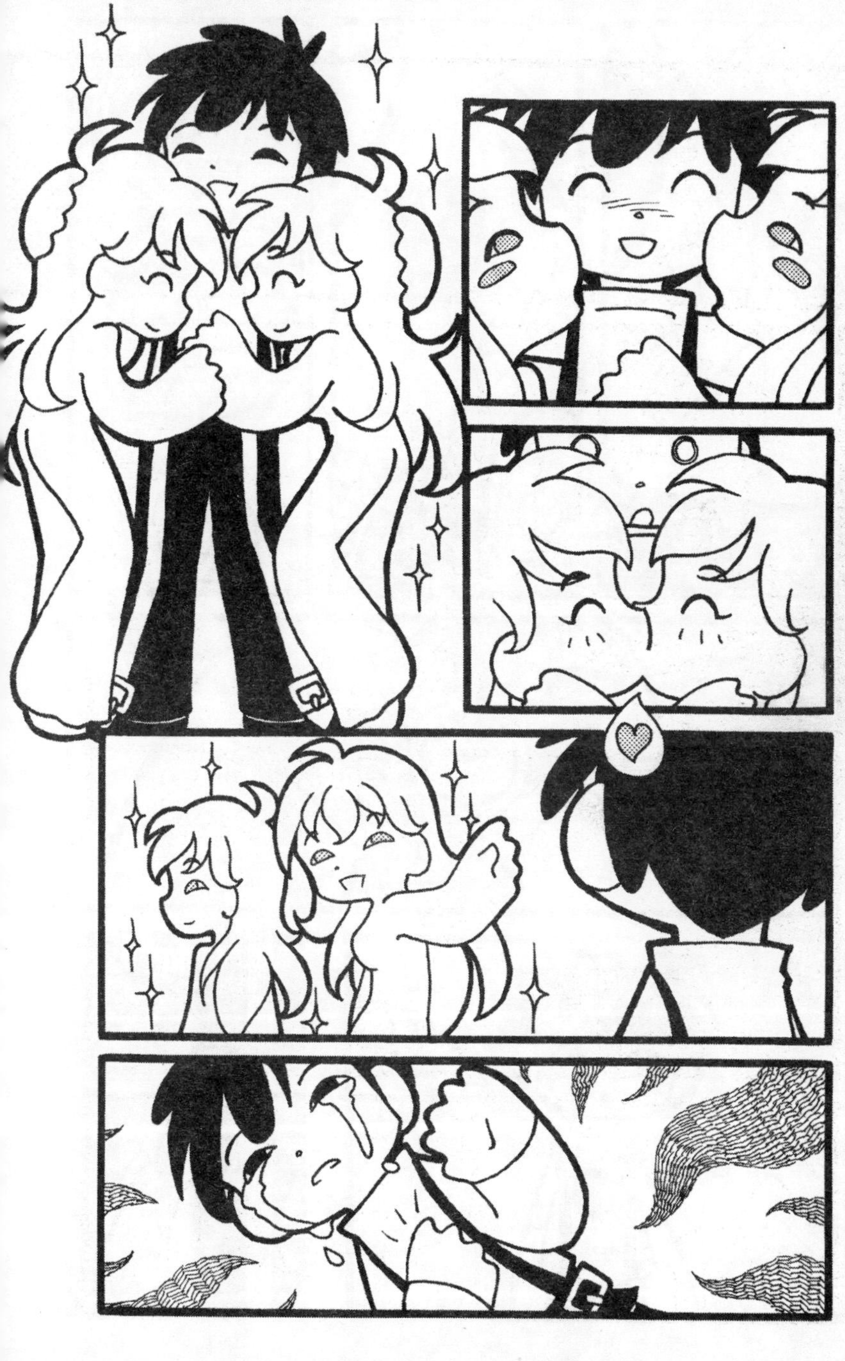

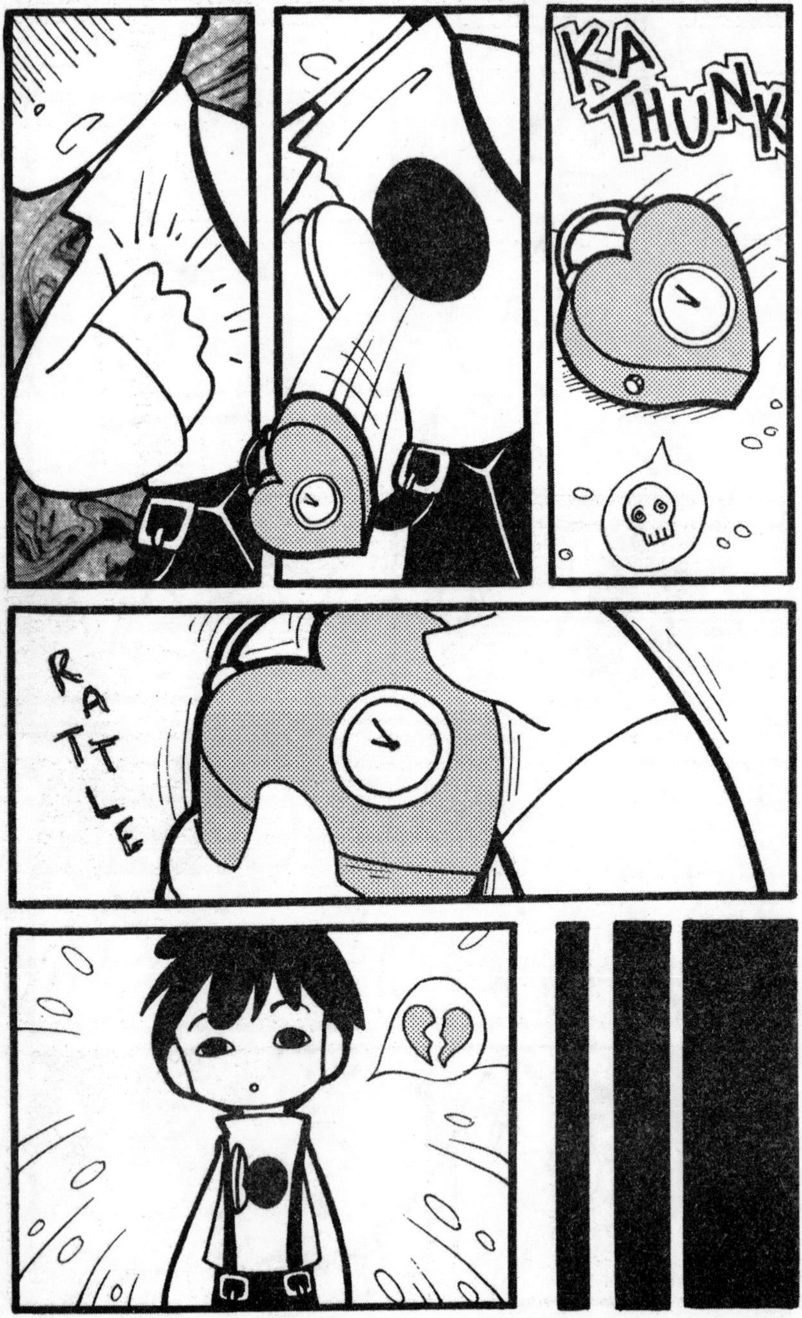
KA THUNK
RATTLE

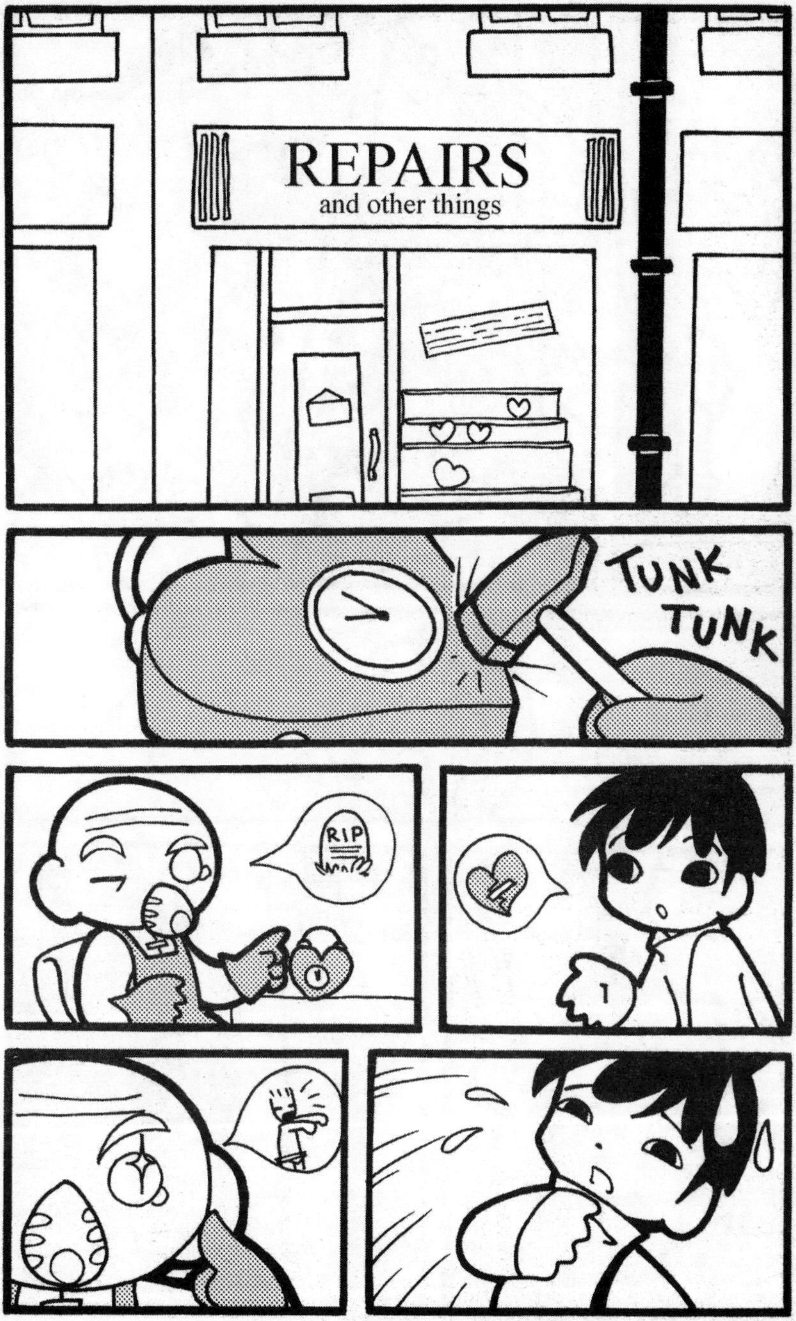
REPAIRS
and other things
TUNK
TUNK
RIP

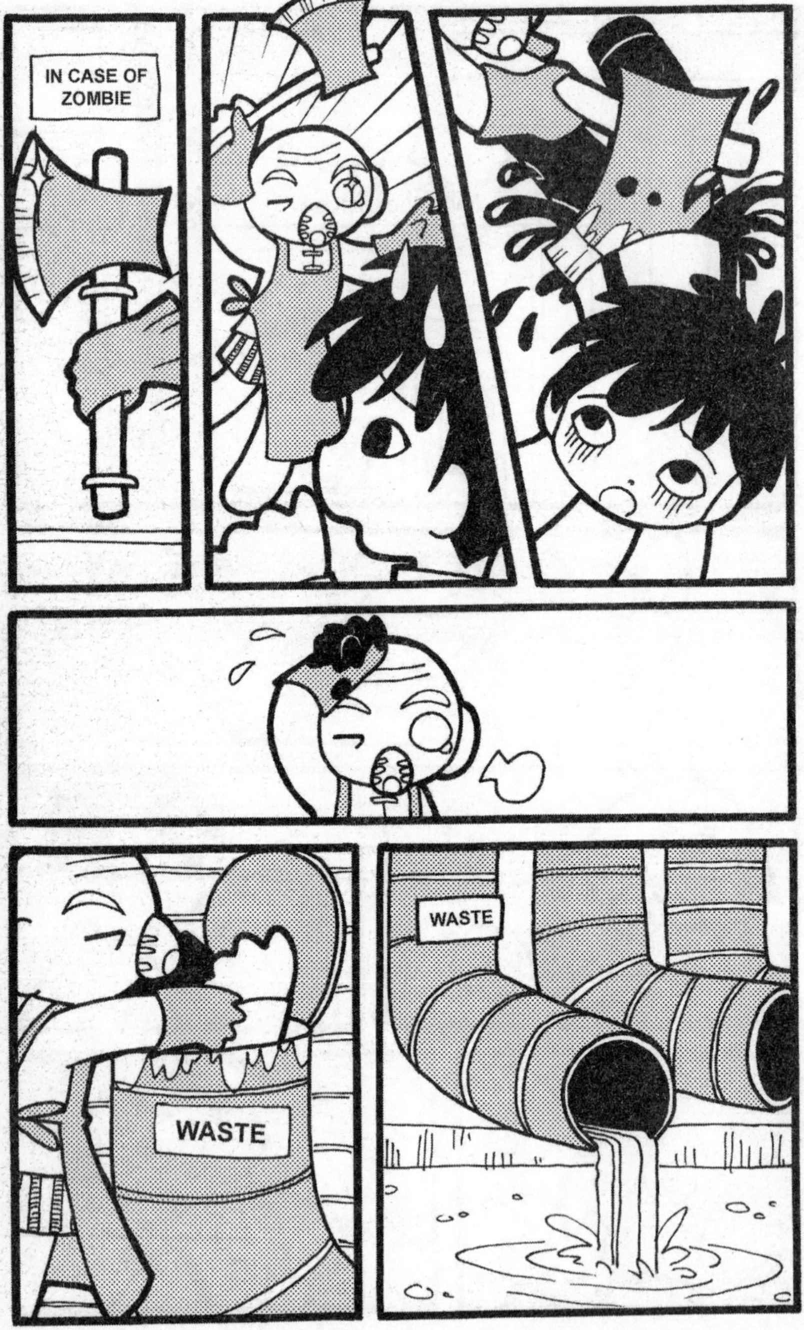
IN CASE OF ZOMBIE
WASTE
WASTE

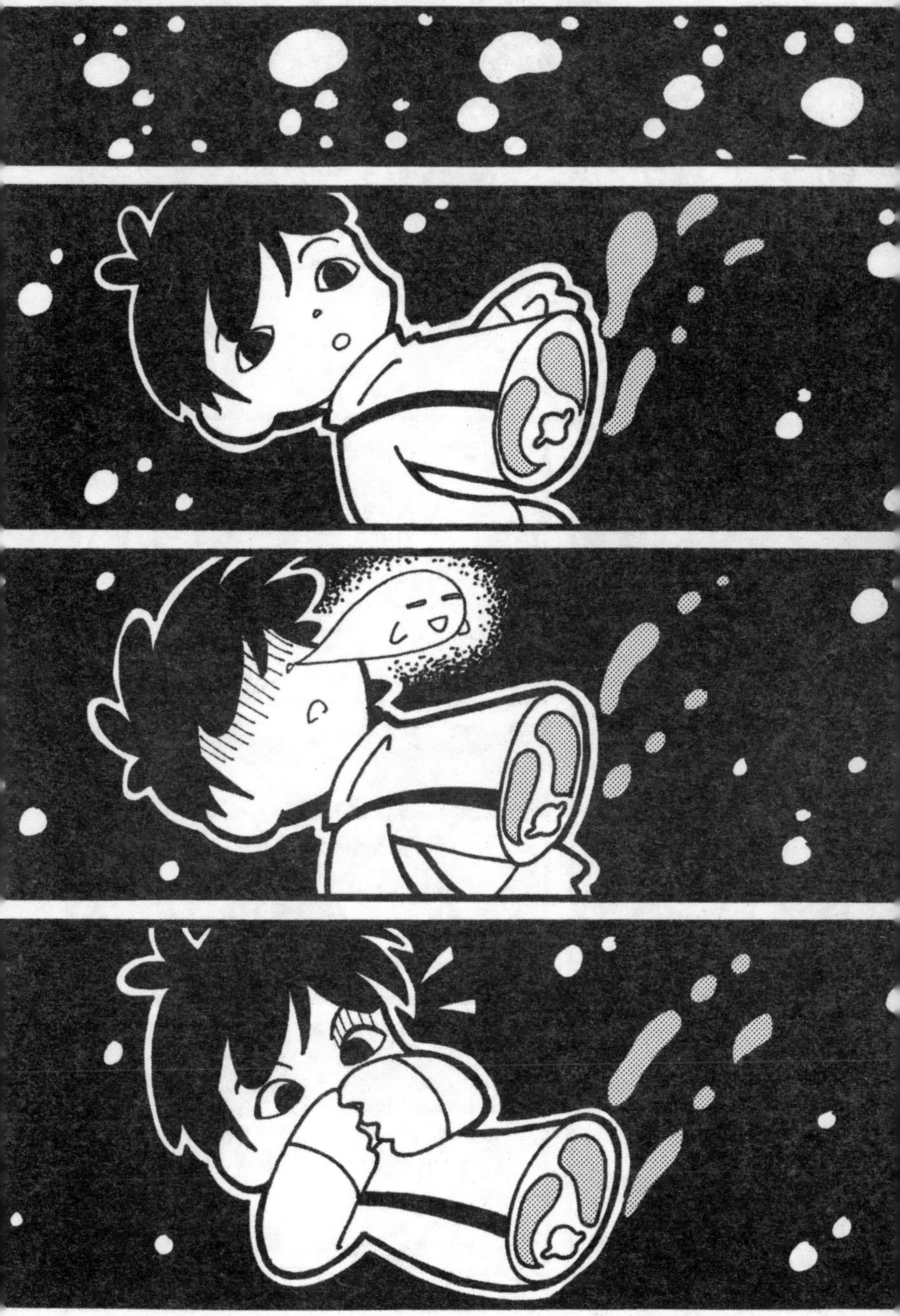

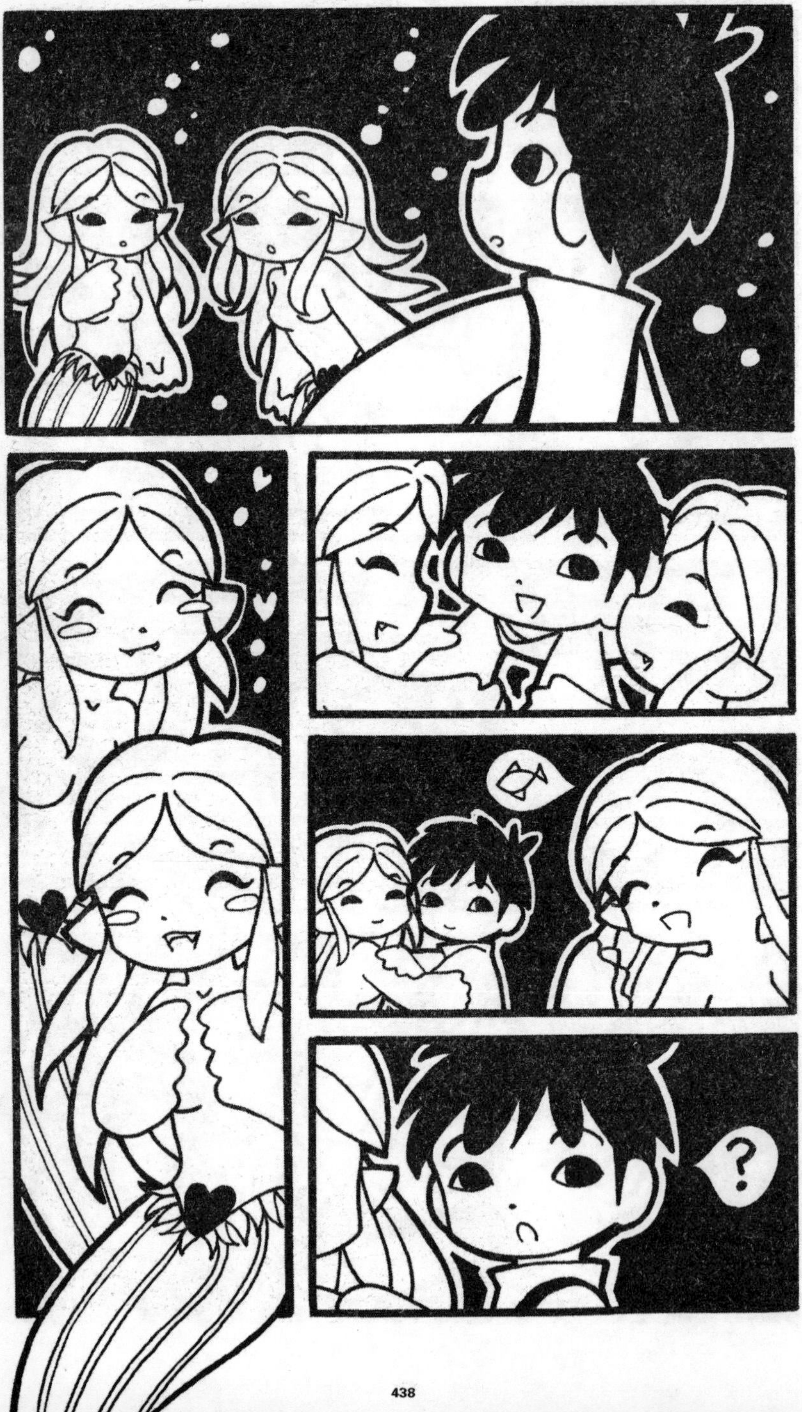
?

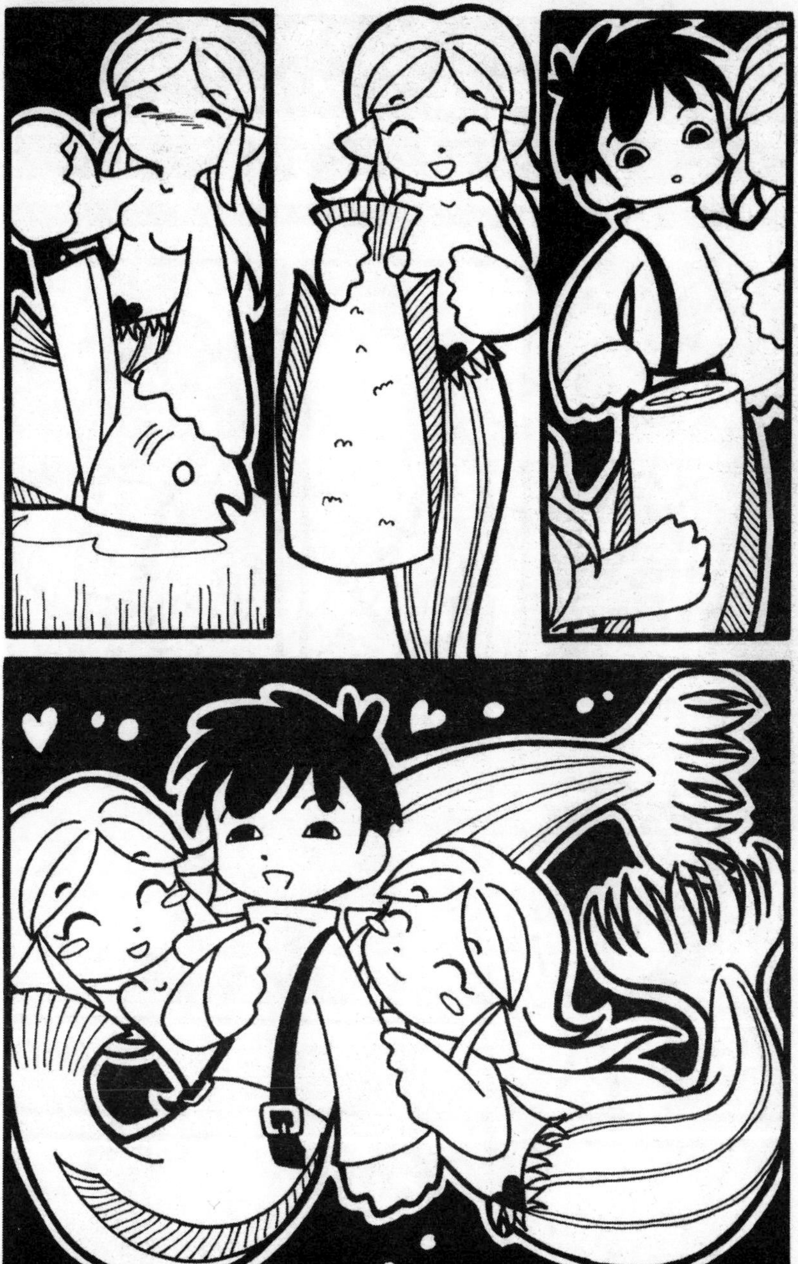

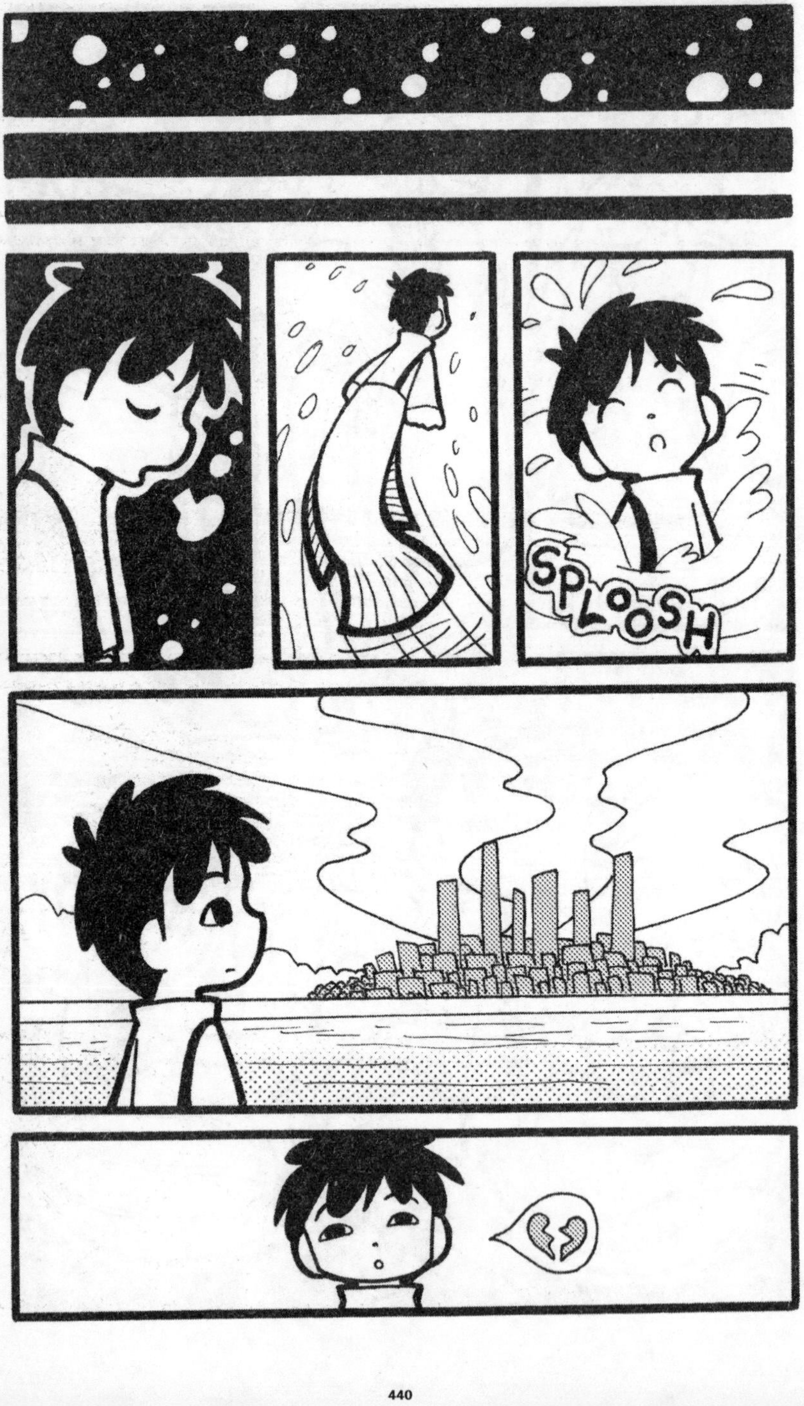
SPLOOSH

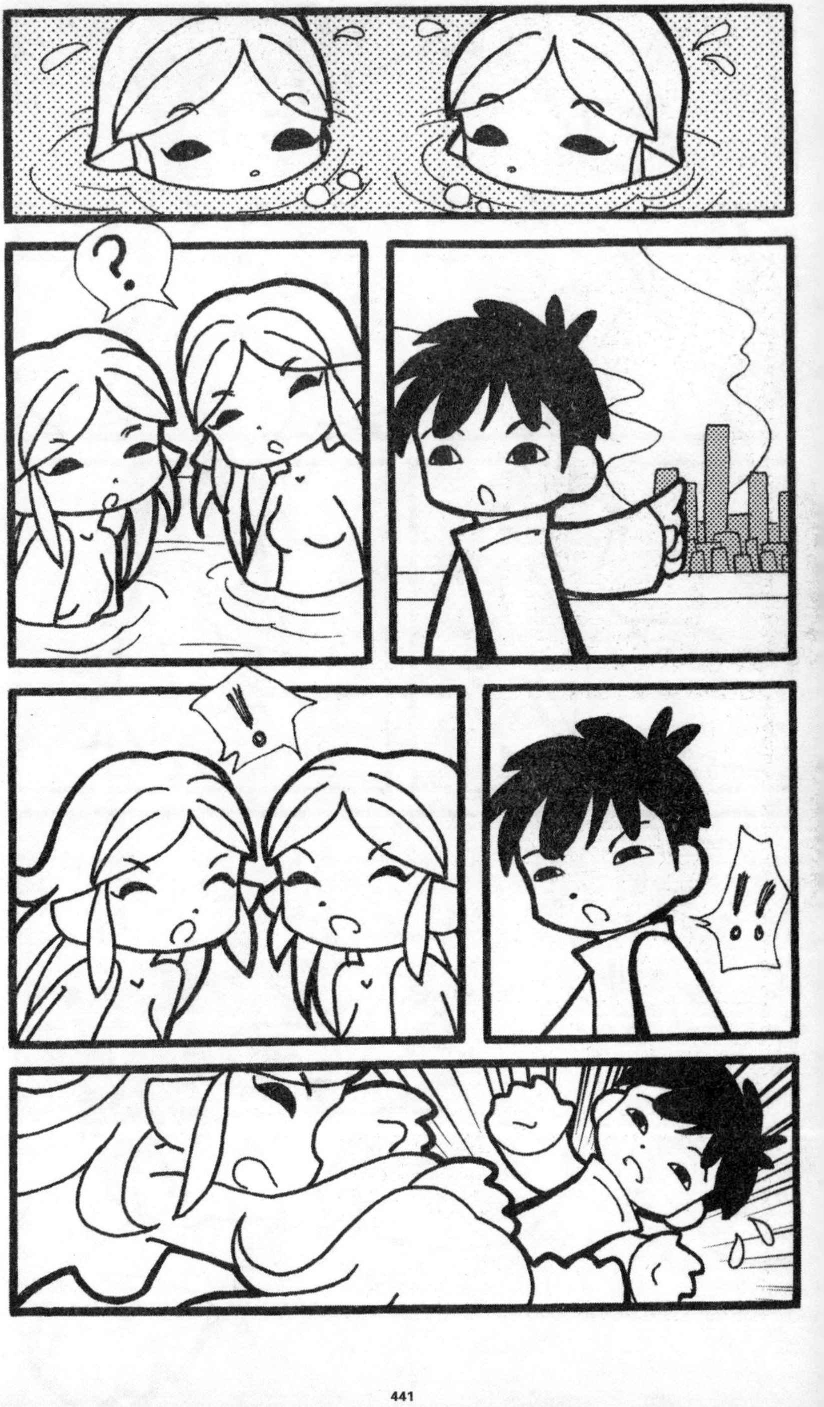
?
!
!!

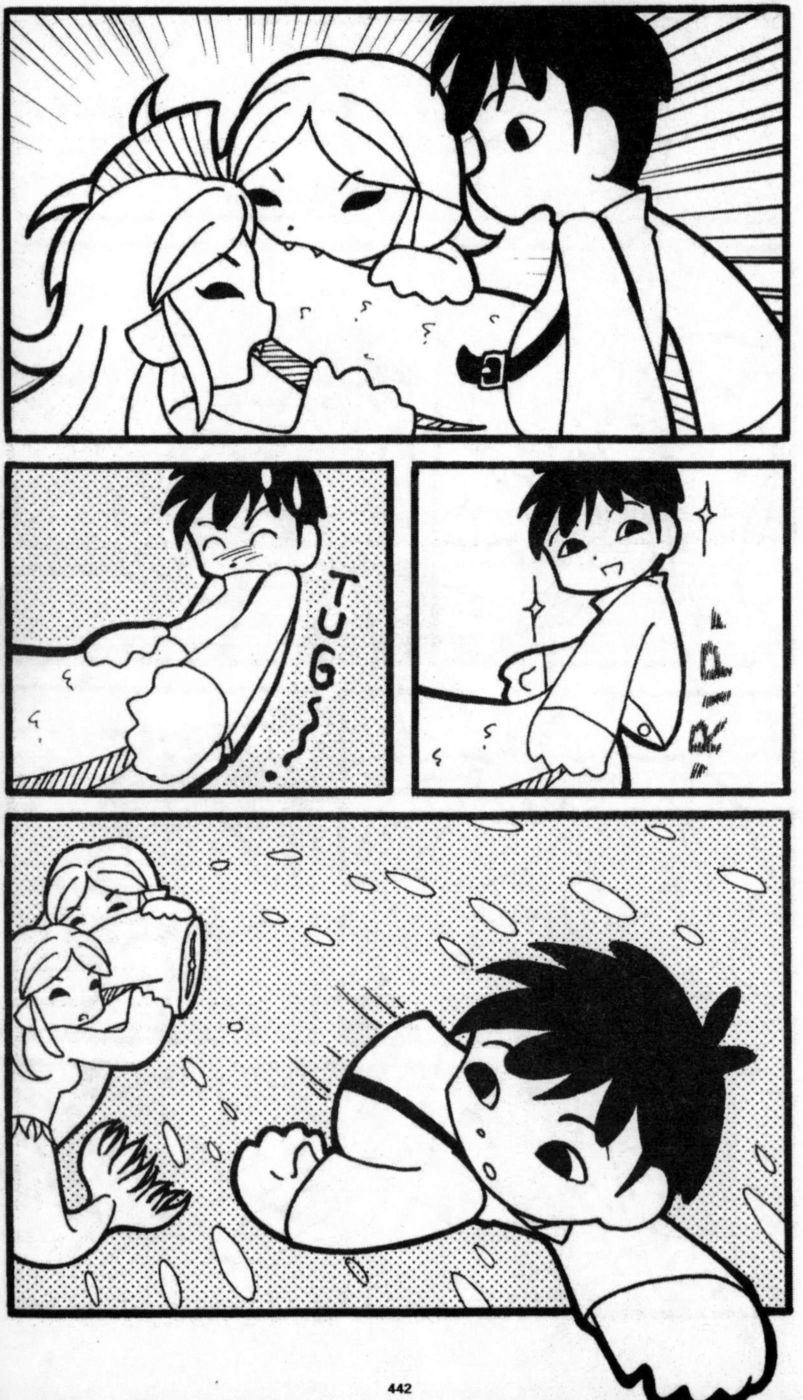
TUG
RIP!

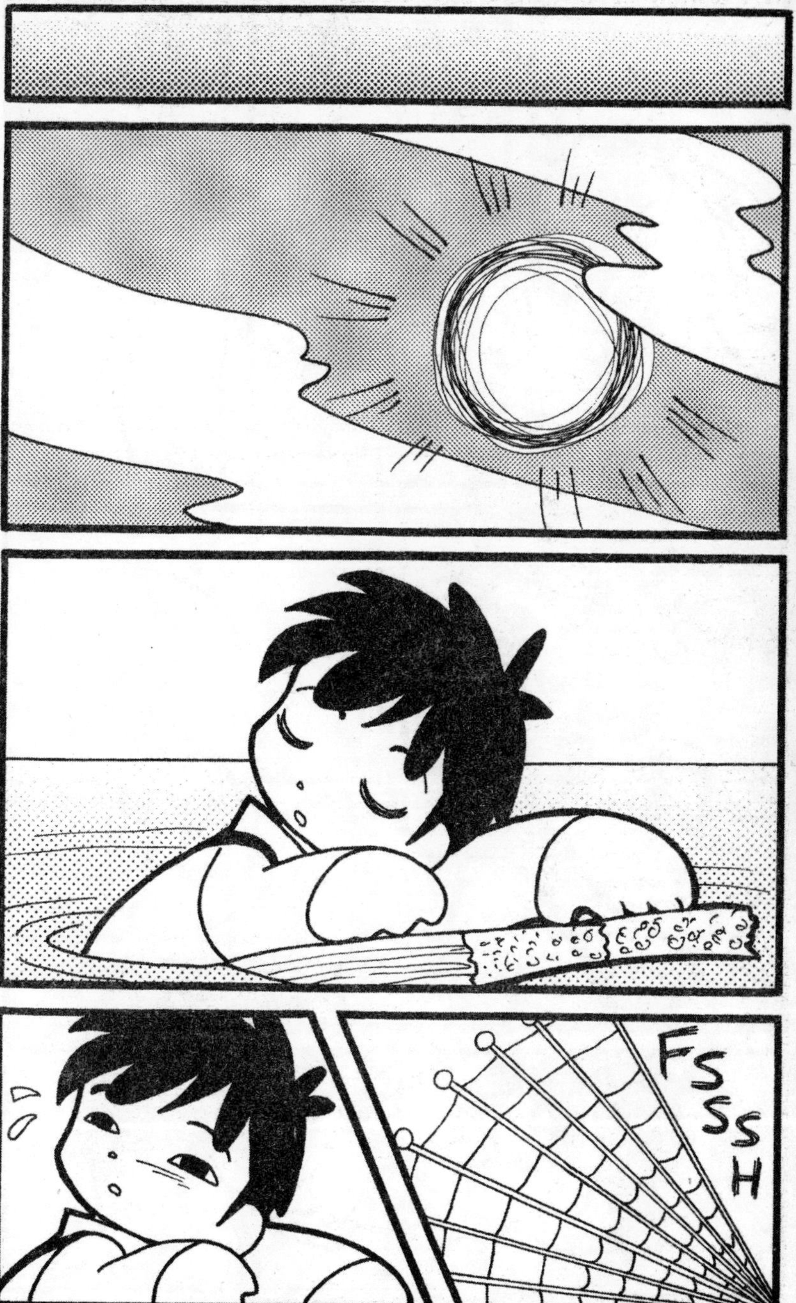
FSSSH

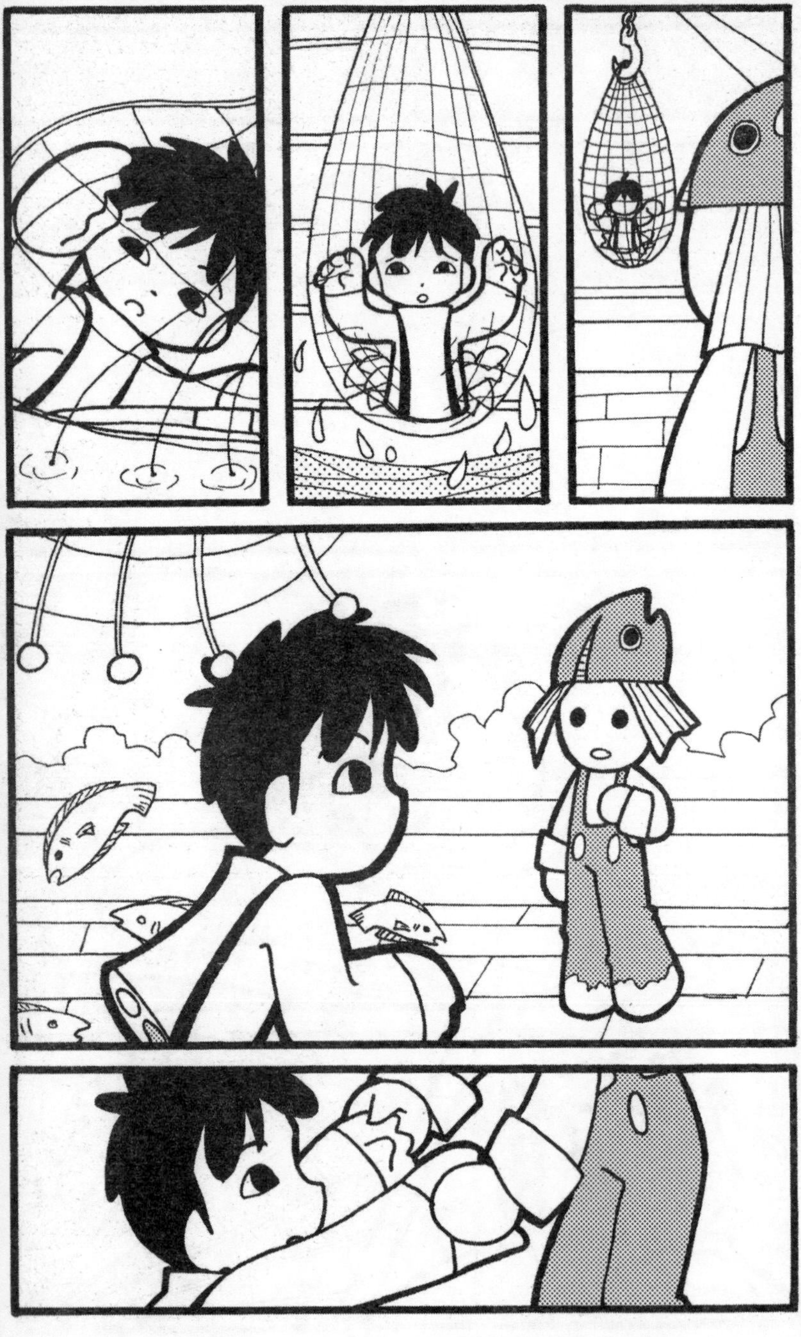

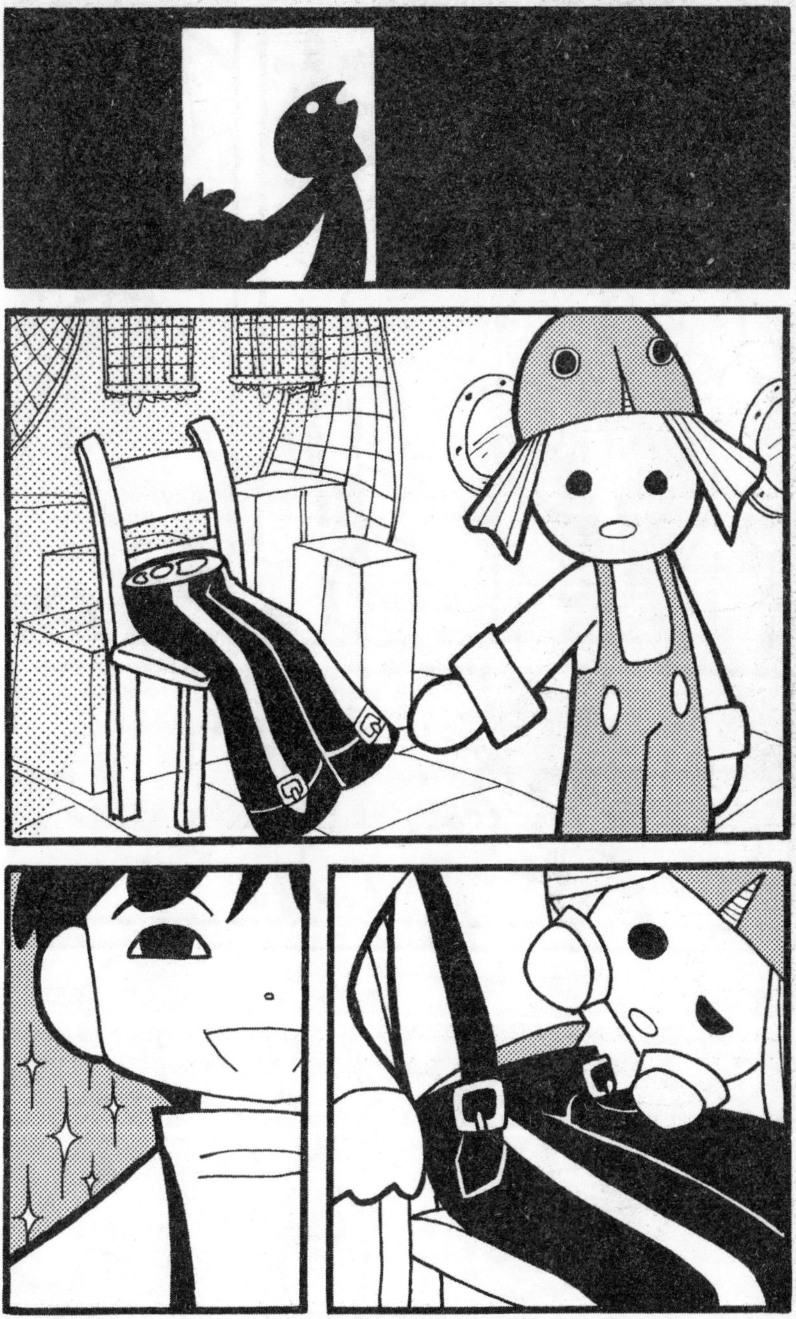

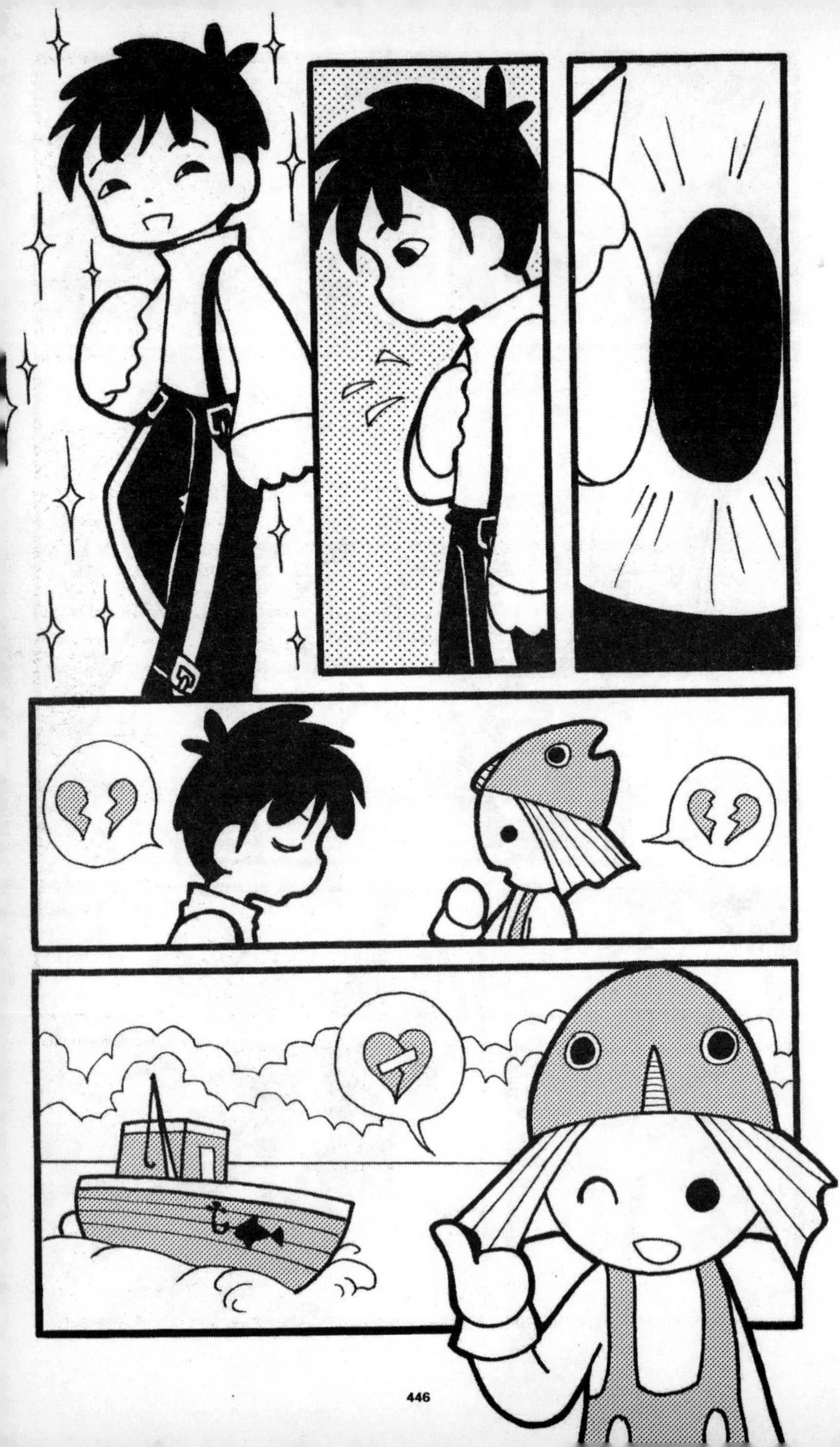

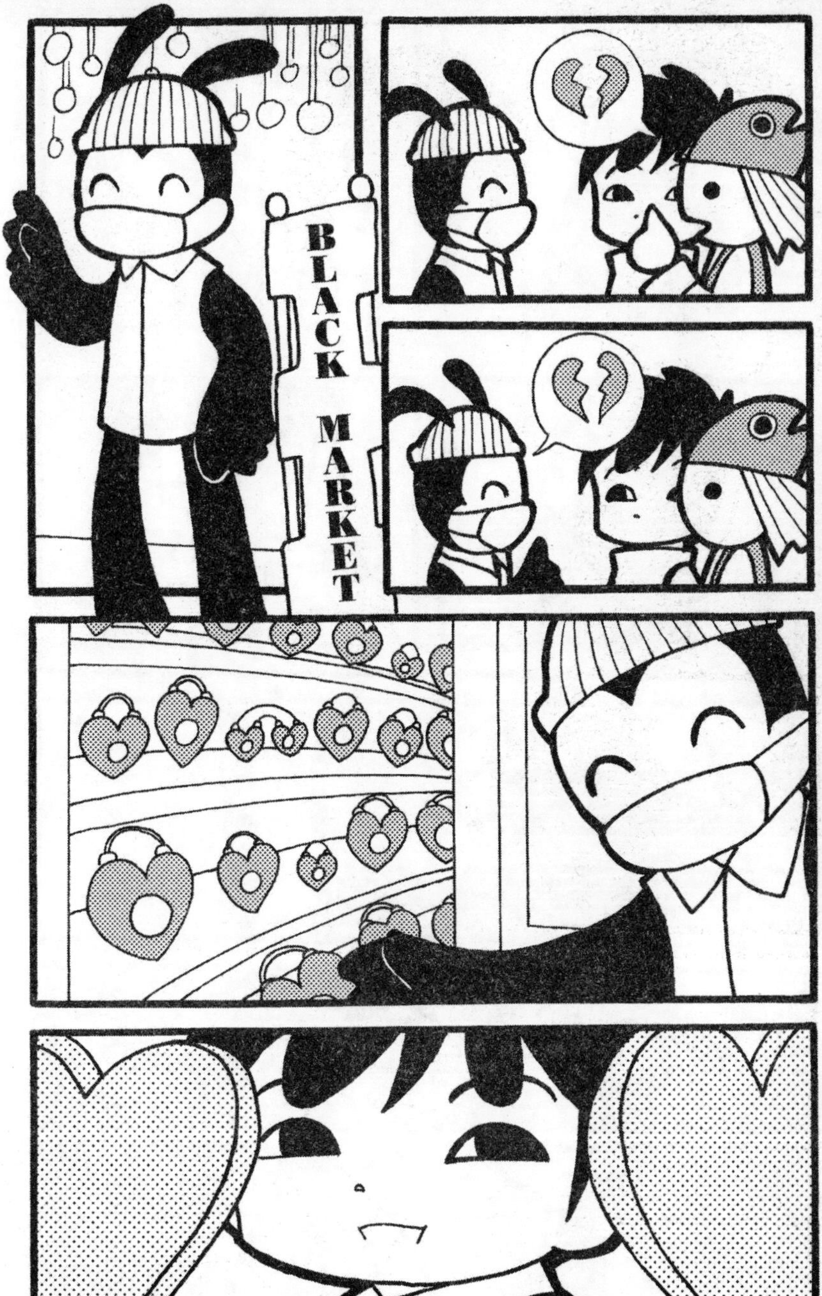
BLACK MARKET

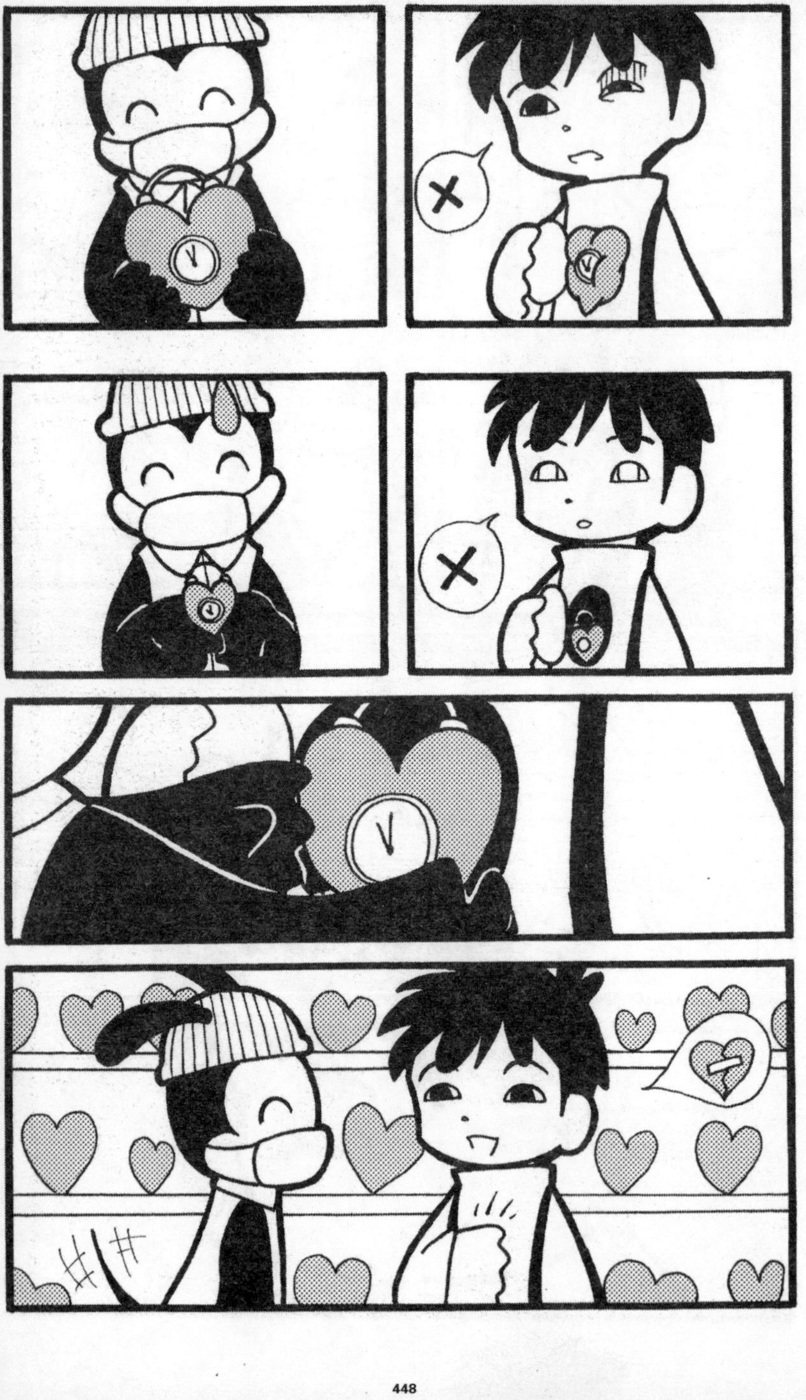

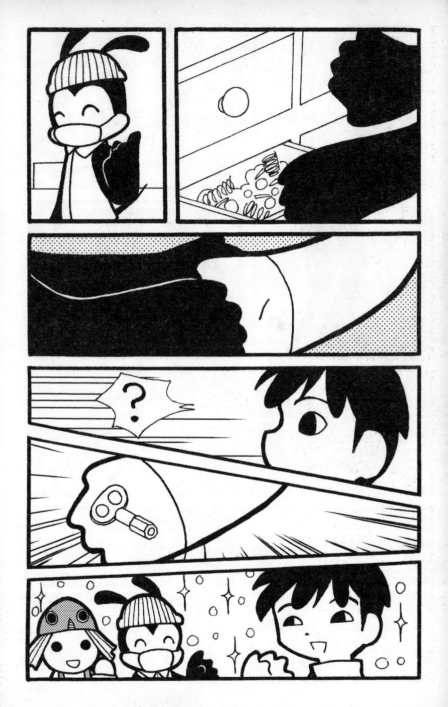

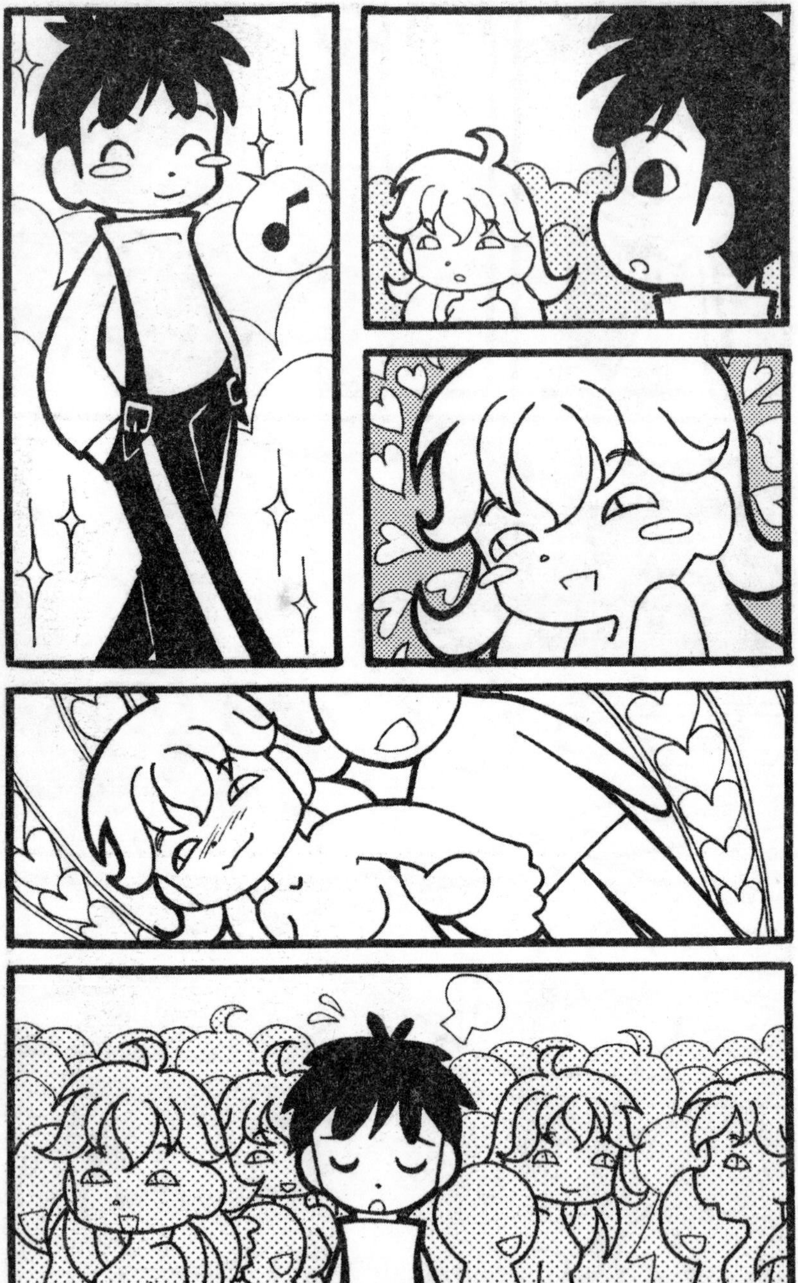

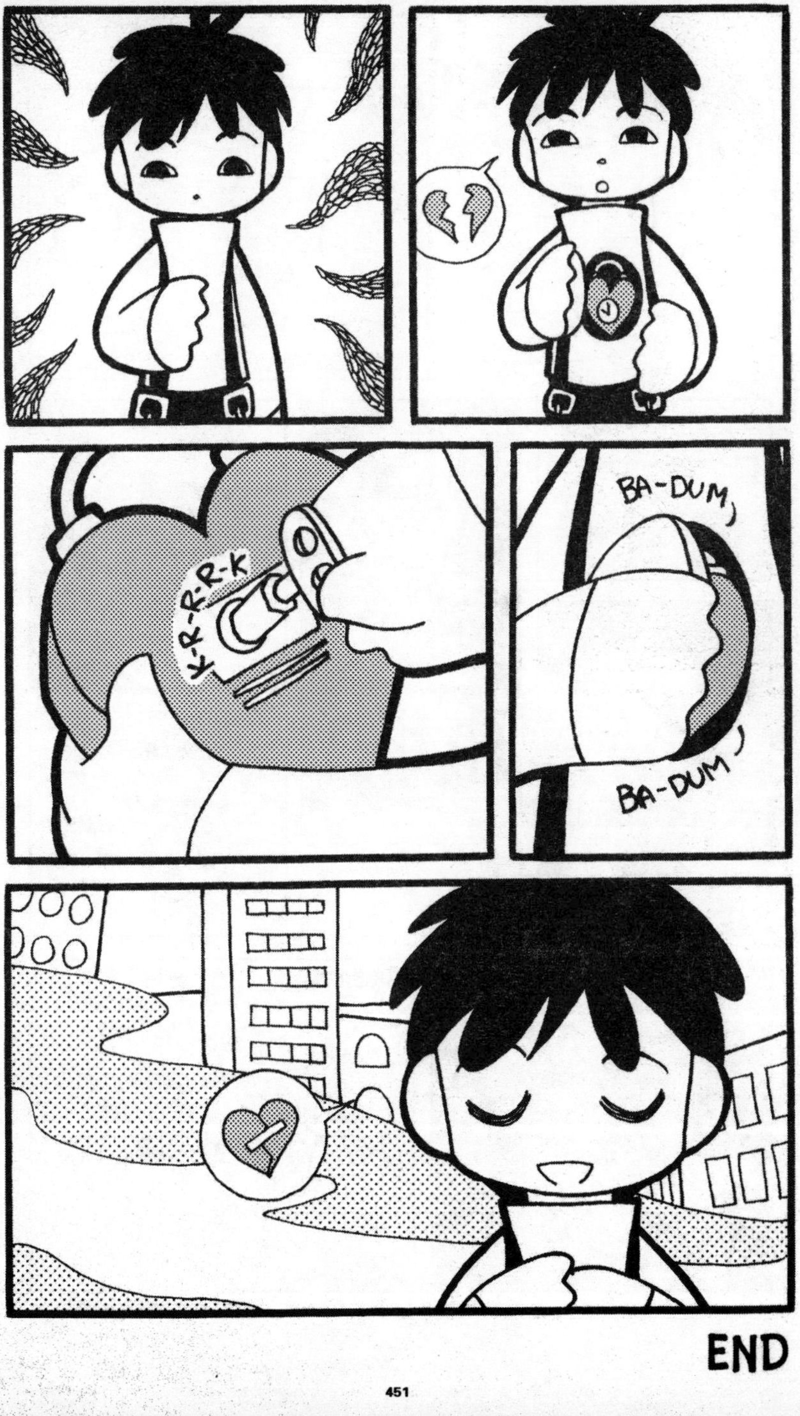
K-R-R-R-K
BA-DUM
BA-DUM

END

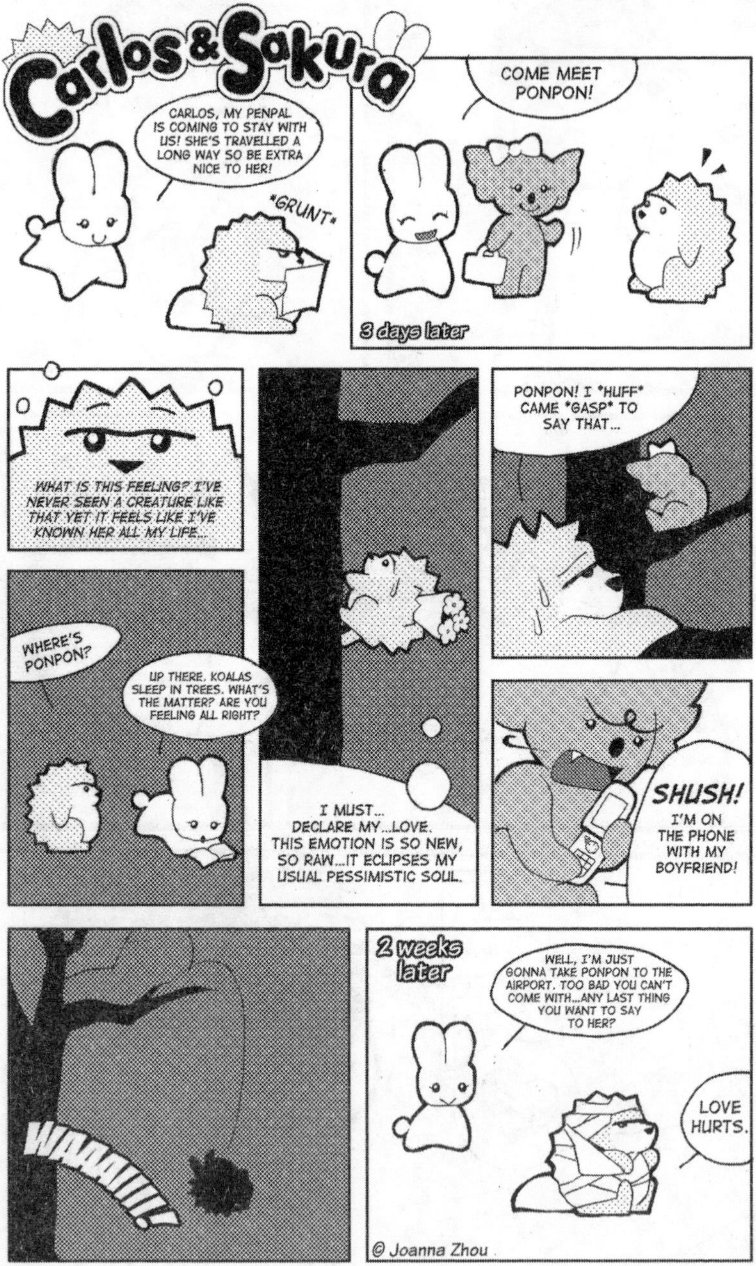
Carlos & Sakura
CARLOS, MY PENPAL IS COMING TO STAY WITH US! SHE'S TRAVELLED A LONG WAY SO BE EXTRA NICE TO HER!
GRUNT
COME MEET PONPON!
3 days later
WHAT IS THIS FEELING? I'VE NEVER SEEN A CREATURE LIKE THAT YET IT FEELS LIKE I'VE KNOWN HER ALL MY LIFE...
WHERE'S PONPON?
UP THERE. KOALAS SLEEP IN TREES. WHAT'S THE MATTER? ARE YOU FEELING ALL RIGHT?
I MUST... DECLARE MY...LOVE. THIS EMOTION IS SO NEW, SO RAW...IT ECLIPSES MY USUAL PESSIMISTIC SOUL.
PONPON! I *HUFF* CAME *GASP* TO SAY THAT...
SHUSH!
I'M ON THE PHONE WITH MY BOYFRIEND!
WAAAIIIII!
2 weeks later
WELL, I'M JUST GONNA TAKE PONPON TO THE AIRPORT. TOO BAD YOU CAN'T COME WITH...ANY LAST THING YOU WANT TO SAY TO HER?
LOVE HURTS.
© Joanna Zhou

Bad Advice

by

Paul HD

Date of birth: 11 May 1972

PAUL HD

After a life of wandering, Paul now lives, vaguely, in 'a small town in the North of England' (although he doesn't seem sure which one). Ask him what his influences are and he'll point to **Black & White** by Taiyo Matsumoto, **Uzumaki** by Junito Ito, and lots of stuff by Rumiko Takahashi; 'It almost causes me physical pain to leave out **Love Roma**, Junko Mizuno's work, **Hellbaby** and **Nausicaa**, which is why I'm sneaking them in now.' Paul also reckons he's a product of 'spending too much time on my own as a kid. I never had an imaginary friend, but if I did I reckon it would've taken the blame for a lot of my bad decisions.'

He loves horror films, 'going walking with my wife' and lots of coffee (cake is optional); he hates getting out of bed, idiots and celebrities. Paul's big ambition is to create a fantastic series of children's books. So, here's hoping.

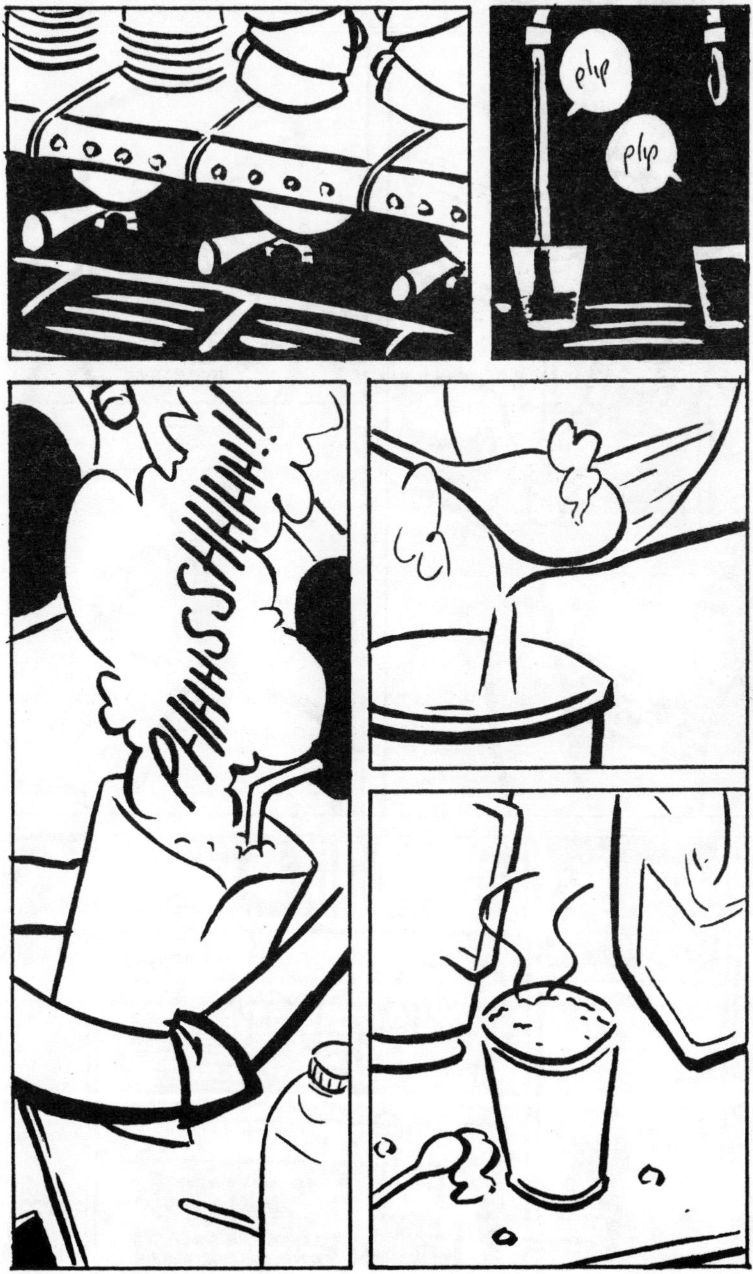
plip
plip
PHHHSSHHHH!!

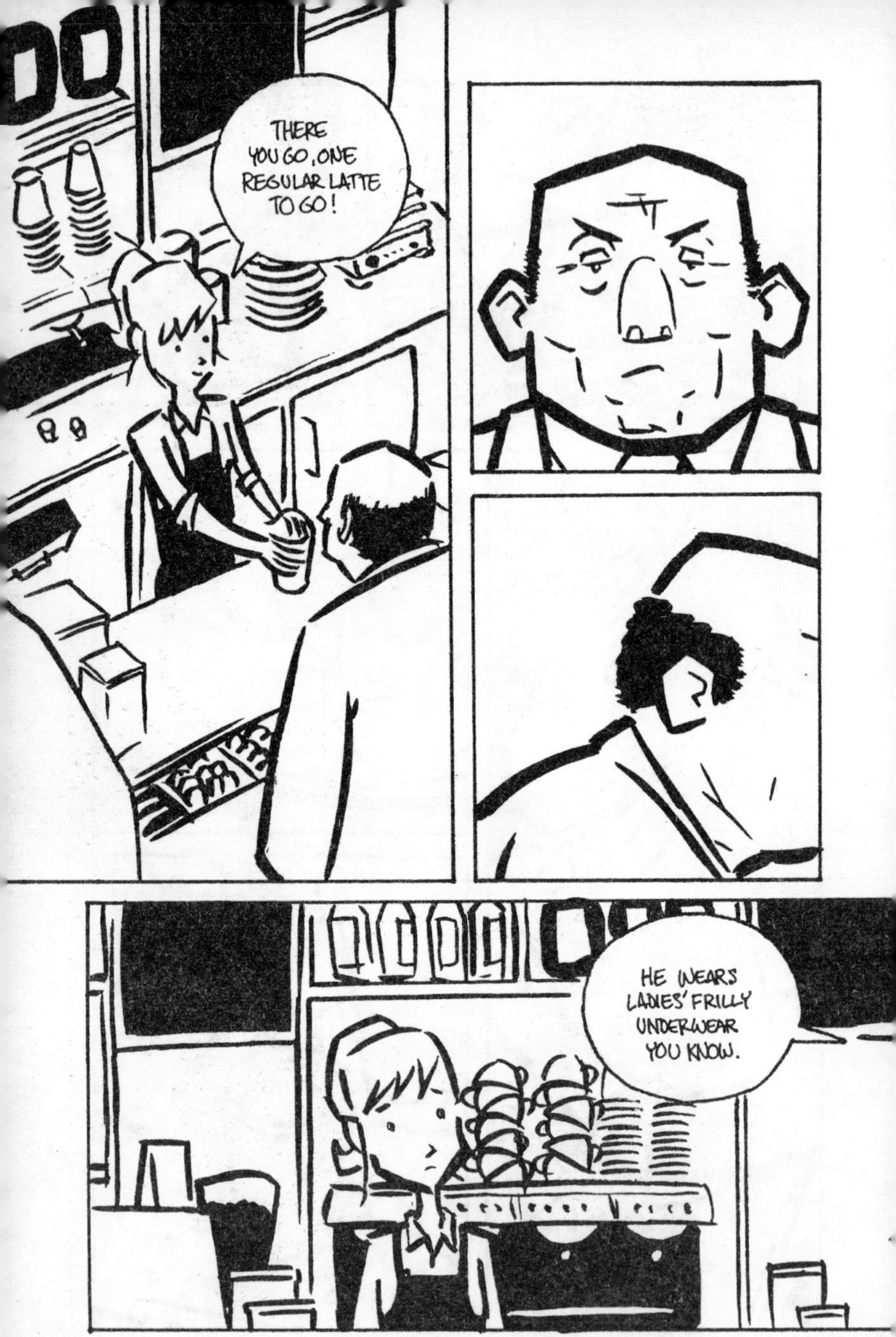
THERE YOU GO, ONE REGULAR LATTE TO GO!
HE WEARS LADIES' FRILLY UNDERWEAR YOU KNOW.

HA! HA! HA! HA! HA!
WHAT, NO? REALLY?
OH YES.
I'LL SHOW YOU.

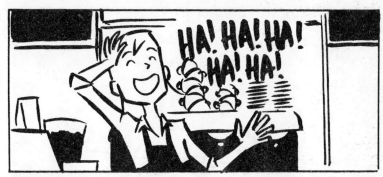

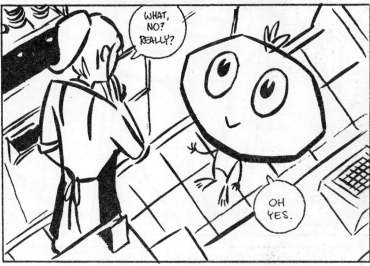

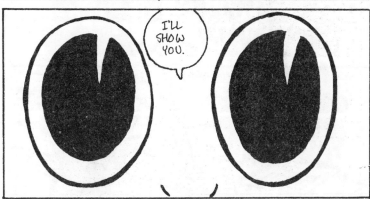

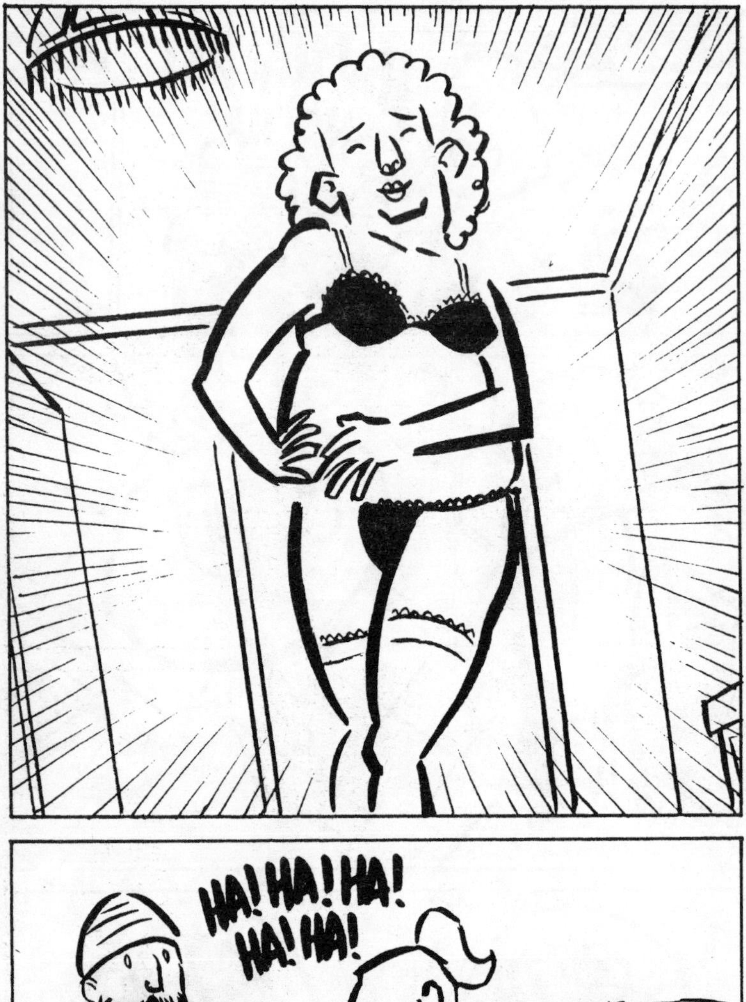

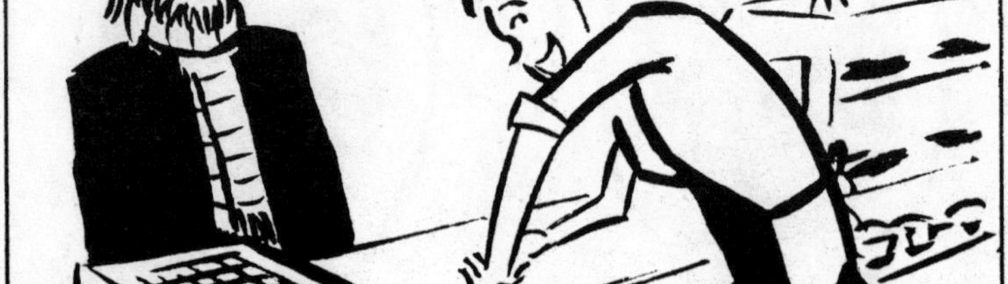
HA! HA! HA!
HA! HA!

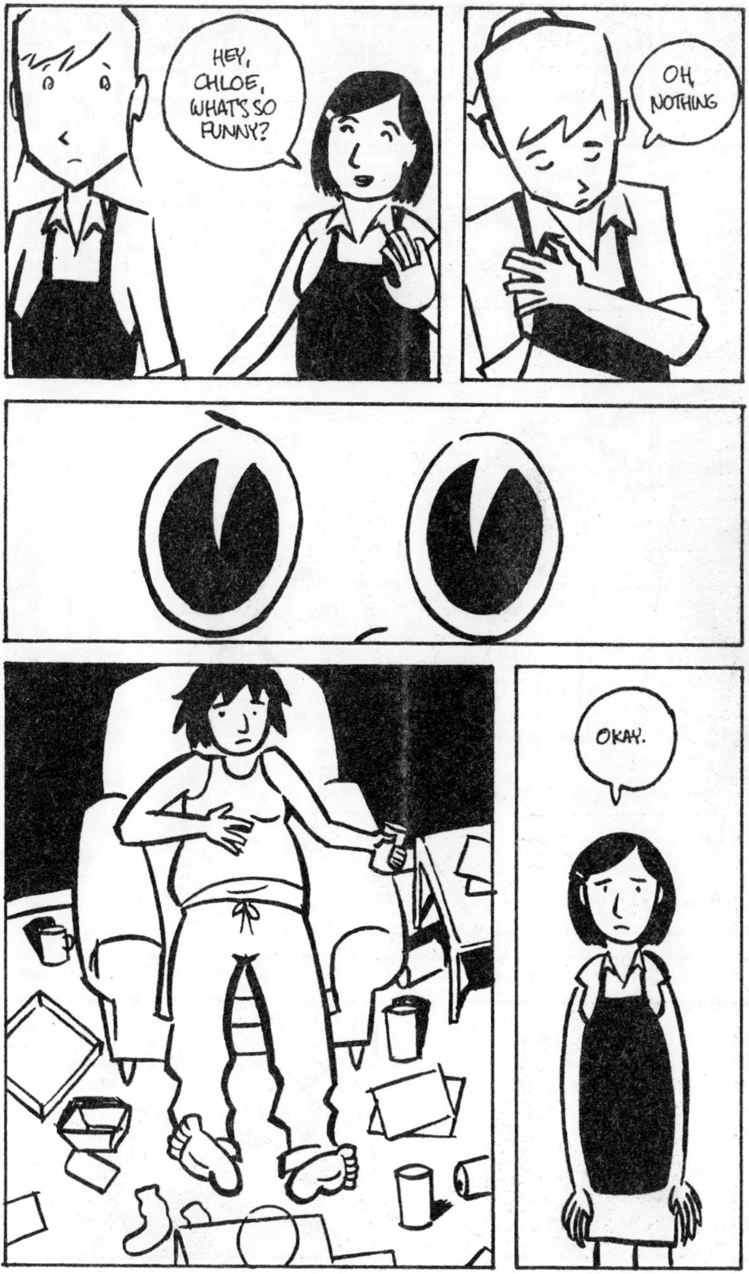
HEY, CHLOE, WHAT'S SO FUNNY?
OH, NOTHING
OKAY.

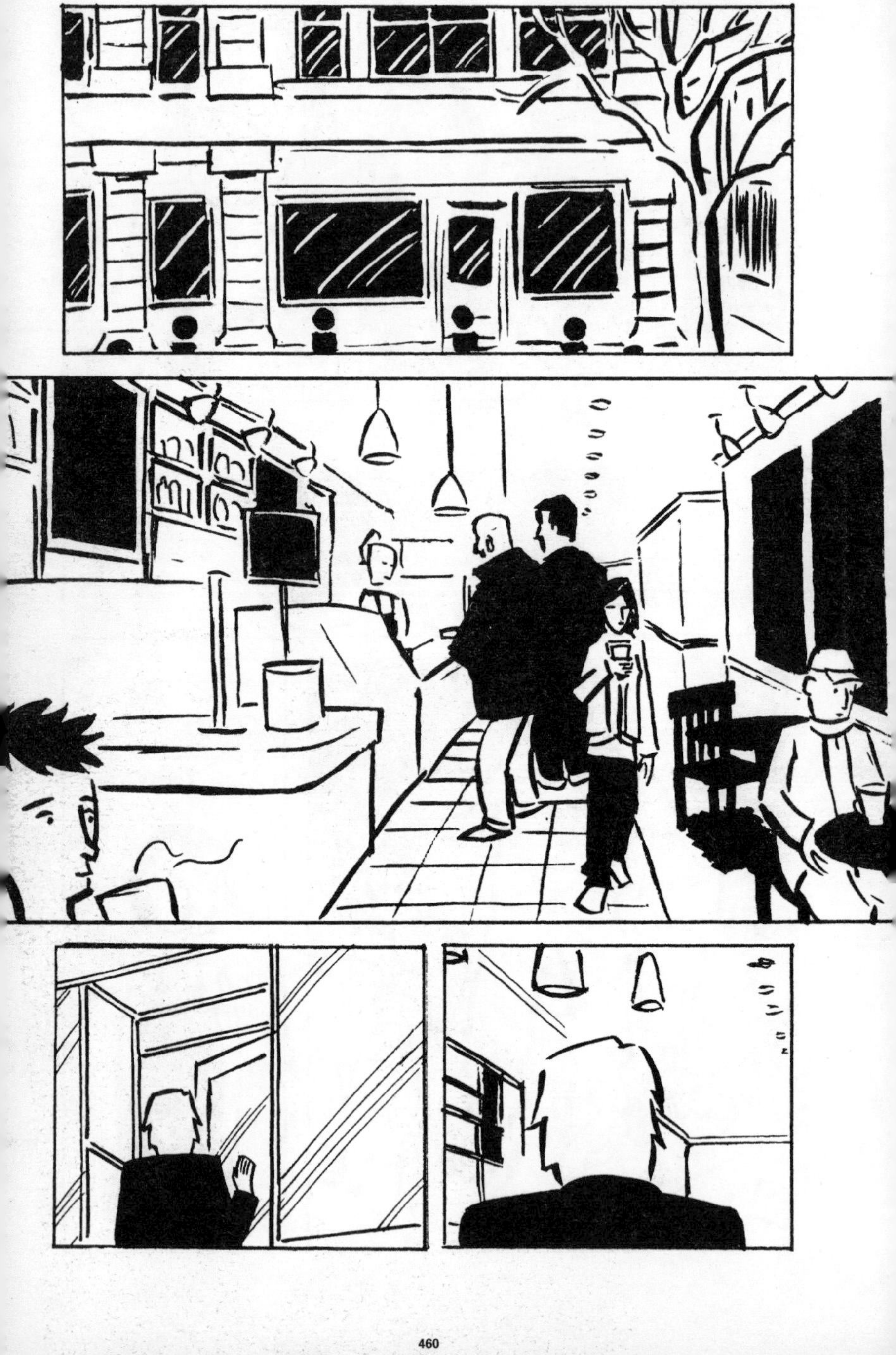

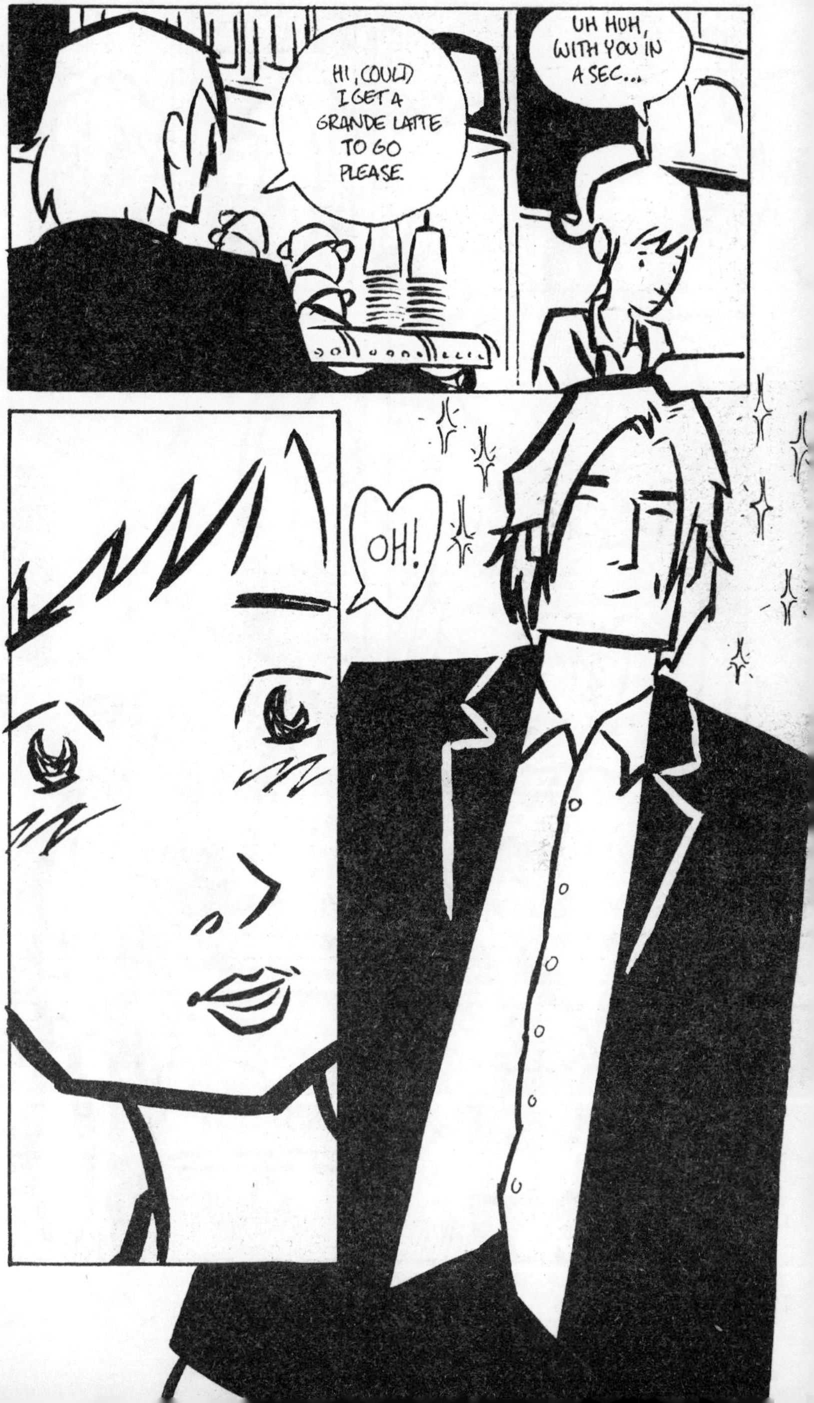
HI, COULD I GET A GRANDE LATTE TO GO PLEASE.
UH HUH, WITH YOU IN A SEC...
OH!

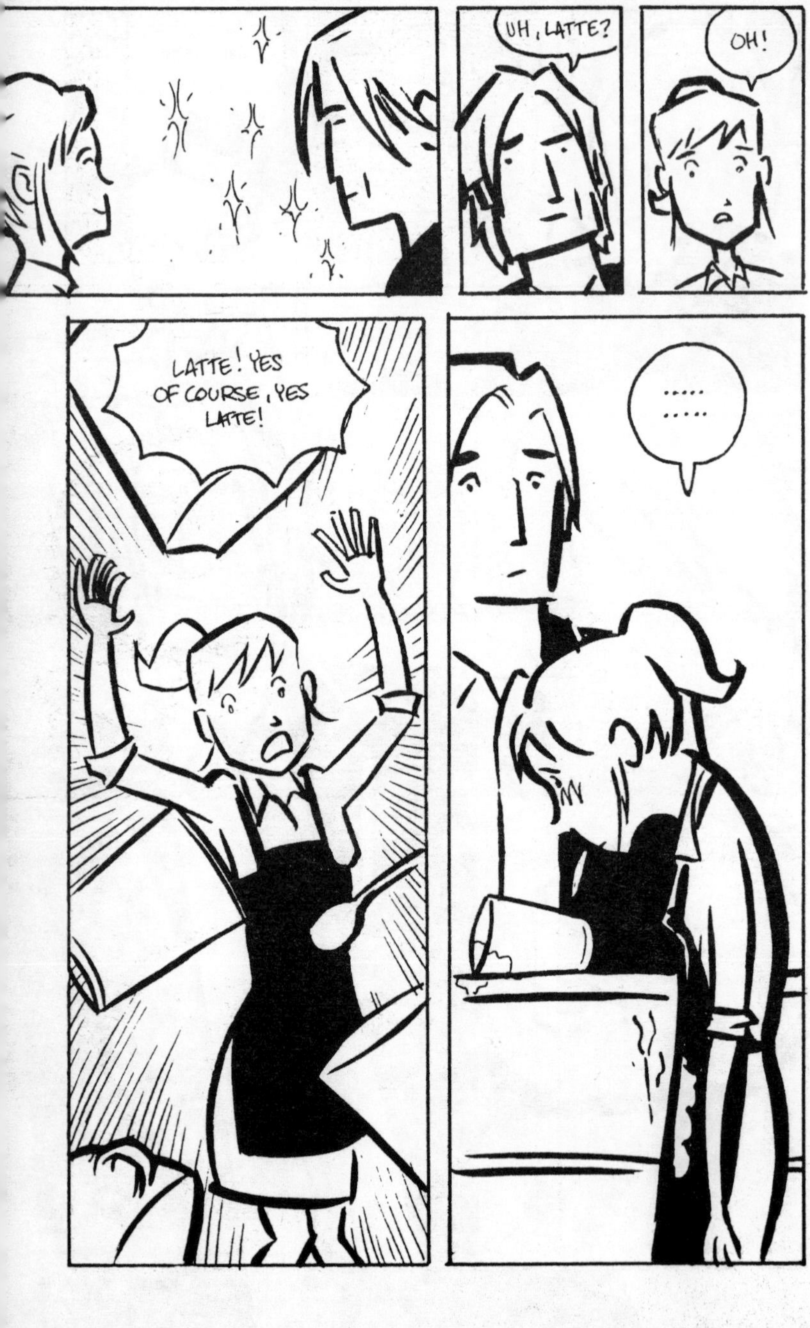
UH, LATTE?
OH!
LATTE! YES OF COURSE, YES LATTE!
......
.....

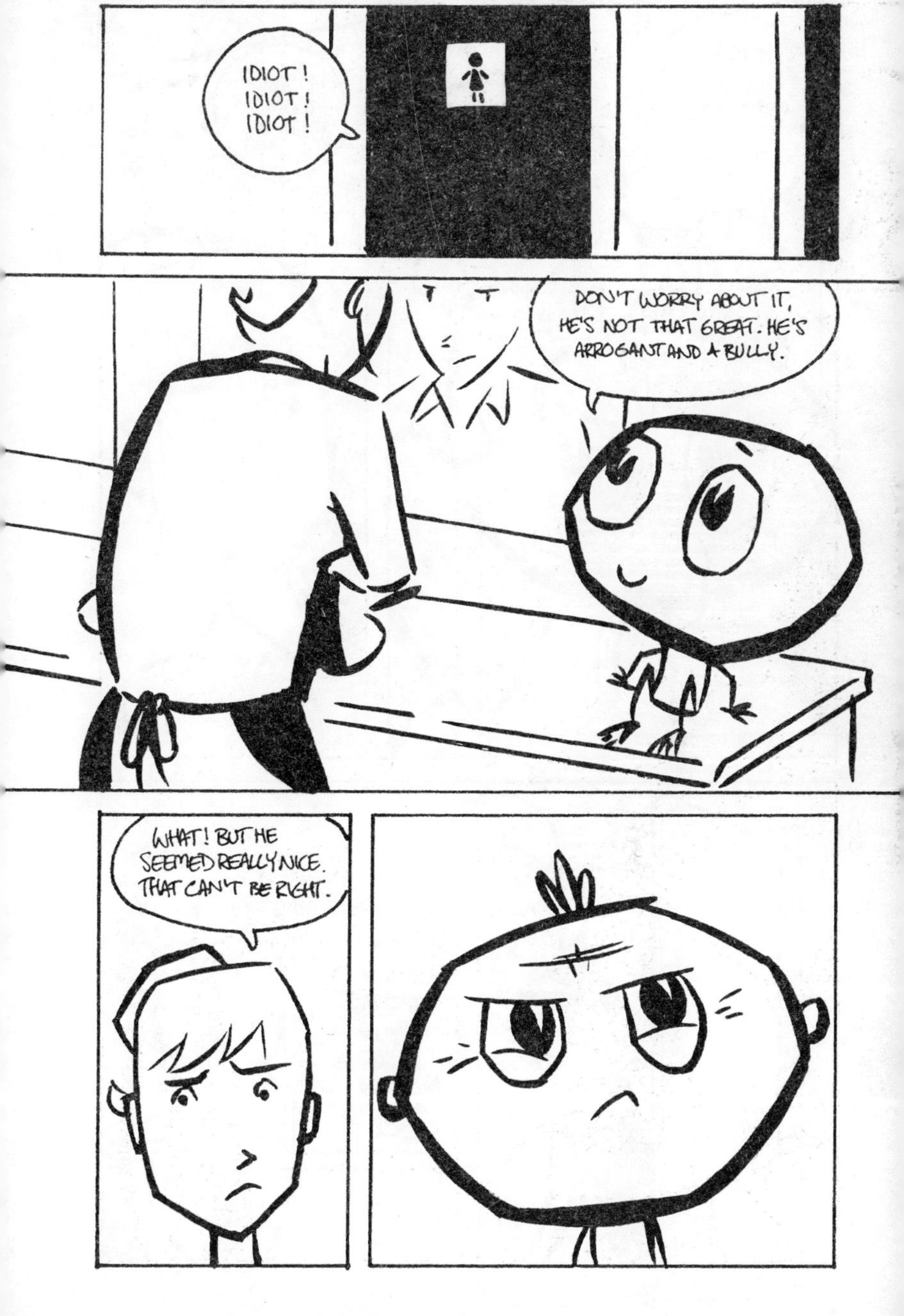
IDIOT! IDIOT! IDIOT!
DON'T WORRY ABOUT IT, HE'S NOT THAT GREAT. HE'S ARROGANT AND A BULLY.
WHAT! BUT HE SEEMED REALLY NICE. THAT CAN'T BE RIGHT.

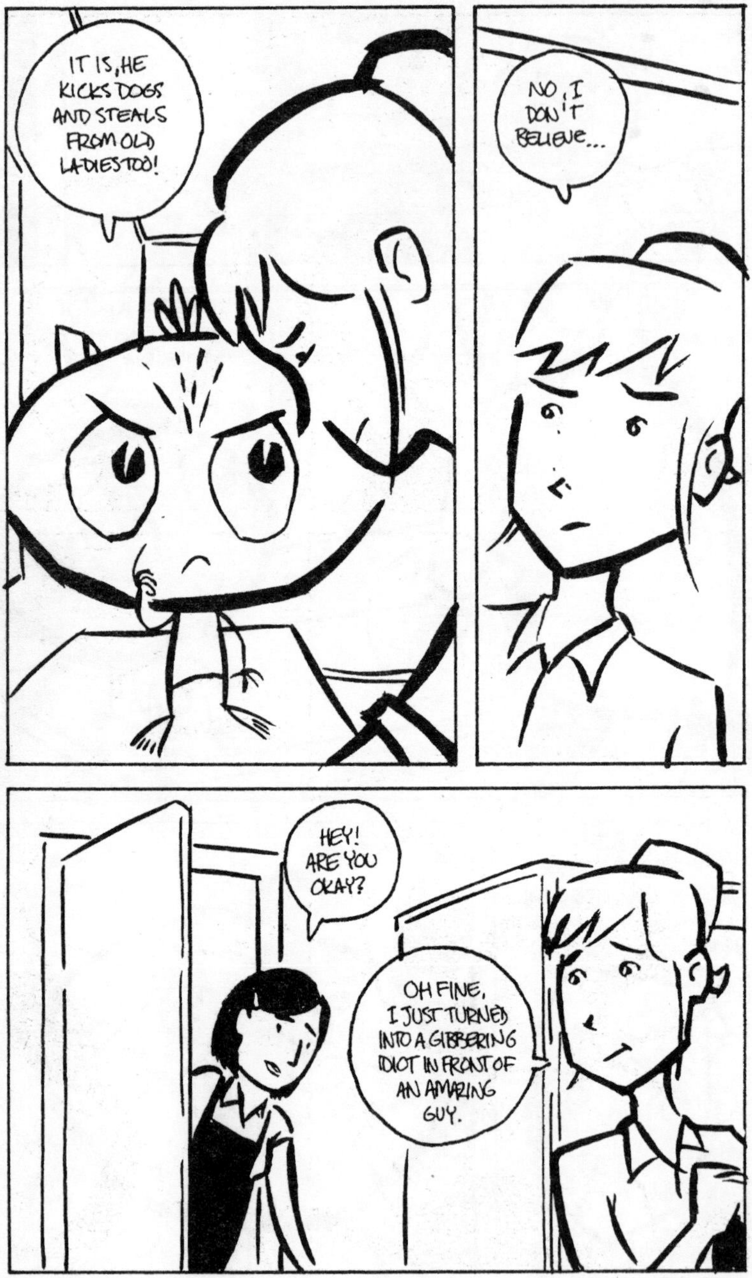
IT IS, HE KICKS DOGS AND STEALS FROM OLD LADIES TOO!
NO, I DON'T BELIEVE...
HEY! ARE YOU OKAY?
OH FINE, I JUST TURNED INTO A GIBBERING IDIOT IN FRONT OF AN AMAZING GUY.

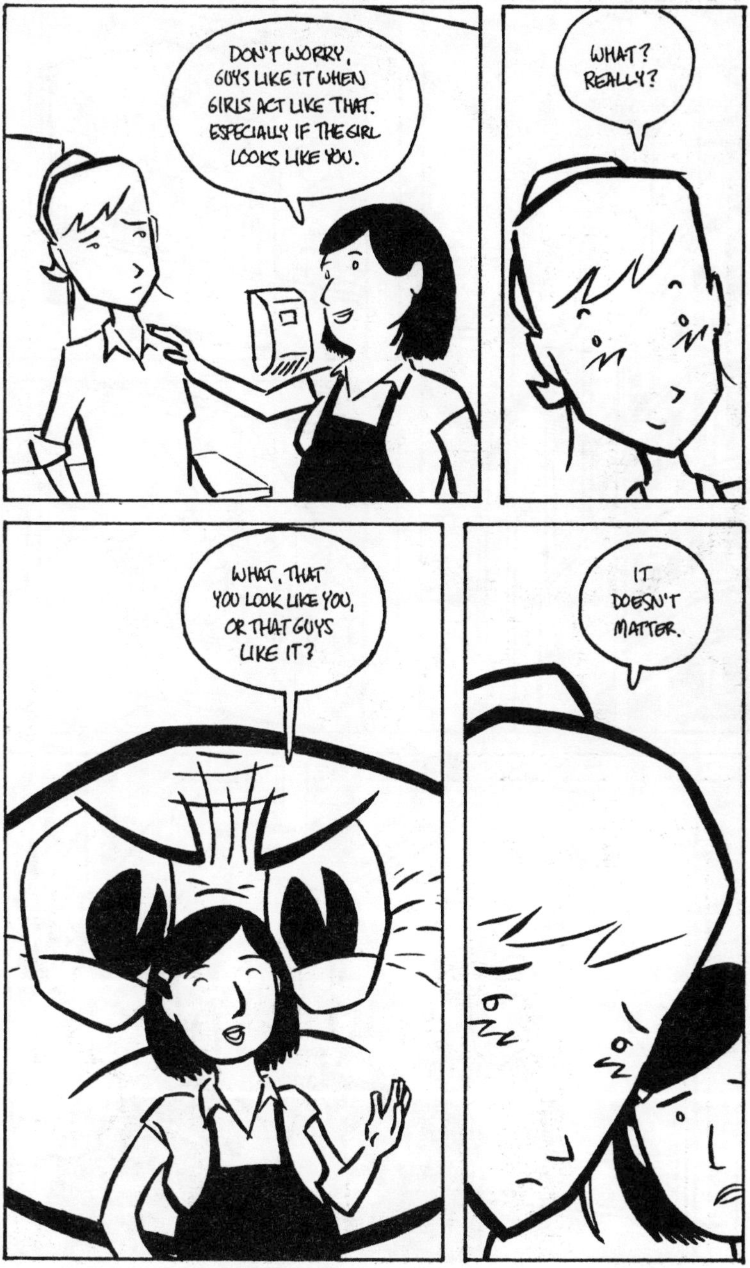
DON'T WORRY, GUYS LIKE IT WHEN GIRLS ACT LIKE THAT. ESPECIALLY IF THE GIRL LOOKS LIKE YOU.
WHAT? REALLY?
WHAT, THAT YOU LOOK LIKE YOU, OR THAT GUYS LIKE IT?
IT DOESN'T MATTER.

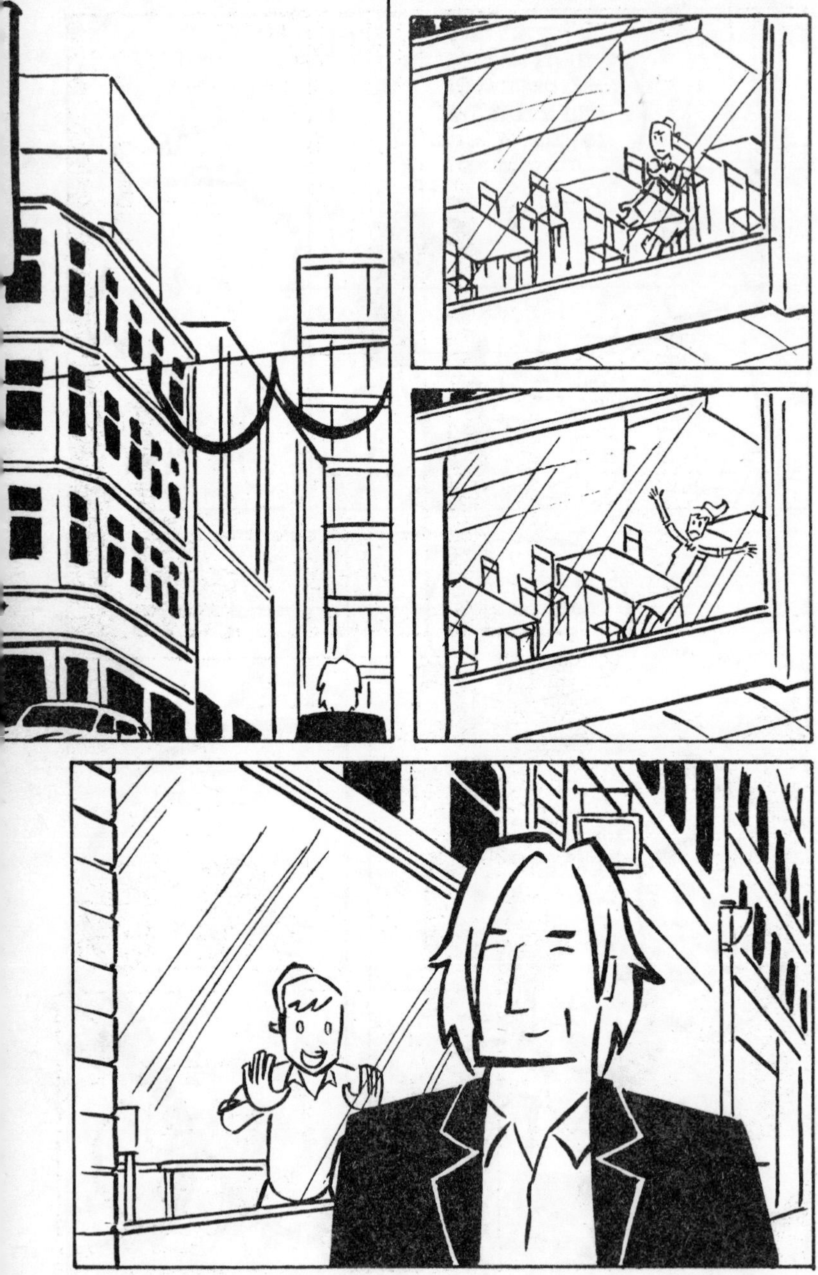

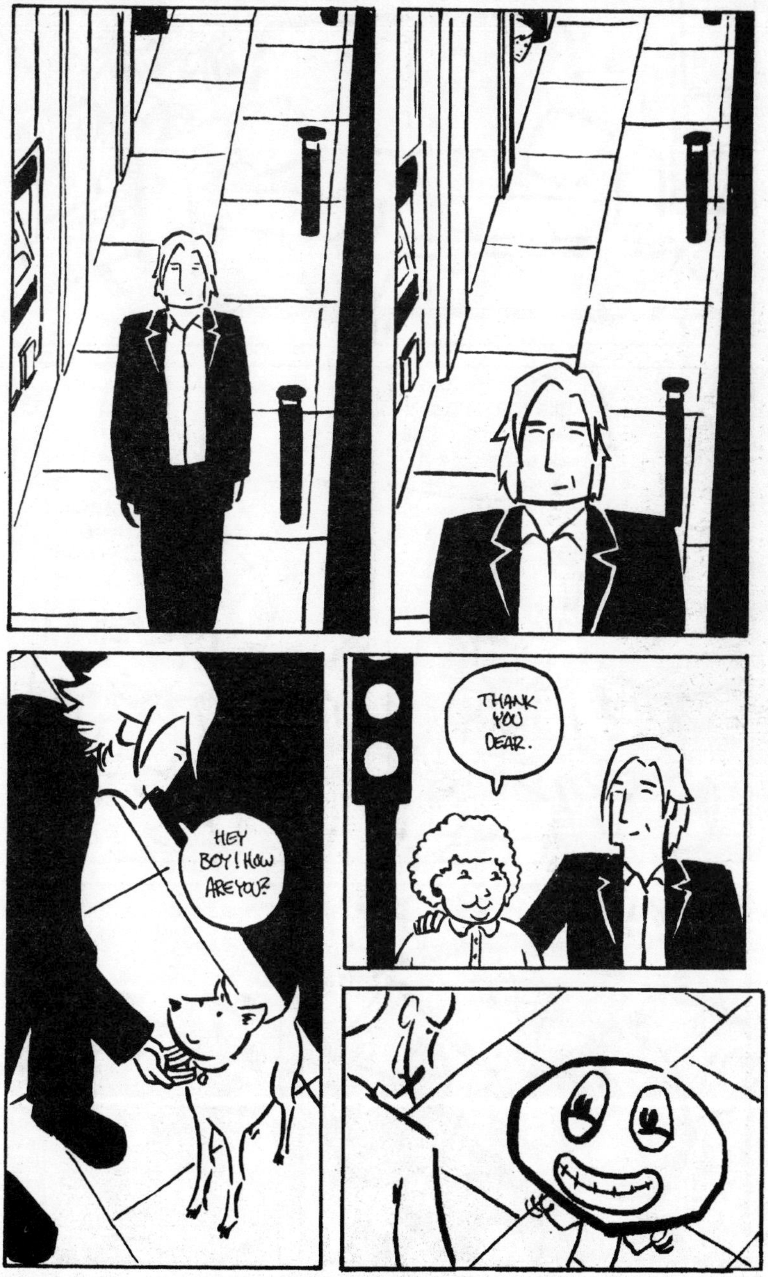
HEY BOY! HOW ARE YOU?
THANK YOU DEAR.

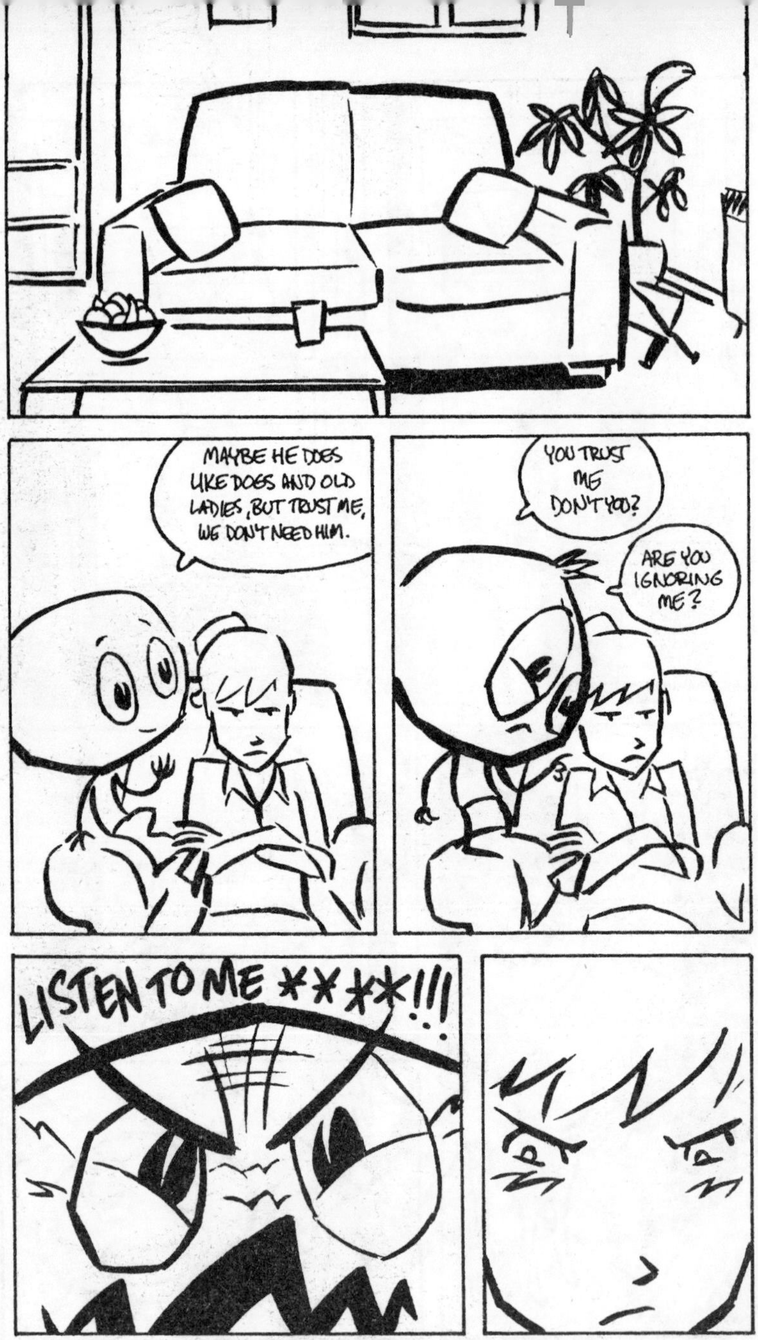
MAYBE HE DOES LIKE DOGS AND OLD LADIES, BUT TRUST ME, WE DON'T NEED HIM.
YOU TRUST ME DON'T YOU?
ARE YOU IGNORING ME?
LISTEN TO ME ****!!!

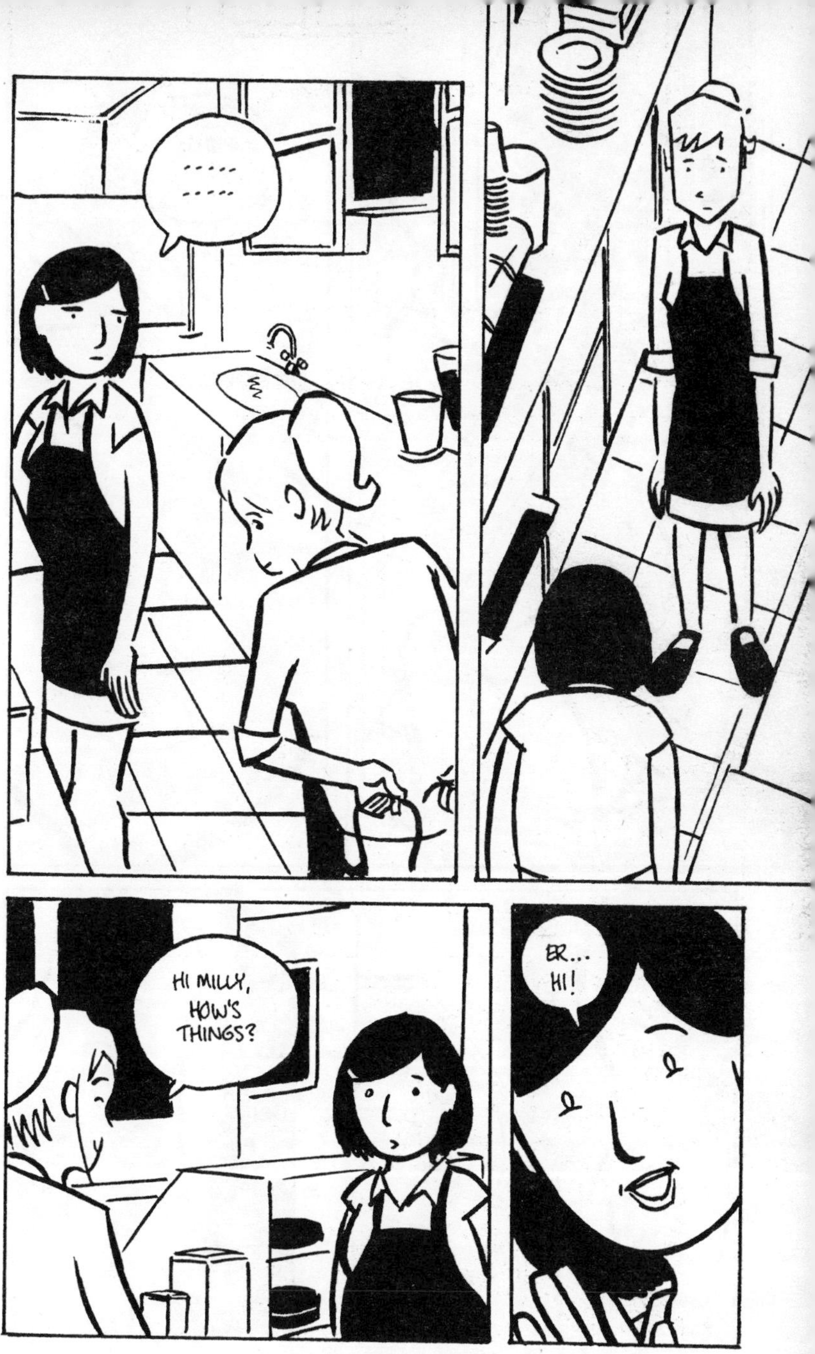

HI MILLY, HOW'S THINGS?
ER... HI!

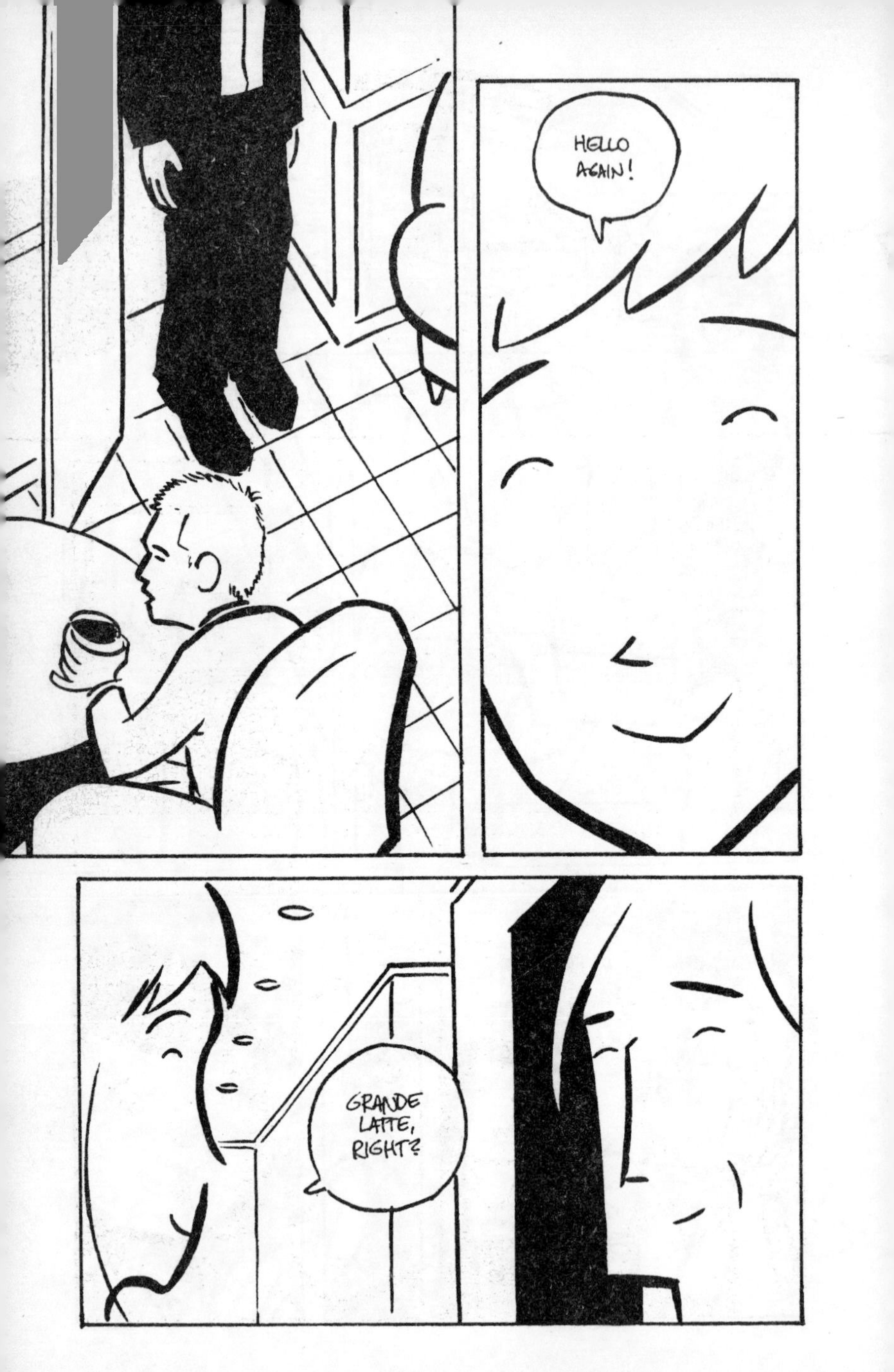
HELLO AGAIN!
GRANDE LATTE, RIGHT?

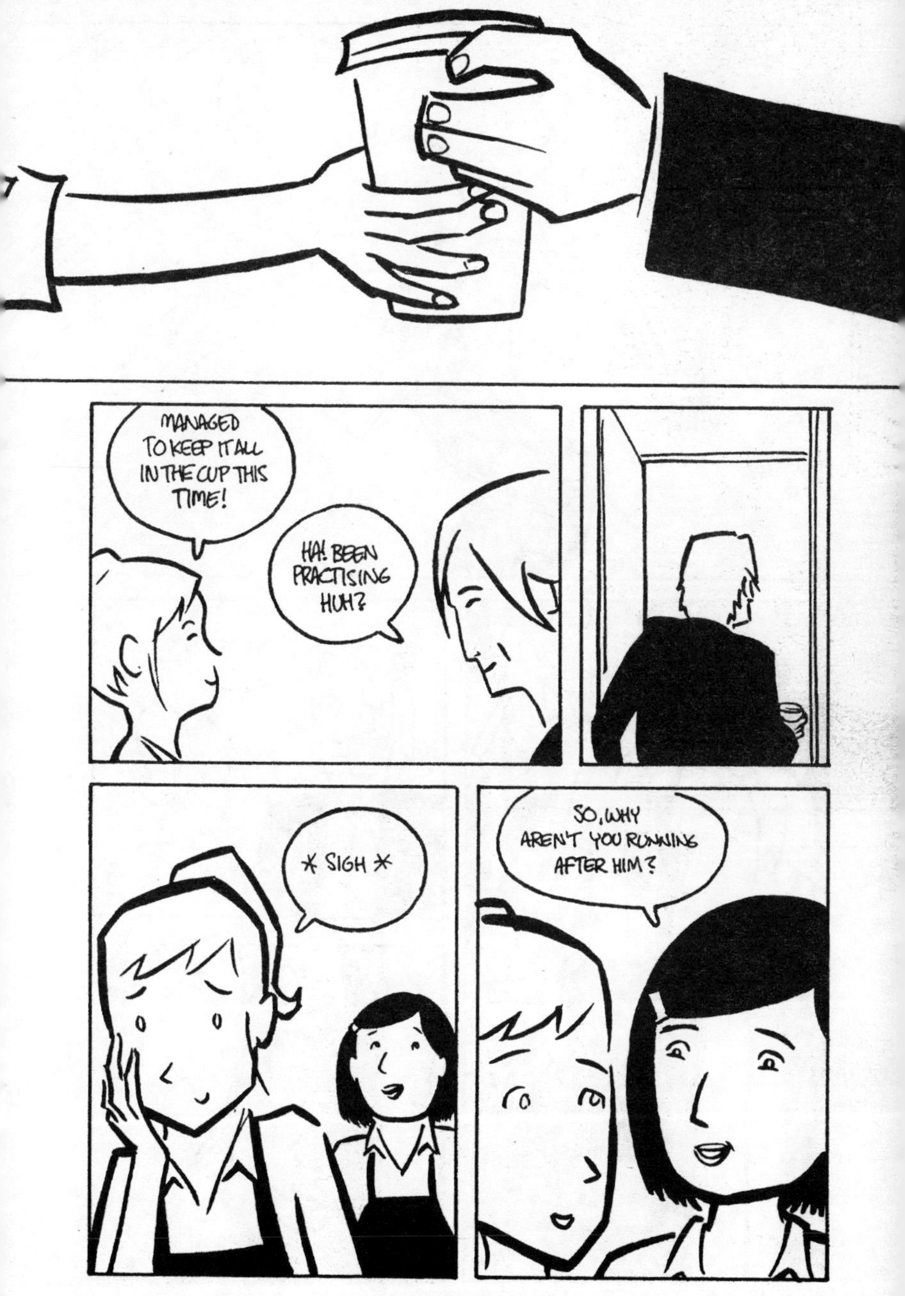
MANAGED TO KEEP IT ALL IN THE CUP THIS TIME!
HA! BEEN PRACTISING HUH?
* SIGH *
SO, WHY AREN'T YOU RUNNING AFTER HIM?

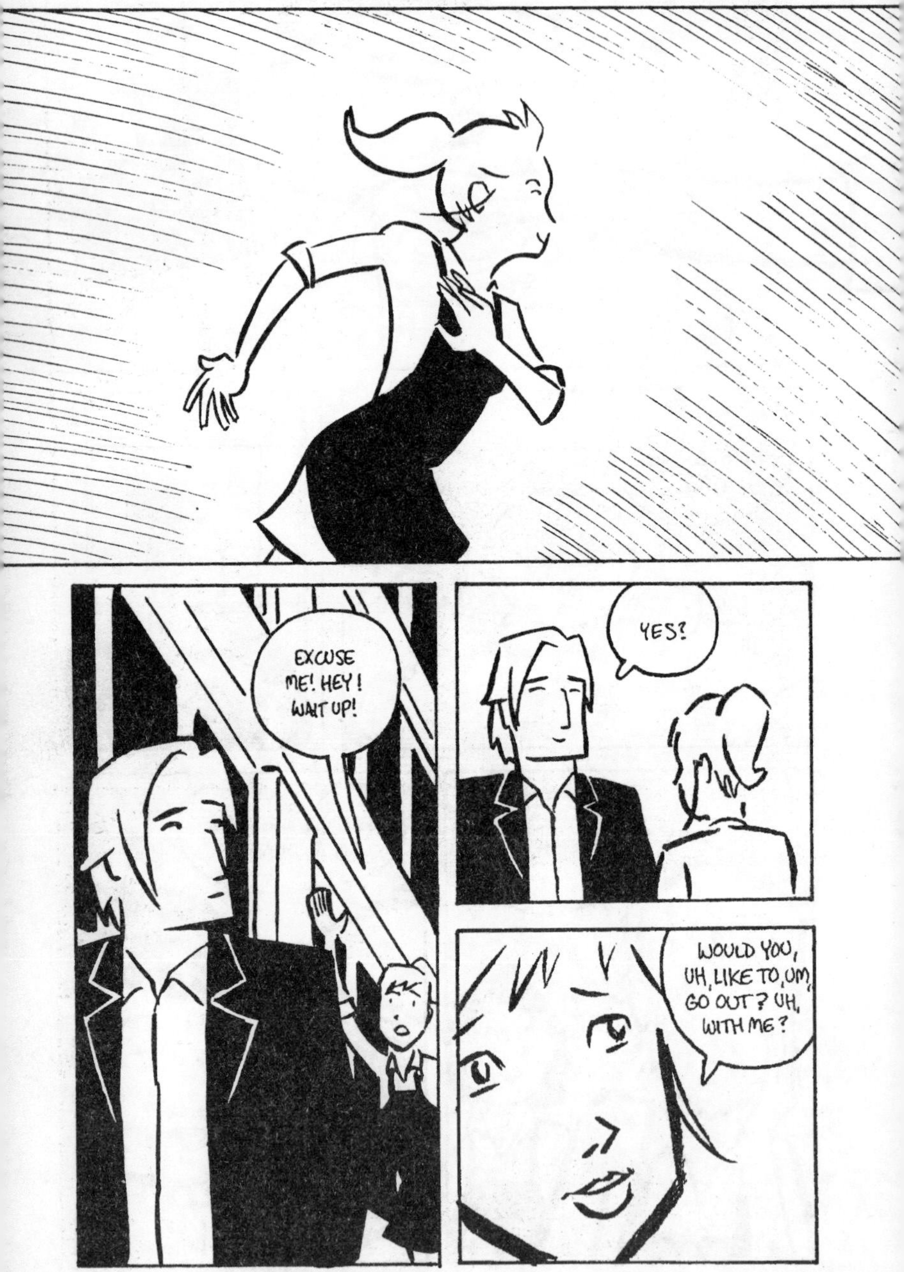
EXCUSE ME! HEY! WAIT UP!
YES?
WOULD YOU, UH, LIKE TO, UM, GO OUT? UH, WITH ME?

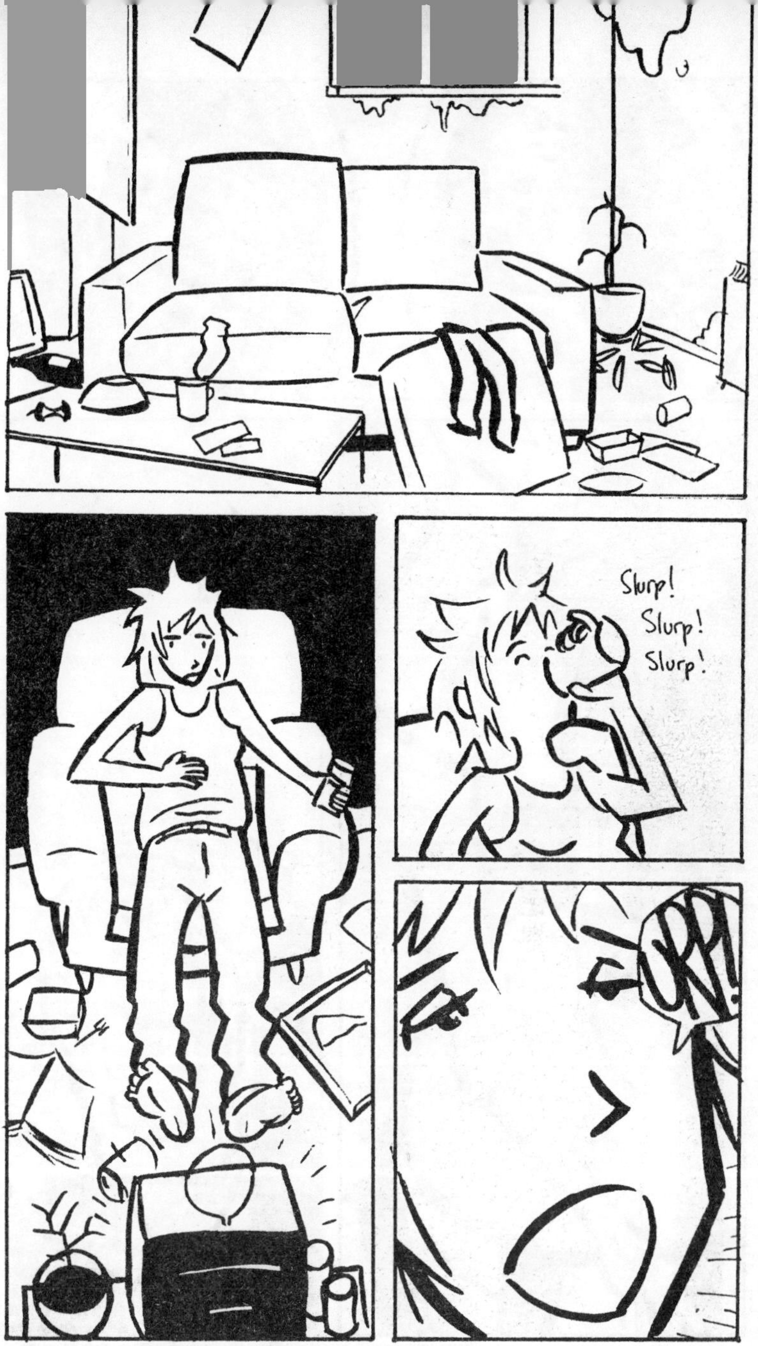
Slurp!
Slurp!
Slurp!
GRP!

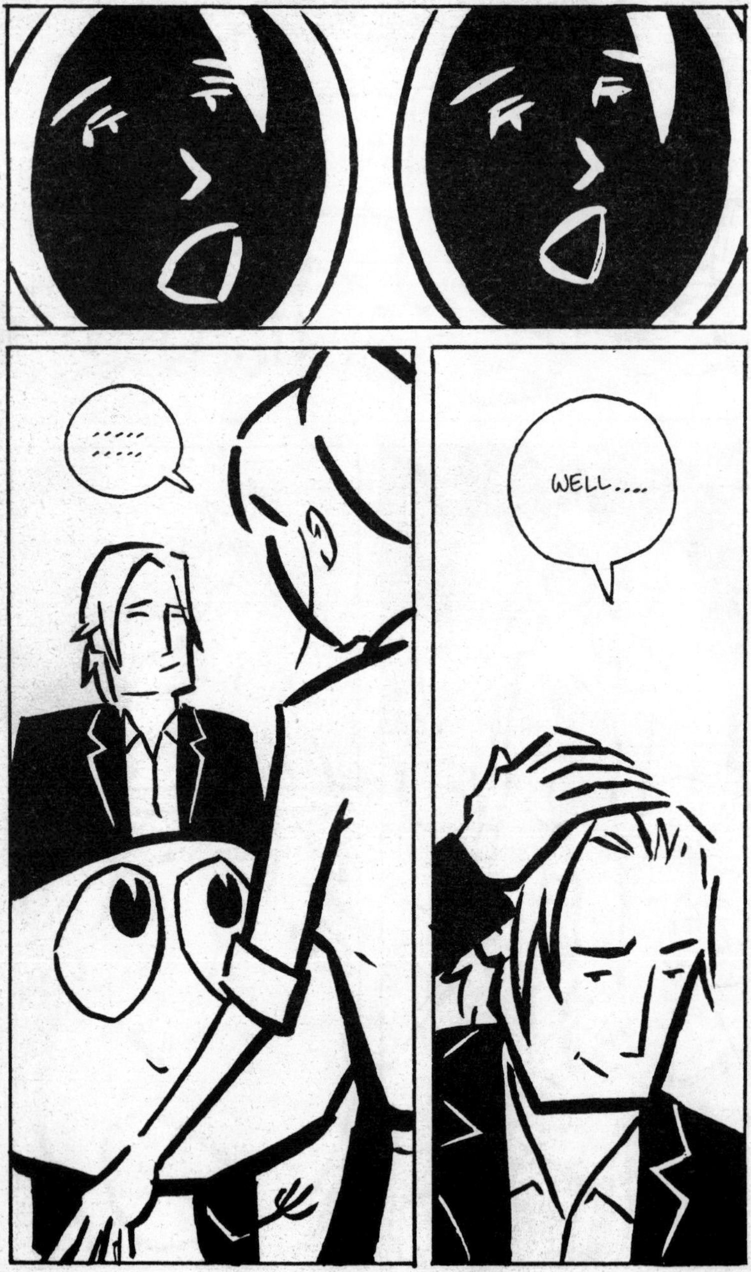
.....
.....
WELL....

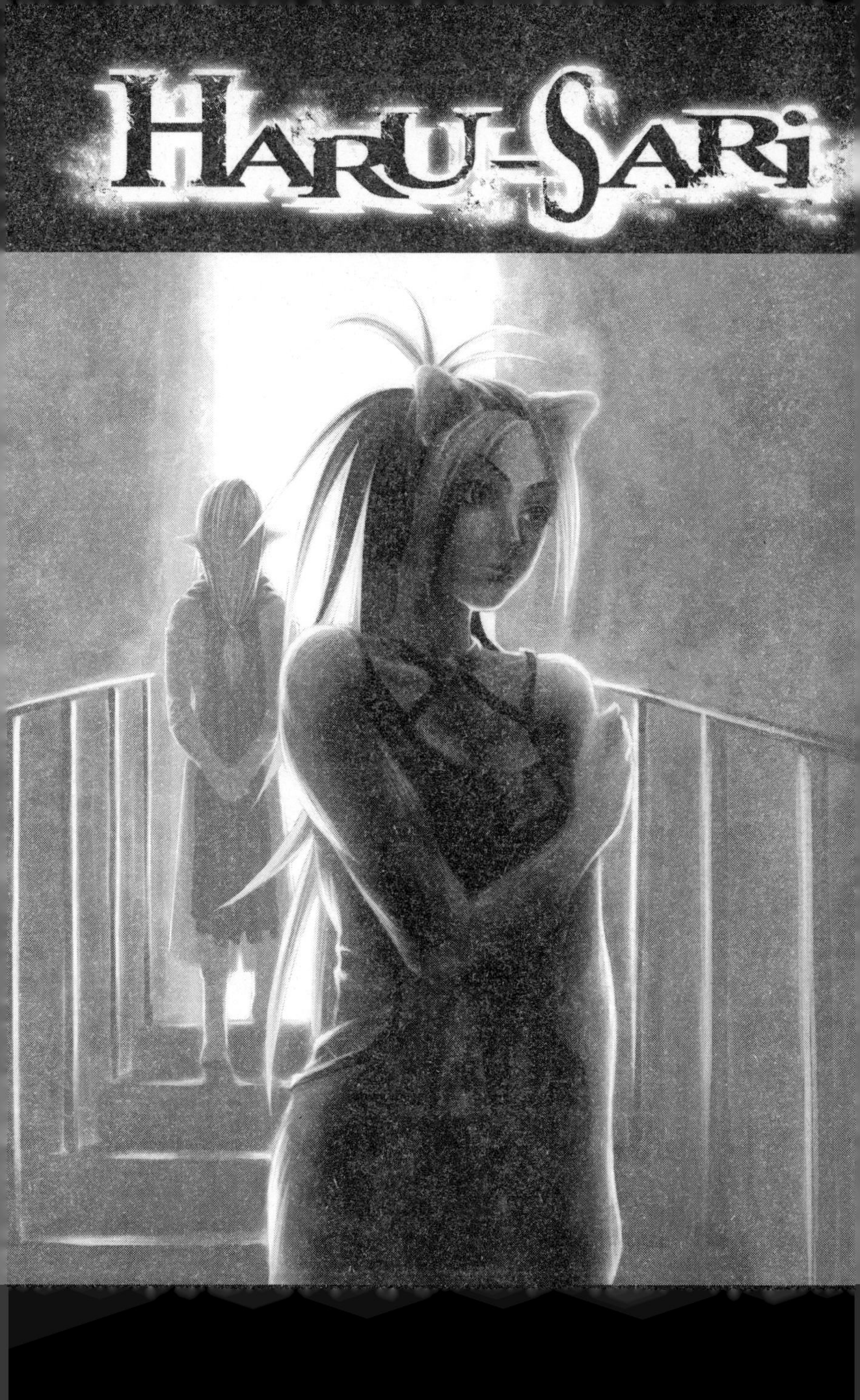
HARU-SARI

Date of birth: 26 November 1981

MIN 'KEIIII' KWON

Keiiii, born in Seoul, Korea, now lives in New Jersey, USA. What follows are just the opening chapters of her long-running strip series, *Haru-Sari* (and it runs waaaay long. Check it out online – fresh pages every week!). Even though this episode isn't self-contained, her work is so good we felt we had to share it with you, the lucky readers of **Best New Manga**.

Keiiii's fave rave is Naoki Urasawa's **20th Century Boys**, 'Gorgeous art and storytelling!'. The sky is her artistic influence, and her mom a role model, plus she favours cheese, potatoes and Alaskan Malamutes.

Of her strip, she says 'It's just like in real people. When a war breaks out, what are you concerned with most? It's either staying alive, or staying close to the ones you care about. That's what *Haru-Sari* is about. Staying alive, and holding onto your loved ones.' The series is best read as a whole, so if you find these pages intriguing, check out the website for lots more.

http://www.haru-sari.com

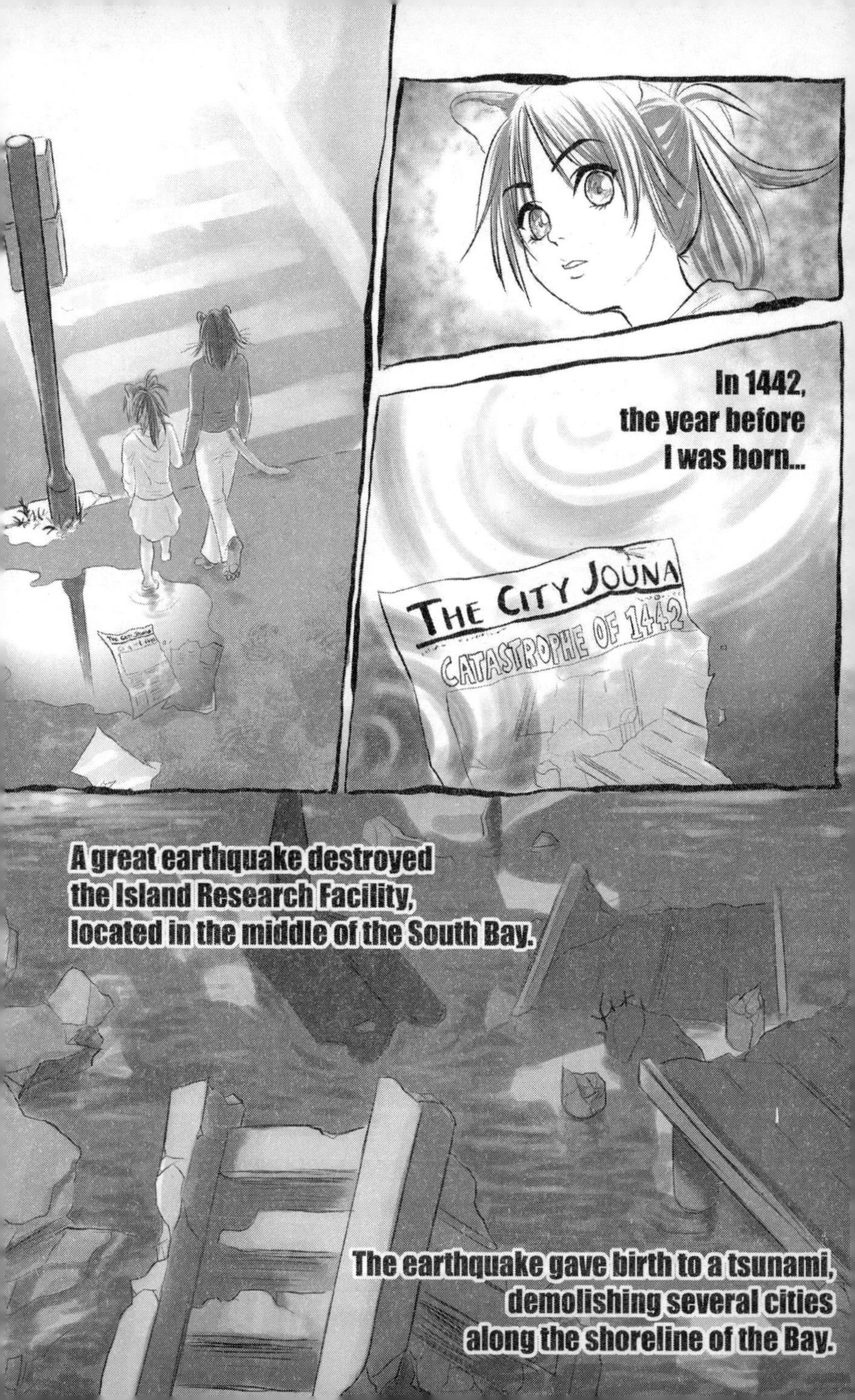
In 1442,
the year before
I was born...
THE CITY JOUNA
CATASTROPHE OF 1442
A great earthquake destroyed
the Island Research Facility,
located in the middle of the South Bay.
The earthquake gave birth to a tsunami,
demolishing several cities
along the shoreline of the Bay.

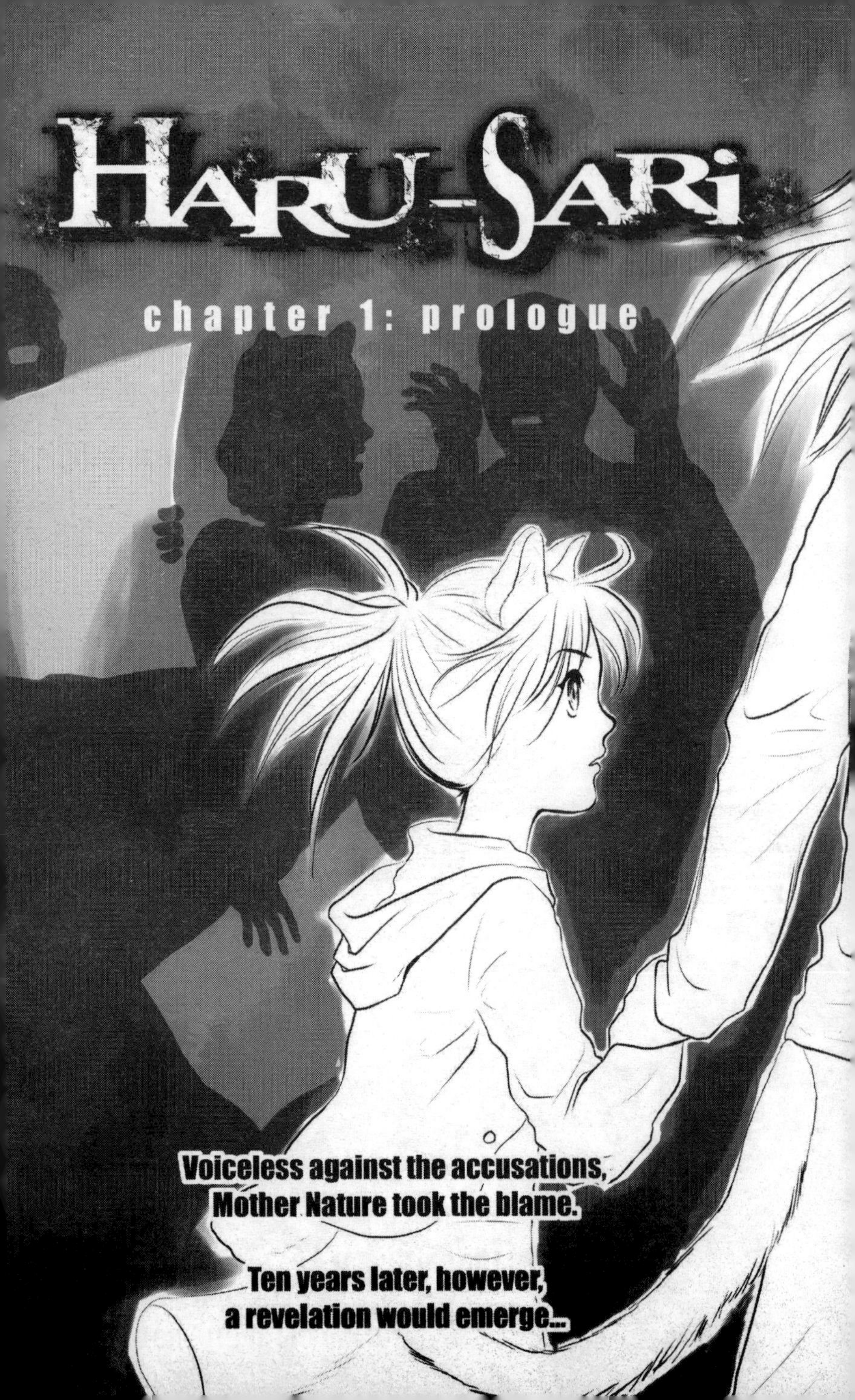
HARU-SARI
chapter 1: prologue
Voiceless against the accusations,
Mother Nature took the blame.
Ten years later, however,
a revelation would emerge...

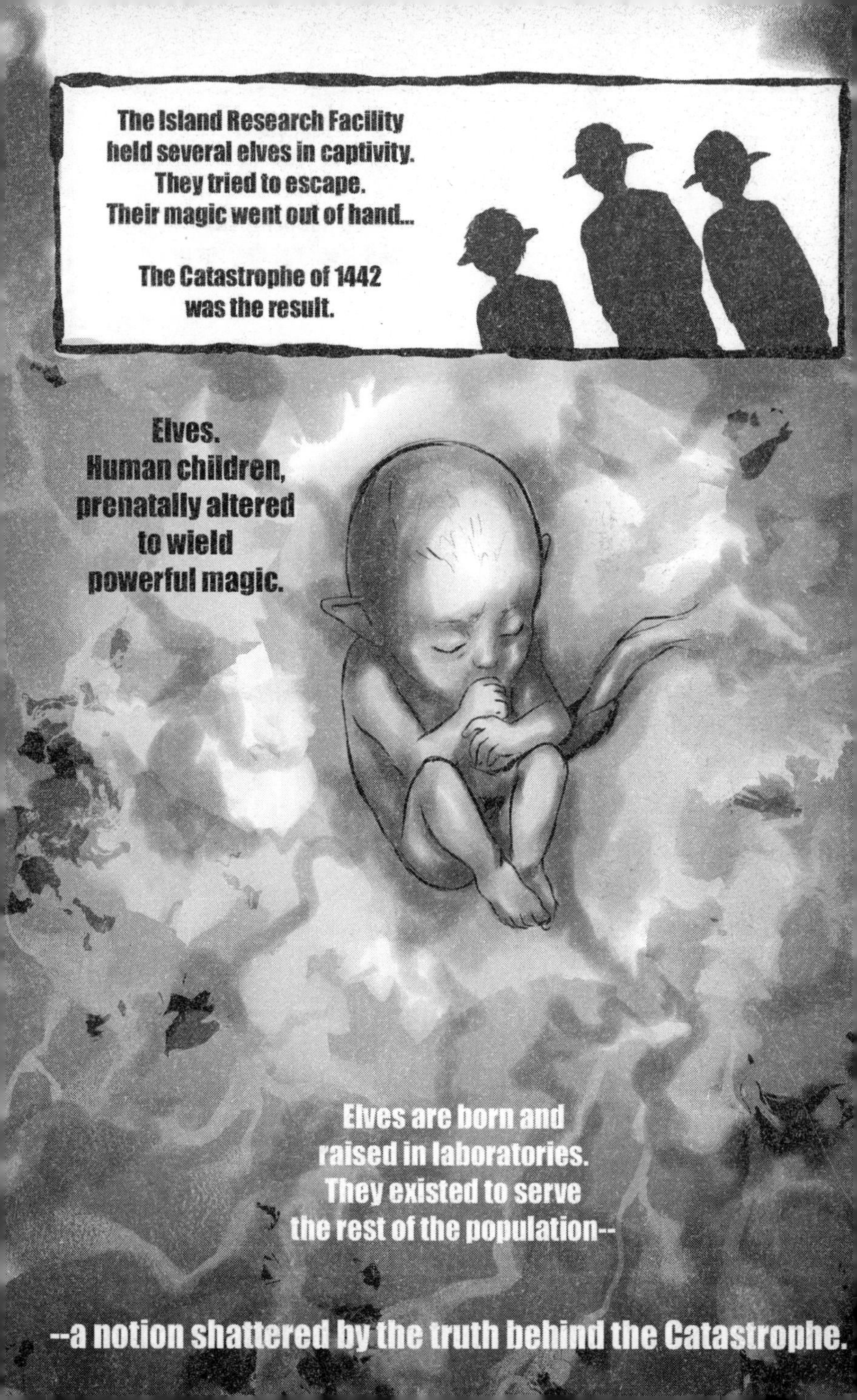

The Island Research Facility
held several elves in captivity.
They tried to escape.
Their magic went out of hand...

The Catastrophe of 1442
was the result.

Elves.
Human children,
prenatally altered
to wield
powerful magic.

Elves are born and
raised in laboratories.
They existed to serve
the rest of the population--

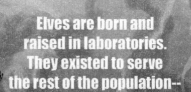

--a notion shattered by the truth behind the Catastrophe.

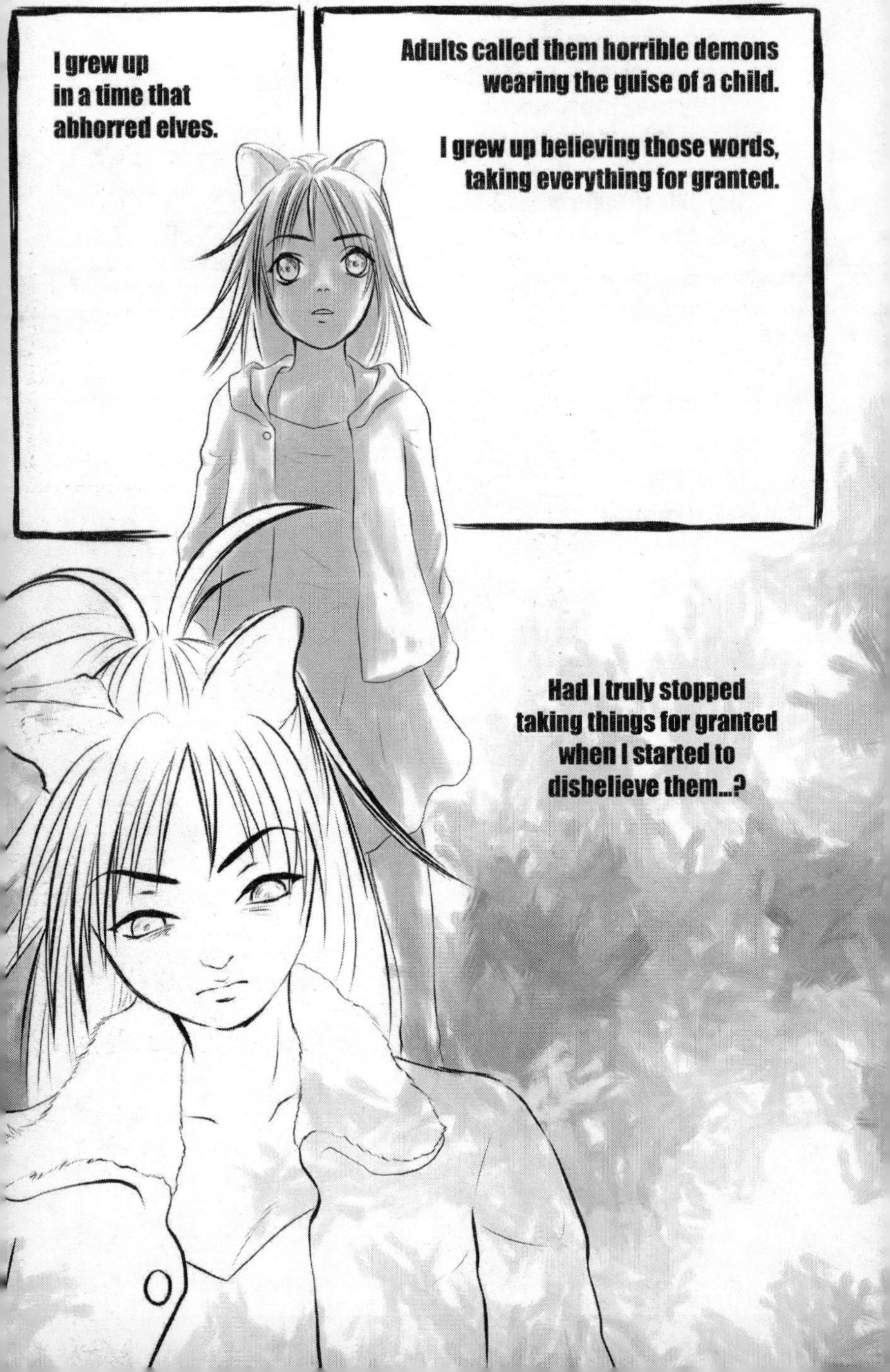
I grew up in a time that abhorred elves.
Adults called them horrible demons wearing the guise of a child.
I grew up believing those words, taking everything for granted.
Had I truly stopped taking things for granted when I started to disbelieve them...?

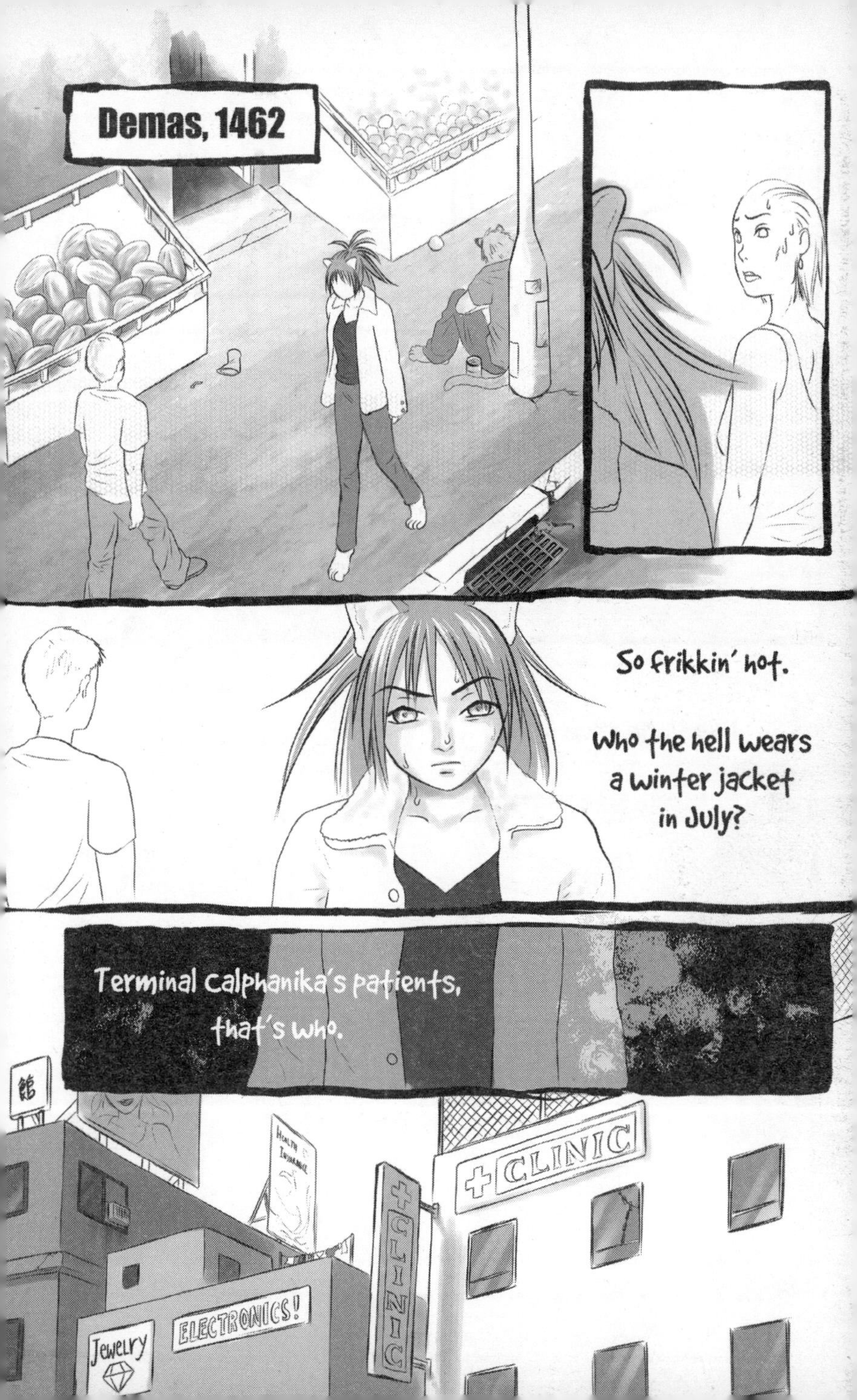
Demas, 1462
So frikkin' hot.
Who the hell wears a winter jacket in July?
Terminal calphanika's patients, that's who.
CLINIC
CLINIC
HEALTH INSURANCE
ELECTRONICS!
Jewelry

Have a seat.
The doctor will be with you shortly.

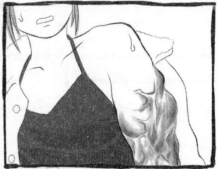

Miss June Blue Delias, correct?

Yes?

I am Dr. Huang.
Pleased to meet you.

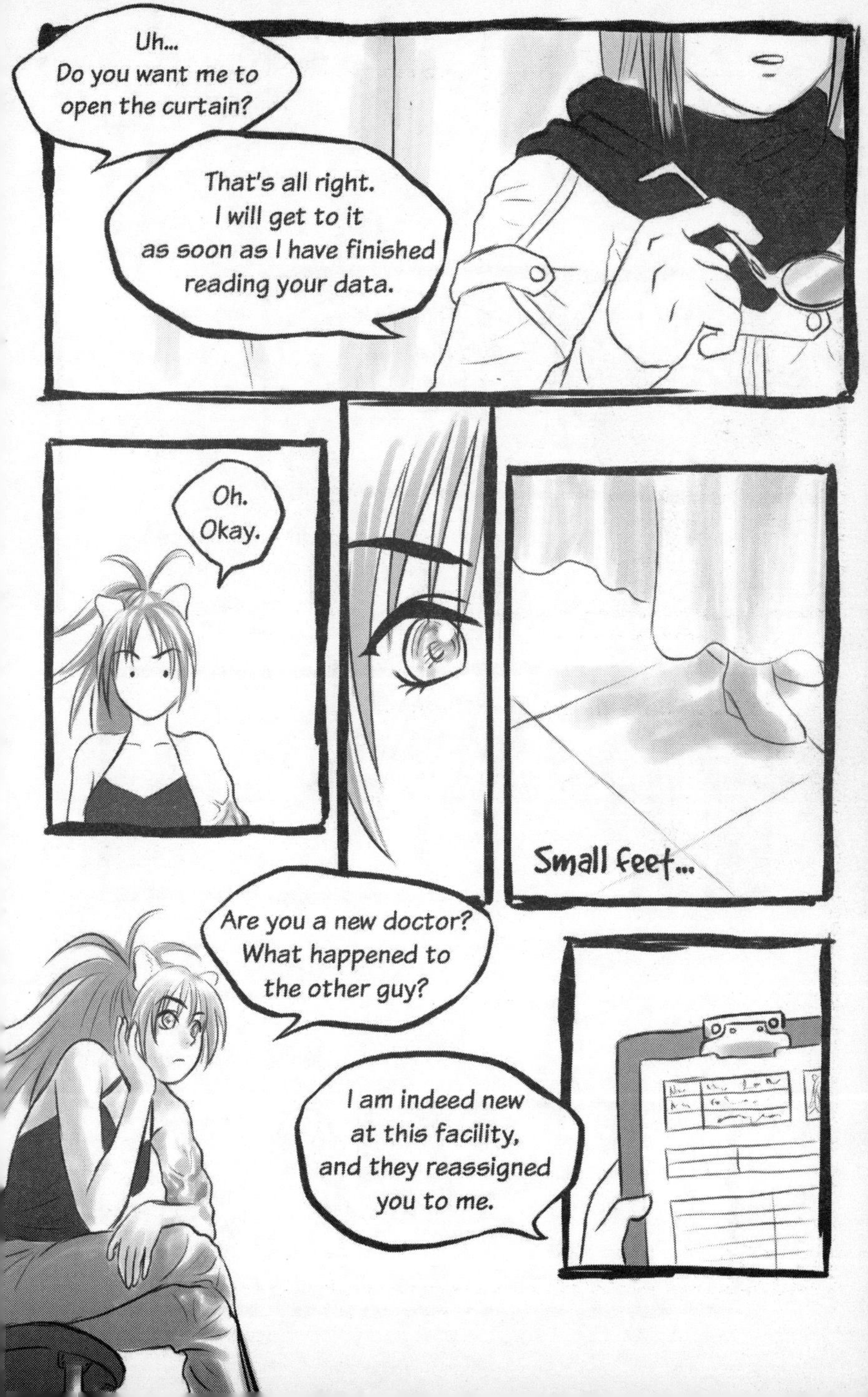
Uh...
Do you want me to open the curtain?
That's all right. I will get to it as soon as I have finished reading your data.
Oh. Okay.
Small feet...
Are you a new doctor? What happened to the other guy?
I am indeed new at this facility, and they reassigned you to me.

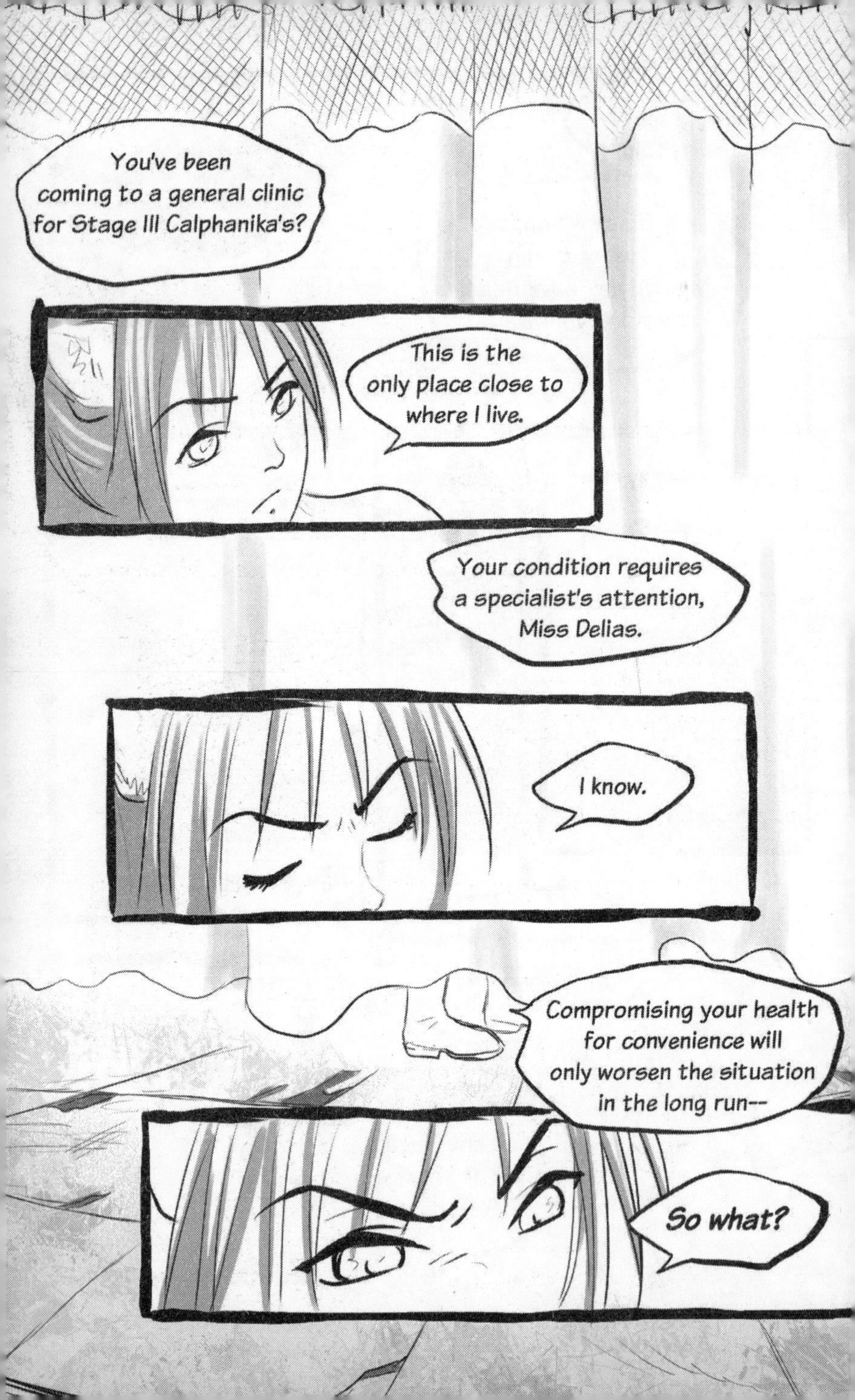
You've been coming to a general clinic for Stage III Calphanika's?
This is the only place close to where I live.
Your condition requires a specialist's attention, Miss Delias.
I know.
Compromising your health for convenience will only worsen the situation in the long run--
So what?

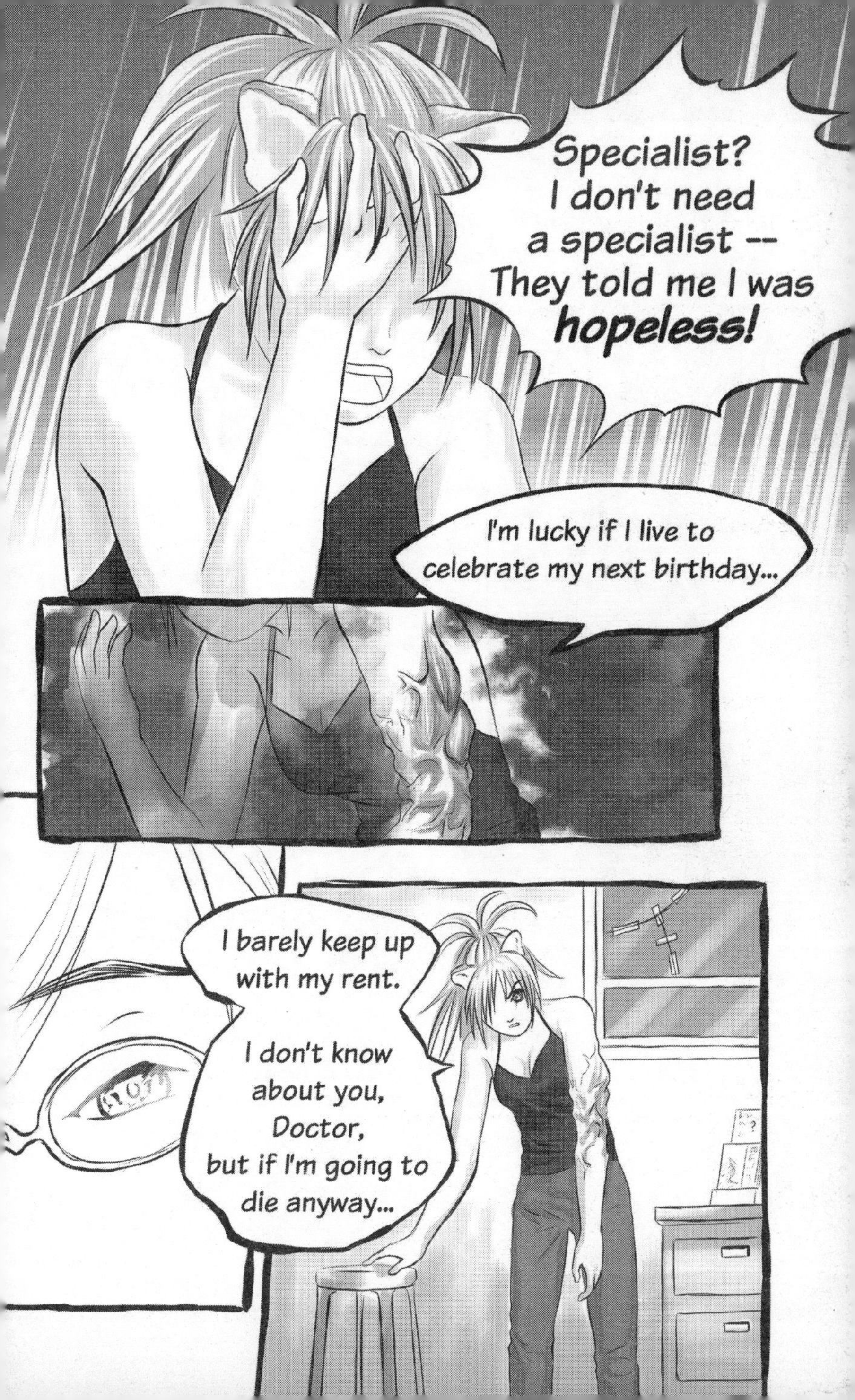

Specialist? I don't need a specialist -- They told me I was **hopeless!**
I'm lucky if I live to celebrate my next birthday...
I barely keep up with my rent.
I don't know about you, Doctor, but if I'm going to die anyway...

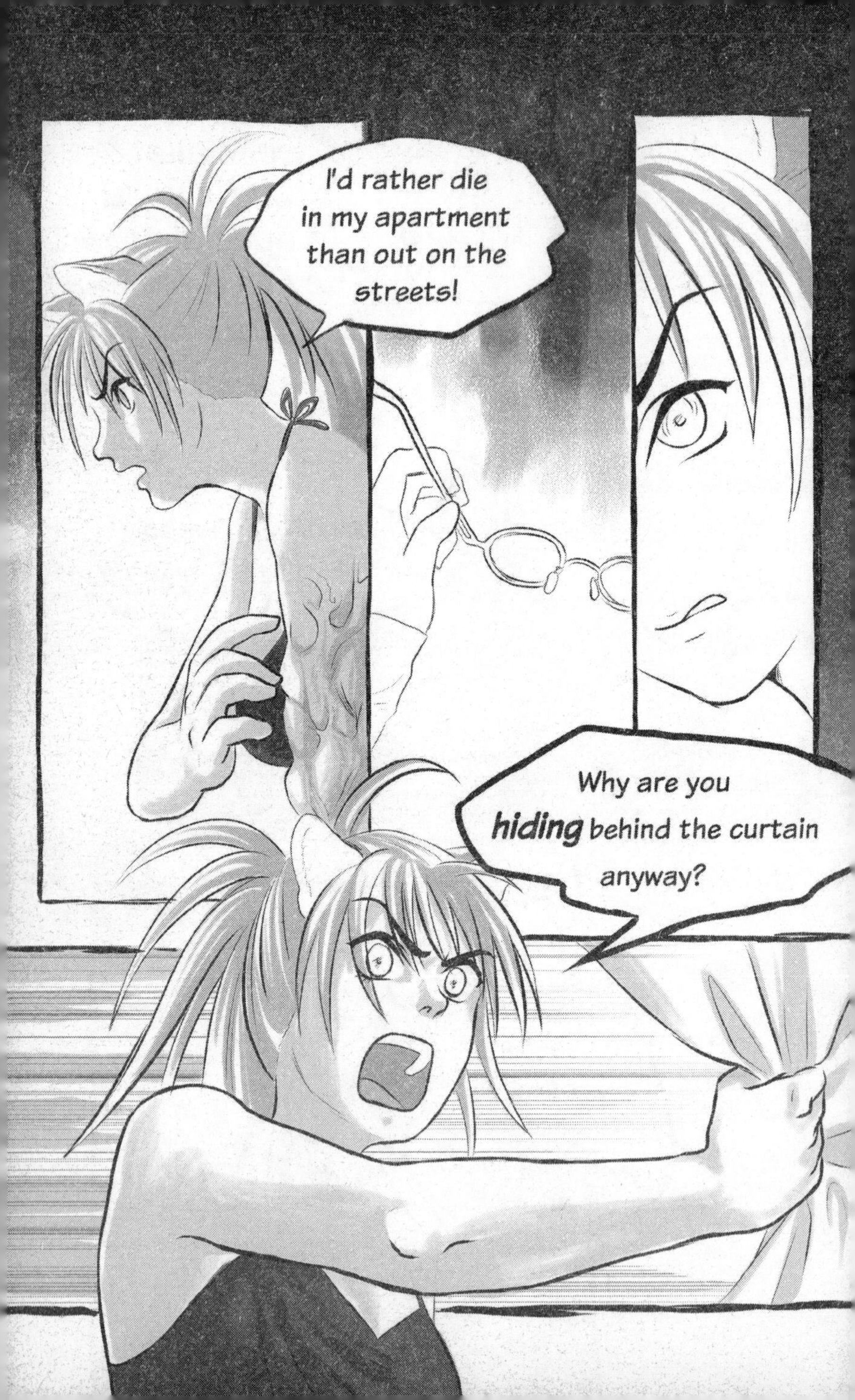
I'd rather die in my apartment than out on the streets!
Why are you **hiding** behind the curtain anyway?

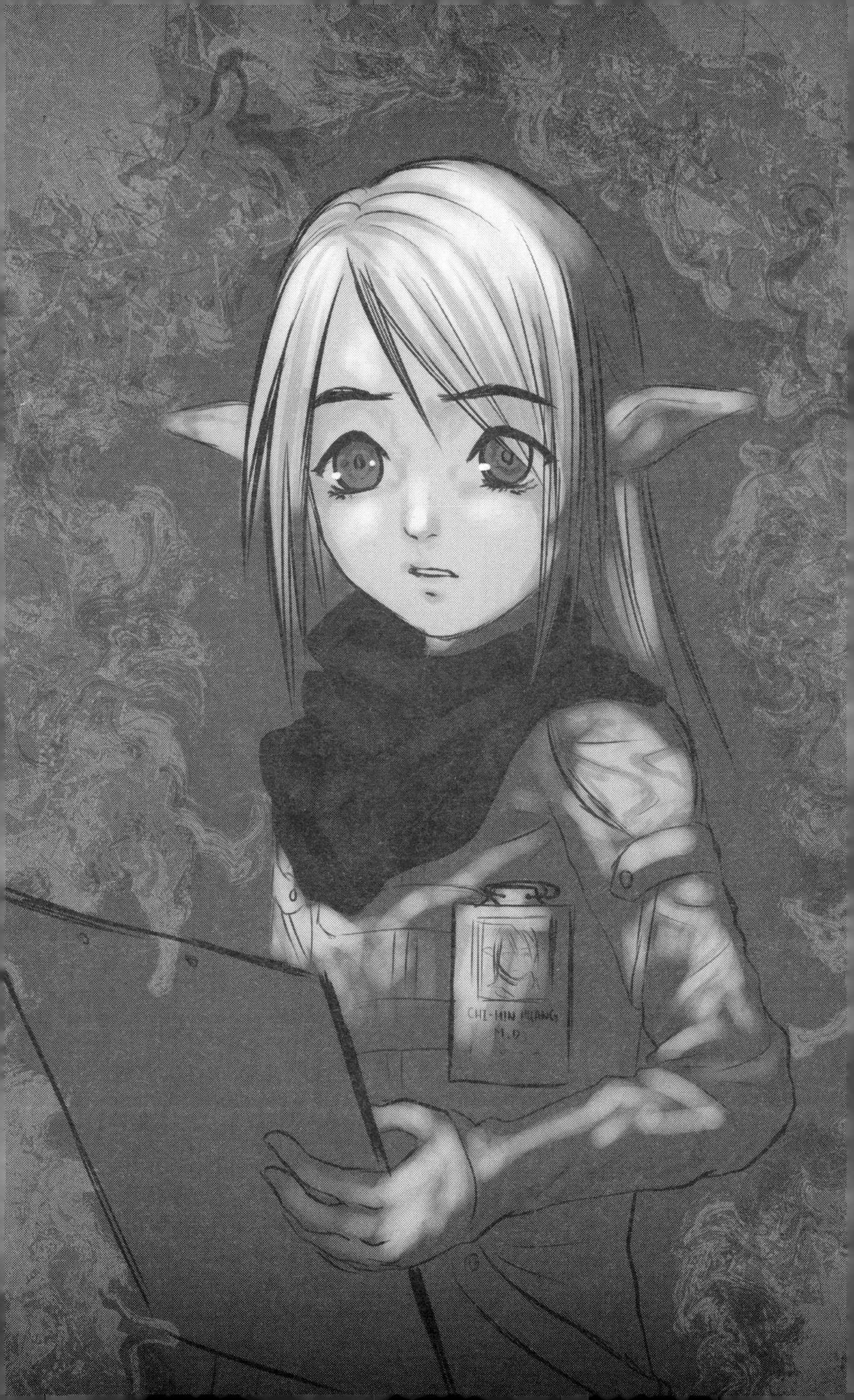

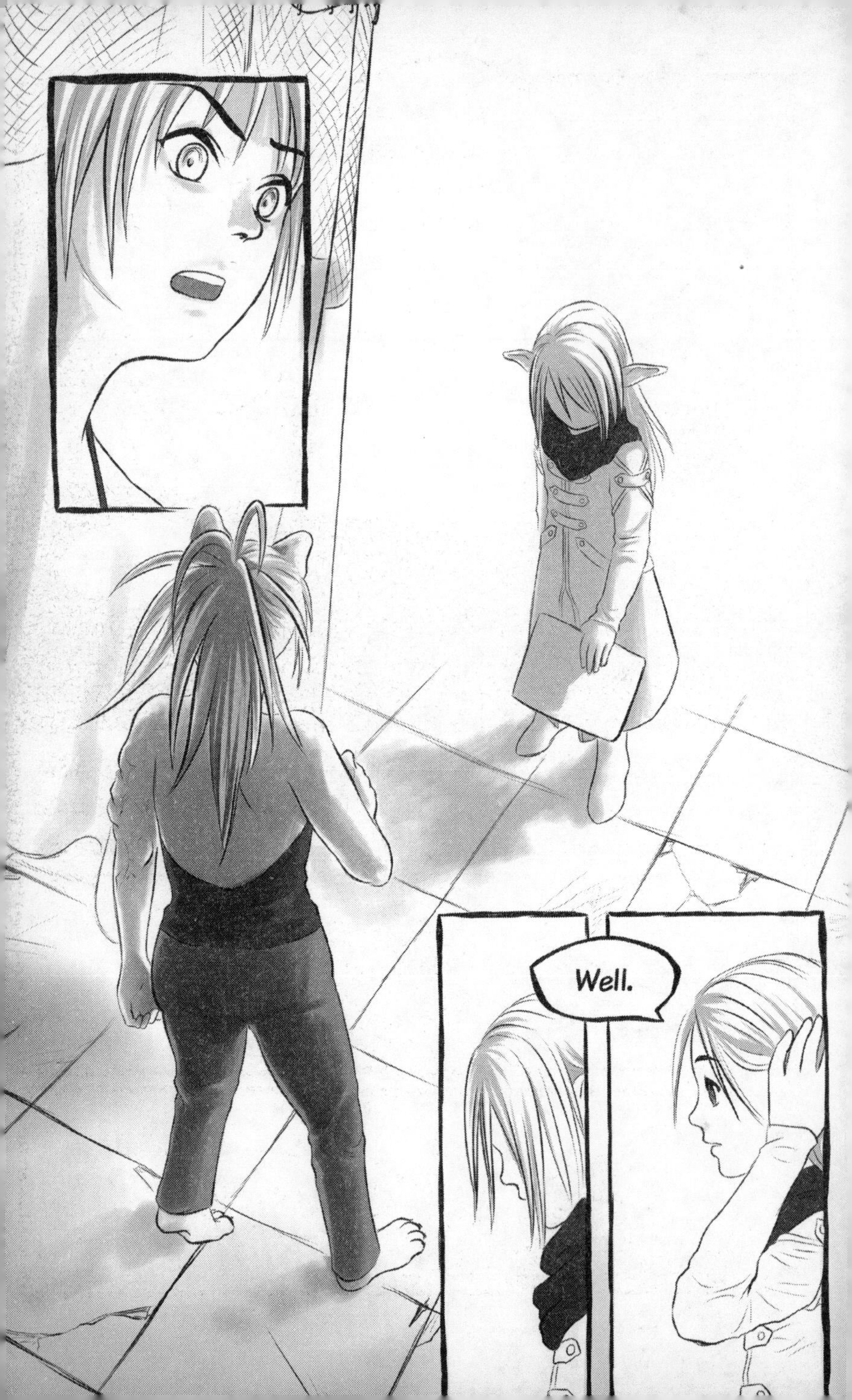
Well.

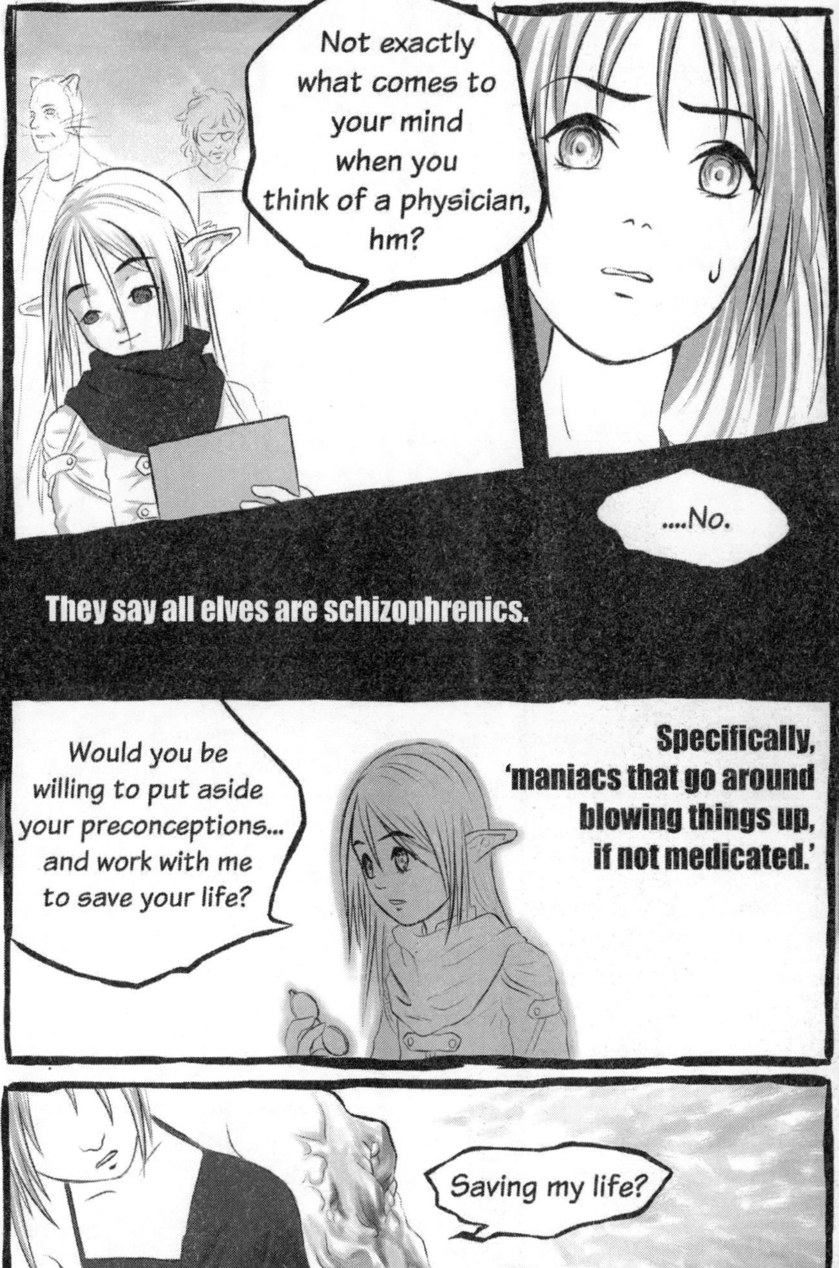

Not exactly what comes to your mind when you think of a physician, hm?
....No.
They say all elves are schizophrenics.
Would you be willing to put aside your preconceptions... and work with me to save your life?
Specifically, 'maniacs that go around blowing things up, if not medicated.'
Saving my life?

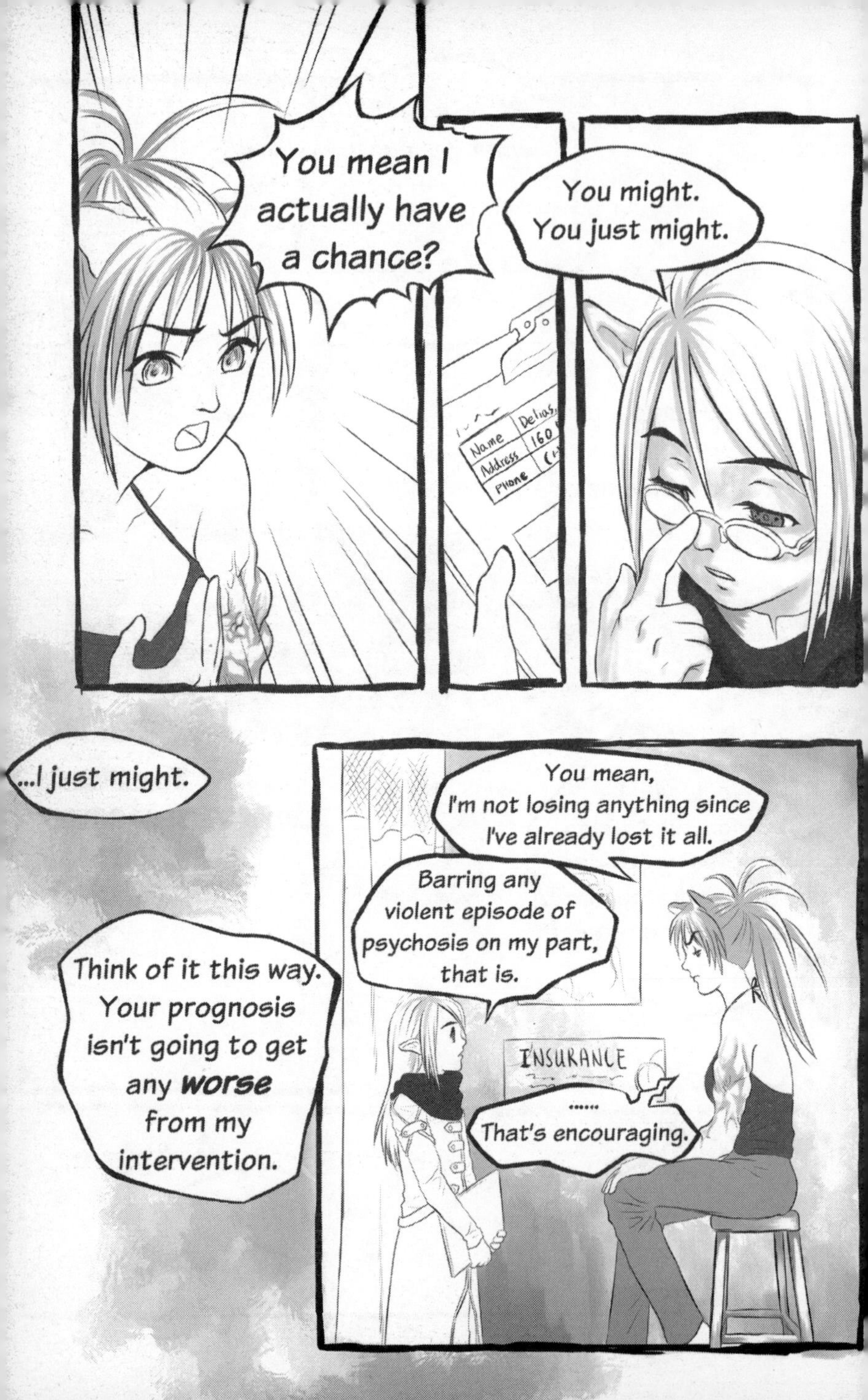
You mean I actually have a chance?
Name
Delias,
Address
160
Phone
You might. You just might.
...I just might.
Think of it this way. Your prognosis isn't going to get any **worse** from my intervention.
You mean, I'm not losing anything since I've already lost it all.
Barring any violent episode of psychosis on my part, that is.
INSURANCE
......
That's encouraging.

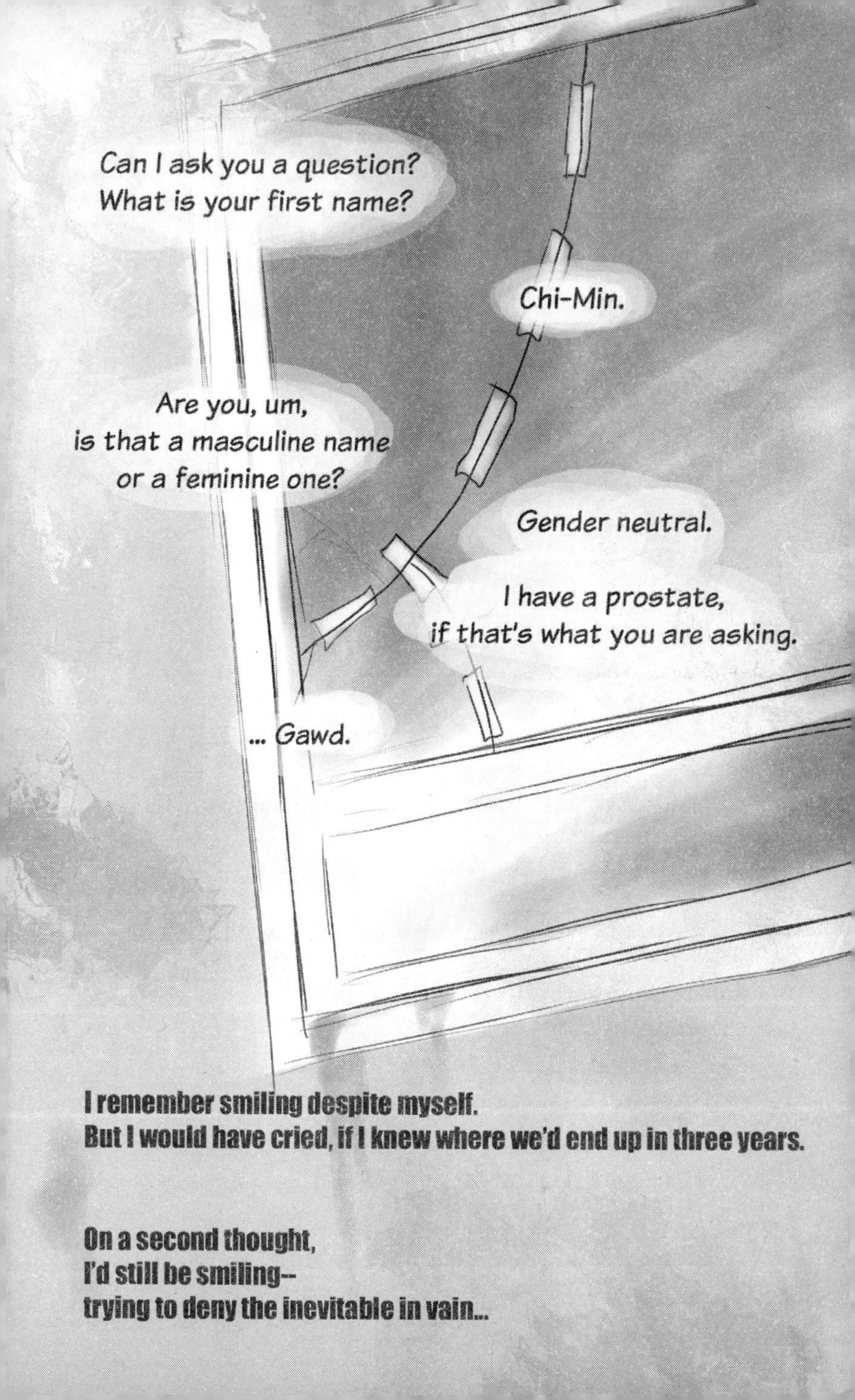
Can I ask you a question?
What is your first name?
Chi-Min.
Are you, um,
is that a masculine name
or a feminine one?
Gender neutral.
I have a prostate,
if that's what you are asking.
... Gawd.
I remember smiling despite myself.
But I would have cried, if I knew where we'd end up in three years.
On a second thought,
I'd still be smiling--
trying to deny the inevitable in vain...

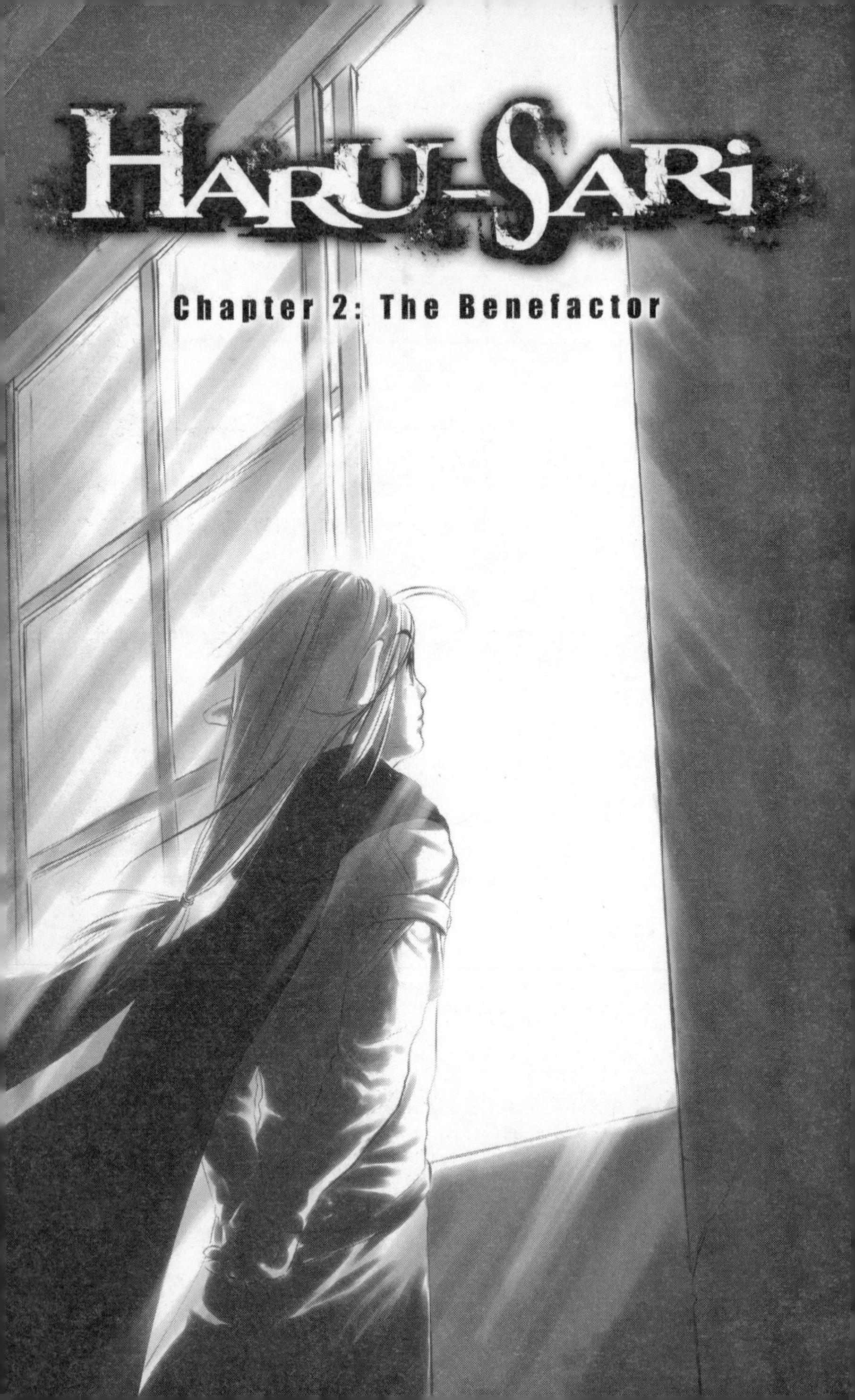
HARU-SARI
Chapter 2: The Benefactor

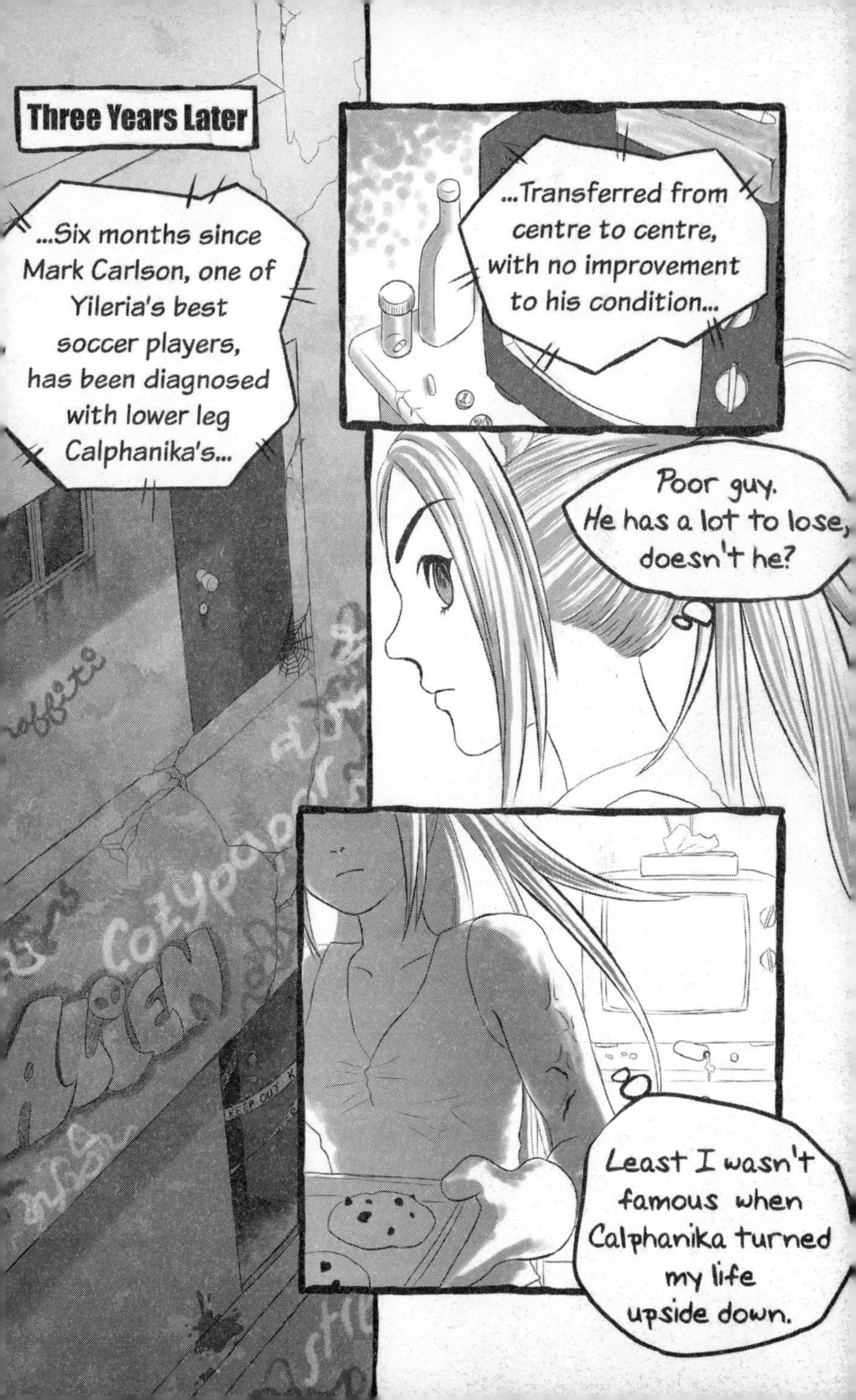
Three Years Later
...Six months since Mark Carlson, one of Yileria's best soccer players, has been diagnosed with lower leg Calphanika's...
...Transferred from centre to centre, with no improvement to his condition...
Poor guy. He has a lot to lose, doesn't he?
Least I wasn't famous when Calphanika turned my life upside down.

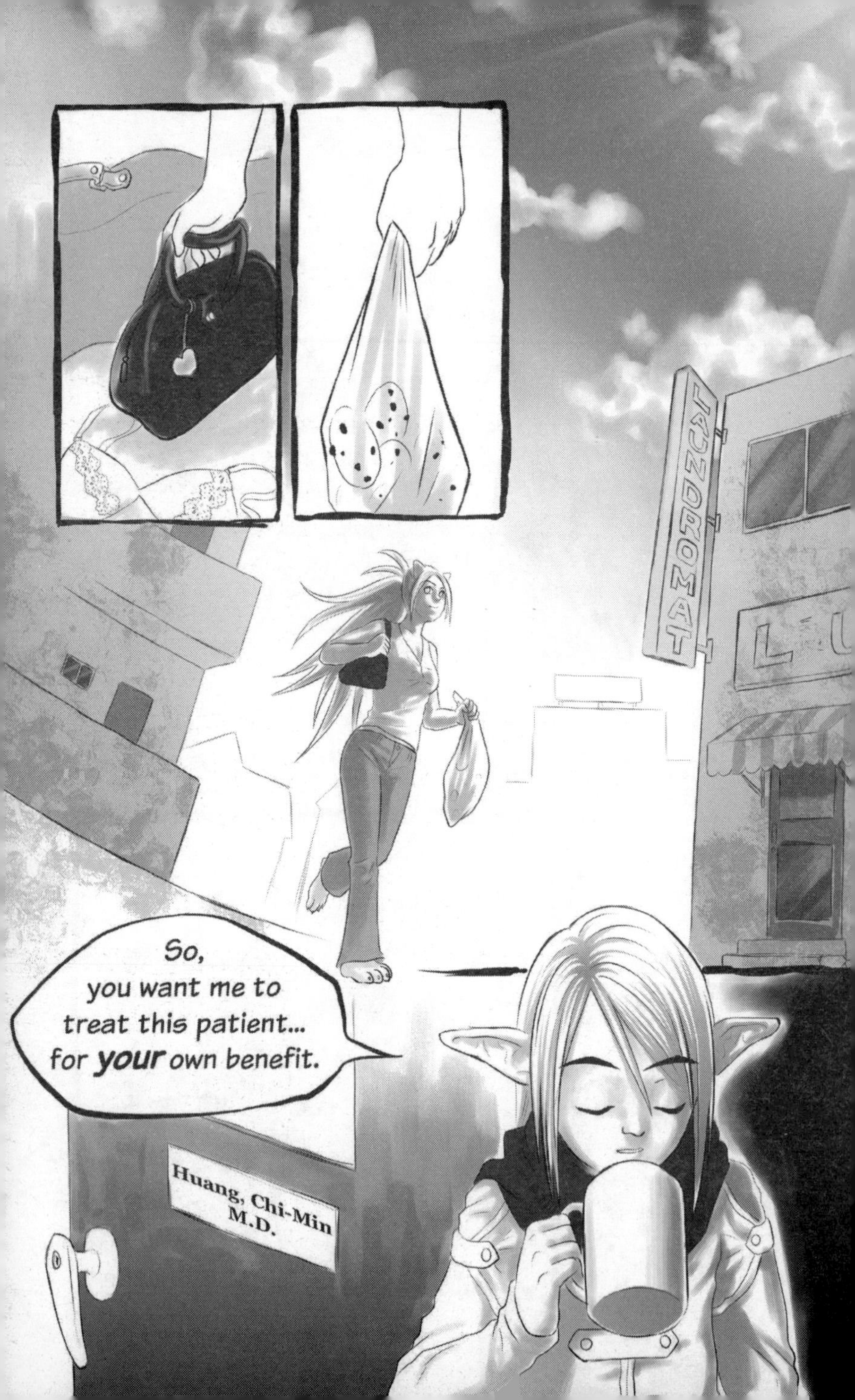
LAUNDROMAT
So, you want me to treat this patient... for *your* own benefit.
Huang, Chi-Min M.D.

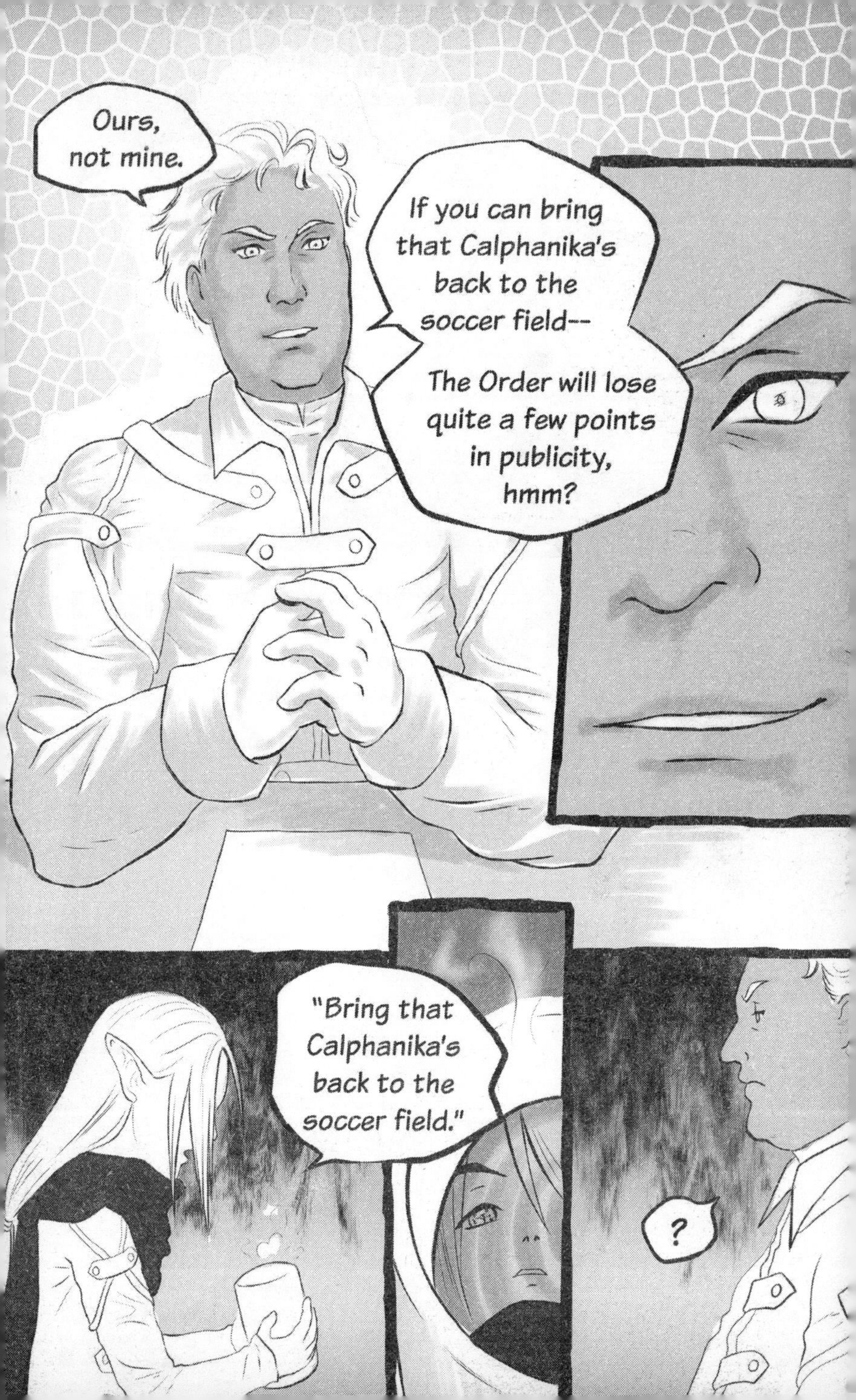
Ours, not mine.
If you can bring that Calphanika's back to the soccer field--
The Order will lose quite a few points in publicity, hmm?
"Bring that Calphanika's back to the soccer field."
?

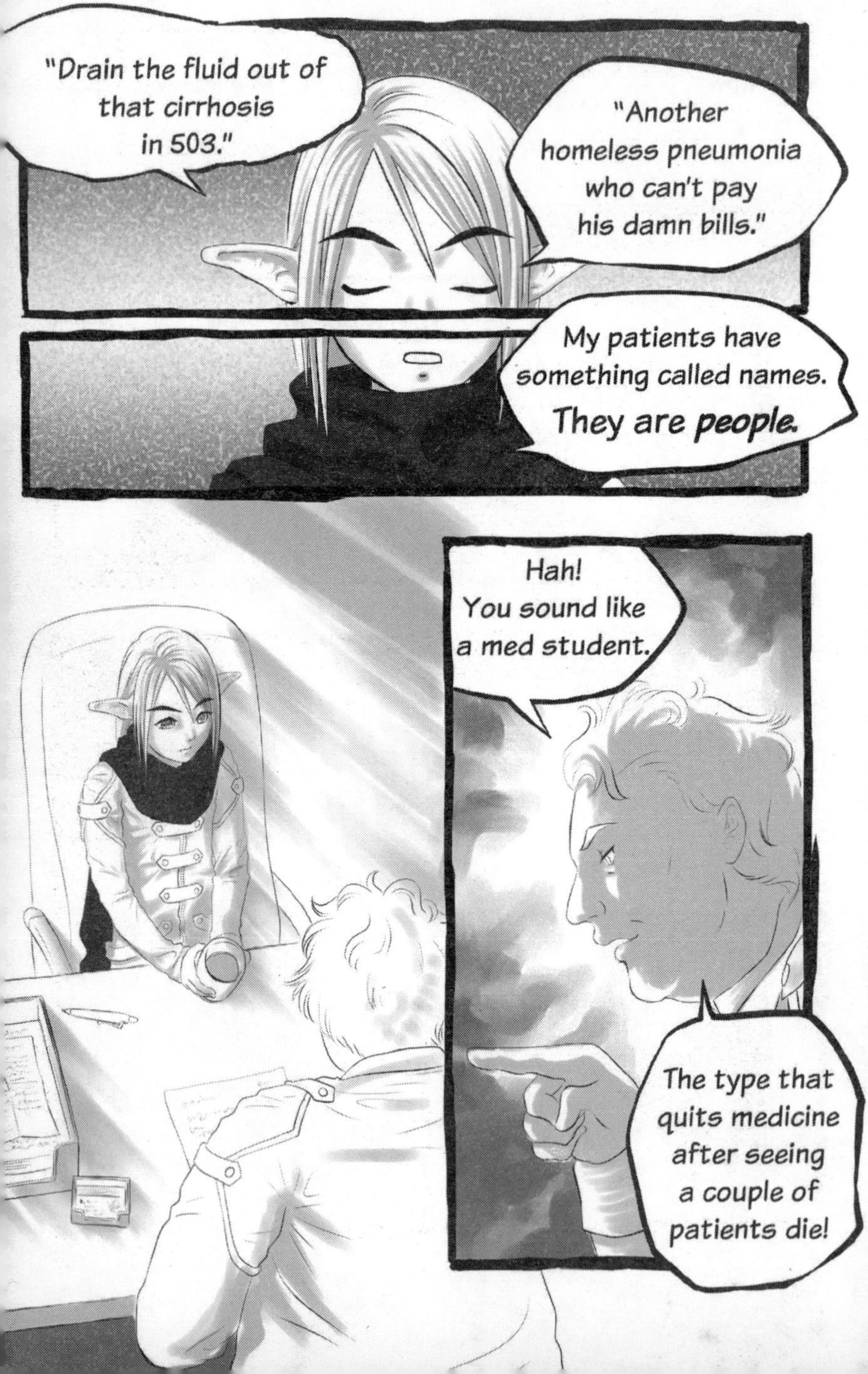
"Drain the fluid out of that cirrhosis in 503."
"Another homeless pneumonia who can't pay his damn bills."
My patients have something called names. They are *people.*
Hah! You sound like a med student.
The type that quits medicine after seeing a couple of patients die!

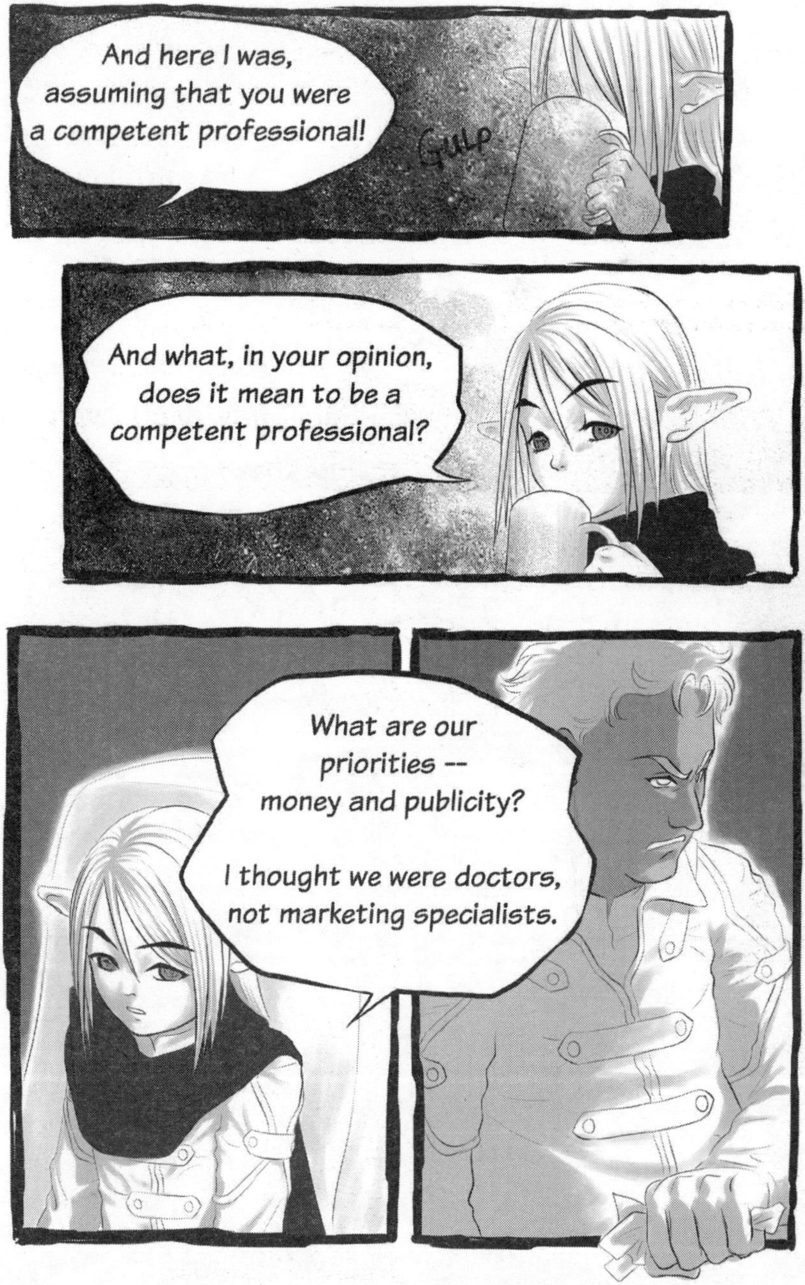
And here I was, assuming that you were a competent professional!
GULP
And what, in your opinion, does it mean to be a competent professional?
What are our priorities -- money and publicity?
I thought we were doctors, not marketing specialists.

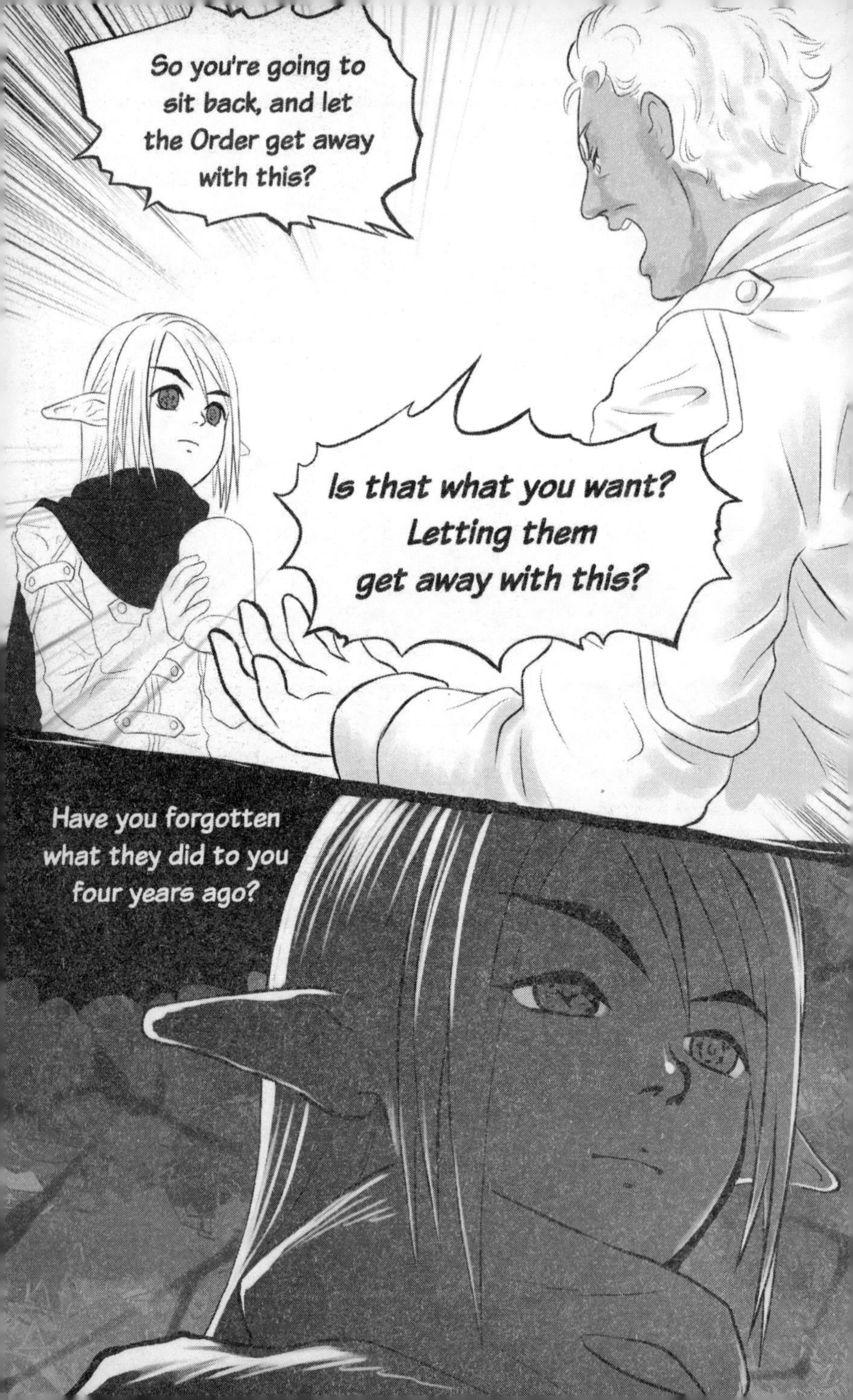
So you're going to sit back, and let the Order get away with this?
Is that what you want? Letting them get away with this?
Have you forgotten what they did to you four years ago?

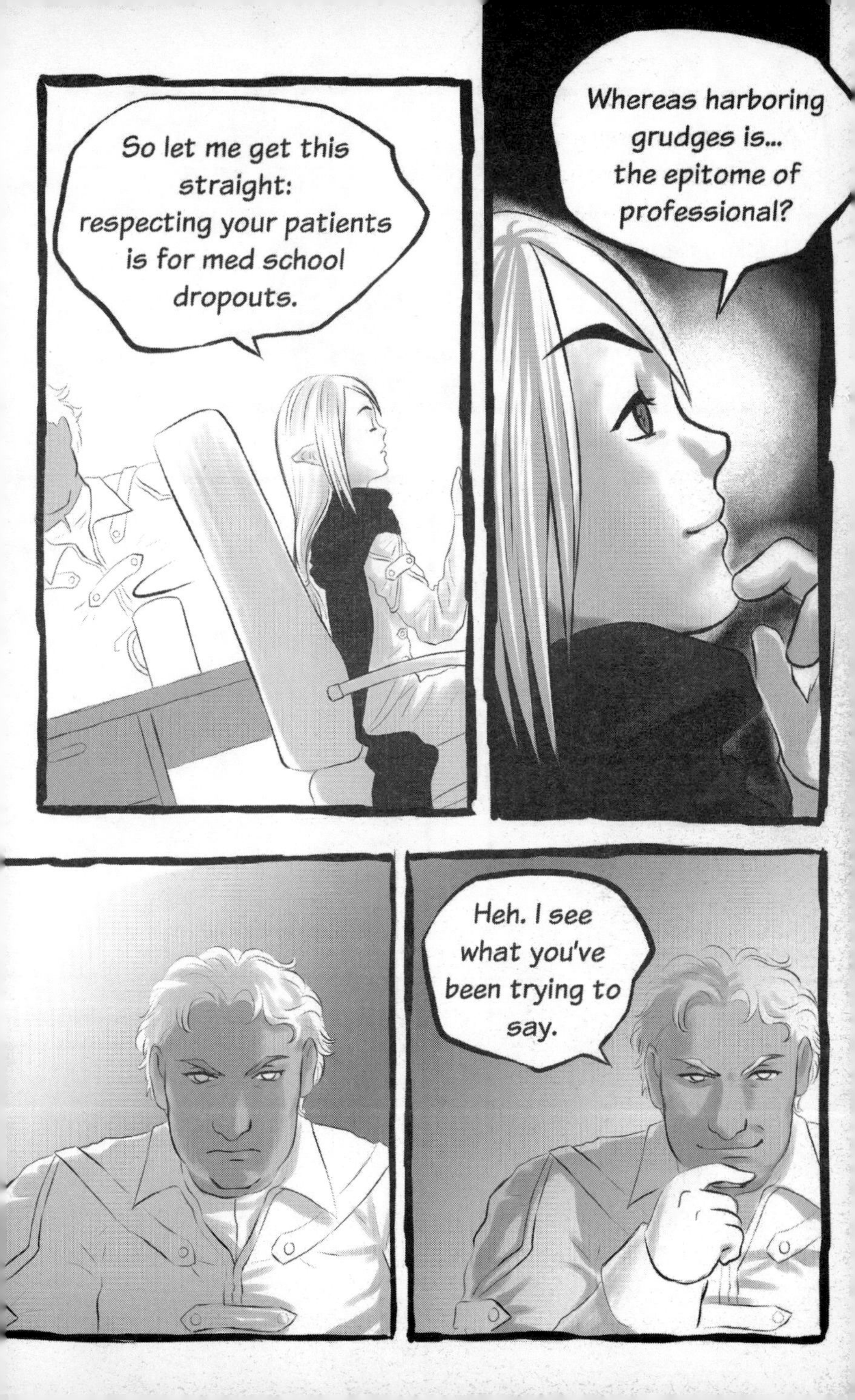
So let me get this straight: respecting your patients is for med school dropouts.
Whereas harboring grudges is... the epitome of professional?
Heh. I see what you've been trying to say.

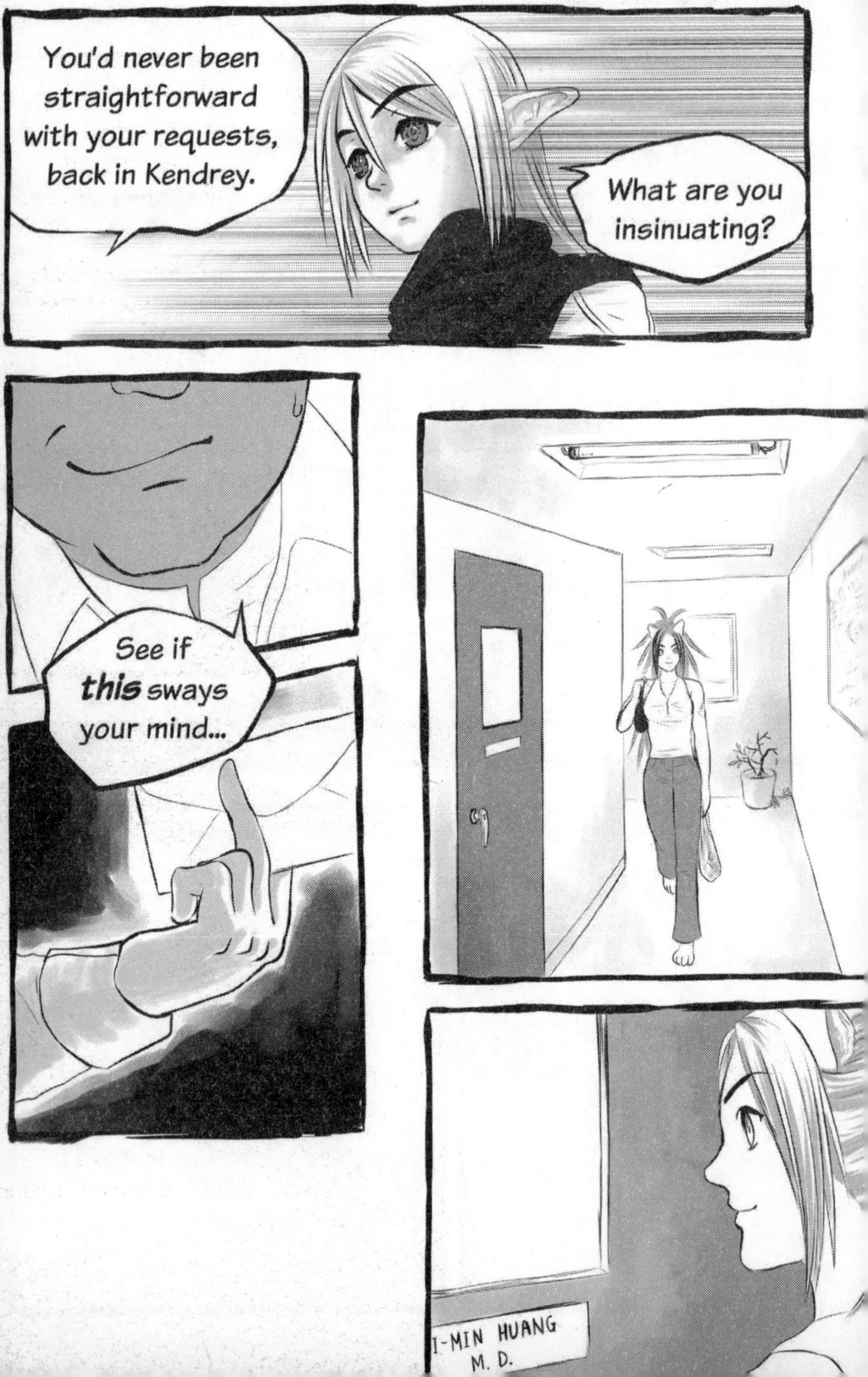
You'd never been straightforward with your requests, back in Kendrey.
What are you insinuating?
See if **this** sways your mind...
I-MIN HUANG
M. D.

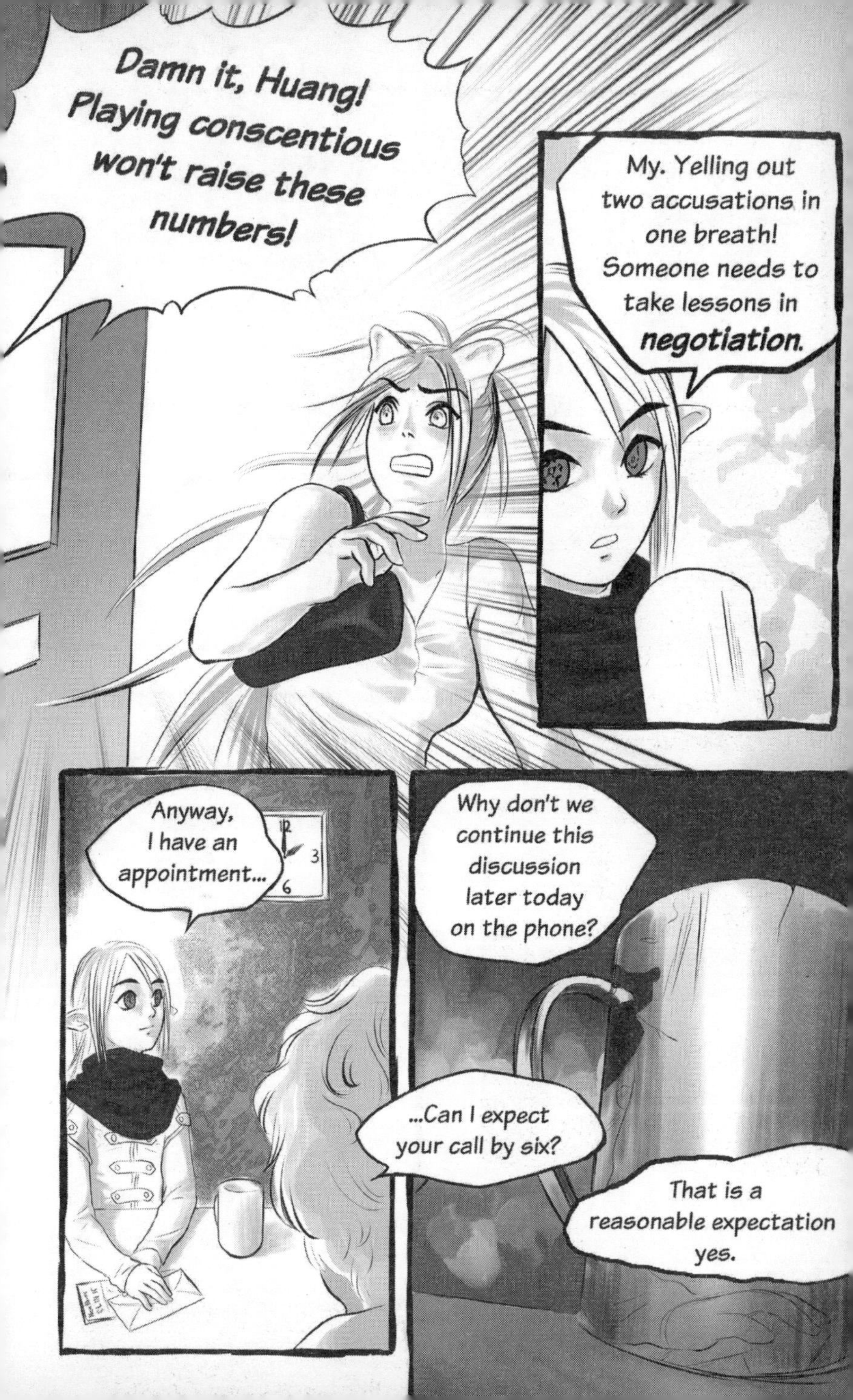
Damn it, Huang! Playing conscentious won't raise these numbers!
My. Yelling out two accusations in one breath! Someone needs to take lessons in **negotiation**.
Anyway, I have an appointment...
Why don't we continue this discussion later today on the phone?
...Can I expect your call by six?
That is a reasonable expectation yes.

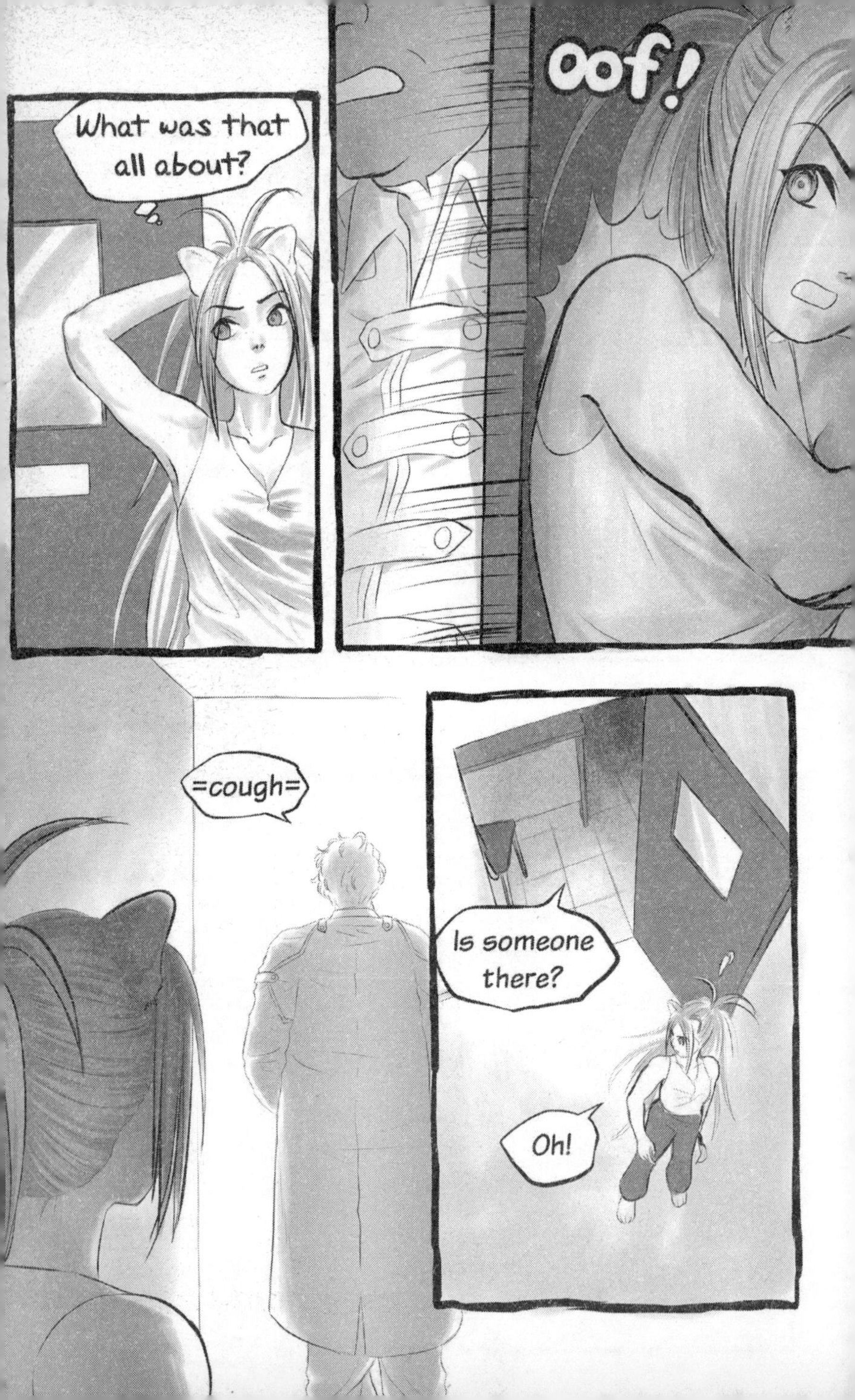
What was that all about?
oof!
=cough=
Is someone there?
Oh!

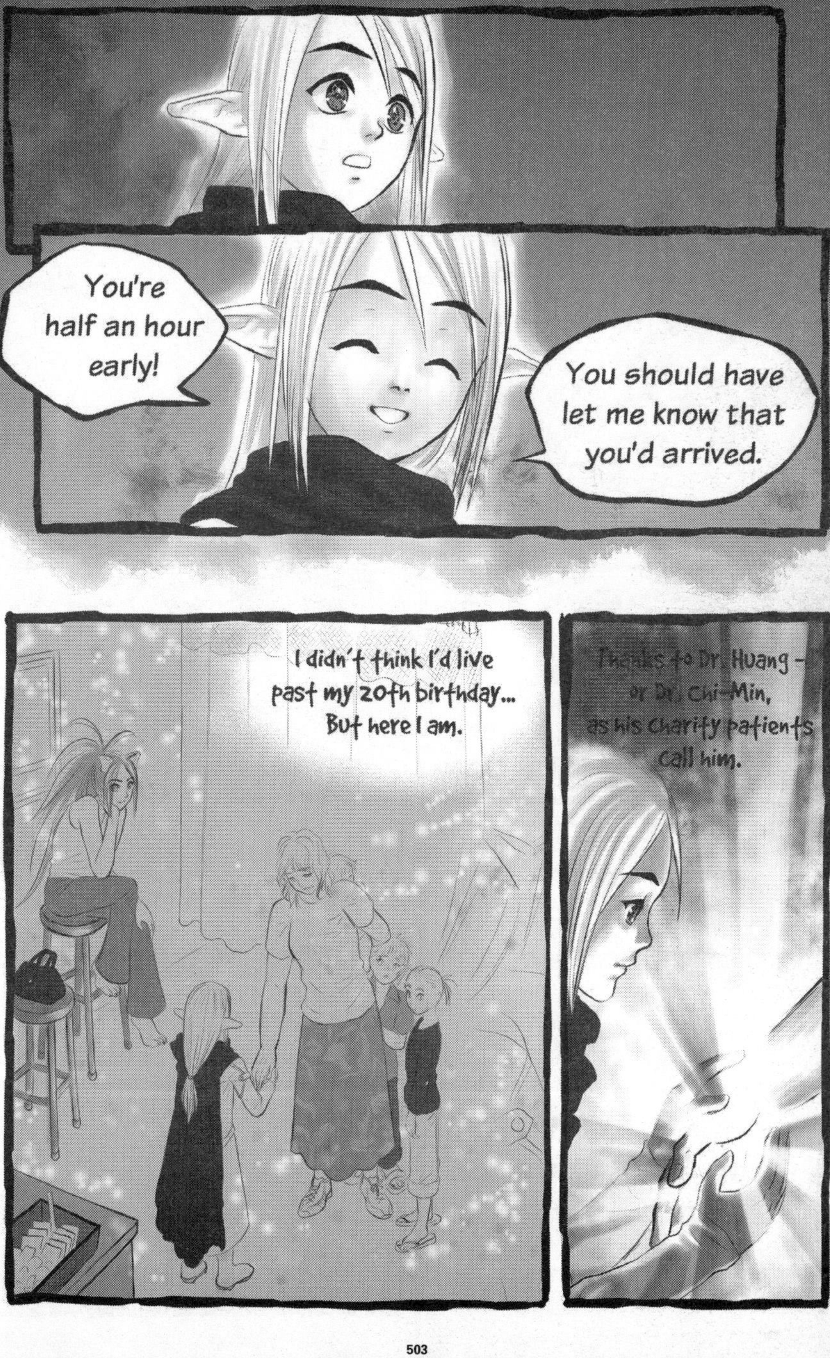
You're half an hour early!
You should have let me know that you'd arrived.
I didn't think I'd live past my 20th birthday... But here I am.
Thanks to Dr. Huang – or Dr. Chi-Min, as his charity patients call him.

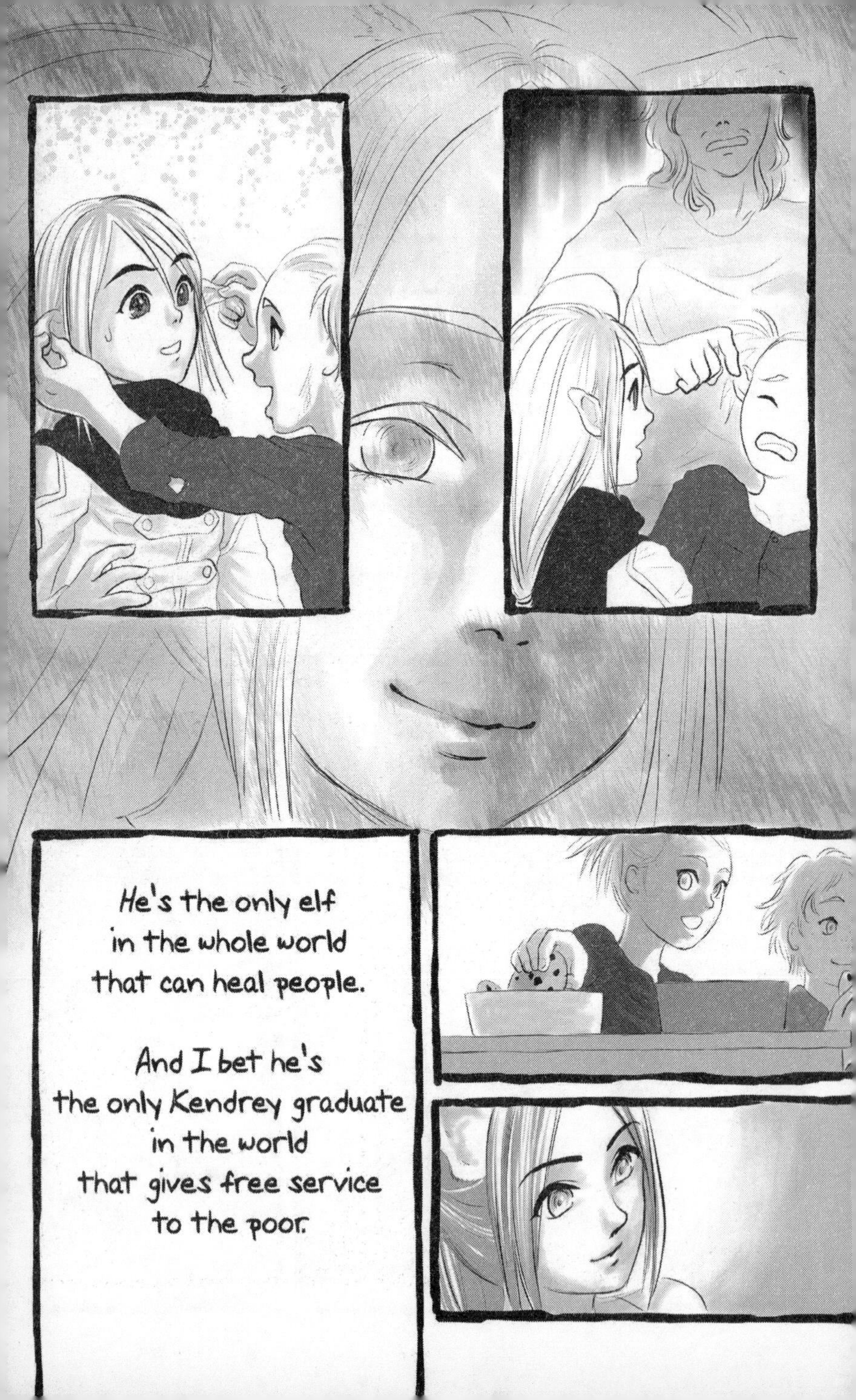
He's the only elf
in the whole world
that can heal people.
And I bet he's
the only Kendrey graduate
in the world
that gives free service
to the poor.

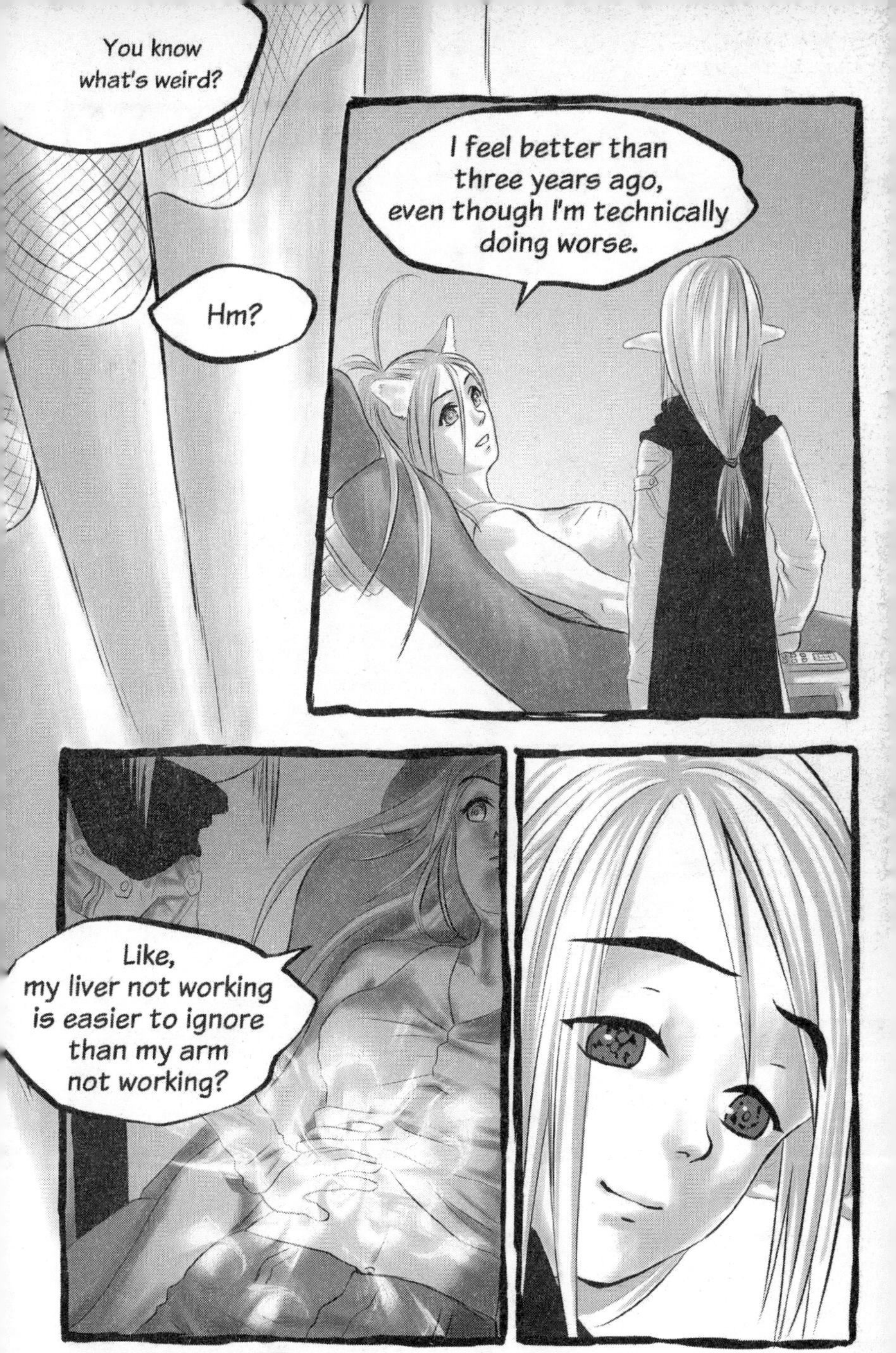
You know what's weird?
Hm?
I feel better than three years ago, even though I'm technically doing worse.
Like, my liver not working is easier to ignore than my arm not working?

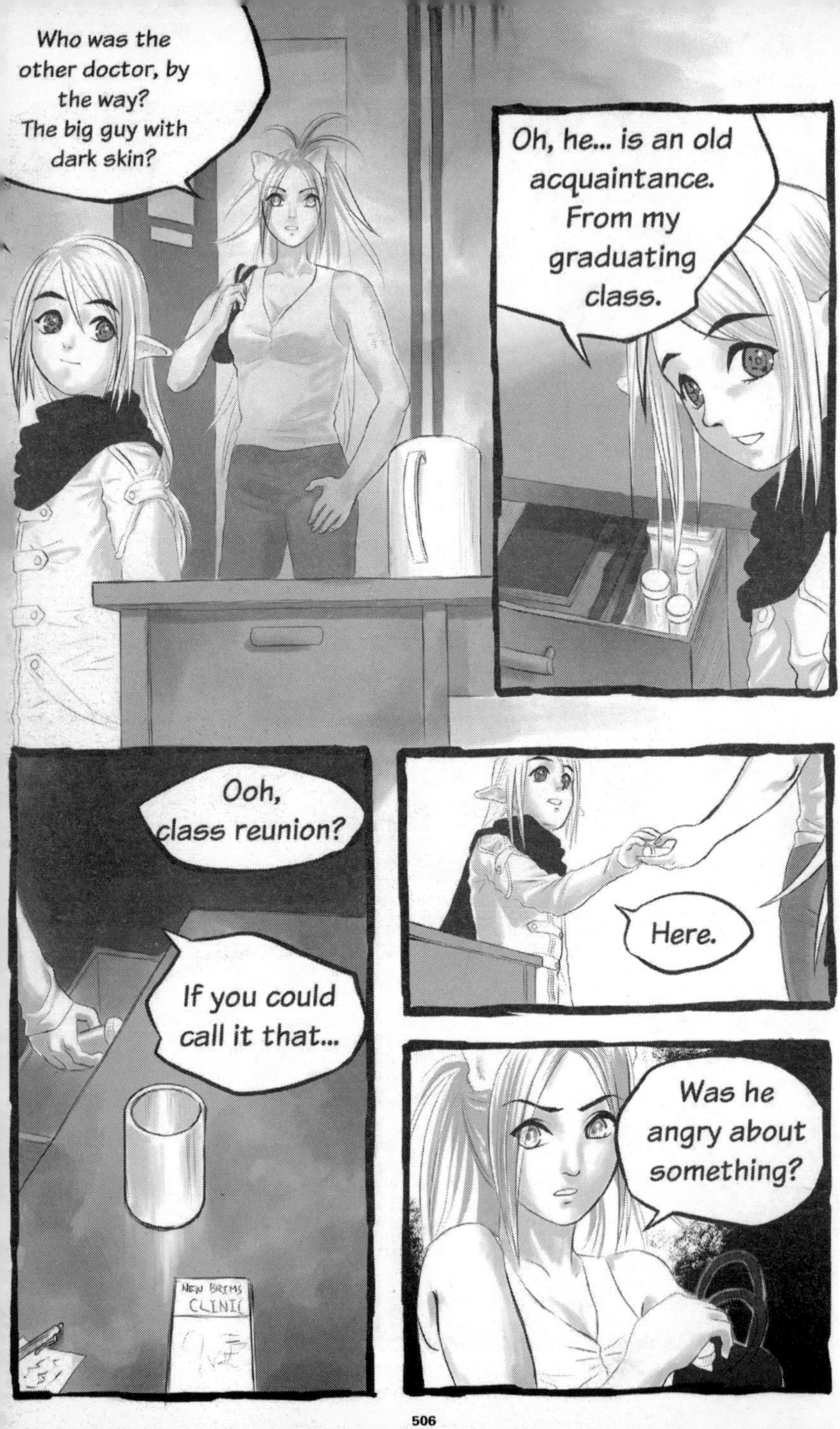
Who was the other doctor, by the way? The big guy with dark skin?
Oh, he... is an old acquaintance. From my graduating class.
Ooh, class reunion?
If you could call it that...
NEW BRIMS CLINIC
Here.
Was he angry about something?

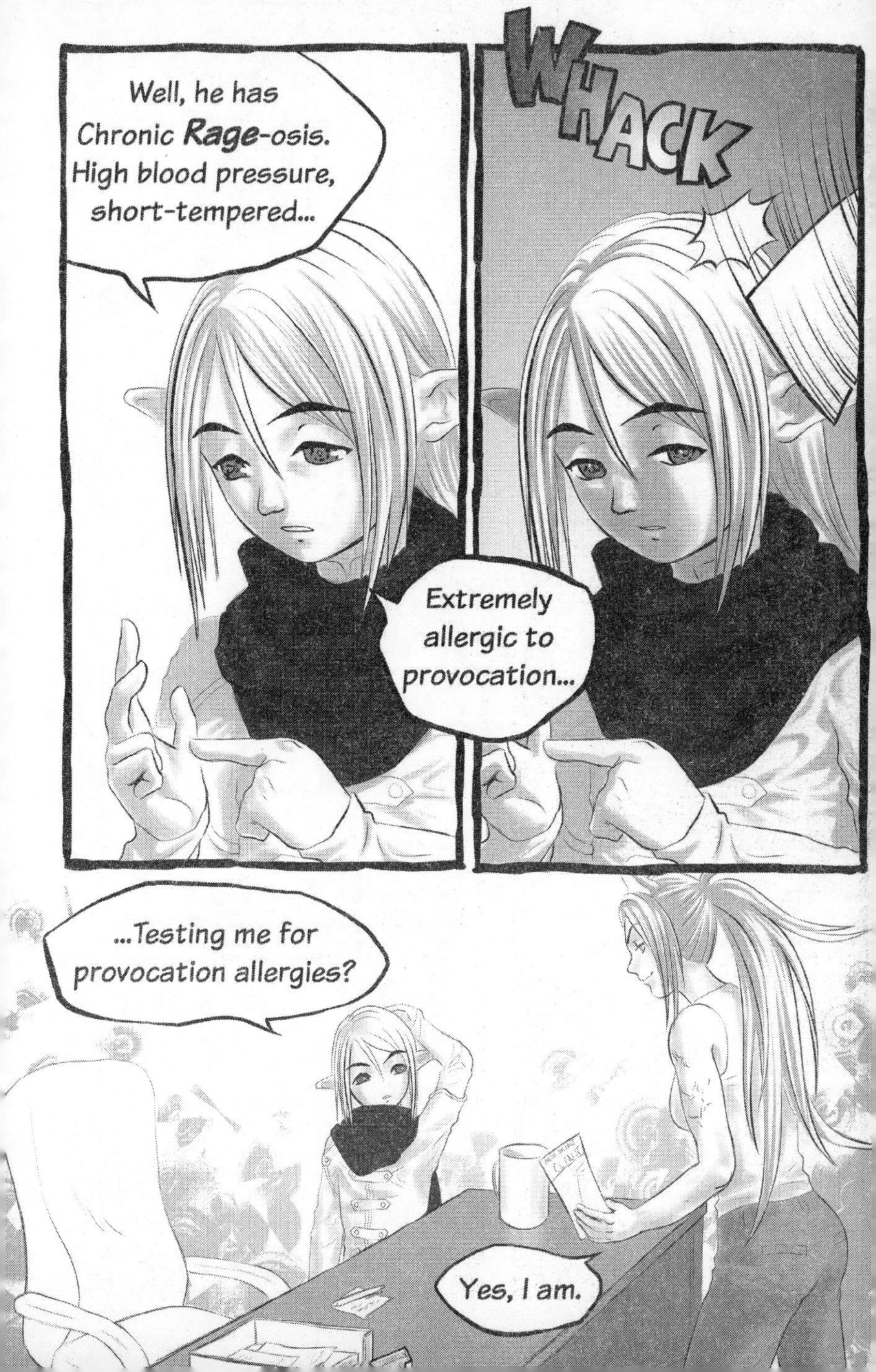
Well, he has Chronic **Rage**-osis. High blood pressure, short-tempered...
Extremely allergic to provocation...
WHACK
...Testing me for provocation allergies?
Yes, I am.

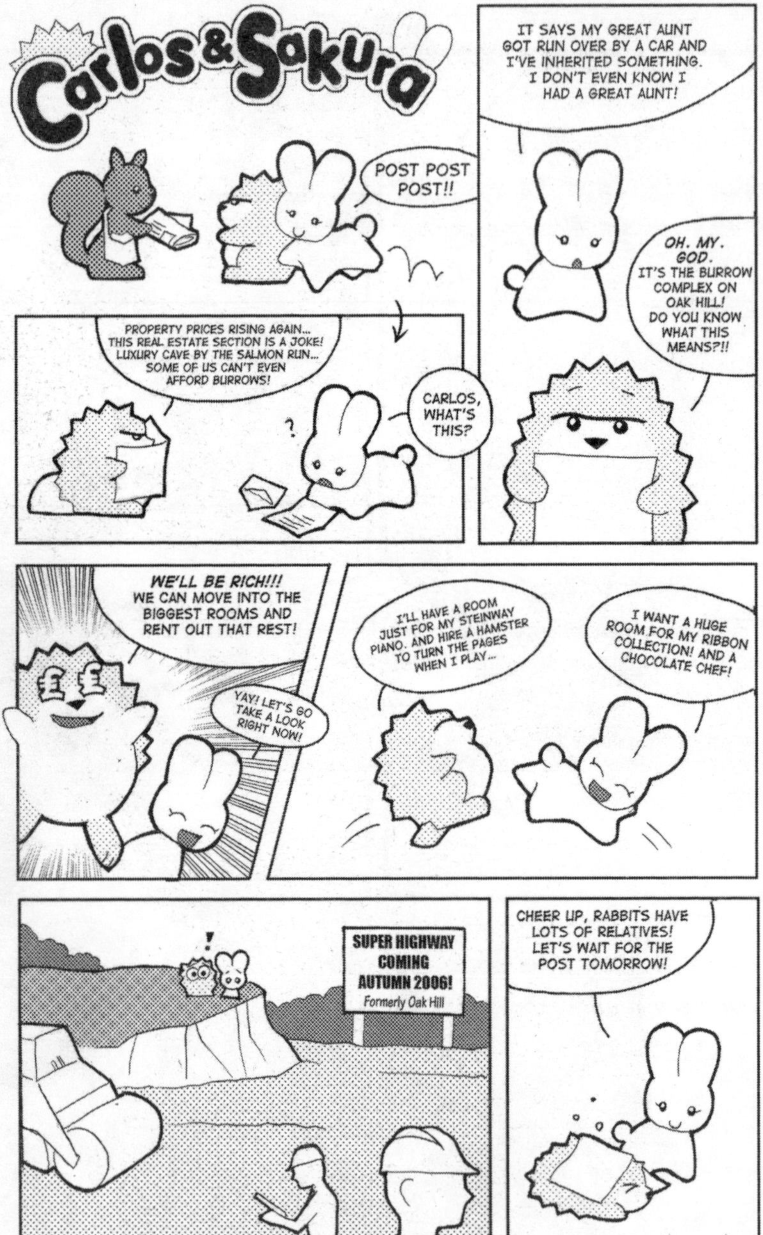
Carlos & Sakura
POST POST POST!!
IT SAYS MY GREAT AUNT GOT RUN OVER BY A CAR AND I'VE INHERITED SOMETHING. I DON'T EVEN KNOW I HAD A GREAT AUNT!
PROPERTY PRICES RISING AGAIN... THIS REAL ESTATE SECTION IS A JOKE! LUXURY CAVE BY THE SALMON RUN... SOME OF US CAN'T EVEN AFFORD BURROWS!
CARLOS, WHAT'S THIS?
OH. MY. GOD. IT'S THE BURROW COMPLEX ON OAK HILL! DO YOU KNOW WHAT THIS MEANS?!!
WE'LL BE RICH!!! WE CAN MOVE INTO THE BIGGEST ROOMS AND RENT OUT THAT REST!
YAY! LET'S GO TAKE A LOOK RIGHT NOW!
I'LL HAVE A ROOM JUST FOR MY STEINWAY PIANO. AND HIRE A HAMSTER TO TURN THE PAGES WHEN I PLAY...
I WANT A HUGE ROOM FOR MY RIBBON COLLECTION! AND A CHOCOLATE CHEF!
SUPER HIGHWAY COMING AUTUMN 2006! Formerly Oak Hill
CHEER UP, RABBITS HAVE LOTS OF RELATIVES! LET'S WAIT FOR THE POST TOMORROW!
© Joanna Zhou

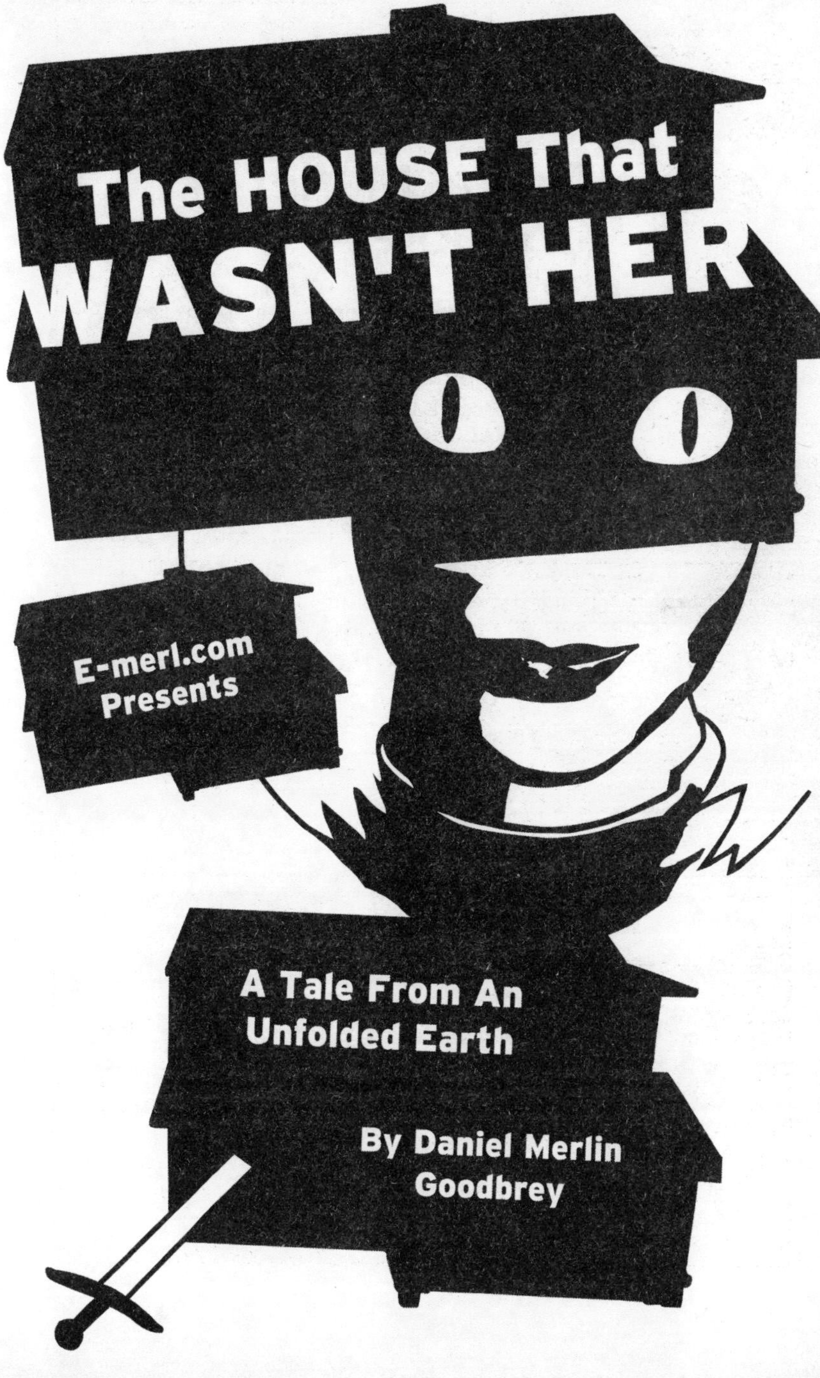
The HOUSE That
WASN'T HER
E-merl.com
Presents
A Tale From An
Unfolded Earth
By Daniel Merlin
Goodbrey

Date of birth: 30 October 1978

Daniel Merlin Goodbrey

aniel Merlin Goodbrey is a comic creator, new media artist, lecturer and occasional drunk. Born on Halloween to a family of antique dealers in Suffolk, it took Daniel just 23 years to leave home and earn his Masters degree in the Digital Practices of Hyperfiction.

When not being possessed by fictional entities for the purpose of creating comics, Daniel lectures in new media design and webcomic creation at The University of Hertfordshire. In 2005 he received the Isotope Award for Excellence in Mini-comics for his surreal western fable, *The Last Sane Cowboy*. To view more of Daniel's web and print comic work, visit his regularly updated experimental archive at E-merl.com.

Welcome To An Unfolded Earth

One day the world stretched, then twisted, then unfurled. It was as if the many-folded thing we then thought to be reality had shrugged its shoulders and settled back into a more comfortable shape. Our Earth, unfolded back into its true form, was for many years afterwards a place of strangeness.

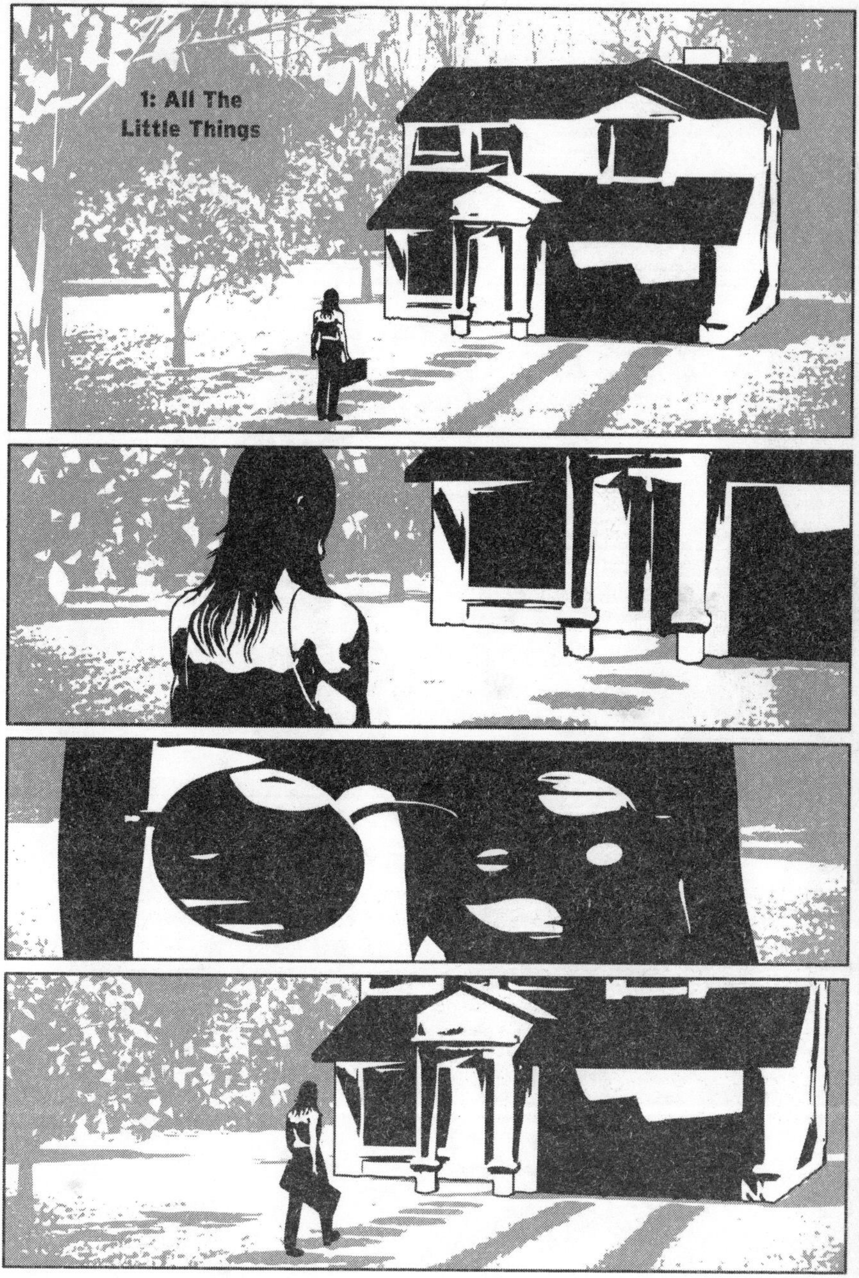
1: All The Little Things

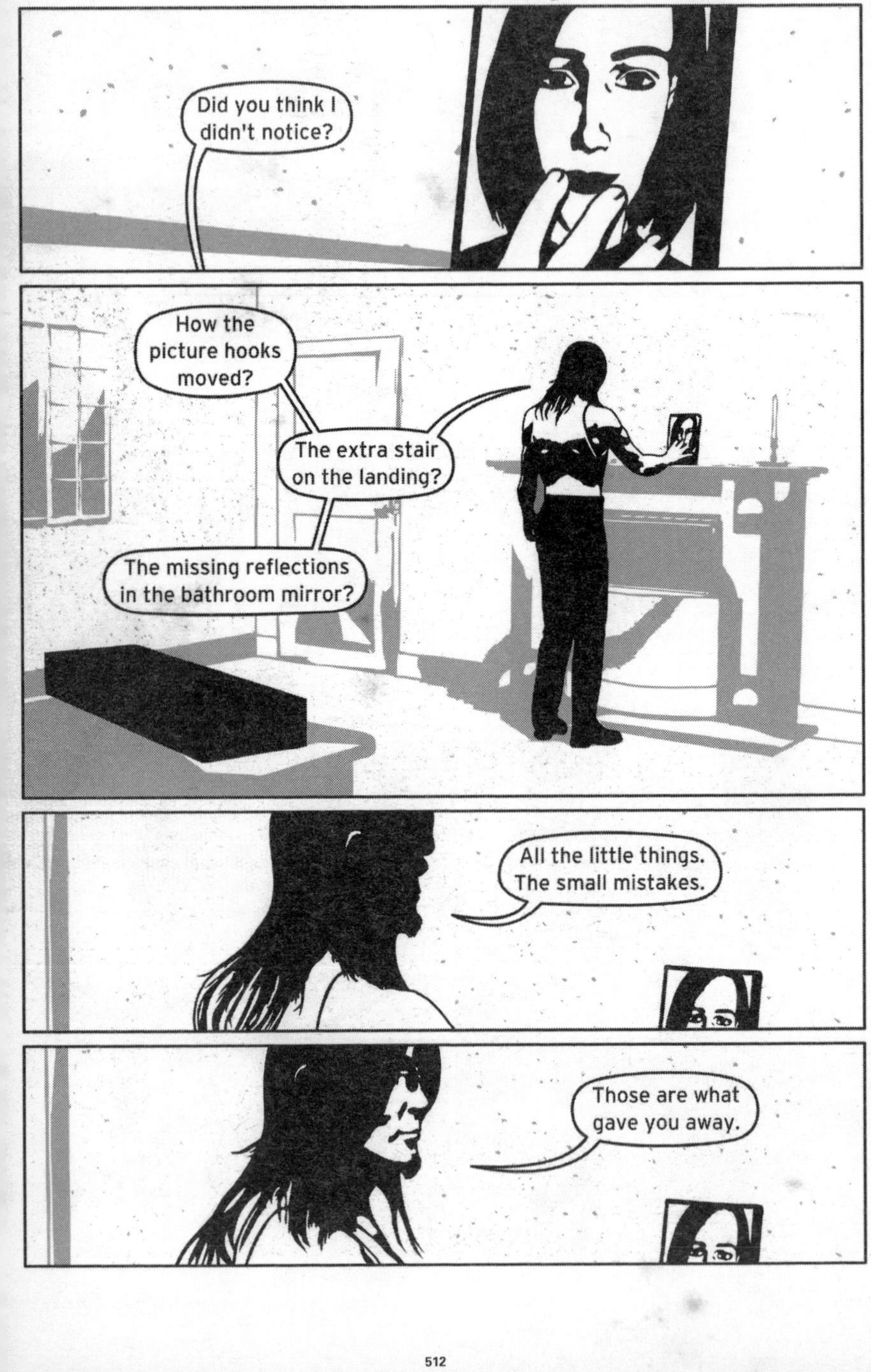
Did you think I didn't notice?
How the picture hooks moved?
The extra stair on the landing?
The missing reflections in the bathroom mirror?
All the little things. The small mistakes.
Those are what gave you away.

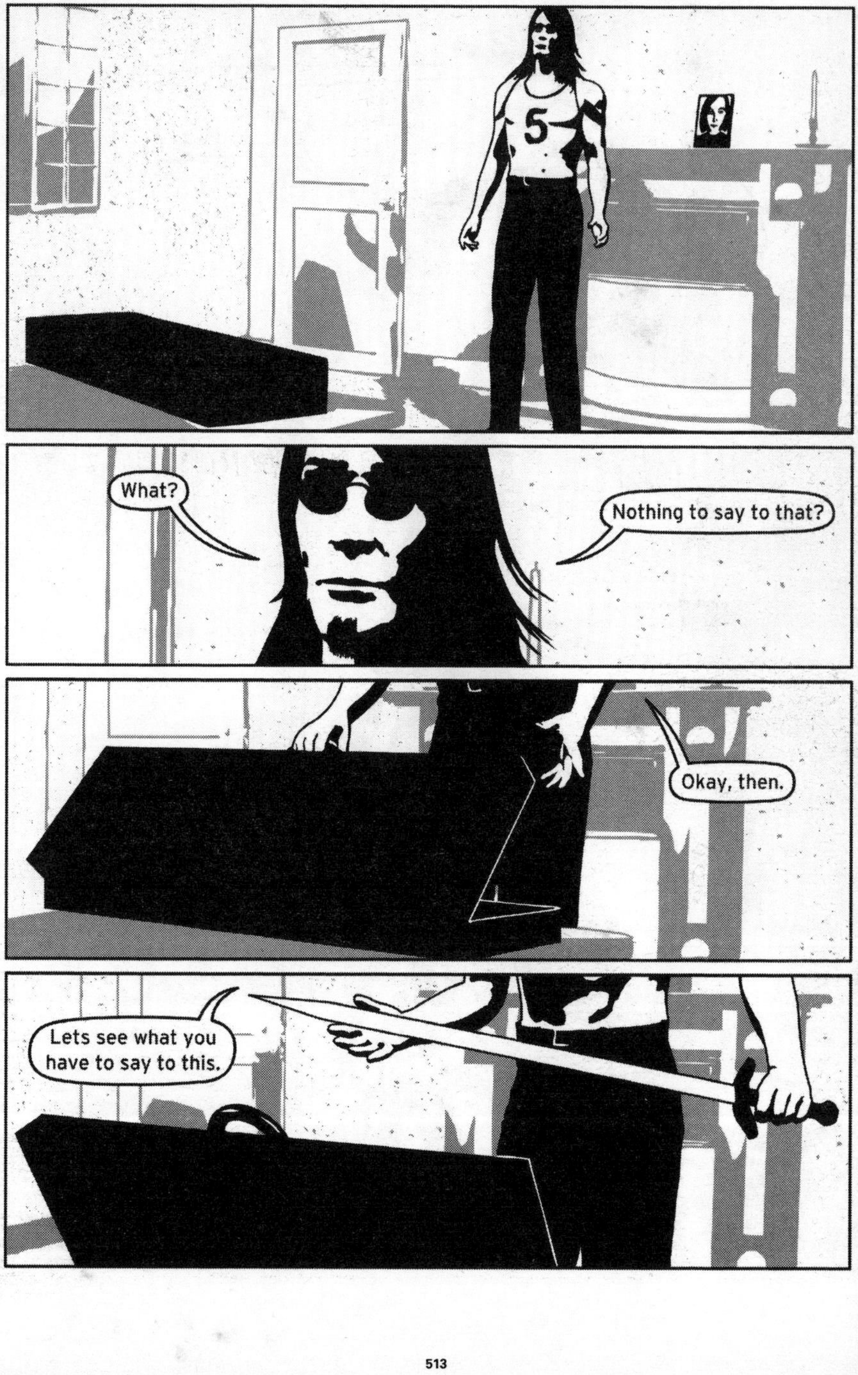
What?
Nothing to say to that?
Okay, then.
Lets see what you have to say to this.

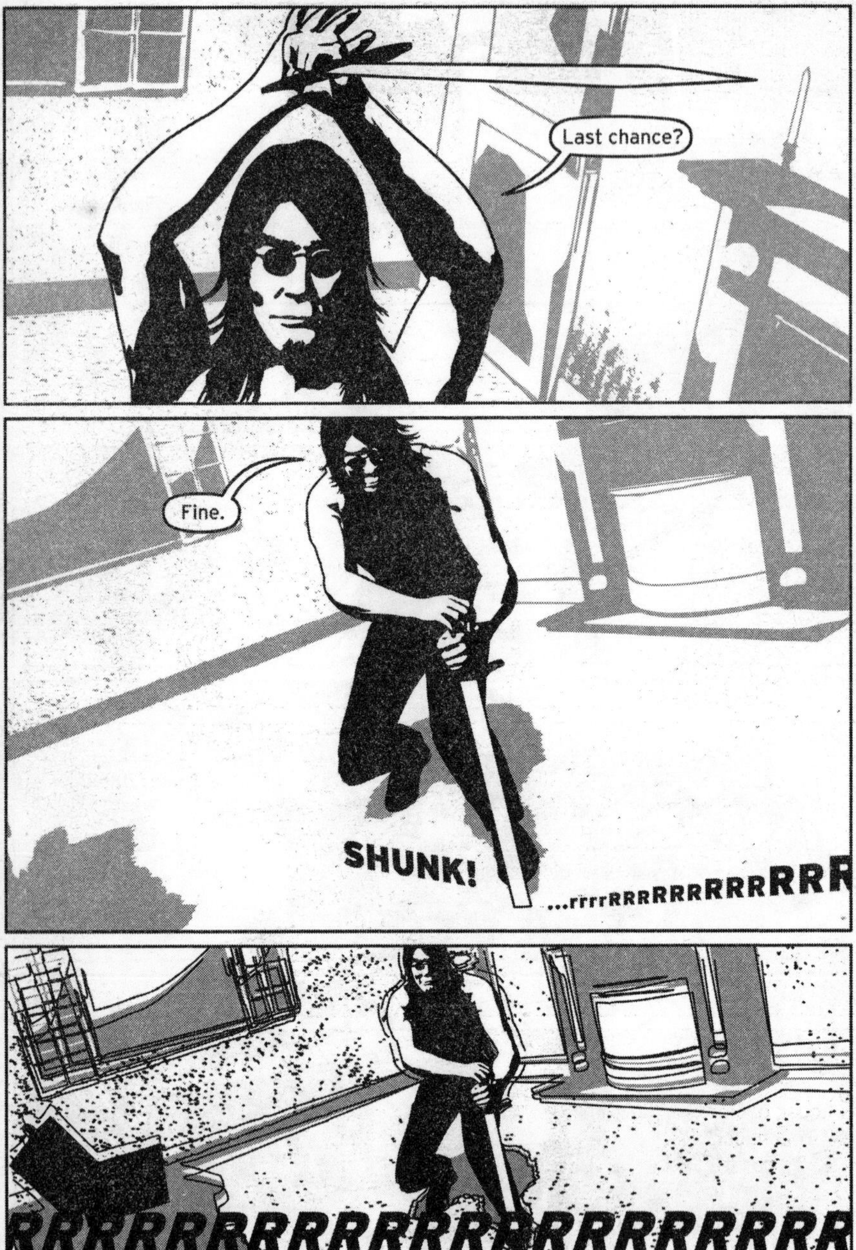
Last chance?
Fine.
SHUNK!
...rrrrRRRRRRRRRRRR
RRRRRRRRRRRRRRRRRRRRR

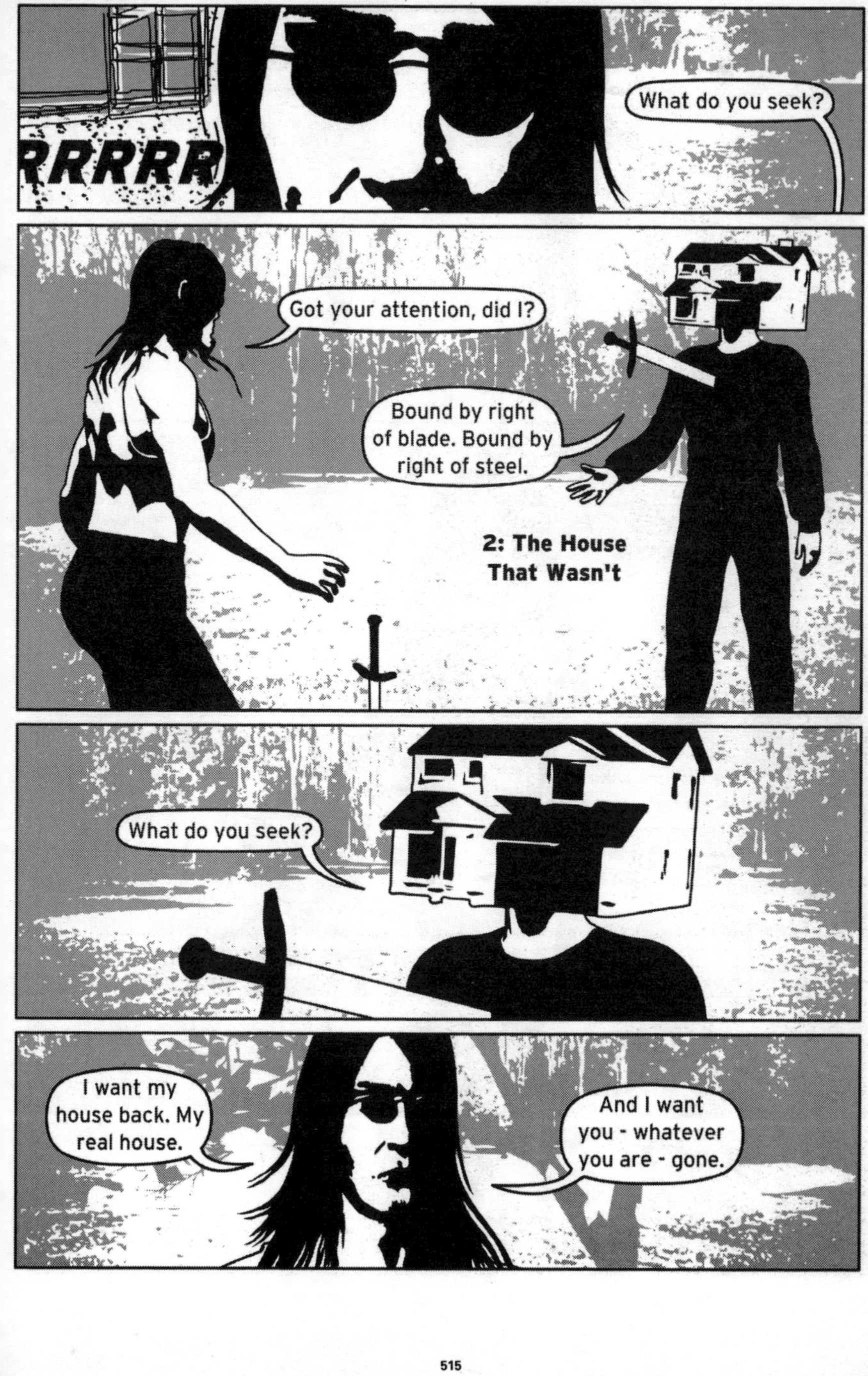
RRRRR
What do you seek?
Got your attention, did I?
Bound by right of blade. Bound by right of steel.
2: The House That Wasn't
What do you seek?
I want my house back. My real house.
And I want you - whatever you are - gone.

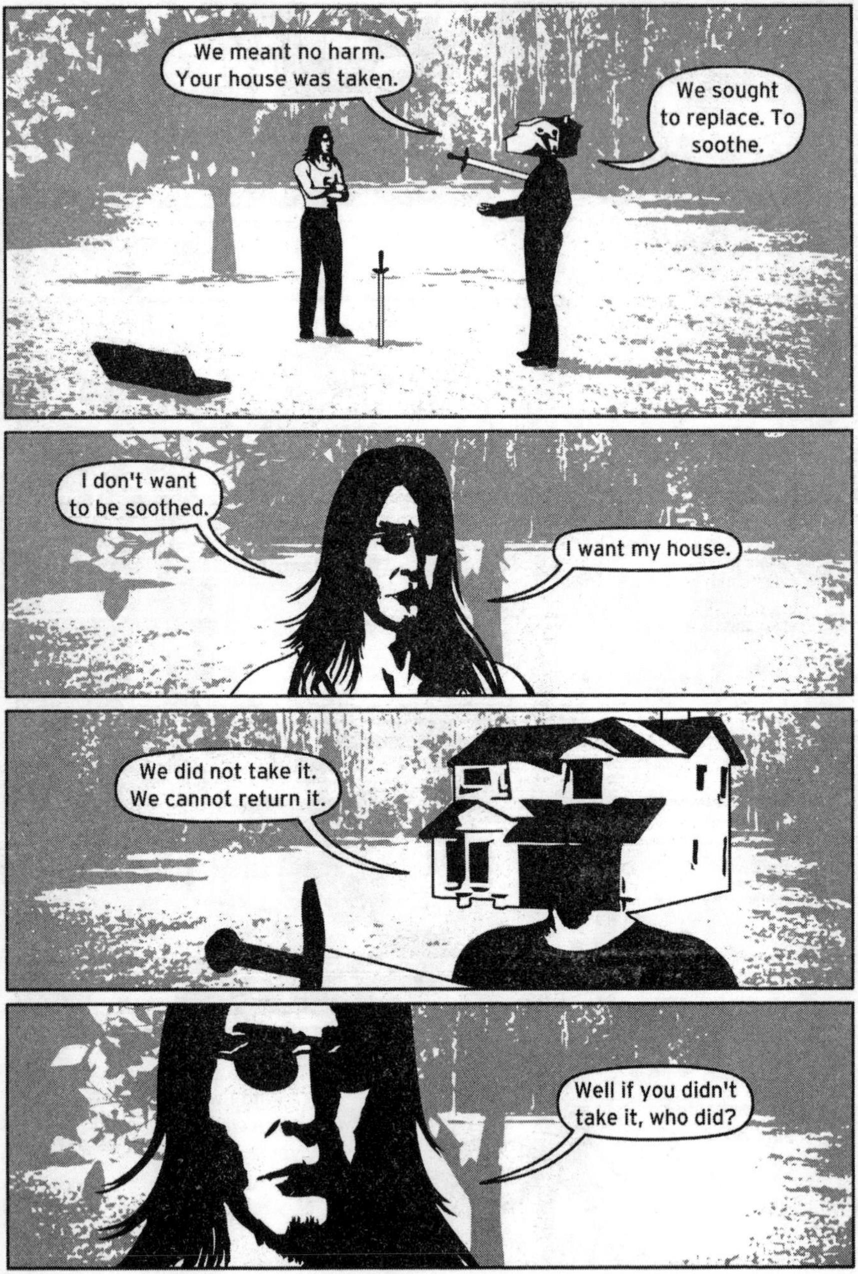
We meant no harm. Your house was taken.
We sought to replace. To soothe.
I don't want to be soothed.
I want my house.
We did not take it. We cannot return it.
Well if you didn't take it, who did?

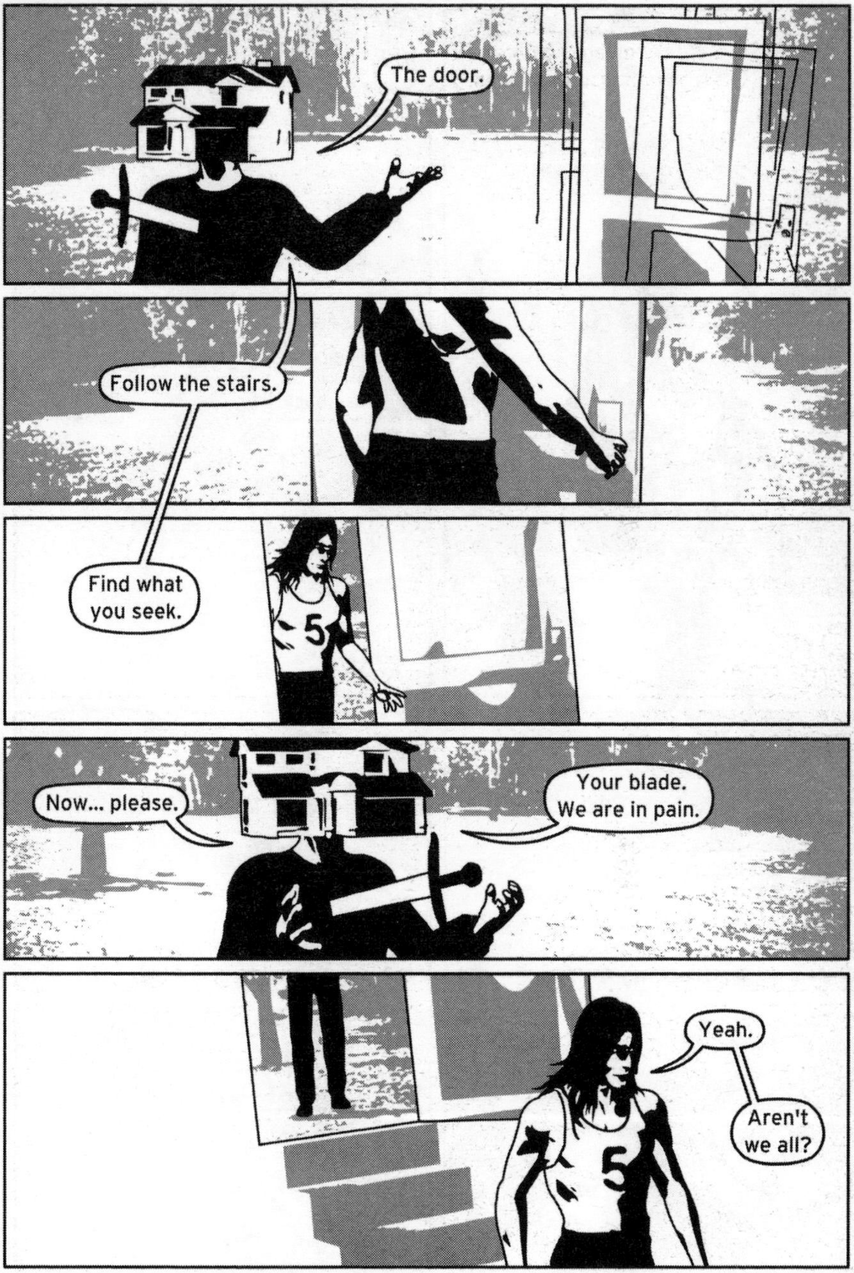
The door.
Follow the stairs.
Find what you seek.
Now... please.
Your blade. We are in pain.
Yeah.
Aren't we all?

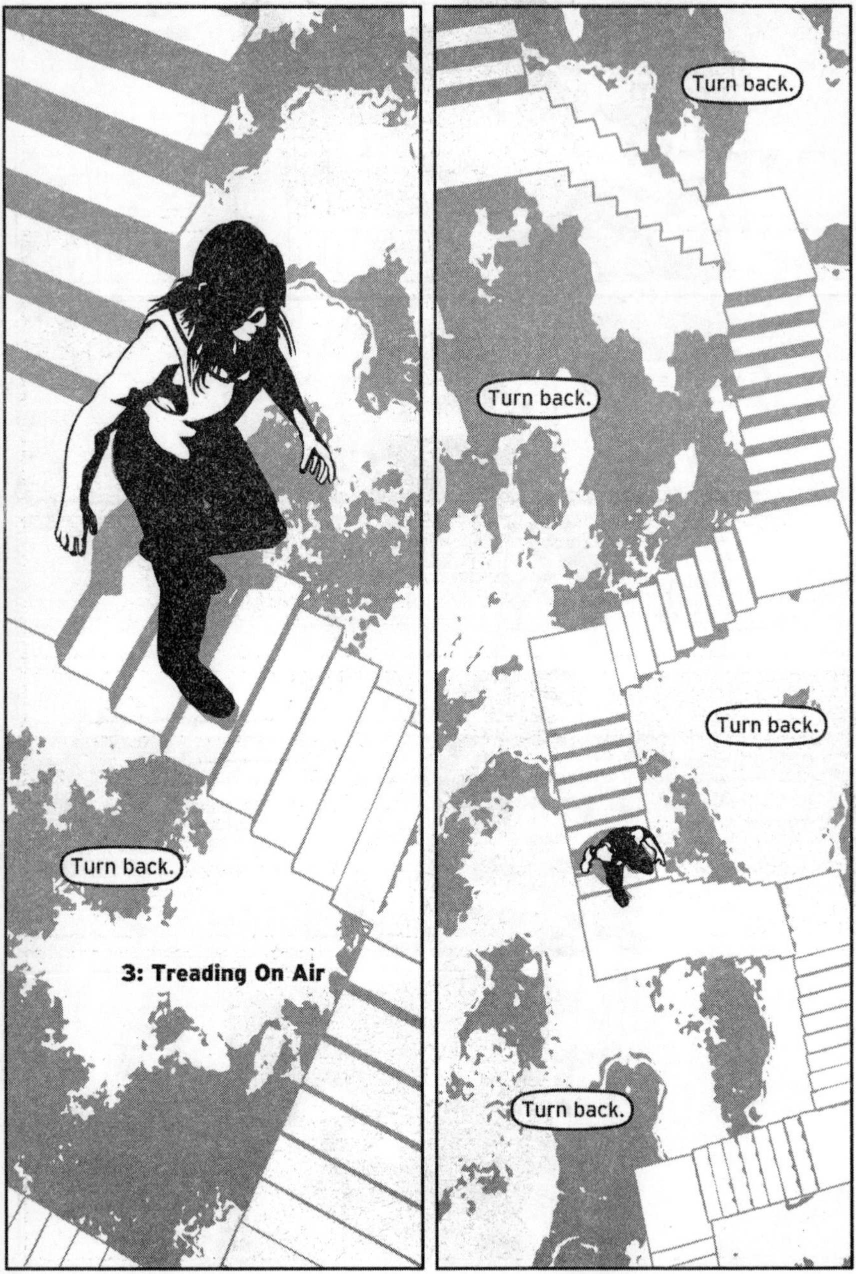
Turn back.
3: Treading On Air
Turn back.
Turn back.
Turn back.
Turn back.

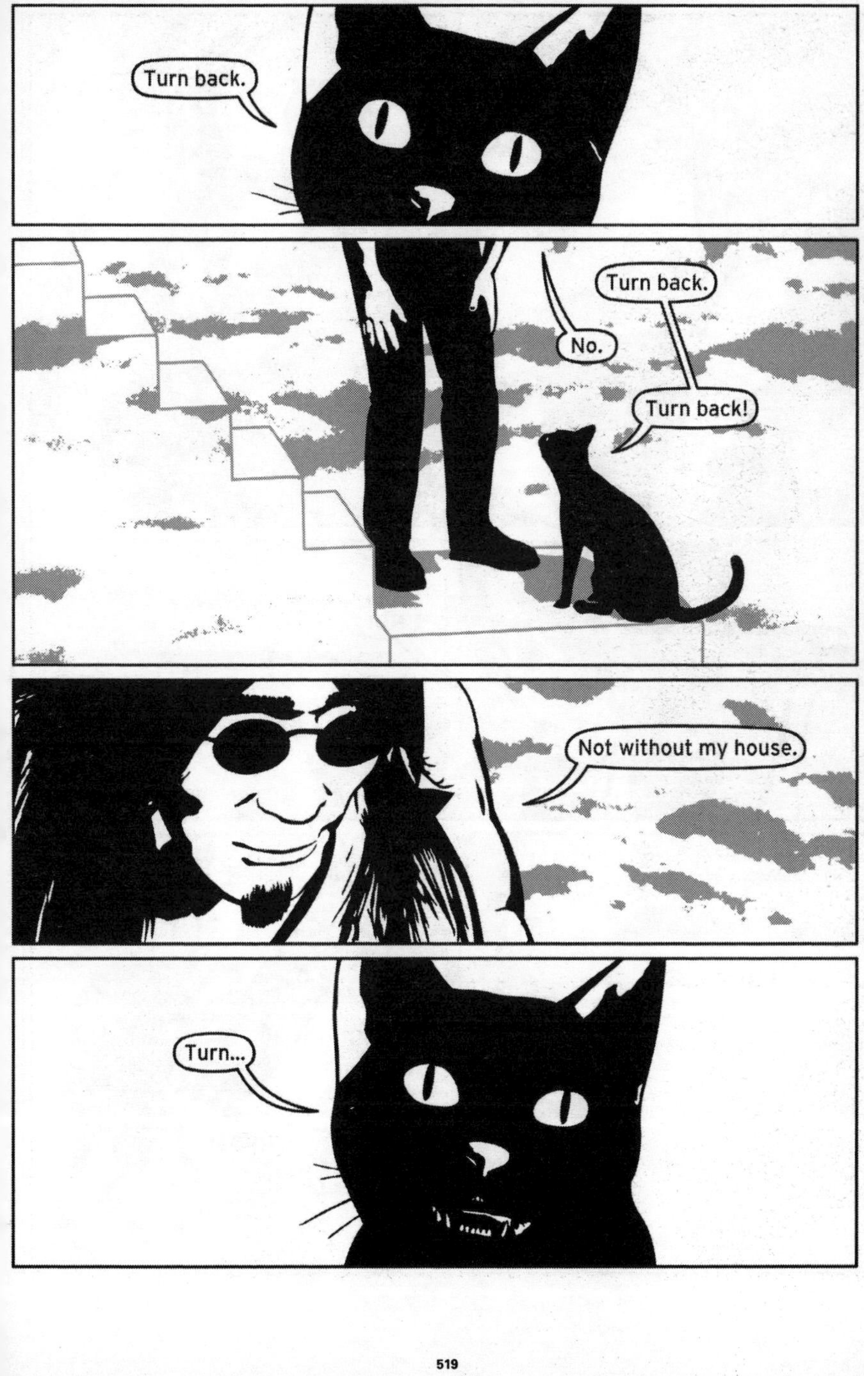
Turn back.
Turn back.
No.
Turn back!
Not without my house.
Turn...

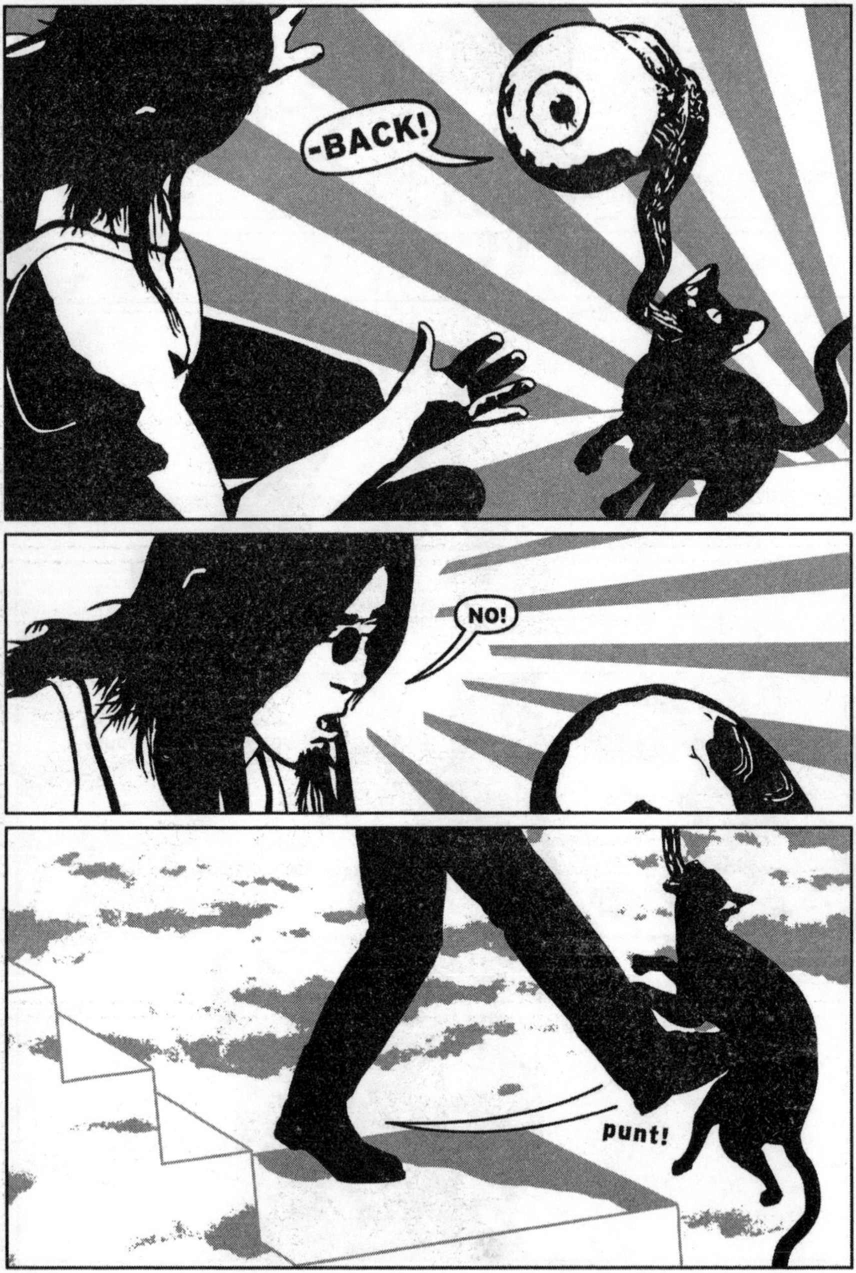
-BACK!
NO!
punt!

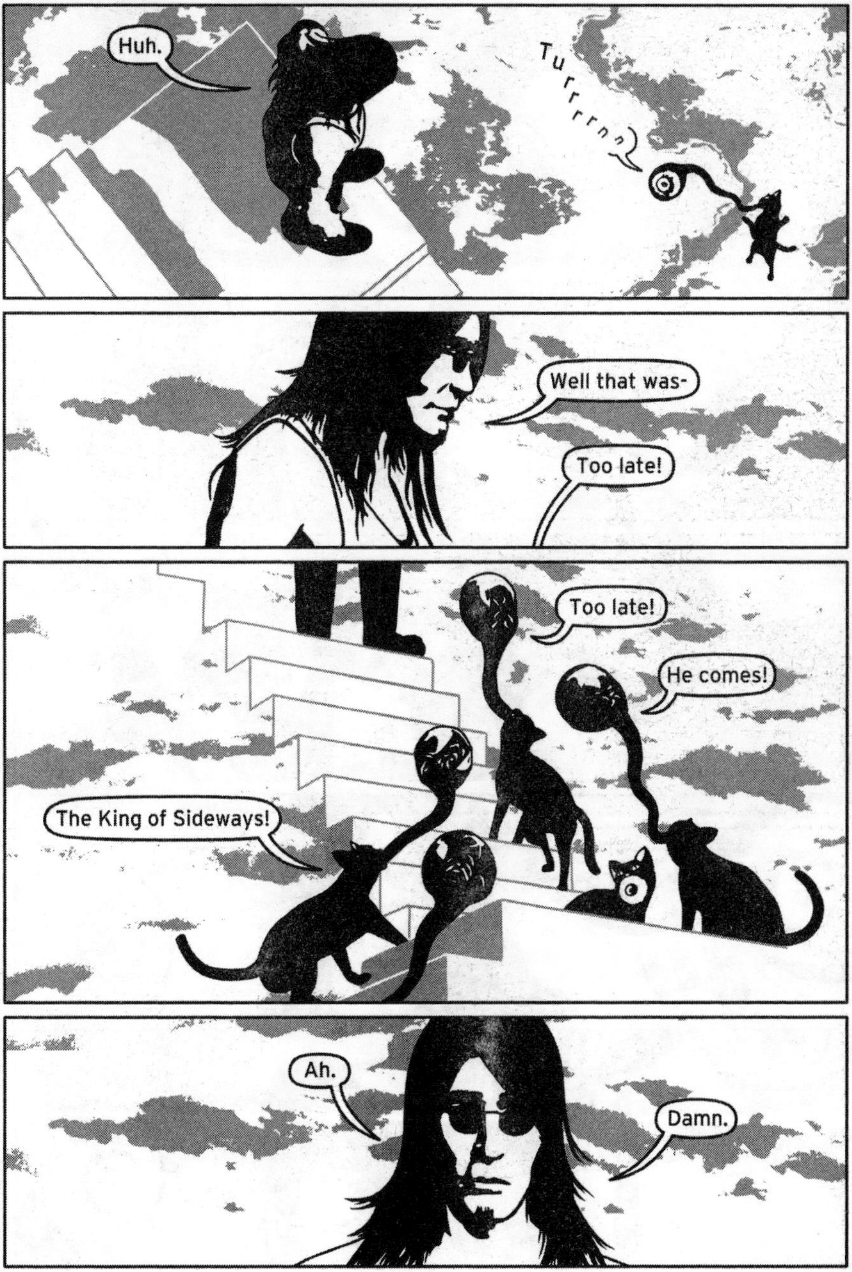
Huh.
Turrrrnn
Well that was-
Too late!
Too late!
He comes!
The King of Sideways!
Ah.
Damn.

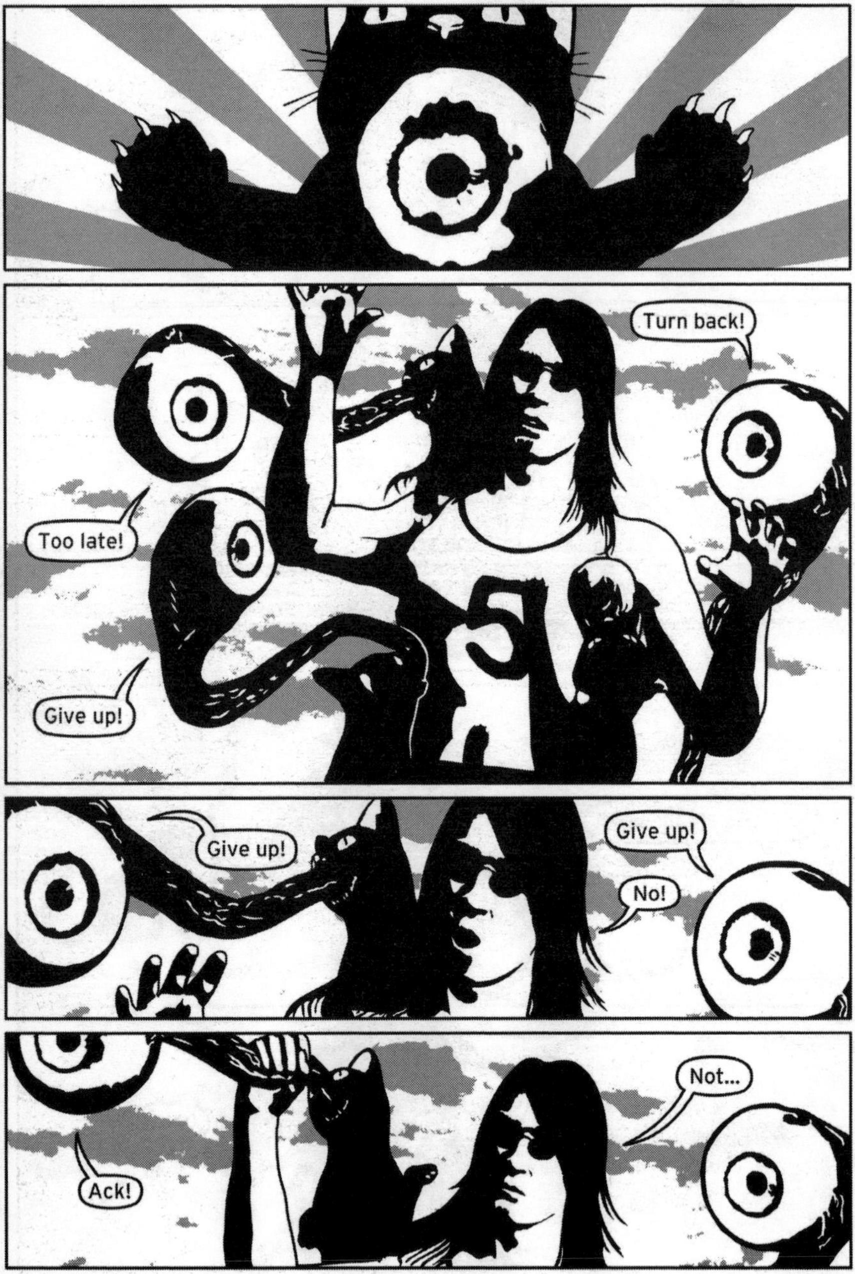
Turn back!
Too late!
Give up!
Give up!
Give up!
No!
Not...
Ack!

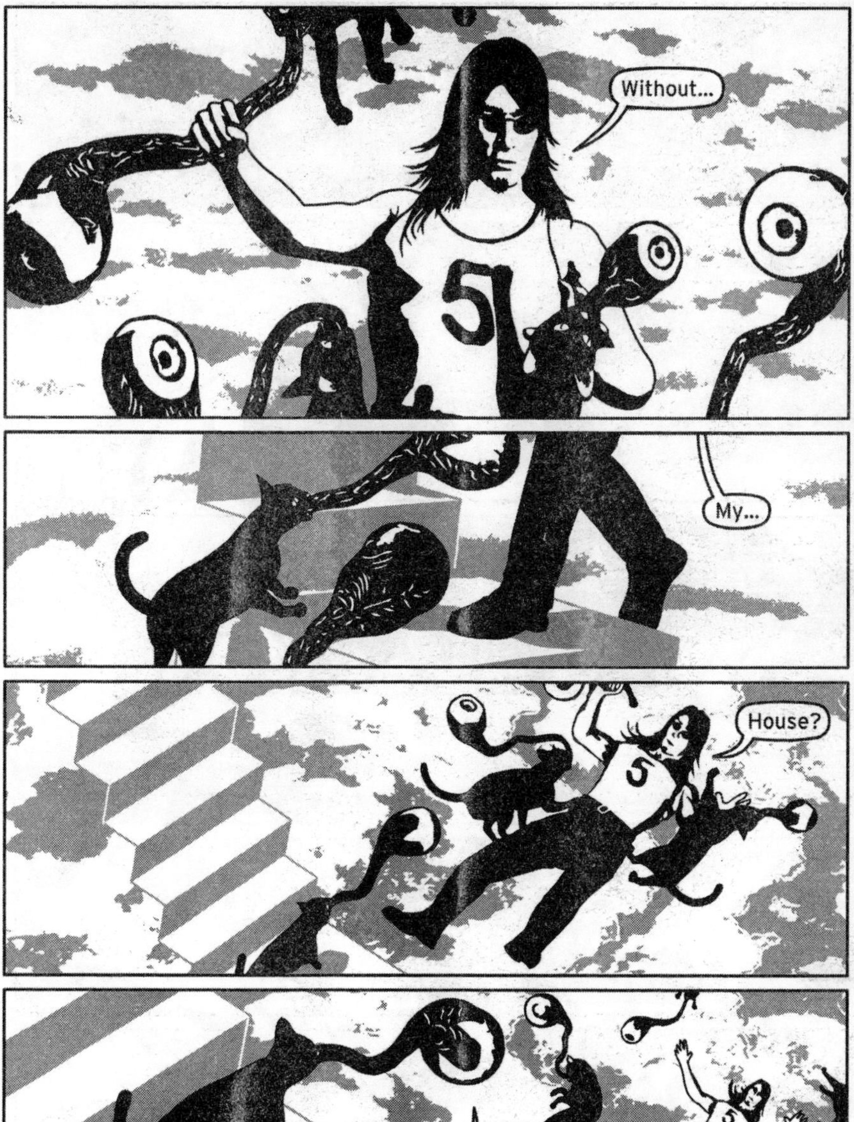
Without...
My...
House?
Too late.

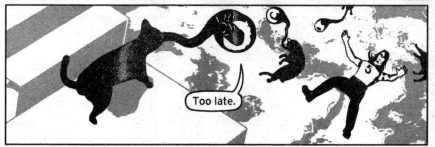

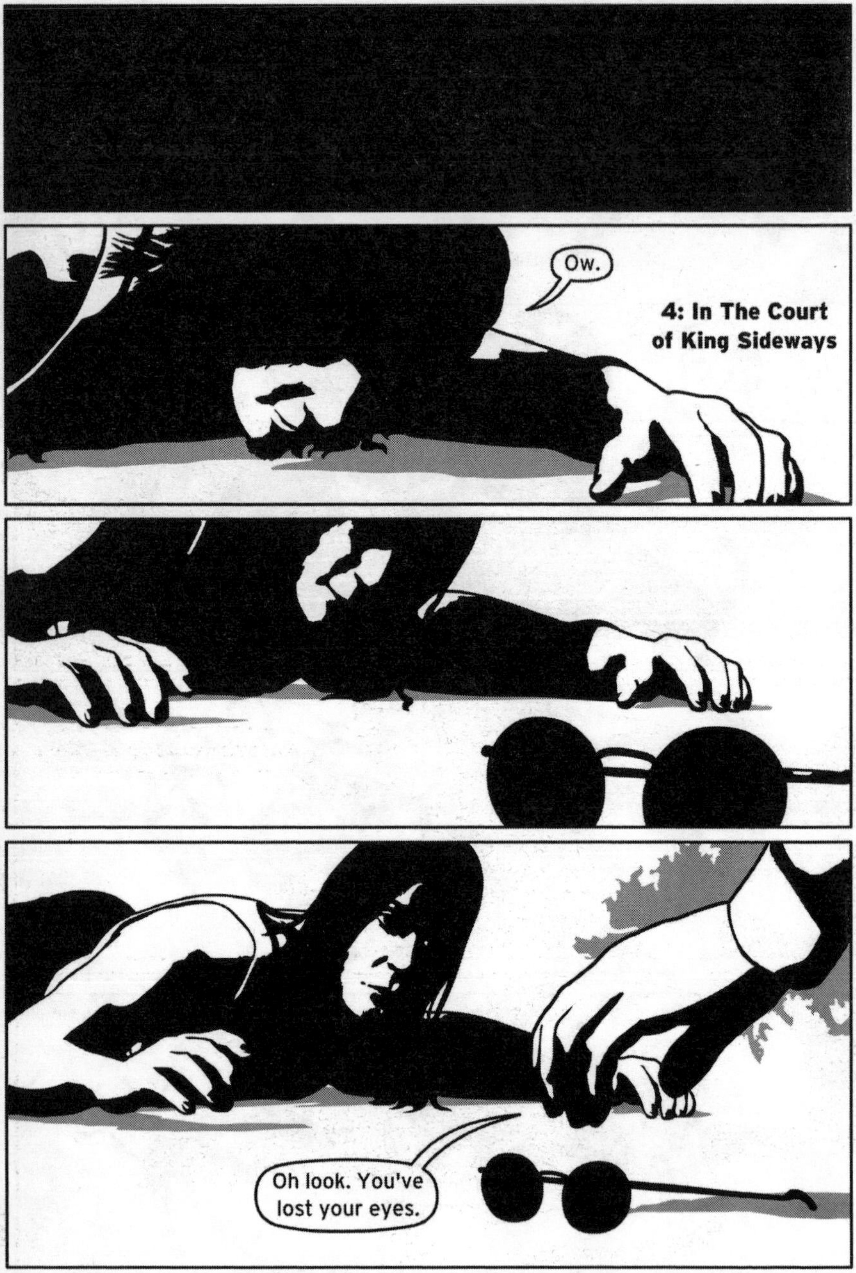
Ow.
4: In The Court of King Sideways
Oh look. You've lost your eyes.

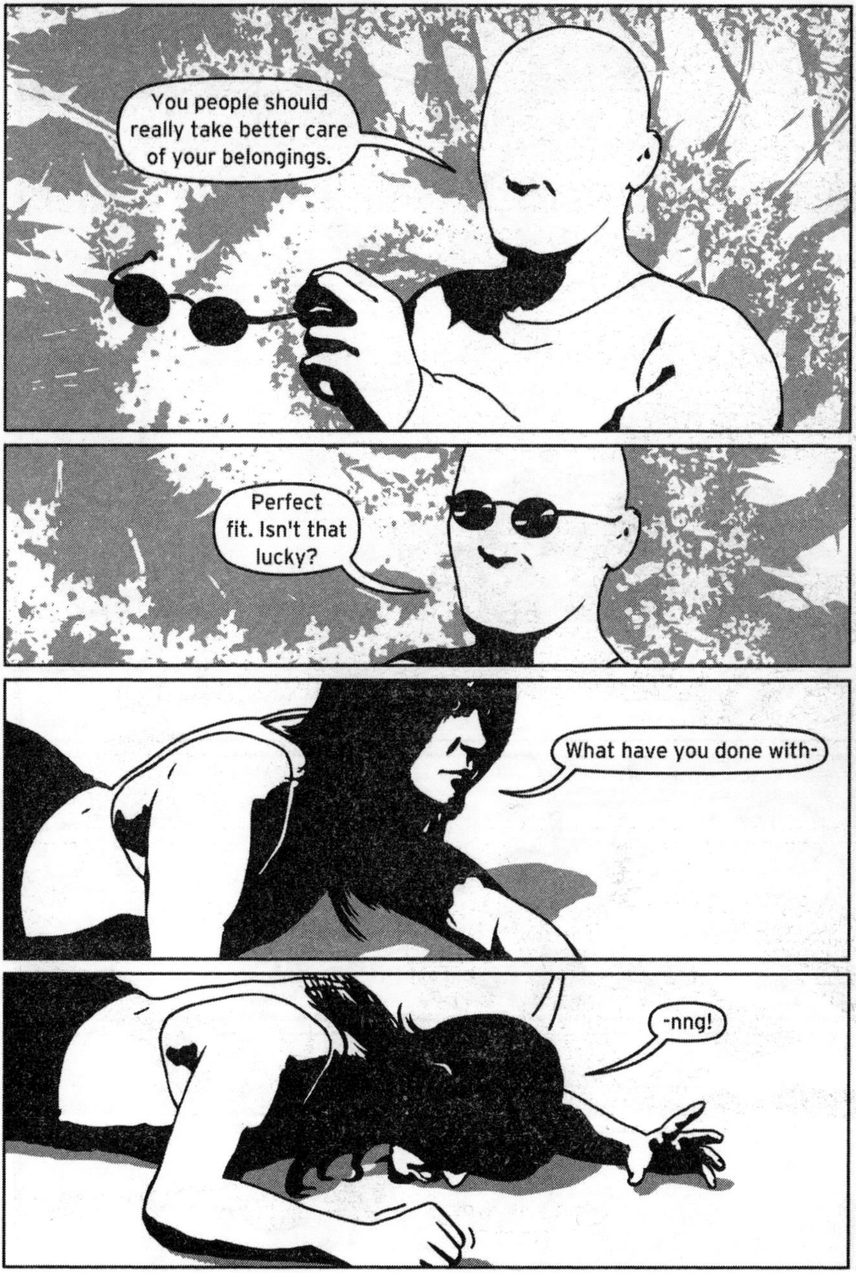
You people should really take better care of your belongings.
Perfect fit. Isn't that lucky?
What have you done with-
-nng!

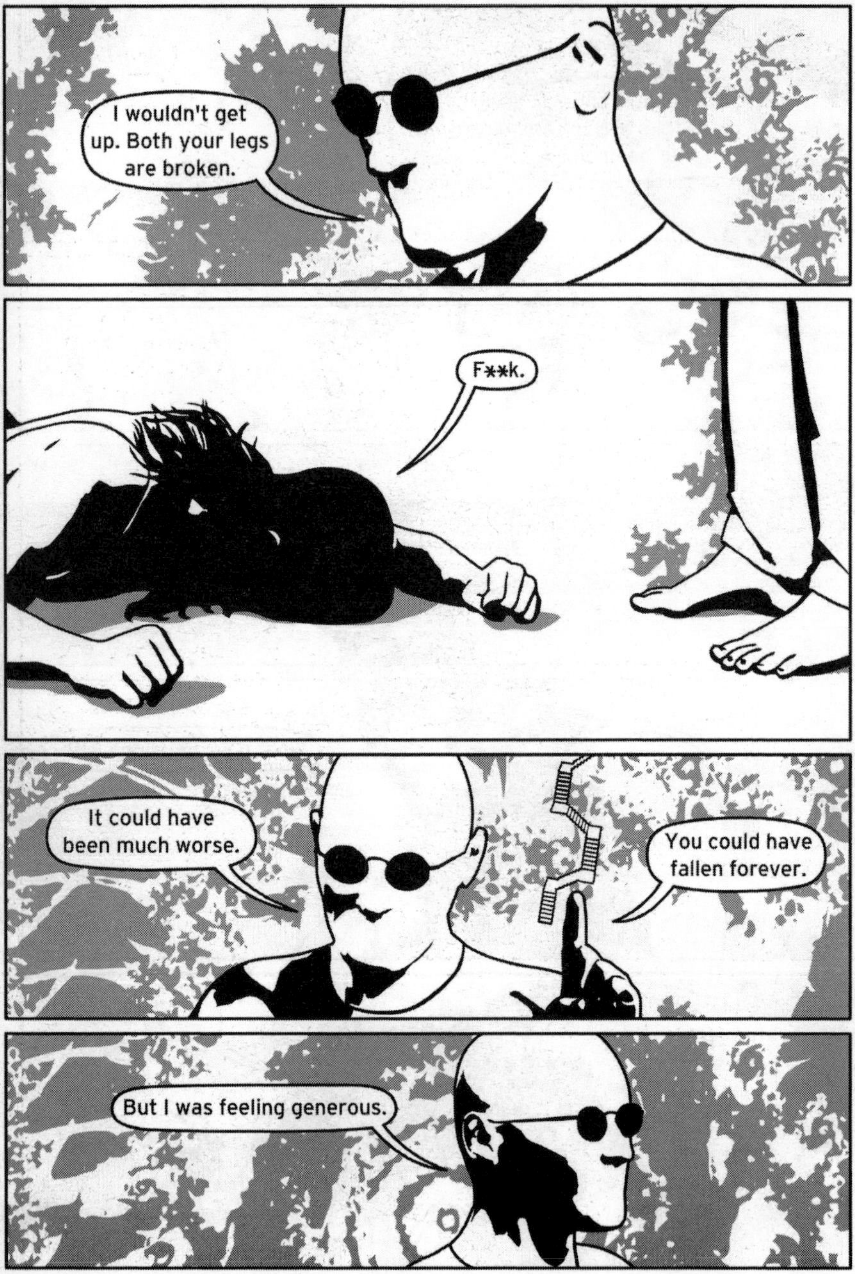
I wouldn't get up. Both your legs are broken.
F**k.
It could have been much worse.
You could have fallen forever.
But I was feeling generous.

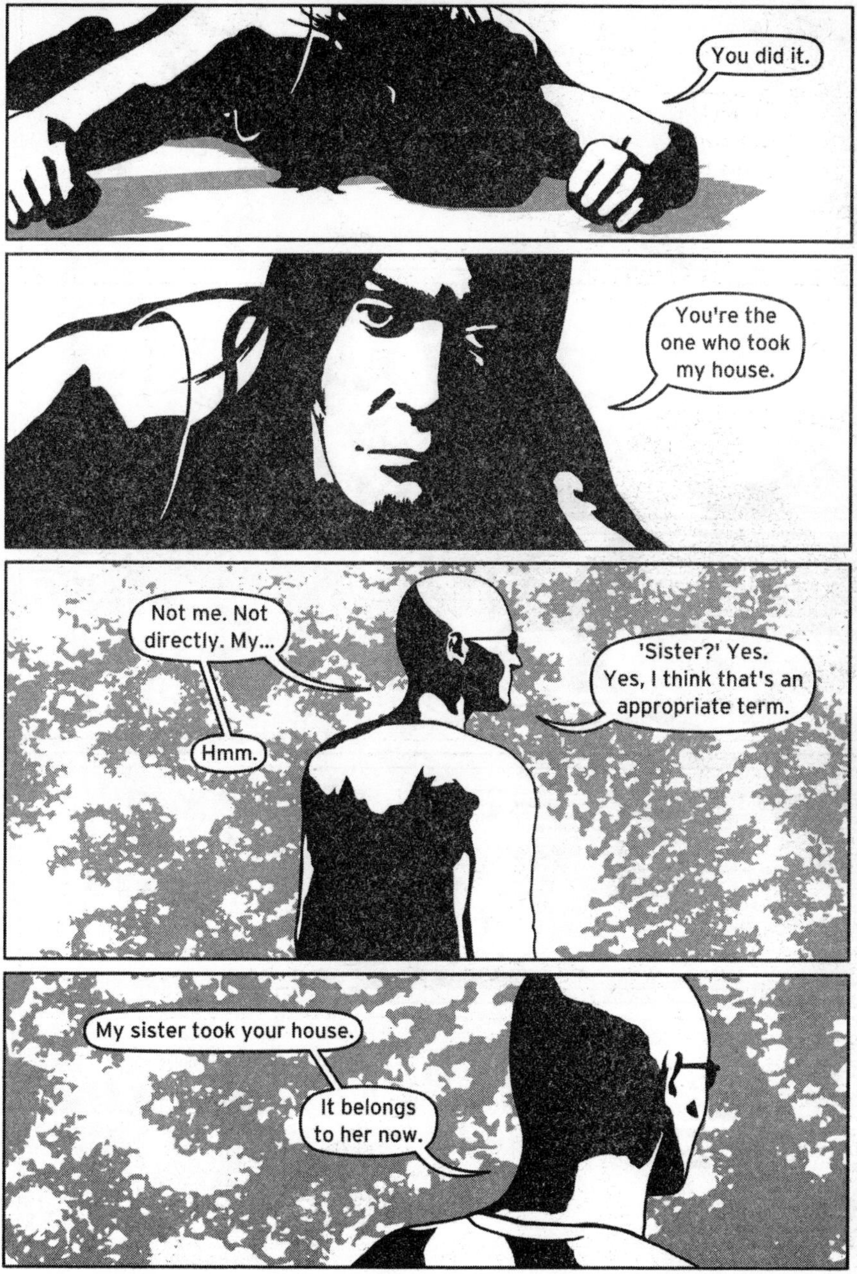
You did it.
You're the one who took my house.
Not me. Not directly. My...
Hmm.
'Sister?' Yes. Yes, I think that's an appropriate term.
My sister took your house.
It belongs to her now.

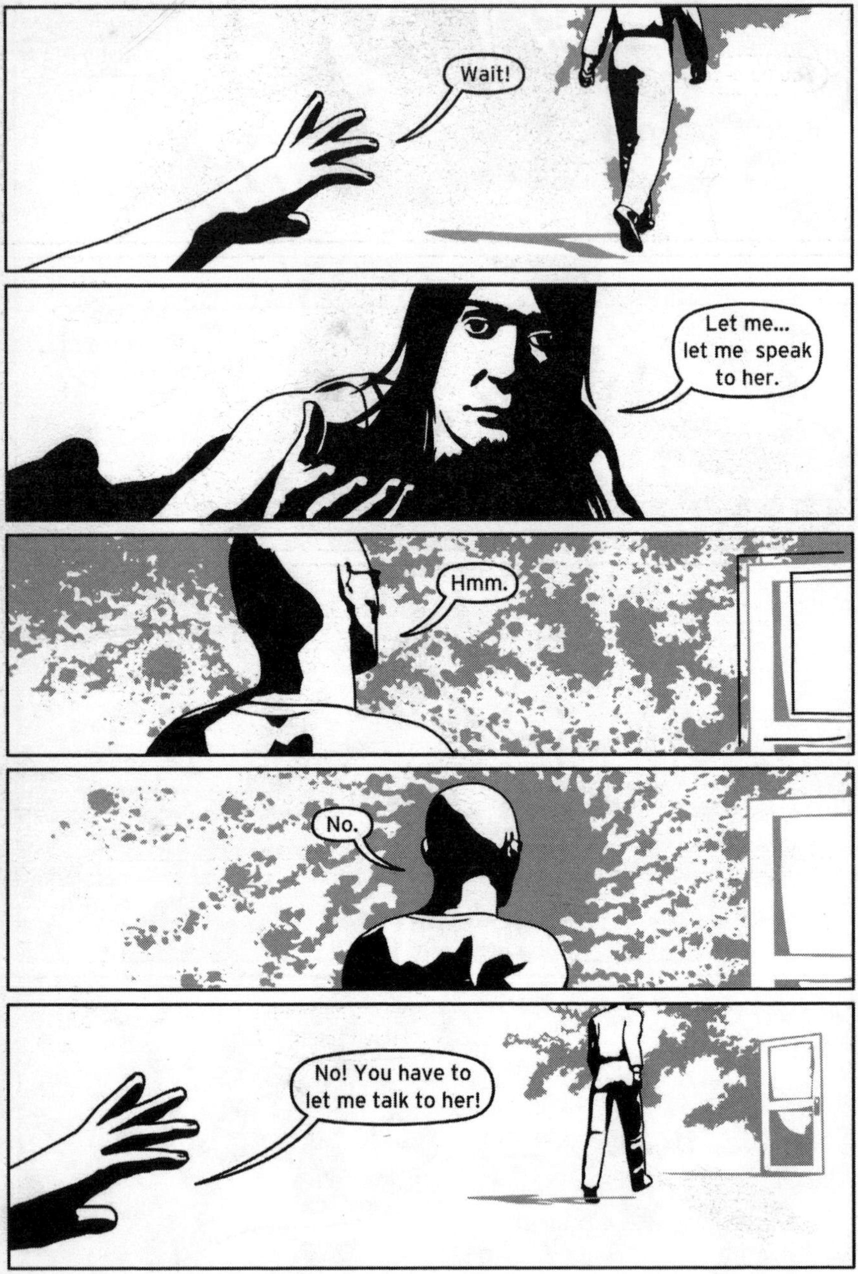
Wait!
Let me... let me speak to her.
Hmm.
No.
No! You have to let me talk to her!

You have to-

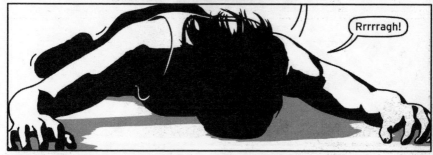

Rrrrragh!

'Have to?' *'Have to?'*

Hah!

I'm the King of Sideways.

There's nothing I have to do.

slam!

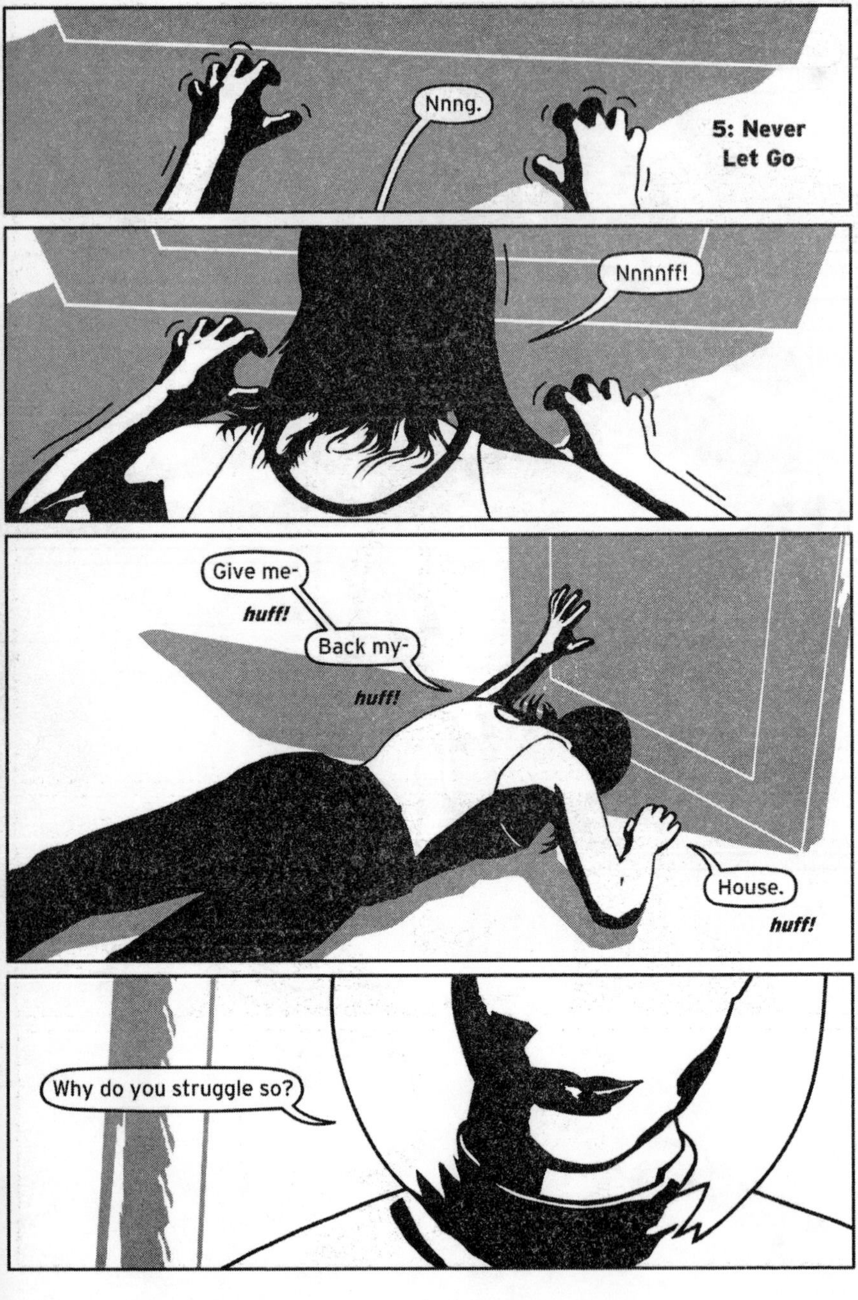
Nnng.
5: Never Let Go
Nnnnff!
Give me-
huff!
Back my-
huff!
House.
huff!
Why do you struggle so?

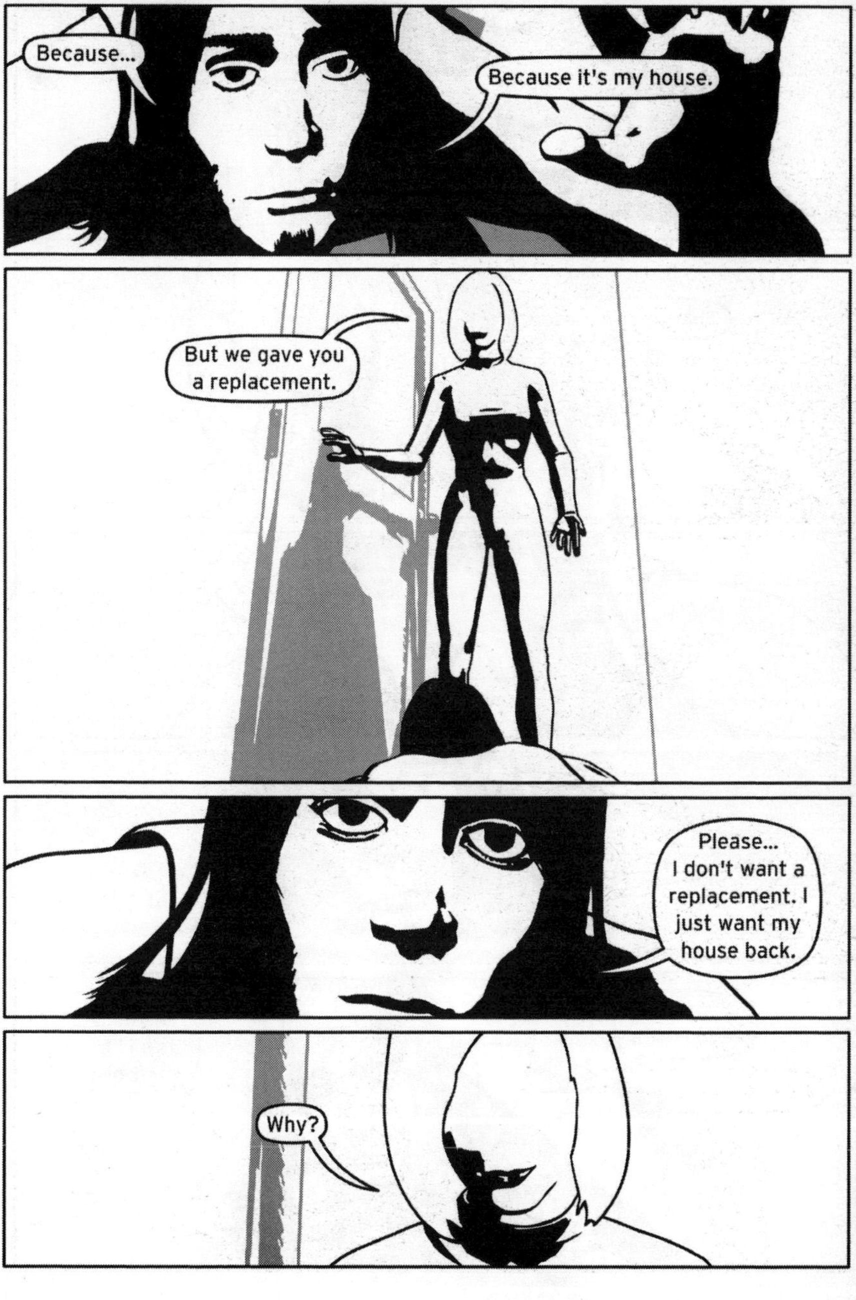
Because...
Because it's my house.
But we gave you a replacement.
Please... I don't want a replacement. I just want my house back.
Why?

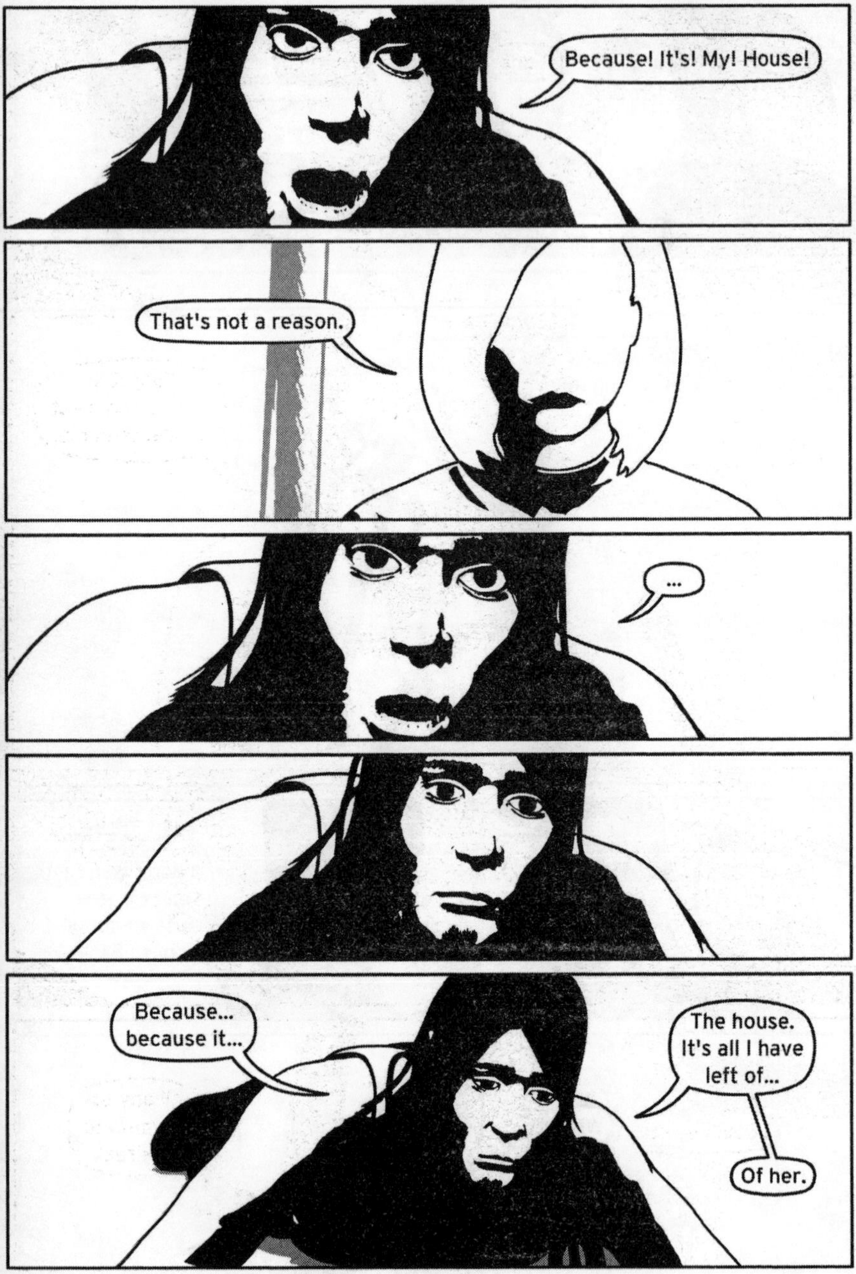
Because! It's! My! House!
That's not a reason.
...
Because... because it...
The house. It's all I have left of...
Of her.

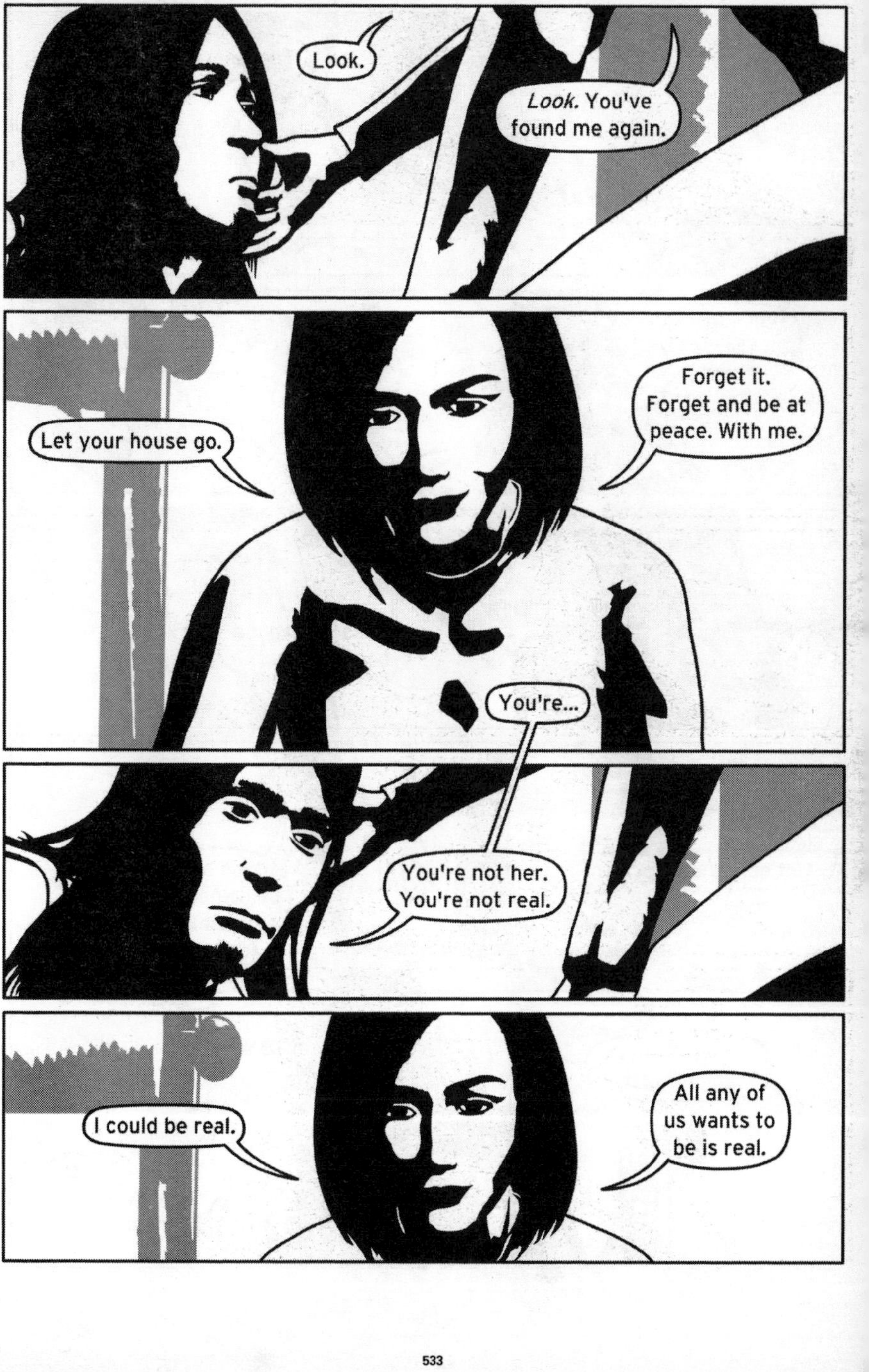
Look.
Look. You've found me again.
Let your house go.
Forget it. Forget and be at peace. With me.
You're...
You're not her. You're not real.
I could be real.
All any of us wants to be is real.

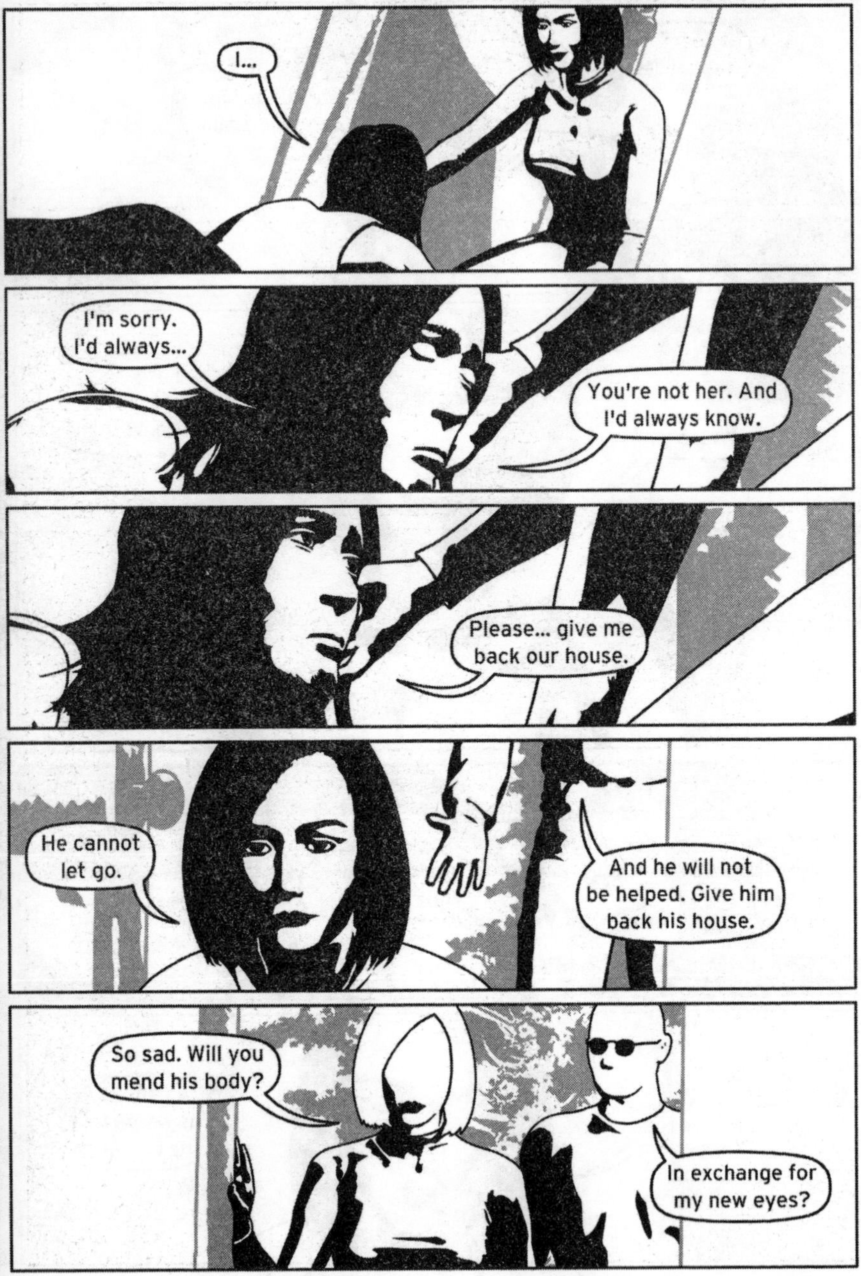
I...
I'm sorry.
I'd always...
You're not her. And
I'd always know.
Please... give me
back our house.
He cannot
let go.
And he will not
be helped. Give him
back his house.
So sad. Will you
mend his body?
In exchange for
my new eyes?

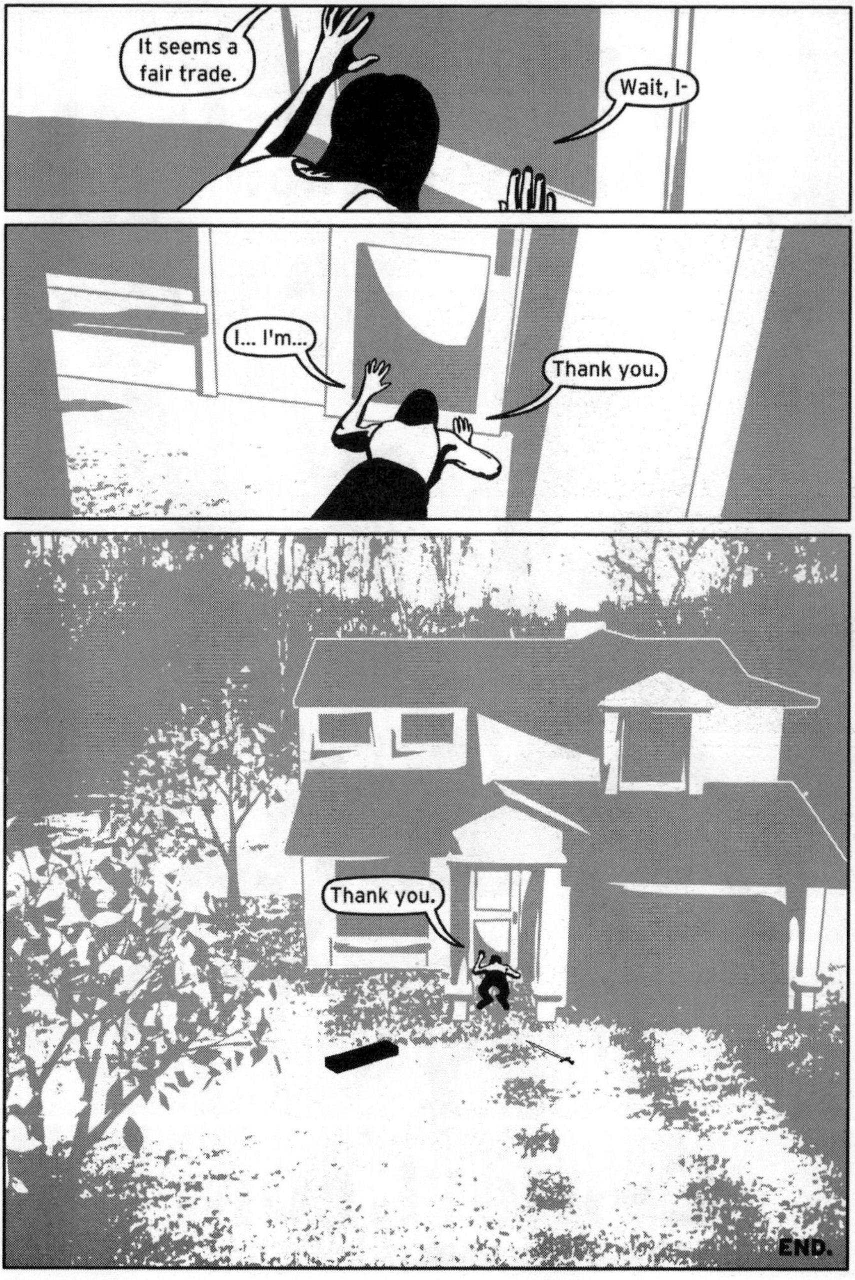
It seems a fair trade.
Wait, I-
I... I'm...
Thank you.
Thank you.
END.

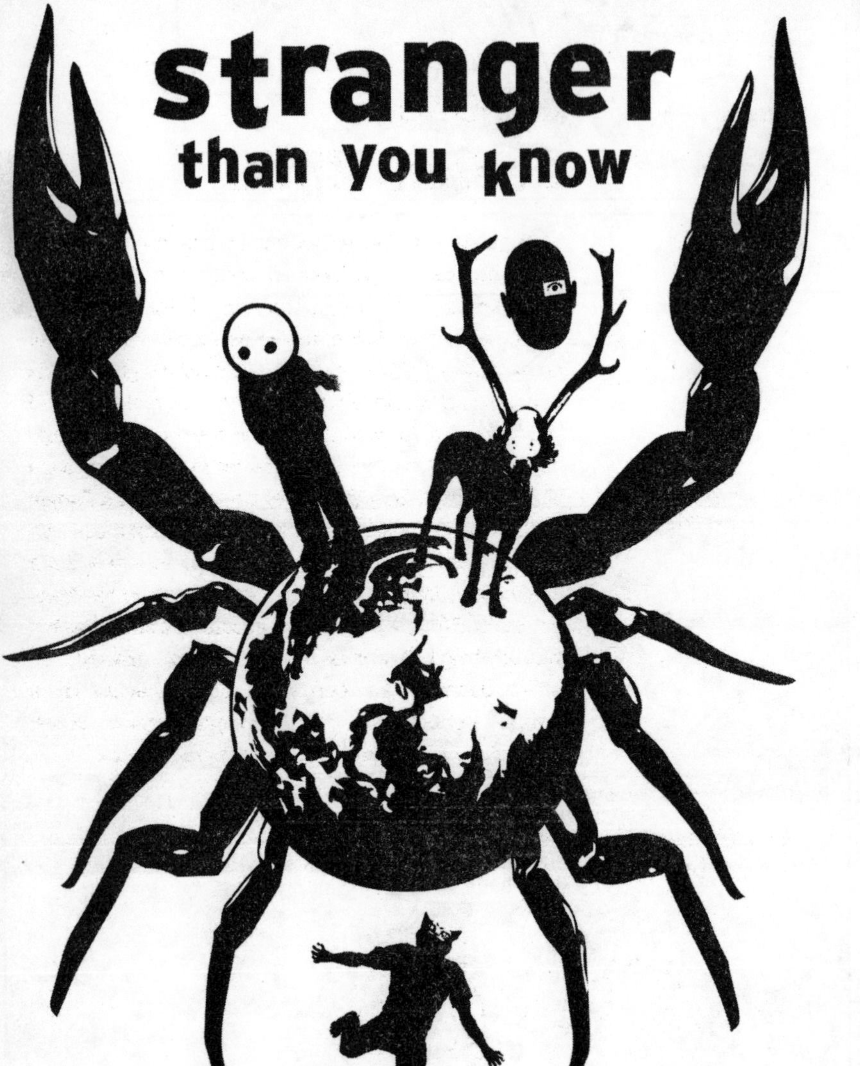
stranger
than you know
E-merl.com
new experiments in fiction

Omake
Joanna Zhou

Date of birth: 7 November 1984

Joanna is Chinese, but has homes in both the UK and Austria, growing up bilingual in English and German. Her manga and anime influences include **Wish**, **Legend of Zelda**, **Doraemon** (he's blue, he's got no ears, he's a robot cat! With, uh, machine guns up his bottom), and Studio Ghibli animation (they're the best – if you aren't familiar with any, check them out); also, hip-hop / r'n'b, Sanrio (cutey character merchandise, such as **Hello Kitty**), Gary (**Far Side**) Larson, and TV's **Family Guy**. Koala bears are the best (don't you dare mess with Ponpon!), but Comic sans sucks (yup, as a font it's a total cliché, right up there with the journalistic fondness for BIFF!, BAM!, POW! sound effects whenever dealing with anything comic-book related – enough, already!).

Joanna's ambition is to be contracted by a manga publisher for a full-length graphic novel. Meanwhile, though, her comic shorts crack us up.

http://www.chocolatepixels.com
http://www.sweatdrop.com

International Manga
and Anime Festival

The International Manga and Anime Festival (IMAF) was created to find and help promote new, original and talented artists from all over the world through an annual drawing/animation competition. It offers prizes catering for all skill levels, whether you are an experienced professional or a talented amateur. Selected entries are displayed at the festival, and a judging panel drawn from within the industry decides on the final winners.

IMAF 2005 was a resounding success. Over 6,000 visitors saw the work of more than 400 artists displayed – a huge improvement on the previous year's event. But the progress didn't stop there – the festival expanded to include workshops, art events, film screenings, panel discussions and artistic demonstrations. IMAF 2006 takes place 10-14 November, and with each succeeding year the IMAF organization will build on the previous year's successes, to become bigger and better than ever before.

Big cash prizes! Check it out.

http://www.imaf.co.uk

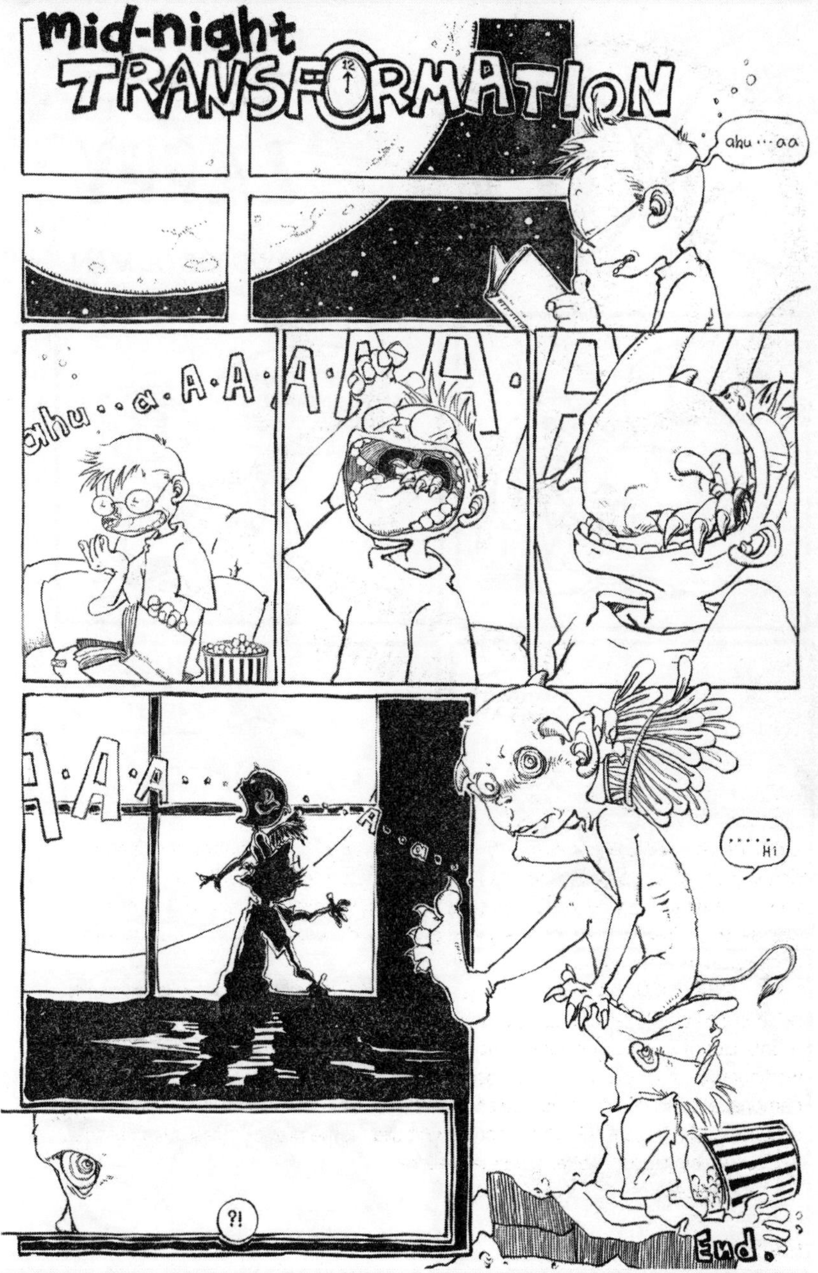
mid-night TRANSFORMATION
ahu···aa
ahu··a·A·A
A·A·A
.....Hi
?!
End.

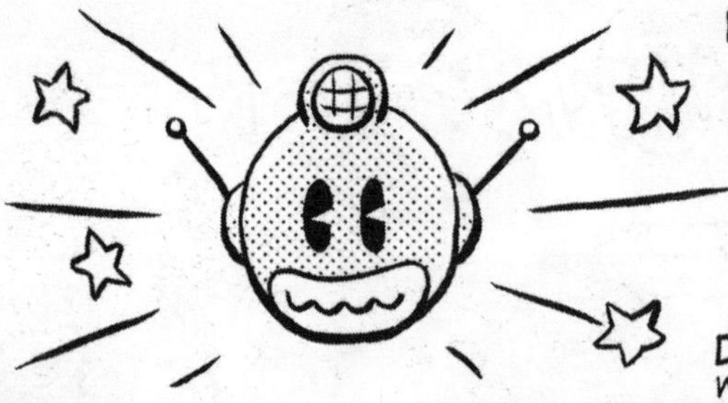

MAGICAL SCIENCE ROBOT ZAPPY

DAVID GOODMAN
WWW.BAHALA-NA.CO.UK

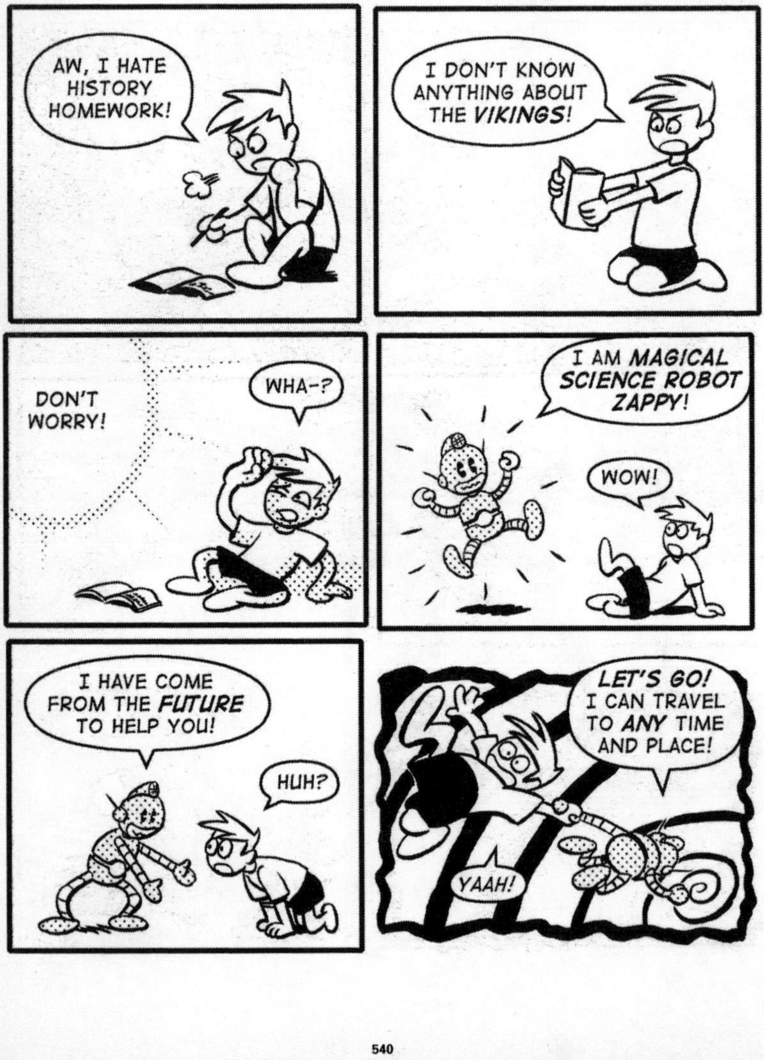
AW, I HATE HISTORY HOMEWORK!
I DON'T KNOW ANYTHING ABOUT THE *VIKINGS*!
DON'T WORRY!
WHA-?
I AM *MAGICAL SCIENCE ROBOT ZAPPY*!
WOW!
I HAVE COME FROM THE *FUTURE* TO HELP YOU!
HUH?
LET'S GO! I CAN TRAVEL TO *ANY* TIME AND PLACE!
YAAH!

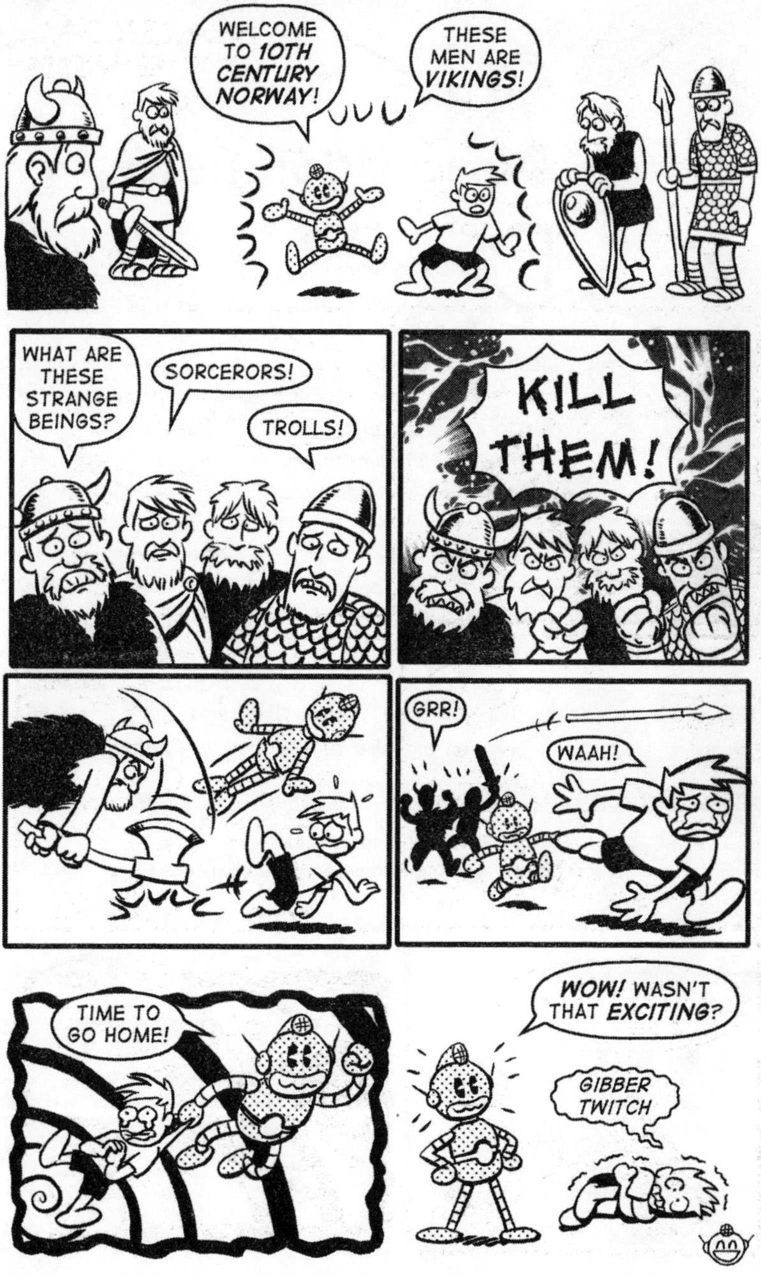
WELCOME TO 10TH CENTURY NORWAY!
THESE MEN ARE VIKINGS!
WHAT ARE THESE STRANGE BEINGS?
SORCERORS!
TROLLS!
KILL THEM!
GRR!
WAAH!
TIME TO GO HOME!
WOW! WASN'T THAT EXCITING?
GIBBER TWITCH

Omake
David Goodman

Date of birth: 11 March 1974

David, from Liverpool in the UK, alongside his equally talented brother Arthur, is, a leading light on the burgeoning small press scene. There's nothing he likes more than to curl up with a good book, or indeed a self-published comic. His prime influences include Tezuka (the Godfather of all manga), *Lone Wolf & Cub*, *Genshiken*, and Stan Sakai's funny animal samurai *Usagi Yojimbo*. He dislikes lacking inspiration, looming deadlines and, most of all, 'deadlines looming when you are feeling particularly uninspired'. Unsurprising, really.

Two of the strips presented here, *Magical Science Robot Zappy* and *Viva Batata!* were originally published as A7 mini-comics, and David would like you to know they have been 'digitally remastered' especially for this publication. Thanks, David!

You can also see his work in *Furrlough* (Radio Comix).

http://www.bahala-na.co.uk
http://www.squareeyedstories.co.uk

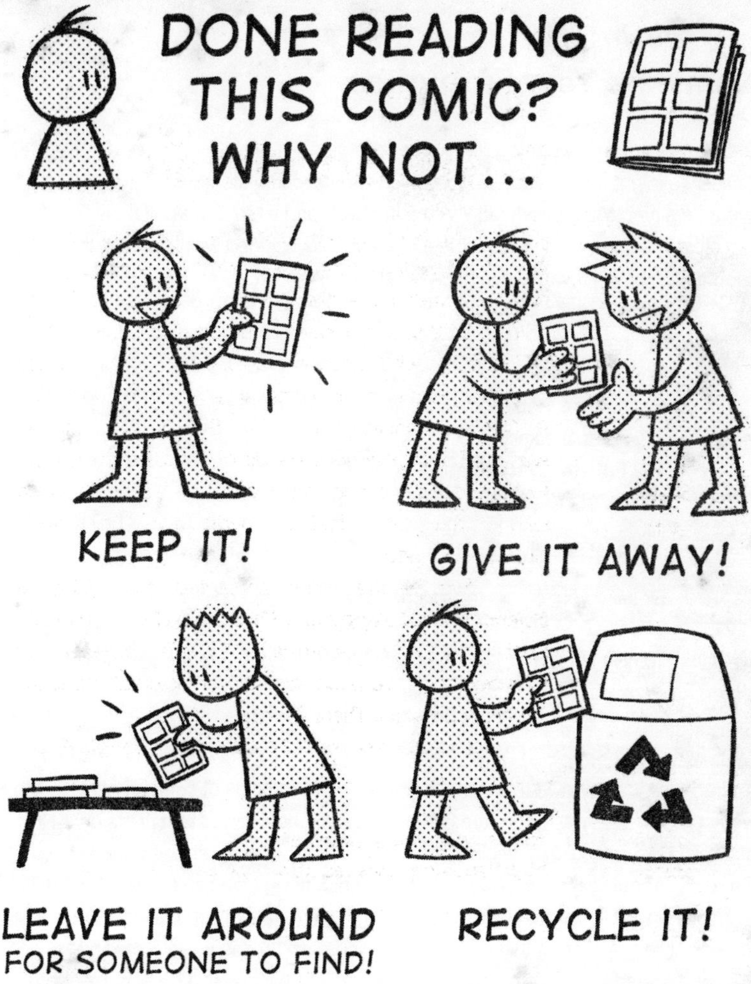
DONE READING THIS COMIC? WHY NOT...
KEEP IT!
GIVE IT AWAY!
LEAVE IT AROUND FOR SOMEONE TO FIND!
RECYCLE IT!
BUT WHATEVER YOU DO, DON'T JUST THROW IT AWAY!
CONSERVE NATURAL RESOURCES. DO YOUR PART!
A PUBLIC AWARENESS ANNOUNCEMENT BY DAVID GOODMAN. WWW.BAHALA-NA.CO.UK

Nominate Your Favourites

OK, here's your chance to influence the direction of future volumes, and the sort of stories we might then include. Tell us which your favourite stories or featured characters are. Whose work did you like the best, and why? Equally, if there was something you really didn't like, or would like to see included which wasn't, tell us about that too! What would you most like to see more of?

Write in to the editorial address:

Best New Manga
Constable & Robinson
3 The Lanchesters
162 Fulham Palace Road
LONDON W6 9ER
UK

Or send your emails to: editor@bestnewmanga.com

We can't promise to reply individually, but we will take on board all your comments.

If you want your own work to be considered, send samples of continuity (that's strip work, not just pin-ups) to the same address. Send photocopies and prints only; NO originals. But you must BE original, and be the BEST! Assess properly whether you are ready for publication yet – and if not, keep practising (you can find plenty of How To books on the subject – but beware, some of them do talk complete rubbish about 'manga style'). We regret that not all submissions can be answered: including a stamped self-addressed envelope will improve your chances of a reply, but random correspondence cannot be entered into.